The Cambridge Poets

General Editor, BLISS PERRY

Edited by

BROWNING	HORACE E. SCUDDER
MRS. BROWNING	HARRIET WATERS PRESTON
BURNS	W. E. HENLEY
BYRON	PAUL E. MORE
DRYDEN	GEORGE R. NOYES
ENGLISH AND SCOTTISH ⎱	HELEN CHILD SARGENT
POPULAR BALLADS ⎰	GEORGE L. KITTREDGE
HOLMES	HORACE E. SCUDDER
KEATS	HORACE E. SCUDDER
LONGFELLOW	HORACE E. SCUDDER
LOWELL	HORACE E. SCUDDER
MILTON	WILLIAM VAUGHN MOODY
POPE	HENRY W. BOYNTON
SCOTT	HORACE E. SCUDDER
SHAKESPEARE	W. A. NEILSON
SHELLEY	GEORGE E. WOODBERRY
SPENSER	R. E. NEIL DODGE
TENNYSON	WILLIAM J. ROLFE
WHITTIER	HORACE E. SCUDDER
WORDSWORTH	A. J. GEORGE

In Preparation

CHAUCER	F. N. ROBINSON

HOUGHTON MIFFLIN COMPANY
BOSTON AND NEW YORK

The Cambridge Edition of the Poets

EDITED BY

HORACE E. SCUDDER

SCOTT

BY THE EDITOR

THE
COMPLETE POETICAL WORKS OF
SIR WALTER SCOTT

Cambridge Edition

Ashestiel

BOSTON AND NEW YORK
HOUGHTON MIFFLIN COMPANY
The Riverside Press, Cambridge

PR
5305
.FOO

EDITOR'S NOTE

WHEN Dr. Rolfe edited *The Poetical Works of Sir Walter Scott, Baronet*, in 1887, he made a critical examination of the several texts, with the result of discovering many errors and inconsistencies in the current editions. The text which he thus established may be regarded as accurate and trustworthy. It has been adopted, so far as it goes, in the present *Cambridge Edition*. Dr. Rolfe, however, was preparing a volume which, by calling in the aid of new and faithful illustrations, should appeal through its beauty and choiceness to lovers of Scott who might be supposed to know their author and to desire a fit and convenient edition of his poems. He excluded purposely a number of less important poems, and grouped all the minor poems in sections following the series of long narrative poems. At the close he added a body of notes and prefaces, drawn from Scott's own editions.

In accordance with the general plan of the *Cambridge* series, the present editor has undertaken to give the entire body of Sir Walter's poetry and to arrange it with as close an approach to strict chronological order as was possible without pedantry. He has prefaced each poem or group of poems with notes describing the origin or circumstance of composition, and in these notes has included Scott's own Introductions, and such references as occur in Lockhart, in Scott's *Letters*, and in his *Journal*. In this way he has undertaken to separate the history of a poem from the explication of its parts.

For the latter, he has had recourse for the most part in the *Notes and Illustrations* to the notes written and gathered by Scott for his collective edition. Scott's unfailing interest in everything Scottish led him to great lengths in his annotation and especially to the accumulation of a great deal of antiquarian and sometimes rather remote material. He forgot his poem and even now and then apparently the subject itself as he heaped up illustrations. The editor therefore has found it expedient, while retaining Scott's own notes, to omit some of the discursive portions drawn from other writers. The annotation, moreover, is made in one respect more convenient and compact by the explanation of rare and local words in a *Glossary* which is an enlargement of the one accompanying Dr. Rolfe's volume.

In his *Biographical Sketch*, the Editor has had in view more especially that portion of Scott's life which closed with the great poetical period, since it is Scott the poet who is especially under consideration. He was glad to avail himself of the admirable and suggestive interpretation of the poet's life made by Ruskin in *Fors Clavigera*.

CAMBRIDGE, March, 1900.

TWO BALLADS FROM THE GERMAN OF BÜRGER

The first publication by Scott was a translation or imitation of two German ballads, and bore the following title-page : ' THE CHASE and WILLIAM AND HELEN. Two Ballads from the German of Gottfried Augustus Bürger, Edinburgh : Printed by Mundell and Son, Royal Bank Close, for Manners and Miller, Parliament Square ; and sold by T. Cadell, junr, and W. Davies, in the Strand, London, 1796.' It was a thin quarto, and, as seen, did not bear the name of the translator. Scott owed his copy of Bürger's works to the daughter of the Saxon Ambassador at the court of St. James, who had married his kinsman, Mr. Scott of Harden. She interested herself in his German studies and lent him aid in correcting his versions. But the immediate occasion of his translating Bürger was the interest excited in the autumn of 1795 by the reading of William Taylor's unpublished version of Bürger's Lenoré, at a party at Dugald Stewart's, by Mrs. Barbauld, then on a visit to Edinburgh. Scott was not present at the reading, but one of his friends who heard it, told him the story, and repeated the chorus, —

'Tramp ! tramp ! across the land they speede,
    Splash ! splash ! across the sea ;
Hurrah ! the dead can ride apace !
Dost fear to ride with me ? '

Scott eagerly laid hold of the original and beginning the task after supper did not go to bed till he had finished it, a good illustration of the impetuosity of his literary labor his life long.

The ballad of *The Wild Huntsman* (*Wilde Jäger*) Scott appears to have written to accompany the other ballad for the little volume The book attracted some attention in Edinburgh, where the author was known, but his friends were disappointed that it received slight notice in London, but translations of *Lenoré*, which had caught the public ear, were abundant enough to keep in tolerable obscurity any single one of them. ' My adventure,' Scott wrote thirty-six years later, when he was famous, ' where so many pushed off to sea, proved a dead loss, and a great part of the edition was condemned to the service of the trunk-maker. This failure did not operate in any unpleasant degree either on my feelings or spirits. I was coldly received by strangers, but my reputation began rather to increase among my own friends, and on the whole I was more bent to show the world that it had neglected something worth notice, than to be affronted by its indifference ; or rather, to speak candidly, I found pleasure in the literary labors in which I had almost by accident become engaged, and labored less in the hope of pleasing others, though certainly without despair of doing so, than in a pursuit of a new and agreeable amusement to myself.' And this may be taken as the most significant element in Scott's first literary venture, made when he was twenty-five years of age, and fairly started in the practice of law. One other interesting fact connected with the little volume is that James Ballantyne, with whom Scott was to have such momentous relations, reprinted it, at Scott's suggestion, a little enlarged, three years later, in order to show Edinburgh society how well he could print.

WILLIAM AND HELEN

FROM heavy dreams fair Helen rose,
    And eyed the dawning red :
' Alas, my love, thou tarriest long !
    O art thou false or dead ? '

With gallant Frederick's princely power
    He sought the bold Crusade,

But not a word from Judah's wars
    Told Helen how he sped.

With Paynim and with Saracen
    At length a truce was made,   10
And every knight returned to dry
    The tears his love had shed.

Our gallant host was homeward bound
    With many a song of joy ;

TABLE OF CONTENTS

NOTE. The frontispiece is a photogravure made by John Andrew and Son from a painting made in 1824 by C. R. Leslie, R. A., once in the possession of the late George Ticknor, Esq., and now the property of the Museum of Fine Arts, Boston.

The vignette is after a drawing by J. M. W. Turner, R. A., engraved in an edition of Scott's Poetical Works published by Adam and Charles Black, 1874.

BIOGRAPHICAL SKETCH

It is a happy fortune that made the two Scotsmen who stand as the highest spiritual representatives of their race to bear names so significant as Burns and Scott. The little streams that catch the sunlight as they spring down the slopes of the Scottish hills are as free in their nature and as limpid in their depths as are the songs with which Burns has given perennial freshness to Scottish life. And it was singularly fortunate that the man of all men who was to interpret his country to the world should himself have been named Scott. If we could reproduce earlier conditions, philologists in some future era of the world's history might be querying whether the little country of the north was named Scotland from the native poet, Walter Scott, or the poet took his name from the country of which he sang.

Walter Scott was born 15 August, 1771, in his father's house at the head of the College Wynd, Edinburgh. He was of the purest Border race. Walter Scott — Wat of Harden — was the grandfather of his father's grandfather and was married to Mary Scott, the Flower of Yarrow, two personages whom Sir Walter honored with more than one reference in his verse. Wat of Harden's eldest son was Sir William Scott, a stout Jacobite who saved his life when making an unsuccessful foray on the lands of Sir Gideon Murray of Elibank, by accepting the alternative of marrying the plainest of the daughters of Sir Gideon, a marriage which by no means turned out ill, but seems to have created a genuine alliance between the two houses.

The third son of Sir William was Walter Scott, the first laird of Raeburn. He and his wife were willing converts to the doctrines of George Fox, the Quaker apostle, but the elder brother, a sturdy Jacobite, would have no such nonsense in the family, and caused Walter and his wife to be clapped into prison and their children educated apart from such pestilential associations as the peace-loving, non-resisting Friends. So effective was the procedure that Walter's son Walter finally intrigued in the cause of the exiled Stuarts, lost pretty much all he had in the world, even his head being in great jeopardy, and wore his beard unclipped to the day of his death under vow that no razor should touch it till the return of the Stuarts, and so got the name of Beardie ; vows, razors, and beards always appear to have had some occult connection. In the Introduction to the sixth canto of *Marmion* he half puts on Beardie's coat as he writes to Richard Heber. Beardie was Scott's great-grandsire. His grandfather was Beardie's second son Robert Scott of Sandy-Knowe, and as this ancestor came to have a large part in Scott's early life, it is worth while to attend to Sir Walter's own narrative concerning him.

'My grandfather,' he writes, in the effective bit of autobiography preserved by Lockhart, ' was originally bred to the sea ; but, being shipwrecked near Dundee in his trial voyage, he took such a sincere dislike to that element that he could not be persuaded to a second attempt. This occasioned a quarrel between him and his father, who left him to shift for himself. Robert was one of those active spirits to whom this was no misfortune. He turned Whig upon the spot, and fairly abjured his father's politics, and his learned poverty. His chief and relative, Mr. Scott of Harden, gave him a lease of the farm of Sandy-Knowe, comprehending the rocks in the centre of which Smailholm or Sandy-Knowe tower is situated. He took for his shepherd an old man called Hogg, who willingly lent him, out of respect to his family, his whole savings, about £30, to stock the new farm. With this sum, which it seems was at the time sufficient for the purpose, the master and servant set off to purchase a stock of sheep at Whitsun-Tryste, a fair held on a hill near Wooler in Northumberland. The old shepherd went carefully from drove to drove, till he found a *hirsel* likely to answer their purpose, and then returned to tell his master to come up and conclude the bargain. But what was his surprise to see him galloping a mettled hunter about the race-course, and to find he had expended the whole stock in this extraordinary purchase ! — Moses's bargain of green spectacles did not strike more dismay into the Vicar of Wakefield's family than my grandfather's rashness into the poor old shepherd. The thing, however, was irretrievable, and they returned without the sheep. In the course of a few days, however, my grandfather, who was one of the best horsemen of his time, attended John Scott of Harden's hounds on this same horse, and displayed him to such advantage that he sold him for double the original price. The farm was now stocked in earnest; and the rest of my grandfather's career was that of successful industry. He was one of the first who were active in the cattle-trade, afterward carried to such extent between the Highlands of Scotland and the leading counties in England, and by his droving transactions acquired a considerable sum of money. He was a man of middle stature, extremely active, quick, keen, and fiery in his temper, stubbornly honest, and so distinguished for his skill in country matters that he was the general referee in all points of dispute which occurred in the neighborhood. His birth being admitted as gentle, gave him access to the best society in the county, and his dexterity in country sports, particularly hunting, made him an acceptable companion in the field as well as at the table.'

This Robert Scott of Sandy-Knowe married Barbara Haliburton, who brought to her husband that part of Dryburgh which included the ruined Abbey. By a misfortune in the family of Barbara Scott, this property was sold, yet the right of burial remained, and was, as we shall see, availed of by Scott himself. The eldest of the large family of Robert and Barbara Scott was Walter the father of Walter. He was educated to the profession of a Writer to the Signet, which is Scots equivalent for attorney. 'He had a zeal for his clients,' writes his son, 'which was almost ludicrous: far from coldly discharging the duties of his employment toward them, he thought for them, felt for their honor as for his own, and rather risked disobliging them than neglecting anything to which he conceived their duty bound them.' For the rest, he was a religious man of the stricter sort, a steady friend to freedom, yet holding fast by the monarchical element, which he thought somewhat jeoparded, a great stickler for etiquette in all the social forms, and a most hearty host. He married Anne, the daughter of Dr. John Rutherford, professor of medicine in the University of Edinburgh.

Such was the inheritance with which Walter Scott came into the world, and at every step one counts a strong strain of that Scottish temper which, twisted and knotted in generations of hardihood, issues in a robust nature, delighting in the hunt and the free coursing over hill and plain, and finding in the stern country a meet nurse for a poetic child. But the conditions of life which developed an inherited power are none the less interesting to observe. His mother could not nurse him, and his first nurse had consumption. One after another of the little family of which he was a member had died in the close air of the wynd, and Walter was snatched from a like end by the wisdom of his father, who moved his household to a meadow district sloping to the south from the old town; but when he was eighteen months old a childish fever cost the boy the full use of his right leg, and all his life long he limped, — a sorry privation to so outdoor a nature; yet as the loss or disability of a member seems to have the effect on resolute persons of making them do the very things for which these members, one would say, were indispensable, making that armless men paint and blind men watch bees, so Scott became mountain climber and bold dragoon.

The enfeeblement which came led Dr. Rutherford, his mother's father, to send the child to his other grandfather's farm at Sandy-Knowe, and there, with some intervals, he lived as a shepherd's child might live for five years, from 1774 to 1779; from three years old, that is, till eight. Here he came into the hands of the housekeeper, old Alison Wilson, whom he has immortalized, even to the name, in his tale of *Old Mortality*. His grandfather, meanwhile, the rugged cattle-dealer, took him in hand with a treatment which brought the little fellow into very close contact with nature. 'Among the odd remedies recurred to to aid my lameness,' says Scott in his autobiography, 'some one had recommended that so often as a sheep was killed for the use of the family, I should be stripped, and swathed up in the skin, warm as it was flayed from the carcase of the animal. In this Tartar-like habiliment I well remember lying upon the floor of the little parlor in the farm-house, while my grandfather, a venerable old man with white hair, used every excitement to make me try to crawl.' Whatever may have been the virtue in this contagion, there can be no hesitation in applauding the brave treatment which later was employed. When he was in his fourth year and it was thought best to try the waters of Bath, Walter had begun to show the results of his life at Sandy-Knowe. 'My health,' he says, 'was by this time a good deal confirmed by the country air, and the influence of that imperceptible and unfatiguing exercise to which the good sense of my grandfather had subjected me ; for when the day was fine, I was usually carried out and laid down beside the old shepherd, among the crags or rocks round which he fed his sheep. The impatience of a child soon inclined me to struggle with my infirmity, and I began by degrees to stand, to walk, and to run. Although the limb affected was much shrunk and contracted, my general health, which was of more importance, was much strengthened by being frequently in the open air, and, in a word, I, who in a city had probably been condemned to hopeless and helpless decrepitude, was now a healthy, high-spirited, and, my lameness apart, a sturdy child.' In another place he says that 'he delighted to roll about in the grass all day long in the midst of the flock, and the sort of fellowship he formed with the sheep and lambs impressed his mind with a degree of affectionate feeling towards them which lasted through life.'

The year he spent at Bath left little impression on his mind, save an experience at the theatre when he saw *As You Like It*, and was so scandalized at the quarrel between Orlando and his brother in the first scene that he screamed, out ' Ain't they brothers ? ' so sheltered had his little life been thus far from anything which savored of strife in the household. He had a little schooling at Bath, where he was under the watch and ward of his aunt Janet Scott, but at Sandy-Knowe both before his excursion and after his return for three years more, he had a more natural and vital introduction to literature in the tales which he heard from his grandmother, whose own recollections went back to the days of Border raids. Thus he came, in the course of nature, as it were, into possession of an inexhaustible treasury from which later he drew forth things new and old.

The years at Sandy-Knowe were the years of conscious awakening to life, and the early impressions made on his mind were so indelible, that when he first began to put pen to paper it was from the scenes he then had known that the images arose. From these scenes sprang the 'Eve of St. John' and *Marmion ;* near at hand was Dryburgh; the Tweed, which flows through his song like an enchanted stream, flowed with an embracing sweep about Melrose; and the Eildon Hills, the Cheviot range, and the wilderness of Lammermoor all mingled with his childish memories and fancies.

As one reads on in Scott's Autobiography, and in the records and letters which supplement it, the experiences begin to call up scenes in the novels and even familiar names offer themselves. Thus, when in his eighth year he abode for a while with his aunt at Prestonpans, to get the benefit of sea-bathing, he formed a youthful intimacy with an old military veteran, Dalgetty by name, ' who had pitched his tent in that little village, after all his campaigns, subsisting upon an ensign's half-pay, though called by courtesy a Captain. As this old gentleman, who had been in all the German wars, found very few to listen to his tales of military feats, he formed a sort of alliance with me, and I used invariably to attend him for the pleasure of hearing those communications.' At Prestonpans, too, he fell in with George Constable, an old friend of his father, and portrayed him afterward so vividly, while unconscious of it, in the character of Jonathan Oldbuck in *The Antiquary* as to fix suspicion on himself as the author of the book.

But now, thanks to the generous course of nature-treatment, he was ready for schooling, and a Scottish boy would be a strange lad, indeed, if he were not given over into the hands of the schoolmaster at a tender age; the schoolmaster himself ranking in the social scale with the minister and the doctor. Thanks too to his mother and his aunt Janet, he began his school life with his head well stocked with stories of the real happenings in his own country, and with a portrait gallery of stalwart figures of history and poetry. The boy lived at home in his father's house in Edinburgh, and went to the High School for five years, from 1778 to 1783. Here he learned Latin and tried his own skill at making versified translations of Virgil and Horace, and here he made friendships that lasted through his life. He had, besides, a tutor at home, and he went, as the custom was, to a separate school for writing and arithmetic. At this school young girls also went, and one of them later in life set down in this wise her remembrance of her schoolfellow : —

' He attracted the regard and fondness of all his companions, for he was ever rational, fanciful, lively, and possessed of that urbane gentleness of manner which makes its way to the heart. His imagination was constantly at work, and he often so engrossed the attention of those who learnt with him that little could be done — Mr. Morton himself being forced to laugh as much as the little scholars at the odd turns and devices he fell upon ; for he did nothing in the ordinary way, but for example, even when he wanted ink to his pen, would get up some ludicrous story about sending his doggie to the mill again. He used also to interest us in a more serious way, by telling us the *visions*, as he called them, which he had lying alone on the floor or sofa, when kept from going to church on a Sunday by ill health. Child as I was, I could not help being highly delighted with his description of the glories he had seen — his misty and sublime sketches of the regions above, which he had visited in his trance. Recollecting these descriptions, radiant and not gloomy as they were, I have often thought since that there must have been a bias in his mind to superstition — the marvellous seemed to have such power over him, though the mere offspring of his own imagination, that the expression of his face, habitually that of genuine benevolence, mingled with a shrewd innocent humor, changed greatly while he was speaking of these things, and showed a deep intenseness of feeling, as if he were awed even by his own recital. . . . I may add, that in walking he used always to keep his eyes turned downwards as if thinking, but with a pleasing expression of countenance, as if enjoying his thoughts. Having once known him, it was impossible ever to forget him.'

But familiar as was the boy's intercourse with companions of his own age, Scott himself plainly lays great emphasis on the affectionate relation he held with his elders. After his studies at the High School and before he entered college, he lived for a while, and afterward frequently visited, with his aunt Janet at Kelso. Here he kept up some schooling with the village schoolmaster, who appears to have been the original of Dominie Sampson, but he also read voraciously in Spenser and Shakespeare, in the older novelists, and here he made the acquaintance of Percy's *Reliques of Ancient Poetry*. 'I remember well,' he records in later life, 'the spot where I read these volumes for the first time. It was beneath a huge platanus-tree, in the ruins of what had been intended for an old-fashioned arbor in the garden. The summer-day sped onward so fast, that notwithstanding the sharp appetite of thirteen, I forgot the hour of dinner, was sought for with anxiety, and was found still entranced in my intellectual banquet. To read and to remember was in this instance the same thing, and henceforth I overwhelmed my school-fellows and all who would hearken to me with tragical recitations from the ballads of Bishop Percy.' Among these school-fellows was James Ballantyne, so closely identified with his later fortunes. 'He soon discovered,' says Ballantyne in a reminiscence, 'that I was as fond of listening as he himself was of relating ; and I remembered it was a thing of daily occurrence, that after he had made himself master of his own lesson, I, alas ! being still sadly to seek in mine, he used to whisper to me : "come, slink over beside me, Jamie, and I'll tell you a story."' And stories in abundance he afterward told to the listening Jamie.

If at Sandy-Knowe nature had stolen into his mind, as well as sent her healing messages into his body, at Kelso he entered upon that hearty, enthusiastic love of natural beauty, and especially of the mingling of man's deeds with nature's elements, which glows through his poems and his novels. 'The meeting,' there, he says, 'of two superb rivers, the Tweed and the Teviot, both renowned in song — the ruins of an ancient Abbey — the more distant vestiges of Roxburgh Castle — the modern mansion of Fleurs, which is so situated as to combine the ideas of ancient baronial grandeur with those of modern taste — are in themselves objects of the first class ; yet are so mixed, united, and melted among a thousand other beauties of a less prominent description, that they harmonize into one general picture, and please rather by unison than by concord. I believe I have written unintelligibly upon this subject, but it is fitter for the pencil than the pen. The romantic feelings which I have described as predominating in any mind, naturally rested upon and associated themselves with these grand features of the landscape around me ; and the historical incidents, or traditional legends connected with many of them, gave to my admiration a sort of intense impression of reverence, which at times made my heart feel too big for its bosom. From this time the love of natural beauty, more especially when combined with ancient ruins, or remains of our fathers' piety or splendor, became with me an insatiable passion, which if circumstances had permitted, I would willingly have gratified by travelling over half the globe.'

In 1783, when he was twelve years old, he entered college at Edinburgh, after the manner of Scottish boys, and had three years of college life, such as it was, for he let Greek sink out of knowledge, kept up a smattering only of Latin, heard a little philosophy under Dugald Stewart, and attended a class in history. His health was not confirmed, and he had recourse more than once to the healing of Kelso, and by the time he was fifteen and had done with college, he was poorly enough equipped with learning. But the flame of poetry and romance which had been kindled burned steadily within him and was fed with large draughts from literature, with delightfully free renderings amongst his chosen friends, and with now and then little exercises with his pen. It is, however, noticeable throughout the formative period of Scott's life, how little he was affected with the *cacoethes scribendi*. He had the healthier appetite which is appeased though never satiated with literature, and the natural gift which finds expression in improvised story-telling, or the free recital of what one has read. A friend recalling the delightful Saturday excursions to Salisbury Crags, Arthur's Seat, or Blackford Hill, when they carried books from the circulating library to read on the rocks in the intervals of hardy climbing, adds : 'After we had continued this practice of reading for two years or more together, he proposed that we should recite to each other alternately such adventures of knight-errants as we could ourselves contrive ; and we continued to do so a long while. He found no difficulty in it, and used to recite for half an hour or more at a time, while I seldom continued half that space. The stories we told were, as Sir Walter has said, interminable — for we were unwilling to have any of our favorite knights killed. Our passion for romance led us to learn Italian together ; after a time we could both read it with fluency, and we then copied such tales as we had met with in that language, being a continued succession of battles and enchantments. He began early to collect old ballads, and as my mother could repeat a great many, he used to come and learn those she could recite to him. He used to get all the copies of these ballads he could, and select the best.' Scott himself, never given to subjective analysis, repeatedly stood off and looked at himself, boy and man, to sketch the figure in some of one of his characters, and thus he has portrayed with great accuracy in the person of Waverley the course of voluntary study which he had followed up to this time.

'He had read, and stored in a memory of uncommon tenacity, much curious, though ill-arranged and miscellaneous information. In English literature he was master of Shakespeare and Milton, of our earlier dramatic authors, of many picturesque and interesting passages from our old historical chronicles, and was particularly well acquainted with Spenser, Drayton, and other poets, who have exercised themselves on romantic fiction, — of all themes the most fascinating to a youthful imagination, before the passions have roused themselves, and demand poetry of a more sentimental description.'

In 1786 Scott was apprenticed to his father, and for five years he served his time; five more years were spent in the scanty practice of the law, before the first volume appeared of that long row which, compress it as we may, must always take up a great deal of shelf-room with the complete writings of Sir Walter Scott. These ten years witnessed the strengthening of a nature which, with all the early promise to be traced in the outlines we have drawn, had nothing in it of the forced ripening of a stimulated brain. Scott was twenty-five years old when he printed the thin volume of translations from the German; he was over thirty when he edited the *Border Minstrelsy* with the first essays into his own field of romantic verse, and he had entered upon the second of man's generations before he wrote *The Lay of the Last Minstrel*. There is nothing of the prodigy in this. Scott's industry was great. His productiveness was notable, especially when one takes into account the great body of letters and journal-writing, and remembers how popular he was in society; but before he entered on his career as an author, he was simply a full-blooded young Scotsman, delighting in excursions, with a capacious memory in which he stored and assimilated the records in prose and verse of Scottish achievements, an omnivorous reader, and a hearty companion. He was not even regarded as a leading figure in the literary society affected by the ingenious youth of Edinburgh. His essays in literature were not very effective. As he himself humorously puts it, ' I never attempted them unless compelled to do so by the regulations of the society, and then I was like the Lord of Castle Rackrent, who was obliged to cut down a tree to get a few fagots to boil the kettle; for the quantity of ponderous and miscellaneous knowledge which I really possessed on many subjects was not easily condensed, or brought to bear upon the object I wished particularly to become master of. Yet there occurred opportunities when this odd lumber of my brain, especially that which was connected with the recondite parts of history, did me, as Hamlet says, " yeoman's service." My memory of events was like one of the large, old-fashioned stone-cannons of the Turks, — very difficult to load well and discharge, but making a powerful effect when by good chance any object did come within range of its shot.'

It was at the beginning of this period that Scott caught a glimpse of that other great Scotsman, Burns, with whom, though he did not know it, he was to share the bench which Scotland owns on the slope of Parnassus. Quite as notable was the acquaintance which he first made about the same time with the Highlands. Though business for his father took him into this region, his delight in the scenery and the people took precedence of his occupation with affairs, and long after he had forgotten the trivial errands in the interest of the law, he remembered the tales he had heard, and his imagination built upon his experience those characters and scenes which live in the lines of *The Lady of the Lake* and in the pages of *Rob Roy*.

The record of Scott's life during the ten years of his legal training and early practice is delightfully varied with narratives of these excursions. The ardor of the young Scotsman carried him into the midst of scenes which were to prove the unfailing quarry from which he was to draw the material for his work of romance and fiction; and when one looks back upon his years of adolescence from the vantage ground of a full knowledge of his career, it would seem as if never did a writer qualify himself for his work of creation in so thorough and direct a fashion. Yet happily this preparation was unpremeditated and unconscious, for the naturalness which is the supreme characteristic of Sir Walter's verse and prose was due to the integrity and simplicity of his nature expending itself during these years of preparation upon occupations and interests which were ends in themselves. His healthy spirit found outlet in this hearty enjoyment of nature and history and human life, with apparently no thought of what use he should put his acquisitions to; it was enough for the time that he should share his enjoyment with his cherished friends, or at the most shape his knowledge into some amateur essay for his literary club.

In the midst of this active, wholesome life he entered upon an experience which made a deep furrow in his soul. It is witness to the sincerity of his first real passion — we may pass over the youthful excitement which gave him a constancy of affection for a girl when he was in his twentieth year — that it should have found expression in the earliest of his own poems, ' The Violet,' have risen into view more than once in direct and indirect reference in poems and novels, and even late in life should have called out a deep note of yearning regret in his journal. The tale of his disappointment in love has been spread before the world recently with sufficient detail in Mr. Adam Scott's book [1] and in Miss Skene's magazine article. As we have intimated, it was an experience of no idle sort, but the outcome is another tribute, if one were needed, to the

---

[1] *The Story of Sir Walter Scott's First Love, with illustrative passages from his Life and Works,* and portraits of Sir Walter and Lady Scott, and of Sir William and Lady Forbes. By Adam Scott. Edinburgh : Macniven & Wallace, 1896.

wholesomeness and freedom from morbid self-love which make Scott in these latter days so eminently the friend in literature of the young and whole hearted. It is a comment on the absence of bitterness in his nature that he did not disengage himself from his kind, but threw himself into the affairs of the hour and organized the Edinburgh Light-horse, of which he became quartermaster, writing a spirited war song, and using his pen thus as an instrument of service, before he was regarded as a man of the pen at all.

There is something very consonant with our largest knowledge of Scott's temper in the incidents which led up to his marriage. The story in its beginning shall be told by Lockhart : ' Riding one day with Fergusson, they met, some miles from Gilsland, a young lady taking the air on horseback, whom neither of them had previously remarked, and whose appearance instantly struck both so much, that they kept her in view until they had satisfied themselves that she also was one of the party at Gilsland [the watering-place where they had halted]. The same evening there was a ball, at which Captain [John] Scott produced himself in his regimentals, and Fergusson also thought proper to be equipped in the uniform of the Edinburgh Volunteers. There was no little rivalry among the young travellers as to who should first get presented to the unknown beauty of the morning's ride; but though both the gentlemen in scarlet had the advantage of being dancing partners, their friend succeeded in handing the fair stranger to supper — and such was his first introduction to Charlotte Margaret Carpenter.

' Without the features of a regular beauty, she was rich in personal attractions ; "a form that was fashioned as light as a fay's ; " a complexion of the clearest and lightest olive ; eyes large, deep-set and dazzling, of the finest Italian brown ; and a profusion of silken tresses, black as the raven's wing ; her address hovering between the reserve of a pretty young English woman who has not mingled largely in general society, and a certain natural archness and gaiety that suited well with the accompaniment of a French accent. A lovelier vision, as all who remember her in the bloom of her days have assured me, could hardly have been imagined ; and from that hour the fate of the young poet was fixed.' The lady was a daughter of a French royalist who had died at the beginning of the revolution, but who had foreseen the approaching perils and had secured a moderate sum in English securities, so that his widow and her family at once fled across the channel and made their home in London. Miss Carpenter at the time was making a summer tour under the direction of a Scotswoman who had been her governess.

Here was a young fellow just emerging from a bitter disappointment, who falls head over ears in love with a saucy, piquant girl whose letters, after the acquaintance had ripened swiftly into passion, disclose a capricious, teasing nature. Scott could write to his mother and to Lord Downshire, who was a sort of guardian of Miss Carpenter, in a reasonable manner, but it is clear from his impetuous love-making and the eagerness he showed to bring matters to a head, that he was swept away by his zeal and impatient of all obstacles. It is just possible that in all this there was something of a reaction from the hurt he had suffered, and that Miss Carpenter's winsomeness and little imperious ways blinded him to all considerations of a prudent sort. He was ready at one time to throw aside all other considerations and take his bride to one of the colonies, there to win a place by the sheer force of energy in a new land. But his impetuousness shows the gay spirit with which he threw himself into all his enterprises, and the ardor with which he pursued an end which he thought he must attain. He removed one difficulty after another, and the sudden encounter in July was followed by marriage on the eve of Christmas, 1797. Lady Scott bore Sir Walter four children, who lived and grew to maturity, two sons and two daughters. It is not easy to escape the impression that though she was lively and volatile, there was a certain lack of profound sympathy between husband and wife ; that with all her love of society, Lady Scott was not able to bring to her husband the kind of appreciation of his genius which he found in such friends as Lady Louisa Stuart, the Duchess of Buccleuch, and the Marchioness of Abercorn. But it would be a mistake to infer that there was any lack of loyalty and tenderness on the part of either ; and when Scott, broken in his fortunes, is obliged also to see his wife pass out of his life, the pathos of his utterance shows how intimately their interests had been blended. Yet Scott's own frank expression of the relation between them (see below, p. 152) must stand as indicating the limitations of their union.

The young couple at first set up their home in Edinburgh not far from the residence of Scott's mother and father, who were now feeble and soon to leave them. Scott was shortly appointed sheriff of Selkirk, an office which carried no very heavy duties and a moderate salary. With this and such other property as he and his wife enjoyed, they were able to live modestly and cheerfully, and Scott let slip the practice of his profession, never very congenial to him, and turned with zest to the semi-literary occupations which had begun to engross his attention.

For shortly before his marriage he had made a little venture in the field of books by publishing his translation of a couple of German ballads that were then highly popular, and not a great while after his marriage, he made a similar effort in the same direction by translating Goethe's drama of *Goetz von Berlichengen ;* but his more zealous pursuit was in the collection of Scottish ballads, and by a natural sequence in patching these where they were broken, and by making very good imitations. Thus, stimulated also by a group of similar collectors, he published in 1802 and 1803 the three volumes of *Minstrelsy of the Scottish Border,* and by the most natural transition took up a theme suggested by his ballad studies and wrought with great celerity *The Lay of the Last Minstrel.*

The Introductory Note to that poem, including as it does Scott's own Introduction, describes in some detail the origin of the poem and the motives which led Scott to undertake it. With the frankness always characteristic of him in his addresses to the public and his letters to his friends, he spoke as if he was moved chiefly by the need to better his circumstances, and the same confession is very openly made in connection with the writing of *Rokeby,* when he was full of the notion of realizing his dreams in the establishment of Abbotsford. But it is given to us with our large knowledge of Scott's career to place motives in a more just relation ; and though it is entirely true that Scott wanted money and found his want an incentive to the writing of poems and novels, it is equally true that the whole course of his life up to the time of writing *The Lay of the Last Minstrel* was a direct preparation for this form of expression, and that his generous enthusiasm and warm imagination found this outlet with a simplicity and directness which explain how truly this writer, though a deliberate maker of books, had yet always that delightful quality which we recognize most surely in the improvisatore. It was his nature to write just such poetry as the free, swinging lines of his long poems.

Before the *Lay* was completed and published, Scott moved with his little family to Ashestiel, a country farm seven miles from the small town of Selkirk, and having a beautiful setting on the Tweedside with green hills all about. Here he lived as a tenant of the Buccleuch estate for seven of the happiest years of his life. It was here that he wrote the poems preceding *Rokeby* and here that he began the *Waverley,* and tossed the fragment aside. His income, which, at the beginning of his poetical career, was from all sources about £1000 a year, enabled him to live at ease, and the successive productions greatly augmented his property. Mr. Morritt, one of his closest friends, visited him at

Ashestiel in 1808, and an extract from a memorandum which he gave Lockhart gives a most agreeable picture of the poet in his home.

'There he was the cherished friend and kind neighbor of every middling Selkirkshire yeoman, just as easily as in Edinburgh he was the companion of clever youth and narrative old age in refined society. He carried us one day to Melrose Abbey or Newark; another, to course with mountain greyhounds by Yarrow braes or St. Mary's loch, repeating every ballad or legendary tale connected with the scenery; and on a third, we must all go to a farmer's *kirn*, or harvest home, to dance with Border lasses on a barn floor, drink whiskey punch, and enter with him into all the gossip and good fellowship of his neighbors, on a complete footing of unrestrained conviviality, equality, and mutual respect. His wife and happy young family were clustered round him, and the cordiality of his reception would have unbent a misanthrope. At this period his conversation was more equal and animated than any man's that I ever knew. It was most characterized by the extreme felicity and fun of his illustrations, drawn from the whole encyclopædia of life and nature, in a style somewhat too exuberant for written narrative, but which to him was natural and spontaneous. A hundred stories, always apposite and often interesting the mind by strong pathos, or eminently ludicrous, were daily told, which, with many more, have since been transplanted, almost in the same language, into the Waverley Novels and his other writings. These and his recitations of poetry, which can never be forgotten by those who knew him, made up the charm that his boundless memory enabled him to exert to the wonder of the gaping lover of wonders. But equally impressive and powerful was the language of his warm heart, and equally wonderful were the conclusions of his vigorous understanding, to those who could return or appreciate either. Among a number of such recollections, I have seen many of the thoughts which then passed through his mind embodied in the delightful prefaces annexed late in life to his poetry and novels.'

Shortly after the publication of *The Lay of the Last Minstrel*, and when he was pleasantly established at Ashestiel, James Ballantyne, who had already been helped by Scott with a loan, applied to his old school friend and the now successful author for further aid in his business. Scott took the opportunity to make an investment in Ballantyne's printing business. He became a silent partner with a third interest. It seemed a most reasonable move. He had practically retired from the bar, though he was making an effort to secure a salaried position as a clerk of the court. He had a fair income, but his real capital he perceived was in his fertile brain, and by allying himself with a printing-office he would be in a position to get far more than an author's ordinary share in the productions of his pen. There was not the same wide gulf in Edinburgh between trade and profession which existed in London; and though Scott, with the natural pride of an author, did not make public his connection with Ballantyne, he was doubtless led to keep his engagement private quite as much by the advantage which privacy gave him in the influence he could use to turn business into Ballantyne's hands. It is possible that if the Ballantynes had been better business men and cooler headed, — for James Ballantyne's brother John shortly set up as a publisher, and after that the affairs of author, printer, and publisher became inextricably interdependent, — the venture might not have turned out ill, but all the men engaged were of a speculative turn of mind, and Scott's marvellous fecundity and versatility seemed to promise an inexhaustible spring from which the currents of manufacture and trade would flow clearly and steadily. All sorts of enterprises were projected and carried out, beyond and beside Scott's creative work. Editions of standard works, magazines, collections of poetry, rushed forth, and capital was shortly locked up, so that an early bankruptcy would have been inevitable, except for the sudden discovery of a new source of wealth. This lay in the invention of the Waverley Novels, at first anonymous, which swept the reading world like a freshet swelling into a flood and seeming for a while to be almost a new force in nature. The Waverley Novels for a while saved this mad combination of author, printer, and publisher from going to pieces, and there might possibly have been no catastrophe had not a new element come into action.

Scott, when he formed the partnership with James Ballantyne, took the money which he contributed from a fund with which he had intended buying Broadmeadows, a small estate on the northern bank of the Yarrow. He abandoned at the time this design, but the strong passion which could not fail to possess a man with Scott's deep love of the soil, and his imagination ever busy with historic traditions, still held him; and when the opportunity came, with the rising tide of his own fortunes, to buy a farm a few miles from Ashestiel, he seized it with alacrity. Nor was his venture an unwise one. He was tenant at will at Ashestiel, and had the natural desire of a man with a growing family to establish himself in a permanent home. 'The farm,' says Lockhart, 'consisted of a rich meadow or haugh along the banks of the river, and about a hundred acres of undulated ground behind, all in a neglected state, undrained, wretchedly enclosed, much of it covered with nothing better than the native heath. The farm-house itself was small and poor, with a common kail-yard on one flank, and a staring barn on the other, while in front appeared a filthy pond covered with ducks and duckweed, from which the whole tenement had derived the unharmonious designation of *Clarty Hole.* But the Tweed was everything to him — a beautiful river, flowing broad and bright over a bed of milk-white pebbles, unless here and there where it darkened into a deep pool, overhung as yet only by the birches and alders which had survived the statelier growth of the primitive forest; and the first hour that he took possession he claimed for his farm the name of the adjoining *ford,* situated just above the influx of the classical tributary Gala. As might be guessed from the name of Abbotsford, these lands had all belonged of old to the great Abbey of Melrose.'

Abbotsford was in the heart of a country already dear to Scott by reason of its teeming historic memories, and here he began and continued through his working days to enrich a creation which was the embodiment in stone and wood and forest and field of the imagination which at the same time was finding vent in poem and novel and history and essay. The characteristics of the estate which he thus formed were the characteristics of his work as an author also. There is the free nature, the trees planted with a fine sense of landscape effect; there is the reproduction in miniature of the life of a bygone age, and there is the suggestion of the stage with its pasteboard properties, its structures all front, and its men and women acting a part.

Ruskin has said with penetrating criticism: ' Scott's work is always epic, and it is contrary to his very nature to treat any subject dramatically.' In explication of this dictum, Ruskin defines dramatic poetry as ' the expression by the poet of other people's feelings, his own not being told,' and epic poetry as an ' account given by the poet of other people's external circumstances, and of events happening to them, with only such expression either of their feelings, or his own, as he thinks may be conveniently added.' We must not confound the dramatic with the theatrical. To Scott, who never wrote a successful play, his figures were nevertheless quite distinctly theatrical. That is to say, he placed them before his readers not only vividly, but with the make-up which would bring into conspicuous light rather the outward show than the inward reality. Not that his persons had not clearly conceived characters, and not that he merely missed the modern analytic presentation, but his persons interested him chiefly by their doing things, and these things were the incidents and accidents of life rather than the inevitable consequences of their nature, the irresistible effects of causes lying deep in their constitution. Hence the delight which he takes in battle and adventure of all sorts, and the emphasis which he lays upon the common, elemental qualities of human nature, male and female, rather than upon the individual and eccentric. There is no destiny in his poems or novels, no inevitable drawing to a climax of forces which are moving beyond the power of restraint which the author may in his own mind exercise.

It is not to be wondered at that Scott, breathing the fresh air of the ballads of the border, should make his first leap into the saddle of verse and ride heartily down his short, bounding lines. It is quite as natural that, as his material grew more and more historical in its character, and greater complexities crept in, he should find the narrative of verse too simple, and should resort to the greater range and diversity of prose ; and that once having found his power in novel writing, he should have abandoned poetry as a vehicle for epic narrative, contenting himself thenceforth with lyric snatches, and with brief flights of verse. Moreover, in poetry, though he had a delighted audience, and never has failed since to draw a large following entirely satisfied with his form, he shared at the time the throne with that mightier, more dramatic artist, Byron, and knew also that men were beginning to turn their eyes toward Wordsworth and Coleridge. But in fiction he held quite undisputed sway. The fashion in fiction changes perhaps more quickly than in poetry ; its representation of the manner of the day, even when it is consciously antiquarian and historic, renders it largely dependent on contemporaneous interest. In Scott's day, Fielding, Smollett, and Richardson were read more because they had not been supplanted than because they appealed strongly to the reader of the time. A more genuine attention was given to Miss Edgeworth, Miss Ferrier, Mackenzie and Galt. But these became at once minor writers when Scott took the field, and he called into existence a great multitude of readers of fiction, establishing thereby a habit of novel reading which was of the greatest service to the later novelists, like Dickens and Thackeray, when they came in with newer appeal to the changing taste of a newer generation.

To all these considerations must be added the incessant demands made upon Scott's brain by the need of keeping on its base the commercial house of cards which he had helped to build and in which he was living, and of carrying farther and farther into reality the dream of a baronial estate which was Rokeby done in plaster. Thus the years went by, full of active occupation, with brilliant pageant indeed, and with social excitement. It is a pleasure, in the midst of it all, to see the real Scott, Sir Walter to the world of display but the genuine master to Tom Purdie and Will Laidlaw, to note the wholesome pride of the firm-footed treader on his own acres, the generous care of others, the absence of cant, religious or social. And when the supreme test came, the test of overwhelming misfortune, the genuineness of this great nature was made plain in the high courage with which he set about the task of paying his creditors, in the toil of year after year, and in those moving passages in his diary when he sat in his loneliness and looked fortune in the face. Listen to the entry in his diary under date December 18, 1825.

" Ballantyne called on me this morning. *Venit illa suprema dies.* My extremity is come. Cadell has received letters from London which all but positively announce the failure of Hurst and Robinson, so that Constable & Co. must follow, and I must go with poor James Ballantyne for company. I suppose it will involve my all. But if they leave me £500, I can still make it £1000 or £1200 a year. And if they take my salaries of £1300 and £300, they cannot but give me something out of them. I have been rash in anticipating funds to buy land, but then I made from £5000 to £10,000 a year, and land was my temptation. I think nobody can lose a penny — that is one comfort. Men will think pride has had a fall. Let them indulge their own pride in thinking that my fall makes them higher, or seems so at least. I have the satisfaction to recollect that my prosperity has been of advantage to many, and that some at least will forgive my transient wealth on account of the innocence of my intentions, and my real wish to do good to the poor. The news will make sad hearts at Darwick, and in the cottages at Abbotsford, which I do not nourish the least hope of preserving. It has been my Delilah, and so I have often termed it ; and now the recollection of the extensive woods I planted, and the walks I have formed, from which strangers must derive both the pleasure and the profit, will excite feelings likely to sober my gayest moments. I have half resolved never to see the place again. How could I tread my hall with such a diminished crest ? How live a poor indebted man where I was once the wealthy, the honored ? My children are provided ; thank God for that. I was to have gone there on Saturday in joy and prosperity to receive my friends. My dogs will wait for me in vain. It is foolish — but the thoughts of parting from these dumb creatures have moved me more than any of the painful reflections I have put down. Poor things, I must get them kind masters ; there may be yet those who loving me may love my dog because it has been mine. I must end this, or I shall lose the tone of mind with which men should meet distress.

' I find my dogs' feet on my knees. I hear them whining and seeking me everywhere — this is nonsense, but it is what they would do could they know how things are. Poor Will Laidlaw ! poor Tom Purdie ! this will be news to wring your heart, and many a poor fellow's besides to whom my prosperity was daily bread. . . . For myself the magic wand of the Unknown is shivered in his grasp. He must henceforth be termed the Too-well-known. The feast of fancy is over with the feeling of independence. I can no longer have the delight of waking in the morning with bright ideas in my mind, haste to commit them to paper, and count them monthly, as the means of planting such groves, and purchasing such wastes ; replacing my dreams of fiction by other prospective visions of walks by —

" Fountain heads, and pathless groves,
Places which pale passion loves."

This cannot be ; but I may work substantial husbandry, work history, and such concerns. They will not be received with the same enthusiasm. . . . To save Abbotsford I would attempt all that was possible. My heart clings to the place I have created. There is scarce a tree on it that does not owe its being to me, and the pain of leaving it is greater than I can tell.'

Here we close our study of Scott's career. Thenceforth his energy was devoted to a painful clearing away of the ruins of his fortune. With patience and with many gleams of his sunny temperament, he labored on. In the end the debts were settled, Abbotsford was saved to his family, and there on the 21st of September, 1832, Scott died. ' It was a beautiful day,' says Lockhart, ' so warm, that every window was wide open — and so perfectly still, that the sound of all others most delicious to his ear, the gentle ripple of the Tweed over its pebbles, was distinctly audible as we knelt around the bed, and his eldest son kissed and closed his eyes.'

H. E. S.

Green waved the laurel in each plume,
  The badge of victory.

And old and young, and sire and son,
  To meet them crowd the way,
With shouts and mirth and melody,
  The debt of love to pay.   20

Full many a maid her true-love met,
  And sobbed in his embrace,
And fluttering joy in tears and smiles
  Arrayed full many a face.

Nor joy nor smile for Helen sad,
  She sought the host in vain ;
For none could tell her William's fate,
  If faithless or if slain.

The martial band is past and gone ;
  She rends her raven hair,   30
And in distraction's bitter mood
  She weeps with wild despair.

' O, rise, my child,' her mother said,
  ' Nor sorrow thus in vain ;
A perjured lover's fleeting heart
  No tears recall again.'

' O mother, what is gone is gone,
  What 's lost forever lorn :
Death, death alone can comfort me ;
  O had I ne'er been born !   40

' O, break, my heart, O, break at once !
  Drink my life-blood, Despair !
No joy remains on earth for me,
  For me in heaven no share.'

' O, enter not in judgment, Lord !'
  The pious mother prays ;
' Impute not guilt to thy frail child !
  She knows not what she says.

' O, say thy pater-noster, child !
  O, turn to God and grace !   50
His will, that turned thy bliss to bale,
  Can change thy bale to bliss.'

' O mother, mother, what is bliss ?
  O mother, what is bale ?
My William's love was heaven on earth,
  Without it earth is hell.

' Why should I pray to ruthless Heaven,
  Since my loved William 's slain ?

I only prayed for William's sake,
  And all my prayers were vain.'   6o

' O, take the sacrament, my child,
  And check these tears that flow ;
By resignation's humble prayer,
  O, hallowed be thy woe !'

' No sacrament can quench this fire,
  Or slake this scorching pain ;
No sacrament can bid the dead
  Arise and live again.

' O, break, my heart, O, break at once !
  Be thou my god, Despair !   7o
Heaven's heaviest blow has fallen on me,
  And vain each fruitless prayer.'

' O, enter not in judgment, Lord,
  With thy frail child of clay !
She knows not what her tongue has spoke ;
  Impute it not, I pray !

' Forbear, my child, this desperate woe,
  And turn to God and grace ;
Well can devotion's heavenly glow
  Convert thy bale to bliss.'   8o

' O mother, mother, what is bliss ?
  O mother, what is bale ?
Without my William what were heaven,
  Or with him what were hell ?'

Wild she arraigns the eternal doom,
  Upbraids each sacred power,
Till, spent, she sought her silent room,
  All in the lonely tower.

She beat her breast, she wrung her hands,
  Till sun and day were o'er,   9o
And through the glimmering lattice shone
  The twinkling of the star.

Then, crash ! the heavy drawbridge fell
  That o'er the moat was hung ;
And, clatter ! clatter ! on its boards
  The hoof of courser rung.

The clank of echoing steel was heard
  As off the rider bounded ;
And slowly on the winding stair
  A heavy footstep sounded.   100

And hark ! and hark ! a knock — tap ! tap !
  A rustling stifled noise ; —

Door-latch and tinkling staples ring ; —
At length a whispering voice.

'Awake, awake, arise, my love !
How, Helen, dost thou fare ?
Wak'st thou, or sleep'st ? laugh'st thou, or
    weep'st ?
Hast thought on me, my fair ? '

'My love ! my love ! — so late by night ! —
I waked, I wept for thee :   110
Much have I borne since dawn of morn ;
Where, William, couldst thou be ? '

'We saddle late — from Hungary
I rode since darkness fell ;
And to its bourne we both return
Before the matin-bell.'

'O, rest this night within my arms,
And warm thee in their fold !
Chill howls through hawthorn bush the
    wind : —
My love is deadly cold.'   120

'Let the wind howl through hawthorn bush !
This night we must away ;
The steed is wight, the spur is bright ;
I cannot stay till day.

'Busk, busk, and boune ! Thou mount'st
    behind
Upon my black barb steed :
O'er stock and stile, a hundred miles,
We haste to bridal bed.'

'To-night — to-night a hundred miles ! —
O dearest William, stay !   130
The bell strikes twelve — dark, dismal hour !
O, wait, my love, till day ! '

'Look here, look here — the moon shines
    clear —
Full fast I ween we ride ;
Mount and away ! for ere the day
We reach our bridal bed.

'The black barb snorts, the bridle rings ;
Haste, busk, and boune, and seat thee !
The feast is made, the chamber spread,
The bridal guests await thee.'   140

Strong love prevailed : she busks, she
    bounes,
She mounts the barb behind,

And round her darling William's waist
Her lily arms she twined.

And, hurry ! hurry ! off they rode,
As fast as fast might be ;
Spurned from the courser's thundering
    heels
The flashing pebbles flee.

And on the right and on the left,
Ere they could snatch a view,   150
Fast, fast each mountain, mead, and plain,
And cot and castle flew.

'Sit fast — dost fear ? — The moon shines
    clear —
Fleet goes my barb — keep hold !
Fear'st thou ? ' — 'O no !' she faintly
    said ;
'But why so stern and cold ?

'What yonder rings ? what yonder sings ?
Why shrieks the owlet gray ? '
''T is death-bells' clang, 't is funeral song,
The body to the clay.   160

'With song and clang at morrow's dawn
Ye may inter the dead :
To-night I ride with my young bride
To deck our bridal bed.

'Come with thy choir, thou coffined guest,
To swell our nuptial song !
Come, priest, to bless our marriage feast !
Come all, come all along ! '

Ceased clang and song ; down sunk the
    bier ;
The shrouded corpse arose :   170
And hurry ! hurry ! all the train
The thundering steed pursues.

And forward ! forward ! on they go ;
High snorts the straining steed ;
Thick pants the rider's laboring breath,
As headlong on they speed.

'O William, why this savage haste ?
And where thy bridal bed ? '
''T is distant far, low, damp, and chill,
And narrow, trustless maid.'   180

'No room for me ? ' — 'Enough for
    both ; —
Speed, speed, my barb, thy course ! '

O'er thundering bridge, through boiling
surge,
He drove the furious horse.

Tramp ! tramp ! along the land they rode,
Splash ! splash ! along the sea ;
The scourge is wight, the spur is bright,
The flashing pebbles flee.

Fled past on right and left how fast
Each forest, grove, and bower !   190
On right and left fled past how fast
Each city, town, and tower !

' Dost fear ? dost fear ? The moon shines
clear,
Dost fear to ride with me ? —
Hurrah ! hurrah ! the dead can ride !' —
' O William, let them be ! —

' See there, see there ! What yonder
swings
And creaks mid whistling rain ?' —
' Gibbet and steel, the accursed wheel ;
A murderer in his chain. —   200

' Hollo ! thou felon, follow here :
To bridal bed we ride ;
And thou shalt prance a fetter dance
Before me and my bride.'

And, hurry ! hurry ! clash, clash, clash !
The wasted form descends ;
And fleet as wind through hazel bush
The wild career attends.

Tramp ! tramp ! along the land they rode,
Splash ! splash ! along the sea ;   210
The scourge is red, the spur drops blood,
The flashing pebbles flee.

How fled what moonshine faintly showed !
How fled what darkness hid !
How fled the earth beneath their feet,
The heaven above their head !

' Dost fear ? dost fear ? The moon shines
clear,
And well the dead can ride ;
Dost faithful Helen fear for them ?' —
' O leave in peace the dead ?' —   220

' Barb ! Barb ! methinks I hear the cock ;
The sand will soon be run :

Barb ! Barb ! I smell the morning air ;
The race is well-nigh done.'

Tramp ! tramp ! along the land they
rode,
Splash ! splash ! along the sea ;
The scourge is red, the spur drops blood,
The flashing pebbles flee.

' Hurrah ! hurrah ! well ride the dead ;
The bride, the bride is come ;   230
And soon we reach the bridal bed,
For, Helen, here 's my home.'

Reluctant on its rusty hinge
Revolved an iron door,
And by the pale moon's setting beam
Were seen a church and tower.

With many a shriek and cry whiz round
The birds of midnight scared ;
And rustling like autumnal leaves
Unhallowed ghosts were heard.   240

O'er many a tomb and tombstone pale
He spurred the fiery horse,
Till sudden at an open grave
He checked the wondrous course.

The falling gauntlet quits the rein,
Down drops the casque of steel,
The cuirass leaves his shrinking side,
The spur his gory heel.

The eyes desert the naked skull,
The mouldering flesh the bone,   250
Till Helen's lily arms entwine
A ghastly skeleton.

The furious barb snorts fire and foam,
And with a fearful bound
Dissolves at once in empty air,
And leaves her on the ground.

Half seen by fits, by fits half heard,
Pale spectres flit along,
Wheel round the maid in dismal dance,
And howl the funeral song ;   260

' E'en when the heart 's with anguish
cleft
Revere the doom of Heaven,
Her soul is from her body reft ;
Her spirit be forgiven !'

THE WILD HUNTSMAN

THE Wildgrave winds his bugle-horn,
To horse, to horse ! halloo, halloo !
His fiery courser snuffs the morn,
And thronging serfs their lord pursue.

The eager pack from couples freed
Dash through the bush, the brier, the
brake ;
While answering hound and horn and steed
The mountain echoes startling wake.

The beams of God's own hallowed day
Had painted yonder spire with gold,   10
And, calling sinful man to pray,
Loud, long, and deep the bell had tolled ;

But still the Wildgrave onward rides ;
Halloo, halloo ! and, hark again !
When, spurring from opposing sides,
Two stranger horsemen join the train.

Who was each stranger, left and right,
Well may I guess, but dare not tell;
The right-hand steed was silver white,
The left the swarthy hue of hell.   20

The right-hand horseman, young and fair,
His smile was like the morn of May;
The left from eye of tawny glare
Shot midnight lightning's lurid ray.

He waved his huntsman's cap on high,
Cried, ' Welcome, welcome, noble lord !
What sport can earth, or sea, or sky,
To match the princely chase, afford ? '

' Cease thy loud bugle's changing knell,'
Cried the fair youth with silver voice;   30
' And for devotion's choral swell
Exchange the rude unhallowed noise.

' To-day the ill-omened chase forbear,
Yon bell yet summons to the fane ;
To-day the Warning Spirit hear,
To-morrow thou mayst mourn in vain.'

' Away, and sweep the glades along ! '
The sable hunter hoarse replies ;
' To muttering monks leave matin-song,
And bells and books and mysteries.'   40

The Wildgrave spurred his ardent steed,
And, launching forward with a bound,

' Who, for thy drowsy priestlike rede,
Would leave the jovial horn and hound ?

' Hence, if our manly sport offend !
With pious fools go chant and pray : —
Well hast thou spoke, my dark-browed
friend ;
Halloo, halloo ! and hark away ! '

The Wildgrave spurred his courser light,
O'er moss and moor, o'er holt and hill ;
And on the left and on the right,   51
Each stranger horseman followed still.

Up springs from yonder tangled thorn
A stag more white than mountain snow ;
And louder rung the Wildgrave's horn,
' Hark forward, forward ! holla, ho ! '

A heedless wretch has crossed the way ;
He gasps the thundering hoofs below ; —
But live who can, or die who may,
Still, ' Forward, forward!' on they go.   60

See, where yon simple fences meet,
A field with autumn's blessings crowned ;
See, prostrate at the Wildgrave's feet,
A husbandman with toil embrowned :

' O mercy, mercy, noble lord !
Spare the poor's pittance,' was his cry,
' Earned by the sweat these brows have
poured
In scorching hour of fierce July.'

Earnest the right-hand stranger pleads,
The left still cheering to the prey ;   70
The impetuous Earl no warning heeds,
But furious holds the onward way.

' Away, thou hound so basely born,
Or dread the scourge's echoing blow ! '
Then loudly rung his bugle-horn,
' Hark forward, forward ! holla, ho ! '

So said, so done : —A single bound
Clears the poor laborer's humble pale ;
Wild follows man and horse and hound,
Like dark December's stormy gale.   80

And man and horse, and hound and horn,
Destructive sweep the field along ;
While, joying o'er the wasted corn,
Fell Famine marks the maddening
throng.

Again uproused the timorous prey
  Scours moss and moor, and holt and hill ;
Hard run, he feels his strength decay,
  And trusts for life his simple skill.

Too dangerous solitude appeared ;
  He seeks the shelter of the crowd ;   90
Amid the flock's domestic herd
  His harmless head he hopes to shroud.

O'er moss and moor, and holt and hill,
  His track the steady blood-hounds trace ;
O'er moss and moor, unwearied still,
  The furious Earl pursues the chase.

Full lowly did the herdsman fall :
  'O spare, thou noble baron, spare
These herds, a widow's little all ;
  These flocks, an orphan's fleecy care !'   100

Earnest the right-hand stranger pleads,
  The left still cheering to the prey ;
The Earl nor prayer nor pity heeds,
  But furious keeps the onward way.

'Unmannered dog ! To stop my sport
  Vain were thy cant and beggar whine,
Though human spirits of thy sort
  Were tenants of these carrion kine !'

Again he winds his bugle-horn,
  'Hark forward, forward, holla, ho !'   110
And through the herd in ruthless scorn
  He cheers his furious hounds to go.

In heaps the throttled victims fall ;
  Down sinks their mangled herdsman
      near ;
The murderous cries the stag appall, —
  Again he starts, new-nerved by fear.

With blood besmeared and white with foam,
  While big the tears of anguish pour,
He seeks amid the forest's gloom
  The humble hermit's hallowed bower.   120

But man and horse, and horn and hound,
  Fast rattling on his traces go ;
The sacred chapel rung around
  With, 'Hark away ! and, holla, ho !

All mild, amid the rout profane,
  The holy hermit poured his prayer ;
'Forbear with blood God's house to stain ;
  Revere His altar and forbear !

'The meanest brute has rights to plead,
  Which, wronged by cruelty or pride,   130
Draw vengeance on the ruthless head : —
  Be warned at length and turn aside.'

Still the fair horseman anxious pleads ;
  The black, wild whooping, points the
      prey : —
Alas ! the Earl no warning heeds,
  But frantic keeps the forward way.

'Holy or not, or right or wrong,
  Thy altar and its rites I spurn ;
Not sainted martyrs' sacred song,
  Not God himself shall make me turn !'   140

He spurs his horse, he winds his horn,
  'Hark forward, forward, holla, ho !'
But off, on whirlwind's pinions borne,
  The stag, the hut, the hermit, go.

And horse and man, and horn and hound,
  And clamor of the chase, was gone ;
For hoofs and howls and bugle-sound,
  A deadly silence reigned alone.

Wild gazed the affrighted Earl around ;
  He strove in vain to wake his horn,   150
In vain to call ; for not a sound
  Could from his anxious lips be borne.

He listens for his trusty hounds,
  No distant baying reached his ears ;
His courser, rooted to the ground,
  The quickening spur unmindful bears.

Still dark and darker frown the shades,
  Dark as the darkness of the grave ;
And not a sound the still invades,
  Save what a distant torrent gave.   160

High o'er the sinner's humbled head
  At length the solemn silence broke ;
And from a cloud of swarthy red
  The awful voice of thunder spoke.

'Oppressor of creation fair !
  Apostate Spirits' hardened tool !
Scorner of God ! Scourge of the poor !
  The measure of thy cup is full.

'Be chased forever through the wood,
  Forever roam the affrighted wild ;   170
And let thy fate instruct the proud,
  God's meanest creature is His child.'

'T was hushed : — One flash of sombre
   glare
With yellow tinged the forests brown ;
Uprose the Wildgrave's bristling hair,
   And horror chilled each nerve and bone.

Cold poured the sweat in freezing rill ;
   A rising wind began to sing,
And louder, louder, louder still,   179
   Brought storm and tempest on its wing.

Earth heard the call ; — her entrails rend;
   From yawning rifts, with many a yell,
Mixed with sulphureous flames, ascend
   The misbegotten dogs of hell.

What ghastly huntsman next arose
   Well may I guess, but dare not tell ;
His eye like midnight lightning glows,
   His steed the swarthy hue of hell.

The Wildgrave flies o'er bush and thorn
   With many a shriek of helpless woe ; 190

Behind him hound and horse and horn,
   And, 'Hark away, and holla, ho !'

With wild despair's reverted eye,
   Close, close behind, he marks the throng,
With bloody fangs and eager cry ;
   In frantic fear he scours along. —

Still, still shall last the dreadful chase
   Till time itself shall have an end ;
By day they scour earth's caverned space,
   At midnight's witching hour ascend. 200

This is the horn and hound and horse
   That oft the lated peasant hears ;
Appalled he signs the frequent cross,
   When the wild din invades his ears.

The wakeful priest oft drops a tear
   For human pride, for human woe,
When at his midnight mass he hears
   The infernal cry of ' Holla, ho !'

EARLY BALLADS AND LYRICS

Scott followed his translations from Bürger
with other efforts in the same direction. The
first book, indeed, which bore his name, was a
prose rendering of Goethe's tragedy of *Goetz von
Berlichingen*, published in 1799, and he translated near the same time, but did not publish
till thirty years later, the *House of Aspen*, a free
adaptation of *Der Heilige Vehmé*, by a pseu-
donymous German author of the day. The Ger-
manic influence was curiously blended with an
antiquarian zeal which had an early birth and
now sent him eagerly abroad among Scottish
legends and half-mythical tales for subjects.
Moreover, he was drawn into the service of
Monk Lewis, who persuaded him to contribute
to his collection of *Tales of Wonder*, themselves touched with the prevailing temper of
eeriness imported freely from Germany.
But the most substantial result of his labors
in these experimental years was the publication in 1802 and 1803 of the three volumes of
Minstrelsy of The Scottish Border. Scott had
now become so enamored of the native legends,
so skilful as an imitator, and, much more, so
informed with the spirit of the old ballads,
that his own contributions harmonized with
the antiquities he had gathered, and these
showed in every line, as well as in the rich ap-
paratus of notes with which they were illustrated, a mastery of the ballad literature, and
a mind thoroughly at home in material which
was soon to be the quarry for the author and
editor's most noble edifices in verse.
The present group contains, in as nearly
exact chronological order as is practicable,
Scott's experiments and performances in original verse, with scattered translations and imitations, before he leaped into fame with *The
Lay of the Last Minstrel*.

THE VIOLET

These slight verses have an interest derived
from the fact that they were written by Scott
in 1797 in connection with that suppressed
passion for Williamina Stuart which never
found direct expression to her, but remained
deep in the poet's heart long after her marriage to Sir William Forbes, and Scott's to
Miss Carpenter; so that thirty years later
Scott could write in his Journal, just after
waiting on Lady Jane Stuart, the aged mother
of Williamina : 'I went to make another visit,
and fairly softened myself like an old fool,
with recalling old stories, till I was fit for nothing but shedding tears and repeating verses

for the whole night. This is sad work. The very grave gives up its dead, and time rolls back thirty years to add to my perplexities. I don't care. Yet what a romance to tell, and told I fear it will one day be. And then my three years of dreaming and my two years of wakening will be chronicled, doubtless. But the dead will feel no pain.' The story of this disappointment is told without names in the eighth chapter of Lockhart's *Life*, and has recently been repeated with greater explicitness by Miss Skene in *The Century* for July, 1899.

THE violet in her green-wood bower,
  Where birchen boughs with hazels mingle,
May boast itself the fairest flower
  In glen or copse or forest dingle.

Though fair her gems of azure hue,
  Beneath the dewdrop's weight reclining ;
I 've seen an eye of lovelier blue,
  More sweet through watery lustre shining.

The summer sun that dew shall dry
  Ere yet the day be past its morrow,
Nor longer in my false love's eye
  Remained the tear of parting sorrow.

TO A LADY

WITH FLOWERS FROM A ROMAN WALL

1797

TAKE these flowers which, purple waving,
  On the ruined rampart grew,
Where, the sons of freedom braving,
  Rome's imperial standards flew.

Warriors from the breach of danger
  Pluck no longer laurels there ;
They but yield the passing stranger
  Wild-flower wreaths for Beauty's hair.

THE ERL-KING

FROM THE GERMAN OF GOETHE

Scott, in sending this in a letter to a friend, makes the comment : ' The Erl-King is a goblin that haunts the Black Forest in Thuringia. — To be read by a candle particularly long in the snuff.' The translation was made in 1797.

O, WHO rides by night thro' the woodland
    so wild ?
It is the fond father embracing his child ;
And close the boy nestles within his loved
    arm,
To hold himself fast and to keep himself
    warm.

' O father, see yonder ! see yonder ! ' he
    says ;
' My boy, upon what dost thou fearfully
    gaze ? ' —
' O, 't is the Erl-King with his crown and
    his shroud.' —
' No, my son, it is but a dark wreath of
    the cloud.'

THE ERL-KING SPEAKS

' O, come and go with me, thou loveliest
    child ;
By many a gay sport shall thy time be
    beguiled ;
My mother keeps for thee full many a fair
    toy,
And many a fine flower shall she pluck for
    my boy.'

' O father, my father, and did you not
    hear
The Erl-King whisper so low in my
    ear ? ' —
' Be still, my heart's darling — my child, be
    at ease ;
It was but the wild blast as it sung thro'
    the trees.'

ERL-KING

' O, wilt thou go with me, thou loveliest
    boy ?
My daughter shall tend thee with care and
    with joy ;
She shall bear thee so lightly thro' wet
    and thro' wild,
And press thee and kiss thee and sing to
    my child.'

' O father, my father, and saw you not
    plain,
The Erl-King's pale daughter glide past
    through the rain ? ' —
' O yes, my loved treasure, I knew it full
    soon ;
It was the gray willow that danced to the
    moon.'

ERL-KING

'O, come and go with me, no longer delay,
Or else, silly child, I will drag thee
   away.' —
'O father ! O father ! now, now keep your
   hold,
The Erl-King has seized me — his grasp is
   so cold !'

Sore trembled the father ; he spurred thro'
   the wild,
Clasping close to his bosom his shuddering
   child ;
He reaches his dwelling in doubt and in
   dread,
But, clasped to his bosom, the infant was
   dead !

WAR-SONG

OF THE ROYAL EDINBURGH LIGHT
DRAGOONS

In 1797 Scott's ardor led to the formation of
the Royal Edinburgh Light Dragoons, and he
served in it as quartermaster. In 1798, when
a French invasion was threatened, Mr. Skene
was one day reciting the German *Kriegslied*
'Der Abschied's Tag ist Da,' and the next
morning Scott showed the following piece
which was adopted as the troop-song.

To horse ! to horse ! the standard flies,
   The bugles sound the call ;
The Gallic navy stems the seas,
The voice of battle 's on the breeze,
   Arouse ye, one and all !

From high Dunedin's towers we come,
   A band of brothers true ;
Our casques the leopard's spoils surround,
With Scotland's hardy thistle crowned ;
   We boast the red and blue.

Though tamely crouch to Gallia's frown
   Dull Holland's tardy train ;
Their ravished toys though Romans
   mourn ;
Though gallant Switzers vainly spurn,
   And, foaming, gnaw the chain ;

Oh ! had they marked the avenging call
   Their brethren's murder gave,
Disunion ne'er their ranks had mown,

Nor patriot valor, desperate grown,
   Sought freedom in the grave !

Shall we, too, bend the stubborn head,
   In Freedom's temple born,
Dress our pale cheek in timid smile,
To hail a master in our isle,
   Or brook a victor's scorn ?

No ! though destruction o'er the land
   Come pouring as a flood,
The sun, that sees our falling day,
Shall mark our sabres' deadly sway,
   And set that night in blood.

For gold let Gallia's legions fight,
   Or plunder's bloody gain ;
Unbribed, unbought, our swords we draw,
To guard our king, to fence our law,
   Nor shall their edge be vain.

If ever breath of British gale
   Shall fan the tri-color,
Or footstep of invader rude,
With rapine foul, and red with blood,
   Pollute our happy shore, —

Then farewell home ! and farewell friends !
   Adieu each tender tie !
Resolved, we mingle in the tide,
Where charging squadrons furious ride,
   To conquer or to die.

To horse ! to horse ! the sabres gleam ;
   High sounds our bugle call ;
Combined by honor's sacred tie,
Our word is *Laws and Liberty !*
   March forward, one and all !

SONG

FROM GOETZ VON BERLICHINGEN

It was a little naughty page,
   Ha ! ha !
Would catch a bird was closed in cage.
   Sa ! sa !
   Ha ! ha !
   Sa ! sa !
He seized the cage, the latch did draw,
   Ha ! ha !
And in he thrust his knavish paw.
   Sa ! sa !
   Ha ! ha !
   Sa ! sa !

The bird dashed out, and gained the thorn,
    Ha ! ha !
And laughed the silly fool to scorn !
      Sa ! sa !
      Ha ! ha !
      Sa ! sa !

SONGS

FROM THE HOUSE OF ASPEN

Lockhart calls attention to the fact that the first of these lyrics has the metre, and not a little of the spirit, of the boat-song of Roderick Dhu and Clan Alpin ; and that the second is the first draft of ' The Maid of Toro.'

I

Joy to the victors, the sons of old Aspen !
Joy to the race of the battle and scar !
Glory's proud garland triumphantly grasp-
    ing,
Generous in peace, and victorious in war.
    Honor acquiring,
    Valor inspiring,
Bursting, resistless, through foemen they
    go ;
    War-axes wielding,
    Broken ranks yielding,
Till from the battle proud Roderic re-
    tiring,
Yields in wild rout the fair palm to his foe.

Joy to each warrior, true follower of As-
    pen !
Joy to the heroes that gained the bold
    day !
Health to our wounded, in agony gasping ;
    Peace to our brethren that fell in the
    fray !
    Boldly this morning,
    Roderic's power scorning,
Well for their chieftain their blades did
    they wield :
    Joy blest them dying,
    As Maltingen flying,
Low laid his banners, our conquest
    adorning,
Their death-clouded eye-balls descried on
    the field !

Now to our home, the proud mansion of
    Aspen
Bend we, gay victors, triumphant away.

There each fond damsel, her gallant youth
    clasping,
Shall wipe from his forehead the stains
    of the fray.
    Listening the prancing
    Of horses advancing ;
E'en now on the turrets our maidens ap-
    pear.
    Love our hearts warming,
    Songs the night charming,
Round goes the grape in the goblet gay
    dancing ;
Love, wine, and song, our blithe evening
    shall cheer !

II

Sweet shone the sun on the fair lake of
    Toro,
Weak were the whispers that waved the
    dark wood,
As a fair maiden, bewildered in sorrow,
    Sighed to the breezes and wept to the
    flood. —
' Saints, from the mansion of bliss lowly
    bending,
Virgin, that hear'st the poor suppliant's
    cry,
Grant my petition, in anguish ascending,
    My Frederick restore, or let Eleanor die.'

Distant and faint were the sounds of the
    battle ;
    With the breezes they rise, with the
    breezes they fail,
Till the shout, and the groan, and the con-
    flict's dread rattle,
    And the chase's wild clamor came load-
    ing the gale.
Breathless she gazed through the wood-
    land so dreary,
    Slowly approaching, a warrior was seen ;
Life's ebbing tide marked his footsteps so
    weary,
    Cleft was his helmet, and woe was his
    mien.

' Save thee, fair maid, for our armies are
    flying ;
Save thee, fair maid, for thy guardian is
    low ;
Cold on yon heath thy bold Frederick is
    lying,
    Fast through the woodland approaches
    the foe.'

III

RHEIN-WEIN LIED

What makes the troopers' frozen courage
    muster ?
The grapes of juice divine.
Upon the Rhine, upon the Rhine they
    cluster :
Oh, blessed be the Rhine !

Let fringe and furs, and many a rabbit
    skin, sirs,
Bedeck your Saracen ;
He 'll freeze without what warms our
    heart within, sirs,
When the night-frost crusts the fen.

But on the Rhine, but on the Rhine they
    cluster,
The grapes of juice divine,
That makes our troopers' frozen courage
    muster :
Oh, blessed be the Rhine !

GLENFINLAS ;

OR

LORD RONALD'S CORONACH

This ballad, written in the summer of 1799,
and first published in Monk Lewis's *Tales of
Wonder*, was provided by Scott with a preface
which is here reproduced because of the suggestion that Scott, in making thus his first use
of native, Scottish material, was affected by
his German studies and translations. The prose
preface, it has been held, where he speaks in
his natural voice, ' is more affecting than the
lofty and sonorous stanzas themselves ; that
the vague tenor of the original dream loses,
instead of gaining, by the expanded elaboration of the detail.' Be that as it may, here is
Scott's preface : —

' The simple tradition, upon which the following stanzas are founded, runs thus : While two
Highland hunters were passing the night in a
solitary *bothy*, (a hut, built for the purpose of
hunting,) and making merry over their venison
and whiskey, one of them expressed a wish
that they had pretty lasses to complete their
party. The words were scarcely uttered, when
two beautiful young women, habited in green,
entered the hut, dancing and singing. One of
the hunters was seduced by the siren who attached herself particularly to him, to leave the
hut : the other remained, and, suspicious of

the fair seducers, continued to play upon a
trump, or Jew's harp, some strain, consecrated
to the Virgin Mary. Day at length came, and
the temptress vanished. Searching in the
forest, he found the bones of his unfortunate
friend, who had been torn to pieces and devoured by the fiend into whose toils he had
fallen. The place was from thence called the
Glen of the Green Women.

' Glenfinlas is a tract of forest-ground, lying
in the Highlands of Perthshire, not far from
Callender, in Menteith. It was formerly a
royal forest, and now belongs to the Earl of
Moray. This country, as well as the adjacent district of Balquidder, was, in times of
yore, chiefly inhabited by the Macgregors. To
the west of the Forest of Glenfinlas lies Loch
Katrine, and its romantic avenue, called the
Troshachs. Benledi, Benmore, and Benvoirlich, are mountains in the same district, and
at no great distance from Glenfinlas. The
River Teith passes Callender and the Castle of
Doune, and joins the Forth near Stirling. The
Pass of Lenny is immediately above Callender,
and is the principal access to the Highlands,
from that town. Glenartney is a forest, near
Benvoirlich. The whole forms a sublime tract
of Alpine scenery.'

It may be observed that the scenery of the
ballad reappears in *The Lady of the Lake*, as
also in *Waverley* and *Rob Roy*.

For them the viewless forms of air obey,
    Their bidding heed, and at their beck repair ;
They know what spirit brews the stormful day,
    And heartless oft, like moody madness stare,
To see the phantom-train their secret work prepare.
        COLLINS.

' O HONE a rie' ! O hone a rie' !
The pride of Albin's line is o'er,
And fallen Glenartney's stateliest tree ;
  We ne'er shall see Lord Ronald more !'

O ! sprung from great Macgillianore,
  The chief that never feared a foe,
How matchless was thy broad claymore,
  How deadly thine unerring bow !

Well can the Saxon widows tell
  How on the Teith's resounding shore   10
The boldest Lowland warriors fell,
  As down from Lenny's pass you bore.

But o'er his hills in festal day
  How blazed Lord Ronald's beltane-tree,
While youths and maids the light strath-
    spey
So nimbly danced with Highland glee !

Cheered by the strength of Ronald's shell,
  E'en age forgot his tresses hoar ;
But now the loud lament we swell,
  O, ne'er to see Lord Ronald more !   20

From distant isles a chieftain came
  The joys of Ronald's halls to find,
And chase with him the dark-brown game
  That bounds o'er Albin's hills of wind.

'T was Moy ; whom in Columba's isle
  The seer's prophetic spirit found,
As, with a minstrel's fire the while,
  He waked his harp's harmonious sound.

Full many a spell to him was known
  Which wandering spirits shrink to hear;
And many a lay of potent tone   31
  Was never meant for mortal ear.

For there, 't is said, in mystic mood
  High converse with the dead they hold,
And oft espy the fated shroud
  That shall the future corpse enfold.

O, so it fell that on a day,
  To rouse the red deer from their den,
The chiefs have ta'en their distant way,
  And scoured the deep Glenfinlas glen.

No vassals wait their sports to aid,   41
  To watch their safety, deck their board;
Their simple dress the Highland plaid,
  Their trusty guard the Highland sword.

Three summer days through brake and dell
  Their whistling shafts successful flew;
And still when dewy evening fell
  The quarry to their hut they drew.

In gray Glenfinlas' deepest nook
  The solitary cabin stood,   50
Fast by Moneira's sullen brook,
  Which murmurs through that lonely
    wood.

Soft fell the night, the sky was calm,
  When three successive days had flown ;
And summer mist in dewy balm
  Steeped heathy bank and mossy stone.

The moon, half-hid in silvery flakes,
  Afar her dubious radiance shed,
Quivering on Katrine's distant lakes,
  And resting on Benledi's head.   60

Now in their hut in social guise
  Their sylvan fare the chiefs enjoy;
And pleasure laughs in Ronald's eyes,
  As many a pledge he quaffs to Moy.

' What lack we here to crown our bliss,
  While thus the pulse of joy beats high ?
What but fair woman's yielding kiss,
  Her panting breath and melting eye ?

' To chase the deer of yonder shades,
  This morning left their father's pile   70
The fairest of our mountain maids,
  The daughters of the proud Glengyle.

' Long have I sought sweet Mary's heart,
  And dropped the tear and heaved the
    sigh :
But vain the lover's wily art
  Beneath a sister's watchful eye.

' But thou mayst teach that guardian fair,
  While far with Mary I am flown,
Of other hearts to cease her care,
  And find it hard to guard her own.   80

' Touch but thy harp, thou soon shalt see
  The lovely Flora of Glengyle,
Unmindful of her charge and me,
  Hang on thy notes 'twixt tear and smile.

' Or, if she choose a melting tale,
  All underneath the greenwood bough,
Will good Saint Oran's rule prevail,
  Stern huntsman of the rigid brow ? '

' Since Enrick's fight, since Morna's death,
  No more on me shall rapture rise,   90
Responsive to the panting breath,
  Or yielding kiss or melting eyes.

' E'en then, when o'er the heath of woe
  Where sunk my hopes of love and fame,
I bade my harp's wild wailings flow,
  On me the Seer's sad spirit came.

' The last dread curse of angry heaven,
  With ghastly sights and sounds of woe
To dash each glimpse of joy was given —
  The gift the future ill to know.   100

' The bark thou saw'st, yon summer morn,
  So gayly part from Oban's bay,
My eye beheld her dashed and torn
  Far on the rocky Colonsay.

'Thy Fergus too — thy sister's son,
  Thou saw'st with pride the gallant's
    power,
As marching 'gainst the Lord of Downe
He left the skirts of huge Benmore.

'Thou only saw'st their tartans wave 109
  As down Benvoirlich's side they wound,
Heard'st but the pibroch answering brave
To many a target clanking round.

'I heard the groans, I marked the tears,
  I saw the wound his bosom bore,
When on the serried Saxon spears
He poured his clan's resistless roar.

'And thou, who bidst me think of bliss,
  And bidst my heart awake to glee,
And court like thee the wanton kiss —
That heart, O Ronald, bleeds for thee ! 120

'I see the death-damps chill thy brow :
  I hear thy Warning Spirit cry ;
The corpse-lights dance — they 're gone,
    and now —
No more is given to gifted eye !'

'Alone enjoy thy dreary dreams,
  Sad prophet of the evil hour !
Say, should we scorn joy's transient beams
Because to-morrow's storm may lour ?

'Or false or sooth thy words of woe, 129
  Clangillian's Chieftain ne'er shall fear ;
His blood shall bound at rapture's glow,
Though doomed to stain the Saxon spear.

'E'en now, to meet me in yon dell,
  My Mary's buskins brush the dew.'
He spoke, nor bade the chief farewell,
But called his dogs and gay withdrew.

Within an hour returned each hound,
  In rushed the rousers of the deer ;
They howled in melancholy sound,
Then closely couched beside the Seer. 140

No Ronald yet, though midnight came,
  And sad were Moy's prophetic dreams,
As, bending o'er the dying flame,
He fed the watch-fire's quivering gleams.

Sudden the hounds erect their ears,
  And sudden cease their moaning howl,

Close pressed to Moy, they mark their fears
By shivering limbs and stifled growl.

Untouched the harp began to ring
  As softly, slowly, oped the door ; 150
And shook responsive every string
As light a footstep pressed the floor.

And by the watch-fire's glimmering light
  Close by the minstrel's side was seen
An huntress maid, in beauty bright,
All dropping wet her robes of green.

All dropping wet her garments seem ;
  Chilled was her cheek, her bosom bare,
As, bending o'er the dying gleam,
She wrung the moisture from her hair. 160

With maiden blush she softly said,
  'O gentle huntsman, hast thou seen,
In deep Glenfinlas' moonlight glade,
  A lovely maid in vest of green :

'With her a chief in Highland pride ;
  His shoulders bear the hunter's bow,
The mountain dirk adorns his side,
  Far on the wind his tartans flow ?' —

'And who art thou ? and who are they ?'
  All ghastly gazing, Moy replied : 170
'And why, beneath the moon's pale ray,
  Dare ye thus roam Glenfinlas' side ?'

'Where wild Loch Katrine pours her tide,
  Blue, dark, and deep, round many an isle,
Our father's towers o'erhang her side,
  The castle of the bold Glengyle.

'To chase the dun Glenfinlas deer
  Our woodland course this morn we bore,
And haply met while wandering here
  The son of great Macgillianore. 180

'O, aid me then to seek the pair,
  Whom, loitering in the woods, I lost ;
Alone I dare not venture there,
  Where walks, they say, the shrieking
    ghost.'

'Yes, many a shrieking ghost walks there ;
  Then first, my own sad vow to keep,
Here will I pour my midnight prayer,
  Which still must rise when mortals
    sleep.'

'O, first, for pity's gentle sake,
  Guide a lone wanderer on her way !   190
For I must cross the haunted brake,
  And reach my father's towers ere day.'

'First, three times tell each Ave-bead,
  And thrice a Pater-noster say ;
Then kiss with me the holy rede ;
  So shall we safely wend our way.'

'O, shame to knighthood, strange and foul !
  Go, doff the bonnet from thy brow,
And shroud thee in the monkish cowl,
  Which best befits thy sullen vow.   200

'Not so, by high Dunlathmon's fire,
  Thy heart was froze to love and joy,
When gayly rung thy raptured lyre
  To wanton Morna's melting eye.'

Wild stared the minstrel's eyes of flame
  And high his sable locks arose,
And quick his color went and came
  As fear and rage alternate rose.

'And thou ! when by the blazing oak
  I lay, to her and love resigned,   210
Say, rode ye on the eddying smoke,
  Or sailed ye on the midnight wind ?

'Not thine a race of mortal blood,
  Nor old Glengyle's pretended line ;
Thy dame, the Lady of the Flood —
  Thy sire, the Monarch of the Mine.'

He muttered thrice Saint Oran's rhyme,
  And thrice Saint Fillan's powerful
    prayer ;
Then turned him to the eastern clime,
  And sternly shook his coal-black hair.   220

And, bending o'er his harp, he flung
  His wildest witch-notes on the wind ;
And loud and high and strange they rung,
  As many a magic change they find.

Tall waxed the Spirit's altering form,
  Till to the roof her stature grew ;
Then, mingling with the rising storm,
  With one wild yell away she flew.

Rain beats, hail rattles, whirlwinds tear :
  The slender hut in fragments flew ;   230
But not a lock of Moy's loose hair
  Was waved by wind or wet by dew.

Wild mingling with the howling gale,
  Loud bursts of ghastly laughter rise ;
High o'er the minstrel's head they sail
  And die amid the northern skies.

The voice of thunder shook the wood,
  As ceased the more than mortal yell ;
And spattering foul a shower of blood
  Upon the hissing firebrands fell.   240

Next dropped from high a mangled arm ;
  The fingers strained an half-drawn blade :
And last, the life-blood streaming warm,
  Torn from the trunk, a gasping head.

Oft o'er that head in battling field
  Streamed the proud crest of high Ben-
    more ;
That arm the broad claymore could wield
  Which dyed the Teith with Saxon gore.

Woe to Moneira's sullen rills !
  Woe to Glenfinlas' dreary glen !   250
There never son of Albin's hills
  Shall draw the hunter's shaft agen !

E'en the tired pilgrim's burning feet
  At noon shall shun that sheltering den,
Lest, journeying in their rage, he meet
  The wayward Ladies of the Glen.

And we — behind the chieftain's shield
  No more shall we in safety dwell ;
None leads the people to the field —
  And we the loud lament must swell.   260

O hone a rie' !   O hone a rie' !
  The pride of Albin's line is o'er !
And fallen Glenartney's stateliest tree ;
  We ne'er shall see Lord Ronald more !

THE EVE OF SAINT JOHN

This ballad was written in the autumn of 1799
at Mertoun House, and was first published in
Monk Lewis's *Tales of Wonder*. Lockhart
points out that it is the first of Scott's original
pieces in which he uses the measure of his own
favorite minstrels. The ballad was written at
the playful request of Scott of Harden, who
was the owner of the tower of Smailholm, when
Walter Scott begged him not to destroy it.

THE Baron of Smaylho'me rose with day,
  He spurred his courser on,

Without stop or stay, down the rocky way,
That leads to Brotherstone.

He went not with the bold Buccleuch
His banner broad to rear ;
He went not 'gainst the English yew
To lift the Scottish spear.

Yet his plate-jack was braced and his hel-
met was laced,
And his vaunt-brace of proof he wore ; 10
At his saddle - gerthe was a good steel
sperthe,
Full ten pound weight and more.

The baron returned in three days' space,
And his looks were sad and sour ;
And weary was his courser's pace
As he reached his rocky tower.

He came not from where Ancram Moor
Ran red with English blood ;
Where the Douglas true and the bold
Buccleuch
'Gainst keen Lord Evers stood.   20

Yet was his helmet hacked and hewed,
His acton pierced and tore,
His axe and his dagger with blood im-
brued, —
But it was not English gore.

He lighted at the Chapellage,
He held him close and still ;
And he whistled thrice for his little foot-
page,
His name was English Will.

'Come thou hither, my little foot-page,
Come hither to my knee ;   30
Though thou art young and tender of
age,
I think thou art true to me.

'Come, tell me all that thou hast seen,
And look thou tell me true !
Since I from Smaylho'me tower have been,
What did thy lady do ? '

'My lady, each night, sought the lonely
light
That burns on the wild Watchfold ;
For from height to height the beacons
bright
Of the English foemen told.   40

'The bittern clamored from the moss,
The wind blew loud and shrill ;
Yet the craggy pathway she did cross
To the eiry Beacon Hill.

'I watched her steps, and silent came
Where she sat her on a stone ; —
No watchman stood by the dreary flame,
It burnèd all alone.

'The second night I kept her in sight
Till to the fire she came,   50
And, by Mary's might ! an armed knight
Stood by the lonely flame.

'And many a word that warlike lord
Did speak to my lady there ;
But the rain fell fast and loud blew the
blast,
And I heard not what they were.

'The third night there the sky was fair,
And the mountain-blast was still,
As again I watched the secret pair
On the lonesome Beacon Hill.   60

'And I heard her name the midnight
hour,
And name this holy eve ;
And say, "Come this night to thy lady's
bower ;
Ask no bold baron's leave.

'"He lifts his spear with the bold Buc-
cleuch ;
His lady is all alone ;
The door she 'll undo to her knight so true
On the eve of good Saint John."

'"I cannot come ; I must not come ;
I dare not come to thee ;   70
On the eve of Saint John I must wander
alone :
In thy bower I may not be."

'"Now, out on thee, faint-hearted knight !
Thou shouldst not say me nay ;
For the eve is sweet, and when lovers
meet
Is worth the whole summer's day.

'"And I 'll chain the blood-hound, and the
warder shall not sound,
And rushes shall be strewed on the
stair ;

So, by the black rood-stone and by holy
    Saint John,
I conjure thee, my love, to be there!" 80

' "Though the blood-hound be mute and
    the rush beneath my foot,
And the warder his bugle should not
    blow,
Yet there sleepeth a priest in the chamber
    to the east,
And my footstep he would know."

' "O, fear not the priest who sleepeth to
    the east,
For to Dryburgh the way he has
    ta'en ;
And there to say mass, till three days do
    pass,
For the soul of a knight that is slayne."

' He turned him around and grimly he
    frowned ;
Then he laughed right scornfully —   90
" He who says the mass-rite for the soul
    of that knight
May as well say mass for me:

' "At the lone midnight hour when bad
    spirits have power
In thy chamber will I be." —
With that he was gone and my lady left
    alone,
And no more did I see.'

Then changed, I trow, was that bold
    baron's brow
From the dark to the blood-red high ;
' Now, tell me the mien of the knight thou
    hast seen,
For, by Mary, he shall die !'   100

' His arms shone full bright in the beacon's
    red light;
His plume it was scarlet and blue;
On his shield was a hound in a silver leash
    bound,
And his crest was a branch of the
    yew.'

' Thou liest, thou liest, thou little foot-
    page,
Loud dost thou lie to me !
For that knight is cold and low laid in the
    mould,
All under the Eildon-tree.'

' Yet hear but my word, my noble lord !
For I heard her name his name ;   110
And that lady bright, she called the
    knight
Sir Richard of Coldinghame.'

The bold baron's brow then changed, I
    trow,
From high blood-red to pale —
' The grave is deep and dark — and the
    corpse is stiff and stark —
So I may not trust thy tale.

' Where fair Tweed flows round holy Mel-
    rose,
And Eildon slopes to the plain,
Full three nights ago by some secret foe
That gay gallant was slain.   120

' The varying light deceived thy sight,
And the wild winds drowned the name;
For the Dryburgh bells ring and the white
    monks do sing
For Sir Richard of Coldinghame !'

He passed the court-gate and he oped the
    tower-gate,
And he mounted the narrow stair
To the bartizan-seat where, with maids
    that on her wait,
He found his lady fair.

That lady sat in mournful mood;
Looked over hill and vale ;   130
Over Tweed's fair flood and Mertoun's
    wood,
And all down Teviotdale.

' Now hail, now hail, thou lady bright!'
' Now hail, thou baron true !
What news, what news, from Ancram
    fight ?
What news from the bold Buccleuch ? '

' The Ancram moor is red with gore,
For many a Southern fell ;
And Buccleuch has charged us evermore
To watch our beacons well.'   140

The lady blushed red, but nothing she
    said :
Nor added the baron a word :
Then she stepped down the stair to her
    chamber fair,
And so did her moody lord.

In sleep the lady mourned, and the baron
  tossed and turned,
  And oft to himself he said, —
'The worms around him creep, and his
  bloody grave is deep —
  It cannot give up the dead!'

It was near the ringing of matin-bell,
  The night was well-nigh done,   150
When a heavy sleep on that baron fell,
  On the eve of good Saint John.

The lady looked through the chamber fair,
  By the light of a dying flame;
And she was aware of a knight stood
  there —
  Sir Richard of Coldinghame!

'Alas! away, away!' she cried,
  'For the holy Virgin's sake!'
'Lady, I know who sleeps by thy side;
  But, lady, he will not awake.   160

'By Eildon-tree for long nights three
  In bloody grave have I lain;
The mass and the death-prayer are said
  for me,
  But, lady, they are said in vain.

'By the baron's brand, near Tweed's fair
  strand,
  Most foully slain I fell;
And my restless sprite on the beacon's
  height
  For a space is doomed to dwell.

'At our trysting-place, for a certain space,
  I must wander to and fro;   170
But I had not had power to come to thy
  bower
  Hadst thou not conjured me so.'

Love mastered fear — her brow she crossed;
  'How, Richard, hast thou sped?
And art thou saved or art thou lost?'
  The vision shook his head!

'Who spilleth life shall forfeit life;
  So bid thy lord believe:
That lawless love is guilt above,
  This awful sign receive.'   180

He laid his left palm on an oaken beam,
  His right upon her hand;

The lady shrunk and fainting sunk,
  For it scorched like a fiery brand.

The sable score of fingers four
  Remains on that board impressed;
And forevermore that lady wore
  A covering on her wrist.

There is a nun in Dryburgh bower
  Ne'er looks upon the sun;   190
There is a monk in Melrose tower
  He speaketh word to none.

That nun who ne'er beholds the day,
  That monk who speaks to none —
That nun was Smaylho'me's lady gay,
  That monk the bold baron.

THE GRAY BROTHER

A fragment written in 1799. 'The tradition,'
says Scott, 'upon which the tale is founded,
regards a house upon the barony of Gilmerton,
near Lasswade, in Mid-lothian. This building,
now called Gilmerton Grange, was originally
named Burndale, from the following tragic
adventure. The barony of Gilmerton belonged,
of yore, to a gentleman named Heron, who
had one beautiful daughter. This young lady
was seduced by the Abbot of Newbattle, a
richly endowed abbey upon the banks of the
South Esk, now a seat of the Marquis of Lothian. Heron came to the knowledge of this
circumstance, and learned also that the lovers
carried on their guilty intercourse by the connivance of the lady's nurse, who lived at this
house of Gilmerton Grange, or Burndale. He
formed a resolution of bloody vengeance, un-
deterred by the supposed sanctity of the clerical character or by the stronger claims of
natural affection. Choosing, therefore, a dark
and windy night, when the objects of his vengeance were engaged in a stolen interview, he
set fire to a stack of dried thorns, and other
combustibles, which he had caused to be piled
against the house, and reduced to a pile of
glowing ashes the dwelling, with all its inmates.'

THE Pope he was saying the high, high
  mass
  All on Saint Peter's day,
With the power to him given by the saints
  in heaven
  To wash men's sins away.

The Pope he was saying the blessed mass,
    And the people kneeled around,
And from each man's soul his sins did pass,
    As he kissed the holy ground.

And all among the crowded throng
    Was still, both limb and tongue,   10
While through vaulted roof and aisles aloof
    The holy accents rung.

At the holiest word he quivered for fear,
    And faltered in the sound —
And when he would the chalice rear
    He dropped it to the ground.

' The breath of one of evil deed
    Pollutes our sacred day ;
He has no portion in our creed,
    No part in what I say.   20

' A being whom no blessed word
    To ghostly peace can bring,
A wretch at whose approach abhorred
    Recoils each holy thing.

' Up, up, unhappy ! haste, arise !
    My adjuration fear !
I charge thee not to stop my voice,
    Nor longer tarry here ! '

Amid them all a pilgrim kneeled
    In gown of sackcloth gray ;   30
Far journeying from his native field,
    He first saw Rome that day.

For forty days and nights so drear
    I ween he had not spoke,
And, save with bread and water clear,
    His fast he ne'er had broke.

Amid the penitential flock,
    Seemed none more bent to pray ;
But when the Holy Father spoke
    He rose and went his way.   40

Again unto his native land
    His weary course he drew,
To Lothian's fair and fertile strand,
    And Pentland's mountains blue.

His unblest feet his native seat
    Mid Eske's fair woods regain ;
Through woods more fair no stream more
        sweet
    Rolls to the eastern main.

And lords to meet the pilgrim came,
    And vassals bent the knee ;   50
For all mid Scotland's chiefs of fame
    Was none more famed than he.

And boldly for his country still
    In battle he had stood,
Ay, even when on the banks of Till
    Her noblest poured their blood.

Sweet are the paths, O passing sweet !
    By Eske's fair streams that run,
O'er airy steep through copsewood deep,
    Impervious to the sun.   60

There the rapt poet's step may rove,
    And yield the muse the day ;
There Beauty, led by timid Love,
    May shun the telltale ray ;

From that fair dome where suit is paid
    By blast of bugle free,
To Auchendinny's hazel glade
    And haunted Woodhouselee.

Who knows not Melville's beechy grove
    And Roslin's rocky glen,   70
Dalkeith, which all the virtues love,
    And classic Hawthornden ?

Yet never a path from day to day
    The pilgrim's footsteps range,
Save but the solitary way
    To Burndale's ruined grange.

A woful place was that, I ween,
    As sorrow could desire ;
For nodding to the fall was each crumbling
        wall,
    And the roof was scathed with fire.   80

It fell upon a summer's eve,
    While on Carnethy's head
The last faint gleams of the sun's low
        beams
    Had streaked the gray with red,

And the convent bell did vespers tell
    Newbattle's oaks among,
And mingled with the solemn knell
    Our Ladye's evening song ;

The heavy knell, the choir's faint swell,
    Came slowly down the wind,   90

And on the pilgrim's ear they fell,
As his wonted path he did find.

Deep sunk in thought, I ween, he was,
Nor ever raised his eye,
Until he came to that dreary place
Which did all in ruins lie.

He gazed on the walls, so scathed with
fire,
With many a bitter groan —
And there was aware of a Gray Friar
Resting him on a stone.   100

'Now, Christ thee save!' said the Gray
Brother ;
'Some pilgrim thou seemest to be.'
But in sore amaze did Lord Albert gaze,
Nor answer again made he.

'O, come ye from east or come ye from
west,
Or bring reliques from over the sea ;
Or come ye from the shrine of Saint James
the divine,
Or Saint John of Beverley ?'

'I come not from the shrine of Saint James
the divine,
Nor bring reliques from over the sea ;   110
I bring but a curse from our father, the
Pope,
Which forever will cling to me.'

'Now, woful pilgrim, say not so !
But kneel thee down to me,
And shrive thee so clean of thy deadly sin
That absolved thou mayst be.'

'And who art thou, thou Gray Brother,
That I should shrive to thee,
When He to whom are given the keys of
earth and heaven
Has no power to pardon me ?'   120

'O, I am sent from a distant clime,
Five thousand miles away,
And all to absolve a foul, foul crime,
Done *here* 'twixt night and day.'

The pilgrim kneeled him on the sand,
And thus began his saye —
When on his neck an ice-cold hand
Did that Gray Brother laye.

.   .   .   .

THE FIRE-KING

The blessings of the evil Genii, which are curses, were
upon him. — *Eastern Tale.*

This ballad, written in 1799, was published
in *Tales of Wonder.* 'The story,' Scott says,
'is partly historical, for it is recorded that, during the struggles of the Latin kingdom of Jerusalem, a Knight Templar called Saint-Alban
deserted to the Saracens, and defeated the
Christians in many combats, till he was finally
routed and slain in a conflict with King Baldwin, under the walls of Jerusalem.'

BOLD knights and fair dames, to my harp
give an ear,
Of love and of war and of wonder to hear ;
And you haply may sigh in the midst of
your glee
At the tale of Count Albert and fair Rosalie.

O, see you that castle, so strong and so
high ?
And see you that lady, the tear in her eye ?
And see you that palmer from Palestine's
land,
The shell on his hat and the staff in his
hand ? —

'Now, palmer, gray palmer, O, tell unto me,
What news bring you home from the Holy
Countrie ?   10
And how goes the warfare by Galilee's
strand ?
And how fare our nobles, the flower of the
land ?'

'O, well goes the warfare by Galilee's
wave,
For Gilead and Nablous and Ramah we
have ;
And well fare our nobles by Mount Lebanon,
For the heathen have lost and the Christians have won.'

A fair chain of gold mid her ringlets there
hung ;
O'er the palmer's gray locks the fair chain
has she flung:
'O palmer, gray palmer, this chain be thy
fee
For the news thou hast brought from the
Holy Countrie.   20

'And, palmer, good palmer, by Galilee's
　　wave,
O, saw ye Count Albert, the gentle and
　　brave ?
When the Crescent went back and the Red-
　　cross rushed on,
O, saw ye him foremost on Mount Leba-
　　non ?'

'O lady, fair lady, the tree green it grows ;
O lady, fair lady, the stream pure it flows ;
Your castle stands strong and your hopes
　　soar on high,
But, lady, fair lady, all blossoms to die.

'The green boughs they wither, the thun-
　　derbolt falls,
It leaves of your castle but levin-scorched
　　walls:　　　　　　　　　　　　　　30
The pure stream runs muddy ; the gay
　　hope is gone ;
Count Albert is prisoner on Mount Leba-
　　non.'

O, she 's ta'en a horse should be fleet at
　　her speed ;
And she 's ta'en a sword should be sharp
　　at her need;
And she has ta'en shipping for Palestine's
　　land,
To ransom Count Albert from Soldanrie's
　　hand.

Small thought had Count Albert on fair
　　Rosalie,
Small thought on his faith or his knight-
　　hood had he:
A heathenish damsel his light heart had
　　won,
The Soldan's fair daughter of Mount Le-
　　banon.　　　　　　　　　　　　　　40

'O Christian, brave Christian, my love
　　wouldst thou be,
Three things must thou do ere I hearken
　　to thee:
Our laws and our worship on thee shalt
　　thou take ;
And this thou shalt first do for Zulema's
　　sake.

'And next, in the cavern where burns ever-
　　more
The mystical flame which the Curdmans
　　adore,

Alone and in silence three nights shalt
　　thou wake ;
And this thou shalt next do for Zulema's
　　sake.

'And last, thou shalt aid us with counsel
　　and hand,
To drive the Frank robber from Palestine's
　　land ;　　　　　　　　　　　　　　50
For my lord and my love then Count
　　Albert I 'll take,
When all this is accomplished for Zulema's
　　sake.'

He has thrown by his helmet and cross-
　　handled sword,
Renouncing his knighthood, denying his
　　Lord ;
He has ta'en the green caftan, and turban
　　put on,
For the love of the maiden of fair Lebanon.

And in the dread cavern, deep deep under
　　ground,
Which fifty steel gates and steel portals
　　surround,
He has watched until daybreak, but sight
　　saw he none,
Save the flame burning bright on its altar
　　of stone.　　　　　　　　　　　　　60

Amazed was the Princess, the Soldan
　　amazed,
Sore murmured the priests as on Albert
　　they gazed ;
They searched all his garments, and under
　　his weeds
They found and took from him his rosary
　　beads.

Again in the cavern, deep deep under
　　ground,
He watched the lone night, while the winds
　　whistled round ;
Far off was their murmur, it came not
　　more nigh,
The flame burned unmoved and naught
　　else did he spy.

Loud murmured the priests and amazed
　　was the king,
While many dark spells of their witchcraft
　　they sing ;　　　　　　　　　　　　70
They searched Albert's body, and, lo ! on
　　his breast

Was the sign of the Cross by his father
   impressed.

The priests they erase it with care and
   with pain,
And the recreant returned to the cavern
   again;
But as he descended a whisper there fell :
It was his good angel, who bade him farewell !

High bristled his hair, his heart fluttered
   and beat,
And he turned him five steps, half resolved
   to retreat ;
But his heart it was hardened, his purpose
   was gone,
When he thought of the maiden of fair
   Lebanon.   80

Scarce passed he the archway, the thresh-
   old scarce trode,
When the winds from the four points of
   heaven were abroad,
They made each steel portal to rattle and
   ring,
And borne on the blast came the dread
   Fire-King.

Full sore rocked the cavern whene'er he
   drew nigh,
The fire on the altar blazed bickering and
   high ;
In volcanic explosions the mountains pro-
   claim
The dreadful approach of the Monarch of
   Flame.

Unmeasured in height, undistinguished in
   form,
His breath it was lightning, his voice it was
   storm ;   90
I ween the stout heart of Count Albert was
   tame,
When he saw in his terrors the Monarch of
   Flame.

In his hand a broad falchion blue-glim-
   mered through smoke,
And Mount Lebanon shook as the monarch
   he spoke:
'With this brand shalt thou conquer, thus
   long and no more,
Till thou bend to the Cross and the Virgin
   adore.'

The cloud-shrouded arm gives the weapon;
   and see !
The recreant receives the charmed gift on
   his knee:
The thunders growl distant and faint
   gleam the fires,
As, borne on the whirlwind, the phantom
   retires.   100

Count Albert has armed him the Paynim
   among,
Though his heart it was false, yet his arm
   it was strong ;
And the Red-cross waxed faint and the
   Crescent came on,
From the day he commanded on Mount
   Lebanon.

From Lebanon's forests to Galilee's wave,
The sands of Samaar drank the blood of
   the brave ;
Till the Knights of the Temple and
   Knights of Saint John,
With Salem's King Baldwin, against him
   came on.

The war-cymbals clattered, the trumpets
   replied,
The lances were couched, and they closed
   on each side ;   110
And horseman and horses Count Albert
   o'erthrew,
Till he pierced the thick tumult King
   Baldwin unto.

Against the charmed blade which Count
   Albert did wield,
The fence had been vain of the king's Red-
   cross shield ;
But a page thrust him forward the mon-
   arch before,
And cleft the proud turban the renegade
   wore.

So fell was the dint that Count Albert
   stooped low
Before the crossed shield to his steel
   saddlebow ;
And scarce had he bent to the Red-cross
   his head, —
'Bonne Grace, Notre Dame!' he unwittingly said.   120

Sore sighed the charmed sword, for its
   virtue was o'er,

It sprung from his grasp and was never
    seen more;
But true men have said that the light-
    ning's red wing
Did waft back the brand to the dread Fire-
    King.

He clenched his set teeth and his gaunt-
    leted hand ;
He stretched with one buffet that page on
    the strand;
As back from the stripling the broken
    casque rolled,
You might see the blue eyes and the ring-
    lets of gold.

Short time had Count Albert in horror to
    stare
On those death-swimming eyeballs and
    blood-clotted hair ;   130
For down came the Templars, like Cedron
    in flood,
And dyed their long lances in Saracen
    blood.

The Saracens, Curdmans, and Ishmaelites
    yield
To the scallop, the saltier, and crossleted
    shield;
And the eagles were gorged with the in-
    fidel dead
From Bethsaida's fountains to Naphthali's
    head.

The battle is over on Bethsaida's plain. —
O, who is yon Paynim lies stretched mid
    the slain ?
And who is yon page lying cold at his
    knee ? —
O, who but Count Albert and fair Rosa-
    lie ?   140

The lady was buried in Salem's blest
    bound,
The count he was left to the vulture and
    hound :
Her soul to high mercy Our Lady did
    bring ;
His went on the blast to the dread Fire-
    King.

Yet many a minstrel in harping can tell
How the Red-cross it conquered, the Cres-
    cent it fell:

And lords and gay ladies have sighed mid
    their glee
At the tale of Count Albert and fair Rosa-
    lie.

BOTHWELL CASTLE

A FRAGMENT

1799

WHEN fruitful Clydesdale's apple-bowers
    Are mellowing in the noon ;
When sighs round Pembroke's ruined
    towers
    The sultry breath of June ;

When Clyde, despite his sheltering wood,
    Must leave his channel dry,
And vainly o'er the limpid flood
    The angler guides his fly ;

If chance by Bothwell's lovely braes
    A wanderer thou hast been,
Or hid thee from the summer's blaze
    In Blantyre's bowers of green,

Full where the copsewood opens wild
    Thy pilgrim step hath staid,
Where Bothwell's towers in ruin piled
    O'erlook the verdant glade ;

And many a tale of love and fear
    Hath mingled with the scene —
Of Bothwell's banks that bloomed so dear,
    And Bothwell's bonny Jean.

O, if with rugged minstrel lays
    Unsated be thy ear,
And thou of deeds of other days
    Another tale wilt hear, —

Then all beneath the spreading beech,
    Flung careless on the lea,
The Gothic muse the tale shall teach
    Of Bothwell's sisters three.

Wight Wallace stood on Deckmont head,
    He blew his bugle round,
Till the wild bull in Cadyow wood
    Has started at the sound.

Saint George's cross, o'er Bothwell hung,
    Was waving far and wide,

And from the lofty turret flung
  Its crimson blaze on Clyde ;

And rising at the bugle blast
  That marked the Scottish foe,
Old England's yeomen mustered fast,
  And bent the Norman bow.

Tall in the midst Sir Aylmer rose,
  Proud Pembroke's Earl was he —
While — . . . . . .

THE SHEPHERD'S TALE

A FRAGMENT

1799

. . . .
AND ne'er but once, my son, he says,
  Was yon sad cavern trod,
In persecution's iron days
  When the land was left by God.

From Bewlie bog with slaughter red
  A wanderer hither drew,
And oft he stopt and turned his head,
  As by fits the night wind blew ;

For trampling round by Cheviot edge
  Were heard the troopers keen,   10
And frequent from the Whitelaw ridge
  The death-shot flashed between.

The moonbeams through the misty shower
  On yon dark cavern fell ;
Through the cloudy night the snow gleamed
    white,
  Which sunbeam ne'er could quell.

' Yon cavern dark is rough and rude,
  And cold its jaws of snow ;
But more rough and rude are the men of
    blood
  That hunt my life below !   20

' Yon spell-bound den, as the aged tell,
  Was hewn by demon's hands;
But I had lourd melle with the fiends of
    hell
  Than with Clavers and his band.'

He heard the deep-mouthed bloodhound
    bark,
  He heard the horses neigh,

He plunged him in the cavern dark,
  And downward sped his way.

Now faintly down the winding path
  Came the cry of the faulting hound,   30
And the muttered oath of balked wrath
  Was lost in hollow sound.

He threw him on the flinted floor,
  And held his breath for fear ;
He rose and bitter cursed his foes,
  As the sounds died on his ear.

' O, bare thine arm, thou battling Lord,
  For Scotland's wandering band ;
Dash from the oppressor's grasp the sword,
  And sweep him from the land !   40

' Forget not thou thy people's groans
  From dark Dunnotter's tower,
Mixed with the sea-fowl's shrilly moans
  And ocean's bursting roar !

' O, in fell Clavers' hour of pride,
  Even in his mightiest day,
As bold he strides through conquest's tide,
  O, stretch him on the clay !

' His widow and his little ones,
  O, may their tower of trust   50
Remove its strong foundation stones,
  And crush them in the dust ! '

' Sweet prayers to me,' a voice replied,
  ' Thrice welcome, guest of mine ! '
And glimmering on the cavern side
  A light was seen to shine.

An aged man in amice brown
  Stood by the wanderer's side,
By powerful charm a dead man's arm
  The torch's light supplied.   60

From each stiff finger stretched upright
  Arose a ghastly flame,
That waved not in the blast of night
  Which through the cavern came.

O, deadly blue was that taper's hue
  That flamed the cavern o'er,
But more deadly blue was the ghastly hue
  Of his eyes who the taper bore.

He laid on his head a hand like lead,
  As heavy, pale, and cold —   70

' Vengeance be thine, thou guest of mine,
　　If thy heart be firm and bold.

' But if faint thy heart, and caitiff fear
　　Thy recreant sinews know,
The mountain erne thy heart shall tear,
　　Thy nerves the hooded crow.'

The wanderer raised him undismayed :
　　' My soul, by dangers steeled,
Is stubborn as my Border blade,
　　Which never knew to yield.　　　80

' And if thy power can speed the hour
　　Of vengeance on my foes,
Theirs be the fate from bridge and gate
　　To feed the hooded crows.'

The Brownie looked him in the face,
　　And his color fled with speed —
' I fear me,' quoth he, ' uneath it will be
　　To match thy word and deed.

' In ancient days when English bands
　　Sore ravaged Scotland fair,　　　90
The sword and shield of Scottish land
　　Was valiant Halbert Kerr.

' A warlock loved the warrior well,
　　Sir Michael Scott by name,
And he sought for his sake a spell to make,
　　Should the Southern foemen tame.

' " Look thou," he said, " from Cessford
　　head
As the July sun sinks low,
And when glimmering white on Cheviot's
　　height
Thou shalt spy a wreath of snow,　　　100
The spell is complete which shall bring to
　　thy feet
The haughty Saxon foe."

' For many a year wrought the wizard here
　　In Cheviot's bosom low,
Till the spell was complete and in July's
　　heat
Appeared December's snow ;
But Cessford's Halbert never came
　　The wondrous cause to know.

' For years before in Bowden aisle
　　The warrior's bones had lain,　　　110
And after short while by female guile
　　Sir Michael Scott was slain.

' But me and my brethren in this cell
　　His mighty charms retain, —
And he that can quell the powerful spell
　　Shall o'er broad Scotland reign.'

He led him through an iron door
　　And up a winding stair,
And in wild amaze did the wanderer gaze
　　On the sight which opened there.　　　120

Through the gloomy night flashed ruddy
　　light,
　　A thousand torches glow ;
The cave rose high, like the vaulted sky,
　　O'er stalls in double row.

In every stall of that endless hall
　　Stood a steed in barding bright ;
At the foot of each steed, all armed save
　　the head,
　　Lay stretched a stalwart knight.

In each mailed hand was a naked brand ;
　　As they lay on the black bull's hide,　　　130
Each visage stern did upwards turn
　　With eyeballs fixed and wide.

A launcegay strong, full twelve ells long,
　　By every warrior hung ;
At each pommel there for battle yare
　　A Jedwood axe was slung.

The casque hung near each cavalier ;
　　The plumes waved mournfully
At every tread which the wanderer made
　　Through the hall of gramarye.　　　140

The ruddy beam of the torches' gleam,
　　That glared the warriors on,
Reflected light from armor bright,
　　In noontide splendor shone.

And onward seen in lustre sheen,
　　Still lengthening on the sight,
Through the boundless hall stood steeds in
　　stall,
　　And by each lay a sable knight.

Still as the dead lay each horseman dread,
　　And moved nor limb nor tongue;　　　150
Each steed stood stiff as an earthfast cliff,
　　Nor hoof nor bridle rung.

No sounds through all the spacious hall
　　The deadly still divide,

Save where echoes aloof from the vaulted
    roof
To the wanderer's step replied.

At length before his wondering eyes,
    On an iron column borne,
Of antique shape and giant size
    Appeared a sword and horn.   160

'Now choose thee here,' quoth his leader,
    'Thy venturous fortune try;
Thy woe and weal, thy boot and bale,
    In yon brand and bugle lie.'

To the fatal brand he mounted his hand,
    But his soul did quiver and quail;
The life-blood did start to his shuddering
    heart,
    And left him wan and pale.

The brand he forsook, and the horn he
    took
    To 'say a gentle sound;   170
But so wild a blast from the bugle brast
    That the Cheviot rocked around.

From Forth to Tees, from seas to seas,
    The awful bugle rung;
On Carlisle wall and Berwick withal
    To arms the warders sprung.

With clank and clang the cavern rang,
    The steeds did stamp and neigh;
And loud was the yell as each warrior
    fell
Sterte up with whoop and cry.   180

'Woe, woe,' they cried, 'thou caitiff cow-
    ard,
    That ever thou wert born!
Why drew ye not the knightly sword
    Before ye blew the horn?'

The morning on the mountain shone
    And on the bloody ground,
Hurled from the cave with shivered bone,
    The mangled wretch was found.

And still beneath the cavern dread
    Among the glidders gray,   190
A shapeless stone with lichens spread
    Marks where the wanderer lay.

. . . .

CHEVIOT

A FRAGMENT

1799

. . . .
Go sit old Cheviot's crest below,
And pensive mark the lingering snow
    In all his scaurs abide,
And slow dissolving from the hill
In many a sightless, soundless rill,
    Feed sparkling Bowmont's tide.

Fair shines the stream by bank and lea,
As wimpling to the eastern sea
    She seeks Till's sullen bed,
Indenting deep the fatal plain
Where Scotland's noblest, brave in vain,
    Around their monarch bled.

And westward hills on hills you see,
Even as old Ocean's mightiest sea
    Heaves high her waves of foam,
Dark and snow-ridged from Cutsfeld's
    wold
To the proud foot of Cheviot rolled,
    Earth's mountain billows come.

. . . .

FREDERICK AND ALICE

This tale, written in 1801, and published in
Tales of Wonder, is imitated, rather than
translated, says Scott, 'from a fragment introduced in Goethe's "Claudina von Villa Bella,"
where it is sung by a member of a gang of
banditti, to engage the attention of the family,
while his companions break into the castle.'

FREDERICK leaves the land of France,
    Homeward hastes his steps to measure,
Careless casts the parting glance
    On the scene of former pleasure.

Joying in his prancing steed,
    Keen to prove his untried blade,
Hope's gay dreams the soldier lead
    Over mountain, moor, and glade.

Helpless, ruined, left forlorn,
    Lovely Alice wept alone,   10
Mourned o'er love's fond contract torn,
    Hope, and peace, and honor flown.

Mark her breast's convulsive throbs !
　See, the tear of anguish flows ! —
Mingling soon with bursting sobs,
　Loud the laugh of frenzy rose.

Wild she cursed, and wild she prayed ;
　Seven long days and nights are o'er:
Death in pity brought his aid,
　As the village bell struck four.　20

Far from her, and far from France,
　Faithless Frederick onward rides ;
Marking blithe the morning's glance
　Mantling o'er the mountains' sides.

Heard ye not the boding sound,
　As the tongue of yonder tower,
Slowly to the hills around
　Told the fourth, the fated hour ?

Starts the steed and snuffs the air,
　Yet no cause of dread appears ;　30
Bristles high the rider's hair,
　Struck with strange mysterious fears.

Desperate, as his terrors rise,
　In the steed the spur he hides;
From himself in vain he flies;
　Anxious, restless, on he rides.

Seven long days and seven long nights,
　Wild he wandered, woe the while !
Ceaseless care and causeless fright
　Urge his footsteps many a mile.　40

Dark the seventh sad night descends ;
　Rivers swell and rain-streams pour,
While the deafening thunder lends
　All the terrors of its roar.

Weary, wet, and spent with toil,
　Where his head shall Frederick hide ?
Where, but in yon ruined aisle,
　By the lightning's flash descried.

To the portal, dank and low,
　Fast his steed the wanderer bound :　50
Down a ruined staircase slow,
　Next his darkling way he wound.

Long drear vaults before him lie !
　Glimmering lights are seen to glide ! —
'Blessed Mary, hear my cry !
　Deign a sinner's steps to guide ! '

Often lost their quivering beam,
　Still the lights move slow before,
Till they rest their ghastly gleam
　Right against an iron door.　60

Thundering voices from within,
　Mixed with peals of laughter, rose ;
As they fell, a solemn strain
　Lent its wild and wondrous close !

Midst the din he seemed to hear
　Voice of friends, by death removed; —
Well he knew that solemn air,
　'T was the lay that Alice loved. —

Hark ! for now a solemn knell
　Four times on the still night broke;　70
Four times at its deaden'd swell,
　Echoes from the ruins spoke.

As the lengthened clangors die,
　Slowly opes the iron door !
Straight a banquet met his eye,
　But a funeral's form it wore !

Coffins for the seats extend;
　All with black the board was spread ;
Girt by parent, brother, friend,
　Long since number'd with the dead !　80

Alice, in her grave-clothes bound,
　Ghastly smiling, points a seat ;
All arose with thundering sound ;
　All the expected stranger greet.

High their meagre arms they wave,
　Wild their notes of welcome swell ; —
' Welcome, traitor, to the grave !
　Perjured, bid the light farewell ! '

CADYOW CASTLE

ADDRESSED TO THE RIGHT HONORABLE
LADY ANNE HAMILTON

This ballad was written in 1801 and included in the third volume of *Minstrelsy of the Scottish Border.*

WHEN princely Hamilton's abode
　Ennobled Cadyow's Gothic towers,
The song went round, the goblet flowed,
　And revel sped the laughing hours.

Then, thrilling to the harp's gay sound,
  So sweetly rung each vaulted wall,
And echoed light the dancer's bound,
  As mirth and music cheered the hall.

But Cadyow's towers in ruins laid,
  And vaults by ivy mantled o'er,   10
Thrill to the music of the shade,
  Or echo Evan's hoarser roar.

Yet still of Cadyow's faded fame
  You bid me tell a minstrel tale,
And tune my harp of Border frame
  On the wild banks of Evandale.

For thou, from scenes of courtly pride,
  From pleasure's lighter scenes, canst
        turn,
To draw oblivion's pall aside
  And mark the long-forgotten urn.   20

Then, noble maid! at thy command
  Again the crumbled halls shall rise;
Lo! as on Evan's banks we stand,
  The past returns — the present flies.

Where with the rock's wood-covered side
  Were blended late the ruins green,
Rise turrets in fantastic pride
  And feudal banners flaunt between:

Where the rude torrent's brawling course
  Was shagged with thorn and tangling
        sloe,   30
The ashler buttress braves its force
  And ramparts frown in battled row.

'T is night — the shade of keep and spire
  Obscurely dance on Evan's stream;
And on the wave the warder's fire
  Is checkering the moonlight beam.

Fades slow their light; the east is gray;
  The weary warder leaves his tower;
Steeds snort, uncoupled stag-hounds bay,
  And merry hunters quit the bower.   40

The drawbridge falls — they hurry out —
  Clatters each plank and swinging chain,
As, dashing o'er, the jovial rout
  Urge the shy steed and slack the rein.

First of his troop, the chief rode on;
  His shouting merry-men throng behind;

The steed of princely Hamilton
  Was fleeter than the mountain wind.

From the thick copse the roebucks bound,
  The startled red-deer scuds the plain,   50
For the hoarse bugle's warrior-sound
  Has roused their mountain haunts again.

Through the huge oaks of Evandale,
  Whose limbs a thousand years have worn,
What sullen roar comes down the gale
  And drowns the hunter's pealing horn?

Mightiest of all the beasts of chase
  That roam in woody Caledon,
Crashing the forest in his race,   59
  The Mountain Bull comes thundering on.

Fierce on the hunter's quivered band
  He rolls his eyes of swarthy glow,
Spurns with black hoof and horn the sand,
  And tosses high his mane of snow.

Aimed well the chieftain's lance has flown;
  Struggling in blood the savage lies;
His roar is sunk in hollow groan —
  Sound, merry huntsmen! sound the
        pryse!

'T is noon — against the knotted oak
  The hunters rest the idle spear;   70
Curls through the trees the slender smoke,
  Where yeomen dight the woodland cheer.

Proudly the chieftain marked his clan,
  On greenwood lap all careless thrown,
Yet missed his eye the boldest man
  That bore the name of Hamilton.

'Why fills not Bothwellhaugh his place,
  Still wont our weal and woe to share?
Why comes he not our sport to grace?
  Why shares he not our hunter's fare?'   80

Stern Claud replied with darkening face —
  Gray Paisley's haughty lord was he —
'At merry feast or buxom chase
  No more the warrior wilt thou see.

'Few suns have set since Woodhouselee
  Saw Bothwellhaugh's bright goblets
        foam,
When to his hearths in social glee
  The war-worn soldier turned him home.

' There, wan from her maternal throes,
His Margaret, beautiful and mild,   90
Sate in her bower, a pallid rose,
   And peaceful nursed her new-born child.

' O change accursed ! past are those days ;
   False Murray's ruthless spoilers came,
And, for the hearth's domestic blaze,
   Ascends destruction's volumed flame.

' What sheeted phantom wanders wild
   Where mountain Eske through woodland
      flows,
Her arms enfold a shadowy child —
   O ! is it she, the pallid rose ?   100

' The wildered traveller sees her glide,
   And hears her feeble voice with awe —
" Revenge," she cries, " on Murray's pride !
   And woe for injured Bothwellhaugh ! " '

He ceased — and cries of rage and grief
   Burst mingling from the kindred band,
And half arose the kindling chief,
   And half unsheathed his Arran brand.

But who o'er bush, o'er stream and rock,
   Rides headlong with resistless speed, 110
Whose bloody poniard's frantic stroke
   Drives to the leap his jaded steed ;

Whose cheek is pale, whose eyeballs glare,
   As one some visioned sight that saw,
Whose hands are bloody, loose his hair ? —
   'T is he ! 't is he ! 't is Bothwellhaugh.

From gory selle and reeling steed
   Sprung the fierce horseman with a bound,
And, reeking from the recent deed,
   He dashed his carbine on the ground. 120

Sternly he spoke — ' 'T is sweet to hear
   In good greenwood the bugle blown,
But sweeter to Revenge's ear
   To drink a tyrant's dying groan.

' Your slaughtered quarry proudly trode
   At dawning morn o'er dale and down,
But prouder base-born Murray rode
   Through old Linlithgow's crowded town.

' From the wild Border's humbled side,
   In haughty triumph marched he,   130
While Knox relaxed his bigot pride
   And smiled the traitorous pomp to see.

' But can stern Power, with all his vaunt,
   Or Pomp, with all her courtly glare,
The settled heart of Vengeance daunt,
   Or change the purpose of Despair ?

' With hackbut bent, my secret stand,
   Dark as the purposed deed, I chose,
And marked where mingling in his band
   Trooped Scottish pipes and English
      bows.   140

' Dark Morton, girt with many a spear,
   Murder's foul minion, led the van ;
And clashed their broadswords in the
      rear
   The wild Macfarlanes' plaided clan.

' Glencairn and stout Parkhead were nigh,
   Obsequious at their Regent's rein,
And haggard Lindesay's iron eye,
   That saw fair Mary weep in vain.

' Mid pennoned spears, a steely grove, 149
   Proud Murray's plumage floated high;
Scarce could his trampling charger move,
   So close the minions crowded nigh.

' From the raised vizor's shade his eye,
   Dark-rolling, glanced the ranks along,
And his steel truncheon, waved on high,
   Seemed marshalling the iron throng.

' But yet his saddened brow confessed
   A passing shade of doubt and awe ;
Some fiend was whispering in his breast,
   " Beware of injured Bothwellhaugh ! " 160

' The death - shot parts ! the charger
      springs ;
Wild rises tumult's startling roar !
And Murray's plumy helmet rings —
   Rings on the ground to rise no more.

' What joy the raptured youth can feel,
   To hear her love the loved one tell —
Or he who broaches on his steel
   The wolf by whom his infant fell !

' But dearer to my injured eye
   To see in dust proud Murray roll ; 170
And mine was ten times trebled joy
   To hear him groan his felon soul.

' My Margaret's spectre glided near,
   With pride her bleeding victim saw,

And shrieked in his death-deafened ear,
  "Remember injured Bothwellhaugh!"

'Then speed thee, noble Chatlerault!
  Spread to the wind thy bannered tree!
Each warrior bend his Clydesdale bow! —
  Murray is fallen and Scotland free!' 180

Vaults every warrior to his steed;
  Loud bugles join their wild acclaim —
'Murray is fallen and Scotland freed!
  Couch, Arran, couch thy spear of flame!'

But see! the minstrel vision fails —
  The glimmering spears are seen no
    more;
The shouts of war die on the gales,
  Or sink in Evan's lonely roar.

For the loud bugle pealing high,
  The blackbird whistles down the vale, 190
And sunk in ivied ruins lie
  The bannered towers of Evandale.

For chiefs intent on bloody deed,
  And Vengeance shouting o'er the slain,
Lo! high-born Beauty rules the steed,
  Or graceful guides the silken rein.

And long may Peace and Pleasure own
  The maids who list the minstrel's tale;
Nor e'er a ruder guest be known
  On the fair banks of Evandale! 200

THE REIVER'S WEDDING

A FRAGMENT

1802

O, WILL ye hear a mirthful bourd?
  Or will ye hear of courtesie?
Or will ye hear how a gallant lord
  Was wedded to a gay ladye?

'Ca' out the kye,' quo' the village herd,
  As he stood on the knowe,
'Ca' this ane's nine and that ane's ten,
  And bauld Lord William's cow.'

'Ah! by my sooth,' quoth William then,
  'And stands it that way now, 10
When knave and churl have nine and ten,
  That the lord has but his cow?

'I swear by the light of the Michaelmas
    moon,
  And the might of Mary high,
And by the edge of my braidsword brown,
  They shall soon say Harden's kye.'

He took a bugle frae his side,
  With names carved o'er and o'er —
Full many a chief of meikle pride
  That Border bugle bore — 20

He blew a note baith sharp and hie
  Till rock and water ran around —
Threescore of moss-troopers and three
  Have mounted at that bugle sound.

The Michaelmas moon had entered then,
  And ere she wan the full
Ye might see by her light in Harden
    glen
  A bow o' kye and a bassened bull.

And loud and loud in Harden tower
  The quaigh gaed round wi' meikle glee;
For the English beef was brought in
    bower 31
  And the English ale flowed merrilie.

And mony a guest from Teviotside
  And Yarrow's braes was there;
Was never a lord in Scotland wide
  That made more dainty fare.

They ate, they laughed, they sang and
    quaffed,
  Till naught on board was seen,
When knight and squire were boune to
    dine,
  But a spur of silver sheen. 40

Lord William has ta'en his berry-brown
    steed —
  A sore shent man was he;
'Wait ye, my guests, a little speed —
  Weel feasted ye shall be.'

He rode him down by Falsehope burn,
  His cousin dear to see,
With him to take a riding turn —
  Wat-draw-the-Sword was he.

And when he came to Falsehope glen,
  Beneath the trysting-tree, 50
On the smooth green was carved plain,
  'To Lochwood bound are we.'

'O, if they be gane to dark Lochwood
　To drive the Warden's gear,
Betwixt our names, I ween, there 's feud ;
　I 'll go and have my share :

'For little reck I for Johnstone's feud,
　The Warden though he be.'
So Lord William is away to dark Loch-
　　wood
With riders barely three.   60

The Warden's daughters in Lochwood sate,
　Were all both fair and gay,
All save the Lady Margaret,
　And she was wan and wae.

The sister Jean had a full fair skin,
　And Grace was bauld and braw ;
But the leal-fast heart her breast within
　It weel was worth them a'.

Her father 's pranked her sisters twa
　With meikle joy and pride ;   70
But Margaret maun seek Dundrennan's
　　wa' —
She ne'er can be a bride.

On spear and casque by gallants gent
　Her sisters' scarfs were borne,
But never at tilt or tournament
　Were Margaret's colors worn.

Her sisters rode to Thirlstane bower,
　But she was left at hame
To wander round the gloomy tower,
　And sigh young Harden's name   80

'Of all the knights, the knight most fair
　From Yarrow to the Tyne,'
Soft sighed the maid, 'is Harden's heir,
　But ne'er can he be mine ;

'Of all the maids, the foulest maid
　From Teviot to the Dee,
Ah !' sighing sad, that lady said,
　'Can ne'er young Harden's be.'

She looked up the briery glen,
　And up the mossy brae,   90
And she saw a score of her father's men
　Yclad in the Johnstone gray.

O, fast and fast they downwards sped
　The moss and briers among,

And in the midst the troopers led
　A shackled knight along.

．　　．　　．　　．　　．　　．

CHRISTIE'S WILL

The origin of this ballad is thus delivered by Scott : ' In the reign of Charles I., when the moss-trooping practices were not entirely discontinued, the tower of Gilnockie, in the parish of Cannoby, was occupied by William Armstrong, called, for distinction's sake, *Christie's Will*, a lineal descendant of the famous John Armstrong, of Gilnockie, executed by James V. The hereditary love of plunder had descended to this person with the family mansion ; and upon some marauding party, he was seized, and imprisoned in the tolbooth of Jedburgh. The Earl of Traquair, Lord High Treasurer, happening to visit Jedburgh, and knowing Christie's Will, inquired the cause of his confinement. Will replied, he was imprisoned for stealing two *tethers* (halters) ; but, upon being more closely interrogated, acknowledged that there were two *delicate colts* at the end of them. The joke, such as it was, amused the Earl, who exerted his interest, and succeeded in releasing Christie's Will from bondage. Some time afterwards, a lawsuit, of importance to Lord Traquair, was to be decided in the Court of Session ; and there was every reason to believe that the judgment would turn upon the voice of the presiding judge, who has a casting vote, in case of an equal division among his brethren. The opinion of the president was unfavorable to Lord Traquair ; and the point was, therefore, to keep him out of the way when the question should be tried. In this dilemma, the Earl had recourse to Christie's Will ; who, at once, offered his service to kidnap the president. Upon due scrutiny, he found it was the judge's practice frequently to take the air, on horseback, on the sands of Leith, without an attendant. In one of these excursions, Christie's Will, who had long watched his opportunity, ventured to accost the president, and engage him in conversation. His address and language were so amusing, that he decoyed the president into an unfrequented and furzy common, called the Frigate Whins, where, riding suddenly up to him, he pulled him from his horse, muffled him in a large cloak, which he had provided, and rode off, with the luckless judge trussed up behind him. Will crossed the country with great expedition, by paths known only to persons of his description, and deposited his weary and terrified burden in an old castle, in Annandale, called the Tower of Graham. The judge's horse being found, it was concluded he had thrown his rider into the sea ; his friends went into mourning, and a successor was appointed to his office. Meanwhile, the poor president spent a heavy time in the vault of the castle. He was imprisoned, and solitary ; receiving his food through an aperture in the wall, and never hearing the sound of a human voice, save when a shepherd called his dog, by the name of *Batty*, and when a female domestic called upon *Maudge*, the cat. These, he concluded, were invocations of spirits ; for he held himself to be in the dungeon of a sorcerer. At length, after three months had elapsed, the lawsuit was decided in favor of Lord Traquair ; and Will was directed to set the president at liberty. Accordingly, he entered the vault at dead of night, seized the president, muffled him once more in the cloak, without speaking a single word, and, using the same mode of transportation, conveyed him to Leith sands, and set down the astonished judge on the very spot where he had taken him up. The joy of his friends, and the less agreeable surprise of his successor, may be easily conceived, when he appeared in court, to reclaim his office and honors. All embraced his own persuasion, that he had been spirited away by witchcraft ; nor could he himself be convinced of the contrary, until, many years afterwards, happening to travel in Annandale, his ears were saluted once more with the sounds of *Maudge* and *Batty* — the only notes which had solaced his long confinement. This led to a discovery of the whole story ; but, in those disorderly times, it was only laughed at, as a fair *ruse de guerre.*

'Wild and strange as this tradition may seem, there is little doubt of its foundation in fact. The judge, upon whose person this extraordinary stratagem was practised, was Sir Alexander Gibson, Lord Durie, collector of the reports, well known in the Scottish law, under the title of *Durie's Decisions.* He was advanced to the station of an ordinary Lord of Session, 10th July, 1621, and died, at his own house of Durie, July, 1646. Betwixt these periods this whimsical adventure must have happened ; a date which corresponds with that of the tradition.' . . .

The ballad thus patched and embroidered was included by Scott in that section of *Minstrelsy of the Scottish Border*, which was given to modern imitations. The date may be set down as 1802.

TRAQUAIR has ridden up Chapelhope,
 And sae has he down by the Grey Mare's
  Tail ;
He never stinted the light gallop,
 Until he speered for Christie's Will.

Now Christie's Will peeped frae the tower,
 And out at the shot-hole keeked he ;
'And ever unlucky,' quo' he, 'is the hour,
 That the Warden comes to speer for
  me !'

'Good Christie's Will, now, have nae fear !
 Nae harm, good Will, shall hap to thee :
I saved thy life at the Jeddart air,   11
 At the Jeddart air frae the justice tree.

'Bethink how ye sware, by the salt and the
  bread,
 By the lightning, the wind, and the rain,
That if ever of Christie's Will I had need,
 He would pay me my service again.'

'Gramercy, my lord,' quo' Christie's Will,
 'Gramercy, my lord, for your grace to
  me !
When I turn my cheek, and claw my
  neck,
 I think of Traquair and the Jeddart
  tree.'   20

And he has opened the fair tower yate,
 To Traquair and a' his companie ;
The spule o' the deer on the board he has
  set,
 The fattest that ran on the Hutton Lee.

'Now, wherefore sit ye sad, my lord ?
 And wherefore sit ye mournfullie ?
And why eat ye not of the venison I
  shot,
 At the dead of night on Hutton Lee ?'

'O weel may I stint of feast and sport,
 And in my mind be vexed sair !   30
A vote of the canker'd Session Court,
 Of land and living will make me bare.

'But if auld Durie to heaven were flown,
 Or if auld Durie to hell were gane,
Or . . . if he could be but ten days
  stoun . . .
 My bonny braid lands would still be my
  ain.'

'O, mony a time, my lord,' he said,
 'I 've stown the horse frae the sleeping
  loon ;
But for you I 'll steal a beast as braid,
 For I 'll steal Lord Durie frae Edinburgh
  toun.   40

'O, mony a time, my lord,' he said,
  ' I've stown a kiss frae a sleeping wench ;
But for you I 'll do as kittle a deed,
  For I 'll steal an auld lurdane aff the
    bench.'

And Christie's Will is to Edinburgh gane ;
  At the Borough Muir then entered he ;
And as he passed the gallow-stane,
  He crossed his brow and he bent his
    knee.

He lighted at Lord Durie's door,   49
  And there he knocked most manfullie ;
And up and spake Lord Durie sae stour,
  ' What tidings, thou stalward groom, to
    me ? '

' The fairest lady in Teviotdale
  Has sent, maist reverent sir, for thee ;
She pleas at the Session for her land, a'
    haill,
  And fain she wad plead her cause to
    thee.'

' But how can I to that lady ride,
  With saving of my dignitie ? '
' O a curch and mantle ye may wear,
  And in my cloak ye sall muffled be.'   60

Wi' curch on head, and cloak ower face,
  He mounted the judge on a palfrey fyne ;
He rode away, a right round pace,
  And Christie's Will held the bridle reyn.

The Lothian Edge they were not o'er,
  When they heard bugles bauldly ring,
And, hunting over Middleton Moor,
  They met, I ween, our noble King.

When Willie looked upon our King,
  I wot a frighted man was he !   70
But ever auld Durie was startled mair,
  For tyning of his dignitie.

The King he crossed himself, iwis,
  When as the pair came riding bye —
' An uglier crone, and a sturdier loon,
  I think, were never seen with eye ! '

Willie has hied to the tower of Græme,
  He took auld Durie on his back,
He shot him down to the dungeon deep,
  Which garred his auld banes gie mony a
    crack.   80

For nineteen days, and nineteen nights,
  Of sun, or moon, or midnight stern,
Auld Durie never saw a blink,
  The lodging was sae dark and dern.

He thought the warlocks o' the rosy cross,
  Had fanged him in their nets sae fast ;
Or that the gipsies' glamoured gang
  Had laired his learning at the last.

' Hey ! Batty, lad ! far yaud ! far yaud ! '
  These were the morning sounds heard
    he ;   90
And ever ' Alack ! ' auld Durie cried,
  ' The de'il is hounding his tykes on
    me ! ' —

And whiles a voice on *Baudrons* cried,
  With sound uncouth, and sharp, and hie ;
' I have tar-barrelled mony a witch,
  But now, I think, they'll clear scores wi'
    me ! '

The King has caused a bill be wrote,
  And he has set it on the Tron, —
' He that will bring Lord Durie back,   99
  Shall have five hundred merks and one.'

Traquair has written a privie letter,
  And he has sealed it wi' his seal, —
' Ye may let the auld brock out o' the
    poke ;
  The land 's my ain, and a's gane weel.'

O Will has mounted his bonny black,
  And to the tower of Græme did trudge,
And once again, on his sturdy back,
  Has he hente up the weary judge.

He brought him to the council stairs,
  And there full loudly shouted he,   110
' Gie me my guerdon, my sovereign liege,
  And take ye back your auld Durie ! '

THOMAS THE RHYMER

When Scott was engaged upon the *Minstrelsy of the Scottish Border*, he had a long and animated correspondence with the antiquarians Leyden and Ellis, over the productions of Thomas of Ercildoune, known by the appellation of *The Rhymer*. He purposed, at first, including the ballad of *Sir Tristrem* in the *Minstrelsy*, but the material illustrative and interpretative of it swelled to such dimensions that he finally issued in 1804, after the *Minstrelsy* had been completed, *The Metrical Romance of Sir Tristrem.* Meanwhile, he had included in the *Minstrelsy* the following ballads under the general head of *Thomas the Rhymer.* Although the third only is wholly Scott's, it seems best to print in their sequence Part First, which is a traditional version, Part Second, which is altered from ancient prophesies, and Part Third, which is modern and Scott's own.

PART FIRST

TRADITIONAL VERSION

TRUE Thomas lay on Huntlie bank;
  A ferlie he spied wi' his ee ;
And there he saw a ladye bright,
  Come riding down by the Eildon Tree.

Her shirt was o' the grass-green silk,
  Her mantle o' the velvet fyne ;
At ilka tett of her horse's mane,
  Hung fifty siller bells and nine.

True Thomas, he pulled aff his cap,
  And louted low down to his knee,   10
' All hail, thou mighty Queen of Heaven !
  For thy peer on earth I never did see.' —

' O no, O no, Thomas,' she said,
  ' That name does not belang to me ;
I am but the queen of fair Elfland,
  That am hither come to visit thee.

' Harp and carp, Thomas,' she said;
  ' Harp and carp along wi' me ;
And if ye dare to kiss my lips,
  Sure of your bodie I will be.' —   20

' Betide me weal, betide me woe,
  That weird shall never daunton me.' —
Syne he has kissed her rosy lips,
  All underneath the Eildon Tree.

' Now, ye maun go wi' me,' she said ;
  ' True Thomas, ye maun go wi' me ;
And ye maun serve me seven years,
  Thro' weal or woe as may chance to
    be.'

She mounted on her milk-white steed ;
  She 's ta'en true Thomas up behind :   30
And aye, whene'er her bridle rung,
  The steed flew swifter than the wind.

O they rade on, and farther on ;
  The steed gaed swifter than the wind ;
Until they reached a desert wide,
  And living land was left behind.

' Light down, light down, now, true
    Thomas,
  And lean your head upon my knee ;
Abide and rest a little space,
  And I will shew you ferlies three.   40

' O see ye not yon narrow road,
  So thick beset with thorns and briers ?
That is the path of righteousness,
  Though after it but few enquires.

' And see ye not that braid braid road,
  That lies across that lily leven ?
That is the path of wickedness,
  Though some call it the road to heaven.

' And see not ye that bonny road,
  That winds about the fernie brae ?   50
That is the road to fair Elfland,
  Where thou and I this night maun gae.

' But, Thomas, ye maun hold your tongue,
  Whatever ye may hear or see ;
For, if you speak word in Elflyn land,
  Ye 'll ne'er get back to your ain coun-
    trie.'

O they rade on, and farther on,
  And they waded through rivers aboon
    the knee,
And they saw neither sun nor moon,
  But they heard the roaring of the sea.   60

It was mirk mirk night, and there was nae
    stern light,
  And they waded through red blude to
    the knee ;
For a' the blude that 's shed on earth
  Rins through the springs o' that countrie.

Syne they came on to a garden green,
  And she pu'd an apple frae a tree —
' Take this for thy wages, true Thomas;
  It will give thee the tongue that can
    never lie.'

' My tongue is mine ain,' true Thomas said;
  ' A gudely gift ye wad gie to me !   70
I neither dought to buy nor sell,
  At fair or tryst where I may be.

'I dought neither speak to prince or peer,
  Nor ask of grace from fair ladye.'
'Now hold thy peace !' the lady said,
  'For as I say, so must it be.'

He has gotten a coat of the even cloth,
  And a pair of shoes of velvet green ;
And till seven years were gane and past,
  True Thomas on earth was never seen. 80

PART SECOND

ALTERED FROM ANCIENT PROPHECIES

When seven years were come and gane,
  The sun blinked fair on pool and stream;
And Thomas lay on Huntlie bank,
  Like one awakened from a dream.

He heard the trampling of a steed,
  He saw the flash of armor flee,
And he beheld a gallant knight
  Come riding down by the Eildon-Tree.

He was a stalwart knight, and strong ;
  Of giant make he 'peared to be :   10
He stirred his horse, as he were wode,
  Wi' gilded spurs, of faushion free.

Says — 'Well met, well met, true Thomas !
  Some uncouth ferlies show to me.'
Says — 'Christ thee save, Corspatrick
      brave
  Thrice welcome, good Dunbar, to me !

'Light down, light down, Corspatrick
      brave !
  And I will show thee curses three,
Shall gar fair Scotland greet and grane,
  And change the green to the black
      livery.   20

'A storm shall roar this very hour,
  From Ross's Hills to Solway sea;'
'Ye lied, ye lied, ye warlock hoar !
  For the sun shines sweet on fauld and
      lea.'

He put his hand on the Earlie's head ;
  He showed him a rock beside the sea,
Where a king lay stiff beneath his steed,
  And steel-dight nobles wiped their ee.

'The neist curse lights on Branxton hills :
  By Flodden's high and heathery side,   30
Shall wave a banner red as blude,
  And chieftains throng wi' meikle pride.

'A Scottish King shall come full keen,
  The ruddy lion beareth he ;
A feathered arrow sharp, I ween,
  Shall make him wink and warre to see.

'When he is bloody, and all to bledde,
  Thus to his men he still shall say —
"For God's sake, turn ye back again,
  And give yon southern folk a fray !   40
Why should I lose the right is mine ?
  My doom is not to die this day."

'Yet turn ye to the eastern hand,
  And woe and wonder ye sall see ;
How forty thousand spearmen stand,
  Where yon rank river meets the sea.

'There shall the lion lose the gylte,
  And the libbards bear it clean away ;
At Pinkyn Cleuch there shall be spilt
  Much gentil bluid that day.'   50

'Enough, enough, of curse and ban ;
  Some blessings show thou now to me,
Or, by the faith o' my bodie,' Corspatrick
      said,
  'Ye shall rue the day ye e'er saw me !'

'The first of blessings I shall thee show,
  Is by a burn, that 's called of bread ;
Where Saxon men shall tine the bow,
  And find their arrows lack the head.

'Beside that brigg, out ower that burn,
  Where the water bickereth bright and
      sheen   60
Shall many a falling courser spurn,
  And knights shall die in battle keen.

'Beside a headless cross of stone,
  The libbards there shall lose the gree;
The raven shall come, the erne shall go,
  And drink the Saxon bluid sae free.
The cross of stone they shall not know,
  So thick the corses there shall be.'

'But tell me now,' said brave Dunbar,
  'True Thomas, tell now unto me,   70

What man shall rule the isle Britain,
  Even from the north to the southern
    sea ? '

' A French Queen shall bear the son,
  Shall rule all Britain to the sea;
He of the Bruce's blood shall come,
  As near as in the ninth degree.

' The waters worship shall his race;
  Likewise the waves of the farthest
    sea;
For they shall ride over ocean wide, 79
  With hempen bridles, and horse of tree.'

PART THIRD

When seven years more were come and
    gone,
  Was war through Scotland spread,
And Ruberslaw showed high Dunyon
  His beacon blazing red.

Then all by bonny Coldingknow,
  Pitched palliouns took their room,
And crested helms, and spears a-rowe,
  Glanced gaily through the broom.

The Leader, rolling to the Tweed,
  Resounds the ensenzie;   10
They roused the deer from Caddenhead,
  To distant Torwoodlee.

The feast was spread in Ercildoune,
  In Learmont's high and ancient hall:
And there were knights of great renown,
  And ladies, laced in pall.

Nor lacked they, while they sat at dine,
  The music nor the tale,
Nor goblets of the blood-red wine,
  Nor mantling quaighs of ale.   20

True Thomas rose, with harp in hand,
  When as the feast was done:
(In minstrel strife, in Fairy Land,
  The elfin harp he won.)

Hushed were the throng, both limb and
    tongue,
  And harpers for envy pale;
And armed lords leaned on their swords,
  And hearkened to the tale.

In numbers high, the witching tale
  The prophet poured along;   30
No after bard might e'er avail
  Those numbers to prolong.

Yet fragments of the lofty strain
  Float down the tide of years,
As, buoyant on the stormy main,
  A parted wreck appears.

He sung King Arthur's Table Round:
  The Warrior of the Lake;
How courteous Gawaine met the wound,
  And bled for ladies' sake.   40

But chief, in gentle Tristrem's praise,
  The notes melodious swell;
Was none excelled in Arthur's days,
  The knight of Lionelle.

For Marke, his cowardly uncle's right,
  A venomed wound he bore;
When fierce Morholde he slew in fight,
  Upon the Irish shore.

No art the poison might withstand;
  No medicine could be found,   50
Till lovely Isolde's lily hand
  Had probed the rankling wound.

With gentle hand and soothing tongue
  She bore the leech's part;
And, while she o'er his sick-bed hung,
  He paid her with his heart.

O fatal was the gift, I ween !
  For, doomed in evil tide,
The maid must be rude Cornwall's queen,
  His cowardly uncle's bride.   60

Their loves, their woes, the gifted bard
  In fairy tissue wove;
Where lords, and knights, and ladies
    bright,
  In gay confusion strove.

The Garde Joyeuse, amid the tale,
  High reared its glittering head;
And Avalon's enchanted vale
  In all its wonders spread.

Brangwain was there, and Segramore,
  And fiend-born Merlin's gramarye; 70
Of that famed wizard's mighty lore,
  O who could sing but he ?

Through many a maze the winning song
  In changeful passion led,
Till bent at length the listening throng
  O'er Tristrem's dying bed.

His ancient wounds their scars expand,
  With agony his heart is wrung:
O where is Isolde's lilye hand,
  And where her soothing tongue ?   80

She comes ! she comes ! — like flash of
    flame
  Can lovers' footsteps fly:
She comes ! she comes ! — she only came
  To see her Tristrem die.

She saw him die; her latest sigh
  Joined in a kiss his parting breath;
The gentlest pair, that Britain bare,
  United are in death.

There paused the harp: its lingering sound
  Died slowly on the ear;   90
The silent guests still bent around,
  For still they seemed to hear.

Then woe broke forth in murmurs weak,
  Nor ladies heaved alone the sigh;
But, half ashamed, the rugged cheek
  Did many a gauntlet dry.

On Leader's stream, and Learmont's tower,
  The mists of evening close;
In camp, in castle, or in bower,
  Each warrior sought repose.   100

Lord Douglas, in his lofty tent,
  Dreamed o'er the woful tale;
When footsteps light, across the bent,
  The warrior's ear assail.

He starts, he wakes; — 'What, Richard, ho!
  Arise, my page, arise !
What venturous wight, at dead of night,
  Dare step where Douglas lies !' —

Then forth they rushed: by Leader's tide,
  A selcouth sight they see —   110
A hart and hind pace side by side,
  As white as snow on Fairnalie.

Beneath the moon, with gesture proud,
  They stately move and slow;

Nor scare they at the gathering crowd,
  Who marvel as they go.

To Learmont's tower a message sped,
  As fast as page might run;
And Thomas started from his bed,
  And soon his clothes did on.   120

First he woxe pale, and then woxe red;
  Never a word he spake but three; —
'My sand is run; my thread is spun;
  This sign regardeth me.'

The elfin harp his neck around,
  In minstrel guise, he hung;
And on the wind, in doleful sound,
  Its dying accents rung.

Then forth he went; yet turned him oft
  To view his ancient hall: 130
On the grey tower, in lustre soft,
  The autumn moonbeams fall;

And Leader's waves, like silver sheen,
  Danced shimmering in the ray;
In deepening mass, at distance seen,
  Broad Soltra's mountains lay.

'Farewell, my father's ancient tower !
  A long farewell,' said he:
'The scene of pleasure, pomp, or power,
  Thou never more shalt be.   140

'To Learmont's name no foot of earth
  Shall here again belong,
And, on thy hospitable hearth,
  The hare shall leave her young.

'Adieu ! adieu !' again he cried,
  All as he turned him roun' —
'Farewell to Leader's silver tide !
  Farewell to Ercildoune !'

The hart and hind approached the place,
  As lingering yet he stood ;   150
And there, before Lord Douglas' face,
  With them he crossed the flood.

Lord Douglas leaped on his berry-brown
    steed,
  And spurred him the Leader o'er;
But, though he rode with lightning speed,
  He never saw them more.

Some said to hill, and some to glen,
  Their wondrous course had been;
But ne'er in haunts of living men
  Again was Thomas seen.   160

THE BARD'S INCANTATION

In the autumn of 1804, Scott was with his wife at Gilsland, where they had first met, when he received intelligence which led him to believe that a French force was about to land in Scotland. He at once rode, within twenty-four hours, a hundred miles to Dalkeith, where his troop was to rendezvous, and it was on this ride that he composed the following poem.

THE forest of Glenmore is drear,
  It is all of black pine and the dark oak-
    tree;
And the midnight wind to the mountain
    deer
Is whistling the forest lullaby:
The moon looks through the drifting
    storm,
But the troubled lake reflects not her form,
For the waves roll whitening to the land,
And dash against the shelvy strand.

There is a voice among the trees
  That mingles with the groaning oak —
That mingles with the stormy breeze,
  And the lake-waves dashing against the
    rock; —
There is a voice within the wood,
The voice of the bard in fitful mood;
His song was louder than the blast,
As the bard of Glenmore through the for-
    est past.

' Wake ye from your sleep of death,
  Minstrels and bards of other days !
For the midnight wind is on the heath,
  And the midnight meteors dimly blaze:
The Spectre with his Bloody Hand
Is wandering through the wild wood-
    land;
The owl and the raven are mute for
    dread,
And the time is meet to awake the dead !

' Souls of the mighty, wake and say
  To what high strain your harps were
    strung,
When Lochlin ploughed her billowy way

And on your shores her Norsemen
    flung ?
Her Norsemen trained to spoil and blood,
Skilled to prepare the raven's food,
All by your harpings doomed to die
On bloody Largs and Loncarty.

' Mute are ye all ? No murmurs strange
  Upon the midnight breeze sail by,
Nor through the pines with whistling
    change
  Mimic the harp's wild harmony !
Mute are ye now ? — Ye ne'er were mute
When Murder with his bloody foot,
And Rapine with his iron hand,
Were hovering near yon mountain
    strand.

' O, yet awake the strain to tell,
  By every deed in song enrolled,
By every chief who fought or fell,
  For Albion's weal in battle bold : —
From Coilgach, first who rolled his car
Through the deep ranks of Roman war,
To him of veteran memory dear
Who victor died on Aboukir.

' By all their swords, by all their scars,
  By all their names, a mighty spell !
By all their wounds, by all their wars,
  Arise, the mighty strain to tell !
For fiercer than fierce Hengist's strain,
More impious than the heathen Dane,
More grasping than all-grasping Rome,
Gaul's ravening legions hither come ! '

The wind is hushed and still the lake —
  Strange murmurs fill my tinkling ears,
Bristles my hair, my sinews quake,
  At the dread voice of other years —
' When targets clashed and bugles rung,
And blades round warriors' heads were
    flung,
The foremost of the band were we
And hymned the joys of Liberty ! '

HELLVELLYN

' In the spring of 1805,' says Scott, ' a young gentleman of talents, and of a most amiable disposition, perished by losing his way on the mountain Hellvellyn. His remains were not discovered till three months afterwards, when they were found guarded by a faithful terrier-bitch, his constant attendant during frequent solitary rambles through the wilds of Cumberland and Westmoreland.' The poem was written at the time.

I CLIMBED the dark brow of the mighty Hellvellyn,
　Lakes and mountains beneath me gleamed misty and wide;
All was still save by fits, when the eagle was yelling,
　And starting around me the echoes replied.
On the right, Striden-edge round the Red-tarn was bending,
And Catchedicam its left verge was defending,
One huge nameless rock in the front was ascending,
　When I marked the sad spot where the wanderer had died.

Dark green was that spot mid the brown mountain heather,
　Where the Pilgrim of Nature lay stretched in decay,
Like the corpse of an outcast abandoned to weather
　Till the mountain-winds wasted the tenantless clay.
Nor yet quite deserted, though lonely extended,
For, faithful in death, his mute favorite attended,
The much-loved remains of her master defended,
　And chased the hill-fox and the raven away.

How long didst thou think that his silence was slumber?
　When the wind waved his garment, how oft didst thou start?
How many long days and long weeks didst thou number,

Ere he faded before thee, the friend of thy heart?
And O, was it meet that — no requiem read o'er him,
No mother to weep and no friend to deplore him,
And thou, little guardian, alone stretched before him —
　Unhonored the Pilgrim from life should depart?

When a prince to the fate of the peasant has yielded,
　The tapestry waves dark round the dim-lighted hall;
With scutcheons of silver the coffin is shielded,
　And pages stand mute by the canopied pall:
Through the courts at deep midnight the torches are gleaming;
In the proudly arched chapel the banners are beaming;
Far adown the long aisle sacred music is streaming,
　Lamenting a chief of the people should fall.

But meeter for thee, gentle lover of nature,
　To lay down thy head like the meek mountain lamb,
When wildered he drops from some cliff huge in stature,
　And draws his last sob by the side of his dam.
And more stately thy couch by this desert lake lying,
Thy obsequies sung by the gray plover flying,
With one faithful friend but to witness thy dying
　In the arms of Hellvellyn and Catchedicam.

THE LAY OF THE LAST MINSTREL

INTRODUCTORY NOTE

When Scott was collecting material for the third volume of *The Border Minstrelsy*, he wrote to Miss Seward that he meant to include in it a 'sort of Romance of Border chivalry and Enchantment,' and when giving the same information to Mr. George Ellis, he adds that it 'is in a light-horseman sort of stanza.' In his *Introduction* which follows below, Scott gives an account of the genesis of the poem and the circumstances of attending the first trial. He was wont to speak lightly of his verse, and it was with no affectation of modesty that he wrote to Miss Seward: 'Was all the time I wasted upon the *Lay* put together, — for it was laid aside for long intervals, — I am sure it would not exceed six weeks. The last canto was written in three forenoons when I was lying in quarters with our yeomanry. I leave it with yourself to guess how little I can have it in my most distant imagination to place myself upon a level with the great Bards you have mentioned, the very latchets of whose shoes neither Southey nor I are worthy to unloose.' As the first considerable poem of Scott's own composition, it has a further interest, often attaching to first productions, from the veiled autobiographic element, for Lockhart says that it distinctly refers to a secret attachment which Scott cherished 'from almost the dawn of the passion.' 'This — (however he may have disguised the story by mixing it up with the Quixotic adventure of the damsel in the green mantle) — this was the early and innocent affection to which we owe the tenderest pages, not only of *Redgauntlet*, but of *The Lay of the Last Minstrel*, and of *Rokeby*, and which found its first poetic expression in the little poem 'The Violet.' In all of these works the heroine has certain distinctive features, drawn from one and the same haunting dream of his manly adolescence.' A more explicit reference will be found in the head-note to 'The Violet,' page 7.

In his *Introduction* Scott treats the poem as a part of his literary history. He wrote the account a quarter of a century after the publication of the poem, and it is a pleasure to read and compare with it the more familiar comment on the *Lay* which he sends at the time of its publication in the freedom of correspondence to Miss Seward.

'EDINBURGH, 21st March, 1805.

'MY DEAR MISS SEWARD, — I am truly happy that you found any amusement in *The Lay of the Last Minstrel*. It has great faults, of which no one can be more sensible than I am myself. Above all, it is deficient in that sort of continuity which a story ought to have, and which, were it to write again, I would endeavour to give it. But I began and wandered forward, like one in a pleasant country, getting to the top of one hill to see a prospect, and to the bottom of another to enjoy a shade ; and what wonder if my course has been devious and desultory, and many of my excursions altogether unprofitable to the advance of my journey ? The Dwarf Page is also an excrescence, and I plead guilty to all the censures concerning him. The truth is he has a history, and it is this : The story of Gilpin Horner was told by an old gentleman to Lady Dalkeith, and she, much diverted with his act, really believing so grotesque a tale, insisted that I should make it into a Border ballad. I don't know if ever you saw my lovely chieftainess — if you have, you must be aware that it is *impossible* for any one to refuse her request, as she has more of the angel in face and temper than any one alive ; so that if she had asked me to write a ballad on a broomstick, I must have attempted it. I began a few verses to be called "The Goblin Page ; " and they lay long by me, till the applause of some friends whose judgment I valued induced me to resume the poem ; so on I wrote, knowing no more than the man in the moon how I was to end. At length the story appeared so uncouth, that I was fain to put it into the mouth of my old Minstrel — lest the nature of it should be misunderstood, and I should be suspected of setting up a new school of poetry, instead of a feeble attempt to imitate the old. In the process of the romance, the page, intended to be a principal person in the work, contrived (from the baseness of his natural propensities, I suppose) to slink down stairs into the kitchen, and now he must e'en abide there.

'I mention these circumstances to you, and to any one whose applause I value, because I am unwilling you should suspect me of trifling with the public in *malice prepense*. As to the herd of critics, it is impossible for me to pay much attention to them, for, as they do not understand what I call poetry, we talk in a foreign language to each other. Indeed, many of these gentlemen appear to me to be a sort of tinkers, who, unable to *make* pots and pans, set up for *menders* of them, and, God knows, often make two holes in patching one. The sixth canto is altogether redundant; for the poem should certainly have closed with the union of the lovers, when the interest, if any, was at an end. But what could I do? I had my book and my page still on my hands, and must get rid of them at all events. Manage them as I would, their catastrophe must have been insufficient to occupy an entire canto; so I was fain to eke it out with the songs of the minstrels. I will now descend from the confessional, which I think I have occupied long enough for the patience of my fair confessor. I am happy you are disposed to give me absolution, notwithstanding all my sins.' . . .

Scott refers in his *Introduction* to the immediate success of his venture, and Lockhart supplies details which substantiate his statement that 'in the history of British Poetry nothing had ever equalled the demand for *The Lay of the Last Minstrel.*' The success unquestionably confirmed Scott in his resolution to devote himself to the literary life, yet it is interesting to note how persistently he held to his theoretical doctrine that literature should be a subsidiary means of support, or as he puts it, a staff and not a crutch. It was while urging again this doctrine in a letter to Crabbe in 1812 that he lets fall the fact, nowhere else referred to by him, that he wrote 'The Lay of the Last Minstrel for the purpose of buying a new horse for the Volunteer Cavalry.'

When first published early in January, 1805, the poem was introduced by the following Preface : —

'The poem, now offered to the Public, is intended to illustrate the customs and manners which anciently prevailed on the Borders of England and Scotland. The inhabitants living in a state partly pastoral and partly warlike, and combining habits of constant depredation with the influence of a rude spirit of chivalry, were often engaged in scenes highly susceptible of poetical ornament. As the description of scenery and manners was more the object of the Author than a combined and regular narrative, the plan of the Ancient Metrical Romance was adopted, which allows greater latitude, in this respect, than would be consistent with the dignity of a regular Poem. The same model offered other facilities, as it permits an occasional alteration of measure, which, in some degree, authorizes the change of rhythm in the text. The machinery, also, adopted from popular belief, would have seemed puerile in a Poem which did not partake of the rudeness of the old Ballad, or Metrical Romance.

'For these reasons, the Poem was put into the mouth of an ancient Minstrel, the last of the race, who, as he is supposed to have survived the Revolution, might have caught somewhat of the refinement of modern poetry, without losing the simplicity of his original model. The date of the Tale itself is about the middle of the sixteenth century, when most of the personages actually flourished. The time occupied by the action is Three Nights and Three Days.'

When Cadell took hold of the publication of Sir Walter's writings he projected that reissue in uniform style of the prose and poetry, with introductions by the author, which resulted in the extraordinary sale, by which Scott's debts were paid and the fortunes of the author put on a firm foundation. It was for this edition of 1830 that Scott furnished the following —

INTRODUCTION

A poem of nearly thirty years' standing may be supposed hardly to need an Introduction, since, without one, it has been able to keep itself afloat through the best part of a generation. Nevertheless, as, in the edition of the Waverley Novels now in course of publication [1830], I have imposed on myself the task of saying something concerning the purpose and history of each, in their turn, I am desirous that the Poems for which I first received some marks of the public favor should also be accompanied with such scraps of their literary

history as may be supposed to carry interest along with them. Even if I should be mistaken in thinking that the secret history of what was once so popular may still attract public attention and curiosity, it seems to me not without its use to record the manner and circumstances under which the present, and other Poems on the same plan, attained for a season an extensive reputation.

I must resume the story of my literary labors at the period at which I broke off in the *Essay on the Imitation of Popular Poetry,*[1]

---

[1] In this essay, printed in the 1830 edition of the *Border Minstrelsy,* Scott gives an account of his schoolboy attempts at writing verse, of his translations of Bürger's 'Lenoré' and *Der Wilde Jaeger* (brought out in 1796 under the title of *William and Helen,* but 'a dead loss' to the publishers), of his subsequent versions of

when I had enjoyed the first gleam of public favor, by the success of the first edition of the *Minstrelsy of the Scottish Border.* The second edition of that work, published in 1803, proved, in the language of the trade, rather a heavy concern. The demand in Scotland had been supplied by the first edition, and the curiosity of the English was not much awakened by poems in the rude garb of antiquity, accompanied with notes referring to the obscure feuds of barbarous clans, of whose very names civilized history was ignorant. It was, on the whole, one of those books which are more praised than they are read.

At this time I stood personally in a different position from that which I occupied when I first dipt my desperate pen in ink for other purposes than those of my profession. In 1796, when I first published the translations from Bürger, I was an insulated individual, with only my own wants to provide for, and having, in a great measure, my own inclinations alone to consult. In 1803, when the second edition of the *Minstrelsy* appeared, I had arrived at a period of life when men, however thoughtless, encounter duties and circumstances which press consideration and plans of life upon the most careless minds. I had been for some time married, — was the father of a rising family, and, though fully enabled to meet the consequent demands upon me, it was my duty and desire to place myself in a situation which would enable me to make honorable provision against the various contingencies of life.

It may be readily supposed that the attempts which I had made in literature had been unfavorable to my success at the bar. The goddess Themis is, at Edinburgh, and I suppose everywhere else, of a peculiarly jealous disposition. She will not readily consent to share her authority, and sternly demands from her votaries, not only that real duty be carefully attended to and discharged, but that a certain air of business shall be observed even in the midst of total idleness. It is prudent, if not absolutely necessary, in a young barrister, to appear completely engrossed by his profession; however destitute of employment he may in reality be, he ought to preserve, if possible, the appearance of full occupation. He should, therefore, seem perpetually engaged among his law-papers, dusting them, as it were; and, as Ovid advises the fair,

'Si nullus erit pulvis, tamen excute nullum.' [1]

Perhaps such extremity of attention is more especially required, considering the great number of counsellors who are called to the bar, and how very small a proportion of them are finally disposed, or find encouragement, to follow the law as a profession. Hence the number of deserters is so great that the least lingering look behind occasions a young novice to be set down as one of the intending fugitives. Certain it is, that the Scottish Themis was at this time peculiarly jealous of any flirtation with the Muses, on the part of those who had ranged themselves under her banners. This was probably owing to her consciousness of the superior attractions of her rivals. Of late, however, she has relaxed in some instances in this particular, an eminent example of which has been shown in the case of my friend Mr. Jeffrey, who, after long conducting one of the most influential literary periodicals of the age with unquestionable ability, has been, by the general consent of his brethren, recently elected to be their Dean of Faculty, or President, — being the highest acknowledgment of his professional talents which they had it in their power to offer.[2] But this is an incident much beyond the ideas of a period of thirty years' distance, when a barrister who really possessed any turn for lighter literature was at as much pains to conceal it as if it had in reality been something to be ashamed of; and I could mention more than one instance in which literature and society have suffered much loss that jurisprudence might be enriched.

Such, however, was not my case; for the reader will not wonder that my open interference with matters of light literature diminished my employment in the weightier matters of the law. Nor did the solicitors, upon whose choice the counsel takes rank in his profession, do me less than justice, by regarding others among my contemporaries as fitter to discharge the duty due to their clients, than a young man who was taken up with running after ballads, whether Teutonic or national. My profession and I, therefore, came to stand nearly upon the footing which honest Slender consoled himself on having established with Mistress Anne Page : ' There was no great love between us at the beginning, and it pleased Heaven to decrease it on farther acquaintance.' I became sensible that the time was come when I must either buckle myself resolutely to the ' toil by day, the lamp by night,' renouncing all the Delilahs of my imagination, or bid adieu to the profession of the law, and hold another course.

---

[1] ' If dust be none, yet brush that none away.'

[2] [Jeffrey conducted the *Edinburgh Review* for twenty-seven years. He retired the year before Scott wrote the above, and was elected Dean of the Faculty of Advocates.]

sundry German dramas, of his first attempts at ballad writing (' Glenfinlas and The Eve of St. John,' included in ' Monk' Lewis's *Tales of Wonder* in 1801), and of his first literary success in the *Border Minstrelsy* of 1802.   **W. J. R.**

I confess my own inclination revolted from the more severe choice, which might have been deemed by many the wiser alternative. As my transgressions had been numerous, my repentance must have been signalized by unusual sacrifices. I ought to have mentioned that since my fourteenth or fifteenth year my health, originally delicate, had become extremely robust. From infancy I had labored under the infirmity of a severe lameness; but, as I believe is usually the case with men of spirit who suffer under personal inconveniences of this nature, I had, since the improvement of my health, in defiance of this incapacitating circumstance, distinguished myself by the endurance of toil on foot or horseback, having often walked thirty miles a day, and rode upwards of a hundred, without resting. In this manner I made many pleasant journeys through parts of the country then not very accessible, gaining more amusement and instruction than I have been able to acquire since I have travelled in a more commodious manner. I practised most sylvan sports also, with some success and with great delight. But these pleasures must have been all resigned, or used with great moderation, had I determined to regain my station at the bar. It was even doubtful whether I could, with perfect character as a jurisconsult, retain a situation in a volunteer corps of cavalry, which I then held. The threats of invasion were at this time instant and menacing; the call by Britain on her children was universal, and was answered by some, who like myself, consulted rather their desire than their ability to bear arms. My services, however, were found useful in assisting to maintain the discipline of the corps, being the point on which their constitution rendered them most amenable to military criticism. In other respects the squadron was a fine one, consisting chiefly of handsome men, well mounted and armed at their own expense. My attention to the corps took up a good deal of time; and while it occupied many of the happiest hours of my life, it furnished an additional reason for my reluctance again to encounter the severe course of study indispensable to success in the juridical profession.

On the other hand, my father, whose feelings might have been hurt by my quitting the bar, had been for two or three years dead, so that I had no control to thwart my own inclination; and my income being equal to all the comforts, and some of the elegancies, of life, I was not pressed to an irksome labor by necessity, that most powerful of motives; consequently, I was the more easily seduced to choose the employment which was most agreeable to me. This was yet the easier, that in 1800 I had obtained the preferment of Sheriff of Selkirkshire, about £300 a year in value, and which was the more agreeable to me as in that county I had several friends and relations. But I did not abandon the profession to which I had been educated without certain prudential resolutions, which, at the risk of some egotism, I will here mention; not without the hope that they may be useful to young persons who may stand in circumstances similar to those in which I then stood.

In the first place, upon considering the lives and fortunes of persons who had given themselves up to literature, or to the task of pleasing the public, it seemed to me that the circumstances which chiefly affected their happiness and character were those from which Horace has bestowed upon authors the epithet of the Irritable Race. It requires no depth of philosophic reflection to perceive that the petty warfare of Pope with the Dunces of his period could not have been carried on without his suffering the most acute torture, such as a man must endure from mosquitoes, by whose stings he suffers agony, although he can crush them in his grasp by myriads. Nor is it necessary to call to memory the many humiliating instances in which men of the greatest genius have, to avenge some pitiful quarrel, made themselves ridiculous during their lives, to become the still more degraded objects of pity to future times.

Upon the whole, as I had no pretension to the genius of the distinguished persons who had fallen into such errors, I concluded there could be no occasion for imitating them in their mistakes, or what I considered as such; and, in adopting literary pursuits as the principal occupation of my future life, I resolved, if possible, to avoid those weaknesses of temper which seemed to have most easily beset my more celebrated predecessors.

With this view, it was my first resolution to keep as far as was in my power abreast of society, continuing to maintain my place in general company, without yielding to the very natural temptation of narrowing myself to what is called literary society. By doing so, I imagined I should escape the besetting sin of listening to language which, from one motive or other, is apt to ascribe a very undue degree of consequence to literary pursuits, as if they were, indeed, the business, rather than the amusement, of life. The opposite course can only be compared to the injudicious conduct of one who pampers himself with cordial and luscious draughts, until he is unable to endure wholesome bitters. Like Gil Blas, therefore, I resolved to stick by the society of my *commis*, instead of seeking that of a more literary cast, and to maintain my general interest in what was going on around me, reserving the man of letters for the desk and the library.

My second resolution was a corollary from the first. I determined that, without shutting my ears to the voice of true criticism, I would pay no regard to that which assumes the form of satire. I therefore resolved to arm myself with that triple brass of Horace, of which those of my profession are seldom held deficient, against all the roving warfare of satire, parody, and sarcasm; to laugh if the jest was a good one; or, if otherwise, to let it hum and buzz itself to sleep.

It is to the observance of these rules (according to my best belief) that, after a life of thirty years engaged in literary labors of various kinds, I attribute my never having been entangled in any literary quarrel or controversy; and, which is a still more pleasing result, that I have been distinguished by the personal friendship of my most approved contemporaries of all parties.

I adopted, at the same time, another resolution, on which it may doubtless be remarked that it was well for me that I had it in my power to do so, and that, therefore, it is a line of conduct which, depending upon accident, can be less generally applicable in other cases. Yet I fail not to record this part of my plan, convinced that, though it may not be in every one's power to adopt exactly the same resolution, he may nevertheless, by his own exertions, in some shape or other, attain the object on which it was founded, namely, to secure the means of subsistence, without relying exclusively on literary talents. In this respect, I determined that literature should be my staff, but not my crutch, and that the profits of my literary labor, however convenient otherwise, should not, if I could help it, become necessary to my ordinary expenses. With this purpose I resolved, if the interest of my friends could so far favor me, to retire upon any of the respectable offices of the law, in which persons of that profession are glad to take refuge, when they feel themselves, or are judged by others, incompetent to aspire to its higher honors. Upon such a post an author might hope to retreat, without any perceptible alteration of circumstances, whenever the time should arrive that the public grew weary of his endeavors to please, or he himself should tire of the pen. At this period of my life, I possessed so many friends capable of assisting me in this object of ambition, that I could hardly overrate my own prospects of obtaining the preferment to which I limited my wishes; and, in fact, I obtained, in no long period, the reversion of a situation which completely met them.

Thus far all was well, and the Author had been guilty, perhaps, of no great imprudence,

when he relinquished his forensic practice with the hope of making some figure in the field of literature. But an established character with the public, in my new capacity, still remained to be acquired. I have noticed that the translations from Bürger had been unsuccessful, nor had the original poetry which appeared under the auspices of Mr. Lewis, in the *Tales of Wonder*, in any great degree raised my reputation. It is true, I had private friends disposed to second me in my efforts to obtain popularity. But I was sportsman enough to know, that if the greyhound does not run well, the halloos of his patrons will not obtain the prize for him.

Neither was I ignorant that the practice of ballad-writing was for the present out of fashion, and that any attempt to revive it, or to found a poetical character upon it, would certainly fail of success. The ballad measure itself, which was once listened to as to an enchanting melody, had become hackneyed and sickening, from its being the accompaniment of every grinding hand-organ; and besides, a long work in quatrains, whether those of the common ballad, or such as are termed elegiac, has an effect upon the mind like that of the bed of Procrustes upon the human body; for, as it must be both awkward and difficult to carry on a long sentence from one stanza to another, it follows that the meaning of each period must be comprehended within four lines, and equally so that it must be extended so as to fill that space. The alternate dilation and contraction thus rendered necessary is singularly unfavorable to narrative composition; and the 'Gondibert' of Sir William D'Avenant, though containing many striking passages, has never become popular, owing chiefly to its being told in this species of elegiac verse.

In the dilemma occasioned by this objection, the idea occurred to the Author of using the measured short line, which forms the structure of so much minstrel poetry, that it may be properly termed the Romantic stanza, by way of distinction; and which appears so natural to our language, that the very best of our poets have not been able to protract it into the verse properly called Heroic, without the use of epithets which are, to say the least, unnecessary.[1] But, on the other hand, the extreme facility of the short couplet, which seems congenial to our language, and was, doubtless for that reason,

two syllables forming a superfluous word in each line, as may be observed by attending to such words as are printed in Italics.

' Achilles' wrath, to Greece the *direful* spring
Of woes unnumber'd, *heavenly* goddess, sing;
That wrath which sent to Pluto's' *gloomy* reign,
The souls of *mighty* chiefs in battle slain,
Whose bones, unburied on the *desert* shore,
Devouring dogs and *hungry* vultures tore.'

---

[1] Thus it has been often remarked, that, in the opening couplets of Pope's translation of the Iliad, there are

so popular with our old minstrels, is, for the same reason, apt to prove a snare to the composer who uses it in more modern days, by encouraging him in a habit of slovenly composition. The necessity of occasional pauses often forces the young poet to pay more attention to sense, as the boy's kite rises highest when the train is loaded by a due counterpoise. The Author was therefore intimidated by what Byron calls the 'fatal facility' of the octosyllabic verse, which was otherwise better adapted to his purpose of imitating the more ancient poetry.

I was not less at a loss for a subject which might admit of being treated with the simplicity and wildness of the ancient ballad. But accident dictated both a theme and measure which decided the subject as well as the structure of the poem.

The lovely young Countess of Dalkeith, afterwards Harriet Duchess of Buccleuch, had come to the land of her husband with the desire of making herself acquainted with its traditions and customs, as well as its manners and history. All who remember this lady will agree that the intellectual character of her extreme beauty, the amenity and courtesy of her manners, the soundness of her understanding, and her unbounded benevolence, gave more the idea of an angelic visitant than of a being belonging to this nether world ; and such a thought was but too consistent with the short space she was permitted to tarry among us.[1] Of course, where all made it a pride and pleasure to gratify her wishes, she soon heard enough of Border lore ; among others, an aged gentleman of property,[2] near Langholm, communicated to her ladyship the story of Gilpin Horner, a tradition in which the narrator, and many more of that country, were firm believers. The young Countess, much delighted with the legend, and the gravity and full confidence with which it was told, enjoined on me as a task to compose a ballad on the subject. Of course, to hear was to obey ; and thus the goblin story objected to by several critics as an excrescence upon the poem was, in fact, the occasion of its being written.

A chance similar to that which dictated the subject gave me also the hint of a new mode of treating it. We had at that time the lease of a pleasant cottage near Lasswade, on the romantic banks of the Esk, to which we es-

caped when the vacations of the Court permitted me so much leisure. Here I had the pleasure to receive a visit from Mr. Stoddart (now Sir John Stoddart, Judge-Advocate at Malta), who was at that time collecting the particulars which he afterwards embodied in his Remarks on Local Scenery in Scotland. I was of some use to him in procuring the information which he desired, and guiding him to the scenes which he wished to see. In return, he made me better acquainted than I had hitherto been with the poetic effusions which have since made the Lakes of Westmoreland, and the authors by whom they have been sung, so famous wherever the English tongue is spoken.

I was already acquainted with the 'Joan of Arc,' the 'Thalaba,' and the 'Metrical Ballads' of Mr. Southey, which had found their way to Scotland, and were generally admired. But Mr. Stoddart, who had the advantage of personal friendship with the authors, and who possessed a strong memory with an excellent taste, was able to repeat to me many long specimens of their poetry, which had not yet appeared in print. Amongst others, was the striking fragment called 'Christabel,' by Mr. Coleridge, which, from the singularly irregular structure of the stanzas, and the liberty which it allowed the author to adapt the sound to the sense, seemed to be exactly suited to such an extravaganza as I meditated on the subject of Gilpin Horner. As applied to comic and humorous poetry, this mescolanza of measures had been already used by Anthony Hall, Anstey, Dr. Wolcott, and others ; but it was in 'Christabel' that I first found it used in serious poetry, and it is to Mr. Coleridge that I am bound to make the acknowledgment due from the pupil to his master. I observe that Lord Byron, in noticing my obligations to Mr. Coleridge, which I have been always most ready to acknowledge, expressed, or was understood to express, a hope that I did not write an unfriendly review on Mr. Coleridge's productions. On this subject I have only to say that I do not even know the review which is alluded to ; and were I ever to take the unbecoming freedom of censuring a man of Mr. Coleridge's extraordinary talents, it would be on account of the caprice and indolence with which he has thrown from him, as if in mere wantonness, those unfinished scraps of poetry, which, like the Torso of an-

---

[1] [The Duchess of Buccleuch died in August, 1814.]
[2] This was Mr Beattie of Mickledale, a man then considerably upwards of eighty, of a shrewd and sarcastic temper, which he did not at all times suppress, as the following anecdote will show : A worthy clergyman, now deceased, with better good-will than tact, was endeavoring to push the senior forward in his recollection of Border ballads and legends, by expressing reiterated

surprise at his wonderful memory. 'No, sir,' said old Mickledale ; 'my memory is good for little, for it cannot retain what ought to be preserved. I can remember all these stories about the auld riding days, which are of no earthly importance ; but were you, reverend sir, to repeat your best sermon in this drawing-room, I could not tell you half an hour afterwards what you had been speaking about.'

tiquity, defy the skill of his poetical brethren to complete them. The charming fragments which the author abandons to their fate, are surely too valuable to be treated like the proofs of careless engravers, the sweepings of whose studios often make the fortune of some painstaking collector.

I did not immediately proceed upon my projected labor, though I was now furnished with a subject, and with a structure of verse which might have the effect of novelty to the public ear, and afford the Author an opportunity of varying his measure with the variations of a romantic theme. On the contrary, it was, to the best of my recollection, more than a year after Mr. Stoddart's visit, that, by way of experiment, I composed the first two or three stanzas of *The Lay of the Last Minstrel*. I was shortly afterwards visited by two intimate friends, one of whom still survives. They were men whose talents might have raised them to the highest station in literature, had they not preferred exerting them in their own profession of the law, in which they attained equal preferment. I was in the habit of consulting them on my attempts at composition, having equal confidence in their sound taste and friendly sincerity.[1] In this specimen I had, in the phrase of the Highland servant, packed all that was my own *at least*, for I had also included a line of invocation, a little softened, from Coleridge —

'Mary, mother, shield us well.'

As neither of my friends said much to me on the subject of the stanzas I showed them before their departure, I had no doubt that their disgust had been greater than their good-nature chose to express. Looking upon them, therefore, as a failure, I threw the manuscript into the fire, and thought as little more as I could of the matter. Some time afterwards I met one of my two counsellors, who inquired, with considerable appearance of interest, about the progress of the romance I had commenced, and was greatly surprised at learning its fate. He confessed that neither he nor our mutual friend had been at first able to give a precise opinion on a poem so much out of the common road; but that as they walked home together to the city, they had talked much on the subject, and the result was an earnest desire that I would proceed with the composition. He also added, that some sort of prologue might be necessary, to place the mind of the hearers in the situation to understand and enjoy the poem, and recommended the adoption of such quaint

mottoes as Spenser has used to announce the contents of the chapters of the *Faery Queen*, such as —

'Babe's bloody hands may not be cleansed.
    The face of golden Mean :
Her sisters two, Extremities,
    Strive her to banish clean.'

I entirely agreed with my friendly critic in the necessity of having some sort of pitch-pipe, which might make readers aware of the object, or rather the tone, of the publication. But I doubted whether, in assuming the oracular style of Spenser's mottoes, the interpreter might not be censured as the harder to be understood of the two. I therefore introduced the Old Minstrel, as an appropriate prolocutor by whom the lay might be sung or spoken, and the introduction of whom betwixt the cantos might remind the reader at intervals of the time, place, and circumstances of the recitation. This species of *cadre*, or frame, afterwards afforded the poem its name of *The Lay of the Last Minstrel*.

The work was subsequently shown to other friends during its progress, and received the *imprimatur* of Mr. Francis Jeffrey, who had been already for some time distinguished by his critical talent.

The poem, being once licensed by the critics as fit for the market, was soon finished, proceeding at about the rate of a canto per week. There was, indeed, little occasion for pause or hesitation, when a troublesome rhyme might be accommodated by an alteration of the stanza, or where an incorrect measure might be remedied by a variation of the rhyme. It was finally published in 1805, and may be regarded as the first work in which the writer, who has been since so voluminous, laid his claim to be considered as an original author.

The book was published by Longman and Company, and Archibald Constable and Company. The principal of the latter firm was then commencing that course of bold and liberal industry which was of so much advantage to his country, and might have been so to himself, but for causes which it is needless to enter into here. The work, brought out on the usual terms of division of profits between the author and publishers, was not long after purchased by them for £500, to which Messrs. Longman and Company afterwards added £100, in their own unsolicited kindness, in consequence of the uncommon success of the work. It was handsomely given to supply the loss of a fine horse, which broke down suddenly while the Author was riding with one of the worthy publishers. It would be great affectation not to own

[1] One of these, William Erskine, esq. (Lord Kinnedder), I have often had occasion to mention, and though I may hardly be thanked for disclosing the name of the other, yet I cannot but state that the second is George Cranstoun, esq., now a Senator of the College of Justice by the title of Lord Corehouse.

frankly, that the Author expected some success from *The Lay of the Last Minstrel*. The attempt to return to a more simple and natural style of poetry was likely to be welcomed, at a time when the public had become tired of heroic hexameters, with all the buckram and binding which belong to them of later days. But whatever might have been his expectations, whether moderate or unreasonable, the result left them far behind, for among those who smiled on the adventurous Minstrel were numbered the great names of William Pitt and Charles Fox. Neither was the extent of the sale inferior to the character of the judges who received the poem with approbation. Upwards of thirty thousand copies of the Lay were disposed of by the trade; and the Author had to perform a task difficult to human vanity, when called upon to make the necessary deductions from his own merits, in a calm attempt to account for his popularity.

A few additional remarks on the Author's literary attempts after this period, will be found in the Introduction to the Poem of *Marmion*.

ABBOTSFORD, April, 1830.

THE LAY OF THE LAST MINSTREL

Dum relego, scripsisse pudet ; quia plurima cerno,
Me quoque qui feci judice, digna lini.

TO THE

RIGHT HONORABLE

CHARLES, EARL OF DALKEITH,

THIS POEM IS INSCRIBED BY

THE AUTHOR

INTRODUCTION

THE way was long, the wind was cold,
The Minstrel was infirm and old;
His withered cheek and tresses gray
Seemed to have known a better day;
The harp, his sole remaining joy,
Was carried by an orphan boy.
The last of all the bards was he,
Who sung of Border chivalry;
For, well-a-day ! their date was fled,
His tuneful brethren all were dead;   10
And he, neglected and oppressed,
Wished to be with them and at rest.
No more on prancing palfrey borne,
He carolled, light as lark at morn;
No longer courted and caressed,
High placed in hall, a welcome guest,
He poured, to lord and lady gay,
The unpremeditated lay:
Old times were changed, old manners gone;
A stranger filled the Stuarts' throne;   20
The bigots of the iron time
Had called his harmless art a crime.
A wandering harper, scorned and poor,

He begged his bread from door to door,
And tuned, to please a peasant's ear,
The harp a king had loved to hear.
He passed where Newark's stately tower
Looks out from Yarrow's birchen bower:
The Minstrel gazed with wishful eye—
No humbler resting-place was nigh.   30
With hesitating step at last
The embattled portal arch he passed,
Whose ponderous grate and massy bar
Had oft rolled back the tide of war,
But never closed the iron door
Against the desolate and poor.
The Duchess marked his weary pace,
His timid mien, and reverend face,
And bade her page the menials tell
That they should tend the old man well: 40
For she had known adversity,
Though born in such a high degree;
In pride of power, in beauty's bloom,
Had wept o'er Monmouth's bloody tomb !

When kindness had his wants supplied,
And the old man was gratified,
Began to rise his minstrel pride;

And he began to talk anon
Of good Earl Francis, dead and gone,
And of Earl Walter, rest him God ! 50
A braver ne'er to battle rode;
And how full many a tale he knew
Of the old warriors of Buccleuch:
And, would the noble Duchess deign
To listen to an old man's strain,
Though stiff his hand, his voice though weak,
He thought even yet, the sooth to speak,
That, if she loved the harp to hear,
He could make music to her ear.

The humble boon was soon obtained; 60
The aged Minstrel audience gained.
But when he reached the room of state
Where she with all her ladies sate,
Perchance he wished his boon denied:
For, when to tune his harp he tried,
His trembling hand had lost the ease
Which marks security to please;
And scenes, long past, of joy and pain
Came wildering o'er his aged brain —
He tried to tune his harp in vain. 70
The pitying Duchess praised its chime,
And gave him heart, and gave him time,
Till every string's according glee
Was blended into harmony.
And then, he said, he would full fain
He could recall an ancient strain
He never thought to sing again.,
It was not framed for village churls,
But for high dames and mighty earls;
He had played it to King Charles the
Good 80
When he kept court in Holyrood;
And much he wished, yet feared, to try
The long-forgotten melody.
Amid the strings his fingers strayed,
And an uncertain warbling made,
And oft he shook his hoary head.
But when he caught the measure wild,
The old man raised his face and smiled;
And lightened up his faded eye
With all a poet's ecstasy ! 90
In varying cadence, soft or strong,
He swept the sounding chords along:
The present scene, the future lot,
His toils, his wants, were all forgot;
Cold diffidence and age's frost
In the full tide of song were lost;
Each blank, in faithless memory void,
The poet's glowing thought supplied;
And, while his harp responsive rung,
'T was thus the LATEST MINSTREL sung. 100

CANTO FIRST

I

THE feast was over in Branksome tower,
And the Ladye had gone to her secret
    bower,
Her bower that was guarded by word and
    by spell,
Deadly to hear, and deadly to tell —
Jesu Maria, shield us well !
No living wight, save the Ladye alone,
Had dared to cross the threshold stone.

II

The tables were drawn, it was idlesse
    all;
    Knight and page and household squire
Loitered through the lofty hall, 10
    Or crowded round the ample fire:
The stag-hounds, weary with the chase,
    Lay stretched upon the rushy floor,
And urged in dreams the forest race,
    From Teviot-stone to Eskdale-moor.

III

Nine-and-twenty knights of fame
    Hung their shields in Branksome Hall;
Nine-and-twenty squires of name
    Brought them their steeds to bower from
        stall;
    Nine-and-twenty yeomen tall 20
    Waited duteous on them all:
    They were all knights of mettle true,
    Kinsmen to the bold Buccleuch.

IV

Ten of them were sheathed in steel,
With belted sword and spur on heel;
They quitted not their harness bright,
Neither by day nor yet by night:
    They lay down to rest,
    With corselet laced,
Pillowed on buckler cold and hard; 30
    They carved at the meal
    With gloves of steel,
And they drank the red wine through the
    helmet barred.

V

Ten squires, ten yeomen, mail-clad men,
Waited the beck of the warders ten;
Thirty steeds, both fleet and wight,
Stood saddled in stable day and night,
Barded with frontlet of steel, I trow,
And with Jedwood-axe at saddle-bow;

A hundred more fed free in stall:— 40
Such was the custom of Branksome Hall.

VI

Why do these steeds stand ready dight ?
Why watch these warriors armed by night?
They watch to hear the bloodhound bay-
   ing ;
They watch to hear the war-horn bray-
   ing;
To see Saint George's red cross stream-
   ing,
To see the midnight beacon gleaming;
They watch against Southern force and
   guile,
   Lest Scroop or Howard or Percy's pow-
   ers
   Threaten Branksome's lordly towers, 50
From Warkworth or Naworth or merry
   Carlisle.

VII

Such is the custom of Branksome Hall.
   Many a valiant knight is here;
But he, the chieftain of them all,
His sword hangs rusting on the wall
   Beside his broken spear.
Bards long shall tell
How Lord Walter fell !
When startled burghers fled afar
The furies of the Border war, 60
When the streets of high Dunedin
Saw lances gleam and falchions redden,
And heard the slogan's deadly yell, —
Then the Chief of Branksome fell.

VIII

Can piety the discord heal,
   Or stanch the death-feud's enmity ?
Can Christian lore, can patriot zeal,
   Can love of blessed charity ?
No ! vainly to each holy shrine,
   In mutual pilgrimage they drew, 70
Implored in vain the grace divine
   For chiefs their own red falchions slew.
While Cessford owns the rule of Carr,
   While Ettrick boasts the line of Scott,
The slaughtered chiefs, the mortal jar,
The havoc of the feudal war,
   Shall never, never be forgot !

IX

In sorrow o'er Lord Walter's bier
   The warlike foresters had bent,

And many a flower and many a tear 80
   Old Teviot's maids and matrons lent;
But o'er her warrior's bloody bier
The Ladye dropped nor flower nor tear !
Vengeance, deep-brooding o'er the slain,
   Had locked the source of softer woe,
And burning pride and high disdain
   Forbade the rising tear to flow;
Until, amid his sorrowing clan,
   Her son lisped from the nurse's knee,
' And if I live to be a man, 90
   My father's death revenged shall be ! '
Then fast the mother's tears did seek
To dew the infant's kindling cheek.

X

All loose her negligent attire,
   All loose her golden hair,
Hung Margaret o'er her slaughtered sire
   And wept in wild despair.
But not alone the bitter tear
   Had filial grief supplied,
For hopeless love and anxious fear 100
   Had lent their mingled tide;
Nor in her mother's altered eye
Dared she to look for sympathy.
Her lover 'gainst her father's clan
   With Carr in arms had stood,
When Mathouse-burn to Melrose ran
   All purple with their blood;
And well she knew her mother dread,
Before Lord Cranstoun she should wed,
Would see her on her dying bed. 110

XI

Of noble race the Ladye came;
Her father was a clerk of fame
   Of Bethune's line of Picardie:
He learned the art that none may name
   In Padua, far beyond the sea.
Men said he changed his mortal frame
   By feat of magic mystery;
For when in studious mood he paced
   Saint Andrew's cloistered hall,
His form no darkening shadow traced 120
   Upon the sunny wall !

XII

And of his skill, as bards avow,
He taught that Ladye fair,
Till to her bidding she could bow
   The viewless forms of air.
And now she sits in secret bower
In old Lord David's western tower,

And listens to a heavy sound
That moans the mossy turrets round.
Is it the roar of Teviot's tide,   130
That chafes against the scaur's red side ?
Is it the wind, that swings the oaks ?
Is it the echo from the rocks ?
What may it be, the heavy sound,
That moans old Branksome's turrets
    round ?

XIII

At the sullen, moaning sound
    The ban-dogs bay and howl,
And from the turrets round
    Loud whoops the startled owl.
In the hall, both squire and knight   140
    Swore that a storm was near,
And looked forth to view the night;
    But the night was still and clear !

XIV

From the sound of Teviot's tide,
Chafing with the mountain's side,
From the groan of the wind-swung oak,
From the sullen echo of the rock,
From the voice of the coming storm,
    The Ladye knew it well !
It was the Spirit of the Flood that
    spoke,   150
    And he called on the Spirit of the Fell.

XV

RIVER SPIRIT
' Sleep'st thou, brother ? '

MOUNTAIN SPIRIT
                    ' Brother, nay —
On my hills the moonbeams play.
From Craik-cross to Skelfhill-pen,
By every rill, in every glen,
Merry elves their morris pacing,
    To aërial minstrelsy,
Emerald rings on brown heath tracing,
    Trip it deft and merrily.
Up, and mark their nimble feet !   160
Up, and list their music sweet !

XVI

RIVER SPIRIT
' Tears of an imprisoned maiden
    Mix with my polluted stream;
Margaret of Branksome, sorrow-laden,
    Mourns beneath the moon's pale beam.
Tell me, thou who view'st the stars,
When shall cease these feudal jars ?

What shall be the maiden's fate ?
Who shall be the maiden's mate ? '

XVII

MOUNTAIN SPIRIT
' Arthur's slow wain his course doth
    roll   170
In utter darkness round the pole;
The Northern Bear lowers black and grim,
Orion's studded belt is dim;
Twinkling faint, and distant far,
Shimmers through mist each planet star;
    Ill may I read their high decree:
But no kind influence deign they shower
On Teviot's tide and Branksome's tower
    Till pride be quelled and love be free.'

XVIII

The unearthly voices ceased,   180
    And the heavy sound was still;
It died on the river's breast,
    It died on the side of the hill.
But round Lord David's tower
    The sound still floated near;
For it rung in the Ladye's bower,
    And it rung in the Ladye's ear.
She raised her stately head,
    And her heart throbbed high with pride:
' Your mountains shall bend   190
And your streams ascend,
    Ere Margaret be our foeman's bride !'

XIX

The Ladye sought the lofty hall,
    Where many a bold retainer lay,
And with jocund din among them all
    Her son pursued his infant play.
A fancied moss-trooper, the boy
    The truncheon of a spear bestrode,
And round the hall right merrily
    In mimic foray rode.   200
Even bearded knights, in arms grown old,
    Share in his frolic gambles bore,
Albeit their hearts of rugged mold
    Were stubborn as the steel they wore.
For the gray warriors prophesied
    How the brave boy in future war
Should tame the Unicorn's pride,
    Exalt the Crescents and the Star.

XX

The Ladye forgot her purpose high
    One moment and no more,   210
One moment gazed with a mother's eye
    As she paused at the arched door;

Then from amid the armed train
She called to her William of Deloraine.

XXI

A stark moss-trooping Scott was he
As e'er couched Border lance by knee:
Through Solway Sands, through Tarras
   Moss,
Blindfold he knew the paths to cross;
By wily turns, by desperate bounds,
Had baffled Percy's best bloodhounds; 220
In Eske or Liddel fords were none
But he would ride them, one by one;
Alike to him was time or tide,
December's snow or July's pride;
Alike to him was tide or time,
Moonless midnight or matin prime:
Steady of heart and stout of hand
As ever drove prey from Cumberland;
Five times outlawed had he been 229
By England's king and Scotland's queen.

XXII

' Sir William of Deloraine, good at need,
Mount thee on the wightest steed;
Spare not to spur nor stint to ride
Until thou come to fair Tweedside;
And in Melrose's holy pile
Seek thou the Monk of Saint Mary's aisle.
Greet the father well from me;
  Say that the fated hour is come,
And to-night he shall watch with thee,
  To win the treasure of the tomb: 240
For this will be Saint Michael's night,
And though stars be dim the moon is bright,
And the cross of bloody red
Will point to the grave of the mighty
   dead.

XXIII

' What he gives thee, see thou keep;
Stay not thou for food or sleep:
Be it scroll or be it book,
Into it, knight, thou must not look;
If thou readest, thou art lorn !
Better hadst thou ne'er been born ! ' 250

XXIV

' O swiftly can speed my dapple-gray steed,
  Which drinks of the Teviot clear;
Ere break of day,' the warrior gan say,
  ' Again will I be here:
And safer by none may thy errand be done
  Than, noble dame, by me;

Letter nor line know I never one,
  Were 't my neck-verse at Hairibee.'

XXV

Soon in his saddle sate he fast,
And soon the steep descent he passed, 260
Soon crossed the sounding barbican,
And soon the Teviot side he won.
Eastward the wooded path he rode,
Green hazels o'er his basnet nod;
He passed the Peel of Goldiland,
And crossed old Borthwick's roaring
   strand;
Dimly he viewed the Moat-hill's mound,
Where Druid shades still flitted round:
In Hawick twinkled many a light;
Behind him soon they set in night; 270
And soon he spurred his courser keen
Beneath the tower of Hazeldean.

XXVI

The clattering hoofs the watchmen mark:
' Stand, ho ! thou courier of the dark.'
' For Branksome, ho ! ' the knight rejoined,
And left the friendly tower behind.
He turned him now from Teviotside,
  And, guided by the tinkling rill,
Northward the dark ascent did ride,
  And gained the moor at Horseliehill; 280
Broad on the left before him lay
For many a mile the Roman way.

XXVII

A moment now he slacked his speed,
A moment breathed his panting steed,
Drew saddle-girth and corselet-band,
And loosened in the sheath his brand.
On Minto-crags the moonbeams glint,
Where Barnhill hewed his bed of flint,
Who flung his outlawed limbs to rest
Where falcons hang their giddy nest 290
Mid cliffs from whence his eagle eye
For many a league his prey could spy;
Cliffs doubling, on their echoes borne,
The terrors of the robber's horn;
Cliffs which for many a later year
The warbling Doric reed shall hear,
When some sad swain shall teach the grove
Ambition is no cure for love.

XXVIII

Unchallenged, thence passed Deloraine
To ancient Riddel's fair domain, 300
  Where Aill, from mountains freed,

Down from the lakes did raving come;
Each wave was crested with tawny foam,
Like the mane of a chestnut steed.
In vain ! no torrent, deep or broad,
Might bar the bold moss-trooper's road.

XXIX

At the first plunge the horse sunk low,
And the water broke o'er the saddle-bow:
Above the foaming tide, I ween,   309
Scarce half the charger's neck was seen;
For he was barded from counter to tail,
And the rider was armed complete in mail;
Never heavier man and horse
Stemmed a midnight torrent's force.
The warrior's very plume, I say,
Was daggled by the dashing spray;
Yet, through good heart and Our Ladye's
    grace,
At length he gained the landing-place.

XXX

Now Bowden Moor the march-man won,
    And sternly shook his plumed head,   320
As glanced his eye o'er Halidon;
    For on his soul the slaughter red
Of that unhallowed morn arose,
When first the Scott and Carr were foes;
When royal James beheld the fray,
Prize to the victor of the day;
When Home and Douglas in the van
Bore down Buccleuch's retiring clan,
Till gallant Cessford's heart-blood dear
Reeked on dark Elliot's Border spear.   330

XXXI

In bitter mood he spurred fast,
And soon the hated heath was past;
And far beneath, in lustre wan,
Old Melros' rose and fair Tweed ran:
Like some tall rock with lichens gray,
Seemed, dimly huge, the dark Abbaye.
When Hawick he passed had curfew rung,
Now midnight lauds were in Melrose sung.
The sound upon the fitful gale
In solemn wise did rise and fail,   340
Like that wild harp whose magic tone
Is wakened by the winds alone.
But when Melrose he reached 't was silence
    all;
He meetly stabled his steed in stall,
And sought the convent's lonely wall.

HERE paused the harp; and with its swell
The Master's fire and courage fell:
Dejectedly and low he bowed,
And, gazing timid on the crowd,
He seemed to seek in every eye
If they approved his minstrelsy;   350
And, diffident of present praise,
Somewhat he spoke of former days,
And how old age and wandering long
Had done his hand and harp some wrong.
The Duchess, and her daughters fair,
And every gentle lady there,
Each after each, in due degree,
Gave praises to his melody;
His hand was true, his voice was clear,   360
And much they longed the rest to hear.
Encouraged thus, the aged man
After meet rest again began.

CANTO SECOND

I

IF thou wouldst view fair Melrose aright,
Go visit it by the pale moonlight;
For the gay beams of lightsome day
Gild but to flout the ruins gray.
When the broken arches are black in
    night,
And each shafted oriel glimmers white;
When the cold light's uncertain shower
Streams on the ruined central tower;
When buttress and buttress, alternately,
Seem framed of ebon and ivory;   10
When silver edges the imagery,
And the scrolls that teach thee to live and
    die;
When distant Tweed is heard to rave,
And the owlet to hoot o'er the dead man's
    grave,
Then go — but go alone the while —
Then view Saint David's ruined pile;
And, home returning, soothly swear
Was never scene so sad and fair !

II

Short halt did Deloraine make there;
Little recked he of the scene so fair: 20
With dagger's hilt on the wicket strong
He struck full loud, and struck full long.
The porter hurried to the gate:
'Who knocks so loud, and knocks so late?'
'From Branksome I,' the warrior cried;
And straight the wicket opened wide:

For Branksome's chiefs had in battle stood
  To fence the rights of fair Melrose;
And lands and livings, many a rood,
  Had gifted the shrine for their souls' re-
    pose.   30

III

Bold Deloraine his errand said;
The porter bent his humble head;
With torch in hand, and feet unshod,
And noiseless step, the path he trod:
The arched cloister, far and wide,
Rang to the warrior's clanking stride,
Till, stooping low his lofty crest,
He entered the cell of the ancient priest,
And lifted his barred aventayle
To hail the Monk of Saint Mary's aisle.   40

IV

'The Ladye of Branksome greets thee by
    me,
  Says that the fated hour is come,
And that to-night I shall watch with thee,
  To win the treasure of the tomb.'
From sackcloth couch the monk arose,
  With toil his stiffened limbs he reared;
A hundred years had flung their snows
  On his thin locks and floating beard.

V

And strangely on the knight looked he,
  And his blue eyes gleamed wild and
    wide: 50
' And darest thou, warrior, seek to see
  What heaven and hell alike would hide ?
My breast in belt of iron pent,
  With shirt of hair and scourge of thorn,
For threescore years, in penance spent,
  My knees those flinty stones have worn;
Yet all too little to atone
For knowing what should ne'er be known.
Wouldst thou thy every future year
  In ceaseless prayer and penance drie,   60
Yet wait thy latter end with fear —
  Then, daring warrior, follow me ! '

VI

' Penance, father, will I none;
Prayer know I hardly one;
For mass or prayer can I rarely tarry,
Save to patter an Ave Mary,
When I ride on a Border foray.
Other prayer can I none;
So speed me my errand, and let me be
  gone.'

VII

Again on the knight looked the churchman
    old,   70
  And again he sighed heavily;
For he had himself been a warrior bold,
  And fought in Spain and Italy.
And he thought on the days that were long
    since by,
When his limbs were strong and his cour-
    age was high:
Now, slow and faint, he led the way
Where, cloistered round, the garden lay;
The pillared arches were over their head,
And beneath their feet were the bones of
    the dead.

VIII

Spreading herbs and flowerets bright   80
Glistened with the dew of night;
Nor herb nor floweret glistened there
But was carved in the cloister-arches as
    fair.
The monk gazed long on the lovely moon,
  Then into the night he looked forth;
And red and bright the streamers light
  Were dancing in the glowing north.
So had he seen, in fair Castile,
  The youth in glittering squadrons start,
Sudden the flying jennet wheel,   90
  And hurl the unexpected dart.
He knew, by the streamers that shot so
    bright,
That spirits were riding the northern light.

IX

By a steel-clenched postern door
  They entered now the chancel tall;
The darkened roof rose high aloof
  On pillars lofty and light and small:
The keystone that locked each ribbed
    aisle
Was a fleur-de-lys or a quatre-feuille;
The corbels were carved grotesque and
    grim;   100
And the pillars, with clustered shafts so
    trim,
With base and with capital flourished
    around,
Seemed bundles of lances which garlands
    had bound.

X

Full many a scutcheon and banner riven
Shook to the cold night-wind of heaven,
  Around the screened altar's pale;

And there the dying lamps did burn
Before thy low and lonely urn,
O gallant Chief of Otterburne !
　And thine, dark Knight of Liddes-
　　dale !　　　　　　　　　　　110
O fading honors of the dead !
O high ambition lowly laid !

XI

The moon on the east oriel shone
Through slender shafts of shapely stone,
　By foliaged tracery combined;
Thou wouldst have thought some fairy's
　hand
'Twixt poplars straight the osier wand
　In many a freakish knot had twined,
Then framed a spell when the work was
　done,
And changed the willow wreaths to
　stone.　　　　　　　　　　　120
The silver light, so pale and faint,
Showed many a prophet and many a saint,
　Whose image on the glass was dyed;
Full in the midst, his cross of red
Triumphant Michael brandished,
　And trampled the Apostate's pride.
The moonbeam kissed the holy pane,
And threw on the pavement a bloody stain.

XII

They sate them down on a marble stone —
　A Scottish monarch slept below;　130
Thus spoke the monk in solemn tone:
' I was not always a man of woe;
For Paynim countries I have trod,
And fought beneath the Cross of God:
Now, strange to my eyes thine arms ap-
　pear,
And their iron clang sounds strange to my
　ear.

XIII

' In these far climes it was my lot
To meet the wondrous Michael Scott;
　A wizard of such dreaded fame
That when, in Salamanca's cave,　140
Him listed his magic wand to wave,
　The bells would ring in Notre Dame !
Some of his skill he taught to me;
And, warrior, I could say to thee
The words that cleft Eildon Hills in three,
　And bridled the Tweed with a curb of
　　stone:
But to speak them were a deadly sin,

And for having but thought them my heart
　within
　A treble penance must be done.

XIV

' When Michael lay on his dying bed,　150
His conscience was awakened;
He bethought him of his sinful deed,
And he gave me a sign to come with speed:
I was in Spain when the morning rose,
But I stood by his bed ere evening close.
The words may not again be said
That he spoke to me, on death-bed laid;
They would rend this Abbaye's massy nave,
And pile it in heaps above his grave.

XV

' I swore to bury his Mighty Book,　160
That never mortal might therein look;
And never to tell where it was hid,
Save at his Chief of Branksome's need;
And when that need was past and o'er,
Again the volume to restore.
I buried him on Saint Michael's night,
When the bell tolled one and the moon
　was bright,
And I dug his chamber among the dead,
When the floor of the chancel was stained
　red,
That his patron's cross might over him
　wave,　　　　　　　　　　　170
And scare the fiends from the wizard's
　grave.

XVI

' It was a night of woe and dread
When Michael in the tomb I laid;
Strange sounds along the chancel passed,
The banners waved without a blast ' —
Still spoke the monk, when the bell tolled
　one ! —
I tell you, that a braver man
Than William of Deloraine, good at need,
Against a foe ne'er spurred a steed;
Yet somewhat was he chilled with
　dread,　　　　　　　　　　　180
And his hair did bristle upon his head.

XVII

' Lo, warrior ! now, the cross of red
Points to the grave of the mighty dead:
Within it burns a wondrous light,
To chase the spirits that love the night;
That lamp shall burn unquenchably,
Until the eternal doom shall be.'

Slow moved the monk to the broad flag-
stone
Which the bloody cross was traced upon:
He pointed to a secret nook;   190
An iron bar the warrior took;
And the monk made a sign with his with-
ered hand,
The grave's huge portal to expand.

XVIII

With beating heart to the task he went,
His sinewy frame o'er the gravestone
bent,
With bar of iron heaved amain
Till the toil-drops fell from his brows like
rain.
It was by dint of passing strength
That he moved the massy stone at length.
I would you had been there to see   200
How the light broke forth so gloriously,
Streamed upward to the chancel roof,
And through the galleries far aloof !
No earthly flame blazed e'er so bright;
It shone like heaven's own blessed light,
  And, issuing from the tomb,
Showed the monk's cowl and visage pale,
Danced on the dark-browed warrior's mail,
  And kissed his waving plume.

XIX

Before their eyes the wizard lay,   210
As if he had not been dead a day.
His hoary beard in silver rolled,
He seemed some seventy winters old;
A palmer's amice wrapped him round,
With a wrought Spanish baldric bound,
  Like a pilgrim from beyond the sea:
His left hand held his Book of Might,
A silver cross was in his right;
  The lamp was placed beside his knee.
High and majestic was his look,   220
At which the fellest fiends had shook,
And all unruffled was his face:
They trusted his soul had gotten grace.

XX

Often had William of Deloraine
Rode through the battle's bloody plain,
And trampled down the warriors slain,
  And neither known remorse nor awe,
Yet now remorse and awe he owned;
His breath came thick, his head swam
round,
  When this strange scene of death he
  saw.   230

Bewildered and unnerved he stood,
And the priest prayed fervently and loud:
With eyes averted prayed he;
He might not endure the sight to see
Of the man he had loved so brotherly.

XXI

And when the priest his death-prayer had
prayed,
Thus unto Deloraine he said:
' Now, speed thee what thou hast to do,
Or, warrior, we may dearly rue;
For those thou mayst not look upon   240
Are gathering fast round the yawning
stone ! '
Then Deloraine in terror took
From the cold hand the Mighty Book,
With iron clasped and with iron bound:
He thought, as he took it, the dead man
frowned;
But the glare of the sepulchral light
Perchance had dazzled the warrior's sight.

XXII

When the huge stone sunk o'er the tomb,
The night returned in double gloom,
For the moon had gone down and the stars
were few;   250
And as the knight and priest withdrew,
With wavering steps and dizzy brain,
They hardly might the postern gain.
'T is said, as through the aisles they
passed,
They heard strange noises on the blast;
And through the cloister-galleries small,
Which at mid-height thread the chancel
wall,
Loud sobs, and laughter louder, ran,
And voices unlike the voice of man,
As if the fiends kept holiday   260
Because these spells were brought to-day.
I cannot tell how the truth may be;
I say the tale as 't was said to me.

XXIII

' Now, hie thee hence,' the father said,
' And when we are on death-bed laid,
O may our dear Ladye and sweet Saint
John
Forgive our souls for the deed we have
done ! '
The monk returned him to his cell,
  And many a prayer and penance sped;
When the convent met at the noontide
bell,   270

The Monk of Saint Mary's aisle was
    dead !
Before the cross was the body laid,
With hands clasped fast, as if still he
    prayed.

XXIV

The knight breathed free in the morning
    wind,
And strove his hardihood to find :
He was glad when he passed the tomb-
    stones gray
Which girdle round the fair Abbaye;
For the mystic book, to his bosom pressed,
Felt like a load upon his breast,
And his joints, with nerves of iron
    twined,   280
Shook like the aspen-leaves in wind.
Full fain was he when the dawn of day
Began to brighten Cheviot gray;
He joyed to see the cheerful light,
And he said Ave Mary as well as he might.

XXV

The sun had brightened Cheviot gray,
    The sun had brightened the Carter's
    side;
And soon beneath the rising day
    Smiled Branksome towers and Teviot's
    tide.
The wild birds told their warbling tale, 290
    And wakened every flower that blows;
And peeped forth the violet pale,
    And spread her breast the mountain
    rose.
And lovelier than the rose so red,
    Yet paler than the violet pale,
She early left her sleepless bed,
    The fairest maid of Teviotdale.

XXVI

Why does fair Margaret so early awake,
    And don her kirtle so hastilie;
And the silken knots, which in hurry she
    would make,   300
    Why tremble her slender fingers to
    tie ?
Why does she stop and look often around,
    As she glides down the secret stair;
And why does she pat the shaggy blood-
    hound,
    As he rouses him up from his lair;
And, though she passes the postern alone,
Why is not the watchman's bugle blown ?

XXVII

The ladye steps in doubt and dread
Lest her watchful mother hear her tread;
The ladye caresses the rough bloodhound
Lest his voice should waken the castle
    round;   311
The watchman's bugle is not blown,
For he was her foster father's son;
And she glides through the greenwood at
    dawn of light
To meet Baron Henry, her own true knight.

XXVIII

The knight and ladye fair are met,
And under the hawthorn's boughs are
    set.
A fairer pair were never seen
To meet beneath the hawthorn green.
He was stately and young and tall,   320
Dreaded in battle and loved in hall;
And she, when love, scarce told, scarce
    hid,
Lent to her cheek a livelier red,
When the half sigh her swelling breast
Against the silken ribbon pressed,
When her blue eyes their secret told,
Though shaded by her locks of gold —
Where would you find the peerless fair
With Margaret of Branksome might com-
    pare !

XXIX

And now, fair dames, methinks I see   330
You listen to my minstrelsy;
Your waving locks ye backward throw,
And sidelong bend your necks of snow.
Ye ween to hear a melting tale
Of two true lovers in a dale;
And how the knight, with tender fire,
    To paint his faithful passion strove,
Swore he might at her feet expire,
    But never, never cease to love;
And how she blushed, and how she
    sighed,   340
And, half consenting, half denied,
And said that she would die a maid; —
Yet, might the bloody feud be stayed,
Henry of Cranstoun, and only he,
Margaret of Branksome's choice should be.

XXX

Alas ! fair dames, your hopes are vain !
My harp has lost the enchanting strain;
    Its lightness would my age reprove:
My hairs are gray, my limbs are old,

My heart is dead, my veins are cold: 350
I may not, must not, sing of love.

XXXI

Beneath an oak, mossed o'er by eld,
The Baron's dwarf his courser held,
  And held his crested helm and spear:
That dwarf was scarce an earthly man,
If the tales were true that of him ran
  Through all the Border far and near.
'T was said, when the Baron a-hunting
    rode
Through Reedsdale's glens, but rarely trod,
He heard a voice cry, 'Lost! lost!
    lost!'   360
And, like tennis-ball by racket tossed,
  A leap of thirty feet and three
Made from the gorse this elfin shape,
Distorted like some dwarfish ape,
  And lighted at Lord Cranstoun's knee.
Lord Cranstoun was some whit dismayed;
'T is said that five good miles he rade,
  To rid him of his company;
But where he rode one mile, the dwarf ran
    four,   369
And the dwarf was first at the castle door.

XXXII

Use lessens marvel, it is said:
This elfish dwarf with the Baron staid;
Little he ate, and less he spoke,
Nor mingled with the menial flock;
And oft apart his arms he tossed,
And often muttered, 'Lost! lost! lost!'
  He was waspish, arch, and litherlie,
  But well Lord Cranstoun served he:
And he of his service was full fain;
For once he had been ta'en or slain,   380
  An it had not been for his ministry.
All between Home and Hermitage
Talked of Lord Cranstoun's Goblin Page.

XXXIII

For the Baron went on pilgrimage,
And took with him this elfish page, ,
  To Mary's Chapel of the Lowes;
For there, beside Our Ladye's lake,
An offering he had sworn to make,
  And he would pay his vows.
But the Ladye of Branksome gathered a
    band   390
Of the best that would ride at her com-
    mand;
  The trysting-place was Newark Lee.

Wat of Harden came thither amain,
And thither came John of Thirlestane,
And thither came William of Deloraine;
  They were three hundred spears and
    three.
Through Douglas-burn, up Yarrow stream,
Their horses prance, their lances gleam.
They came to Saint Mary's lake ere day,
But the chapel was void and the Baron
    away.   400
They burned the chapel for very rage,
And cursed Lord Cranstoun's Goblin Page.

XXXIV

And now, in Branksome's good green-
    wood,
As under the aged oak he stood,
The Baron's courser pricks his ears,
As if a distant noise he hears.
The dwarf waves his long lean arm on
    high,
And signs to the lovers to part and fly;
No time was then to vow or sigh.
Fair Margaret through the hazel-grove   410
Flew like the startled cushat-dove:
The dwarf the stirrup held and rein;
Vaulted the knight on his steed amain,
And, pondering deep that morning's scene,
Rode eastward through the hawthorns
    green.

While thus he poured the lengthened
    tale,
The Minstrel's voice began to fail.
Full slyly smiled the observant page,
And gave the withered hand of age
A goblet, crowned with mighty wine,   420
The blood of Velez' scorched vine.
He raised the silver cup on high,
And, while the big drop filled his eye,
Prayed God to bless the Duchess long,
And all who cheered a son of song.
The attending maidens smiled to see
How long, how deep, how zealously,
The precious juice the Minstrel quaffed;
And he, emboldened by the draught,
Looked gayly back to them and laughed.
The cordial nectar of the bowl   431
Swelled his old veins and cheered his
    soul;
A lighter, livelier prelude ran,
Ere thus his tale again began.

CANTO THIRD

I

AND said I that my limbs were old,
And said I that my blood was cold,
And that my kindly fire was fled,
And my poor withered heart was dead,
    And that I might not sing of love ? —
How could I to the dearest theme
That ever warmed a minstrel's dream,
    So foul, so false a recreant prove ?
How could I name love's very name,
Nor wake my heart to notes of flame ?   10

II

In peace, Love tunes the shepherd's
    reed;
In war, he mounts the warrior's steed;
In halls, in gay attire is seen;
In hamlets, dances on the green.
Love rules the court, the camp, the grove,
And men below, and saints above;
For love is heaven, and heaven is love.

III

So thought Lord Cranstoun, as I ween,
While, pondering deep the tender scene,
He rode through Branksome's hawthorn
    green.   20
But the page shouted wild and shrill,
    And scarce his helmet could he don,
When downward from the shady hill
    A stately knight came pricking on.
That warrior's steed, so dapple-gray,
Was dark with sweat and splashed with
    clay,
    His armor red with many a stain:
He seemed in such a weary plight,
As if he had ridden the livelong night;
    For it was William of Deloraine.   30

IV

But no whit weary did he seem,
When, dancing in the sunny beam,
He marked the crane on the Baron's crest;
For his ready spear was in his rest.
Few were the words, and stern and high,
    That marked the foemen's feudal hate;
For question fierce and proud reply
    Gave signal soon of dire debate.
Their very coursers seemed to know
That each was other's mortal foe,   40
And snorted fire when wheeled around
To give each knight his vantage-ground.

V

In rapid round the Baron bent;
    He sighed a sigh and breathed a prayer;
The prayer was to his patron saint,
    The sigh was to his ladye fair.
Stout Deloraine nor sighed nor prayed,
Nor saint nor ladye called to aid;
But he stooped his head, and couched his
    spear,
And spurred his steed to full career.   50
The meeting of these champions proud
Seemed like the bursting thunder-cloud.

VI

Stern was the dint the Borderer lent !
The stately Baron backwards bent,
Bent backwards to his horse's tail,
And his plumes went scattering on the
    gale;
The tough ash spear, so stout and true,
Into a thousand flinders flew.
But Cranstoun's lance, of more avail,
Pierced through, like silk, the Borderer's
    mail;   60
Through shield and jack and acton passed,
Deep in his bosom broke at last.
Still sate the warrior saddle-fast,
Till, stumbling in the mortal shock,
Down went the steed, the girthing broke,
Hurled on a heap lay man and horse.
The Baron onward passed his course,
Nor knew — so giddy rolled his brain —
His foe lay stretched upon the plain.

VII

But when he reined his courser round,   70
And saw his foeman on the ground
    Lie senseless as the bloody clay,
He bade his page to stanch the wound,
    And there beside the warrior stay,
And tend him in his doubtful state,
And lead him to Branksome castle-gate:
His noble mind was inly moved
For the kinsman of the maid he loved.
'This shalt thou do without delay:
No longer here myself may stay;   80
Unless the swifter I speed away,
Short shrift will be at my dying day.

VIII

Away in speed Lord Cranstoun rode;
The Goblin Page behind abode;
His lord's command he ne'er withstood,
Though small his pleasure to do good.

As the corselet off he took,
The dwarf espied the Mighty Book !
Much he marvelled a knight of pride
Like a book-bosomed priest should ride: 90
He thought not to search or stanch the
    wound
Until the secret he had found.

IX

The iron band, the iron clasp,
Resisted long the elfin grasp;
For when the first he had undone,
It closed as he the next begun.
Those iron clasps, that iron band,
Would not yield to unchristened hand
Till he smeared the cover o'er
With the Borderer's curdled gore;   100
A moment then the volume spread,
And one short spell therein he read.
It had much of glamour might,
Could make a ladye seem a knight,
The cobwebs on a dungeon wall
Seem tapestry in lordly hall,
A nutshell seem a gilded barge,
A sheeling seem a palace large,
And youth seem age, and age seem
    youth —
All was delusion, nought was truth.   110

X

He had not read another spell,
When on his cheek a buffet fell,
So fierce, it stretched him on the plain
Beside the wounded Deloraine.
From the ground he rose dismayed,
And shook his huge and matted head;
One word he muttered and no more,
'Man of age, thou smitest sore !'
No more the elfin page durst try
Into the wondrous book to pry;   120
The clasps, though smeared with Christian
    gore,
Shut faster than they were before.
He hid it underneath his cloak. —
Now, if you ask who gave the stroke,
I cannot tell, so mot I thrive;
It was not given by man alive.

XI

Unwillingly himself he addressed
To do his master's high behest:
He lifted up the living corse,
And laid it on the weary horse;   130
He led him into Branksome Hall
Before the beards of the warders all,

And each did after swear and say
There only passed a wain of hay.
He took him to Lord David's tower,
Even to the Ladye's secret bower;
And, but that stronger spells were spread,
And the door might not be opened,
He had laid him on her very bed.
Whate'er he did of gramarye   140
Was always done maliciously;
He flung the warrior on the ground,
And the blood welled freshly from the
    wound.

XII

As he repassed the outer court,
He spied the fair young child at sport:
He thought to train him to the wood;
For, at a word, be it understood,
He was always for ill, and never for good.
Seemed to the boy some comrade gay
Led him forth to the woods to play;   150
On the drawbridge the warders stout
Saw a terrier and lurcher passing out.

XIII

He led the boy o'er bank and fell,
    Until they came to a woodland brook;
The running stream dissolved the spell,
    And his own elfish shape he took.
Could he have had his pleasure vilde,
He had crippled the joints of the noble
    child,
Or, with his fingers long and lean,
Had strangled him in fiendish spleen: 160
But his awful mother he had in dread,
And also his power was limited;
So he but scowled on the startled child,
And darted through the forest wild;
The woodland brook he bounding crossed,
And laughed, and shouted, 'Lost ! lost !
    lost !'

XIV

Full sore amazed at the wondrous change,
    And frightened, as a child might be,
At the wild yell and visage strange,
    And the dark words of gramarye,   170
The child, amidst the forest bower,
Stood rooted like a lily flower;
And when at length, with trembling pace,
    He sought to find where Branksome lay,
He feared to see that grisly face
    Glare from some thicket on his way.
Thus, starting oft, he journeyed on,
And deeper in the wood is gone, —

For aye the more he sought his way,
The farther still he went astray, — 180
Until he heard the mountains round
Ring to the baying of a hound.

XV

And hark ! and hark ! the deep-mouthed
    bark
    Comes nigher still and nigher;
Bursts on the path a dark bloodhound,
His tawny muzzle tracked the ground,
    And his red eye shot fire.
Soon as the wildered child saw he,
He flew at him right furioslie.
I ween you would have seen with joy 190
The bearing of the gallant boy,
When, worthy of his noble sire,
His wet cheek glowed 'twixt fear and ire !
He faced the bloodhound manfully,
And held his little bat on high;
So fierce he struck, the dog, afraid,
At cautious distance hoarsely bayed,
    But still in act to spring;
When dashed an archer through the glade,
And when he saw the hound was stayed, 200
    He drew his tough bowstring;
But a rough voice cried, 'Shoot not, hoy !
Ho ! shoot not, Edward, — 't is a boy !'

XVI

The speaker issued from the wood,
And checked his fellow's surly mood,
    And quelled the ban-dog's ire:
He was an English yeoman good
    And born in Lancashire.
Well could he hit a fallow-deer
    Five hundred feet him fro ; 210
With hand more true and eye more clear
    No archer bended bow.
His coal-black hair, shorn round and close,
Set off his sun-burned face;
Old England's sign, Saint George's cross,
    His barret-cap did grace;
His bugle-horn hung by his side,
    All in a wolf-skin baldric tied;
And his short falchion, sharp and clear,
Had pierced the throat of many a deer. 220

XVII

His kirtle, made of forest green,
    Reached scantly to his knee;
And, at his belt, of arrows keen
    A furbished sheaf bore he;
His buckler scarce in breadth a span,
    No longer fence had he;

He never counted him a man,
    Would strike below the knee:
His slackened bow was in his hand,
And the leash that was his bloodhound's
    band. 230

XVIII

He would not do the fair child harm,
But held him with his powerful arm,
That he might neither fight nor flee;
For when the red cross spied he,
The boy strove long and violently.
' Now, by Saint George,' the archer cries,
' Edward, methinks we have a prize !
This boy's fair face and courage free
Show he is come of high degree.'

XIX

' Yes ! I am come of high degree, 240
    For I am the heir of bold Buccleuch;
And, if thou dost not set me free,
    False Southron, thou shalt dearly rue !
For Walter of Harden shall come with
    speed,
And William of Deloraine, good at need,
And every Scott from Esk to Tweed;
And, if thou dost not let me go,
Despite thy arrows and thy bow,
I 'll have thee hanged to feed the crow !'

XX

' Gramercy for thy good-will, fair boy ! 250
My mind was never set so high;
But if thou art chief of such a clan,
And art the son of such a man,
And ever comest to thy command,
    Our wardens had need to keep good
    order:
My bow of yew to a hazel wand,
    Thou 'lt make them work upon the
    Border !
Meantime, be pleased to come with me,
For good Lord Dacre shalt thou see;
I think our work is well begun, 260
When we have taken thy father's son.'

XXI

Although the child was led away,
In Branksome still he seemed to stay,
For so the Dwarf his part did play;
And, in the shape of that young boy,
He wrought the castle much annoy.
The comrades of the young Buccleuch
He pinched and beat and overthrew;
Nay, some of them he well-nigh slew.

He tore Dame Maudlin's silken tire,   270
And, as Sym Hall stood by the fire,
He lighted the match of his bandelier,
And wofully scorched the hackbuteer.
It may be hardly thought or said,
The mischief that the urchin made,
Till many of the castle guessed
That the young baron was possessed !

XXII

Well I ween the charm he held
The noble Ladye had soon dispelled,
But she was deeply busied then   280
To tend the wounded Deloraine.
Much she wondered to find him lie
  On the stone threshold stretched along:
She thought some spirit of the sky
  Had done the bold moss-trooper wrong,
Because, despite her precept dread,
Perchance he in the book had read;
But the broken lance in his bosom stood,
And it was earthly steel and wood.

XXIII

She drew the splinter from the wound,   290
  And with a charm she stanched the
    blood.
She bade the gash be cleansed and bound:
  No longer by his couch she stood;
But she has ta'en the broken lance,
  And washed it from the clotted gore,
  And salved the splinter o'er and o'er.
William of Deloraine, in trance,
Whene'er she turned it round and round,
Twisted as if she galled his wound.
  Then to her maidens she did say,   300
That he should be whole man and sound
  Within the course of a night and day.
Full long she toiled, for she did rue
Mishap to friend so stout and true.

XXIV

So passed the day — the evening fell,
'T was near the time of curfew bell;
The air was mild, the wind was calm,
The stream was smooth, the dew was balm;
E'en the rude watchman on the tower
Enjoyed and blessed the lovely hour.   310
Far more fair Margaret loved and blessed
The hour of silence and of rest.
On the high turret sitting lone,
She waked at times the lute's soft tone,
Touched a wild note, and all between
Thought of the bower of hawthorns green.

Her golden hair streamed free from band,
Her fair cheek rested on her hand,
Her blue eyes sought the west afar,
For lovers love the western star.   320

XXV

Is yon the star, o'er Penchryst Pen,
That rises slowly to her ken,
And, spreading broad its wavering light,
Shakes its loose tresses on the night ?
Is yon red glare the western star ? —
O, 't is the beacon-blaze of war !
Scarce could she draw her tightened
    breath,
For well she knew the fire of death !

XXVI

The warder viewed it blazing strong,
And blew his war-note loud and long,   330
Till, at the high and haughty sound,
Rock, wood, and river rung around.
The blast alarmed the festal hall,
And startled forth the warriors all;
Far downward in the castle-yard
Full many a torch and cresset glared;
And helms and plumes, confusedly tossed,
Were in the blaze half seen, half lost;
And spears in wild disorder shook,
Like reeds beside a frozen brook.   340

XXVII

The seneschal, whose silver hair
Was reddened by the torches' glare,
Stood in the midst, with gesture proud,
And issued forth his mandates loud:
' On Penchryst glows a bale of fire,
And three are kindling on Priesthaughs-
    wire;
    Ride out, ride out,
    The foe to scout !
Mount, mount for Branksome, every man !
Thou, Todrig, warn the Johnstone clan,   350
    That ever are true and stout.
Ye need not send to Liddesdale,
For when they see the blazing bale
Elliots and Armstrongs never fail. —
Ride, Alton, ride, for death and life,
And warn the warden of the strife ! —
Young Gilbert, let our beacon blaze,
Our kin and clan and friends to raise ! '

XXVIII

Fair Margaret from the turret head
Heard far below the coursers' tread,   360

While loud the harness rung,
As to their seats with clamor dread
    The ready horsemen sprung:
And trampling hoofs, and iron coats,
And leaders' voices, mingled notes,
        And out ! and out !
    In hasty rout,
    The horsemen galloped forth;
Dispersing to the south to scout,
    And east, and west, and north,   370
To view their coming enemies,
And warn their vassals and allies.

XXIX

The ready page with hurried hand
Awaked the need-fire's slumbering brand,
    And ruddy blushed the heaven;
For a sheet of flame from the turret high
Waved like a blood-flag on the sky,
    All flaring and uneven.
And soon a score of fires, I ween,   379
From height and hill and cliff were seen,
    Each with warlike tidings fraught;
Each from each the signal caught;
Each after each they glanced to sight,
    As stars arise upon the night.
They gleamed on many a dusky tarn,
    Haunted by the lonely earn;
On many a cairn's gray pyramid,
Where urns of mighty chiefs lie hid;
Till high Dunedin the blazes saw
From Soltra and Dumpender Law,   390
And Lothian heard the Regent's order
That all should bowne them for the Border.

XXX

The livelong night in Branksome rang
    The ceaseless sound of steel;
The castle-bell with backward clang
    Sent forth the larum peal.
Was frequent heard the heavy jar,
Where massy stone and iron bar
Were piled on echoing keep and tower,
To whelm the foe with deadly shower;   400
Was frequent heard the changing guard,
And watchword from the sleepless ward;
While, wearied by the endless din,
Bloodhound and ban-dog yelled within.

XXXI

The noble dame, amid the broil,
Shared the gray seneschal's high toil,
And spoke of danger with a smile,
Cheered the young knights, and council
    sage

Held with the chiefs of riper age.
No tidings of the foe were brought,   410
Nor of his numbers knew they aught,
Nor what in time of truce he sought.
    Some said that there were thousands
        ten;
And others weened that it was nought
    But Leven Clans or Tynedale men,
Who came to gather in black-mail;
And Liddesdale, with small avail,
    Might drive them lightly back agen.
So passed the anxious night away,
And welcome was the peep of day.   420

CEASED the high sound — the listening
        throng
Applaud the Master of the Song;
And marvel much, in helpless age,
So hard should be his pilgrimage.
Had he no friend — no daughter dear,
His wandering toil to share and cheer ?
No son to be his father's stay,
And guide him on the rugged way ?
' Ay, once he had — but he was dead ! ' —
Upon the harp he stooped his head,   430
And busied himself the strings withal,
To hide the tear that fain would fall.
In solemn measure, soft and slow,
Arose a father's notes of woe.

CANTO FOURTH

I

SWEET Teviot ! on thy silver tide
    The glaring bale-fires blaze no more;
No longer steel-clad warriors ride
    Along thy wild and willowed shore;
Where'er thou wind'st by dale or hill,
All, all is peaceful, all is still,
    As if thy waves, since time was born,
Since first they rolled upon the Tweed,
Had only heard the shepherd's reed,
    Nor startled at the bugle-horn.   10

II

Unlike the tide of human time,
    Which, though it change in ceaseless
        flow,
Retains each grief, retains each crime,
    Its earliest course was doomed to know,
And, darker as it downward bears,

Is stained with past and present tears.
    Low as that tide has ebbed with me,
It still reflects to memory's eye
The hour my brave, my only boy
    Fell by the side of great Dundee.   20
Why, when the volleying musket played
Against the bloody Highland blade,
Why was not I beside him laid ? —
Enough — he died the death of fame;
Enough — he died with conquering Græme.

III

Now over Border dale and fell
    Full wide and far was terror spread;
For pathless marsh and mountain cell
    The peasant left his lowly shed.
The frightened flocks and herds were pent 30
Beneath the peel's rude battlement;
And maids and matrons dropped the tear,
While ready warriors seized the spear.
From Branksome's towers the watchman's
        eye
Dun wreaths of distant smoke can spy,
Which, curling in the rising sun,
Showed Southern ravage was begun.

IV

Now loud the heedful gate-ward cried:
    ' Prepare ye all for blows and blood !
Watt Tinlinn, from the Liddel-side,   40
    Comes wading through the flood.
Full oft the Tynedale snatchers knock
At his lone gate and prove the lock;
It was but last Saint Barnabright
They sieged him a whole summer night,
But fled at morning; well they knew,
In vain he never twanged the yew.
Right sharp has been the evening shower
That drove him from his Liddel tower;
And, by my faith,' the gate-ward said,   50
' I think 't will prove a Warden-raid.'

V

While thus he spoke, the bold yeoman
Entered the echoing barbican.
He led a small and shaggy nag,
That through a bog, from hag to hag,
Could bound like any Billhope stag.
It bore his wife and children twain;
A half-clothed serf was all their train:
His wife, stout, ruddy, and dark-browed,
Of silver brooch and bracelet proud,   60
Laughed to her friends among the crowd.
He was of stature passing tall,
But sparely formed and lean withal:

A battered morion on his brow;
A leathern jack, as fence enow,
On his broad shoulders loosely hung;
A Border axe behind was slung;
    His spear, six Scottish ells in length,
Seemed newly dyed with gore;
    His shafts and bow, of wondrous
        strength,   70
His hardy partner bore.

VI

Thus to the Ladye did Tinlinn show
The tidings of the English foe:
' Belted Will Howard is marching here,
And hot Lord Dacre, with many a spear,
And all the German hackbut-men
Who have long lain at Askerten.
They crossed the Liddel at curfew hour,
And burned my little lonely tower —
The fiend receive their souls therefor ! 80
It had not been burnt this year and more.
Barnyard and dwelling, blazing bright,
Served to guide me on my flight,
But I was chased the livelong night.
Black John of Akeshaw and Fergus
        Græme
Fast upon my traces came,
Until I turned at Priesthaugh Scrogg,
And shot their horses in the bog,
Slew Fergus with my lance outright —
I had him long at high despite;   90
He drove my cows last Fastern's night.'

VII

Now weary scouts from Liddesdale,
Fast hurrying in, confirmed the tale;
As far as they could judge by ken,
    Three hours would bring to Teviot's
        strand
Three thousand armed Englishmen.
    Meanwhile, full many a warlike band,
From Teviot, Aill, and Ettrick shade,
Came in, their chief's defence to aid.
There was saddling and mounting in
        haste,   100
    There was pricking o'er moor and lea;
He that was last at the trysting-place
    Was but lightly held of his gay ladye.

VIII

From fair Saint Mary's silver wave,
    From dreary Gamescleuch's dusky
        height,
His ready lances Thirlestane brave
    Arrayed beneath a banner bright.

The tressured fleur-de-luce he claims
To wreathe his shield, since royal James,
Encamped by Fala's mossy wave,   110
The proud distinction grateful gave
  For faith mid feudal jars;
What time, save Thirlestane alone,
Of Scotland's stubborn barons none
  Would march to southern wars;
And hence, in fair remembrance worn,
Yon sheaf of spears his crest has borne;
Hence his high motto shines revealed,
' Ready, aye ready,' for the field.

IX

An aged knight, to danger steeled,   120
  With many a moss-trooper, came on;
And, azure in a golden field,
The stars and crescent graced his shield,
  Without the bend of Murdieston.
Wide lay his lands round Oakwood Tower,
And wide round haunted Castle-Ower;
High over Borthwick's mountain flood
His wood-embosomed mansion stood;
In the dark glen, so deep below,
The herds of plundered England low,   130
  His bold retainers' daily food,
And bought with danger, blows, and blood.
Marauding chief! his sole delight
The moonlight raid, the morning fight;
Not even the Flower of Yarrow's charms
In youth might tame his rage for arms;
And still in age he spurned at rest,
And still his brows the helmet pressed,
  Albeit the blanched locks below
Were white as Dinlay's spotless snow.   140
Five stately warriors drew the sword
  Before their father's band;
A braver knight than Harden's lord
  Ne'er belted on a brand.

X

Scotts of Eskdale, a stalwart band,
  Came trooping down the Todshawhill;
By the sword they won their land,
  And by the sword they hold it still.
Hearken, Ladye, to the tale
How thy sires won fair Eskdale.   150
Earl Morton was lord of that valley fair,
The Beattisons were his vassals there.
The earl was gentle and mild of mood,
The vassals were warlike and fierce and
  rude;
High of heart and haughty of word,
Little they recked of a tame liege-lord.
The earl into fair Eskdale came,

Homage and seigniory to claim:
Of Gilbert the Galliard a heriot he sought,
Saying, 'Give thy best steed, as a vassal
  ought.'   160
' Dear to me is my bonny white steed,
Oft has he helped me at pinch of need;
Lord and earl though thou be, I trow,
I can rein Bucksfoot better than thou.'
Word on word gave fuel to fire,
Till so high blazed the Beattison's ire,
But that the earl the flight had ta'en,
The vassals there their lord had slain.
Sore he plied both whip and spur,
As he urged his steed through Eskdale
  muir;   170
And it fell down a weary weight,
Just on the threshold of Branksome gate.

XI

The earl was a wrathful man to see,
Full fain avenged would he be.
In haste to Branksome's lord he spoke,
Saying, ' Take these traitors to thy yoke;
For a cast of hawks, and a purse of gold,
All Eskdale I'll sell thee, to have and
  hold:
Beshrew thy heart, of the Beattisons' clan
If thou leavest on Eske a landed man!   180
But spare Woodkerrick's lands alone,
For he lent me his horse to escape upon.'
A glad man then was Branksome bold,
Down he flung him the purse of gold,
To Eskdale soon he spurred amain,
And with him five hundred riders has
  ta'en.
He left his merrymen in the midst of the
  hill,
And bade them hold them close and still;
And alone he wended to the plain,
To meet with the Galliard and all his
  train.   190
To Gilbert the Galliard thus he said:
' Know thou me for thy liege-lord and
  head;
Deal not with me as with Morton tame,
For Scotts play best at the roughest game.
Give me in peace my heriot due,
Thy bonny white steed, or thou shalt rue.
If my horn I three times wind,
Eskdale shall long have the sound in
  mind.'

XII

Loudly the Beattison laughed in scorn;
' Little care we for thy winded horn.   200

Ne'er shall it be the Galliard's lot
To yield his steed to a haughty Scott.
Wend thou to Branksome back on foot,
With rusty spur and miry boot.'
He blew his bugle so loud and hoarse
That the dun deer started at far Craik-
    cross;
He blew again so loud and clear,
Through the gray mountain-mist there did
    lances appear;
And the third blast rang with such a
    din
That the echoes answered from Pentoun-
    linn,   210
And all his riders came lightly in.
Then had you seen a gallant shock,
When saddles were emptied and lances
    broke !
For each scornful word the Galliard had
    said
A Beattison on the field was laid.
His own good sword the chieftain drew,
And he bore the Gailliard through and
    through;
Where the Beattisons' blood mixed with
    the rill,
The Galliard's Haugh men call it still.
The Scotts have scattered the Beattison
    clan,   220
In Eskdale they left but one landed man.
The valley of Eske, from the mouth to the
    source,
Was lost and won for that bonny white
    horse.

XIII

Whitslade the Hawk, and Headshaw
    came,
And warriors more than I may name;
From Yarrow-cleugh to Hindhaugh-swair,
    From Woodhouselie to Chester-glen,
Trooped man and horse, and bow and
    spear;
    Their gathering word was Bellenden.
And better hearts o'er Border sod   230
To siege or rescue never rode.
The Ladye marked the aids come in,
    And high her heart of pride arose;
She bade her youthful son attend,
That he might know his Father's friend,
    And learn to face his foes:
'The boy is ripe to look on war;
    I saw him draw a cross-bow stiff,
And his true arrow struck afar
    The raven's nest upon the cliff;   240

The red cross on a Southern breast
Is broader than the raven's nest:
Thou, Whitslade, shall teach him his
    weapon to wield,
And o'er him hold his father's shield.'

XIV

Well may you think the wily page
Cared not to face the Ladye sage.
He counterfeited childish fear,
And shrieked, and shed full many a tear,
And moaned, and plained in manner wild.
    The attendants to the Ladye told,   250
Some fairy, sure, had changed the child,
    That wont to be so free and bold.
Then wrathful was the noble dame;
She blushed blood-red for very shame:
'Hence ! ere the clan his faintness view;
Hence with the weakling to Buccleugh ! —
Watt Tinlinn, thou shalt be his guide
To Rangleburn's lonely side. —
Sure, some fell fiend has cursed our line,
That coward should e'er be son of
    mine ! '   260

XV

A heavy task Watt Tinlinn had,
To guide the counterfeited lad.
Soon as the palfrey felt the weight
Of that ill-omened elfish freight,
He bolted, sprung, and reared amain,
Nor heeded bit nor curb nor rein.
It cost Watt Tinlinn mickle toil
To drive him but a Scottish mile;
    But as a shallow brook they crossed,
The elf, amid the running stream,   270
His figure changed, like form in dream,
    And fled, and shouted, 'Lost ! lost !
    lost ! '
Full fast the urchin ran and laughed,
But faster still a cloth-yard shaft
Whistled from startled Tinlinn's yew,
And pierced his shoulder through and
    through.
Although the imp might not be slain,
And though the wound soon healed again,
Yet, as he ran, he yelled for pain;
And Watt of Tinlinn, much aghast,   280
Rode back to Branksome fiery fast.

XVI

Soon on the hill's steep verge he stood,
That looks o'er ·Branksome's towers and
    wood;

And martial murmurs from below
Proclaimed the approaching Southern foe.
Through the dark wood, in mingled tone,
Were border pipes and bugles blown;
The coursers' neighing he could ken,
A measured tread of marching men;
While broke at times the solemn hum, 290
The Almayn's sullen kettle-drum;
And banners tall, of crimson sheen,
  Above the copse appear;
And, glistening through the hawthorns
    green,
  Shine helm and shield and spear.

XVII

Light forayers first, to view the ground,
Spurred their fleet coursers loosely round;
Behind, in close array, and fast,
  The Kendal archers, all in green,
Obedient to the bugle blast, 300
  Advancing from the wood were seen.
To back and guard the archer band,
Lord Dacre's billmen were at hand:
A hardy race, on Irthing bred,
With kirtles white and crosses red,
Arrayed beneath the banner tall
That streamed o'er Acre's conquered wall;
And minstrels, as they marched in order,
Played, 'Noble Lord Dacre, he dwells on
    the Border.'

XVIII

Behind the English bill and bow 310
The mercenaries, firm and slow,
  Moved on to fight in dark array,
By Conrad led of Wolfenstein,
Who brought the band from distant Rhine,
  And sold their blood for foreign pay.
The camp their home, their law the sword,
They knew no country, owned no lord:
They were not armed like England's sons,
But bore the levin-darting guns;
Buff coats, all frounced and broidered
    o'er, 320
And morsing-horns and scarfs they wore;
Each better knee was bared, to aid
The warriors in the escalade;
All as they marched, in rugged tongue
Songs of Teutonic feuds they sung.

XIX

But louder still the clamor grew,
And louder still the minstrels blew,
When, from beneath the greenwood tree,
Rode forth Lord Howard's chivalry;

His men-at-arms, with glaive and spear, 330
Brought up the battle's glittering rear.
There many a youthful knight, full keen
To gain his spurs, in arms was seen,
With favor in his crest, or glove,
Memorial of his ladye-love.
So rode they forth in fair array,
Till full their lengthened lines display;
Then called a halt, and made a stand,
And cried, 'Saint George for merry Eng-
    land!'

XX

Now every English eye intent 340
On Branksome's armed towers was bent;
So near they were that they might know
The straining harsh of each cross-bow;
On battlement and bartizan
Gleamed axe and spear and partisan;
Falcon and culver on each tower
Stood prompt their deadly hail to shower;
And flashing armor frequent broke
From eddying whirls of sable smoke,
Where upon tower and turret head 350
The seething pitch and molten lead
Reeked like a witch's caldron red.
While yet they gaze, the bridges fall,
The wicket opes, and from the wall
Rides forth the hoary seneschal.

XXI

Armed he rode, all save the head,
His white beard o'er his breastplate spread;
Unbroke by age, erect his seat,
He ruled his eager courser's gait,
Forced him with chastened fire to
    prance, 360
And, high curvetting, slow advance:
In sign of truce, his better hand
Displayed a peeled willow wand;
His squire, attending in the rear,
Bore high a gauntlet on his spear.
When they espied him riding out,
Lord Howard and Lord Dacre stout
Sped to the front of their array,
To hear what this old knight should say.

XXII

'Ye English warden lords, of you 370
Demands the ladye of Buccleuch,
Why, 'gainst the truce of Border tide,
In hostile guise ye dare to ride,
With Kendal bow and Gilsland brand,
And all yon mercenary band,
Upon the bounds of fair Scotland?

My Ladye reads you swith return;
And, if but one poor straw you burn,
Or do our towers so much molest
As scare one swallow from her nest,   380
Saint Mary ! but we 'll light a brand
Shall warm your hearths in Cumber-
    land.' —

XXIII

A wrathful man was Dacre's lord,
But calmer Howard took the word:
' May 't please thy dame, Sir Seneschal,
To seek the castle's outward wall,
Our pursuivant-at-arms shall show
Both why we came and when we go.'
The message sped, the noble dame
To the wall's outward circle came;   390
Each chief around leaned on his spear,
To see the pursuivant appear.
All in Lord Howard's livery dressed,
The lion argent decked his breast;
He led a boy of blooming hue —
O sight to meet a mother's view !
It was the heir of great Buccleuch.
Obeisance meet the herald made,
And thus his master's will he said:

XXIV

' It irks, high dame, my noble lords,   400
'Gainst ladye fair to draw their swords;
But yet they may not tamely see,
All through the Western Wardenry,
Your law-contemning kinsmen ride,
And burn and spoil the Border-side;
And ill beseems your rank and birth
To make your towers a flemens-firth.
We claim from thee William of Delo-
    raine,
That he may suffer march-treason pain.
It was but last Saint Cuthbert's even   410
He pricked to Stapleton on Leven,
Harried the lands of Richard Musgrave,
And slew his brother by dint of glaive.
Then, since a lone and widowed dame
These restless riders may not tame,
Either receive within thy towers
Two hundred of my master's powers,
Or straight they sound their warrison,
And storm and spoil thy garrison;
And this fair boy, to London led,   420
Shall good King Edward's page be bred.'

XXV

He ceased — and loud the boy did cry,
And stretched his little arms on high,

Implored for aid each well-known face,
And strove to seek the dame's embrace.
A moment changed that Ladye's cheer,
Gushed to her eye the unbidden tear;
She gazed upon the leaders round,
And dark and sad each warrior frowned;
Then deep within her sobbing breast   430
She locked the struggling sigh to rest,
Unaltered and collected stood,
And thus replied in dauntless mood:

XXVI

' Say to your lords of high emprise
Who war on women and on boys,
That either William of Deloraine
Will cleanse him by oath of march-treason
    stain,
Or else he will the combat take
'Gainst Musgrave for his honor's sake.
No knight in Cumberland so good   440
But William may count with him kin and
    blood.
Knighthood he took of Douglas' sword,
When English blood swelled Ancram ford;
And but Lord Dacre's steed was wight,
And bare him ably in the flight,
Himself had seen him dubbed a knight.
For the young heir of Branksome's line,
God be his aid, and God be mine !
Through me no friend shall meet his doom;
Here, while I live, no foe finds room.   450
Then, if thy lords their purpose urge,
    Take our defiance loud and high;
Our slogan is their lyke-wake dirge,
    Our moat the grave where they shall lie.'

XXVII

Proud she looked round, applause to
    claim —
Then lightened Thirlestane's eye of flame;
    His bugle Wat of Harden blew;
Pensils and pennons wide were flung,
To heaven the Border slogan rung,   459
    ' Saint Mary for the young Buccleuch ! '
The English war-cry answered wide,
    And forward bent each Southern spear;
Each Kendal archer made a stride,
    And drew the bowstring to his ear;
Each minstrel's war-note loud was blown; —
But, ere a gray-goose shaft had flown,
    A horseman galloped from the rear.

XXVIII

' Ah ! noble lords ! ' he breathless said,
' What treason has your march betrayed ?

What make you here from aid so far,   470
Before you walls, around you war?
Your foemen triumph in the thought
That in the toils the lion's caught.
Already on dark Ruberslaw
The Douglas holds his weapon-schaw;
The lances, waving in his train,
Clothe the dun heath like autumn grain;
And on the Liddel's northern strand,
To bar retreat to Cumberland,   479
Lord Maxwell ranks his merrymen good
Beneath the eagle and the rood;
And Jedwood, Eske, and Teviotdale,
  Have to proud Angus come;
And all the Merse and Lauderdale
  Have risen with haughty Home.
An exile from Northumberland,
  In Liddesdale I've wandered long,
But still my heart was with merry Eng-
    land,
And cannot brook my country's wrong;
And hard I've spurred all night, to show 490
The mustering of the coming foe.'

XXIX

' And let them come!' fierce Dacre cried;
' For soon yon crest, my father's pride,
That swept the shores of Judah's sea,
And waved in gales of Galilee,
From Branksome's highest towers dis-
    played,
Shall mock the rescue's lingering aid! —
Level each harquebuss on row;
Draw, merry archers, draw the bow;
Up, billmen, to the walls, and cry,   500
Dacre for England, win or die!' —

XXX

' Yet hear,' quoth Howard, 'calmly hear,
Nor deem my words the words of fear:
For who, in field or foray slack,
Saw the Blanche Lion e'er fall back?
But thus to risk our Border flower
In strife against a kingdom's power,
Ten thousand Scots 'gainst thousands three,
Certes, were desperate policy.
Nay, take the terms the Ladye made   510
Ere conscious of the advancing aid:
Let Musgrave meet fierce Deloraine
In single fight, and if he gain,
He gains for us; but if he's crossed,
'T is but a single warrior lost:
The rest, retreating as they came,
Avoid defeat and death and shame.'

XXXI

Ill could the haughty Dacre brook
His brother warden's sage rebuke;
And yet his forward step he stayed,   520
And slow and sullenly obeyed.
But ne'er again the Border side
Did these two lords in friendship ride;
And this slight discontent, men say,
Cost blood upon another day.

XXXII

The pursuivant-at-arms again
  Before the castle took his stand;
His trumpet called with parleying strain
  The leaders of the Scottish band;
And he defied, in Musgrave's right,   530
Stout Deloraine to single fight.
A gauntlet at their feet he laid,
And thus the terms of fight he said:
' If in the lists good Musgrave's sword
  Vanquish the Knight of Deloraine,
Your youthful chieftain, Branksome's lord,
  Shall hostage for his clan remain;
If Deloraine foil good Musgrave,
The boy his liberty shall have.
Howe'er it falls, the English band,   540
Unharming Scots, by Scots unharmed,
In peaceful march, like men unarmed,
  Shall straight retreat to Cumberland.'

XXXIII

Unconscious of the near relief,
The proffer pleased each Scottish chief,
  Though much the Ladye sage gain-
    said;
For though their hearts were brave and
    true,
From Jedwood's recent sack they knew
  How tardy was the Regent's aid:
And you may guess the noble dame   550
  Durst not the secret prescience own,
Sprung from the art she might not name,
  By which the coming help was known.
Closed was the compact, and agreed
That lists should be enclosed with speed
  Beneath the castle on a lawn:
They fixed the morrow for the strife,
On foot, with Scottish axe and knife,
  At the fourth hour from peep of dawn;
When Deloraine, from sickness freed,   560
Or else a champion in his stead,
Should for himself and chieftain stand
Against stout Musgrave, hand to hand.

XXXIV

I know right well that in their lay
Full many minstrels sing and say
    Such combat should be made on horse,
On foaming steed, in full career,
With brand to aid, whenas the spear
    Should shiver in the course:
But he, the jovial harper, taught   570
Me, yet a youth, how it was fought,
    In guise which now I say ;
He knew each ordinance and clause
Of Black Lord Archibald's battle-laws,
    In the old Douglas' day.
He brooked not, he, that scoffing tongue
Should tax his minstrelsy with wrong,
    Or call his song untrue:
For this, when they the goblet plied,
And such rude taunt had chafed his
        pride,   580
    The bard of Reull he slew.
On Teviot's side in fight they stood,
And tuneful hands were stained with
        blood,
Where still the thorn's white branches
        wave,
Memorial o'er his rival's grave.

XXXV

Why should I tell the rigid doom
That dragged my master to his tomb;
    How Ousenam's maidens tore their
        hair,
Wept till their eyes were dead and dim,
And wrung their hands for love of him   590
    Who died at Jedwood Air ?
He died ! — his scholars, one by one,
To the cold silent grave are gone;
And I, alas ! survive alone,
To muse o'er rivalries of yore,
And grieve that I shall hear no more
The strains, with envy heard before;
For, with my minstrel brethren fled,
My jealousy of song is dead.

He paused: the listening dames again   600
Applaud the hoary Minstrel's strain.
With many a word of kindly cheer, —
In pity half, and half sincere, —
Marvelled the Duchess how so well
His legendary song could tell
Of ancient deeds, so long forgot;
Of feuds, whose memory was not;

Of forests, now laid waste and bare;
Of towers, which harbor now the hare;
Of manners, long since changed and
        gone;   610
Of chiefs, who under their gray stone
So long had slept that fickle Fame
Had blotted from her rolls their name,
And twined round some new minion's head
The fading wreath for which they bled:
In sooth, 't was strange this old man's verse
Could call them from their marble hearse.

The harper smiled, well pleased; for ne'er
Was flattery lost on poet's ear.
A simple race ! they waste their toil   620
For the vain tribute of a smile;
E'en when in age their flame expires,
Her dulcet breath can fan its fires:
Their drooping fancy wakes at praise,
And strives to trim the short-lived blaze.

Smiled then, well pleased, the aged man,
And thus his tale continued ran.

CANTO FIFTH

I

CALL it not vain: — they do not err,
    Who say that when the poet dies
Mute Nature mourns her worshipper
    And celebrates his obsequies;
Who say tall cliff and cavern lone
For the departed bard make moan;
That mountains weep in crystal rill;
That flowers in tears of balm distil;
Through his loved groves that breezes
        sigh,
And oaks in deeper groan reply,   10
And rivers teach their rushing wave
To murmur dirges round his grave.

II

Not that, in sooth, o'er mortal urn
Those things inanimate can mourn,
But that the stream, the wood, the gale,
Is vocal with the plaintive wail
Of those who, else forgotten long,
Lived in the poet's faithful song,
And, with the poet's parting breath,
Whose memory feels a second death.   20
The maid's pale shade, who wails her lot,
That love, true love, should be forgot,
From rose and hawthorn shakes the tear
Upon the gentle minstrel's bier:

The phantom knight, his glory fled,
Mourns o'er the field he heaped with dead,
Mounts the wild blast that sweeps amain
And shrieks along the battle-plain;
The chief, whose antique crownlet long
Still sparkled in the feudal song, 30
Now, from the mountain's misty throne,
Sees, in the thanedom once his own,
His ashes undistinguished lie,
His place, his power, his memory die;
His groans the lonely caverns fill,
His tears of rage impel the rill;
All mourn the minstrel's harp unstrung,
Their name unknown, their praise un-
sung.

III

Scarcely the hot assault was stayed,
The terms of truce were scarcely made, 40
When they could spy, from Branksome's
towers,
The advancing march of martial powers.
Thick clouds of dust afar appeared,
And trampling steeds were faintly heard;
Bright spears above the columns dun
Glanced momentary to the sun;
And feudal banners fair displayed
The bands that moved to Branksome's aid.

IV

Vails not to tell each hardy clan,
From the fair Middle Marches came; 50
The Bloody Heart blazed in the van,
Announcing Douglas, dreaded name !
Vails not to tell what steeds did spurn,
Where the Seven Spears of Wedderburne
Their men in battle-order set,
And Swinton laid the lance in rest
That tamed of yore the sparkling crest
Of Clarence's Plantagenet.
Nor list I say what hundreds more,
From the rich Merse and Lammermore, 60
And Tweed's fair borders, to the war,
Beneath the crest of old Dunbar
And Hepburn's mingled banners, come
Down the steep mountain glittering far,
And shouting still, ' A Home ! a Home ! '

V

Now squire and knight, from Branksome
sent,
On many a courteous message went:
To every chief and lord they paid
Meet thanks for prompt and powerful aid,
And told them how a truce was made, 70

And how a day of fight was ta'en
'Twixt Musgrave and stout Deloraine;
And how the Ladye prayed them dear
That all would stay the fight to see,
And deign, in love and courtesy,
To taste of Branksome cheer.
Nor, while they bade to feast each Scot,
Were England's noble lords forgot.
Himself, the hoary seneschal,
Rode forth, in seemly terms to call 80
Those gallant foes to Branksome Hall.
Accepted Howard, than whom knight
Was never dubbed, more bold in fight,
Nor, when from war and armor free,
More famed for stately courtesy;
But angry Dacre rather chose
In his pavilion to repose.

VI

Now, noble dame, perchance you ask
How these two hostile armies met,
Deeming it were no easy task 90
To keep the truce which here was set;
Where martial spirits, all on fire,
Breathed only blood and mortal ire.
By mutual inroads, mutual blows,
By habit, and by nation, foes,
They met on Teviot's strand;
They met and sate them mingled down,
Without a threat, without a frown,
As brothers meet in foreign land:
The hands, the spear that lately grasped, 100
Still in the mailed gauntlet clasped,
Were interchanged in greeting dear;
Visors were raised and faces shown,
And many a friend, to friend made known,
Partook of social cheer.
Some drove the jolly bowl about;
With dice and draughts some chased the
day;
And some, with many a merry shout,
In riot, revelry, and rout,
Pursued the football play. 110

VII

Yet, be it known, had bugles blown
Or sign of war been seen,
Those bands, so fair together ranged,
Those hands, so frankly interchanged,
Had dyed with gore the green:
The merry shout by Teviot-side
Had sunk in war-cries wild and wide,
And in the groan of death;
And whingers, now in friendship bare,

The social meal to part and share,   120
  Had found a bloody sheath.
'Twixt truce and war, such sudden change
Was not infrequent, nor held strange,
  In the old Border-day;
But yet on Branksome's towers and town,
In peaceful merriment, sunk down
  The sun's declining ray.

VIII

The blithesome signs of wassail gay
Decayed not with the dying day;
Soon through the latticed windows tall   130
Of lofty Branksome's lordly hall,
Divided square by shafts of stone,
Huge flakes of ruddy lustre shone;
Nor less the gilded rafters rang
With merry harp and beakers' clang;
And frequent, on the darkening plain,
  Loud hollo, whoop, or whistle ran,
As bands, their stragglers to regain,
  Give the shrill watchword of their clan;
And revellers, o'er their bowls, proclaim 140
Douglas' or Dacre's conquering name.

IX

Less frequent heard, and fainter still,
  At length the various clamors died,
And you might hear from Branksome hill
  No sound but Teviot's rushing tide;
Save when the changing sentinel
The challenge of his watch could tell;
And save where, through the dark profound,
The clanging axe and hammer's sound
  Rung from the nether lawn;   150
For many a busy hand toiled there,
Strong pales to shape and beams to square,
The lists' dread barriers to prepare
Against the morrow's dawn.

X

Margaret from hall did soon retreat,
  Despite the dame's reproving eye;
Nor marked she, as she left her seat,
  Full many a stifled sigh:
For many a noble warrior strove
To win the Flower of Teviot's love,   160
  And many a bold ally.
With throbbing head and anxious heart,
All in her lonely bower apart,
  In broken sleep she lay.
By times, from silken couch she rose;
While yet the bannered hosts repose,
  She viewed the dawning day:

Of all the hundreds sunk to rest,
First woke the loveliest and the best.

XI

She gazed upon the inner court,   170
  Which in the tower's tall shadow lay,
Where coursers' clang and stamp and snort
  Had rung the livelong yesterday:
Now still as death; till stalking slow, —
  The jingling spurs announced his
    tread, —
A stately warrior passed below;
  But when he raised his plumed head —
  Blessed Mary! can it be? —
Secure, as if in Ousenam bowers,
He walks through Branksome's hostile
    towers,   180
  With fearless step and free.
She dared not sign, she dared not speak —
O, if one page's slumbers break,
  His blood the price must pay!
Not all the pearls Queen Mary wears,
Not Margaret's yet more precious tears,
  Shall buy his life a day.

XII

Yet was his hazard small; for well
You may bethink you of the spell
  Of that sly urchin page: 190
This to his lord he did impart,
And made him seem, by glamour art,
  A knight from Hermitage.
Unchallenged, thus, the warder's post,
The court, unchallenged, thus he crossed,
  For all the vassalage;
But O, what magic's quaint disguise
Could blind fair Margaret's azure eyes!
  She started from her seat;
While with surprise and fear she strove, 200
And both could scarcely master love —
  Lord Henry's at her feet.

XIII

Oft have I mused what purpose bad
That foul malicious urchin had
  To bring this meeting round,
For happy love's a heavenly sight,
And by a vile malignant sprite
  In such no joy is found;
And oft I've deemed, perchance he
    thought
      209
Their erring passion might have wrought
  Sorrow and sin and shame,
And death to Cranstoun's gallant Knight,

And to the gentle Ladye bright
　　Disgrace and loss of fame.
But earthly spirit could not tell
The heart of them that loved so well.
True love 's the gift which God has given
To man alone beneath the heaven:
It is not fantasy's hot fire,
　　Whose wishes soon as granted fly;　220
It liveth not in fierce desire,
　　With dead desire it doth not die;
It is the secret sympathy,
The silver link, the silken tie,
Which heart to heart, and mind to mind,
In body and in soul can bind. —
Now leave we Margaret and her knight,
To tell you of the approaching fight.

XIV

Their warning blasts the bugles blew,
　　The pipe's shrill port aroused each
　　　clan;　230
In haste the deadly strife to view,
　　The trooping warriors eager ran:
Thick round the lists their lances stood,
Like blasted pines in Ettrick wood;
To Branksome many a look they threw,
The combatants' approach to view,
And bandied many a word of boast
About the knight each favored most.

XV

Meantime full anxious was the dame;
For now arose disputed claim　240
Of who should fight for Deloraine,
'Twixt Harden and 'twixt Thirlestane.
They gan to reckon kin and rent,
And frowning brow on brow was bent;
　　But yet not long the strife — for, lo!
Himself, the Knight of Deloraine,
Strong, as it seemed, and free from pain,
　　In armor sheathed from top to toe,
Appeared and craved the combat due.
The dame her charm successful knew,　250
And the fierce chiefs their claims withdrew.

XVI

When for the lists they sought the plain,
The stately Ladye's silken rein
　　Did noble Howard hold;
Unarmed by her side he walked,
And much in courteous phrase they talked
　　Of feats of arms of old.
Costly his garb — his Flemish ruff
Fell o'er his doublet, shaped of buff,
　　With satin slashed and lined;　260

Tawny his boot, and gold his spur,
His cloak was all of Poland fur,
　　His hose with silver twined;
His Bilboa blade, by Marchmen felt,
Hung in a broad and studded belt;
Hence, in rude phrase, the Borderers still
Called noble Howard Belted Will.

XVII

Behind Lord Howard and the dame
Fair Margaret on her palfrey came,
　　Whose footcloth swept the ground;　270
White was her wimple and her veil,
And her loose locks a chaplet pale
　　Of whitest roses bound;
The lordly Angus, by her side,
In courtesy to cheer her tried;
Without his aid, her hand in vain
Had strove to guide her broidered rein.
He deemed she shuddered at the sight
Of warriors met for mortal fight;
But cause of terror, all unguessed,　280
Was fluttering in her gentle breast,
When, in their chairs of crimson placed,
The dame and she the barriers graced.

XVIII

Prize of the field, the young Buccleuch
An English knight led forth to view;
Scarce rued the boy his present plight,
So much he longed to see the fight.
Within the lists in knightly pride
High Home and haughty Dacre ride;
Their leading staffs of steel they wield,　290
As marshals of the mortal field,
While to each knight their care assigned
Like vantage of the sun and wind.
Then heralds hoarse did loud proclaim,
In King and Queen and Warden's name,
　　That none, while lasts the strife,
Should dare, by look or sign or word,
Aid to a champion to afford,
　　On peril of his life;
And not a breath the silence broke　300
Till thus the alternate heralds spoke: —

XIX

ENGLISH HERALD

' Here standeth Richard of Musgrave,
　　Good knight and true, and freely born,
Amends from Deloraine to crave,
　　For foul despiteous scathe and scorn.
He sayeth that William of Deloraine
　　Is traitor false by Border laws;

This with his sword he will maintain,
    So help him God and his good cause ! '

XX

SCOTTISH HERALD

' Here standeth William of Deloraine,   310
Good knight and true, of noble strain,
Who sayeth that foul treason's stain,
Since he bore arms ne'er soiled his coat;
    And that, so help him God above !
He will on Musgrave's body prove
He lies most foully in his throat.'

LORD DACRE

' Forward, brave champions, to the fight !
Sound trumpets ! '

LORD HOME
                ' God defend the right ! ' —
Then, Teviot, how thine echoes rang,
When bugle-sound and trumpet-clang   320
    Let loose the martial foes,
And in mid-list, with shield poised high,
And measured step and wary eye,
    The combatants did close !

XXI

Ill would it suit your gentle ear,
Ye lovely listeners, to hear
How to the axe the helms did sound,
And blood poured down from many a
    wound;
For desperate was the strife and long,
And either warrior fierce and strong.   330
But, were each dame a listening knight,
I well could tell how warriors fight;
For I have seen war's lightning flashing,
Seen the claymore with bayonet clashing,
Seen through red blood the war-horse
    dashing,
And scorned, amid the reeling strife,
To yield a step for death or life.

XXII

'T is done, 't is done ! that fatal blow
    Has stretched him on the bloody plain;
He strives to rise — brave Musgrave,
    no !   340
Thence never shalt thou rise again !
He chokes in blood — some friendly hand
Undo the visor's barred band,
Unfix the gorget's iron clasp,
And give him room for life to gasp ! —

O, bootless aid ! — haste, holy friar,
Haste, ere the sinner shall expire !
Of all his guilt let him be shriven,
And smooth his path from earth to heaven !

XXIII

In haste the holy friar sped; —   350
His naked foot was dyed with red,
    As through the lists he ran;
Unmindful of the shouts on high
That hailed the conqueror's victory,
    He raised the dying man;
Loose waved his silver beard and hair,
As o'er him he kneeled down in prayer;
And still the crucifix on high
He holds before his darkening eye;
And still he bends an anxious ear,   360
His faltering penitence to hear;
    Still props him from the bloody sod,
Still, even when soul and body part,
Pours ghostly comfort on his heart,
    And bids him trust in God !
Unheard he prays; — the death-pang's
    o'er !
Richard of Musgrave breathes no more.

XXIV

As if exhausted in the fight,
Or musing o'er the piteous sight,
    The silent victor stands;   370
His beaver did he not unclasp,
Marked not the shouts, felt not the grasp
    Of gratulating hands.
When lo ! strange cries of wild surprise,
Mingled with seeming terror, rise
    Among the Scottish bands;
And all, amid the thronged array,
In panic haste gave open way
To a half-naked ghastly man,
Who downward from the castle ran: 380
He crossed the barriers at a bound,
And wild and haggard looked around,
    As dizzy and in pain;
And all upon the armed ground
    Knew William of Deloraine !
Each ladye sprung from seat with speed;
Vaulted each marshal from his steed;
    ' And who art thou,' they cried,
' Who hast this battle fought and won ? '
His plumed helm was soon undone —   390
    ' Cranstoun of Teviot-side !
For this fair prize I 've fought and won,' —
And to the Ladye led her son.

XXV

Full oft the rescued boy she kissed,
And often pressed him to her breast,
For, under all her dauntless show,
Her heart had throbbed at every blow;
Yet not Lord Cranstoun deigned she greet,
Though low he kneeled at her feet.
Me lists not tell what words were made, 400
What Douglas, Home, and Howard said —
For Howard was a generous foe —
And how the clan united prayed
The Ladye would the feud forego,
And deign to bless the nuptial hour
Of Cranstoun's lord and Teviot's Flower.

XXVI

She looked to river, looked to hill,
    Thought on the Spirit's prophecy,
Then broke her silence stern and still: 409
    'Not you, but Fate, has vanquished
    me;
Their influence kindly stars may shower
On Teviot's tide and Branksome's tower,
    For pride is quelled and love is free.'
She took fair Margaret by the hand,
Who, breathless, trembling, scarce might
    stand;
    That hand to Cranstoun's lord gave she:
'As I am true to thee and thine,
Do thou be true to me and mine!
    This clasp of love our bond shall be,
For this is your betrothing day, 420
And all these noble lords shall stay,
    To grace it with their company.'

XXVII

All as they left the listed plain,
Much of the story she did gain:
How Cranstoun fought with Deloraine,
And of his page, and of the book
Which from the wounded knight he took;
And how he sought her castle high,
That morn, by help of gramarye;
How, in Sir William's armor dight, 430
Stolen by his page, while slept the knight,
He took on him the single fight.
But half his tale he left unsaid,
And lingered till he joined the maid. —
Cared not the Ladye to betray
Her mystic arts in view of day;
But well she thought, ere midnight came,
Of that strange page the pride to tame,
From his foul hands the book to save,
And send it back to Michael's grave. — 440

Needs not to tell each tender word
'Twixt Margaret and 'twixt Cranstoun's
    lord;
Nor how she told of former woes,
And how her bosom fell and rose
While he and Musgrave bandied blows. —
Needs not these lovers' joys to tell;
One day, fair maids, you'll know them
    well.

XXVIII

William of Deloraine some chance
Had wakened from his deathlike trance,
    And taught that in the listed plain 450
Another, in his arms and shield,
Against fierce Musgrave axe did wield,
    Under the name of Deloraine.
Hence to the field unarmed he ran,
And hence his presence scared the clan,
Who held him for some fleeting wraith,
And not a man of blood and breath.
Not much this new ally he loved,
Yet, when he saw what hap had proved,
    He greeted him right heartilie: 460
He would not waken old debate,
For he was void of rancorous hate,
    Though rude and scant of courtesy;
In raids he spilt but seldom blood,
Unless when men-at-arms withstood,
Or, as was meet, for deadly feud.
He ne'er bore grudge for stalwart blow,
Ta'en in fair fight from gallant foe.
And so 't was seen of him e'en now,
    When on dead Musgrave he looked
    down: 470
Grief darkened on his rugged brow,
    Though half disguised with a frown;
And thus, while sorrow bent his head,
His foeman's epitaph he made:

XXIX

'Now, Richard Musgrave, liest thou here,
    I ween, my deadly enemy;
For, if I slew thy brother dear,
    Thou slew'st a sister's son to me;
And when I lay in dungeon dark
    Of Naworth Castle long months three, 480
Till ransomed for a thousand mark,
    Dark Musgrave, it was long of thee.
And, Musgrave, could our fight be tried,
    And thou wert now alive, as I,
No mortal man should us divide,
    Till one, or both of us, did die:
Yet rest thee God! for well I know
I ne'er shall find a nobler foe.

In all the northern counties here,
Whose word is Snaffle, spur, and spear,   490
Thou wert the best to follow gear.
'T was pleasure, as we looked behind,
To see how thou the chase couldst wind,
Cheer the dark bloodhound on his way,
And with the bugle rouse the fray!
I 'd give the lands of Deloraine,
Dark Musgrave were alive again.'

XXX

So mourned he till Lord Dacre's band
Were bowning back to Cumberland.
They raised brave Musgrave from the
        field   500
And laid him on his bloody shield;
On levelled lances, four and four,
By turns, the noble burden bore.
Before, at times, upon the gale
Was heard the Minstrel's plaintive wail;
Behind, four priests in sable stole
Sung requiem for the warrior's soul;
Around, the horsemen slowly rode;
With trailing pikes the spearmen trode;
And thus the gallant knight they bore 510
Through Liddesdale to Leven's shore,
Thence to Holme Coltrame's lofty nave,
And laid him in his father's grave.

THE harp's wild notes, though hushed the
        song,
The mimic march of death prolong;
Now seems it far, and now a-near,
Now meets, and now eludes the ear,
Now seems some mountain side to sweep,
Now faintly dies in valley deep,
Seems now as if the Minstrel's wail,   520
Now the sad requiem, loads the gale;
Last, o'er the warrior's closing grave,
Rung the full choir in choral stave.

After due pause, they bade him tell
Why he, who touched the harp so well,
Should thus, with ill-rewarded toil,
Wander a poor and thankless soil,
When the more generous Southern Land
Would well requite his skilful hand.

The aged harper, howsoe'er   530
His only friend, his harp, was dear,
Liked not to hear it ranked so high
Above his flowing poesy:

Less liked he still that scornful jeer
Misprized the land he loved so dear;
High was the sound as thus again
The bard resumed his minstrel strain.

CANTO SIXTH

I

BREATHES there the man, with soul so
        dead,
Who never to himself hath said,
    This is my own, my native land?
Whose heart hath ne'er within him burned,
As home his footsteps he hath turned
    From wandering on a foreign strand?
If such there breathe, go, mark him well;
For him no minstrel raptures swell;
High though his titles, proud his name,   9
Boundless his wealth as wish can claim, —
Despite those titles, power, and pelf,
The wretch, concentred all in self,
Living, shall forfeit fair renown,
And, doubly dying, shall go down
To the vile dust from whence he sprung,
Unwept, unhonored, and unsung.

II

O Caledonia, stern and wild,
Meet nurse for a poetic child!
Land of brown heath and shaggy wood,
Land of the mountain and the flood,   20
Land of my sires! what mortal hand
Can e'er untie the filial band
That knits me to thy rugged strand!
Still, as I view each well-known scene,
Think what is now and what hath been,
Seems as to me, of all bereft,
Sole friends thy woods and streams were
        left;
And thus I love them better still,
Even in extremity of ill.
By Yarrow's stream still let me stray, 30
Though none should guide my feeble way;
Still feel the breeze down Ettrick break,
Although it chill my withered cheek;
Still lay my head by Teviot-stone,
Though there, forgotten and alone,
The bard may draw his parting groan.

III

Not scorned like me, to Branksome Hall
The minstrels came at festive call;
Trooping they came from near and far,

The jovial priests of mirth and war; 40
Alike for feast and fight prepared,
Battle and banquet both they shared.
Of late, before each martial clan
They blew their death-note in the van,
But now for every merry mate
Rose the portcullis' iron grate;
They sound the pipe, they strike the string,
They dance, they revel, and they sing,
Till the rude turrets shake and ring.

IV

Me lists not at this tide declare 50
The splendor of the spousal rite,
How mustered in the chapel fair
Both maid and matron, squire and
knight;
Me lists not tell of owches rare,
Of mantles green, and braided hair,
And kirtles furred with miniver;
What plumage waved the altar round,
How spurs and ringing chainlets sound:
And hard it were for bard to speak
The changeful hue of Margaret's cheek, 60
That lovely hue which comes and flies,
As awe and shame alternate rise!

V

Some bards have sung, the Ladye high
Chapel or altar came not nigh,
Nor durst the rites of spousal grace,
So much she feared each holy place.
False slanders these: — I trust right well,
She wrought not by forbidden spell,
For mighty words and signs have power
O'er sprites in planetary hour; 70
Yet scarce I praise their venturous part
Who tamper with such dangerous art.
But this for faithful truth I say, —
The Ladye by the altar stood,
Of sable velvet her array,
And on her head a crimson hood,
With pearls embroidered and entwined,
Guarded with gold, with ermine lined;
A merlin sat upon her wrist,
Held by a leash of silken twist. 80

VI

The spousal rites were ended soon;
'T was now the merry hour of noon,
And in the lofty arched hall
Was spread the gorgeous festival.
Steward and squire, with heedful haste,
Marshalled the rank of every guest;

Pages, with ready blade, were there,
The mighty meal to carve and share:
O'er capon, heron-shew, and crane,
And princely peacock's gilded train, 90
And o'er the boar-head, garnished brave,
And cygnet from Saint Mary's wave,
O'er ptarmigan and venison,
The priest had spoke his benison.
Then rose the riot and the din,
Above, beneath, without, within!
For, from the lofty balcony,
Rung trumpet, shalm, and psaltery:
Their clanging bowls old warriors quaffed,
Loudly they spoke and loudly laughed; 100
Whispered young knights, in tone more
mild,
To ladies fair, and ladies smiled.
The hooded hawks, high perched on beam,
The clamor joined with whistling scream,
And flapped their wings and shook their
bells,
In concert with the stag-hounds' yells.
Round go the flasks of ruddy wine,
From Bordeaux, Orleans, or the Rhine;
Their tasks the busy sewers ply,
And all is mirth and revelry. 110

VII

The Goblin Page, omitting still
No opportunity of ill,
Strove now, while blood ran hot and high,
To rouse debate and jealousy;
Till Conrad, Lord of Wolfenstein,
By nature fierce, and warm with wine,
And now in humor highly crossed
About some steeds his band had lost,
High words to words succeeding still,
Smote with his gauntlet stout Hunthill, 120
A hot and hardy Rutherford,
Whom men called Dickon Draw-the-Sword.
He took it on the page's saye,
Hunthill had driven these steeds away.
Then Howard, Home, and Douglas rose,
The kindling discord to compose;
Stern Rutherford right little said,
But bit his glove and shook his head.
A fortnight thence, in Inglewood, 129
Stout Conrad, cold, and drenched in blood,
His bosom gored with many a wound,
Was by a woodman's lyme-dog found:
Unknown the manner of his death,
Gone was his brand, both sword and sheath;
But ever from that time, 't was said,
That Dickon wore a Cologne blade.

VIII

The dwarf, who feared his master's eye
Might his foul treachery espie,
Now sought the castle buttery,
Where many a yeoman, bold and free,   140
Revelled as merrily and well
As those that sat in lordly selle.
Watt Tinlinn there did frankly raise
The pledge to Arthur Fire-the-Braes;
And he, as by his breeding bound,
To Howard's merrymen sent it round.
To quit them, on the English side,
Red Roland Forster loudly cried,
' A deep carouse to yon fair bride! '
At every pledge, from vat and pail,   150
Foamed forth in floods the nut-brown ale,
While shout the riders every one;
Such day of mirth ne'er cheered their
        clan,
Since old Buccleuch the name did gain,
When in the cleuch the buck was ta'en.

IX

The wily page, with vengeful thought,
    Remembered him of Tinlinn's yew,
And swore it should be dearly bought
    That ever he the arrow drew.
First, he the yeoman did molest   160
With bitter gibe and taunting jest;
Told how he fled at Solway strife,
And how Hob Armstrong cheered his
        wife;
Then, shunning still his powerful arm,
At unawares he wrought him harm;
From trencher stole his choicest cheer,
Dashed from his lips his can of beer;
Then, to his knee sly creeping on,
With bodkin pierced him to the bone:
The venomed wound and festering joint 170
Long after rued that bodkin's point.
The startled yeoman swore and spurned,
And board and flagons overturned.
Riot and clamor wild began;
Back to the hall the urchin ran,
Took in a darkling nook his post,
And grinned, and muttered, ' Lost ! lost !
    lost ! '

X

By this, the dame, lest farther fray
Should mar the concord of the day,
Had bid the minstrels tune their lay.   180
And first stepped forth old Albert Græme,
The minstrel of that ancient name:

Was none who struck the harp so well
Within the Land Debatable;
Well friended too, his hardy kin,
Whoever lost, were sure to win;
They sought the beeves that made their
        broth
In Scotland and in England both.
In homely guise, as nature bade,
His simple song the Borderer said.   190

XI

ALBERT GRÆME

It was an English ladye bright,
    (The sun shines fair on Carlisle wall)
And she would marry a Scottish knight,
    For Love will still be lord of all.

Blithely they saw the rising sun,
    When he shone fair on Carlisle wall;
But they were sad ere day was done,
    Though Love was still the lord of all.

Her sire gave brooch and jewel fine,
    Where the sun shines fair on Carlisle
        wall;   200
Her brother gave but a flask of wine,
    For ire that Love was lord of all.

For she had lands both meadow and lea,
    Where the sun shines fair on Carlisle
        wall;
And he swore her death, ere he would
        see
    A Scottish knight the lord of all !

XII

That wine she had not tasted well,
    (The sun shines fair on Carlisle wall)
When dead, in her true love's arms, she
        fell,
    For Love was still the lord of all.   210

He pierced her brother to the heart,
    Where the sun shines fair on Carlisle
        wall; —
So perish all would true love part,
    That Love may still be lord of all !

And then he took the cross divine,
    Where the sun shines fair on Carlisle
        wall,
And died for her sake in Palestine,
    So Love was still the lord of all.

Now all ye lovers, that faithful prove,
  (The sun shines fair on Carlisle wall) 220
Pray for their souls who died for love,
  For Love shall still be lord of all !

XIII

As ended Albert's simple lay,
  Arose a bard of loftier port,
For sonnet, rhyme, and roundelay
  Renowned in haughty Henry's court:
There rung thy harp, unrivalled long,
Fitztraver of the silver song !
The gentle Surrey loved his lyre —   229
  Who has not heard of Surrey's fame ?
His was the hero's soul of fire,
  And his the bard's immortal name,
And his was love, exalted high
By all the glow of chivalry.

XIV

They sought together climes afar,
  And oft, within some olive grove,
When even came with twinkling star,
  They sung of Surrey's absent love.
His step the Italian peasant stayed,   239
  And deemed that spirits from on high,
Round where some hermit saint was laid,
  Were breathing heavenly melody;
So sweet did harp and voice combine
To praise the name of Geraldine.

XV

Fitztraver, O, what tongue may say
  The pangs thy faithful bosom knew,
When Surrey of the deathless lay
  Ungrateful Tudor's sentence slew ?
Regardless of the tyrant's frown,
His harp called wrath and vengeance
    down.   250
He left, for Naworth's iron towers,
Windsor's green glades and courtly bowers,
And, faithful to his patron's name,
With Howard still Fitztraver came;
Lord William's foremost favorite he,
And chief of all his minstrelsy.

XVI

FITZTRAVER

'T was All-souls' eve, and Surrey's heart
  beat high;
  He heard the midnight bell with anx-
    ious start,
  Which told the mystic hour, approaching
  nigh,

When wise Cornelius promised by his
  art   260
To show to him the ladye of his heart,
Albeit betwixt them roared the ocean
  grim;
Yet so the sage had hight to play his
  part,
That he should see her form in life and
  limb,
And mark if still she loved and still she
  thought of him.

XVII

Dark was the vaulted room of grama-
  rye,
  To which the wizard led the gallant
  knight,
Save that before a mirror, huge and
  high,
  A hallowed taper shed a glimmering
  light
  On mystic implements of magic
  might,   270
On cross, and character, and talisman,
  And almagest, and altar, nothing
  bright;
For fitful was the lustre, pale and wan,
As watch-light by the bed of some depart-
  ing man.

XVIII

But soon, within that mirror huge and
  high,
  Was seen a self-emitted light to
  gleam;
And forms upon its breast the earl 'gan
  spy,
  Cloudy and indistinct as feverish
  dream;
Till, slow arranging and defined, they
  seem
To form a lordly and a lofty room,   280
  Part lighted by a lamp with silver
  beam,
Placed by a couch of Agra's silken loom,
And part by moonshine pale, and part was
  hid in gloom.

XIX

Fair all the pageant — but how passing
  fair
  The slender form which lay on couch
  of Ind !
O'er her white bosom strayed her hazel
  hair,

Pale her dear cheek, as if for love she
  pined;
All in her night-robe loose she lay reclined,
And pensive read from tablet eburnine
Some strain that seemed her inmost
  soul to find: 290
That favored strain was Surrey's raptured line,
That fair and lovely form the Lady Geraldine.

XX

Slow rolled the clouds upon the lovely
  form,
  And swept the goodly vision all
    away —
So royal envy rolled the murky storm
  O'er my beloved Master's glorious
    day.
Thou jealous, ruthless tyrant! Hea-
  ven repay
On thee, and on thy children's latest
  line,
The wild caprice of thy despotic sway,
The gory bridal bed, the plundered
  shrine,   300
The murdered Surrey's blood, the tears of
  Geraldine!

XXI

Both Scots and Southern chiefs prolong
Applauses of Fitztraver's song;
These hated Henry's name as death,
And those still held the ancient faith.
Then from his seat with lofty air
Rose Harold, bard of brave Saint Clair, —
Saint Clair, who, feasting high at Home,
Had with that lord to battle come.
Harold was born where restless seas   310
Howl round the storm-swept Orcades ;
Where erst Saint Clairs held princely sway
O'er isle and islet, strait and bay ;—
Still nods their palace to its fall,
Thy pride and sorrow, fair Kirkwall ! —
Thence oft he marked fierce Pentland rave,
As if grim Odin rode her wave,
And watched the whilst, with visage pale
And throbbing heart, the struggling sail ;
For all of wonderful and wild   320
Had rapture for the lonely child.

XXII

And much of wild and wonderful
In these rude isles might Fancy cull;

For thither came in times afar
Stern Lochlin's sons of roving war,
The Norsemen, trained to spoil and blood,
Skilled to prepare the raven's food,
Kings of the main their leaders brave,
Their barks the dragons of the wave ;
And there, in many a stormy vale,   330
The Scald had told his wondrous tale,
And many a Runic column high
Had witnessed grim idolatry.
And thus had Harold in his youth
Learned many a Saga's rhyme uncouth, —
Of that Sea-Snake, tremendous curled,
Whose monstrous circle girds the world;
Of those dread Maids whose hideous yell
Maddens the battle's bloody swell;
Of chiefs who, guided through the
  gloom   340
By the pale death-lights of the tomb,
Ransacked the graves of warriors old,
Their falchions wrenched from corpses'
  hold,
Waked the deaf tomb with war's alarms,
And bade the dead arise to arms !
With war and wonder all on flame,
To Roslin's bowers young Harold came,
Where, by sweet glen and greenwood tree,
He learned a milder minstrelsy;
Yet something of the Northern spell   350
Mixed with the softer numbers well.

XXIII

HAROLD

O, listen, listen, ladies gay !
  No haughty feat of arms I tell;
Soft is the note, and sad the lay,
  That mourns the lovely Rosabelle.

'Moor, moor the barge, ye gallant crew !
  And, gentle ladye, deign to stay !
Rest thee in Castle Ravensheuch,
  Nor tempt the stormy firth to-day.

'The blackening wave is edged with
  white;   360
  To inch and rock the sea-mews fly;
The fishers have heard the Water Sprite,
  Whose screams forebode that wreck is
    nigh.

'Last night the gifted Seer did view
  A wet shroud swathed round ladye gay;
Then stay thee, fair, in Ravensheuch:
  Why cross the gloomy firth to-day ? '

' 'T is not because Lord Lindesay's heir
  To-night at Roslin leads the ball,
But that my ladye-mother there   370
  Sits lonely in her castle-hall.

' 'T is not because the ring they ride,
  And Lindesay at the ring rides well,
But that my sire the wine will chide,
  If 't is not filled by Rosabelle.'

O'er Roslin all that dreary night
  A wondrous blaze was seen to gleam;
'T was broader than the watch-fire light,
  And redder than the bright moonbeam.

It glared on Roslin's castled rock,   380
  It ruddied all the copsewood glen;
'T was seen from Dreyden's groves of oak,
  And seen from caverned Hawthornden.

Seemed all on fire that chapel proud
  Where Roslin's chiefs uncoffined lie,
Each baron, for a sable shroud,
  Sheathed in his iron panoply.

Seemed all on fire within, around,
  Deep sacristy and altar's pale;
Shone every pillar foliage-bound,   390
  And glimmered all the dead men's mail.

Blazed battlement and pinnet high,
  Blazed every rose-carved buttress fair —
So still they blaze when fate is nigh
  The lordly line of high Saint Clair.

There are twenty of Roslin's barons bold
  Lie buried within that proud chapelle;
Each one the holy vault doth hold —
  But the sea holds lovely Rosabelle !

And each Saint Clair was buried there,   400
  With candle, with book, and with knell;
But the sea-caves rung and the wild winds
    sung
  The dirge of lovely Rosabelle.

XXIV

So sweet was Harold's piteous lay,
  Scarce marked the guests the darkened
    hall,
Though, long before the sinking day,
  A wondrous shade involved them all.
It was not eddying mist or fog,
Drained by the sun from fen or bog;
  Of no eclipse had sages told;   410

And yet, as it came on apace,
Each one could scarce his neighbor's face,
  Could scarce his own stretched hand be-
    hold.
A secret horror checked the feast,
And chilled the soul of every guest;
Even the high dame stood half aghast,
She knew some evil on the blast;
The elfish page fell to the ground,
And, shuddering, muttered, 'Found !
    found ! found !'

XXV

Then sudden through the darkened air   420
  A flash of lightning came;
So broad, so bright, so red the glare,
  The castle seemed on flame.
Glanced every rafter of the hall,
Glanced every shield upon the wall:
Each trophied beam, each sculptured stone,
Were instant seen and instant gone;
Full through the guests' bedazzled band
Resistless flashed the levin-brand,
And filled the hall with smouldering
    smoke,   430
As on the elfish page it broke.
It broke with thunder long and loud,
Dismayed the brave, appalled the proud, —
  From sea to sea the larum rung;
On Berwick wall, and at Carlisle withal,
  To arms the startled warders sprung.
When ended was the dreadful roar,
The elfish dwarf was seen no more !

XXVI

Some heard a voice in Branksome Hall,
Some saw a sight, not seen by all;   440
That dreadful voice was heard by some
Cry, with loud summons, 'GYLBIN, COME !'
  And on the spot where burst the brand,
Just where the page had flung him down,
  Some saw an arm, and some a hand,
And some the waving of a gown.
The guests in silence prayed and shook,
And terror dimmed each lofty look.
But none of all the astonished train
Was so dismayed as Deloraine: 450
His blood did freeze, his brain did burn,
'T was feared his mind would ne'er return;
For he was speechless, ghastly, wan,
Like him of whom the story ran,
Who spoke the spectre-hound in Man.
At length by fits he darkly told,
With broken hint and shuddering cold,
  That he had seen right certainly

A shape with amice wrapped around,
With a wrought Spanish baldric bound,   460
  Like pilgrim from beyond the sea;
And knew — but how it mattered not —
It was the wizard, Michael Scott.

XXVII

The anxious crowd, with horror pale,
All trembling heard the wondrous tale:
No sound was made, no word was spoke,
Till noble Angus silence broke;
  And he a solemn sacred plight
Did to Saint Bride of Douglas make,
That he a pilgrimage would take   470
To Melrose Abbey, for the sake
  Of Michael's restless sprite.
Then each, to ease his troubled breast,
To some blest saint his prayers addressed:
Some to Saint Modan made their vows,
Some to Saint Mary of the Lowes,
Some to the Holy Rood of Lisle,
Some to Our Lady of the Isle;
Each did his patron witness make
That he such pilgrimage would take,   480
And monks should sing and bells should toll,
All for the weal of Michael's soul.
While vows were ta'en and prayers were
        prayed,
'T is said the noble dame, dismayed,
Renounced for aye dark magic's aid.

XXVIII

Nought of the bridal will I tell,
Which after in short space befell;
Nor how brave sons and daughters fair
Blessed Teviot's Flower and Cranstoun's
        heir:
After such dreadful scene 't were vain   490
To wake the note of mirth again.
More meet it were to mark the day
  Of penitence and prayer divine,
When pilgrim-chiefs, in sad array,
  Sought Melrose' holy shrine.

XXIX

With naked foot, and sackcloth vest,
And arms enfolded on his breast,
  Did every pilgrim go;
The standers-by might hear uneath
Footstep, or voice, or high-drawn breath, 500
  Through all the lengthened row:
No lordly look nor martial stride,
Gone was their glory, sunk their pride,
  Forgotten their renown;
Silent and slow, like ghosts, they glide

To the high altar's hallowed side,
  And there they knelt them down.
Above the suppliant chieftains wave
The banners of departed brave;
Beneath the lettered stones were laid   510
The ashes of their fathers dead;
From many a garnished niche around
Stern saints and tortured martyrs frowned.

XXX

And slow up the dim aisle afar,
With sable cowl and scapular,
And snow-white stoles, in order due,
The holy fathers, two and two,
  In long procession came;
Taper and host and book they bare,
And holy banner, flourished fair   520
  With the Redeemer's name.
Above the prostrate pilgrim band
The mitred abbot stretched his hand,
  And blessed them as they kneeled;
With holy cross he signed them all,
And prayed they might be sage in hall
  And fortunate in field.
Then mass was sung, and prayers were
        said,
And solemn requiem for the dead;
And bells tolled out their mighty peal   530
For the departed spirit's weal;
And ever in the office close
The hymn of intercession rose;
And far the echoing aisles prolong
The awful burden of the song,
  DIES IRÆ, DIES ILLA,
  SOLVET SÆCLUM IN FAVILLA,
While the pealing organ rung.
  Were it meet with sacred strain
  To close my lay, so light and vain,   540
Thus the holy fathers sung:

HYMN FOR THE DEAD

That day of wrath, that dreadful day,
When heaven and earth shall pass away,
What power shall be the sinner's stay ?
How shall he meet that dreadful day ?

When, shrivelling like a parched scroll,
The flaming heavens together roll,
When louder yet, and yet more dread,
Swells the high trump that wakes the dead !

O, on that day, that wrathful day,   550
When man to judgment wakes from clay,

Be THOU the trembling sinner's stay,
Though heaven and earth shall pass away !

HUSHED is the harp — the Minstrel gone.
And did he wander forth alone ?
Alone, in indigence and age,
To linger out his pilgrimage ?
No: close beneath proud Newark's tower
Arose the Minstrel's lowly bower,
A simple hut; but there was seen   560
The little garden hedged with green,
The cheerful hearth, and lattice clean.
There sheltered wanderers, by the blaze,
Oft heard the tale of other days;
For much he loved to ope his door,

And give the aid he begged before.
So passed the winter's day; but still,
When summer smiled on sweet Bowhill,
And July's eve, with balmy breath,
Waved the blue-bells on Newark heath,   570
When throstles sung in Harehead-shaw,
And corn was green on Carterhaugh,
And flourished, broad, Blackandro's oak,
The aged harper's soul awoke !
Then would he sing achievements high
And circumstance of chivalry,
Till the rapt traveller would stay,
Forgetful of the closing day;
And noble youths, the strain to hear,
Forsook the hunting of the deer;   580
And Yarrow, as he rolled along,
Bore burden to the Minstrel's song.

MARMION

A TALE OF FLODDEN FIELD

INTRODUCTORY NOTE

In August, 1791, when Scott was twenty years of age, and shortly before he was called to the bar, he made an excursion to Northumberland, ostensibly for fishing; but with the keen scent for things and places historical which possessed him from his earliest years, he revelled especially in the associations which rose to mind in all the neighborhood. 'We are amidst places,' he writes to his friend Clerk, ' renowned by the feats of former days; each hill is crowned with a tower or camp, or cairn, and in no situation can you be near more fields of battle: Flodden, Otterburn, Chevy Chase, Ford Castle, Chillingham Castle, Copland Castle, and many another scene of blood are within the compass of a forenoon's ride. . . . Often as I have wished for your company, I never did it more earnestly than when I rode over Flodden Edge. I knew your taste for these things, and could have undertaken to demonstrate, that never was an affair more completely bungled than that day's work was. Suppose one army posted upon the face of a hill, and secured by high grounds projecting on each flank, with the river Till in front, a deep and still river, winding through a very extensive valley called Milfield Plain, and the only passage over it by a narrow bridge, which the Scots artillery, from the hill, could in a moment have demolished. Add, that the English must have hazarded a battle while their troops, which were tumultuously levied, remained together; and that the Scots, behind whom the country was opened to Scotland, had nothing to do but to wait for the attack as they were posted. Yet, did two thirds of the army, actuated by the perfervidium ingenium Scotorum, rush down and give an opportunity to Stanley to occupy the ground they had quitted, by coming over the shoulder of the hill, while the other third, under Lord Home, kept their ground, and having seen their king and about 10,000 of their countrymen cut to pieces, retired into Scotland without loss. For the reason of the bridge not being destroyed while the English passed, I refer you to Pitscottie, who narrates at large, and to whom I give credit for a most accurate and clear description, agreeing perfectly with the ground.'

Seventeen years later Scott availed himself of this visit to make the battle on Flodden Field the culminating scene of the second great poem which he gave the public. As he states in his Introduction, printed below, he had retired from his profession, and since the publication of *The Lay of the Last Minstrel* had been engaged in editing Dryden. But he was also now the quarry at which the publishers were flying, and Constable especially was spreading his wings for that large enterprise in which Scott was to play so prominent a part. As Scott further states in his Introduction, Constable made him a munificent offer of a thousand guineas for the as yet un-

finished poem of *Marmion*, and the offer came
just as Scott was in special need of money to
aid his brother Thomas, then withdrawing
from his profession as Writer to the Signet.

The first reference which Scott makes to his
poem is in a letter to Miss Seward dated Edinburgh, 20 February, 1807 : ' I have at length
fixed on the title of my new poem, which is to
be christened, from the principal character,
Marmion, or A Tale of Flodden Field.   There
are to be six Cantos, and an introductory Epistle to each, in the style of that which I send
to you as a specimen.   In the legendary part
of the work, " Knights, Squires and Steeds
shall enter on the stage."   I am not at all
afraid of my patriotism being a sufferer in the
course of the tale.   It is very true that my
friend Leyden has said : —

> ' " Alas ! that Scottish maid should sing
> The combat where her lover fell,
> That Scottish Bard should wake the string
> The triumph of our foes to tell."

But we may say with Francis I. " that at Flodden all was lost *but our honor*," — an exception
which includes everything that is desirable for
a poet.'

The difficulties into which his brother
Thomas had fallen were connected with the
business affairs of the Marquis of Abercorn, for
whom Thomas Scott had been manager. ' The
consequence of my brother's failure,' Scott
wrote later to Miss Seward, ' was that the whole
affairs of these extensive estates were thrown
upon my hands in a state of unutterable confusion, so that to save myself from ruin [he
was security for his brother] I was obliged to
lend my constant and unremitting attention
to their reëstablishment.'   All this, however,
though it delayed his poem, produced no estrangement from Lord and Lady Abercorn,
and on 10 September, 1807, he writes to the
latter from Ashestiel, ' I have deferred writing
from day to day, my dear Lady Abercorn,
until I should be able to make good my promise of sending you the first two cantos of *Marmion ;* ' and on 22 January, 1808, he writes to
the same, ' I have finished *Marmion*, and your
Ladyship will do me the honor, I hope, to accept a copy very soon.   In the sixth and last
canto I have succeeded better than I had ventured to hope, for I had a battle to fight, and
I dread hard blows almost as much in poetry
as in common life.'   He had thought of asking
Lord Abercorn to let him dedicate *Marmion* to
him, but was deterred by hearing him express
his general dislike to dedications.

Lockhart points out that Scott was doubtless indebted for the death scene in *Marmion*
to Goethe's *Goetz von Berlichingen of the Iron
Hand*, which Scott had translated ten years

before ; but Scott himself, as was his wont,
made but few allusions to the origin of any
parts of the poem.   He did, indeed, in a letter
to Miss Seward, 23 November, 1807, give a
slight explanation of one point, when he wrote,
' My reason for transporting Marmion from
Lichfield was to make good the minstrel prophecy of Constance's song.   Why I should
ever have taken him there I cannot very well
say.   Attachment to the place, its locality
with respect to Tamworth, the ancient seat of
the Marmions, partly, perhaps, the whim of
taking a slap at Lord Brooke *en passant*, joined
in suggesting the idea which I had not time to
bring out or finish.'   And in a letter to Lady
Louisa Stuart from Edinburgh, 3 March, 1808,
he writes this unusually full explanation of
one passage in the poem : —

' I have thought on your reading about the
death of Constance, and with all the respect
which (*sans* phrase) I entertain for everything
you honor me with, I have not made up my
mind to the alteration, and here are my reasons.   Clare has no wish to embitter Marmion's
last moments, and is only induced to mention
the death of Constance because she observes
that the wounded man's anxiety for her deliverance prevents his attending to his own
spiritual affairs.   It seems natural, however,
that knowing by the Abbess, or however you
please, the share which Marmion had in the
fate of Constance, she should pronounce the
line assigned to her in such a manner as perfectly conveyed to his conscience the whole
truth, although her gentleness avoided conveying it in direct terms.   We are to consider,
too, that Marmion had from various workings
of his own mind been led to suspect the fate
of Constance, so that, the train being ready
laid, the slightest hint of her fate communicated
the whole tale of terror to his conviction.
Were I to read the passage, I would hesitate a
little, like one endeavoring to seek a soft mode
of conveying painful intelligence : —

> ' " In vain for Constance is your zeal ;
> She — died at Holy Isle."

Perhaps after all this is too fine spun, and requires more from my gentle readers to fill up
my sketch than I am entitled to exact.   But
I would rather put in an explanatory couplet
describing Clare's manner of speaking the
words, than make her communication more
full and specific.'   But the couplet he did not
add.

Lockhart in his *Life* throws a little further
light on the construction of *Marmion* by quoting from a narrative by Mr. Guthrie Wright,
who had succeeded Thomas Scott in the
charge of the Abercorn estate. ' In the summer of 1807,' he writes, ' I had the pleasure of

making a trip with Sir Walter to Dumfries, for the purpose of meeting the late Lord Abercorn on his way with his family to Ireland. His Lordship did not arrive for two or three days after we reached Dumfries, and we employed the interval in visiting Sweetheart Abbey, Caerlaverock Castle, and some other ancient buildings in the neighborhood. . . . [Sir Walter] recited poetry and old legends from morn till night, and in short it is impossible that anything could be more delightful than his society; but what I particularly allude to is the circumstance, that at that time he was writing *Marmion*, the three or four first cantos of which he had with him, and which he was so good as to read to me. It is unnecessary to say how much I was enchanted with them; but as he good-naturedly asked me to state any observations that occurred to me, I said in joke that it appeared to me he had brought his hero by a very strange route into Scotland. "Why," says I, "did ever mortal coming from England to Edinburgh go by Gifford, Crichton Castle, Borthwick Castle, and over the top of Blackford Hill? Not only is it a circuitous *détour*, but there never was a road that way since the world was created!" "That is a most irrelevant objection," said Sir Walter; "it was my good pleasure to bring Marmion by that route, for the purpose of describing the places you have mentioned, and the view from Blackford Hill — it was his business to find his road and pick his steps the best way he could. But, pray, how would you have me bring him? Not by the post-road, surely, as if he had been travelling in a mail-coach?" "No," I replied; "there were neither post - roads nor mail-coaches in those days; but I think you might have brought him with a less chance of getting into a swamp, by allowing him to travel the natural route by Dunbar and the sea-coast; and then he might have tarried for a space with the famous Earl of Angus, surnamed Bell-the-Cat, at his favorite residence of Tantallon Castle, by which means you would have had not only that fortress with all his feudal followers, but the Castle of Dunbar, the Bass, and all the beautiful scenery of the Forth, to describe." This observation seemed to strike him much, and after a pause he exclaimed — "By Jove, you are right! I ought to have brought him that way;" and he added, "but before he and I part, depend upon it he shall visit Tantallon." He then asked me if I had ever been there, and upon saying I had frequently, he desired me to describe it, which I did; and I verily believe it is from what I then said, that the accurate description contained in the fifth canto was given — at least I never heard him say he had afterwards gone

to visit the castle; and when the poem was published, I remember he laughed, and asked me how I liked Tantallon.'

The dating of the several poetical Introductions gives a hint of Scott's abodes when he was engaged upon *Marmion*. The first four are from Ashestiel, and the scenes about that spot became identified in his mind with the composition of the poem. 'I well remember his saying,' writes Lockhart, 'as I rode with him across the hills from Ashestiel to Newark one day in his declining years — "Oh, man, I had many a grand gallop among these braes when I was thinking of *Marmion*, but a trotting canny pony must serve me now." His friend, Mr. Skene, however, informs me that many of the more energetic descriptions, and particularly that of the battle of Flodden, were struck out while he was in quarters again with his cavalry, in the autumn of 1807. " In the intervals of drilling," he says, "Scott used to delight in walking his powerful black steed up and down by himself upon the Portobello sands, within the beating of the surge; and now and then you would see him plunge in his spurs, and go off as if at the charge, with the spray dashing about him. As we rode back to Musselburgh, he often came and placed himself beside me, to repeat the verses that he had been composing during these pauses of our exercise." '

It was a year after he began the poem that he wrote the Introductory Epistle for Canto IV. at Ashestiel. The next month he wrote the fifth introduction in Edinburgh; the last was written during the Christmas festivities of Mertoun house, where, as Lockhart says, 'from the first days of his ballad-rhyming, down to the close of his life, he, like his bearded ancestor, usually spent that season with the immediate head of the race.'

These epistles, it should be remarked, were not designed in the first instance to be inwoven with the romance. They were, in fact, announced early in 1807 in an advertisement as *Six Epistles from Ettrick Forest*, and were to have been published in an independent volume. It is perhaps a happier fortune for readers of this day than for the first readers of *Marmion* that the epistles were thus inwoven, since they serve so emphatically to connect Scott's friendships with his poetry; the personal side of authorship in Scott's case is written thus indelibly in the poem.

Marmion was published February 23, 1808, and was seized with avidity by Scott's personal friends, and by the public, which called for new editions in rapid succession. Every one naturally compared it with *The Lay of the Last Minstrel*. Southey wrote frankly: 'The story is made of better materials than the *Lay*, yet they are not so well fitted together. As a whole, it has not pleased me so much — in parts, it has pleased me more. There is nothing so finely conceived in your former poem as the death of Marmion : there is nothing finer in its conception anywhere. The introductory epistles I did not wish away, because, as poems, they gave me great pleasure ; but I wished them at the end of the volume, or at the beginning — anywhere except where they were. My taste is perhaps peculiar in disliking all interruptions in narrative poetry.'

Wordsworth, too, wrote with the freedom of an accepted friend, and the frankness of these brother poets implies the candor also of Scott's nature. ' I think your end has been attained. That it is not the end which I should wish you to propose to yourself, you will be well aware, from what you know of my notions of composition, both as to matter and manner. In the circle of my acquaintance, it seems as well liked as the Lay, though I have heard that in the world it is not so. Had the poem been much better than the Lay, it could scarcely have satisfied the public, which has too much of the monster, the moral monster, in its composition.'

Mr. George Ellis, the accomplished antiquarian scholar who had made the acquaintance of Scott in the days of the Border Minstrelsy, also wrote at length, reflecting in his leisurely letter the best judgment of the men of letters of the day. After balancing the opinions of critics respecting the two poems, he concludes : ' My own opinion is, that both the productions are equally good in their different ways : yet, upon the whole, I had rather be the author of Marmion than of the Lay, because I think its species of excellence of much more difficult attainment. What degree of bulk may be essentially necessary to the corporeal part of an Epic poem, I know not ; but sure I am that the story of Marmion might have furnished twelve books as easily as six — that the masterly character of Constance would not have been less bewitching had it been much more minutely painted — and that De Wilton might have been dilated with great ease, and even to considerable advantage ; — in short, that had it been your intention merely to exhibit a spirited romantic story, instead of making that story subservient to the delineation of the manners which prevailed at a certain period of our history, the number and variety of your characters would have suited any scale of painting.'

Scott himself in a letter to Surtees, who had offered him the subject of Prince Charlie, says : ' When you have read over Marmion, which has more individuality of character than the Lay, although it wants a sort of tenderness which the personage of the old minstrel gave to my first-born romance, you will be a better judge whether I should undertake a work which will depend less on incident and description than on the power of distinguishing and marking the dramatis personæ.' And it is a commentary on the confusion of literature and politics so characteristic of the day, that we find him writing to Lady Abercorn : ' All the Whigs here (in Edinburgh) are in arms against Marmion. If I had satirized Fox, they could have borne it, but a secondary place for the god of their idolatry puts them beyond the slender degree of patience which displaced patriots usually possess. I make them welcome to cry till they are hoarse against both the book and author, as they are not in the habit of having majorities upon their side. I suppose the crossed critics of Holland House will take the same tone in your Metropolis.' The allusion, of course, is to the lines in the Introduction to Canto I., beginning with line 126. In illustration of the asperity of politics at the time, Scott writes to the same correspondent : ' The Morning Chronicle of the 29th March [1808] has made a pretty story of the cancel of page 10th of Marmion which your Ladyship cannot but recollect was reprinted for the sole purpose of inserting the lines suggested so kindly by the Marquis : —

> ' " For talents mourn, untimely lost,
>   When best employed and wanted most ; "

I suppose from the carelessness of those who arranged the book for binding, this sheet may not in a copy or two have been right placed, and the worthy Editor affirms kindly that this was done that I might have copies to send to Mr. Pitt's friends in which these lines do not occur ! ! ! My publishers here, who forwarded the books, have written in great wrath to contradict the story, and were surprised to find I had more inclination to laugh at it. This is a punishment for appropriating my neighbor's goods. I suppose it would surprise Mr. Morning Chronicle considerably to know that the couplet in question was written by so distinguished a friend of Mr. Pitt as Lord Abercorn.'

We noted how Scott's youthful excursion into the Cheviot Hills found expression later in Marmion. It is pleasant to recall that later journey made with his family when Marmion had made Flodden Field famous. ' Halting at Flodden,' is Lockhart's narrative, ' to expound the field of battle to his young folks, he found that Marmion had, as might have been expected, benefited the keeper of the public house there very largely ; and the village Boniface, overflowing with gratitude, expressed his anxiety to have a Scott's Head for his sign-post.

The poet demurred to this proposal, and assured mine host that nothing could be more appropriate than the portraiture of a foaming tankard, which already surmounted his doorway. "Why, the painter-man has not made an ill job," said the landlord, "but I would fain have something more connected with the book that has brought me so much good custom." He produced a well-thumbed copy, and handing it to the author, begged he would at least suggest a motto from the tale of Flodden Field. Scott opened the book at the death scene of the hero, and his eye was immediately caught by the " inscription " in black.letter —

   '"Drink, weary pilgrim, drink, and pray
   For the kind soul of Sibyl Grey," etc.

"Well, my friend," said he, "what more would you have? You need but strike out one letter in the first of these lines, and make your painter-man, the next time he comes this way, print between the jolly tankard and your own name —

   '"Drink, weary pilgrim, drink and pay."

Scott was delighted to find, on his return, that this suggestion had been adopted, and for aught I know, the romantic legend may still be visible.'

The poem when first published was prefaced by the following

ADVERTISEMENT

'It is hardly to be expected that an author whom the public have honored with some degree of applause should not be again a trespasser on their kindness. Yet the author of Marmion must be supposed to feel some anxiety concerning its success, since he is sensible that he hazards, by this second intrusion, any reputation which his first poem may have procured him. The present story turns upon the private adventures of a fictitious character, but is called a Tale of Flodden Field, because the hero's fate is connected with that memorable defeat and the causes which led to it. The design of the author was, if possible, to apprise his readers, at the outset, of the date of his story, and to prepare them for the manners of the age in which it is laid. Any historical narrative, far more an attempt at epic composition, exceeded his plan of a romantic tale; yet he may be permitted to hope, from the popularity of The Lay of the Last Minstrel, that an attempt

to paint the manners of the feudal times, upon a broader scale, and in the course of a more interesting story, will not be unacceptable to the public.

'The poem opens about the commencement of August, and concludes with the defeat of Flodden, 9th September, 1513.

'ASHESTIEL, 1808.'

The poem, as Scott wrote to Lady Abercorn, in consequence of an unexampled demand was hurried through the press again and a second edition was quickly issued; but second editions in those days were not second impressions from the same type or from plates, and the author had an opportunity to make corrections. Scott heeded Lady Abercorn's criticism on the speech of Constance, but after much consideration placed a single dash in the line, as it now stands (page 105, line 522), to express her confusion. A few weeks after, when he could look back deliberately on the whole poem, he wrote his friend from Edinburgh 9 June, 1808: 'No one is so sensible as I am of what deficiencies occur in my poetry from the want of judicious criticism and correction, above all from the extreme hurry in which it has hitherto been composed. The worst is that I take the pet at the things myself after they are finished, and I fear I shall never be able to muster up the courage necessary to revise Marmion as he should be revised. But if I ever write another poem, I am determined to make every single couplet of it as perfect as my uttermost care and attention can possibly effect. In order to ensure the accomplishment of these good resolutions, I will consider the whole story in humble prose, and endeavor to make it as interesting as I can before I begin to write it out in verse, and thus I shall have at least the satisfaction to know where I am going, my narrative having been hitherto much upon the plan of blind man's buff. Secondly, having made my story, I will write my poem with all deliberation, and when finished lay it aside for a year at least, during which quarantine I would be most happy if it were suffered to remain in your escritoire or in that of the Marquis, who has the best ear for English versification of any person whom, in a pretty extensive acquaintance with literary characters, I have ever had the fortune to meet with; nor is his taste at all inferior to his power of appreciating the harmony of verse.'

When Marmion was reissued in the collective edition of 1830, it carried the following —

INTRODUCTION

What I have to say respecting this poem may be briefly told. In the Introduction to the *Lay of the Last Minstrel* I have mentioned the circumstances, so far as my literary life is concerned, which induced me to resign the active pursuit of an honorable profession for the more precarious resources of literature. My appointment to the Sheriffdom of Selkirk called for a change of residence. I left, therefore, the pleasant cottage I had upon the side of the Esk, for the 'pleasanter banks of the Tweed,' in order to comply with the law, which requires that the sheriff shall be resident, at least during a certain number of months, within his jurisdiction. We found a delightful retirement, by my becoming the tenant of my intimate friend and cousin-german, Colonel Russel, in his mansion of Ashestiel, which was unoccupied during his absence on military service in India. The house was adequate to our accommodation and the exercise of a limited hospitality. The situation is uncommonly beautiful, by the side of a fine river whose streams are there very favorable for angling, surrounded by the remains of natural woods, and by hills abounding in game. In point of society, according to the heartfelt phrase of Scripture, we dwelt 'amongst our own people;' and as the distance from the metropolis was only thirty miles, we were not out of reach of our Edinburgh friends, in which city we spent the terms of the summer and winter sessions of the court, that is, five or six months in the year.

An important circumstance had, about the same time, taken place in my life. Hopes had been held out to me from an influential quarter, of a nature to relieve me from the anxiety which I must have otherwise felt, as one upon the precarious tenure of whose own life rested the principal prospects of his family, and especially as one who had necessarily some dependence upon the favor of the public, which is proverbially capricious; though it is but justice to add that in my own case I have not found it so. Mr. Pitt had expressed a wish to my personal friend, the Right Honorable William Dundas, now Lord Clerk Register of Scotland, that some fitting opportunity should be taken to be of service to me; and as my views and wishes pointed to a future rather than an immediate provision, an opportunity of accomplishing this was soon found. One of the Principal Clerks of Session, as they are called (official persons who occupy an important and responsible situation, and enjoy a considerable income), who had served upwards of thirty years, felt himself, from age and the infirmity of deafness with which it was accompanied, desirous of retiring from his official situation. As the law then stood, such official persons were entitled to bargain with their successors, either for a sum of money, which was usually a considerable one, or for an interest in the emoluments of the office during their life. My predecessor, whose services had been unusually meritorious, stipulated for the emoluments of his office during his life, while I should enjoy the survivorship on the condition that I discharged the duties of the office in the mean time. Mr. Pitt, however, having died in the interval, his administration was dissolved, and was succeeded by that known by the name of the Fox and Grenville Ministry. My affair was so far completed that my commission lay in the office subscribed by his Majesty; but, from hurry or mistake, the interest of my predecessor was not expressed in it, as had been usual in such cases. Although, therefore, it only required payment of the fees, I could not in honor take out the commission in the present state, since, in the event of my dying before him, the gentleman whom I succeeded must have lost the vested interest which he had stipulated to retain. I had the honor of an interview with Earl Spencer on the subject, and he, in the most handsome manner, gave directions that the commission should issue as originally intended; adding, that the matter having received the royal assent, he regarded only as a claim of justice what he would have willingly done as an act of favor. I never saw Mr. Fox on this or on any other occasion, and never made any application to him, conceiving that in doing so I might have been supposed to express political opinions contrary to those which I had always professed. In his private capacity, there is no man to whom I would have been more proud to owe an obligation, had I been so distinguished.

By this arrangement I obtained the survivorship of an office the emoluments of which were fully adequate to my wishes; and as the law respecting the mode of providing for superannuated officers was, about five or six years after, altered from that which admitted the arrangement of assistant and successor, my colleague very handsomely took the opportunity of the alteration to accept of the retiring annuity provided in such cases, and admitted me to the full benefit of the office.

But although the certainty of succeeding to a considerable income, at the time I obtained it, seemed to assure me of a quiet harbor in my old age, I did not escape my share of inconvenience from the contrary tides and currents by which we are so often encountered in our journey through life. Indeed, the publication of my next poetical attempt was prematurely accelerated, from one of those unpleasant accidents which can neither be foreseen nor avoided.

I had formed the prudent resolution to endeavor to bestow a little more labor than I had yet done on my productions, and to be in no hurry again to announce myself as a candidate for literary fame. Accordingly, particular passages of a poem which was finally called *Marmion* were labored with a good deal of care by one by whom much care was seldom bestowed. Whether the work was worth the labor or not, I am no competent judge ; but I may be permitted to say that the period of its composition was a very happy one in my life ; so much so, that I remember with pleasure, at this moment, some of the spots in which particular passages were composed. It is probably owing to this that the Introductions to the several cantos assumed the form of familiar epistles to my intimate friends, in which I alluded, perhaps more than was necessary or graceful, to my domestic occupations and amusements, — a loquacity which may be excused by those who remember that I was still young, light-headed, and happy, and that 'out of the abundance of the heart the mouth speaketh.'

The misfortunes of a near relation and friend, which happened at this time, led me to alter my prudent determination, which had been to use great precaution in sending this poem into the world ; and made it convenient at least, if not absolutely necessary, to hasten its publication. The publishers of *The Lay of the Last Minstrel*, emboldened by the success of that poem, willingly offered a thousand pounds for *Marmion*. The transaction, being no secret, afforded Lord Byron, who was then at general war with all who blacked paper, an apology for including me in his satire entitled *English Bards and Scotch Reviewers*.[1] I never could conceive how an arrangement between an author and his publishers, if satisfactory to the persons concerned, could afford matter of censure to any third party. I had taken no unusual or ungenerous means of enhancing the value of my merchandise, — I had never higgled a moment about the bargain, but accepted at once what I considered the handsome offer

of my publishers. These gentlemen, at least, were not of opinion that they had been taken advantage of in the transaction, which indeed was one of their own framing ; on the contrary, the sale of the poem was so far beyond their expectation as to induce them to supply the author's cellars with what is always an acceptable present to a young Scottish housekeeper, namely, a hogshead of excellent claret.

The poem was finished in too much haste to allow me an opportunity of softening down, if not removing, some of its most prominent defects. The nature of Marmion's guilt, although similar instances were found, and might be quoted, as existing in feudal times, was nevertheless not sufficiently peculiar to be indicative of the character of the period, forgery being the crime of a commercial rather than a proud and warlike age. This gross defect ought to have been remedied or palliated. Yet I suffered the tree to lie as it had fallen. I remember my friend, Dr. Leyden, then in the East, wrote me a furious remonstrance on the subject. I have, nevertheless, always been of opinion that corrections, however in themselves judicious, have a bad effect — after publication. An author is never so decidedly condemned as on his own confession, and may long find apologists and partisans until he gives up his own cause. I was not, therefore, inclined to afford matter for censure out of my own admissions ; and, by good fortune, the novelty of the subject and, if I may say so, some force and vivacity of description, were allowed to atone for many imperfections. Thus the second experiment on the public patience, generally the most perilous, — for the public are then most apt to judge with rigor what in the first instance they had received perhaps with imprudent generosity, — was in my case decidedly successful. I had the good fortune to pass this ordeal favorably, and the return of sales before me makes the copies amount to thirty-six thousand printed between 1808 and 1825, besides a considerable sale since that period. I shall here pause upon the subject of *Marmion*, and, in a few prefatory words to *The Lady of the Lake*, the last poem of mine which obtained eminent success, I will continue the task which I have imposed on myself respecting the origin of my productions.

ABBOTSFORD, April, 1830.

---

[1] Lockhart quotes the passage, which is as follows :—

' Next view in state, proud prancing on his roan,
The golden-crested haughty Marmion,
Now forging scrolls, now foremost in the fight,
Not quite a felon, yet but half a knight,
The gibbet or the field prepared to grace ;
A mighty mixture of the great and base.
And think'st thou, Scott ! by vain conceit perchance,
On public taste to foist thy stale romance,
Though Murray with his Miller may combine

To yield thy muse just half a crown per line ?
No ! when the sons of song descend to trade,
Their bays are sear, their former laurels fade.
Let such forego the poet's sacred name,
Who rack their brains for lucre, not for fame ;
Still for stern Mammon may they toil in vain !
And sadly gaze on gold they cannot gain !
Such be their meed, such still the just reward
Of prostituted muse and hireling bard !
For this we spurn Apollo's venal son,
And bid a long " Good-night to Marmion." '

MARMION

A TALE OF FLODDEN FIELD

> Alas! that Scottish maid should sing
> The combat where her lover fell!
> That Scottish Bard should wake the string,
> The triumph of our foes to tell!
> LEYDEN's *Ode on Visiting Flodden*

TO THE

RIGHT HONORABLE HENRY, LORD MONTAGUE,

&c., &c., &c.,

THIS ROMANCE IS INSCRIBED BY

THE AUTHOR.

INTRODUCTION TO CANTO FIRST

TO WILLIAM STEWART ROSE, ESQ.

Ashestiel, Ettrick Forest

NOVEMBER's sky is chill and drear,
November's leaf is red and sear:
Late, gazing down the steepy linn
That hems our little garden in,
Low in its dark and narrow glen,
You scarce the rivulet might ken,
So thick the tangled greenwood grew,
So feeble trilled the streamlet through;
Now, murmuring hoarse, and frequent seen   9
Through bush and brier, no longer green,
An angry brook, it sweeps the glade,
Brawls over rock and wild cascade,
And, foaming brown with double speed,
Hurries its waters to the Tweed.

No longer autumn's glowing red
Upon our Forest hills is shed;
No more, beneath the evening beam,
Fair Tweed reflects their purple gleam.
Away hath passed the heather-bell
That bloomed so rich on Needpath-fell;   20
Sallow his brow, and russet bare
Are now the sister-heights of Yair.
The sheep, before the pinching heaven,
To sheltered dale and down are driven,
Where yet some faded herbage pines,
And yet a watery sunbeam shines;
In meek despondency they eye
The withered sward and wintry sky,
And far beneath their summer hill
Stray sadly by Glenkinnon's rill.   30
The shepherd shifts his mantle's fold,
And wraps him closer from the cold;
His dogs no merry circles wheel,
But shivering follow at his heel;
A cowering glance they often cast,
As deeper moans the gathering blast.

My imps, though hardy, bold, and wild,
As best befits the mountain child,
Feel the sad influence of the hour,
And wail the daisy's vanished flower,   40
Their summer gambols tell, and mourn,
And anxious ask, — Will spring return,
And birds and lambs again be gay,
And blossoms clothe the hawthorn spray?

Yes, prattlers, yes. The daisy's flower
Again shall paint your summer bower;
Again the hawthorn shall supply
The garlands you delight to tie;
The lambs upon the lea shall bound,
The wild birds carol to the round;   50
And while you frolic light as they,
Too short shall seem the summer day.

To mute and to material things
New life revolving summer brings;

The genial call dead Nature hears,
And in her glory reappears.
But oh ! my country's wintry state
What second spring shall renovate ?
What powerful call shall bid arise
The buried warlike and the wise,   60
The mind that thought for Britain's weal,
The hand that grasped the victor steel ?
The vernal sun new life bestows
Even on the meanest flower that blows;
But vainly, vainly may he shine
Where Glory weeps o'er NELSON's shrine,
And vainly pierce the solemn gloom
That shrouds, O PITT, thy hallowed tomb !

Deep graved in every British heart,
Oh, never let those names depart !   70
Say to your sons, — Lo, here his grave
Who victor died on Gadite wave !
To him, as to the burning levin,
Short, bright, resistless course was given;
Where'er his country's foes were found,
Was heard the fated thunder's sound,
Till burst the bolt on yonder shore,
Rolled, blazed, destroyed, — and was no
        more.

Nor mourn ye less his perished worth
Who bade the conqueror go forth,   80
And launched that thunderbolt of war
On Egypt, Hafnia, Trafalgar;
Who, born to guide such high emprise,
For Britain's weal was early wise;
Alas ! to whom the Almighty gave,
For Britain's sins, an early grave!
His worth who, in his mightiest hour,
A bauble held the pride of power,
Spurned at the sordid lust of pelf,
And served his Albion for herself;   90
Who, when the frantic crowd amain
Strained at subjection's bursting rein,
O'er their wild mood full conquest gained,
The pride, he would not crush, restrained,
Showed their fierce zeal a worthier cause,
And brought the freeman's arm to aid the
        freeman's laws.

Hadst thou but lived, though stripped of
        power,
A watchman on the lonely tower,
Thy thrilling trump had roused the land,
When fraud or danger were at hand;   100
By thee, as by the beacon-light,
Our pilots had kept course aright;
As some proud column, though alone,

Thy strength had propped the tottering
        throne.
Now is the stately column broke,
The beacon-light is quenched in smoke,
The trumpet's silver sound is still,
The warder silent on the hill !

Oh, think, how to his latest day,
When Death, just hovering, claimed his
        prey,   110
With Palinure's unaltered mood,
Firm at his dangerous post he stood,
Each call for needful rest repelled,
With dying hand the rudder held,
Till, in his fall, with fateful sway,
The steerage of the realm gave way !
Then, while on Britain's thousand plains
One unpolluted church remains,
Whose peaceful bells ne'er sent around
The bloody tocsin's maddening sound,   120
But still, upon the hallowed day,
Convoke the swains to praise and pray;
While faith and civil peace are dear,
Grace this cold marble with a tear,
He who preserved them, PITT, lies here.

Nor yet suppress the generous sigh
Because his rival slumbers nigh,
Nor be thy *requiescat* dumb
Lest it be said o'er Fox's tomb;
For talents mourn, untimely lost,   130
When best employed and wanted most;
Mourn genius high, and lore profound,
And wit that loved to play, not wound;
And all the reasoning powers divine,
To penetrate, resolve, combine;
And feelings keen, and fancy's glow,
They sleep with him who sleeps below:
And, if thou mourn'st they could not save
From error him who owns this grave,
Be every harsher thought suppressed,   140
And sacred be the last long rest.
Here, where the end of earthly things
Lays heroes, patriots, bards, and kings;
Where stiff the hand, and still the tongue,
Of those who fought, and spoke, and
        sung;
Here, where the fretted aisles prolong
The distant notes of holy song,
As if some angel spoke again,
' All peace on earth, good-will to men;'
If ever from an English heart,   150
Oh, *here* let prejudice depart,
And, partial feeling cast aside,
Record that Fox a Briton died !

When Europe crouched to France's yoke,
And Austria bent, and Prussia broke,
And the firm Russian's purpose brave
Was bartered by a timorous slave,
Even then dishonor's peace he spurned,
The sullied olive-branch returned,
Stood for his country's glory fast,   160
And nailed her colors to the mast !
Heaven, to reward his firmness, gave
A portion in this honored grave,
And ne'er held marble in its trust
Of two such wondrous men the dust.

With more than mortal powers endowed,
How high they soared above the crowd !
Theirs was no common party race,
Jostling by dark intrigue for place;
Like fabled Gods, their mighty war   170
Shook realms and nations in its jar;
Beneath each banner proud to stand,
Looked up the noblest of the land,
Till through the British world were known
The names of PITT and FOX alone.
Spells of such force no wizard grave
E'er framed in dark Thessalian cave,
Though his could drain the ocean dry,
And force the planets from the sky.
These spells are spent, and, spent with   180
          these,
The wine of life is on the lees,
Genius and taste and talent gone,
Forever tombed beneath the stone,
Where — taming   thought   to   human
          pride ! —
The mighty chiefs sleep side by side.
Drop upon Fox's grave the tear,
'T will trickle to his rival's bier;
O'er PITT'S the mournful requiem sound,
And Fox's shall the notes rebound.
The solemn echo seems to cry, —   190
' Here let their discord with them die.
Speak not for those a separate doom
Whom Fate made brothers in the tomb;
But search the land, of living men,
Where wilt thou find their like again ? '

Rest, ardent spirits, till the cries
Of dying nature bid you rise !
Not even your Britain's groans can pierce
The leaden silence of your hearse;
Then, oh, how impotent and vain   200
This grateful tributary strain !
Though not unmarked from northern
          clime,
Ye heard the Border Minstrel's rhyme:

His Gothic harp has o'er you rung;
The Bard you deigned to praise, your
          deathless names has sung.

Stay yet, illusion, stay a while,
My wildered fancy still beguile !
From this high theme how can I part,
Ere half unloaded is my heart !
For all the tears e'er sorrow drew,   210
And all the raptures fancy knew,
And all the keener rush of blood
That throbs through bard in bardlike mood,
Were here a tribute mean and low,
Though all their mingled streams could
          flow —
Woe, wonder, and sensation high,
In one spring-tide of ecstacy ! —
It will not be — it may not last —
The vision of enchantment 's past:
Like frostwork in the morning ray,   220
The fancy fabric melts away;
Each Gothic arch, memorial-stone,
And long, dim, lofty aisle are gone;
And, lingering last, deception dear,
The choir's high sounds die on my ear.
Now slow return the lonely down,
The silent pastures bleak and brown,
The farm begirt with copsewood wild,
The gambols of each frolic child,
Mixing their shrill cries with the tone   230
Of Tweed's dark waters rushing on.

Prompt on unequal tasks to run,
Thus Nature disciplines her son:
Meeter, she says, for me to stray,
And waste the solitary day
In plucking from yon fen the reed,
And watch it floating down the Tweed,
Or idly list the shrilling lay
With which the milkmaid cheers her
          way.
Marking its cadence rise and fail,   240
As from the field, beneath her pail,
She trips it down the uneven dale;
Meeter for me, by yonder cairn,
The ancient shepherd's tale to learn,
Though oft he stop in rustic fear,
Lest his old legends tire the ear
Of one who, in his simple mind,
May boast of book-learned taste refined.

But thou, my friend, canst fitly tell —
For few have read romance so well —   250
How still the legendary lay
O'er poet's bosom holds its sway;

How on the ancient minstrel strain
Time lays his palsied hand in vain;
And how our hearts at doughty deeds,
By warriors wrought in steely weeds,
Still throb for fear and pity's sake;
As when the Champion of the Lake
Enters Morgan's fated house,
Or in the Chapel Perilous,   260
Despising spells and demons' force,
Holds converse with the unburied corse;
Or when, Dame Ganore's grace to move —
Alas, that lawless was their love ! —
He sought proud Tarquin in his den,
And freed full sixty knights; or when,
A sinful man and unconfessed,
He took the Sangreal's holy quest,
And slumbering saw the vision high
He might not view with waking eye.   270

The mightiest chiefs of British song
Scorned not such legends to prolong.
They gleam through Spenser's elfin dream,
And mix in Milton's heavenly theme;
And Dryden, in immortal strain,
Had raised the Table Round again,
But that a ribald king and court
Bade him toil on, to make them sport;
Demanded for their niggard pay,
Fit for their souls, a looser lay,   280
Licentious satire, song, and play;
The world defrauded of the high design,
Profaned the God - given strength, and
    marred the lofty line.

Warmed by such names, well may we
    then,
Though dwindled sons of little men,
Essay to break a feeble lance
In the fair fields of old romance;
Or seek the moated castle's cell,
Where long through talisman and spell,
While tyrants ruled and damsels wept,   290
Thy Genius, Chivalry, hath slept.
There sound the harpings of the North,
Till he awake and sally forth,
On venturous quest to prick again,
In all his arms, with all his train,
Shield, lance, and brand, and plume, and
    scarf,
Fay, giant, dragon, squire, and dwarf,
And wizard with his wand of might,
And errant maid on palfrey white.
Around the Genius weave their spells,   300
Pure Love, who scarce his passion tells;
Mystery, half veiled and half revealed;

And Honor, with his spotless shield;
Attention, with fixed eye; and Fear,
That loves the tale she shrinks to hear;
And gentle Courtesy; and Faith,
Unchanged by sufferings, time, or death;
And Valor, lion-mettled lord,
Leaning upon his own good sword.

Well has thy fair achievement shown   310
A worthy meed may thus be won:
Ytene's oaks — beneath whose shade
Their theme the merry minstrels made,
Of Ascapart, and Bevis bold,
And that Red King, who, while of old
Through Boldrewood the chase he led,
By his loved huntsman's arrow bled —
Ytene's oaks have heard again
Renewed such legendary strain;
For thou hast sung, how he of Gaul,   320
That Amadis so famed in hall,
For Oriana, foiled in fight
The Necromancer's felon might;
And well in modern verse hast wove
Partenopex's mystic love:
Hear, then, attentive to my lay,
A knightly tale of Albion's elder day.

CANTO FIRST

THE CASTLE

I

DAY set on Norham's castled steep,
And Tweed's fair river, broad and deep,
    And Cheviot's mountains lone;
The battled towers, the donjon keep,
The loophole grates where captives weep,
The flanking walls that round it sweep,
    In yellow lustre shone.
The warriors on the turrets high,
Moving athwart the evening sky,
    Seemed forms of giant height;   10
Their armor, as it caught the rays,
Flashed back again the western blaze,
    In lines of dazzling light.

II

Saint George's banner, broad and gay,
Now faded, as the fading ray
    Less bright, and less, was flung;
The evening gale had scarce the power
To wave it on the donjon tower,
    So heavily it hung.

The scouts had parted on their search, 20
  The castle gates were barred;
Above the gloomy portal arch,
Timing his footsteps to a march,
  The warder kept his guard,
Low humming, as he paced along,
Some ancient Border gathering song.

III

A distant trampling sound he hears;
He looks abroad, and soon appears,
O'er Horncliff-hill, a plump of spears
  Beneath a pennon gay; 30
A horseman, darting from the crowd
Like lightning from a summer cloud,
Spurs on his mettled courser proud,
  Before the dark array.
Beneath the sable palisade
That closed the castle barricade,
  His bugle-horn he blew;
The warder hasted from the wall,
And warned the captain in the hall,
  For well the blast he knew; 40
And joyfully that knight did call
To sewer, squire, and seneschal.

IV

' Now broach ye a pipe of Malvoisie,
  Bring pasties of the doe,
And quickly make the entrance free,
And bid my heralds ready be,
And every minstrel sound his glee,
  And all our trumpets blow;
And, from the platform, spare ye not
To fire a noble salvo-shot; 50
  Lord Marmion waits below ! '
Then to the castle's lower ward
  Sped forty yeomen tall,
The iron-studded gates unbarred,
Raised the portcullis' ponderous guard,
The lofty palisade unsparred,
  And let the drawbridge fall.

V

Along the bridge Lord Marmion rode,
Proudly his red-roan charger trode,
His helm hung at the saddle bow; 60
Well by his visage you might know
He was a stalworth knight and keen,
And had in many a battle been;
The scar on his brown cheek revealed
A token true of Bosworth field;
His eyebrow dark and eye of fire
Showed spirit proud and prompt to ire,

Yet lines of thought upon his cheek
Did deep design and counsel speak.
His forehead, by his casque worn bare, 70
His thick moustache and curly hair,
Coal-black, and grizzled here and there,
  But more through toil than age,
His square-turned joints and strength of
    limb,
Showed him no carpet knight so trim,
But in close fight a champion grim,
  In camps a leader sage.

VI

Well was he armed from head to heel,
In mail and plate of Milan steel;
But his strong helm, of mighty cost, 80
Was all with burnished gold embossed.
Amid the plumage of the crest
A falcon hovered on her nest,
With wings outspread and forward breast;
E'en such a falcon, on his shield,
Soared sable in an azure field:
The golden legend bore aright,
' Who checks at me, to death is dight.'
Blue was the charger's broidered rein;
Blue ribbons decked his arching mane; 90
The knightly housing's ample fold
Was velvet blue and trapped with gold.

VII

Behind him rode two gallant squires,
Of noble name and knightly sires:
They burned the gilded spurs to claim,
For well could each a war-horse tame,
Could draw the bow, the sword could
    sway,
And lightly bear the ring away;
Nor less with courteous precepts stored,
Could dance in hall, and carve at board,
And frame love-ditties passing rare, 101
And sing them to a lady fair.

VIII

Four men-at-arms came at their backs,
With halbert, bill, and battle-axe;
They bore Lord Marmion's lance so strong,
And led his sumpter-mules along,
And ambling palfrey, when at need
Him listed ease his battle-steed.
The last and trustiest of the four
On high his forky pennon bore; 110
Like swallow's tail in shape and hue.
Fluttered the streamer glossy blue,
Where, blazoned sable, as before,
The towering falcon seemed to soar.

Last, twenty yeomen, two and two
In hosen black and jerkins blue,
With falcons broidered on each breast,
Attended on their lord's behest.
Each, chosen for an archer good,
Knew hunting-craft by lake or wood;   120
Each one a six-foot bow could bend,
And far a cloth-yard shaft could send;
Each held a boar-spear tough and strong,
And at their belts their quivers rung.
Their dusty palfreys and array
Showed they had marched a weary way.

IX

'T is meet that I should tell you now,
How fairly armed, and ordered how,
  The soldiers of the guard,
With musket, pike, and morion,   130
To welcome noble Marmion,
  Stood in the castle-yard;
Minstrels and trumpeters were there,
The gunner held his linstock yare,
  For welcome-shot prepared:
Entered the train, and such a clang
As then through all his turrets rang
  Old Norham never heard.

X

The guards their morrice-pikes advanced,
  The trumpets flourished brave,   140
The cannon from the ramparts glanced,
  And thundering welcome gave.
A blithe salute, in martial sort,
  The minstrels well might sound,
For, as Lord Marmion crossed the court,
  He scattered angels round.
'Welcome to Norham, Marmion!
  Stout heart and open hand!
Well dost thou brook thy gallant roan,
  Thou flower of English land!'   150

XI

Two pursuivants, whom tabards deck,
With silver scutcheon round their neck,
  Stood on the steps of stone
By which you reach the donjon gate,
And there, with herald pomp and state,
  They hailed Lord Marmion:
They hailed him Lord of Fontenaye,
Of Lutterward, and Scrivelbaye,
  Of Tamworth tower and town;
And he, their courtesy to requite,   160
Gave them a chain of twelve marks'
    weight,
  All as he lighted down.

'Now, largesse, largesse, Lord Marmion,
  Knight of the crest of gold!
A blazoned shield, in battle won,
  Ne'er guarded heart so bold.'

XII

They marshalled him to the castle-hall,
  Where the guests stood all aside,
And loudly flourished the trumpet-call,
  And the heralds loudly cried,—   170
'Room, lordlings, room for Lord Marmion,
  With the crest and helm of gold!
Full well we know the trophies won
  In the lists at Cottiswold:
There, vainly Ralph de Wilton strove
  'Gainst Marmion's force to stand;
To him he lost his lady-love,
  And to the king his land.
Ourselves beheld the listed field,
  A sight both sad and fair;   180
We saw Lord Marmion pierce his shield,
  And saw his saddle bare;
We saw the victor win the crest
  He wears with worthy pride,
And on the gibbet-tree, reversed,
  His foeman's scutcheon tied.
Place, nobles, for the Falcon-Knight!
  Room, room, ye gentles gay,
For him who conquered in the right,
  Marmion of Fontenaye!'   190

XIII

Then stepped, to meet that noble lord,
  Sir Hugh the Heron bold,
Baron of Twisell and of Ford,
  And Captain of the Hold;
He led Lord Marmion to the deas,
  Raised o'er the pavement high,
And placed him in the upper place—
  They feasted full and high:
The whiles a Northern harper rude
Chanted a rhyme of deadly feud,   200
'How the fierce Thirwalls, and Ridleys
    all,
  Stout Willimondswick,
  And Hardriding Dick,
And Hughie of Hawdon, and Will o' the
    Wall,
Have set on Sir Albany Featherstonhaugh,
And taken his life at the Dead-man's-
    shaw.'
Scantly Lord Marmion's ear could brook
  The harper's barbarous lay,
Yet much he praised the pains he took,
  And well those pains did pay;   210

For lady's suit and minstrel's strain
By knight should ne'er be heard in vain.

XIV

' Now, good Lord Marmion,' Heron says,
  ' Of your fair courtesy,
I pray you bide some little space
  In this poor tower with me.
Here may you keep your arms from rust,
  May breathe your war-horse well;
Seldom hath passed a week but joust
  Or feat of arms befell.   220
The Scots can rein a mettled steed,
  And love to couch a spear; —
Saint George ! a stirring life they lead
  That have such neighbors near !
Then stay with us a little space,
  Our Northern wars to learn;
I pray you for your lady's grace ! '
  Lord Marmion's brow grew stern.

XV

The captain marked his altered look,
  And gave the squire the sign;   230
A mighty wassail-bowl he took,
  And crowned it high with wine.
' Now pledge me here, Lord Marmion;
  But first I pray thee fair,
Where hast thou left that page of thine
That used to serve thy cup of wine,
  Whose beauty was so rare ?
When last in Raby-towers we met,
  The boy I closely eyed,
And often marked his cheeks were wet 240
  With tears he fain would hide.
His was no rugged horse-boy's hand,
To burnish shield or sharpen brand,
  Or saddle battle-steed,
But meeter seemed for lady fair,
To fan her cheek, or curl her hair,
Or through embroidery, rich and rare,
  The slender silk to lead;
His skin was fair, his ringlets gold,
  His bosom — when he sighed,   250
The russet doublet's rugged fold
  Could scarce repel its pride !
Say, hast thou given that lovely youth
  To serve in lady's bower ?
Or was the gentle page, in sooth,
  A gentle paramour ? '

XVI

Lord Marmion ill could brook such jest;
  He rolled his kindling eye,

With pain his rising wrath suppressed,
  Yet made a calm reply: 260
' That boy thou thought so goodly fair,
He might not brook the Northern air.
More of his fate if thou wouldst learn,
I left him sick in Lindisfarne.
Enough of him. — But, Heron, say,
Why does thy lovely lady gay
Disdain to grace the hall to-day ?
Or has that dame, so fair and sage,
Gone on some pious pilgrimage ? ' —
He spoke in covert scorn, for fame   270
Whispered light tales of Heron's dame.

XVII

Unmarked, at least unrecked, the taunt,
  Careless the knight replied:
' No bird whose feathers gayly flaunt
  Delights in cage to bide;
Norham is grim and grated close,
Hemmed in by battlement and fosse,
  And many a darksome tower,
And better loves my lady bright
To sit in liberty and light   280
  In fair Queen Margaret's bower.
We hold our greyhound in our hand,
  Our falcon on our glove,
But where shall we find leash or band
  For dame that loves to rove ?
Let the wild falcon soar her swing,
She 'll stoop when she has tired her
  wing.' —

XVIII

' Nay, if with Royal James's bride
  The lovely Lady Heron bide,
Behold me here a messenger,   290
  Your tender greetings prompt to bear;
For, to the Scottish court addressed,
  I journey at our king's behest,
And pray you, of your grace, provide
  For me and mine a trusty guide.
I have not ridden in Scotland since
James backed the cause of that mock
  prince
Warbeck, that Flemish counterfeit,
Who on the gibbet paid the cheat.
Then did I march with Surrey's power, 300
What time we razed old Ayton tower.' —

XIX

' For such-like need, my lord, I trow,
Norham can find you guides enow;
For here be some have pricked as far
On Scottish ground as to Dunbar,

Have drunk the monks of Saint Bothan's
          ale,
And driven the beeves of Lauderdale,
Harried the wives of Greenlaw's goods,
And given them light to set their hoods.' —

XX

'Now, in good sooth,' Lord Marmion
          cried,   310
' Were I in warlike wise to ride,
A better guard I would not lack
Than your stout forayers at my back;
But as in form of peace I go,
A friendly messenger, to know,
Why, through all Scotland, near and far,
Their king is mustering troops for war,
The sight of plundering Border spears
Might justify suspicious fears,
And deadly feud or thirst of spoil   320
Break out in some unseemly broil.
A herald were my fitting guide;
Or friar, sworn in peace to bide;
Or pardoner, or travelling priest,
Or strolling pilgrim, at the least.'

XXI

The captain mused a little space,
And passed his hand across his face. —
' Fain would I find the guide you want,
But ill may spare a pursuivant,
The only men that safe can ride   330
Mine errands on the Scottish side:
And though a bishop built this fort,
Few holy brethren here resort;
Even our good chaplain, as I ween,
Since our last siege we have not seen.
The mass he might not sing or say
Upon one stinted meal a day;
So, safe he sat in Durham aisle,
And prayed for our success the while.
Our Norham vicar, woe betide,   340
Is all too well in case to ride;
The priest of Shoreswood — he could rein
The wildest war-horse in your train,
But then no spearman in the hall
Will sooner swear, or stab, or brawl.
Friar John of Tillmouth were the man;
A blithesome brother at the can,
A welcome guest in hall and bower,
He knows each castle, town, and tower,
In which the wine and ale is good,   350
'Twixt Newcastle and Holy-Rood.
But that good man, as ill befalls,
Hath seldom left our castle walls,

Since, on the vigil of Saint Bede,
In evil hour he crossed the Tweed,
To teach Dame Alison her creed.
Old Bughtrig found him with his wife,
And John, an enemy to strife,
Sans frock and hood, fled for his life.
The jealous churl hath deeply swore   360
That, if again he venture o'er,
He shall shrieve penitent no more.
Little he loves such risks, I know,
Yet in your guard perchance will go.'

XXII

Young Selby, at the fair hall-board,
Carved to his uncle and that lord,
And reverently took up the word:
' Kind uncle, woe were we each one,
If harm should hap to brother John.
He is a man of mirthful speech,   370
Can many a game and gambol teach;
Full well at tables can he play,
And sweep at bowls the stake away.
None can a lustier carol bawl,
The needfullest among us all,
When time hangs heavy in the hall,
And snow comes thick at Christmas tide,
And we can neither hunt nor ride
A foray on the Scottish side.
The vowed revenge of Bughtrig rude   380
May end in worse than loss of hood.
Let friar John in safety still
In chimney-corner snore his fill,
Roast hissing crabs, or flagons swill;
Last night, to Norham there came one
Will better guide Lord Marmion.' —
' Nephew,' quoth Heron, ' by my fay,
Well hast thou spoke; say forth thy say.' —

XXIII

' Here is a holy Palmer come,
From Salem first, and last from Rome;   390
One that hath kissed the blessed tomb,
And visited each holy shrine
In Araby and Palestine;
On hills of Armenie hath been,
Where Noah's ark may yet be seen;
By that Red Sea, too, hath he trod,
Which parted at the Prophet's rod;
In Sinai's wilderness he saw
The Mount where Israel heard the law,
Mid thunder-dint, and flashing levin,   400
And shadows, mists, and darkness, given.
He shows Saint James's cockle-shell,
Of fair Montserrat, too, can tell;

And of that Grot where Olives nod,
Where, darling of each heart and eye,
From all the youth of Sicily,
　　Saint Rosalie retired to God.

XXIV

' To stout Saint George of Norwich merry,
Saint Thomas, too, of Canterbury,
Cuthbert of Durham and Saint Bede,   410
For his sins' pardon hath he prayed.
He knows the passes of the North,
And seeks far shrines beyond the Forth;
Little he eats, and long will wake,
And drinks but of the stream or lake.
This were a guide o'er moor and dale;
But when our John hath quaffed his ale,
As little as the wind that blows,
And warms itself against his nose,
Kens he, or cares, which way he goes.' — 420

XXV

' Gramercy ! ' quoth Lord Marmion,
' Full loath were I that Friar John,
That venerable man, for me
Were placed in fear or jeopardy:
If this same Palmer will me lead
　　From hence to Holy-Rood,
Like his good saint, I 'll pay his meed,
Instead of cockle-shell or bead,
　　With angels fair and good.
I love such holy ramblers; still   430
They know to charm a weary hill
　　With song, romance, or lay:
Some jovial tale, or glee, or jest,
Some lying legend, at the least,
　　They bring to cheer the way.' —

XXVI

' Ah ! noble sir,' young Selby said,
And finger on his lip he laid,
' This man knows much, perchance e'en
　　more
Than he could learn by holy lore.
Still to himself he 's muttering,   440
And shrinks as at some unseen thing.
Last night we listened at his cell;
Strange sounds we heard, and, sooth to tell,
He murmured on till morn, howe'er
No living mortal could be near.
Sometimes I thought I heard it plain,
As other voices spoke again.
I cannot tell — I like it not —
Friar John hath told us it is wrote,
No conscience clear and void of wrong   450
Can rest awake and pray so long.

Himself still sleeps before his beads
Have marked ten aves and two creeds.' —

XXVII

' Let pass,' quoth Marmion ; ' by my fay,
This man shall guide me on my way,
Although the great arch-fiend and he
Had sworn themselves of company.
So please you, gentle youth, to call
This Palmer to the castle-hall.'
The summoned Palmer came in place: 460
His sable cowl o'erhung his face;
In his black mantle was he clad,
With Peter's keys, in cloth of red,
　　On his broad shoulders wrought;
The scallop shell his cap did deck;
The crucifix around his neck
　　Was from Loretto brought;
His sandals were with travel tore,
Staff, budget, bottle, scrip, he wore;
The faded palm-branch in his hand   470
Showed pilgrim from the Holy Land.

XXVIII

Whenas the Palmer came in hall,
Nor lord nor knight was there more tall,
Or had a statelier step withal,
　　Or looked more high and keen;
For no saluting did he wait,
But strode across the hall of state,
And fronted Marmion where he sate,
　　As he his peer had been.   479
But his gaunt frame was worn with toil;
His cheek was sunk, alas the while !
And when he struggled at a smile
　　His eye looked haggard wild:
Poor wretch, the mother that him bare,
If she had been in presence there,
In his wan face and sunburnt hair
　　She had not known her child.
Danger, long travel, want, or woe,
Soon change the form that best we know —
For deadly fear can time outgo,   490
　　And blanch at once the hair;
Hard toil can roughen form and face,
And want can quench the eye's bright
　　grace,
Nor does old age a wrinkle trace
　　More deeply than despair.
Happy whom none of these befall,
But this poor Palmer knew them all.

XXIX

Lord Marmion then his boon did ask;
The Palmer took on him the task,

So he would march with morning tide, 500
To Scottish court to be his guide.
'But I have solemn vows to pay,
And may not linger by the way,
  To fair Saint Andrew's bound,
Within the ocean-cave to pray,
Where good Saint Rule his holy lay,
From midnight to the dawn of day,
  Sung to the billows' sound;
Thence to Saint Fillan's blessed well, 509
Whose spring can frenzied dreams dispel,
  And the crazed brain restore.
Saint Mary grant that cave or spring
Could back to peace my bosom bring,
  Or bid it throb no more ! '

XXX

And now the midnight draught of sleep,
Where wine and spices richly steep,
In massive bowl of silver deep,
  The page presents on knee.
Lord Marmion drank a fair good rest,
The captain pledged his noble guest, 520
The cup went through among the rest,
  Who drained it merrily;
Alone the Palmer passed it by,
Though Selby pressed him courteously.
This was a sign the feast was o'er;
It hushed the merry wassail roar,
  The minstrels ceased to sound.
Soon in the castle nought was heard
But the slow footstep of the guard
  Pacing his sober round. 530

XXXI

With early dawn Lord Marmion rose:
And first the chapel doors unclose;
Then, after morning rites were done —
A hasty mass from Friar John —
And knight and squire had broke their
  fast
On rich substantial repast,
Lord Marmion's bugles blew to horse.
Then came the stirrup-cup in course:
Between the baron and his host,
No point of courtesy was lost; 540
High thanks were by Lord Marmion paid,
Solemn excuse the captain made,
Till, filing from the gate, had passed
That noble train, their lord the last.
Then loudly rung the trumpet call;
Thundered the cannon from the wall,
  And shook the Scottish shore;
Around the castle eddied slow
Volumes of smoke as white as snow

And hid its turrets hoar, 550
Till they rolled forth upon the air,
And met the river breezes there,
Which gave again the prospect fair.

INTRODUCTION TO CANTO SECOND

TO THE REV. JOHN MARRIOTT, A.M.

Ashestiel, Ettrick Forest

THE scenes are desert now and bare,
Where flourished once a forest fair,
When these waste glens with copse were
  lined,
And peopled with the hart and hind.
Yon thorn — perchance whose prickly
  spears
Have fenced him for three hundred years,
While fell around his green compeers —
Yon lonely thorn, would he could tell
The changes of his parent dell,
Since he, so gray and stubborn now, 10
Waved in each breeze a sapling bough !
Would he could tell how deep the shade
A thousand mingled branches made;
How broad the shadows of the oak,
How clung the rowan to the rock,
And through the foliage showed his head,
With narrow leaves and berries red;
What pines on every mountain sprung,
O'er every dell what birches hung,
In every breeze what aspens shook, 20
What alders shaded every brook !

'Here, in my shade,' methinks he 'd say,
'The mighty stag at noontide lay;
The wolf I 've seen, a fiercer game, —
The neighboring dingle bears his name, —
With lurching step around me prowl,
And stop, against the moon to howl;
The mountain-boar, on battle set,
His tusks upon my stem would whet;
While doe, and roe, and red-deer good, 30
Have bounded by through gay greenwood.
Then oft from Newark's riven tower
Sallied a Scottish monarch's power:
A thousand vassals mustered round,
With horse, and hawk, and horn, and
  hound;
And I might see the youth intent
Guard every pass with crossbow bent;
And through the brake the rangers stalk,

And falconers hold the ready hawk;
And foresters, in Greenwood trim,   40
Lead in the leash the gazehounds grim,
Attentive, as the bratchet's bay
From the dark covert drove the prey,
To slip them as he broke away.
The startled quarry bounds amain,
As fast the gallant greyhounds strain;
Whistles the arrow from the bow,
Answers the harquebuss below;
While all the rocking hills reply
To hoof-clang, hound, and hunters' cry,   50
And bugles ringing lightsomely.'

Of such proud huntings many tales
Yet linger in our lonely dales,
Up pathless Ettrick and on Yarrow,
Where erst the outlaw drew his arrow.
But not more blithe that sylvan court,
Than we have been at humbler sport;
Though small our pomp and mean our
         game,
Our mirth, dear Marriott, was the same.
Remember'st thou my greyhounds true ?
O'er holt or hill there never flew,   61
From slip or leash there never sprang,
More fleet of foot or sure of fang.
Nor dull, between each merry chase,
Passed by the intermitted space;
For we had fair resource in store,
In Classic and in Gothic lore:
We marked each memorable scene,
And held poetic talk between;
Nor hill, nor brook, we paced along,   70
But had its legend or its song.
All silent now — for now are still
Thy bowers, untenanted Bowhill !
No longer from thy mountains dun
The yeoman hears the well-known gun,
And while his honest heart glows warm
At thought of his paternal farm,
Round to his mates a brimmer fills,
And drinks, ' The Chieftain of the Hills !'
No fairy forms, in Yarrow's bowers,   80
Trip o'er the walks or tend the flowers,
Fair as the elves whom Janet saw
By moonlight dance on Carterhaugh;
No youthful Baron 's left to grace
The Forest-Sheriff's lonely chace,
And ape, in manly step and tone,
The majesty of Oberon:
And she is gone whose lovely face
Is but her least and lowest grace;   89
Though if to Sylphid Queen 't were given
To show our earth the charms of heaven,

She could not glide along the air
With form more light or face more fair.
No more the widow's deafened ear
Grows quick that lady's step to hear:
At noontide she expects her not,
Nor busies her to trim the cot;
Pensive she turns her humming wheel,
Or pensive cooks her orphans' meal,
Yet blesses, ere she deals their bread,   100
The gentle hand by which they 're fed.

From Yair — which hills so closely bind,
Scarce can the Tweed his passage find,
Though much he fret, and chafe, and toil,
Till all his eddying currents boil —
Her long-descended lord is gone,
And left us by the stream alone.
And much I miss those sportive boys,
Companions of my mountain joys,
Just at the age 'twixt boy and youth,   110
When thought is speech, and speech is
         truth.
Close to my side with what delight
They pressed to hear of Wallace wight,
When, pointing to his airy mound,
I called his ramparts holy ground !
Kindled their brows to hear me speak;
And I have smiled, to feel my cheek,
Despite the difference of our years,
Return again the glow of theirs.
Ah, happy boys ! such feelings pure,   120
They will not, cannot long endure;
Condemned to stem the world's rude tide,
You may not linger by the side;
For Fate shall thrust you from the shore
And Passion ply the sail and oar.
Yet cherish the remembrance still
Of the lone mountain and the rill;
For trust, dear boys, the time will come,
When fiercer transport shall be dumb,
And you will think right frequently,   130
But, well I hope, without a sigh,
On the free hours that we have spent
Together on the brown hill's bent.

When, musing on companions gone,
We doubly feel ourselves alone,
Something, my friend, we yet may gain;
There is a pleasure in this pain:
It soothes the love of lonely rest,
Deep in each gentler heart impressed.
'T is silent amid worldly toils,   140
And stifled soon by mental broils;
But, in a bosom thus prepared,
Its still small voice is often heard,

Whispering a mingled sentiment
'Twixt resignation and content.
Oft in my mind such thoughts awake
By lone Saint Mary's silent lake:
Thou know'st it well, — nor fen nor sedge
Pollute the pure lake's crystal edge;
Abrupt and sheer, the mountains sink   150
At once upon the level brink,
And just a trace of silver sand
Marks where the water meets the land.
Far in the mirror, bright and blue,
Each hill's huge outline you may view;
Shaggy with heath, but lonely bare,
Nor tree, nor bush, nor brake is there,
Save where of land yon slender line
Bears thwart the lake the scattered pine.
Yet even this nakedness has power,   160
And aids the feeling of the hour:
Nor thicket, dell, nor copse you spy,
Where living thing concealed might lie;
Nor point retiring hides a dell
Where swain or woodman lone might
    dwell.
There's nothing left to fancy's guess,
You see that all is loneliness:
And silence aids — though the steep hills
Send to the lake a thousand rills;
In summer tide so soft they weep,   170
The sound but lulls the ear asleep;
Your horse's hoof-tread sounds too rude,
So stilly is the solitude.

Nought living meets the eye or ear,
But well I ween the dead are near;
For though, in feudal strife, a foe
Hath laid Our Lady's chapel low,
Yet still, beneath the hallowed soil,
The peasant rests him from his toil,
And dying bids his bones be laid   180
Where erst his simple fathers prayed.

If age had tamed the passions' strife,
And fate had cut my ties to life,
Here have I thought 't were sweet to
    dwell,
And rear again the chaplain's cell,
Like that same peaceful hermitage,
Where Milton longed to spend his age.
'T were sweet to mark the setting day
On Bourhope's lonely top decay,
And, as it faint and feeble died   190
On the broad lake and mountain's side,
To say, 'Thus pleasures fade away;
Youth, talents, beauty, thus decay,
And leave us dark, forlorn, and gray;'

Then gaze on Dryhope's ruined tower,
And think on Yarrow's faded Flower;
And when that mountain-sound I heard,
Which bids us be for storm prepared,
The distant rustling of his wings,
As up his force the Tempest brings,   200
'T were sweet, ere yet his terrors rave,
To sit upon the Wizard's grave,
That Wizard Priest's whose bones are
    thrust
From company of holy dust;
On which no sunbeam ever shines —
So superstition's creed divines —
Thence view the lake with sullen roar
Heave her broad billows to the shore;
And mark the wild-swans mount the gale,
Spread wide through mist their snowy
    sail,   210
And ever stoop again, to lave
Their bosoms on the surging wave;
Then, when against the driving hail
No longer might my plaid avail,
Back to my lonely home retire,
And light my lamp and trim my fire;
There ponder o'er some mystic lay,
Till the wild tale had all its sway,
And, in the bittern's distant shriek,
I heard unearthly voices speak,   220
And thought the Wizard Priest was come
To claim again his ancient home !
And bade my busy fancy range,
To frame him fitting shape and strange,
Till from the task my brow I cleared,
And smiled to think that I had feared.

But chief 't were sweet to think such
    life —
Though but escape from fortune's strife —
Something most matchless good and wise,
A great and grateful sacrifice,   230
And deem each hour to musing given
A step upon the road to heaven.

Yet him whose heart is ill at ease
Such peaceful solitudes displease;
He loves to drown his bosom's jar
Amid the elemental war:
And my black Palmer's choice had been
Some ruder and more savage scene,
Like that which frowns round dark Loch-
    skene.
There eagles scream from isle to shore;   240
Down all the rocks the torrents roar;
O'er the black waves incessant driven,
Dark mists infect the summer heaven;

Through the rude barriers of the lake,
Away its hurrying waters break,
Faster and whiter dash and curl,
Till down yon dark abyss they hurl.
Rises the fog-smoke white as snow,
Thunders the viewless stream below,
Diving, as if condemned to lave   250
Some demon's subterranean cave,
Who, prisoned by enchanter's spell,
Shakes the dark rock with groan and
        yell.
And well that Palmer's form and mien
Had suited with the stormy scene,
Just on the edge, straining his ken
To view the bottom of the den,
Where, deep deep down, and far within,
Toils with the rocks the roaring linn;
Then, issuing forth one foamy wave,   260
And wheeling round the Giant's Grave,
White as the snowy charger's tail,
Drives down the pass of Moffatdale.

Marriott, thy harp, on Isis strung,
To many a Border theme has rung :
Then list to me, and thou shalt know
Of this mysterious Man of Woe.

CANTO SECOND

THE CONVENT

I

THE breeze which swept away the smoke
    Round Norham Castle rolled,
When all the loud artillery spoke
With lightning-flash and thunder-stroke,
    As Marmion left the hold, —
It curled not Tweed alone, that breeze,
For, far upon Northumbrian seas,
    It freshly blew and strong,
Where, from high Whitby's cloistered pile,
Bound to Saint Cuthbert's Holy Isle,   10
    It bore a bark along.
Upon the gale she stooped her side,
And bounded o'er the swelling tide,
    As she were dancing home;
The merry seamen laughed to see
Their gallant ship so lustily
    Furrow the green sea-foam.
Much joyed they in their honored freight;
For on the deck, in chair of state,
The Abbess of Saint Hilda placed,   20
With five fair nuns, the galley graced.

II

'T was sweet to see these holy maids,
Like birds escaped to greenwood shades,
    Their first flight from the cage,
How timid, and how curious too,
For all to them was strange and new,
And all the common sights they view
    Their wonderment engage.
One eyed the shrouds and swelling sail,
    With many a benedicite;   30
One at the rippling surge grew pale,
    And would for terror pray,
Then shrieked because the sea-dog nigh
His round black head and sparkling eye
    Reared o'er the foaming spray;
And one would still adjust her veil,
Disordered by the summer gale,
Perchance lest some more worldly eye
Her dedicated charms might spy,
Perchance because such action graced   40
Her fair-turned arm and slender waist.
Light was each simple bosom there,
Save two, who ill might pleasure share, —
The Abbess and the Novice Clare.

III

The Abbess was of noble blood,
But early took the veil and hood,
Ere upon life she cast a look,
Or knew the world that she forsook.
Fair too she was, and kind had been
As she was fair, but ne'er had seen   50
For her a timid lover sigh,
Nor knew the influence of her eye.
Love to her ear was but a name,
Combined with vanity and shame;
Her hopes, her fears, her joys, were all
Bounded within the cloister wall;
The deadliest sin her mind could reach
Was of monastic rule the breach,
And her ambition's highest aim
To emulate Saint Hilda's fame.   60
For this she gave her ample dower
To raise the convent's eastern tower;
For this, with carving rare and quaint,
She decked the chapel of the saint,
And gave the relic-shrine of cost,
With ivory and gems embossed.
The poor her convent's bounty blest,
The pilgrim in its halls found rest.

IV

Black was her garb, her rigid rule
Reformed on Benedictine school;   70

Her cheek was pale, her form was spare;
Vigils and penitence austere
Had early quenched the light of youth:
But gentle was the dame, in sooth;
Though, vain of her religious sway,
She loved to see her maids obey,
Yet nothing stern was she in cell,
And the nuns loved their Abbess well.
Sad was this voyage to the dame;
Summoned to Lindisfarne, she came, 80
There, with Saint Cuthbert's Abbot old
And Tynemouth's Prioress, to hold
A chapter of Saint Benedict,
For inquisition stern and strict
On two apostates from the faith,
And, if need were, to doom to death.

V

Nought say I here of Sister Clare,
Save this, that she was young and fair;
As yet a novice unprofessed,
Lovely and gentle, but distressed. 90
She was betrothed to one now dead,
Or worse, who had dishonored fled.
Her kinsmen bade her give her hand
To one who loved her for her land;
Herself, almost heart-broken now,
Was bent to take the vestal vow,
And shroud within Saint Hilda's gloom
Her blasted hopes and withered bloom.

VI

She sate upon the galley's prow,
And seemed to mark the waves below; 100
Nay, seemed, so fixed her look and eye,
To count them as they glided by.
She saw them not — 't was seeming all —
Far other scene her thoughts recall, —
A sun-scorched desert, waste and bare,
Nor waves nor breezes murmured there;
There saw she where some careless hand
O'er a dead corpse had heaped the sand,
To hide it till the jackals come
To tear it from the scanty tomb. — 110
See what a woful look was given,
As she raised up her eyes to heaven!

VII

Lovely, and gentle, and distressed —
These charms might tame the fiercest breast:
Harpers have sung and poets told
That he, in fury uncontrolled,
The shaggy monarch of the wood,
Before a virgin, fair and good,

Hath pacified his savage mood.
But passions in the human frame 120
Oft put the lion's rage to shame;
And jealousy, by dark intrigue,
With sordid avarice in league,
Had practised with their bowl and knife
Against the mourner's harmless life.
This crime was charged 'gainst those who lay
Prisoned in Cuthbert's islet gray.

VIII

And now the vessel skirts the strand
Of mountainous Northumberland;
Towns, towers, and halls successive rise, 130
And catch the nuns' delighted eyes.
Monk-Wearmouth soon behind them lay,
And Tynemouth's priory and bay;
They marked amid her trees the hall
Of lofty Seaton-Delaval;
They saw the Blythe and Wansbeck floods
Rush to the sea through sounding woods;
They passed the tower of Widderington,
Mother of many a valiant son;
At Coquet-isle their beads they tell 140
To the good saint who owned the cell;
Then did the Alne attention claim,
And Warkworth, proud of Percy's name;
And next they crossed themselves to hear
The whitening breakers sound so near,
Where, boiling through the rocks, they roar
On Dunstanborough's caverned shore;
Thy tower, proud Bamborough, marked they there,
King Ida's castle, huge and square,
From its tall rock look grimly down, 150
And on the swelling ocean frown;
Then from the coast they bore away,
And reached the Holy Island's bay.

IX

The tide did now its flood-mark gain,
And girdled in the Saint's domain;
For, with the flow and ebb, its style
Varies from continent to isle;
Dry shod, o'er sands, twice every day
The pilgrims to the shrine find way;
Twice every day the waves efface 160
Of staves and sandalled feet the trace.
As to the port the galley flew,
Higher and higher rose to view
The castle with its battled walls,
The ancient monastery's halls,
A solemn, huge, and dark-red pile,
Placed on the margin of the isle.

X

In Saxon strength that abbey frowned,
With massive arches broad and round,
　That rose alternate, row and row,　170
On ponderous columns, short and low,
　Built ere the art was known,
By pointed aisle and shafted stalk
The arcades of an alleyed walk
　To emulate in stone.
On the deep walls the heathen Dane
Had poured his impious rage in vain;
And needful was such strength to these,
Exposed to the tempestuous seas,
Scourged by the winds' eternal sway,　180
Open to rovers fierce as they,
Which could　twelve hundred years with-
　　stand
Winds, waves, and northern pirates' hand.
Not but that portions of the pile,
Rebuilded in a later style,
Showed where the spoiler's hand had been;
Not but the wasting sea-breeze keen
Had worn the pillar's carving quaint,
And mouldered in his niche the saint,
And rounded with consuming power　190
The pointéd angles of each tower;
Yet still entire the abbey stood,
Like veteran, worn, but unsubdued.

XI

Soon as they neared his turrets strong,
The maidens raised Saint Hilda's song,
And with the sea-wave and the wind
Their voices, sweetly shrill, combined,
　And made harmonious close;
Then, answering from the sandy shore,
Half-drowned amid the breakers' roar,　200
　According chorus rose:
Down to the haven of the Isle
The monks and nuns in order file
　From Cuthbert's cloisters grim;
Banner, and cross, and relics there,
To meet Saint Hilda's maids, they bare;
And, as they caught the sounds on air,
　They echoed back the hymn.
The islanders in joyous mood
Rushed emulously through the flood　210
　To hale the bark to land;
Conspicuous by her veil and hood,
Signing the cross, the Abbess stood,
　And blessed them with her hand.

XII

Suppose we now the welcome said,
Suppose the convent banquet made:

All through the holy dome,
Through cloister, aisle, and gallery,
Wherever vestal maid might pry,
Nor risk to meet unhallowed eye,　220
　The stranger sisters roam;
Till fell the evening damp with dew,
And the sharp sea-breeze coldly blew,
For there even summer night is chill.
Then, having strayed and gazed their fill,
　They closed around the fire;
And all, in turn, essayed to paint
The rival merits of their saint,
　A theme that ne'er can tire
A holy maid, for be it known　230
That their saint's honor is their own.

XIII

Then Whitby's nuns exulting told
How to their house three barons bold
　Must menial service do,
While horns blow out a note of shame,
And monks cry, ' Fie upon your name !
In wrath, for loss of sylvan game,
　Saint Hilda's priest ye slew.' —
' This, on Ascension-day, each year
While laboring on our harbor-pier,　240
Must Herbert, Bruce, and Percy hear.' —
They told how in their convent-cell
A Saxon princess once did dwell,
　The lovely Edelfled;
And how, of thousand snakes, each one
Was changed into a coil of stone
　When holy Hilda prayed;
Themselves, within their holy bound,
Their stony folds had often found.
They told how sea-fowls' pinions fail,　250
As over Whitby's towers they sail,
And, sinking down, with flutterings faint,
They do their homage to the saint.

XIV

Nor did Saint Cuthbert's daughters fail
To vie with these in holy tale;
His body's resting-place, of old,
How oft their patron changed, they told;
How, when the rude Dane burned their pile,
The monks fled forth from Holy Isle;　259
O'er northern mountain, marsh, and moor,
From sea to sea, from shore to shore,
Seven years Saint Cuthbert's corpse they
　　bore.
They rested them in fair Melrose;
　But though, alive, he loved it well,
Not there his relics might repose;
　For, wondrous tale to tell !

In his stone coffin forth he rides,
A ponderous bark for river tides,
Yet light as gossamer it glides
    Downward to Tilmouth cell.   270
Nor long was his abiding there,
For southward did the saint repair;
Chester-le-Street and Ripon saw
His holy corpse ere Wardilaw
Hailed him with joy and fear;
And, after many wanderings past,
He chose his lordly seat at last
Where his cathedral, huge and vast,
    Looks down upon the Wear.
There, deep in Durham's Gothic shade, 280
His relics are in secret laid;
    But none may know the place,
Save of his holiest servants three,
Deep sworn to solemn secrecy,
    Who share that wondrous grace.

XV

Who may his miracles declare?
Even Scotland's dauntless king and heir —
    Although with them they led
Galwegians, wild as ocean's gale,   289
And Loden's knights, all sheathed in mail,
And the bold men of Teviotdale —
    Before his standard fled.
'T was he, to vindicate his reign,
Edged Alfred's falchion on the Dane,
And turned the Conqueror back again,
When, with his Norman bowyer band,
He came to waste Northumberland.

XVI

But fain Saint Hilda's nuns would learn
If on a rock, by Lindisfarne,
Saint Cuthbert sits, and toils to frame 300
The sea-born beads that bear his name:
Such tales had Whitby's fishers told,
And said they might his shape behold,
    And hear his anvil sound;
A deadened clang, — a huge dim form,
Seen but, and heard, when gathering storm
    And night were closing round.
But this, as tale of idle fame,
The nuns of Lindisfarne disclaim.

XVII

While round the fire such legends go, 310
Far different was the scene of woe
Where, in a secret aisle beneath,
Council was held of life and death.
It was more dark and lone, that vault,
    Than the worst dungeon cell;

Old Colwulf built it, for his fault
    In penitence to dwell,
When he for cowl and beads laid down
The Saxon battle-axe and crown.
This den, which, chilling every sense 320
    Of feeling, hearing, sight,
Was called the Vault of Penitence,
    Excluding air and light,
Was by the prelate Sexhelm made
A place of burial for such dead
As, having died in mortal sin,
Might not be laid the church within.
'T was now a place of punishment;
Whence if so loud a shriek were sent
    As reached the upper air,   330
The hearers blessed themselves, and said
The spirits of the sinful dead
    Bemoaned their torments there.

XVIII

But though, in the monastic pile,
Did of this penitential aisle
    Some vague tradition go,
Few only, save the Abbot, knew
Where the place lay, and still more few
Were those who had from him the clew
    To that dread vault to go.   340
Victim and executioner
Were blindfold when transported there.
In low dark rounds the arches hung,
From the rude rock the side-walls sprung;
The gravestones, rudely sculptured o'er,
Half sunk in earth, by time half wore,
Were all the pavement of the floor;
The mildew-drops fell one by one,
With tinkling plash, upon the stone.
A cresset, in an iron chain,   350
Which served to light this drear domain,
With damp and darkness seemed to strive,
As if it scarce might keep alive;
And yet it dimly served to show
.The awful conclave met below.

XIX

There, met to doom in secrecy,
Were placed the heads of convents three,
All servants of Saint Benedict,
The statutes of whose order strict
    On iron table lay;   360
In long black dress, on seats of stone,
Behind were these three judges shown
    By the pale cresset's ray.
The Abbess of Saint Hilda's there
Sat for a space with visage bare,

Until, to hide her bosom's swell,
And tear-drops that for pity fell,
  She closely drew her veil;
Yon shrouded figure, as I guess,
By her proud mien and flowing dress,   370
Is Tynemouth's haughty Prioress,
  And she with awe looks pale;
And he, that ancient man, whose sight
Has long been quenched by age's night,
Upon whose wrinkled brow alone
Nor ruth nor mercy's trace is shown,
  Whose look is hard and stern, —
Saint Cuthbert's Abbot is his style,
For sanctity called through the isle
  The Saint of Lindisfarne.   380

XX

Before them stood a guilty pair;
But, though an equal fate they share,
Yet one alone deserves our care.
Her sex a page's dress belied;
The cloak and doublet, loosely tied,
Obscured her charms, but could not hide.
  Her cap down o'er her face she drew;
    And, on her doublet breast,
  She tried to hide the badge of blue,
    Lord Marmion's falcon crest.   390
But, at the prioress' command,
A monk undid the silken band
  That tied her tresses fair,
And raised the bonnet from her head,
And down her slender form they spread
  In ringlets rich and rare.
Constance de Beverley they know,
Sister professed of Fontevraud,
Whom the Church numbered with the dead,
For broken vows and convent fled.   400

XXI

When thus her face was given to view, —
Although so pallid was her hue,
It did a ghastly contrast bear
To those bright ringlets glistering fair, —
Her look composed, and steady eye,
Bespoke a matchless constancy;
And there she stood so calm and pale
That, but her breathing did not fail,
And motion slight of eye and head,
And of her bosom, warranted   410
That neither sense nor pulse she lacks,
You might have thought a form of wax,
Wrought to the very life, was there;
So still she was, so pale, so fair.

XXII

Her comrade was a sordid soul,
  Such as does murder for a meed;
Who, but of fear, knows no control,
Because his conscience, seared and foul,
  Feels not the import of his deed;
One whose brute-feeling ne'er aspires   420
Beyond his own more brute desires.
Such tools the Tempter ever needs
To do the savagest of deeds;
For them no visioned terrors daunt,
Their nights no fancied spectres haunt;
One fear with them, of all most base,
The fear of death, alone finds place.
This wretch was clad in frock and cowl,
And shamed not loud to moan and howl,
His body on the floor to dash,   430
And crouch, like hound beneath the lash;
While his mute partner, standing near,
Waited her doom without a tear.

XXIII

Yet well the luckless wretch might shriek,
Well might her paleness terror speak !
For there were seen in that dark wall
Two niches, narrow, deep, and tall; —
Who enters at such grisly door
Shall ne'er, I ween, find exit more.
In each a slender meal was laid,   440
Of roots, of water, and of bread;
By each, in Benedictine dress,
Two haggard monks stood motionless,
Who, holding high a blazing torch,
Showed the grim entrance of the porch;
Reflecting back the smoky beam,
The dark-red walls and arches gleam.
Hewn stones and cement were displayed,
And building tools in order laid.

XXIV

These executioners were chose   450
As men who were with mankind foes,
And, with despite and envy fired,
Into the cloister had retired,
Or who, in desperate doubt of grace,
Strove by deep penance to efface
  Of some foul crime the stain;
For, as the vassals of her will,
Such men the Church selected still
  As either joyed in doing ill,
    Or thought more grace to gain   460
If in her cause they wrestled down
Feelings their nature strove to own.

By strange device were they brought
   there,
They knew not how, and knew not where.

XXV

And now that blind old abbot rose,
  To speak the Chapter's doom
On those the wall was to enclose
  Alive within the tomb,
But stopped because that woful maid,
Gathering her powers, to speak essayed; 470
Twice she essayed, and twice in vain,
Her accents might no utterance gain;
Nought but imperfect murmurs slip
From her convulsed and quivering lip:
  'Twixt each attempt all was so still,
  You seemed to hear a distant rill —
    'T was ocean's swells and falls;
For though this vault of sin and fear
Was to the sounding surge so near,   479
A tempest there you scarce could hear,
  So massive were the walls.

XXVI

At length, an effort sent apart
The blood that curdled to her heart,
  And light came to her eye,
And color dawned upon her cheek,
A hectic and a fluttered streak,
Like that left on the Cheviot peak
  By Autumn's stormy sky;
And when her silence broke at length,
Still as she spoke she gathered strength,
  And armed herself to bear.   491
It was a fearful sight to see
Such high resolve and constancy
  In form so soft and fair.

XXVII

' I speak not to implore your grace,
Well know I for one minute's space
  Successless might I sue?
Nor do I speak your prayers to gain;
For if a death of lingering pain
To cleanse my sins be penance vain,   500
  Vain are your masses too. —
I listened to a traitor's tale,
I left the convent and the veil;
For three long years I bowed my pride,
A horse-boy in his train to ride;
And well my folly's meed he gave,
Who forfeited, to be his slave,
All here, and all beyond the grave.
He saw young Clara's face more fair,

He knew her of broad lands the heir,   510
Forgot his vows, his faith forswore,
And Constance was beloved no more.
  'T is an old tale, and often told;
    But did my fate and wish agree,
Ne'er had been read, in story old,
Of maiden true betrayed for gold,
  That loved, or was avenged, like me !

XXVIII

' The king approved his favorite's aim;
In vain a rival barred his claim,
  Whose fate with Clare's was plight,   520
For he attaints that rival's fame
With treason's charge — and on they came
  In mortal lists to fight.
    Their oaths are said,
    Their prayers are prayed,
    Their lances in the rest are laid,
  They meet in mortal shock;
And hark ! the throng, with thundering
    cry,
Shout "Marmion, Marmion ! to the sky,
  De Wilton to the block ! "   530
Say, ye who preach Heaven shall decide
When in the lists two champions ride,
  Say, was Heaven's justice here ?
When, loyal in his love and faith,
Wilton found overthrow or death
  Beneath a traitor's spear ?
How false the charge, how true he fell,
This guilty packet best can tell.'
Then drew a packet from her breast,
Paused, gathered voice, and spoke the
  rest.   540

XXIX

' Still was false Marmion's bridal stayed;
To Whitby's convent fled the maid,
  The hated match to shun.
"Ho ! shifts she thus ? " King Henry
    cried,
"Sir Marmion, she shall be thy bride,
  If she were sworn a nun."
One way remained — the king's command
Sent Marmion to the Scottish land;
I lingered here, and rescue planned
  For Clara and for me: 550
This caitiff monk for gold did swear
He would to Whitby's shrine repair,
And by his drugs my rival fair
  A saint in heaven should be ;
But ill the dastard kept his oath,
Whose cowardice hath undone us both.

XXX

'And now my tongue the secret tells,
Not that remorse my bosom swells,
But to assure my soul that none
Shall ever wed with Marmion.   560
Had fortune my last hope betrayed,
This packet, to the king conveyed,
Had given him to the headsman's stroke,
Although my heart that instant broke. —
Now, men of death, work forth your will,
For I can suffer, and be still;
And come he slow, or come he fast,
It is but Death who comes at last.

XXXI

'Yet dread me from my living tomb,
Ye vassal slaves of bloody Rome !   570
If Marmion's late remorse should wake,
Full soon such vengeance will he take
That you shall wish the fiery Dane
Had rather been your guest again.
Behind, a darker hour ascends !
The altars quake, the crosier bends,
The ire of a despotic king
Rides forth upon destruction's wing;
Then shall these vaults, so strong and deep,
Burst open to the sea-winds' sweep;   580
Some traveller then shall find my bones
Whitening amid disjointed stones,
And, ignorant of priests' cruelty,
Marvel such relics here should be.'

XXXII

Fixed was her look and stern her air:
Back from her shoulders streamed her hair;
The locks that wont her brow to shade
Stared up erectly from her head;
Her figure seemed to rise more high;
Her voice despair's wild energy   590
Had given a tone of prophecy.
Appalled the astonished conclave sate;
With stupid eyes, the men of fate
Gazed on the light inspired form,
And listened for the avenging storm;
The judges felt the victim's dread;
No hand was moved, no word was said,
  Till thus the abbot's doom was given,
Raising his sightless balls to heaven:
'Sister, let thy sorrows cease;   600
Sinful brother, part in peace !'
  From that dire dungeon, place of doom,
  Of execution too, and tomb,
    Paced forth the judges three;

Sorrow it were and shame to tell
The butcher-work that there befell,
When they had glided from the cell
  Of sin and misery.

XXXIII

An hundred winding steps convey
That conclave to the upper day;   610
But ere they breathed the fresher air
They heard the shriekings of despair,
  And many a stifled groan.
With speed their upward way they take, —
Such speed as age and fear can make, —
And crossed themselves for terror's sake,
  As hurrying, tottering on,
Even in the vesper's heavenly tone
They seemed to hear a dying groan,
And bade the passing knell to toll   620
For welfare of a parting soul.
Slow o'er the midnight wave it swung,
Northumbrian rocks in answer rung;
To Warkworth cell the echoes rolled,
His beads the wakeful hermit told;
The Bamborough peasant raised his head,
But slept ere half a prayer he said;
So far was heard the mighty knell,
The stag sprung up on Cheviot Fell,
Spread his broad nostril to the wind,   630
Listed before, aside, behind,
Then couched him down beside the hind,
And quaked among the mountain fern,
To hear that sound so dull and stern.

INTRODUCTION TO CANTO THIRD

TO WILLIAM ERSKINE, ESQ.

Ashestiel, Ettrick Forest

LIKE April morning clouds, that pass
With varying shadow o'er the grass,
And imitate on field and furrow
Life's checkered scene of joy and sorrow;
Like streamlet of the mountain north,
Now in a torrent racing forth,
Now winding slow its silver train,
And almost slumbering on the plain;
Like breezes of the autumn day,
Whose voice inconstant dies away,   10
And ever swells again as fast
When the ear deems its murmur past;
Thus various, my romantic theme
Flits, winds, or sinks, a morning dream.

Yet pleased, our eye pursues the trace
Of Light and Shade's inconstant race;
Pleased, views the rivulet afar,
Weaving its maze irregular;
And pleased, we listen as the breeze
Heaves its wild sigh through Autumn
    trees: 20
Then, wild as cloud, or stream, or gale,
Flow on, flow unconfined, my tale !

Need I to thee, dear Erskine, tell
I love the license all too well,
In sounds now lowly, now more strong,
To raise the desultory song ?
Oft, when mid such capricious chime
Some transient fit of loftier rhyme
To thy kind judgment seemed excuse
For many an error of the muse, 30
Oft hast thou said, ' If, still misspent,
Thine hours to poetry are lent,
Go, and to tame thy wandering course,
Quaff from the fountain at the source;
Approach those masters o'er whose tomb
Immortal laurels ever bloom:
Instructive of the feebler bard,
Still from the grave their voice is heard;
From them, and from the paths they
    showed,
Choose honored guide and practised
    road; 40
Nor ramble on through brake and maze,
With harpers rude of barbarous days.

' Or deem'st thou not our later time
Yields topic meet for classic rhyme ?
Hast thou no elegiac verse
For BRUNSWICK'S venerable hearse ?
What ! not a line, a tear, a sigh,
When valor bleeds for liberty ? —
Oh, hero of that glorious time,
When, with unrivalled light sublime, — 50
Though martial Austria, and though all
The might of Russia, and the Gaul,
Though banded Europe stood her foes —
The star of Brandenburg arose !
Thou couldst not live to see her beam
Forever quenched in Jena's stream.
Lamented chief ! — it was not given
To thee to change the doom of Heaven,
And crush that dragon in its birth,
Predestined scourge of guilty earth. 60
Lamented chief ! — not thine the power
To save in that presumptuous hour
When Prussia hurried to the field,
And snatched the spear, but left the shield !

Valor and skill 't was thine to try,
And, tried in vain, 't was thine to die.
Ill had it seemed thy silver hair
The last, the bitterest pang to share,
For princedoms reft, and scutcheons riven,
And birthrights to usurpers given; 70
Thy land's, thy children's wrongs to feel,
And witness woes thou couldst not heal !
On thee relenting Heaven bestows
For honored life an honored close;
And when revolves, in time's sure change,
The hour of Germany's revenge,
When, breathing fury for her sake,
Some new Arminius shall awake,
Her champion, ere he strike, shall come
To whet his sword on BRUNSWICK'S tomb.

' Or of the Red-Cross hero teach, 81
Dauntless in dungeon as on breach.
Alike to him the sea, the shore,
The brand, the bridle, or the oar:
Alike to him the war that calls
Its votaries to the shattered walls
Which the grim Turk, besmeared with
    blood,
Against the Invincible made good;
Or that whose thundering voice could wake
The silence of the polar lake, 90
When stubborn Russ and mettled Swede
On the warped wave their death-game
    played;
Or that where Vengeance and Affright
Howled round the father of the fight,
Who snatched on Alexandria's sand
The conqueror's wreath with dying hand.

' Or if to touch such chord be thine,
Restore the ancient tragic line,
And emulate the notes that rung
From the wild harp which silent hung 100
By silver Avon's holy shore
Till twice an hundred years rolled o'er;
When she, the bold Enchantress, came,
With fearless hand and heart on flame,
From the pale willow snatched the treasure,
And swept it with a kindred measure,
Till Avon's swans, while rung the grove
With Montfort's hate and Basil's love,
Awakening at the inspired strain,
Deemed their own Shakespeare lived
    again.' 110

Thy friendship thus thy judgment
    wronging
With praises not to me belonging,

In task more meet for mightiest powers
Wouldst thou engage my thriftless hours.
But say, my Erskine, hast thou weighed
That secret power by all obeyed,
Which warps not less the passive mind,
Its source concealed or undefined;
Whether an impulse, that has birth
Soon as the infant wakes on earth,   120
One with our feelings and our powers,
And rather part of us than ours;
Or whether fitlier termed the sway
Of habit, formed in early day ?
Howe'er derived, its force confessed
Rules with despotic sway the breast,
And drags us on by viewless chain,
While taste and reason plead in vain.
Look east, and ask the Belgian why,
Beneath Batavia's sultry sky,   130
He seeks not eager to inhale
The freshness of the mountain gale,
Content to rear his whitened wall
Beside the dank and dull canal ?
He 'll say, from youth he loved to see
The white sail gliding by the tree.
Or see yon weather-beaten hind,
Whose sluggish herds before him wind,
Whose tattered plaid and rugged cheek
His northern clime and kindred speak;   140
Through England's laughing meads he
      goes,
And England's wealth around him flows;
Ask if it would content him well,
At ease in those gay plains to dwell,
Where hedge - rows spread a verdant
      screen,
And spires and forests intervene,
And the neat cottage peeps between ?
No ! not for these will he exchange
His dark Lochaber's boundless range,
Not for fair Devon's meads forsake   150
Ben Nevis gray and Garry's lake.

Thus while I ape the measure wild
Of tales that charmed me yet a child,
Rude though they be, still with the chime
Return the thoughts of early time;
And feelings, roused in life's first day,
Glow in the line and prompt the lay.
Then rise those crags, that mountain tower,
Which charmed my fancy's wakening hour.
Though no broad river swept along,   160
To claim, perchance, heroic song,
Though sighed no groves in summer gale,
To prompt of love a softer tale,
Though scarce a puny streamlet's speed

Claimed homage from a shepherd's reed,
Yet was poetic impulse given
By the green hill and clear blue heaven.
It was a barren scene and wild,
Where naked cliffs were rudely piled,
But ever and anon between   170
Lay velvet tufts of loveliest green;
And well the lonely infant knew
Recesses where the wall-flower grew,
And honeysuckle loved to crawl
Up the low crag and ruined wall.
I deemed such nooks the sweetest shade
The sun in all its round surveyed;
And still I thought that shattered tower
The mightiest work of human power,
And marvelled as the aged hind   180
With some strange tale bewitched my
      mind
Of forayers, who with headlong force
Down from that strength had spurred their
      horse,
Their southern rapine to renew
Far in the distant Cheviots blue,
And, home returning, filled the hall
With revel, wassail-rout, and brawl.
Methought that still with trump and clang
The gateway's broken arches rang;
Methought grim features, seamed with
      scars,   190
Glared through the window's rusty bars,
And ever, by the winter hearth,
Old tales I heard of woe or mirth,
Of lovers' sleights, of ladies' charms,
Of witches' spells, of warriors' arms;
Of patriot battles, won of old
By Wallace wight and Bruce the bold;
Of later fields of feud and fight,
When, pouring from their Highland
      height,
The Scottish clans in headlong sway   200
Had swept the scarlet ranks away.
While stretched at length upon the floor,
Again I fought each combat o'er,
Pebbles and shells, in order laid,
The mimic ranks of war displayed;
And onward still the Scottish Lion bore,
And still the scattered Southron fled be-
      fore.

Still, with vain fondness, could I trace
Anew each kind familiar face
That brightened at our evening fire !   210
From the thatched mansion's gray-haired
      sire,
Wise without learning, plain and good,

And sprung of Scotland's gentler blood;
Whose eye in age, quick, clear, and keen,
Showed what in youth its glance had been;
Whose doom discording neighbors sought,
Content with equity unbought;
To him the venerable priest,
Our frequent and familiar guest, 219
Whose life and manners well could paint
Alike the student and the saint,
Alas! whose speech too oft I broke
With gambol rude and timeless joke:
For I was wayward, bold, and wild,
A self-willed imp, a grandame's child,
But half a plague, and half a jest,
Was still endured, beloved, caressed.

From me, thus nurtured, dost thou ask
The classic poet's well-conned task?
Nay, Erskine, nay — on the wild hill 230
Let the wild heath-bell flourish still;
Cherish the tulip, prune the vine,
But freely let the woodbine twine,
And leave untrimmed the eglantine:
Nay, my friend, nay — since oft thy praise
Hath given fresh vigor to my lays,
Since oft thy judgment could refine
My flattened thought or cumbrous line,
Still kind, as is thy wont, attend,
And in the minstrel spare the friend. 240
Though wild as cloud, as stream, as gale,
Flow forth, flow unrestrained, my tale!

CANTO THIRD

THE HOSTEL, OR INN

I

THE livelong day Lord Marmion rode;
The mountain path the Palmer showed
By glen and streamlet winded still,
Where stunted birches hid the rill.
They might not choose the lowland road,
For the Merse forayers were abroad,
Who, fired with hate and thirst of prey,
Had scarcely failed to bar their way;
Oft on the trampling band from crown
Of some tall cliff the deer looked down; 10
On wing of jet from his repose
In the deep heath the blackcock rose;
Sprung from the gorse the timid roe,
Nor waited for the bending bow;
And when the stony path began
By which the naked peak they wan,
Up flew the snowy ptarmigan.

The noon had long been passed before
They gained the height of Lammermoor;
Thence winding down the northern way, 20
Before them at the close of day
Old Gifford's towers and hamlet lay.

II

No summons calls them to the tower,
To spend the hospitable hour.
To Scotland's camp the lord was gone;
His cautious dame, in bower alone,
Dreaded her castle to unclose,
So late, to unknown friends or foes.
On through the hamlet as they paced,
Before a porch whose front was graced,
With bush and flagon trimly placed, 31
Lord Marmion drew his rein:
The village inn seemed large, though rude;
Its cheerful fire and hearty food
Might well relieve his train.
Down from their seats the horsemen sprung,
With jingling spurs the court-yard rung;
They bind their horses to the stall,
For forage, food, and firing call,
And various clamor fills the hall: 40
Weighing the labor with the cost,
Toils everywhere the bustling host.

III

Soon, by the chimney's merry blaze,
Through the rude hostel might you gaze,
Might see where in dark nook aloof
The rafters of the sooty roof
Bore wealth of winter cheer;
Of sea-fowl dried, and solands store,
And gammons of the tusky boar,
And savory haunch of deer. 50
The chimney arch projected wide;
Above, around it, and beside,
Were tools for housewives' hand;
Nor wanted, in that martial day,
The implements of Scottish fray,
The buckler, lance, and brand.
Beneath its shade, the place of state,
On oaken settle Marmion sate,
And viewed around the blazing hearth
His followers mix in noisy mirth; 60
Whom with brown ale, in jolly tide,
From ancient vessels ranged aside
Full actively their host supplied.

IV

Theirs was the glee of martial breast,
And laughter theirs at little jest;

And oft Lord Marmion deigned to aid,
And mingle in the mirth they made;
For though, with men of high degree,
The proudest of the proud was he,
Yet, trained in camps, he knew the art   70
To win the soldier's hardy heart.
They love a captain to obey,
Boisterous as March, yet fresh as May;
With open hand and brow as free,
Lover of wine and minstrelsy;
Ever the first to scale a tower,
As venturous in a lady's bower: —
Such buxom chief shall lead his host
From India's fires to Zembla's frost.

V

Resting upon his pilgrim staff,   80
  Right opposite the Palmer stood,
His thin dark visage seen but half,
  Half hidden by his hood.
Still fixed on Marmion was his look,
Which he, who ill such gaze could brook,
  Strove by a frown to quell;
But not for that, though more than once
Full met their stern encountering glance,
  The Palmer's visage fell.

VI

By fits less frequent from the crowd   90
Was heard the burst of laughter loud;
For still, as squire and archer stared
On that dark face and matted beard,
  Their glee and game declined.
All gazed at length in silence drear,
Unbroke save when in comrade's ear
Some yeoman, wondering in his fear,
  Thus whispered forth his mind:
'Saint Mary! saw'st thou e'er such sight?
How pale his cheek, his eye how bright, 100
Whene'er the firebrand's fickle light
  Glances beneath his cowl!
Full on our lord he sets his eye;
For his best palfrey would not I
  Endure that sullen scowl.'

VII

But Marmion, as to chase the awe
Which thus had quelled their hearts who
    saw
The ever-varying firelight show
That figure stern and face of woe,
  Now called upon a squire: 110
'Fitz-Eustace, know'st thou not some lay,
To speed the lingering night away?
  We slumber by the fire.'

VIII

'So please you,' thus the youth rejoined,
'Our choicest minstrel's left behind.
Ill may we hope to please your ear,
Accustomed Constant's strains to hear.
The harp full deftly can he strike,
And wake the lover's lute alike;
To dear Saint Valentine no thrush   120
Sings livelier from a springtide bush,
No nightingale her lovelorn tune
More sweetly warbles to the moon.
Woe to the cause, whate'er it be,
Detains from us his melody,
Lavished on rocks and billows stern,
Or duller monks of Lindisfarne.
Now must I venture as I may,
To sing his favorite roundelay.'

IX

A mellow voice Fitz-Eustace had,   130
The air he chose was wild and sad;
Such have I heard in Scottish land
Rise from the busy harvest band,
When falls before the mountaineer
On Lowland plains the ripened ear.
Now one shrill voice the notes prolong,
Now a wild chorus swells the song:
Oft have I listened and stood still
As it came softened up the hill,
And deemed it the lament of men   140
Who languished for their native glen,
And thought how sad would be such sound
On Susquehanna's swampy ground,
Kentucky's wood-encumbered brake,
Or wild Ontario's boundless lake,
Where heart-sick exiles in the strain
Recalled fair Scotland's hills again!

X

SONG

Where shall the lover rest,
  Whom the fates sever
From his true maiden's breast,   150
  Parted forever?
Where, through groves deep and high,
  Sounds the far billow,
Where early violets die,
  Under the willow.

CHORUS

Eleu loro, etc. Soft shall be his pillow.

There, through the summer day,
  Cool streams are laving;

There, while the tempests sway,
  Scarce are boughs waving;   160
There thy rest shalt thou take,
  Parted forever,
Never again to wake,
  Never, O never !

Eleu loro, etc.   Never, O never !

XI

Where shall the traitor rest,
  He the deceiver,
Who could win maiden's breast,
  Ruin and leave her ?
In the lost battle,   170
  Borne down by the flying,
Where mingles war's rattle
  With groans of the dying.

Eleu loro, etc.   There shall he be lying.

Her wing shall the eagle flap
  O'er the false-hearted;
His warm blood the wolf shall lap,
  Ere life be parted.
Shame and dishonor sit
  By his grave ever;   180
Blessing shall hallow it, —
  Never, O never !

Eleu loro, etc.   Never, O never !

XII

It ceased, the melancholy sound,
And silence sunk on all around.
The air was sad; but sadder still
  It fell on Marmion's ear,
And plained as if disgrace and ill,
  And shameful death, were near.
He drew his mantle past his face,   190
  Between it and the band,
And rested with his head a space
  Reclining on his hand.
His thoughts I scan not; but I ween
That, could their import have been seen,
The meanest groom in all the hall,
That e'er tied courser to a stall,
Would scarce have wished to be their prey,
For Lutterward and Fontenaye.

XIII

High minds, of native pride and force,   200
Most deeply feel thy pangs, Remorse !

Fear for their scourge mean villains have,
Thou art the torturer of the brave !
Yet fatal strength they boast to steel
Their minds to bear the wounds they feel,
Even while they writhe beneath the smart
Of civil conflict in the heart.
For soon Lord Marmion raised his head,
And smiling to Fitz-Eustace said:
' Is it not strange that, as ye sung,   210
Seemed in mine ear a death-peal rung,
Such as in nunneries they toll
For some departing sister's soul ?
  Say, what may this portend ? '
Then first the Palmer silence broke, —
The livelong day he had not spoke, —
  ' The death of a dear friend.'

XIV

Marmion, whose steady heart and eye
Ne'er changed in worst extremity,   219
Marmion, whose soul could scantly brook
Even from his king a haughty look,
Whose accent of command controlled
In camps the boldest of the bold —
Thought, look, and utterance failed him
  now,
Fallen was his glance and flushed his brow:
  For either in the tone,
Or something in the Palmer's look,
So full upon his conscience strook
  That answer he found none.
Thus oft it haps that when within   230
They shrink at sense of secret sin,
  A feather daunts the brave;
A fool's wild speech confounds the wise,
And proudest princes vail their eyes
  Before their meanest slave.

XV

Well might he falter ! — By his aid
Was Constance Beverley betrayed.
Not that he augured of the doom
Which on the living closed the tomb:
But, tired to hear the desperate maid   240
Threaten by turns, beseech, upbraid,
And wroth because in wild despair
She practised on the life of Clare,
Its fugitive the Church he gave,
Though not a victim, but a slave,
And deemed restraint in convent strange
Would hide her wrongs and her revenge.
Himself, proud Henry's favorite peer,
Held Romish thunders idle fear;
Secure his pardon he might hold   250
For some slight mulct of penance-gold.
Thus judging, he gave secret way

When the stern priests surprised their prey.
His train but deemed the favorite page
Was left behind to spare his age;
Or other if they deemed, none dared
To mutter what he thought and heard:
Woe to the vassal who durst pry
Into Lord Marmion's privacy !

XVI

His conscience slept — he deemed her well,
And safe secured in distant cell;   261
But, wakened by her favorite lay,
And that strange Palmer's boding say
That fell so ominous and drear
Full on the object of his fear,
To aid remorse's venomed throes,
Dark tales of convent-vengeance rose;
And Constance, late betrayed and scorned,
All lovely on his soul returned;
Lovely as when at treacherous call   270
She left her convent's peaceful wall,
Crimsoned with shame, with terror mute,
Dreading alike escape, pursuit,
Till love, victorious o'er alarms,
Hid fears and blushes in his arms.

XVII

' Alas !' he thought, ' how changed that
        mien !
How changed these timid looks have been,
Since years of guilt and of disguise
Have steeled her brow and armed her eyes !
No more of virgin terror speaks   280
The blood that mantles in her cheeks;
Fierce and unfeminine are there,
Frenzy for joy, for grief despair;
And I the cause — for whom were given
Her peace on earth, her hopes in heaven ! —
Would,' thought he, as the picture grows,
' I on its stalk had left the rose !
Oh, why should man's success remove
The very charms that wake his love ? —
Her convent's peaceful solitude   290
Is now a prison harsh and rude;
And, pent within the narrow cell,
How will her spirit chafe and swell !
How brook the stern monastic laws !
The penance how — and I the cause ! —
Vigil and scourge — perchance even worse !'
And twice he rose to cry, ' To horse !'
And twice his sovereign's mandate came,
Like damp upon a kindling flame;   299
And twice he thought, ' Gave I not charge
She should be safe, though not at large ?

They durst not, for their island, shred
One golden ringlet from her head.'

XVIII

While thus in Marmion's bosom strove
Repentance and reviving love,
Like whirlwinds whose contending sway
I 've seen Loch Vennachar obey,
Their host the Palmer's speech had heard,
And talkative took up the word:
    ' Ay, reverend pilgrim, you who stray   310
    From Scotland's simple land away,
        To visit realms afar,
    Full often learn the art to know
    Of future weal or future woe,
        By word, or sign, or star;
Yet might a knight his fortune hear,
If, knight-like, he despises fear,
Not far from hence; — if fathers old
Aright our hamlet legend told.'
These broken words the menials move, —   320
For marvels still the vulgar love, —
And, Marmion giving license cold,
His tale the host thus gladly told: —

XIX

THE HOST'S TALE

' A clerk could tell what years have flown
Since Alexander filled our throne, —
Third monarch of that warlike name, —
And eke the time when here he came
To seek Sir Hugo, then our lord:
A braver never drew a sword;
A wiser never, at the hour   330
Of midnight, spoke the word of power;
The same whom ancient records call
The founder of the Goblin-Hall.
I would, Sir Knight, your longer stay
Gave you that cavern to survey.
Of lofty roof and ample size,
Beneath the castle deep it lies:
To hew the living rock profound,
The floor to pave, the arch to round,
There never toiled a mortal arm,   340
It all was wrought by word and charm;
And I have heard my grandsire say
That the wild clamor and affray
Of those dread artisans of hell,
Who labored under Hugo's spell,
Sounded as loud as ocean's war
Among the caverns of Dunbar.

XX

' The king Lord Gifford's castle sought,
Deep laboring with uncertain thought.

Even then he mustered all his host,   350
To meet upon the western coast;
For Norse and Danish galleys plied
Their oars within the Firth of Clyde.
There floated Haco's banner trim
Above Norweyan warriors grim,
Savage of heart and large of limb,
Threatening both continent and isle,
Bute, Arran, Cunninghame, and Kyle.
Lord Gifford, deep beneath the ground,
Heard Alexander's bugle sound,   360
And tarried not his garb to change,
But, in his wizard habit strange,
Came forth, — a quaint and fearful sight:
His mantle lined with fox-skins white;
His high and wrinkled forehead bore
A pointed cap, such as of yore
Clerks say that Pharaoh's Magi wore;
His shoes were marked with cross and spell,
Upon his breast a pentacle;
His zone of virgin parchment thin,   370
Or, as some tell, of dead man's skin,
Bore many a planetary sign,
Combust, and retrograde, and trine;
And in his hand he held prepared
A naked sword without a guard.

XXI

' Dire dealings with the fiendish race
Had marked strange lines upon his face;
Vigil and fast had worn him grim,
His eyesight dazzled seemed and dim,
As one unused to upper day;   380
Even his own menials with dismay
Beheld, Sir Knight, the grisly sire
In this unwonted wild attire;
Unwonted, for traditions run
He seldom thus beheld the sun.
" I know," he said, — his voice was hoarse,
And broken seemed its hollow force, —
" I know the cause, although untold,
Why the king seeks his vassal's hold:
Vainly from me my liege would know   390
His kingdom's future weal or woe;
But yet, if strong his arm and heart,
His courage may do more than art.

XXII

' " Of middle air the demons proud,
Who ride upon the racking cloud,
Can read in fixed or wandering star
The issue of events afar,
But still their sullen aid withhold,
Save when by mightier force controlled.
Such late I summoned to my hall;   400

And though so potent was the call
That scarce the deepest nook of hell
I deemed a refuge from the spell,
Yet, obstinate in silence still,
The haughty demon mocks my skill.
But thou, — who little know'st thy might
As born upon that blessed night
When yawning graves and dying groan
Proclaimed hell's empire overthrown, —
With untaught valor shalt compel   410
Response denied to magic spell."
" Gramercy," quoth our monarch free,
" Place him but front to front with me,
And, by this good and honored brand,
The gift of Cœur-de-Lion's hand,
Soothly I swear that, tide what tide,
The demon shall a buffet bide."
His bearing bold the wizard viewed,
And thus, well pleased, his speech renewed:
" There spoke the blood of Malcolm ! —
mark: 420
Forth pacing hence at midnight dark,
The rampart seek whose circling crown
Crests the ascent of yonder down:
A southern entrance shalt thou find;
There halt, and there thy bugle wind,
And trust thine elfin foe to see
In guise of thy worst enemy.
Couch then thy lance and spur thy steed —
Upon him ! and Saint George to speed !
If he go down, thou soon shalt know   430
Whate'er these airy sprites can show;
If thy heart fail thee in the strife,
I am no warrant for thy life."

XXIII

' Soon as the midnight bell did ring,
Alone and armed, forth rode the king
To that old camp's deserted round.
Sir Knight, you well might mark the mound
Left hand the town, — the Pictish race
The trench, long since, in blood did trace;
The moor around is brown and bare,   440
The space within is green and fair.
The spot our village children know,
For there the earliest wild-flowers grow;
But woe betide the wandering wight
That treads its circle in the night !
The breadth across, a bowshot clear,
Gives ample space for full career;
Opposed to the four points of heaven,
By four deep gaps are entrance given.
The southernmost our monarch passed,   450
Halted, and blew a gallant blast;
And on the north, within the ring,

Appeared the form of England's king,
Who then, a thousand leagues afar,
In Palestine waged holy war:
Yet arms like England's did he wield;
Alike the leopards in the shield,
Alike his Syrian courser's frame,
The rider's length of limb the same.
Long afterwards did Scotland know   460
Fell Edward was her deadliest foe.

XXIV

'The vision made our monarch start,
But soon he manned his noble heart,
And in the first career they ran,
The Elfin Knight fell, horse and man;
Yet did a splinter of his lance
Through Alexander's visor glance,
And razed the skin — a puny wound.
The king, light leaping to the ground,
With naked blade his phantom foe   470
Compelled the future war to show.
Of Largs he saw the glorious plain,
  Where still gigantic bones remain,
    Memorial of the Danish war;
Himself he saw, amid the field,
On high his brandished war-axe wield
    And strike proud Haco from his car,
While all around the shadowy kings
Denmark's grim ravens cowered their
        wings.
'T is said that in that awful night   480
Remoter visions met his sight,
Foreshowing future conquest far,
When our sons' sons wage Northern war;
A royal city, tower and spire,
Reddened the midnight sky with fire,
And shouting crews her navy bore
Triumphant to the victor shore.
Such signs may learned clerks explain,
They pass the wit of simple swain.

XXV

'The joyful king turned home again,   490
Headed his host, and quelled the Dane;
But yearly, when returned the night
Of his strange combat with the sprite,
  His wound must bleed and smart;
Lord Gifford then would gibing say,
"Bold as ye were, my liege, ye pay
  The penance of your start."
Long since, beneath Dunfermline's nave,
King Alexander fills his grave,
  Our Lady give him rest !   500
Yet still the knightly spear and shield

The Elfin Warrior doth wield
  Upon the brown hill's breast,
And many a knight hath proved his chance
In the charmed ring to break a lance,
  But all have foully sped;
Save two, as legends tell, and they
Were Wallace wight and Gilbert Hay. —
Gentles, my tale is said.'   509

XXVI

The quaighs were deep, the liquor strong,
And on the tale the yeoman-throng
Had made a comment sage and long,
  But Marmion gave a sign:
And with their lord the squires retire,
The rest around the hostel fire
  Their drowsy limbs recline;
For pillow, underneath each head
The quiver and the targe were laid.
Deep slumbering on the hostel floor,
Oppressed with toil and ale, they snore;   520
The dying flame, in fitful change,
Threw on the group its shadows strange.

XXVII

Apart, and nestling in the hay
Of a waste loft, Fitz-Eustace lay;
Scarce by the pale moonlight were seen
The foldings of his mantle green:
Lightly he dreamt, as youth will dream,
Of sport by thicket, or by stream,
Of hawk or hound, or ring or glove,
Or, lighter yet, of lady's love.   530
A cautious tread his slumber broke,
And, close beside him when he woke,
In moonbeam half, and half in gloom,
Stood a tall form with nodding plume;
But, ere his dagger Eustace drew,
His master Marmion's voice he knew:

XXVIII

' Fitz-Eustace ! rise, — I cannot rest;
Yon churl's wild legend haunts my breast,
And graver thoughts have chafed my mood;
The air must cool my feverish blood,   540
And fain would I ride forth to see
The scene of elfin chivalry.
Arise, and saddle me my steed;
And, gentle Eustace, take good heed
Thou dost not rouse these drowsy slaves;
I would not that the prating knaves
Had cause for saying, o'er their ale,
That I could credit such a tale.'
Then softly down the steps they slid,

Eustace the stable door undid,   550
And, darkling, Marmion's steed arrayed,
While, whispering, thus the baron said: —

XXIX

'Didst never, good my youth, hear tell
  That on the hour when I was born
Saint George, who graced my sire's cha-
      pelle,
Down from his steed of marble fell,
  A weary wight forlorn ?
The flattering chaplains all agree
The champion left his steed to me.
I would, the omen's truth to show,   560
  That I could meet this elfin foe !
Blithe would I battle for the right
To ask one question at the sprite. —
Vain thought ! for elves, if elves there
      be,
An empty race, by fount or sea
To dashing waters dance and sing,
Or round the green oak wheel their ring.'
Thus speaking, he his steed bestrode,
And from the hostel slowly rode.

XXX

Fitz-Eustace followed him abroad,   570
And marked him pace the village road,
  And listened to his horse's tramp,
    Till, by the lessening sound,
  He judged that of the Pictish camp
    Lord Marmion sought the round.
Wonder it seemed, in the squire's eyes,
That one, so wary held and wise, —
Of whom 't was said, he scarce received
For gospel what the Church believed, —
  Should, stirred by idle tale,   580
Ride forth in silence of the night,
As hoping half to meet a sprite,
  Arrayed in plate and mail.
For little did Fitz-Eustace know
That passions in contending flow
  Unfix the strongest mind;
Wearied from doubt to doubt to flee,
We welcome fond credulity,
  Guide confident, though blind.

XXXI

Little for this Fitz-Eustace cared,   590
But patient waited till he heard
At distance, pricked to utmost speed,
The foot-tramp of a flying steed
  Come townward rushing on;
First, dead, as if on turf it trode,
Then, clattering on the village road, —

In other pace than forth he yode,
  Returned Lord Marmion.
Down hastily he sprung from selle,
And in his haste wellnigh he fell;   600
To the squire's hand the rein he threw,
And spoke no word as he withdrew:
But yet the moonlight did betray
The falcon-crest was soiled with clay;
And plainly might Fitz-Eustace see,
By stains upon the charger's knee
And his left side, that on the moor
He had not kept his footing sure.
Long musing on these wondrous signs,
At length to rest the squire reclines,   610
Broken and short; for still between
Would dreams of terror intervene:
Eustace did ne'er so blithely mark
The first notes of the morning lark.

INTRODUCTION TO CANTO FOURTH

TO JAMES SKENE, ESQ.

Ashestiel, Ettrick Forest

An ancient Minstrel sagely said,
' Where is the life which late we led ? '
That motley clown in Arden wood,
Whom humorous Jaques with envy viewed,
Not even that clown could amplify
On this trite text so long as I.
Eleven years we now may tell
Since we have known each other well,
Since, riding side by side, our hand
First drew the voluntary brand;   10
And sure, through many a varied scene,
Unkindness never came between.
Away these winged years have flown,
To join the mass of ages gone;
And though deep marked, like all below,
With checkered shades of joy and woe,
Though thou o'er realms and seas hast
      ranged,
Marked cities lost and empires changed,
While here at home my narrower ken
Somewhat of manners saw and men;   20
Though varying wishes, hopes, and fears
Fevered the progress of these years,
Yet now, days, weeks, and months but
      seem
The recollection of a dream,
So still we glide down to the sea
Of fathomless eternity.

Even now it scarcely seems a day
Since first I tuned this idle lay;
A task so often thrown aside,
When leisure graver cares denied,   30
That now November's dreary gale,
Whose voice inspired my opening tale,
That same November gale once more
Whirls the dry leaves on Yarrow shore.
Their vexed boughs streaming to the sky,
Once more our naked birches sigh,
And Blackhouse heights and Ettrick Pen
Have donned their wintry shrouds again,
And mountain dark and flooded mead
Bid us forsake the banks of Tweed.   40
Earlier than wont along the sky,
Mixed with the rack, the snow mists fly;
The shepherd who, in summer sun,
Had something of our envy won,
As thou with pencil, I with pen,
The features traced of hill and glen, —
He who, outstretched the livelong day,
At ease among the heath-flowers lay,
Viewed the light clouds with vacant look,
Or slumbered o'er his tattered book,   50
Or idly busied him to guide
His angle o'er the lessened tide, —
At midnight now the snowy plain
Finds sterner labor for the swain.

When red hath set the beamless sun
Through heavy vapors dank and dun,
When the tired ploughman, dry and warm,
Hears, half asleep, the rising storm
Hurling the hail and sleeted rain
Against the casement's tinkling pane;   60
The sounds that drive wild deer and fox
To shelter in the brake and rocks
Are warnings which the shepherd ask
To dismal and to dangerous task.
Oft he looks forth, and hopes, in vain,
The blast may sink in mellowing rain;
Till, dark above and white below,
Decided drives the flaky snow,
And forth the hardy swain must go.
Long, with dejected look and whine,   70
To leave the hearth his dogs repine;
Whistling and cheering them to aid,
Around his back he wreathes the plaid:
His flock he gathers and he guides
To open downs and mountain-sides,
Where fiercest though the tempest blow,
Least deeply lies the drift below.
The blast that whistles o'er the fells
Stiffens his locks to icicles;
Oft he looks back while, streaming far,   80

His cottage window seems a star, —
Loses its feeble gleam, — and then
Turns patient to the blast again,
And, facing to the tempest's sweep,
Drives through the gloom his lagging
     sheep.
If fails his heart, if his limbs fail,
Benumbing death is in the gale;
His paths, his landmarks, all unknown,
Close to the hut, no more his own,
Close to the aid he sought in vain,   90
The morn may find the stiffened swain:
The widow sees, at dawning pale,
His orphans raise their feeble wail;
And, close beside him in the snow,
Poor Yarrow, partner of their woe,
Couches upon his master's breast,
And licks his cheek to break his rest.

Who envies now the shepherd's lot,
His healthy fare, his rural cot,
His summer couch by greenwood tree,   100
His rustic kirn's loud revelry,
His native hill-notes tuned on high
To Marion of the blithesome eye,
His crook, his scrip, his oaten reed,
And all Arcadia's golden creed?

Changes not so with us, my Skene,
Of human life the varying scene?
Our youthful summer oft we see
Dance by on wings of game and glee,
While the dark storm reserves its rage   110
Against the winter of our age;
As he, the ancient chief of Troy,
His manhood spent in peace and joy,
But Grecian fires and loud alarms
Called ancient Priam forth to arms.
Then happy those, since each must drain
His share of pleasure, share of pain, —
Then happy those, beloved of Heaven,
To whom the mingled cup is given;
Whose lenient sorrows find relief;   120
Whose joys are chastened by their grief.
And such a lot, my Skene, was thine,
When thou of late wert doomed to twine —
Just when thy bridal hour was by —
The cypress with the myrtle tie.
Just on thy bride her sire had smiled,
And blessed the union of his child,
When love must change its joyous cheer,
And wipe affection's filial tear.
Nor did the actions next his end   130
Speak more the father than the friend:
Scarce had lamented Forbes paid

The tribute to his minstrel's shade,
The tale of friendship scarce was told,
Ere the narrator's heart was cold —
Far may we search before we find
A heart so manly and so kind !
But not around his honored urn
Shall friends alone and kindred mourn;
The thousand eyes his care had dried   140
Pour at his name a bitter tide,
And frequent falls the grateful dew
For benefits the world ne'er knew.
If mortal charity dare claim
The Almighty's attributed name,
Inscribe above his mouldering clay,
' The widow's shield, the orphan's stay.'
Nor, though it wake thy sorrow, deem
My verse intrudes on this sad theme,
For sacred was the pen that wrote,   150
' Thy father's friend forget thou not;'
And grateful title may I plead,
For many a kindly word and deed,
To bring my tribute to his grave: —
'T is little — but 't is all I have.

To thee, perchance, this rambling strain
Recalls our summer walks again;
When, doing nought, — and, to speak true,
Not anxious to find aught to do, —
The wild unbounded hills we ranged,   160
While oft our talk its topic changed,
And, desultory as our way,
Ranged unconfined from grave to gay.
Even when it flagged, as oft will chance,
No effort made to break its trance,
We could right pleasantly pursue
Our sports in social silence too;
Thou gravely laboring to portray
The blighted oak's fantastic spray,
I spelling o'er with much delight   170
The legend of that antique knight,
Tirante by name, ycleped the White.
At either's feet a trusty squire,
Pandour and Camp, with eyes of fire,
Jealous each other's motions viewed,
And scarce suppressed their ancient feud.
The laverock whistled from the cloud;
The stream was lively, but not loud;
From the white thorn the May-flower shed
Its dewy fragrance round our head: 180
Not Ariel lived more merrily
Under the blossomed bough than we.

And blithesome nights, too, have been
  ours,
When Winter stript the Summer's bowers.

Careless we heard, what now I hear,
The wild blast sighing deep and drear,
When fires were bright and lamps beamed
  gay,
And ladies tuned the lovely lay,
And he was held a laggard soul
Who shunned to quaff the sparkling
  bowl.   190
Then he whose absence we deplore,
Who breathes the gales of Devon's shore,
The longer missed, bewailed the more,
And thou, and I, and dear-loved Rae,
And one whose name I may not say, —
For not mimosa's tender tree
Shrinks sooner from the touch than he, —
In merry chorus well combined,
With laughter drowned the whistling wind.
Mirth was within, and Care without   200
Might gnaw her nails to hear our shout.
Not but amid the buxom scene
Some grave discourse might intervene —
Of the good horse that bore him best,
His shoulder, hoof, and arching crest;
For, like mad Tom's, our chiefest care
Was horse to ride and weapon wear.
Such nights we 've had; and, though the
  game
Of manhood be more sober tame,
And though the field-day or the drill   210
Seem less important now, yet still
Such may we hope to share again.
The sprightly thought inspires my strain !
And mark how, like a horseman true,
Lord Marmion's march I thus renew.

CANTO FOURTH

THE CAMP

I

EUSTACE, I said, did blithely mark
The first notes of the merry lark.
The lark sang shrill, the cock he crew,
And loudly Marmion's bugles blew,
And with their light and lively call
Brought groom and yeoman to the stall.
  Whistling they came and free of heart,
    But soon their mood was changed;
  Complaint was heard on every part
    Of something disarranged.   10
Some clamored loud for armor lost;
Some brawled and wrangled with the host;
' By Becket's bones,' cried one, ' I fear
That some false Scot has stolen my spear !'

Young Blount, Lord Marmion's second
    squire,
Found his steed wet with sweat and mire,
Although the rated horseboy sware
Last night he dressed him sleek and fair.
While chafed the impatient squire like
    thunder,
Old Hubert shouts in fear and wonder, — 20
'Help, gentle Blount ! help, comrades all !
Bevis lies dying in his stall ;
To Marmion who the plight dare tell
Of the good steed he loves so well ? '
Gaping for fear and ruth, they saw
The charger panting on his straw ;
Till one, who would seem wisest, cried,
'What else but evil could betide,
With that cursed Palmer for our guide ?
Better we had through mire and bush   30
Been lantern-led by Friar Rush.'

II

Fitz-Eustace, who the cause but guessed,
    Nor wholly understood,
His comrades' clamorous plaints sup-
    pressed ;
He knew Lord Marmion's mood.
Him, ere he issued forth, he sought,
And found deep plunged in gloomy thought,
    And did his tale display
Simply, as if he knew of nought
    To cause such disarray.   40
Lord Marmion gave attention cold,
Nor marvelled at the wonders told, —
Passed them as accidents of course,
And bade his clarions sound to horse.

III

Young Henry Blount, meanwhile, the cost
Had reckoned with their Scottish host ;
And, as the charge he cast and paid,
'Ill thou deserv'st thy hire,' he said ;
'Dost see, thou knave, my horse's plight ?
Fairies have ridden him all the night,   50
    And left him in a foam !
I trust that soon a conjuring band,
With English cross and blazing brand,
Shall drive the devils from this land
    To their infernal home ;
For in this haunted den, I trow,
All night they trampled to and fro.'
The laughing host looked on the hire :
'Gramercy, gentle southern squire,
And if thou com'st among the rest,   60
With Scottish broadsword to be blest,
Sharp be the brand, and sure the blow,
And short the pang to undergo.'

Here stayed their talk, for Marmion
Gave now the signal to set on.
The Palmer showing forth the way,
They journeyed all the morning-day.

IV

The greensward way was smooth and good,
Through Humbie's and through Saltoun's
    wood ;
A forest glade, which, varying still,   70
Here gave a view of dale and hill,
There narrower closed till overhead
A vaulted screen the branches made.
'A pleasant path,' Fitz-Eustace said ;
'Such as where errant-knights might see
Adventures of high chivalry,
Might meet some damsel flying fast,
With hair unbound and looks aghast ;
And smooth and level course were here,
In her defence to break a spear.   80
Here, too, are twilight nooks and dells ;
And oft in such, the story tells,
The damsel kind, from danger freed,
Did grateful pay her champion's meed.'
He spoke to cheer Lord Marmion's mind,
Perchance to show his lore designed ;
    For Eustace much had pored
Upon a huge romantic tome,
In the hall-window of his home,
Imprinted at the antique dome   90
    Of Caxton or de Worde.
Therefore he spoke, — but spoke in vain,
For Marmion answered nought again.

V

Now sudden, distant trumpets shrill,
In notes prolonged by wood and hill,
    Were heard to echo far ;
Each ready archer grasped his bow,
But by the flourish soon they know
    They breathed no point of war.
Yet cautious, as in foeman's land,   100
Lord Marmion's order speeds the band
    Some opener ground to gain ;
And scarce a furlong had they rode,
When thinner trees receding showed
    A little woodland plain.
Just in that advantageous glade
The halting troop a line had made,
As forth from the opposing shade
    Issued a gallant train.   109

VI

First came the trumpets, at whose clang
So late the forest echoes rang ;
On prancing steeds they forward pressed,

With scarlet mantle, azure vest;
Each at his trump a banner wore,
Which Scotland's royal scutcheon bore:
Heralds and pursuivants, by name
Bute, Islay, Marchmount, Rothsay, came,
In painted tabards, proudly showing
Gules, argent, or, and azure glowing,
  Attendant on a king-at-arms,   120
Whose hand the armorial truncheon held
That feudal strife had often quelled
  When wildest its alarms.

VII

He was a man of middle age,
In aspect manly, grave, and sage,
  As on king's errand come;
But in the glances of his eye
A penetrating, keen, and sly
  Expression found its home;
The flash of that satiric rage   130
Which, bursting on the early stage,
Branded the vices of the age,
  And broke the keys of Rome.
On milk-white palfrey forth he paced;
His cap of maintenance was graced
  With the proud heron-plume.
From his steed's shoulder, loin, and breast,
Silk housings swept the ground,
With Scotland's arms, device, and crest,
  Embroidered round and round.   140
The double tressure might you see,
First by Achaius borne,
The thistle and the fleur-de-lis,
  And gallant unicorn.
So bright the king's armorial coat
That scarce the dazzled eye could note,
In living colors blazoned brave,
The Lion, which his title gave;
A train, which well beseemed his state,
But all unarmed, around him wait.   150
  Still is thy name in high account,
    And still thy verse has charms,
  Sir David Lindesay of the Mount,
    Lord Lion King-at-arms!

VIII

Down from his horse did Marmion spring
Soon as he saw the Lion-King;
For well the stately baron knew
To him such courtesy was due
Whom royal James himself had crowned,
And on his temples placed the round   160
  Of Scotland's ancient diadem,
And wet his brow with hallowed wine,
And on his finger given to shine

  The emblematic gem.
Their mutual greetings duly made,
The Lion thus his message said: —
'Though Scotland's King hath deeply
    swore
Ne'er to knit faith with Henry more,
And strictly hath forbid resort
From England to his royal court,   170
Yet, for he knows Lord Marmion's name
And honors much his warlike fame,
My liege hath deemed it shame and lack
Of courtesy to turn him back;
And by his order I, your guide,
Must lodging fit and fair provide
Till finds King James meet time to see
The flower of English chivalry.'

IX

Though inly chafed at this delay,
Lord Marmion bears it as he may.   180
The Palmer, his mysterious guide,
Beholding thus his place supplied,
  Sought to take leave in vain;
Strict was the Lion-King's command
That none who rode in Marmion's band
  Should sever from the train.
'England has here enow of spies
In Lady Heron's witching eyes:'
To Marchmount thus apart he said,
But fair pretext to Marmion made.   190
The right-hand path they now decline,
And trace against the stream the Tyne.

X

At length up that wild dale they wind,
  Where Crichtoun Castle crowns the bank;
For there the Lion's care assigned
  A lodging meet for Marmion's rank.
That castle rises on the steep
  Of the green vale of Tyne;
And far beneath, where slow they creep
From pool to eddy, dark and deep,   200
Where alders moist and willows weep,
  You hear her streams repine.
The towers in different ages rose,
Their various architecture shows
  The builders' various hands;
A mighty mass, that could oppose,
When deadliest hatred fired its foes,
  The vengeful Douglas bands.

XI

Crichtoun! though now thy miry court
  But pens the lazy steer and sheep,   210
  Thy turrets rude and tottered keep

Have been the minstrel's loved resort.
Oft have I traced, within thy fort,
  Of mouldering shields the mystic sense,
  Scutcheons of honor or pretence,
Quartered in old armorial sort,
  Remains of rude magnificence.
Nor wholly yet hath time defaced
  Thy lordly gallery fair,
Nor yet the stony cord unbraced   220
Whose twisted knots, with roses laced,
  Adorn thy ruined stair.
Still rises unimpaired below
The court-yard's graceful portico;
Above its cornice, row and row
Of fair-hewn facets richly show
  Their pointed diamond form,
Though there but houseless cattle go,
  To shield them from the storm.
And, shuddering, still may we explore, 230
  Where oft whilom were captives pent,
The darkness of thy Massy More,
  Or, from thy grass-grown battlement,
May trace in undulating line
The sluggish mazes of the Tyne.

XII

Another aspect Crichtoun showed
As through its portal Marmion rode;
But yet 't was melancholy state
Received him at the outer gate,
For none were in the castle then   240
But women, boys, or aged men.
With eyes scarce dried, the sorrowing
    dame
To welcome noble Marmion came;
Her son, a stripling twelve years old,
Proffered the baron's rein to hold:
For each man that could draw a sword
Had marched that morning with their
    lord,
Earl Adam Hepburn, — he who died
On Flodden by his sovereign's side.
Long may his lady look in vain !   250
She ne'er shall see his gallant train
Come sweeping back through Crichtoun-
    Dean.
'T was a brave race before the name
Of hated Bothwell stained their fame.

XIII

And here two days did Marmion rest,
  With every right that honor claims,
Attended as the king's own guest; —
  Such the command of Royal James,
Who marshalled then his land's array,

Upon the Borough-moor that lay.   260
Perchance he would not foeman's eye
Upon his gathering host should pry,
Till full prepared was every band
To march against the English land.
Here while they dwelt, did Lindesay's wit
Oft cheer the baron's moodier fit;
And, in his turn, he knew to prize
Lord Marmion's powerful mind and
    wise, —
Trained in the lore of Rome and Greece,
And policies of war and peace.   270

XIV

It chanced, as fell the second night,
  That on the battlements they walked,
And by the slowly fading light
  Of varying topics talked;
And, unaware, the herald-bard
Said Marmion might his toil have spared
  In travelling so far,
For that a messenger from heaven
In vain to James had counsel given
  Against the English war;   280
And, closer questioned, thus he told
A tale which chronicles of old
In Scottish story have enrolled: —

XV

SIR DAVID LINDESAY'S TALE

'Of all the palaces so fair,
  Built for the royal dwelling
In Scotland, far beyond compare
  Linlithgow is excelling;
And in its park, in jovial June,
How sweet the merry linnet's tune,
  How blithe the blackbird's lay !   290
The wild buck bells from ferny brake,
The coot dives merry on the lake,
The saddest heart might pleasure take
  To see all nature gay.
But June is to our sovereign dear
The heaviest month in all the year;
Too well his cause of grief you know,
June saw his father's overthrow.
Woe to the traitors who could bring
The princely boy against his king !   300
Still in his conscience burns the sting.
In offices as strict as Lent
King James's June is ever spent.

XVI

' When last this ruthful month was come,
And in Linlithgow's holy dome
  The king, as wont, was praying;

While for his royal father's soul
The chanters sung, the bells did toll,
  The bishop mass was saying —
For now the year brought round again   310
The day the luckless king was slain —
In Catherine's aisle the monarch knelt,
With sackcloth shirt and iron belt,
  And eyes with sorrow streaming;
Around him in their stalls of state
The Thistle's Knight-Companions sate,
  Their banners o'er them beaming.
I too was there, and, sooth to tell,
Bedeafened with the jangling knell,   319
Was watching where the sunbeams fell,
  Through the stained casement gleam-
    ing;
But while I marked what next befell
  It seemed as I were dreaming.
Stepped from the crowd a ghostly wight,
In azure gown, with cincture white;
His forehead bald, his head was bare,
Down hung at length his yellow hair. —
Now, mock me not when, good my lord,
I pledge to you my knightly word
That when I saw his placid grace,   330
His simple majesty of face,
His solemn bearing, and his pace
  So stately gliding on, —
Seemed to me ne'er did limner paint
So just an image of the saint
Who propped the Virgin in her faint,
  The loved Apostle John !

XVII

' He stepped before the monarch's chair,
And stood with rustic plainness there,
  And little reverence made;   340
Nor head, nor body, bowed, nor bent,
But on the desk his arm he leant,
  And words like these he said,
In a low voice, — but never tone
So thrilled through vein, and nerve, and
    bone: —
" My mother sent me from afar,
Sir King, to warn thee not to war, —
  Woe waits on thine array;
If war thou wilt, of woman fair,
Her witching wiles and wanton snare,   350
James Stuart, doubly warned, beware:
  God keep thee as He may ! " —
The wondering monarch seemed to seek
  For answer, and found none;
And when he raised his head to speak,
  The monitor was gone.
The marshal and myself had cast

To stop him as he outward passed;
But, lighter than the whirlwind's blast,
  He vanished from our eyes,   360
Like sunbeam on the billow cast,
  That glances but, and dies.'

XVIII

While Lindesay told his marvel strange
  The twilight was so pale,
He marked not Marmion's color change
  While listening to the tale;
But, after a suspended pause,
The baron spoke: ' Of Nature's laws
  So strong I held the force,
That never superhuman cause   370
  Could e'er control their course,
And, three days since, had judged your aim
Was but to make your guest your game;
But I have seen, since past the Tweed,
What much has changed my sceptic creed,
And made me credit aught.' — He stayed,
And seemed to wish his words unsaid,
But, by that strong emotion pressed
Which prompts us to unload our breast
  Even when discovery's pain,   380
To Lindesay did at length unfold
The tale his village host had told,
  At Gifford, to his train.
Nought of the Palmer says he there,
And nought of Constance or of Clare;
The thoughts which broke his sleep he seems
To mention but as feverish dreams.

XIX

' In vain,' said he, ' to rest I spread
My burning limbs, and couched my head;
  Fantastic thoughts returned,   390
And, by their wild dominion led,
  My heart within me burned.
So sore was the delirious goad,
I took my steed and forth I rode,
And, as the moon shone bright and cold,
Soon reached the camp upon the wold.
The southern entrance I passed through,
And halted, and my bugle blew.
Methought an answer met my ear, —
Yet was the blast so low and drear,   400
So hollow, and so faintly blown,
It might be echo of my own.

XX

' Thus judging, for a little space
I listened ere I left the place,
  But scarce could trust my eyes,
Nor yet can think they serve me true,

When sudden in the ring I view,
In form distinct of shape and hue,
  A mounted champion rise. —
I 've fought, Lord-Lion, many a day,   410
In single fight and mixed affray,
And ever, I myself may say,
  Have borne me as a knight;
But when this unexpected foe
Seemed starting from the gulf below, —
I care not though the truth I show, —
  I trembled with affright;
And as I placed in rest my spear,
My hand so shook for very fear,
  I scarce could couch it right.   420

XXI

' Why need my tongue the issue tell ?
We ran our course, — my charger fell; —
What could he 'gainst the shock of hell ?
  I rolled upon the plain.
High o'er my head with threatening hand
The spectre shook his naked brand, —
  Yet did the worst remain:
My dazzled eyes I upward cast, —
Not opening hell itself could blast
  Their sight like what I saw !   430
Full on his face the moonbeam strook ! —
A face could never be mistook !
I knew the stern vindictive look,
  And held my breath for awe.
I saw the face of one who, fled
To foreign climes, has long been dead, —
  I well believe the last;
For ne'er from visor raised did stare
A human warrior with a glare
  So grimly and so ghast.   440
Thrice o'er my head he shook the blade;
But when to good Saint George I
    prayed, —
The first time e'er I asked his aid, —
  He plunged it in the sheath,
And, on his courser mounting light,
He seemed to vanish from my sight:
The moonbeam drooped, and deepest night
  Sunk down upon the heath. —
'T were long to tell what cause I have
  To know his face that met me there,   450
Called by his hatred from the grave
  To cumber upper air;
Dead or alive, good cause had he
To be my mortal enemy.'

XXII

Marvelled Sir David of the Mount;
Then, learned in story, gan recount

Such chance had happed of old,
When once, near Norham, there did fight
A spectre fell of fiendish might,
In likeness of a Scottish knight,   460
  With Brian Bulmer bold,
And trained him nigh to disallow
The aid of his baptismal vow.
' And such a phantom, too, 't is said,
With Highland broadsword, targe, and
    plaid,
  And fingers red with gore,
Is seen in Rothiemurcus glade,
Or where the sable pine-trees shade
Dark Tomantoul, and Auchnaslaid,
  Dromouchty, or Glenmore.   470
And yet, whate'er such legends say
Of warlike demon, ghost, or fay,
  On mountain, moor, or plain,
Spotless in faith, in bosom bold,
True son of chivalry should hold
  These midnight terrors vain;
For seldom have such spirits power
To harm, save in the evil hour
When guilt we meditate within
Or harbor unrepented sin.' —   480
Lord Marmion turned him half aside,
And twice to clear his voice he tried,
  Then pressed Sir David's hand, —
But nought, at length, in answer said;
And here their further converse stayed,
  Each ordering that his band
Should bowne them with the rising day,
To Scotland's camp to take their way, —
  Such was the king's command.

XXIII

Early they took Dun-Edin's road,   490
And I could trace each step they trode;
Hill, brook, nor dell, nor rock, nor stone,
Lies on the path to me unknown.
Much might it boast of storied lore;
But, passing such digression o'er,
Suffice it that their route was laid
Across the furzy hills of Braid.
They passed the glen and scanty rill,
And climbed the opposing bank, until
They gained the top of Blackford Hill.   500

XXIV

Blackford ! on whose uncultured breast,
  Among the broom and thorn and whin,
A truant-boy, I sought the nest,
Or listed, as I lay at rest,
  While rose on breezes thin
The murmur of the city crowd,

And, from his steeple jangling loud,
  Saint Giles's mingling din.
Now, from the summit to the plain,
Waves all the hill with yellow grain;   510
  And o'er the landscape as I look,
Nought do I see unchanged remain,
  Save the rude cliffs and chiming brook.
To me they make a heavy moan
Of early friendships past and gone.

XXV

But different far the change has been,
  Since Marmion from the crown
Of Blackford saw that martial scene
  Upon the bent so brown:
Thousand pavilions, white as snow,   520
Spread all the Borough-moor below,
  Upland, and dale, and down.
A thousand did I say? I ween,
Thousands on thousands there were seen,
That checkered all the heath between
  The streamlet and the town,
In crossing ranks extending far,
  Forming a camp irregular;
Oft giving way where still there stood
Some relics of the old oak wood,   530
  That darkly huge did intervene
And tamed the glaring white with green:
In these extended lines there lay
A martial kingdom's vast array.

XXVI

For from Hebudes, dark with rain,
To eastern Lodon's fertile plain,
And from the southern Redswire edge
To furthest Rosse's rocky ledge,
From west to east, from south to north,
Scotland sent all her warriors forth.   540
Marmion might hear the mingled hum
Of myriads up the mountain come, —
The horses' tramp and tinkling clank,
Where chiefs reviewed their vassal rank,
  And charger's shrilling neigh, —
And see the shifting lines advance,
While frequent flashed from shield and lance
  The sun's reflected ray.

XXVII

Thin curling in the morning air,
The wreaths of failing smoke declare   550
To embers now the brands decayed,
Where the night - watch their fires had made.
They saw, slow rolling on the plain,

Full many a baggage-cart and wain,
And dire artillery's clumsy car,
By sluggish oxen tugged to war;
And there were Borthwick's Sisters Seven,
And culverins which France had given.
Ill-omened gift! the guns remain
The conqueror's spoil on Flodden plain. 560

XXVIII

Nor marked they less where in the air
A thousand streamers flaunted fair;
  Various in shape, device, and hue,
  Green, sanguine, purple, red, and blue,
Broad, narrow, swallow-tailed, and square,
Scroll, pennon, pencil, bandrol, there
  O'er the pavilions flew.
Highest and midmost, was descried
The royal banner floating wide;
  The staff, a pine-tree, strong and straight,   570
  Pitched deeply in a massive stone,
  Which still in memory is shown,
  Yet bent beneath the standard's weight,
  Whene'er the western wind unrolled
  With toil the huge and cumbrous fold,
And gave to view the dazzling field,
Where in proud Scotland's royal shield
The ruddy lion ramped in gold.

XXIX

Lord Marmion viewed the landscape bright,
He viewed it with a chief's delight,   580
  Until within him burned his heart,
  And lightning from his eye did part,
  As on the battle-day;
Such glance did falcon never dart
  When stooping on his prey.
' Oh! well, Lord-Lion, hast thou said,
Thy king from warfare to dissuade
  Were but a vain essay;
For, by Saint George, were that host mine,
Not power infernal nor divine   590
Should once to peace my soul incline,
Till I had dimmed their armor's shine
  In glorious battle-fray!'
Answered the bard, of milder mood:
' Fair is the sight, — and yet 't were good
  That kings would think withal,
When peace and wealth their land has blessed,
'T is better to sit still at rest
  Than rise, perchance to fall.'

XXX

Still on the spot Lord Marmion stayed, 600
For fairer scene he ne'er surveyed.
When sated with the martial show
That peopled all the plain below,
The wandering eye could o'er it go,
And mark the distant city glow
  With gloomy splendor red;
For on the smoke-wreaths, huge and slow,
That round her sable turrets flow,
  The morning beams were shed,
And tinged them with a lustre proud, 610
Like that which streaks a thunder-cloud.
Such dusky grandeur clothed the height
Where the huge castle holds its state,
  And all the steep slope down,
Whose ridgy back heaves to the sky,
Piled deep and massy, close and high,
  Mine own romantic town!
But northward far, with purer blaze,
On Ochil mountains fell the rays,
And as each heathy top they kissed, 620
  It gleamed a purple amethyst.
Yonder the shores of Fife you saw,
Here Preston-Bay and Berwick-Law;
  And, broad between them rolled,
The gallant Firth the eye might note,
Whose islands on its bosom float,
  Like emeralds chased in gold.
Fitz-Eustace's heart felt closely pent;
As if to give his rapture vent,
The spur he to his charger lent, 630
  And raised his bridle hand,
And making demi-volt in air,
Cried, 'Where 's the coward that would
      not dare
  To fight for such a land!'
The Lindesay smiled his joy to see,
Nor Marmion's frown repressed his glee.

XXXI

Thus while they looked, a flourish proud,
Where mingled trump, and clarion loud,
  And fife, and kettle-drum,
And sackbut deep, and psaltery, 640
And war-pipe with discordant cry,
And cymbal clattering to the sky,
Making wild music bold and high,
  Did up the mountain come;
The whilst the bells with distant chime
Merrily tolled the hour of prime,
  And thus the Lindesay spoke:
'Thus clamor still the war-notes when
The king to mass his way has ta'en,
Or to Saint Catherine's of Sienne, 650

Or Chapel of Saint Rocque.
To you they speak of martial fame,
But me remind of peaceful game,
  When blither was their cheer,
Thrilling in Falkland-woods the air,
In signal none his steed should spare,
But strive which foremost might repair
  To the downfall of the deer.

XXXII

'Nor less,' he said, 'when looking forth
I view yon Empress of the North 660
  Sit on her hilly throne,
Her palace's imperial bowers,
Her castle, proof to hostile powers,
Her stately halls and holy towers —
  Nor less,' he said, 'I moan
To think what woe mischance may bring,
And how these merry bells may ring
The death-dirge of our gallant king,
  Or with their larum call
The burghers forth to watch and ward, 670
'Gainst Southern sack and fires to guard
  Dun-Edin's leaguered wall.—
But not for my presaging thought,
Dream conquest sure or cheaply bought!
Lord Marmion, I say nay:
God is the guider of the field,
He breaks the champion's spear and shield;
  But thou thyself shalt say,
When joins yon host in deadly stowre, 679
That England's dames must weep in bower,
  Her monks the death-mass sing;
For never saw'st thou such a power
  Led on by such a king.'
And now, down winding to the plain,
The barriers of the camp they gain,
  And there they made a stay. —
There stays the Minstrel, till he fling
His hand o'er every Border string,
And fit his harp the pomp to sing
Of Scotland's ancient court and king, 690
  In the succeeding lay.

INTRODUCTION TO CANTO FIFTH

TO GEORGE ELLIS, ESQ.

Edinburgh

WHEN dark December glooms the day,
And takes our autumn joys away;
When short and scant the sunbeam throws
Upon the weary waste of snows

A cold and profitless regard,
Like patron on a needy bard;
When sylvan occupation's done,
And o'er the chimney rests the gun,
And hang in idle trophy near,
The game-pouch, fishing-rod, and spear;   10
When wiry terrier, rough and grim,
And greyhound, with his length of limb,
And pointer, now employed no more,
Cumber our parlor's narrow floor;
When in his stall the impatient steed
Is long condemned to rest and feed;
When from our snow-encircled home
Scarce cares the hardiest step to roam,
Since path is none, save that to bring
The needful water from the spring;   20
When wrinkled news-page, thrice conned
      o'er,
Beguiles the dreary hour no more,
And darkling politician, crossed,
Inveighs against the lingering post,
And answering housewife sore complains
Of carriers' snow-impeded wains; —
When such the country-cheer, I come
Well pleased to seek our city home;
For converse and for books to change
The forest's melancholy range,   30
And welcome with renewed delight
The busy day and social night.

Not here need my desponding rhyme
Lament the ravages of time,
As erst by Newark's riven towers,
And Ettrick stripped of forest bowers.
True, Caledonia's Queen is changed
Since on her dusky summit ranged,
Within its steepy limits pent
By bulwark, line, and battlement,   40
And flanking towers, and laky flood,
Guarded and garrisoned she stood,
Denying entrance or resort
Save at each tall embattled port,
Above whose arch, suspended, hung
Portcullis spiked with iron prong.
That long is gone, — but not so long
Since, early closed and opening late,
Jealous revolved the studded gate,
Whose task, from eve to morning tide,   50
A wicket churlishly supplied.
Stern then and steel-girt was thy brow,
Dun-Edin ! Oh, how altered now,
When safe amid thy mountain court
Thou sitt'st, like empress at her sport,
And liberal, unconfined, and free,
Flinging thy white arms to the sea,

For thy dark cloud, with umbered lower,
That hung o'er cliff and lake and tower,
Thou gleam'st against the western ray   60
Ten thousand lines of brighter day !

Not she, the championess of old,
In Spenser's magic tale enrolled,
She for the charmed spear renowned,
Which forced each knight to kiss the
      ground, —
Not she more changed, when, placed at
      rest,
What time she was Malbecco's guest,
She gave to flow her maiden vest,
When, from the corselet's grasp relieved,
Free to the sight her bosom heaved: 70
Sweet was her blue eye's modest smile,
Erst hidden by the aventayle,
And down her shoulders graceful rolled
Her locks profuse of paly gold.
They who whilom in midnight fight
Had marvelled at her matchless might,
No less her maiden charms approved,
But looking liked, and liking loved.
The sight could jealous pangs beguile,
And charm Malbecco's cares awhile;   80
And he, the wandering Squire of Dames,
Forgot his Columbella's claims,
And passion, erst unknown, could gain
The breast of blunt Sir Satyrane;
Nor durst light Paridell advance,
Bold as he was, a looser glance.
She charmed, at once, and tamed the heart,
Incomparable Britomart !

So thou, fair City ! disarrayed
Of battled wall and rampart's aid,   90
As stately seem'st, but lovelier far
Than in that panoply of war.
Nor deem that from thy fenceless throne
Strength and security are flown;
Still as of yore, Queen of the North !
Still canst thou send thy children forth.
Ne'er readier at alarm-bell's call
Thy burghers rose to man thy wall
Than now, in danger, shall be thine,
Thy dauntless voluntary line;   100
For fosse and turret proud to stand,
Their breasts the bulwarks of the land.
Thy thousands, trained to martial toil,
Full red would stain their native soil,
Ere from thy mural crown there fell
The slightest knosp or pinnacle.
And if it come, as come it may,
Dun-Edin ! that eventful day,

Renowned for hospitable deed,   109
That virtue much with Heaven may plead,
In patriarchal times whose care
Descending angels deigned to share;
That claim may wrestle blessings down
On those who fight for the Good Town,
Destined in every age to be
Refuge of injured royalty;
Since first, when conquering York arose,
To Henry meek she gave repose,
Till late, with wonder, grief, and awe,
Great Bourbon's relics sad she saw.   120

Truce to these thoughts ! — for, as they
          rise,
How gladly I avert mine eyes,
Bodings, or true or false, to change
For Fiction's fair romantic range,
Or for tradition's dubious light,
That hovers 'twixt the day and night:
Dazzling alternately and dim,
Her wavering lamp I 'd rather trim,
Knights, squires, and lovely dames to see,
Creation of my fantasy,   130
Than gaze abroad on reeky fen,
And make of mists invading men. —
Who loves not more the night of June
Than dull December's gloomy noon ?
The moonlight than the fog of frost ?
And can we say which cheats the most ?

But who shall teach my harp to gain
A sound of the romantic strain
Whose Anglo-Norman tones whilere
Could win the royal Henry's ear,   140
Famed Beauclerk called, for that he loved
The minstrel and his lay approved ?
Who shall these lingering notes redeem,
Decaying on Oblivion's stream;
Such notes as from the Breton tongue
Marie translated, Blondel sung ? —
Oh ! born Time's ravage to repair,
And make the dying Muse thy care;
Who, when his scythe her hoary foe
Was poising for the final blow,   150
The weapon from his hand could ring,
And break his glass and shear his wing,
And bid, reviving in his strain,
The gentle poet live again;
Thou, who canst give to lightest lay
An unpedantic moral gay,
Nor less the dullest theme bid flit
On wings of unexpected wit;
In letters as in life approved,
Example honored and beloved, —   160

Dear ELLIS ! to the bard impart
A lesson of thy magic art,
To win at once the head and heart, —
At once to charm, instruct, and mend,
My guide, my pattern, and my friend !

Such minstrel lesson to bestow
Be long thy pleasing task, — but, oh !
No more by thy example teach
What few can practise, all can preach, —
With even patience to endure   170
Lingering disease and painful cure,
And boast affliction's pangs subdued
By mild and manly fortitude.
Enough, the lesson has been given:
Forbid the repetition, Heaven !

Come listen, then ! for thou hast known
And loved the Minstrel's varying tone,
Who, like his Border sires of old,
Waked a wild measure rude and bold,
Till Windsor's oaks and Ascot plain   180
With wonder heard the Northern strain.
Come listen ! bold in thy applause,
The bard shall scorn pedantic laws;
And, as the ancient art could stain
Achievements on the storied pane,
Irregularly traced and planned,
But yet so glowing and so grand,
So shall he strive, in changeful hue,
Field, feast, and combat to renew,
And loves, and arms, and harpers' glee,   190
And all the pomp of chivalry.

CANTO FIFTH

THE COURT

I

THE train has left the hills of Braid;
The barrier guard have open made —
So Lindesay bade — the palisade
     That closed the tented ground;
Their men the warders backward drew,
And carried pikes as they rode through
     Into its ample bound.
Fast ran the Scottish warriors there,
Upon the Southern band to stare,
And envy with their wonder rose,   10
To see such well-appointed foes;
Such length of shafts, such mighty bows,
So huge that many simply thought
But for a vaunt such weapons wrought,
And little deemed their force to feel

Through links of mail and plates of steel
When, rattling upon Flodden vale,
The cloth-yard arrows flew like hail.

II

Nor less did Marmion's skilful view
Glance every line and squadron through, 20
And much he marvelled one small land
Could marshal forth such various band;
  For men-at-arms were here,
Heavily sheathed in mail and plate,
Like iron towers for strength and weight,
On Flemish steeds of bone and height,
  With battle-axe and spear.
Young knights and squires, a lighter
  train,
Practised their chargers on the plain,
By aid of leg, of hand, and rein, 30
  Each warlike feat to show,
To pass, to wheel, the croupe to gain,
And high curvet, that not in vain
The sword-sway might descend amain
  On foeman's casque below.
He saw the hardy burghers there
March armed on foot with faces bare,
  For visor they wore none,
Nor waving plume, nor crest of knight;
But burnished were their corselets bright, 40
Their brigantines and gorgets light
  Like very silver shone.
Long pikes they had for standing fight,
  Two-handed swords they wore,
And many wielded mace of weight,
  And bucklers bright they bore.

III

On foot the yeoman too, but dressed
In his steel-jack, a swarthy vest,
  With iron quilted well;
Each at his back — a slender store — 50
His forty days' provision bore,
  As feudal statutes tell.
His arms were halbert, axe, or spear,
A crossbow there, a hagbut here,
  A dagger-knife, and brand.
Sober he seemed and sad of cheer,
As loath to leave his cottage dear
  And march to foreign strand,
Or musing who would guide his steer
  To till the fallow land. 60
Yet deem not in his thoughtful eye
Did aught of dastard terror lie;
  More dreadful far his ire
Than theirs who, scorning danger's name,
In eager mood to battle came,

Their valor like light straw on flame,
  A fierce but fading fire.

IV

Not so the Borderer: — bred to war,
He knew the battle's din afar,
  And joyed to hear it swell. 70
His peaceful day was slothful ease;
Nor harp nor pipe his ear could please
  Like the loud slogan yell.
On active steed, with lance and blade,
The light-armed pricker plied his trade, —
  Let nobles fight for fame;
Let vassals follow where they lead,
Burghers, to guard their townships, bleed,
  But war's the Borderers' game.
Their gain, their glory, their delight, 80
To sleep the day, maraud the night,
  O'er mountain, moss, and moor;
Joyful to fight they took their way,
Scarce caring who might win the day,
  Their booty was secure.
These, as Lord Marmion's train passed by,
Looked on at first with careless eye,
Nor marvelled aught, well taught to know
The form and force of English bow.
But when they saw the lord arrayed 90
In splendid arms and rich brocade,
Each Borderer to his kinsman said, —
' Hist, Ringan! seest thou there!
Canst guess which road they 'll homeward
  ride?
Oh! could we but on Border side,
By Eusedale glen, or Liddell's tide,
  Beset a prize so fair!
That fangless Lion, too, their guide,
Might chance to lose his glistering hide;
Brown Maudlin of that doublet pied 100
  Could make a kirtle rare.'

V

Next, Marmion marked the Celtic race,
Of different language, form, and face,
  A various race of man;
Just then the chiefs their tribes arrayed,
And wild and garish semblance made
The checkered trews and belted plaid,
And varying notes the war-pipes brayed
  To every varying clan.
Wild through their red or sable hair 110
Looked out their eyes with savage stare
  On Marmion as he passed;
Their legs above the knee were bare;
Their frame was sinewy, short, and spare,
  And hardened to the blast;

Of taller race, the chiefs they own
Were by the eagle's plumage known.
The hunted red-deer's undressed hide
Their hairy buskins well supplied;
The graceful bonnet decked their head; 120
Back from their shoulders hung the plaid;
A broadsword of unwieldy length,
A dagger proved for edge and strength,
  A studded targe they wore,
And quivers, bows, and shafts, — but, oh !
Short was the shaft and weak the bow
  To that which England bore.
The Isles-men carried at their backs
The ancient Danish battle-axe.
They raised a wild and wondering cry, 130
As with his guide rode Marmion by.
Loud were their clamoring tongues, as when
The clanging sea-fowl leave the fen,
And, with their cries discordant mixed,
Grumbled and yelled the pipes betwixt.

VI

Thus through the Scottish camp they passed,
And reached the city gate at last,
Where all around, a wakeful guard,
Armed burghers kept their watch and ward.
Well had they cause of jealous fear, 140
When lay encamped in field so near
The Borderer and the Mountaineer.
As through the bustling streets they go,
All was alive with martial show;
At every turn with dinning clang
The armorer's anvil clashed and rang,
Or toiled the swarthy smith to wheel
The bar that arms the charger's heel,
Or axe or falchion to the side
Of jarring grindstone was applied. 150
Page, groom, and squire, with hurrying pace,
Through street and lane and market-place,
  Bore lance or casque or sword;
While burghers, with important face,
Described each new-come lord,
Discussed his lineage, told his name,
His following, and his warlike fame.
The Lion led to lodging meet,
Which high o'erlooked the crowded street;
  There must the baron rest 160
Till past the hour of vesper tide,
And then to Holy-Rood must ride, —
  Such was the king's behest.
Meanwhile the Lion's care assigns

A banquet rich and costly wines
  To Marmion and his train;
And when the appointed hour succeeds,
The baron dons his peaceful weeds,
And following Lindesay as he leads,
  The palace halls they gain. 170

VII

Old Holy-Rood rung merrily
That night with wassail, mirth, and glee:
King James within her princely bower
Feasted the chiefs of Scotland's power,
Summoned to spend the parting hour;
For he had charged that his array
Should southward march by break of day.
Well loved that splendid monarch aye
  The banquet and the song,
By day the tourney, and by night 180
The merry dance, traced fast and light,
The maskers quaint, the pageant bright,
  The revel loud and long.
This feast outshone his banquets past;
It was his blithest — and his last.
The dazzling lamps from gallery gay
Cast on the court a dancing ray;
Here to the harp did minstrels sing,
There ladies touched a softer string;
With long-eared cap and motley vest, 190
The licensed fool retailed his jest;
His magic tricks the juggler plied;
At dice and draughts the gallants vied;
While some, in close recess apart,
Courted the ladies of their heart,
  Nor courted them in vain;
For often in the parting hour
Victorious Love asserts his power
  O'er coldness and disdain;
And flinty is her heart can view 200
To battle march a lover true —
Can hear, perchance, his last adieu,
  Nor own her share of pain.

VIII

Through this mixed crowd of glee and game
The king to greet Lord Marmion came,
  While, reverent, all made room.
An easy task it was, I trow,
King James's manly form to know,
Although, his courtesy to show,
He doffed to Marmion bending low 210
  His broidered cap and plume.
For royal were his garb and mien:

His cloak of crimson velvet piled,
  Trimmed with the fur of marten wild,
His vest of changeful satin sheen,
  The dazzled eye beguiled;
His gorgeous collar hung adown,
Wrought with the badge of Scotland's
    crown,
The thistle brave of old renown;
His trusty blade, Toledo right,   220
Descended from a baldric bright;
White were his buskins, on the heel
His spurs inlaid of gold and steel;
His bonnet, all of crimson fair,
Was buttoned with a ruby rare:
And Marmion deemed he ne'er had seen
A prince of such a noble mien.

IX

The monarch's form was middle size,
For feat of strength or exercise
  Shaped in proportion fair;   230
And hazel was his eagle eye,
And auburn of the darkest dye
  His short curled beard and hair.
Light was his footstep in the dance,
  And firm his stirrup in the lists;
And, oh! he had that merry glance
  That seldom lady's heart resists.
Lightly from fair to fair he flew,
And loved to plead, lament, and sue, —
Suit lightly won and short-lived pain,   240
For monarchs seldom sigh in vain.
  I said he joyed in banquet bower;
But, mid his mirth, 't was often strange
How suddenly his cheer would change,
  His look o'ercast and lower,
If in a sudden turn he felt
The pressure of his iron belt,
That bound his breast in penance pain,
In memory of his father slain.
Even so 't was strange how evermore,   250
Soon as the passing pang was o'er,
Forward he rushed with double glee
Into the stream of revelry.
Thus dim-seen object of affright
Startles the courser in his flight,
And half he halts, half springs aside,
But feels the quickening spur applied,
And, straining on the tightened rein,
Scours doubly swift o'er hill and plain.

X

O'er James's heart, the courtiers say,   260
Sir Hugh the Heron's wife held sway;
  To Scotland's court she came,

To be a hostage for her lord,
Who Cessford's gallant heart had gored,
And with the king to make accord
  Had sent his lovely dame.
Nor to that lady free alone
Did the gay king allegiance own;
  For the fair Queen of France
Sent him a turquoise ring and glove,   270
And charged him, as her knight and love,
  For her to break a lance,
And strike three strokes with Scottish
    brand,
And march three miles on Southron land
And bid the banners of his band
  In English breezes dance.
And thus for France's queen he drest
His manly limbs in mailed vest,
And thus admitted English fair
His inmost councils still to share,   280
And thus for both he madly planned
The ruin of himself and land!
  And yet, the sooth to tell,
Nor England's fair nor France's queen
Were worth one pearl-drop, bright and
    sheen,
  From Margaret's eyes that fell, —
His own Queen Margaret, who in Lith-
    gow's bower
All lonely sat and wept the weary hour.

XI

The queen sits lone in Lithgow pile,
  And weeps the weary day   290
The war against her native soil,
  Her monarch's risk in battle broil, —
And in gay Holy-Rood the while
Dame Heron rises with a smile
  Upon the harp to play.
Fair was her rounded arm, as o'er
  The strings her fingers flew;
And as she touched and tuned them all,
Ever her bosom's rise and fall
  Was plainer given to view;   300
For, all for heat, was laid aside
Her wimple, and her hood untied.
And first she pitched her voice to sing,
Then glanced her dark eye on the king,
And then around the silent ring,
And laughed, and blushed, and oft did say
Her pretty oath, by yea and nay,
She could not, would not, durst not play!
At length, upon the harp, with glee,
Mingled with arch simplicity,   310
A soft yet lively air she rung,
While thus the wily lady sung: —

XII

LOCHINVAR

LADY HERON'S SONG

Oh! young Lochinvar is come out of the
    west,
Through all the wide Border his steed was
    the best;
And save his good broadsword he weapons
    had none,
He rode all unarmed and he rode all
    alone.
So faithful in love and so dauntless in
    war,
There never was knight like the young
    Lochinvar.

He stayed not for brake and he stopped
    not for stone,
He swam the Eske river where ford there
    was none;   320
But ere he alighted at Netherby gate
The bride had consented, the gallant came
    late:
For a laggard in love and a dastard in
    war
Was to wed the fair Ellen of brave Loch-
    invar.

So boldly he entered the Netherby Hall,
Among bridesmen, and kinsmen, and bro-
    thers, and all:
Then spoke the bride's father, his hand on
    his sword, —
For the poor craven bridegroom said never
    a word, —
'Oh! come ye in peace here, or come ye
    in war,
Or to dance at our bridal, young Lord
    Lochinvar?' —   330

'I long wooed your daughter, my suit you
    denied;
Love swells like the Solway, but ebbs like
    its tide —
And now am I come, with this lost love of
    mine,
To lead but one measure, drink one cup of
    wine.
There are maidens in Scotland more lovely
    by far,
That would gladly be bride to the young
    Lochinvar.'

The bride kissed the goblet; the knight
    took it up,
He quaffed off the wine, and he threw
    down the cup.
She looked down to blush, and she looked
    up to sigh,
With a smile on her lips and a tear in her
    eye.   340
He took her soft hand ere her mother could
    bar, —
'Now tread we a measure!' said young
    Lochinvar.

So stately his form, and so lovely her
    face,
That never a hall such a galliard did
    grace;
While her mother did fret, and her father
    did fume,
And the bridegroom stood dangling his
    bonnet and plume;
And the bride-maidens whispered, ''T were
    better by far
To have matched our fair cousin with
    young Lochinvar.'

One touch to her hand and one word in
    her ear,
When they reached the hall-door, and the
    charger stood near;   350
So light to the croupe the fair lady he
    swung,
So light to the saddle before her he
    sprung!
'She is won! we are gone, over bank,
    bush, and scaur;
They'll have fleet steeds that follow,' quoth
    young Lochinvar.

There was mounting 'mong Græmes of the
    Netherby clan;
Forsters, Fenwicks, and Musgraves, they
    rode and they ran:
There was racing and chasing on Cannobie
    Lee,
But the lost bride of Netherby ne'er did
    they see.
So daring in love and so dauntless in war,
Have ye e'er heard of gallant like young
    Lochinvar?   360

XIII

The monarch o'er the siren hung,
And beat the measure as she sung;
And, pressing closer and more near,

He whispered praises in her ear.
In loud applause the courtiers vied,
And ladies winked and spoke aside.
The witching dame to Marmion threw
A glance, where seemed to reign
The pride that claims applauses due,
And of her royal conquest too   370
A real or feigned disdain:
Familiar was the look, and told
Marmion and she were friends of old.
The king observed their meeting eyes
With something like displeased surprise;
For monarchs ill can rivals brook,
Even in a word, or smile, or look.
Straight took he forth the parchment broad
Which   Marmion's   high   commission showed:
'Our Borders sacked by many a raid,   380
Our peaceful liege-men robbed,' he said,
'On day of truce our warden slain,
Stout Barton killed, his vessels ta'en —
Unworthy were we here to reign,
Should these for vengeance cry in vain;
Our full defiance, hate, and scorn,
Our herald has to Henry borne.'

XIV

He paused, and led where Douglas stood
And with stern eye the pageant viewed;
I mean that Douglas, sixth of yore,   390
Who coronet of Angus bore,
And, when his blood and heart were high,
Did the third James in camp defy,
And all his minions led to die
On Lauder's dreary flat.
Princes and favorites long grew tame,
And trembled at the homely name
Of Archibald Bell-the-Cat;
The same who left the dusky vale
Of Hermitage in Liddisdale,   400
Its dungeons and its towers,
Where Bothwell's turrets brave the air,
And Bothwell bank is blooming fair,
To fix his princely bowers.
Though now in age he had laid down
His armor for the peaceful gown,
And for a staff his brand,
Yet often would flash forth the fire
That could in youth a monarch's ire
And minion's pride withstand;   410
And even that day at council board,
Unapt to soothe his sovereign's mood,
Against the war had Angus stood,
And chafed his royal lord.

XV

His giant-form, like ruined tower,
Though fallen its muscles' brawny vaunt,
Huge - boned, and tall, and grim, and gaunt,
Seemed o'er the gaudy scene to lower;
His locks and beard in silver grew,
His eyebrows kept their sable hue.   420
Near Douglas when the monarch stood,
His bitter speech he thus pursued:
'Lord Marmion, since these letters say
That in the North you needs must stay
While slightest hopes of peace remain,
Uncourteous speech it were and stern
To say — Return to Lindisfarne,
Until my herald come again.
Then rest you in Tantallon hold;
Your host shall be the Douglas bold, —   430
A chief unlike his sires of old.
He wears their motto on his blade,
Their blazon o'er his towers displayed,
Yet loves his sovereign to oppose
More than to face his country's foes.
And, I bethink me, by Saint Stephen,
But e'en this morn to me was given
A prize, the first fruits of the war,
Ta'en by a galley from Dunbar,
A bevy of the maids of heaven.   440
Under your guard these holy maids
Shall safe return to cloister shades,
And, while they at Tantallon stay,
Requiem for Cochran's soul may say.'
And with the slaughtered favorite's name
Across the monarch's brow there came
A cloud of ire, remorse, and shame.

XVI

In answer nought could Angus speak,
His proud heart swelled well-nigh to break;
He turned aside, and down his cheek   450
A burning tear there stole.
His hand the monarch sudden took,
That sight his kind heart could not brook:
'Now, by the Bruce's soul,
Angus, my hasty speech forgive !
For sure as doth his spirit live,
As he said of the Douglas old,
I well may say of you, —
That never king did subject hold,
In speech more free, in war more bold,   460
More tender and more true;
Forgive me, Douglas, once again.' —
And, while the king his hand did strain,
The old man's tears fell down like rain.
To seize the moment Marmion tried,

And whispered to the king aside:
'Oh ! let such tears unwonted plead
For respite short from dubious deed !
A child will weep a bramble's smart,
A maid to see her sparrow part,   470
A stripling for a woman's heart;
But woe awaits a country when
She sees the tears of bearded men.
Then, oh ! what omen, dark and high,
When Douglas wets his manly eye !'

XVII

Displeased was James that stranger viewed
And tampered with his changing mood.
'Laugh those that can, weep those that
          may,'
Thus did the fiery monarch say,
'Southward I march by break of day;   480
And if within Tantallon strong
The good Lord Marmion tarries long,
Perchance our meeting next may fall
At Tamworth in his castle-hall.' —
The haughty Marmion felt the taunt,
And answered grave the royal vaunt:
'Much honored were my humble home,
If in its halls King James should come;
But Nottingham has archers good,
And Yorkshire men are stern of mood,   490
Northumbrian prickers wild and rude.
On Derby Hills the paths are steep,
In Ouse and Tyne the fords are deep;
And many a banner will be torn,
And many a knight to earth be borne,
And many a sheaf of arrows spent,
Ere Scotland's king shall cross the Trent:
Yet pause, brave prince, while yet you
          may !' —
The monarch lightly turned away,
And to his nobles loud did call,   500
'Lords, to the dance, — a hall ! a hall !'
Himself his cloak and sword flung by,
And led Dame Heron gallantly;
And minstrels, at the royal order,
Rung out 'Blue Bonnets o'er the Border.'

XVIII

Leave we these revels now to tell
What to Saint Hilda's maids befell,
Whose galley, as they sailed again
To Whitby, by a Scot was ta'en.
Now at Dun-Edin did they bide   510
Till James should of their fate decide,
          And soon by his command
Were gently summoned to prepare
To journey under Marmion's care,

As escort honored, safe, and fair,
          Again to English land.
The abbess told her chaplet o'er,
Nor knew which Saint she should implore;
For, when she thought of Constance, sore
          She feared Lord Marmion's mood.   520
And judge what Clara must have felt !
The sword that hung in Marmion's belt
          Had drunk De Wilton's blood.
Unwittingly King James had given,
          As guard to Whitby's shades,
The man most dreaded under heaven
          By these defenceless maids;
Yet what petition could avail,
Or who would listen to the tale
Of woman, prisoner, and nun,   530
Mid bustle of a war begun ?
They deemed it hopeless to avoid
The convoy of their dangerous guide.

XIX

Their lodging, so the king assigned,
To Marmion's, as their guardian, joined;
And thus it fell that, passing nigh,
The Palmer caught the abbess' eye,
          Who warned him by a scroll
She had a secret to reveal
That much concerned the Church's weal
          And health of sinner's soul;   541
And, with deep charge of secrecy,
          She named a place to meet
Within an open balcony,
That hung from dizzy pitch and high
          Above the stately street,
To which, as common to each home,
At night they might in secret come.

XX

At night in secret there they came,
The Palmer and the holy dame.   550
The moon among the clouds rode high,
And all the city hum was by.
Upon the street, where late before
Did din of war and warriors roar,
          You might have heard a pebble fall,
A beetle hum, a cricket sing,
An owlet flap his boding wing
          On Giles's steeple tall.
The antique buildings, climbing high,
Whose Gothic frontlets sought the sky,   560
          Were here wrapt deep in shade;
There on their brows the moonbeam broke,
Through the faint wreaths of silvery
          smoke,
          And on the casements played.

And other light was none to see,
  Save torches gliding far,
Before some chieftain of degree
Who left the royal revelry
  To bowne him for the war. —
A solemn scene the abbess chose,   570
A solemn hour, her secret to disclose.

XXI

'O holy Palmer!' she began, —
'For sure he must be sainted man,
Whose blessed feet have trod the ground
Where the Redeemer's tomb is found, —
For his dear Church's sake, my tale
Attend, nor deem of light avail,
Though I must speak of worldly love, —
How vain to those who wed above! —
De Wilton and Lord Marmion wooed   580
Clara de Clare, of Gloster's blood; —
Idle it were of Whitby's dame
To say of that same blood I came; —
And once, when jealous rage was high,
Lord Marmion said despiteously,
Wilton was traitor in his heart,
And had made league with Martin Swart
When he came here on Simnel's part,
And only cowardice did restrain   .
His rebel aid on Stokefield's plain, —   590
And down he threw his glove. The thing
Was tried, as wont, before the king;
Where frankly did De Wilton own
That Swart in Guelders he had known,
And that between them then there went
Some scroll of courteous compliment.
For this he to his castle sent;
But when his messenger returned,
Judge how De Wilton's fury burned!
For in his packet there were laid   600
Letters that claimed disloyal aid
And proved King Henry's cause betrayed.
His fame, thus blighted, in the field
He strove to clear by spear and shield; —
To clear his fame in vain he strove,
For wondrous are His ways above!
Perchance some form was unobserved,
Perchance in prayer or faith he swerved,
Else how could guiltless champion quail,
Or how the blessed ordeal fail?   610

XXII

'His squire, who now De Wilton saw
As recreant doomed to suffer law,
  Repentant, owned in vain
That while he had the scrolls in care
A stranger maiden, passing fair,

Had drenched him with a beverage rare;
  His words no faith could gain.
With Clare alone he credence won,
Who, rather than wed Marmion,
Did to Saint Hilda's shrine repair,   620
To give our house her livings fair
And die a vestal votaress there.
The impulse from the earth was given,
But bent her to the paths of heaven.
A purer heart, a lovelier maid,
Ne'er sheltered her in Whitby's shade,
No, not since Saxon Edelfled;
Only one trace of earthly stain,
  That for her lover's loss
She cherishes a sorrow vain,   630
  And murmurs at the cross. —
And then her heritage: — it goes
Along the banks of Tame;
Deep fields of grain the reaper mows,
In meadows rich the heifer lows,
The falconer and huntsman knows
  Its woodlands for the game.
Shame were it to Saint Hilda dear,
And I, her humble votaress here,
  Should do a deadly sin,   640
Her temple spoiled before mine eyes,
If this false Marmion such a prize
  By my consent should win;
Yet hath our boisterous monarch sworn
That Clare shall from our house be torn,
And grievous cause have I to fear
Such mandate doth Lord Marmion bear.

XXIII

'Now, prisoner, helpless, and betrayed
To evil power, I claim thine aid,
  By every step that thou hast trod   650
To holy shrine and grotto dim,
By every martyr's tortured limb,
By angel, saint, and seraphim,
  And by the Church of God!
For mark: when Wilton was betrayed,
And with his squire forged letters laid,
She was, alas! that sinful maid
  By whom the deed was done, —
Oh! shame and horror to be said!
  She was — a perjured nun!   660
No clerk in all the land like her
Traced quaint and varying character.
Perchance you may a marvel deem,
  That Marmion's paramour —
For such vile thing she was — should
    scheme
  Her lover's nuptial hour;
But o'er him thus she hoped to gain,

As privy to his honor's stain,
  Illimitable power.
For this she secretly retained   670
  Each proof that might the plot reveal,
  Instructions with his hand and seal;
And thus Saint Hilda deigned,
  Through sinners' perfidy impure,
  Her house's glory to secure
  And Clare's immortal weal.

XXIV

'' 'T were long and needless here to tell
How to my hand these papers fell;
  With me they must not stay.
Saint Hilda keep her abbess true!   680
Who knows what outrage he might do
  While journeying by the way? —
O blessed Saint, if e'er again
I venturous leave thy calm domain,
To travel or by land or main,
  Deep penance may I pay! —
Now, saintly Palmer, mark my prayer:
I give this packet to thy care,
For thee to stop they will not dare;
  And oh! with cautious speed   690
To Wolsey's hand the papers bring,
That he may show them to the king:
  And for thy well-earned meed,
Thou holy man, at Whitby's shrine
A weekly mass shall still be thine
  While priests can sing and read. —
What ail'st thou? — Speak!' — For as he took
The charge a strong emotion shook
  His frame, and ere reply
They heard a faint yet shrilly tone,   700
Like distant clarion feebly blown,
  That on the breeze did die;
And loud the abbess shrieked in fear,
' Saint Withold, save us! — What is here!
  Look at yon City Cross!
See on its battled tower appear
Phantoms, that scutcheons seem to rear
  And blazoned banners toss!' —

XXV

Dun-Edin's Cross, a pillared stone,
Rose on a turret octagon; —   710
But now is razed that monument,
  Whence royal edict rang,
And voice of Scotland's law was sent
  In glorious trumpet-clang.
Oh! be his tomb as lead to lead
Upon its dull destroyer's head! —
A minstrel's malison is said. —

Then on its battlements they saw
A vision, passing Nature's law,
  Strange, wild, and dimly seen;   720
Figures that seemed to rise and die,
Gibber and sign, advance and fly,
While nought confirmed could ear or eye
  Discern of sound or mien.
Yet darkly did it seem as there
Heralds and pursuivants prepare,
With trumpet sound and blazon fair,
  A summons to proclaim;
But indistinct the pageant proud,
As fancy forms of midnight cloud   730
When flings the moon upon her shroud
  A wavering tinge of flame;
It flits, expands, and shifts, till loud,
From midmost of the spectre crowd,
  This awful summons came: —

XXVI

' Prince, prelate, potentate, and peer,
  Whose names I now shall call,
Scottish or foreigner, give ear!
Subjects of him who sent me here,
At his tribunal to appear   740
  I summon one and all:
I cite you by each deadly sin
That e'er hath soiled your hearts within;
I cite you by each brutal lust
That e'er defiled your earthly dust, —
  By wrath, by pride, by fear,
By each o'ermastering passion's tone,
By the dark grave and dying groan!
When forty days are passed and gone,
I cite you, at your monarch's throne   750
  To answer and appear.'
Then thundered forth a roll of names: —
The first was thine, unhappy James!
  Then all thy nobles came;
Crawford, Glencairn, Montrose, Argyle,
Ross, Bothwell, Forbes, Lennox, Lyle, —
Why should I tell their separate style?
  Each chief of birth and fame,
Of Lowland, Highland, Border, Isle,
Foredoomed to Flodden's carnage pile,   760
  Was cited there by name;
And Marmion, Lord of Fontenaye,
Of Lutterward, and Scrivelbaye;
De Wilton, erst of Aberley,
The self-same thundering voice did say. —
  But then another spoke:
' Thy fatal summons I deny
And thine infernal lord defy,
Appealing me to Him on high
  Who burst the sinner's yoke.'   770

At that dread accent, with a scream,
Parted the pageant like a dream,
  The summoner was gone.
Prone on her face the abbess fell,
And fast, and fast, her beads did tell;
Her nuns came, startled by the yell,
  And found her there alone.
She marked not, at the scene aghast,
What time or how the Palmer passed.

XXVII

Shift we the scene. — The camp doth
  move;   780
  Dun-Edin's streets are empty now,
Save when, for weal of those they love,
  To pray the prayer and vow the vow,
The tottering child, the anxious fair,
The gray-haired sire, with pious care,
To chapels and to shrines repair. —
Where is the Palmer now ? and where
The abbess, Marmion, and Clare ? —
Bold Douglas ! to Tantallon fair
  They journey in thy charge: 790
Lord Marmion rode on his right hand,
The Palmer still was with the band;
Angus, like Lindesay, did command
  That none should roam at large.
But in that Palmer's altered mien
A wondrous change might now be seen;
  Freely he spoke of war,
Of marvels wrought by single hand
When lifted for a native land,
And still looked high, as if he planned   800
  Some desperate deed afar.
His courser would he feed and stroke,
And, tucking up his sable frock,
  Would first his mettle bold provoke,
  Then soothe or quell his pride.
Old Hubert said that never one
He saw, except Lord Marmion,
  A steed so fairly ride.

XXVIII

Some half-hour's march behind there came,
  By Eustace governed fair,   810
A troop escorting Hilda's dame,
  With all her nuns and Clare.
No audience had Lord Marmion sought;
Ever he feared to aggravate
Clara de Clare's suspicious hate;
And safer 't was, he thought,
  To wait till, from the nuns removed,
  The influence of kinsmen loved,
  And suit by Henry's self approved,
Her slow consent had wrought.   820

His was no flickering flame, that dies
Unless when fanned by looks and sighs
And lighted oft at lady's eyes;
He longed to stretch his wide command
O'er luckless Clara's ample land:
Besides, when Wilton with him vied,
Although the pang of humbled pride
The place of jealousy supplied,
Yet conquest, by that meanness won
He almost loathed to think upon,   830
Led him, at times, to hate the cause
Which made him burst through honor's
  laws.
If e'er he loved, 't was her alone
Who died within that vault of stone.

XXIX

And now, when close at hand they saw
North Berwick's town and lofty Law,
Fitz-Eustace bade them pause awhile
Before a venerable pile
  Whose turrets viewed afar
The lofty Bass, the Lambie Isle,   840
  The ocean's peace or war.
At tolling of a bell, forth came
The convent's venerable dame,
And prayed Saint Hilda's abbess rest
With her, a loved and honored guest,
Till Douglas should a bark prepare
To waft her back to Whitby fair.
Glad was the abbess, you may guess,
And thanked the Scottish prioress;
And tedious were to tell, I ween,   850
The courteous speech that passed be-
  tween.
O'erjoyed the nuns their palfreys leave;
But when fair Clara did intend,
Like them, from horseback to descend,
  Fitz-Eustace said: ' I grieve,
Fair lady, grieve e'en from my heart,
Such gentle company to part; —
  Think not discourtesy,
But lords' commands must be obeyed,
And Marmion and the Douglas said   860
  That you must wend with me.
Lord Marmion hath a letter broad,
Which to the Scottish earl he showed,
Commanding that beneath his care
Without delay you shall repair
To your good kinsman, Lord Fitz-Clare.'

XXX

The startled abbess loud exclaimed;
But she at whom the blow was aimed
Grew pale as death and cold as lead, —

She deemed she heard her death - doom
   read.   870
' Cheer thee, my child ! ' the abbess said,
' They dare not tear thee from my hand,
To ride alone with armed band.' —
   ' Nay, holy mother, nay,'
Fitz-Eustace said, ' the lovely Clare
Will be in Lady Angus' care,
   In Scotland while we stay;
And when we move an easy ride
Will bring us to the English side,
Female attendance to provide   880
   Befitting Gloster's heir;
Nor thinks nor dreams my noble lord,
By slightest look, or act, or word,
   To harass Lady Clare.
Her faithful guardian he will be,
Nor sue for slightest courtesy
   That e'en to stranger falls,
Till he shall place her safe and free
   Within her kinsman's halls.'   889
He spoke, and blushed with earnest grace;
His faith was painted on his face,
   And Clare's worst fear relieved.
The Lady Abbess loud exclaimed
On Henry, and the Douglas blamed,
   Entreated, threatened, grieved,
To martyr, saint, and prophet prayed
Against Lord Marmion inveighed,
And called the prioress to aid,
To curse with candle, bell, and book.
Her head the grave Cistertian shook: 900
' The Douglas and the king,' she said,
' In their commands will be obeyed;
Grieve not, nor dream that harm can
   fall
The maiden in Tantallon Hall.'

XXXI

The abbess, seeing strife was vain,
Assumed her wonted state again, —
   For much of state she had, —
Composed her veil, and raised her head,
And ' Bid,' in solemn voice she said,
   ' Thy master, bold and bad,   910
The records of his house turn o'er,
   And, when he shall there written see
That one of his own ancestry
   Drove the monks forth of Coventry,
Bid him his fate explore !
   Prancing in pride of earthly trust,
His charger hurled him to the dust,
   And, by a base plebeian thrust,
He died his band before.

God judge 'twixt Marmion and me: 920
   He is a chief of high degree,
And I a poor recluse,
   Yet oft in holy writ we see
   Even such weak minister as me
May the oppressor bruise;
   For thus, inspired, did Judith slay
   The mighty in his sin,
   And Jael thus, and Deborah ' —
   Here hasty Blount broke in: 929
' Fitz-Eustace, we must march our band;
Saint Anton' fire thee ! wilt thou stand
All day, with bonnet in thy hand,
   To hear the lady preach ?
By this good light ! if thus we stay,
Lord Marmion for our fond delay
   Will sharper sermon teach.
Come, don thy cap and mount thy horse;
The dame must patience take perforce.'

XXXII

' Submit we then to force,' said Clare,
' But let this barbarous lord despair   940
   His purposed aim to win;
Let him take living, land, and life,
But to be Marmion's wedded wife
   In me were deadly sin:
And if it be the king's decree
That I must find no sanctuary
   In that inviolable dome
Where even a homicide might come
   And safely rest his head,
Though at its open portals stood,   950
Thirsting to pour forth blood for blood,
   The kinsmen of the dead,
Yet one asylum is my own
   Against the dreaded hour, —
A low, a silent, and a lone,
   Where kings have little power.
One victim is before me there. —
Mother, your blessing, and in prayer
Remember your unhappy Clare ! '
Loud weeps the abbess, and bestows   960
   Kind blessings many a one;
Weeping and wailing loud arose,
Round patient Clare, the clamorous woes
   Of every simple nun.
His eyes the gentle Eustace dried,
And scarce rude Blount the sight could
   bide.
   Then took the squire her rein,
And gently led away her steed,
And by each courteous word and deed
   To cheer her strove in vain.   970

XXXIII

But scant three miles the band had rode,
  When o'er a height they passed,
And, sudden, close before them showed
  His towers Tantallon vast,
Broad, massive, high, and stretching far,
And held impregnable in war.
On a projecting rock they rose,
And round three sides the ocean flows.
The fourth did battled walls enclose
  And double mound and fosse.   980
By narrow drawbridge, outworks strong,
Through studded gates, an entrance long,
  To the main court they cross.
It was a wide and stately square;
Around were lodgings fit and fair,
  And towers of various form,
Which on the court projected far
And broke its lines quadrangular.
Here was square keep, there turret high,
Or pinnacle that sought the sky,   990
Whence oft the warder could descry
  The gathering ocean-storm.

XXXIV

Here did they rest. — The princely care
Of Douglas why should I declare,
Or say they met reception fair?
Or why the tidings say,
Which varying to Tantallon came,
By hurrying posts or fleeter fame,
  With every varying day?
And, first, they heard King James had
  won   1000
  Etall, and Wark, and Ford; and then,
  That Norham Castle strong was ta'en.
At that sore marvelled Marmion,
And Douglas hoped his monarch's hand
Would soon subdue Northumberland;
  But whispered news there came,
That while his host inactive lay,
And melted by degrees away,
King James was dallying off the day
  With Heron's wily dame.   1010
Such acts to chronicles I yield;
  Go seek them there and see:
Mine is a tale of Flodden Field,
  And not a history. —
At length they heard the Scottish host
On that high ridge had made their post
  Which frowns o'er Millfield Plain;
And that brave Surrey many a band
Had gathered in the Southern land,
And marched into Northumberland,   1020
  And camp at Wooler ta'en.

Marmion, like charger in the stall,
That hears, without, the trumpet-call,
  Began to chafe and swear: —
' A sorry thing to hide my head
In castle, like a fearful maid,
  When such a field is near.
Needs must I see this battle-day;
Death to my fame if such a fray
Were fought, and Marmion away!   1030
  The Douglas, too, I wot not why,
  Hath bated of his courtesy;
No longer in his halls I'll stay:'
Then bade his band they should array
For march against the dawning day.

INTRODUCTION TO CANTO SIXTH

TO RICHARD HEBER, ESQ.

Mertoun House, Christmas

HEAP on more wood! — the wind is chill;
But let it whistle as it will,
We'll keep our Christmas merry still.
Each age has deemed the new-born year
The fittest time for festal cheer:
Even, heathen yet, the savage Dane
At Iol more deep the mead did drain,
High on the beach his galleys drew,
And feasted all his pirate crew;
Then in his low and pine-built hall,   10
Where shields and axes decked the wall,
They gorged upon the half-dressed steer,
Caroused in seas of sable beer,
While round in brutal jest were thrown
The half-gnawed rib and marrowbone,
Or listened all in grim delight
While scalds yelled out the joys of fight.
Then forth in frenzy would they hie,
While wildly loose their red locks fly,
And dancing round the blazing pile,   20
They make such barbarous mirth the
  while
As best might to the mind recall
The boisterous joys of Odin's hall.

And well our Christian sires of old
Loved when the year its course had rolled,
And brought blithe Christmas back again
With all his hospitable train.
Domestic and religious rite
Gave honor to the holy night;
On Christmas eve the bells were rung,   30
On Christmas eve the mass was sung:

That only night in all the year
Saw the stoled priest the chalice rear.
The damsel donned her kirtle sheen;
The hall was dressed with holly green;
Forth to the wood did merrymen go,
To gather in the mistletoe.
Then opened wide the baron's hall
To vassal, tenant, serf, and all;
Power laid his rod of rule aside,   40
And Ceremony doffed his pride.
The heir, with roses in his shoes,
That night might village partner choose;
The lord, underogating, share
The vulgar game of ' post and pair.'
All hailed, with uncontrolled delight
And general voice, the happy night
That to the cottage, as the crown,
Brought tidings of salvation down.

The fire, with well-dried logs supplied, 50
Went roaring up the chimney wide;
The huge hall-table's oaken face,
Scrubbed till it shone, the day to grace,
Bore then upon its massive board
No mark to part the squire and lord.
Then was brought in the lusty brawn
By old blue-coated serving-man;
Then the grim boar's - head frowned on
        high,
Crested with bays and rosemary.
Well can the green-garbed ranger tell   60
How, when, and where, the monster fell,
What dogs before his death he tore,
And all the baiting of the boar.
The wassail round, in good brown bowls
Garnished with ribbons, blithely trowls.
There the huge sirloin reeked; hard by
Plum-porridge stood and Christmas pie;
Nor failed old Scotland to produce
At such high tide her savory goose.
Then came the merry maskers in,   70
And carols roared with blithesome din;
If unmelodious was the song,
It was a hearty note and strong.
Who lists may in their mumming see
Traces of ancient mystery;
White shirts supplied the masquerade,
And smutted cheeks the visors made;
But oh ! what maskers, richly dight,
Can boast of bosoms half so light !
England was merry England when   80
Old Christmas brought his sports again.
'T was Christmas broached the mightiest
        ale,
'T was Christmas told the merriest tale;

A Christmas gambol oft could cheer
The poor man's heart through half the
        year.

Still linger in our northern clime
Some remnants of the good old time,
And still within our valleys here
We hold the kindred title dear,
Even when, perchance, its far - fetched
        claim   90
To Southron ear sounds empty name;
For course of blood, our proverbs deem,
Is warmer than the mountain-stream.
And thus my Christmas still I hold
Where my great-grandsire came of old,
With amber beard and flaxen hair
And reverent apostolic air,
The feast and holy-tide to share,
And mix sobriety with wine,
And honest mirth with thoughts divine: 100
Small thought was his, in after time
E'er to be hitched into a rhyme.
The simple sire could only boast
That he was loyal to his cost,
The banished race of kings revered,
And lost his land, — but kept his beard.

In these dear halls, where welcome kind
Is with fair liberty combined,
Where cordial friendship gives the hand,
And flies constraint the magic wand   110
Of the fair dame that rules the land,
Little we heed the tempest drear,
While music, mirth, and social cheer
Speed on their wings the passing year.
And Mertoun's halls are fair e'en now,
When not a leaf is on the bough.
Tweed loves them well, and turns again,
As loath to leave the sweet domain,
And holds his mirror to her face,
And clips her with a close embrace: — 120
Gladly as he we seek the dome,
And as reluctant turn us home.

How just that at this time of glee
My thoughts should, Heber, turn to thee !
For many a merry hour we 've known,
And heard the chimes of midnight's tone.
Cease, then, my friend ! a moment cease,
And leave these classic tomes in peace !
Of Roman and of Grecian lore
Sure mortal brain can hold no more.   130
These ancients, as Noll Bluff might say,
' Were pretty fellows in their day,'
But time and tide o'er all prevail —

On Christmas eve a Christmas tale —
Of wonder and of war — ' Profane !
What ! leave the lofty Latian strain,
Her stately prose, her verse's charms,
To hear the clash of rusty arms;
In Fairy-land or Limbo lost,
To jostle conjurer and ghost,   140
Goblin and witch ! ' — Nay, Heber dear,
Before you touch my charter, hear;
Though Leyden aids, alas! no more,
My cause with many-languaged lore,
This may I say: — in realms of death
Ulysses meets Alcides' *wraith*,
Æneas upon Thracia's shore
The ghost of murdered Polydore;
For omens, we in Livy cross
At every turn *locutus Bos*.   150
As grave and duly speaks that ox
As if he told the price of stocks,
Or held in Rome republican
The place of Common-councilman.

All nations have their omens drear,
Their legends wild of woe and fear.
To Cambria look — the peasant see
Bethink him of Glendowerdy
And shun 'the Spirit's Blasted Tree.' —
The Highlander, whose red claymore   160
The battle turned on Maida's shore,
Will on a Friday morn look pale,
If asked to tell a fairy tale:
He fears the vengeful Elfin King,
Who leaves that day his grassy ring;
Invisible to human ken,
He walks among the sons of men.

Didst e'er, dear Heber, pass along
Beneath the towers of Franchémont,
Which, like an eagle's nest in air,   170
Hang o'er the stream and hamlet fair ?
Deep in their vaults, the peasants say,
A mighty treasure buried lay,
Amassed through rapine and through
    wrong
By the last Lord of Franchémont.
The iron chest is bolted hard,
A huntsman sits its constant guard;
Around his neck his horn is hung,
His hanger in his belt is slung;
Before his feet his bloodhounds lie: 180
An 't were not for his gloomy eye,
Whose withering glance no heart can
    brook,
As true a huntsman doth he look

As bugle e'er in brake did sound,
Or ever hallooed to a hound.
To chase the fiend and win the prize
In that same dungeon ever tries
An aged necromantic priest:
It is an hundred years at least
Since 'twixt them first the strife begun, 190
And neither yet has lost nor won.
And oft the conjurer's words will make
The stubborn demon groan and quake;
And oft the bands of iron break,
Or bursts one lock that still amain
Fast as 't is opened, shuts again.
That magic strife within the tomb
May last until the day of doom,
Unless the adept shall learn to tell
The very word that clenched the spell   200
When Franch'mont locked the treasure
    cell.
An hundred years are passed and gone,
And scarce three letters has he won.

Such general superstition may
Excuse for old Pitscottie say,
Whose gossip history has given
My song the messenger from heaven
That warned, in Lithgow, Scotland's king,
Nor less the infernal summoning;
May pass the Monk of Durham's tale,   210
Whose demon fought in Gothic mail;
May pardon plead for Fordun grave,
Who told of Gifford's Goblin-Cave.
But why such instances to you,
Who in an instant can renew
Your treasured hoards of various lore,
And furnish twenty thousand more ?
Hoards, not like theirs whose volumes
    rest
Like treasures in the Franch'mont chest,
While gripple owners still refuse   220
To others what they cannot use;
Give them the priest's whole century,
They shall not spell you letters three, —
Their pleasure in the books the same
The magpie takes in pilfered gem.
Thy volumes, open as thy heart,
Delight, amusement, science, art,
To every ear and eye impart;
Yet who, of all who thus employ them,
Can like the owner's self enjoy them ? — 230
But, hark ! I hear the distant drum !
The day of Flodden Field is come. —
Adieu, dear Heber ! life and health,
And store of literary wealth.

CANTO SIXTH

THE BATTLE

I

WHILE great events were on the gale,
And each hour brought a varying tale,
And the demeanor, changed and cold,
Of Douglas fretted Marmion bold,
And, like the impatient steed of war,
He snuffed the battle from afar,
And hopes were none that back again
Herald should come from Terouenne,
Where England's king in leaguer lay,
Before decisive battle-day, —   10
While these things were, the mournful Clare
Did in the dame's devotions share;
For the good countess ceaseless prayed
To Heaven and saints her sons to aid,
And with short interval did pass
From prayer to book, from book to mass,
And all in high baronial pride, —
A life both dull and dignified:
Yet, as Lord Marmion nothing pressed
Upon her intervals of rest,   20
Dejected Clara well could bear
The formal state, the lengthened prayer,
Though dearest to her wounded heart
The hours that she might spend apart.

II

I said Tantallon's dizzy steep
Hung o'er the margin of the deep.
Many a rude tower and rampart there
Repelled the insult of the air,
Which, when the tempest vexed the sky,
Half breeze, half spray, came whistling by.   30
Above the rest a turret square
Did o'er its Gothic entrance bear,
Of sculpture rude, a stony shield;
The Bloody Heart was in the field,
And in the chief three mullets stood,
The cognizance of Douglas blood.
The turret held a narrow stair,
Which, mounted, gave you access where
A parapet's embattled row
Did seaward round the castle go.   40
Sometimes in dizzy steps descending,
Sometimes in narrow circuit bending,
Sometimes in platform broad extending,
Its varying circle did combine
Bulwark, and bartizan, and line,
And bastion, tower, and vantage-coign.

Above the booming ocean leant
The far-projecting battlement;
The billows burst in ceaseless flow
Upon the precipice below.   50
Where'er Tantallon faced the land,
Gate - works and walls were strongly manned;
No need upon the sea-girt side:
The steepy rock and frantic tide
Approach of human step denied,
And thus these lines and ramparts rude
Were left in deepest solitude.

III

And, for they were so lonely, Clare
Would to these battlements repair,
And muse upon her sorrows there,   60
And list the sea-bird's cry,
Or slow, like noontide ghost, would glide
Along the dark-gray bulwarks' side,
And ever on the heaving tide
Look down with weary eye.
Oft did the cliff and swelling main
Recall the thoughts of Whitby's fane, —
A home she ne'er might see again;
For she had laid adown,
So Douglas bade, the hood and veil,   70
And frontlet of the cloister pale,
And Benedictine gown:
It were unseemly sight, he said,
A novice out of convent shade. —
Now her bright locks with sunny glow
Again adorned her brow of snow;
Her mantle rich, whose borders round
A deep and fretted broidery bound,
In golden foldings sought the ground;
Of holy ornament, alone   80
Remained a cross with ruby stone;
And often did she look
On that which in her hand she bore,
With velvet bound and broidered o'er,
Her breviary book.
In such a place, so lone, so grim,
At dawning pale or twilight dim,
It fearful would have been
To meet a form so richly dressed,
With book in hand, and cross on breast,   90
And such a woful mien.
Fitz-Eustace, loitering with his bow,
To practise on the gull and crow,
Saw her at distance gliding slow,
And did by Mary swear
Some lovelorn fay she might have been,
Or in romance some spell-bound queen,

For ne'er in work-day world was seen
A form so witching fair.

IV

Once walking thus at evening tide 100
It chanced a gliding sail she spied,
And sighing thought — ' The abbess there
Perchance does to her home repair;
Her peaceful rule, where Duty free
Walks hand in hand with Charity,
Where oft Devotion's tranced glow
Can such a glimpse of heaven bestow
That the enraptured sisters see
High vision and deep mystery, —
The very form of Hilda fair, 110
Hovering upon the sunny air
And smiling on her votaries' prayer.
Oh! wherefore to my duller eye
Did still the Saint her form deny?
Was it that, seared by sinful scorn,
My heart could neither melt nor burn?
Or lie my warm affections low
With him that taught them first to glow?
Yet, gentle abbess, well I knew
To pay thy kindness grateful due, 120
And well could brook the mild command
That ruled thy simple maiden band.
How different now, condemned to bide
My doom from this dark tyrant's pride! —
But Marmion has to learn ere long
That constant mind and hate of wrong
Descended to a feeble girl
From Red de Clare, stout Gloster's Earl:
Of such a stem a sapling weak,
He ne'er shall bend, although he break. 130

V

' But see! — what makes this armor
here?' —
For in her path there lay
Targe, corselet, helm; she viewed them
near. —
' The breastplate pierced! — Ay, much I
fear,
Weak fence wert thou 'gainst foeman's
spear,
That hath made fatal entrance here,
As these dark blood-gouts say. —
Thus Wilton! — Oh! not corselet's ward,
Not truth, as diamond pure and hard,
Could be thy manly bosom's guard 140
On yon disastrous day!' —
She raised her eyes in mournful mood, —
Wilton himself before her stood!
It might have seemed his passing ghost,

For every youthful grace was lost,
And joy unwonted and surprise
Gave their strange wildness to his eyes. —
Expect not, noble dames and lords,
That I can tell such scene in words:
What skilful limner e'er would choose 150
To paint the rainbow's varying hues,
Unless to mortal it were given
To dip his brush in dyes of heaven?
Far less can my weak line declare
Each changing passion's shade:
Brightening to rapture from despair,
Sorrow, surprise, and pity there,
And joy with her angelic air,
And hope that paints the future fair,
Their varying hues displayed; 160
Each o'er its rival's ground extending,
Alternate conquering, shifting, blending,
Till all fatigued the conflict yield,
And mighty love retains the field.
Shortly I tell what then he said,
By many a tender word delayed,
And modest blush, and bursting sigh,
And question kind, and fond reply: —

VI

DE WILTON'S HISTORY

' Forget we that disastrous day
When senseless in the lists I lay. 170
    Thence dragged, — but how I cannot
    know,
    For sense and recollection fled, —
I found me on a pallet low
    Within my ancient beadsman's shed.
Austin, — remember'st thou, my Clare,
How thou didst blush when the old man,
When first our infant love began,
    Said we would make a matchless pair? —
Menials and friends and kinsmen fled
From the degraded traitor's bed, — 180
He only held my burning head,
And tended me for many a day
While wounds and fever held their sway.
But far more needful was his care
When sense returned to wake despair;
    For I did tear the closing wound,
    And dash me frantic on the ground,
If e'er I heard the name of Clare.
At length, to calmer reason brought,
Much by his kind attendance wrought, 190
    With him I left my native strand,
And, in a palmer's weeds arrayed,
My hated name and form to shade,
    I journeyed many a land,

No more a lord of rank and birth,
But mingled with the dregs of earth.
  Oft Austin for my reason feared,
When I would sit, and deeply brood
On dark revenge and deeds of blood,
  Or wild mad schemes upreared.   200
My friend at length fell sick, and said
  God would remove him soon;
And while upon his dying bed
  He begged of me a boon —
If e'er my deadliest enemy
Beneath my brand should conquered lie,
Even then my mercy should awake
And spare his life for Austin's sake.

VII

'Still restless as a second Cain,
To Scotland next my route was ta'en,   210
  Full well the paths I knew.
Fame of my fate made various sound,
That death in pilgrimage I found,
That I had perished of my wound, —
  None cared which tale was true;
And living eye could never guess
De Wilton in his palmer's dress,
For now that sable slough is shed,
And trimmed my shaggy beard and head,
  I scarcely know me in the glass.   220
A chance most wondrous did provide
That I should be that baron's guide —
  I will not name his name ! —
Vengeance to God alone belongs;
But, when I think on all my wrongs,
  My blood is liquid flame !
And ne'er the time shall I forget
When, in a Scottish hostel set,
  Dark looks we did exchange:
What were his thoughts I cannot tell, 230
But in my bosom mustered Hell
  Its plans of dark revenge.

VIII

'A word of vulgar augury
That broke from me, I scarce knew why,
  Brought on a village tale,
Which wrought upon his moody sprite,
And sent him armed forth by night.
  I borrowed steed and mail
And weapons from his sleeping band;
  And, passing from a postern door,   240
We met and 'countered, hand to hand, —
  He fell on Gifford-moor.
For the death-stroke my brand I drew, —
Oh ! then my helmed head he knew,
  The palmer's cowl was gone, —

Then had three inches of my blade
The heavy debt of vengeance paid, —
My hand the thought of Austin stayed;
  I left him there alone. —
O good old man ! even from the grave   250
Thy spirit could thy master save:
If I had slain my foeman, ne'er
Had Whitby's abbess in her fear
Given to my hand this packet dear,
Of power to clear my injured fame
And vindicate De Wilton's name. —
Perchance you heard the abbess tell
Of the strange pageantry of hell
  That broke our secret speech —
It rose from the infernal shade,   260
Or featly was some juggle played,
  A tale of peace to teach.
Appeal to Heaven I judged was best
When my name came among the rest.

IX

' Now here within Tantallon hold
To Douglas late my tale I told,
To whom my house was known of old.
Won by my proofs, his falchion bright
This eve anew shall dub me knight.
These were the arms that once did turn 270
The tide of fight on Otterburne,
And Harry Hotspur forced to yield
When the Dead Douglas won the field.
These Angus gave — his armorer's care
Ere morn shall every breach repair;
For nought, he said, was in his halls
But ancient armor on the walls,
And aged chargers in the stalls,
And women, priests, and gray - haired
      men;
The rest were all in Twisel glen.   280
And now I watch my armor here,
By law of arms, till midnight 's near;
Then, once again a belted knight,
Seek Surrey's camp with dawn of light.

X

' There soon again we meet, my Clare !
This baron means to guide thee there:
Douglas reveres his king's command,
Else would he take thee from his band.
And there thy kinsman Surrey, too,
Will give De Wilton justice due.   290
Now meeter far for martial broil,
Firmer my limbs and strung by toil,
Once more ' — ' O Wilton ! must we then
Risk new-found happiness again,
  Trust fate of arms once more ?

And is there not an humble glen
  Where we, content and poor,
Might build a cottage in the shade,
A shepherd thou, and I to aid
  Thy task on dale and moor ? —   300
That reddening brow ! — too well I know
Not even thy Clare can peace bestow
  While falsehood stains thy name:
Go then to fight !   Clare bids thee go !
Clare can a warrior's feelings know
  And weep a warrior's shame,
Can Red Earl Gilbert's spirit feel,
Buckle the spurs upon thy heel
And belt thee with thy brand of steel,
  And send thee forth to fame !'   310

XI

That night upon the rocks and bay
The midnight moonbeam slumbering lay,
And poured its silver light and pure
Through loophole and through embra-
    sure
  Upon Tantallon tower and hall;
But chief where arched windows wide
Illuminate the chapel's pride
  The sober glances fall.
Much was there need; though seamed with
    scars,
Two veterans of the Douglas' wars,   320
  Though two gray priests were there,
And each a blazing torch held high,
You could not by their blaze descry
  The chapel's carving fair.
Amid that dim and smoky light,
Checkering the silvery moonshine bright,
  A bishop by the altar stood,
  A noble lord of Douglas blood,
With mitre sheen and rochet white.   329
Yet showed his meek and thoughtful eye
But little pride of prelacy;
More pleased that in a barbarous age
He gave rude Scotland Virgil's page
Than that beneath his rule he held
The bishopric of fair Dunkeld.
Beside him ancient Angus stood,
Doffed his furred gown and sable hood;
O'er his huge form and visage pale
He wore a cap and shirt of mail,   339
And leaned his large and wrinkled hand
Upon the huge and sweeping brand
Which wont of yore in battle fray
His foeman's limbs to shred away,
As wood-knife lops the sapling spray.
  He seemed as, from the tombs around
  Rising at judgment-day,

Some giant Douglas may be found
  In all his old array;
So pale his face, so huge his limb,
So old his arms, his look so grim.   350

XII

Then at the altar Wilton kneels,
And Clare the spurs bound on his heels;
And think what next he must have felt
At buckling of the falchion belt !
  And judge how Clara changed her hue
While fastening to her lover's side
A friend, which, though in danger tried,
  He once had found untrue !
Then Douglas struck him with his blade:
'Saint Michael and Saint Andrew aid,   360
  I dub thee knight.
Arise, Sir Ralph, De Wilton's heir !
For king, for church, for lady fair,
  See that thou fight.'
And Bishop Gawain, as he rose,
Said: 'Wilton ! grieve not for thy woes,
  Disgrace, and trouble;
For He who honor best bestows
  May give thee double.'
De Wilton sobbed, for sob he must: 370
'Where'er I meet a Douglas, trust
  That Douglas is my brother !'
'Nay, nay,' old Angus said, 'not so;
To Surrey's camp thou now must go,
  Thy wrongs no longer smother.
I have two sons in yonder field;
And, if thou meet'st them under shield,
Upon them bravely — do thy worst,
And foul fall him that blenches first !'

XIII

Not far advanced was morning day   380
When Marmion did his troop array
  To Surrey's camp to ride;
He had safe-conduct for his band
Beneath the royal seal and hand,
  And Douglas gave a guide.
The ancient earl with stately grace
Would Clara on her palfrey place,
And whispered in an undertone,
'Let the hawk stoop, his prey is flown.'
The train from out the castle drew,   390
But Marmion stopped to bid adieu:
  'Though something I might plain,' he
    said,
'Of cold respect to stranger guest,
Sent hither by your king's behest,
  While in Tantallon's towers I stayed,
Part we in friendship from your land,

And, noble earl, receive my hand.' —
But Douglas round him drew his cloak,
Folded his arms, and thus he spoke: — 399
' My manors, halls, and bowers shall still
Be open at my sovereign's will
To each one whom he lists, howe'er
Unmeet to be the owner's peer.
My castles are my king's alone,
From turret to foundation-stone —
The hand of Douglas is his own,
And never shall in friendly grasp
The hand of such as Marmion clasp.'

XIV

Burned Marmion's swarthy cheek like fire
And shook his very frame for ire,   410
    And — ' This to me ! ' he said,
' An 't were not for thy hoary beard,
Such hand as Marmion's had not spared
    To cleave the Douglas' head !
And first I tell thee, haughty peer,
He who does England's message here,
Although the meanest in her state,
May well, proud Angus, be thy mate;
And, Douglas, more I tell thee here,
    Even in thy pitch of pride,   420
Here in thy hold, thy vassals near, —
Nay, never look upon your lord,
And lay your hands upon your sword, —
    I tell thee, thou 'rt defied !
And if thou saidst I am not peer
To any lord in Scotland here,
Lowland or Highland, far or near,
    Lord Angus, thou hast lied ! '
On the earl's cheek the flush of rage
O'ercame the ashen hue of age: 430
Fierce he broke forth, — ' And darest thou
    then
To beard the lion in his den,
    The Douglas in his hall ?
And hopest thou hence unscathed to go ? —
No, by Saint Bride of Bothwell, no !
Up drawbridge, grooms — what, warder, ho !
    Let the portcullis fall.' —
Lord Marmion turned, — well was his
    need, —
And dashed the rowels in his steed,   439
Like arrow through the archway sprung,
The ponderous grate behind him rung;
To pass there was such scanty room,
The bars descending razed his plume.

XV

The steed along the drawbridge flies
Just as it trembled on the rise;

Not lighter does the swallow skim
Along the smooth lake's level brim:
And when Lord Marmion reached his
    band,
He halts, and turns with clenched hand,
And shout of loud defiance pours,   450
And shook his gauntlet at the towers.
' Horse ! horse ! ' the Douglas cried, ' and
    chase ! '
But soon he reined his fury's pace:
' A royal messenger he came,
Though most unworthy of the name. —
A letter forged ! Saint Jude to speed !
Did ever knight so foul a deed ?
At first in heart it liked me ill
When the king praised his clerkly skill.
Thanks to Saint Bothan, son of mine,   460
Save Gawain, ne'er could pen a line;
So swore I, and I swear it still,
Let my boy-bishop fret his fill. —
Saint Mary mend my fiery mood !
Old age ne'er cools the Douglas blood,
I thought to slay him where he stood.
'T is pity of him too,' he cried:
' Bold can he speak and fairly ride,
I warrant him a warrior tried.'
With this his mandate he recalls,   470
And slowly seeks his castle halls.

XVI

The day in Marmion's journey wore;
Yet, ere his passion's gust was o'er,
They crossed the heights of Stanrig-moor.
His troop more closely there he scanned,
And missed the Palmer from the band.
' Palmer or not,' young Blount did say,
' He parted at the peep of day;
Good sooth, it was in strange array.'
' In what array ? ' said Marmion quick.   480
' My lord, I ill can spell the trick;
But all night long with clink and bang
Close to my couch did hammers clang;
At dawn the falling drawbridge rang,
And from a loophole while I peep,
Old Bell-the-Cat came from the keep,
Wrapped in a gown of sables fair,
As fearful of the morning air;
Beneath, when that was blown aside,
A rusty shirt of mail I spied,   490
By Archibald won in bloody work
Against the Saracen and Turk:
Last night it hung not in the hall;
I thought some marvel would befall.
And next I saw them saddled lead
Old Cheviot forth, the earl's best steed,

A matchless horse, though something old,
Prompt in his paces, cool and bold.
I heard the Sheriff Sholto say
The earl did much the Master pray   500
To use him on the battle-day,
But he preferred ' — ' Nay, Henry, cease !
Thou sworn horse - courser, hold thy
      peace. —
Eustace, thou bear'st a brain — I pray,
What did Blount see at break of day ? ' —

XVII

' In brief, my lord, we both descried —
For then I stood by Henry's side —
The Palmer mount and outwards ride
Upon the earl's own favorite steed.
All sheathed he was in armor bright,   510
And much resembled that same knight
Subdued by you in Cotswold fight;
   Lord Angus wished him speed.' —
The instant that Fitz-Eustace spoke,
A sudden light on Marmion broke: —
' Ah ! dastard fool, to reason lost ! '
He muttered; ''T was nor fay nor ghost
I met upon the moonlight wold,
But living man of earthly mould.
   O dotage blind and gross !   520
Had I but fought as wont, one thrust
Had laid De Wilton in the dust,
   My path no more to cross. —
How stand we now ? — he told his tale
To Douglas, and with some avail;
   'T was therefore gloomed his rugged
      brow. —
Will Surrey dare to entertain
'Gainst Marmion charge disproved and
      vain ?
   Small risk of that, I trow.   529
Yet Clare's sharp questions must I shun,
Must separate Constance from the nun —
Oh ! what a tangled web we weave
When first we practise to deceive !
A Palmer too ! — no wonder why
I felt rebuked beneath his eye;
I might have known there was but one
Whose look could quell Lord Marmion.'

XVIII

Stung with these thoughts, he urged to
      speed
His troop, and reached at eve the Tweed,
Where Lennel's convent closed their
      march.   540
There now is left but one frail arch,
   Yet mourn thou not its cells;

Our time a fair exchange has made:
Hard by, in hospitable shade,
   A reverend pilgrim dwells,
Well worth the whole Bernardine brood
That e'er wore sandal, frock, or hood. —
Yet did Saint Bernard's abbot there
Give Marmion entertainment fair,
And lodging for his train and Clare.   550
Next morn the baron climbed the tower,
To view afar the Scottish power,
   Encamped on Flodden edge;
The white pavilions made a show
Like remnants of the winter snow
   Along the dusky ridge.
Long Marmion looked: — at length his eye
Unusual movement might descry
   Amid the shifting lines;
The Scottish host drawn out appears,   560
For, flashing on the hedge of spears,
   The eastern sunbeam shines.
Their front now deepening, now extending,
Their flank inclining, wheeling, bending,
Now drawing back, and now descending,
The skilful Marmion well could know
They watched the motions of some foe
Who traversed on the plain below.

XIX

Even so it was.   From Flodden ridge
   The Scots beheld the English host   570
   Leave Barmore-wood, their evening post,
   And heedful watched them as they
      crossed
The Till by Twisel Bridge.
   High sight it is and haughty, while
   They dive into the deep defile;
   Beneath the caverned cliff they fall,
   Beneath the castle's airy wall.
By rock, by oak, by hawthorn-tree,
   Troop after troop are disappearing;
   Troop after troop their banners rear-
      ing   580
Upon the eastern bank you see;
Still pouring down the rocky den
   Where flows the sullen Till,
And rising from the dim-wood glen,
Standards on standards, men on men,
   In slow succession still,
And sweeping o'er the Gothic arch,
And pressing on, in ceaseless march,
   To gain the opposing hill.
That morn, to many a trumpet clang,   590
Twisel ! thy rock's deep echo rang,
And many a chief of birth and rank,
Saint Helen ! at thy fountain drank.

Thy hawthorn glade, which now we see
In spring-tide bloom so lavishly,
Had then from many an axe its doom,
To give the marching columns room.

XX

And why stands Scotland idly now,
Dark Flodden! on thy airy brow,
Since England gains the pass the while, 600
And struggles through the deep defile?
What checks the fiery soul of James?
Why sits that champion of the dames
    Inactive on his steed,
And sees, between him and his land,
Between him and Tweed's southern strand,
    His host Lord Surrey lead?
What   vails   the   vain   knight - errant's
    brand? —
O Douglas, for thy leading wand!
    Fierce Randolph, for thy speed!   610
Oh! for one hour of Wallace wight,
Or well-skilled Bruce, to rule the fight
And cry, 'Saint Andrew and our right!'
Another sight had seen that morn,
From Fate's dark book a leaf been torn,
And Flodden had been Bannockbourne! —
The precious hour has passed in vain,
And England's host has gained the plain,
Wheeling their march and circling still
Around the base of Flodden hill.   620

XXI

Ere yet the bands met Marmion's eye,
Fitz-Eustace shouted loud and high,
'Hark! hark! my lord, an English drum!
And see ascending squadrons come
    Between Tweed's river and the hill,
Foot, horse, and cannon! Hap what hap,
My basnet to a prentice cap,
    Lord Surrey's o'er the Till! —
Yet more! yet more! — how fair arrayed
They file from out the hawthorn shade, 630
    And sweep so gallant by!
With all their banners bravely spread,
    And all their armor flashing high,
Saint George might waken from the dead,
    To see fair England's standards fly.' —
'Stint in thy prate,' quoth Blount, 'thou 'dst
    best,
And listen to our lord's behest.' —
With kindling brow Lord Marmion said,
'This instant be our band arrayed;
The river must be quickly crossed,   640
That we may join Lord Surrey's host.
If fight King James, — as well I trust

That fight he will, and fight he must, —
The Lady Clare behind our lines
Shall tarry while the battle joins.'

XXII

Himself he swift on horseback threw,
Scarce to the abbot bade adieu,
Far less would listen to his prayer
To leave behind the helpless Clare.
Down to the Tweed his band he drew,   650
And muttered as the flood they view,
'The pheasant in the falcon's claw,
He scarce will yield to please a daw;
Lord Angus may the abbot awe,
    So Clare shall bide with me.'
Then on that dangerous ford and deep
Where to the Tweed Leat's eddies creep,
    He ventured desperately:
And not a moment will he bide
Till squire or groom before him ride;   660
Headmost of all he stems the tide,
    And stems it gallantly.
Eustace held Clare upon her horse,
    Old Hubert led her rein,
Stoutly they braved the current's course,
And, though far downward driven perforce,
    The southern bank they gain.
Behind them straggling came to shore,
    As best they might, the train:
Each o'er his head his yew-bow bore,   670
    A caution not in vain:
Deep need that day that every string,
By wet unharmed, should sharply ring.
A moment then Lord Marmion stayed,
And breathed his steed, his men arrayed,
    Then forward moved his band,
Until, Lord Surrey's rear-guard won,
He halted by a cross of stone,
That on a hillock standing lone
    Did all the field command.   680

XXIII

Hence might they see the full array
Of either host for deadly fray;
Their marshalled lines stretched east and
    west,
    And fronted north and south,
And distant salutation passed
    From the loud cannon mouth;
Not in the close successive rattle
That breathes the voice of modern battle,
    But slow and far between.
The hillock gained, Lord Marmion stayed:
'Here, by this cross,' he gently said,   691
    'You well may view the scene.

Here shalt thou tarry, lovely Clare:
Oh ! think of Marmion in thy prayer ! —
Thou wilt not ? — well, no less my care
Shall, watchful, for thy weal prepare. —
You, Blount and Eustace, are her guard,
    With ten picked archers of my train;
With England if the day go hard,
    To Berwick speed amain. —   700
But if we conquer, cruel maid,
My spoils shall at your feet be laid,
    When here we meet again.'
He waited not for answer there,
And would not mark the maid's despair,
    Nor heed the discontented look
From either squire, but spurred amain,
And, dashing through the battle-plain,
    His way to Surrey took.

XXIV

' The good Lord Marmion, by my life ! 710
    Welcome to danger's hour ! —
Short greeting serves in time of strife. —
    Thus have I ranged my power:
Myself will rule this central host,
    Stout Stanley fronts their right,
My sons command the vaward post,
    With Brian Tunstall, stainless knight;
Lord Dacre, with his horsemen light,
Shall be in rearward of the fight,
    And succor those that need it most. 720
    Now, gallant Marmion, well I know,
    Would gladly to the vanguard go;
Edmund, the Admiral, Tunstall there,
With thee their charge will blithely share;
There fight thine own retainers too
Beneath De Burg, thy steward true.'
' Thanks, noble Surrey !' Marmion said,
Nor further greeting there he paid,
But, parting like a thunderbolt,
    First in the vanguard made a halt, 730
    Where such a shout there rose
Of ' Marmion ! Marmion !' that the cry,
Up Flodden mountain shrilling high,
    Startled the Scottish foes.

XXV

Blount and Fitz-Eustace rested still
With Lady Clare upon the hill,
On which — for far the day was spent —
The western sunbeams now were bent;
The cry they heard, its meaning knew,
Could plain their distant comrades view: 740
    Sadly to Blount did Eustace say,
' Unworthy office here to stay !
No hope of gilded spurs to-day. —

But see ! look up — on Flodden bent
The Scottish foe has fired his tent.'
    And sudden, as he spoke,
From the sharp ridges of the hill,
All downward to the banks of Till,
    Was wreathed in sable smoke.
Volumed and vast, and rolling far,   750
The cloud enveloped Scotland's war
    As down the hill they broke;
Nor martial shout, nor minstrel tone,
Announced their march; their tread alone,
At times one warning trumpet blown,
    At times a stifled hum,
Told England, from his mountain-throne
King James did rushing come.
Scarce could they hear or see their foes
Until at weapon-point they close. —   760
They close in clouds of smoke and dust,
With sword-sway and with lance's thrust;
    And such a yell was there,
Of sudden and portentous birth,
As if men fought upon the earth,
    And fiends in upper air:
Oh ! life and death were in the shout,
Recoil and rally, charge and rout,
    And triumph and despair.   769
Long looked the anxious squires; their
    eye
Could in the darkness nought descry.

XXVI

At length the freshening western blast
Aside the shroud of battle cast;
And first the ridge of mingled spears
Above the brightening cloud appears,
And in the smoke the pennons flew,
As in the storm the white seamew.
Then marked they, dashing broad and far,
The broken billows of the war,
And plumed crests of chieftains brave   780
Floating like foam upon the wave;
    But nought distinct they see:
Wide raged the battle on the plain;
Spears shook and falchions flashed amain;
Fell England's arrow-flight like rain;
Crests rose, and stooped, and rose again,
    Wild and disorderly.
Amid the scene of tumult, high
They saw Lord Marmion's falcon fly;
And stainless Tunstall's banner white,   790
And Edmund Howard's lion bright,
Still bear them bravely in the fight,
    Although against them come
Of gallant Gordons many a one,
And many a stubborn Badenoch-man,

And many a rugged Border clan,
  With Huntly and with Home.—

XXVII

Far on the left, unseen the while,
Stanley broke Lennox and Argyle,
Though there the western mountaineer 800
Rushed with bare bosom on the spear,
And flung the feeble targe aside,
And with both hands the broadsword plied.
'T was vain. — But Fortune, on the right,
With fickle smile cheered Scotland's fight.
Then fell that spotless banner white,
  The Howard's lion fell;
Yet still Lord Marmion's falcon flew
With wavering flight, while fiercer grew
  Around the battle-yell. 810
The Border slogan rent the sky !
A Home ! a Gordon ! was the cry:
Loud were the clanging blows;
Advanced, — forced back, — now low, now
    high,
  The pennon sunk and rose;
As bends the bark's-mast in the gale,
When rent are rigging, shrouds, and sail,
  It wavered mid the foes.
No longer Blount the view could bear:
' By heaven and all its saints ! I swear 820
I will not see it lost !
Fitz-Eustace, you with Lady Clare
May bid your beads and patter prayer, —
  I gallop to the host.'
And to the fray he rode amain,
Followed by all the archer train.
The fiery youth, with desperate charge,
Made for a space an opening large, —
  The rescued banner rose, —
But darkly closed the war around, 830
Like pine-tree rooted from the ground
  It sank among the foes.
Then Eustace mounted too, — yet stayed,
As loath to leave the helpless maid,
When, fast as shaft can fly,
Bloodshot his eyes, his nostrils spread,
The loose rein dangling from his head,
Housing and saddle bloody red,
Lord Marmion's steed rushed by;
And Eustace, maddening at the sight, 840
  A look and sign to Clara cast
  To mark he would return in haste,
Then plunged into the fight.

XXVIII

Ask me not what the maiden feels,
Left in that dreadful hour alone:

Perchance her reason stoops or reels;
  Perchance a courage, not her own,
  Braces her mind to desperate tone. —
The scattered van of England wheels; —
  She only said, as loud in air 850
The tumult roared, ' Is Wilton there ? ' —
They fly, or, maddened by despair,
Fight but to die, — ' Is Wilton there ? '
With that, straight up the hill there rode
  Two horsemen drenched with gore,
And in their arms, a helpless load,
  A wounded knight they bore.
His hand still strained the broken brand;
His arms were smeared with blood and
    sand.
Dragged from among the horses' feet, 860
With dinted shield and helmet beat,
The falcon-crest and plumage gone,
Can that be haughty Marmion ! . . .
Young Blount his armor did unlace,
  And, gazing on his ghastly face,
  Said, ' By Saint George, he 's gone !
That spear-wound has our master sped,
And see the deep cut on his head !
  Good-night to Marmion.' — 869
' Unnurtured Blount ! thy brawling cease:
He opes his eyes,' said Eustace; ' peace ! '

XXIX

When, doffed his casque, he felt free air,
Around gan Marmion wildly stare:
' Where 's Harry Blount ? Fitz - Eustace
    where ?
Linger ye here, ye hearts of hare !
Redeem my pennon, — charge again !
Cry, " Marmion to the rescue ! " — Vain !
Last of my race, on battle-plain
That shout shall ne'er be heard again ! —
Yet my last thought is England's — fly, 880
  To Dacre bear my signet-ring;
  Tell him his squadrons up to bring. —
Fitz-Eustace, to Lord Surrey hie:
  Tunstall lies dead upon the field,
  His lifeblood stains the spotless shield;
  Edmund is down; my life is reft;
  The Admiral alone is left.
Let Stanley charge with spur of fire, —
With Chester charge, and Lancashire,
Full upon Scotland's central host, 890
Or victory and England 's lost. —
Must I bid twice ? — hence, varlets ! fly ! —
  Leave Marmion here alone — to die.'
  They parted, and alone he lay;
Clare drew her from the sight away,
Till pain wrung forth a lowly moan,

And half he murmured, ' Is there none
Of all my halls have nurst,
Page, squire, or groom, one cup to bring
Of blessed water from the spring,   900
To slake my dying thirst ! '

XXX

O Woman ! in our hours of ease
Uncertain, coy, and hard to please,
And variable as the shade
By the light quivering aspen made;
When pain and anguish wring the brow,
A ministering angel thou ! —
Scarce were the piteous accents said,
When with the baron's casque the maid
To the nigh streamlet ran: 910
Forgot were hatred, wrongs, and fears;
The plaintive voice alone she hears,
Sees but the dying man.
She stooped her by the runnel's side,
But in abhorrence backward drew;
For, oozing from the mountain's side
Where raged the war, a dark-red tide
Was curdling in the streamlet blue.
Where shall she turn ? — behold her mark
A little fountain cell,   920
Where water, clear as diamond spark,
In a stone basin fell.
Above, some half-worn letters say,
Drink. weary. pilgrim. drink. and. pray.
For. the. kind. soul. of. Sibyl. Grey.
Who. built. this. cross. and. well.
She filled the helm and back she hied,
And with surprise and joy espied
A monk supporting Marmion's head;
A pious man, whom duty brought   930
To dubious verge of battle fought,
To shrive the dying, bless the dead.

XXXI

Deep drank Lord Marmion of the wave,
And, as she stooped his brow to lave —
' Is it the hand of Clare,' he said,
' Or injured Constance, bathes my head ? '
Then, as remembrance rose, —
' Speak not to me of shrift or prayer !
I must redress her woes.   939
Short space, few words, are mine to spare;
Forgive and listen, gentle Clare ! ' —
' Alas ! ' she said, ' the while, —
Oh ! think of your immortal weal !
In vain for Constance is your zeal;
She — died at Holy Isle.' —
Lord Marmion started from the **ground**
As light as if he felt no wound,

Though in the action burst the tide
In torrents from his wounded side.   949
' Then it was truth,' he said — ' I knew
That the dark presage must be true. —
I would the Fiend, to whom belongs
The vengeance due to all her wrongs,
Would spare me but a day!
For wasting fire, and dying groan,
And priests slain on the altar stone,
Might bribe him for delay.
It may not be ! — this dizzy trance —
Curse on yon base marauder's lance,
And doubly cursed my failing brand !   960
A sinful heart makes feeble hand.'
Then fainting down on earth he sunk,
Supported by the trembling monk.

XXXII

With fruitless labor Clara bound
And strove to stanch the gushing wound;
The monk with unavailing cares
Exhausted all the Church's prayers.
Ever, he said, that, close and near,
A lady's voice was in his ear,
And that the priest he could not hear;   970
For that she ever sung,
' In the lost battle, borne down by the flying,
Where mingles war's rattle with groans of the
dying ! '
So the notes rung. —
' Avoid thee, Fiend ! — with cruel hand
Shake not the dying sinner's sand ! —
Oh ! look, my son, upon yon sign
Of the Redeemer's grace divine;
Oh ! think on faith and bliss ! —
By many a death-bed I have been,   980
And many a sinner's parting seen,
But never aught like this.' —
The war, that for a space did fail,
Now trebly thundering swelled the gale,
And ' Stanley ! ' was the cry. —
A light on Marmion's visage spread,
And fired his glazing eye;
With dying hand above his head
He shook the fragment of his blade,
And shouted ' Victory !   990
Charge, Chester, charge !   On, Stanley,
on ! '
Were the last words of Marmion.

XXXIII

By this, though deep the evening fell,
Still rose the battle's deadly swell,
For still the Scots around their king,
Unbroken, fought in desperate ring.

Where's now their victor vaward wing,
  Where Huntley, and where Home ? —
Oh ! for a blast of that dread horn,
On Fontarabian echoes borne,   1000
  That to King Charles did come,
When Rowland brave, and Olivier,
And every paladin and peer,
  On Roncesvalles died !
Such blasts might warn them, not in vain,
To quit the plunder of the slain
And turn the doubtful day again,
  While yet on Flodden side
Afar the Royal Standard flies,
And round it toils and bleeds and dies   1010
  Our Caledonian pride !
In vain the wish — for far away,
While spoil and havoc mark their way,
Near Sibyl's Cross the plunderers stray. —
'O lady,' cried the monk, ' away !'
And placed her on her steed,
And led her to the chapel fair
  Of Tilmouth upon Tweed.
There all the night they spent in prayer,
And at the dawn of morning there   1020
She met her kinsman, Lord Fitz-Clare.

XXXIV

But as they left the darkening heath
More desperate grew the strife of death.
The English shafts in volleys hailed,
In headlong charge their horse assailed;
Front, flank, and rear, the squadrons sweep
To break the Scottish circle deep
  That fought around their king.
But yet, though thick the shafts as snow,
Though charging knights like whirlwinds
  go,   1030
Though billmen ply the ghastly blow,
  Unbroken was the ring;
The stubborn spearmen still made good
  Their dark impenetrable wood,
Each stepping where his comrade stood
  The instant that he fell.
No thought was there of dastard flight;
Linked in the serried phalanx tight,
Groom fought like noble, squire like knight,
  As fearlessly and well,   1040
Till utter darkness closed her wing
O'er their thin host and wounded king.
Then skilful Surrey's sage commands
Led back from strife his shattered bands;
  And from the charge they drew,
As mountain-waves from wasted lands
  Sweep back to ocean blue.
Then did their loss his foemen know;

Their king, their lords, their mightiest
  low,
They melted from the field, as snow,   1050
When streams are swoln and southwinds
  blow,
  Dissolves in silent dew.
Tweed's echoes heard the ceaseless plash,
  While many a broken band
Disordered through her currents dash,
  To gain the Scottish land;
To town and tower, to down and dale,
To tell red Flodden's dismal tale,
And raise the universal wail.
Tradition, legend, tune, and song   1060
Shall many an age that wail prolong;
Still from the sire the son shall hear
Of the stern strife and carnage drear
  Of Flodden's fatal field,
Where shivered was fair Scotland's spear
  And broken was her shield !

XXXV

Day dawns upon the mountain's side. —
There, Scotland ! lay thy bravest pride,
Chiefs, knights, and nobles, many a one;
The sad survivors all are gone. —   1070
View not that corpse mistrustfully,
Defaced and mangled though it be;
Nor to yon Border castle high
Look northward with upbraiding eye;
  Nor cherish hope in vain
That, journeying far on foreign strand,
The Royal Pilgrim to his land
  May yet return again.
He saw the wreck his rashness wrought;
Reckless of life, he desperate fought,   1080
  And fell on Flodden plain:
And well in death his trusty brand,
Firm clenched within his manly hand,
  Beseemed the monarch slain.
But oh ! how changed since yon blithe
  night ! —
Gladly I turn me from the sight
  Unto my tale again.

XXXVI

Short is my tale: — Fitz-Eustace' care
A pierced and mangled body bare
To moated Lichfield's lofty pile;   1090
And there, beneath the southern aisle,
A tomb with Gothic sculpture fair
Did long Lord Marmion's image bear. —
Now vainly for its site you look;
'T was levelled when fanatic Brook
The fair cathedral stormed and took,

But, thanks to Heaven and good Saint
    Chad,
A guerdon meet the spoiler had ! —
There erst was martial Marmion found,
His feet upon a couchant hound,   1100
   His hands to heaven upraised;
And all around, on scutcheon rich,
And tablet carved, and fretted niche,
   His arms and feats were blazed.
And yet, though all was carved so fair,
And priest for Marmion breathed the
    prayer,
The last Lord Marmion lay not there.
From Ettrick woods a peasant swain
Followed his lord to Flodden plain, —
One of those flowers whom plaintive lay 1110
In Scotland mourns as ' wede away:'
Sore wounded, Sibyl's Cross he spied,
And dragged him to its foot, and died
Close by the noble Marmion's side.
The spoilers stripped and gashed the slain,
And thus their corpses were mista'en;
And thus in the proud baron's tomb
The lowly woodsman took the room.

XXXVII

Less easy task it were to show
Lord Marmion's nameless grave and low.
They dug his grave e'en where he lay, 1121
   But every mark is gone:
Time's wasting hand has done away
The simple Cross of Sibyl Grey,
   And broke her font of stone;
But yet from out the little hill
Oozes the slender springlet still.
   Oft halts the stranger there,
For thence may best his curious eye
The memorable field descry;   1130
   And shepherd boys repair
To seek the water-flag and rush,
And rest them by the hazel bush,
   And plait their garlands fair,
Nor dream they sit upon the grave
That holds the bones of Marmion brave. —
When thou shalt find the little hill,
With thy heart commune and be still.
If ever in temptation strong
Thou left'st the right path for the
    wrong,   1140
If every devious step thus trod
Still led thee further from the road,
Dread thou to speak presumptuous doom
On noble Marmion's lowly tomb;
But say, ' He died a gallant knight,
With sword in hand, for England's right.'

XXXVIII

I do not rhyme to that dull elf
Who cannot image to himself
That all through Flodden's dismal night
Wilton was foremost in the fight,   1150
That when brave Surrey's steed was slain
'T was Wilton mounted him again;
'T was Wilton's brand that deepest hewed
Amid the spearmen's stubborn wood:
Unnamed by Holinshed or Hall,
He was the living soul of all;
That, after fight, his faith made plain,
He won his rank and lands again,
And charged his old paternal shield
With bearings won on Flodden Field. 1160
Nor sing I to that simple maid
To whom it must in terms be said
That king and kinsmen did agree
To bless fair Clara's constancy;
Who cannot, unless I relate,
Paint to her mind the bridal's state, —
That Wolsey's voice the blessing spoke,
More, Sands, and Denny, passed the joke;
That bluff King Hal the curtain drew, 1169
And Katherine's hand the stocking threw;
And afterwards, for many a day,
That it was held enough to say,
In blessing to a wedded pair,
' Love they like Wilton and like Clare !'

L'ENVOY

TO THE READER

WHY then a final note prolong,
Or lengthen out a closing song,
Unless to bid the gentles speed,
Who long have listed to my rede ?
To statesmen grave, if such may deign
To read the minstrel's idle strain,
Sound head, clean hand, and piercing wit,
And patriotic heart — as PITT !
A garland for the hero's crest,
And twined by her he loves the best !
To every lovely lady bright,
What can I wish but faithful knight ?
To every faithful lover too,
What can I wish but lady true ?
And knowledge to the studious sage,
And pillow soft to head of age !
To thee, dear school-boy, whom my lay
Has cheated of thy hour of play,
Light task and merry holiday !
To all, to each, a fair good-night,
And pleasing dreams, and slumbers light !

THE LADY OF THE LAKE

INTRODUCTORY NOTE

The Lady of the Lake, Scott says, was a very sudden thought. It was begun in the fall of 1809, when *Marmion* had enjoyed a year and a half of popularity. 'The first hundred lines,' he writes to Lady Abercorn, 'were written, I think, in October, 1809, and the first canto was sent to your Ladyship in Ireland so soon as it was complete, and you were the first who saw them, excepting one friend and the printer, Mr. Ballantyne, who is a great critic as well as an excellent printer. I have been always, God help me, too poor and too impatient to let my poems lie by me for years, or for months either; on the contrary, they have hitherto been always sent to the press before they were a third part finished. This is, to be sure, a very reprehensible practice in many respects, and I hope I shall get the better of it the next time.'

He had by this time separated from Constable and made Ballantyne's interests his own. In his 'Introduction' given below, Scott details in lively fashion the effect which the reading of the poem, while in course of composition, had upon the friend who started in to 'heeze up his hope.' Lockhart quotes also from the recollection of Robert Cadell an account of the interest excited by the poem before it was published. 'James Ballantyne read the cantos from time to time to select coteries, as they advanced at press. Common fame was loud in their favor; a great poem was on all hands anticipated. I do not recollect that any of all the author's works was ever looked for with more intense anxiety, or that any one of them excited a more extraordinary sensation when it did appear. The whole country rang with the praises of the poet — crowds set off to view the scenery of Loch Katrine, till then comparatively unknown; and as the book came out just before the season for excursions, every house and inn in that neighborhood was crammed with a constant succession of visitors.' 'I have tried,' writes Scott to Lady Abercorn, 'according to promise, to make "a knight of love who never broke a vow." But welladay, though I have succeeded tolerably with the damsel, my lover, spite of my best exertions, is like to turn out what the players call a *walking gentleman.* It is incredible the pains it has cost me to give him a little dignity.' And then follows this curious and rueful reflection. 'Notwithstanding this, I have had

in my time melancholy cause to paint from experience, for I gained no advantage from three years' constancy, except the said experience and some advantage to my conversation and manners. Mrs. Scott's match and mine was of our own making, and proceeded from the most sincere affection on both sides, which has rather increased than diminished during twelve years' marriage. But it was something short of love in all its forms, which I suspect people only *feel* once in their lives; folks who have been nearly drowned in bathing rarely venturing a second time out of their depth.' In a later letter written to the same lady, he returns to the subject, which plainly gave him some uneasiness. 'As for my lover, I find with deep regret that, however interesting lovers are to each other, it is no easy matter to render them generally interesting. There was, however, another reason for keeping Malcolm Græme's character a little *under,* as the painters say, for it must otherwise have interfered with that of the king, which I was more anxious to bring forward in splendor, or something like it.'

Once again, in a letter to Miss Smith, who took the part of Ellen in a dramatization of the poem, he wrote: 'You must know this Malcolm Græme was a great plague to me from the beginning. You ladies can hardly comprehend how very stupid lovers are to everybody but mistresses. I gave him that dip in the lake by way of making him do something; but wet or dry I could make nothing of him. His insignificance is the greatest defect among many others in the poem; but the canvas was not broad enough to include him, considering I had to group the king, Roderick, and Douglas.'

On another point, Scott had been criticised by his vigilant friend Morritt. 'The only disappointment,' writes Morritt, 'I felt in the poem is your own fault. The character and terrific birth of Brian is so highly wrought that I expected him to appear again in the *dénouement,* and wanted to hear something more of him; but as we do not hear of his death, it is your own fault for introducing us to an acquaintance of so much promise and not telling us how he was afterwards disposed of.' To this Scott replied: 'Your criticism is quite just as to the Son of the dry bone, Brian. Truth is, I had intended the battle should have been more detailed, and that some of the persons mentioned in the third canto, and Brian in particular, should have been commemorated. I intended he should have been shot like a *corbie on a craig* as he was excommunicating and anathematizing the Saxons from some of the predominant peaks in the Trosachs. But I found the battle in itself too much displaced to admit of being prolonged by any details which could be spared. For it was in the first place *episodical*, and then all the principal characters had been disposed of before it came on, and were absent at the time of action, and nothing hinged upon the issue of consequence to the fable. So I e'en left it to the judgment of my reader whether Brian was worried in the Trosachs, or escaped to take earth in his old retreat in Benharrow, near Ardkinlas.'

The Lady of the Lake came out early in May, 1810, and its popularity is shown by the haste with which the dramatists laid hold of it, three separate versions being attempted. 'That Mr. Siddons is bringing it out,' Scott writes to the actress, Miss Smith, ' is very certain, but it is equally so that I have not seen and do not intend to see a line of it, because I would not willingly have the public of this place [Edinburgh] suppose that I was in any degree responsible for the success of the piece; it would be like submitting to be twice tried for the same offence. My utmost knowledge has been derived from chatting with Mrs. Siddons and Mrs. Young in the green-room, where I have been an occasional lounger since our company has been put on a respectable footing. . . . Whether the dialogue is in verse or prose I really do not know. There is a third *Lady of the Lake* on the *tapis* at Covent Garden, dramatized by no less genius than the united firm of Reynolds and Morton. But

though I have these theatrical grandchildren, as I may call them, I have seen none of them. I shall go to the Edinburgh piece when it is rehearsed with lights and scenes, and if I see anything that I think worth your adopting I will write to you. The strength will probably lie in the dumb show, music and decorations, for I have no idea that the language can be rendered very dramatic. If any person can make aught of it, I am sure you will. The mad Lowland captive if well played, should, I think, answer. I wish I could give you an idea of the original, whom I really saw in the Pass of Glencoe many years ago. It is one of the wildest and most tremendous passes in the Highlands, winding through huge masses of rock without a pile of verdure, and between mountains that seem rent asunder by an earthquake. This poor woman had placed herself in the wildest attitude imaginable, upon the very top of one of these huge fragments; she had scarce any covering but a tattered plaid, which left her arms, legs, and neck bare to the weather. Her long shaggy black hair was streaming backwards in the wind, and exposed a face rather wild and wasted than ugly, and bearing a very peculiar expression of frenzy. She had a handful of eagle's feathers in her hand. . . . The lady who plays this part should beware of singing with too stiff regularity; even her music, or rather her style of singing it, should be a little mad.'

Scott summed up his own analysis of the three long poems thus far published, when he wrote in 1812 : 'The force in the *Lay* is thrown on style ; in *Marmion*, on description, and in *The Lady of the Lake*, on incident.' When reissuing the poem in the collective edition of 1830, he prefixed the following

INTRODUCTION.

After the success of *Marmion*, I felt inclined to exclaim with Ulysses in the *Odyssey* : —

Οὗτος μὲν δὴ ἄεθλος ἀάατος ἐκτετέλεσται·
Νῦν αὖτε σκοπὸν ἄλλον.

Odys. x. 5.

' One venturous game my hand has won to-day —
Another, gallants, yet remains to play.'

The ancient manners, the habits and customs of the aboriginal race by whom the Highlands of Scotland were inhabited, had always appeared to me peculiarly adapted to poetry. The change in their manners, too, had taken place almost within my own time, or at least I had learned many particulars concerning the ancient state of the Highlands from the old

men of the last generation. I had always thought the old Scottish Gael highly adapted for poetical composition. The feuds and political dissensions which, half a century earlier, would have rendered the richer and wealthier part of the kingdom indisposed to countenance a poem, the scene of which was laid in the Highlands, were now sunk in the generous compassion which the English, more than any other nation, feel for the misfortunes of an honorable foe. The Poems of Ossian had by their popularity sufficiently shown that if writings on Highland subjects were qualified to interest the reader, mere national prejudices were, in the present day, very unlikely to interfere with their success.

I had also read a great deal, seen much, and heard more, of that romantic country where I was in the habit of spending some time every autumn ; and the scenery of Loch Katrine was connected with the recollection of many a dear friend and merry expedition of former days. This poem, the action of which lay among scenes so beautiful and so deeply imprinted on my recollections, was a labor of love, and it was no less so to recall the manners and incidents introduced. The frequent custom of James IV., and particularly of James V., to walk through their kingdom in disguise, afforded me the hint of an incident which never fails to be interesting if managed with the slightest address or dexterity.

I may now confess, however, that the employment, though attended with great pleasure, was not without its doubts and anxieties. A lady, to whom I was nearly related, and with whom I lived, during her whole life, on the most brotherly terms of affection, was residing with me at the time when the work was in progress, and used to ask me what I could possibly do to rise so early in the morning (that happening to be the most convenient to me for composition). At last I told her the subject of my meditations ; and I can never forget the anxiety and affection expressed in her reply. ‘ Do not be so rash,’ she said, ‘ my dearest cousin. You are already popular, — more so, perhaps, than you yourself will believe, or than even I, or other partial friends, can fairly allow to your merit. You stand high, — do not rashly attempt to climb higher, and incur the risk of a fall ; for, depend upon it, a favorite will not be permitted even to stumble with impunity.’ I replied to this affectionate expostulation in the words of Montrose, —

> ‘ “ He either fears his fate too much,
> 　Or his deserts are small,
> Who dares not put it to the touch
> 　To gain or lose it all.”

‘ If I fail,’ I said, for the dialogue is strong in my recollection, ‘ it is a sign that I ought never to have succeeded, and I will write prose for life : you shall see no change in my temper, nor will I eat a single meal the worse. But if I succeed, —

> ‘ “ Up with the bonnie blue bonnet,
> 　The dirk, and the feather, and a’ ! ”

Afterwards I showed my affectionate and anxious critic the first canto of the poem, which reconciled her to my imprudence. Nevertheless, although I answered thus confidently, with the obstinacy often said to be proper to those who bear my surname, I acknowledge that my confidence was considerably shaken by the warning of her excellent taste and unbiassed friendship. Nor was I much comforted by her retractation of the unfavorable judgment, when I recollected how likely a natural partiality was to effect that change of opinion. In such cases affection rises like a light on the canvas, improves any favorable tints which it formerly exhibited, and throws its defects into the shade.

I remember that about the same time a friend started in to ‘ heeze up my hope,’ like the ‘ sportsman with his cutty gun,’ in the old song. He was bred a farmer, but a man of powerful understanding, natural good taste, and warm poetical feeling, perfectly competent to supply the wants of an imperfect or irregular education. He was a passionate admirer of field-sports, which we often pursued together.

As this friend happened to dine with me at Ashestiel one day, I took the opportunity of reading to him the first canto of *The Lady of the Lake*, in order to ascertain the effect the poem was likely to produce upon a person who was but too favorable a representative of readers at large. It is of course to be supposed that I determined rather to guide my opinion by what my friend might appear to feel, than by what he might think fit to say. His reception of my recitation, or prelection, was rather singular. He placed his hand across his brow, and listened with great attention, through the whole account of the stag-hunt, till the dogs threw themselves into the lake to follow their master, who embarks with Ellen Douglas. He then started up with a sudden exclamation, struck his hand on the table, and declared, in a voice of censure calculated for the occasion, that the dogs must have been totally ruined by being permitted to take the water after such a severe chase. I own I was much encouraged by the species of revery which had possessed so zealous a follower of the sports of the ancient Nimrod, who had been completely surprised out of all doubts of the reality of the tale. Another of his remarks gave me less pleasure. He detected the identity of the king with the wandering knight, Fitz-James, when he winds his bugle to summon his attendants. He was probably thinking of the lively, but somewhat licentious, old ballad, in which the *dénouement* of a royal intrigue takes place as follows : —

> ‘ He took a bugle frae his side,
> 　He blew both loud and shrill,
> And four and twenty belted knights
> 　Came skipping ower the hill ;
> Then he took out a little knife,
> 　Let a’ his duddies fa’,
> And he was the brawest gentleman
> 　That was amang them a’.
> 　　And we ’ll go no more a roving,’ etc.

This discovery, as Mr. Pepys says of the rent in his camlet cloak, was but a trifle, yet it troubled me ; and I was at a good deal of pains to efface any marks by which I thought my secret could be traced before the conclusion, when I relied on it with the same hope of producing effect, with which the Irish post-boy is said to reserve a ' trot for the avenue.'

I took uncommon pains to verify the accuracy of the local circumstances of this story. I recollect, in particular, that to ascertain whether I was telling a probable tale I went into Perthshire, to see whether King James could actually have ridden from the banks of Loch Vennachar to Stirling Castle within the time supposed in the poem, and had the pleasure to satisfy myself that it was quite practicable.

After a considerable delay, *The Lady of the Lake* appeared in June, 1810 ; and its success was certainly so extraordinary as to induce me for the moment to conclude that I had at last fixed a nail in the proverbially inconstant wheel of Fortune, whose stability in behalf of an individual who had so boldly courted her favors for three successive times had not as yet been shaken. I had attained, perhaps, that degree of reputation at which prudence, or certainly timidity, would have made a halt, and discontinued efforts by which I was far more likely to diminish my fame than to increase it. But, as the celebrated John Wilkes is said to have explained to his late Majesty, that he himself, amid his full tide of popularity, was never a Wilkite, so I can, with honest truth, exculpate myself from having been at any time a partisan of my own poetry, even when it was in the highest fashion with the million. It must not be supposed that I was either so ungrateful or so superabundantly candid as to despise or scorn the value of those whose voice had elevated me so much higher than my own opinion told me I deserved. I felt, on the contrary, the more grateful to the public, as receiving that from partiality to me, which I could not have claimed from merit ; and I endeavored to deserve the partiality by continuing such exertions as I was capable of for their amusement.

It may be that I did not, in this continued course of scribbling, consult either the interest of the public or my own. But the former had effectual means of defending themselves, and could, by their coldness, sufficiently check any approach to intrusion ; and for myself, I had now for several years dedicated my hours so much to literary labor that I should have felt difficulty in employing myself otherwise ; and so, like Dogberry, I generously bestowed all my tediousness on the public, comforting myself with the reflection that, if posterity should think me undeserving of the favor with which I was regarded by my contemporaries, ' they could not but say I *had* the crown,' and had enjoyed for a time that popularity which is so much coveted.

I conceived, however, that I held the distinguished situation I had obtained, however unworthily, rather like the champion of pugilism, on the condition of being always ready to show proofs of my skill, than in the manner of the champion of chivalry, who performs his duties only on rare and solemn occasions. I was in any case conscious that I could not long hold a situation which the caprice rather than the judgment of the public had bestowed upon me, and preferred being deprived of my precedence by some more worthy rival, to sinking into contempt for my indolence, and losing my reputation by what Scottish lawyers call the *negative prescription.* Accordingly, those who choose to look at the Introduction to *Rokeby,* will be able to trace the steps by which I declined as a poet to figure as a novelist ; as the ballad says, Queen Eleanor sunk at Charing Cross to rise again at Queenhithe.

It only remains for me to say that, during my short preëminence of popularity, I faithfully observed the rules of moderation which I had resolved to follow before I began my course as a man of letters. If a man is determined to make a noise in the world, he is as sure to encounter abuse and ridicule, as he who gallops furiously through a village must reckon on being followed by the curs in full cry. Experienced persons know that in stretching to flog the latter, the rider is very apt to catch a bad fall ; nor is an attempt to chastise a malignant critic attended with less danger to the author. On this principle, I let parody, burlesque, and squibs find their own level ; and while the latter hissed most fiercely, I was cautious never to catch them up, as schoolboys do, to throw them back against the naughty boy who fired them off, wisely remembering that they are in such cases apt to explode in the handling. Let me add that my reign (since Byron has so called it) was marked by some instances of good-nature as well as patience. I never refused a literary person of merit such services in smoothing his way to the public as were in my power ; and I had the advantage — rather an uncommon one with our irritable race — to enjoy general favor without incurring permanent ill-will, so far as is known to me, among any of my contemporaries.

ABBOTSFORD, April, 1830.

THE LADY OF THE LAKE

TO

THE MOST NOBLE

JOHN JAMES, MARQUIS OF ABERCORN

&c., &c., &c.,

THIS POEM IS INSCRIBED BY

THE AUTHOR.

ARGUMENT

THE scene of the following Poem is laid chiefly in the vicinity of Loch Katrine, in the Western Highlands of Perthshire. The time of Action includes Six Days, and the transactions of each Day occupy a Canto.

CANTO FIRST

THE CHASE

HARP of the North ! that mouldering long
hast hung
On the witch-elm that shades Saint Fillan's spring,
And down the fitful breeze thy numbers
flung,
Till envious ivy did around thee cling,
Muffling with verdant ringlet every
string, —
O Minstrel Harp, still must thine accents
sleep ?
Mid rustling leaves and fountains murmuring,
Still must thy sweeter sounds their
silence keep,
Nor bid a warrior smile, nor teach a maid
to weep ?

Not thus, in ancient days of Caledon,   10
Was thy voice mute amid the festal
crowd,
When lay of hopeless love, or glory won,
Aroused the fearful or subdued the
proud.
At each according pause was heard aloud
Thine ardent symphony sublime and high !
Fair dames and crested chiefs attention
bowed;
For still the burden of thy minstrelsy
Was Knighthood's dauntless deed, and
Beauty's matchless eye.

O, wake once more ! how rude soe'er the
hand
That ventures o'er thy magic maze to
stray;   20
O, wake once more ! though scarce my
skill command
Some feeble echoing of thine earlier lay:
Though harsh and faint, and soon to die
away,
And all unworthy of thy nobler strain,
Yet if one heart throb higher at its sway,
The wizard note has not been touched in
vain.
Then silent be no more ! Enchantress,
wake again !

I

The stag at eve had drunk his fill,
Where danced the moon on Monan's rill,
And deep his midnight lair had made   30
In lone Glenartney's hazel shade;
But when the sun his beacon red
Had kindled on Benvoirlich's head,
The deep-mouthed bloodhound's heavy bay
Resounded up the rocky way,
And faint, from farther distance borne,
Were heard the clanging hoof and horn.

II

As Chief, who hears his warder call,
'To arms ! the foemen storm the wall,'
The antlered monarch of the waste   40
Sprung from his heathery couch in haste.
But ere his fleet career he took,
The dew-drops from his flanks he shook;

Like crested leader proud and high
Tossed his beamed frontlet to the sky;
A moment gazed adown the dale,
A moment snuffed the tainted gale,
A moment listened to the cry,
That thickened as the chase drew nigh;
Then, as the headmost foes appeared,   50
With one brave bound the copse he cleared,
And, stretching forward free and far,
Sought the wild heaths of Uam-Var.

III

Yelled on the view the opening pack;
Rock, glen, and cavern paid them back;
To many a mingled sound at once
The awakened mountain gave response.
A hundred dogs bayed deep and strong,
Clattered a hundred steeds along,
Their peal the merry horns rung out,   60
A hundred voices joined the shout;
With hark and whoop and wild halloo,
No rest Benvoirlich's echoes knew.
Far from the tumult fled the roe,
Close in her covert cowered the doe,
The falcon, from her cairn on high,
Cast on the rout a wondering eye,
Till far beyond her piercing ken
The hurricane had swept the glen.
Faint, and more faint, its failing din   70
Returned from cavern, cliff, and linn,
And silence settled, wide and still,
On the lone wood and mighty hill.

IV

Less loud the sounds of sylvan war
Disturbed the heights of Uam-Var,
And roused the cavern where, 't is told,
A giant made his den of old;
For ere that steep ascent was won,
High in his pathway hung the sun,
And many a gallant, stayed perforce,   80
Was fain to breathe his faltering horse,
And of the trackers of the deer
Scarce half the lessening pack was near;
So shrewdly on the mountain-side
Had the bold burst their mettle tried.

V

The noble stag was pausing now
Upon the mountain's southern brow,
Where broad extended, far beneath,
The varied realms of fair Menteith.
With anxious eye he wandered o'er   90
Mountain and meadow, moss and moor,

And pondered refuge from his toil,
By far Lochard or Aberfoyle.
But nearer was the copsewood gray
That waved and wept on Loch Achray,
And mingled with the pine-trees blue
On the bold cliffs of Benvenue.
Fresh vigor with the hope returned,
With flying foot the heath he spurned,
Held westward with unwearied race,   100
And left behind the panting chase.

VI

'T were long to tell what steeds gave o'er,
As swept the hunt through Cambusmore;
What reins were tightened in despair,
When rose Benledi's ridge in air;
Who flagged upon Bochastle's heath,
Who shunned to stem the flooded Teith, —
For twice that day, from shore to shore,
The gallant stag swam stoutly o'er.
Few were the stragglers, following far,   110
That reached the lake of Vennachar;
And when the Brigg of Turk was won,
The headmost horseman rode alone.

VII

Alone, but with unbated zeal,
That horseman plied the scourge and steel;
For jaded now, and spent with toil,
Embossed with foam, and dark with soil,
While every gasp with sobs he drew,
The laboring stag strained full in view.
Two dogs of black Saint Hubert's breed,   120
Unmatched for courage, breath, and speed,
Fast on his flying traces came,
And all but won that desperate game;
For, scarce a spear's length from his haunch,
Vindictive toiled the bloodhounds stanch;
Nor nearer might the dogs attain,
Nor farther might the quarry strain.
Thus up the margin of the lake,
Between the precipice and brake,
O'er stock and rock their race they take.   130

VIII

The Hunter marked that mountain high,
The lone lake's western boundary,
And deemed the stag must turn to bay,
Where that huge rampart barred the way;
Already glorying in the prize,
Measured his antlers with his eyes;
For the death-wound and death-halloo
Mustered his breath, his whinyard drew: —
But thundering as he came prepared,

With ready arm and weapon bared,   140
The wily quarry shunned the shock,
And turned him from the opposing rock;
Then, dashing down a darksome glen,
Soon lost to hound and Hunter's ken,
In the deep Trosachs' wildest nook
His solitary refuge took.
There, while close couched the thicket shed
Cold dews and wild flowers on his head,
He heard the baffled dogs in vain
Rave through the hollow pass amain,   150
Chiding the rocks that yelled again.

IX

Close on the hounds the Hunter came,
To cheer them on the vanished game;
But, stumbling in the rugged dell,
The gallant horse exhausted fell.
The impatient rider strove in vain
To rouse him with the spur and rein,
For the good steed, his labors o'er,
Stretched his stiff limbs, to rise no more;
Then, touched with pity and remorse,   160
He sorrowed o'er the expiring horse.
' I little thought, when first thy rein
I slacked upon the banks of Seine,
That Highland eagle e'er should feed
On thy fleet limbs, my matchless steed!
Woe worth the chase, woe worth the day,
That costs thy life, my gallant gray!'

X

Then through the dell his horn resounds,
From vain pursuit to call the hounds.   169
Back limped, with slow and crippled pace,
The sulky leaders of the chase;
Close to their master's side they pressed,
With drooping tail and humbled crest;
But still the dingle's hollow throat
Prolonged the swelling bugle-note.
The owlets started from their dream,
The eagles answered with their scream,
Round and around the sounds were cast,
Till echo seemed an answering blast;
And on the Hunter hied his way,   180
To join some comrades of the day,
Yet often paused, so strange the road,
So wondrous were the scenes it showed.

XI

The western waves of ebbing day
Rolled o'er the glen their level way;
Each purple peak, each flinty spire,
Was bathed in floods of living fire.
But not a setting beam could glow

Within the dark ravines below,
Where twined the path in shadow hid,   190
Round many a rocky pyramid,
Shooting abruptly from the dell
Its thunder-splintered pinnacle;
Round many an insulated mass,
The native bulwarks of the pass,
Huge as the tower which builders vain
Presumptuous piled on Shinar's plain.
The rocky summits, split and rent,
Formed turret, dome, or battlement,
Or seemed fantastically set   200
With cupola or minaret,
Wild crests as pagod ever decked,
Or mosque of Eastern architect.
Nor were these earth-born castles bare,
Nor lacked they many a banner fair;
For, from their shivered brows displayed,
Far o'er the unfathomable glade,
All twinkling with the dewdrop sheen,
The brier-rose fell in streamers green,
And creeping shrubs of thousand dyes   210
Waved in the west-wind's summer sighs.

XII

Boon nature scattered, free and wild,
Each plant or flower, the mountain's child.
Here eglantine embalmed the air,
Hawthorn and hazel mingled there;
The primrose pale and violet flower
Found in each clift a narrow bower;
Foxglove and nightshade, side by side,
Emblems of punishment and pride,   219
Grouped their dark hues with every stain
The weather-beaten crags retain.
With boughs that quaked at every breath,
Gray birch and aspen wept beneath;
Aloft, the ash and warrior oak
Cast anchor in the rifted rock;
And, higher yet, the pine-tree hung
His shattered trunk, and frequent flung,
Where seemed the cliffs to meet on high,
His boughs athwart the narrowed sky.   229
Highest of all, where white peaks glanced,
Where glistening streamers waved and
          danced,
The wanderer's eye could barely view
The summer heaven's delicious blue;
So wondrous wild, the whole might seem
The scenery of a fairy dream.

XIII

Onward, amid the copse 'gan peep
A narrow inlet, still and deep,
Affording scarce such breadth of brim

As served the wild duck's brood to swim. 239
Lost for a space, through thickets veering,
But broader when again appearing,
Tall rocks and tufted knolls their face
Could on the dark-blue mirror trace;
And farther as the Hunter strayed,
Still broader sweep its channels made.
The shaggy mounds no longer stood,
Emerging from entangled wood,
But, wave-encircled, seemed to float,
Like castle girdled with its moat;
Yet broader floods extending still   250
Divide them from their parent hill,
Till each, retiring, claims to be
An islet in an inland sea.

XIV

And now, to issue from the glen,
No pathway meets the wanderer's ken,
Unless he climb with footing nice
A far-projecting precipice.
The broom's tough roots his ladder made,
The hazel saplings lent their aid;
And thus an airy point he won,   260
Where, gleaming with the setting sun,
One burnished sheet of living gold,
Loch Katrine lay beneath him rolled,
In all her length far winding lay,
With promontory, creek, and bay,
And islands that, empurpled bright,
Floated amid the livelier light,
And mountains that like giants stand
To sentinel enchanted land.
High on the south, huge Benvenue   270
Down to the lake in masses threw
Crags, knolls, and mounds, confusedly
    hurled,
The fragments of an earlier world;
A wildering forest feathered o'er
His ruined sides and summit hoar,
While on the north, through middle air,
Ben-an heaved high his forehead bare.

XV

From the steep promontory gazed
The stranger, raptured and amazed;   279
And, ' What a scene were here,' he cried,
' For princely pomp or churchman's pride !
On this bold brow, a lordly tower;
In that soft vale, a lady's bower;
On yonder meadow far away,
The turrets of a cloister gray;
How blithely might the bugle-horn
Chide on the lake the lingering morn !
How sweet at eve the lover's lute

Chime when the groves were still and
    mute !
And when the midnight moon should lave
Her forehead in the silver wave,   291
How solemn on the ear would come
The holy matins' distant hum,
While the deep peal's commanding tone
Should wake, in yonder islet lone,
A sainted hermit from his cell,
To drop a bead with every knell !
And bugle, lute, and bell, and all,
Should each bewildered stranger call
To friendly feast and lighted hall.   300

XVI

' Blithe were it then to wander here !
But now — beshrew yon nimble deer —
Like that same hermit's, thin and spare,
The copse must give my evening fare;
Some mossy bank my couch must be,
Some rustling oak my canopy.
Yet pass we that; the war and chase
Give little choice of resting-place; —
A summer night in greenwood spent
Were but to-morrow's merriment: 310
But hosts may in these wilds abound,
Such as are better missed than found;
To meet with Highland plunderers here
Were worse than loss of steed or deer. —
I am alone; — my bugle-strain
May call some straggler of the train;
Or, fall the worst that may betide,
Ere now this falchion has been tried.'

XVII

But scarce again his horn he wound,
When lo ! forth starting at the sound,   320
From underneath an aged oak
That slanted from the islet rock,
A damsel guider of its way,
A little skiff shot to the bay,
That round the promontory steep
Led its deep line in graceful sweep,
Eddying, in almost viewless wave,
The weeping willow twig to lave,
And kiss, with whispering sound and slow,
The beach of pebbles bright as snow.   330
The boat had touched this silver strand
Just as the Hunter left his stand,
And stood concealed amid the brake,
To view this Lady of the Lake.
The maiden paused, as if again
She thought to catch the distant strain.
With head upraised, and look intent,
And eye and ear attentive bent,

And locks flung back, and lips apart,
Like monument of Grecian art,   340
In listening mood, she seemed to stand,
The guardian Naiad of the strand.

XVIII

And ne'er did Grecian chisel trace
A Nymph, a Naiad, or a Grace,
Of finer form or lovelier face !
What though the sun, with ardent frown,
Had slightly tinged her cheek with
    brown, —
The sportive toil, which, short and light,
Had dyed her glowing hue so bright,
Served too in hastier swell to show   350
Short glimpses of a breast of snow:
What though no rule of courtly grace
To measured mood had trained her pace, —
A foot more light, a step more true,
Ne'er from the heath-flower dashed the dew;
E'en the slight harebell raised its head,
Elastic from her airy tread:
What though upon her speech there hung
The accents of the mountain tongue, —
Those silver sounds, so soft, so dear,   360
The listener held his breath to hear !

XIX

A chieftain's daughter seemed the maid;
Her satin snood, her silken plaid,
Her golden brooch, such birth betrayed.
And seldom was a snood amid
Such wild luxuriant ringlets hid,
Whose glossy black to shame might bring
The plumage of the raven's wing;
And seldom o'er a breast so fair
Mantled a plaid with modest care,   370
And never brooch the folds combined
Above a heart more good and kind.
Her kindness and her worth to spy,
You need but gaze on Ellen's eye;
Not Katrine in her mirror blue
Gives back the shaggy banks more true,
Than every free-born glance confessed
The guileless movements of her breast;
Whether joy danced in her dark eye,
Or woe or pity claimed a sigh,   380
Or filial love was glowing there,
Or meek devotion poured a prayer,
Or tale of injury called forth
The indignant spirit of the North.
One only passion unrevealed
With maiden pride the maid concealed,
Yet not less purely felt the flame; —
O, need I tell that passion's name ?

XX

Impatient of the silent horn,
Now on the gale her voice was borne: — 390
'Father !' she cried; the rocks around
Loved to prolong the gentle sound.
Awhile she paused, no answer came; —
'Malcolm, was thine the blast ?' the name
Less resolutely uttered fell,
The echoes could not catch the swell.
'A stranger I,' the Huntsman said,
Advancing from the hazel shade.
The maid, alarmed, with hasty oar
Pushed her light shallop from the shore, 400
And when a space was gained between,
Closer she drew her bosom's screen; —
So forth the startled swan would swing,
So turn to prune his ruffled wing.
Then safe, though fluttered and amazed,
She paused, and on the stranger gazed.
Not his the form, nor his the eye,
That youthful maidens wont to fly.

XXI

On his bold visage middle age
Had slightly pressed its signet sage,   410
Yet had not quenched the open truth
And fiery vehemence of youth;
Forward and frolic glee was there,
The will to do, the soul to dare,
The sparkling glance, soon blown to fire,
Of hasty love or headlong ire.
His limbs were cast in manly mould
For hardy sports or contest bold;
And though in peaceful garb arrayed,
And weaponless except his blade,   420
His stately mien as well implied
A high-born heart, a martial pride,
As if a baron's crest he wore,
And sheathed in armor trode the shore.
Slighting the petty need he showed,
He told of his benighted road;
His ready speech flowed fair and free,
In phrase of gentlest courtesy,
Yet seemed that tone and gesture bland
Less used to sue than to command   430

XXII

Awhile the maid the stranger eyed,
And, reassured, at length replied,
That Highland halls were open still
To wildered wanderers of the hill.
'Nor think you unexpected come
To yon lone isle, our desert home;
Before the heath had lost the dew,
This morn, a couch was pulled for you;

On yonder mountain's purple head
Have ptarmigan and heath-cock bled,   440
And our broad nets have swept the mere,
To furnish forth your evening cheer.' —
' Now, by the rood, my lovely maid,
Your courtesy has erred,' he said;
' No right have I to claim, misplaced,
The welcome of expected guest.
A wanderer, here by fortune tost,
My way, my friends, my courser lost,
I ne'er before, believe me, fair,
Have ever drawn your mountain air,   450
Till on this lake's romantic strand
I found a fay in fairy land ! ' —

XXIII

' I well believe,' the maid replied,
As her light skiff approached the side, —
' I well believe, that ne'er before
Your foot has trod Loch Katrine's shore;
But yet, as far as yesternight,
Old Allan-bane foretold your plight, —
A gray-haired sire, whose eye intent
Was on the visioned future bent.   460
He saw your steed, a dappled gray,
Lie dead beneath the birchen way;
Painted exact your form and mien,
Your hunting-suit of Lincoln green,
That tasselled horn so gayly gilt,
That falchion's crooked blade and hilt,
That cap with heron plumage trim,
And you two hounds so dark and grim.
He bade that all should ready be
To grace a guest of fair degree;   470
But light I held his prophecy,
And deemed it was my father's horn
Whose echoes o'er the lake were borne.'

XXIV

The stranger smiled: — ' Since to your home
A destined errant-knight I come,
Announced by prophet sooth and old,
Doomed, doubtless, for achievement bold,
I 'll lightly front each high emprise
For one kind glance of those bright eyes.
Permit me first the task to guide   480
Your fairy frigate o'er the tide.'
The maid, with smile suppressed and sly,
The toil unwonted saw him try;
For seldom, sure, if e'er before,
His noble hand had grasped an oar:
Yet with main strength his strokes he drew,
And o'er the lake the shallop flew;

With heads erect and whimpering cry,
The hounds behind their passage ply.
Nor frequent does the bright oar break   490
The darkening mirror of the lake,
Until the rocky isle they reach,
And moor their shallop on the beach.

XXV

The stranger viewed the shore around;
'T was all so close with copsewood bound,
Nor track nor pathway might declare
That human foot frequented there,
Until the mountain maiden showed
A clambering unsuspected road,   499
That winded through the tangled screen,
And opened on a narrow green,
Where weeping birch and willow round
With their long fibres swept the ground.
Here, for retreat in dangerous hour,
Some chief had framed a rustic bower.

XXVI

It was a lodge of ample size,
But strange of structure and device;
Of such materials as around
The workman's hand had readiest found.
Lopped of their boughs, their hoar trunks
bared,   510
And by the hatchet rudely squared,
To give the walls their destined height,
The sturdy oak and ash unite;
While moss and clay and leaves combined
To fence each crevice from the wind.
The lighter pine-trees overhead
Their slender length for rafters spread,
And withered heath and rushes dry
Supplied a russet canopy.
Due westward, fronting to the green,   520
A rural portico was seen,
Aloft on native pillars borne,
Of mountain fir with bark unshorn,
Where Ellen's hand had taught to twine
The ivy and Idæan vine,
The clematis, the favored flower
Which boasts the name of virgin-bower,
And every hardy plant could bear
Loch Katrine's keen and searching air.
An instant in this porch she stayed,   530
And gayly to the stranger said:
' On heaven and on thy lady call,
And enter the enchanted hall ! '

XXVII

' My hope, my heaven, my trust must be,
My gentle guide, in following thee ! ' —

He crossed the threshold, — and a clang
Of angry steel that instant rang.
To his bold brow his spirit rushed,
But soon for vain alarm he blushed,
When on the floor he saw displayed,　540
Cause of the din, a naked blade
Dropped from the sheath, that careless
　　　flung
Upon a stag's huge antlers swung;
For all around, the walls to grace,
Hung trophies of the fight or chase:
A target there, a bugle here,
A battle-axe, a hunting-spear,
And broadswords, bows, and arrows store,
With the tusked trophies of the boar.
Here grins the wolf as when he died,　550
And there the wild-cat's brindled hide
The frontlet of the elk adorns,
Or mantles o'er the bison's horns;
Pennons and flags defaced and stained,
That blackening streaks of blood retained,
And deer-skins, dappled, dun, and white,
With otter's fur and seal's unite,
In rude and uncouth tapestry all,
To garnish forth the sylvan hall.　559

XXVIII

The wondering stranger round him gazed,
And next the fallen weapon raised: —
Few were the arms whose sinewy strength
Sufficed to stretch it forth at length.
And as the brand he poised and swayed,
'I never knew but one,' he said,
'Whose stalwart arm might brook to wield
A blade like this in battle-field.'
She sighed, then smiled and took the word;
'You see the guardian champion's sword;
As light it trembles in his hand　570
As in my grasp a hazel wand:
My sire's tall form might grace the part
Of Ferragus or Ascabart,
But in the absent giant's hold
Are women now, and menials old.'

XXIX

The mistress of the mansion came,
Mature of age, a graceful dame,
Whose easy step and stately port
Had well become a princely court,
To whom, though more than kindred
　　　knew,　580
Young Ellen gave a mother's due.
Meet welcome to her guest she made,
And every courteous rite was paid,
That hospitality could claim,

Though all unasked his birth and name.
Such then the reverence to a guest,
That fellest foe might join the feast,
And from his deadliest foeman's door
Unquestioned turn, the banquet o'er.
At length his rank the stranger names,　590
'The Knight of Snowdoun, James Fitz-
　　　James;
Lord of a barren heritage,
Which his brave sires, from age to age,
By their good swords had held with toil;
His sire had fallen in such turmoil,
And he, God wot, was forced to stand
Oft for his right with blade in hand.
This morning with Lord Moray's train
He chased a stalwart stag in vain,　599
Outstripped his comrades, missed the deer,
Lost his good steed, and wandered here.'

XXX

Fain would the Knight in turn require
The name and state of Ellen's sire.
Well showed the elder lady's mien
That courts and cities she had seen;
Ellen, though more her looks displayed
The simple grace of sylvan maid,
In speech and gesture, form and face,
Showed she was come of gentle race.
'T were strange in ruder rank to find　610
Such looks, such manners, and such mind.
Each hint the Knight of Snowdoun gave,
Dame Margaret heard with silence grave;
Or Ellen, innocently gay,
Turned all inquiry light away: —
'Weird women we ! by dale and down
We dwell, afar from tower and town.
We stem the flood, we ride the blast,　618
On wandering knights our spells we cast;
While viewless minstrels touch the string,
'T is thus our charmed rhymes we sing.'
She sung, and still a harp unseen
Filled up the symphony between.

XXXI
SONG

'Soldier, rest ! thy warfare o'er,
　Sleep the sleep that knows not break-
　　　ing;
Dream of battled fields no more,
　Days of danger, nights of waking.
In our isle's enchanted hall,
　Hands unseen thy couch are strewing,
Fairy strains of music fall,　630
　Every sense in slumber dewing.
Soldier, rest ! thy warfare o'er,

Dream of fighting fields no more;
Sleep the sleep that knows not breaking,
Morn of toil, nor night of waking.

'No rude sound shall reach thine ear,
 Armor's clang of war-steed champing,
Trump nor pibroch summon here
 Mustering clan or squadron tramping.
Yet the lark's shrill fife may come   640
 At the daybreak from the fallow,
And the bittern sound his drum,
 Booming from the sedgy shallow.
Ruder sounds shall none be near,
Guards nor warders challenge here,
Here's no war-steed's neigh and champ-
 ing,
Shouting clans or squadrons stamping.'

XXXII

She paused, — then, blushing, led the lay,
To grace the stranger of the day.
Her mellow notes awhile prolong   650
The cadence of the flowing song,
Till to her lips in measured frame
The minstrel verse spontaneous came.

SONG CONTINUED

'Huntsman, rest! thy chase is done;
 While our slumbrous spells assail ye,
Dream not, with the rising sun,
 Bugles here shall sound reveillé.
Sleep! the deer is in his den;
Sleep! thy hounds are by thee lying:
Sleep! nor dream in yonder glen   660
How thy gallant steed lay dying.
Huntsman, rest! thy chase is done;
Think not of the rising sun,
For at dawning to assail ye
Here no bugles sound reveillé.'

XXXIII

The hall was cleared, — the stranger's bed
Was there of mountain heather spread,
Where oft a hundred guests had lain,
And dreamed their forest sports again.
But vainly did the heath-flower shed   670
Its moorland fragrance round his head;
Not Ellen's spell had lulled to rest
The fever of his troubled breast.
In broken dreams the image rose
Of varied perils, pains, and woes:
His steed now flounders in the brake,
Now sinks his barge upon the lake;
Now leader of a broken host,
His standard falls, his honor's lost.

Then, — from my couch may heavenly
 might   680
Chase that worst phantom of the night! —
Again returned the scenes of youth,
Of confident, undoubting truth;
Again his soul he interchanged
With friends whose hearts were long es-
 tranged.
They come, in dim procession led,
The cold, the faithless, and the dead;
As warm each hand, each brow as gay,
As if they parted yesterday.
And doubt distracts him at the view, — 690
O were his senses false or true?
Dreamed he of death or broken vow,
Or is it all a vision now?

XXXIV

At length, with Ellen in a grove
He seemed to walk and speak of love;
She listened with a blush and sigh,
His suit was warm, his hopes were high.
He sought her yielded hand to clasp,
And a cold gauntlet met his grasp:
The phantom's sex was changed and
 gone,   700
Upon its head a helmet shone;
Slowly enlarged to giant size,
With darkened cheek and threatening eyes,
The grisly visage, stern and hoar,
To Ellen still a likeness bore. —
He woke, and, panting with affright,
Recalled the vision of the night.
The hearth's decaying brands were red,
And deep and dusky lustre shed,
Half showing, half concealing, all   710
The uncouth trophies of the hall.
Mid those the stranger fixed his eye
Where that huge falchion hung on high,
And thoughts on thoughts, a countless
 throng,
Rushed, chasing countless thoughts along,
Until, the giddy whirl to cure,
He rose and sought the moonshine pure.

XXXV

The wild rose, eglantine, and broom
Wasted around their rich perfume;
The birch-trees wept in fragrant balm; 720
The aspens slept beneath the calm;
The silver light, with quivering glance,
Played on the water's still expanse, —
Wild were the heart whose passion's sway
Could rage beneath the sober ray!
He felt its calm, that warrior guest,

While thus he communed with his
   breast: —
'Why is it, at each turn I trace
Some memory of that exiled race ?
Can I not mountain maiden spy,   730
But she must bear the Douglas eye ?
Can I not view a Highland brand,
But it must match the Douglas hand ?
Can I not frame a fevered dream,
But still the Douglas is the theme ?
I 'll dream no more, — by manly mind
Not even in sleep is will resigned.
My midnight orisons said o'er,
I 'll turn to rest, and dream no more.'
His midnight orisons he told,   740
A prayer with every bead of gold,
Consigned to heaven his cares and woes,
And sunk in undisturbed repose,
Until the heath-cock shrilly crew,
And morning dawned on Benvenue.

CANTO SECOND

THE ISLAND

I

At morn the black-cock trims his jetty
   wing,
'T is morning prompts the linnet's blith-
   est lay,
All Nature's children feel the matin spring
Of life reviving, with reviving day;
And while yon little bark glides down the
   bay,
Wafting the stranger on his way again,
Morn's genial influence roused a minstrel
   gray,
And sweetly o'er the lake was heard thy
   strain,
Mixed with the sounding harp, O white-
   haired Allan-bane !

II

SONG

'Not faster yonder rowers' might   10
   Flings from their oars the spray,
Not faster yonder rippling bright,
That tracks the shallop's course in light,
   Melts in the lake away,
Than men from memory erase
The benefits of former days;
Then, stranger, go ! good speed the while,
Nor think again of the lonely isle.

'High place to thee in royal court,
   High place in battled line,   20
Good hawk and hound for sylvan sport !
Where beauty sees the brave resort,
   The honored meed be thine !
True be thy sword, thy friend sincere,
Thy lady constant, kind, and dear,
And lost in love's and friendship's smile
Be memory of the lonely isle !

III

SONG CONTINUED

'But if beneath yon southern sky
   A plaided stranger roam,
Whose drooping crest and stifled sigh,   30
And sunken cheek and heavy eye,
   Pine for his Highland home;
Then, warrior, then be thine to show
The care that soothes a wanderer's woe;
Remember then thy hap erewhile,
A stranger in the lonely isle.

'Or if on life's uncertain main
   Mishap shall mar thy sail;
If faithful, wise, and brave in vain,
Woe, want, and exile thou sustain   40
   Beneath the fickle gale;
Waste not a sigh on fortune changed,
On thankless courts, or friends estranged,
But come where kindred worth shall
   smile,
To greet thee in the lonely isle.'

IV

As died the sounds upon the tide,
The shallop reached the mainland side,
And ere his onward way he took,
The stranger cast a lingering look,
Where easily his eye might reach   50
The Harper on the islet beach,
Reclined against a blighted tree,
As wasted, gray, and worn as he.
To minstrel meditation given,
His reverend brow was raised to heaven,
As from the rising sun to claim
A sparkle of inspiring flame.
His hand, reclined upon the wire,
Seemed watching the awakening fire;
So still he sat as those who wait   60
Till judgment speak the doom of fate;
So still, as if no breeze might dare
To lift one lock of hoary hair;
So still, as life itself were fled
In the last sound his harp had sped.

V

Upon a rock with lichens wild,
Beside him Ellen sat and smiled. —
Smiled she to see the stately drake
Lead forth his fleet upon the lake,
While her vexed spaniel from the beach 70
Bayed at the prize beyond his reach ?
Yet tell me, then, the maid who knows,
Why deepened on her cheek the rose ? —
Forgive, forgive, Fidelity !
Perchance the maiden smiled to see
Yon parting lingerer wave adieu,
And stop and turn to wave anew;
And, lovely ladies, ere your ire
Condemn the heroine of my lyre,
Show me the fair would scorn to spy 80
And prize such conquest of her eye !

VI

While yet he loitered on the spot,
It seemed as Ellen marked him not;
But when he turned him to the glade,
One courteous parting sign she made;
And after, oft the knight would say,
That not when prize of festal day
Was dealt him by the brightest fair
Who e'er wore jewel in her hair,
So highly did his bosom swell 90
As at that simple mute farewell.
Now with a trusty mountain-guide,
And his dark stag-hounds by his side,
He parts, — the maid, unconscious still,
Watched him wind slowly round the hill;
But when his stately form was hid,
The guardian in her bosom chid, —
'Thy Malcolm ! vain and selfish maid !'
'T was thus upbraiding conscience said, —
'Not so had Malcolm idly hung 100
On the smooth phrase of Southern tongue;
Not so had Malcolm strained his eye
Another step than thine to spy.' —
'Wake, Allan-bane,' aloud she cried
To the old minstrel by her side, —
'Arouse thee from thy moody dream !
I 'll give thy harp heroic theme,
And warm thee with a noble name;
Pour forth the glory of the Græme !'
Scarce from her lip the word had rushed, 110
When deep the conscious maiden blushed;
For of his clan, in hall and bower,
Young Malcolm Græme was held the flower.

VII

The minstrel waked his harp, — three times
Arose the well-known martial chimes,
And thrice their high heroic pride
In melancholy murmurs died.
'Vainly thou bidst, O noble maid,'
Clasping his withered hands, he said,
'Vainly thou bidst me wake the strain, 120
Though all unwont to bid in vain.
Alas ! than mine a mightier hand
Has tuned my harp, my strings has spanned !
I touch the chords of joy, but low
And mournful answer notes of woe;
And the proud march which victors tread
Sinks in the wailing for the dead.
O, well for me, if mine alone
That dirge's deep prophetic tone !
If, as my tuneful fathers said, 130
This harp, which erst Saint Modan swayed,
Can thus its master's fate foretell,
Then welcome be the minstrel's knell !

VIII

'But ah ! dear lady, thus it sighed,
The eve thy sainted mother died;
And such the sounds which, while I strove
To wake a lay of war or love,
Came marring all the festal mirth,
Appalling me who gave them birth,
And, disobedient to my call, 140
Wailed loud through Bothwell's bannered hall,
Ere Douglases, to ruin driven,
Were exiled from their native heaven. —
O ! if yet worse mishap and woe
My master's house must undergo,
Or aught but weal to Ellen fair
Brood in these accents of despair,
No future bard, sad Harp ! shall fling
Triumph or rapture from thy string;
One short, one final strain shall flow, 150
Fraught with unutterable woe,
Then shivered shall thy fragments lie,
Thy master cast him down and die !'

IX

Soothing she answered him: 'Assuage,
Mine honored friend, the fears of age;
All melodies to thee are known
That harp has rung or pipe has blown,
In Lowland vale or Highland glen,
From Tweed to Spey — what marvel, then,
At times unbidden notes should rise, 160

Confusedly bound in memory's ties,
Entangling, as they rush along,
The war-march with the funeral song ? —
Small ground is now for boding fear;
Obscure, but safe, we rest us here.
My sire, in native virtue great,
Resigning lordship, lands, and state,
Not then to fortune more resigned
Than yonder oak might give the wind;
The graceful foliage storms may reave,   170
The noble stem they cannot grieve.
For me ' — she stooped, and, looking round,
Plucked   a   blue   harebell   from   the
    ground, —
' For me, whose memory scarce conveys
An image of more splendid days,
This little flower that loves the lea
May well my simple emblem be;
It drinks heaven's dew as blithe as rose
That in the King's own garden grows;
And when I place it in my hair,   180
Allan, a bard is bound to swear
He ne'er saw coronet so fair.'
Then playfully the chaplet wild
She   wreathed   in   her   dark   locks, and
    smiled.

X

Her smile, her speech, with winning sway,
Wiled the old Harper's mood away.
With such a look as hermits throw,
When angels stoop to soothe their woe,
He gazed, till fond regret and pride
Thrilled to a tear, then thus replied: 190
' Loveliest and best ! thou little know'st
The rank, the honors, thou hast lost !
O, might I live to see thee grace,
In Scotland's court, thy birthright place,
To see my favorite's step advance
The lightest in the courtly dance,
The cause of every gallant's sigh,
And leading star of every eye,
And theme of every minstrel's art,
The Lady of the Bleeding Heart !'   200

XI

'Fair   dreams   are   these,' the   maiden
    cried, —
Light was her accent, yet she sighed, —
'Yet is this mossy rock to me
Worth splendid chair and canopy;
Nor would my footstep spring more gay
In courtly dance than blithe strathspey,
Nor half so pleased mine ear incline
To royal minstrel's lay as thine.

And then for suitors proud and high,
To bend before my conquering eye, —   210
Thou, flattering bard ! thyself wilt say,
That grim Sir Roderick owns its sway.
The Saxon scourge, Clan-Alpine's pride,
The terror of Loch Lomond's side,
Would, at my suit, thou know'st, delay
A Lennox foray — for a day.' —

XII

The ancient bard her glee repressed:
' Ill hast thou chosen theme for jest !
For who, through all this western wild,
Named   Black   Sir   Roderick   e'er, and
    smiled ?   220
In Holy-Rood a knight he slew ;
I saw, when back the dirk he drew,
Courtiers give place before the stride
Of the undaunted homicide;
And since, though outlawed, hath his hand
Full sternly kept his mountain land.
Who else dared give — ah ! woe the day,
That I such hated truth should say ! —
The Douglas, like a stricken deer,
Disowned by every noble peer,   230
Even the rude refuge we have here ?
Alas, this wild marauding Chief
Alone might hazard our relief,
And now thy maiden charms expand,
Looks for his guerdon in thy hand;
Full soon may dispensation sought,
To back his suit, from Rome be brought.
Then, though an exile on the hill,
Thy father, as the Douglas, still
Be held in reverence and fear;   240
And though to Roderick thou 'rt so dear
That thou mightst guide with silken thread,
Slave of thy will, this chieftain dread,
Yet, O loved maid, thy mirth refrain !
Thy hand is on a lion's mane.' —

XIII

' Minstrel,' the maid replied, and high
Her father's soul glanced from her eye,
' My debts to Roderick's house I know:
All that a mother could bestow
To Lady Margaret's care I owe,   250
Since first an orphan in the wild
She sorrowed o'er her sister's child;
To her brave chieftain son, from ire
Of Scotland's king who shrouds my sire,
A deeper, holier debt is owed;
And, could I pay it with my blood,
Allan ! Sir Roderick should command
My blood, my life, — but not my hand.

Rather will Ellen Douglas dwell
A votaress in Maronnan's cell; 260
Rather through realms beyond the sea,
Seeking the world's cold charity,
Where ne'er was spoke a Scottish word,
And ne'er the name of Douglas heard,
An outcast pilgrim will she rove,
Than wed the man she cannot love.

XIV

'Thou shak'st, good friend, thy tresses
 gray, —
That pleading look, what can it say
But what I own ? — I grant him brave, 269
But wild as Bracklinn's thundering wave;
And generous, — save vindictive mood
Or jealous transport chafe his blood:
I grant him true to friendly band,
As his claymore is to his hand;
But O ! that very blade of steel
More mercy for a foe would feel:
I grant him liberal, to fling
Among his clan the wealth they bring,
When back by lake and glen they wind,
And in the Lowland leave behind, 280
Where once some pleasant hamlet stood,
A mass of ashes slaked with blood.
The hand that for my father fought
I honor, as his daughter ought;
But can I clasp it reeking red
From peasants slaughtered in their shed ?
No ! wildly while his virtues gleam,
They make his passions darker seem,
And flash along his spirit high,
Like lightning o'er the midnight sky. 290
While yet a child, — and children know,
Instinctive taught, the friend and foe, —
I shuddered at his brow of gloom,
His shadowy plaid and sable plume;
A maiden grown, I ill could bear
His haughty mien and lordly air:
But, if thou join'st a suitor's claim,
In serious mood, to Roderick's name,
I thrill with anguish ! or, if e'er
A Douglas knew the word, with fear. 300
To change such odious theme were best, —
What think'st thou of our stranger
 guest ? ' —

XV

'What think I of him ? — woe the while
That brought such wanderer to our isle !
Thy father's battle-brand, of yore
For Tine-man forged by fairy lore,
What time he leagued, no longer foes,

His Border spears with Hotspur's bows,
Did, self-unscabbarded, foreshow
The footstep of a secret foe. 310
If courtly spy hath harbored here,
What may we for the Douglas fear ?
What for this island, deemed of old
Clan-Alpine's last and surest hold ?
If neither spy nor foe, I pray
What yet may jealous Roderick say ? —
Nay, wave not thy disdainful head !
Bethink thee of the discord dread
That kindled when at Beltane game
Thou ledst the dance with Malcolm Græme;
Still, though thy sire the peace renewed, 321
Smoulders in Roderick's breast the feud:
Beware ! — But hark ! what sounds are
 these ?
My dull ears catch no faltering breeze,
No weeping birch nor aspens wake,
Nor breath is dimpling in the lake;
Still is the canna's hoary beard,
Yet, by my minstrel faith, I heard —
And hark again ! some pipe of war
Sends the bold pibroch from afar.' 330

XVI

Far up the lengthened lake were spied
Four darkening specks upon the tide,
That, slow enlarging on the view,
Four manned and masted barges grew,
And, bearing downwards from Glengyle,
Steered full upon the lonely isle;
The point of Brianchoil they passed,
And, to the windward as they cast,
Against the sun they gave to shine
The bold Sir Roderick's bannered Pine. 340
Nearer and nearer as they bear,
Spears, pikes, and axes flash in air.
Now might you see the tartans brave,
And plaids and plumage dance and wave:
Now see the bonnets sink and rise,
As his tough oar the rower plies;
See, flashing at each sturdy stroke,
The wave ascending into smoke;
See the proud pipers on the bow,
And mark the gaudy streamers flow 350
From their loud chanters down, and sweep
The furrowed bosom of the deep,
As, rushing through the lake amain,
They plied the ancient Highland strain.

XVII

Ever, as on they bore, more loud
And louder rung the pibroch proud.
At first the sounds, by distance tame,

Mellowed along the waters came,
And, lingering long by cape and bay,
Wailed every harsher note away,   360
Then bursting bolder on the ear,
The clan's shrill Gathering they could hear,
Those thrilling sounds that call the might
Of old Clan-Alpine to the fight.
Thick beat the rapid notes, as when
The mustering hundreds shake the glen,
And hurrying at the signal dread,
The battered earth returns their tread.
Then prelude light, of livelier tone,
Expressed their merry marching on,   370
Ere peal of closing battle rose,
With mingled outcry, shrieks, and blows;
And mimic din of stroke and ward,
As broadsword upon target jarred;
And groaning pause, ere yet again,
Condensed, the battle yelled amain:
The rapid charge, the rallying shout,
Retreat borne headlong into rout,
And bursts of triumph, to declare
Clan-Alpine's conquest — all were there. 380
Nor ended thus the strain, but slow
Sunk in a moan prolonged and low,
And changed the conquering clarion swell
For wild lament o'er those that fell.

XVIII

The war-pipes ceased, but lake and hill
Were busy with their echoes still;
And, when they slept, a vocal strain
Bade their hoarse chorus wake again,
While loud a hundred clansmen raise
Their voices in their Chieftain's praise.   390
Each boatman, bending to his oar,
With measured sweep the burden bore,
In such wild cadence as the breeze
Makes through December's leafless trees.
The chorus first could Allan know,
'Roderick Vich Alpine, ho! iro!'
And near, and nearer as they rowed,
Distinct the martial ditty flowed.

XIX
BOAT SONG

Hail to the Chief who in triumph advances!
  Honored and blessed be the ever-green
    Pine!   400
Long may the tree, in his banner that
    glances,
  Flourish, the shelter and grace of our
    line!
    Heaven send it happy dew,
    Earth lend it sap anew,

Gayly to bourgeon and broadly to grow,
    While every Highland glen
    Sends our shout back again,
  'Roderigh Vich Alpine dhu, ho! ieroe!'

Ours is no sapling, chance-sown by the
    fountain,
  Blooming at Beltane, in winter to
    fade;   410
When the whirlwind has stripped every
    leaf on the mountain,
  The more shall Clan-Alpine exult in her
    shade.
    Moored in the rifted rock,
    Proof to the tempest's shock,
  Firmer he roots him the ruder it blow;
    Menteith and Breadalbane, then,
    Echo his praise again,
  'Roderigh Vich Alpine dhu, ho! ieroe!'

XX

Proudly our pibroch has thrilled in Glen
    Fruin,
  And Bannochar's groans to our slogan
    replied;   420
Glen-Luss and Ross-dhu, they are smoking
    in ruin,
  And the best of Loch Lomond lie dead
    on her side.
    Widow and Saxon maid
    Long shall lament our raid,
  Think of Clan-Alpine with fear and with
    woe;
    Lennox and Leven-glen
    Shake when they hear again,
  'Roderigh Vich Alpine dhu, ho! ieroe!'

Row, vassals, row, for the pride of the
    Highlands!
  Stretch to your oars for the ever-green
    Pine!   430
O that the rosebud that graces yon islands
  Were wreathed in a garland around him
    to twine!
    O that some seedling gem,
    Worthy such noble stem,
  Honored and blessed in their shadow
    might grow!
    Loud should Clan-Alpine then
    Ring from her deepmost glen,
  'Roderigh Vich Alpine dhu, ho! ieroe!'

XXI

With all her joyful female band
Had Lady Margaret sought the strand.   440

Loose on the breeze their tresses flew,
And high their snowy arms they threw,
As echoing back with shrill acclaim,
And chorus wild, the Chieftain's name;
While, prompt to please, with mother's art,
The darling passion of his heart,
The Dame called Ellen to the strand,
To greet her kinsman ere he land:
' Come, loiterer, come ! a Douglas thou,
And shun to wreathe a victor's brow ? ' 450
Reluctantly and slow, the maid
The unwelcome summoning obeyed,
And when a distant bugle rung,
In the mid-path aside she sprung: —
' List, Allan-bane ! From mainland cast
I hear my father's signal blast.
Be ours,' she cried, ' the skiff to guide,
And waft him from the mountain-side.'
Then, like a sunbeam, swift and bright,
She darted to her shallop light, 460
And, eagerly while Roderick scanned,
For her dear form, his mother's band,
The islet far behind her lay,
And she had landed in the bay.

XXII

Some feelings are to mortals given
With less of earth in them than heaven;
And if there be a human tear
From passion's dross refined and clear,
A tear so limpid and so meek
It would not stain an angel's cheek, 470
'T is that which pious fathers shed
Upon a duteous daughter's head !
And as the Douglas to his breast
His darling Ellen closely pressed,
Such holy drops her tresses steeped,
Though 't was an hero's eye that weeped.
Nor while on Ellen's faltering tongue
Her filial welcomes crowded hung,
Marked she that fear — affection's proof —
Still held a graceful youth aloof; 480
No ! not till Douglas named his name,
Although the youth was Malcom Græme.

XXIII

Allan, with wistful look the while,
Marked Roderick landing on the isle;
His master piteously he eyed,
Then gazed upon the Chieftain's pride,
Then dashed with hasty hand away
From his dimmed eye the gathering spray;
And Douglas, as his hand he laid
On Malcolm's shoulder, kindly said: 490
' Canst thou, young friend, no meaning spy

In my poor follower's glistening eye ?
I 'll tell thee: — he recalls the day
When in my praise he led the lay
O'er the arched gate of Bothwell proud,
While many a minstrel answered loud,
When Percy's Norman pennon, won
In bloody field, before me shone,
And twice ten knights, the least a name
As mighty as yon Chief may claim, 500
Gracing my pomp, behind me came.
Yet trust me, Malcolm, not so proud
Was I of all that marshalled crowd,
Though the waned crescent owned my
might,
And in my train trooped lord and knight,
Though Blantyre hymned her holiest lays,
And Bothwell's bards flung back my praise,
As when this old man's silent tear,
And this poor maid's affection dear,
A welcome give more kind and true 510
Than aught my better fortunes knew.
Forgive, my friend, a father's boast, —
O, it out-beggars all I lost !'

XXIV

Delightful praise ! — like summer rose,
That brighter in the dew-drop glows,
The bashful maiden's cheek appeared,
For Douglas spoke, and Malcolm heard.
The flash of shame-faced joy to hide,
The hounds, the hawk, her cares divide;
The loved caresses of the maid 520
The dogs with crouch and whimper paid;
And, at her whistle, on her hand
The falcon took his favorite stand,
Closed his dark wing, relaxed his eye,
Nor, though unhooded, sought to fly.
And, trust, while in such guise she stood,
Like fabled Goddess of the wood,
That if a father's partial thought
O'erweighed her worth and beauty aught,
Well might the lover's judgment fail 530
To balance with a juster scale;
For with each secret glance he stole,
The fond enthusiast sent his soul.

XXV

Of stature fair, and slender frame,
But firmly knit, was Malcolm Græme.
The belted plaid and tartan hose
Did ne'er more graceful limbs disclose ;
His flaxen hair, of sunny hue,
Curled closely round his bonnet blue.
Trained to the chase, his eagle eye 540
The ptarmigan in snow could spy;

Each pass, by mountain, lake, and heath,
He knew, through Lennox and Menteith;
Vain was the bound of dark-brown doe
When Malcolm bent his sounding bow,
And scarce that doe, though winged with
    fear,
Outstripped in speed the mountaineer:
Right up Ben Lomond could he press,
And not a sob his toil confess.
His form accorded with a mind   550
Lively and ardent, frank and kind;
A blither heart, till Ellen came,
Did never love nor sorrow tame;
It danced as lightsome in his breast
As played the feather on his crest.
Yet friends, who nearest knew the youth,
His scorn of wrong, his zeal for truth,
And bards, who saw his features bold
When kindled by the tales of old,
Said, were that youth to manhood grown, 560
Not long should Roderick Dhu's renown
Be foremost voiced by mountain fame,
But quail to that of Malcolm Græme.

XXVI

Now back they wend their watery way,
And, ' O my sire !' did Ellen say,
' Why urge thy chase so far astray ?
And why so late returned ?   And why ' —
The rest was in her speaking eye.
' My child, the chase I follow far,
'T is mimicry of noble war;   570
And with that gallant pastime reft
Were all of Douglas I have left.
I met young Malcolm as I strayed
Far eastward, in Glenfinlas' shade;
Nor strayed I safe, for all around
Hunters and horsemen scoured the ground.
This youth, though still a royal ward,
Risked life and land to be my guard,
And through the passes of the wood
Guided my steps, not unpursued;   580
And Roderick shall his welcome make,
Despite old spleen, for Douglas' sake.
Then must he seek Strath-Endrick glen,
Nor peril aught for me again.'

XXVII

Sir Roderick, who to meet them came,
Reddened at sight of Malcolm Græme,
Yet, not in action, word, or eye,
Failed aught in hospitality.
In talk and sport they whiled away
The morning of that summer day;   590
But at high noon a courier light

Held secret parley with the knight,
Whose moody aspect soon declared
That evil were the news he heard.
Deep thought seemed toiling in his head;
Yet was the evening banquet made
Ere he assembled round the flame
His mother, Douglas, and the Græme,
And Ellen too; then cast around
His eyes, then fixed them on the ground, 600
As studying phrase that might avail
Best to convey unpleasant tale.
Long with his dagger's hilt he played,
Then raised his haughty brow, and said: —

XXVIII

' Short be my speech; — nor time affords,
Nor my plain temper, glozing words.
Kinsman and father, — if such name
Douglas vouchsafe to Roderick's claim;
Mine honored mother; — Ellen, — why,
My cousin, turn away thine eye ? —   610
And Græme, in whom I hope to know
Full soon a noble friend or foe,
When age shall give thee thy command,
And leading in thy native land, —
List all ! — The King's vindictive pride
Boasts to have tamed the Border-side,
Where chiefs, with hound and hawk who
    came
To share their monarch's sylvan game,
Themselves in bloody toils were snared,
And when the banquet they prepared,   620
And wide their loyal portals flung,
O'er their own gateway struggling hung.
Loud cries their blood from Meggat's
    mead,
From Yarrow braes and banks of Tweed,
Where the lone streams of Ettrick glide,
And from the silver Teviot's side;
The dales, where martial clans did ride,
Are now one sheep-walk, waste and wide.
This tyrant of the Scottish throne,
So faithless and so ruthless known,   630
Now hither comes; his end the same,
The same pretext of sylvan game.
What grace for Highland Chiefs, judge ye
By fate of Border chivalry.
Yet more; amid Glenfinlas' green,
Douglas, thy stately form was seen.
This by espial sure I know:
Your counsel in the streight I show.'

XXIX

Ellen and Margaret fearfully
Sought comfort in each other's eye,   640

Then turned their ghastly look, each one,
This to her sire, that to her son.
The hasty color went and came
In the bold cheek of Malcolm Græme,
But from his glance it well appeared
'T was but for Ellen that he feared;
While, sorrowful, but undismayed,
The Douglas thus his counsel said:
' Brave Roderick, though the tempest roar,
It may but thunder and pass o'er;   650
Nor will I here remain an hour,
To draw the lightning on thy bower;
For well thou know'st, at this gray head
The royal bolt were fiercest sped.
For thee, who, at thy King's command,
Canst aid him with a gallant band,
Submission, homage, humbled pride,
Shall turn the Monarch's wrath aside.
Poor remnants of the Bleeding Heart,
Ellen and I will seek apart   660
The refuge of some forest cell;
There, like the hunted quarry, dwell,
Till on the mountain and the moor
The stern pursuit be passed and o'er.' —

XXX

' No, by mine honor,' Roderick said,
' So help me Heaven, and my good blade !
No, never ! Blasted be yon Pine,
My father's ancient crest and mine,
If from its shade in danger part
The lineage of the Bleeding Heart !   670
Hear my blunt speech: grant me this maid
To wife, thy counsel to mine aid;
To Douglas, leagued with Rhoderick Dhu,
Will friends and allies flock enow;
Like cause of doubt, distrust, and grief,
Will bind to us each Western Chief.
When the loud pipes my bridal tell,
The Links of Forth shall hear the knell,
The guards shall start in Stirling's porch;
And when I light the nuptial torch,   680
A thousand villages in flames
Shall scare the slumbers of King James ! —
Nay, Ellen, blench not thus away,
And, mother, cease these signs, I pray;
I meant not all my heat might say. —
Small need of inroad or of fight,
When the sage Douglas may unite
Each mountain clan in friendly band,
To guard the passes of their land,
Till the foiled King from pathless glen   690
Shall bootless turn him home again.'

XXXI

There are who have, at midnight hour,
In slumber scaled a dizzy tower,
And, on the verge that beetled o'er
The ocean tide's incessant roar,
Dreamed calmly out their dangerous
    dream,
Till wakened by the morning beam;
When, dazzled by the eastern glow,
Such startler cast his glance below,
And saw unmeasured depth around,   700
And heard unintermitted sound,
And thought the battled fence so frail,
It waved like cobweb in the gale; —
Amid his senses' giddy wheel,
Did he not desperate impulse feel,
Headlong to plunge himself below,
And meet the worst his fears foreshow ? —
Thus Ellen, dizzy and astound,
As sudden ruin yawned around,
By crossing terrors wildly tossed,   710
Still for the Douglas fearing most,
Could scarce the desperate thought with-
    stand,
To buy his safety with her hand.

XXXII

Such purpose dread could Malcolm spy
In Ellen's quivering lip and eye,
And eager rose to speak, — but ere
His tongue could hurry forth his fear,
Had Douglas marked the hectic strife,
Where death seemed combating with life;
For to her cheek, in feverish flood,   720
One instant rushed the throbbing blood,
Then ebbing back, with sudden sway,
Left its domain as wan as clay.
' Roderick, enough ! enough !' he cried,
' My daughter cannot be thy bride;
Not that the blush to wooer dear,
Nor paleness that of maiden fear.
It may not be, — forgive her, Chief,
Nor hazard aught for our relief.
Against his sovereign, Douglas ne'er   730
Will level a rebellious spear.
'T was I that taught his youthful hand
To rein a steed and wield a brand;
I see him yet, the princely boy !
Not Ellen more my pride and joy;
I love him still, despite my wrongs
By hasty wrath and slanderous tongues.
O, seek the grace you well may find,
Without a cause to mine combined !'

XXXIII

Twice through the hall the Chieftain
        strode;   740
The waving of his tartans broad,
And darkened brow, where wounded pride
With ire and disappointment vied,
Seemed, by the torch's gloomy light,
Like the ill Demon of the night,
Stooping his pinions' shadowy sway
Upon the nighted pilgrim's way:
But, unrequited Love ! thy dart
Plunged deepest its envenomed smart,   749
And Roderick, with thine anguish stung,
At length the hand of Douglas wrung,
While eyes that mocked at tears before
With bitter drops were running o'er.
The death-pangs of long-cherished hope
Scarce in that ample breast had scope,
But, struggling with his spirit proud,
Convulsive heaved its checkered shroud,
While every sob — so mute were all —
Was heard distinctly through the hall.
The son's despair, the mother's look,   760
Ill might the gentle Ellen brook;
She rose, and to her side there came,
To aid her parting steps, the Græme.

XXXIV

Then Roderick from the Douglas broke —
As flashes flame through sable smoke,
Kindling its wreaths, long, dark, and low,
To one broad blaze of ruddy glow,
So the deep anguish of despair
Burst, in fierce jealousy, to air.
With stalwart grasp his hand he laid   770
On Malcolm's breast and belted plaid:
' Back, beardless boy !' he sternly said,
' Back, minion ! holdst thou thus at nought
The lesson I so lately taught ?
This roof, the Douglas, and that maid,
Thank thou for punishment delayed.'
Eager as greyhound on his game,
Fiercely with Roderick grappled Græme.
' Perish my name, if aught afford
Its Chieftain safety save his sword !'   780
Thus as they strove their desperate hand
Griped to the dagger or the brand,
And death had been — but Douglas rose,
And thrust between the struggling foes
His giant strength: — ' Chieftains, forego !
I hold the first who strikes my foe. —
Madmen, forbear your frantic jar !
What ! is the Douglas fallen so far,
His daughter's hand is deemed the spoil
Of such dishonorable broil ? '   790

Sullen and slowly they unclasp,
As struck with shame, their desperate
        grasp,
And each upon his rival glared,
With foot advanced and blade half bared.

XXXV

Ere yet the brands aloft were flung,
Margaret on Roderick's mantle hung,
And Malcolm heard his Ellen's scream,
As faltered through terrific dream.
Then Roderick plunged in sheath his sword,
And veiled his wrath in scornful word: 800
' Rest safe till morning; pity 't were
Such cheek should feel the midnight air !
Then mayst thou to James Stuart tell,
Roderick will keep the lake and fell,
Nor lackey with his freeborn clan
The pageant pomp of earthly man.
More would he of Clan-Alpine know,
Thou canst our strength and passes show.—
Malise, what ho ! ' — his henchman came:
' Give our safe-conduct to the Græme.' 810
Young Malcolm answered, calm and bold:
' Fear nothing for thy favorite hold;
The spot an angel deigned to grace
Is blessed, though robbers haunt the place.
Thy churlish courtesy for those
Reserve, who fear to be thy foes.
As safe to me the mountain way
At midnight as in blaze of day,
Though with his boldest at his back
Even Roderick Dhu beset the track. —   820
Brave Douglas, — lovely Ellen, — nay,
Nought here of parting will I say.
Earth does not hold a lonesome glen
So secret but we meet again. —
Chieftain ! we too shall find an hour,' —
He said, and left the sylvan bower.

XXXVI

Old Allan followed to the strand —
Such was the Douglas's command —
And anxious told, how, on the morn,   829
The stern Sir Roderick deep had sworn,
The Fiery Cross should circle o'er
Dale, glen, and valley, down and moor.
Much were the peril to the Græme
From those who to the signal came;
Far up the lake 't were safest land,
Himself would row him to the strand.
He gave his counsel to the wind,
While Malcolm did, unheeding, bind,
Round dirk and pouch and broadsword
        rolled,

His ample plaid in tightened fold,   840
And stripped his limbs to such array
As best might suit the watery way, —

XXXVII

Then spoke abrupt: ' Farewell to thee,
Pattern of old fidelity ! '
The Minstrel's hand he kindly pressed, —
' O, could I point a place of rest !
My sovereign holds in ward my land,
My uncle leads my vassal band;
To tame his foes, his friends to aid,
Poor Malcolm has but heart and blade. 850
Yet, if there be one faithful Græme
Who loves the chieftain of his name,
Not long shall honored Douglas dwell
Like hunted stag in mountain cell;
Nor, ere yon pride-swollen robber dare, —
I may not give the rest to air !
Tell Roderick Dhu I owed him nought,
Not the poor service of a boat,
To waft me to yon mountain-side.'
Then plunged he in the flashing tide.   860
Bold o'er the flood his head he bore,
And stoutly steered him from the shore;
And Allan strained his anxious eye,
Far mid the lake his form to spy,
Darkening across each puny wave,
To which the moon her silver gave.
Fast as the cormorant could skim,
The swimmer plied each active limb;
Then landing in the moonlight dell,
Loud shouted of his weal to tell.   870
The Minstrel heard the far halloo,
And joyful from the shore withdrew.

CANTO THIRD

THE GATHERING

I

TIME rolls his ceaseless course. The race
of yore,
Who danced our infancy upon their
knee,
And told our marvelling boyhood legends
store
Of their strange ventures happed by land
or sea,
How are they blotted from the things that
be !
How few, all weak and withered of their
force,
Wait on the verge of dark eternity,

Like stranded wrecks, the tide returning
hoarse,
To sweep them from our sight ! Time
rolls his ceaseless course.

Yet live there still who can remember
well,   10
How, when a mountain chief his bugle
blew,
Both field and forest, dingle, cliff, and dell,
And solitary heath, the signal knew;
And fast the faithful clan around him
drew,
What time the warning note was keenly
wound,
What time aloft their kindred banner flew,
While clamorous war-pipes yelled the
gathering sound,
And while the Fiery Cross glanced, like a
meteor, round.

II

The Summer dawn's reflected hue
To purple changed Loch Katrine blue;   20
Mildly and soft the western breeze
Just kissed the lake, just stirred the trees,
And the pleased lake, like maiden coy,
Trembled but dimpled not for joy:
The mountain-shadows on her breast
Were neither broken nor at rest;
In bright uncertainty they lie,
Like future joys to Fancy's eye.
The water-lily to the light
Her chalice reared of silver bright;   30
The doe awoke, and to the lawn,
Begemmed with dew-drops, led her fawn;
The gray mist left the mountain-side,
The torrent showed its glistening pride;
Invisible in flecked sky
The lark sent down her revelry;
The blackbird and the speckled thrush
Good-morrow gave from brake and bush;
In answer cooed the cushat dove
Her notes of peace and rest and love.   40

III

No thought of peace, no thought of rest,
Assuaged the storm in Roderick's breast.
With sheathed broadsword in his hand,
Abrupt he paced the islet strand,
And eyed the rising sun, and laid
His hand on his impatient blade.
Beneath a rock, his vassals' care
Was prompt the ritual to prepare,
With deep and deathful meaning fraught;

For such Antiquity had taught   50
Was preface meet, ere yet abroad
The Cross of Fire should take its road.
The shrinking band stood oft aghast
At the impatient glance he cast; —
Such glance the mountain eagle threw,
As, from the cliffs of Benvenue,
She spread her dark sails on the wind,
And, high in middle heaven reclined,
With her broad shadow on the lake,
Silenced the warblers of the brake.   60

IV

A heap of withered boughs was piled,
Of juniper and rowan wild,
Mingled with shivers from the oak,
Rent by the lightning's recent stroke.
Brian the Hermit by it stood,
Barefooted, in his frock and hood.
His grizzled beard and matted hair
Obscured a visage of despair;
His naked arms and legs, seamed o'er,
The scars of frantic penance bore.   70
That monk, of savage form and face,
The impending danger of his race
Had drawn from deepest solitude,
Far in Benharrow's bosom rude.
Not his the mien of Christian priest,
But Druid's, from the grave released,
Whose hardened heart and eye might brook
On human sacrifice to look;
And much, 't was said, of heathen lore
Mixed in the charms he muttered o'er.   80
The hallowed creed gave only worse
And deadlier emphasis of curse.
No peasant sought that Hermit's prayer,
His cave the pilgrim shunned with care;
The eager huntsman knew his bound,
And in mid chase called off his hound;
Or if, in lonely glen or strath,
The desert-dweller met his path,
He prayed, and signed the cross between,
While terror took devotion's mien.   90

V

Of Brian's birth strange tales were told.
His mother watched a midnight fold,
Built deep within a dreary glen,
Where scattered lay the bones of men
In some forgotten battle slain,
And bleached by drifting wind and rain.
It might have tamed a warrior's heart
To view such mockery of his art !
The knot-grass fettered there the hand
Which once could burst an iron band;   100

Beneath the broad and ample bone,
That bucklered heart to fear unknown,
A feeble and a timorous guest,
The fieldfare framed her lowly nest;
There the slow blindworm left his slime
On the fleet limbs that mocked at time;
And there, too, lay the leader's skull,
Still wreathed with chaplet, flushed and
        full,
For heath-bell with her purple bloom
Supplied the bonnet and the plume.   110
All night, in this sad glen, the maid
Sat shrouded in her mantle's shade:
She said no shepherd sought her side,
No hunter's hand her snood untied,
Yet ne'er again to braid her hair
The virgin snood did Alice wear;
Gone was her maiden glee and sport,
Her maiden girdle all too short,
Nor sought she, from that fatal night,
Or holy church or blessed rite,   120
But locked her secret in her breast,
And died in travail, unconfessed.

VI

Alone, among his young compeers,
Was Brian from his infant years;
A moody and heart-broken boy,
Estranged from sympathy and joy,
Bearing each taunt which careless tongue
On his mysterious lineage flung.
Whole nights he spent by moonlight pale,
To wood and stream his hap to wail,   130
Till, frantic, he as truth received
What of his birth the crowd believed,
And sought, in mist and meteor fire,
To meet and know his Phantom Sire !
In vain, to soothe his wayward fate,
The cloister oped her pitying gate;
In vain the learning of the age
Unclasped the sable-lettered page;
Even in its treasures he could find
Food for the fever of his mind.   140
Eager he read whatever tells
Of magic, cabala, and spells,
And every dark pursuit allied
To curious and presumptuous pride;
Till with fired brain and nerves o'erstrung,
And heart with mystic horrors wrung,
Desperate he sought Benharrow's den,
And hid him from the haunts of men.

VII

The desert gave him visions wild,
Such as might suit the spectre's child.   150

Where with black cliffs the torrents toil,
He watched the wheeling eddies boil,
Till from their foam his dazzled eyes
Beheld the River Demon rise:
The mountain mist took form and limb
Of noontide hag or goblin grim;
The midnight wind came wild and dread,
Swelled with the voices of the dead;
Far on the future battle-heath
His eye beheld the ranks of death;   160
Thus the lone Seer, from mankind hurled,
Shaped forth a disembodied world.
One lingering sympathy of mind
Still bound him to the mortal kind;
The only parent he could claim
Of ancient Alpine's lineage came.
Late had he heard, in prophet's dream,
The fatal Ben-Shie's boding scream;
Sounds, too, had come in midnight blast
Of charging steeds, careering fast   170
Along Benharrow's shingly side,
Where mortal horseman ne'er might ride;
The thunderbolt had split the pine, —
All augured ill to Alpine's line.
He girt his loins, and came to show
The signals of impending woe,
And now stood prompt to bless or ban,
As bade the Chieftain of his clan.

VIII

'T was all prepared; — and from the rock
A goat, the patriarch of the flock,   180
Before the kindling pile was laid,
And pierced by Roderick's ready blade.
Patient the sickening victim eyed
The life-blood ebb in crimson tide
Down his clogged beard and shaggy limb,
Till darkness glazed his eyeballs dim.
The grisly priest, with murmuring prayer,
A slender crosslet framed with care,
A cubit's length in measure due;
The shaft and limbs were rods of yew,   190
Whose parents in Inch-Cailliach wave
Their shadows o'er Clan-Alpine's grave,
And, answering Lomond's breezes deep,
Soothe many a chieftain's endless sleep.
The Cross thus formed he held on high,
With wasted hand and haggard eye,
And strange and mingled feelings woke,
While his anathema he spoke: —

IX

'Woe to the clansman who shall view
This symbol of sepulchral yew,   200
Forgetful that its branches grew

Where weep the heavens their holiest dew
On Alpine's dwelling low!
Deserter of his Chieftain's trust,
He ne'er shall mingle with their dust,
But, from his sires and kindred thrust,
Each clansman's execration just
Shall doom him wrath and woe.'
He paused; — the word the vassals took,
With forward step and fiery look,   210
On high their naked brands they shook,
Their clattering targets wildly strook;
And first in murmur low,
Then, like the billow in his course,
That far to seaward finds his source,
And flings to shore his mustered force,
Burst with loud roar their answer hoarse,
'Woe to the traitor, woe!'
Ben-an's gray scalp the accents knew,
The joyous wolf from covert drew,   220
The exulting eagle screamed afar, —
They knew the voice of Alpine's war.

X

The shout was hushed on lake and fell,
The Monk resumed his muttered spell:
Dismal and low its accents came,
The while he scathed the Cross with flame;
And the few words that reached the air,
Although the holiest name was there,
Had more of blasphemy than prayer.
But when he shook above the crowd   230
Its kindled points, he spoke aloud: —
'Woe to the wretch who fails to rear
At this dread sign the ready spear!
For, as the flames this symbol sear,
His home, the refuge of his fear,
A kindred fate shall know;
Far o'er its roof the volumed flame
Clan-Alpine's vengeance shall proclaim,
While maids and matrons on his name
Shall call down wretchedness and shame,   240
And infamy and woe.'
Then rose the cry of females, shrill
As goshawk's whistle on the hill,
Denouncing misery and ill,
Mingled with childhood's babbling trill
Of curses stammered slow;
Answering with imprecation dread,
'Sunk be his home in embers red!
And cursed be the meanest shed
That e'er shall hide the houseless head   250
We doom to want and woe!'
A sharp and shrieking echo gave,
Coir-Uriskin, thy goblin cave!

And the gray pass where birches wave
  On Beala-nam-bo.

XI

Then deeper paused the priest anew,
And hard his laboring breath he drew,
While, with set teeth and clenched hand,
And eyes that glowed like fiery brand,
He meditated curse more dread,   260
And deadlier, on the clansman's head
Who, summoned to his chieftain's aid,
The signal saw and disobeyed.
The crosslet's points of sparkling wood
He quenched among the bubbling blood,
And, as again the sign he reared,
Hollow and hoarse his voice was heard:
' When flits this Cross from man to man,
Vich-Alpine's summons to his clan,
Burst be the ear that fails to heed !   270
Palsied the foot that shuns to speed !
May ravens tear the careless eyes,
Wolves make the coward heart their prize!
As sinks that blood-stream in the earth,
So may his heart's-blood drench his hearth !
As dies in hissing gore the spark,
Quench thou his light, Destruction dark !
And be the grace to him denied,
Bought by this sign to all beside ! '
He ceased; no echo gave again   280
The murmur of the deep Amen.

XII

Then Roderick with impatient look
From Brian's hand the symbol took:
' Speed, Malise, speed ! ' he said, and gave
The crosslet to his henchman brave.
' The muster-place be Lanrick mead —
Instant the time — speed, Malise, speed ! '
Like heath-bird, when the hawks pursue,
A barge across Loch Katrine flew:
High stood the henchman on the prow;   290
So rapidly the barge-men row,
The bubbles, where they launched the boat,
Were all unbroken and afloat,
Dancing in foam and ripple still,
When it had neared the mainland hill;
And from the silver beach's side
Still was the prow three fathom wide,
When lightly bounded to the land
The messenger of blood and brand.   299

XIII

Speed, Malise, speed ! the dun deer's hide
On fleeter foot was never tied.
Speed, Malise, speed ! such cause of haste

Thine active sinews never braced.
Bend 'gainst the steepy hill thy breast,
Burst down like torrent from its crest;
With short and springing footstep pass
The trembling bog and false morass;
Across the brook like roebuck bound,
And thread the brake like questing hound;
The crag is high, the scaur is deep,   310
Yet shrink not from the desperate leap:
Parched are thy burning lips and brow,
Yet by the fountain pause not now;
Herald of battle, fate, and fear,
Stretch onward in thy fleet career !
The wounded hind thou track'st not now,
Pursuest not maid through greenwood
  bough,
Nor pliest thou now thy flying pace
With rivals in the mountain race;
But danger, death, and warrior deed   320
Are in thy course — speed, Malise, speed !

XIV

Fast as the fatal symbol flies,
In arms the huts and hamlets rise;
From winding glen, from upland brown,
They poured each hardy tenant down.
Nor slacked the messenger his pace;
He showed the sign, he named the place,
And, pressing forward like the wind,
Left clamor and surprise behind.
The fisherman forsook the strand,   330
The swarthy smith took dirk and brand;
With changed cheer, the mower blithe
Left in the half-cut swath his scythe;
The herds without a keeper strayed,
The plough was in mid-furrow stayed,
The falconer tossed his hawk away,
The hunter left the stag at bay;
Prompt at the signal of alarms,
Each son of Alpine rushed to arms;
So swept the tumult and affray   340
Along the margin of Achray.
Alas, thou lovely lake ! that e'er
Thy banks should echo sounds of fear !
The rocks, the bosky thickets, sleep
So stilly on thy bosom deep,
The lark's blithe carol from the cloud
Seems for the scene too gayly loud.

XV

Speed, Malise, speed ! The lake is past,
Duncraggan's huts appear at last,
And peep, like moss-grown rocks, half
  seen,   350
Half hidden in the copse so green;

There mayst thou rest, thy labor done,
Their lord shall speed the signal on. —
As stoops the hawk upon his prey,
The henchman shot him down the way.
What woeful accents load the gale ?
The funeral yell, the female wail !
A gallant hunter's sport is o'er,
A valiant warrior fights no more.
Who, in the battle or the chase,   360
At Roderick's side shall fill his place ! —
Within the hall, where torch's ray
Supplies the excluded beams of day,
Lies Duncan on his lowly bier,
And o'er him streams his widow's tear.
His stripling son stands mournful by,
His youngest weeps, but knows not why;
The village maids and matrons round
The dismal coronach resound.

XVI

CORONACH

He is gone on the mountain,   370
   He is lost to the forest,
Like a summer-dried fountain,
   When our need was the sorest.
The font, reappearing,
   From the rain-drops shall borrow,
But to us comes no cheering,
   To Duncan no morrow !

The hand of the reaper
   Takes the ears that are hoary,
But the voice of the weeper   380
   Wails manhood in glory.
The autumn winds rushing
   Waft the leaves that are searest,
But our flower was in flushing,
   When blighting was nearest.

Fleet foot on the correi,
   Sage counsel in cumber,
Red hand in the foray,
   How sound is thy slumber !
Like the dew on the mountain,   390
   Like the foam on the river,
Like the bubble on the fountain,
   Thou art gone, and forever !

XVII

See Stumah, who, the bier beside,
His master's corpse with wonder eyed,
Poor Stumah ! whom his least halloo
Could send like lightning o'er the dew,
Bristles his crest, and points his ears,

As if some stranger step he hears.
'T is not a mourner's muffled tread,   400
Who comes to sorrow o'er the dead,
But headlong haste or deadly fear
Urge the precipitate career.
All stand aghast: — unheeding all,
The henchman bursts into the hall;
Before the dead man's bier he stood,
Held forth the Cross besmeared with
      blood;
' The muster-place is Lanrick mead;
Speed forth the signal ! clansmen, speed !'

XVIII

Angus, the heir of Duncan's line,   410
Sprung forth and seized the fatal sign.
In haste the stripling to his side
His father's dirk and broadsword tied;
But when he saw his mother's eye
Watch him in speechless agony,
Back to her opened arms he flew,
Pressed on her lips a fond adieu, —
' Alas !' she sobbed, — ' and yet be gone,
And speed thee forth, like Duncan's son !'
One look he cast upon the bier,   420
Dashed from his eye the gathering tear,
Breathed deep to clear his laboring breast,
And tossed aloft his bonnet crest,
Then, like the high-bred colt when, freed,
First he essays his fire and speed,
He vanished, and o'er moor and moss
Sped forward with the Fiery Cross.
Suspended was the widow's tear
While yet his footsteps she could hear;
And when she marked the henchman's
      eye   430
Wet with unwonted sympathy,
' Kinsman,' she said, ' his race is run
That should have sped thine errand on;
The oak has fallen, — the sapling bough
Is all Duncraggan's shelter now.
Yet trust I well, his duty done,
The orphan's God will guard my son. —
And you, in many a danger true,
At Duncan's hest your blades that drew,
To arms, and guard that orphan's head !
Let babes and women wail the dead.'   441
Then weapon-clang and martial call
Resounded through the funeral hall,
While from the walls the attendant band
Snatched sword and targe with hurried
      hand;
And short and flitting energy
Glanced from the mourner's sunken eye,
As if the sounds to warrior dear

Might rouse her Duncan from his bier.
But faded soon that borrowed force;   450
Grief claimed his right, and tears their
    course.

XIX

Benledi saw the Cross of Fire,
It glanced like lightning up Strath-Ire.
O'er dale and hill the summons flew,
Nor rest nor pause young Angus knew;
The tear that gathered in his eye
He left the mountain-breeze to dry;
Until, where Teith's young waters roll
Betwixt him and a wooded knoll   459
That graced the sable strath with green,
The chapel of Saint Bride was seen.
Swoln was the stream, remote the bridge,
But Angus paused not on the edge;
Though the dark waves danced dizzily,
Though reeled his sympathetic eye,
He dashed amid the torrent's roar:
His right hand high the crosslet bore,
His left the pole-axe grasped, to guide
And stay his footing in the tide.
He stumbled twice, — the foam splashed
    high,   470
With hoarser swell the stream raced by;
And had he fallen, — forever there,
Farewell Duncraggan's orphan heir !
But still, as if in parting life,
Firmer he grasped the Cross of strife,
Until the opposing bank he gained,
And up the chapel pathway strained.

XX

A blithesome rout that morning-tide
Had sought the chapel of Saint Bride.
Her troth Tombea's Mary gave   480
To Norman, heir of Armandave,
And, issuing from the Gothic arch,
The bridal now resumed their march.
In rude but glad procession came
Bonneted sire and coif-clad dame;
And plaided youth, with jest and jeer,
Which snooded maiden would not hear;
And children, that, unwitting why,
Lent the gay shout their shrilly cry;
And minstrels, that in measures vied   490
Before the young and bonny bride,
Whose downcast eye and cheek disclose
The tear and blush of morning rose.
With virgin step and bashful hand
She held the kerchief's snowy band.
The gallant bridegroom by her side

Beheld his prize with victor's pride,
And the glad mother in her ear
Was closely whispering word of cheer.   499

XXI

Who meets them at the churchyard gate ?
The messenger of fear and fate !
Haste in his hurried accent lies,
And grief is swimming in his eyes.
All dripping from the recent flood,
Panting and travel-soiled he stood,
The fatal sign of fire and sword
Held forth, and spoke the appointed word:
' The muster-place is Lanrick mead;
Speed forth the signal ! Norman, speed ! '
And must he change so soon the hand   510
Just linked to his by holy band,
For the fell Cross of blood and brand ?
And must the day so blithe that rose,
And promised rapture in the close,
Before its setting hour, divide
The bridegroom from the plighted bride ?
O fatal doom ! — it must ! it must !
Clan-Alpine's cause, her Chieftain's trust,
Her summons dread, brook no delay;
Stretch to the race, — away ! away !   520

XXII

Yet slow he laid his plaid aside,
And lingering eyed his lovely bride,
Until he saw the starting tear
Speak woe he might not stop to cheer;
Then, trusting not a second look,
In haste he sped him up the brook,
Nor backward glanced till on the heath
Where Lubnaig's lake supplies the Teith.—
What in the racer's bosom stirred ?
The sickening pang of hope deferred,   530
And memory with a torturing train
Of all his morning visions vain.
Mingled with love's impatience, came
The manly thirst for martial fame;
The stormy joy of mountaineers
Ere yet they rush upon the spears;
And zeal for Clan and Chieftain burning,
And hope, from well-fought field return-
    ing,
With war's red honors on his crest,
To clasp his Mary to his breast.   540
Stung by such thoughts, o'er bank and
    brae,
Like fire from flint he glanced away,
While high resolve and feeling strong
Burst into voluntary song.

XXIII

SONG

The heath this night must be my bed,
The bracken curtain for my head,
My lullaby the warder's tread,
 Far, far, from love and thee, Mary;
To-morrow eve, more stilly laid,
My couch may be my bloody plaid, 550
My vesper song thy wail, sweet maid!
 It will not waken me, Mary!

I may not, dare not, fancy now
The grief that clouds thy lovely brow,
I dare not think upon thy vow,
 And all it promised me, Mary.
No fond regret must Norman know;
When bursts Clan-Alpine on the foe,
His heart must be like bended bow,
 His foot like arrow free, Mary. 560

A time will come with feeling fraught,
For, if I fall in battle fought,
Thy hapless lover's dying thought
 Shall be a thought on thee, Mary.
And if returned from conquered foes,
How blithely will the evening close,
How sweet the linnet sing repose,
 To my young bride and me, Mary!

XXIV

Not faster o'er thy heathery braes,
Balquidder, speeds the midnight blaze, 570
Rushing in conflagration strong
Thy deep ravines and dells along,
Wrapping thy cliffs in purple glow,
And reddening the dark lakes below;
Nor faster speeds it, nor so far,
As o'er thy heaths the voice of war.
The signal roused to martial coil
The sullen margin of Loch Voil,
Waked still Loch Doine, and to the source
Alarmed, Balvaig, thy swampy course; 580
Thence southward turned its rapid road
Adown Strath-Gartney's valley broad,
Till rose in arms each man might claim
A portion in Clan-Alpine's name,
From the gray sire, whose trembling hand
Could hardly buckle on his brand,
To the raw boy, whose shaft and bow
Were yet scarce terror to the crow.
Each valley, each sequestered glen,
Mustered its little horde of men, 590
That met as torrents from the height
In highland dales their streams unite,

Still gathering, as they pour along,
A voice more loud, a tide more strong,
Till at the rendezvous they stood
By hundreds prompt for blows and blood,
Each trained to arms since life began,
Owning no tie but to his clan,
No oath but by his chieftain's hand,
No law but Roderick Dhu's command. 600

XXV

That summer morn had Roderick Dhu
Surveyed the skirts of Benvenue,
And sent his scouts o'er hill and heath,
To view the frontiers of Menteith.
All backward came with news of truce;
Still lay each martial Græme and Bruce,
In Rednock courts no horsemen wait,
No banner waved on Cardross gate,
On Duchray's towers no beacon shone,
Nor scared the herons from Loch Con; 610
All seemed at peace. — Now wot ye why
The Chieftain with such anxious eye,
Ere to the muster he repair,
This western frontier scanned with care? —
In Benvenue's most darksome cleft,
A fair though cruel pledge was left;
For Douglas, to his promise true,
That morning from the isle withdrew,
And in a deep sequestered dell
Had sought a low and lonely cell. 620
By many a bard in Celtic tongue
Has Coir-nan-Uriskin been sung;
A softer name the Saxons gave,
And called the grot the Goblin Cave.

XXVI

It was a wild and strange retreat,
As e'er was trod by outlaw's feet.
The dell, upon the mountain's crest,
Yawned like a gash on warrior's breast;
Its trench had stayed full many a rock,
Hurled by primeval earthquake shock 630
From Benvenue's gray summit wild,
And here, in random ruin piled,
They frowned incumbent o'er the spot,
And formed the rugged sylvan grot.
The oak and birch with mingled shade
At noontide there a twilight made,
Unless when short and sudden shone
Some straggling beam on cliff or stone,
With such a glimpse as prophet's eye
Gains on thy depth, Futurity. 640
No murmur waked the solemn still,
Save tinkling of a fountain rill;
But when the wind chafed with the lake,

A sullen sound would upward break,
With dashing hollow voice, that spoke
The incessant war of wave and rock.
Suspended cliffs with hideous sway
Seemed nodding o'er the cavern gray.
From such a den the wolf had sprung,
In such the wild-cat leaves her young;   650
Yet Douglas and his daughter fair
Sought for a space their safety there.
Gray Superstition's whisper dread
Debarred the spot to vulgar tread;
For there, she said, did fays resort,
And satyrs hold their sylvan court,
By moonlight tread their mystic maze,
And blast the rash beholder's gaze.

XXVII

Now eve, with western shadows long,
Floated on Katrine bright and strong,   660
When Roderick with a chosen few
Repassed the heights of Benvenue.
Above the Goblin Cave they go,
Through the wild pass of Beal-nam-bo;
The prompt retainers speed before,
To launch the shallop from the shore,
For 'cross Loch Katrine lies his way
To view the passes of Achray,
And place his clansmen in array.
Yet lags the Chief in musing mind,   670
Unwonted sight, his men behind.
A single page, to bear his sword,
Alone attended on his lord;
The rest their way through thickets break,
And soon await him by the lake.
It was a fair and gallant sight,
To view them from the neighboring height,
By the low-levelled sunbeam's light !
For strength and stature, from the clan
Each warrior was a chosen man,   680
As even afar might well be seen,
By their proud step and martial mien.
Their feathers dance, their tartans float,
Their targets gleam, as by the boat
A wild and warlike group they stand,
That well became such mountain-strand.

XXVIII

Their Chief with step reluctant still
Was lingering on the craggy hill,
Hard by where turned apart the road
To Douglas's obscure abode.   690
It was but with that dawning morn
That Roderick Dhu had proudly sworn
To drown his love in war's wild roar,
Nor think of Ellen Douglas more;

But he who stems a stream with sand,
And fetters flame with flaxen band,
Has yet a harder task to prove, —
By firm resolve to conquer love !
Eve finds the Chief, like restless ghost,
Still hovering near his treasure lost;   700
For though his haughty heart deny
A parting meeting to his eye,
Still fondly strains his anxious ear
The accents of her voice to hear,
And inly did he curse the breeze
That waked to sound the rustling trees.
But hark ! what mingles in the strain ?
It is the harp of Allan-bane,
That wakes its measure slow and high,
Attuned to sacred minstrelsy.   710
What melting voice attends the strings ?
'T is Ellen, or an angel, sings.

XXIX
HYMN TO THE VIRGIN

Ave Maria ! maiden mild !
  Listen to a maiden's prayer !
Thou canst hear though from the wild,
  Thou canst save amid despair.
Safe may we sleep beneath thy care,
  Though banished, outcast, and reviled —
Maiden ! hear a maiden's prayer;
  Mother, hear a suppliant child !   720
      Ave Maria !

Ave Maria ! undefiled !
  The flinty couch we now must share
Shall seem with down of eider piled,
  If thy protection hover there.
The murky cavern's heavy air
  Shall breathe of balm if thou hast
    smiled;
Then, Maiden ! hear a maiden's prayer,
  Mother, list a suppliant child !
      Ave Maria !

Ave Maria ! stainless styled !
  Foul demons of the earth and air,   730
From this their wonted haunt exiled,
  Shall flee before thy presence fair.
We bow us to our lot of care,
  Beneath thy guidance reconciled:
Hear for a maid a maiden's prayer,
  And for a father hear a child !
      Ave Maria !

XXX

Died on the harp the closing hymn, —
Unmoved in attitude and limb,

As listening still, Clan-Alpine's lord
Stood leaning on his heavy sword,
Until the page with humble sign   740
Twice pointed to the sun's decline.
Then while his plaid he round him cast,
' It is the last time — 't is the last,'
He muttered thrice, — ' the last time e'er
That angel-voice shall Roderick hear !'
It was a goading thought, — his stride
Hied hastier down the mountain-side;
Sullen he flung him in the boat,
An instant 'cross the lake it shot.   750
They landed in that silvery bay,
And eastward held their hasty way,
Till, with the latest beams of light,
The band arrived on Lanrick height,
Where mustered in the vale below
Clan-Alpine's men in martial show.

XXXI

A various scene the clansmen made:
Some sat, some stood, some slowly strayed;
But most, with mantles folded round,   760
Were couched to rest upon the ground,
Scarce to be known by curious eye
From the deep heather where they lie,
So well was matched the tartan screen
With heath-bell dark and brackens green;
Unless where, here and there, a blade
Or lance's point a glimmer made,
Like glow-worm twinkling through the
        shade.
But when, advancing through the gloom,
They saw the Chieftain's eagle plume,
Their shout of welcome, shrill and wide, 770
Shook the steep mountain's steady side.
Thrice it arose, and lake and fell
Three times returned the martial yell;
It died upon Bochastle's plain,
And Silence claimed her evening reign.

CANTO FOURTH

THE PROPHECY

I

' THE rose is fairest when 't is budding
        new,
    And hope is brightest when it dawns
        from fears;
The rose is sweetest washed with morning
        dew,
    And love is loveliest when embalmed in
        tears.

O wilding rose, whom fancy thus endears,
    I bid your blossoms in my bonnet wave,
Emblem of hope and love through future
        years !'
    Thus spoke young Norman, heir of Ar-
        mandave,
What time the sun arose on Vennachar's
        broad wave.

II

Such fond conceit, half said, half sung,   10
Love prompted to the bridegroom's tongue.
All while he stripped the wild-rose spray,
His axe and bow beside him lay,
For on a pass 'twixt lake and wood
A wakeful sentinel he stood.
Hark ! — on the rock a footstep rung,
And instant to his arms he sprung.
' Stand, or thou diest ! — What, Malise ? —
        soon
Art thou returned from Braes of Doune.
By thy keen step and glance I know,   20
Thou bring'st us tidings of the foe.' —
For while the Fiery Cross hied on,
On distant scout had Malise gone. —
' Where sleeps the Chief ? ' the henchman
        said.
' Apart, in yonder misty glade;
To his lone couch I 'll be your guide.' —
Then called a slumberer by his side,
And stirred him with his slackened bow, —
' Up, up, Glentarkin ! rouse thee, ho !
We seek the Chieftain; on the track   30
Keep eagle watch till I come back.'

III

Together up the pass they sped:
' What of the foeman ? ' Norman said. —
' Varying reports from near and far;
This certain, — that a band of war
Has for two days been ready boune,
At prompt command to march from
        Doune;
King James the while, with princely
        powers,
Holds revelry in Stirling towers.
Soon will this dark and gathering cloud 40
Speak on our glens in thunder loud.
Inured to bide such bitter bout,
The warrior's plaid may bear it out;
But, Norman, how wilt thou provide
A shelter for thy bonny bride ? ' —
' What ! know ye not that Roderick's care
To the lone isle hath caused repair
Each maid and matron of the clan,

And every child and aged man
Unfit for arms; and given his charge,   50
Nor skiff nor shallop, boat nor barge,
Upon these lakes shall float at large,
But all beside the islet moor,
That such dear pledge may rest se-
    cure ? ' —

IV

' 'T is well advised, — the Chieftain's plan
Bespeaks the father of his clan.
But wherefore sleeps Sir Roderick Dhu
Apart from all his followers true ? '
' It is because last evening-tide
Brian an augury hath tried,   60
Of that dread kind which must not be
Unless in dread extremity,
The Taghairm called; by which, afar,
Our sires foresaw the events of war.
Duncraggan's milk-white bull they slew.' —

MALISE

' Ah ! well the gallant brute I knew !
The choicest of the prey we had
When swept our merrymen Gallangad.
His hide was snow, his horns were dark,
His red eye glowed like fiery spark;   70
So fierce, so tameless, and so fleet,
Sore did he cumber our retreat,
And kept our stoutest kerns in awe,
Even at the pass of Beal 'maha.
But steep and flinty was the road,
And sharp the hurrying pikeman's goad,
And when we came to Dennan's Row
A child might scathless stroke his brow.'

V

NORMAN

' That bull was slain; his reeking hide
They stretched the cataract beside,   80
Whose waters their wild tumult toss
Adown the black and craggy boss
Of that huge cliff whose ample verge
Tradition calls the Hero's Targe.
Couched on a shelf beneath its brink,
Close where the thundering torrents sink,
Rocking beneath their headlong sway,
And drizzled by the ceaseless spray,
Midst groan of rock and roar of stream,
The wizard waits prophetic dream.   90
Nor distant rests the Chief; — but hush !
See, gliding slow through mist and bush,
The hermit gains yon rock, and stands
To gaze upon our slumbering bands.
Seems he not, Malise, like a ghost,

That hovers o'er a slaughtered host ?
Or raven on the blasted oak,
That, watching while the deer is broke,
His morsel claims with sullen croak ? '

MALISE

' Peace ! peace ! to other than to me   100
Thy words were evil augury;
But still I hold Sir Roderick's blade
Clan-Alpine's omen and her aid,
Not aught that, gleaned from heaven or
    hell,
Yon fiend-begotten Monk can tell.
The Chieftain joins him, see — and now
Together they descend the brow.'

VI

And, as they came, with Alpine's Lord
The Hermit Monk held solemn word: —
' Roderick ! it is a fearful strife,   110
For man endowed with mortal life,
Whose shroud of sentient clay can still
Feel feverish pang and fainting chill,
Whose eye can stare in stony trance,
Whose hair can rouse like warrior's
    lance, —
'T is hard for such to view, unfurled,
The curtain of the future world.
Yet, witness every quaking limb,
My sunken pulse, mine eyeballs dim,
My soul with harrowing anguish torn,   120
This for my Chieftain have I borne ! —
The shapes that sought my fearful couch
A human tongue may ne'er avouch;
No mortal man — save he, who, bred
Between the living and the dead,
Is gifted beyond nature's law —
Had e'er survived to say he saw.
At length the fateful answer came
In characters of living flame !
Not spoke in word, nor blazed in scroll,   130
But borne and branded on my soul: —
WHICH SPILLS THE FOREMOST FOEMAN'S
    LIFE,
THAT PARTY CONQUERS IN THE STRIFE.'

VII

' Thanks, Brian, for thy zeal and care !
Good is thine augury, and fair.
Clan-Alpine ne'er in battle stood
But first our broadswords tasted blood.
A surer victim still I know,
Self-offered to the auspicious blow:
A spy has sought my land this morn, —   140
No eve shall witness his return !

My followers guard each pass's mouth,
To east, to westward, and to south;
Red Murdoch, bribed to be his guide,
Has charge to lead his steps aside,
Till in deep path or dingle brown
He light on those shall bring him down. —
But see, who comes his news to show !
Malise ! what tidings of the foe ? '   149

VIII

' At Doune, o'er many a spear and glaive,
Two Barons proud their banners wave.
I saw the Moray's silver star,
And marked the sable pale of Mar.'
' By Alpine's soul, high tidings those !
I love to hear of worthy foes.
When move they on ? ' ' To-morrow's noon
Will see them here for battle boune.'
' Then shall it see a meeting stern !
But, for the place, — say, couldst thou
        learn
Nought of the friendly clans of Earn ?   160
Strengthened by them, we well might bide
The battle on Benledi's side.
Thou couldst not ? — well ! Clan-Alpine's
        men
Shall man the Trosachs' shaggy glen;
Within Loch Katrine's gorge we 'll fight,
All in our maids' and matrons' sight,
Each for his hearth and household fire,
Father for child, and son for sire,
Lover for maid beloved ! — But why —
Is it the breeze affects mine eye ?   170
Or dost thou come, ill-omened tear !
A messenger of doubt or fear ?
No ! sooner may the Saxon lance
Unfix Benledi from his stance,
Than doubt or terror can pierce through
The unyielding heart of Roderick Dhu !
'T is stubborn as his trusty targe.
Each to his post ! — all know their charge.'
The pibroch sounds, the bands advance,
The broadswords gleam, the banners
        dance,   180
Obedient to the Chieftain's glance. —
I turn me from the martial roar,
And seek Coir-Uriskin once more.

IX

Where is the Douglas ? — he is gone;
And Ellen sits on the gray stone
Fast by the cave, and makes her moan,
While vainly Allan's words of cheer
Are poured on her unheeding ear.
' He will return — dear lady, trust ! —

With joy return; — he will — he must.   190
Well was it time to seek afar
Some refuge from impending war,
When e'en Clan-Alpine's rugged swarm
Are cowed by the approaching storm.
I saw their boats with many a light,
Floating the livelong yesternight,
Shifting like flashes darted forth
By the red streamers of the north;
I marked at morn how close they ride,
Thick moored by the lone islet's side,   200
Like wild ducks couching in the fen
When stoops the hawk upon the glen.
Since this rude race dare not abide
The peril on the mainland side,
Shall not thy noble father's care
Some safe retreat for thee prepare ? '

X
ELLEN

' No, Allan, no !   Pretext so kind
My wakeful terrors could not blind.
When in such tender tone, yet grave,
Douglas a parting blessing gave,   210
The tear that glistened in his eye
Drowned not his purpose fixed and high.
My soul, though feminine and weak,
Can image his; e'en as the lake,
Itself disturbed by slightest stroke,
Reflects the invulnerable rock.
He hears report of battle rife,
He deems himself the cause of strife.
I saw him redden when the theme
Turned, Allan, on thine idle dream   220
Of Malcolm Græme in fetters bound,
Which I, thou saidst, about him wound.
Think'st thou he trowed thine omen aught ?
O no ! 't was apprehensive thought
For the kind youth, — for Roderick too —
Let me be just — that friend so true;
In danger both, and in our cause !
Minstrel, the Douglas dare not pause.
Why else that solemn warning given,
" If not on earth, we meet in heaven ! "   230
Why else, to Cambus-kenneth's fane,
If eve return him not again,
Am I to hie and make me known ?
Alas ! he goes to Scotland's throne,
Buys his friends' safety with his own;
He goes to do — what I had done,
Had Douglas' daughter been his son ! '

XI

' Nay, lovely Ellen ! — dearest, nay !
If aught should his return delay,

He only named yon holy fane   240
As fitting place to meet again.
Be sure he 's safe, and for the Græme, —
Heaven's blessing on his gallant name ! —
My visioned sight may yet prove true,
Nor bode of ill to him or you.
When did my gifted dream beguile ?
Think of the stranger at the isle,
And think upon the harpings slow
That presaged this approaching woe !
Sooth was my prophecy of fear;   250
Believe it when it augurs cheer.
Would we had left this dismal spot !
Ill luck still haunts a fairy grot.
Of such a wondrous tale I know —
Dear lady, change that look of woe,
My harp was wont thy grief to cheer.'

ELLEN

' Well, be it as thou wilt; I hear,
But cannot stop the bursting tear.'
The Minstrel tried his simple art,
But distant far was Ellen's heart.   260

XII

BALLAD

ALICE BRAND

Merry it is in the good greenwood,
    When the mavis and merle are singing,
When the deer sweeps by, and the hounds
    are in cry,
    And the hunter's horn is ringing.

' O Alice Brand, my native land
    Is lost for love of you;
And we must hold by wood and wold,
    As outlaws wont to do.

' O Alice, 't was all for thy locks so bright,
    And 't was all for thine eyes so blue,   270
That on the night of our luckless flight
    Thy brother bold I slew.

' Now must I teach to hew the beech
    The hand that held the glaive,
For leaves to spread our lowly bed,
    And stakes to fence our cave.

' And for vest of pall, thy fingers small,
    That wont on harp to stray,
A cloak must shear from the slaughtered
    deer,
    To keep the cold away.'   280

' O Richard ! if my brother died,
    'T was but a fatal chance;
For darkling was the battle tried,
    And fortune sped the lance.

' If pall and vair no more I wear,
    Nor thou the crimson sheen,
As warm, we 'll say, is the russet gray,
    As gay the forest-green.

' And, Richard, if our lot be hard,
    And lost thy native land,   290
Still Alice has her own Richard,
    And he his Alice Brand.'

XIII

BALLAD CONTINUED

'T is merry, 't is merry, in good greenwood;
    So blithe Lady Alice is singing;
On the beech's pride, and oak's brown side,
    Lord Richard's axe is ringing.

Up spoke the moody Elfin King,
    Who woned within the hill, —
Like wind in the porch of a ruined church,
    His voice was ghostly shrill.   300

' Why sounds yon stroke on beech and
    oak,
    Our moonlight circle's screen ?
Or who comes here to chase the deer,
    Beloved of our Elfin Queen ?
Or who may dare on wold to wear
    The fairies' fatal green ?

' Up, Urgan, up ! to yon mortal hie,
    For thou wert christened man;
For cross or sign thou wilt not fly,
    For muttered word or ban.   310

' Lay on him the curse of the withered heart,
    The curse of the sleepless eye;
Till he wish and pray that his life would
    part,
    Nor yet find leave to die.'

XIV

BALLAD CONTINUED

'T is merry, 't is merry, in good green-
    wood,
    Though the birds have stilled their sing-
    ing;
The evening blaze doth Alice raise,
    And Richard is fagots bringing.

Up Urgan starts, that hideous dwarf,
    Before Lord Richard stands,   320
And, as he crossed and blessed himself,
'I fear not sign,' quoth the grisly elf,
    'That is made with bloody hands.'

But out then spoke she, Alice Brand,
    That woman void of fear, —
'And if there 's blood upon his hand,
    'T is but the blood of deer.'

'Now loud thou liest, thou bold of mood!
    It cleaves unto his hand,
The stain of thine own kindly blood,   330
    The blood of Ethert Brand.'

Then forward stepped she, Alice Brand,
    And made the holy sign, —
'And if there 's blood on Richard's hand,
    A spotless hand is mine.

'And I conjure thee, demon elf,
    By Him whom demons fear,
To show us whence thou art thyself,
    And what thine errand here?'

XV

BALLAD CONTINUED

''T is merry, 't is merry, in Fairy-land,   340
    When fairy birds are singing,
When the court doth ride by their monarch's
        side,
    With bit and bridle ringing:

'And gayly shines the Fairy-land —
    But all is glistening show,
Like the idle gleam that December's beam
    Can dart on ice and snow.

'And fading, like that varied gleam,
    Is our inconstant shape,
Who now like knight and lady seem,   350
    And now like dwarf and ape.

'It was between the night and day,
    When the Fairy King has power,
That I sunk down in a sinful fray,
And 'twixt life and death was snatched away
    To the joyless Elfin bower.

'But wist I of a woman bold,
    Who thrice my brow durst sign,
I might regain my mortal mould,
    As fair a form as thine.'   360

She crossed him once — she crossed him
        twice —
    That lady was so brave;
The fouler grew his goblin hue,
    The darker grew the cave.

She crossed him thrice, that lady bold;
    He rose beneath her hand
The fairest knight on Scottish mould,
    Her brother, Ethert Brand!

Merry it is in good greenwood,
    When the mavis and merle are sing-
        ing,   370
But merrier were they in Dunfermline gray,
    When all the bells were ringing.

XVI

Just as the minstrel sounds were stayed,
A stranger climbed the steepy glade;
His martial step, his stately mien,
His hunting-suit of Lincoln green,
His eagle glance, remembrance claims —
'T is Snowdoun's Knight, 't is James Fitz-
        James.
Ellen beheld as in a dream,
Then, starting, scarce suppressed a
        scream: 380
'O stranger! in such hour of fear
What evil hap has brought thee here?'
'An evil hap how can it be
That bids me look again on thee?
By promise bound, my former guide
Met me betimes this morning-tide,
And marshalled over bank and bourne
The happy path of my return.'
'The happy path! — what! said he
        nought
Of war, of battle to be fought,   390
Of guarded pass?' 'No, by my faith!
Nor saw I aught could augur scathe.'
'O haste thee, Allan, to the kern:
Yonder his tartans I discern;
Learn thou his purpose, and conjure
That he will guide the stranger sure! —
What prompted thee, unhappy man?
The meanest serf in Roderick's clan
Had not been bribed, by love or fear,
Unknown to him to guide thee here.'   400

XVII

'Sweet Ellen, dear my life must be,
Since it is worthy care from thee;
Yet life I hold but idle breath
When love or honor 's weighed with death.

Then let me profit by my chance,
And speak my purpose bold at once.
I come to bear thee from a wild
Where ne'er before such blossom smiled,
By this soft hand to lead thee far
From frantic scenes of feud and war.   410
Near Bochastle my horses wait;
They bear us soon to Stirling gate.
I 'll place thee in a lovely bower,
I 'll guard thee like a tender flower — '
' O hush, Sir Knight ! 't were female art,
To say I do not read thy heart;
Too much, before, my selfish ear
Was idly soothed my praise to hear.
That fatal bait hath lured thee back,
In deathful hour, o'er dangerous track;   420
And how, O how, can I atone
The wreck my vanity brought on ! —
One way remains — I 'll tell him all —
Yes ! struggling bosom, forth it shall !
Thou, whose light folly bears the blame,
Buy thine own pardon with thy shame !
But first — my father is a man
Outlawed and exiled, under ban;
The price of blood is on his head,
With me, 't were infamy to wed.   430
Still wouldst thou speak ? — then hear the
        truth !
Fitz-James, there is a noble youth
If yet he is ! — exposed for me
And mine to dread extremity —
Thou hast the secret of my heart;
Forgive, be generous, and depart ! '

XVIII

Fitz-James knew every wily train
A lady's fickle heart to gain,
But here he knew and felt them vain.
There shot no glance from Ellen's eye,   440
To give her steadfast speech the lie;
In maiden confidence she stood,
Though mantled in her cheek the blood,
And told her love with such a sigh
Of deep and hopeless agony,
As death had sealed her Malcolm's doom
And she sat sorrowing on his tomb.
Hope vanished from Fitz-James's eye,
But not with hope fled sympathy.
He proffered to attend her side,   450
As brother would a sister guide.
' O little know'st thou Roderick's heart !
Safer for both we go apart.
O haste thee, and from Allan learn
If thou mayst trust yon wily kern.'
With hand upon his forehead laid,

The conflict of his mind to shade,
A parting step or two he made;
Then, as some thought had crossed his
        brain,
He paused, and turned, and came again.   460

XIX

' Hear, lady, yet a parting word ! —
It chanced in fight that my poor sword
Preserved the life of Scotland's lord.
This ring the grateful Monarch gave,
And bade, when I had boon to crave,
To bring it back, and boldly claim
The recompense that I would name.
Ellen, I am no courtly lord,
But one who lives by lance and sword,
Whose castle is his helm and shield,   470
His lordship the embattled field.
What from a prince can I demand,
Who neither reck of state nor land ?
Ellen, thy hand — the ring is thine;
Each guard and usher knows the sign.
Seek thou the King without delay;
This signet shall secure thy way:
And claim thy suit, whate'er it be,
As ransom of his pledge to me.'
He placed the golden circlet on,   480
Paused — kissed her hand — and then was
        gone.
The aged Minstrel stood aghast,
So hastily Fitz-James shot past.
He joined his guide, and wending down
The ridges of the mountain brown,
Across the stream they took their way
That joins Loch Katrine to Achray.

XX

All in the Trosachs' glen was still,
Noontide was sleeping on the hill: 489
Sudden his guide whooped loud and high —
' Murdoch ! was that a signal cry ? ' —
He stammered forth, ' I shout to scare
Yon raven from his dainty fare.'
He looked — he knew the raven's prey,
His own brave steed: ' Ah ! gallant gray !
For thee — for me, perchance —'t were well
We ne'er had seen the Trosachs' dell. —
Murdoch, move first — but silently;
Whistle or whoop, and thou shalt die ! '
Jealous and sullen on they fared,   500
Each silent, each upon his guard.

XXI

Now wound the path its dizzy ledge
Around a precipice's edge,

When lo ! a wasted female form,
Blighted by wrath of sun and storm,
In tattered weeds and wild array,
Stood on a cliff beside the way,
And glancing round her restless eye,
Upon the wood, the rock, the sky,
Seemed nought to mark, yet all to spy. 510
Her brow was wreathed with gaudy
        broom;
With gesture wild she waved a plume
Of feathers, which the eagles fling
To crag and cliff from dusky wing;
Such spoils her desperate step had sought,
Where scarce was footing for the goat.
The tartan plaid she first descried,
And shrieked till all the rocks replied;
As loud she laughed when near they
        drew,
For then the Lowland garb she knew; 520
And then her hands she wildly wrung,
And then she wept, and then she sung —
She sung ! — the voice, in better time,
Perchance to harp or lute might chime;
And now, though strained and roughened,
        still
Rung wildly sweet to dale and hill.

XXII
SONG

They bid me sleep, they bid me pray,
    They say my brain is warped and
        wrung —
I cannot sleep on Highland brae,
    I cannot pray in Highland tongue. 530
But were I now where Allan glides,
Or heard my native Devan's tides,
So sweetly would I rest, and pray
That Heaven would close my wintry day !

'T was thus my hair they bade me braid,
    They made me to the church repair;
It was my bridal morn, they said,
    And my true love would meet me there.
But woe betide the cruel guile 539
That drowned in blood the morning smile !
And woe betide the fairy dream !
I only waked to sob and scream.

XXIII

' Who is this maid ? what means her lay ?
She hovers o'er the hollow way,
And flutters wide her mantle gray,
As the lone heron spreads his wing,
By twilight, o'er a haunted spring.'
' 'T is Blanche of Devan,' Murdoch said,

' A crazed and captive Lowland maid,
Ta'en on the morn she was a bride, 550
When Roderick forayed Devan-side.
The gay bridegroom resistance made,
And felt our Chief's unconquered blade.
I marvel she is now at large,
But oft she 'scapes from Maudlin's
        charge. —
Hence, brain-sick fool ! ' — He raised his
        bow : —
' Now, if thou strik'st her but one blow,
I 'll pitch thee from the cliff as far
As ever peasant pitched a bar ! '
' Thanks, champion, thanks ! ' the Maniac
        cried, 560
And pressed her to Fitz-James's side.
' See the gray pennons I prepare,
To seek my true love through the air !
I will not lend that savage groom,
To break his fall, one downy plume !
No ! — deep amid disjointed stones,
The wolves shall batten on his bones,
And then shall his detested plaid,
By bush and brier in mid-air stayed,
Wave forth a banner fair and free, 570
Meet signal for their revelry.'

XXIV

' Hush thee, poor maiden, and be still ! '
' O ! thou look'st kindly, and I will.
Mine eye has dried and wasted been,
But still it loves the Lincoln green;
And, though mine ear is all unstrung,
Still, still it loves the Lowland tongue.

' For O my sweet William was forester
        true,
    He stole poor Blanche's heart away ! 579
His coat it was all of the greenwood hue,
    And so blithely he trilled the Lowland
        lay !

' It was not that I meant to tell . . .
But thou art wise and guessest well.'
Then, in a low and broken tone,
And hurried note, the song went on.
Still on the Clansman fearfully
She fixed her apprehensive eye,
Then turned it on the Knight, and then
Her look glanced wildly o'er the glen.

XXV

' The toils are pitched, and the stakes are
        set, — 590
    Ever sing merrily, merrily;

The bows they bend, and the knives they
  whet,
Hunters live so cheerily.

' It was a stag, a stag of ten,
  Bearing its branches sturdily;
He came stately down the glen, —
  Ever sing hardily, hardily.

' It was there he met with a wounded
  doe,
  She was bleeding deathfully;
She warned him of the toils below,   600
  O, so faithfully, faithfully !

' He had an eye, and he could heed, —
  Ever sing warily, warily;
He had a foot, and he could speed, —
  Hunters watch so narrowly.'

XXVI

Fitz-James's mind was passion-tossed,
When Ellen's hints and fears were lost;
But Murdoch's shout suspicion wrought,
And Blanche's song conviction brought.
Not like a stag that spies the snare,   610
But lion of the hunt aware,
He waved at once his blade on high,
' Disclose thy treachery, or die ! '
Forth at full speed the Clansman flew,
But in his race his bow he drew.
The shaft just grazed Fitz-James's crest,
And thrilled in Blanche's faded breast. —
Murdoch of Alpine ! prove thy speed,
For ne'er had Alpine's son such need;
With heart of fire, and foot of wind,   620
The fierce avenger is behind !
Fate judges of the rapid strife —
The forfeit death — the prize is life;
Thy kindred ambush lies before,
Close couched upon the heathery moor;
Them couldst thou reach ! — it may not
  be —
Thine ambushed kin thou ne'er shalt see,
The fiery Saxon gains on thee ! —
Resistless speeds the deadly thrust,
As lightning strikes the pine to dust;   630
With foot and hand Fitz-James must
  strain
Ere he can win his blade again.
Bent o'er the fallen with falcon eye,
He grimly smiled to see him die,
Then slower wended back his way,
Where the poor maiden bleeding lay.

XXVII

She sat beneath the birchen tree,
Her elbow resting on her knee;
She had withdrawn the fatal shaft,
And gazed on it, and feebly laughed;   640
Her wreath of broom and feathers gray,
Daggled with blood, beside her lay.
The Knight to stanch the life-stream
  tried, —
' Stranger, it is in vain ! ' she cried.
' This hour of death has given me more
Of reason's power than years before;
For, as these ebbing veins decay,
My frenzied visions fade away.
A helpless injured wretch I die,
And something tells me in thine eye   650
That thou wert mine avenger born.
Seest thou this tress ? — O, still I 've worn
This little tress of yellow hair,
Through danger, frenzy, and despair !
It once was bright and clear as thine,
But blood and tears have dimmed its shine.
I will not tell thee when 't was shred,
Nor from what guiltless victim's head, —
My brain would turn ! — but it shall wave
Like plumage on thy helmet brave,   660
Till sun and wind shall bleach the stain,
And thou wilt bring it me again.
I waver still. — O God ! more bright
Let reason beam her parting light ! —
O, by thy knighthood's honored sign,
And for thy life preserved by mine,
When thou shalt see a darksome man,
Who boasts him Chief of Alpine's Clan,
With tartans broad and shadowy plume,
And hand of blood, and brow of gloom,   670
Be thy heart bold, thy weapon strong,
And wreak poor Blanche of Devan's
  wrong ! —
They watch for thee by pass and fell . . .
Avoid the path . . . O God ! . . . fare-
  well !'

XXVIII

A kindly heart had brave Fitz-James;
Fast poured his eyes at pity's claims;
And now, with mingled grief and ire,
He saw the murdered maid expire.
' God, in my need, be my relief,
As I wreak this on yonder Chief !'   680
A lock from Blanche's tresses fair
He blended with her bridegroom's hair;
The mingled braid in blood he dyed,
And placed it on his bonnet-side:

' By Him whose word is truth, I swear,
No other favor will I wear,
Till this sad token I imbrue
In the best blood of Roderick Dhu ! —
But hark ! what means yon faint halloo ?
The chase is up, — but they shall know, 690
The stag at bay 's a dangerous foe.'
Barred from the known but guarded way,
Through copse and cliffs Fitz-James must stray,
And oft must change his desperate track,
By stream and precipice turned back.
Heartless, fatigued, and faint, at length,
From lack of food and loss of strength,
He couched him in a thicket hoar,
And thought his toils and perils o'er: —
Of all my rash adventures past,   700
This frantic feat must prove the last !
Who e'er so mad but might have guessed
That all this Highland hornet's nest
Would muster up in swarms so soon
As e'er they heard of bands at Doune ? —
Like bloodhounds now they search me out, —
Hark, to the whistle and the shout ! —
If farther through the wilds I go,
I only fall upon the foe:
I 'll couch me here till evening gray,   710
Then darkling try my dangerous way.'

XXIX

The shades of eve come slowly down,
The woods are wrapt in deeper brown,
The owl awakens from her dell,
The fox is heard upon the fell;
Enough remains of glimmering light
To guide the wanderer's steps aright,
Yet not enough from far to show
His figure to the watchful foe.
With cautious step and ear awake,   720
He climbs the crag and threads the brake;
And not the summer solstice there
Tempered the midnight mountain air,
But every breeze that swept the wold
Benumbed his drenched limbs with cold.
In dread, in danger, and alone,
Famished and chilled, through ways unknown,
Tangled and steep, he journeyed on;
Till, as a rock's huge point he turned,
A watch-fire close before him burned.   730

XXX

Beside its embers red and clear,
Basked in his plaid a mountaineer;

And up he sprung with sword in hand, —
'Thy name and purpose ! Saxon, stand !'
' A stranger.'   ' What dost thou require ? '
' Rest and a guide, and food and fire.
My life 's beset, my path is lost,
The gale has chilled my limbs with frost.'
' Art thou a friend to Roderick ? '   ' No.'
' Thou dar'st not call thyself a foe ? '   740
' I dare ! to him and all the band
He brings to aid his murderous hand.'
' Bold words ! — but, though the beast of game
The privilege of chase may claim,
Though space and law the stag we lend,
Ere hound we slip or bow we bend,
Who ever recked, where, how, or when,
The prowling fox was trapped or slain ?
Thus treacherous scouts, — yet sure they lie,
Who say thou cam'st a secret spy !' —   750
' They do, by heaven ! — come Roderick Dhu,
And of his clan the boldest two,
And let me but till morning rest,
I write the falsehood on their crest.'
' If by the blaze I mark aright,
Thou bear'st the belt and spur of Knight.'
' Then by these tokens mayst thou know
Each proud oppressor's mortal foe.'
' Enough, enough; sit down and share
A soldier's couch, a soldier's fare.'   760

XXXI

He gave him of his Highland cheer,
The hardened flesh of mountain deer;
Dry fuel on the fire he laid,
And bade the Saxon share his plaid.
He tended him like welcome guest,
Then thus his further speech addressed: —
' Stranger, I am to Roderick Dhu
A clansman born, a kinsman true:
Each word against his honor spoke
Demands of me avenging stroke;   770
Yet more, — upon thy fate, 't is said,
A mighty augury is laid.
It rests with me to wind my horn, —
Thou art with numbers overborne;
It rests with me, here, brand to brand,
Worn as thou art, to bid thee stand:
But, not for clan, nor kindred's cause,
Will I depart from honor's laws;
To assail a wearied man were shame,
And stranger is a holy name;   780
Guidance and rest, and food and fire,
In vain he never must require.

Then rest thee here till dawn of day;
Myself will guide thee on the way,
O'er stock and stone, through watch and
    ward,
Till past Clan-Alpine's outmost guard,
As far as Coilantogle's ford;
From thence thy warrant is thy sword.'
' I take thy courtesy, by heaven,
As freely as 't is nobly given ! '   790
' Well, rest thee; for the bittern's cry
Sings us the lake's wild lullaby.'
With that he shook the gathered heath,
And spread his plaid upon the wreath;
And the brave foemen, side by side,
Lay peaceful down like brothers tried,
And slept until the dawning beam
Purpled the mountain and the stream.

CANTO FIFTH

THE COMBAT

I

FAIR as the earliest beam of eastern light,
    When first, by the bewildered pilgrim
      spied,
It smiles upon the dreary brow of night,
    And silvers o'er the torrent's foaming
      tide,
And lights the fearful path on mountain-
    side, —
    Fair as that beam, although the fairest
      far,
Giving to horror grace, to danger pride,
    Shine martial Faith, and Courtesy's
      bright star,
Through all the wreckful storms that cloud
    the brow of War.

II

That early beam, so fair and sheen,   10
Was twinkling through the hazel screen,
When, rousing at its glimmer red,
The warriors left their lowly bed,
Looked out upon the dappled sky,
Muttered their soldier matins by,
And then awaked their fire, to steal,
As short and rude, their soldier meal.
That o'er, the Gael around him threw
His graceful plaid of varied hue,
And, true to promise, led the way,   20
By thicket green and mountain gray.
A wildering path ! — they winded now
Along the precipice's brow,

Commanding the rich scenes beneath,
The windings of the Forth and Teith,
And all the vales between that lie,
Till Stirling's turrets melt in sky;
Then, sunk in copse, their farthest glance
Gained not the length of horseman's lance.
'T was oft so steep, the foot was fain   30
Assistance from the hand to gain;
So tangled oft that, bursting through,
Each hawthorn shed her showers of
    dew, —
That diamond dew, so pure and clear,
It rivals all but Beauty's tear !

III

At length they came where, stern and
    steep,
The hill sinks down upon the deep.
Here Vennachar in silver flows,
There, ridge on ridge, Benledi rose;
Ever the hollow path twined on,   40
Beneath steep bank and threatening stone;
A hundred men might hold the post
With hardihood against a host.
The rugged mountain's scanty cloak
Was dwarfish shrubs of birch and oak,
With shingles bare, and cliffs between,
And patches bright of bracken green,
And heather black, that waved so high,
It held the copse in rivalry.
But where the lake slept deep and still, 50
Dank osiers fringed the swamp and hill;
And oft both path and hill were torn,
Where wintry torrent down had borne,
And heaped upon the cumbered land
Its wreck of gravel, rocks, and sand.
So toilsome was the road to trace,
The guide, abating of his pace,
Led slowly through the pass's jaws,
And asked Fitz-James by what strange
    cause   59
He sought these wilds, traversed by few,
Without a pass from Roderick Dhu.

IV

' Brave Gael, my pass, in danger tried,
Hangs in my belt and by my side;
Yet, sooth to tell,' the Saxon said,
' I dreamt not now to claim its aid.
When here, but three days since, I came,
Bewildered in pursuit of game,
All seemed as peaceful and as still
As the mist slumbering on yon hill;
Thy dangerous Chief was then afar,   70
Nor soon expected back from war.

Thus said, at least, my mountain-guide,
Though deep perchance the villain lied.'
' Yet why a second venture try ? '
' A warrior thou, and ask me why ! —
Moves our free course by such fixed cause
As gives the poor mechanic laws ?
Enough, I sought to drive away
The lazy hours of peaceful day;
Slight cause will then suffice to guide   80
A Knight's free footsteps far and wide, —
A falcon flown, a greyhound strayed,
The merry glance of mountain maid;
Or, if a path be dangerous known,
The danger's self is lure alone.'

V

' Thy secret keep, I urge thee not; —
Yet, ere again ye sought this spot,
Say, heard ye nought of Lowland war,
Against Clan-Alpine, raised by Mar ? '
' No, by my word; — of bands prepared   90
To guard King James's sports I heard;
Nor doubt I aught, but, when they hear
This muster of the mountaineer,
Their pennons will abroad be flung,
Which else in Doune had peaceful hung.'
' Free be they flung ! for we were loath
Their silken folds should feast the moth.
Free be they flung ! — as free shall wave
Clan-Alpine's pine in banner brave.
But, stranger, peaceful since you came,   100
Bewildered in the mountain-game,
Whence the bold boast by which you show
Vich-Alpine's vowed and mortal foe ? '
' Warrior, but yester-morn I knew
Nought of thy Chieftain, Roderick Dhu,
Save as an outlawed desperate man,
The chief of a rebellious clan,
Who, in the Regent's court and sight,
With ruffian dagger stabbed a knight;
Yet this alone might from his part   110
Sever each true and loyal heart.'

VI

Wrathful at such arraignment foul,
Dark lowered the clansman's sable scowl,
A space he paused, then sternly said,
' And heardst thou why he drew his blade ?
Heardst thou that shameful word and blow
Brought Roderick's vengeance on his foe ?
What recked the Chieftain if he stood
On Highland heath or Holy-Rood ?
He rights such wrong where it is given,   120
If it were in the court of heaven.'
' Still was it outrage; — yet, 't is true,

Not then claimed sovereignty his due;
While Albany with feeble hand
Held borrowed truncheon of command,
The young King, mewed in Stirling tower,
Was stranger to respect and power.
But then, thy Chieftain's robber life ! —
Winning mean prey by causeless strife,
Wrenching from ruined Lowland swain   130
His herds and harvest reared in vain, —
Methinks a soul like thine should scorn
The spoils from such foul foray borne.'

VII

The Gael beheld him grim the while,
And answered with disdainful smile:
' Saxon, from yonder mountain high,
I marked thee send delighted eye
Far to the south and east, where lay,
Extended in succession gay,
Deep waving fields and pastures green,   140
With gentle slopes and groves between: —
These fertile plains, that softened vale,
Were once the birthright of the Gael;
The stranger came with iron hand,
And from our fathers reft the land.
Where dwell we now ?   See, rudely swell
Crag over crag, and fell o'er fell.
Ask we this savage hill we tread
For fattened steer or household bread,
Ask we for flocks these shingles dry,   150
And well the mountain might reply, —
" To you, as to your sires of yore,
Belong the target and claymore !
I give you shelter in my breast,
Your own good blade must win the rest."
Pent in this fortress of the North,
Think'st thou we will not sally forth,
To spoil the spoiler as we may,
And from the robber rend the prey ?
Ay, by my soul ! — While on yon plain   160
The Saxon rears one shock of grain,
While of ten thousand herds there strays
But one along yon river's maze, —
The Gael, of plain and river heir,
Shall with strong hand redeem his share.
Where live the mountain Chiefs who hold
That plundering Lowland field and fold
Is aught but retribution true ?
Seek other cause 'gainst Roderick Dhu.'

VIII

Answered Fitz-James: ' And, if I sought,
Think'st thou no other could be brought ?
What deem ye of my path waylaid ?   172
My life given o'er to ambuscade ? '

'As of a meed to rashness due:
Hadst thou sent warning fair and true, —
I seek my hound or falcon strayed,
I seek, good faith, a Highland maid, —
Free hadst thou been to come and go;
But secret path marks secret foe.
Nor yet for this, even as a spy,   180
Hadst thou, unheard, been doomed to die,
Save to fulfil an augury.'
'Well, let it pass; nor will I now
Fresh cause of enmity avow,
To chafe thy mood and cloud thy brow.
Enough, I am by promise tied
To match me with this man of pride:
Twice have I sought Clan-Alpine's glen
In peace; but when I come again,
I come with banner, brand, and bow,   190
As leader seeks his mortal foe.
For love-lorn swain in lady's bower
Ne'er panted for the appointed hour,
As I, until before me stand
This rebel Chieftain and his band!'

IX

'Have then thy wish!' — He whistled
          shrill,
And he was answered from the hill;
Wild as the scream of the curlew,
From crag to crag the signal flew.
Instant, through copse and heath, arose   200
Bonnets and spears and bended bows;
On right, on left, above, below,
Sprung up at once the lurking foe;
From shingles gray their lances start,
The bracken bush sends forth the dart,
The rushes and the willow-wand
Are bristling into axe and brand,
And every tuft of broom gives life
To plaided warrior armed for strife.
That whistle garrisoned the glen   210
At once with full five hundred men,
As if the yawning hill to heaven
A subterranean host had given.
Watching their leader's beck and will,
All silent there they stood and still.
Like the loose crags whose threatening mass
Lay tottering o'er the hollow pass,
As if an infant's touch could urge
Their headlong passage down the verge,
With step and weapon forward flung,   220
Upon the mountain-side they hung.
The Mountaineer cast glance of pride
Along Benledi's living side,
Then fixed his eye and sable brow
Full on Fitz-James: 'How say'st thou now?

These are Clan-Alpine's warriors true;
And, Saxon, — I am Roderick Dhu!'

X

Fitz-James was brave: — though to his
          heart
The life-blood thrilled with sudden start,
He manned himself with dauntless air,   230
Returned the Chief his haughty stare,
His back against a rock he bore,
And firmly placed his foot before: —
'Come one, come all! this rock shall fly
From its firm base as soon as I.'
Sir Roderick marked, — and in his eyes
Respect was mingled with surprise,
And the stern joy which warriors feel
In foeman worthy of their steel.
Short space he stood — then waved his
          hand: 240
Down sunk the disappearing band;
Each warrior vanished where he stood,
In broom or bracken, heath or wood;
Sunk brand and spear and bended bow,
In osiers pale and copses low;
It seemed as if their mother Earth
Had swallowed up her warlike birth.
The wind's last breath had tossed in air
Pennon and plaid and plumage fair, —
The next but swept a lone hill-side,   250
Where heath and fern were waving wide:
The sun's last glance was glinted back
From spear and glaive, from targe and
          jack;
The next, all unreflected, shone
On bracken green and cold gray stone.

XI

Fitz-James looked round, — yet scarce be-
          lieved
The witness that his sight received;
Such apparition well might seem
Delusion of a dreadful dream.
Sir Roderick in suspense he eyed,   260
And to his look the Chief replied:
'Fear nought — nay, that I need not say —
But — doubt not aught from mine array.
Thou art my guest; — I pledged my word
As far as Coilantogle ford:
Nor would I call a clansman's brand
For aid against one valiant hand,
Though on our strife lay every vale
Rent by the Saxon from the Gael.
So move we on; — I only meant   270
To show the reed on which you leant,
Deeming this path you might pursue

Without a pass from Roderick Dhu.'
They moved; — I said Fitz-James was
    brave
As ever knight that belted glaive,
Yet dare not say that now his blood
Kept on its wont and tempered flood,
As, following Roderick's stride, he drew
That seeming lonesome pathway through,
Which yet by fearful proof was rife   280
With lances, that, to take his life,
Waited but signal from a guide,
So late dishonored and defied.
Ever, by stealth, his eye sought round
The vanished guardians of the ground,
And still from copse and heather deep
Fancy saw spear and broadsword peep,
And in the plover's shrilly strain
The signal whistle heard again.
Nor breathed he free till far behind   290
The pass was left; for then they wind
Along a wide and level green,
Where neither tree nor tuft was seen,
Nor rush nor bush of broom was near,
To hide a bonnet or a spear.

XII

The Chief in silence strode before,
And reached that torrent's sounding shore,
Which, daughter of three mighty lakes,
From Vennachar in silver breaks,
Sweeps through the plain, and ceaseless
    mines   300
On Bochastle the mouldering lines,
Where Rome, the Empress of the world,
Of yore her eagle wings unfurled.
And here his course the Chieftain stayed,
Threw down his target and his plaid,
And to the Lowland warrior said:
'Bold Saxon! to his promise just,
Vich-Alpine has discharged his trust.
This murderous Chief, this ruthless man,
This head of a rebellious clan,   310
Hath led thee safe, through watch and
    ward,
Far past Clan-Alpine's outmost guard.
Now, man to man, and steel to steel,
A Chieftain's vengeance thou shalt feel.
See, here all vantageless I stand,
Armed like thyself with single brand;
For this is Coilantogle ford,
And thou must keep thee with thy sword.'

XIII

The Saxon paused: ' I ne'er delayed,
When foeman bade me draw my blade;   320

Nay more, brave Chief, I vowed thy death;
Yet sure thy fair and generous faith,
And my deep debt for life preserved,
A better meed have well deserved:
Can nought but blood our feud atone?
Are there no means?' — 'No, stranger,
    none!
And hear, — to fire thy flagging zeal, —
The Saxon cause rests on thy steel;
For thus spoke Fate by prophet bred
Between the living and the dead: 330
"Who spills the foremost foeman's life,
His party conquers in the strife."'
'Then, by my word,' the Saxon said,
' The riddle is already read.
Seek yonder brake beneath the cliff, —
There lies Red Murdoch, stark and stiff.
Thus Fate hath solved her prophecy;
Then yield to Fate, and not to me.
To James at Stirling let us go,
When, if thou wilt be still his foe,   340
Or if the King shall not agree
To grant thee grace and favor free,
I plight mine honor, oath, and word
That, to thy native strengths restored,
With each advantage shalt thou stand
That aids thee now to guard thy land.'

XIV

Dark lightning flashed from Roderick's eye:
'Soars thy presumption, then, so high,
Because a wretched kern ye slew,
Homage to name to Roderick Dhu?   350
He yields not, he, to man nor Fate!
Thou add'st but fuel to my hate; —
My clansman's blood demands revenge.
Not yet prepared? — By heaven, I change
My thought, and hold thy valor light
As that of some vain carpet knight,
Who ill deserved my courteous care,
And whose best boast is but to wear
A braid of his fair lady's hair.'
'I thank thee, Roderick, for the word!   360
It nerves my heart, it steels my sword;
For I have sworn this braid to stain
In the best blood that warms thy vein.
Now, truce, farewell! and, ruth, begone! —
Yet think not that by thee alone,
Proud Chief! can courtesy be shown;
Though not from copse, or heath, or cairn,
Start at my whistle clansmen stern,
Of this small horn one feeble blast
Would fearful odds against thee cast.   370
But fear not — doubt not — which thou
    wilt —

We try this quarrel hilt to hilt.'
Then each at once his falchion drew,
Each on the ground his scabbard threw,
Each looked to sun and stream and plain
As what they ne'er might see again;
Then foot and point and eye opposed,
In dubious strife they darkly closed.

XV

Ill fared it then with Roderick Dhu,
That on the field his targe he threw,   380
Whose brazen studs and tough bull-hide
Had death so often dashed aside;
For, trained abroad his arms to wield,
Fitz-James's blade was sword and shield.
He practised every pass and ward,
To thrust, to strike, to feint, to guard;
While less expert, though stronger far,
The Gael maintained unequal war.
Three times in closing strife they stood,
And thrice the Saxon blade drank blood; 390
No stinted draught, no scanty tide,
The gushing flood the tartans dyed.
Fierce Roderick felt the fatal drain,
And showered his blows like wintry rain;
And, as firm rock or castle-roof
Against the winter shower is proof,
The foe, invulnerable still,
Foiled his wild rage by steady skill;
Till, at advantage ta'en, his brand   399
Forced Roderick's weapon from his hand,
And backward borne upon the lea,
Brought the proud Chieftain to his knee.

XVI

' Now yield thee, or by Him who made
The world, thy heart's blood dyes my
      blade ! '
' Thy threats, thy mercy, I defy !
Let recreant yield, who fears to die.'
Like adder darting from his coil,
Like wolf that dashes through the toil,
Like mountain-cat who guards her young,
Full at Fitz-James's throat he sprung;   410
Received, but recked not of a wound,
And locked his arms his foeman round. —
Now, gallant Saxon, hold thine own !
No maiden's hand is round thee thrown !
That desperate grasp thy frame might feel
Through bars of brass and triple steel !
They tug, they strain ! down, down they go,
The Gael above, Fitz-James below.
The Chieftain's gripe his throat com-
      pressed, .

His knee was planted on his breast;   420
His clotted locks he backward threw,
Across his brow his hand he drew,
From blood and mist to clear his sight,
Then gleamed aloft his dagger bright !
But hate and fury ill supplied
The stream of life's exhausted tide,
And all too late the advantage came,
To turn the odds of deadly game;
For, while the dagger gleamed on high,
Reeled soul and sense, reeled brain and
      eye.   430
Down came the blow ! but in the heath
The erring blade found bloodless sheath.
The struggling foe may now unclasp
The fainting Chief's relaxing grasp;
Unwounded from the dreadful close,
But breathless all, Fitz-James arose.

XVII

He faltered thanks to Heaven for life,
Redeemed, unhoped, from desperate strife:
Next on his foe his look he cast,
Whose every gasp appeared his last;   440
In Roderick's gore he dipped the braid, —
' Poor Blanche ! thy wrongs are dearly
      paid;
Yet with thy foe must die, or live,
The praise that faith and valor give.'
With that he blew a bugle note,
Undid the collar from his throat,
Unbonneted, and by the wave
Sat down his brow and hands to lave.
Then faint afar are heard the feet
Of rushing steeds in gallop fleet;   450
The sounds increase, and now are seen
Four mounted squires in Lincoln green;
Two who bear lance, and two who lead
By loosened rein a saddled steed;
Each onward held his headlong course,
And by Fitz-James reined up his horse, —
With wonder viewed the bloody spot. —
' Exclaim not, gallants ! question not. —
You, Herbert and Luffness, alight,
And bind the wounds of yonder knight;   460
Let the gray palfrey bear his weight,
We destined for a fairer freight,
And bring him on to Stirling straight;
I will before at better speed,
To seek fresh horse and fitting weed.
The sun rides high: — I must be boune
To see the archer-game at noon;
But lightly Bayard clears the lea. —
De Vaux and Herries, follow me.

XVIII

'Stand, Bayard, stand!'—the steed
    obeyed,   470
With arching neck and bended head,
And glancing eye and quivering ear,
As if he loved his lord to hear.
No foot Fitz-James in stirrup stayed,
No grasp upon the saddle laid,
But wreathed his left hand in the mane,
And lightly bounded from the plain,
Turned on the horse his armed heel,
And stirred his courage with the steel.
Bounded the fiery steed in air,   480
The rider sat erect and fair,
Then like a bolt from steel crossbow
Forth launched, along the plain they go.
They dashed that rapid torrent through,
And up Carhonie's hill they flew;
Still at the gallop pricked the Knight,
His merrymen followed as they might.
Along thy banks, swift Teith, they ride,
And in the race they mock thy tide;
Torry and Lendrick now are past,   490
And Deanstown lies behind them cast;
They rise, the bannered towers of Doune,
They sink in distant woodland soon;
Blair-Drummond sees the hoofs strike fire,
They sweep like breeze through Ochter-
    tyre;
They mark just glance and disappear
The lofty brow of ancient Kier;
They bathe their coursers' sweltering sides,
Dark Forth! amid thy sluggish tides,
And on the opposing shore take ground, 500
With plash, with scramble, and with bound.
Right-hand they leave thy cliffs, Craig-
    Forth!
And soon the bulwark of the North,
Gray Stirling, with her towers and town,
Upon their fleet career look down.

XIX

As up the flinty path they strained,
Sudden his steed the leader reined;
A signal to his squire he flung,
Who instant to his stirrup sprung:—
'Seest thou, De Vaux, yon woodsman
    gray,   510
Who townward holds the rocky way,
Of stature tall and poor array?
Mark'st thou the firm yet active stride,
With which he scales the mountain side?
Know'st thou from whence he comes, or
    whom?'
'No, by my word;—a burly groom

He seems, who in the field or chase
A baron's train would nobly grace'—
'Out, out, De Vaux! can fear supply,
And jealousy, no sharper eye?   520
Afar, ere to the hill he drew,
That stately form and step I knew;
Like form in Scotland is not seen,
Treads not such step on Scottish green.
'T is James of Douglas, by Saint Serle!
The uncle of the banished Earl.
Away, away, to court, to show
The near approach of dreaded foe:
The King must stand upon his guard;
Douglas and he must meet prepared.'   530
Then right-hand wheeled their steeds, and
    straight
They won the Castle's postern gate.

XX

The Douglas who had bent his way
From Cambus-kenneth's abbey gray,
Now, as he climbed the rocky shelf,
Held sad communion with himself:—
'Yes! all is true my fears could frame;
A prisoner lies the noble Græme,
And fiery Roderick soon will feel
The vengeance of the royal steel.   540
I, only I, can ward their fate,—
God grant the ransom come not late!
The Abbess hath her promise given,
My child shall be the bride of Heaven;—
Be pardoned one repining tear!
For He who gave her knows how dear,
How excellent!—but that is by,
And now my business is—to die.—
Ye towers! within whose circuit dread
A Douglas by his sovereign bled;   550
And thou, O sad and fatal mound!
That oft hast heard the death-axe sound,
As on the noblest of the land
Fell the stern headsman's bloody hand,—
The dungeon, block, and nameless tomb
Prepare—for Douglas seeks his doom!
But hark! what blithe and jolly peal
Makes the Franciscan steeple reel?
And see! upon the crowded street,
In motley groups what masquers
    meet!   560
Banner and pageant, pipe and drum,
And merry morrice-dancers come.
I guess, by all this quaint array,
The burghers hold their sports to-day.
James will be there; he loves such show,
Where the good yeoman bends his bow,
And the tough wrestler foils his foe,

As well as where, in proud career,
The high-born tilter shivers spear.
I 'll follow to the Castle-park,   570
And play my prize; — King James shall
        mark
If age has tamed these sinews stark,
Whose force so oft in happier days
His boyish wonder loved to praise.'

XXI

The Castle gates were open flung,
The quivering drawbridge rocked and
        rung,
And echoed loud the flinty street
Beneath the courser's clattering feet,
As slowly down the steep descent
Fair Scotland's King and nobles went,   580
While all along the crowded way
Was jubilee and loud huzza.
And ever James was bending low
To his white jennet's saddle-bow,
Doffing his cap to city dame,
Who smiled and blushed for pride and
        shame.
And well the simperer might be vain, —
He chose the fairest of the train.
Gravely he greets each city sire,
Commends each pageant's quaint attire, 590
Gives to the dancers thanks aloud,
And smiles and nods upon the crowd,
Who rend the heavens with their ac-
        claims, —
'Long live the Commons' King, King
        James!'
Behind the King thronged peer and knight,
And noble dame and damsel bright,
Whose fiery steeds ill brooked the stay
Of the steep street and crowded way.
But in the train you might discern
Dark lowering brow and visage stern;   600
There nobles mourned their pride restrained,
And the mean burgher's joys disdained;
And chiefs, who, hostage for their clan,
Were each from home a banished man,
There thought upon their own gray tower,
Their waving woods, their feudal power,
And deemed themselves a shameful part
Of pageant which they cursed in heart.

XXII

Now, in the Castle-park, drew out
Their checkered bands the joyous rout. 610
There morricers, with bell at heel
And blade in hand, their mazes wheel;
But chief, beside the butts, there stand

Bold Robin Hood and all his band, —
Friar Tuck with quarterstaff and cowl,
Old Scathelocke with his surly scowl,
Maid Marian, fair as ivory bone,
Scarlet, and Mutch, and Little John;
Their bugles challenge all that will,
In archery to prove their skill.   620
The Douglas bent a bow of might, —
His first shaft centred in the white,
And when in turn he shot again,
His second split the first in twain.
From the King's hand must Douglas take
A silver dart, the archer's stake;
Fondly he watched, with watery eye,
Some answering glance of sympathy, —
No kind emotion made reply !
Indifferent as to archer wight,   630
The monarch gave the arrow bright.

XXIII

Now, clear the ring ! for, hand to hand,
The manly wrestlers take their stand.
Two o'er the rest superior rose,
And proud demanded mightier foes, —
Nor called in vain, for Douglas came. —
For life is Hugh of Larbert lame;
Scarce better John of Alloa's fare,
Whom senseless home his comrades bare.
Prize of the wrestling match, the King 640
To Douglas gave a golden ring,
While coldly glanced his eye of blue,
As frozen drop of wintry dew.
Douglas would speak, but in his breast
His struggling soul his words suppressed;
Indignant then he turned him where
Their arms the brawny yeomen bare,
To hurl the massive bar in air.
When each his utmost strength had shown,
The Douglas rent an earth-fast stone   650
From its deep bed, then heaved it high,
And sent the fragment through the sky
A rood beyond the farthest mark;
And still in Stirling's royal park,
The gray-haired sires, who know the past,
To strangers point the Douglas cast,
And moralize on the decay
Of Scottish strength in modern day.

XXIV

The vale with loud applauses rang,
The Ladies' Rock sent back the clang.   660
The King, with look unmoved, bestowed
A purse well filled with pieces broad.
Indignant smiled the Douglas proud,
And threw the gold among the crowd,

Who now with anxious wonder scan,
And sharper glance, the dark gray man;
Till whispers rose among the throng,
That heart so free, and hand so strong,
Must to the Douglas blood belong.   669
The old men marked and shook the head,
To see his hair with silver spread,
And winked aside, and told each son
Of feats upon the English done,
Ere Douglas of the stalwart hand
Was exiled from his native land.
The women praised his stately form,
Though wrecked by many a winter's storm;
The youth with awe and wonder saw   •
His strength surpassing Nature's law.
Thus judged, as is their wont, the crowd, 680
Till murmurs rose to clamors loud.
But not a glance from that proud ring
Of peers who circled round the King
With Douglas held communion kind,
Or called the banished man to mind;
No, not from those who at the chase
Once held his side the honored place,
Begirt his board, and in the field
Found safety underneath his shield;
For he whom royal eyes disown,   690
When was his form to courtiers known !

XXV

The Monarch saw the gambols flag,
And bade let loose a gallant stag,
Whose pride, the holiday to crown,
Two favorite greyhounds should pull down,
That venison free and Bourdeaux wine
Might serve the archery to dine.
But Lufra, — whom from Douglas' side
Nor bribe nor threat could e'er divide,
The fleetest hound in all the North, —   700
Brave Lufra saw, and darted forth.
She left the royal hounds midway,
And dashing on the antlered prey,
Sunk her sharp muzzle in his flank,
And deep the flowing life-blood drank.
The king's stout huntsman saw the sport
By strange intruder broken short,
Came up, and with his leash unbound
In anger struck the noble hound.
The Douglas had endured, that morn,   710
The King's cold look, the nobles' scorn,
And last, and worst to spirit proud,
Had borne the pity of the crowd;
But Lufra had been fondly bred,
To share his board, to watch his bed,
And oft would Ellen Lufra's neck
In maiden glee with garlands deck;

They were such playmates that with name
Of Lufra Ellen's image came.
His stifled wrath is brimming high,   720
In darkened brow and flashing eye;
As waves before the bark divide,
The crowd gave way before his stride;
Needs but a buffet and no more,
The groom lies senseless in his gore.
Such blow no other hand could deal,
Though gauntleted in glove of steel.

XXVI

Then clamored loud the royal train,
And brandished swords and staves amain,
But stern the Baron's warning: 'Back ! 730
Back, on your lives, ye menial pack !
Beware the Douglas. — Yes ! behold,
King James ! The Douglas, doomed of
      old,
And vainly sought for near and far,
A victim to atone the war,
A willing victim, now attends,
Nor craves thy grace but for his friends.' —
' Thus is my clemency repaid ?
Presumptuous Lord !' the Monarch said:
' Of thy misproud ambitious clan,   740
Thou, James of Bothwell, wert the man,
The only man, in whom a foe
My woman-mercy would not know;
But shall a Monarch's presence brook
Injurious blow and haughty look ? —
What ho ! the Captain of our Guard !
Give the offender fitting ward. —
Break off the sports ! ' — for tumult rose,
And yeomen 'gan to bend their bows, —
' Break off the sports ! ' he said and
      frowned,
      750
' And bid our horsemen clear the ground.'

XXVII

Then uproar wild and misarray
Marred the fair form of festal day.
The horsemen pricked among the crowd,
Repelled by threats and insult loud;
To earth are borne the old and weak,
The timorous fly, the women shriek;
With flint, with shaft, with staff, with bar,
The hardier urge tumultuous war.
At once round Douglas darkly sweep   760
The royal spears in circle deep,
And slowly scale the pathway steep,
While on the rear in thunder pour
The rabble with disordered roar.
With grief the noble Douglas saw
The Commons rise against the law,

And to the leading soldier said:
'Sir John of Hyndford, 't was my blade,
That knighthood on thy shoulder laid;
For that good deed permit me then   770
A word with these misguided men. —

XXVIII

'Hear, gentle friends, ere yet for me
Ye break the bands of fealty.
My life, my honor, and my cause,
I tender free to Scotland's laws.
Are these so weak as must require
The aid of your misguided ire ?
Or if I suffer causeless wrong,
Is then my selfish rage so strong,
My sense of public weal so low,   780
That, for mean vengeance on a foe,
Those cords of love I should unbind
Which knit my country and my kind ?
O no ! Believe, in yonder tower
It will not soothe my captive hour,
To know those spears our foes should dread
For me in kindred gore are red:
To know, in fruitless brawl begun,
For me that mother wails her son,
For me that widow's mate expires,   790
For me that orphans weep their sires,
That patriots mourn insulted laws,
And curse the Douglas for the cause.
O let your patience ward such ill,
And keep your right to love me still ! '

XXIX

The crowd's wild fury sunk again
In tears, as tempests melt in rain.
With lifted hands and eyes, they prayed
For blessings on his generous head
Who for his country felt alone,   800
And prized her blood beyond his own.
Old men upon the verge of life
Blessed him who stayed the civil strife;
And mothers held their babes on high,
The self-devoted Chief to spy,
Triumphant over wrongs and ire,
To whom the prattlers owed a sire.
Even the rough soldier's heart was moved;
As if behind some bier beloved,
With trailing arms and drooping head,   810
The Douglas up the hill he led,
And at the Castle's battled verge,
With sighs resigned his honored charge.

XXX

The offended Monarch rode apart,
With bitter thought and swelling heart,

And would not now vouchsafe again
Through Stirling streets to lead his train.
'O Lenox, who would wish to rule
This changeling crowd, this common fool ?
Hear'st thou,' he said, 'the loud acclaim 820
With which they shout the Douglas name ?
With like acclaim the vulgar throat
Strained for King James their morning
          note;
With like acclaim they hailed the day
When first I broke the Douglas sway;
And like acclaim would Douglas greet
If he could hurl me from my seat.
Who o'er the herd would wish to reign,
Fantastic, fickle, fierce, and vain ?
Vain as the leaf upon the stream,   830
And fickle as a changeful dream;
Fantastic as a woman's mood,
And fierce as Frenzy's fevered blood.
Thou many-headed monster-thing,
O who would wish to be thy king ? —

XXXI

'But soft ! what messenger of speed
Spurs hitherward his panting steed ?
I guess his cognizance afar —
What from our cousin, John of Mar ? '
'He prays, my liege, your sports keep
          bound   840
Within the safe and guarded ground;
For some foul purpose yet unknown, —
Most sure for evil to the throne, —
The outlawed Chieftain, Roderick Dhu,
Has summoned his rebellious crew;
'T is said, in James of Bothwell's aid
These loose banditti stand arrayed.
The Earl of Mar this morn from Doune
To break their muster marched, and soon
Your Grace will hear of battle fought; 850
But earnestly the Earl besought,
Till for such danger he provide,
With scanty train you will not ride.'

XXXII

'Thou warn'st me I have done amiss, —
I should have earlier looked to this;
I lost it in this bustling day. —
Retrace with speed thy former way;
Spare not for spoiling of thy steed,
The best of mine shall be thy meed.
Say to our faithful Lord of Mar,   860
We do forbid the intended war;
Roderick this morn in single fight
Was made our prisoner by a knight,
And Douglas hath himself and cause

Submitted to our kingdom's laws.
The tidings of their leaders lost
Will soon dissolve the mountain host,
Nor would we that the vulgar feel,
For their Chief's crimes, avenging steel.
Bear Mar our message, Braco, fly!'   870
He turned his steed, — 'My liege, I hie,
Yet ere I cross this lily lawn
I fear the broadswords will be drawn.'
The turf the flying courser spurned,
And to his towers the King returned.

XXXIII

Ill with King James's mood that day
Suited gay feast and minstrel lay;
Soon were dismissed the courtly throng,
And soon cut short the festal song.
Nor less upon the saddened town   880
The evening sunk in sorrow down.
The burghers spoke of civil jar,
Of rumored feuds and mountain war,
Of Moray, Mar, and Roderick Dhu,
All up in arms; — the Douglas too,
They mourned him pent within the hold,
'Where stout Earl William was of old.' —
And there his word the speaker stayed,
And finger on his lip he laid,
Or pointed to his dagger blade.   890
But jaded horsemen from the west
At evening to the Castle pressed,
And busy talkers said they bore
Tidings of fight on Katrine's shore;
At noon the deadly fray begun,
And lasted till the set of sun.
Thus giddy rumor shook the town,
Till closed the Night her pennons brown.

CANTO SIXTH

THE GUARD-ROOM

I

THE sun, awakening, through the smoky air
  Of the dark city casts a sullen glance,
Rousing each caitiff to his task of care,
  Of sinful man the sad inheritance;
Summoning revellers from the lagging
    dance,
  Scaring the prowling robber to his den;
Gilding on battled tower the warder's
    lance,
  And warning student pale to leave his
    pen,
And yield his drowsy eyes to the kind
    nurse of men.

What various scenes, and O, what scenes
    of woe,   10
  Are witnessed by that red and strug-
    gling beam!
The fevered patient, from his pallet low,
  Through crowded hospital beholds it
    stream;
The ruined maiden trembles at its gleam,
  The debtor wakes to thought of gyve
    and jail,
The love-lorn wretch starts from torment-
    ing dream;
  The wakeful mother, by the glimmering
    pale,
Trims her sick infant's couch, and soothes
    his feeble wail.

II

At dawn the towers of Stirling rang
With soldier-step and weapon-clang,   20
While drums with rolling note foretell
Relief to weary sentinel.
Through narrow loop and casement barred,
The sunbeams sought the Court of Guard,
And, struggling with the smoky air,
Deadened the torches' yellow glare.
In comfortless alliance shone
The lights through arch of blackened stone,
And showed wild shapes in garb of war,
Faces deformed with beard and scar,   30
All haggard from the midnight watch,
And fevered with the stern debauch;
For the oak table's massive board,
Flooded with wine, with fragments stored,
And beakers drained, and cups o'erthrown,
Showed in what sport the night had flown.
Some, weary, snored on floor and bench;
Some labored still their thirst to quench;
Some, chilled with watching, spread their
    hands
O'er the huge chimney's dying brands,   40
While round them, or beside them flung,
At every step their harness rung.

III

These drew not for their fields the sword,
Like tenants of a feudal lord,
Nor owned the patriarchal claim
Of Chieftain in their leader's name;
Adventurers they, from far who roved,
To live by battle which they loved.
There the Italian's clouded face,
The swarthy Spaniard's there you trace;   50
The mountain-loving Switzer there
More freely breathed in mountain-air;
The Fleming there despised the soil

That paid so ill the laborer's toil;
Their rolls showed French and German
    name;
And merry England's exiles came,
To share, with ill-concealed disdain,
Of Scotland's pay the scanty gain.
All brave in arms, well trained to wield
The heavy halberd, brand, and shield; 60
In camps licentious, wild, and bold;
In pillage fierce and uncontrolled;
And now, by holytide and feast,
From rules of discipline released.

IV

They held debate of bloody fray,
Fought 'twixt Loch Katrine and Achray.
Fierce was their speech, and mid their
    words
Their hands oft grappled to their swords;
Nor sunk their tone to spare the ear
Of wounded comrades groaning near, 70
Whose mangled limbs and bodies gored
Bore token of the mountain sword,
Though, neighboring to the Court of
    Guard,
Their prayers and feverish wails were
    heard, —
Sad burden to the ruffian joke,
And savage oath by fury spoke ! —
At length up started John of Brent,
A yeoman from the banks of Trent;
A stranger to respect or fear,
In peace a chaser of the deer, 80
In host a hardy mutineer,
But still the boldest of the crew
When deed of danger was to do.
He grieved that day their games cut
    short,
And marred the dicer's brawling sport,
And shouted loud, 'Renew the bowl !
And, while a merry catch I troll,
Let each the buxom chorus bear,
Like brethren of the brand and spear.'

V

SOLDIER'S SONG

Our vicar still preaches that Peter and
    Poule 90
Laid a swinging long curse on the bonny
    brown bowl,
That there 's wrath and despair in the
    jolly black-jack,
And the seven deadly sins in a flagon of
    sack;

Yet whoop, Barnaby ! off with thy liquor,
Drink upsees out, and a fig for the vicar !

Our vicar he calls it damnation to sip
The ripe ruddy dew of a woman's dear
    lip,
Says that Beelzebub lurks in her kerchief
    so sly,
And Apollyon shoots darts from her merry
    black eye; 99
Yet whoop, Jack ! kiss Gillian the quicker,
Till she bloom like a rose, and a fig for the
    vicar !

Our vicar thus preaches, — and why should
    he not ?
For the dues of his cure are the placket
    and pot;
And 't is right of his office poor laymen to
    lurch
Who infringe the domains of our good
    Mother Church.
Yet whoop, bully-boys ! off with your
    liquor,
Sweet Marjorie 's the word, and a fig for
    the vicar !

VI

The warder's challenge, heard without,
Stayed in mid-roar the merry shout.
A soldier to the portal went, — 110
'Here is old Bertram, sirs, of Ghent;
And — beat for jubilee the drum ! —
A maid and minstrel with him come.'
Bertram, a Fleming, gray and scarred,
Was entering now the Court of Guard,
A harper with him, and, in plaid
All muffled close, a mountain maid,
Who backward shrunk to 'scape the view
Of the loose scene and boisterous crew.
'What news ?' they roared: — 'I only
    know, 120
From noon till eve we fought with foe,
As wild and as untamable
As the rude mountains where they dwell;
On both sides store of blood is lost,
Nor much success can either boast.' —
'But whence thy captives, friend ? such
    spoil
As theirs must needs reward thy toil.
Old dost thou wax, and wars grow sharp;
Thou now hast glee-maiden and harp !
Get thee an ape, and trudge the land, 130
The leader of a juggler band.'

VII

'No, comrade; — no such fortune mine.
After the fight these sought our line,
That aged harper and the girl,
And, having audience of the Earl,
Mar bade I should purvey them steed,
And bring them hitherward with speed.
Forbear your mirth and rude alarm,
For none shall do them shame or harm. — '
'Hear ye his boast?' cried John of
     Brent,   140
Ever to strife and jangling bent;
'Shall he strike doe beside our lodge,
And yet the jealous niggard grudge
To pay the forester his fee?
I 'll have my share howe'er it be,
Despite of Moray, Mar, or thee.'
Bertram his forward step withstood;
And, burning in his vengeful mood,
Old Allan, though unfit for strife,
Laid hand upon his dagger-knife;   150
But Ellen boldly stepped between,
And dropped at once the tartan screen: —
So, from his morning cloud, appears
The sun of May through summer tears.
The savage soldiery, amazed,
As on descended angel gazed;
Even hardy Brent, abashed and tamed,
Stood half admiring, half ashamed.

VIII

Boldly she spoke: 'Soldiers, attend!
My father was the soldier's friend,   160
Cheered him in camps, in marches led,
And with him in the battle bled.
Not from the valiant or the strong
Should exile's daughter suffer wrong.'
Answered De Brent, most forward still
In every feat or good or ill:
'I shame me of the part I played;
And thou an outlaw's child, poor maid!
An outlaw I by forest laws,
And merry Needwood knows the cause. 170
Poor Rose, — if Rose be living now,' —
He wiped his iron eye and brow, —
'Must bear such age, I think, as thou. —
Hear ye, my mates! I go to call
The Captain of our watch to hall:
There lies my halberd on the floor;
And he that steps my halberd o'er,
To do the maid injurious part,
My shaft shall quiver in his heart!
Beware loose speech, or jesting rough;   180
Ye all know John de Brent. Enough.'

IX

Their Captain came, a gallant young, —
Of Tullibardine's house he sprung, —
Nor wore he yet the spurs of knight;
Gay was his mien, his humor light,
And, though by courtesy controlled,
Forward his speech, his bearing bold.
The high-born maiden ill could brook
The scanning of his curious look
And dauntless eye: — and yet, in sooth, 190
Young Lewis was a generous youth;
But Ellen's lovely face and mien,
Ill suited to the garb and scene,
Might lightly bear construction strange,
And give loose fancy scope to range.
'Welcome to Stirling towers, fair maid!
Come ye to seek a champion's aid,
On palfrey white, with harper hoar,
Like errant damosel of yore?
Does thy high quest a knight require, 200
Or may the venture suit a squire?'
Her dark eye flashed; — she paused and
     sighed: —
'O what have I to do with pride! —
Through scenes of sorrow, shame, and
     strife,
A suppliant for a father's life,
I crave an audience of the King.
Behold, to back my suit, a ring,
The royal pledge of grateful claims,
Given by the Monarch to Fitz-James.'

X

The signet-ring young Lewis took   210
With deep respect and altered look,
And said: 'This ring our duties own;
And pardon, if to worth unknown,
In semblance mean obscurely veiled,
Lady, in aught my folly failed.
Soon as the day flings wide his gates,
The King shall know what suitor waits.
Please you meanwhile in fitting bower
Repose you till his waking hour;
Female attendance shall obey   220
Your hest, for service or array.
Permit I marshal you the way.'
But, ere she followed, with the grace
And open bounty of her race,
She bade her slender purse be shared
Among the soldiers of the guard.
The rest with thanks their guerdon took,
But Brent, with shy and awkward look,
On the reluctant maiden's hold   229
Forced bluntly back the proffered gold: —
'Forgive a haughty English heart,

And O, forget its ruder part !
The vacant purse shall be my share,
Which in my barret-cap I 'll bear,
Perchance, in jeopardy of war,
Where gayer crests may keep afar.'
With thanks — 't was all she could — the maid
His rugged courtesy repaid.

XI

When Ellen forth with Lewis went,
Allan made suit to John of Brent: —   240
' My lady safe, O let your grace
Give me to see my master's face !
His minstrel I, — to share his doom
Bound from the cradle to the tomb.
Tenth in descent, since first my sires
Waked for his noble house their lyres,
Nor one of all the race was known
But prized its weal above their own.
With the Chief's birth begins our care;
Our harp must soothe the infant heir,   250
Teach the youth tales of fight, and grace
His earliest feat of field or chase;
In peace, in war, our rank we keep,
We cheer his board, we soothe his sleep,
Nor leave him till we pour our verse —
A doleful tribute ! — o'er his hearse.
Then let me share his captive lot;
It is my right, — deny it not ! '
' Little we reck,' said John of Brent,
' We Southern men, of long descent;   260
Nor wot we how a name — a word —
Makes clansmen vassals to a lord:
Yet kind my noble landlord's part, —
God bless the house of Beaudesert !
And, but I loved to drive the deer
More than to guide the laboring steer,
I had not dwelt an outcast here.
Come, good old Minstrel, follow me;
Thy Lord and Chieftain shalt thou see.'

XII

Then, from a rusted iron hook,   270
A bunch of ponderous keys he took,
Lighted a torch, and Allan led
Through grated arch and passage dread.
Portals they passed, where, deep within,
Spoke prisoner's moan and fetters' din;
Through rugged vaults, where, loosely stored,
Lay wheel, and axe, and headsman's sword,
And many a hideous engine grim,
For wrenching joint and crushing limb,

By artists formed who deemed it shame   280
And sin to give their work a name.
They halted at a low-browed porch,
And Brent to Allan gave the torch,
While bolt and chain he backward rolled,
And made the bar unhasp its hold.
They entered: — 't was a prison-room
Of stern security and gloom,
Yet not a dungeon; for the day
Through lofty gratings found its way,
And rude and antique garniture   290
Decked the sad walls and oaken floor,
Such as the rugged days of old
Deemed fit for captive noble's hold.
' Here,' said De Brent, ' thou mayst remain
Till the Leech visit him again.
Strict is his charge, the warders tell,
To tend the noble prisoner well.'
Retiring then the bolt he drew,
And the lock's murmurs growled anew.
Roused at the sound, from lowly bed   300
A captive feebly raised his head;
The wondering Minstrel looked, and knew —
Not his dear lord, but Roderick Dhu !
For, come from where Clan-Alpine fought,
They, erring, deemed the Chief he sought.

XIII

As the tall ship, whose lofty prore
Shall never stem the billows more,
Deserted by her gallant band,
Amid the breakers lies astrand, —
So on his couch lay Roderick Dhu !   310
And oft his fevered limbs he threw
In toss abrupt, as when her sides
Lie rocking in the advancing tides,
That shake her frame with ceaseless beat,
Yet cannot heave her from her seat; —
O, how unlike her course at sea !
Or his free step on hill and lea ! —
Soon as the Minstrel he could scan, —
' What of thy lady ? — of my clan ? —   319
My mother ? — Douglas ? — tell me all !
Have they been ruined in my fall ?
Ah, yes ! or wherefore art thou here ?
Yet speak, — speak boldly, — do not fear.'
For Allan, who his mood well knew,
Was choked with grief and terror too.
' Who fought ? — who fled ? — Old man, be brief; —
Some might, — for they had lost their Chief.
Who basely live ? — who bravely died ? '

' O, calm thee, Chief ! ' the Minstrel cried,
' Ellen is safe ! ' ' For that thank Heaven ! '
' And hopes are for the Douglas given; —
The Lady Margaret, too, is well;   332
And, for thy clan, — on field or fell,
Has never harp of minstrel told
Of combat fought so true and bold.
Thy stately Pine is yet unbent,
Though many a goodly bough is rent.'

XIV

The Chieftain reared his form on high,
And fever's fire was in his eye;
But ghastly, pale, and livid streaks   340
Checkered his swarthy brow and cheeks.
' Hark, Minstrel ! I have heard thee play,
With measure bold on festal day,
In yon lone isle, — again where ne'er
Shall harper play or warrior hear ! —
That stirring air that peals on high,
O'er Dermid's race our victory. —
Strike it ! — and then, — for well thou
      canst, —
Free from thy minstrel-spirit glanced,
Fling me the picture of the fight,   350
When met my clan the Saxon might.
I 'll listen, till my fancy hears
The clang of swords, the crash of spears !
These grates, these walls, shall vanish then
For the fair field of fighting men,
And my free spirit burst away,
As if it soared from battle fray.'
The trembling Bard with awe obeyed, —
Slow on the harp his hand he laid;
But soon remembrance of the sight   360
He witnessed from the mountain's height,
With what old Bertram told at night,
Awakened the full power of song,
And bore him in career along; —
As shallop launched on river's tide,
That slow and fearful leaves the side,
But, when it feels the middle stream,
Drives downward swift as lightning's
      beam.

XV

BATTLE OF BEAL' AN DUINE

' The Minstrel came once more to view
The eastern ridge of Benvenue,   370
For ere he parted he would say
Farewell to lovely Loch Achray —
Where shall he find, in foreign land,
So lone a lake, so sweet a strand ! —
   There is no breeze upon the fern,
      No ripple on the lake,

Upon her eyry nods the erne,
   The deer has sought the brake;
The small birds will not sing aloud,
   The springing trout lies still,   380
So darkly glooms yon thunder-cloud,
That swathes, as with a purple shroud,
   Benledi's distant hill.
Is it the thunder's solemn sound,
   That mutters deep and dread,
Or echoes from the groaning ground
   The warrior's measured tread ?
Is it the lightning's quivering glance
   That on the thicket streams,
Or do they flash on spear and lance   390
   The sun's retiring beams ? —
I see the dagger-crest of Mar,
I see the Moray's silver star,
Wave o'er the cloud of Saxon war,
That up the lake comes winding far !
   To hero boune for battle-strife,
      Or bard of martial lay,
'T were worth ten years of peaceful
      life,
      One glance at their array !

XVI

' Their light - armed archers far and
      near   400
   Surveyed the tangled ground,
Their centre ranks, with pike and spear,
   A twilight forest frowned,
Their barded horsemen in the rear
   The stern battalia crowned.
No symbol clashed, no clarion rang,
   Still were the pipe and drum;
Save heavy tread, and armor's clang,
   The sullen march was dumb.
There breathed no wind their crests to
      shake,   410
   Or wave their flags abroad;
Scarce the frail aspen seemed to quake,
   That shadowed o'er their road.
Their vaward scouts no tidings bring,
   Can rouse no lurking foe,
Nor spy a trace of living thing,
   Save when they stirred the roe;
The host moves like a deep-sea wave,
Where rise no rocks its pride to brave,
   High-swelling, dark, and slow.   420
The lake is passed, and now they gain
A narrow and a broken plain,
Before the Trosachs' rugged jaws;
And here the horse and spearmen pause,
While, to explore the dangerous glen,
Dive through the pass the archer-men.

XVII

' At once there rose so wild a yell
Within that dark and narrow dell,
As all the fiends from heaven that fell
Had pealed the banner-cry of hell !   430
  Forth from the pass in tumult driven,
  Like chaff before the wind of heaven,
    The archery appear:
  For life ! for life ! their flight they
    ply —
And shriek, and shout, and battle-cry,
And plaids and bonnets waving high,
And broadswords flashing to the sky,
Are maddening in the rear.
Onward they drive in dreadful race,
  Pursuers and pursued;   440
Before that tide of flight and chase,
How shall it keep its rooted place,
  The spearmen's twilight wood ? —
" Down, down," cried Mar, " your lances
    down !
  Bear back both friend and foe ! " —
Like reeds before the tempest's frown,
That serried grove of lances brown
  At once lay levelled low;
And closely shouldering side to side,
The bristling ranks the onset bide. —   450
" We 'll quell the savage mountaineer,
  As their Tinchel cows the game !
They come as fleet as forest deer,
We 'll drive them back as tame."

XVIII

' Bearing before them in their course
The relics of the archer force,
Like wave with crest of sparkling foam,
Right onward did Clan-Alpine come.
  Above the tide, each broadsword bright
Was brandishing like beam of light,   460
    Each targe was dark below;
And with the ocean's mighty swing,
When heaving to the tempest's wing,
  They hurled them on the foe.
I heard the lance's shivering crash,
As when the whirlwind rends the ash;
I heard the broadsword's deadly clang,
As if a hundred anvils rang !
But Moray wheeled his rearward rank
Of horsemen on Clan-Alpine's flank, —   470
  " My banner-men, advance !
I see," he cried, " their column shake.
Now, gallants ! for your ladies' sake,
  Upon them with the lance ! " —
The horsemen dashed among the rout,
  As deer break through the broom;

Their steeds are stout, their swords are
    out,
  They soon make lightsome room.
Clan-Alpine's best are backward borne —
  Where, where was Roderick then ! 480
One blast upon his bugle-horn
  Were worth a thousand men.
And refluent through the pass of fear
  The battle's tide was poured;
Vanished the Saxon's struggling spear,
  Vanished the mountain-sword.
As Bracklinn's chasm, so black and steep,
  Receives her roaring linn,
As the dark caverns of the deep
  Suck the wild whirlpool in,   490
So did the deep and darksome pass
Devour the battle's mingled mass;
None linger now upon the plain,
Save those who ne'er shall fight again.

XIX

' Now westward rolls the battle's din,
That deep and doubling pass within. —
Minstrel, away ! the work of fate
Is bearing on; its issue wait,
Where the rude Trosachs' dread defile
Opens on Katrine's lake and isle.   500
Gray Benvenue I soon repassed,
Loch Katrine lay beneath me cast.
  The sun is set; — the clouds are met,
    The lowering scowl of heaven
  An inky hue of livid blue
    To the deep lake has given;
Strange gusts of wind from mountain glen
Swept o'er the lake, then sunk again.
I heeded not the eddying surge,
Mine eye but saw the Trosachs' gorge,   510
Mine ear but heard that sullen sound,
Which like an earthquake shook the
    ground,
And spoke the stern and desperate strife
That parts not but with parting life,
Seeming, to minstrel ear, to toll
The dirge of many a passing soul.
  Nearer it comes — the dim-wood glen
  The martial flood disgorged again,
    But not in mingled tide;
  The plaided warriors of the North   520
  High on the mountain thunder forth
    And overhang its side,
  While by the lake below appears
  The darkening cloud of Saxon spears.
At weary bay each shattered band,
Eying their foemen, sternly stand;
Their banners stream like tattered sail,

That flings its fragments to the gale,
And broken arms and disarray
Marked the fell havoc of the day.   530

XX

'Viewing the mountain's ridge askance,
The Saxons stood in sullen trance,
Till Moray pointed with his lance,
          And cried: "Behold yon isle ! —
See ! none are left to guard its strand
But women weak, that wring the hand:
'T is there of yore the robber band
          Their booty wont to pile; —
My purse, with bonnet-pieces store,
To him will swim a bow-shot o'er,   540
And loose a shallop from the shore.
Lightly we 'll tame the war-wolf then,
Lords of his mate, and brood, and den."
Forth from the ranks a spearman sprung,
On earth his casque and corselet rung,
          He plunged him in the wave: —
All saw the deed, — the purpose knew,
And to their clamors Benvenue
          A mingled echo gave;
The Saxons shout, their mate to cheer,   550
The helpless females scream for fear,
And yells for rage the mountaineer.
'T was then, as by the outcry riven,
Poured down at once the lowering heaven:
A whirlwind swept Loch Katrine's breast,
Her billows reared their snowy crest.
Well for the swimmer swelled they high,
To mar the Highland marksman's eye;
For round him showered, mid rain and hail,
The vengeful arrows of the Gael.   560
In vain. — He nears the isle — and lo !
His hand is on a shallop's bow.
Just then a flash of lightning came,
It tinged the waves and strand with flame;
I marked Duncraggan's widowed dame,
Behind an oak I saw her stand,
A naked dirk gleamed in her hand: —
It darkened, — but amid the moan
Of waves I heard a dying groan; —
Another flash ! — the spearman floats   570
A weltering corse beside the boats,
And the stern matron o'er him stood,
Her hand and dagger streaming blood.

XXI

'"Revenge ! revenge !" the Saxons cried,
The Gaels' exulting shout replied.
Despite the elemental rage,
Again they hurried to engage;
But, ere they closed in desperate fight,

Bloody with spurring came a knight,
Sprung from his horse, and from a crag   580
Waved 'twixt the hosts a milk-white flag.
Clarion and trumpet by his side
Rung forth a truce-note high and wide,
While, in the Monarch's name, afar
A herald's voice forbade the war,
For Bothwell's lord and Roderick bold
Were both, he said, in captive hold.' —
But here the lay made sudden stand,
The harp escaped the Minstrel's hand !
Oft had he stolen a glance, to spy   590
How Roderick brooked his minstrelsy:
At first, the Chieftain, to the chime,
With lifted hand kept feeble time;
That motion ceased, — yet feeling strong
Varied his look as changed the song;
At length, no more his deafened ear
The minstrel melody can hear;
His face grows sharp, — his hands are clenched,
As if some pang his heart-strings wrenched;
Set are his teeth, his fading eye   600
Is sternly fixed on vacancy;
Thus, motionless and moanless drew,
His parting breath stout Roderick Dhu ! —
Old Allan-bane looked on aghast,
While grim and still his spirit passed;
But when he saw that life was fled,
He poured his wailing o'er the dead.

XXII

LAMENT

'And art thou cold and lowly laid,
Thy foeman's dread, thy people's aid,   609
Breadalbane's boast, Clan-Alpine's shade !
For thee shall none a requiem say ? —
For thee, who loved the minstrel's lay,
For thee, of Bothwell's house the stay,
The shelter of her exiled line,
E'en in this prison-house of thine,
I 'll wail for Alpine's honored Pine !

'What groans shall yonder valleys fill !
What shrieks of grief shall rend yon hill !
What tears of burning rage shall thrill,
When mourns thy tribe thy battles done,
Thy fall before the race was won,   621
Thy sword ungirt ere set of sun !
There breathes not clansman of thy line,
But would have given his life for thine.
O, woe for Alpine's honored Pine !

'Sad was thy lot on mortal stage ! —
The captive thrush may brook the cage,

The prisoned eagle dies for rage.
Brave spirit, do not scorn my strain !
And, when its notes awake again,   630
Even she, so long beloved in vain,
Shall mix with my harp her voice combine,
And mix her woe and tears with mine,
To wail Clan-Alpine's honored Pine.'

XXIII

Ellen the while, with bursting heart,
Remained in lordly bower apart,
Where played, with many-colored gleams,
Through storied pane the rising beams.
In vain on gilded roof they fall,
And lightened up a tapestried wall,   640
And for her use a menial train
A rich collation spread in vain.
The banquet proud, the chamber gay,
Scarce drew one curious glance astray;
Or if she looked, 't was but to say,
With better omen dawned the day
In that lone isle, where waved on high
The dun-deer's hide for canopy;
Where oft her noble father shared
The simple meal her care prepared,   650
While Lufra, crouching by her side,
Her station claimed with jealous pride,
And Douglas, bent on woodland game,
Spoke of the chase to Malcolm Græme,
Whose answer, oft at random made,
The wandering of his thoughts betrayed.
Those who such simple joys have known
Are taught to prize them when they 're
        gone.
But sudden, see, she lifts her head,
The window seeks with cautious tread.   660
What distant music has the power
To win her in this woful hour ?
'T was from a turret that o'erhung
Her latticed bower, the strain was sung.

XXIV

LAY OF THE IMPRISONED HUNTSMAN

' My hawk is tired of perch and hood,
My idle greyhound loathes his food,
My horse is weary of his stall,
And I am sick of captive thrall.
I wish I were as I have been,
Hunting the hart in forest green,   670
With bended bow and bloodhound free,
For that 's the life is meet for me.
' I hate to learn the ebb of time
From yon dull steeple's drowsy chime,
Or mark it as the sunbeams crawl,
Inch after inch, along the wall.

The lark was wont my matins ring,
The sable rook my vespers sing,
These towers, although a king's they be,
Have not a hall of joy for me.   680

' No more at dawning morn I rise,
And sun myself in Ellen's eyes,
Drive the fleet deer the forest through,
And homeward wend with evening dew;
A blithesome welcome blithely meet,
And lay my trophies at her feet,
While fled the eve on wing of glee, —
That life is lost to love and me ! '

XXV

The heart-sick lay was hardly said,
The listener had not turned her head,   690
It trickled still, the starting tear,
When light a footstep struck her ear,
And Snowdoun's graceful Knight was near.
She turned the hastier, lest again
The prisoner should renew his strain.
' O welcome, brave Fitz-James ! ' she said;
' How may an almost orphan maid
Pay the deep debt — ' ' O say not so !
To me no gratitude you owe.
Not mine, alas ! the boon to give,   700
And bid thy noble father live;
I can but be thy guide, sweet maid,
With Scotland's King thy suit to aid.
No tyrant he, though ire and pride
May lay his better mood aside.
Come, Ellen, come ! 't is more than time,
He holds his court at morning prime.'
With beating heart, and bosom wrung,
As to a brother's arm she clung.
Gently he dried the falling tear,   710
And gently whispered hope and cheer;
Her faltering steps half led, half stayed,
Through gallery fair and high arcade,
Till at his touch its wings of pride
A portal arch unfolded wide.

XXVI

Within 't was brilliant all and light,
A thronging scene of figures bright;
It glowed on Ellen's dazzled sight,
As when the setting sun has given
Ten thousand hues to summer even,   720
And from their tissue fancy frames
Aerial knights and fairy dames.
Still by Fitz-James her footing staid;
A few faint steps she forward made,
Then slow her drooping head she raised,
And fearful round the presence gazed;

For him she sought who owned this state,
The dreaded Prince whose will was fate ! —
She gazed on many a princely port
Might well have ruled a royal court;   730
On many a splendid garb she gazed, —
Then turned bewildered and amazed,
For all stood bare; and in the room
Fitz-James alone wore cap and plume.
To him each lady's look was lent,
On him each courtier's eye was bent;
Midst furs and silks and jewels sheen,
He stood, in simple Lincoln green,
The centre of the glittering ring, —
And Snowdoun's Knight is Scotland's
    King !   740

XXVII

As wreath of snow on mountain-breast
Slides from the rock that gave it rest,
Poor Ellen glided from her stay,
And at the Monarch's feet she lay;
No word her choking voice commands, —
She showed the ring, — she clasped her
    hands.
O, not a moment could he brook,
The generous Prince, that suppliant look !
Gently he raised her, — and, the while,
Checked with a glance the circle's smile; 750
Graceful, but grave, her brow he kissed,
And bade her terrors be dismissed: —
' Yes, fair; the wandering poor Fitz-James
The fealty of Scotland claims.
To him thy woes, thy wishes, bring;
He will redeem his signet ring.
Ask nought for Douglas; — yester even,
His Prince and he have much forgiven;
Wrong hath he had from slanderous
    tongue,
I, from his rebel kinsmen, wrong.   760
We would not, to the vulgar crowd,
Yield what they craved with clamor loud;
Calmly we heard and judged his cause,
Our council aided and our laws.
I stanched thy father's death-feud stern
With stout De Vaux and gray Glencairn;
And Bothwell's Lord henceforth we own
The friend and bulwark of our throne. —
But, lovely infidel, how now ?
What clouds thy misbelieving brow ?   770
Lord James of Douglas, lend thine aid;
Thou must confirm this doubting maid.'

XXVIII

Then forth the noble Douglas sprung,
And on his neck his daughter hung.

The Monarch drank, that happy hour,
The sweetest, holiest draught of Power, —
When it can say with godlike voice,
Arise, sad Virtue, and rejoice !
Yet would not James the general eye
On nature's raptures long should pry;   780
He stepped between — ' Nay, Douglas,
    nay,
Steal not my proselyte away !
The riddle 't is my right to read,
That brought this happy chance to speed.
Yes, Ellen, when disguised I stray
In life's more low but happier way,
'T is under name which veils my power,
Nor falsely veils, — for Stirling's tower
Of yore the name of Snowdoun claims,   789
And Normans call me James Fitz-James.
Thus watch I o'er insulted laws,
Thus learn to right the injured cause.'
Then, in a tone apart and low, —
' Ah, little traitress ! none must know
What idle dream, what lighter thought,
What vanity full dearly bought,
Joined to thine eye's dark witchcraft, drew
My spell-bound steps to Benvenue
In dangerous hour, and all but gave   799
Thy Monarch's life to mountain glaive !'
Aloud he spoke: ' Thou still dost hold
That little talisman of gold,
Pledge of my faith, Fitz-James's ring, —
What seeks fair Ellen of the King ?'

XXIX

Full well the conscious maiden guessed
He probed the weakness of her breast;
But with that consciousness there came
A lightening of her fears for Græme,
And more she deemed the Monarch's ire
Kindled 'gainst him who for her sire   810
Rebellious broadsword boldly drew;
And, to her generous feeling true,
She craved the grace of Roderick Dhu.
' Forbear thy suit; — the King of kings
Alone can stay life's parting wings.
I know his heart, I know his hand,
Have shared his cheer, and proved his
    brand; —
My fairest earldom would I give
To bid Clan-Alpine's Chieftain live ! —
Hast thou no other boon to crave ?   820
No other captive friend to save ?'
Blushing, she turned her from the King,
And to the Douglas gave the ring,
As if she wished her sire to speak
The suit that stained her glowing cheek.

' Nay, then, my pledge has lost its force,
And stubborn justice holds her course.
Malcolm, come forth!' — and, at the
    word,
Down kneeled the Græme to Scotland's
    Lord.   829
' For thee, rash youth, no suppliant sues,
From thee may Vengeance claim her
    dues,
Who, nurtured underneath our smile,
Hast paid our care by treacherous wile,
And sought amid thy faithful clan
A refuge for an outlawed man,
Dishonoring thus thy loyal name. —
Fetters and warder for the Græme!'
His chain of gold the King unstrung,
The links o'er Malcolm's neck he flung,
Then gently drew the glittering band,   840
And laid the clasp on Ellen's hand.

HARP of the North, farewell! The hills
    grow dark,
  On purple peaks a deeper shade de-
    scending;
In twilight copse the glow-worm lights her
    spark,
  The deer, half-seen, are to the covert
    wending.
Resume thy wizard elm! the fountain
    lending,
  And the wild breeze, thy wilder min-
    strelsy;
Thy numbers sweet with nature's vespers
    blending,

With distant echo from the fold and lea,
And herd-boy's evening pipe, and hum
    of housing bee.   850

Yet, once again, farewell, thou Minstrel
    Harp!
Yet, once again, forgive my feeble sway,
And little reck I of the censure sharp
    May idly cavil at an idle lay.
Much have I owed thy strains on life's
    long way,
  Through secret woes the world has never
    known,
When on the weary night dawned wearier
    day,
  And bitterer was the grief devoured
    alone. —
That I o'erlive such woes, Enchantress! is
    thine own.

Hark! as my lingering footsteps slow
    retire,   860
  Some Spirit of the Air has waked thy
    string!
'T is now a seraph bold, with touch of fire,
  'T is now the brush of Fairy's frolic
    wing.
Receding now, the dying numbers ring
  Fainter and fainter down the rugged
    dell;
And now the mountain breezes scarcely
    bring
  A wandering witch-note of the distant
    spell —
And now, 't is silent all! — Enchantress,
    fare thee well!

THE VISION OF DON RODERICK

INTRODUCTORY NOTE

THE foundation of *The Vision of Don Roderick* is given by Scott in the Preface printed below and referred to again in the Notes, but there was no further Introduction in 1830, and it is to the Dedication, Scott's *Letters*, and to Lockhart's *Life* that we must turn for an explanation of the occasion which produced the poem. In a letter to Lady Abercorn, dated Ashestiel, 30th April, 1811, Scott writes : —

' I promised I would not write any poetry without letting you know, and I make all sort of haste to tell you of my sudden determina-

tion to write a sort of rhapsody upon the affairs of the Peninsula. It is to be called *The Vision of Don Roderick*, and is founded upon the apparition explanatory of the future events in Spain, said to be seen by the last King of the Gothic race, in a vault beneath the great church of Toledo. I believe your Ladyship will find something of the story in the Comtesse D'Aunois' travels into Spain, but I find it at most length in an old Spanish history of the aforesaid Don Roderick, professing to be translated from the Arabic, but being in truth a mere romance of the reign of Ferdinand and

Isabella. It will serve my purpose, however, *tout de même.* The idea of forming a short lyric piece upon this subject has often glided through my mind, but I should never, I fear, have had the grace to turn it to practice if it were not that groping in my pockets to find some guineas for the suffering Portuguese, and detecting very few to spare, I thought I could only have recourse to the apostolic benediction, "Silver and gold have I none, but that which I have I will give unto you." My friends and booksellers, the Ballantynes of Edinburgh, have very liberally promised me a hundred guineas for this trifle, which I intend to send to the fund for relieving the sufferers in Portugal. I have come out to this wilderness to write my poem, and so soon as it is finished I will send you, my dear Lady Marchioness, a copy, — not that it will be worth your acceptance, but merely that you may be assured I am doing nothing that I would not you knew of sooner than any one. I intend to write to the Chairman of the Committee by to-morrow's post. I would give them a hundred drops of my blood with the same pleasure, would it do them service, for my heart is a soldier's, and always has been, though my lameness rendered me unfit for the profession, which, old as I am, I would rather follow than any other. But these are waking dreams, in which I seldom indulge even to my kindest friends.'

The poem, which was published July 15, 1811, called out two criticisms, — one for the adoption of the Spenserian stanza, the other for the omission of any reference to Sir John Moore, Scott's countryman who had just fallen in battle in the cause which Scott was celebrating, and whose memory is kept alive in many readers' minds by Wolfe's martial verses on his burial, —

'Not a drum was heard, not a funeral note,
As his corse to the rampart we hurried.'

Scott meets both criticisms in a letter to Morritt, September, 1811 : —

'The Edinburgh Reviewers have been down on my poor *Don Roderick*, hand to fist ; but truly, as they are too fastidious to approve of the campaign, I should be very unreasonable if I expected them to like the celebration thereof. I agree with you respecting the lumbering weight of the stanza, and I shrewdly suspect it would require a very great poet indeed to prevent the tedium arising from the frequent recurrence of rhymes. Our language is unable to support the expenditure of so many for each stanza ; even Spenser himself, with all the licenses of using obsolete words and uncommon spelling, sometimes fatigues the ear. They are also very wroth with me

for omitting the merits of Sir John Moore ; but as I never exactly discovered in what they lay, unless in conducting his advance and retreat upon a plan the most likely to verify the desponding speculations of the foresaid reviewers, I must hold myself excused for not giving praise where I was unable to see that much was due.'

The poem was both published in quarto form and included in the Edinburgh *Annual Register* for 1809, which was not however published till 1811. It had the following : —

PREFACE

The following Poem is founded upon a Spanish Tradition, particularly detailed in the Notes ; but bearing, in general, that Don Roderick, the last Gothic King of Spain, when the Invasion of the Moors was impending, had the temerity to descend into an ancient vault, near Toledo, the opening of which had been denounced as fatal to the Spanish Monarchy. The legend adds, that his rash curiosity was mortified by an emblematical representation of those Saracens who, in the year 714, defeated him in battle, and reduced Spain under their dominion. I have presumed to prolong the Vision of the Revolutions of Spain down to the present eventful crisis of the Peninsula ; and to divide it, by a supposed change of scene, into Three Periods. The First of these represents the Invasion of the Moors, the Defeat and Death of Roderick, and closes with the peaceful occupation of the country by the Victors. The Second Period embraces the state of the Peninsula, when the conquests of the Spaniards and Portuguese in the East and West Indies had raised to the highest pitch the renown of their arms ; sullied, however, by superstition and cruelty. An allusion to the inhumanities of the Inquisition terminates this picture. The Last Part of the Poem opens with the state of Spain previous to the unparalleled treachery of Bonaparte ; gives a sketch of the usurpation attempted upon that unsuspicious and friendly kingdom, and terminates with the arrival of the British succors. It may be further proper to mention that the object of the Poem is less to commemorate or detail particular incidents, than to exhibit a general and impressive picture of the several periods brought upon the stage.

I am too sensible of the respect due to the Public, especially by one who has already experienced more than ordinary indulgence, to offer any apology for the inferiority of the poetry to the subject it is chiefly designed to commemorate. Yet I think it proper to mention that while I was hastily executing a work, written for a temporary purpose, and on passing events, the task was most cruelly interrupted by the successive deaths of Lord President Blair and Lord Viscount Melville. In those distinguished characters I had not only to regret persons whose lives were most important to Scotland, but also whose notice and patronage honored my entrance upon active life ; and, I may add, with melancholy pride, who permitted my more advanced age to claim no common share in their friendship. Under such interruptions, the following verses, which my best and happiest efforts must have left far unworthy of their theme, have, I am myself sensible, an appearance of negligence and incoherence, which, in other circumstances, I might have been able to remove.

EDINBURGH, June 24, 1811.

THE VISION OF DON RODERICK

Quid dignum memorare tuis, Hispania, terris,
Vox humana valet ! — CLAUDIAN.

TO

JOHN WHITMORE, ESQ.,

AND TO THE

COMMITTEE OF SUBSCRIBERS FOR RELIEF OF THE PORTUGUESE SUFFERERS

IN WHICH HE PRESIDES,

THIS POEM,

COMPOSED FOR THE BENEFIT OF THE FUND UNDER THEIR MANAGEMENT,

IS RESPECTFULLY INSCRIBED BY

WALTER SCOTT.

INTRODUCTION

I

LIVES there a strain whose sounds of
    mounting fire
  May rise distinguished o'er the din of
    war;
Or died it with yon Master of the Lyre,
  Who sung beleaguered Ilion's evil
    star ?
Such, WELLINGTON, might reach thee
    from afar,
  Wafting its descant wide o'er Ocean's
    range;
Nor shouts, nor clashing arms, its mood
    could mar,
  All as it swelled 'twixt each loud trumpet-change,
That clangs to Britain victory, to Portugal
    revenge !

II

Yes ! such a strain, with all o'erpowering measure,   10
  Might melodize with each tumultuous
    sound,
Each voice of fear or triumph, woe or
    pleasure,
  That rings Mondego's ravaged shores
    around;
The thundering cry of hosts with conquest crowned,
  The female shriek, the ruined peasant's
    moan,
The shout of captives from their chains
    unbound,
  The foiled oppressor's deep and sullen
    groan,
A Nation's choral hymn for tyranny o'erthrown.

III

But we, weak minstrels of a laggard
    day,   19
    Skilled but to imitate an elder page,
Timid and raptureless, can we repay
    The debt thou claim'st in this ex-
    hausted age ?
Thou givest our lyres a theme, that
    might engage
    Those that could send thy name o'er
    sea and land,
While sea and land shall last; for Ho-
    mer's rage
    A theme; a theme for Milton's mighty
    hand —
How much unmeet for us, a faint degener-
    ate band !

IV

Ye mountains stern ! within whose rug-
    ged breast
    The friends of Scottish freedom found
    repose;
Ye torrents ! whose hoarse sounds have
    soothed their rest,   30
    Returning from the field of vanquished
    foes;
Say, have ye lost each wild majestic
    close,
    That erst the choir of Bards or Druids
    flung;
What time their hymn of victory arose,
    And Cattreath's glens with voice of
    triumph rung,
And mystic Merlin harped, and gray-haired
    Llywarch sung ?

V

O, if your wilds such minstrelsy re-
    tain,
    As sure your changeful gales seem oft
    to say,
When sweeping wild and sinking soft
    again,
    Like trumpet-jubilee or harp's wild
    sway;   40
If ye can echo such triumphant lay,
    Then lend the note to him has loved
    you long !
Who pious gathered each tradition
    gray,
    That floats your solitary wastes
    along,
And with affection vain gave them new
    voice in song.

VI

For not till now, how oft soe'er the task
    Of truant verse hath lightened graver
    care,
From Muse or Sylvan was he wont to ask,
    In phrase poetic, inspiration fair;   49
Careless he gave his numbers to the air,
    They came unsought for, if applauses
    came;
Nor for himself prefers he now the
    prayer:
    Let but his verse befit a hero's fame,
Immortal be the verse ! — forgot the poet's
    name !

VII

Hark, from yon misty cairn their answer
    tost:
    ' Minstrel ! the fame of whose roman-
    tic lyre,
Capricious-swelling now, may soon be
    lost,
    Like the light flickering of a cottage fire;
If to such task presumptuous thou aspire
    Seek not from us the meed to warrior
    due: 60
Age after age has gathered son to sire,
    Since our gray cliffs the din of conflict
    knew,
Or, pealing through our vales, victorious
    bugles blew.

VIII

' Decayed our old traditionary lore,
    Save where the lingering fays renew
    their ring,
By milkmaid seen beneath the hawthorn
    hoar,
    Or round the marge of Minchmore's
    haunted spring;
Save where their legends gray-haired
    shepherds sing,
    That now scarce win a listening ear
    but thine,   69
Of feuds obscure and Border ravaging,
    And rugged deeds recount in rugged
    line
Of moonlight foray made on Teviot, Tweed,
    or Tyne.

IX

' No ! search romantic lands, where the
    near Sun
    Gives with unstinted boon ethereal
    flame,

Where the rude villager, his labor done,
In verse spontaneous chants some fa-
    vored name,
Whether Olalia's charms his tribute
    claim,
Her eye of diamond and her locks of
    jet,
Or whether, kindling at the deeds of
    Græme,   79
He sing, to wild Morisco measure set,
Old Albin's red claymore, green Erin's
    bayonet !

X

'Explore those regions, where the flinty
    crest
Of wild Nevada ever gleams with
    snows,
Where in the proud Alhambra's ruined
    breast
Barbaric monuments of pomp repose;
Or where the banners of more ruthless
    foes
Than the fierce Moor float o'er Toledo's
    fane,
From whose tall towers even now the
    patriot throws
An anxious glance, to spy upon the
    plain
The blended ranks of England, Portugal,
    and Spain.   90

XI

'There, of Numantian fire a swarthy
    spark
Still lightens in the sunburnt native's
    eye;
The stately port, slow step, and visage
    dark
Still mark enduring pride and con-
    stancy.
And, if the glow of feudal chivalry
Beam not, as once, thy nobles' dearest
    pride,
Iberia ! oft thy crestless peasantry
Have seen the plumed Hidalgo quit
    their side,
Have seen, yet dauntless stood — 'gainst
    fortune fought and died.

XII

' And cherished still by that unchanging
    race,   100
Are themes for minstrelsy more high
    than thine;

Of strange tradition many a mystic trace,
    Legend and vision, prophecy and sign;
Where wonders wild of Arabesque com-
    bine
With Gothic imagery of darker shade.
Forming a model meet for minstrel line,
    Go, seek such theme !' — The Moun-
    tain Spirit said:
With filial awe I heard — I heard, and I
    obeyed.

THE VISION OF DON RODERICK

I

REARING their crests amid the cloudless
    skies,
    And darkly clustering in the pale moon-
    light,
Toledo's holy towers and spires arise,
    As from a trembling lake of silver
    white.
Their mingled shadows intercept the
    sight
    Of the broad burial - ground out-
    stretched below,
And nought disturbs the silence of the
    night;
    All sleeps in sullen shade, or silver
    glow,
All save the heavy swell of Teio's ceaseless
    flow.   9

II

All save the rushing swell of Teio's tide,
    Or, distant heard, a courser's neigh or
    tramp,
Their changing rounds as watchful horse-
    men ride,
    To guard the limits of King Roderick's
    camp.
For, through the river's night-fog rolling
    damp,
    Was many a proud pavilion dimly seen,
Which glimmered back, against the
    moon's fair lamp,
Tissues of silk and silver twisted sheen,
And standards proudly pitched, and warders
    armed between.

III

But of their monarch's person keeping
    ward,
    Since last the deep-mouthed bell of
    vespers tolled,   20

The chosen soldiers of the royal guard
  The post beneath the proud cathedral
    hold:
A band unlike their Gothic sires of old,
  Who, for the cap of steel and iron mace,
Bear slender darts and casques bedecked
    with gold,
  While silver-studded belts their shoul-
    ders grace,
Where ivory quivers ring in the broad fal-
    chion's place.

IV

In the light language of an idle court,
  They murmured at their master's long
    delay,   29
And held his lengthened orisons in sport:
  'What! will Don Roderick here till
    morning stay,
To wear in shrift and prayer the night
    away?
  And are his hours in such dull penance
    past,
For fair Florinda's plundered charms to
    pay?'
  Then to the east their weary eyes they
    cast,
And wished the lingering dawn would glim-
    mer forth at last.

V

But, far within, Toledo's prelate lent
  An ear of fearful wonder to the king;
The silver lamp a fitful lustre sent,   39
  So long that sad confession witnessing:
For Roderick told of many a hidden
    thing,
  Such as are lothly uttered to the air,
When Fear, Remorse, and Shame the
    bosom wring,
  And Guilt his secret burden cannot
    bear,
And Conscience seeks in speech a respite
    from Despair.

VI

Full on the prelate's face and silver hair
  The stream of failing light was feebly
    rolled;
But Roderick's visage, though his head
    was bare,
  Was shadowed by his hand and mantle's
    fold.
While of his hidden soul the sins he
    told,   50

Proud Alaric's descendant could not
    brook
That mortal man his bearing should   *
    behold,
  Or boast that he had seen, when con-
    science shook,
Fear tame a monarch's brow, remorse a
    warrior's look.

VII

The old man's faded cheek waxed yet
    more pale,
  As many a secret sad the king be-
    wrayed;
As sign and glance eked out the unfin-
    ished tale,
  When in the midst his faltering whisper
    staid. —
'Thus royal Witiza was slain,' he said;
  'Yet, holy father, deem not it was I.' 60
Thus still Ambition strives her crimes
    to shade. —
  'O, rather deem 't was stern necessity!
Self-preservation bade, and I must kill or
    die.

VIII

'And if Florinda's shrieks alarmed the
    air,
  If she invoked her absent sire in vain
And on her knees implored that I would
    spare,
  Yet, reverend priest, thy sentence rash
    refrain!
All is not as it seems — the female train
  Know by their bearing to disguise their
    mood:' —
But Conscience here, as if in high dis-
    dain,
  Sent to the Monarch's cheek the burn- 70
    ing blood —
He stayed his speech abrupt — and up the
    prelate stood.

IX

'O hardened offspring of an iron race!
  What of thy crimes, Don Roderick,
    shall I say?
What alms or prayers or penance can
    efface
  Murder's dark spot, wash treason's
    stain away!
For the foul ravisher how shall I pray,
  Who, scarce repentant, makes his
    crime his boast?

How hope Almighty vengeance shall
delay, 79
Unless, in mercy to yon Christian host,
He spare the shepherd lest the guiltless
sheep be lost.'

X

Then kindled the dark tyrant in his mood,
And to his brow returned its dauntless
gloom;
'And welcome then,' he cried, 'be blood
for blood,
For treason treachery, for dishonor
doom!
Yet will I know whence come they or by
whom.
Show, for thou canst — give forth the
fated key,
And guide me, priest, to that mysterious
room
Where, if aught true in old tradition
be,
His nation's future fates a Spanish king
shall see.' 90

XI

'Ill-fated Prince! recall the desperate
word,
Or pause ere yet the omen thou obey!
Bethink, yon spell-bound portal would
afford
Never to former monarch entrance-
way;
Nor shall it ever ope, old records say,
Save to a king, the last of all his line,
What time his empire totters to decay,
And treason digs beneath her fatal
mine,
And high above impends avenging wrath
divine.' —

XII

'Prelate! a monarch's fate brooks no
delay; 100
Lead on!' — The ponderous key the
old man took,
And held the winking lamp, and led the
way,
By winding stair, dark aisle, and secret
nook,
Then on an ancient gateway bent his look;
And, as the key the desperate king
essayed,
Low muttered thunders the cathedral
shook,

And twice he stopped and twice new
effort made,
Till the huge bolts rolled back and the
loud hinges brayed.

XIII

Long, large, and lofty was that vaulted
hall;
Roof, walls, and floor were all of marble stone, 110
Of polished marble, black as funeral
pall,
Carved o'er with signs and characters
unknown.
A paly light, as of the dawning, shone
Through the sad bounds, but whence
they could not spy,
For window to the upper air was
none;
Yet by that light Don Roderick could
descry
Wonders that ne'er till then were seen by
mortal eye.

XIV

Grim sentinels, against the upper wall,
Of molten bronze, two Statues held
their place;
Massive their naked limbs, their stature
tall, 120
Their frowning foreheads golden
circles grace.
Moulded they seemed for kings of giant
race,
That lived and sinned before the
avenging flood;
This grasped a scythe, that rested on a
mace;
This spread his wings for flight, that
pondering stood,
Each stubborn seemed and stern, immu-
table of mood.

XV

Fixed was the right-hand giant's brazen
look
Upon his brother's glass of shifting
sand,
As if its ebb he measured by a book,
Whose iron volume loaded his huge
hand; 130
In which was wrote of many a fallen
land,
Of empires lost, and kings to exile
driven:

And o'er that pair their names in scroll
    expand —
'Lo, DESTINY and TIME! to whom
    by Heaven
The guidance of the earth is for a season
    given.' —

XVI

Even while they read, the sand-glass
    wastes away;
And, as the last and lagging grains
    did creep,
That right-hand giant 'gan his club up-
    sway,
    As one that startles from a heavy
    sleep.
Full on the upper wall the mace's
    sweep   140
At once descended with the force of
    thunder,
And, hurtling down at once in crumbled
    heap,
    The marble boundary was rent asun-
    der,
And gave to Roderick's view new sights of
    fear and wonder.

XVII

For they might spy beyond that mighty
    breach
    Realms as of Spain in visioned pro-
    spect laid,
Castles and towers, in due proportion
    each,
    As by some skilful artist's hand por-
    trayed:
Here, crossed by many a wild Sierra's
    shade
    And boundless plains that tire the
    traveller's eye;   150
There, rich with vineyard and with olive
    glade,
    Or deep-embrowned by forests huge
    and high,
Or washed by mighty streams that slowly
    murmured by.

XVIII

And here, as erst upon the antique stage
    Passed forth the band of masquers
    trimly led,
In various forms and various equipage,
    While fitting strains the hearer's fancy
    fed;
So, to sad Roderick's eye in order spread,

Successive pageants filled that mystic
    scene,
Showing the fate of battles ere they
    bled,   160
    And issue of events that had not been;
And ever and anon strange sounds were
    heard between.

XIX

First shrilled an unrepeated female
    shriek! —
    It seemed as if Don Roderick knew
    the call,
For the bold blood was blanching in his
    cheek. —
    Then answered kettle-drum and at-
    abal,
Gong-peal and cymbal-clank the ear ap-
    pall,
    The Tecbir war-cry and the Lelie's
    yell
Ring wildly dissonant along the hall.
    Needs not to Roderick their dread im-
    port tell —   170
'The Moor!' he cried, 'the Moor! — ring
    out the tocsin bell!

XX

'They come! they come! I see the
    groaning lands
    White with the turbans of each Arab
    horde;
Swart Zaarah joins her misbelieving
    bands,
    Alla and Mahomet their battle-word,
The choice they yield, the Koran or the
    sword. —
    See how the Christians rush to arms
    amain! —
In yonder shout the voice of conflict
    roared,
    The shadowy hosts are closing on the
    plain —
Now, God and Saint Iago strike for the
    good cause of Spain!   180

XXI

'By Heaven, the Moors prevail! the
    Christians yield!
    Their coward leader gives for flight
    the sign!
The sceptred craven mounts to quit the
    field —
    Is not yon steed Orelia? — Yes, 't is
    mine!

But never was she turned from battle-
    line:
Lo ! where the recreant spurs o'er
    stock and stone ! —
Curses pursue the slave, and wrath di-
    vine !
Rivers ingulf him ! ' — 'Hush,' in
    shuddering tone,
The prelate said; 'rash prince, yon vis-
    ioned form 's thine own.'

XXII

Just then, a torrent crossed the flier's
    course;   190
    The dangerous ford the kingly likeness
    tried;
But the deep eddies whelmed both man
    and horse,
    Swept like benighted peasant down
    the tide;
And the proud Moslemah spread far and
    wide,
    As numerous as their native locust
    band;
Berber and Ismael's sons the spoils di-
    vide,
    With naked scimitars mete out the
    land,
And for the bondsmen base the free-born
    natives brand.

XXIII

Then rose the grated Harem, to enclose
    The loveliest maidens of the Christian
    line;   200
Then, menials, to their misbelieving
    foes
    Castile's young nobles held forbidden
    wine;
Then, too, the holy Cross, salvation's
    sign,
    By impious hands was from the altar
    thrown,
And the deep aisles of the polluted shrine
    Echoed, for holy hymn and organ-tone,
The Santon's frantic dance, the Fakir's
    gibbering moan.

XXIV

How fares Don Roderick ? — E'en as
    one who spies
    Flames dart their glare o'er midnight's
    sable woof,
And hears around his children's piercing
    cries,   210

And sees the pale assistants stand
    aloof;
While cruel Conscience brings him bitter
    proof
    His folly or his crime have caused his
    grief;
And while above him nods the crumbling
    roof,
    He curses earth and Heaven — him-
    self in chief —
Desperate of earthly aid, despairing Hea-
    ven's relief !

XXV

That scythe-armed Giant turned his fatal
    glass
    And twilight on the landscape closed
    her wings;
Far to Asturian hills the war-sounds pass,
    And in their stead rebeck or timbrel
    rings;   220
And to the sound the bell-decked dancer
    springs,
    Bazars resound as when their marts
    are met,
In tourney light the Moor his jerrid
    flings,
    And on the land as evening seemed to
    set,
The Imaum's chant was heard from mosque
    or minaret.

XXVI

So passed that pageant. Ere another
    came,
    The visionary scene was wrapped in
    smoke,
Whose sulphurous wreaths were crossed
    by sheets of flame;
    With every flash a bolt explosive
    broke,
Till Roderick deemed the fiends had
    burst their yoke   230
    And waved 'gainst heaven the infer-
    nal gonfalone !
For War a new and dreadful language
    spoke,
    Never by ancient warrior heard or
    known;
Lightning and smoke her breath, and
    thunder was her tone.

XXVII

From the dim landscape roll the clouds
    away —

The Christians have regained their
heritage;
Before the Cross has waned the Cres-
cent's ray,
And many a monastery decks the
stage,
And lofty church and low-browed her-
mitage.
The land obeys a Hermit and a
Knight, —   240
The Genii these of Spain for many an
age;
This clad in sackcloth, that in armor
bright,
And that was VALOR named, this BIGOTRY
was hight.

XXVIII

VALOR was harnessed like a chief of
old,
Armed at all points, and prompt for
knightly gest;
His sword was tempered in the Ebro
cold,
Morena's eagle plume adorned his
crest,
The spoils of Afric's lion bound his
breast.
Fierce he stepped forward and flung
down his gage;   249
As if of mortal kind to brave the best.
Him followed his companion, dark and
sage
As he my Master sung, the dangerous
Archimage.

XXIX

Haughty of heart and brow the warrior
came,
In look and language proud as proud
might be,
Vaunting his lordship, lineage, fights,
and fame:
Yet was that barefoot monk more
proud than he;
And as the ivy climbs the tallest tree,
So round the loftiest soul his toils he
wound,
And with his spells subdued the fierce
and free,
Till ermined Age and Youth in arms
renowned,   260
Honoring his scourge and haircloth, meekly
kissed the ground.

XXX

And thus it chanced that VALOR, peer-
less knight,
Who ne'er to King or Kaiser veiled his
crest,
Victorious still in bull-feast or in fight,
Since first his limbs with mail he did
invest,
Stooped ever to that anchoret's behest;
Nor reasoned of the right nor of the
wrong,
But at his bidding laid the lance in
rest,
And wrought fell deeds the troubled
world along,
For he was fierce as brave and pitiless as
strong.   270

XXXI

Oft his proud galleys sought some new-
found world,
That latest sees the sun or first the
morn;
Still at that wizard's feet their spoils he
hurled, —
Ingots of ore from rich Potosi borne,
Crowns by Caciques, aigrettes by Om-
rahs worn,
Wrought of rare gems, but broken,
rent, and foul;
Idols of gold from heathen temples torn,
Bedabbled all with blood. — With
grisly scowl
The hermit marked the stains and smiled
beneath his cowl.

XXXII

Then did he bless the offering, and bade
make   280
Tribute to Heaven of gratitude and
praise;
And at his word the choral hymns awake,
And many a hand the silver censer
sways,
But with the incense-breath these censers
raise
Mix steams from corpses smouldering
in the fire;
The groans of prisoned victims mar the
lays,
And shrieks of agony confound the
quire;
While, 'mid the mingled sounds, the darkened scenes expire.

XXXIII

Preluding light, were strains of music
heard,
As once again revolved that measured
sand: 290
Such sounds as when, for sylvan dance
prepared,
Gay Xeres summons forth her vintage
band;
When for the light bolero ready stand
The mozo blithe, with gay muchacha
met,
He conscious of his broidered cap and
band,
She of her netted locks and light cor-
sette,
Each tiptoe perched to spring and shake
the castanet.

XXXIV

And well such strains the opening scene
became;
For VALOR had relaxed his ardent
look,
And at a lady's feet, like lion tame, 300
Lay stretched, full loath the weight
of arms to brook;
And softened BIGOTRY upon his book
Pattered a task of little good or
ill:
But the blithe peasant plied his pruning-
hook,
Whistled the muleteer o'er vale and
hill,
And rung from village-green the merry
seguidille.

XXXV

Gray Royalty, grown impotent of toil,
Let the grave sceptre slip his lazy
hold;
And careless saw his rule become the
spoil
Of a loose female and her minion
bold.   310
But peace was on the cottage and the
fold,
From court intrigue, from bickering
faction far;
Beneath the chestnut-tree love's tale was
told,
And to the tinkling of the light gui-
tar
Sweet stooped the western sun, sweet rose
the evening star.

XXXVI

As that sea-cloud, in size like human
hand
When first from Carmel by the Tishbite
seen,
Came slowly overshadowing Israel's land,
Awhile perchance bedecked with colors
sheen,
While yet the sunbeams on its skirts had
been,   320
Limning with purple and with gold its
shroud,
Till darker folds obscured the blue serene
And blotted heaven with one broad sa-
ble cloud,
Then sheeted rain burst down and whirl-
winds howled aloud: —

XXXVII

Even so, upon that peaceful scene was
poured,
Like gathering clouds, full many a foreign band,
And HE, their leader, wore in sheath his
sword,
And offered peaceful front and open
hand,
Veiling the perjured treachery he
planned,
By friendship's zeal and honor's specious guise,   330
Until he won the passes of the land;
Then burst were honor's oath and
friendship's ties !
He clutched his vulture grasp and called
fair Spain his prize.

XXXVIII

An iron crown his anxious forehead bore:
And well such diadem his heart became
Who ne'er his purpose for remorse gave
o'er,
Or checked his course for piety or
shame;
Who, trained a soldier, deemed a soldier's
fame
Might flourish in the wreath of battles
won,
Though neither truth nor honor decked
his name;   340
Who, placed by fortune on a monarch's
throne,
Recked not of monarch's faith or mercy's
kingly tone.

XXXIX

From a rude isle his ruder lineage came:
  The spark that, from a suburb-hovel's
    hearth
Ascending, wraps some capital in flame,
  Hath not a meaner or more sordid
    birth.
And for the soul that bade him waste the
    earth —
  The sable land-flood from some swamp
    obscure,
That poisons the glad husband-field with
    dearth,
  And by destruction bids its fame en-
    dure,   350
Hath not a source more sullen, stagnant,
  and impure.

XL

Before that leader strode a shadowy
    form;
  Her limbs like mist, her torch like
    meteor showed,
With which she beckoned him through
    fight and storm,
  And all he crushed that crossed his
    desperate road,
Nor thought, nor feared, nor looked on
    what he trode.
  Realms could not glut his pride, blood
    could not slake,
So oft as e'er she shook her torch abroad:
  It was AMBITION bade his terrors
    wake,
Nor deigned she, as of yore, a milder form
  to take.   360

XLI

No longer now she spurned at mean re-
    venge,
  Or staid her hand for conquered foe-
    man's moan,
As when, the fates of aged Rome to
    change,
  By Cæsar's side she crossed the Ru-
    bicon.
Nor joyed she to bestow the spoils she
    won,
  As when the banded powers of Greece
    were tasked
To war beneath the Youth of Macedon:
  No seemly veil her modern minion
    asked,
He saw her hideous face and loved the fiend
  unmasked.

XLII

That prelate marked his march — on ban-
    ners blazed   370
  With battles won in many a distant
    land,
On eagle-standards and on arms he gazed;
  'And hopest thou, then,' he said, 'thy
    power shall stand?
O, thou hast builded on the shifting sand
  And thou hast tempered it with slaugh-
    ter's flood;
And know, fell scourge in the Almighty's
    hand,
  Gore-moistened trees shall perish in
    the bud,
And by a bloody death shall die the Man of
  Blood!'

XLIII

The ruthless leader beckoned from his
    train
  A wan fraternal shade, and bade him
    kneel,
And paled his temples with the crown of   380
    Spain,
  While trumpets rang and heralds cried
    'Castile!'
Not that he loved him — No! — In no
    man's weal,
  Scarce in his own, e'er joyed that sullen
    heart;
Yet round that throne he bade his war-
    riors wheel,
  That the poor puppet might perform
    his part
And be a sceptred slave, at his stern beck
  to start.

XLIV

But on the natives of that land misused
  Not long the silence of amazement
    hung,
Nor brooked they long their friendly faith
    abused;
  For with a common shriek the general   390
    tongue
Exclaimed, 'To arms!' and fast to arms
    they sprung.
  And VALOR woke, that Genius of the
    land!
Pleasure and ease and sloth aside he flung,
  As burst the awakening Nazarite his
    band
When 'gainst his treacherous foes he
  clenched his dreadful hand.

XLV

That mimic monarch now cast anxious
  eye
  Upon the satraps that begirt him
  round,
Now doffed his royal robe in act to fly,
  And from his brow the diadem un-
  bound.   400
So oft, so near, the Patriot bugle wound,
  From Tarik's walls to Bilboa's moun-
  tains blown,
These martial satellites hard labor found,
  To guard awhile his substituted throne;
Light recking of his cause, but battling for
  their own.

XLVI

From Alpuhara's peak that bugle rung,
  And it was echoed from Corunna's
  wall;
Stately Seville responsive war-shout
  flung,
  Grenada caught it in her Moorish hall;
Galicia bade her children fight or fall, 410
  Wild Biscay shook his mountain-coro-
  net,
Valencia roused her at the battle-call,
  And, foremost still where Valor's sons
  are met,
Fast started to his gun each fiery Miquelet.

XLVII

But unappalled and burning for the fight,
  The invaders march, of victory secure,
Skilful their force to sever or unite,
  And trained alike to vanquish or
  endure.
Nor skilful less, cheap conquest to insure,
  Discord to breathe and jealousy to sow,
To quell by boasting and by bribes to
  lure;   421
  While nought against them bring the
  unpractised foe,
Save hearts for freedom's cause and hands
  for freedom's blow.

XLVIII

Proudly they march — but, O, they march
  not forth
  By one hot field to crown a brief campaign,
As when their eagles, sweeping through
  the North,
  Destroyed at every stoop an ancient
  reign!

Far other fate had Heaven decreed for
  Spain;
  In vain the steel, in vain the torch was
  plied,
New Patriot armies started from the
  slain,   430
  High blazed the war, and long, and far,
  and wide,
And oft the God of Battles blest the right-
  eous side.

XLIX

Nor unatoned, where Freedom's foes
  prevail,
  Remained their savage waste. With
  blade and brand
By day the invaders ravaged hill and
  dale,
  But with the darkness the Guerilla
  band
Came like night's tempest and avenged
  the land,
  And claimed for blood the retribution
  due,
Probed the hard heart and lopped the
  murd'rous hand;
  And Dawn, when o'er the scene her
  beams she threw,   440
Midst ruins they had made the spoilers'
  corpses knew.

L

What minstrel verse may sing or tongue
  may tell,
  Amid the visioned strife from sea to
  sea,
How oft the Patriot banners rose or
  fell,
  Still honored in defeat as victory?
For that sad pageant of events to be
  Showed every form of fight by field
  and flood;
Slaughter and Ruin, shouting forth their
  glee,
  Beheld, while riding on the tempest
  scud,
The waters choked with slain, the earth
  bedrenched with blood!   450

LI

Then Zaragoza — blighted be the tongue
  That names thy name without the
  honor due!
For never hath the harp of minstrel rung
  Of faith so felly proved, so firmly true!

Mine, sap, and bomb thy shattered ruins
    knew,
Each art of war's extremity had room,
Twice from thy half-sacked streets the
    foe withdrew,
And when at length stern Fate de-
    creed thy doom,
They won not Zaragoza but her children's
    bloody tomb.

LII

Yet raise thy head, sad city! Though
    in chains,   460
    Enthralled thou canst not be! Arise,
    and claim
Reverence from every heart where Free-
    dom reigns,
    For what thou worshippest! — thy
    sainted dame,
She of the Column, honored be her name
By all, whate'er their creed, who
    honor love!
And like the sacred relics of the flame
    That gave some martyr to the blessed
    above,
To every loyal heart may thy sad embers
    prove!

LIII

Nor thine alone such wreck. Gerona
    fair!
    Faithful to death thy heroes should be
    sung,   470
Manning the towers, while o'er their
    heads the air
Swart as the smoke from raging fur-
    nace hung;
Now thicker darkening where the mine
    was sprung,
    Now briefly lightened by the cannon's
    flare,
Now arched with fire-sparks as the bomb
    was flung,
    And reddening now with conflagra-
    tion's glare,
While by the fatal light the foes for storm
    prepare.

LIV

While all around was danger, strife, and
    fear,
    While the earth shook and darkened
    was the sky,
And wide destruction stunned the listen-
    ing ear,   480

Appalled the heart, and stupefied the
    eye, —
Afar was heard that thrice-repeated cry,
    In which old Albion's heart and tongue
    unite,
Whene'er her soul is up and pulse beats
    high,
    Whether it hail the wine-cup or the fight,
And bid each arm be strong or bid each
    heart be light.

LV

Don Roderick turned him as the shout
    grew loud —
    A varied scene the changeful vision
    showed,
For, where the ocean mingled with the
    cloud,
    A gallant navy stemmed the billows
    broad.   490
From mast and stern Saint George's
    symbol flowed,
    Blent with the silver cross to Scotland
    dear;
Mottling the sea their landward barges
    rowed,
    And flashed the sun on bayonet, brand,
    and spear,
And the wild beach returned the seamen's
    jovial cheer.

LVI

It was a dread yet spirit-stirring sight!
    The billows foamed beneath a thou-
    sand oars,
Fast as they land the red-cross ranks
    unite,
    Legions on legions brightening all the
    shores.
Then banners rise and cannon - signal
    roars,
    Then peals the warlike thunder of the
    drum,   500
Thrills the loud fife, the trumpet-flourish
    pours,
    And patriot hopes awake and doubts
    are dumb,
For, bold in Freedom's cause, the bands of
    Ocean come!

LVII

A various host they came — whose ranks
    display
    Each mode in which the warrior meets
    the fight:

The deep battalion locks its firm array,
And meditates his aim the marksman light;
Far glance the lines of sabres flashing bright,
Where mounted squadrons shake the echoing mead;   510
Lacks not artillery breathing flame and night,
Nor the fleet ordnance whirled by rapid steed,
That rivals lightning's flash in ruin and in speed.

LVIII

A various host — from kindred realms they came,
Brethren in arms but rivals in renown —
For yon fair bands shall merry England claim,
And with their deeds of valor deck her crown.
Hers their bold port, and hers their martial frown,
And hers their scorn of death in freedom's cause,
Their eyes of azure, and their locks of brown,   520
And the blunt speech that bursts without a pause,
And freeborn thoughts which league the soldier with the laws.

LIX

And, O loved warriors of the minstrel's land !
Yonder your bonnets nod, your tartans wave !
The rugged form may mark the mountain band,
And harsher features, and a mien more grave;
But ne'er in battle-field throbbed heart so brave
As that which beats beneath the Scottish plaid;
And when the pibroch bids the battle rave,
And level for the charge your arms are laid,   530
Where lives the desperate foe that for such onset staid ?

LX

Hark ! from yon stately ranks what laughter rings,
Mingling wild mirth with war's stern minstrelsy,
His jest while each blithe comrade round him flings
And moves to death with military glee:
Boast, Erin, boast them ! tameless, frank, and free,
In kindness warm and fierce in danger known,
Rough nature's children, humorous as she:
And HE, yon Chieftain — strike the proudest tone
Of thy bold harp, green Isle ! — the hero is thine own.   540

LXI

Now on the scene Vimeira should be shown,
On Talavera's fight should Roderick gaze,
And hear Corunna wail her battle won,
And see Busaco's crest with lightning blaze: —
But shall fond fable mix with heroes' praise ?
Hath Fiction's stage for Truth's long triumphs room ?
And dare her wild-flowers mingle with the bays
That claim a long eternity to bloom
Around the warrior's crest and o'er the warrior's tomb !   549

LXII

Or may I give adventurous Fancy scope,
And stretch a bold hand to the awful veil
That hides futurity from anxious hope,
Bidding beyond it scenes of glory hail,
And painting Europe rousing at the tale
Of Spain's invaders from her confines hurled,
While kindling nations buckle on their mail,
And Fame, with clarion - blast and wings unfurled,
To freedom and revenge awakes an injured world ?

LXIII

O vain, though anxious, is the glance I
    cast,
    Since Fate has marked futurity her
      own: 560
Yet Fate resigns to worth the glorious
    past,
    The deeds recorded and the laurels
      won.
Then, though the Vault of Destiny be
    gone,
    King, prelate, all the phantasms of my
      brain,
Melted away like mist-wreaths in the
    sun,
    Yet grant for faith, for valor, and for
      Spain,
One note of pride and fire, a patriot's part-
    ing strain !

CONCLUSION

I

' Who shall command Estrella's moun-
    tain-tide
    Back to the source, when tempest-
      chafed, to hie ?
Who, when Gascogne's vexed gulf is
    raging wide,
    Shall hush it as a nurse her infant's
      cry ?
His magic power let such vain boaster
    try,
    And when the torrent shall his voice
      obey,
And Biscay's whirlwinds list his lullaby,
    Let him stand forth and bar mine
      eagles' way,
And they shall heed his voice and at his
    bidding stay.

II

' Else ne'er to stoop till high on Lisbon's
    towers   10
    They close their wings, the symbol of
      our yoke,
And their own sea hath whelmed yon
    red-cross powers ! '
    Thus, on the summit of Alverca's
      rock,
To marshal, duke, and peer Gaul's leader
    spoke.
    While downward on the land his le-
    gions press,

Before them it was rich with vine and
    flock,
    And smiled like Eden in her summer
    dress ; —
Behind their wasteful march a reeking wil-
    derness.

III

And shall the boastful chief maintain his
    word,
    Though Heaven hath heard the wail-
      ings of the land,   20
Though Lusitania whet her vengeful
    sword,
    Though Britons arm and Welling-
    ton command ?
No ! grim Busacos' iron ridge shall
    stand
    An adamantine barrier to his force;
And from its base shall wheel his shat-
    tered band,
    As from the unshaken rock the torrent
    hoarse
Bears off its broken waves and seeks a
    devious course.

IV

Yet not because Alcoba's mountain-hawk
    Hath on his best and bravest made
      her food,
In numbers confident, yon chief shall
    balk   30
    His lord's imperial thirst for spoil and
      blood:
For full in view the promised conquest
    stood,
    And Lisbon's matrons from their walls
    might sum
The myriads that had half the world sub-
    dued,
    And hear the distant thunders of the
    drum
That bids the bands of France to storm
    and havoc come.

V

Four moons have heard these thunders
    idly rolled,
    Have seen these wistful myriads eye
      their prey,
As famished wolves survey a guarded
    fold —
    But in the middle path a Lion lay !   40
At length they move — but not to battle-
    fray,

Nor blaze yon fires where meets the
    manly fight;
Beacons of infamy, they light the way
    Where cowardice and cruelty unite
To damn with double shame their ignomini-
    ous flight !

VI

O triumph for the fiends of lust and
    wrath !
Ne'er to be told, yet ne'er to be forgot,
What wanton horrors marked their
    wrackful path !
The peasant butchered in his ruined
    cot,
The hoary priest even at the altar shot, 50
    Childhood and age given o'er to sword
    and flame,
Woman to infamy; — no crime forgot,
    By which inventive demons might pro-
    claim
Immortal hate to man and scorn of God's
    great name !

VII

The rudest sentinel in Britain born
    With horror paused to view the havoc
    done,
Gave his poor crust to feed some wretch
    forlorn,
    Wiped his stern eye, then fiercer
    grasped his gun.
Nor with less zeal shall Britain's peace-
    ful son
Exult the debt of sympathy to pay; 60
Riches nor poverty the tax shall shun,
    Nor prince nor peer, the wealthy nor
    the gay,
Nor the poor peasant's mite, nor bard's
    more worthless lay.

VIII

But thou — unfoughten wilt thou yield to
    Fate,
    Minion of Fortune, now miscalled in
    vain !
Can vantage-ground no confidence cre-
    ate,
    Marcella's pass, nor Guarda's moun-
    tain-chain ?
Vainglorious fugitive, yet turn again !
    Behold, where, named by some pro-
    phetic seer,
Flows Honor's Fountain, as foredoomed
    the stain   70

From thy dishonored name and arms
    to clear —
Fallen child of Fortune, turn, redeem her
    favor here !

IX

Yet, ere thou turn'st, collect each distant
    aid;
    Those chief that never heard the lion
    roar !
Within whose souls lives not a trace por-
    trayed
    Of Talavera or Mondego's shore !
Marshal each band thou hast and sum-
    mon more;
    Of war's fell stratagems exhaust the
    whole;
Rank upon rank, squadron on squadron
    pour,
    Legion on legion on thy foeman
    roll,   80
And weary out his arm — thou canst not
    quell his soul.

X

O vainly gleams with steel Agueda's
    shore,
    Vainly thy squadrons hide Assuava's
    plain,
And front the flying thunders as they
    roar,
    With frantic charge and tenfold odds,
    in vain !
And what avails thee that for CAMERON
    slain
    Wild from his plaided ranks the yell
    was given ?
Vengeance and grief gave mountain-rage
    the rein,
    And, at the bloody spear-point head-
    long driven,
Thy despot's giant guards fled like the rack
    of heaven.   90

XI

Go, baffled boaster ! teach thy haughty
    mood
    To plead at thine imperious master's
    throne !
Say, thou hast left his legions in their
    blood,
    Deceived his hopes and frustrated
    thine own;
Say, that thine utmost skill and valor
    shown

By British skill and valor were out-
vied;
Last say, thy conqueror was WELLING-
TON !
And if he chafe, be his own fortune
tried —
God and our cause to friend, the venture
we 'll abide.

XII

But you, the heroes of that well-fought
day,   100
How shall a bard unknowing and un-
known
His meed to each victorious leader pay,
Or bind on every brow the laurels
won ?
Yet fain my harp would wake its boldest
tone,
O'er the wide sea to hail CADOGAN
brave;
And he perchance the minstrel-note
might own,
Mindful of meeting brief that Fortune
gave
Mid yon far western isles that hear the
Atlantic rave.

XIII

Yes ! hard the task, when Britons wield
the sword
To give each chief and every field its
fame: 110
Hark ! Albuera thunders BERESFORD,
And red Barosa shouts for dauntless
GRÆME !
O for a verse of tumult and of flame,
Bold as the bursting of their cannon
sound,
To bid the world re-echo to their fame !
For never upon gory battle-ground
With conquest's well-bought wreath were
braver victors crowned !

XIV

O who shall grudge him Albuera's bays
Who brought a race regenerate to the
field,
Roused them to emulate their fathers'
praise,   120
Tempered their headlong rage, their
courage steeled,
And raised fair Lusitania's fallen shield,
And gave new edge to Lusitania's
sword,

And taught her sons forgotten arms to
wield —
Shivered my harp and burst its every
chord,
If it forget thy worth, victorious BERES-
FORD !

XV

Not on that bloody field of battle
won,
Though Gaul's proud legions rolled
like mist away,
Was half his self-devoted valor shown, —
He gaged but life on that illustrious
day;   130
But when he toiled those squadrons to
array
Who fought like Britons in the bloody
game,
Sharper than Polish pike or assagay,
He braved the shafts of censure and
of shame,
And, dearer far than life, he pledged a
soldier's fame.

XVI

Nor be his praise o'erpast who strove to
hide
Beneath the warrior's vest affection's
wound,
Whose wish Heaven for his country's
weal denied;
Danger and fate he sought, but glory
found.
From clime to clime, where'er war's
trumpets sound,   140
The wanderer went; yet, Caledonia !
still
Thine was his thought in march and
tented ground;
He dreamed mid Alpine cliffs of Athole's hill,
And heard in Ebro's roar his Lyndoch's
lovely rill.

XVII

O hero of a race renowned of old,
Whose war-cry oft has waked the
battle-swell,
Since first distinguished in the onset
bold,
Wild sounding when the Roman rampart fell !
By Wallace' side it rung the Southron's
knell,

Alderne, Kilsythe, and Tibber owned
   its fame,   150
Tummell's rude pass can of its terrors
   tell,
But ne'er from prouder field arose the
   name
Than when wild Ronda learned the conquering shout of GRÆME !

XVIII

But all too long, through seas unknown
   and dark, —
   With Spenser's parable I close my
   tale, —

By shoal and rock hath steered my venturous bark,
   And landward now I drive before the
   gale.
And now the blue and distant shore I
   hail,
   And nearer now I see the port expand,
And now I gladly furl my weary
   sail,   160
   And as the prow light touches on the
   strand,
I strike my red-cross flag and bind my
   skiff to land.

ROKEBY

INTRODUCTORY NOTE

Mr. Morritt, to whom Scott dedicates
Rokeby, and in whose beautiful estate the
scene of the poem is laid, was introduced to
the poet in the early summer of 1808, and an
intimacy began which was one of the most
agreeable elements in Scott's life. Twenty
years later when paying him a visit, Scott recorded in his *Journal* (ii. 195): ' He is now
one of my oldest, and, I believe, one of my
most sincere friends, a man unequalled in the
mixture of sound good sense, high literary cul-
tivation, and the kindest and sweetest temper
that ever graced a human bosom.' The intimacy led to a long correspondence and to
frequent interchange of visits. Mr. Morritt's
own recollections of Scott form a delightful
contribution in Lockhart's *Life*. He visited
Scott in Edinburgh when he first made his acquaintance, and Scott returned the visit a year
later. The beauty of Rokeby made a great
impression upon him, as may be seen by his
letter to George Ellis, July 8, 1809, and it is
most probable that in taking the step which
led to the purchase of Abbotsford, and re-
moval from Ashestiel, Scott was influenced by
his admiration for his friend's estate. At any
rate, Scott palpably connected the writing of
the poem *Rokeby* with the enlargement of his
domain, and asked eagerly Morritt to aid him
in his poetical venture.

' I have a grand project to tell you of,' he
writes December 20, 1811. " Nothing less than
a fourth romance, in verse ; the theme, during
the English civil wars of Charles I., and the
scene, your own domain of Rokeby. I want
to build my cottage a little better than my
limited finances will permit out of my ordinary

income ; and although it is very true that an
author should not hazard his reputation, yet,
as Bob Acres says, I really think Reputation
should take some care of the gentleman in return. Now, I have all your scenery deeply
imprinted in my memory, and moreover, be it
known to you, I intend to refresh its traces
this ensuing summer, and to go as far as the
borders of Lancashire, and the caves of Yorkshire, and so perhaps on to Derbyshire. I
have sketched a story which pleases me, and I
am only anxious to keep my theme quiet, for
its being piddled upon by some of your *Ready-
to-catch* literati, as John Bunyan calls them,
would be a serious misfortune to me. I am
not without hope of seducing you to be my
guide a little way on my tour. Is there not
some book (sense or nonsense I care not) on
the beauties of Teesdale — I mean a descriptive work ? If you can point it out or lend it
me, you will do me a great favour, and no less
if you can tell me any traditions of the period.
By which party was Barnard castle occupied ?
It strikes me that it should be held for the
Parliament. Pray help me in this, by truth,
or fiction, or tradition, — I care not which if
it be picturesque. What the deuce is the
name of that wild glen, where we had such
a clamber on horseback up a stone staircase ?
— Cat's Cradle, or Cat's Castle, I think it
was. I wish also to have the true edition of
the traditionary tragedy of your old house at
Mortham, and the ghost thereunto appertaining, and you will do me yeoman's service in
compiling the relics of so valuable a legend.
Item — Do you know anything of a striking
ancient castle, belonging, I think, to the Duke

of Leeds, called Coningsburgh? Grose notices it, but in a very flimsy manner. I once flew past it on the mail-coach, when its round tower and flying buttresses had a most romantic effect in the morning dawn.'

Whereupon Mr. Morritt girded himself and addressed himself thoroughly to the task of supplying Scott with the needed material, and of making suggestions for the construction of the poem which were clearly heeded by the poet. The correspondence between the two friends continued during the winter and spring of 1812, and Morritt furnished further memorabilia in answer to questions, and Scott divided his time between his poem and the estate which it was to help pay for. 'My work *Rokeby* does and must go forward,' he writes March 2, 1812, ' or my trees and enclosures might, perchance, stand still. But I destroyed the first canto after I had written it fair out, because it did not quite please me. I shall keep off people's kibes if I can, for my plan, though laid during the civil wars, has little to do with the politics of either party, being very much confined to the adventures and distresses of a particular family.'

In the same letter he says that he must certainly refresh his memory with the scenery, in spite of the serviceable memoranda of Mr. Morritt, and in the autumn of 1812 he went with Mrs. Scott, Walter, and Sophia to Rokeby, remaining there about a week. It was while he was on this visit that Mr. Morritt made that interesting note on Scott's habits of observation which has often been quoted for the light it throws on the poet's attitude toward his work.

'I observed him,' says Morritt, ' noting down even the peculiar little wild flowers and herbs that accidentally grew round and on the side of a bold crag near his intended cave of Guy Denzil; and could not help saying, that as he was not to be on oath in his work, daisies, violets, and primroses would be as poetical as any of the humble plants he was examining. I laughed, in short, at his scrupulousness ; but I understood him when he replied, "that in nature herself no two scenes were exactly alike, and that whoever copied truly what was before his eyes, would possess the same variety in his descriptions, and exhibit apparently an imagination as boundless as the range of nature in the scenes he recorded; whereas — whoever trusted to imagination, would soon find his own mind circumscribed, and contracted to a few favorite images, and the repetition of these would sooner or later produce that very monotony and barrenness which had always haunted descriptive poetry in the hands of any but the patient worshippers of truth. Besides which,"

he said, " local names and peculiarities make a fictitious story book look so much better in the face." '

The poem gave its author a good deal of trouble, since he was unwontedly anxious to do it well, and he destroyed his work and re-attacked it, finally pushing it to a conclusion in the three months at the close of 1812. As usual, during the process of composition and when it was completed he sought the criticism of his friends. 'There are two or three songs,' he wrote Morritt, ' and particularly one in praise of Brignal Banks, which I trust you will like — because, *entre nous*, I like them myself. One of them is a little dashing banditti song, called and entitled Allen-a-Dale.' Scott, indeed, gives Joanna Baillie a curious coincidence in the discovery, on reading her 'Passion of Fear,' that she had an outlaw's song of which the chorus was almost verbatim that which he had written for his outlaw's song in *Rokeby*, so that he was forced to re-write that song. Miss Baillie herself repaid him with an enthusiastic letter after reading *Rokeby*. 'I wish you could have seen me,' she writes, ' when it arrived. My sister was from home, so I stirred my fire, swept the hearth, chased the cat out of the room, lighted my candles, and began upon it immediately. It is written with wonderful power both as to natural objects and human character ; and your magnificent bandit, Bertram, is well entitled to your partiality ; for it is a masterly picture, and true to nature in all its parts, according to my conceptions of nature. Your Lady and both her lovers are very pleasing and beautifully drawn, her conduct and behavior to them both is so natural and delicate ; and so is theirs to each other. How many striking passages there are which take a hold of the imagination that can never be unloosed! The burning of the castle in all its progress is very sublime ; the final scene, also, when Bertram rides into the church, is grand and terrific; the scene between him and Edmund, when he weeps to find that there is any human being that will shed a tear for him, is very touching and finely imagined. I say nothing of what struck me so much in the three first cantos. And besides those higher beauties, there are those of a softer kind that are wonderfully attractive ; for instance, the account of the poor Irishman's death, after he had delivered the child to the Lord of Rokeby, which made me weep freely, and the stealing of Edmund back to the cave by night with all the indications of his silent path, the owlet ceasing its cry, the otter leaping into the stream, etc., is delightful. Your images and similes too, with which the work is not overloaded (like a lady with a few jewels, but of the best water), are excellent. Your songs are good, particularly those of Wilfrid; but they have struck me less, somehow or other, than the rest of the poem. As to the invention of your story, I praise that more sparingly, for tho' the leading circumstances are well imagined, the conducting of it seems to me too dramatic for a lyrical narrative, and there are too many complex contrivances to the bringing about the catastrophe.'

Miss Baillie proceeded, with some sagacity, to predict that Scott's mind was working toward dramatic composition. Her criticism of *Rokeby* indeed implies that the story would have lent itself better to a form which permitted a greater elaboration of character and plot. Only the next year, Scott was to perfect his *Waverley*. In truth, in *Rokeby*, Scott's interest, though largely in the presentation of his friend's domain, was specifically in character, and the heroine especially was the reflection, in imaginative form, of that early love, whose influence had already been felt in *The Lay of the Last Minstrel*. Writing to Miss Edgeworth, five years after the appearance of *Rokeby*, he says: 'This much of Matilda I recollect — (for that is not so easily forgotten) — that she was attempted for the existing person of a lady who is now no more, so that I am particularly flattered with your distinguishing it from the others, which are in general mere shadows.' And Lockhart, quoting this, adds: 'I can have no doubt that the lady he here alludes to, was the object of his own unfortunate first love; and as little, that in the romantic generosity, both of the youthful poet who fails to win her higher favor, and of his chivalrous competitor, we have before us something more than "a mere shadow." '

Rokeby was published the first week in January, 1813, and bore the dedication to Mr. Morritt. When the poem was issued in the collective edition of 1830, it was preceded by the following Introduction.

INTRODUCTION

Between the publication of *The Lady of the Lake*, which was so eminently successful, and that of *Rokeby*, in 1813, three years had intervened. I shall not, I believe, be accused of ever having attempted to usurp a superiority over many men of genius, my contemporaries; but, in point of popularity, not of actual talent, the caprice of the public had certainly given me such a temporary superiority over men, of whom, in regard to poetical fancy and feeling, I scarcely thought myself worthy to loose the shoe-latch. On the other hand, it would be absurd affectation in me to deny, that I conceived myself to understand, more perfectly than many of my contemporaries, the manner most likely to interest the great mass of mankind. Yet, even with this belief, I must truly and fairly say that I always considered myself rather as one who held the bets in time to be paid over to the winner, than as having any pretence to keep them in my own right.

In the mean time years crept on, and not without their usual depredations on the passing generation. My sons had arrived at the age when the paternal home was no longer their best abode, as both were destined to active life. The field-sports, to which I was peculiarly attached, had now less interest, and were replaced by other amusements of a more quiet character; and the means and opportunity of pursuing these were to be sought for. I had, indeed, for some years attended to farming, a knowledge of which is, or at least was then, indispensable to the comfort of a family residing in a solitary country-house; but although this was the favorite amusement of many of my friends, I have never been able to consider it as a source of pleasure. I never could think it a matter of passing importance, that my cattle or crops were better or more plentiful than those of my neighbors, and nevertheless I began to feel the necessity of some more quiet out-door occupation, different from those I had hitherto pursued. I purchased a small farm of about one hundred acres, with the purpose of planting and improving it, to which property circumstances afterwards enabled me to make considerable additions; and thus an era took place in my life, almost equal to the important one mentioned by the Vicar of Wakefield, when he removed from the Blue-room to the Brown. In point of neighborhood, at least, the change of residence made little *more* difference. Abbotsford, to which we removed, was only six or seven miles down the Tweed, and lay on the same beautiful stream. It did not possess the romantic character of Ashestiel, my former residence; but it had a stretch of meadow-land along the river, and possessed, in the phrase of the landscape-gardener, considerable capabilities. Above all, the land was my own, like Uncle Toby's Bowling-green, to do what I would with. It had been, though the gratification was long postponed, an early wish of mine to connect myself with my mother earth, and prosecute those experiments by which a species of creative power is exercised over the face of nature. I can trace, even to childhood, a pleasure derived from Dodsley's account of Shenstone's Lea-sowes, and I envied the poet much more for the pleasure of accomplishing the objects de-tailed in his friend's sketch of his grounds, than for the possession of pipe, crook, flock, and Phillis to boot. My memory, also, tena-cious of quaint expressions, still retained a phrase which it had gathered from an old almanac of Charles the Second's time (when everything down to almanacs affected to be smart), in which the reader, in the month of June, is advised for health's sake to walk a mile or two every day before breakfast, and, if he can possibly so manage, to let his exer-cise be taken upon his own land.

With the satisfaction of having attained the fulfilment of an early and long-cherished hope, I commenced my improvements, as delight-ful in their progress as those of the child who first makes a dress for a new doll. The naked-ness of the land was in time hidden by wood-lands of considerable extent — the smallest of possible cottages was progressively expanded into a sort of dream of a mansion-house, whim-sical in the exterior, but convenient within. Nor did I forget what is the natural pleasure of every man who has been a reader; I mean the filling the shelves of a tolerably large library. All these objects I kept in view, to be executed as convenience should serve; and although I knew many years must elapse be-fore they could be attained, I was of a dispo-sition to comfort myself with the Spanish proverb, 'Time and I against any two.'

The difficult and indispensable point of finding a permanent subject of occupation was now at length attained; but there was an-nexed to it the necessity of becoming again a candidate for public favor; for as I was turned improver on the earth of the every-day world it was under condition that the small tenement of Parnassus, which might be access-ible to my labors, should not remain unculti-vated.

I meditated, at first, a poem on the subject of Bruce, in which I made some progress, but afterwards judged it advisable to lay it aside, supposing that an English story might have more novelty; in consequence, the precedence was given to *Rokeby*.

If subject and scenery could have influ-enced the fate of a poem, that of *Rokeby* should have been eminently distinguished; for the grounds belonged to a dear friend, with whom I had lived in habits of intimacy for many years, and the place itself united the romantic beauties of the wilds of Scotland with the rich and smiling aspect of the southern portion of the island. But the Cavaliers and

Roundheads, whom I attempted to summon up to tenant this beautiful region, had for the public neither the novelty nor the peculiar interest of the primitive Highlanders. This, perhaps, was scarcely to be expected, consider-ing that the general mind sympathizes read-ily and at once with the stamp which nature herself has affixed upon the manners of a peo-ple living in a simple and patriarchal state; whereas it has more difficulty in understand-ing or interesting itself in manners founded upon those peculiar habits of thinking or act-ing which are produced by the progress of so-ciety. We could read with pleasure the tale of the adventures of a Cossack or a Mongol Tartar, while we only wonder and stare over those of the lovers in the *Pleasing Chinese His-tory*, where the embarrassments turn upon difficulties arising out of unintelligible deli-cacies peculiar to the customs and manners of that affected people.

'The cause of my failure had, however, a far deeper root. The manner, or style, which, by its novelty, attracted the public in an un-usual degree, had now, after having been three times before them, exhausted the patience of the reader, and began in the fourth to lose its charms. The reviewers may be said to have apostrophized the author in the language of Parnell's *Edwin*: —

'And here reverse the charm, he cries,
And let it fairly now suffice,
The gambol has been shown.'

The licentious combination of rhymes, in a manner perhaps not very congenial to our lan-guage, had not been confined to the author. Indeed, in most similar cases, the inventors of such novelties have their reputation destroyed by their own imitators, as Actæon fell under the fury of his own dogs. The present author, like Bobadil, had taught his trick of fence to a hundred gentlemen (and ladies), who could fence very nearly or quite as well as himself. For this there was no remedy; the harmony became tiresome and ordinary, and both the original inventor and his invention must have fallen into contempt if he had not found out another road to public favor. What has been said of the metre only, must be considered to apply equally to the structure of the Poem and of the style. The very best passages of any popular style are not, perhaps, susceptible of imitation, but they may be approached by men of talent; and those who are less able to copy them, at least lay hold of their peculiar fea-tures, so as to produce a strong burlesque. In either way, the effect of the manner is rendered cheap and common; and, in the latter case, ridiculous to boot. The evil consequences to an author's reputation are at least as fatal as those which come upon the musical composer when his melody falls into the hands of the street ballad-singer.

Of the unfavorable species of imitation, the author's style gave room to a very large number, owing to an appearance of facility to which some of those who used the measure unquestionably leaned too far. The effect of the more favorable imitations, composed by persons of talent, was almost equally unfortunate to the original minstrel, by showing that they could overshoot him with his own bow. In short, the popularity which once attended the *School*, as it was called, was now fast decaying.

Besides all this, to have kept his ground at the crisis when *Rokeby* appeared, its author ought to have put forth his utmost strength, and to have possessed at least all his original advantages, for a mighty and unexpected rival was advancing on the stage, — a rival not in poetical powers only, but in that art of attracting popularity, in which the present writer had hitherto preceded better men than himself. The reader will easily see that Byron is here meant, who, after a little velitation of no great promise, now appeared as a serious candidate, in the first two cantos of *Childe Harold*. I was astonished at the power evinced by that work, which neither the *Hours of Idleness*, nor the *English Bards and Scotch Reviewers*, had prepared me to expect from its author. There was a depth in his thought, an eager abundance in his diction, which argued full confidence in the inexhaustible resources of which he felt himself possessed, and there was some appearance of that labor of the file, which indicates that the author is conscious of the necessity of doing every justice to his work, that it may pass warrant. Lord Byron was also a traveller, a man whose ideas were fired by having seen, in distant scenes of difficulty and danger, the places whose very names are recorded in our bosoms as the shrines of ancient poetry. For his own misfortune, perhaps, but certainly to the high increase of his poetical character, nature had mixed in Lord Byron's system those passions which agitate the human heart with most violence, and which may be said to have hurried his bright career to an early close. There would have been little wisdom in measuring my force with so formidable an antagonist; and I was as likely to tire of playing the second fiddle in the concert, as my audience of hearing me. Age also was advancing. I was growing insensible to those subjects of excitation by which

youth is agitated. I had around me the most pleasant but least exciting of all society, that of kind friends and an affectionate family. My circle of employments was a narrow one; it occupied me constantly, and it became daily more difficult for me to interest myself in poetical composition: —

' How happily the days of Thalaba went by ! '

Yet, though conscious that I must be, in the opinion of good judges, inferior to the place I had for four or five years held in letters, and feeling alike that the latter was one to which I had only a temporary right, I could not brook the idea of relinquishing literary occupation, which had been so long my chief diversion. Neither was I disposed to choose the alternative of sinking into a mere editor and commentator, though that was a species of labor which I had practised, and to which I was attached. But I could not endure to think that I might not, whether known or concealed, do something of more importance. My inmost thoughts were those of the Trojan Captain in the galley race:

' Non jam, prima peto, Mnestheus, neque vincere certo,
Quanquam O ! — sed superent, quibus hoc, Neptune, dedisti;
Extremos pudeat rediisse : hoc vincite, cives,
Et prohibete nefas.' [1]

Æn. lib. v. 194.

I had, indeed, some private reasons for my ' Quanquam O ! ' which were not worse than those of Mnestheus. I have already hinted that the materials were collected for a poem on the subject of Bruce, and fragments of it had been shown to some of my friends, and received with applause. Notwithstanding, therefore, the eminent success of Byron, and the great chance of his taking the wind out of my sails, there was, I judged, a species of cowardice in desisting from the task which I had undertaken, and it was time enough to retreat when the battle should be more decidedly lost. The sale of *Rokeby*, excepting as compared with that of *The Lady of the Lake*, was in the highest degree respectable ; and as it included fifteen hundred quartos, in those quarto-reading days, the trade had no reason to be dissatisfied.

ABBOTSFORD, April, 1830.

[1] I seek not now the foremost palm to gain;
Though yet — but ah ! that haughty wish is vain !
Let those enjoy it whom the gods ordain.
But to be last, the lags of all the race ! —
Redeem yourselves and me from that disgrace.
DRYDEN.

ROKEBY

A POEM IN SIX CANTOS

TO

JOHN B. S. MORRITT, ESQ.,

THIS POEM

THE SCENE OF WHICH IS LAID IN HIS BEAUTIFUL DEMESNE OF ROKEBY,

IS INSCRIBED, IN TOKEN OF SINCERE FRIENDSHIP, BY

WALTER SCOTT.

ADVERTISEMENT

The Scene of this Poem is laid at Rokeby, near Greta Bridge, in Yorkshire, and shifts to the adjacent fortress of Barnard Castle, and to other places in that Vicinity.

The Time occupied by the Action is a space of Five Days, Three of which are supposed to elapse between the end of the Fifth and the beginning of the Sixth Canto.

The date of the supposed events is immediately subsequent to the great Battle of Marston Moor, 3d July, 1644. This period of public confusion has been chosen without any purpose of combining the Fable with the Military or Political Events of the Civil War, but only as affording a degree of probability to the Fictitious Narrative now presented to the Public.

CANTO FIRST

I

THE moon is in her summer glow,
But hoarse and high the breezes blow,
And, racking o'er her face, the cloud
Varies the tincture of her shroud;
On Barnard's towers and Tees's stream,
She changes as a guilty dream,
When Conscience with remorse and fear
Goads sleeping Fancy's wild career.
Her light seems now the blush of shame,
Seems now fierce anger's darker flame,   10
Shifting that shade to come and go,
Like apprehension's hurried glow;
Then sorrow's livery dims the air,
And dies in darkness, like despair.
Such varied hues the warder sees
Reflected from the Woodland Tees,
Then from old Baliol's tower looks forth,
Sees the clouds mustering in the north,
Hears upon turret-roof and wall
By fits the plashing rain-drop fall,   20
Lists to the breeze's boding sound,
And wraps his shaggy mantle round.

II

Those towers, which in the changeful gleam
Throw murky shadows on the stream,
Those towers of Barnard hold a guest,
The emotions of whose troubled breast,
In wild and strange confusion driven,
Rival the flitting rack of heaven.
Ere sleep stern OSWALD'S senses tied,
Oft had he changed his weary side,   30
Composed his limbs, and vainly sought
By effort strong to banish thought.
Sleep came at length, but with a train
Of feelings true and fancies vain,
Mingling, in wild disorder cast,
The expected future with the past.
Conscience, anticipating time,
Already rues the enacted crime,
And calls her furies forth to shake
The sounding scourge and hissing snake;   40
While her poor victim's outward throes
Bear witness to his mental woes,
And show what lesson may be read
Beside a sinner's restless bed.

III

Thus Oswald's laboring feelings trace
Strange changes in his sleeping face,
Rapid and ominous as these
With which the moonbeams tinge the Tees.
There might be seen of shame the blush,
There anger's dark and fiercer flush,   50
While the perturbed sleeper's hand
Seemed grasping dagger-knife or brand.
Relaxed that grasp, the heavy sigh,
The tear in the half-opening eye,
The pallid cheek and brow, confessed
That grief was busy in his breast:
Nor paused that mood — a sudden start
Impelled the life-blood from the heart;
Features convulsed and mutterings dread
Show terror reigns in sorrow's stead.   60
That pang the painful slumber broke,
And Oswald with a start awoke.

IV

He woke, and feared again to close
His eyelids in such dire repose;
He woke, — to watch the lamp, and tell
From hour to hour the castle-bell,
Or listen to the owlet's cry,
Or the sad breeze that whistles by,
Or catch by fits the tuneless rhyme
With which the warder cheats the time,   70
And envying think how, when the sun
Bids the poor soldier's watch be done,
Couched on his straw and fancy-free,
He sleeps like careless infancy.

V

Far townward sounds a distant tread,
And Oswald, starting from his bed,
Hath caught it, though no human ear,
Unsharpened by revenge and fear,
Could e'er distinguish horse's clank,
Until it reached the castle bank.   80
Now nigh and plain the sound appears,
The warder's challenge now he hears,
Then clanking chains and levers tell
That o'er the moat the drawbridge fell,
And, in the castle court below,
Voices are heard, and torches glow,
As marshalling the stranger's way
Straight for the room where Oswald lay;
The cry was, 'Tidings from the host,
Of weight — a messenger comes post.'   90
Stifling the tumult of his breast,
His answer Oswald thus expressed,
'Bring food and wine, and trim the fire;
Admit the stranger and retire.'

VI

The stranger came with heavy stride;
The morion's plumes his visage hide,
And the buff-coat in ample fold
Mantles his form's gigantic mould.
Full slender answer deigned he
To Oswald's anxious courtesy,   100
But marked by a disdainful smile
He saw and scorned the petty wile,
When Oswald changed the torch's place,
Anxious that on the soldier's face
Its partial lustre might be thrown,
To show his looks yet hide his own.
His guest the while laid slow aside
The ponderous cloak of tough bull's hide,
And to the torch glanced broad and clear
The corselet of a cuirassier;   110
Then from his brows the casque he drew
And from the dank plume dashed the dew,
From gloves of mail relieved his hands
And spread them to the kindling brands,
And, turning to the genial board,
Without a health or pledge or word
Of meet and social reverence said,
Deeply he drank and fiercely fed,
As free from ceremony's sway
As famished wolf that tears his prey.   120

VII

With deep impatience, tinged with fear,
His host beheld him gorge his cheer,
And quaff the full carouse that lent
His brow a fiercer hardiment.
Now Oswald stood a space aside,
Now paced the room with hasty stride,
In feverish agony to learn
Tidings of deep and dread concern,
Cursing each moment that his guest
Protracted o'er his ruffian feast,   130
Yet, viewing with alarm at last
The end of that uncouth repast,
Almost he seemed their haste to rue
As at his sign his train withdrew,
And left him with the stranger, free
To question of his mystery.
Then did his silence long proclaim
A struggle between fear and shame.

VIII

Much in the stranger's mien appears
To justify suspicious fears.   140
On his dark face a scorching clime
And toil had done the work of time,
Roughened the brow, the temples bared,
And sable hairs with silver shared,

Yet left — what age alone could tame —
The lip of pride, the eye of flame;
The full-drawn lip that upward curled,
The eye that seemed to scorn the world.
That lip had terror never blanched;   149
Ne'er in that eye had tear-drop quenched
The flash severe of swarthy glow
That mocked at pain and knew not woe.
Inured to danger's direst form,
Tornado and earthquake, flood and storm,
Death had he seen by sudden blow,
By wasting plague, by tortures slow,
By mine or breach, by steel or ball,
Knew all his shapes and scorned them all.

IX

But yet, though BERTRAM'S hardened look
Unmoved could blood and danger brook,
Still worse than apathy had place   161
On his swart brow and callous face;
For evil passions cherished long
Had ploughed them with impressions
   strong.
All that gives gloss to sin, all gay
Light folly, past with youth away,
But rooted stood in manhood's hour
The weeds of vice without their flower.
And yet the soil in which they grew,
Had it been tamed when life was new,   170
Had depth and vigor to bring forth
The hardier fruits of virtuous worth.
Not that e'en then his heart had known
The gentler feelings' kindly tone;
But lavish waste had been refined
To bounty in his chastened mind,
And lust of gold, that waste to feed,
Been lost in love of glory's meed,
And, frantic then no more, his pride
Had ta'en fair virtue for its guide.   180

X

Even now, by conscience unrestrained,
Clogged by gross vice, by slaughter stained,
Still knew his daring soul to soar,
And mastery o'er the mind he bore;
For meaner guilt or heart less hard
Quailed beneath Bertram's bold regard.
And this felt Oswald, while in vain
He strove by many a winding train
To lure his sullen guest to show
Unasked the news he longed to know,   190
While on far other subject hung
His heart than faltered from his tongue.
Yet nought for that his guest did deign
To note or spare his secret pain,

But still in stern and stubborn sort
Returned him answer dark and short,
Or started from the theme to range
In loose digression wild and strange,
And forced the embarrassed host to buy
By query close direct reply.   200

XI

Awhile he glozed upon the cause
Of Commons, Covenant, and Laws,
And Church reformed — but felt rebuke
Beneath grim Bertram's sneering look,
Then stammered — 'Has a field been
   fought ?
Has Bertram news of battle brought ?
For sure a soldier, famed so far
In foreign fields for feats of war,
On eve of fight ne'er left the host
Until the field were won and lost.'   210
' Here, in your towers by circling Tees,
You, Oswald Wycliffe, rest at ease;
Why deem it strange that others come
To share such safe and easy home,
From fields where danger, death, and
   toil
Are the reward of civil broil ? ' —
' Nay, mock not, friend ! since well we
   know
The near advances of the foe,
To mar our northern army's work,
Encamped before beleaguered York   220
Thy horse with valiant Fairfax lay,
And must have fought — how went the
   day ? '

XII

' Wouldst hear the tale ? — On Marston
   heath
Met front to front the ranks of death;
Flourished the trumpets fierce, and now
Fired was each eye and flushed each brow;
On either side loud clamors ring,
" God and the Cause ! " — " God and the
   King ! "
Right English all, they rushed to blows,
With nought to win and all to lose.   230
I could have laughed — but lacked the
   time —
To see, in phrenesy sublime,
How the fierce zealots fought and bled
For king or state, as humor led;
Some for a dream of public good,
Some for church-tippet, gown, and hood,
Draining their veins, in death to claim
A patriot's or a martyr's name. —

Led Bertram Risingham the hearts
That countered there on adverse parts, 240
No superstitious fool had I
Sought El Dorados in the sky !
Chili had heard me through her states,
And Lima oped her silver gates,
Rich Mexico I had marched through,
And sacked the splendors of Peru,
Till sunk Pizarro's daring name,
And, Cortez, thine, in Bertram's fame.' —
'Still from the purpose wilt thou stray !
Good gentle friend, how went the day ?' 250

XIII

'Good am I deemed at trumpet sound,
And good where goblets dance the round,
Though gentle ne'er was joined till now
With rugged Bertram's breast and brow. —
But I resume.   The battle's rage
Was like the strife which currents wage
Where Orinoco in his pride
Rolls to the main no tribute tide,
But 'gainst broad ocean urges far
A rival sea of roaring war; 260
While, in ten thousand eddies driven,
The billows fling their foam to heaven,
And the pale pilot seeks in vain
Where rolls the river, where the main
Even thus upon the bloody field
The eddying tides of conflict wheeled
Ambiguous, till that heart of flame,
Hot Rupert, on our squadrons came,
Hurling against our spears a line
Of gallants fiery as their wine; 270
Then ours, though stubborn in their zeal,
In zeal's despite began to reel.
What wouldst thou more ? — in tumult tost,
Our leaders fell, our ranks were lost.
A thousand men who drew the sword
For both the Houses and the Word,
Preached forth from hamlet, grange, and down,
To curb the crosier and the crown,
Now, stark and stiff, lie stretched in gore,
And ne'er shall rail at mitre more. — 280
Thus fared it when I left the fight
With the good Cause and Commons' right.' —

XIV

'Disastrous news !' dark Wycliffe said;
Assumed despondence bent his head,
While troubled joy was in his eye,
The well-feigned sorrow to belie. —

'Disastrous news ! — when needed most,
Told ye not that your chiefs were lost ?
Complete the woful tale and say
Who fell upon that fatal day, 290
What leaders of repute and name
Bought by their death a deathless fame.
If such my direst foeman's doom,
My tears shall dew his honored tomb. —
No answer ? — Friend, of all our host,
Thou know'st whom I should hate the most,
Whom thou too once wert wont to hate,
Yet leavest me doubtful of his fate.' —
With look unmoved — ' Of friend or foe,
Aught,' answered Bertram, ' wouldst thou know, 300
Demand in simple terms and plain,
A soldier's answer shalt thou gain;
For question dark or riddle high
I have nor judgment nor reply.'

XV

The wrath his art and fear suppressed
Now blazed at once in Wycliffe's breast,
And brave from man so meanly born
Roused his hereditary scorn.
' Wretch ! hast thou paid thy bloody debt ?
PHILIP OF MORTHAM, lives he yet ? 310
False to thy patron or thine oath,
Traitorous or perjured, one or both.
Slave ! hast thou kept thy promise plight,
To slay thy leader in the fight ?'
Then from his seat the soldier sprung,
And Wycliffe's hand he strongly wrung;
His grasp, as hard as glove of mail,
Forced the red blood-drop from the nail —
'A health !' he cried; and ere he quaffed
Flung from him Wycliffe's hand and laughed — 320
'Now, Oswald Wycliffe, speaks thy heart !
Now play'st thou well thy genuine part !
Worthy, but for thy craven fear,
Like me to roam a buccaneer.
What reck'st thou of the Cause divine,
If Mortham's wealth and lands be thine ?
What carest thou for beleaguered York,
If this good hand have done its work ?
Or what though Fairfax and his best
Are reddening Marston's swarthy breast, 330
If Philip Mortham with them lie,
Lending his life-blood to the dye ? —
Sit, then ! and as mid comrades free
Carousing after victory,
When tales are told of blood and fear
That boys and women shrink to hear,

From point to point I frankly tell
The deed of death as it befell.

XVI

‘ When purposed vengeance I forego,
Term me a wretch, nor deem me foe; 340
And when an insult I forgive,
Then brand me as a slave and live ! —
Philip of Mortham is with those
Whom Bertram Risingham calls foes;
Or whom more sure revenge attends,
If numbered with ungrateful friends.
As was his wont, ere battle glowed,
Along the marshalled ranks he rode,
And wore his visor up the while.
I saw his melancholy smile 350
When, full opposed in front, he knew
Where ROKEBY’S kindred banner flew.
“And thus,” he said, “ will friends divide ! ” —
I heard, and thought how side by side
We two had turned the battle’s tide
In many a well-debated field
Where Bertram’s breast was Philip’s shield.
I thought on Darien’s deserts pale
Where death bestrides the evening gale;
How o’er my friend my cloak I threw, 360
And fenceless faced the deadly dew;
I thought on Quariana’s cliff
Where, rescued from our foundering skiff,
Through the white breakers’ wrath I bore
Exhausted Mortham to the shore;
And, when his side an arrow found,
I sucked the Indian’s venomed wound.
These thoughts like torrents rushed along,
To sweep away my purpose strong.

XVII

‘ Hearts are not flint, and flints are rent; 370
Hearts are not steel, and steel is bent.
When Mortham bade me, as of yore,
Be near him in the battle’s roar,
I scarcely saw the spears laid low,
I scarcely heard the trumpets blow;
Lost was the war in inward strife,
Debating Mortham’s death or life.
’T was then I thought how, lured to come
As partner of his wealth and home,
Years of piratic wandering o’er, 380
With him I sought our native shore.
But Mortham’s lord grew far estranged
From the bold heart with whom he ranged;
Doubts, horrors, superstitious fears,
Saddened and dimmed descending years;

The wily priests their victim sought,
And damned each free-born deed and thought.
Then must I seek another home,
My license shook his sober dome;
If gold he gave, in one wild day 390
I revelled thrice the sum away.
An idle outcast then I strayed,
Unfit for tillage or for trade.
Deemed, like the steel of rusted lance,
Useless and dangerous at once.
The women feared my hardy look,
At my approach the peaceful shook;
The merchant saw my glance of flame,
And locked his hoards when Bertram came;
Each child of coward peace kept far 400
From the neglected son of war.

XVIII

‘ But civil discord gave the call,
And made my trade the trade of all.
By Mortham urged, I came again
His vassals to the fight to train.
What guerdon waited on my care ?
I could not cant of creed or prayer;
Sour fanatics each trust obtained,
And I, dishonored and disdained,
Gained but the high and happy lot 410
In these poor arms to front the shot ! —
All this thou know’st, thy gestures tell;
Yet hear it o’er and mark it well.
’T is honor bids me now relate
Each circumstance of Mortham’s fate.

XIX

‘ Thoughts, from the tongue that slowly part,
Glance quick as lightning through the heart.
As my spur pressed my courser’s side,
Philip of Mortham’s cause was tried,
And ere the charging squadrons mixed 420
His plea was cast, his doom was fixed.
I watched him through the doubtful fray,
That changed as March’s moody day,
Till, like a stream that bursts its bank,
Fierce Rupert thundered on our flank.
’T was then, midst tumult, smoke, and strife,
Where each man fought for death or life,
’T was then I fired my petronel,
And Mortham, steed and rider, fell.
One dying look he upward cast, 430
Of wrath and anguish — ’t was his last.
Think not that there I stopped, to view
What of the battle should ensue;

But ere I cleared that bloody press,
Our northern horse ran masterless;
Monckton and Mitton told the news
How troops of Roundheads choked the
    Ouse,
And many a bonny Scot aghast,
Spurring his palfrey northward, past,
Cursing the day when zeal or meed   440
First lured their Lesley o'er the Tweed.
Yet when I reached the banks of Swale,
Had rumor learned another tale;
With his barbed horse, fresh tidings say,
Stout Cromwell has redeemed the day:
But whether false the news or true,
Oswald, I reck as light as you.'

XX

Not then by Wycliffe might be shown
How his pride startled at the tone
In which his complice, fierce and free,   450
Asserted guilt's equality.
In smoothest terms his speech he wove
Of endless friendship, faith, and love;
Promised and vowed in courteous sort,
But Bertram broke professions short.
' Wycliffe, be sure not here I stay,
No, scarcely till the rising day;
Warned by the legends of my youth,
I trust not an associate's truth.
Do not my native dales prolong   460
Of Percy Rede the tragic song,
Trained forward to his bloody fall,
By Girsonfield, that treacherous Hall ?
Oft by the Pringle's haunted side
The shepherd sees his spectre glide.
And near the spot that gave me name,
The moated mound of Risingham,
Where Reed her margin sees
Sweet Woodburne's cottages and trees,
Some ancient sculptor's art has shown   470
An outlaw's image on the stone;
Unmatched in strength, a giant he,
With quivered back and kirtled knee.
Ask how he died, that hunter bold,
The tameless monarch of the wold,
And age and infancy can tell
By brother's treachery he fell.
Thus warned by legends of my youth,
I trust to no associate's truth.

XXI

' When last we reasoned of this deed,   480
Nought, I bethink me, was agreed,
Or by what rule, or when, or where,
The wealth of Mortham we should share;

Then list while I the portion name
Our differing laws give each to claim.
Thou, vassal sworn to England's throne,
Her rules of heritage must own;
They deal thee, as to nearest heir,
Thy kinsman's lands and livings fair,
And these I yield: — do thou revere   490
The statutes of the buccaneer.
Friend to the sea, and foeman sworn
To all that on her waves are borne,
When falls a mate in battle broil
His comrade heirs his portioned spoil;
When dies in fight a daring fôe
He claims his wealth who struck the
    blow;
And either rule to me assigns
Those spoils of Indian seas and mines
Hoarded in Mortham's caverns dark;   500
Ingot of gold and diamond spark,
Chalice and plate from churches borne,
And gems from shrieking beauty torn,
Each string of pearl, each silver bar,
And all the wealth of western war.
I go to search where, dark and deep,
Those trans-Atlantic treasures sleep.
Thou must along — for, lacking thee,
The heir will scarce find entrance free;
And then farewell.   I haste to try   510
Each varied pleasure wealth can buy;
When cloyed each wish, these wars afford
Fresh work for Bertram's restless sword.'

XXII

An undecided answer hung
On Oswald's hesitating tongue.
Despite his craft, he heard with awe
This ruffian stabber fix the law;
While his own troubled passions veer
Through hatred, joy, regret, and fear: —
Joyed at the soul that Bertram flies,   520
He grudged the murderer's mighty prize,
Hated his pride's presumptuous tone,
And feared to wend with him alone.
At length, that middle course to steer
To cowardice and craft so dear,
' His charge,' he said, ' would ill allow
His absence from the fortress now;
WILFRID on Bertram should attend,
His son should journey with his friend.'

XXIII

Contempt kept Bertram's anger down,   530
And wreathed to savage smile his frown.
' Wilfrid, or thou — 't is one to me,
Whichever bears the golden key.

Yet think not but I mark, and smile
To mark, thy poor and selfish wile !
If injury from me you fear,
What, Oswald Wycliffe, shields thee here ?
I 've sprung from walls more high than
    these,
I 've swam through deeper streams than
    Tees.
Might I not stab thee ere one yell   540
Could rouse the distant sentinel ?
Start not — it is not my design,
But, if it were, weak fence were thine;
And, trust me that in time of need
This hand hath done more desperate
    deed.
Go, haste and rouse thy slumbering son;
Time calls, and I must needs be gone.'

XXIV

Nought of his sire's ungenerous part
Polluted Wilfrid's gentle heart,
A heart too soft from early life
To hold with fortune needful strife.   550
His sire, while yet a hardier race
Of numerous sons were Wycliffe's grace,
On Wilfrid set contemptuous brand
For feeble heart and forceless hand;
But a fond mother's care and joy
Were centred in her sickly boy.
No touch of childhood's frolic mood
Showed the elastic spring of blood;
Hour after hour he loved to pore
On Shakespeare's rich and varied lore,   560
But turned from martial scenes and light,
From Falstaff's feast and Percy's fight,
To ponder Jaques' moral strain,
And muse with Hamlet, wise in vain,
And weep himself to soft repose
O'er gentle Desdemona's woes.

XXV

In youth he sought not pleasures found
By youth in horse and hawk and hound,
But loved the quiet joys that wake   570
By lonely stream and silent lake;
In Deepdale's solitude to lie,
Where all is cliff and copse and sky;
To climb Catcastle's dizzy peak,
Or lone Pendragon's mound to seek.
Such was his wont; and there his dream
Soared on some wild fantastic theme
Of faithful love or ceaseless spring,
Till Contemplation's wearied wing
The enthusiast could no more sustain,   580
And sad he sunk to earth again.

XXVI

He loved — as many a lay can tell,
Preserved in Stanmore's lonely dell;
For his was minstrel's skill, he caught
The art unteachable, untaught;
He loved — his soul did nature frame
For love, and fancy nursed the flame;
Vainly he loved — for seldom swain
Of such soft mould is loved again;
Silent he loved — in every gaze   590
Was passion, friendship in his phrase;
So mused his life away — till died
His brethren all, their father's pride.
Wilfrid is now the only heir
Of all his stratagems and care,
And destined darkling to pursue
Ambition's maze by Oswald's clue.

XXVII

Wilfrid must love and woo the bright
Matilda, heir of Rokeby's knight.
To love her was an easy hest,   600
The secret empress of his breast;
To woo her was a harder task
To one that durst not hope or ask.
Yet all Matilda could she gave
In pity to her gentle slave;
Friendship, esteem, and fair regard,
And praise, the poet's best reward !
She read the tales his taste approved,
And sung the lays he framed or loved;
Yet, loath to nurse the fatal flame   610
Of hopeless love in friendship's name,
In kind caprice she oft withdrew
The favoring glance to friendship due,
Then grieved to see her victim's pain,
And gave the dangerous smiles again.

XXVIII

So did the suit of Wilfrid stand
When war's loud summons waked the
    land.
Three banners, floating o'er the Tees,
The woe-foreboding peasant sees;
In concert oft they braved of old   620
The bordering Scot's incursion bold:
Frowning defiance in their pride,
Their vassals now and lords divide.
From his fair hall on Greta banks,
The Knight of Rokeby led his ranks,
To aid the valiant northern earls
Who drew the sword for royal Charles.
Mortham, by marriage near allied, —
His sister had been Rokeby's bride,
Though long before the civil fray   630

In peaceful grave the lady lay, —
Philip of Mortham raised his band,
And marched at Fairfax's command;
While Wycliffe, bound by many a train
Of kindred art with wily Vane,
Less prompt to brave the bloody field,
Made Barnard's battlements his shield,
Secured them with his Lunedale powers,
And for the Commons held the towers.

XXIX

The lovely heir of Rokeby's Knight   640
Waits in his halls the event of fight;
For England's war revered the claim
Of every unprotected name,
And spared amid its fiercest rage
Childhood and womanhood and age.
But Wilfrid, son to Rokeby's foe,
Must the dear privilege forego,
By Greta's side in evening gray,
To steal upon Matilda's way,
Striving with fond hypocrisy   650
For careless step and vacant eye;
Calming each anxious look and glance,
To give the meeting all to chance,
Or framing as a fair excuse
The book, the pencil, or the muse;
Something to give, to sing, to say,
Some modern tale, some ancient lay.
Then, while the longed-for minutes last, —
Ah! minutes quickly over-past! —
Recording each expression free   660
Of kind or careless courtesy,
Each friendly look, each softer tone,
As food for fancy when alone.
All this is o'er — but still unseen
Wilfrid may lurk in Eastwood green,
To watch Matilda's wonted round,
While springs his heart at every sound.
She comes! — 't is but a passing sight,
Yet serves to cheat his weary night;
She comes not — he will wait the hour   670
When her lamp lightens in the tower;
'T is something yet if, as she past,
Her shade is o'er the lattice cast.
'What is my life, my hope?' he said;
'Alas! a transitory shade.'

XXX

Thus wore his life, though reason strove
For mastery in vain with love,
Forcing upon his thoughts the sum
Of present woe and ills to come,
While still he turned impatient ear   680
From Truth's intrusive voice severe.

Gentle, indifferent, and subdued,
In all but this unmoved he viewed
Each outward change of ill and good:
But Wilfrid, docile, soft, and mild,
Was Fancy's spoiled and wayward child;
In her bright car she bade him ride,
With one fair form to grace his side,
Or, in some wild and lone retreat,
Flung her high spells around his seat,   690
Bathed in her dews his languid head,
Her fairy mantle o'er him spread,
For him her opiates gave to flow,
Which he who tastes can ne'er forego,
And placed him in her circle, free
From every stern reality,
Till to the Visionary seem
Her day-dreams truth, and truth a dream.

XXXI

Woe to the youth whom Fancy gains,
Winning from Reason's hand the reins,   700
Pity and woe! for such a mind
Is soft, contemplative, and kind;
And woe to those who train such youth,
And spare to press the rights of truth,
The mind to strengthen and anneal
While on the stithy glows the steel!
O teach him while your lessons last
To judge the present by the past;
Remind him of each wish pursued,
How rich it glowed with promised good;   710
Remind him of each wish enjoyed,
How soon his hopes possession cloyed!
Tell him we play unequal game
Whene'er we shoot by Fancy's aim;
And, ere he strip him for her race,
Show the conditions of the chase:
Two sisters by the goal are set,
Cold Disappointment and Regret;
One disenchants the winner's eyes,
And strips of all its worth the prize.   720
While one augments its gaudy show,
More to enhance the loser's woe.
The victor sees his fairy gold
Transformed when won to drossy mould,
But still the vanquished mourns his loss,
And rues as gold that glittering dross.

XXXII

More wouldst thou know — yon tower sur-
        vey,
Yon couch unpressed since parting day,
Yon untrimmed lamp, whose yellow gleam
Is mingling with the cold moonbeam,   730
And yon thin form! — the hectic red

On his pale cheek unequal spread;
The head reclined, the loosened hair,
The limbs relaxed, the mournful air. —
See, he looks up; — a woful smile
Lightens his woe-worn cheek a while, —
'T is Fancy wakes some idle thought,
To gild the ruin she has wrought;
For, like the bat of Indian brakes,
Her pinions fan the wound she makes,   740
And, soothing thus the dreamer's pain,
She drinks his life-blood from the vein.
Now to the lattice turn his eyes,
Vain hope ! to see the sun arise.
The moon with clouds is still o'ercast,
Still howls by fits the stormy blast;
Another hour must wear away
Ere the east kindle into day,
And hark ! to waste that weary hour,
He tries the minstrel's magic power.   750

XXXIII

SONG

TO THE MOON

Hail to thy cold and clouded beam,
    Pale pilgrim of the troubled sky !
Hail, though the mists that o'er thee stream
    Lend to thy brow their sullen dye !
How should thy pure and peaceful eye
    Untroubled view our scenes below,
Or how a tearless beam supply
    To light a world of war and woe !

Fair Queen ! I will not blame thee now,
    As once by Greta's fairy side;   760
Each little cloud that dimmed thy brow
    Did then an angel's beauty hide.
And of the shades I then could chide,
    Still are the thoughts to memory dear,
For, while a softer strain I tried,
    They hid my blush and calmed my fear.

Then did I swear thy ray serene
    Was formed to light some lonely dell,
By two fond lovers only seen,
    Reflected from the crystal well;   770
Or sleeping on their mossy cell,
    Or quivering on the lattice bright,
Or glancing on their couch, to tell
    How swiftly wanes the summer night !

XXXIV

He starts — a step at this lone hour !
A voice ! — his father seeks the tower,
With haggard look and troubled sense,
Fresh from his dreadful conference.
'Wilfrid ! — what, not to sleep addressed ?
Thou hast no cares to chase thy rest.   780
Mortham has fallen on Marston-moor;
Bertram brings warrant to secure
His treasures, bought by spoil and blood,
For the state's use and public good.
The menials will thy voice obey;
Let his commission have its way,
In every point, in every word.'
Then, in a whisper, — 'Take thy sword !
Bertram is — what I must not tell.
I hear his hasty step — farewell !'   790

CANTO SECOND

I

FAR in the chambers of the west,
The gale had sighed itself to rest;
The moon was cloudless now and clear,
But pale and soon to disappear.
The thin gray clouds waxed dimly light
On Brusleton and Houghton height;
And the rich dale that eastward lay
Waited the wakening touch of day,
To give its woods and cultured plain,
And towers and spires, to light again.   10
But, westward, Stanmore's shapeless swell,
And Lunedale wild, and Kelton-fell,
And rock-begirdled Gilmanscar,
And Arkingarth, lay dark afar;
While as a livelier twilight falls,
Emerge proud Barnard's bannered walls.
High crowned he sits in dawning pale,
The sovereign of the lovely vale.

II

What prospects from his watch-tower high
Gleam gradual on the warder's eye !   —   20
Far sweeping to the east, he sees
Down his deep woods the course of Tees,
And tracks his wanderings by the steam
Of summer vapors from the stream;
And ere he pace his destined hour
By Brackenbury's dungeon-tower,
These silver mists shall melt away
And dew the woods with glittering spray.
Then in broad lustre shall be shown
That mighty trench of living stone,   30
And each huge trunk that from the side
Reclines him o'er the darksome tide
Where Tees, full many a fathom low,

Wears with his rage no common foe;
For pebbly bank, nor sand-bed here,
Nor clay-mound, checks his fierce career,
Condemned to mine a channelled way
O'er solid sheets of marble gray.

III

Nor Tees alone in dawning bright
Shall rush upon the ravished sight;   40
But many a tributary stream
Each from its own dark cell shall gleam :
Staindrop, who from her sylvan bowers
Salutes proud Raby's battled towers;
The rural brook of Egliston,
And Balder, named from Odin's son;
And Greta, to whose banks ere long
We lead the lovers of the song;
And silver Lune from Stanmore wild,
And fairy Thorsgill's murmuring child,   50
And last and least, but loveliest still,
Romantic Deepdale's slender rill.
Who in that dim-wood glen hath strayed,
Yet longed for Roslin's magic glade ?
Who, wandering there, hath sought to
          change
Even for that vale so stern and strange
Where Cartland's crags, fantastic rent,
Through her green copse like spires are
          sent ?
Yet, Albin, yet the praise be thine,
Thy scenes and story to combine !   60
Thou bid'st him who by Roslin strays
List to the deeds of other days;
Mid Cartland's crags thou show'st the
          cave,
The refuge of thy champion brave;
Giving each rock its storied tale,
Pouring a lay for every dale,
Knitting, as with a moral band,
Thy native legends with thy land,
To lend each scene the interest high
Which genius beams from Beauty's eye.   70

IV

Bertram awaited not the sight
Which sunrise shows from Barnard's
          height,
But from the towers, preventing day,
With Wilfrid took his early way,
While misty dawn and moonbeam pale
Still mingled in the silent dale.
By Barnard's bridge of stately stone
The southern bank of Tees they won;
Their winding path then eastward cast,
And Egliston's gray ruins passed;   80

Each on his own deep visions bent,
Silent and sad they onward went.
Well may you think that Bertram's mood
To Wilfrid savage seemed and rude;
Well may you think bold Risingham
Held Wilfrid trivial, poor, and tame;
And small the intercourse, I ween,
Such uncongenial souls between.

V

Stern Bertram shunned the nearer way
Through Rokeby's park and chase that
          lay,   90
And, skirting high the valley's ridge,
They crossed by Greta's ancient bridge,
Descending where her waters wind
Free for a space and unconfined
As, 'scaped from Brignall's dark-wood glen,
She seeks wild Mortham's deeper den.
There, as his eye glanced o'er the mound
Raised by that Legion long renowned
Whose votive shrine asserts their claim
Of pious, faithful, conquering fame,   100
' Stern sons of war ! ' sad Wilfrid sighed,
' Behold the boast of Roman pride !
What now of all your toils are known ?
A grassy trench, a broken stone ! ' —
This to himself; for moral strain
To Bertram were addressed in vain.

VI

Of different mood a deeper sigh
Awoke when Rokeby's turrets high
Were northward in the dawning seen
To rear them o'er the thicket green.   110
O then, though Spenser's self had strayed
Beside him through the lovely glade,
Lending his rich luxuriant glow
Of fancy all its charms to show,
Pointing the stream rejoicing free
As captive set at liberty,
Flashing her sparkling waves abroad,
And clamoring joyful on her road;
Pointing where, up the sunny banks,
The trees retire in scattered ranks,   120
Save where, advanced before the rest,
On knoll or hillock rears his crest,
Lonely and huge, the giant Oak,
As champions when their band is broke
Stand forth to guard the rearward post,
The bulwark of the scattered host —
All this and more might Spenser say,
Yet waste in vain his magic lay,
While Wilfrid eyed the distant tower
Whose lattice lights Matilda's bower.   130

VII

The open vale is soon passed o'er,
Rokeby, though nigh, is seen no more;
Sinking mid Greta's thickets deep,
A wild and darker course they keep,
A stern and lone yet lovely road
As e'er the foot of minstrel trode !
Broad shadows o'er their passage fell,
Deeper and narrower grew the dell;
It seemed some mountain, rent and riven,
A channel for the stream had given,   140
So high the cliffs of limestone gray
Hung beetling o'er the torrent's way,
Yielding along their rugged base
A flinty footpath's niggard space,
Where he who winds 'twixt rock and
      wave
May hear the headlong torrent rave,
And like a steed in frantic fit,
That flings the froth from curb and bit,
May view her chafe her waves to spray
O'er every rock that bars her way,   150
Till foam-globes on her eddies ride,
Thick as the schemes of human pride
That down life's current drive amain,
As frail, as frothy, and as vain !

VIII

The cliffs that rear their haughty head
High o'er the river's darksome bed
Were now all naked, wild, and gray,
Now waving all with greenwood spray;
Here trees to every crevice clung
And o'er the dell their branches hung;   160
And there, all splintered and uneven,
The shivered rocks ascend to heaven;
Oft, too, the ivy swathed their breast
And wreathed its garland round their
      crest,
Or from the spires bade loosely flare
Its tendrils in the middle air.
As pennons wont to wave of old
O'er the high feast of baron bold,
When revelled loud the feudal rout   169
And the arched halls returned their shout,
Such and more wild is Greta's roar,
And such the echoes from her shore,
And so the ivied banners gleam,
Waved wildly o'er the brawling stream.

IX

Now from the stream the rocks recede,
But leave between no sunny mead,
No, nor the spot of pebbly sand
Oft found by such a mountain strand.

Forming such warm and dry retreat
As fancy deems the lonely seat   180
Where hermit, wandering from his cell,
His rosary might love to tell.
But here 'twixt rock and river grew
A dismal grove of sable yew,
With whose sad tints were mingled seen
The blighted fir's sepulchral green.
Seemed that the trees their shadows cast
The earth that nourished them to blast;
For never knew that swarthy grove
The verdant hue that fairies love,   190
Nor wilding green nor woodland flower
Arose within its baleful bower:
The dank and sable earth receives
Its only carpet from the leaves
That, from the withering branches cast,
Bestrewed the ground with every blast.
Though now the sun was o'er the hill,
In this dark spot 't was twilight still,
Save that on Greta's farther side
Some straggling beams through copsewood
      glide;   200
And wild and savage contrast made
That dingle's deep and funeral shade
With the bright tints of early day,
Which, glimmering through the ivy spray,
On the opposing summit lay.

X

The lated peasant shunned the dell;
For Superstition wont to tell
Of many a grisly sound and sight,
Scaring its path at dead of night.   209
When Christmas logs blaze high and wide
Such wonders speed the festal tide,
While Curiosity and Fear,
Pleasure and Pain, sit crouching near,
Till childhood's cheek no longer glows,
And village maidens lose the rose.
The thrilling interest rises higher,
The circle closes nigh and nigher,
And shuddering glance is cast behind,
As louder moans the wintry wind.
Believe that fitting scene was laid   22c
For such wild tales in Mortham glade;
For who had seen on Greta's side
By that dim light fierce Bertram stride,
In such a spot, at such an hour, —
If touched by Superstition's power,
Might well have deemed that Hell had
      given
A murderer's ghost to upper heaven,
While Wilfrid's form had seemed to glide
Like his pale victim by his side.

XI

Nor think to village swains alone 230
Are these unearthly terrors known,
For not to rank nor sex confined
Is this vain ague of the mind;
Hearts firm as steel, as marble hard,
'Gainst faith and love and pity barred,
Have quaked, like aspen leaves in May,
Beneath its universal sway.
Bertram had listed many a tale
Of wonder in his native dale,
That in his secret soul retained 240
The credence they in childhood gained:
Nor less his wild adventurous youth
Believed in every legend's truth;
Learned when beneath the tropic gale
Full swelled the vessel's steady sail,
And the broad Indian moon her light
Poured on the watch of middle night,
When seamen love to hear and tell
Of portent, prodigy, and spell: 249
What gales are sold on Lapland's shore,
How whistle rash bids tempests roar,
Of witch, of mermaid, and of sprite,
Of Erick's cap and Elmo's light;
Or of that Phantom Ship whose form
Shoots like a meteor through the storm
When the dark scud comes driving hard,
And lowered is every top-sail yard,
And canvas wove in earthly looms
No more to brave the storm presumes !
Then mid the war of sea and sky, 260
Top and top-gallant hoisted high,
Full spread and crowded every sail,
The Demon Frigate braves the gale,
And well the doomed spectators know
The harbinger of wreck and woe.

XII

Then, too, were told in stifled tone
Marvels and omens all their own;
How, by some desert isle or key,
Where Spaniards wrought their cruelty,
Or where the savage pirate's mood 270
Repaid it home in deeds of blood,
Strange nightly sounds of woe and fear
Appalled the listening buccaneer,
Whose light-armed shallop anchored lay
In ambush by the lonely bay.
The groan of grief, the shriek of pain,
Ring from the moonlight groves of cane;
The fierce adventurer's heart they scare,
Who wearies memory for a prayer,
Curses the roadstead, and with gale 280
Of early morning lifts the sail,

To give, in thirst of blood and prey,
A legend for another bay.

XIII

Thus, as a man, a youth, a child,
Trained in the mystic and the wild,
With this on Bertram's soul at times
Rushed a dark feeling of his crimes;
Such to his troubled soul their form
As the pale Death-ship to the storm,
And such their omen dim and dread 290
As shrieks and voices of the dead.
That pang, whose transitory force
Hovered 'twixt horror and remorse —
That pang, perchance, his bosom pressed
As Wilfrid sudden he addressed:
' Wilfrid, this glen is never trod
Until the sun rides high abroad,
Yet twice have I beheld to-day
A form that seemed to dog our way;
Twice from my glance it seemed to flee 300
And shroud itself by cliff or tree.
How think'st thou ? — Is our path way-
laid ?
Or hath thy sire my trust betrayed ?
If so ' — Ere, starting from his dream
That turned upon a gentler theme,
Wilfrid had roused him to reply,
Bertram sprung forward, shouting high,
' Whate'er thou art, thou now shalt stand ! '
And forth he darted, sword in hand.

XIV

As bursts the levin in its wrath, 310
He shot him down the sounding path;
Rock, wood, and stream rang wildly out
To his loud step and savage shout.
Seems that the object of his race
Hath scaled the cliffs; his frantic chase
Sidelong he turns, and now 't is bent
Right up the rock's tall battlement;
Straining each sinew to ascend,
Foot, hand, and knee their aid must lend.
Wilfrid, all dizzy with dismay, 320
Views from beneath his dreadful way:
Now to the oak's warped roots he clings,
Now trusts his weight to ivy strings,
Now, like the wild-goat, must he dare
An unsupported leap in air;
Hid in the shrubby rain-course now,
You mark him by the crashing bough,
And by his corselet's sullen clank,
And by the stones spurned from the bank,
And by the hawk scared from her nest, 330
And raven's croaking o'er their guest,

Who deem his forfeit limbs shall pay
The tribute of his bold essay.

XV

See, he emerges ! — desperate now
All farther course — yon beetling brow,
In craggy nakedness sublime,
What heart or foot shall dare to climb ?
It bears no tendril for his clasp,
Presents no angle to his grasp:
Sole stay his foot may rest upon   340
Is yon earth-bedded jetting stone.
Balanced on such precarious prop,
He strains his grasp to reach the top.
Just as the dangerous stretch he makes,
By heaven, his faithless footstool shakes !
Beneath his tottering bulk it bends,
It sways, it loosens, it descends,
And downward holds its headlong way,
Crashing o'er rock and copsewood spray !
Loud thunders shake the echoing dell !   350
Fell it alone ? — alone it fell.
Just on the very verge of fate,
The hardy Bertram's falling weight
He trusted to his sinewy hands,
And on the top unharmed, he stands !

XVI

Wilfrid a safer path pursued,
At intervals where, roughly hewed,
Rude steps ascending from the dell
Rendered the cliffs accessible.
By circuit slow he thus attained
The height that Risingham had gained,   360
And when he issued from the wood
Before the gate of Mortham stood.
'T was a fair scene ! the sunbeam lay
On battled tower and portal gray;
And from the grassy slope he sees
The Greta flow to meet the Tees
Where, issuing from her darksome bed,
She caught the morning's eastern red,
And through the softening vale below   370
Rolled her bright waves in rosy glow,
All blushing to her bridal bed,
Like some shy maid in convent bred,
While linnet, lark, and blackbird gay
Sing forth her nuptial roundelay.

XVII

'T was sweetly sung that roundelay,
That summer morn shone blithe and gay;
But morning beam and wild-bird's call
Awaked not Mortham's silent hall.

No porter by the low-browed gate   380
Took in the wonted niche his seat;
To the paved court no peasant drew;
Waked to their toil no menial crew;
The maiden's carol was not heard,
As to her morning task she fared:
In the void offices around
Rung not a hoof nor bayed a hound;
Nor eager steed with shrilling neigh
Accused the lagging groom's delay;
Untrimmed, undressed, neglected now,   390
Was alleyed walk and orchard bough;
All spoke the master's absent care,
All spoke neglect and disrepair.
South of the gate an arrow flight,
Two mighty elms their limbs unite,
As if a canopy to spread
O'er the lone dwelling of the dead;
For their huge boughs in arches bent
Above a massive monument,
Carved o'er in ancient Gothic wise   400
With many a scutcheon and device:
There, spent with toil and sunk in gloom,
Bertram stood pondering by the tomb.

XVIII

' It vanished like a flitting ghost !
Behind this tomb,' he said, ' 't was lost —
This tomb where oft I deemed lies stored
Of Mortham's Indian wealth the hoard.
'T is true, the aged servants said
Here his lamented wife is laid;
But weightier reasons may be guessed   410
For their lord's strict and stern behest
That none should on his steps intrude
Whene'er he sought this solitude.
An ancient mariner I knew,
What time I sailed with Morgan's crew,
Who oft mid our carousals spake
Of Raleigh, Frobisher, and Drake;
Adventurous hearts ! who bartered, bold,
Their English steel for Spanish gold.
Trust not, would his experience say,   420
Captain or comrade with your prey,
But seek some charnel, when, at full,
The moon gilds skeleton and skull:
There dig and tomb your precious heap,
And bid the dead your treasure keep;
Sure stewards they, if fitting spell
Their service to the task compel.
Lacks there such charnel ? — kill a slave
Or prisoner on the treasure-grave,
And bid his discontented ghost   430
Stalk nightly on his lonely post.

Such was his tale. Its truth, I ween,
Is in my morning vision seen.'

XIX

Wilfrid, who scorned the legend wild,
In mingled mirth and pity smiled,
Much marvelling that a breast so bold
In such fond tale belief should hold,
But yet of Bertram sought to know
The apparition's form and show.
The power within the guilty breast,   440
Oft vanquished, never quite suppressed,
That unsubdued and lurking lies
To take the felon by surprise
And force him, as by magic spell,
In his despite his guilt to tell —
That power in Bertram's breast awoke;
Scarce conscious he was heard, he spoke;
' 'T was Mortham's form, from foot to
head !
His morion with the plume of red,
His shape, his mien — 't was Mortham,
right   450
As when I slew him in the fight.' —
' Thou slay him ? — thou ? ' — With con-
scious start
He heard, them manned his haughty
heart —
' I slew him ? — I ! — I had forgot
Thou, stripling, knew'st not of the plot.
But it is spoken — nor will I
Deed done or spoken word deny.
I slew him; I ! for thankless pride;
'T was by this hand that Mortham died.'

XX

Wilfrid, of gentle hand and heart,   460
Averse to every active part,
But most adverse to martial broil,
From danger shrunk and turned from
toil;
Yet the meek lover of the lyre
Nursed one brave spark of noble fire;
Against injustice, fraud, or wrong
His blood beat high, his hand waxed strong.
Not his the nerves that could sustain,
Unshaken, danger, toil, and pain;   469
But, when that spark blazed forth to flame,
He rose superior to his frame.
And now it came, that generous mood;
And, in full current of his blood,
On Bertram he laid desperate hand,
Placed firm his foot, and drew his brand.
' Should every fiend to whom thou 'rt sold
Rise in thine aid, I keep my hold. —

Arouse there, ho ! take spear and sword !
Attach the murderer of your lord ! '

XXI

A moment, fixed as by a spell,   480
Stood Bertram — it seemed miracle,
That one so feeble, soft, and tame
Set grasp on warlike Risingham.
But when he felt a feeble stroke
The fiend within the ruffian woke !
To wrench the sword from Wilfrid's hand,
To dash him headlong on the sand,
Was but one moment's work, — one more
Had drenched the blade in Wilfrid's gore.
But in the instant it arose   490
To end his life, his love, his woes,
A warlike form that marked the scene
Presents his rapier sheathed between,
Parries the fast-descending blow,
And steps 'twixt Wilfrid and his foe;
Nor then unscabbarded his brand,
But, sternly pointing with his hand,
With monarch's voice forbade the fight,
And motioned Bertram from his sight.
' Go, and repent,' he said, ' while time   500
Is given thee; add not crime to crime.'

XXII

Mute and uncertain and amazed,
As on a vision Bertram gazed !
'T was Mortham's bearing, bold and high,
His sinewy frame, his falcon eye,
His look and accent of command,
The martial gesture of his hand,
His stately form, spare-built and tall,
His war-bleached locks — 't was Mortham
all.
Through Bertram's dizzy brain career   510
A thousand thoughts, and all of fear;
His wavering faith received not quite
The form he saw as Mortham's sprite,
But more he feared it if it stood
His lord in living flesh and blood.
What spectre can the charnel send,
So dreadful as an injured friend ?
Then, too, the habit of command,
Used by the leader of the band
When Risingham for many a day   520
Had marched and fought beneath his sway,
Tamed him — and with reverted face
Backwards he bore his sullen pace,
Oft stopped, and oft on Mortham stared,
And dark as rated mastiff glared,
But when the tramp of steeds was heard
Plunged in the glen and disappeared;

Nor longer there the warrior stood,
Retiring eastward through the wood,
But first to Wilfrid warning gives,   530
'Tell thou to none that Mortham lives.'

XXIII

Still rung these words in Wilfrid's ear,
Hinting he knew not what of fear,
When nearer came the coursers' tread,
And, with his father at their head,
Of horsemen armed a gallant power
Reined up their steeds before the tower.
'Whence these pale looks, my son?' he
      said:
'Where's Bertram? Why that naked
      blade?'
Wilfrid ambiguously replied —   540
For Mortham's charge his honor tied —
'Bertram is gone — the villain's word
Avouched him murderer of his lord!
Even now we fought — but when your
      tread
Announced you nigh, the felon fled.'
In Wycliffe's conscious eye appear
A guilty hope, a guilty fear;
On his pale brow the dew-drop broke,
And his lip quivered as he spoke:

XXIV

'A murderer! — Philip Mortham died   550
Amid the battle's wildest tide.
Wilfrid, or Bertram raves or you!
Yet, grant such strange confession true,
Pursuit were vain — let him fly far —
Justice must sleep in civil war.'
A gallant youth rode near his side,
Brave Rokeby's page, in battle tried;
That morn an embassy of weight
He brought to Barnard's castle gate,
And followed now in Wycliffe's train   560
An answer for his lord to gain.
His steed, whose arched and sable neck
An hundred wreaths of foam bedeck,
Chafed not against the curb more high
Than he at Oswald's cold reply;
He bit his lip, implored his saint —
His the old faith — then burst restraint:

XXV

'Yes! I beheld his bloody fall
By that base traitor's dastard ball,
Just when I thought to measure sword,   570
Presumptuous hope! with Mortham's lord.
And shall the murderer 'scape who slew

His leader, generous, brave, and true?
Escape, while on the dew you trace
The marks of his gigantic pace?
No! ere the sun that dew shall dry,
False Risingham shall yield or die. —
Ring out the castle larum bell!
Arouse the peasants with the knell!   579
Meantime disperse — ride, gallants, ride!
Beset the wood on every side.
But if among you one there be
That honors Mortham's memory,
Let him dismount and follow me!
Else on your crests sit fear and shame,
And foul suspicion dog your name!'

XXVI

Instant to earth young REDMOND sprung;
Instant on earth the harness rung
Of twenty men of Wycliffe's band,
Who waited not their lord's command.   590
Redmond his spurs from buskins drew,
His mantle from his shoulders threw,
His pistols in his belt he placed,
The green-wood gained, the footsteps
      traced,
Shouted like huntsman to his hounds,
'To cover, hark!'—and in he bounds.
Scarce heard was Oswald's anxious cry,
'Suspicion! yes — pursue him — fly —
But venture not in useless strife
On ruffian desperate of his life;   600
Whoever finds him shoot him dead!
Five hundred nobles for his head!'

XXVII

The horsemen galloped to make good
Each path that issued from the wood.
Loud from the thickets rung the shout
Of Redmond and his eager rout;
With them was Wilfrid, stung with ire,
And envying Redmond's martial fire,
And emulous of fame. — But where
Is Oswald, noble Mortham's heir?   610
He, bound by honor, law, and faith,
Avenger of his kinsman's death? —
Leaning against the elmin tree,
With drooping head and slackened knee,
And clenched teeth, and close-clasped
      hands,
In agony of soul he stands!
His downcast eye on earth is bent,
His soul to every sound is lent;
For in each shout that cleaves the air
May ring discovery and despair.   620

XXVIII

What 'vailed it him that brightly played
The morning sun on Mortham's glade ?
All seems in giddy round to ride,
Like objects on a stormy tide
Seen eddying by the moonlight dim,
Imperfectly to sink and swim.
What 'vailed it that the fair domain,
Its battled mansion, hill, and plain,
On which the sun so brightly shone,
Envied so long, was now his own ?   630
The lowest dungeon, in that hour,
Of Brackenbury's dismal tower,
Had been his choice, could such a doom
Have opened Mortham's bloody tomb !
Forced, too, to turn unwilling ear
To each surmise of hope or fear,
Murmured among the rustics round,
Who gathered at the larum sound,
He dare not turn his head away,
Even to look up to heaven to pray,   640
Or call on hell in bitter mood
For one sharp death-shot from the wood !

XXIX

At length o'erpast that dreadful space,
Back straggling came the scattered chase;
Jaded and weary, horse and man,
Returned the troopers one by one.
Wilfrid the last arrived to say
All trace was lost of Bertram's way,
Though Redmond still up Brignall wood
The hopeless quest in vain pursued.   650
O, fatal doom of human race !
What tyrant passions passions chase !
Remorse from Oswald's brow is gone,
Avarice and pride resume their throne;
The pang of instant terror by,
They dictate thus their slave's reply:

XXX

' Ay — let him range like hasty hound !
And if the grim wolf's lair be found,
Small is my care how goes the game
With Redmond or with Risingham. —   660
Nay, answer not, thou simple boy !
Thy fair Matilda, all so coy
To thee, is of another mood
To that bold youth of Erin's blood.
Thy ditties will she freely praise,
And pay thy pains with courtly phrase;
In a rough path will oft command —
Accept at least — thy friendly hand;
His she avoids, or, urged and prayed,
Unwilling takes his proffered aid,   670

While conscious passion plainly speaks
In downcast look and blushing cheeks.
Whene'er he sings will she glide nigh,
And all her soul is in her eye;
Yet doubts she still to tender free
The wonted words of courtesy.
These are strong signs ! — yet wherefore
      sigh,
And wipe, effeminate, thine eye ?
Thine shall she be, if thou attend
The counsels of thy sire and friend.   680

XXXI

' Scarce wert thou gone, when peep of
      light
Brought genuine news of Marston's fight.
Brave Cromwell turned the doubtful tide,
And conquest blessed the rightful side;
Three thousand cavaliers lie dead,
Rupert and that bold Marquis fled;
Nobles and knights, so proud of late,
Must fine for freedom and estate.
Of these committed to my charge
Is Rokeby, prisoner at large;   690
Redmond his page arrived to say
He reaches Barnard's towers to-day.
Right heavy shall his ransom be
Unless that maid compound with thee !
Go to her now — be bold of cheer
While her soul floats 'twixt hope and fear;
It is the very change of tide,
When best the female heart is tried —
Pride, prejudice, and modesty,
Are in the current swept to sea,   700
And the bold swain who plies his oar
May lightly row his bark to shore.'

CANTO THIRD

I

THE hunting tribes of air and earth
Respect the brethren of their birth;
Nature, who loves the claim of kind,
Less cruel chase to each assigned.
The falcon, poised on soaring wing,
Watches the wild-duck by the spring;
The slow-hound wakes the fox's lair;
The greyhound presses on the hare;
The eagle pounces on the lamb;
The wolf devours the fleecy dam: 10
Even tiger fell and sullen bear
Their likeness and their lineage spare;
Man only mars kind Nature's plan,
And turns the fierce pursuit on man,

Plying war's desultory trade,
Incursion, flight, and ambuscade,
Since Nimrod, Cush's mighty son,
At first the bloody game begun.

II

The Indian, prowling for his prey,
Who hears the settlers track his way,   20
And knows in distant forest far
Camp his red brethren of the war —
He, when each double and disguise
To baffle the pursuit he tries,
Low crouching now his head to hide
Where swampy streams through rushes glide,
Now covering with the withered leaves
The foot-prints that the dew receives —
He, skilled in every sylvan guile,
Knows not, nor tries, such various wile   30
As Risingham when on the wind
Arose the loud pursuit behind.
In Redesdale his youth had heard
Each art her wily dalesman dared,
When Rooken-edge and Redswair high
To bugle rung and blood-hound's cry,
Announcing Jedwood-axe and spear,
And Lid'sdale riders in the rear;
And well his venturous life had proved
The lessons that his childhood loved.   40

III

Oft had he shown in climes afar
Each attribute of roving war;
The sharpened ear, the piercing eye,
The quick resolve in danger nigh;
The speed that in the flight or chase
Outstripped the Charib's rapid race;
The steady brain, the sinewy limb,
To leap, to climb, to dive, to swim;
The iron frame, inured to bear
Each dire inclemency of air,   50
Nor less confirmed to undergo
Fatigue's faint chill and famine's throe.
These arts he proved, his life to save,
In peril oft by land and wave,
On Arawaca's desert shore,
Or where La Plata's billows roar,
When oft the sons of vengeful Spain
Tracked the marauder's steps in vain.
These arts, in Indian warfare tried,
Must save him now by Greta's side.   60

IV

'T was then, in hour of utmost need,
He proved his courage, art, and speed.

Now slow he stalked with stealthy pace,
Now started forth in rapid race,
Oft doubling back in mazy train
To blind the trace the dews retain;
Now clomb the rocks projecting high
To baffle the pursuer's eye;
Now sought the stream, whose brawling sound
The echo of his footsteps drowned.   70
But if the forest verge he nears,
There trample steeds, and glimmer spears;
If deeper down the copse he drew,
He heard the rangers' loud halloo,
Beating each cover while they came,
As if to start the sylvan game.
'T was then — like tiger close beset
At every pass with toil and net,
'Countered where'er he turns his glare
By clashing arms and torches' flare,   80
Who meditates with furious bound
To burst on hunter, horse and hound —
'T was then that Bertram's soul arose,
Prompting to rush upon his foes:
But as that crouching tiger, cowed
By brandished steel and shouting crowd,
Retreats beneath the jungle's shroud,
Bertram suspends his purpose stern,
And crouches in the brake and fern,
Hiding his face lest foemen spy   90
The sparkle of his swarthy eye.

V

Then Bertram might the bearing trace
Of the bold youth who led the chase;
Who paused to list for every sound,
Climbed every height to look around,
Then rushing on with naked sword,
Each dingle's bosky depths explored.
'T was Redmond — by the azure eye;
'T was Redmond — by the locks that fly
Disordered from his glowing cheek;   100
Mien, face, and form young Redmond speak.
A form more active, light, and strong,
Ne'er shot the ranks of war along;
The modest yet the manly mien
Might grace the court of maiden queen;
A face more fair you well might find,
For Redmond's knew the sun and wind,
Nor boasted, from their tinge when free,
The charm of regularity;
But every feature had the power   110
To aid the expression of the hour:
Whether gay wit and humor sly
Danced laughing in his light-blue eye,

Or bended brow and glance of fire
And kindling cheek spoke Erin's ire,
Or soft and saddened glances show
Her ready sympathy with woe;
Or in that wayward mood of mind
When various feelings are combined,
When joy and sorrow mingle near,   120
And hope's bright wings are checked by
          fear,
And rising doubts keep transport down,
And anger lends a short-lived frown;
In that strange mood which maids approve
Even when they dare not call it love —
With every change his features played,
As aspens show the light and shade.

VI

Well Risingham young Redmond knew,
And much he marvelled that the crew
Roused to revenge bold Mortham dead   130
Were by that Mortham's foeman led;
For never felt his soul the woe
That wails a generous foeman low,
Far less that sense of justice strong
That wreaks a generous foeman's wrong.
But small his leisure now to pause;
Redmond is first, whate'er the cause:
And twice that Redmond came so near
Where Bertram couched like hunted deer,
The very boughs his steps displace   140
Rustled against the ruffian's face,
Who desperate twice prepared to start,
And plunge his dagger in his heart!
But Redmond turned a different way,
And the bent boughs resumed their sway,
And Bertram held it wise, unseen,
Deeper to plunge in coppice green.
Thus, circled in his coil, the snake,
When roving hunters beat the brake,
Watches with red and glistening eye,   150
Prepared, if heedless step draw nigh,
With forked tongue and venomed fang
Instant to dart the deadly pang;
But if the intruders turn aside,
Away his coils unfolded glide,
And through the deep savannah wind,
Some undisturbed retreat to find.

VII

But Bertram, as he backward drew,
And heard the loud pursuit renew,
And Redmond's hollo on the wind,   160
Oft muttered in his savage mind —
'Redmond O'Neale! were thou and I
Alone this day's event to try,

With not a second here to see
But the gray cliff and oaken tree,
That voice of thine that shouts so loud
Should ne'er repeat its summons proud!
No! nor e'er try its melting power
Again in maiden's summer bower.'
Eluded, now behind him die   170
Faint and more faint each hostile cry;
He stands in Scargill wood alone,
Nor hears he now a harsher tone
Than the hoarse cushat's plaintive cry,
Or Greta's sound that murmurs by;
And on the dale, so lone and wild,
The summer sun in quiet smiled.

VIII

He listened long with anxious heart,
Ear bent to hear and foot to start,
And, while his stretched attention glows, 180
Refused his weary frame repose.
'T was silence all — he laid him down,
Where purple heath profusely strown,
And throatwort with its azure bell,
And moss and thyme his cushion swell.
There, spent with toil, he listless eyed
The course of Greta's playful tide;
Beneath her banks now eddying dun,
Now brightly gleaming to the sun,
As, dancing over rock and stone,   190
In yellow light her currents shone,
Matching in hue the favorite gem
Of Albin's mountain-diadem.
Then, tired to watch the currents play,
He turned his weary eyes away
To where the bank opposing showed
Its huge, square cliffs through shaggy
          wood.
One, prominent above the rest,
Reared to the sun its pale gray breast;
Around its broken summit grew   200
The hazel rude and sable yew;
A thousand varied lichens dyed
Its waste and weather-beaten side,
And round its rugged basis lay,
By time or thunder rent away,
Fragments that from its frontlet torn
Were mantled now by verdant thorn.
Such was the scene's wild majesty
That filled stern Bertram's gazing eye.

IX

In sullen mood he lay reclined,   210
Revolving in his stormy mind
The felon deed, the fruitless guilt,
His patron's blood by treason spilt;

A crime, it seemed, so dire and dread
That it had power to wake the dead.
Then, pondering on his life betrayed
By Oswald's art to Redmond's blade,
In treacherous purpose to withhold,
So seemed it, Mortham's promised gold,
A deep and full revenge he vowed   220
On Redmond, forward, fierce, and proud;
Revenge on Wilfrid — on his sire
Redoubled vengeance, swift and dire ! —
If, in such mood — as legends say,
And well believed that simple day —
The Enemy of Man has power
To profit by the evil hour,
Here stood a wretch prepared to change
His soul's redemption for revenge !
But though his vows with such a fire   230
Of earnest and intense desire
For vengeance dark and fell were made
As well might reach hell's lowest shade,
No deeper clouds the grove embrowned,
No nether thunders shook the ground;
The demon knew his vassal's heart,
And spared temptation's needless art.

X

Oft, mingled with the direful theme,
Came Mortham's form — was it a dream ?
Or had he seen in vision true   240
That very Mortham whom he slew ?
Or had in living flesh appeared
The only man on earth he feared ? —
To try the mystic cause intent,
His eyes that on the cliff were bent
'Countered at once a dazzling glance,
Like sunbeam flashed from sword or lance.
At once he started as for fight,
But not a foeman was in sight;
He heard the cushat's murmur hoarse,   250
He heard the river's sounding course;
The solitary woodlands lay,
As slumbering in the summer ray.
He gazed, like lion roused, around,
Then sunk again upon the ground.
'T was but, he thought, some fitful beam,
Glanced sudden from the sparkling stream;
Then plunged him in his gloomy train
Of ill-connected thoughts again,
Until a voice behind him cried,   260
' Bertram ! well met on Greta side.'

XI

Instant his sword was in his hand,
As instant sunk the ready brand;

Yet, dubious still, opposed he stood
To him that issued from the wood:
' Guy Denzil ! — is it thou ? ' he said;
' Do we two meet in Scargill shade ! —
Stand back a space ! — thy purpose show,
Whether thou comest as friend or foe.
Report hath said, that Denzil's name   270
From Rokeby's band was razed with
shame ' —
' A shame I owe that hot O'Neale,
Who told his knight in peevish zeal
Of my marauding on the clowns
Of Calverley and Bradford downs.
I reck not. In a war to strive,
Where save the leaders none can thrive,
Suits ill my mood; and better game
Awaits us both, if thou 'rt the same
Unscrupulous, bold Risingham   280
Who watched with me in midnight dark
To snatch a deer from Rokeby-park.
How think'st thou ? ' — ' Speak thy pur-
pose out;
I love not mystery or doubt.' —

XII

' Then list. — Not far there lurk a crew
Of trusty comrades stanch and true,
Gleaned from both factions — Roundheads,
freed
From cant of sermon and of creed,
And Cavaliers, whose souls like mine
Spurn at the bonds of discipline.   290
Wiser, we judge, by dale and wold
A warfare of our own to hold
Than breathe our last on battle-down
For cloak or surplice, mace or crown.
Our schemes are laid, our purpose set,
A chief and leader lack we yet.
Thou art a wanderer, it is said,
For Mortham's death thy steps waylaid,
Thy head at price — so say our spies,
Who ranged the valley in disguise.   300
Join then with us: though wild debate
And wrangling rend our infant state,
Each, to an equal loath to bow,
Will yield to chief renowned as thou.' —

XIII

' Even now,' thought Bertram, passion-
stirred,
' I called on hell, and hell has heard !
What lack I, vengeance to command,
But of stanch comrades such a band ?
This Denzil, vowed to every evil,
Might read a lesson to the devil.   310

Well, be it so ! each knave and fool
Shall serve as my revenge's tool.' —
Aloud, ' I take thy proffer, Guy,
But tell me where thy comrades lie.'
' Not far from hence,' Guy Denzil said;
' Descend and cross the river's bed
Where rises yonder cliff so gray.'
' Do thou,' said Bertram, ' lead the way.'
Then muttered, ' It is best make sure;
Guy Denzil's faith was never pure.'   320
He followed down the steep descent,
Then through the Greta's streams they
            went;
And when they reached the farther shore
They stood the lonely cliff before.

XIV

With wonder Bertram heard within
The flinty rock a murmured din;
But when Guy pulled the wilding spray
And brambles from its base away,
He saw appearing to the air
A little entrance low and square,   330
Like opening cell of hermit lone,
Dark winding through the living stone.
Here entered Denzil, Bertram here;
And loud and louder on their ear,
As from the bowels of the earth,
Resounded shouts of boisterous mirth.
Of old the cavern strait and rude
In slaty rock the peasant hewed;
And Brignall's woods and Scargill's wave
E'en now o'er many a sister cave,   340
Where, far within the darksome rift,
The wedge and lever ply their thrift.
But war had silenced rural trade,
And the deserted mine was made
The banquet-hall and fortress too
Of Denzil and his desperate crew.
There Guilt his anxious revel kept,
There on his sordid pallet slept
Guilt-born Excess, the goblet drained
Still in his slumbering grasp retained;   350
Regret was there, his eye still cast
With vain repining on the past;
Among the feasters waited near
Sorrow and unrepentant Fear,
And Blasphemy, to frenzy driven,
With his own crimes reproaching Heaven;
While Bertram showed amid the crew
The Master-Fiend that Milton drew.

XV

Hark ! the loud revel wakes again
To greet the leader of the train.   360

Behold the group by the pale lamp
That struggles with the earthy damp.
By what strange features Vice hath known
To single out and mark her own !
Yet some there are whose brows retain
Less deeply stamped her brand and stain.
See yon pale stripling ! when a boy,
A mother's pride, a father's joy !
Now, 'gainst the vault's rude walls reclined,
An early image fills his mind: 370
The cottage once his sire's he sees,
Embowered upon the banks of Tees;
He views sweet Winston's woodland scene,
And shares the dance on Gainford-green.
A tear is springing — but the zest
Of some wild tale or brutal jest
Hath to loud laughter stirred the rest.
On him they call, the aptest mate
For jovial song and merry feat:
Fast flies his dream — with dauntless
            air,   380
As one victorious o'er despair,
He bids the ruddy cup go round
Till sense and sorrow both are drowned;
And soon in merry wassail he,
The life of all their revelry,
Peals his loud song ! — The muse has
            found
Her blossoms on the wildest ground,
Mid noxious weeds at random strewed,
Themselves all profitless and rude. —
With desperate merriment he sung,   390
The cavern to the chorus rung,
Yet mingled with his reckless glee
Remorse's bitter agony.

XVI

SONG

O, Brignall banks are wild and fair,
    And Greta woods are green,
And you may gather garlands there
    Would grace a summer queen.
And as I rode by Dalton-hall,
    Beneath the turrets high,
A maiden on the castle wall   400
    Was singing merrily, —

CHORUS

' O, Brignall banks are fresh and fair,
    And Greta woods are green;
I 'd rather rove with Edmund there
    Than reign our English queen.'
' If, maiden, thou wouldst wend with me,
    To leave both tower and town,

Thou first must guess what life lead we
  That dwell by dale and down?
And if thou canst that riddle read,   410
  As read full well you may,
Then to the greenwood shalt thou speed,
  As blithe as Queen of May.'

CHORUS

Yet sung she, 'Brignall banks are fair,
  And Greta woods are green;
I'd rather rove with Edmund there
  Than reign our English queen.

XVII

'I read you, by your bugle horn,
  And by your palfrey good,
I read you for a ranger sworn
  To keep the king's greenwood.'   420
'A ranger, lady, winds his horn,
  And 'tis at peep of light;
His blast is heard at merry morn,
  And mine at dead of night.'

CHORUS

Yet sung she, 'Brignall banks are fair,
  And Greta woods are gay;
I would I were with Edmund there,
  To reign his Queen of May!

'With burnished brand and musketoon   430
  So gallantly you come,
I read you for a bold dragoon,
  That lists the tuck of drum.'
'I list no more the tuck of drum,
  No more the trumpet hear;
But when the beetle sounds his hum,
  My comrades take the spear.

CHORUS

'And O, though Brignall banks be fair,
  And Greta woods be gay,
Yet mickle must the maiden dare   440
  Would reign my Queen of May!

XVIII

'Maiden! a nameless life I lead,
  A nameless death I'll die;
The fiend whose lantern lights the mead
  Were better mate than I!
And when I'm with my comrades met
  Beneath the greenwood bough,
What once we were we all forget,
  Nor think what we are now.

CHORUS

'Yet Brignall banks are fresh and fair,   450
  And Greta woods are green,
And you may gather garlands there
  Would grace a summer queen.'

When Edmund ceased his simple song,
Was silence on the sullen throng.
Till waked some ruder mate their glee
With note of coarser minstrelsy.
But far apart in dark divan,
Denzil and Bertram many a plan
Of import foul and fierce designed,   460
While still on Bertram's grasping mind
The wealth of murdered Mortham hung;
Though half he feared his daring tongue,
When it should give his wishes birth,
Might raise a spectre from the earth!

XIX

At length his wondrous tale he told;
When scornful smiled his comrade bold,
For, trained in license of a court,
Religion's self was Denzil's sport;
Then judge in what contempt he held   470
The visionary tales of eld!
His awe for Bertram scarce repressed
The unbeliever's sneering jest,
''T were hard,' he said, 'for sage or seer
To spell the subject of your fear;
Nor do I boast the art renowned
Vision and omen to expound.
Yet, faith if I must needs afford
To spectre watching treasured hoard,
As ban-dog keeps his master's roof,   480
Bidding the plunderer stand aloof,
This doubt remains — thy goblin gaunt
Hath chosen ill his ghostly haunt;
For why his guard on Mortham hold,
When Rokeby castle hath the gold
Thy patron won on Indian soil
By stealth, by piracy and spoil?'—

XX

At this he paused — for angry shame
Lowered on the brow of Risingham.   489
He blushed to think, that he should seem
Asserter of an airy dream,
And gave his wrath another theme.
'Denzil,' he says, 'though lowly laid,
Wrong not the memory of the dead;
For while he lived at Mortham's look
Thy very soul, Guy Denzil, shook!
And when he taxed thy breach of word
To yon fair rose of Allenford,

I saw thee crouch like chastened hound
Whose back the huntsman's lash hath
    found.   500
Nor dare to call his foreign wealth
The spoil of piracy or stealth;
He won it bravely with his brand
When Spain waged warfare with our land.
Mark, too — I brook no idle jeer,
Nor couple Bertram's name with fear;
Mine is but half the demon's lot,
For I believe, but tremble not.
Enough of this.   Say, why this hoard
Thou deem'st at Rokeby castle stored;   510
Or think'st that Mortham would bestow
His treasure with his faction's foe ? '

XXI

Soon   quenched   was   Denzil's   ill - timed
    mirth;
Rather he would have seen the earth
Give to ten thousand spectres birth
Than venture to awake to flame
The deadly wrath of Risingham.
Submiss he answered, ' Mortham's mind,
Thou know'st, to joy was ill inclined.
In youth, 't is said, a gallant free,   520
A lusty reveller was he;
But since returned from over sea,
A sullen and a silent mood
Hath numbed the current of his blood.
Hence he refused each kindly call
To Rokeby's hospitable hall,
And our stout knight, at dawn or morn
Who loved to hear the bugle-horn,
Nor less, when eve his oaks embrowned,
To see the ruddy cup go round,   530
Took umbrage that a friend so near
Refused to share his chase and cheer;
Thus did the kindred barons jar
Ere they divided in the war.
Yet, trust me, friend, Matilda fair
Of Mortham's wealth is destined heir.'

XXII

' Destined to her ! to yon slight maid !
The prize my life had wellnigh paid
When 'gainst Laroche by Cayo's wave
I fought my patron's wealth to save ! — 540
Denzil, I knew him long, yet ne'er
Knew him that joyous cavalier
Whom youthful friends and early fame
Called soul of gallantry and game.
A moody man he sought our crew,
Desperate and dark, whom no one knew,

And rose, as men with us must rise,
By scorning life and all its ties.
On each adventure rash he roved,
As danger for itself he loved;   550
On his sad brow nor mirth nor wine
Could ere one wrinkled knot untwine;
Ill was the omen if he smiled,
For 't was in peril stern and wild;
But when he laughed each luckless mate
Might hold our fortune desperate.
Foremost he fought in every broil,
Then scornful turned him from the spoil,
Nay, often strove to bar the way
Between his comrades and their prey;   560
Preaching even then to such as we,
Hot with our dear-bought victory,
Of mercy and humanity.

XXIII

' I loved him well — his fearless part,
His gallant leading, won my heart.
And after each victorious fight,
'T was I that wrangled for his right,
Redeemed his portion of the prey
That greedier mates had torn away,
In field and storm thrice saved his life, 570
And once amid our comrades' strife. —
Yes, I have loved thee ! Well hath proved
My toil, my danger, how I loved !
Yet will I mourn no more thy fate,
Ingrate in life, in death ingrate.
Rise if thou canst ! ' he looked around
And sternly stamped upon the ground —
' Rise, with thy bearing proud and high,
Even as this morn it met mine eye,
And give me, if thou darest, the lie ! ' 580
He paused — then, calm and passion-freed,
Bade Denzil with his tale proceed.

XXIV

' Bertram, to thee I need not tell,
What thou hast cause to wot so well,
How superstition's nets were twined
Around the Lord of Mortham's mind;
But since he drove thee from his tower,
A maid he found in Greta's bower
Whose speech, like David's harp, had sway
To charm his evil fiend away.   590
I know not if her features moved
Remembrance of the wife he loved,
But he would gaze upon her eye,
Till his mood softened to a sigh.
He, whom no living mortal sought
To question of his secret thought,

Now every thought and care confessed
To his fair niece's faithful breast;
Nor was there aught of rich and rare,
In earth, in ocean, or in air,   600
But it must deck Matilda's hair.
Her love still bound him unto life;
But then awoke the civil strife,
And menials bore by his commands
Three coffers with their iron bands
From Mortham's vault at midnight deep
To her lone bower in Rokeby-Keep,
Ponderous with gold and plate of pride,
His gift, if he in battle died.'

XXV

' Then Denzil, as I guess, lays train   610
These iron-banded chests to gain,
Else wherefore should he hover here
Where many a peril waits him near
For all his feats of war and peace,
For plundered boors, and harts of greese ?
Since through the hamlets as he fared
What hearth has Guy's marauding spared,
Or where the chase that hath not rung
With Denzil's bow at midnight strung ? '
' I hold my wont — my rangers go,   620
Even now to track a milk-white doe.
By Rokeby-hall she takes her lair,
In Greta wood she harbors fair,
And when my huntsman marks her way,
What think'st thou, Bertram, of the prey ?
Were Rokeby's daughter in our power,
We rate her ransom at her dower.'

XXVI

' 'T is well ! — there 's vengeance in the
          thought,
Matilda is by Wilfrid sought;
And hot-brained Redmond too, 't is said,   630
Pays lover's homage to the maid.
Bertram she scorned — if met by chance
She turned from me her shuddering glance,
Like a nice dame that will not brook
On what she hates and loathes to look;
She told to Mortham she could ne'er
Behold me without secret fear,
Foreboding evil: — she may rue
To find her prophecy fall true ! —
The war has weeded Rokeby's train,   640
Few followers in his halls remain;
If thy scheme miss, then, brief and bold,
We are enow to storm the hold,
Bear off the plunder and the dame,
And leave the castle all in flame.'

XXVII

' Still art thou Valor's venturous son !
Yet ponder first the risk to run:
The menials of the castle, true
And stubborn to their charge, though
          few —
The wall to scale —the moat to cross —   650
The wicket-grate — the inner fosse '—
' Fool ! if we blench for toys like these,
On what fair guerdon can we seize ?
Our hardiest venture, to explore
Some wretched peasant's fenceless door,
And the best prize we bear away,
The earnings of his sordid day.'
' A while thy hasty taunt forbear:
In sight of road more sure and fair
Thou wouldst not choose, in blindfold
          wrath   660
Or wantonness a desperate path ?
List, then; — for vantage or assault,
From gilded vane to dungeon vault,
Each pass of Rokeby-house I know:
There is one postern dark and low
That issues at a secret spot,
By most neglected or forgot.
Now, could a spial of our train
On fair pretext admittance gain,
That sally-port might be unbarred;   670
Then, vain were battlement and ward !'

XXVIII

' Now speak'st thou well: to me the same
If force or art shall urge the game;
Indifferent if like fox I wind,
Or spring like tiger on the hind. —
But, hark ! our merry men so gay
Troll forth another roundelay.'

SONG

' A weary lot is thine, fair maid,
    A weary lot is thine !
To pull the thorn thy brow to braid,   680
    And press the rue for wine !
A lightsome eye, a soldier's mien,
    A feather of the blue,
A doublet of the Lincoln green, —
    No more of me you knew,
                    My love !
No more of me you knew.

'This morn is merry June, I trow,
    The rose is budding fain;
But she shall bloom in winter snow   690
    Ere we two meet again.'

He turned his charger as he spake
Upon the river shore,
He gave his bridle-reins a shake,
Said, 'Adieu for evermore,
                              My love !
And adieu for evermore.'

XXIX

'What youth is this your band among
The best for minstrelsy and song ?
In his wild notes seem aptly met   700
A strain of pleasure and regret.' —
'Edmund of Winston is his name;
The hamlet sounded with the fame
Of early hopes his childhood gave, —
Now centred all in Brignall cave !
I watch him well — his wayward course
Shows oft a tincture of remorse.
Some early love-shaft grazed his heart,
And oft the scar will ache and smart.
Yet is he useful; — of the rest   710
By fits the darling and the jest,
His harp, his story, and his lay,
Oft aid the idle hours away:
When unemployed, each fiery mate
Is ripe for mutinous debate.
He tuned his strings e'en now — again
He wakes them with a blither strain.'

XXX

SONG

ALLEN-A-DALE

Allen-a-Dale has no fagot for burning,
Allen-a-Dale has no furrow for turning,
Allen-a-Dale has no fleece for the spin-
    ning,   720
Yet Allen-a-Dale has red gold for the
    winning.
Come, read me my riddle ! come, hearken
    my tale !
And tell me the craft of bold Allen-a-
    Dale.

The Baron of Ravensworth prances in
    pride,
And he views his domains upon Arkindale
    side.
The mere for his net and the land for his
    game,
The chase for the wild and the park for
    the tame;

Yet the fish of the lake and the deer of the
    vale
Are less free to Lord Dacre than Allen-a-
    Dale !

Allen-a-Dale was ne'er belted a knight, 730
Though his spur be as sharp and his blade
    be as bright;
Allen-a-Dale is no baron or lord,
Yet twenty tall yeomen will draw at his
    word;
And the best of our nobles his bonnet will
    vail,
Who at Rere-cross on Stanmore meets
    Allen-a-Dale !

Allen-a-Dale to his wooing is come;
The mother, she asked of his household
    and home:
'Though the castle of Richmond stand fair
    on the hill,
My hall,' quoth bold Allen, 'shows gallanter
    still;
'T is the blue vault of heaven, with its cres-
    cent so pale   740
And with all its bright spangles !' said
    Allen-a-Dale.

The father was steel and the mother was
    stone;
They lifted the latch and they bade him be
    gone;
But loud on the morrow their wail and their
    cry:
He had laughed on the lass with his bonny
    black eye,
And she fled to the forest to hear a love-
    tale,
And the youth it was told by was Allen-a-
    dale !

XXXI

'Thou see'st that, whether sad or gay,
Love mingles ever in his lay.
But when his boyish wayward fit   750
Is o'er, he hath address and wit;
O, 't is a brain of fire, can ape
Each dialect, each various shape !' —
'Nay then, to aid thy project, Guy —
Soft ! who comes here ?' — 'My trusty
    spy.
Speak, Hamlin ! hast thou lodged our
    deer ?' —
'I have — but two fair stags are near.

I watched her as she slowly strayed
From Egliston up Thorsgill glade,
But Wilfrid Wycliffe sought her side,   760
And then young Redmond in his pride
Shot down to meet them on their way;
Much, as it seemed, was theirs to say:
There 's time to pitch both toil and net
Before their path be homeward set.'
A hurried and a whispered speech
Did Bertram's will to Denzil teach,
Who, turning to the robber band,
Bade four, the bravest, take the brand.

CANTO FOURTH

I

WHEN Denmark's raven soared on high,
Triumphant through Northumbrian sky,
The hovering near her fatal croak
Bade Reged's Britons dread the yoke,
And the broad shadow of her wing
Blackened each cataract and spring
Where Tees in tumult leaves his source,
Thundering o'er Caldron and High-Force;
Beneath the shade the Northmen came,
Fixed on each vale a Runic name,   10
Reared high their altar's rugged stone,
And gave their gods the land they won.
Then, Balder, one bleak garth was thine
And one sweet brooklet's silver line,
And Woden's Croft did title gain
From the stern Father of the Slain;
But to the Monarch of the Mace,
That held in fight the foremost place,
To Odin's son and Sifia's spouse,   19
Near Startforth high they paid their vows,
Remembered Thor's victorious fame,
And gave the dell the Thunderer's name.

II

Yet Scald or Kemper erred, I ween,
Who gave that soft and quiet scene,
With all its varied light and shade,
And every little sunny glade,
And the blithe brook that strolls along
Its pebbled bed with summer song,
To the grim God of blood and scar,
The grisly King of Northern War.   30
O, better were its banks assigned
To spirits of a gentler kind !
For where the thicket-groups recede
And the rath primrose decks the mead,
The velvet grass seems carpet meet

For the light fairies' lively feet.
Yon tufted knoll with daisies strown
Might make proud Oberon a throne,
While, hidden in the thicket nigh,
Puck should brood o'er his frolic sly;   40
And where profuse the wood-vetch clings
Round ash and elm in verdant rings,
Its pale and azure-pencilled flower
Should canopy Titania's bower.

III

Here rise no cliffs the vale to shade;
But, skirting every sunny glade,
In fair variety of green
The woodland lends its sylvan screen.
Hoary yet haughty, frowns the oak,
Its boughs by weight of ages broke;   50
And towers erect in sable spire
The pine-tree scathed by lightning-fire;
The drooping ash and birch between
Hang their fair tresses o'er the green,
And all beneath at random grow
Each coppice dwarf of varied show,
Or, round the stems profusely twined,
Fling summer odors on the wind.
Such varied group Urbino's hand
Round Him of Tarsus nobly planned,   60
What time he bade proud Athens own
On Mars's Mount the God Unknown !
Then gray Philosophy stood nigh,
Though bent by age, in spirit high:
There rose the scar-seamed veteran's spear,
There Grecian Beauty bent to hear,
While Childhood at her foot was placed,
Or clung delighted to her waist.

IV

'And rest we here,' Matilda said,
And sat her in the varying shade.   70
'Chance-met, we well may steal an hour,
To friendship due from fortune's power.
Thou, Wilfrid, ever kind, must lend
Thy counsel to thy sister-friend;
And, Redmond, thou, at my behest,
No farther urge thy desperate quest.
For to my care a charge is left,
Dangerous to one of aid bereft,
Wellnigh an orphan and alone,
Captive her sire, her house o'erthrown.'   80
Wilfrid, with wonted kindness graced,
Beside her on the turf she placed;
Then paused with downcast look and eye,
Nor bade young Redmond seat him nigh.
Her conscious diffidence he saw,
Drew backward as in modest awe,

And sat a little space removed,
Unmarked to gaze on her he loved.

V

Wreathed in its dark-brown rings, her hair
Half hid Matilda's forehead fair,   90
Half hid and half revealed to view
Her full dark eye of hazel hue.
The rose with faint and feeble streak
So slightly tinged the maiden's cheek
That you had said her hue was pale;
But if she faced the summer gale,
Or spoke, or sung, or quicker moved,
Or heard the praise of those she loved,
Or when of interest was expressed
Aught that waked feeling in her breast, 100
The mantling blood in ready play
Rivalled the blush of rising day.
There was a soft and pensive grace,
A cast of thought upon her face,
That suited well the forehead high,
The eyelash dark and downcast eye;
The mild expression spoke a mind
In duty firm, composed, resigned; —
'T is that which Roman art has given,
To mark their maiden Queen of Heaven. 110
In hours of sport that mood gave way
To Fancy's light and frolic play;
And when the dance, or tale, or song
In harmless mirth sped time along,
Full oft her doting sire would call
His Maud the merriest of them all.
But days of war and civil crime
Allowed but ill such festal time,
And her soft pensiveness of brow
Had deepened into sadness now.   120
In Marston field her father ta'en,
Her friends dispersed, brave Mortham
    slain,
While every ill her soul foretold
From Oswald's thirst of power and gold,
And boding thoughts that she must part
With a soft vision of her heart, —
All lowered around the lovely maid,
To darken her dejection's shade.

VI

Who has not heard — while Erin yet
Strove 'gainst the Saxon's iron bit —   130
Who has not heard how brave O'Neale
In English blood imbrued his steel,
Against Saint George's cross blazed high
The banners of his Tanistry,
To fiery Essex gave the foil,
And reigned a prince on Ulster's soil ?

But chief arose his victor pride
When that brave Marshal fought and died,
And Avon-Duff to ocean bore
His billows red with Saxon gore.   140
'T was first in that disastrous fight
Rokeby and Mortham proved their might.
There had they fallen amongst the rest,
But pity touched a chieftain's breast;
The Tanist he to great O'Neale,
He checked his followers' bloody zeal,
To quarter took the kinsmen bold,
And bore them to his mountain-hold,
Gave them each sylvan joy to know
Slieve-Donard's cliffs and woods could
    show,   150
Shared with them Erin's festal cheer,
Showed them the chase of wolf and deer,
And, when a fitting time was come,
Safe and unransomed sent them home,
Loaded with many a gift to prove
A generous foe's respect and love.

VII

Years speed away.   On Rokeby's head
Some touch of early snow was shed;
Calm he enjoyed by Greta's wave   159
The peace which James the Peaceful gave,
While Mortham far beyond the main
Waged his fierce wars on Indian Spain. —
It chanced upon a wintry night
That whitened Stanmore's stormy height,
The chase was o'er, the stag was killed,
In Rokeby hall the cups were filled,
And by the huge stone chimney sate
The knight in hospitable state.
Moonless the sky, the hour was late,
When a loud summons shook the gate,   170
And sore for entrance and for aid
A voice of foreign accent prayed.
The porter answered to the call,
And instant rushed into the hall
A man whose aspect and attire
Startled the circle by the fire.

VIII

His plaited hair in elf-locks spread
Around his bare and matted head;
On leg and thigh, close stretched and trim,
His vesture showed the sinewy limb;   180
In saffron dyed, a linen vest
Was frequent folded round his breast;
A mantle long and loose he wore,
Shaggy with ice and stained with gore.
He clasped a burden to his heart,
And, resting on a knotted dart,

The snow from hair and beard he shook,
And round him gazed with wildered look.
Then up the hall with staggering pace
He hastened by the blaze to place,   190
Half lifeless from the bitter air,
His load, a boy of beauty rare.
To Rokeby next he louted low,
Then stood erect his tale to show
With wild majestic port and tone,
Like envoy of some barbarous throne.
'Sir Richard, Lord of Rokeby, hear!
Turlough O'Neale salutes thee dear;
He graces thee, and to thy care   199
Young Redmond gives, his grandson fair.
He bids thee breed him as thy son,
For Turlough's days of joy are done,
And other lords have seized his land,
And faint and feeble is his hand,
And all the glory of Tyrone
Is like a morning vapor flown.
To bind the duty on thy soul,
He bids thee think on Erin's bowl!
If any wrong the young O'Neale,
He bids thee think of Erin's steel.   210
Tò Mortham first this charge was due,
But in his absence honors you. —
Now is my master's message by,
And Ferraught will contented die.'

IX

His look grew fixed, his cheek grew pale,
He sunk when he had told his tale;
For, hid beneath his mantle wide,
A mortal wound was in his side.
Vain was all aid — in terror wild
And sorrow screamed the orphan child.   220
Poor Ferraught raised his wistful eyes,
And faintly strove to soothe his cries;
All reckless of his dying pain,
He blest and blest him o'er again,
And kissed the little hands outspread,
And kissed and crossed the infant head,
And in his native tongue and phrase
Prayed to each saint to watch his days;
Then all his strength together drew
The charge to Rokeby to renew.   230
When half was faltered from his breast,
And half by dying signs expressed,
'Bless thee, O'Neale!' he faintly said,
And thus the faithful spirit fled.

X

'T was long ere soothing might prevail
Upon the child to end the tale:

And then he said that from his home
His grandsire had been forced to roam,
Which had not been if Redmond's hand
Had but had strength to draw the brand,
The brand of Lenaugh More the Red,   241
That hung beside the gray wolf's head. —
'T was from his broken phrase descried,
His foster father was his guide,
Who in his charge from Ulster bore
Letters and gifts a goodly store;
But ruffians met them in the wood,
Ferraught in battle boldly stood,
Till wounded and o'erpowered at length,
And stripped of all, his failing strength   25(
Just bore him here — and then the child
Renewed again his moaning wild.

XI

The tear down childhood's cheek that flows
Is like the dew-drop on the rose;
When next the summer breeze comes by
And waves the bush, the flower is dry.
Won by their care, the orphan child
Soon on his new protector smiled,
With dimpled cheek and eye so fair,
Through his thick curls of flaxen hair,   260
But blithest laughed that cheek and eye,
When Rokeby's little maid was nigh;
'T was his with elder brother's pride
Matilda's tottering steps to guide;
His native lays in Irish tongue
To soothe her infant ear he sung,
And primrose twined with daisy fair
To form a chaplet for her hair.
By lawn, by grove, by brooklet's strand,
The children still were hand in hand,   270
And good Sir Richard smiling eyed
The early knot so kindly tied.

XII

But summer months bring wilding shoot
From bud to bloom, from bloom to fruit;
And years draw on our human span
From child to boy, from boy to man;
And soon in Rokeby's woods is seen
A gallant boy in hunter's green.
He loves to wake the felon boar
In his dark haunt on Greta's shore,   28(
And loves against the deer so dun
To draw the shaft, or lift the gun:
Yet more he loves in autumn prime
The hazel's spreading boughs to climb,
And down its clustered stores to hail
Where young Matilda holds her veil.

And she whose veil receives the shower
Is altered too and knows her power,
Assumes a monitress's pride   289
Her Redmond's dangerous sports to chide,
Yet listens still to hear him tell
How the grim wild-boar fought and fell,
How at his fall the bugle rung,
Till rock and greenwood answer flung;
Then blesses her that man can find
A pastime of such savage kind !

XIII

But Redmond knew to weave his tale
So well with praise of wood and dale,
And knew so well each point to trace
Gives living interest to the chase,   300
And knew so well o'er all to throw
His spirit's wild romantic glow,
That, while she blamed and while she
          feared,
She loved each venturous tale she heard.
Oft, too, when drifted snow and rain
To bower and hall their steps restrain,
Together they explored the page
Of glowing bard or gifted sage;
Oft, placed the evening fire beside,
The minstrel art alternate tried,   310
While gladsome harp and lively lay
Bade winter night flit fast away:
Thus, from their childhood blending still
Their sport, their study, and their skill,
An union of the soul they prove,
But must not think that it was love.
But though they dared not, envious Fame
Soon dared to give that union name;
And when so often side by side
From year to year the pair she eyed,   320
She sometimes blamed the good old knight
As dull of ear and dim of sight,
Sometimes his purpose would declare
That young O'Neale should wed his heir.

XIV

The suit of Wilfrid rent disguise
And bandage from the lovers' eyes;
'T was plain that Oswald for his son
Had Rokeby's favor wellnigh won.
Now must they meet with change of cheer,
With mutual looks of shame and fear;   330
Now must Matilda stray apart
To school her disobedient heart,
And Redmond now alone must rue
The love he never can subdue.
But factions rose, and Rokeby sware
No rebel's son should wed his heir;

And Redmond, nurtured while a child
In many a bard's traditions wild,
Now sought the lonely wood or stream,
To cherish there a happier dream   340
Of maiden won by sword or lance,
As in the regions of romance;
And count the heroes of his line,
Great Nial of the Pledges Nine,
Shane-Dymas wild, and Geraldine,
And Connan-more, who vowed his race
For ever to the fight and chase,
And cursed him of his lineage born
Should sheathe the sword to reap the
          corn,
Or leave the mountain and the wold   350
To shroud himself in castled hold.
From such examples hope he drew,
And brightened as the trumpet blew.

XV

If brides were won by heart and blade,
Redmond had both his cause to aid,
And all beside of nurture rare
That might beseem a baron's heir.
Turlough O'Neale in Erin's strife
On Rokeby's Lord bestowed his life,
And well did Rokeby's generous knight   360
Young Redmond for the deed requite.
Nor was his liberal care and cost
Upon the gallant stripling lost:
Seek the North Riding broad and wide,
Like Redmond none could steed bestride;
From Tynemouth search to Cumberland,
Like Redmond none could wield a brand;
And then, of humor kind and free,
And bearing him to each degree
With frank and fearless courtesy,   370
There never youth was formed to steal
Upon the heart like brave O'Neale.

XVI

Sir Richard loved him as his son;
And when the days of peace were done,
And to the gales of war he gave
The banner of his sires to wave,
Redmond, distinguished by his care,
He chose that honored flag to bear,
And named his page, the next degree
In that old time to chivalry.   380
In five pitched fields he well maintained
The honored place his worth obtained,
And high was Redmond's youthful name
Blazed in the roll of martial fame.
Had fortune smiled on Marston fight,
The eve had seen him dubbed a knight;

Twice mid the battle's doubtful strife
Of Rokeby's Lord he saved the life,
But when he saw him prisoner made,
He kissed and then resigned his blade,   390
And yielded him an easy prey
To those who led the knight away,
Resolved Matilda's sire should prove
In prison, as in fight, his love.

XVII

When lovers meet in adverse hour,
'T is like a sun-glimpse through a shower,
A watery ray an instant seen
The darkly closing clouds between.
As Redmond on the turf reclined,
The past and present filled his mind: 400
' It was not thus,' Affection said,
' I dreamed of my return, dear maid !
Not thus when from thy trembling hand
I took the banner and the brand,
When round me, as the bugles blew,
Their blades three hundred warriors drew,
And, while the standard I unrolled,
Clashed their bright arms, with clamor bold.
Where is that banner now ? — its pride
Lies whelmed in Ouse's sullen tide !   410
Where now these warriors ? — in their gore
They cumber Marston's dismal moor !
And what avails a useless brand,
Held by a captive's shackled hand,
That only would his life retain
To aid thy sire to bear his chain !'
Thus Redmond to himself apart,
Nor lighter was his rival's heart;
For Wilfrid, while his generous soul
Disdained to profit by control,   420
By many a sign could mark too plain,
Save with such aid, his hopes were vain.
But now Matilda's accents stole
On the dark visions of their soul,
And bade their mournful musing fly,
Like mist before the zephyr's sigh.

XVIII

' I need not to my friends recall,
How Mortham shunned my father's hall,
A man of silence and of woe,
Yet ever anxious to bestow   430
On my poor self whate'er could prove
A kinsman's confidence and love.
My feeble aid could sometimes chase
The clouds of sorrow for a space;
But oftener, fixed beyond my power,
I marked his deep despondence lower.

One dismal cause, by all unguessed,
His fearful confidence confessed;
And twice it was my hap to see
Examples of that agony   440
Which for a season can o'erstrain
And wreck the structure of the brain.
He had the awful power to know
The approaching mental overthrow,
And while his mind had courage yet
To struggle with the dreadful fit,
The victim writhed against its throes,
Like wretch beneath a murderer's blows.
This malady, I well could mark,
Sprung from some direful cause and dark,   450
But still he kept its source concealed,
Till arming for the civil field;
Then in my charge he bade me hold
A treasure huge of gems and gold,
With this disjointed dismal scroll
That tells the secret of his soul
In such wild words as oft betray
A mind by anguish forced astray.'

XIX

MORTHAM'S HISTORY

' Matilda ! thou hast seen me start,
As if a dagger thrilled my heart,   460
When it has happed some casual phrase
Waked memory of my former days.
Believe that few can backward cast
Their thought with pleasure on the past;
But I ! — my youth was rash and vain,
And blood and rage my manhood stain,
And my gray hairs must now descend
To my cold grave without a friend !
Even thou, Matilda, wilt disown
Thy kinsman when his guilt is known.   470
And must I lift the bloody veil
That hides my dark and fatal tale ?
I must — I will — Pale phantom, cease !
Leave me one little hour in peace !
Thus haunted, think'st thou I have skill
Thine own commission to fulfil ?
Or, while thou point'st with gesture fierce
Thy blighted cheek, thy bloody hearse,
How can I paint thee as thou wert,
So fair in face, so warm in heart ! —   480

XX

' Yes, she was fair ! — Matilda, thou
Hast a soft sadness on thy brow;
But hers was like the sunny glow,
That laughs on earth and all below !

We wedded secret — there was need —
Differing in country and in creed;
And when to Mortham's tower she came,
We mentioned not her race and name,
Until thy sire, who fought afar,   489
Should turn him home from foreign war,
On whose kind influence we relied
To soothe her father's ire and pride.
Few months we lived retired, unknown
To all but one dear friend alone,
One darling friend — I spare his shame,
I will not write the villain's name !
My trespasses I might forget,
And sue in vengeance for the debt
Due by a brother worm to me,
Ungrateful to God's clemency,   500
That spared me penitential time,
Nor cut me off amid my crime. —

XXI

' A kindly smile to all she lent,
But on her husband's friend 't was bent
So kind that from its harmless glee
The wretch misconstrued villany.
Repulsed in his presumptuous love,
A vengeful snare the traitor wove.
Alone we sat — the flask had flowed,
My blood with heat unwonted glowed,   510
When through the alleyed walk we spied
With hurried step my Edith glide,
Cowering beneath the verdant screen,
As one unwilling to be seen.
Words cannot paint the fiendish smile
That curled the traitor's cheek the while !
Fiercely I questioned of the cause;
He made a cold and artful pause,
Then prayed it might not chafe my mood —
" There was a gallant in the wood ! "   520
We had been shooting at the deer;
My cross-bow — evil chance ! — was near:
That ready weapon of my wrath
I caught and, hasting up the path,
In the yew grove my wife I found;
A stranger's arms her neck had bound !
I marked his heart — the bow I drew —
I loosed the shaft — 't was more than true !
I found my Edith's dying charms   529
Locked in her murdered brother's arms !
He came in secret to inquire
Her state and reconcile her sire.

XXII

' All fled my rage — the villain first
Whose craft my jealousy had nursed;

He sought in far and foreign clime
To 'scape the vengeance of his crime.
The manner of the slaughter done
Was known to few, my guilt to none;
Some tale my faithful steward framed —
I know not what — of shaft mis-aimed;   540
And even from those the act who knew
He hid the hand from which it flew.
Untouched by human laws I stood,
But God had heard the cry of blood !
There is a blank upon my mind,
A fearful vision ill-defined
Of raving till my flesh was torn,
Of dungeon-bolts and fetters worn —
And when I waked to woe more mild
And questioned of my infant child —   550
Have I not written that she bare
A boy, like summer morning fair ? —
With looks confused my menials tell
That armed men in Mortham dell
Beset the nurse's evening way,
And bore her with her charge away.
My faithless friend, and none but he,
Could profit by this villany;
Him then I sought with purpose dread
Of treble vengeance on his head !   560
He 'scaped me — but my bosom's wound
Some faint relief from wandering found,
And over distant land and sea
I bore my load of misery.

XXIII

' 'T was then that fate my footsteps led
Among a daring crew and dread,
With whom full oft my hated life
I ventured in such desperate strife
That even my fierce associates saw
My frantic deeds with doubt and awe.   570
Much then I learned and much can show
Of human guilt and human woe,
Yet ne'er have in my wanderings known
A wretch whose sorrows matched my
            own !
It chanced that after battle fray
Upon the bloody field we lay;
The yellow moon her lustre shed
Upon the wounded and the dead,
While, sense in toil and wassail drowned,
My ruffian comrades slept around,   580
There came a voice — its silver tone
Was soft, Matilda, as thine own —
" Ah, wretch ! " it said, " what mak'st thou
            here,
While unavenged my bloody bier,

While unprotected lives mine heir
Without a father's name and care ? "

XXIV

' I heard — obeyed — and homeward drew;
The fiercest of our desperate crew
I brought, at time of need to aid
My purposed vengeance long delayed. 590
But humble be my thanks to Heaven
That better hopes and thoughts has given,
And by our Lord's dear prayer has taught
Mercy by mercy must be bought ! —
Let me in misery rejoice —
I 've seen his face — I 've heard his
    voice —
I claimed of him my only child —
As he disowned the theft, he smiled !
That very calm and callous look,
That fiendish sneer his visage took, 600
As when he said, in scornful mood,
" There is a gallant in the wood ! " —
I did not slay him as he stood —
All praise be to my Maker given !
Long suffrance is one path to heaven.'

XXV

Thus far the woful tale was heard
When something in the thicket stirred.
Up Redmond sprung; the villain Guy —
For he it was that lurked so nigh —
Drew back — he durst not cross his steel 610
A moment's space with brave O'Neale
For all the treasured gold that rests
In Mortham's iron-banded chests.
Redmond resumed his seat; — he said
Some roe was rustling in the shade.
Bertram laughed grimly when he saw
His timorous comrade backward draw;
' A trusty mate art thou, to fear
A single arm, and aid so near !
Yet have I seen thee mark a deer. 620
Give me thy carabine — I 'll show
An art that thou wilt gladly know,
How thou mayst safely quell a foe.'

XXVI

On hands and knees fierce Bertram drew
The spreading birch and hazels through,
Till he had Redmond full in view;
The gun he levelled — Mark like this
Was Bertram never known to miss,
When fair opposed to aim their sate
An object of his mortal hate. 630
That day young Redmond's death had seen,
But twice Matilda came between

The carabine and Redmond's breast
Just ere the spring his finger pressed.
A deadly oath the ruffian swore,
But yet his fell design forbore:
' It ne'er,' he muttered, ' shall be said
That thus I scathed thee, haughty maid ! '
Then moved to seek more open aim,
When to his side Guy Denzil came: 640
' Bertram, forbear ! — we are undone
For ever, if thou fire the gun.
By all the fiends, an armed force
Descends the dell of foot and horse !
We perish if they hear a shot —
Madman ! we have a safer plot —
Nay, friend, be ruled, and bear thee
    back !
Behold, down yonder hollow track
The warlike leader of the band
Comes with his broadsword in his hand.' 650
Bertram looked up; he saw, he knew
That Denzil's fears had counselled true,
Then cursed his fortune and withdrew,
Threaded the woodlands undescried,
And gained the cave on Greta side.

XXVII

They whom dark Bertram in his wrath
Doomed to captivity or death,
Their thoughts to one sad subject lent,
Saw not nor heard the ambushment.
Heedless and unconcerned they sate 660
While on the very verge of fate,
Heedless and unconcerned remained
When Heaven the murderer's arm re-
    strained;
As ships drift darkling down the tide,
Nor see the shelves o'er which they glide.
Uninterrupted thus they heard
What Mortham's closing tale declared.
He spoke of wealth as of a load
By fortune on a wretch bestowed,
In bitter mockery of hate, 670
His cureless woes to aggravate;
But yet he prayed Matilda's care
Might save that treasure for his heir —
His Edith's son — for still he raved
As confident his life was saved;
In frequent vision, he averred,
He saw his face, his voice he heard,
Then argued calm — had murder been,
The blood, the corpses, had been seen;
Some had pretended, too, to mark 680
On Windermere a stranger bark,
Whose crew, with jealous care yet mild,
Guarded a female and a child.

While these faint proofs he told and
    pressed,
Hope seemed to kindle in his breast;
Though inconsistent, vague, and vain,
It warped his judgment and his brain.

XXVIII

These solemn words his story close: —
' Heaven witness for me that I chose
My part in this sad civil fight   690
Moved by no cause but England's right.
My country's groans have bid me draw
My sword for gospel and for law; —
These righted, I fling arms aside
And seek my son through Europe wide.
My wealth, on which a kinsman nigh
Already casts a grasping eye,
With thee may unsuspected lie.
When of my death Matilda hears,
Let her retain her trust three years;   700
If none from me the treasure claim,
Perished is Mortham's race and name.
Then let it leave her generous hand,
And flow in bounty o'er the land,
Soften the wounded prisoner's lot,
Rebuild the peasant's ruined cot;
So spoils, acquired by fight afar,
Shall mitigate domestic war.'

XXIX

The generous youths, who well had known
Of Mortham's mind the powerful tone, 710
To that high mind by sorrow swerved
Gave sympathy his woes deserved;
But Wilfrid chief, who saw revealed
Why Mortham wished his life concealed,
In secret, doubtless, to pursue
The schemes his wildered fancy drew.
Thoughtful he heard Matilda tell
That she would share her father's cell,
His partner of captivity,
Where'er his prison-house should be;   720
Yet grieved to think that Rokeby-hall,
Dismantled and forsook by all,
Open to rapine and to stealth,
Had now no safeguard for the wealth
Intrusted by her kinsman kind
And for such noble use designed.
' Was Barnard Castle then her choice,'
Wilfrid inquired with hasty voice,
' Since there the victor's laws ordain
Her father must a space remain ? '   730
A fluttered hope his accent shook,
A fluttered joy was in his look.

Matilda hastened to reply,
For anger flashed in Redmond's eye; —
' Duty,' she said, with gentle grace,
' Kind Wilfrid, has no choice of place;
Else had I for my sire assigned
Prison less galling to his mind
Than that his wild-wood haunts which sees
And hears the murmur of the Tees,   740
Recalling thus with every glance
What captive's sorrow can enhance;
But where those woes are highest, there
Needs Rokeby most his daughter's care.'

XXX

He felt the kindly check she gave,
And stood abashed — then answered grave:
' I sought thy purpose, noble maid,
Thy doubts to clear, thy schemes to aid.
I have beneath mine own command,
So wills my sire, a gallant band,   750
And well could send some horsemen wight
To bear the treasure forth by night,
And so bestow it as you deem
In these ill days may safest seem.'
' Thanks, gentle Wilfrid, thanks,' she said:
' O, be it not one day delayed !
And, more thy sister-friend to aid,
Be thou thyself content to hold
In thine own keeping Mortham's gold, 759
Safest with thee.' — While thus she spoke,
Armed soldiers on their converse broke,
The same of whose approach afraid
The ruffians left their ambuscade.
Their chief to Wilfrid bended low,
Then looked around as for a foe.
' What mean'st thou, friend,' young Wy-
    cliffe said,
' Why thus in arms beset the glade ? ' —
' That would I gladly learn from you;
For up my squadron as I drew
To exercise our martial game   770
Upon the moor of Barninghame,
A stranger told you were waylaid,
Surrounded, and to death betrayed.
He had a leader's voice, I ween,
A falcon glance, a warrior's mien.
He bade me bring you instant aid;
I doubted not and I obeyed.'

XXXI

Wilfrid changed color, and amazed
Turned short and on the speaker gazed,
While Redmond every thicket round 780
Tracked earnest as a questing hound,

And Denzil's carabine he found;
Sure evidence by which they knew
The warning was as kind as true.
Wisest it seemed with cautious speed
To leave the dell. It was agreed
That Redmond with Matilda fair
And fitting guard should home repair;
At nightfall Wilfrid should attend
With a strong band his sister-friend,   790
To bear with her from Rokeby's bowers
To Barnard Castle's lofty towers
Secret and safe the banded chests
In which the wealth of Mortham rests.
This hasty purpose fixed, they part,
Each with a grieved and anxious heart.

CANTO FIFTH

I

THE sultry summer day is done,
The western hills have hid the sun,
But mountain peak and village spire
Retain reflection of his fire.
Old Barnard's towers are purple still
To those that gaze from Toller-hill;
Distant and high, the tower of Bowes
Like steel upon the anvil glows;
And Stanmore's ridge behind that lay
Rich with the spoils of parting day,   10
In crimson and in gold arrayed,
Streaks yet awhile the closing shade,
Then slow resigns to darkening heaven
The tints which brighter hours had given.
Thus aged men full loath and slow
The vanities of life forego,
And count their youthful follies o'er
Till memory lends her light no more.

II

The eve that slow on upland fades
Has darker closed on Rokeby's glades   20
Where, sunk within their banks profound,
Her guardian streams to meeting wound.
The stately oaks, whose sombre frown
Of noontide made a twilight brown,
Impervious now to fainter light,
Of twilight make an early night.
Hoarse into middle air arose
The vespers of the roosting crows,
And with congenial murmurs seem
To wake the Genii of the stream;   30
For louder clamored Greta's tide,
And Tees in deeper voice replied,

And fitful waked the evening wind,
Fitful in sighs its breath resigned.
Wilfrid, whose fancy-nurtured soul
Felt in the scene a soft control,
With lighter footstep pressed the ground,
And often paused to look around;
And, though his path was to his love,
Could not but linger in the grove,   40
To drink the thrilling interest dear
Of awful pleasure checked by fear.
Such inconsistent moods have we,
Even when our passions strike the key.

III

Now, through the wood's dark mazes past,
The opening lawn he reached at last
Where, silvered by the moonlight ray,
The ancient Hall before him lay.
Those martial terrors long were fled
That frowned of old around its head: 50
The battlements, the turrets gray,
Seemed half abandoned to decay;
On barbican and keep of stone
Stern Time the foeman's work had done.
Where banners the invader braved,
The harebell now and wallflower waved;
In the rude guard-room where of yore
Their weary hours the warders wore,
Now, while the cheerful fagots blaze,
On the paved floor the spindle plays;   60
The flanking guns dismounted lie,
The moat is ruinous and dry,
The grim portcullis gone — and all
The fortress turned to peaceful Hall.

IV

But yet precautions lately ta'en
Showed danger's day revived again;
The court-yard wall showed marks of care
The fall'n defences to repair,
Lending such strength as might withstand
The insult of marauding band.   70
The beams once more were taught to bear
The trembling drawbridge into air,
And not till questioned o'er and o'er
For Wilfrid oped the jealous door,
And when he entered bolt and bar
Resumed their place with sullen jar;
Then, as he crossed the vaulted porch,
The old gray porter raised his torch,
And viewed him o'er from foot to head
Ere to the hall his steps he led.   80
That huge old hall of knightly state
Dismantled seemed and desolate.

The moon through transom-shafts of stone
Which crossed the latticed oriels shone,
And by the mournful light she gave
The Gothic vault seemed funeral cave.
Pennon and banner waved no more
O'er beams of stag and tusks of boar,
Nor glimmering arms were marshalled
    seen
To glance those sylvan spoils between.   90
Those arms, those ensigns, borne away,
Accomplished Rokeby's brave array,
But all were lost on Marston's day !
Yet here and there the moonbeams fall
Where armor yet adorns the wall,
Cumbrous of size, uncouth to sight,
And useless in the modern fight,
Like veteran relic of the wars
Known only by neglected scars.

V

Matilda soon to greet him came,   100
And bade them light the evening flame;
Said all for parting was prepared,
And tarried but for Wilfrid's guard.
But then, reluctant to unfold
His father's avarice of gold,
He hinted that lest jealous eye
Should on their precious burden pry,
He judged it best the castle gate
To enter when the night wore late;
And therefore he had left command   110
With those he trusted of his band
That they should be at Rokeby met
What time the midnight-watch was set.
Now Redmond came, whose anxious care
Till then was busied to prepare
All needful, meetly to arrange
The mansion for its mournful change.
With Wilfrid's care and kindness pleased,
His cold unready hand he seized,
And pressed it till his kindly strain   120
The gentle youth returned again.
Seemed as between them this was said,
'Awhile let jealousy be dead,
And let our contest be whose care
Shall best assist this helpless fair.'

VI

There was no speech the truce to bind;
It was a compact of the mind,
A generous thought at once impressed
On either rival's generous breast.
Matilda well the secret took   130
From sudden change of mien and look,

And — for not small had been her fear
Of jealous ire and danger near —
Felt even in her dejected state
A joy beyond the reach of fate.
They closed beside the chimney's blaze,
And talked, and hoped for happier days,
And lent their spirits' rising glow
Awhile to gild impending woe —
High privilege of youthful time,   140
Worth all the pleasures of our prime !
The bickering fagot sparkled bright
And gave the scene of love to sight,
Bade Wilfrid's cheek more lively glow,
Played on Matilda's neck of snow,
Her nut-brown curls and forehead high,
And laughed in Redmond's azure eye.
Two lovers by the maiden sate
Without a glance of jealous hate;
The maid her lovers sat between   150
With open brow and equal mien;
It is a sight but rarely spied,
Thanks to man's wrath and woman's pride.

VII

While thus in peaceful guise they sate
A knock alarmed the outer gate,
And ere the tardy porter stirred
The tinkling of a harp was heard.
A manly voice of mellow swell
Bore burden to the music well: —

SONG

'Summer eve is gone and past,   160
  Summer dew is falling fast;
  I have wandered all the day,
  Do not bid me farther stray !
  Gentle hearts of gentle kin,
  Take the wandering harper in !'

But the stern porter answer gave,
With 'Get thee hence, thou strolling knave !
The king wants soldiers; war, I trow,
Were meeter trade for such as thou.'
At this unkind reproof again   170
Answered the ready Minstrel's strain:

SONG RESUMED

'Bid not me, in battle-field,
  Buckler lift or broadsword wield !
  All my strength and all my art
  Is to touch the gentle heart
  With the wizard notes that ring
  From the peaceful minstrel-string.'

The porter, all unmoved, replied, —
'Depart in peace, with Heaven to guide;
If longer by the gate thou dwell,   180
Trust me, thou shalt not part so well.'

VIII

With somewhat of appealing look
The harper's part young Wilfrid took:
'These notes so wild and ready thrill,
They show no vulgar minstrel's skill;
Hard were his task to seek a home
More distant, since the night is come;
And for his faith I dare engage —
Your Harpool's blood is soured by age;
His gate, once readily displayed   190
To greet the friend, the poor to aid,
Now even to me though known of old
Did but reluctantly unfold.' —
'O blame not as poor Harpool's crime
An evil of this evil time.
He deems dependent on his care
The safety of his patron's heir,
Nor judges meet to ope the tower
To guest unknown at parting hour,
Urging his duty to excess   200
Of rough and stubborn faithfulness.
For this poor harper, I would fain
He may relax: — hark to his strain!'

IX

SONG RESUMED

'I have song of war for knight,
Lay of love for lady bright,
Fairy tale to lull the heir,
Goblin grim the maids to scare.
Dark the night and long till day,
Do not bid me farther stray!

'Rokeby's lords of martial fame,   210
I can count them name by name;
Legends of their line there be,
Known to few but known to me;
If you honor Rokeby's kin,
Take the wandering harper in!

'Rokeby's lords had fair regard
For the harp and for the bard;
Baron's race throve never well
Where the curse of minstrel fell.
If you love that noble kin,
Take the weary harper in!'   220

'Hark! Harpool parleys — there is hope,'
Said Redmond, 'that the gate will ope.' —

'For all thy brag and boast, I trow,
Nought knowest thou of the Felon Sow,'
Quoth Harpool, 'nor how Greta-side
She roamed and Rokeby forest wide;
Nor how Ralph Rokeby gave the beast
To Richmond's friars to make a feast.
Of Gilbert Griffinson the tale   230
Goes, and of gallant Peter Dale
That well could strike with sword amain,
And of the valiant son of Spain,
Friar Middleton, and blithe Sir Ralph;
There were a jest to make us laugh!
If thou canst tell it, in yon shed,
Thou 'st won thy supper and thy bed.'

X

Matilda smiled; 'Cold hope,' said she,
'From Harpool's love of minstrelsy!
But for this harper may we dare,   240
Redmond, to mend his couch and fare?' —
'O, ask me not! — At minstrel-string
My heart from infancy would spring;
Nor can I hear its simplest strain
But it brings Erin's dream again,
When placed by Owen Lysagh's knee —
The Filea of O'Neale was he,
A blind and bearded man whose eld
Was sacred as a prophet's held —
I 've seen a ring of rugged kerne,   250
With aspects shaggy, wild, and stern,
Enchanted by the master's lay,
Linger around the livelong day,
Shift from wild rage to wilder glee,
To love, to grief, to ecstasy,
And feel each varied change of soul
Obedient to the bard's control. —
Ah! Clandeboy! thy friendly floor
Slieve-Donard's oak shall light no more;
Nor Owen's harp beside the blaze   260
Tell maiden's love or hero's praise!
The mantling brambles hide thy hearth,
Centre of hospitable mirth;
All undistinguished in the glade,
My sires' glad home is prostrate laid,
Their vassals wander wide and far,
Serve foreign lords in distant war,
And now the stranger's sons enjoy
The lovely woods of Clandeboy!'
He spoke, and proudly turned aside   270
The starting tear to dry and hide.

XI

Matilda's dark and softened eye
Was glistening ere O'Neale's was dry.

Her hand upon his arm she laid, —
'It is the will of Heaven,' she said.
'And think'st thou, Redmond, I can part
From this loved home with lightsome
    heart,
Leaving to wild neglect whate'er
Even from my infancy was dear?
For in this calm domestic bound   280
Were all Matilda's pleasures found.
That hearth my sire was wont to grace
Full soon may be a stranger's place;
This hall in which a child I played
Like thine, dear Redmond, lowly laid,
The bramble and the thorn may braid;
Or, passed for aye from me and mine,
It ne'er may shelter Rokeby's line.
Yet is this consolation given,   289
My Redmond, — 't is the will of Heaven.'
Her word, her action, and her phrase
Were kindly as in early days;
For cold reserve had lost its power
In sorrow's sympathetic hour.
Young Redmond dared not trust his voice;
But rather had it been his choice
To share that melancholy hour
Than, armed with all a chieftain's power,
In full possession to enjoy
Slieve-Donard wide and Clandeboy.   300

XII

The blood left Wilfrid's ashen cheek,
Matilda sees and hastes to speak. —
'Happy in friendship's ready aid,
Let all my murmurs here be staid!
And Rokeby's maiden will not part
From Rokeby's hall with moody heart.
This night at least for Rokeby's fame
The hospitable hearth shall flame,
And ere its native heir retire
Find for the wanderer rest and fire,   310
While this poor harper by the blaze
Recounts the tale of other days.
Bid Harpool ope the door with speed,
Admit him and relieve each need. —
Meantime, kind Wycliffe, wilt thou try
Thy minstrel skill? — Nay, no reply —
And look not sad! — I guess thy thought;
Thy verse with laurels would be bought,
And poor Matilda, landless now,
Has not a garland for thy brow.   320
True, I must leave sweet Rokeby's glades,
Nor wander more in Greta shades;
But sure, no rigid jailer, thou
Wilt a short prison-walk allow
Where summer flowers grow wild at will

On Marwood-chase and Toller Hill;
Then holly green and lily gay
Shall twine in guerdon of thy lay.'
The mournful youth a space aside
To tune Matilda's harp applied,   330
And then a low sad descant rung
As prelude to the lay he sung.

XIII

THE CYPRESS WREATH

'O, lady, twine no wreath for me,
Or twine it of the cypress-tree!
Too lively glow the lilies light,
The varnished holly's all too bright,
The May-flower and the eglantine
May shade a brow less sad than mine;
But, lady, weave no wreath for me,
Or weave it of the cypress-tree!   340

'Let dimpled Mirth his temples twine
With tendrils of the laughing vine;
The manly oak, the pensive yew,
To patriot and to sage be due;
The myrtle bough bids lovers live,
But that Matilda will not give;
Then, lady, twine no wreath for me,
Or twine it of the cypress-tree!

'Let merry England proudly rear
Her blended roses bought so dear;   350
Let Albin bind her bonnet blue
With heath and harebell dipped in dew;
On favored Erin's crest be seen
The flower she loves of emerald green —
But, lady, twine no wreath for me,
Or twine it of the cypress-tree.

'Strike the wild harp while maids pre-
    pare
The ivy meet for minstrel's hair;
And, while his crown of laurel-leaves
With bloody hand the victor weaves,   360
Let the loud trump his triumph tell;
But when you hear the passing-bell,
Then, lady, twine a wreath for me,
And twine it of the cypress-tree.

'Yes! twine for me the cypress-bough;
But, O Matilda, twine not now!
Stay till a few brief months are past,
And I have looked and loved my last!
When villagers my shroud bestrew
With pansies, rosemary, and rue, —   370

Then, lady, weave a wreath for me,
And weave it of the cypress-tree.'

XIV

O'Neale observed the starting tear,
And spoke with kind and blithesome
cheer —
' No, noble Wilfrid ! ere the day
When mourns the land thy silent lay,
Shall many a wreath be freely wove
By hand of friendship and of love.
I would not wish that rigid Fate
Had doomed thee to a captive's state,   380
Whose hands are bound by honor's law,
Who wears a sword he must not draw;
But were it so, in minstrel pride
The land together would we ride
On prancing steeds, like harpers old,
Bound for the halls of barons bold;
Each lover of the lyre we 'd seek
From Michael's Mount to Skiddaw's Peak,
Survey wild Albin's mountain strand,
And roam green Erin's lovely land,   390
While thou the gentler souls should move
With lay of pity and of love,
And I, thy mate, in rougher strain
Would sing of war and warriors slain.
Old England's bards were vanquished
then,
And Scotland's vaunted Hawthornden,
And, silenced on Iernian shore,
M'Curtin's harp should charm no more ! '
In lively mood he spoke to wile
From Wilfrid's woe - worn cheek a
smile.   400

XV

' But,' said Matilda, ' ere thy name,
Good Redmond, gain its destined fame,
Say, wilt thou kindly deign to call
Thy brother-minstrel to the hall ?
Bid all the household too attend,
Each in his rank a humble friend;
I know their faithful hearts will grieve
When their poor mistress takes her leave;
So let the horn and beaker flow
To mitigate their parting woe.'   410
The harper came ; — in youth's first prime
Himself; in mode of olden time
His garb was fashioned, to express
The ancient English minstrel's dress,
A seemly gown of Kendal green
With gorget closed of silver sheen;
His harp in silken scarf was slung,
And by his side an anlace hung.

It seemed some masquer's quaint array
For revel or for holiday.   420

XVI

He made obeisance with a free
Yet studied air of courtesy.
Each look and accent framed to please
Seemed to affect a playful ease;
His face was of that doubtful kind
That wins the eye, but not the mind;
Yet harsh it seemed to deem amiss
Of brow so young and smooth as this.
His was the subtle look and sly
That, spying all, seems nought to spy;   430
Round all the group his glances stole,
Unmarked themselves, to mark the whole.
Yet sunk beneath Matilda's look,
Nor could the eye of Redmond brook.
To the suspicious or the old
Subtle and dangerous and bold
Had seemed this self-invited guest;
But young our lovers, — and the rest,
Wrapt in their sorrow and their fear
At parting of their Mistress dear,   440
Tear-blinded to the castle-hall
Came as to bear her funeral pall.

XVII

All that expression base was gone
When waked the guest his minstrel tone;
It fled at inspiration's call,
As erst the demon fled from Saul.
More noble glance he cast around,
More free-drawn breath inspired the sound,
His pulse beat bolder and more high
In all the pride of minstrelsy !   450
Alas ! too soon that pride was o'er,
Sunk with the lay that bade it soar !
His soul resumed with habit's chain
Its vices wild and follies vain,
And gave the talent with him born
To be a common curse and scorn.
Such was the youth whom Rokeby's maid
With condescending kindness prayed
Here to renew the strains she loved,
At distance heard and well approved.   460

XVIII

SONG

THE HARP

I was a wild and wayward boy,
My childhood scorned each childish toy;

Retired from all, reserved and coy,
    To musing prone,
I wooed my solitary joy,
    My Harp alone.

My youth with bold ambition's mood
Despised the humble stream and wood
Where my poor father's cottage stood,
    To fame unknown; —   470
What should my soaring views make good ?
    My Harp alone !

Love came with all his frantic fire,
And wild romance of vain desire:
The baron's daughter heard my lyre
    And praised the tone; —
What could presumptuous hope inspire ?
    My Harp alone !

At manhood's touch the bubble burst,
And manhood's pride the vision curst,   480
And all that had my folly nursed
    Love's sway to own;
Yet spared the spell that lulled me first,
    My Harp alone !

Woe came with war, and want with woe,
And it was mine to undergo
Each outrage of the rebel foe: —
    Can aught atone
My fields laid waste, my cot laid low ?
    My Harp alone !   490

Ambition's dreams I 've seen depart,
Have rued of penury the smart,
Have felt of love the venomed dart,
    When hope was flown;
Yet rests one solace to my heart, —
    My Harp alone !

Then over mountain, moor, and hill,
My faithful Harp, I 'll bear thee still;
And when this life of want and ill
    Is wellnigh gone,   500
Thy strings mine elegy shall thrill,
    My Harp alone !

XIX

'A pleasing lay !' Matilda said;
But Harpool shook his old gray head,
And took his baton and his torch
To seek his guard-room in the porch.
Edmund observed — with sudden change
Among the strings his fingers range,
Until they waked a bolder glee

Of military melody;   510
Then paused amid the martial sound,
And looked with well - feigned fear
    around;—
'None to this noble house belong,'
He said, 'that would a minstrel wrong
Whose fate has been through good and ill
To love his Royal Master still,
And with your honored leave would fain
Rejoice you with a royal strain.'
Then, as assured by sign and look,
The warlike tone again he took;   520
And Harpool stopped and turned to hear
A ditty of the Cavalier.

XX

SONG

THE CAVALIER

While the dawn on the mountain was misty
    and gray,
My true love has mounted his steed and
    away,
Over hill, over valley, o'er dale, and o'er
    down;
Heaven shield the brave gallant that fights
    for the Crown !

He has doffed the silk doublet the breast-
    plate to bear,
He has placed the steel-cap o'er his long-
    flowing hair,
From his belt to his stirrup his broadsword
    hangs down, —
Heaven shield the brave gallant that fights
    for the Crown !   530

For the rights of fair England that broad-
    sword he draws,
Her King is his leader, her Church is his
    cause;
His watchword is honor, his pay is re-
    nown, —
God strike with the gallant that strikes for
    the Crown !

They may boast of their Fairfax, their
    Waller, and all
The roundheaded rebels of Westminster
    Hall;
But tell these bold traitors of London's
    proud town,
That the spears of the North have encir-
    cled the Crown.

There 's Derby and Cavendish, dread of
    their foes;
There 's Erin's high Ormond and Scotland's
    Montrose !   540
Would you match the base Skippon, and
    Massey, and Brown,
With the Barons of England that fight for
    the Crown ?

Now joy to the crest of the brave Cava-
    lier!
Be his banner unconquered, resistless his
    spear,
Till in peace and in triumph his toils he
    may drown,
In a pledge to fair England, her Church,
    and her Crown.

XXI

' Alas !' Matilda said, ' that strain,
Good harper, now is heard in vain !
The time has been at such a sound
When Rokeby's vassals gathered round, 550
An hundred manly hearts would bound;
But now, the stirring verse we hear
Like trump in dying soldier's ear !
Listless and sad the notes we own,
The power to answer them is flown.
Yet not without his meet applause
Be he that sings the rightful cause,
Even when the crisis of its fate
To human eye seems desperate.
While Rokeby's heir such power retains, 560
Let this slight guerdon pay thy pains: —
And lend thy harp; I fain would try
If my poor skill can aught supply,
Ere yet I leave my fathers' hall,
To mourn the cause in which we fall.'

XXII

The harper with a downcast look
And trembling hand her bounty took.
As yet the conscious pride of art
Had steeled him in his treacherous part;
A powerful spring of force unguessed 570
That hath each gentler mood suppressed,
And reigned in many a human breast,
From his that plans the red campaign
To his that wastes the woodland reign.
The failing wing, the blood-shot eye
The sportsman marks with apathy,
Each feeling of his victim's ill
Drowned in his own successful skill.
The veteran, too, who now no more
Aspires to head the battle's roar, 580

Loves still the triumph of his art,
And traces on the pencilled chart
Some stern invader's destined way
Through blood and ruin to his prey;
Patriots to death, and towns to flame
He dooms, to raise another's name,
And shares the guilt, though not the fame.
What pays him for his span of time
Spent in premeditating crime ?
What against pity arms his heart ? 590
It is the conscious pride of art.

XXIII

But principles in Edmund's mind
Were baseless, vague, and undefined.
His soul, like bark with rudder lost,
On passion's changeful tide was tost;
Nor vice nor virtue had the power
Beyond the impression of the hour;
And O, when passion rules, how rare
The hours that fall to Virtue's share !
Yet now she roused her — for the pride 600
That lack of sterner guilt supplied
Could scarce support him when arose
The lay that mourned Matilda's woes.

SONG

THE FAREWELL

' The sound of Rokeby's woods I hear,
    They mingle with the song:
Dark Greta's voice is in mine ear,
    I must not hear them long.
From every loved and native haunt
    The native heir must stray,
And, like a ghost whom sunbeams daunt, 610
    Must part before the day.

' Soon from the halls my fathers reared,
    Their scutcheons may descend,
A line so long beloved and feared
    May soon obscurely end.
No longer here Matilda's tone
    Shall bid these echoes swell;
Yet shall they hear her proudly own
    The cause in which we fell.'

The lady paused, and then again 620
Resumed the lay in loftier strain. —

XXIV

' Let our halls and towers decay,
    Be our name and line forgot,
Lands and manors pass away, —
    We but share our monarch's lot.

If no more our annals show
    Battles won and banners taken,
Still in death, defeat, and woe,
    Ours be loyalty unshaken !

' Constant still in danger's hour,   630
    Princes owned our fathers' aid ;
Lands and honors, wealth and power,
    Well their loyalty repaid.
Perish wealth and power and pride,
    Mortal boons by mortals given !
But let constancy abide,
    Constancy 's the gift of Heaven.'

XXV

While thus Matilda's lay was heard,
A thousand thoughts in Edmund stirred.
In peasant life he might have known   640
As fair a face, as sweet a tone ;
But village notes could ne'er supply
That rich and varied melody,
And ne'er in cottage maid was seen
The easy dignity of mien,
Claiming respect yet waiving state,
That marks the daughters of the great.
Yet not perchance had these alone
His scheme of purposed guilt o'erthrown ;
But while her energy of mind   650
Superior rose to griefs combined,
Lending its kindling to her eye,
Giving her form new majesty, —
To Edmund's thought Matilda seemed
The very object he had dreamed
When, long ere guilt his soul had known,
In Winston bowers he mused alone,
Taxing his fancy to combine
The face, the air, the voice divine,
Of princess fair by cruel fate   660
Reft of her honors, power, and state,
Till to her rightful realm restored
By destined hero's conquering sword.

XXVI

' Such was my vision !' Edmund thought ;
' And have I then the ruin wrought
Of such a maid that fancy ne'er
In fairest vision formed her peer ?
Was it my hand that could unclose
The postern to her ruthless foes ?
Foes lost to honor, law, and faith,   670
Their kindest mercy sudden death !
Have I done this ? I, who have swore
That if the globe such angel bore,
I would have traced its circle broad
To kiss the ground on which she trode !—

And now — O, would that earth would rive
And close upon me while alive ! —
Is there no hope ? — is all then lost ? —
Bertram 's already on his post !
Even now beside the hall's arched door 680
I saw his shadow cross the floor !
He was to wait my signal strain —
A little respite thus we gain :
By what I heard the menials say,
Young Wycliffe's troop are on their way —
Alarm precipitates the crime !
My harp must wear away the time.' —
And then in accents faint and low
He faltered forth a tale of woe.   689

XXVII
BALLAD

' " And whither would you lead me then ? "
    Quoth the friar of orders gray ;
And the ruffians twain replied again,
    " By a dying woman to pray." —

' " I see," he said, " a lovely sight,
    A sight bodes little harm,
A lady as a lily bright
    With an infant on her arm." —

' " Then do thine office, friar gray,
    And see thou shrive her free !
Else shall the sprite that parts to-night 700
    Fling all its guilt on thee.

' " Let mass be said and trentals read
    When thou 'rt to convent gone,
And bid the bell of Saint Benedict
    Toll out its deepest tone."

' The shrift is done, the friar is gone,
    Blindfolded as he came —
Next morning all in Littlecot Hall
    Were weeping for their dame.

' Wild Darrell is an altered man,   710
    The village crones can tell ;
He looks pale as clay and strives to pray,
    If he hears the convent bell.

' If prince or peer cross Darrell's way,
    He 'll beard him in his pride —
If he meet a friar of orders gray,
    He droops and turns aside.'

XXVIII

' Harper ! methinks thy magic lays,'
Matilda said, ' can goblins raise !

Wellnigh my fancy can discern   720
Near the dark porch a visage stern;
E'en now in yonder shadowy nook
I see it ! — Redmond, Wilfrid, look ! —
A human form distinct and clear —
God, for thy mercy ! — It draws near ! '
She saw too true.   Stride after stride,
The centre of that chamber wide
Fierce Bertram gained; then made a
    stand
And, proudly waving with his hand,   729
Thundered — ' Be still, upon your lives ! —
He bleeds who speaks, he dies who strives.'
Behind their chief the robber crew,
Forth from the darkened portal drew
In silence — save that echo dread
Returned their heavy measured tread.
The lamp's uncertain lustre gave
Their arms to gleam, their plumes to wave;
File after file in order pass,
Like forms on Banquo's mystic glass.
Then, halting at their leader's sign,   740
At once they formed and curved their line,
Hemming within its crescent drear
Their victims like a herd of deer.
Another sign, and to the aim
Levelled at once their muskets came,
As waiting but their chieftain's word
To make their fatal volley heard.

XXIX

Back in a heap the menials drew;
Yet, even in mortal terror true,
Their pale and startled group oppose   750
Between Matilda and the foes.
' O, haste thee, Wilfrid !' Redmond cried;
' Undo that wicket by thy side !
Bear hence Matilda — gain the wood —
The pass may be awhile made good —
Thy band ere this must sure be nigh —
O speak not — dally not — but fly !'
While yet the crowd their motions hide,
Through the low wicket door they glide.
Through vaulted passages they wind,   760
In Gothic intricacy twined;
Wilfrid half led and half he bore
Matilda to the postern door,
And safe beneath the forest tree,
The lady stands at liberty.
The moonbeams, the fresh gale's caress,
Renewed suspended consciousness; —
' Where 's Redmond ? ' eagerly she cries:
' Thou answer'st not — he dies ! he dies !
And thou hast left him all bereft   770
Of mortal aid — with murderers left !

I know it well — he would not yield
His sword to man — his doom is sealed !
For my scorned life, which thou hast
    bought
At price of his, I thank thee not.'

XXX

The unjust reproach, the angry look,
The heart of Wilfrid could not brook.
' Lady,' he said, ' my band so near,
In safety thou mayst rest thee here.   779
For Redmond's death thou shalt not mourn,
If mine can buy his safe return.'
He turned away — his heart throbbed high,
The tear was bursting from his eye;
The sense of her injustice pressed
Upon the maid's distracted breast, —
' Stay, Wilfrid, stay ! all aid is vain !'
He heard but turned him not again !
He reaches now the postern door,
Now enters — and is seen no more.

XXXI

With all the agony that e'er   790
Was gendered 'twixt suspense and fear,
She watched the line of windows tall
Whose Gothic lattice lights the Hall,
Distinguished by the paly red
The lamps in dim reflection shed,
While all beside in wan moonlight
Each grated casement glimmered white.
No sight of harm, no sound of ill,
It is a deep and midnight still.   799
Who looked upon the scene had guessed
All in the castle were at rest —
When sudden on the windows shone
A lightning flash just seen and gone !
A shot is heard — again the flame
Flashed thick and fast — a volley came !
Then echoed wildly from within
Of shout and scream the mingled din,
And weapon-clash and maddening cry,
Of those who kill and those who die ! —
As filled the hall with sulphurous smoke,
More red, more dark, the death-flash broke;
And forms were on the lattice cast   812
That struck or struggled as they past.

XXXII

What sounds upon the midnight wind
Approach so rapidly behind ?
It is, it is, the tramp of steeds,
Matilda hears the sound, she speeds,
Seizes upon the leader's rein —
' O, haste to aid ere aid be vain !

Fly to the postern — gain the hall ! '   820
From saddle spring the troopers all;
Their gallant steeds at liberty
Run wild along the moonlight lea.
But ere they burst upon the scene
Full stubborn had the conflict been.
When Bertram marked Matilda's flight,
It gave the signal for the fight;
And Rokeby's veterans, seamed with scars
Of Scotland's and of Erin's wars,
Their momentary panic o'er,   830
Stood to the arms which then they bore —
For they were weaponed and prepared
Their mistress on her way to guard.
Then cheered them to the fight O'Neale,
Then pealed the shot, and clashed the
    steel;
The war-smoke soon with sable breath
Darkened the scene of blood and death,
While on the few defenders close
The bandits with redoubled blows,
And, twice driven back, yet fierce and
  . fell   840
Renew the charge with frantic yell.

XXXIII

Wilfrid has fallen — but o'er him stood
Young Redmond soiled with smoke and
    blood,
Cheering his mates with heart and hand
Still to make good their desperate stand:
' Up, comrades, up !   In Rokeby halls
Ne'er be it said our courage falls.
What ! faint ye for their savage cry,
Or do the smoke-wreaths daunt your eye ?
These rafters have returned a shout   850
As loud at Rokeby's wassail rout,
As thick a smoke these hearths have given
At Hallow-tide or Christmas-even.
Stand to it yet ! renew the fight
For Rokeby's and Matilda's right !
These slaves ! they dare not hand to hand
Bide buffet from a true man's brand.'
Impetuous, active, fierce, and young,
Upon the advancing foes he sprung.
Woe to the wretch at whom is bent   860
His brandished falchion's sheer descent !
Backward they scattered as he came,
Like wolves before the levin flame,
When, mid their howling conclave driven,
Hath glanced the thunderbolt of heaven.
Bertram rushed on — but Harpool clasped
His knees, although in death he gasped,
His falling corpse before him flung,
And round the trammelled ruffian clung.

Just then the soldiers filled the dome,   870
And shouting charged the felons home
So fiercely that in panic dread
They broke, they yielded, fell, or fled,
Bertram's stern voice they heed no more,
Though heard above the battle's roar;
While, trampling down the dying man,
He strove with volleyed threat and ban
In scorn of odds, in fate's despite,
To rally up the desperate fight.

XXXIV

Soon murkier clouds the hall enfold   880
Than e'er from battle-thunders rolled,
So dense the combatants scarce know
To aim or to avoid the blow.
Smothering and blindfold grows the
    fight —
But soon shall dawn a dismal light !
Mid cries and clashing arms there came
The hollow sound of rushing flame;
New horrors on the tumult dire
Arise — the castle is on fire !
Doubtful if chance had cast the brand   890
Or frantic Bertram's desperate hand,
Matilda saw — for frequent broke
From the dim casements gusts of smoke,
Yon tower, which late so clear defined
On the fair hemisphere reclined
That, pencilled on its azure pure,
The eye could count each embrasure,
Now, swathed within the sweeping cloud,
Seems giant-spectre in his shroud;
Till, from each loop-hole flashing light, 900
A spout of fire shines ruddy bright,
And, gathering to united glare,
Streams high into the midnight air;
A dismal beacon, far and wide
That wakened Greta's slumbering side.
Soon all beneath, through gallery long
And pendent arch, the fire flashed strong,
Snatching whatever could maintain,
Raise, or extend its furious reign;
Startling with closer cause of dread   910
The females who the conflict fled,
And now rushed forth upon the plain,
Filling the air with clamors vain.

XXXV

But ceased not yet the hall within
The shriek, the shout, the carnage-din,
Till bursting lattices give proof
The flames have caught the raftered roof
What ! wait they till its beams amain
Crash on the slayers and the slain ?

The alarm is caught — the drawbridge
    falls,   920
The warriors hurry from the walls,
But by the conflagration's light
Upon the lawn renew the fight.
Each straggling felon down was hewed,
Not one could gain the sheltering wood;
But forth the affrighted harper sprung,
And to Matilda's robe he clung.
Her shriek, entreaty, and command
Stopped the pursuer's lifted hand.
Denzil and he alive were ta'en;   930
The rest save Bertram all are slain.

XXXVI

And where is Bertram ? — Soaring high,
The general flame ascends the sky;
In gathered group the soldiers gaze
Upon the broad and roaring blaze,
When, like infernal demon, sent
Red from his penal element,
To plague and to pollute the air,
His face all gore, on fire his hair,
Forth from the central mass of smoke   940
The giant form of Bertram broke !
His brandished sword on high he rears,
Then plunged among opposing spears;
Round his left arm his mantle trussed,
Received and foiled three lances' thrust;
Nor these his headlong course withstood,
Like reeds he snapped the tough ashwood.
In vain his foes around him clung;
With matchless force aside he flung
Their boldest, — as the bull at bay   950
Tosses the ban-dogs from his way,
Through forty foes his path he made,
And safely gained the forest glade.

XXXVII

Scarce was this final conflict o'er
When from the postern Redmond bore
Wilfrid, who, as of life bereft,
Had in the fatal hall been left,
Deserted there by all his train;
But Redmond saw and turned again.
Beneath an oak he laid him down   960
That in the blaze gleamed ruddy brown,
And then his mantle's clasp undid;
Matilda held his drooping head,
Till, given to breathe the freer air,
Returning life repaid their care.
He gazed on them with heavy sigh, —
'I could have wished even thus to die !'
No more he said, — for now with speed
Each trooper had regained his steed;

The ready palfreys stood arrayed   970
For Redmond and for Rokeby's maid;
Two Wilfrid on his horse sustain,
One leads his charger by the rein.
But oft Matilda looked behind,
As up the vale of Tees they wind,
Where far the mansion of her sires
Beaconed the dale with midnight fires.
In gloomy arch above them spread,
The clouded heaven lowered bloody red;
Beneath in sombre light the flood   980
Appeared to roll in waves of blood.
Then one by one was heard to fall
The tower, the donjon-keep, the hall.
Each rushing down with thunder sound
A space the conflagration drowned;
Till gathering strength again it rose,
Announced its triumph in its close,
Shook wide its light the landscape o'er,
Then sunk — and Rokeby was no more !

CANTO SIXTH

I

THE summer sun, whose early power
Was wont to gild Matilda's bower
And rouse her with his matin ray
Her duteous orisons to pay,
That morning sun has three times seen
The flowers unfold on Rokeby green,
But sees no more the slumbers fly
From fair Matilda's hazel eye;
That morning sun has three times broke
On Rokeby's glades of elm and oak,   10
But, rising from their sylvan screen,
Marks no gray turrets glance between.
A shapeless mass lie keep and tower,
That, hissing to the morning shower,
Can but with smouldering vapor pay
The early smile of summer day.
The peasant, to his labor bound,
Pauses to view the blackened mound,
Striving amid the ruined space
Each well-remembered spot to trace.   20
That length of frail and fire-scorched wall
Once screened the hospitable hall;
When yonder broken arch was whole,
'T was there was dealt the weekly dole;
And where yon tottering columns nod
The chapel sent the hymn to God.
So flits the world's uncertain span !
Nor zeal for God nor love for man
Gives mortal monuments a date
Beyond the power of Time and Fate.   30

The towers must share the builder's doom;
Ruin is theirs, and his a tomb:
But better boon benignant Heaven
To Faith and Charity has given,
And bids the Christian hope sublime
Transcend the bounds of Fate and Time.

II

Now the third night of summer came
Since that which witnessed Rokeby's flame.
On Brignall cliffs and Scargill brake
The owlet's homilies awake,   40
The bittern screamed from rush and flag,
The raven slumbered on his crag,
Forth from his den the otter drew, —
Grayling and trout their tyrant knew,
As between reed and sedge he peers,
With fierce round snout and sharpened
        ears,
Or prowling by the moonbeam cool
Watches the stream or swims the pool; —
Perched on his wonted eyrie high,
Sleep sealed the tercelet's wearied eye,   50
That all the day had watched so well
The cushat dart across the dell.
In dubious beam reflected shone
That lofty cliff of pale gray stone
Beside whose base the secret cave
To rapine late a refuge gave.
The crag's wild crest of copse and yew
On Greta's breast dark shadows threw,
Shadows that met or shunned the sight
With every change of fitful light,   60
As hope and fear alternate chase
Our course through life's uncertain race.

III

Gliding by crag and copsewood green,
A solitary form was seen
To trace with stealthy pace the wold.
Like fox that seeks the midnight fold,
And pauses oft, and cowers dismayed
At every breath that stirs the shade.
He passes now the ivy bush, —
The owl has seen him and is hush;   70
He passes now the doddered oak, —
He heard the startled raven croak;
Lower and lower he descends,
Rustle the leaves, the brushwood bends;
The otter hears him tread the shore,
And dives and is beheld no more;
And by the cliff of pale gray stone
The midnight wanderer stands alone.
Methinks that by the moon we trace
A well-remembered form and face !   80

That stripling shape, that cheek so pale,
Combine to tell a rueful tale,
Of powers misused, of passion's force,
Of guilt, of grief, and of remorse !
'T is Edmund's eye at every sound
That flings that guilty glance around;
'T is Edmund's trembling haste divides
The brushwood that the cavern hides;
And when its narrow porch lies bare
'T is Edmund's form that enters there.   90

IV

His flint and steel have sparkled bright,
A lamp hath lent the cavern light.
Fearful and quick his eye surveys
Each angle of the gloomy maze.
Since last he left that stern abode,
It seemed as none its floor had trode;
Untouched appeared the various spoil,
The purchase of his comrades' toil;
Masks and disguises grimed with mud,
Arms broken and defiled with blood,   100
And all the nameless tools that aid
Night-felons in their lawless trade,
Upon the gloomy walls were hung
Or lay in nooks obscurely flung.
Still on the sordid board appear
The relics of the noontide cheer:
Flagons and emptied flasks were there,
And bench o'erthrown and shattered chair;
And all around the semblance showed,
As when the final revel glowed,   110
When the red sun was setting fast
And parting pledge Guy Denzil past.
'To   Rokeby   treasure - vaults !'   they
        quaffed,
And shouted loud and wildly laughed,
Poured maddening from the rocky door,
And parted — to return no more !
They found in Rokeby vaults their doom, —
A bloody death, a burning tomb !

V

There his own peasant dress he spies,
Doffed to assume that quaint disguise,   120
And shuddering thought upon his glee
When pranked in garb of minstrelsy.
'O, be the fatal art accurst,'
He cried, 'that moved my folly first,
Till, bribed by bandits' base applause,
I burst through God's and Nature's laws !
Three summer days are scantly past
Since I have trod this cavern last,
A thoughtless wretch, and prompt to err —
But O, as yet no murderer !   130

Even now I list my comrades' cheer,
That general laugh is in mine ear
Which raised my pulse and steeled my
  heart,
As I rehearsed my treacherous part —
And would that all since then could seem
The phantom of a fever's dream !
But fatal memory notes too well
The horrors of the dying yell
From my despairing mates that broke
When flashed the fire and rolled the
  smoke,   140
When the avengers shouting came
And hemmed us 'twixt the sword and
  flame !
My frantic flight — the lifted brand —
That angel's interposing hand ! —
If for my life from slaughter freed
I yet could pay some grateful meed !
Perchance this object of my quest
May aid ' — he turned nor spoke the rest.

VI

Due northward from the rugged hearth
With paces five he meets the earth,   150
Then toiled with mattock to explore
The entrails of the cavern floor,
Nor paused till deep beneath the ground
His search a small steel casket found.
Just as he stooped to loose its hasp
His shoulder felt a giant grasp;
He started and looked up aghast,
Then shrieked ! — 'T was Bertram held
  him fast.
' Fear not ! ' he said ; but who could
  hear
That deep stern voice and cease to
  fear ?   160
' Fear not ! — By heaven, he shakes as much
As partridge in the falcon's clutch:'
He raised him and unloosed his hold,
While from the opening casket rolled
A chain and reliquaire of gold.
Bertram beheld it with surprise,
Gazed on its fashion and device,
Then, cheering Edmund as he could,
Somewhat he smoothed his rugged mood,
For still the youth's half-lifted eye   170
Quivered with terror's agony,
And sidelong glanced as to explore
In meditated flight the door.
' Sit,' Bertram said, ' from danger free:
Thou canst not and thou shalt not flee.
Chance brings me hither; hill and plain
I 've sought for refuge-place in vain.

And tell me now, thou aguish boy,
What makest thou here ? what means this
  toy ?
Denzil and thou, I marked, were ta'en;   180
What lucky chance unbound your chain ?
I deemed, long since on Baliol's tower,
Your heads were warped with sun and
  shower.
Tell me the whole — and mark ! nought
  e'er
Chafes me like falsehood or like fear.'
Gathering his courage to his aid
But trembling still, the youth obeyed.

VII

' Denzil and I two nights passed o'er
In fetters on the dungeon floor.
A guest the third sad morrow brought;   190
Our hold, dark Oswald Wycliffe sought,
And eyed my comrade long askance
With fixed and penetrating glance.
"Guy Denzil art thou called ? " — " The
  same."
" At Court who served wild Buckinghame;
Thence banished, won a keeper's place,
So Villiers willed, in Marwood-chase,
That lost — I need not tell thee why —
Thou madest thy wit thy wants supply,
Then fought for Rokeby: — have I
  guessed
My prisoner right ? " — " At thy be-   200
  hest." —
He paused awhile, and then went on
With low and confidential tone; —
Me, as I judge, not then he saw
Close nestled in my couch of straw. —
" List to me, Guy. Thou know'st the great
Have frequent need of what they hate;
Hence, in their favor oft we see
Unscrupled, useful men like thee.
Were I disposed to bid thee live,   210
What pledge of faith hast thou to give ? "

VIII

' The ready fiend who never yet
Hath failed to sharpen Denzil's wit
Prompted his lie — " His only child
Should rest his pledge." — The baron
  smiled,
And turned to me — " Thou art his son ? "
I bowed — our fetters were undone,
And we were led to hear apart
A dreadful lesson of his art.
Wilfrid, he said, his heir and son,   220
Had fair Matilda's favor won;

And long since had their union been
But for her father's bigot spleen,
Whose brute and blindfold party-rage
Would, force perforce, her hand engage
To a base kern of Irish earth,
Unknown his lineage and his birth,
Save that a dying ruffian bore
The infant brat to Rokeby door.
Gentle restraint, he said, would lead   230
Old Rokeby to enlarge his creed;
But fair occasion he must find
For such restraint well meant and kind,
The knight being rendered to his charge
But as a prisoner at large.

IX

'He schooled us in a well-forged tale
Of scheme the castle walls to scale,
To which was leagued each Cavalier
That dwells upon the Tyne and Wear,
That Rokeby, his parole forgot,   240
Had dealt with us to aid the plot.
Such was the charge which Denzil's zeal
Of hate to Rokeby and O'Neale
Proffered as witness to make good,
Even though the forfeit were their blood.
I scrupled until o'er and o'er
His prisoners' safety Wycliffe swore;
And then — alas ! what needs there more ?
I knew I should not live to say
The proffer I refused that day;   250
Ashamed to live, yet loath to die,
I soiled me with their infamy !'
'Poor youth !' said Bertram, 'wavering
   still,
Unfit alike for good or ill !
But what fell next ? ' — ' Soon as at large
Was scrolled and signed our fatal charge,
There never yet on tragic stage
Was seen so well a painted rage
As Oswald's showed ! With loud alarm
He called his garrison to arm;   260
From tower to tower, from post to post,
He hurried as if all were lost;
Consigned to dungeon and to chain
The good old knight and all his train;
Warned each suspected Cavalier
Within his limits to appear
To-morrow at the hour of noon
In the high church of Eglistone.' —

X

'Of Eglistone ! — Even now I passed,'
Said Bertram, ' as the night closed fast;   270

Torches and cressets gleamed around,
I heard the saw and hammer sound,
And I could mark they toiled to raise
A scaffold, hung with sable baize,
Which the grim headsman's scene dis-
   played,
Block, axe, and sawdust ready laid.
Some evil deed will there be done
Unless Matilda wed his son; —
She loves him not — 't is shrewdly guessed
That Redmond rules the damsel's breast. 280
This is a turn of Oswald's skill;
But I may meet, and foil him still ! —
How camest thou to thy freedom ? ' —
   ' There
Lies mystery more dark and rare.
In midst of Wycliffe's well-feigned rage,
A scroll was offered by a page,
Who told a muffled horseman late
Had left it at the Castle-gate.
He broke the seal — his cheek showed
   change,
Sudden, portentous, wild, and strange;   290
The mimic passion of his eye
Was turned to actual agony;
His hand like summer sapling shook,
Terror and guilt were in his look.
Denzil he judged in time of need
Fit counsellor for evil deed;
And thus apart his counsel broke,
While with a ghastly smile he spoke:

XI

' " As in the pageants of the stage
The dead awake in this wild age,   300
Mortham — whom all men deemed decreed
In his own deadly snare to bleed,
Slain by a bravo whom o'er sea
He trained to aid in murdering me, —
Mortham has 'scaped ! The coward shot
The steed but harmed the rider not." '
Here with an execration fell
Bertram leaped up and paced the cell: —
' Thine own gray head or bosom dark,'
He muttered, ' may be surer mark ! '   310
Then sat and signed to Edmund, pale
With terror, to resume his tale.
' Wycliffe went on: — " Mark with what
   flights
Of wildered reverie he writes: —

THE LETTER

' " Ruler of Mortham's destiny !
Though dead, thy victim lives to thee.

Once had he all that binds to life,
A lovely child, a lovelier wife;
Wealth, fame, and friendship were his
 own —
Thou gavest the word and they are flown.
Mark how he pays thee: to thy hand   321
He yields his honors and his land,
One boon premised; — restore his child !
And, from his native land exiled,
Mortham no more returns to claim
His lands, his honors, or his name;
Refuse him this and from the slain
Thou shalt see Mortham rise again." —

XII

' This billet while the baron read,
His faltering accents showed his dread; 330
He pressed his forehead with his palm,
Then took a scornful tone and calm;
" Wild as the winds, as billows wild !
What wot I of his spouse or child ?
Hither he brought a joyous dame,
Unknown her lineage or her name:
Her in some frantic fit he slew;
The nurse and child in fear withdrew.
Heaven be my witness, wist I where
To find this youth, my kinsman's heir,   340
Unguerdoned I would give with joy
The father's arms to fold his boy,
And Mortham's lands and towers resign
To the just heirs of Mortham's line."
Thou know'st that scarcely e'en his fear
Suppresses Denzil's cynic sneer; —
" Then happy is thy vassal's part,"
He said, " to ease his patron's heart !
In thine own jailer's watchful care
Lies Mortham's just and rightful heir; 350
Thy generous wish is fully won, —
Redmond O'Neale is Mortham's son." —

XIII

' Up starting with a frenzied look,
His clenched hand the baron shook:
" Is Hell at work ? or dost thou rave,
Or darest thou palter with me, slave !
Perchance thou wot'st not, Barnard's tow-
 ers
Have racks of strange and ghastly pow-
 ers."
Denzil, who well his safety knew,
Firmly rejoined, " I tell thee true.   360
Thy racks could give thee but to know
The proofs which I, untortured, show.
It chanced upon a winter night
When early snow made Stanmore white,

That very night when first of all
Redmond O'Neale saw Rokeby-hall,
It was my goodly lot to gain
A reliquary and a chain,
Twisted and chased of massive gold.
Demand not how the prize I hold !   370
It was not given nor lent nor sold.
Gilt tablets to the chain were hung
With letters in the Irish tongue.
I hid my spoil, for there was need
That I should leave the land with speed,
Nor then I deemed it safe to bear
On mine own person gems so rare.
Small heed I of the tablets took,
But since have spelled them by the book
When some sojourn in Erin's land   380
Of their wild speech had given command.
But darkling was the sense; the phrase
And language those of other days,
Involved of purpose, as to foil
An interloper's prying toil.
The words but not the sense I knew,
Till fortune gave the guiding clue.

XIV

' " Three days since, was that clue re-
 vealed
In Thorsgill as I lay concealed,
And heard at full when Rokeby's maid 390
Her uncle's history displayed;
And now I can interpret well
Each syllable the tablets tell.
Mark, then: fair Edith was the joy
Of old O'Neale of Clandeboy;
But from her sire and country fled
In secret Mortham's lord to wed.
O'Neale, his first resentment o'er,
Despatched his son to Greta's shore,   399
Enjoining he should make him known —
Until his farther will were shown —
To Edith, but to her alone.
What of their ill-starred meeting fell
Lord Wycliffe knows, and none so well.

XV

' " O'Neale it was who in despair
Robbed Mortham of his infant heir;
He bred him in their nurture wild,
And called him murdered Connel's child.
Soon died the nurse; the clan believed 409
What from their chieftain they received.
His purpose was that ne'er again
The boy should cross the Irish main,
But, like his mountain sires, enjoy
The woods and wastes of Clandeboy.

Then on the land wild troubles came,
And stronger chieftains urged a claim,
And wrested from the old man's hands
His native towers, his father's lands.
Unable then amid the strife
To guard young Redmond's rights or
 life,   420
Late and reluctant he restores
The infant to his native shores,
With goodly gifts and letters stored,
With many a deep conjuring word,
To Mortham and to Rokeby's lord.
Nought knew the clod of Irish earth,
Who was the guide, of Redmond's birth,
But deemed his chief's commands were
 laid
On both, by both to be obeyed.
How he was wounded by the way   430
I need not, and I list not say." —

XVI

' " A wondrous tale ! and, grant it true,
What," Wycliffe answered, " might I do ?
Heaven knows, as willingly as now
I raise the bonnet from my brow,
Would I my kinsman's manors fair
Restore to Mortham or his heir;
But Mortham is distraught — O'Neale
Has drawn for tyranny his steel,
Malignant to our rightful cause   440
And trained in Rome's delusive laws.
Hark thee apart ! " They whispered long,
Till Denzil's voice grew bold and strong:
" My proofs ! I never will," he said,
" Show mortal man where they are laid.
Nor hope discovery to foreclose
By giving me to feed the crows;
For I have mates at large who know
Where I am wont such toys to stow.
Free me from peril and from band,   450
These tablets are at thy command;
Nor were it hard to form some train,
To wile old Mortham o'er the main.
Then, lunatic's nor papist's hand
Should wrest from thine the goodly land."
" I like thy wit," said Wycliffe, " well;
But here in hostage shalt thou dwell.
Thy son, unless my purpose err,
May prove the trustier messenger.
A scroll to Mortham shall he bear   460
From me, and fetch these tokens rare.
Gold shalt thou have, and that good store,
And freedom, his commission o'er;
But if his faith should chance to fail,
The gibbet frees thee from the jail."

XVII

' Meshed in the net himself had twined,
What subterfuge could Denzil find ?
He told me with reluctant sigh
That hidden here the tokens lie,
Conjured my swift return and aid,   470
By all he scoffed and disobeyed,
And looked as if the noose were tied
And I the priest who left his side.
This scroll for Mortham Wycliffe gave,
Whom I must seek by Greta's wave,
Or in the hut where chief he hides,
Where Thorsgill's forester resides. —
Thence chanced it, wandering in the glade,
That he descried our ambuscade. —
I was dismissed as evening fell,   480
And reached but now this rocky cell.'
' Give Oswald's letter.' — Bertram read,
And tore it fiercely shred by shred: —
' All lies and villany ! to blind
His noble kinsman's generous mind,
And train him on from day to day,
Till he can take his life away. —
And now, declare thy purpose, youth,
Nor dare to answer, save the truth;
If aught I mark of Denzil's art,   490
I 'll tear the secret from thy heart ! ' —

XVIII

' It needs not.   I renounce,' he said,
' My tutor and his deadly trade.
Fixed was my purpose to declare
To Mortham, Redmond is his heir;
To tell him in what risk he stands,
And yield these tokens to his hands.
Fixed was my purpose to atone,
Far as I may, the evil done;
And fixed it rests — if I survive   500
This night, and leave this cave alive.' —
' And Denzil ? ' — ' Let them ply the rack,
Even till his joints and sinews crack !
If Oswald tear him limb from limb,
What ruth can Denzil claim from him
Whose thoughtless youth he led astray
And damned to this unhallowed way ?
He schooled me, faith and vows were vain;
Now let my master reap his gain.' —   509
' True,' answered Bertram, ' 't is his meed;
There 's retribution in the deed.
But thou — thou art not for our course,
Hast fear, hast pity, hast remorse;
And he with us the gale who braves
Must heave such cargo to the waves,
Or lag with overloaded prore
While barks unburdened reach the shore.'

XIX

He paused and, stretching him at length,
Seemed to repose his bulky strength.
Communing with his secret mind,   520
As half he sat and half reclined,
One ample hand his forehead pressed,
And one was dropped across his breast.
The shaggy eyebrows deeper came
Above his eyes of swarthy flame;
His lip of pride awhile forebore
The haughty curve till then it wore;
The unaltered fierceness of his look
A shade of darkened sadness took, —
For dark and sad a presage pressed   530
Resistlessly on Bertram's breast, —
And when he spoke, his wonted tone,
So fierce, abrupt, and brief, was gone.
His voice was steady, low, and deep,
Like distant waves when breezes sleep;
And sorrow mixed with Edmund's fear,
Its low unbroken depth to hear.

XX

' Edmund, in thy sad tale I find
The woe that warped my patron's mind;
'T would wake the fountains of the eye   540
In other men, but mine are dry.
Mortham must never see the fool
That sold himself base Wycliffe's tool,
Yet less from thirst of sordid gain
Than to avenge supposed disdain.
Say Bertram rues his fault — a word
Till now from Bertram never heard:
Say, too, that Mortham's lord he prays
To think but on their former days;
On Quariana's beach and rock,   550
On Cayo's bursting battle-shock,
On Darien's sands and deadly dew,
And on the dart Tlatzeca threw; —
Perchance my patron yet may hear
More that may grace his comrade's bier,
My soul hath felt a secret weight,
A warning of approaching fate:
A priest had said, " Return, repent ! "
As well to bid that rock be rent.
Firm as that flint I face mine end;   560
My heart may burst but cannot bend.

XXI

' The dawning of my youth with awe
And prophesy the Dalesmen saw;
For over Redesdale it came,
As bodeful as their beacon-flame.
Edmund, thy years were scarcely mine
When, challenging the Clans of Tyne

To bring their best my brand to prove,
O'er Hexham's altar hung my glove;
But Tynedale, nor in tower nor town,   570
Held champion meet to take it down.
My noontide India may declare;
Like her fierce sun, I fired the air !
Like him, to wood and cave bade fly
Her natives from mine angry eye.
Panama's maids shall long look pale
When Risingham inspires the tale;
Chili's dark matrons long shall tame
The froward child with Bertram's name.
And now, my race of terror run,   580
Mine be the eve of tropic sun !
No pale gradations quench his ray,
No twilight dews his wrath allay;
With disk like battle-target red
He rushes to his burning bed,
Dyes the wide wave with bloody light,
Then sinks at once — and all is night. —

XXII

' Now to thy mission, Edmund. Fly,
Seek Mortham out, and bid him hie   589
To Richmond where his troops are laid,
And lead his force to Redmond's aid.
Say till he reaches Eglistone
A friend will watch to guard his son.
Now, fare - thee - well; for night draws
on,
And I would rest me here alone.'
Despite his ill-dissembled fear,
There swam in Edmund's eye a tear;
A tribute to the courage high
Which stooped not in extremity,
But strove, irregularly great,   600
To triumph o'er approaching fate !
Bertram beheld the dew-drop start,
It almost touched his iron heart:
' I did not think there lived,' he said,
' One who would tear for Bertram shed.'
He loosened then his baldric's hold,
A buckle broad of massive gold; —
' Of all the spoil that paid his pains
But this with Risingham remains;
And this, dear Edmund, thou shalt take, 610
And wear it long for Bertram's sake.
Once more — to Mortham speed amain;
Farewell ! and turn thee not again.'

XXIII

The night has yielded to the morn,
And far the hours of prime are worn.
Oswald, who since the dawn of day
Had cursed his messenger's delay,

Impatient questioned now his train,
'Was Denzil's son returned again?'
It chanced there answered of the crew   620
A menial who young Edmund knew:
'No son of Denzil this,' he said;
'A peasant boy from Winston glade,
For song and minstrelsy renowned
And knavish pranks the hamlets round.'
'Not Denzil's son!—from Winston vale!—
Then it was false, that specious tale;
Or worse—he hath despatched the youth
To show to Mortham's lord its truth.
Fool that I was!—But 't is too late;—   630
This is the very turn of fate!—
The tale, or true or false, relies
On Denzil's evidence!—He dies!—
Ho! Provost Marshal! instantly
Lead Denzil to the gallows-tree!
Allow him not a parting word;
Short be the shrift and sure the cord!
Then let his gory head appall
Marauders from the castle-wall.
Lead forth thy guard, that duty done,   640
With best despatch to Eglistone.—
Basil, tell Wilfrid he must straight
Attend me at the castle-gate.'

XXIV

'Alas!' the old domestic said,
And shook his venerable head,
'Alas, my lord! full ill to-day
May my young master brook the way!
The leech has spoke with grave alarm
Of unseen hurt, of secret harm,
Of sorrow lurking at the heart,   650
That mars and lets his healing art.'
'Tush! tell not me!—Romantic boys
Pine themselves sick for airy toys,
I will find cure for Wilfrid soon;
Bid him for Eglistone be boune,
And quick!—I hear the dull death-drum
Tell Denzil's hour of fate is come.'
He paused with scornful smile, and then
Resumed his train of thought agen.
'Now comes my fortune's crisis near!   660
Entreaty boots not—instant fear,
Nought else, can bend Matilda's pride
Or win her to be Wilfrid's bride.
But when she sees the scaffold placed,
With axe and block and headsman graced,
And when she deems that to deny
Dooms Redmond and her sire to die,
She must give way.—Then, were the
      line
Of Rokeby once combined with mine,

I gain the weather-gage of fate!   670
If Mortham come, he comes too late,
While I, allied thus and prepared,
Bid him defiance to his beard.—
If she prove stubborn, shall I dare
To drop the axe?—Soft! pause we there.
Mortham still lives—yon youth may tell
His tale—and Fairfax loves him well;—
Else, wherefore should I now delay
To sweep this Redmond from my way?—
But she to piety perforce   680
Must yield.—Without there! Sound to
      horse!'

XXV

'T was bustle in the court below,—
'Mount, and march forward!' Forth they
      go;
Steeds neigh and trample all around,
Steel rings, spears glimmer, trumpets
      sound.—
Just then was sung his parting hymn;
And Denzil turned his eyeballs dim,
And, scarcely conscious what he sees,
Follows the horsemen down the Tees;
And scarcely conscious what he hears,   690
The trumpets tingle in his ears.
O'er the long bridge they 're sweeping now,
The van is hid by greenwood bough;
But ere the rearward had passed o'er
Guy Denzil heard and saw no more!
One stroke upon the castle bell
To Oswald rung his dying knell.

XXVI

O, for that pencil, erst profuse
Of chivalry's emblazoned hues,
That traced of old in Woodstock bower   700
The pageant of the Leaf and Flower,
And bodied forth the tourney high
Held for the hand of Emily!
Then might I paint the tumult broad
That to the crowded abbey flowed,
And poured, as with an ocean's sound,
Into the church's ample bound!
Then might I show each varying mien,
Exulting, woful, or serene;
Indifference, with his idiot stare,   710
And Sympathy, with anxious air;
Paint the dejected Cavalier,
Doubtful, disarmed, and sad of cheer;
And his proud foe, whose formal eye
Claimed conquest now and mastery;
And the brute crowd, whose envious zeal
Huzzas each turn of Fortune's wheel,

And loudest shouts when lowest lie
Exalted worth and station high.
Yet what may such a wish avail?   720
'T is mine to tell an onward tale,
Hurrying, as best I can, along
The hearers and the hasty song; —
Like traveller when approaching home,
Who sees the shades of evening come,
And must not now his course delay,
Or choose the fair but winding way:
Nay, scarcely may his pace suspend,
Where o'er his head the wildings bend,
To bless the breeze that cools his brow   730
Or snatch a blossom from the bough.

XXVII

The reverend pile lay wild and waste,
Profaned, dishonored, and defaced.
Through storied lattices no more
In softened light the sunbeams pour,
Gilding the Gothic sculpture rich
Of shrine and monument and niche.
The civil fury of the time
Made sport of sacrilegious crime;
For dark fanaticism rent   740
Altar and screen and ornament,
And peasant hands the tombs o'erthrew
Of Bowes, of Rokeby, and Fitz-Hugh.
And now was seen, unwonted sight,
In holy walls a scaffold dight!
Where once the priest of grace divine
Dealt to his flock the mystic sign,
There stood the block displayed, and there
The headsman grim his hatchet bare,
And for the word of hope and faith   750
Resounded loud a doom of death.
Thrice the fierce trumpet's breath was
        heard,
And echoed thrice the herald's word,
Dooming, for breach of martial laws
And treason to the Commons' cause,
The Knight of Rokeby, and O'Neale,
To stoop their heads to block and steel.
The trumpets flourished high and shrill,
Then was a silence dead and still;
And silent prayers to Heaven were cast,   760
And stifled sobs were bursting fast,
Till from the crowd begun to rise
Murmurs of sorrow or surprise,
And from the distant isles there came
Deep - muttered threats with Wycliffe's
        name.

XXVIII

But Oswald, guarded by his band,
Powerful in evil, waved his hand,

And bade sedition's voice be dead,
On peril of the murmurer's head.
Then first his glance sought Rokeby's
        Knight,   770
Who gazed on the tremendous sight
As calm as if he came a guest
To kindred baron's feudal feast,
As calm as if that trumpet-call
Were summons to the bannered hall;
Firm in his loyalty he stood,
And prompt to seal it with his blood.
With downcast look drew Oswald nigh, —
He durst not cope with Rokeby's eye! —
And said with low and faltering breath,   780
'Thou know'st the terms of life and
        death.'
The knight then turned and sternly smiled:
'The maiden is mine only child,
Yet shall my blessing leave her head
If with a traitor's son she wed.'
Then Redmond spoke: 'The life of one
Might thy malignity atone,
On me be flung a double guilt!
Spare Rokeby's blood, let mine be spilt!'
Wycliffe had listened to his suit,   790
But dread prevailed and he was mute.

XXIX

And now he pours his choice of fear
In secret on Matilda's ear;
'An union formed with me and mine
Ensures the faith of Rokeby's line.
Consent, and all this dread array
Like morning dream shall pass away;
Refuse, and by my duty pressed
I give the word — thou know'st the rest.'
Matilda, still and motionless,   800
With terror heard the dread address,
Pale as the sheeted maid who dies
To hopeless love a sacrifice;
Then wrung her hands in agony,
And round her cast bewildered eye,
Now on the scaffold glanced, and now
On Wycliffe's unrelenting brow.
She veiled her face, and with a voice
Scarce audible, 'I make my choice!
Spare but their lives! — for aught beside
Let Wilfrid's doom my fate decide.   811
He once was generous!' As she spoke,
Dark Wycliffe's joy in triumph broke:
'Wilfrid, where loitered ye so late?
Why upon Basil rest thy weight? —
Art spell-bound by enchanter's wand? —
Kneel, kneel, and take her yielded hand;
Thank her with raptures, simple boy!
Should tears and trembling speak thy joy?'

'O hush, my sire!   To prayer and tear 820
Of mine thou hast refused thine ear;
But now the awful hour draws on
When truth must speak in loftier tone.'

XXX

He took Matilda's hand: 'Dear maid,
Couldst thou so injure me,' he said,
'Of thy poor friend so basely deem
As blend with him this barbarous scheme?
Alas! my efforts made in vain
Might well have saved this added pain.
But now, bear witness earth and heaven 830
That ne'er was hope to mortal given
So twisted with the strings of life
As this — to call Matilda wife!
I bid it now forever part,
And with the effort bursts my heart.'
His feeble frame was worn so low,
With wounds, with watching, and with
        woe
That nature could no more sustain
The agony of mental pain.
He kneeled — his lip her hand had
        pressed,   840
Just then he felt the stern arrest.
Lower and lower sunk his head, —
They raised him, — but the life was fled!
Then first alarmed his sire and train
Tried every aid, but tried in vain.
The soul, too soft its ills to bear,
Had left our mortal hemisphere,
And sought in better world the meed
To blameless life by Heaven decreed.

XXXI

The wretched sire beheld aghast   850
With Wilfrid all his projects past,
All turned and centred on his son,
On Wilfrid all — and he was gone.
'And I am childless now,' he said;
'Childless, through that relentless maid!
A lifetime's arts in vain essayed
Are bursting on their artist's head!
Here lies my Wilfrid dead — and there
Comes hated Mortham for his heir,
Eager to knit in happy band   860
With Rokeby's heiress Redmond's hand.
And shall their triumph soar o'er all
The schemes deep-laid to work their fall?
No! — deeds which prudence might not
        dare
Appall not vengeance and despair.
The murderess weeps upon his bier —
I'll change to real that feigned tear!

They all shall share destruction's shock; —
Ho! lead the captives to the block!'
But ill his provost could divine   870
His feelings, and forbore the sign.
'Slave! to the block! — or I or they
Shall face the judgment-seat this day!'

XXXII

The outmost crowd have heard a sound
Like horse's hoof on hardened ground;
Nearer it came, and yet more near, —
The very death's-men paused to hear.
'T is in the churchyard now — the tread
Hath waked the dwelling of the dead!
Fresh sod and old sepulchral stone   880
Return the tramp in varied tone.
All eyes upon the gateway hung,
When through the Gothic arch there sprung
A horseman armed at headlong speed —
Sable his cloak, his plume, his steed.
Fire from the flinty floor was spurned,
The vaults unwonted clang returned! —
One instant's glance around he threw,
From saddlebow his pistol drew.
Grimly determined was his look!   890
His charger with the spurs he strook —
All scattered backward as he came,
For all knew Bertram Risingham!
Three bounds that noble courser gave;
The first has reached the central nave,
The second cleared the chancel wide,
The third — he was at Wycliffe's side.
Full levelled at the baron's head,
Rung the report — the bullet sped —
And to his long account and last   900
Without a groan dark Oswald past!
All was so quick that it might seem
A flash of lightning or a dream.

XXXIII

While yet the smoke the deed conceals,
Bertram his ready charger wheels;
But floundered on the pavement-floor
The steed and down the rider bore,
And, bursting in the headlong sway,
The faithless saddle-girths gave way.
'T was while he toiled him to be freed, 910
And with the rein to raise the steed,
That from amazement's iron trance
All Wycliffe's soldiers waked at once.
Sword, halberd, musket-butt, their blows
Hailed upon Bertram as he rose;
A score of pikes with each a wound
Bore down and pinned him to the
        ground;

But still his struggling force he rears,
'Gainst hacking brands and stabbing spears,
Thrice from assailants shook him free,   920
Once gained his feet and twice his knee.
By tenfold odds oppressed at length,
Despite his struggles and his strength,
He took a hundred mortal wounds
As mute as fox 'mongst mangling hounds;
And when he died his parting groan
Had more of laughter than of moan !
They gazed as when a lion dies,
And hunters scarcely trust their eyes,
But bend their weapons on the slain   930
Lest the grim king should rouse again !
Then blow and insult some renewed,
And from the trunk the head had hewed,
But Basil's voice the deed forbade;
A mantle o'er the corse he laid : —
' Fell as he was in act and mind,
He left no bolder heart behind :
Then, give him, for a soldier meet,
A soldier's cloak for winding sheet.'

XXXIV

No more of death and dying pang,   940
No more of trump and bugle clang,
Though through the sounding woods there
  come
Banner and bugle, trump and drum.
Armed with such powers as well had
  freed
Young Redmond at his utmost need,
And backed with such a band of horse
As might less ample powers enforce,
Possessed of every proof and sign
That gave an heir to Mortham's line,
And yielded to a father's arms   950
An image of his Edith's charms, —

Mortham is come, to hear and see
Of this strange morn the history.
What saw he ? — not the church's floor,
Cumbered with dead and stained with gore;
What heard he ? — not the clamorous
  crowd,
That shout their gratulations loud :
Redmond he saw and heard alone,
Clasped him and sobbed, ' My son ! my
  son ! '

XXXV

This chanced upon a summer morn,   960
When yellow waved the heavy corn :
But when brown August o'er the land
Called forth the reaper's busy band,
A gladsome sight the sylvan road
From Eglistone to Mortham showed.
Awhile the hardy rustic leaves
The task to bind and pile the sheaves,
And maids their sickles fling aside
To gaze on bridegroom and on bride,
And childhood's wondering group draws
  near,   970
And from the gleaner's hands the ear
Drops while she folds them for a prayer
And blessing on the lovely pair.
'T was then the Maid of Rokeby gave
Her plighted troth to Redmond brave;
And Teesdale can remember yet
How Fate to Virtue paid her debt,
And for their troubles bade them prove
A lengthened life of peace and love.

Time and Tide had thus their sway,   980
Yielding, like an April day,
Smiling noon for sullen morrow,
Years of joy for hours of sorrow !

THE BRIDAL OF TRIERMAIN

INTRODUCTORY NOTE

One of the projects which grew out of the enterprise of the Ballantynes, when Scott was drawn into the toils, was the establishment of the *Edinburgh Annual Register*, which was to be conducted in opposition to Constable's *Edinburgh Review*. It was to be mainly historical and annalistic, and the *Quarterly Review* established shortly after more completely served the purpose of an antagonist of the *Review*, but Scott infused a little literary spirit into the *Register*, and amongst other contributions

inserted in the first volume, for 1809, some imitations of living poets, one of them taking Scott himself for its model !

Meanwhile *Rokeby* had been started on the stocks ; and Scott, who in the ebullition of his active fancy liked to keep two or three varied tasks on hand, bethought himself of one of these fragments, *The Vision of Triermain*, and conceived the notion of expanding it into a poem, to be published anonymously at the same time with *Rokeby*, and fathered upon some one of his friends, to complete the mystification. The fragment taken is nearly identical with Canto First of the *Bridal*, divisions I.–VIII. He hoped especially by this scheme to draw Jeffrey, and elicit from him a criticism which would be unencumbered by the reviewer's relations with the real author.

As Erskine had generally been credited with the authorship of the anonymous fragments in the *Register*, he was asked by Scott to play his part in the plot, and good naturedly lent his aid. 'I shall be very much amused,' he wrote to Scott, 'if the secret is kept and the knowing ones taken in. To prevent any discovery from your prose, what think you of putting down your ideas of what the preface ought to contain, and allowing me to write it over? And perhaps a quizzing review might be concocted.' Scott took the hint, and the *Introduction to The Bridal of Triermain* given below is a mixture of Scott and Erskine, the latter's quotations from the Greek being especially adapted to throwing off the scent those who might naturally attribute the poem to Scott. In his *Introduction* to *The Lord of the Isles*, written in 1830, when the secret had long been out, Scott wrote : 'Being much urged by my intimate friend, now unhappily no more, William Erskine (a Scottish judge, by the title of Lord Kinedder), I agreed to write the little romantic tale called *The Bridal of Triermain*; but it was on the condition that he should make no serious effort to disown the composition, if report should lay it at his door. As he was more than suspected of a taste for poetry, and as I took care, in several places, to mix something which might resemble (as far as was in my power) my friend's feeling and manner, the train easily caught, and two large editions were sold. A third being called for, Lord Kinedder became unwilling to aid any longer a deception which was going farther than he expected or desired, and the real author's name was given.'[1]

Scott had taken Morritt into his confidence, but apparently he had not thus treated his intimate correspondent, Lady Louisa Stuart, or Lady Abercorn. With both of these clever women he kept up a bit of fencing, though it is not quite certain that one or the other did not have an inkling of the truth, and so amused herself with playing a like game of hoodwinking. The little book was published almost on the same day as *Rokeby*, and Scott wrote to Morritt, March 9, 1813 ; 'I wish you would give the said author of *Triermain* a hoist to notice, by speaking of him now and then in those parts where a word spoken is sure to

have a hundred echoes. . . . I hear Jeffrey has really bestowed great praise on the poem, and means to give it a place in his review. It has not, he says, my great artery, but there is more attention to style, more elegance and ornament, etc., etc. We will see, however, what he really will say to it in his review, for there is no sure augury from his private conversation.' A few days later, when writing to Lady Abercorn, Scott threw in a reference to the poem in a careless fashion. He is sending her some books : 'The first and most interesting is a spirited imitation of *my manner* called *The Bridal of Triermain*. The author is unknown, but it makes some noise among us. The other is a little novel,' and so on with a reference shortly to his own *Rokeby*. A month later, writing the same lady again, he says, parenthetically, as it were, ' *The Bridal of Triermain* is the book which has excited the most interest here. Jeffrey lauds it highly, I am informed, and is one day to throw it at my head.' Lady Louisa Stuart on her side intimates that she suspects Scott to have written the *Bridal*, though she reports common rumor to assign it to R. P. Gillies.

It was some time before the authorship was rightly placed. Scott and Morritt were disappointed that Jeffrey did not fall into the trap laid for them, but though Scott's name was often mentioned as that of the probable author, the secret was well kept. As late as January, 1814, Scott was writing to Morritt : 'The fourth edition is at press. The Empress-Dowager of Prussia has expressed such an interest in it, that it will be inscribed to her, in some doggerel sonnet or other, by the unknown author. This is funny enough ;' and again to the same friend : ' As your conscience has very few things to answer for, you must still burthen it with the secret of the *Bridal*. It is spreading very rapidly, and I have one or two little faery romances which will make a second volume, and which I would wish published, but not with my name. The truth is that this sort of muddling work amuses me, and I am something in the condition of Joseph Surface, who was embarrassed by getting himself too good a reputation ; for many things would please people well enough anonymously, which, if they bore me on the title-page, would just give me that sort of ill-name which precedes hanging, and that would be in many respects inconvenient if I thought of again trying a *grande opus*. I will give you a hundred good reasons when we meet for not owning the *Bridal* till I either secede entirely from the field of literature, or from that of life.' It is an amusing comment on Scott's willingness to allow others to carry off his honors, when we find him writing in his Journal a dozen years

[1] A statement somewhat at variance with Scott's to Morritt on occasion of a fourth edition. — See below.

later : 'A long letter from R. P. Gillies. I wonder how ever he could ask me to announce myself as the author of *Annotations on German Novels* which he is to write.' The Introduction prefixed to the first edition, of March, 1813, here follows : —

INTRODUCTION

In the *Edinburgh Annual Register* for the year 1809, Three Fragments were inserted, written in imitation of Living Poets. It must have been apparent that by these prolusions nothing burlesque or disrespectful to the authors was intended, but that they were offered to the public as serious, though certainly very imperfect, imitations of that style of composition by which each of the writers is supposed to be distinguished. As these exercises attracted a greater degree of attention than the author anticipated, he has been induced to complete one of them and present it as a separate publication.

It is not in this place that an examination of the works of the master whom he has here adopted as his model, can, with propriety, be introduced ; since his general acquiescence in the favorable suffrage of the public must necessarily be inferred from the attempt he has now made. He is induced, by the nature of his subject, to offer a few remarks on what has been called *romantic poetry ;* the popularity of which has been revived in the present day, under the auspices, and by the unparalleled success, of one individual.

The original purpose of poetry is either religious or historical, or, as must frequently happen, a mixture of both. To modern readers the poems of Homer have many of the features of pure romance ; but in the estimation of his contemporaries, they probably derived their chief value from their supposed historical authenticity. The same may be generally said of the poetry of all early ages. The marvels and miracles which the poet blends with his song do not exceed in number or extravagance the figments of the historians of the same period of society ; and indeed, the difference betwixt poetry and prose, as the vehicles of historical truth, is always of late introduction. Poets, under various denominations of Bards, Scalds, Chroniclers, and so forth, are the first historians of all nations. Their intention is to relate the events they have witnessed, or the traditions that have reached them ; and they clothe the relation in rhyme, merely as the means of rendering it more solemn in the narrative, or more easily committed to memory. But as the poetical historian improves in the art of conveying information, the authenticity of his narrative unavoidably declines. He is tempted to dilate and dwell upon the events that are interesting to his imagination, and, conscious how indifferent his audience is to the naked truth of his poem, his history gradually becomes a romance.

It is in this situation that those epics are found, which have been generally regarded the standards of poetry ; and it has happened somewhat strangely that the moderns have pointed out as the characteristics and peculiar excellencies of narrative poetry, the very circumstances which the authors themselves adopted, only because their art involved the duties of the historian as well as the poet. It cannot be believed, for example, that Homer selected the siege of Troy as the most appropriate subject for poetry ; his purpose was to write the early history of his country ; the event he has chosen, though not very fruitful in varied incident, nor perfectly well adapted for poetry, was nevertheless combined with traditionary and genealogical anecdotes extremely interesting to those who were to listen to him ; and this he has adorned by the exertions of a genius which, if it has been equalled, has certainly been never surpassed. It was not till comparatively a late period that the general accuracy of his narrative, or his purpose in composing it, was brought into question. Δοκεῖ πρῶτος [ὁ 'Αναξαγόρας] (καθά φησι Φαβορῖνος ἐν παντοδαπῇ 'Ιστορία) τὴν 'Ομήρου ποίησιν ἀποφήνασθαι εἶναι περὶ ἀρετῆς καὶ δικαιοσύνης.[1] But whatever theories might be framed by speculative men, his work was of an historical, not of an allegorical nature. 'Εναυτίλλετο μετὰ τοῦ Μέντεω καὶ ὅπου ἑκάστοτε ἀφίκοιτο, πάντα τὰ ἐπιχώρια διερωτᾶτο, καὶ ἱστορέων ἐπυνθάνετο· εἰκὸς δέ μιν ἦν καὶ μνημοσύνην πάντων γράφεσθαι.[2] Instead of recommending the choice of a subject similar to that of Homer, it was to be expected that critics should have exhorted the poets of these latter days to adopt or invent a narrative in itself more susceptible of poetical ornament, and to avail themselves of that advantage in order to compensate, in some degree, the inferiority of genius. The contrary course has been inculcated by almost all the writers upon the *Epopœia ;* with what success, the fate of Homer's numerous imitators may best show. The *ultimum supplicium* of criticism was in-

[1] Diogenes Laertius, lib. ii. Anaxag. Segm. II.
[2] Homeri Vita, in Herod. *Henr. Steph.* 1570, p. 356.

flicted on the author if he did not choose a subject which at once deprived him of all claim to originality, and placed him, if not in actual contest, at least in fatal comparison, with those giants in the land whom it was most his interest to avoid. The celebrated receipt for writing an epic poem, which appeared in *The Guardian*,[1] was the first instance in which common sense was applied to this department of poetry ; and, indeed, if the question be considered on its own merits, we must be satisfied that narrative poetry, if strictly confined to the great occurrences of history, would be deprived of the individual interest which it is so well calculated to excite.

Modern poets may therefore be pardoned in seeking simpler subjects of verse, more interesting in proportion to their simplicity. Two or three figures, well grouped, suit the artist better than a crowd, for whatever purpose assembled. For the same reason, a scene immediately presented to the imagination, and directly brought home to the feelings, though involving the fate of but one or two persons, is more favorable for poetry than the political struggles and convulsions which influence the fate of kingdoms. The former are within the reach and comprehension of all, and, if depicted with vigor, seldom fail to fix attention : The other if more sublime, are more vague and distant, less capable of being distinctly understood, and infinitely less capable of exciting those sentiments which it is the very purpose of poetry to inspire. To generalize is always to destroy effect. We would, for example, be more interested in the fate of an individual soldier in combat, than in the grand event of a general action ; with the happiness of two lovers raised from misery and anxiety to peace and union, than with the successful exertions of a whole nation. From what causes this may originate, is a separate and obviously an immaterial consideration. Before ascribing this peculiarity to causes decidedly and odiously selfish, it is proper to recollect that while men see only a limited space, and while

¹ *The Guardian*, No. 78. POPE.

their affections and conduct are regulated, not by aspiring to an universal good, but by exerting their power of making themselves and others happy within the limited scale allotted to each individual, so long will individual history and individual virtue be the readier and more accessible road to general interest and attention ; and, perhaps, we may add, that it is the more useful, as well as the more accessible, inasmuch as it affords an example capable of being easily imitated.

According to the author's idea of Romantic Poetry, as distinguished from Epic, the former comprehends a fictitious narrative, framed and combined at the pleasure of the writer ; beginning and ending as he may judge best ; which neither exacts nor refuses the use of supernatural machinery ; which is free from the technical rules of the *Epée ;* and is subject only to those which good sense, good taste, and good morals apply to every species of poetry without exception. The date may be in a remote age, or in the present ; the story may detail the adventures of a prince or of a peasant. In a word, the author is absolute master of his country and its inhabitants, and everything is permitted to him, excepting to be heavy or prosaic, for which, free and unembarrassed as he is, he has no manner of apology. Those, it is probable, will be found the peculiarities of this species of composition ; and before joining the outcry against the vitiated taste that fosters and encourages it, the justice and grounds of it ought to be made perfectly apparent. If the want of sieges and battles and great military evolutions, in our poetry, is complained of, let us reflect that the campaigns and heroes of our days are perpetuated in a record that neither requires nor admits of the aid of fiction ; and if the complaint refers to the inferiority of our bards, let us pay a just tribute to their modesty, limiting them, as it does, to subjects which, however indifferently treated, have still the interest and charm of novelty, and which thus prevents them from adding insipidity to their other more insuperable defects.

THE BRIDAL OF TRIERMAIN

OR

THE VALE OF SAINT JOHN

A LOVER'S TALE

INTRODUCTION

I

COME LUCY ! while 't is morning hour
  The woodland brook we needs must
      pass;
So ere the sun assume his power
We shelter in our poplar bower,
Where dew lies long upon the flower,
  Though vanished from the velvet grass.
Curbing the stream, this stony ridge
May serve us for a sylvan bridge;
  For here compelled to disunite,
    Round petty isles the runnels glide, 10
And chafing off their puny spite,
The shallow murmurers waste their might,
  Yielding to footstep free and light
  A dry-shod pass from side to side.

II

Nay, why this hesitating pause ?
And, Lucy, as thy step withdraws,
Why sidelong eye the streamlet's brim ?
Titania's foot without a slip,
Like thine, though timid, light, and slim,
  From stone to stone might safely trip, 20
  Nor risk the glow-worm clasp to dip
That binds her slipper's silken rim.
Or trust thy lover's strength; nor fear
  That this same stalwart arm of mine,
Which could yon oak's prone trunk up-
    rear,
Shall shrink beneath the burden dear
  Of form so slender, light, and fine. —
So — now, the danger dared at last,
Look back and smile at perils past !

III

And now we reach the favorite glade, 30
  Paled in by copsewood, cliff, and stone,
Where never harsher sounds invade
  To break affection's whispering tone
Than the deep breeze that waves the shade,
  Than the small brooklet's feeble moan.

Come ! rest thee on thy wonted seat;
  Mossed is the stone, the turf is green,
A place where lovers best may meet
  Who would not that their love be seen.
The boughs that dim the summer sky 40
Shall hide us from each lurking spy
  That fain would spread the invidious
    tale,
How Lucy of the lofty eye,
Noble in birth, in fortunes high,
She for whom lords and barons sigh,
  Meets her poor Arthur in the dale.

IV

How deep that blush ! — how deep that
    sigh !
And why does Lucy shun mine eye ?
Is it because that crimson draws
Its color from some secret cause, 50
Some hidden movement of the breast,
She would not that her Arthur guessed ?
O, quicker far is lovers' ken
Than the dull glance of common men,
And by strange sympathy can spell
The thoughts the loved one will not tell !
And mine in Lucy's blush saw met
  The hue of pleasure and regret;
  Pride mingled in the sigh her voice,
    And shared with Love the crimson
      glow, 60
Well pleased that thou art Arthur's
    choice,
    Yet shamed thine own is placed so
      low:
Thou turn'st thy self-confessing cheek,
  As if to meet the breezes cooling;
Then, Lucy, hear thy tutor speak,
  For Love too has his hours of school-
    ing.

V

Too oft my anxious eye has spied
That secret grief thou fain wouldst hide,
The passing pang of humbled pride;

287

Too oft when through the splendid
    hall,   70
  The loadstar of each heart and eye,
My fair one leads the glittering ball,
Will her stolen glance on Arthur fall
  With such a blush and such a sigh!
Thou wouldst not yield for wealth or
    rank
  The heart thy worth and beauty won,
Nor leave me on this mossy bank
  To meet a rival on a throne:
Why then should vain repinings rise,
That to thy lover fate denies   80
A nobler name, a wide domain,
A baron's birth, a menial train,
Since Heaven assigned him for his part
A lyre, a falchion, and a heart?

VI

My sword — its master must be dumb;
  But when a soldier names my name,
Approach, my Lucy! fearless come,
  Nor dread to hear of Arthur's shame.
My heart — mid all yon courtly crew
  Of lordly rank and lofty line,   90
Is there to love and honor true,
  That boasts a pulse so warm as mine?
They praised thy diamonds' lustre rare —
Matched with thine eyes, I thought it
    faded;
They praised the pearls that bound thy
    hair —
I only saw the locks they braided;
They talked of wealthy dower and land,
  And titles of high birth the token —
I thought of Lucy's heart and hand,
  Nor knew the sense of what was
    spoken.   100
And yet, if ranked in Fortune's roll,
  I might have learned their choice un-
    wise
Who rate the dower above the soul
  And Lucy's diamonds o'er her eyes.

VII

My lyre — it is an idle toy
  That borrows accents not its own,
Like warbler of Colombian sky
  That sings but in a mimic tone.
Ne'er did it sound o'er sainted well,
Nor boasts it aught of Border spell;   110
Its strings no feudal slogan pour,
Its heroes draw no broad claymore;
No shouting clans applauses raise
Because it sung their fathers' praise;

On Scottish moor, or English down,
It ne'er was graced with fair renown;
Nor won — best meed to minstrel true —
One favoring smile from fair BUCCLEUCH!
By one poor streamlet sounds its tone,
And heard by one dear maid alone.   120

VIII

But, if thou bid'st, these tones shall tell
Of errant knight, and damoselle;
Of the dread knot a wizard tied
In punishment of maiden's pride,
In notes of marvel and of fear
That best may charm romantic ear.

For Lucy loves — like COLLINS, ill-starred
    name!
Whose lay's requital was that tardy Fame,
Who bound no laurel round his living
    head,
Should hang it o'er his monument when
    dead, —   130
For Lucy loves to tread enchanted strand,
And thread like him the maze of Fairy-
    land;
Of golden battlements to view the gleam,
And slumber soft by some Elysian stream;
Such lays she loves — and, such my Lucy's
    choice,
What other song can claim her Poet's
    voice?

CANTO FIRST

I

WHERE is the maiden of mortal strain
That may match with the Baron of Trier-
    main?
She must be lovely and constant and kind,
Holy and pure and humble of mind,
Blithe of cheer and gentle of mood,
Courteous and generous and noble of
    blood —
Lovely as the sun's first ray
When it breaks the clouds of an April
    day;
Constant and true as the widowed dove,
Kind as a minstrel that sings of love;   10
Pure as the fountain in rocky cave
Where never sunbeam kissed the wave;
Humble as maiden that loves in vain,
Holy as hermit's vesper strain;
Gentle as breeze that but whispers and
    dies,

Yet blithe as the light leaves that dance in
　　its sighs;
Courteous as monarch the morn he is
　　crowned,
Generous as spring-dews that bless the
　　glad ground;
Noble her blood as the currents that met 19
In the veins of the noblest Plantagenet —
Such must her form be, her mood, and her
　　strain,
That shall match with Sir Roland of Trier-
　　main.

II

Sir Roland de Vaux he hath laid him to
　　sleep,
His blood it was fevered, his breathing
　　was deep.
He had been pricking against the Scot,
The foray was long and the skirmish hot;
His dinted helm and his buckler's plight
Bore token of a stubborn fight.
　　All in the castle must hold them still,
Harpers must lull him to his rest　　30
With the slow soft tunes he loves the best
Till sleep sink down upon his breast,
　　Like the dew on a summer hill.

III

It was the dawn of an autumn day;
The sun was struggling with frost-fog gray
That like a silvery crape was spread
Round Skiddaw's dim and distant head,
And faintly gleamed each painted pane
Of the lordly halls of Triermain,
　　When that baron bold awoke.　　40
Starting he woke and loudly did call,
Rousing his menials in bower and hall
　　While hastily he spoke.

IV

' Hearken, my minstrels ! Which of ye all
Touched his harp with that dying fall,
　　So sweet, so soft, so faint,
It seemed an angel's whispered call
　　To an expiring saint ?
And hearken, my merry-men !　What time
　　or where
　　Did she pass, that maid with her heavenly
　　　brow,　　50
With her look so sweet and her eyes so fair,
And her graceful step and her angel air,
And the eagle plume in her dark-brown
　　hair,
　　That passed from my bower e'en now ! '

V

Answered him Richard de Bretville; he
Was chief of the baron's minstrelsy, —
' Silent, noble chieftain, we
　　Have sat since midnight close,
When such lulling sounds as the brooklet
　　sings
Murmured from our melting strings,　　60
　　And hushed you to repose.
Had a harp-note sounded here,
　　It had caught my watchful ear,
Although it fell as faint and shy
As bashful maiden's half-formed sigh
　　When she thinks her lover near.'
Answered Philip of Fasthwaite tall;
He kept guard in the outer-hall, —
' Since at eve our watch took post,
Not a foot has thy portal crossed;　　70
　　Else had I heard the steps, though low
And light they fell as when earth receives
In morn of frost the withered leaves
　　That drop when no winds blow.'

VI

' Then come thou hither, Henry, my page,
Whom I saved from the sack of Hermitage,
When that dark castle, tower, and spire,
Rose to the skies a pile of fire,
　　And reddened all the Nine-stane Hill, 79
And the shrieks of death, that wildly broke
Through devouring flame and smothering
　　smoke,
　　Made the warrior's heart-blood chill.
The trustiest thou of all my train,
My fleetest courser thou must rein,
　　And ride to Lyulph's tower,
And from the Baron of Triermain
　　Greet well that sage of power.
He is sprung from Druid sires
And British bards that tuned their lyres
To Arthur's and Pendragon's praise,　　90
And his who sleeps at Dunmailraise.
Gifted like his gifted race,
He the characters can trace
Graven deep in elder time
Upon Hellvellyn's cliffs sublime;
Sign and sigil well doth he know,
And can bode of weal and woe,
Of kingdoms' fall and fate of wars,
From mystic dreams and course of stars.
He shall tell if middle earth　　100
To that enchanting shape gave birth,
Or if 't was but an airy thing
Such as fantastic slumbers bring,
Framed from the rainbow's varying dyes

Or fading tints of western skies.
For, by the blessed rood I swear,
If that fair form breathe vital air,
No other maiden by my side
Shall ever rest De Vaux's bride !'

VII

The faithful page he mounts his steed, 110
And soon he crossed green Irthing's mead,
Dashed o'er Kirkoswald's verdant plain,
And Eden barred his course in vain.
He passed red Penrith's Table Round,
For feats of chivalry renowned,
Left Mayburgh's mound and stones of
        power,
By Druids raised in magic hour,
And traced the Eamont's winding way
Till Ulfo's lake beneath him lay.

VIII

Onward he rode, the pathway still 120
Winding betwixt the lake and hill;
Till, on the fragment of a rock
Struck from its base by lightning shock,
    He saw the hoary sage:
The silver moss and lichen twined,
With fern and deer - hair checked and
        lined,
    A cushion fit for age;
And o'er him shook the aspen-tree,
A restless rustling canopy.
Then sprung young Henry from his selle 130
    And greeted Lyulph grave,
And then his master's tale did tell,
    And then for counsel crave.
The man of years mused long and deep,
Of time's lost treasures taking keep,
And then, as rousing from a sleep,
    His solemn answer gave.

IX

' That maid is born of middle earth
    And may of man be won,
Though there have glided since her birth 140
    Five hundred years and one.
But where 's the knight in all the north
That dare the adventure follow forth,
So perilous to knightly worth,
    In the valley of Saint John ?
Listen, youth, to what I tell,
And bind it on thy memory well;
Nor muse that I commence the rhyme
Far distant mid the wrecks of time.
The mystic tale by bard and sage 150
Is handed down from Merlin's age.

X

LYULPH'S TALE

' King Arthur has ridden from merry Car-
        lisle
    When Pentecost was o'er:
He journeyed like errant-knight the while
And sweetly the summer sun did smile
    On mountain, moss, and moor.
Above his solitary track
Rose Glaramara's ridgy back,
Amid whose yawning gulfs the sun
Cast umbered radiance red and dun, 160
Though never sunbeam could discern
The surface of that sable tarn,
In whose black mirror you may spy
The stars while noontide lights the sky.
The gallant king he skirted still
The margin of that mighty hill;
Rock upon rocks incumbent hung,
And torrents, down the gullies flung,
Joined the rude river that brawled on,
Recoiling now from crag and stone, 170
Now diving deep from human ken,
And raving down its darksome glen.
The monarch judged this desert wild,
With such romantic ruin piled,
Was theatre by Nature's hand
For feat of high achievement planned.

XI

' O, rather he chose, that monarch bold,
    On venturous quest to ride
In plate and mail by wood and wold
Than, with ermine trapped and cloth of
        gold, 180
    In princely bower to bide;
The bursting crash of a foeman's spear,
    As it shivered against his mail,
Was merrier music to his ear
    Than courtier's whispered tale:
And the clash of Caliburn more dear,
    When on the hostile casque it rung,
        Than all the lays
        To the monarch's praise
That the harpers of Reged sung. 190
He loved better to rest by wood or river
Than in bower of his bride, Dame Guen-
        ever,
For he left that lady so lovely of cheer
To follow adventures of danger and fear;
And the frank-hearted monarch full little
        did wot
That she smiled in his absence on brave
        Lancelot.

XII

'He rode till over down and dell
The shade more broad and deeper fell;
And though around the mountain's head
Flowed streams of purple and gold and
    red,   200
Dark at the base, unblest by beam,
Frowned the black rocks and roared the
    stream.
With toil the king his way pursued
By lonely Threlkeld's waste and wood,
Till on his course obliquely shone
The narrow valley of SAINT JOHN,
Down sloping to the western sky
Where lingering sunbeams love to lie.
Right glad to feel those beams again,
The king drew up his charger's rein;   210
With gauntlet raised he screened his sight,
As dazzled with the level light,
And from beneath his glove of mail
Scanned at his ease the lovely vale,
While 'gainst the sun his armor bright
Gleamed ruddy like the beacon's light.

XIII

'Paled in by many a lofty hill,
The narrow dale lay smooth and still,
And, down its verdant bosom led,
A winding brooklet found its bed.   220
But midmost of the vale a mound
Arose with airy turrets crowned,
Buttress, and rampire's circling bound,
    And mighty keep and tower;
Seemed some primeval giant's hand
The castle's massive walls had planned,
A ponderous bulwark to withstand
    Ambitious Nimrod's power.
Above the moated entrance slung,
The balanced drawbridge trembling
    hung,   230
    As jealous of a foe;
Wicket of oak, as iron hard,
With iron studded, clenched, and barred,
And pronged portcullis, joined to guard
    The gloomy pass below.
But the gray walls no banners crowned,
Upon the watchtower's airy round
No warder stood his horn to sound,
No guard beside the bridge was found,
And where the Gothic gateway frowned 240
    Glanced neither bill nor bow.

XIV

'Beneath the castle's gloomy pride,
In ample round did Arthur ride

Three times; nor living thing he spied,
    Nor heard a living sound,
Save that, awakening from her dream,
The owlet now began to scream
In concert with the rushing stream
    That washed the battled mound.
He lighted from his goodly steed,   250
And he left him to graze on bank and mead;
And slowly he climbed the narrow way
That reached the entrance grim and gray,
And he stood the outward arch below,
And his bugle-horn prepared to blow
    In summons blithe and bold,
Deeming to rouse from iron sleep
The guardian of this dismal keep,
    Which well he guessed the hold
Of wizard stern, or goblin grim,   260
Or pagan of gigantic limb,
    The tyrant of the wold.

XV

'The ivory bugle's golden tip
Twice touched the monarch's manly lip,
    And twice his hand withdrew. —
Think not but Arthur's heart was good !
His shield was crossed by the blessed rood:
Had a pagan host before him stood,
    He had charged them through and
        through;
Yet the silence of that ancient place   270
Sunk on his heart, and he paused a space
    Ere yet his horn he blew.
But, instant as its larum rung,
The castle gate was open flung,
Portcullis rose with crashing groan
Full harshly up its groove of stone;
The balance-beams obeyed the blast,
And down the trembling drawbridge cast;
The vaulted arch before him lay
With nought to bar the gloomy way,   280
And onward Arthur paced with hand
On Caliburn's resistless brand.

XVI

'A hundred torches flashing bright
Dispelled at once the gloomy night
    That loured along the walls,
And showed the king's astonished sight
    The inmates of the halls.
Nor wizard stern, nor goblin grim,
Nor giant huge of form and limb,
    Nor heathen knight, was there;   290
But the cressets which odors flung aloft
Showed by their yellow light and soft
    A band of damsels fair.

Onward they came, like summer wave
  That dances to the shore;
An hundred voices welcome gave,
  And welcome o'er and o'er !
An hundred lovely hands assail
The bucklers of the monarch's mail,
And busy labored to unhasp   300
Rivet of steel and iron clasp.
One wrapped him in a mantle fair,
And one flung odors on his hair;
His short curled ringlets one smoothed
      down,
One wreathed them with a myrtle crown.
A bride upon her wedding-day
Was tended ne'er by troop so gay.

XVII

' Loud laughed they all, — the king in
      vain
With questions tasked the giddy train;
Let him entreat or crave or call,   310
'T was one reply — loud laughed they all.
Then o'er him mimic chains they fling
Framed of the fairest flowers of spring;
While some their gentle force unite
Onward to drag the wondering knight,
Some bolder urge his pace with blows,
Dealt with the lily or the rose.
Behind him were in triumph borne
The warlike arms he late had worn.
Four of the train combined to rear   320
The terrors of Tintagel's spear;
Two, laughing at their lack of strength,
Dragged Caliburn in cumbrous length;
One, while she aped a martial stride,
Placed on her brows the helmet's pride;
Then screamed 'twixt laughter and sur-
      prise
To feel its depth o'erwhelm her eyes.
With revel-shout and triumph-song
Thus gayly marched the giddy throng.

XVIII

' Through many a gallery and hall   330
They led, I ween, their royal thrall;
At length, beneath a fair arcade
Their march and song at once they staid.
The eldest maiden of the band —
    The lovely maid was scarce eighteen —
Raised with imposing air her hand,
And reverent silence did command
    On entrance of their Queen,
And they were mute. — But as a glance
They steal on Arthur's countenance   340
    Bewildered with surprise,

Their smothered mirth again 'gan speak
In archly dimpled chin and cheek
  And laughter-lighted eyes.

XIX

' The attributes of those high days
Now only live in minstrel-lays;
For Nature, now exhausted, still
Was then profuse of good and ill.
Strength was gigantic, valor high,
And wisdom soared beyond the sky,   350
And beauty had such matchless beam
As lights not now a lover's dream.
Yet e'en in that romantic age
  Ne'er were such charms by mortal seen
As Arthur's dazzled eyes engage,
When forth on that enchanted stage
With glittering train of maid and page
  Advanced the castle's queen !
While up the hall she slowly passed,
Her dark eye on the king she cast   360
  That flashed expression strong;
The longer dwelt that lingering look,
Her cheek the livelier color took,
And scarce the shame-faced king could
      brook
  The gaze that lasted long.
A sage who had that look espied,
Where kindling passion strove with pride,
  Had whispered, " Prince, beware !
From the chafed tiger rend the prey,
Rush on the lion when at bay,   370
Bar the fell dragon's blighted way,
  But shun that lovely snare ! "

XX

' At once, that inward strife suppressed,
The dame approached her warlike guest,
With greeting in that fair degree
Where female pride and courtesy
Are blended with such passing art
As awes at once and charms the heart.
A courtly welcome first she gave,
Then of his goodness 'gan to crave   380
  Construction fair and true
Of her light maidens' idle mirth,
Who drew from lonely glens their birth
Nor knew to pay to stranger worth
  And dignity their due;
And then she prayed that he would rest
That night her castle's honored guest.
The monarch meetly thanks expressed;
The banquet rose at her behest,
With lay and tale, and laugh and jest,   390
  Apace the evening flew.

XXI

' The lady sate the monarch by,
Now in her turn abashed and shy,
And with indifference seemed to hear
The toys he whispered in her ear.
Her bearing modest was and fair,
Yet shadows of constraint were there
That showed an over-cautious care
  Some inward thought to hide;
Oft did she pause in full reply,   400
And oft cast down her large dark eye,
Oft checked the soft voluptuous sigh
  That heaved her bosom's pride.
Slight symptoms these, but shepherds
  know
How hot the mid-day sun shall glow
  From the mist of morning sky;
And so the wily monarch guessed
That this assumed restraint expressed
More ardent passions in the breast
  Than ventured to the eye.   410
Closer he pressed while beakers rang,
While maidens laughed and minstrels sang,
  Still closer to her ear —
But why pursue the common tale ?
Or wherefore show how knights prevail
  When ladies dare to hear ?
Or wherefore trace from what slight cause
Its source one tyrant passion draws,
  Till, mastering all within,
Where lives the man that has not tried 420
How mirth can into folly glide
  And folly into sin ! '

CANTO SECOND

LYULPH'S TALE CONTINUED

I

' ANOTHER day, another day,
And yet another, glides away !
The Saxon stern, the pagan Dane,
Maraud on Britain's shores again.
Arthur, of Christendom the flower,
Lies loitering in a lady's bower;
The horn that foemen wont to fear
Sounds but to wake the Cumbrian deer,
And Caliburn, the British pride,
Hangs useless by a lover's side.   10

II

' Another day, another day,
And yet another, glides away.
Heroic plans in pleasure drowned,

He thinks not of the Table Round;
In lawless love dissolved his life,
He thinks not of his beauteous wife:
Better he loves to snatch a flower
From bosom of his paramour
Than from a Saxon knight to wrest
The honors of his heathen crest;   20
Better to wreathe mid tresses brown
The heron's plume her hawk struck down
Than o'er the altar give to flow
The banners of a Paynim foe.
Thus week by week and day by day
His life inglorious glides away;
But she that soothes his dream with fear
Beholds his hour of waking near.

III

' Much force have mortal charms to stay
Our pace in Virtue's toilsome way;   30
But Guendolen's might far outshine
Each maid of merely mortal line.
Her mother was of human birth,
Her sire a Genie of the earth,
In days of old deemed to preside
O'er lovers' wiles and beauty's pride,
By youths and virgins worshipped long
With festive dance and choral song,
Till, when the cross to Britain came,
On heathen altars died the flame.   40
Now, deep in Wastdale solitude,
The downfall of his rights he rued,
And born of his resentment heir,
He trained to guile that lady fair,
To sink in slothful sin and shame
The champions of the Christian name.
Well skilled to keep vain thoughts alive,
And all to promise, nought to give,
The timid youth had hope in store,
The bold and pressing gained no more. 50
As wildered children leave their home
After the rainbow's arch to roam,
Her lovers bartered fair esteem,
Faith, fame, and honor, for a dream.

IV

' Her sire's soft arts the soul to tame
She practised thus — till Arthur came;
Then frail humanity had part,
And all the mother claimed her heart.
Forgot each rule her father gave,
Sunk from a princess to a slave,   60
Too late must Guendolen deplore,
He that has all can hope no more !
Now must she see her lover strain
At every turn her feeble chain,

Watch to new-bind each knot and shrink
To view each fast-decaying link.
Art she invokes to Nature's aid,
Her vest to zone, her locks to braid;
Each varied pleasure heard her call,
The feast, the tourney, and the ball: 70
Her storied lore she next applies,
Taxing her mind to aid her eyes;
Now more than mortal wise and then
In female softness sunk again;
Now raptured with each wish complying,
With feigned reluctance now denying;
Each charm she varied to retain
A varying heart — and all in vain !

V

'Thus in the garden's narrow bound
Flanked by some castle's Gothic round,   80
Fain would the artist's skill provide
The limits of his realms to hide.
The walks in labyrinths he twines,
Shade after shade with skill combines
With many a varied flowery knot,
And copse and arbor, decks the spot,
Tempting the hasty foot to stay
And linger on the lovely way —
Vain art ! vain hope ! 't is fruitless all !
At length we reach the bounding wall !   90
And, sick of flower and trim-dressed tree,
Long for rough glades and forest free.

VI

'Three summer months had scantly flown
When Arthur in embarrassed tone
Spoke of his liegemen and his throne;
Said all too long had been his stay,
And duties which a monarch sway,
Duties unknown to humbler men,
Must tear her knight from Guendolen.
She listened silently the while,   100
Her mood expressed in bitter smile
Beneath her eye must Arthur quail
And oft resume the unfinished tale,
Confessing by his downcast eye
The wrong he sought to justify.
He ceased.   A moment mute she gazed,
And then her looks to heaven she raised;
One palm her temples veiled to hide
The tear that sprung in spite of pride;
The other for an instant pressed   110
The foldings of her silken vest !

VII

'At her reproachful sign and look,
The hint the monarch's conscience took.

Eager he spoke — "No, lady, no !
Deem not of British Arthur so,
Nor think he can deserter prove
To the dear pledge of mutual love.
I swear by sceptre and by sword,
As belted knight and Britain's lord,
That if a boy shall claim my care,   120
That boy is born a kingdom's heir;
But, if a maiden Fate allows,
To choose that mate a fitting spouse,
A summer-day in lists shall strive
My knights — the bravest knights alive —
And he, the best and bravest tried,
Shall Arthur's daughter claim for bride."
He spoke with voice resolved and high —
The lady deigned him not reply.

VIII

'At dawn of morn ere on the brake   130
His matins did a warbler make
Or stirred his wing to brush away
A single dew-drop from the spray,
Ere yet a sunbeam through the mist
The castle-battlements had kissed,
The gates revolve, the drawbridge falls,
And Arthur sallies from the walls.
Doffed his soft garb of Persia's loom,
And steel from spur to helmet plume,
His Lybian steed full proudly trode,   140
And joyful neighed beneath his load.
The monarch gave a passing sigh
To penitence and pleasures by,
When, lo ! to his astonished ken
Appeared the form of Guendolen.

IX

'Beyond the outmost wall she stood,
Attired like huntress of the wood:
Sandalled her feet, her ankles bare,
And eagle-plumage decked her hair;
Firm was her look, her bearing bold,   150
And in her hand a cup of gold.
"Thou goest ! " she said, " and ne'er again
Must we two meet in joy or pain.
Full fain would I this hour delay,
Though weak the wish — yet wilt thou stay ?
No ! thou look'st forward.   Still attend, —
Part we like lover and like friend."
She raised the cup — " Not this the juice
The sluggish vines of earth produce;
Pledge we at parting in the draught   160
Which   Genii   love ! " — she   said   and
        quaffed;
And strange unwonted lustres fly
From her flushed cheek and sparkling eye.

X

'The courteous monarch bent him low
And, stooping down from saddlebow,
Lifted the cup in act to drink.
A drop escaped the goblet's brink —
Intense as liquid fire from hell,
Upon the charger's neck it fell.
Screaming with agony and fright,   170
He bolted twenty feet upright —
The peasant still can show the dint
Where his hoofs lighted on the flint. —
From Arthur's hand the goblet flew,
Scattering a shower of fiery dew
That burned and blighted where it fell !
The frantic steed rushed up the dell,
As whistles from the bow the reed;
Nor bit nor rein could check his speed
  Until he gained the hill;   180
Then breath and sinew failed apace,
And, reeling from the desperate race,
  He stood exhausted, still.
The monarch, breathless and amazed,
Back on the fatal castle gazed —
Nor tower nor donjon could he spy,
Darkening against the morning sky;
But on the spot where once they frowned
The lonely streamlet brawled around
A tufted knoll, where dimly shone   190
Fragments of rock and rifted stone.
Musing on this strange hap the while,
The king wends back to fair Carlisle;
And cares that cumber royal sway
Wore memory of the past away.

XI

'Full fifteen years and more were sped,
Each brought new wreaths to Arthur's head.
Twelve bloody fields with glory fought
The Saxons to subjection brought:
Rython, the mighty giant, slain   200
By his good brand, relieved Bretagne:
The Pictish Gillamore in fight
And Roman Lucius owned his might;
And wide were through the world renowned
The glories of his Table Round.
Each knight who sought adventurous fame
To the bold court of Britain came,
And all who suffered causeless wrong,
From tyrant proud or faitour strong,
Sought Arthur's presence to complain,   210
Nor there for aid implored in vain.

XII

'For this the king with pomp and pride
Held solemn court at Whitsuntide,
And summoned prince and peer,
All who owed homage for their land,
Or who craved knighthood from his hand,
Or who had succour to demand,
  To come from far and near.
At such high tide were glee and game
Mingled with feats of martial fame,   220
For many a stranger champion came
  In lists to break a spear;
And not a knight of Arthur's host,
Save that he trode some foreign coast,
But at this feast of Pentecost
  Before him must appear.
Ah, minstrels ! when the Table Round
Arose with all its warriors crowned,
There was a theme for bards to sound
  In triumph to their string !   230
Five hundred years are past and gone,
But time shall draw his dying groan
Ere he behold the British throne
  Begirt with such a ring !

XIII

'The heralds named the appointed spot,
As Caerleon or Camelot,
  Or Carlisle fair and free.
At Penrith now the feast was set,
And in fair Eamont's vale were met
  The flower of chivalry.   240
There Galaad sate with manly grace,
Yet maiden meekness in his face;
There Morolt of the iron mace,
  And love-lorn Tristrem there;
And Dinadam with lively glance,
And Lanval with the fairy lance,
And Mordred with his look askance,
  Brunor and Bevidere.
Why should I tell of numbers more ?
Sir Cay, Sir Bannier, and Sir Bore,   250
  Sir Carodac the keen,
The gentle Gawain's courteous lore,
Hector de Mares and Pellinore,
And Lancelot, that evermore
  Looked stolen-wise on the queen.

XIV

'When wine and mirth did most abound
And harpers played their blithest round,
A shrilly trumpet shook the ground
  And marshals cleared the ring;
A maiden on a palfrey white,   260
Heading a band of damsels bright,
Paced through the circle to alight
  And kneel before the king.
Arthur with strong emotion saw

Her graceful boldness checked by awe,
Her dress like huntress of the wold,
Her bow and baldric trapped with gold,
Her sandalled feet, her ankles bare,
And the eagle-plume that decked her hair.
Graceful her veil she backward flung — 270
The king, as from his seat he sprung,
　　Almost cried, " Guendolen ! "
But 't was a face more frank and wild,
Betwixt the woman and the child,
Where less of magic beauty smiled
　　Than of the race of men;
And in the forehead's haughty grace
The lines of Britain's royal race,
　　Pendragon's you might ken.

XV

'Faltering, yet gracefully she said —　280
"Great Prince ! behold an orphan maid,
In her departed mother's name,
A father's vowed protection claim !
The vow was sworn in desert lone
In the deep valley of Saint John."
At once the king the suppliant raised,
And kissed her brow, her beauty praised;
His vow, he said, should well be kept,
Ere in the sea the sun was dipped, —
Then conscious glanced upon his queen: 290
But she, unruffled at the scene
Of human frailty construed mild,
Looked upon Lancelot and smiled.

XVI

' "Up ! up ! each knight of gallant crest
Take buckler, spear, and brand !
He that to-day shall bear him best
　　Shall win my Gyneth's hand.
And Arthur's daughter when a bride
　　Shall bring a noble dower,
Both fair Strath-Clyde and Reged wide, 300
　　And Carlisle town and tower."
Then might you hear each valiant knight
　　To page and squire that cried,
"Bring my armor bright and my courser
　　wight;
'T is not each day that a warrior's might
　　May win a royal bride."
Then cloaks and caps of maintenance
　　In haste aside they fling;
The helmets glance and gleams the lance,
　　And the steel-weaved hauberks ring. 310
Small care had they of their peaceful array,
　　They might gather it that wolde;
For brake and bramble glittered gay
　　With pearls and cloth of gold.

XVII

' Within trumpet sound of the Table Round,
　　Were fifty champions free,
And they all arise to fight that prize, —
　　They all arise but three.
Nor love's fond troth nor wedlock's oath
　　One gallant could withhold,　　　　320
For priests will allow of a broken vow
　　For penance or for gold.
But sigh and glance from ladies bright
　　Among the troop were thrown,
To plead their right and true-love plight,
　　And plain of honor flown.
The knights they busied them so fast
　　With buckling spur and belt
That sigh and look by ladies cast
　　Were neither seen nor felt.　　　330
From pleading or upbraiding glance
　　Each gallant turns aside,
And only thought, " If speeds my lance,
　　A queen becomes my bride !
She has fair Strath-Clyde and Reged
　　wide,
　　And Carlisle tower and town;
She is the loveliest maid, beside,
　　That ever heired a crown."
So in haste their coursers they bestride
　　And strike their visors down.　　340

XVIII

' The champions, armed in martial sort,
　　Have thronged into the list,
And but three knights of Arthur's court
　　Are from the tourney missed.
And still these lovers' fame survives
　　For faith so constant shown, —
There were two who loved their neighbors'
　　wives,
　　And one who loved his own.
The first was Lancelot de Lac,
　　The second Tristrem bold,　　　350
The third was valiant Carodac,
　　Who won the cup of gold
What time, of all King Arthur's crew —
　　Thereof came jeer and laugh —
He, as the mate of lady true,
　　Alone the cup could quaff.
Though envy's tongue would fain surmise
　　That, but for very shame,
Sir Carodac to fight that prize
　　Had given both cup and dame,　　360
Yet, since but one of that fair court
　　Was true to wedlock's shrine,
Brand him who will with base report,
　　He shall be free from mine.

XIX

'Now caracoled the steeds in air,
Now plumes and pennons wantoned fair,
As all around the lists so wide
In panoply the champions ride.
King Arthur saw with startled eye
The flower of chivalry march by,   370
The bulwark of the Christian creed,
The kingdom's shield in hour of need.
Too late he thought him of the woe
Might from their civil conflict flow;
For well he knew they would not part
Till cold was many a gallant heart.
His hasty vow he 'gan to rue,
And Gyneth then apart he drew;
To her his leading-staff resigned,
But added caution grave and kind.   380

XX

' " Thou see'st, my child, as promise-bound,
I bid the trump for tourney sound.
Take thou my warder as the queen
And umpire of the martial scene;
But mark thou this: — as Beauty bright
Is polar star to valiant knight,
As at her word his sword he draws,
His fairest guerdon her applause,
So gentle maid should never ask
Of knighthood vain and dangerous task;   390
And Beauty's eyes should ever be
Like the twin stars that soothe the sea,
And Beauty's breath should whisper peace
And bid the storm of battle cease.
I tell thee this lest all too far
These knights urge tourney into war.
Blithe at the trumpet let them go,
And fairly counter blow for blow; —
No striplings these, who succor need
For a razed helm or falling steed.   400
But, Gyneth, when the strife grows warm
And threatens death or deadly harm,
Thy sire entreats, thy king commands,
Thou drop the warder from thy hands.
Trust thou thy father with thy fate,
Doubt not he choose thee fitting mate;
Nor be it said through Gyneth's pride
A rose of Arthur's chaplet died." '

XXI

' A proud and discontented glow
O'ershadowed Gyneth's brow of snow;   410
She put the warder by: —
" Reserve thy boon, my liege," she said,
" Thus chaffered down and limited,
Debased and narrowed for a maid
Of less degree than I.
No petty chief but holds his heir
At a more honored price and rare
Than Britain's King holds me !
Although the sun-burned maid for dower
Has but her father's rugged tower,   420
His barren hill and lee."
King Arthur swore, " By crown and sword,
As belted knight and Britain's lord,
That a whole summer's day should strive
His knights, the bravest knights alive ! "
" Recall thine oath ! and to her glen
Poor Gyneth can return agen;
Not on thy daughter will the stain
That soils thy sword and crown remain.
But think not she will e'er be bride   430
Save to the bravest, proved and tried;
Pendragon's daughter will not fear
For clashing sword or splintered spear,
Nor shrink though blood should flow;
And all too well sad Guendolen
Hath taught the faithlessness of men
That child of hers should pity when
Their meed they undergo." '

XXII

' He frowned and sighed, the monarch bold: —
" I give — what I may not withhold;   440
For, not for danger, dread, or death,
Must British Arthur break his faith.
Too late I mark thy mother's art
Hath taught thee this relentless part.
I blame her not, for she had wrong,
But not to these my faults belong.
Use then the warder as thou wilt;
But trust me that, if life be spilt,
In Arthur's love, in Arthur's grace,
Gyneth shall lose a daughter's place."   450
With that he turned his head aside,
Nor brooked to gaze upon her pride,
As with the truncheon raised she sate
The arbitress of mortal fate;
Nor brooked to mark in ranks disposed
How the bold champions stood opposed,
For shrill the trumpet-flourish fell
Upon his ear like passing bell !
Then first from sight of martial fray
Did Britain's hero turn away.   460

XXIII

' But Gyneth heard the clangor high
As hears the hawk the partridge cry.
O, blame her not ! the blood was hers

That at the trumpet's summons stirs ! —
And e'en the gentlest female eye
Might the brave strife of chivalry
    Awhile untroubled view;
So well accomplished was each knight
To strike and to defend in fight,
Their meeting was a goodly sight   470
    While plate and mail held true.
The lists with painted plumes were strown,
Upon the wind at random thrown,
But helm and breastplate bloodless shone,
It seemed their feathered crests alone
    Should this encounter rue.
And ever, as the combat grows,
The trumpet's cheery voice arose,
Like lark's shrill song the flourish flows,
Heard while the gale of April blows   480
    The merry greenwood through.

XXIV

' But soon to earnest grew their game,
The spears drew blood, the swords struck
        flame,
And, horse and man, to ground there
        came
    Knights who shall rise no more !
Gone was the pride the war that graced,
Gay shields were cleft and crests defaced,
And steel coats riven and helms unbraced,
    And pennons streamed with gore.
Gone too were fence and fair array,   490
And desperate strength made deadly way
At random through the bloody fray,
And blows were dealt with headlong sway,
    Unheeding where they fell;
And now the trumpet's clamors seem
Like the shrill sea-bird's wailing scream
Heard o'er the whirlpool's gulfing stream,
    The sinking seaman's knell !

XXV

' Seemed in this dismal hour that Fate
Would Camlan's ruin antedate,   500
    And spare dark Mordred's crime;
Already gasping on the ground
Lie twenty of the Table Round,
    Of chivalry the prime.
Arthur in anguish tore away
From head and beard his tresses gray,
And she, proud Gyneth, felt dismay
    And quaked with ruth and fear;
But still she deemed her mother's shade
Hung o'er the tumult, and forbade   510
The sign that had the slaughter staid,
    And chid the rising tear.

Then Brunor, Taulas, Mador, fell,
Helias the White, and Lionel,
    And many a champion more;
Rochemont and Dinadam are down,
And Ferrand of the Forest Brown
    Lies gasping in his gore.
Vanoc, by mighty Morolt pressed
Even to the confines of the list,   520
Young Vanoc of the beardless face —
Fame spoke the youth of Merlin's race —
O'erpowered at Gyneth's footstool bled,
His heart's-blood dyed her sandals red.
But then the sky was overcast,
Then howled at once a whirlwind's blast,
    And, rent by sudden throes,
Yawned in mid lists the quaking earth,
And from the gulf — tremendous birth ! —
    The form of Merlin rose.   530

XXVI

' Sternly the Wizard Prophet eyed
The dreary lists with slaughter dyed,
    And sternly raised his hand: —
" Madmen," he said, " your strife for-
        bear !
And thou, fair cause of mischief, hear
The doom thy fates demand !
    Long shall close in stony sleep
    Eyes for ruth that would not weep;
    Iron lethargy shall seal
    Heart that pity scorned to feel.   540
    Yet, because thy mother's art
    Warped thine unsuspicious heart,
    And for love of Arthur's race
    Punishment is blent with grace,
    Thou shalt bear thy penance lone
    In the Valley of Saint John,
    And this weird shall overtake thee;
    Sleep until a knight shall wake thee,
    For feats of arms as far renowned
    As warrior of the Table Round.   550
    Long endurance of thy slumber
    Well may teach the world to number
    All their woes from Gyneth's pride,
    When the Red Cross champions died."

XXVII

' As Merlin speaks, on Gyneth's eye
Slumber's load begins to lie;
Fear and anger vainly strive
Still to keep its light alive.
Twice with effort and with pause
O'er her brow her hand she draws;   560
Twice her strength in vain she tries
From the fatal chair to rise;

Merlin's magic doom is spoken,
Vanoc's death must now be wroken.
Slow the dark-fringed eyelids fall,
Curtaining each azure ball,
Slowly as on summer eves
Violets fold their dusky leaves.
The weighty baton of command
Now bears down her sinking hand,   570
On her shoulder droops her head;
Net of pearl and golden thread
Bursting gave her locks to flow
O'er her arm and breast of snow.
And so lovely seemed she there,
Spell-bound in her ivory chair,
That her angry sire repenting,
Craved stern Merlin for relenting,
And the champions for her sake
Would again the contest wake;   580
Till in necromantic night
Gyneth vanished from their sight.

XXVIII

' Still she bears her weird alone
In the Valley of Saint John;
And her semblance oft will seem,
Mingling in a champion's dream,
Of her weary lot to plain
And crave his aid to burst her chain.
While her wondrous tale was new
Warriors to her rescue drew,   590
East and west, and south and north,
From the Liffy, Thames, and Forth.
Most have sought in vain the glen,
Tower nor castle could they ken;
Not at every time or tide,
Nor by every eye, descried.
Fast and vigil must be borne,
Many a night in watching worn,
Ere an eye of mortal powers
Can discern those magic towers.   600
Of the persevering few
Some from hopeless task withdrew
When they read the dismal threat
Graved upon the gloomy gate.
Few have braved the yawning door,
And those few returned no more.
In the lapse of time forgot,
Wellnigh lost is Gyneth's lot;
Sound her sleep as in the tomb
Till wakened by the trump of doom.   610

END OF LYULPH'S TALE

I

HERE pause, my tale; for all too soon,
My Lucy, comes the hour of noon.

Already from thy lofty dome
Its courtly inmates 'gin to roam,
And each, to kill the goodly day
That God has granted them, his way
    Of lazy sauntering has sought;
    Lordlings and witlings not a few,
    Incapable of doing aught,
    Yet ill at ease with nought to do.   620
Here is no longer place for me;
For, Lucy, thou wouldst blush to see
    Some phantom fashionably thin,
    With limb of lath and kerchiefed chin,
    And lounging gape or sneering grin,
Steal sudden on our privacy.
And how should I, so humbly born,
Endure the graceful spectre's scorn ?
Faith ! ill, I fear, while conjuring wand
Of English oak is hard at hand.   630

II

Or grant the hour be all too soon
For Hessian boot and pantaloon,
And grant the lounger seldom strays
Beyond the smooth and gravelled maze,
Laud we the gods that Fashion's train
Holds hearts of more adventurous strain.
Artists are hers who scorn to trace
Their rules from Nature's boundless grace,
But their right paramount assert
    To limit her by pedant art,   640
Damning whate'er of vast and fair
Exceeds a canvas three feet square.
This thicket, for their *gumption* fit,
    May furnish such a happy *bit*.
Bards too are hers, wont to recite
Their own sweet lays by waxen light,
Half in the salver's tingle drowned,
While the *chasse-café* glides around;
And such may hither secret stray
    To labor an extempore: 650
Or sportsman with his boisterous hollo
May here his wiser spaniel follow,
Or stage-struck Juliet may presume
To choose this bower for tiring-room;
And we alike must shun regard
From painter, player, sportsman, bard.
Insects that skim in fashion's sky,
Wasp, blue-bottle, or butterfly,
Lucy, have all alarms for us,
For all can hum and all can buzz.   660

III

But O, my Lucy, say how long
We still must dread this trifling throng,
And stoop to hide with coward art
The genuine feelings of the heart !

No parents thine whose just command
Should rule their child's obedient hand;
Thy guardians with contending voice
Press each his individual choice.
And which is Lucy's ? — Can it be
That puny fop, trimmed cap-a-pee,   670
Who loves in the saloon to show
The arms that never knew a foe;
Whose sabre trails along the ground,
Whose legs in shapeless boots are drowned;
A new Achilles, sure — the steel
Fled from his breast to fence his heel;
One, for the simple manly grace
That wont to deck our martial race,
  Who comes in foreign trashery
    Of tinkling chain and spur,   680
  A walking haberdashery
    Of feathers, lace, and fur:
In Rowley's antiquated phrase,
Horse-milliner of modern days ?

IV

Or is it he, the wordy youth,
  So early trained for statesman's
    part,
Who talks of honor, faith and truth,
  As themes that he has got by heart;
Whose ethics Chesterfield can teach,   690
Whose logic is from Single-speech;
Who scorns the meanest thought to vent
Save in the phrase of Parliament;
Who, in a tale of cat and mouse,
Calls ' order,' and ' divides the house,'
Who ' craves permission to reply,'
Whose ' noble friend is in his eye;'
Whose loving tender some have reckoned
A *motion* you should gladly *second ?*

V

What, neither ?   Can there be a third,
To such resistless swains preferred ? — 700
O why, my Lucy, turn aside
With that quick glance of injured pride ?
Forgive me, love, I cannot bear
That altered and resentful air.
Were all the wealth of Russel mine
And all the rank of Howard's line,
All would I give for leave to dry
That dew-drop trembling in thine eye.
Think not I fear such fops can wile
From Lucy more than careless smile;   710
But yet if wealth and high degree
Give gilded counters currency,
Must I not fear when rank and birth

Stamp the pure ore of genuine worth ?
Nobles there are whose martial fires
Rival the fame that raised their sires,
And patriots, skilled through storms of
    fate
To guide and guard the reeling state.
Such, such there are — If such should
    come,
Arthur must tremble and be dumb,   720
Self-exiled seek some distant shore,
And mourn till life and grief are o'er.

VI

What sight, what signal of alarm,
That Lucy clings to Arthur's arm ?
Or is it that the rugged way
Makes Beauty lean on lover's stay ?
O, no ! for on the vale and brake
Nor sight nor sounds of danger wake,
And this trim sward of velvet green
Were carpet for the Fairy Queen.   730
That pressure slight was but to tell
That Lucy loves her Arthur well,
And fain would banish from his mind
Suspicious fear and doubt unkind.

VII

But wouldst thou bid the demons fly
Like mist before the dawning sky,
There is but one resistless spell —
Say, wilt thou guess or must I tell ?
'T were hard to name in minstrel phrase
A landaulet and four blood-bays,   740
But bards agree this wizard band
Can but be bound in Northern land.
'T is there — nay, draw not back thy
    hand ! —
'T is there this slender finger round
Must golden amulet be bound,
Which, blessed with many a holy prayer,
Can change to rapture lovers' care,
And doubt and jealousy shall die,
And fears give place to ecstasy.

VIII

Now, trust me, Lucy, all too long   750
Has been thy lover's tale and song.
O, why so silent, love, I pray ?
Have I not spoke the livelong day ?
And will not Lucy deign to say
One word her friend to bless ?
I ask but one — a simple sound,
Within three little letters bound —
  O, let the word be YES !

CANTO THIRD

INTRODUCTION

I

Long loved, long wooed, and lately won,
My life's best hope, and now mine own !
Doth not this rude and Alpine glen
Recall our favorite haunts agen ?
A wild resemblance we can trace,
Though reft of every softer grace,
As the rough warrior's brow may bear
A likeness to a sister fair.
Full well advised our Highland host
That this wild pass on foot be crossed,   10
While round Ben-Cruach's mighty base
Wheel the slow steeds and lingering
    chase.
The keen old carle, with Scottish pride
He praised his glen and mountains wide;
An eye he bears for nature's face,
Ay, and for woman's lovely grace.
Even in such mean degree we find
The subtle Scot's observing mind;
For nor the chariot nor the train
Could gape of vulgar wonder gain,   20
But when old Allan would expound
Of Beal-na-paish the Celtic sound,
His bonnet doffed and bow applied
His legend to my bonny bride;
While Lucy blushed beneath his eye,
Courteous and cautious, shrewd and sly.

II

Enough of him. — Now, ere we lose,
Plunged in the vale, the distant views,
Turn thee, my love ! look back once
    more
To the blue lake's retiring shore.   30
On its smooth breast the shadows seem
Like objects in a morning dream,
What time the slumberer is aware
He sleeps and all the vision 's air:
Even so on yonder liquid lawn,
In hues of bright reflection drawn,
Distinct the shaggy mountains lie,
Distinct the rocks, distinct the sky;
The summer-clouds so plain we note
That we might count each dappled spot: 40
We gaze and we admire, yet know
The scene is all delusive show.
Such dreams of bliss would Arthur draw
When first his Lucy's form he saw,
Yet sighed and sickened as he drew,
Despairing they could e'er prove true !

III

But, Lucy, turn thee now to view
    Up the fair glen our destined way:
The fairy path that we pursue,
Distinguished but by greener hue,   50
    Winds round the purple brae,
While Alpine flowers of varied dye
For carpet serve or tapestry.
See how the little runnels leap
In threads of silver down the steep
    To swell the brooklet's moan !
Seems that the Highland Naiad grieves,
Fantastic while her crown she weaves
Of rowan, birch, and alder leaves,
    So lovely and so lone.   60
There 's no illusion there; these flowers,
That wailing brook, these lovely bowers,
    Are, Lucy, all our own;
And, since thine Arthur called thee wife,
Such seems the prospect of his life,
A lovely path on-winding still
By gurgling brook and sloping hill.
'T is true that mortals cannot tell
What waits them in the distant dell;
But be it hap or be it harm,   70
We tread the pathway arm in arm.

IV

And now, my Lucy, wot'st thou why
I could thy bidding twice deny,
When twice you prayed I would again
Resume the legendary strain
Of the bold knight of Triermain ?
At length yon peevish vow you swore
That you would sue to me no more,
Until the minstrel fit drew near
And made me prize a listening ear.   80
But, loveliest, when thou first didst pray
Continuance of the knightly lay,
Was it not on the happy day
    That made thy hand mine own ?
When, dizzied with mine ecstasy,
Nought past, or present, or to be,
Could I or think on, hear, or see,
    Save, Lucy, thee alone !
A giddy draught my rapture was
As ever chemist's magic gas.   90

V

Again the summons I denied
In yon fair capital of Clyde:
My harp — or let me rather choose
The good old classic form — my Muse —
For harp 's an over-scutched phrase,
Worn out by bards of modern days —

My Muse, then — seldom will she wake,
Save by dim wood and silent lake;
She is the wild and rustic maid
Whose foot unsandalled loves to tread   100
Where the soft greensward is inlaid
  With varied moss and thyme;
And, lest the simple lily-braid,
That coronets her temples, fade,
She hides her still in greenwood shade
  To meditate her rhyme.

VI

And now she comes ! The murmur dear
Of the wild brook hath caught her ear,
  The glade hath won her eye;
She longs to join with each blithe rill   110
That dances down the Highland hill
  Her blither melody.
And now my Lucy's way to cheer
She bids Ben-Cruach's echoes hear
How closed the tale my love whilere
  Loved for its chivalry.
List how she tells in notes of flame
'Child Roland to the dark tower came !'

CANTO THIRD

I

BEWCASTLE now must keep the hold,
Speir-Adam's steeds must bide in stall,
Of Hartley-burn the bowmen bold
  Must only shoot from battled wall;
And Liddesdale may buckle spur,
  And Teviot now may belt the brand,
Tarras and Ewes keep nightly stir,
  And Eskdale foray Cumberland.
Of wasted fields and plundered flocks
  The Borderers bootless may complain;   10
They lack the sword of brave De Vaux,
  There comes no aid from Triermain.
That lord on high adventure bound
  Hath wandered forth alone,
And day and night keeps watchful round
  In the Valley of Saint John.

II

When first began his vigil bold
The moon twelve summer nights was old
  And shone both fair and full;
High in the vault of cloudless blue,   20
O'er streamlet, dale, and rock, she threw
  Her light composed and cool.
Stretched on the brown hill's heathy breast,
  Sir Roland eyed the vale;

Chief where, distinguished from the rest,
Those clustering rocks upreared their
    crest,
The dwelling of the fair distressed,
  As told gray Lyulph's tale.
Thus as he lay, the lamp of night
Was quivering on his armor bright   30
  In beams that rose and fell,
And danced upon his buckler's boss
That lay beside him on the moss
  As on a crystal well.

III

Ever he watched and oft he deemed,
While on the mound the moonlight
    streamed,
  It altered to his eyes;
Fain would he hope the rocks 'gan change
To buttressed walls their shapeless range,
Fain think by transmutation strange   40
  He saw gray turrets rise.
But scarce his heart with hope throbbed
    high
Before the wild illusions fly
  Which fancy had conceived,
Abetted by an anxious eye
  That longed to be deceived.
It was a fond deception all,
Such as in solitary hall
  Beguiles the musing eye
When, gazing on the sinking fire,   50
Bulwark, and battlement, and spire
  In the red gulf we spy.
For, seen by moon of middle night,
Or by the blaze of noontide bright,
Or by the dawn of morning light,
  Or evening's western flame,
In every tide, at every hour,
In mist, in sunshine, and in shower,
  The rocks remained the same.

IV

Oft has he traced the charmed mound,   60
Oft climbed its crest or paced it round,
  Yet nothing might explore,
Save that the crags so rudely piled,
At distance seen, resemblance wild
  To a rough fortress bore.
Yet still his watch the warrior keeps,
Feeds hard and spare, and seldom sleeps,
  And drinks but of the well;
Ever by day he walks the hill,
And when the evening gale is chill   70
  He seeks a rocky cell,
Like hermit poor to bid his bead,

And tell his Ave and his Creed,
Invoking every saint at need
  For aid to burst his spell.

V

And now the moon her orb has hid
And dwindled to a silver thread,
  Dim seen in middle heaven,
While o'er its curve careering fast
Before the fury of the blast
  The midnight clouds are driven.   80
The brooklet raved, for on the hills
The upland showers had swoln the rills
  And down the torrents came;
Muttered the distant thunder dread,
And frequent o'er the vale was spread
  A sheet of lightning flame.
De Vaux within his mountain cave —
No human step the storm durst brave —
  To moody meditation gave   90
  Each faculty of soul,
Till, lulled by distant torrent sound
And the sad winds that whistled round,
  Upon his thoughts in musing drowned
  A broken slumber stole.

VI

'T was then was heard a heavy sound —
  Sound, strange and fearful there to hear,
'Mongst desert hills where leagues around
  Dwelt but the gorcock and the deer.
As, starting from his couch of fern,   100
Again he heard in clangor stern
  That deep and solemn swell,
Twelve times in measured tone it spoke,
Like some proud minster's pealing clock
  Or city's larum-bell.
What thought was Roland's first when
    fell
In that deep wilderness the knell
  Upon his startled ear ?
To slander warrior were I loath,
Yet must I hold my minstrel troth —   110
  It was a thought of fear.

VII

But lively was the mingled thrill
That chased that momentary chill,
  For Love's keen wish was there,
And eager Hope, and Valor high,
And the proud glow of Chivalry
  That burned to do and dare.
Forth from the cave the warrior rushed,
Long ere the mountain-voice was hushed
  That answered to the knell;   120

For long and far the unwonted sound,
Eddying in echoes round and round,
  Was tossed from fell to fell;
And Glaramara answer flung,
And Grisdale-pike responsive rung,
And Legbert heights their echoes swung
  As far as Derwent's dell.

VIII

Forth upon trackless darkness gazed
The knight, bedeafened and amazed,
  Till all was hushed and still,   130
Save the swoln torrent's sullen roar,
And the night-blast that wildly bore
  Its course along the hill.
Then on the northern sky there came
A light as of reflected flame,
  And over Legbert-head,
As if by magic art controlled,
A mighty meteor slowly rolled
  Its orb of fiery red;
Thou wouldst have thought some demon dire
Came mounted on that car of fire   141
  To do his errand dread.
Far on the sloping valley's course,
On thicket, rock, and torrent hoarse,
Shingle and Scrae, and Fell and Force,
  A dusky light arose:
Displayed, yet altered was the scene;
Dark rock, and brook of silver sheen,
Even the gay thicket's summer green,
  In bloody tincture glows.   150

IX

De Vaux had marked the sunbeams set
At eve upon the coronet
  Of that enchanted mound,
And seen but crags at random flung,
That, o'er the brawling torrent hung,
  In desolation frowned.
What sees he by that meteor's lour ? —
A bannered castle, keep, and tower
  Return the lurid gleam,
With battled walls and buttress fast,   160
And barbican and ballium vast,
And airy flanking towers that cast
  Their shadows on the stream.
'T is no deceit ! distinctly clear
Crenell and parapet appear,
While o'er the pile that meteor drear
  Makes momentary pause;
Then forth its solemn path it drew,
And fainter yet and fainter grew
Those gloomy towers upon the view,   170
  As its wild light withdraws.

X

Forth from the cave did Roland rush,
O'er crag and stream, through brier and
    bush;
  Yet far he had not sped
Ere sunk was that portentous light
Behind the hills and utter night
  Was on the valley spread.
He paused perforce and blew his horn,
And, on the mountain-echoes borne,
  Was heard an answering sound,   180
A wild and lonely trumpet note, —
In middle air it seemed to float
  High o'er the battled mound;
And sounds were heard as when a guard
Of some proud castle, holding ward,
  Pace forth their nightly round.
The valiant Knight of Triermain
Rung forth his challenge-blast again,
  But answer came there none;
And mid the mingled wind and rain   190
Darkling he sought the vale in vain,
  Until the dawning shone;
And when it dawned that wondrous
    sight
Distinctly seen by meteor light,
  It all had passed away !
And that enchanted mount once more
A pile of granite fragments bore
  As at the close of day.

XI

Steeled for the deed, De Vaux's heart
Scorned from his vent'rous quest to
    part   200
  He walks the vale once more;
But only sees by night or day
That shattered pile of rocks so gray,
  Hears but the torrent's roar:
Till when, through hills of azure borne,
The moon renewed her silver horn,
Just at the time her waning ray
Had faded in the dawning day,
  A summer mist arose;
Adown the vale the vapors float,   210
And cloudy undulations moat
That tufted mound of mystic note,
  As round its base they close.
And higher now the fleecy tide
Ascends its stern and shaggy side,
Until the airy billows hide
  The rock's majestic isle;
It seemed a veil of filmy lawn,
By some fantastic fairy drawn
  Around enchanted pile.   220

XII

The breeze came softly down the brook,
  And, sighing as it blew,
The veil of silver mist it shook
And to De Vaux's eager look
  Renewed that wondrous view.
For, though the loitering vapor braved
The gentle breeze, yet oft it waved
  Its mantle's dewy fold;
And still when shook that filmy screen
Were towers and bastions dimly seen,   230
And Gothic battlements between
  Their gloomy length unrolled.
Speed, speed, De Vaux, ere on thine eye
Once more the fleeting vision die ! —
  The gallant knight 'gan speed
As prompt and light as, when the hound
Is opening and the horn is wound,
  Careers the hunter's steed.
Down the steep dell his course amain
  Hath rivalled archer's shaft;   240
But ere the mound he could attain
The rocks their shapeless form regain,
And, mocking loud his labor vain,
  The mountain spirits laughed.
Far up the echoing dell was borne
Their wild unearthly shout of scorn.

XIII

Wroth waxed the warrior. — ' Am I then
Fooled by the enemies of men,
Like a poor hind whose homeward way
Is haunted by malicious fay ?   250
Is Triermain become your taunt,
De Vaux your scorn ? False fiends,
    avaunt ! '
A weighty curtal-axe he bare;
The baleful blade so bright and square,
And the tough shaft of heben wood,
Were oft in Scottish gore imbrued.
Backward his stately form he drew,
And at the rocks the weapon threw
Just where one crag's projected crest
Hung proudly balanced o'er the rest.   260
Hurled with main force the weapon's shock
Rent a huge fragment of the rock.
If by mere strength, 't were hard to tell,
Or if the blow dissolved some spell,
But down the headlong ruin came
With cloud of dust and flash of flame.
Down bank, o'er bush, its course was
    borne,
Crushed lay the copse, the earth was torn,
Till staid at length the ruin dread
Cumbered the torrent's rocky bed,   270

And bade the waters' high-swoln tide
Seek other passage for its pride.

XIV

When ceased that thunder Triermain
Surveyed the mound's rude front again;
And lo ! the ruin had laid bare,
Hewn in the stone, a winding stair
Whose mossed and fractured steps might
   lend
The means the summit to ascend;
And by whose aid the brave De Vaux
Began to scale these magic rocks,   280
   And soon a platform won
Where, the wild witchery to close,
Within three lances' length arose
   The Castle of Saint John !
No misty phantom of the air,
No meteor-blazoned show was there;
In morning splendor full and fair
   The massive fortress shone.

XV

Embattled high and proudly towered,
Shaded by ponderous flankers, lowered   290
   The portal's gloomy way.
Though for six hundred years and more
Its strength had brooked the tempest's
   roar,
The scutcheoned emblems which it bore
   Had suffered no decay:
But from the eastern battlement
A turret had made sheer descent,
And, down in recent ruin rent,
   In the mid torrent lay.
Else, o'er the castle's brow sublime,   300
Insults of violence or of time
   Unfelt had passed away.
In shapeless characters of yore,
The gate this stern inscription bore:

XVI

INSCRIPTION

' Patience waits the destined day,
Strength can clear the cumbered way.
Warrior, who hast waited long,
Firm of soul, of sinew strong,
It is given to thee to gaze
On the pile of ancient days.   310
Never mortal builder's hand
This enduring fabric planned;
Sign and sigil, word of power,
From the earth raised keep and tower.
View it o'er and pace it round,

Rampart, turret, battled mound.
Dare no more ! To cross the gate
Were to tamper with thy fate;
Strength and fortitude were vain,
View it o'er — and turn again.'   320

XVII

' That would I,' said the warrior bold,
' If that my frame were bent and old,
And my thin blood dropped slow and cold
   As icicle in thaw;
But while my heart can feel it dance
Blithe as the sparkling wine of France,
And this good arm wields sword or lance,
   I mock these words of awe !'
He said; the wicket felt the sway
Of his strong hand and straight gave
   way,   330
And with rude crash and jarring bray
   The rusty bolts withdraw;
But o'er the threshold as he strode
And forward took the vaulted road,
An unseen arm with force amain
The ponderous gate flung close again,
   And rusted bolt and bar
Spontaneous took their place once more
While the deep arch with sullen roar
   Returned their surly jar.   340
' Now closed is the gin and the prey within,
   By the Rood of Lanercost !
But he that would win the war-wolf's skin
   May rue him of his boast.'
Thus muttering on the warrior went
By dubious light down steep descent.

XVIII

Unbarred, unlocked, unwatched, a port
Led to the castle's outer court:
There the main fortress, broad and tall,
Spread its long range of bower and hall   350
   And towers of varied size,
Wrought with each ornament extreme
That Gothic art in wildest dream
   Of fancy could devise;
But full between the warrior's way
And the main portal arch there lay
   An inner moat;
   Nor bridge nor boat
Affords De Vaux the means to cross
The clear, profound, and silent fosse.   360
His arms aside in haste he flings,
Cuirass of steel and hauberk rings,
And down falls helm and down the shield,
Rough with the dints of many a field.
Fair was his manly form and fair

His keen dark eye and close curled hair,
When all unarmed save that the brand
Of well-proved metal graced his hand,
With nought to fence his dauntless breast
But the close gipon's under-vest,   370
Whose sullied buff the sable stains
Of hauberk and of mail retains, —
Roland De Vaux upon the brim
Of the broad moat stood prompt to swim.

XIX

Accoutred thus he dared the tide,
And soon he reached the farther side
    And entered soon the hold,
And paced a hall whose walls so wide
Were blazoned all with feats of pride
    By warriors done of old.   380
In middle lists they countered here
    While trumpets seemed to blow;
And there in den or desert drear
    They quelled gigantic foe,
Braved the fierce griffon in his ire,
Or faced the dragon's breath of fire.
Strange in their arms and strange in
    face,
Heroes they seemed of ancient race,
Whose deeds of arms and race and name,
Forgotten long by later fame,   390
    Were here depicted to appall
Those of an age degenerate
Whose bold intrusion braved their fate
    In this enchanted hall.
For some short space the venturous knight
With these high marvels fed his sight,
Then sought the chamber's upper end
Where three broad easy steps ascend
    To an arched portal door,
In whose broad folding leaves of state   400
Was framed a wicket window-grate;
    And ere he ventured more,
The gallant knight took earnest view
The grated wicket-window through.

XX

O, for his arms !   Of martial weed
Had never mortal knight such need ! —
He spied a stately gallery; all
Of snow-white marble was the wall,
    The vaulting, and the floor;
And, contrast strange ! on either hand   410
There stood arrayed in sable band
    Four maids whom Afric bore;
And each a Lybian tiger led,
Held by as bright and frail a thread
    As Lucy's golden hair,

For the leash that bound these monsters
    dread
    Was but of gossamer.
Each maiden's short barbaric vest
Left all unclosed the knee and breast
    And limbs of shapely jet;   420
White was their vest and turban's fold,
On arms and ankles rings of gold
    In savage pomp were set;
A quiver on their shoulders lay,
And in their hand an assagay.
Such and so silent stood they there
    That Roland wellnigh hoped
He saw a band of statues rare,
Stationed the gazer's soul to scare;
    But when the wicket oped   430
Each grisly beast 'gan upward draw,
Rolled his grim eye, and spread his claw,
Scented the air, and licked his jaw;
While these weird maids in Moorish
    tongue
A wild and dismal warning sung.

XXI

' Rash adventurer, bear thee back !
    Dread the spell of Dahomay !
Fear the race of Zaharak;
    Daughters of the burning day !

' When the whirlwind's gusts are wheeling,
    Ours it is the dance to braid;   441
Zarah's sands in pillars reeling
    Join the measure that we tread,
When the Moon has donned her cloak
    And the stars are red to see,
Shrill when pipes the sad Siroc,
    Music meet for such as we.

' Where the shattered columns lie,
    Showing Carthage once had been,
If the wandering Santon's eye   450
    Our mysterious rites hath seen, —
Oft he cons the prayer of death,
    To the nations preaches doom,
" Azrael's brand hath left the sheath,
    Moslems, think upon the tomb ! "

' Ours the scorpion, ours the snake,
    Ours the hydra of the fen,
Ours the tiger of the brake,
    All that plague the sons of men.
Ours the tempest's midnight wrack,   460
    Pestilence that wastes by day —
Dread the race of Zaharak !
    Fear the spell of Dahomay ! '

XXII

Uncouth and strange the accents shrill
Rung those vaulted roofs among,
Long it was ere faint and still
Died the far-resounding song.
While yet the distant echoes roll,
The warrior communed with his soul.
  'When first I took this venturous
     quest,   470
    I swore upon the rood
  Neither to stop nor turn nor rest,
    For evil or for good.
My forward path too well I ween
Lies yonder fearful ranks between;
For man unarmed 't is bootless hope
With tigers and with fiends to cope —
Yet, if I turn, what waits me there
Save famine dire and fell despair ? —
Other conclusion let me try,   480
Since, choose howe'er I list, I die.
Forward lies faith and knightly fame;
Behind are perjury and shame.
In life or death I hold my word !'
With that he drew his trusty sword,
Caught down a banner from the wall,
And entered thus the fearful hall.

XXIII

On high each wayward maiden threw
Her swarthy arm with wild halloo !
On either side a tiger sprung —   490
Against the leftward foe he flung
The ready banner to engage
With tangling folds the brutal rage;
The right-hand monster in mid air
He struck so fiercely and so fair
Through gullet and through spinal bone
The trenchant blade hath sheerly gone.
His grisly brethren ramped and yelled,
But the slight leash their rage withheld,
Whilst 'twixt their ranks the dangerous
    road   500
Firmly though swift the champion strode.
Safe to the gallery's bound he drew,
Safe passed an open portal through;
And when against pursuit he flung
The gate, judge if the echoes rung !
Onward his daring course he bore,
While, mixed with dying growl and roar,
Wild jubilee and loud hurra
Pursued him on his venturous way.

XXIV

'Hurra, hurra ! Our watch is done !   510
  We hail once more the tropic sun.

Pallid beams of northern day,
Farewell, farewell ! Hurra, hurra !

'Five hundred years o'er this cold glen
Hath the pale sun come round agen;
Foot of man till now hath ne'er
Dared to cross the Hall of Fear.

'Warrior ! thou whose dauntless heart
Gives us from our ward to part,
Be as strong in future trial   520
Where resistance is denial.

'Now for Afric's glowing sky,
Zwenga wide and Atlas high,
Zaharak and Dahomay ! —
Mount the winds ! Hurra, hurra !'

XXV

The wizard song at distance died,
  As if in ether borne astray,
While through waste halls and chambers
    wide
  The knight pursued his steady way
Till to a lofty dome he came   530
That flashed with such a brilliant flame
As if the wealth of all the world
Were there in rich confusion hurled.
For here the gold in sandy heaps
With duller earth incorporate sleeps;
Was there in ingots piled, and there
Coined badge of empery it bare;
Yonder, huge bars of silver lay,
Dimmed by the diamond's neighboring
    ray,
Like the pale moon in morning day;   540
And in the midst four maidens stand,
The daughters of some distant land.
Their hue was of the dark-red dye
That fringes oft a thunder sky;
Their hands palmetto baskets bare,
And cotton fillets bound their hair;
Slim was their form, their mien was
    shy,
To earth they bent the humbled eye,
Folded their arms, and suppliant kneeled,
And thus their proffered gifts revealed. 550

XXVI

CHORUS

'See the treasures Merlin piled,
Portion meet for Arthur's child.
Bathe in Wealth's unbounded stream,
Wealth that Avarice ne'er could dream !'

FIRST MAIDEN

'See these clots of virgin gold !
Severed from the sparry mould,
Nature's mystic alchemy
In the mine thus bade them lie;
And their orient smile can win
Kings to stoop and saints to sin.'   560

SECOND MAIDEN

'See these pearls that long have slept;
These were tears by Naiads wept
For the loss of Marinel.
Tritons in the silver shell
Treasured them till hard and white
As the teeth of Amphitrite.'

THIRD MAIDEN

'Does a livelier hue delight ?
Here are rubies blazing bright,
Here the emerald's fairy green,
And the topaz glows between;   570
Here their varied hues unite
In the changeful chrysolite.'

FOURTH MAIDEN

'Leave these gems of poorer shine,
Leave them all and look on mine !
While their glories I expand
Shade thine eyebrows with thy hand.
Mid-day sun and diamond's blaze
Blind the rash beholder's gaze.'

CHORUS

'Warrior, seize the splendid store;
Would 't were all our mountains bore ! 580
We should ne'er in future story
Read, Peru, thy perished glory !'

XXVII

Calmly and unconcerned the knight
Waved aside the treasures bright —
'Gentle Maidens, rise, I pray !
Bar not thus my destined way.
Let these boasted brilliant toys
Braid the hair of girls and boys !
Bid your streams of gold expand
O'er proud London's thirsty land. 590
De Vaux of wealth saw never need
Save to purvey him arms and steed,
And all the ore he deigned to hoard
Inlays his helm and hilts his sword.'
Thus gently parting from their hold,
He left unmoved the dome of gold.

XXVIII

And now the morning sun was high,
De Vaux was weary, faint, and dry;
When, lo ! a plashing sound he hears,
A gladsome signal that he nears 600
  Some frolic water-run:
And soon he reached a courtyard square
Where, dancing in the sultry air,
Tossed high aloft a fountain fair
  Was sparkling in the sun.
On right and left a fair arcade
In long perspective view displayed
Alleys and bowers for sun or shade:
  But full in front a door,
Low - browed and dark, seemed as it
  led 610
To the lone dwelling of the dead
  Whose memory was no more.

XXIX

Here stopped De Vaux an instant's space
To bathe his parched lips and face,
  And marked with well-pleased eye,
Refracted on the fountain stream,
In rainbow hues the dazzling beam
  Of that gay summer sky.
His senses felt a mild control,
Like that which lulls the weary soul, 620
  From contemplation high
Relaxing, when the ear receives
The music that the greenwood leaves
  Make to the breezes' sigh.

XXX

And oft in such a dreamy mood
  The half-shut eye can frame
Fair apparitions in the wood,
As if the Nymphs of field and flood
  In gay procession came.
Are these of such fantastic mould, 630
  Seen distant down the fair arcade,
These maids enlinked in sister-fold,
  Who, late at bashful distance staid,
  Now tripping from the greenwood shade,
Nearer the musing champion draw,
And in a pause of seeming awe
  Again stand doubtful now ? —
Ah, that sly pause of witching powers !
That seems to say, 'To please be ours,
  Be yours to tell us how.' 640
Their hue was of the golden glow
That sons of Candahar bestow,
O'er which in slight suffusion flows
A frequent tinge of paly rose;
Their limbs were fashioned fair and free

In nature's justest symmetry;
And, wreathed with flowers, with odors
    graced,
Their raven ringlets reached the waist:
In eastern pomp its gilding pale
The henna lent each shapely nail,   650
And the dark sumah gave the eye
More liquid and more lustrous dye.
The spotless veil of misty lawn,
In studied disarrangement drawn
    The form and bosom o'er,
To win the eye or tempt the touch,
For modesty showed all too much —
    Too much — yet promised more.

XXXI

'Gentle knight, awhile delay,'
Thus they sung, ' thy toilsome way,   660
While we pay the duty due
To our Master and to you.
Over Avarice, over Fear,
Love triumphant led thee here;
Warrior, list to us, for we
Are slaves to Love, are friends to thee.
Though no treasured gems have we
To proffer on the bended knee,
Though we boast nor arm nor heart
For the assagay or dart,   670
Swains allow each simple girl
Ruby lip and teeth of pearl;
Or, if dangers more you prize,
Flatterers find them in our eyes.

'Stay, then, gentle warrior, stay,
Rest till evening steal on day;
Stay, O, stay ! — in yonder bowers
We will braid thy locks with flowers,
Spread the feast and fill the wine,
Charm thy ear with sounds divine,   680
Weave our dances till delight
Yield to languor, day to night.
Then shall she you most approve
Sing the lays that best you love,
Soft thy mossy couch shall spread,
Watch thy pillow, prop thy head,
Till the weary night be o'er —
Gentle warrior, wouldst thou more.
Wouldst thou more, fair warrior, — she
Is slave to Love and slave to thee.'   690

XXXII

O, do not hold it for a crime
In the bold hero of my rhyme,
    For Stoic look
    And meet rebuke
He lacked the heart or time;

As round the band of sirens trip,
He kissed one damsel's laughing lip,
And pressed another's proffered hand,
Spoke to them all in accents bland,
But broke their magic circle through;   700
' Kind maids,' he said, 'adieu, adieu !
My fate, my fortune, forward lies.'
He said and vanished from their eyes;
But, as he dared that darksome way,
Still heard behind their lovely lay:
'Fair Flower of Courtesy, depart !
Go where the feelings of the heart
With the warm pulse in concord move;
Go where Virtue sanctions Love ! '

XXXIII

Downward De Vaux through darksome
    ways   710
    And ruined vaults has gone,
Till issue from their wildered maze
    Or safe retreat seemed none,
And e'en the dismal path he strays
    Grew worse as he went on.
For cheerful sun, for living air,
Foul vapors rise and mine-fires glare,
Whose fearful light the dangers showed
That dogged him on that dreadful road.
Deep pits and lakes of waters dun   720
They showed, but showed not how to
    shun.
These scenes of desolate despair,
These smothering clouds of poisoned air,
How gladly had De Vaux exchanged,
Though 't were to face yon tigers ranged !
    Nay, soothful bards have said,
So perilous his state seemed now
He wished him under arbor bough
    With Asia's willing maid.
When, joyful sound ! at distance near   730
A trumpet flourished loud and clear,
And as it ceased a lofty lay
Seemed thus to chide his lagging way.

XXXIV

' Son of Honor, theme of story,
    Think on the reward before ye !
Danger, darkness, toil despise;
    'T is Ambition bids thee rise.

' He that would her heights ascend,
    Many a weary step must wend;
Hand and foot and knee he tries;   740
    Thus Ambition's minions rise.

' Lag not now, though rough the way,
    Fortune's mood brooks no delay;

Grasp the boon that's spread before ye,
Monarch's power and Conqueror's glory!'

It ceased.   Advancing on the sound,
A steep ascent the wanderer found,
    And then a turret stair:
Nor climbed he far its steepy round
    Till fresher blew the air,   750
And next a welcome glimpse was given
That cheered him with the light of hea-
        ven.
    At length his toil had won
A lofty hall with trophies dressed,
Where as to greet imperial guest
Four maidens stood whose crimson vest
    Was bound with golden zone.

XXXV

Of Europe seemed the damsels all;
The first a nymph of lively Gaul
Whose easy step and laughing eye   760
Her borrowed air of awe belie;
    The next a maid of Spain,
Dark-eyed, dark-haired, sedate yet bold;
White ivory skin and tress of gold
Her shy and bashful comrade told
    For daughter of Almaine.
These maidens bore a royal robe,
With crown, with sceptre, and with globe,
    Emblems of empery;
The fourth a space behind them stood,   770
And leant upon a harp in mood
    Of minstrel ecstasy.
Of merry England she, in dress
Like ancient British Druidess,
    Her hair an azure fillet bound,
Her graceful vesture swept the ground,
    And in her hand displayed
A crown did that fourth maiden hold,
But unadorned with gems and gold,
    Of glossy laurel made.   780

XXXVI

At once to brave De Vaux knelt down
    These foremost maidens three,
And proffered sceptre, robe, and crown,
    Liegedom and seignorie
O'er many a region wide and fair,
Destined, they said, for Arthur's heir;
    But homage would he none: —
' Rather,' he said, ' De Vaux would ride,
A warden of the Border-side
In plate and mail than, robed in pride, 790
    A monarch's empire own;
Rather, far rather, would he be

A free-born knight of England free
    Than sit on despot's throne.'
So passed he on, when that fourth maid,
    As starting from a trance,
Upon the harp her finger laid;
Her magic touch the chords obeyed,
    Their soul awaked at once!

SONG OF THE FOURTH MAIDEN

' Quake to your foundations deep,   800
Stately towers, and bannered keep,
Bid your vaulted echoes moan,
As the dreaded step they own.

' Fiends, that wait on Merlin's spell,
Hear the foot-fall! mark it well!
Spread your dusky wings abroad,
Boune ye for your homeward road!

' It is HIS, the first who e'er
Dared the dismal Hall of Fear;
HIS, who hath the snares defied   810
Spread by Pleasure, Wealth, and Pride.

' Quake to your foundations deep,
Bastion huge, and turret steep!
Tremble, keep! and totter, tower!
This is Gyneth's waking hour.'

XXXVII

Thus while she sung the venturous knight
Has reached a bower where milder light
    Through crimson curtains fell;
Such softened shade the hill receives,
Her purple veil when twilight leaves   820
    Upon its western swell.
That bower, the gazer to bewitch,
Had wondrous store of rare and rich
    As e'er was seen with eye;
For there by magic skill, iwis,
Form of each thing that living is
    Was limned in proper dye.
All seemed to sleep — the timid hare
On form, the stag upon his lair,
The eagle in her eyrie fair   830
    Between the earth and sky.
But what of pictured rich and rare
Could win De Vaux's eye-glance, where,
Deep slumbering in the fatal chair,
    He saw King Arthur's child!
Doubt and anger and dismay
From her brow had passed away,
Forgot was that fell tourney-day,
    For as she slept she smiled:

It seemed that the repentant Seer 840
Her sleep of many a hundred year
  With gentle dreams beguiled.

XXXVIII

That form of maiden loveliness,
  'Twixt childhood and 'twixt youth,
That ivory chair, that sylvan dress,
The arms and ankles bare, express
  Of Lyulph's tale the truth.
Still upon her garment's hem
Vanoc's blood made purple gem,
And the warder of command 850
Cumbered still her sleeping hand;
Still her dark locks dishevelled flow
From net of pearl o'er breast of snow;
And so fair the slumberer seems
That De Vaux impeached his dreams,
Vapid all and void of might,
Hiding half her charms from sight.
Motionless awhile he stands,
Folds his arms and clasps his hands,
Trembling in his fitful joy, 860
Doubtful how he should destroy
  Long-enduring spell;
Doubtful too, when slowly rise
Dark-fringed lids of Gyneth's eyes,
  What these eyes shall tell. —
'Saint George! Saint Mary! can it be
That they will kindly look on me!'

XXXIX

Gently, lo! the warrior kneels,
Soft that lovely hand he steals,
Soft to kiss and soft to clasp — 870
But the warder leaves her grasp;
  Lightning flashes, rolls the thunder!
Gyneth startles from her sleep,
Totters tower, and trembles keep,
  Burst the castle-walls asunder!
Fierce and frequent were the shocks, —
  Melt the magic halls away; —
But beneath their mystic rocks,
In the arms of bold De Vaux
  Safe the princess lay; 880
Safe and free from magic power,
Blushing like the rose's flower
  Opening to the day;
And round the champion's brows were
  bound
The crown that Druidess had wound
  Of the green laurel-bay.
And this was what remained of all
The wealth of each enchanted hall,

The Garland and the Dame:
But where should warrior seek the meed 890
Due to high worth for daring deed
  Except from LOVE and FAME!

CONCLUSION

I

MY Lucy, when the maid is won
The minstrel's task, thou know'st, is done;
  And to require of bard
That to his dregs the tale should run
  Were ordinance too hard.
Our lovers, briefly be it said,
Wedded as lovers wont to wed,
  When tale or play is o'er;
Lived long and blest, loved fond and true,
And saw a numerous race renew 10
  The honors that they bore.
Know too that when a pilgrim strays
In morning mist or evening maze
  Along the mountain lone,
That fairy fortress often mocks
His gaze upon the castled rocks
  Of the Valley of Saint John;
But never man since brave De Vaux
  The charmed portal won.
'T is now a vain illusive show 20
That melts whene'er the sunbeams glow,
  Or the fresh breeze hath blown.

II

But see, my love, where far below
Our lingering wheels are moving slow,
  The whiles, up-gazing still,
Our menials eye our steepy way,
Marvelling perchance what whim can stay
Our steps when eve is sinking gray
  On this gigantic hill.
So think the vulgar — Life and time 30
Ring all their joys in one dull chime
  Of luxury and ease;
And O, beside these simple knaves,
How many better born are slaves
  To such coarse joys as these,
Dead to the nobler sense that glows
When nature's grander scenes unclose!
But, Lucy, we will love them yet,
The mountain's misty coronet,
  The greenwood and the wold; 40
And love the more that of their maze
Adventure high of other days
  By ancient bards is told,

Bringing perchance, like my poor tale,
Some moral truth in fiction's veil:
Nor love them less that o'er the hill
The evening breeze as now comes chill; —

My love shall wrap her warm,
And, fearless of the slippery way
While safe she trips the heathy brae,   50
Shall hang on Arthur's arm.

THE LORD OF THE ISLES

A POEM IN SIX CANTOS

INTRODUCTORY NOTE

When *The Lord of the Isles* was published, Scott wrote of it to Lady Abercorn: ' I think it is my last poetical venture, at least upon a large scale. I swear not, because I do not make any positive resolution, but I think I have written enough, and it is unlikely I shall change my opinion.' With his healthy mind, Scott was not likely to misread the signs of nature, or the movement which his intellectual interest was likely to take. When he wrote these words he had published *Waverley*, and was projecting *Guy Mannering*, and the wider range which fiction could take to include the experiences of life which most appealed to him was too evident to permit him ever to return to any considerable poetic effort.

As in the case of his earlier work, he drove two horses abreast and was at work alternately on this poem and on the novel, whose early draft he stumbled on at this time. The poem, indeed, had been projected earlier, — before *Rokeby* was written, — but in the final heat it was despatched with great rapidity, for, begun at Abbotsford in the autumn of 1814, it was ended at Edinburgh the 16th of December, and published January 2, 1815. ' It may be mentioned,' says the anonymous editor of the British Poets Edition, ' that those parts of the poem which were written at Abbotsford, were composed almost all in the presence of Sir Walter Scott's family, and many in that of casual visitors also : the original cottage which he then occupied not affording him any means of retirement. Neither conversation nor music seemed to disturb him.' When he was in the midst of his work, he wrote to Morritt : ' My literary tormentor is a certain Lord of the Isles, famed for his tyranny of yore, and not unjustly. I am bothering some tale of him I have had long by me into a sort of romance. I think

you will like it: it is Scottified up to the teeth, and somehow I feel myself like the liberated chiefs of the Rolliad, " who boast their native philabeg restored." I believe the frolics one can cut in this loose garb are all set down by you Sassenachs to the real agility of the wearer, and not the brave, free, and independent character of his clothing. It is, in a word, the real Highland fling, and no one is supposed able to dance it but a native.' The poem bore this advertisement when it was printed.

ADVERTISEMENT

The Scene of this Poem lies, at first, in the Castle of Artornish, on the coast of Argyleshire ; and, afterwards, in the Islands of Skye and Arran, and upon the coast of Ayrshire. Finally it is laid near Stirling. The story opens in the spring of the year 1307, when Bruce, who had been driven out of Scotland by the English, and the Barons who adhered to that foreign interest, returned from the Island of Rachrin on the coast of Ireland, again to assert his claims to the Scottish crown. Many of the personages and incidents introduced are of historical celebrity. The authorities used are chiefly those of the venerable Lord Hailes, as well entitled to be called the restorer of Scottish history, as Bruce the restorer of Scottish Monarchy ; and of Archdeacon Barbour ; a correct edition of whose Metrical History of Robert Bruce will soon, I trust, appear, under the care of my learned friend, the Rev. Dr. Jamieson.

ABBOTSFORD, 10th December, 1814.

The edition of 1833 had the following introduction, those passages being omitted here which relate to *The Bridal of Triermain* and *Harold the Dauntless*, since they are printed in connection with those poems.

INTRODUCTION

I could hardly have chosen a subject more popular in Scotland than anything connected with the Bruce's history, unless I had attempted

that of Wallace. But I am decidedly of opinion that a popular, or what is called a *taking*, title, though well qualified to ensure the publishers against loss, and clear their shelves of the original impression, is rather apt to be hazardous than otherwise to the reputation of the author. He who attempts a subject of distinguished popularity has not the privilege of awakening the enthusiasm of his audience; on the contrary, it is already awakened, and glows, it may be, more ardently than that of the author himself. In this case the warmth of the author is inferior to that of the party whom he addresses, who has therefore little chance of being, in Bayes's phrase, ' elevated and surprised ' by what he has thought of with more enthusiasm than the writer. The sense of this risk, joined to the consciousness of striving against wind and tide, made the task of composing the proposed Poem somewhat heavy and hopeless; but, like the prize-fighter in *As You Like It*, I was to wrestle for my reputation, and not neglect any advantage. In a most agreeable pleasure-voyage, which I have tried to commemorate in the Introduction to the new edition of the *Pirate*, I visited, in social and friendly company, the coasts and islands of Scotland, and made myself acquainted with the localities of which I meant to treat. But this voyage, which was in every other effect so delightful, was in its conclusion saddened by one of those strokes of fate which so often mingle themselves with our pleasures. The accomplished and excellent person who had recommended to me the subject for *The Lay of the Last Minstrel*, [Harriet, Duchess of Buc-

cleuch] and to whom I proposed to inscribe what I already suspected might be the close of my poetical labors, was unexpectedly removed from the world, which she seemed only to have visited for purposes of kindness and benevolence. It is needless to say how the author's feelings, or the composition of his trifling work, were affected by a circumstance which occasioned so many tears and so much sorrow. True it is, that *The Lord of the Isles* was concluded, unwillingly and in haste, under the painful feeling of one who has a task which must be finished, rather than with the ardor of one who endeavors to perform that task well. Although the Poem cannot be said to have made a favorable impression on the public, the sale of fifteen thousand copies enabled the Author to retreat from the field with the honors of war.

In the mean time, what was necessarily to be considered as a failure was much reconciled to my feelings by the success attending my attempt in another species of composition. *Waverley* had, under strict incognito, taken its flight from the press, just before I set out upon the voyage already mentioned; it had now made its way to popularity, and the success of that work and the volumes which followed was sufficient to have satisfied a greater appetite for applause than I have at any time possessed.

ABBOTSFORD, April, 1830.

CANTO FIRST

AUTUMN departs — but still his mantle's fold
Rests on the groves of noble Somerville,
Beneath a shroud of russet drooped with gold
Tweed and his tributaries mingle still;
Hoarser the wind and deeper sounds the rill,
Yet lingering notes of sylvan music swell,
The deep-toned cushat and the redbreast shrill;
And yet some tints of summer splendor tell
When the broad sun sinks down on Ettrick's western fell.

Autumn departs — from Gala's fields no more   10
Come rural sounds our kindred banks to cheer;
Blent with the stream and gale that wafts it o'er,
No more the distant reaper's mirth we hear.
The last blithe shout hath died upon our ear,
And harvest-home hath hushed the clanging wain,
On the waste hill no forms of life appear,
Save where, sad laggard of the autumnal strain,
Some age-struck wanderer gleans few ears of scattered grain.

Deem'st thou these saddened scenes have pleasure still,
Lov'st thou through Autumn's fading realms to stray,   20
To see the heath-flower withered on the hill,

To listen to the woods' expiring lay,
To note the red leaf shivering on the spray,
To mark the last bright tints the mountain stain,
On the waste fields to trace the gleaner's way,
And moralize on mortal joy and pain? —
O, if such scenes thou lov'st, scorn not the minstrel strain !

No ! do not scorn, although its hoarser note
Scarce with the cushat's homely song can vie,
Though faint its beauties as the tints remote   30
That gleam through mist in autumn's evening sky,
And few as leaves that tremble, sear and dry,
When wild November hath his bugle wound;
Nor mock my toil — a lonely gleaner I
Through fields time-wasted, on sad inquest bound
Where happier bards of yore have richer harvest found.

So shalt thou list, and haply not unmoved,
To a wild tale of Albyn's warrior day;
In distant lands, by the rough West reproved,
Still live some relics of the ancient lay.   40
For, when on Coolin's hills the lights decay,
With such the Seer of Skye the eve beguiles;
'T is known amid the pathless wastes of Reay,
In Harries known and in Iona's piles,
Where rest from mortal coil the Mighty of the Isles.

I

'Wake, Maid of Lorn !' the minstrels
    sung. —
Thy rugged halls, Artornish, rung,
And the dark seas thy towers that lave
Heaved on the beach a softer wave,
As mid the tuneful choir to keep   50
The diapason of the deep.
Lulled were the winds on Inninmore
And green Loch-Alline's woodland shore,
As if wild woods and waves had pleasure
In listing to the lovely measure.
And ne'er to symphony more sweet
Gave mountain echoes answer meet
Since, met from mainland and from isle,
Ross, Arran, Islay, and Argyle,
Each minstrel's tributary lay   60
Paid homage to the festal day.
Dull and dishonored were the bard,
Worthless of guerdon and regard,
Deaf to the hope of minstrel fame,
Or lady's smiles, his noblest aim,
Who on that morn's resistless call
Was silent in Artornish hall.

II

'Wake, Maid of Lorn !' — 't was thus
    they sung,
And yet more proud the descant rung,   69

'Wake, Maid of Lorn ! high right is ours
To charm dull sleep from Beauty's bowers;
Earth, ocean, air, have nought so shy
But owns the power of minstrelsy.
In Lettermore the timid deer
Will pause the harp's wild chime to hear;
Rude Heiskar's seal through surges dark
Will long pursue the minstrel's bark;
To list his notes the eagle proud
Will poise him on Ben-Cailliach's cloud;
Then let not maiden's ear disdain   80
The summons of the minstrel train,
But while our harps wild music make,
Edith of Lorn, awake, awake !

III

'O, wake while Dawn with dewy shine
Wakes nature's charms to vie with thine !
She bids the mottled thrush rejoice
To mate thy melody of voice;
The dew that on the violet lies
Mocks the dark lustre of thine eyes;
But, Edith, wake, and all we see   90
Of sweet and fair shall yield to thee !' —
'She comes not yet,' gray Ferrand cried;
'Brethren, let softer spell be tried,
Those notes prolonged, that soothing
    theme,
Which best may mix with Beauty's dream,

And whisper with their silvery tone
The hope she loves yet fears to own.'
He spoke, and on the harp-strings died
The strains of flattery and of pride;
More soft, more low, more tender fell   100
The lay of love he bade them tell.

IV

'Wake, Maid of Lorn ! the moments fly
Which yet that maiden-name allow;
Wake, Maiden, wake ! the hour is nigh
When love shall claim a plighted vow.
By Fear, thy bosom's fluttering guest,
By Hope, that soon shall fears remove,
We bid thee break the bonds of rest,
And wake thee at the call of Love !

'Wake, Edith, wake ! in yonder bay   110
Lies many a galley gayly manned,
We hear the merry pibroch's play,
We see the streamers' silken band.
What chieftain's praise these pibrochs swell,
What crest is on these banners wove,
The harp, the minstrel, dare not tell —
The riddle must be read by Love !'

V

Retired her maiden train among,
Edith of Lorn received the song,   119
But tamed the minstrel's pride had been
That had her cold demeanor seen;
For not upon her cheek awoke
The glow of pride when Flattery spoke,
Nor could their tenderest numbers bring
One sigh responsive to the string.
As vainly had her maidens vied
In skill to deck the princely bride.
Her locks in dark-brown length arrayed,
Cathleen of Ulne, 't was thine to braid;
Young Eva with meet reverence drew   130
On the light foot the silken shoe,
While on the ankle's slender round
Those strings of pearl fair Bertha wound
That, bleached Lochryan's depths within,
Seemed dusky still on Edith's skin.
But Einion, of experience old,
Had weightiest task — the mantle's fold
In many an artful plait she tied
To show the form it seemed to hide,
Till on the floor descending rolled   140
Its waves of crimson blent with gold.

VI

O, lives there now so cold a maid,
Who thus in beauty's pomp arrayed,

In beauty's proudest pitch of power,
And conquest won — the bridal hour —
With every charm that wins the heart,
By Nature given, enhanced by Art,
Could yet the fair reflection view
In the bright mirror pictured true,
And not one dimple on her cheek   150
A telltale consciousness bespeak ? —
Lives still such maid ? — Fair damsels, say,
For further vouches not my lay
Save that such lived in Britain's isle
When Lorn's bright Edith scorned to
smile.

VII

But Morag, to whose fostering care
Proud Lorn had given his daughter fair,
Morag, who saw a mother's aid
By all a daughter's love repaid —
Strict was that bond, most kind of all,   160
Inviolate in Highland hall —
Gray Morag sate a space apart,
In Edith's eyes to read her heart.
In vain the attendant's fond appeal
To Morag's skill, to Morag's zeal;
She marked her child receive their care,
Cold as the image sculptured fair —
Form of some sainted patroness —
Which cloistered maids combine to dress;
She marked — and knew her nursling's
heart   170
In the vain pomp took little part.
Wistful awhile she gazed — then pressed
The maiden to her anxious breast
In finished loveliness — and led
To where a turret's airy head,
Slender and steep and battled round,
O'erlooked, dark Mull, thy mighty Sound,
Where thwarting tides with mingled roar
Part thy swarth hills from Morven's shore.

VIII

'Daughter,' she said, 'these seas behold,   180
Round twice a hundred islands rolled,
From Hirt that hears their northern roar
To the green Ilay's fertile shore;
Or mainland turn where many a tower
Owns thy bold brother's feudal power,
Each on its own dark cape reclined
And listening to its own wild wind,
From where Mingarry sternly placed
O'erawes the woodland and the waste,   189
To where Dunstaffnage hears the raging
Of Connal with its rocks engaging.
Think'st thou amid this ample round

A single brow but thine has frowned,
To sadden this auspicious morn
That bids the daughter of high Lorn
Impledge her spousal faith to wed
The heir of mighty Somerled ?
Ronald, from many a hero sprung,
The fair, the valiant, and the young,
LORD OF THE ISLES, whose lofty name   200
A thousand bards have given to fame,
The mate of monarchs, and allied
On equal terms with England's pride. —
From chieftain's tower to bondsman's
     cot,
Who hears the tale, and triumphs not ?
The damsel dons her best attire,
The shepherd lights his beltane fire,
Joy ! joy ! each warder's horn hath sung,
Joy ! joy ! each matin bell hath rung;
The holy priest says grateful mass,   210
Loud shouts each hardy galla-glass,
No mountain den holds outcast boor
Of heart so dull, of soul so poor,
But he hath flung his task aside,
And claimed this morn for holy-tide;
Yet, empress of this joyful day,
Edith is sad while all are gay.'

IX

Proud Edith's soul came to her eye,
Resentment checked the struggling sigh.
Her hurrying hand indignant dried   220
The burning tears of injured pride —
' Morag, forbear ! or lend thy praise
To swell yon hireling harpers' lays;
Make to yon maids thy boast of power,
That they may waste a wondering hour
Telling of banners proudly borne,
Of pealing bell and bugle horn,
Or, theme more dear, of robes of price,
Crownlets and gauds of rare device.
But thou, experienced as thou art,   230
Think'st thou with these to cheat the heart
That, bound in strong affection's chain,
Looks for return and looks in vain ?
No ! sum thine Edith's wretched lot
In these brief words — He loves her not !

X

' Debate it not — too long I strove
To call his cold observance love,
All blinded by the league that styled
Edith of Lorn — while yet a child
She tripped the heath by Morag's
     side —   240
The brave Lord Ronald's destined bride.

Ere yet I saw him, while afar
His broadsword blazed in Scotland's war,
Trained to believe our fates the same,
My bosom throbbed when Ronald's name
Came gracing Fame's heroic tale,
Like perfume on the summer gale.
What pilgrim sought our halls nor told
Of Ronald's deeds in battle bold;
Who touched the harp to heroes' praise   250
But his achievements swelled the lays ?
Even Morag — not a tale of fame
Was hers but closed with Ronald's name.
He came ! and all that had been told
Of his high worth seemed poor and cold,
Tame, lifeless, void of energy,
Unjust to Ronald and to me !

XI

' Since then, what thought had Edith's
     heart
And gave not plighted love its part ! —
And what requital ? cold delay —   260
Excuse that shunned the spousal day. —
It dawns and Ronald is not here ! —
Hunts he Bentalla's nimble deer,
Or loiters he in secret dell
To bid some lighter love farewell,
And swear that though he may not scorn
A daughter of the House of Lorn,
Yet, when these formal rites are o'er,
Again they meet to part no more ? '

XII

' Hush, daughter, hush ! thy doubts re-
     move,   270
More nobly think of Ronald's love.
Look, where beneath the castle gray
His fleet unmoor from Aros bay !
See'st not each galley's topmast bend
As on the yards the sails ascend ?
Hiding the dark-blue land they rise,
Like the white clouds on April skies;
The shouting vassals man the oars,
Behind them sink Mull's mountain shores,
Onward their merry course they keep   280
Through whistling breeze and foaming
     deep.
And mark the headmost, seaward cast,
Stoop to the freshening gale her mast,
As if she veiled its bannered pride
To greet afar her prince's bride !
Thy Ronald comes, and while in speed
His galley mates the flying steed,
He chides her sloth ! ' — Fair Edith sighed,
Blushed, sadly smiled, and thus replied:

XIII

'Sweet thought, but vain ! — No, Morag !
    mark,   290
Type of his course, yon lonely bark,
That oft hath shifted helm and sail
To win its way against the gale.
Since peep of morn my vacant eyes
Have viewed by fits the course she tries;
Now, though the darkening scud comes
    on,
And dawn's fair promises be gone,
And though the weary crew may see
Our sheltering haven on their lee,
Still closer to the rising wind   300
They strive her shivering sail to bind,
Still nearer to the shelves' dread verge
At every tack her course they urge,
As if they feared Artornish more
Than adverse winds and breakers' roar.'

XIV

Sooth spoke the maid. Amid the tide
    The skiff she marked lay tossing sore,
And shifted oft her stooping side,
    In weary tack from shore to shore.
Yet on her destined course no more   310
    She gained of forward way
Than what a minstrel may compare
To the poor meed which peasants share
    Who toil the livelong day;
And such the risk her pilot braves
    That oft, before she wore,
Her boltsprit kissed the broken waves
Where in white foam the ocean raves
    Upon the shelving shore.
Yet, to their destined purpose true,   320
Undaunted toiled her hardy crew,
    Nor looked where shelter lay,
    Nor for Artornish Castle drew,
    Nor steered for Aros bay.

XV

Thus while they strove with wind and seas,
Borne onward by the willing breeze,
    Lord Ronald's fleet swept by,
Streamered with silk and tricked with
    gold,
Manned with the noble and the bold
    Of Island chivalry.   330
Around their prows the ocean roars,
And chafes beneath their thousand oars,
    Yet bears them on their way:
So chafes the war-horse in his might
That fieldward bears some valiant knight,
Champs till both bit and boss are white,

But foaming must obey.
On each gay deck they might behold
Lances of steel and crests of gold,
And hauberks with their burnished fold   340
    That shimmered fair and free;
And each proud galley as she passed
To the wild cadence of the blast
    Gave wilder minstrelsy.
Full many a shrill triumphant note
Saline and Scallastle bade float
    Their misty shores around;
And Morven's echoes answered well,
And Duart heard the distant swell
    Come down the darksome Sound.   350

XVI

So bore they on with mirth and pride,
And if that laboring bark they spied,
    'T was with such idle eye
As nobles cast on lowly boor
When, toiling in his task obscure,
    They pass him careless by.
Let them sweep on with heedless eyes !
But had they known what mighty prize
    In that frail vessel lay,
The famished wolf that prowls the wold   360
Had scathless passed the unguarded fold,
Ere, drifting by these galleys bold,
    Unchallenged were her way !
And thou, Lord Ronald, sweep thou on
With mirth and pride and minstrel tone !
But hadst thou known who sailed so
    nigh,
Far other glance were in thine eye !
Far other flush were on thy brow,
That, shaded by the bonnet, now
Assumes but ill the blithesome cheer   370
Of bridegroom when the bride is near !

XVII

Yes, sweep they on ! — We will not leave,
For them that triumph, those who grieve.
    With that armada gay
Be laughter loud and jocund shout,
And bards to cheer the wassail rout
    With tale, romance, and lay;
And of wild mirth each clamorous art,
Which, if it cannot cheer the heart,
May stupefy and stun its smart   380
    For one loud busy day.
Yes, sweep they on ! — But with that skiff
    Abides the minstrel tale,
Where there was dread of surge and cliff,
Labor that strained each sinew stiff,
    And one sad maiden's wail.

XVIII

All day with fruitless strife they toiled,
With eve the ebbing currents boiled
  More fierce from strait and lake;
And midway through the channel met   390
Conflicting tides that foam and fret,
And high their mingled billows jet,
As spears that in the battle set
  Spring upward as they break.
Then too the lights of eve were past,
And louder sung the western blast
  On rocks of Inninmore;
Rent was the sail, and strained the mast,
And many a leak was gaping fast,
And the pale steersman stood aghast   400
  And gave the conflict o'er.

XIX

'T was then that One whose lofty look
Nor labor dulled nor terror shook
  Thus to the leader spoke: —
'Brother, how hop'st thou to abide
The fury of this wildered tide,
Or how avoid the rock's rude side
  Until the day has broke ?
Didst thou not mark the vessel reel   409
With quivering planks and groaning keel
  At the last billow's shock ?
Yet how of better counsel tell,
Though here thou see'st poor Isabel
  Half dead with want and fear;
For look on sea, or look on land,
Or yon dark sky, on every hand
  Despair and death are near.
For her alone I grieve — on me
Danger sits light by land and sea,
  I follow where thou wilt;   420
Either to bide the tempest's lour,
Or wend to yon unfriendly tower,
Or rush amid their naval power,
With war-cry wake their wassail-hour,
  And die with hand on hilt.'

XX

That elder leader's calm reply
  In steady voice was given,
'In man's most dark extremity
  Oft succor dawns from heaven.
Edward, trim thou the shattered sail,   430
The helm be mine, and down the gale
  Let our free course be driven;
So shall we 'scape the western bay,
The hostile fleet, the unequal fray,
So safely hold our vessel's way

Beneath the castle wall;
For if a hope of safety rest,
'T is on the sacred name of guest,
Who seeks for shelter storm-distressed
  Within a chieftain's hall.   440
If not — it best beseems our worth,
Our name, our right, our lofty birth,
  By noble hands to fall.'

XXI

The helm, to his strong arm consigned,
Gave the reefed sail to meet the wind,
  And on her altered way
Fierce bounding forward sprung the ship,
Like greyhound starting from the slip
  To seize his flying prey.
Awaked before the rushing prow   450
The mimic fires of ocean glow,
  Those lightnings of the wave;
Wild sparkles crest the broken tides,
And flashing round the vessel's sides
  With elfish lustre lave,
While far behind their livid light
To the dark billows of the night
  A gloomy splendor gave,
It seems as if old Ocean shakes
From his dark brow the lucid flakes   46
  In envious pageantry,
To match the meteor-light that streaks
  Grim Hecla's midnight sky.

XXII

Nor lacked they steadier light to keep
Their course upon the darkened deep; —
Artornish, on her frowning steep
  'Twixt cloud and ocean hung,
Glanced with a thousand lights of glee,
And landward far, and far to sea
  Her festal radiance flung.   47c
By that blithe beacon-light they steered,
  Whose lustre mingled well
With the pale beam that now appeared,
As the cold moon her head upreared
  Above the eastern fell.

XXIII

Thus guided, on their course they bore
Until they neared the mainland shore,
When frequent on the hollow blast
Wild shouts of merriment were cast,
And wind and wave and sea-birds' cry   480
With wassail sounds in concert vie,
Like funeral shrieks with revelry,
  Or like the battle-shout
By peasants heard from cliffs on high

When Triumph, Rage, and Agony
 Madden the fight and rout.
Now nearer yet through mist and storm
Dimly arose the castle's form
 And deepened shadow made,
Far lengthened on the main below,   490
Where dancing in reflected glow
 A hundred torches played,
Spangling the wave with lights as vain
As pleasures in this vale of pain,
 That dazzle as they fade.

XXIV

Beneath the castle's sheltering lee
They staid their course in quiet sea.
Hewn in the rock, a passage there
Sought the dark fortress by a stair,
 So strait, so high, so steep,   500
With peasant's staff one valiant hand
Might well the dizzy pass have manned
'Gainst hundreds armed with spear and
     brand
 And plunged them in the deep.
His bugle then the helmsman wound:
Loud answered every echo round
 From turret, rock, and bay;
The postern's hinges crash and groan,
And soon the warder's cresset shone
On those rude steps of slippery stone,   510
 To light the upward way.
' Thrice welcome, holy Sire ! ' he said;
' Full long the spousal train have staid,
 And, vexed at thy delay,
Feared lest amidst these wildering seas
The darksome night and freshening breeze
 Had driven thy bark astray.' —

XXV

' Warder,' the younger stranger said,
' Thine erring guess some mirth had made
In mirthful hour; but nights like these, 520
When the rough winds wake western seas,
Brook not of glee.   We crave some aid
And needful shelter for this maid
 Until the break of day;
For to ourselves the deck's rude plank
Is easy as the mossy bank
 That 's breathed upon by May.
And for our storm-tossed skiff we seek
Short shelter in this leeward creek,   529
Prompt when the dawn the east shall streak
 Again to bear away.'
Answered the warder, ' In what name
Assert ye hospitable claim ?
 Whence come or whither bound ?

Hath Erin seen your parting sails,
Or come ye on Norweyan gales ?
And seek ye England's fertile vales,
 Or Scotland's mountain ground ? '

XXVI

' Warriors — for other title none
For some brief space we list to own,   540
Bound by a vow — warriors are we;
In strife by land and storm by sea
 We have been known to fame;
And these brief words have import dear,
When sounded in a noble ear,
To harbor safe and friendly cheer
 That gives us rightful claim.
Grant us the trivial boon we seek,
And we in other realms will speak
 Fair of your courtesy;   550
Deny — and be your niggard hold
Scorned by the noble and the bold,
Shunned by the pilgrim on the wold
 And wanderer on the lea ! '

XXVII

' Bold   stranger, no — 'gainst claim like
     thine
No bolt revolves by hand of mine,
Though urged in tone that more expressed
A monarch than a suppliant guest.
Be what ye will, Artornish Hall
On this glad eve is free to all.   560
Though ye had drawn a hostile sword
'Gainst our ally, great England's Lord,
Or mail upon your shoulders borne
To battle with the Lord of Lorn,
Or outlawed dwelt by greenwood tree
With the fierce Knight of Ellerslie,
Or aided even the murderous strife
When Comyn fell beneath the knife
Of that fell homicide the Bruce,
This night had been a term of truce. —   570
Ho, vassals ! give these guests your care,
And show the narrow postern stair.'

XXVIII

To land these two bold brethren leapt —
The weary crew their vessel kept —
And, lighted by the torches' flare
That seaward flung their smoky glare,
The younger knight that maiden bare
 Half lifeless up the rock;
On his strong shoulder leaned her head,
And down her long dark tresses shed,   580
As the wild vine in tendrils spread
 Droops from the mountain oak.

Him followed close that elder lord,
And in his hand a sheathed sword
    Such as few arms could wield;
But when he bouned him to such task
Well could it cleave the strongest casque
    And rend the surest shield.

XXIX

The raised portcullis' arch they pass,
The wicket with its bars of brass,   590
    The entrance long and low,
Flanked at each turn by loop-holes strait,
Where bowmen might in ambush wait —
If force or fraud should burst the gate —
    To gall an entering foe.
But every jealous post of ward
Was now defenceless and unbarred,
    And all the passage free
To one low-browed and vaulted room
Where squire and yeoman, page and
        groom,   600
    Plied their loud revelry.

XXX

And 'Rest ye here,' the warder bade,
' Till to our lord your suit is said. —
And, comrades, gaze not on the maid
And on these men who ask our aid,
    As if ye ne'er had seen
A damsel tired of midnight bark
Or wanderers of a moulding stark
    And bearing martial mien.'
    But not for Eachin's reproof   610
Would page or vassal stand aloof,
    But crowded on to stare,
As men of courtesy untaught,
Till Fiery Edward roughly caught
    From one the foremost there
His chequered plaid, and in its shroud,
To hide her from the vulgar crowd,
    Involved his sister fair.
His brother, as the clansman bent
His sullen brow in discontent,   620
    Made brief and stern excuse:
' Vassal, were thine the cloak of pall
That decks thy lord in bridal hall,
    'T were honored by her use.'

XXXI

Proud was his tone but calm; his eye
Had that compelling dignity,
His mien that bearing haught and high,
    Which common spirits fear;
Needed nor word nor signal more,
Nod, wink, and laughter, all were o'er;   630

Upon each other back they bore
    And gazed like startled deer.
But now appeared the seneschal,
Commissioned by his lord to call
The strangers to the baron's hall,
    Where feasted fair and free
That Island Prince in nuptial tide
With Edith there his lovely bride,
And her bold brother by her side,
And many a chief, the flower and pride   640
    Of Western land and sea.

Here pause we, gentles, for a space;
And, if our tale hath won your grace,
Grant us brief patience and again
We will renew the minstrel strain.

CANTO SECOND

I

FILL the bright goblet, spread the festive
        board !
Summon the gay, the noble, and the
        fair !
Through the loud hall in joyous concert
        poured,
Let mirth and music sound the dirge of
        Care !
But ask thou not if Happiness be there,
If the loud laugh disguise convulsive
        throe,
Or if the brow the heart's true livery
        wear;
Lift not the festal mask ! — enough to
        know,
No scene of mortal life but teems with
        mortal woe.

II

With beakers' clang, with harpers' lay,   10
With all that olden time deemed gay,
The Island Chieftain feasted high;
But there was in his troubled eye
A gloomy fire, and on his brow
Now sudden flushed and faded now
Emotions such as draw their birth
From deeper source than festal mirth.
By fits he paused, and harper's strain
And jester's tale went round in vain,
Or fell but on his idle ear   20
Like distant sounds which dreamers hear.
Then would he rouse him, and employ
Each art to aid the clamorous joy,
    And call for pledge and lay,

And, for brief space, of all the crowd,
As he was loudest of the loud,
   Seem gayest of the gay.

III

Yet nought amiss the bridal throng
Marked in brief mirth or musing long;
The vacant brow, the unlistening ear,   30
They gave to thoughts of raptures near,
And his fierce starts of sudden glee
Seemed bursts of bridegroom's ecstasy.
Nor thus alone misjudged the crowd,
Since lofty Lorn, suspicious, proud,
And jealous of his honored line,
And that keen knight, De Argentine —
From England sent on errand high
The western league more firm to tie —
Both deemed in Ronald's mood to find   40
A lover's transport-troubled mind.
But one sad heart, one tearful eye,
Pierced deeper through the mystery,
And watched with agony and fear
Her wayward bridegroom's varied cheer.

IV

She watched — yet feared to meet his
   glance,
And he shunned hers; — till when by
   chance
They met, the point of foeman's lance
   Had given a milder pang !
Beneath the intolerable smart   50
He writhed; — then sternly manned his
   heart
To play his hard but destined part,
   And from the table sprang.
'Fill me the mighty cup,' he said,
'Erst owned by royal Somerled !
Fill it, till on the studded brim
In burning gold the bubbles swim,
And every gem of varied shine
Glow doubly bright in rosy wine !
  To you, brave lord, and brother mine,   60
   Of Lorn, this pledge I drink —
  The Union of Our House with thine,
   By this fair bridal-link !'

V

'Let it pass round !' quoth he of Lorn,
'And in good time — that winded horn
   Must of the abbot tell;
The laggard monk is come at last.'
Lord Ronald heard the bugle-blast,
And on the floor at random cast
   The untasted goblet fell.   70

But when the warder in his car
Tells other news, his blither cheer
   R turns like sun of May
When through a thunder-cloud it beams ! —
Lord of two hundred isles, he seems
   As glad of brief delay
As some poor criminal might feel
When from the gibbet or the wheel
   Respited for a day.

VI

'Brother of Lorn,' with hurried voice   80
He said, 'and you, fair lords, rejoice !
   Here, to augment our glee,
Come wandering knights from travel far,
Well proved, they say, in strife of war
   And tempest on the sea. —
Ho ! give them at your board such place
As best their presences may grace,
   And bid them welcome free !'
With solemn step and silver wand,
The seneschal the presence scanned   90
Of these strange guests, and well he knew
How to assign their rank its due;
   For though the costly furs
That erst had decked their caps were torn,
And their gay robes were over-worn,
   And soiled their gilded spurs,
Yet such a high commanding grace
Was in their mien and in their face
As suited best the princely dais
   And royal canopy;   100
And there he marshalled them their place,
   First of that company.

VII

Then lords and ladies spake aside,
And angry looks the error chide
That gave to guests unnamed, unknown,
A place so near their prince's throne;
   But Owen Erraught said,
'For forty years a seneschal,
To marshal guests in bower and hall
   Has been my honored trade.   110
Worship and birth to me are known,
By look, by bearing, and by tone,
Not by furred robe or broidered zone;
   And 'gainst an oaken bough
I 'll gage my silver wand of state
That these three strangers oft have sate
   In higher place than now.'

VIII

'I too,' the aged Ferrand said,
'Am qualified by minstrel trade

Of rank and place to tell; —   120
Marked ye the younger stranger's eye,
My mates, how quick, how keen, how
      high,
    How fierce its flashes fell,
Glancing among the noble rout
As if to seek the noblest out,
Because the owner might not brook
On any save his peers to look ?
    And yet it moves me more,
That steady, calm, majestic brow,
With which the elder chief even now   130
    Scanned the gay presence o'er,
Like being of superior kind,
In whose high-toned impartial mind
Degrees of mortal rank and state
Seem objects of indifferent weight.
    The lady too — though closely tied
    The mantle veil both face and eye,
Her motions' grace it could not hide,
    Nor cloud her form's fair symme-
      try.'

IX

Suspicious doubt and lordly scorn   140
Loured on the haughty front of Lorn.
From underneath his brows of pride
The stranger guests he sternly eyed,
And whispered closely what the ear
Of Argentine alone might hear;
    Then questioned, high and brief,
If in their voyage aught they knew
Of the rebellious Scottish crew
Who to Rath-Erin's shelter drew
    With Carrick's outlawed Chief ?   150
And if, their winter's exile o'er,
They harbored still by Ulster's shore,
Or launched their galleys on the main
To vex their native land again ?

X

That younger stranger, fierce and high,
At once confronts the chieftain's eye
    With look of equal scorn:
' Of rebels have we nought to show;
But if of royal Bruce thou 'dst know,
    I warn thee he has sworn,   160
Ere thrice three days shall come and go,
His banner Scottish winds shall blow,
Despite each mean or mighty foe,
From England's every bill and bow
    To Allaster of Lorn.'
Kindled the mountain chieftain's ire,
But Ronald quenched the rising fire:
' Brother, it better suits the time

To chase the night with Ferrand's rhyme
Than wake midst mirth and wine the
      jars   170
That flow from these unhappy wars.'
' Content,' said Lorn; and spoke apart
With Ferrand, master of his art,
    Then whispered Argentine,
' The lay I named will carry smart
To these bold strangers' haughty heart,
    If right this guess of mine.'
He ceased, and it was silence all
Until the minstrel waked the hall.

XI

THE BROOCH OF LORN

' Whence the brooch of burning gold   180
That clasps the chieftain's mantle-fold,
On the varied tartans beaming,
Wrought and chased with rare device,
Studded fair with gems of price,
As, through night's pale rainbow gleam-
      ing,
Fainter now, now seen afar,
Fitful shines the northern star ?

' Gem ! ne'er wrought on Highland moun-
      tain,
Did the fairy of the fountain
Or the mermaid of the wave   190
Frame thee in some coral cave ?
Did, in Iceland's darksome mine,
Dwarf's swart hands thy metal twine ?
Or, mortal-moulded, comest thou here
From England's love or France's fear ?

XII

SONG CONTINUED

' No ! — thy splendors nothing tell
Foreign art or faëry spell.
Moulded thou for monarch's use,
By the overweening Bruce,
When the royal robe he tied   200
O'er a heart of wrath and pride;
Thence in triumph wert thou torn
By the victor hand of Lorn !

' When the gem was won and lost,
Widely was the war-cry tossed !
Rung aloud Bendourish fell,
Answered Douchart's sounding dell,
Fled the deer from wild Teyndrum,
When the homicide o'ercome
Hardly 'scaped with scathe and scorn, 210
Left the pledge with conquering Lorn !

XIII

SONG CONCLUDED

'Vain was then the Douglas brand,
Vain the Campbell's vaunted hand,
Vain Kirkpatrick's bloody dirk,
Making sure of murder's work;
Barendown fled fast away,
Fled the fiery De la Haye,
When this brooch triumphant borne
Beamed upon the breast of Lorn.

'Farthest fled its former lord,   220
Left his men to brand and cord,
Bloody brand of Highland steel,
English gibbet, axe, and wheel.
Let him fly from coast to coast,
Dogged by Comyn's vengeful ghost,
While his spoils in triumph worn
Long shall grace victorious Lorn!'

XIV

As glares the tiger on his foes,
Hemmed in by hunters, spears, and bows,
And, ere he bounds upon the ring,   230
Selects the object of his spring, —
Now on the bard, now on his lord,
So Edward glared and grasped his sword —
But stern his brother spoke, 'Be still.
What! art thou yet so wild of will,
After high deeds and sufferings long,
To chafe thee for a menial's song? —
Well hast thou framed, old man, thy
          strains,
To praise the hand that pays thy pains!
Yet something might thy song have told   240
Of Lorn's three vassals, true and bold,
Who rent their lord from Bruce's hold
As underneath his knee he lay,
And died to save him in the fray.
I've heard the Bruce's cloak and clasp
Was clenched within their dying grasp,
What time a hundred foemen more
Rushed in and back the victor bore,
Long after Lorn had left the strife,
Full glad to 'scape with limb and life. — 250
Enough of this — and, minstrel, hold
As minstrel-hire this chain of gold,
For future lays a fair excuse
To speak more nobly of the Bruce.' —

XV

'Now, by Columba's shrine, I swear,
And every saint that's buried there,
'T is he himself!' Lorn sternly cries,

'And for my kinsman's death he dies.'
As loudly Ronald calls, 'Forbear!
Not in my sight while brand I wear,   260
O'ermatched by odds, shall warrior fall,
Or blood of stranger stain my hall!
This ancient fortress of my race
Shall be misfortune's resting-place,
Shelter and shield of the distressed,
No slaughter-house for shipwrecked guest.'
'Talk not to me,' fierce Lorn replied,
'Of odds or match! — when Comyn died,
Three daggers clashed within his side!
Talk not to me of sheltering hall,   270
The Church of God saw Comyn fall!
On God's own altar streamed his blood,
While o'er my prostrate kinsman stood
The ruthless murderer — e'en as now —
With armed hand and scornful brow! —
Up, all who love me! blow on blow!
And lay the outlawed felons low!'

XVI

Then up sprang many a mainland lord,
Obedient to their chieftain's word.
Barcaldine's arm is high in air,   280
And Kinloch-Alline's blade is bare,
Black Murthok's dirk has left its sheath,
And clenched is Dermid's hand of death.
Their muttered threats of vengeance swell
Into a wild and warlike yell;
Onward they press with weapons high,
The affrighted females shriek and fly,
And, Scotland, then thy brightest ray
Had darkened ere its noon of day,
But every chief of birth and fame   290
That from the Isles of Ocean came
At Ronald's side that hour withstood
Fierce Lorn's relentless thirst for blood.

XVII

Brave Torquil from Dunvegan high,
Lord of the misty hills of Skye,
Mac-Niel, wild Bara's ancient thane,
Duart of bold Clan-Gillian's strain,
Fergus of Canna's castled bay,
Mac-Duffith, Lord of Colonsay,   299
Soon as they saw the broadswords glance,
With ready weapons rose at once,
More prompt that many an ancient feud,
Full oft suppressed, full oft renewed,
Glowed 'twixt the chieftains of Argyle,
And many a lord of ocean's isle.
Wild was the scene — each sword was
          bare,
Back streamed each chieftain's shaggy hair,

In gloomy opposition set,
Eyes, hands, and brandished weapons met;
Blue gleaming o'er the social board,   310
Flashed to the torches many a sword;
And soon those bridal lights may shine
On purple blood for rosy wine.

XVIII

While thus for blows and death prepared,
Each heart was up, each weapon bared,
Each foot advanced, — a surly pause
Still reverenced hospitable laws.
All menaced violence, but alike
Reluctant each the first to strike —
For aye accursed in minstrel line   320
Is he who brawls mid song and wine,
And, matched in numbers and in might,
Doubtful and desperate seemed the fight.
Thus threat and murmur died away,
Till on the crowded hall there lay
Such silence as the deadly still
Ere bursts the thunder on the hill.
With blade advanced, each chieftain bold
Showed like the Sworder's form of old,
As wanting still the torch of life   330
To wake the marble into strife.

XIX

That awful pause the stranger maid
And Edith seized to pray for aid.
As to De Argentine she clung,
Away her veil the stranger flung,
And, lovely mid her wild despair,
Fast streamed her eyes, wide flowed her
    hair:
' O thou, of knighthood once the flower,
Sure refuge in distressful hour,
Thou who in Judah well hast fought   340
For our dear faith and oft hast sought
Renown in knightly exercise
When this poor hand has dealt the prize,
Say, can thy soul of honor brook
On the unequal strife to look,
When, butchered thus in peaceful hall,
Those once thy friends, my brethren, fall ! '
To Argentine she turned her word,
But her eye sought the Island Lord.
A flush like evening's setting flame   350
Glowed on his cheek ; his hardy frame
As with a brief convulsion shook:
With hurried voice and eager look,
' Fear not,' he said, ' my Isabel !
What said I — Edith ! — all is well —
Nay, fear not — I will well provide
The safety of my lovely bride —

My bride ? ' — but there the accents clung
In tremor to his faltering tongue.

XX

Now rose De Argentine to claim   360
The prisoners in his sovereign's name
To England's crown, who, vassals sworn,
'Gainst their liege lord had weapon
    borne —
Such speech, I ween, was but to hide
His care their safety to provide;
For knight more true in thought and deed
Than Argentine ne'er spurred a steed —
And Ronald who his meaning guessed
Seemed half to sanction the request.
This purpose fiery Torquil broke: 370
' Somewhat we 've heard of England's
    yoke,'
He said, ' and in our islands Fame
Hath whispered of a lawful claim
That calls the Bruce fair Scotland's lord,
Though dispossessed by foreign sword.
This craves reflection — but though right
And just the charge of England's Knight,
Let England's crown her rebels seize
Where she has power; — in towers like
    these,   379
Midst Scottish chieftains summoned here
To bridal mirth and bridal cheer,
Be sure, with no consent of mine
Shall either Lorn or Argentine
With chains or violence, in our sight,
Oppress a brave and banished knight.'

XXI

Then waked the wild debate again
With brawling threat and clamor vain.
Vassals and menials thronging in
Lent their brute rage to swell the din;
When far and wide a bugle-clang   390
From the dark ocean upward rang.
' The abbot comes ! ' they cry at once,
' The holy man, whose favored glance
    Hath sainted visions known;
    Angels have met him on the way,
    Beside the blessed martyr's bay,
    And by Columba's stone.
His monks have heard their hymnings
    high
Sound from the summit of Dun-Y,
    To cheer his penance lone,   400
When at each cross, on girth and wold —
Their number thrice a hundred-fold —
His prayer he made, his beads he told,
    With Aves many a one —

He comes our feuds to reconcile,
A sainted man from sainted isle;
We will his holy doom abide,
The abbot shall our strife decide.'

XXII

Scarcely this fair accord was o'er
When through the wide revolving door 410
    The black-stoled brethren wind;
Twelve sandalled monks who relics bore,
With many a torch-bearer before
    And many a cross behind.
Then sunk each fierce uplifted hand,
And dagger bright and flashing brand
    Dropped swiftly at the sight;
They vanished from the Churchman's eye,
As shooting stars that glance and die
    Dart from the vault of night. 420

XXIII

The abbot on the threshold stood,
And in his hand the holy rood;
Back on his shoulders flowed his hood,
    The torch's glaring ray
Showed in its red and flashing light
His withered cheek and amice white,
His blue eye glistening cold and bright,
    His tresses scant and gray.
' Fair Lords,' he said, ' Our Lady's love,
And peace be with you from above, 430
    And Benedicite ! —
But what means this ? — no peace is
    here ! —
Do dirks unsheathed suit bridal cheer ?
    Or are these naked brands
A seemly show for Churchman's sight
When he comes summoned to unite
    Betrothed hearts and hands ? '

XXIV

Then, cloaking hate with fiery zeal,
Proud Lorn first answered the appeal:
    ' Thou com'st, O holy man, 440
True sons of blessed church to greet,
But little deeming here to meet
    A wretch beneath the ban
Of Pope and Church for murder done
Even on the sacred altar-stone —
Well mayst thou wonder we should know
Such miscreant here, nor lay him low,
Or dream of greeting, peace, or truce,
    With excommunicated Bruce !
Yet well I grant, to end debate, 450
Thy sainted voice decide his fate.'

XXV

Then Ronald pled the stranger's cause,
And knighthood's oath and honor's laws;
    And Isabel on bended knee
Brought prayers and tears to back the
    plea;
And Edith lent her generous aid,
And wept, and Lorn for mercy prayed.
' Hence,' he exclaimed, ' degenerate maid !
Was 't not enough to Ronald's bower
I brought thee, like a paramour, 460
Or bond-maid at her master's gate,
His careless cold approach to wait ? —
But the bold Lord of Cumberland,
The gallant Clifford, seeks thy hand;
His it shall be — Nay, no reply !
Hence ! till those rebel eyes be dry.'
With grief the abbot heard and saw,
Yet nought relaxed his brow of awe.

XXVI

Then Argentine, in England's name,
So highly urged his sovereign's claim 470
He waked a spark that long suppressed
Had smouldered in Lord Ronald's breast;
And now, as from the flint the fire,
Flashed forth at once his generous ire.
' Enough of noble blood,' he said,
' By English Edward had been shed,
Since matchless Wallace first had been
In mockery crowned with wreaths of green,
And done to death by felon hand
For guarding well his father's land. 480
Where 's Nigel Bruce ? and De la Haye,
And valiant Seton — where are they ?
Where Somerville, the kind and free ?
And Fraser, flower of chivalry ?
Have they not been on gibbet bound,
Their quarters flung to hawk and hound,
And hold we here a cold debate
To yield more victims to their fate ?
What ! can the English Leopard's mood
Never be gorged with northern blood ? 490
Was not the life of Athole shed
To soothe the tyrant's sickened bed ?
And must his word till dying day
Be nought but quarter, hang, and slay ! —
Thou frown'st, De Argentine, — my gage
Is prompt to prove the strife I wage.'

XXVII

' Nor deem,' said stout Dunvegan's knight,
' That thou shalt brave alone the fight !
By saints of isle and mainland both,

By Woden wild — my grandsire's oath —　500
Let Rome and England do their worst,
Howe'er attainted or accursed,
If Bruce shall e'er find friends again
Once more to brave a battle-plain,
If Douglas couch again his lance,
Or Randolph dare another chance,
Old Torquil will not be to lack
With twice a thousand at his back. —
Nay, chafe not at my bearing bold,
Good abbot! for thou know'st of old,　510
Torquil's rude thought and stubborn will
Smack of the wild Norwegian still;
Nor will I barter Freedom's cause
For England's wealth or Rome's ap-
　　plause.'

XXVIII

The abbot seemed with eye severe
The hardy chieftain's speech to hear;
Then on King Robert turned the monk,
But twice his courage came and sunk,
Confronted with the hero's look;
Twice fell his eye, his accents shook;　520
At length, resolved in tone and brow,
Sternly he questioned him — 'And thou,
Unhappy! what hast thou to plead,
Why I denounce not on thy deed
That awful doom which canons tell
Shuts paradise and opens hell;
Anathema of power so dread
It blends the living with the dead,
Bids each good angel soar away
And every ill one claim his prey;　530
Expels thee from the church's care
And deafens Heaven against thy prayer;
Arms every hand against thy life,
Bans all who aid thee in the strife,
Nay, each whose succor, cold and scant,
With meanest alms relieves thy want;
Haunts thee while living, — and when dead
Dwells on thy yet devoted head,
Rends Honor's scutcheon from thy hearse,
Stills o'er thy bier the holy verse,　540
And spurns thy corpse from hallowed
　　ground,
Flung like vile carrion to the hound:
Such is the dire and desperate doom
For sacrilege, decreed by Rome:
And such the well-deserved meed
Of thine unhallowed, ruthless deed.'

XXIX

'Abbot!' the Bruce replied, 'thy charge
It boots not to dispute at large.

This much, howe'er, I bid thee know,
No selfish vengeance dealt the blow,　550
For Comyn died his country's foe.
Nor blame I friends whose ill-timed speed
Fulfilled my soon-repented deed,
Nor censure those from whose stern tongue
The dire anathema has rung.
I only blame mine own wild ire,
By Scotland's wrongs incensed to fire.
Heaven knows my purpose to atone,
Far as I may, the evil done,
And hears a penitent's appeal　560
From papal curse and prelate's zeal.
My first and dearest task achieved,
Fair Scotland from her thrall relieved,
Shall many a priest in cope and stole
Say requiem for Red Comyn's soul,
While I the blessed cross advance
And expiate this unhappy chance
In Palestine with sword and lance.
But, while content the Church should know
My conscience owns the debt I owe,　570
Unto De Argentine and Lorn
The name of traitor I return,
Bid them defiance stern and high,
And give them in their throats the lie!
These brief words spoke, I speak no more.
Do what thou wilt; my shrift is o'er.'

XXX

Like man by prodigy amazed,
Upon the king the abbot gazed;
Then o'er his pallid features glance
Convulsions of ecstatic trance.　580
His breathing came more thick and fast,
And from his pale blue eyes were cast
Strange rays of wild and wandering light;
Uprise his locks of silver white,
Flushed is his brow, through every vein
In azure tide the currents strain,
And undistinguished accents broke
The awful silence ere he spoke.

XXXI

'De Bruce! I rose with purpose dread
To speak my curse upon thy head,　590
And give thee as an outcast o'er
To him who burns to shed thy gore; —
But, like the Midianite of old
Who stood on Zophim, Heaven-controlled,
I feel within mine aged breast
A power that will not be repressed.
It prompts my voice, it swells my veins,
It burns, it maddens, it constrains! —
De Bruce, thy sacrilegious blow

Hath at God's altar slain thy foe: 600
O'ermastered yet by high behest,
I bless thee, and thou shalt be blessed ! '
He spoke, and o'er the astonished throng
Was silence, awful, deep, and long.

XXXII

Again that light has fired his eye,
Again his form swells bold and high,
The broken voice of age is gone,
'T is vigorous manhood's lofty tone:
' Thrice vanquished on the battle-plain,
Thy followers slaughtered, fled, or ta'en, 610
A hunted wanderer on the wild,
On foreign shores a man exiled,
Disowned, deserted, and distressed,
I bless thee, and thou shalt be blessed !
Blessed in the hall and in the field,
Under the mantle as the shield.
Avenger of thy country's shame,
Restorer of her injured fame,
Blessed in thy sceptre and thy sword,
De Bruce, fair Scotland's rightful lord, 620
Blessed in thy deeds and in thy fame,
What lengthened honors wait thy name !
In distant ages sire to son
Shall tell thy tale of freedom won,
And teach his infants in the use
Of earliest speech to falter Bruce.
Go, then, triumphant ! sweep along
Thy course, the theme of many a song !
The Power whose dictates swell my breast
Hath blessed thee, and thou shalt be
    blessed ! — 630
Enough — my short-lived strength de-
    cays,
And sinks the momentary blaze. —
Heaven hath our destined purpose broke,
Not here must nuptial vow be spoke;
Brethren, our errand here is o'er,
Our task discharged. — Unmoor, unmoor ! '
His priests received the exhausted monk,
As breathless in their arms he sunk.
Punctual his orders to obey,
The train refused all longer stay, 640
Embarked, raised sail, and bore away.

CANTO THIRD

I

HAST thou not marked when o'er thy
    startled head
Sudden and deep the thunder-peal has
    rolled,

How, when its echoes fell, a silence dead
Sunk on the wood, the meadow, and the
    wold ?
The rye-grass shakes not on the sod-built
    fold,
The rustling aspen's leaves are mute and
    still,
The wall-flower waves not on the ruined
    hold,
Till, murmuring distant first, then near
    and shrill,
The savage whirlwind wakes and sweeps
    the groaning hill.

II

Artornish ! such a silence sunk 10
Upon thy halls, when that gray monk
    His prophet-speech had spoke;
And his obedient brethren's sail
Was stretched to meet the southern gale
    Before a whisper woke.
Then murmuring sounds of doubt and
    fear,
Close poured in many an anxious ear,
    The solemn stillness broke;
And still they gazed with eager guess
Where in an oriel's deep recess 20
The Island Prince seemed bent to press
What Lorn, by his impatient cheer
And gesture fierce, scarce deigned to hear.

III

Starting at length with frowning look,
His hand he clenched, his head he shook,
    And sternly flung apart:
' And deem'st thou me so mean of mood
As to forget the mortal feud,
And clasp the hand with blood imbrued
    From my dear kinsman's heart ? 30
Is this thy rede ? — a due return
For ancient league and friendship sworn !
But well our mountain proverb shows
The faith of Islesmen ebbs and flows.
Be it even so — believe ere long
He that now bears shall wreak the wrong. —
Call Edith — call the Maid of Lorn !
My sister, slaves ! — for further scorn,
Be sure nor she nor I will stay. —
Away, De Argentine, away ! — 40
We nor ally nor brother know
In Bruce's friend or England's foe.'

IV

But who the chieftain's rage can tell
When, sought from lowest dungeon cell

To highest tower the castle round,
No Lady Edith was there found !
He shouted, 'Falsehood ! —treachery ! —
Revenge and blood ! — a lordly meed
To him that will avenge the deed !
A baron's lands !' — His frantic mood   50
Was scarcely by the news withstood
That Morag shared his sister's flight,
And that in hurry of the night,
'Scaped noteless and without remark,
Two strangers sought the abbot's bark. —
' Man every galley ! — fly — pursue !
The priest his treachery shall rue !
Ay, and the time shall quickly come
When we shall hear the thanks that Rome
Will pay his feigned prophecy !'   60
Such was fierce Lorn's indignant cry;
And Cormac Doil in haste obeyed,
Hoisted his sail, his anchor weighed —
For, glad of each pretext for spoil,
A pirate sworn was Cormac Doil.
But others, lingering, spoke apart,
' The maid has given her maiden heart
  To Ronald of the Isles,
And, fearful lest her brother's word
Bestow her on that English lord,   70
  She seeks Iona's piles,
And wisely deems it best to dwell
A votaress in the holy cell
Until these feuds so fierce and fell
  The abbot reconciles.'

V

As, impotent of ire, the hall
Echoed to Lorn's impatient call —
' My horse, my mantle, and my train !
Let none who honors Lorn remain !' —
Courteous but stern, a bold request   80
To Bruce De Argentine expressed:
' Lord Earl,' he said, ' I cannot chuse
But yield such title to the Bruce,
Though name and earldom both are gone
Since he braced rebel's armor on —
But, earl or serf — rude phrase was thine
Of late, and launched at Argentine;
Such as compels me to demand
Redress of honor at thy hand.
We need not to each other tell   90
That both can wield their weapons well;
  Then do me but the soldier grace
  This glove upon thy helm to place
    Where we may meet in fight;
  And I will say, as still I 've said,
  Though by ambition far misled,
    Thou art a noble knight.'

VI

' And I,' the princely Bruce replied,
' Might term it stain on knighthood's pride
That the bright sword of Argentine   100
Should in a tyrant's quarrel shine;
  But, for your brave request,
Be sure the honored pledge you gave
In every battle-field shall wave
  Upon my helmet-crest;
Believe that if my hasty tongue
Hath done thine honor causeless wrong,
  It shall be well redressed.
Not dearer to my soul was glove
Bestowed in youth by lady's love   110
  Than this which thou hast given !
Thus then my noble foe I greet;
Health and high fortune till we meet,
  And then — what pleases Heaven.'

VII

Thus parted they — for now, with sound
Like waves rolled back from rocky ground,
  The friends of Lorn retire;
Each mainland chieftain with his train
Draws to his mountain towers again,   119
Pondering how mortal schemes prove vain
  And mortal hopes expire.
But through the castle double guard
By Ronald's charge kept wakeful ward,
Wicket and gate were trebly barred
  By beam and bolt and chain;
Then of the guests in courteous sort
He prayed excuse for mirth broke short,
And bade them in Artornish fort
  In confidence remain.
Now torch and menial tendance led   130
Chieftain and knight to bower and bed,
And beads were told and Aves said,
  And soon they sunk away
Into such sleep as wont to shed
Oblivion on the weary head
  After a toilsome day.

VIII

But soon uproused, the monarch cried
To Edward slumbering by his side,
  ' Awake, or sleep for aye !
Even now there jarred a secret door —   140
A taper-light gleams on the floor —
  Up, Edward ! up, I say !
Some one glides in like midnight ghost —
Nay, strike not ! 't is our noble host.'
Advancing then his taper's flame,
Ronald stept forth, and with him came

Dunvegan's chief — each bent the knee
To Bruce in sign of fealty
　And proffered him his sword,
And hailed him in a monarch's style　150
As king of mainland and of isle
　And Scotland's rightful lord.
'And O,' said Ronald, 'Owned of Heaven !
Say, is my erring youth forgiven,
By falsehood's arts from duty driven,
　Who rebel falchion drew,
Yet ever to thy deeds of fame,
Even while I strove against thy claim,
　Paid homage just and true ? ' —
'Alas ! dear youth, the unhappy time,'　160
Answered the Bruce, ' must bear the crime
　Since, guiltier far than you,
Even I ' — he paused; for Falkirk's woes
Upon his conscious soul arose.
The chieftain to his breast he pressed,
And in a sigh concealed the rest.

IX

They proffered aid by arms and might
To repossess him in his right;
But well their counsels must be weighed
Ere banners raised and musters made,　170
For English hire and Lorn's intrigues
Bound many chiefs in southern leagues.
In answer Bruce his purpose bold
To his new vassals frankly told:
' The winter worn in exile o'er,
I longed for Carrick's kindred shore.
I thought upon my native Ayr
And longed to see the burly fare
That Clifford makes, whose lordly call
Now echoes through my father's hall.　180
But first my course to Arran led
Where valiant Lennox gathers head,
And on the sea by tempest tossed,
Our barks dispersed, our purpose crossed,
Mine own, a hostile sail to shun,
Far from her destined course had run,
When that wise will which masters ours
Compelled us to your friendly towers.'

X

Then Torquil spoke : ' The time craves
　　speed !
We must not linger in our deed,　190
But instant pray our sovereign liege
To shun the perils of a siege.
The vengeful Lorn with all his powers
Lies but too near Artornish towers,
And England's light-armed vessels ride
Not distant far the waves of Clyde,

Prompt at these tidings to unmoor,
And sweep each strait and guard each
　　shore.
Then, till this fresh alarm pass by,
Secret and safe my liege must lie　200
In the far bounds of friendly Skye,
Torquil thy pilot and thy guide.' —
' Not so, brave chieftain,' Ronald cried;
' Myself will on my sovereign wait,
And raise in arms the men of Sleate,
Whilst thou, renowned where chiefs debate,
Shalt sway their souls by council sage
And awe them by thy locks of age.' —
' And if my words in weight shall fail,　209
This ponderous sword shall turn the scale.'

XI

' The scheme,' said Bruce, ' contents me
　　well;
Meantime, 't were best that Isabel
For safety with my bark and crew
Again to friendly Erin drew.
There Edward too shall with her wend,
In need to cheer her and defend
And muster up each scattered friend.'
Here seemed it as Lord Ronald's ear
Would other counsel gladlier hear;
But, all achieved as soon as planned,　220
Both barks, in secret armed and manned,
　From out the haven bore;
On different voyage forth they ply,
This for the coast of winged Skye
　And that for Erin's shore.

XII

With Bruce and Ronald bides the tale. —
To favoring winds they gave the sail
Till Mull's dark headlands scarce they
　　knew
And Ardnamurchan's hills were blue.　229
But then the squalls blew close and hard,
And, fain to strike the galley's yard
　And take them to the oar,
With these rude seas in weary plight
They strove the livelong day and night,
Nor till the dawning had a sight
Of Skye's romantic shore.
Where Coolin stoops him to the west,
They saw upon his shivered crest
　The sun's arising gleam;
But such the labor and delay,　240
Ere they were moored in Scavigh bay —
For calmer heaven compelled to stay —
　He shot a western beam.
Then Ronald said, ' If true mine eye,

These are the savage wilds that lie
North of Strathnardill and Dunskye;
    No human foot comes here,
And, since these adverse breezes blow,
If my good liege love hunter's bow,
What hinders that on land we go   250
    And strike a mountain-deer?
Allan, my page, shall with us wend;
A bow full deftly can he bend,
And, if we meet a herd, may send
    A shaft shall mend our cheer.'
Then each took bow and bolts in hand,
Their row-boat launched and leapt to land,
    And left their skiff and train,
Where a wild stream with headlong shock
Came brawling down its bed of rock   260
    To mingle with the main.

XIII

Awhile their route they silent made,
    As men who stalk for mountain-deer,
Till the good Bruce to Ronald said, —
    'Saint Mary! what a scene is here!
I 've traversed many a mountain-strand,
Abroad and in my native land,
And it has been my lot to tread
Where safety more than pleasure led;   269
Thus, many a waste I 've wandered o'er,
Clomb many a crag, crossed many a moor,
    But, by my halidome,
A scene so rude, so wild as this,
Yet so sublime in barrenness,
Ne'er did my wandering footsteps press
    Where'er I happed to roam.'

XIV

No marvel thus the monarch spake;
    For rarely human eye has known
A scene so stern as that dread lake
    With its dark ledge of barren stone. 280
Seems that primeval earthquake's sway
Hath rent a strange and shattered way
    Through the rude bosom of the hill,
And that each naked precipice,
Sable ravine, and dark abyss,
    Tells of the outrage still.
The wildest glen but this can show
Some touch of Nature's genial glow;
On high Benmore green mosses grow,
And heath-bells bud in deep Glencroe,   290
    And copse on Cruchan-Ben;
But here, — above, around, below,
    On mountain or in glen,
Nor tree, nor shrub, nor plant, nor flower,
Nor aught of vegetative power,

    The weary eye may ken.
For all is rocks at random thrown,
Black waves, bare crags, and banks of
        stone,
    As if were here denied   299
The summer sun, the spring's sweet dew,
That clothe with many a varied hue
    The bleakest mountain-side.

XV

And wilder, forward as they wound,
Were the proud cliffs and lake profound.
Huge terraces of granite black
Afforded rude and cumbered track;
    For from the mountain hoar,
Hurled headlong in some night of fear,
When yelled the wolf and fled the deer,
    Loose crags had toppled o'er;   310
And some, chance-poised and balanced, lay
So that a stripling arm might sway
    A mass no host could raise,
In Nature's rage at random thrown
Yet trembling like the Druid's stone
    On its precarious base.
The evening mists with ceaseless change
Now clothed the mountains' lofty range,
    Now left their foreheads bare,   319
And round the skirts their mantle furled,
Or on the sable waters curled,
Or on the eddying breezes whirled,
    Dispersed in middle air.
And oft condensed at once they lower
When, brief and fierce, the mountain
        shower
    Pours like a torrent down,
And when return the sun's glad beams,
Whitened with foam a thousand streams
    Leap from the mountain's crown.

XVI

'This lake,' said Bruce, 'whose barriers
        drear   330
Are precipices sharp and sheer,
Yielding no track for goat or deer
    Save the black shelves we tread,
How term you its dark waves? and how
Yon northern mountain's pathless brow,
    And yonder peak of dread
That to the evening sun uplifts
The griesly gulfs and slaty rifts
    Which seam its shivered head?' —
'Coriskin call the dark lake's name,   340
Coolin the ridge, as bards proclaim,
    From old Cuchullin, chief of fame.
But bards, familiar in our isles

Rather with Nature's frowns than smiles,
Full oft their careless humors please
By sportive names from scenes like these.
I would old Torquil were to show
His Maidens with their breasts of snow,
Or that my noble liege were nigh
To hear his Nurse sing lullaby ! —   350
The Maids — tall cliffs with breakers
   white,
The Nurse — a torrent's roaring might —
Or that your eye could see the mood
Of Corryvrekin's whirlpool rude,
When dons the Hag her whitened hood —
'T is thus our islesmen's fancy frames
For scenes so stern fantastic names.'

XVII

Answered the Bruce, ' And musing mind
Might here a graver moral find.
These mighty cliffs that heave on high   360
Their naked brows to middle sky,
Indifferent to the sun or snow,
Where nought can fade and nought can
   blow
May they not mark a monarch's fate, —
Raised high mid storms of strife and state,
Beyond life's lowlier pleasures placed,
His soul a rock, his heart a waste ?
O'er hope and love and fear aloft
High rears his crowned head — But soft !
Look, underneath yon jutting crag   370
Are hunters and a slaughtered stag.
Who may they be ? But late you said
No steps these desert regions tread ? ' —

XVIII

' So said I — and believed in sooth,'
Ronald replied, ' I spoke the truth.
Yet now I spy, by yonder stone,
Five men — they mark us and come on;
And by their badge on bonnet borne
I guess them of the land of Lorn,
Foes to my liege.' — ' So let it be;   380
I 've faced worse odds than five to three —
But the poor page can little aid;
Then be our battle thus arrayed,
If our free passage they contest;
Cope thou with two, I 'll match the rest.'—
' Not so, my liege — for, by my life,
This sword shall meet the treble strife;
My strength, my skill in arms, more small,
And less the loss should Ronald fall.
But islesmen soon to soldiers grow,   390
Allan has sword as well as bow,
And were my monarch's order given,

Two shafts should make our number
   even.' —
' No ! not to save my life ! ' he said;
' Enough of blood rests on my head
Too rashly spilled — we soon shall know,
Whether they come as friend or foe.'

XIX

Nigh came the strangers and more nigh; —
Still less they pleased the monarch's eye.
Men were they all of evil mien,   400
Down-looked, unwilling to be seen;
They moved with half-resolved pace,
And bent on earth each gloomy face.
The foremost two were fair arrayed
With brogue and bonnet, trews and plaid,
And bore the arms of mountaineers,
Daggers and broadswords, bows and
   spears.
The three that lagged small space behind
Seemed serfs of more degraded kind;
Goat-skins or deer-hides o'er them cast   410
Made a rude fence against the blast;
Their arms and feet and heads were bare,
Matted their beards, unshorn their hair;
For arms the caitiffs bore in hand
A club, an axe, a rusty brand.

XX

Onward still mute, they kept the track; —
' Tell who ye be, or else stand back,'
Said Bruce; ' in deserts when they meet,
Men pass not as in peaceful street.'
Still at his stern command they stood,   420
And proffered greeting brief and rude,
But acted courtesy so ill
As seemed of fear and not of will.
' Wanderers we are, as you may be;
Men hither driven by wind and sea,
Who, if you list to taste our cheer,
Will share with you this fallow deer.' —
' If from the sea, where lies your bark ? ' —
' Ten fathom deep in ocean dark !
Wrecked yesternight: but we are men   430
Who little sense of peril ken.
The shades come down — the day is shut —
Will you go with us to our hut ? ' —
' Our vessel waits us in the bay;
Thanks for your proffer — have good-
   day.' —
' Was that your galley, then, which rode
Not far from shore when evening
   glowed ? ' —
' It was.' — ' Then spare your needless
   pain,

There will she now be sought in vain.
We saw her from the mountain head   440
When, with Saint George's blazon red
A southern vessel bore in sight,
And yours raised sail and took to flight.' —

XXI

'Now, by the rood, unwelcome news!'
Thus with Lord Ronald communed Bruce;
'Nor rests there light enough to show
If this their tale be true or no.
The men seem bred of churlish kind,
Yet mellow nuts have hardest rind;
We will go with them — food and fire   450
And sheltering roof our wants require.
Sure guard 'gainst treachery will we keep,
And watch by turns our comrades' sleep. —
Good fellows, thanks; your guests we 'll be,
And well will pay the courtesy.
Come, lead us where your lodging lies —
Nay, soft! we mix not companies. —
Show us the path o'er crag and stone,
And we will follow you; — lead on.'

XXII

They reached the dreary cabin, made   460
Of sails against a rock displayed,
    And there on entering found
A slender boy, whose form and mien
Ill suited with such savage scene,
    In cap and cloak of velvet green,
    Low seated on the ground.
His garb was such as minstrels wear,
Dark was his hue, and dark his hair,
His youthful cheek was marred by care,
    His eyes in sorrow drowned.   470
'Whence this poor boy?' — As Ronald
    spoke,
The voice his trance of anguish broke;
As if awaked from ghastly dream,
He raised his head with start and scream,
    And wildly gazed around;
Then to the wall his face he turned,
And his dark neck with blushes burned.

XXIII

'Whose is the boy?' again he said.
'By chance of war our captive made;
He may be yours, if you should hold   480
That music has more charms than gold;
For, though from earliest childhood mute,
The lad can deftly touch the lute,
    And on the rote and viol play,
    And well can drive the time away
    For those who love such glee;

For me the favoring breeze, when loud
It pipes upon the galley's shroud,
    Makes blither melody.' —
'Hath he, then, sense of spoken sound?' —
    'Ay; so his mother bade us know,   491
A crone in our late shipwreck drowned,
    And hence the silly stripling's woe.
More of the youth I cannot say,
Our captive but since yesterday;
When wind and weather waxed so grim,
We little listed think of him. —
But why waste time in idle words?
Sit to your cheer — unbelt your swords.'
Sudden the captive turned his head,   500
And one quick glance to Ronald sped.
It was a keen and warning look,
And well the chief the signal took.

XXIV

'Kind host,' he said, 'our needs require
A separate board and separate fire;
For know that on a pilgrimage
Wend I, my comrade, and this page.
And, sworn to vigil and to fast
Long as this hallowed task shall last,
We never doff the plaid or sword,   510
Or feast us at a stranger's board,
And never share one common sleep,
But one must still his vigil keep.
Thus, for our separate use, good friend,
We 'll hold this hut's remoter end.' —
'A churlish vow,' the elder said,
'And hard, methinks, to be obeyed.
How say you, if, to wreak the scorn
That pays our kindness harsh return,
We should refuse to share our meal?' —   520
'Then say we that our swords are steel!
And our vow binds us not to fast
Where gold or force may buy repast.' —
Their host's dark brow grew keen and
    fell,
His teeth are clenched, his features swell;
Yet sunk the felon's moody ire
Before Lord Ronald's glance of fire,
Nor could his craven courage brook
The monarch's calm and dauntless look.
With laugh constrained — 'Let every
    man   530
Follow the fashion of his clan!
Each to his separate quarters keep,
And feed or fast, or wake or sleep.'

XXV

Their fire at separate distance burns,
By turns they eat, keep guard by turns;

For evil seemed that old man's eye,
Dark and designing, fierce yet shy.
Still he avoided forward look,
But slow and circumspectly took
A circling, never-ceasing glance,   540
By doubt and cunning marked at once,
Which shot a mischief-boding ray
From under eyebrows shagged and gray.
The younger, too, who seemed his son,
Had that dark look the timid shun;
The half-clad serfs behind them sate,
And scowled a glare 'twixt fear and hate —
Till all, as darkness onward crept,
Couched down, and seemed to sleep or
      slept.
Nor he, that boy, whose powerless
      tongue   550
Must trust his eyes to wail his wrong,
A longer watch of sorrow made,
But stretched his limbs to slumber laid.

XXVI

Not in his dangerous host confides
The king, but wary watch provides.
Ronald keeps ward till midnight past,
Then wakes the king, young Allan last;
Thus ranked, to give the youthful page
The rest required by tender age.
What is Lord Ronald's wakeful thought 560
To chase the languor toil had brought? —
For deem not that he deigned to throw
Much care upon such coward foe —
He thinks of lovely Isabel
When at her foeman's feet she fell,
Nor less when, placed in princely selle,
She glanced on him with favoring eyes
At Woodstock when he won the prize.
Nor, fair in joy, in sorrow fair,
In pride of place as mid despair,   570
Must she alone engross his care.
His thoughts to his betrothed bride,
To Edith, turn — O, how decide,
When here his love and heart are given,
And there his faith stands plight to
      Heaven !
No drowsy ward 't is his to keep,
For seldom lovers long for sleep.
Till sung his midnight hymn the owl,
Answered the dog-fox with his howl,
Then waked the king — at his request, 580
Lord Ronald stretched himself to rest.

XXVII

What spell was good King Robert's, say,
To drive the weary night away ?

His was the patriot's burning thought
Of freedom's battle bravely fought,
Of castles stormed, of cities freed,
Of deep design and daring deed,
Of England's roses reft and torn,
And Scotland's cross in triumph worn,
Of rout and rally, war and truce, —   590
As heroes think, so thought the Bruce.
No marvel, mid such musings high
Sleep shunned the monarch's thoughtful
      eye.
Now over Coolin's eastern head
The grayish light begins to spread,
The otter to his cavern drew,
And clamored shrill the wakening mew;
Then watched the page — to needful rest
The king resigned his anxious breast.

XXVIII

To Allan's eyes was harder task   600
The weary watch their safeties ask.
He trimmed the fire and gave to shine
With bickering light the splintered pine;
Then gazed awhile where silent laid
Their hosts were shrouded by the plaid.
But little fear waked in his mind,
For he was bred of martial kind,
And, if to manhood he arrive,
May match the boldest knight alive.
Then thought he of his mother's tower, 610
His little sister's greenwood bower,
How there the Easter-gambols pass,
And of Dan Joseph's lengthened mass.
But still before his weary eye
In rays prolonged the blazes die —
Again he roused him — on the lake
Looked forth where now the twilight-flake
Of pale cold dawn began to wake.
On Coolin's cliffs the mist lay furled,
The morning breeze the lake had curled, 620
The short dark waves, heaved to the land,
With ceaseless plash kissed cliff or sand; —
It was a slumbrous sound — he turned
To tales at which his youth had burned,
Of pilgrim's path by demon crossed,
Of sprightly elf or yelling ghost,
Of the wild witch's baneful cot,
And mermaid's alabaster grot,
Who bathes her limbs in sunless well
Deep in Strathaird's enchanted cell.   630
Thither in fancy rapt he flies,
And on his sight the vaults arise;
That hut's dark walls he sees no more,
His foot is on the marble floor,
And o'er his head the dazzling spars

Gleam like a firmament of stars ! —
Hark ! hears he not the sea-nymph speak
Her anger in that thrilling shriek ! —
No ! all too late, with Allan's dream
Mingled the captive's warning scream. 640
As from the ground he strives to start,
A ruffian's dagger finds his heart !
Upwards he casts his dizzy eyes —
Murmurs his master's name — and dies !

XXIX

Not so awoke the king ! his hand
Snatched from the flame a knotted brand,
The nearest weapon of his wrath;
With this he crossed the murderer's path
  And venged young Allan well !
The spattered brain and bubbling blood 650
Hissed on the half-extinguished wood,
  The miscreant gasped and fell !
Nor rose in peace the Island Lord;
One caitiff died upon his sword,
And one beneath his grasp lies prone
In mortal grapple overthrown.
But while Lord Ronald's dagger drank
The life-blood from his panting flank,
The father-ruffian of the band
Behind him rears a coward hand ! —   660
  O for a moment's aid,
Till Bruce, who deals no double blow,
Dash to the earth another foe,
  Above his comrade laid ! —
And it is gained — the captive sprung
On the raised arm and closely clung,
  And, ere he shook him loose,
The mastered felon pressed the ground,
And gasped beneath a mortal wound,
  While o'er him stands the Bruce.   670

XXX

'Miscreant ! while lasts thy flitting spark,
Give me to know the purpose dark
That armed thy hand with murderous
        knife
Against offenceless stranger's life ? ' —
'No stranger thou ! ' with accent fell,
Murmured the wretch; 'I know thee well,
And know thee for the foeman sworn
Of my high chief, the mighty Lorn.' —
'Speak yet again, and speak the truth
For thy soul's sake ! — from whence this
        youth ?   680
His country, birth, and name declare,
And thus one evil deed repair.' —
'Vex me no more ! — my blood runs
        cold —

No more I know than I have told.
We found him in a bark we sought
With different purpose — and I thought ' —
Fate cut him short; in blood and broil,
As he had lived, died Cormac Doil.

XXXI

Then resting on his bloody blade,
The valiant Bruce to Ronald said,   690
'Now shame upon us both ! — that boy
  Lifts his mute face to heaven
And clasps his hands, to testify
His gratitude to God on high
  For strange deliverance given.
His speechless gesture thanks hath paid,
Which our free tongues have left unsaid ! '
He raised the youth with kindly word,
But marked him shudder at the sword:
He cleansed it from its hue of death, 700
And plunged the weapon in its sheath.
'Alas, poor child ! unfitting part
Fate doomed when with so soft a heart
  And form so slight as thine
She made thee first a pirate's slave,
Then in his stead a patron gave
  Of wayward lot like mine;
A landless prince, whose wandering life
Is but one scene of blood and strife —
Yet scant of friends the Bruce shall be, 710
But he 'll find resting-place for thee. —
Come, noble Ronald ! o'er the dead
Enough thy generous grief is paid,
And well has Allan's fate been wroke;
Come, wend we hence — the day has broke.
Seek we our bark — I trust the tale
Was false that she had hoisted sail.'

XXXII

Yet, ere they left that charnel-cell,
The Island Lord bade sad farewell
To Allan: 'Who shall tell this tale,'   720
He said, 'in halls of Donagaile ?
O, who his widowed mother tell
That, ere his bloom, her fairest fell ? —
Rest thee, poor youth ! and trust my care
For mass and knell and funeral prayer;
While o'er those caitiffs where they lie
The wolf shall snarl, the raven cry ! '
And now the eastern mountain's head
On the dark lake threw lustre red;
Bright gleams of gold and purple streak 730
Ravine and precipice and peak —
So earthly power at distance shows;
Reveals his splendor, hides his woes.
O'er sheets of granite, dark and broad,

Rent and unequal, lay the road.
In sad discourse the warriors wind,
And the mute captive moves behind.

CANTO FOURTH

I

STRANGER! if e'er thine ardent step
    hath traced
The northern realms of ancient Caledon,
Where the proud Queen of Wilderness
    hath placed
By lake and cataract her lonely throne,
Sublime but sad delight thy soul hath
    known,
Gazing on pathless glen and mountain
    high,
Listing where from the cliffs the torrents
    thrown
Mingle their echoes with the eagle's cry,
And with the sounding lake and with the
    moaning sky.

Yes! 't was sublime, but sad. — The
    loneliness   10
Loaded thy heart, the desert tired thine
    eye;
And strange and awful fears began to
    press
Thy bosom with a stern solemnity.
Then hast thou wished some woodman's
    cottage nigh,
Something that showed of life, though
    low and mean;
Glad sight, its curling wreath of smoke
    to spy,
Glad sound, its cock's blithe carol would
    have been,
Or children whooping wild beneath the
    willows green.

Such are the scenes where savage gran-
    deur wakes
An awful thrill that softens into sighs; 20
Such feelings rouse them by dim Ran-
    noch's lakes,
In dark Glencoe such gloomy raptures
    rise:
Or farther, where beneath the northern
    skies
Chides wild Loch - Eribol his caverns
    hoar —
But, be the minstrel judge, they yield the
    prize

Of desert dignity to that dread shore
That sees grim Coolin rise and hears Coris-
    kin roar.

II

Through such wild scenes the champion
    passed,
When bold halloo and bugle-blast
Upon the breeze came loud and fast.   30
'There,' said the Bruce, 'rung Edward's
    horn !
What can have caused such brief return ?
And see, brave Ronald, — see him dart
O'er stock and stone like hunted hart,
Precipitate, as is the use,
In war or sport, of Edward Bruce.
He marks us, and his eager cry
Will tell his news ere he be nigh.'

III

Loud Edward shouts, 'What make ye
    here,
Warring upon the mountain-deer,   40
    When Scotland wants her king ?
A bark from Lennox crossed our track,
With her in speed I hurried back,
    These joyful news to bring —
The Stuart stirs in Teviotdale,
And Douglas wakes his native vale;
Thy storm-tossed fleet hath won its way
With little loss to Brodick-Bay,
And Lennox with a gallant band
Waits but thy coming and command   50
To waft them o'er to Carrick strand.
There are blithe news ! — but mark the
    close !
Edward, the deadliest of our foes,
As with his host he northward passed,
Hath on the borders breathed his last.'

IV

Still stood the Bruce — his steady cheek
Was little wont his joy to speak,
    But then his color rose: —
'Now, Scotland ! shortly shalt thou see,
With God's high will, thy children free 60
    And vengeance on thy foes !
Yet to no sense of selfish wrongs,
Bear witness with me, Heaven, belongs
    My joy o'er Edward's bier;
I took my knighthood at his hand,
And lordship held of him and land,
    And well may vouch it here,
That, blot the story from his page
Of Scotland ruined in his rage,

You read a monarch brave and sage   70
  And to his people dear.' —
' Let London's burghers mourn her lord
  And Croydon monks his praise record,'
  The eager Edward said;
' Eternal as his own, my hate
Surmounts the bounds of mortal fate
  And dies not with the dead !
Such hate was his on Solway's strand
When vengeance clenched his palsied hand,
That pointed yet to Scotland's land,   80
  As his last accents prayed
Disgrace and curse upon his heir
If he one Scottish head should spare
Till stretched upon the bloody lair
  Each rebel corpse was laid !
Such hate was his when his last breath
Renounced the peaceful house of death,
And bade his bones to Scotland's coast
Be borne by his remorseless host,
As if his dead and stony eye   90
  Could still enjoy her misery !
Such hate was his — dark, deadly, long;
Mine — as enduring, deep, and strong ! ' —

            V

' Let women, Edward, war with words,
With curses monks, but men with swords:
Nor doubt of living foes to sate
Deepest revenge and deadliest hate.
Now to the sea !   Behold the beach,
And see the galley's pendants stretch
Their fluttering length down favoring
  gale !   100
Aboard, aboard ! and hoist the sail.
Hold we our way for Arran first,
Where meet in arms our friends dispersed;
Lennox the loyal, De la Haye,
And Boyd the bold in battle fray.
I long the hardy band to head,
And see once more my standard spread. —
Does noble Ronald share our course,
Or stay to raise his island force ? ' —
' Come   weal,   come   woe,   by Bruce's
  side,'   110
Replied the chief, ' will Ronald bide.
And since two galleys yonder ride,
Be mine, so please my liege, dismissed
To wake to arms the clans of Uist,
And all who hear the Minche's roar
On the Long Island's lonely shore.
The nearer Isles with slight delay
Ourselves may summon in our way;
And soon on Arran's shore shall meet
With Torquil's aid a gallant fleet,   120

If aught avails their chieftain's hest
Among the islesmen of the west.'

            VI

Thus was their venturous council said.
But, ere their sails the galleys spread,
Coriskin dark and Coolin high
Echoed the dirge's doleful cry.
Along that sable lake passed slow —
Fit scene for such a sight of woe —
The sorrowing islesmen as they bore
The murdered Allan to the shore.   130
At every pause with dismal shout
Their coronach of grief rung out,
And ever when they moved again
The pipes resumed their clamorous strain,
And with the pibroch's shrilling wail
Mourned the young heir of Donagaile.
Round and around, from cliff and cave
His answer stern old Coolin gave,
Till high upon his misty side   139
Languished the mournful notes and died.
For never sounds by mortal made
Attained his high and haggard head,
That echoes but the tempest's moan
Or the deep thunder's rending groan.

            VII

Merrily, merrily bounds the bark,
  She bounds before the gale,
The mountain breeze from Ben-na-darch
  Is joyous in her sail !
With fluttering sound like laughter hoarse
  The cords and canvas strain,   150
The waves, divided by her force,
In rippling eddies chased her course,
  As if they laughed again.
Not down the breeze more blithely flew,
Skimming the wave, the light sea-mew
  Than the gay galley bore
Her course upon that favoring wind,
And Coolin's crest has sunk behind
  And Slapin's caverned shore.
'T was then that warlike signals wake   160
Dunsceaith's dark towers and Eisord's lake,
And soon from Cavilgarrigh's head
Thick wreaths of eddying smoke were
  spread;
A summons these of war and wrath
To the brave clans of Sleat and Strath,
  And ready at the sight
Each warrior to his weapon sprung
And targe upon his shoulder flung,
  Impatient for the fight.
Mac-Kinnon's chief, in warfare gray,   170

Had charge to muster their array
And guide their barks to Brodick Bay.

VIII

Signal of Ronald's high command,
A beacon gleamed o'er sea and land
From Canna's tower, that, steep and gray,
Like falcon-nest o'erhangs the bay.
Seek not the giddy crag to climb
To view the turret scathed by time;
It is a task of doubt and fear
To aught but goat or mountain-deer.   180
But rest thee on the silver beach,
And let the aged herdsman teach
His tale of former day;
His cur's wild clamor he shall chide,
And for thy seat by ocean's side
His varied plaid display;
Then tell how with their chieftain came
In ancient times a foreign dame
To yonder turret gray.
Stern was her lord's suspicious mind   190
Who in so rude a jail confined
So soft and fair a thrall!
And oft when moon on ocean slept
That lovely lady sate and wept
Upon the castle-wall,
And turned her eye to southern climes,
And thought perchance of happier times,
And touched her lute by fits, and sung
Wild ditties in her native tongue.
And still, when on the cliff and bay   200
Placid and pale the moonbeams play,
And every breeze is mute,
Upon the lone Hebridean's ear
Steals a strange pleasure mixed with fear,
While from that cliff he seems to hear
The murmur of a lute
And sounds as of a captive lone
That mourns her woes in tongue un-
        known. —
Strange is the tale — but all too long
Already hath it staid the song —   210
Yet who may pass them by,
That crag and tower in ruins gray,
Nor to their hapless tenant pay
The tribute of a sigh?

IX

Merrily, merrily bounds the bark
O'er the broad ocean driven,
Her path by Ronin's mountains dark
The steersman's hand hath given.
And Ronin's mountains dark have sent
Their hunters to the shore,   220

And each his ashen bow unbent,
And gave his pastime o'er,
And at the Island Lord's command
For hunting spear took warrior's brand.
On Scooreigg next a warning light
Summoned her warriors to the fight;
A numerous race ere stern MacLeod
O'er their bleak shores in vengeance
        strode,
When all in vain the ocean-cave
Its refuge to his victims gave.   230
The chief, relentless in his wrath,
With blazing heath blockades the path;
In dense and stifling volumes rolled,
The vapor filled the caverned hold!
The warrior-threat, the infant's plain,
The mother's screams, were heard in vain;
The vengeful chief maintains his fires
Till in the vault a tribe expires!
The bones which strew that cavern's gloom
Too well attest their dismal doom.   240

X

Merrily, merrily goes the bark
On a breeze from the northward free,
So shoots through the morning sky the lark,
Or the swan through the summer sea.
The shores of Mull on the eastward lay,
And Ulva dark and Colonsay,
And all the group of islets gay
That guard famed Staffa round.
Then all unknown its columns rose
Where dark and undisturbed repose   250
The cormorant had found,
And the shy seal had quiet home
And weltered in that wondrous dome
Where, as to shame the temples decked
By skill of earthly architect,
Nature herself, it seemed, would raise
A minster to her Maker's praise!
Not for a meaner use ascend
Her columns or her arches bend;
Nor of a theme less solemn tells   260
That mighty surge that ebbs and swells,
And still, between each awful pause,
From the high vault an answer draws
In varied tone prolonged and high
That mocks the organ's melody.
Nor doth its entrance front in vain
To old Iona's holy fane,
That Nature's voice might seem to say,
'Well hast thou done, frail child of clay!
Thy humble powers that stately shrine   270
Tasked high and hard — but witness
        mine!'

XI

Merrily, merrily goes the bark,
  Before the gale she bounds;
So darts the dolphin from the shark,
  Or the deer before the hounds.
They left Loch-Tua on their lee,
And they wakened the men of the wild
    Tiree,
  And the chief of the sandy Coll;
They paused not at Columba's isle,   279
Though pealed the bells from the holy
    pile,
  With long and measured toll;
No time for matin or for mass,
And the sounds of the holy summons pass
  Away in the billows' roll.
Lochbuie's fierce and warlike lord
Their signal saw and grasped his sword,
And verdant Islay called her host,
And the clans of Jura's rugged coast
  Lord Ronald's call obey,
And Scarba's isle, whose tortured shore 290
Still rings to Corrievreken's roar,
  And lonely Colonsay; —
Scenes sung by him who sings no more!
His bright and brief career is o'er,
  And mute his tuneful strains;
Quenched is his lamp of varied lore
That loved the light of song to pour;
A distant and a deadly shore
  Has LEYDEN's cold remains!

XII

Ever the breeze blows merrily,   300
But the galley ploughs no more the sea.
Lest, rounding wild Cantyre, they meet
The southern foeman's watchful fleet,
  They held unwonted way;
Up Tarbat's western lake they bore,
Then dragged their bark the isthmus o'er,
  As far as Kilmaconnel's shore
    Upon the eastern bay.
It was a wondrous sight to see
Topmast and pennon glitter free,   310
High raised above the greenwood tree,
As on dry land the galley moves
By cliff and copse and alder groves.
Deep import from that selcouth sign
Did many a mountain seer divine,
For ancient legends told the Gael
That when a royal bark should sail
  O'er Kilmaconnel moss
Old Albyn should in fight prevail,
And every foe should faint and quail   320
  Before her silver Cross.

XIII

Now launched once more, the inland sea
They furrow with fair augury,
  And steer for Arran's isle;
The sun, ere yet he sunk behind
Ben-Ghoil, 'the Mountain of the Wind,'
Gave his grim peaks a greeting kind,
  And bade Loch Ranza smile.
Thither their destined course they drew;
It seemed the isle her monarch knew,   330
So brilliant was the landward view,
  The ocean so serene;
Each puny wave in diamonds rolled
O'er the calm deep where hues of gold
  With azure strove and green.
The hill, the vale, the tree, the tower,
Glowed with the tints of evening's hour,
  The beach was silver sheen,
The wind breathed soft as lover's sigh,
And oft renewed seemed oft to die,   340
  With breathless pause between.
O, who with speech of war and woes
Would wish to break the soft repose
  Of such enchanting scene?

XIV

Is it of war Lord Ronald speaks?
The blush that dyes his manly cheeks,
The timid look, and downcast eye,
And faltering voice the theme deny.
  And good King Robert's brow expressed
  He pondered o'er some high request,   350
    As doubtful to approve;
  Yet in his eye and lip the while,
  Dwelt the half-pitying glance and smile
  Which manhood's graver mood beguile
    When lovers talk of love.
Anxious his suit Lord Ronald pled;
'And for my bride betrothed,' he said,
'My liege has heard the rumor spread
Of Edith from Artornish fled.
Too hard her fate — I claim no right   360
To blame her for her hasty flight;
Be joy and happiness her lot! —
But she hath fled the bridal-knot,
And Lorn recalled his promised plight
In the assembled chieftains' sight. —
  When, to fulfil our fathers' band,
  I proffered all I could — my hand —
    I was repulsed with scorn;
  Mine honor I should ill assert,
  And worse the feelings of my heart,   370
  If I should play a suitor's part
    Again to pleasure Lorn.'

XV

'Young Lord,' the royal Bruce replied,
'That question must the Church decide;
Yet seems it hard, since rumors state
Edith takes Clifford for her mate,
The very tie which she hath broke
To thee should still be binding yoke.
But, for my sister Isabel —
The mood of woman who can tell ?   380
I guess the Champion of the Rock,
Victorious in the tourney shock,
That knight unknown to whom the prize
She dealt, — had favor in her eyes;
But since our brother Nigel's fate,
Our ruined house and hapless state,
From worldly joy and hope estranged,
Much is the hapless mourner changed.
Perchance,' here smiled the noble King,
'This tale may other musings bring.   390
Soon shall we know -- yon mountains hide
The little convent of Saint Bride;
There, sent by Edward, she must stay
Till fate shall give more prosperous day;
And thither will I bear thy suit,
Nor will thine advocate be mute.'

XVI

As thus they talked in earnest mood,
That speechless boy beside them stood.
He stooped his head against the mast,
And bitter sobs came thick and fast,   400
A grief that would not be repressed
But seemed to burst his youthful breast.
His hands against his forehead held
As if by force his tears repelled,
But through his fingers long and slight
Fast trilled the drops of crystal bright.
Edward, who walked the deck apart,
First spied this conflict of the heart.
Thoughtless as brave, with bluntness kind
He sought to cheer the sorrower's mind; 410
By force the slender hand he drew
From those poor eyes that streamed with
          dew.
As in his hold the stripling strove —
'T was a rough grasp, though meant in
          love —
Away his tears the warrior swept,
And bade shame on him that he wept.
'I would to Heaven thy helpless tongue
Could tell me who hath wrought thee
          wrong !
For, were he of our crew the best,
The insult went not unredressed.   420
Come, cheer thee; thou art now of age

To be a warrior's gallant page;
Thou shalt be mine ! — a palfrey fair
O'er hill and holt my boy shall bear,
To hold my bow in hunting grove,
Or speed on errand to my love;
For well I wot thou wilt not tell
The temple where my wishes dwell.'

XVII

Bruce interposed, 'Gay Edward, no,
This is no youth to hold thy bow,   430
To fill thy goblet, or to bear
Thy message light to lighter fair.
Thou art a patron all too wild
And thoughtless for this orphan child.
See'st thou not how apart he steals,
Keeps lonely couch, and lonely meals ?
Fitter by far in yon calm cell
To tend our sister Isabel,
With father Augustine to share
The peaceful change of convent prayer, 440
Than wander wild adventures through
With such a reckless guide as you.' —
'Thanks,   brother ! '   Edward   answered
          gay,
'For the high laud thy words convey !
But we may learn some future day,
If thou or I can this poor boy
Protect the best or best employ.
Meanwhile, our vessel nears the strand;
Launch we the boat and seek the land.'

XVIII

To land King Robert lightly sprung,   450
And thrice aloud his bugle rung
With note prolonged and varied strain
Till bold Ben-Ghoil replied again.
Good Douglas then and De la Haye
Had in a glen a hart at bay,
And Lennox cheered the laggard hounds,
When   waked that horn the greenwood
          bounds.
'It is the foe !' cried Boyd, who came
In breathless haste with eye of flame, —
'It is the foe ! — Each valiant lord   460
Fling by his bow and grasp his sword ! '
'Not so,' replied the good Lord James,
'That blast no English bugle claims.
Oft have I heard it fire the fight,
Cheer the pursuit, or stop the flight.
Dead were my heart and deaf mine ear,
If Bruce should call nor Douglas hear !
Each to Loch Ranza's margin spring;
That blast was winded by the king ! '

XIX

Fast to their mates the tidings spread, 470
And fast to shore the warriors sped.
Bursting from glen and greenwood tree,
High waked their loyal jubilee !
Around the royal Bruce they crowd,
And clasped his hands, and wept aloud.
Veterans of early fields were there,
Whose helmets pressed their hoary hair,
Whose swords and axes bore a stain
From life-blood of the red-haired Dane;
And boys whose hands scarce brooked to
    wield 480
The heavy sword or bossy shield.
Men too were there that bore the scars
Impressed in Albyn's woful wars,
At Falkirk's fierce and fatal fight,
Teyndrum's dread rout, and Methven's
    flight;
The might of Douglas there was seen,
There Lennox with his graceful mien;
Kirkpatrick, Closeburn's dreadèd Knight;
The Lindsay, fiery, fierce, and light;
The heir of murdered De la Haye, 490
And Boyd the grave, and Seton gay.
Around their king regained they pressed,
Wept, shouted, clasped him to their breast,
And young and old, and serf and lord,
And he who ne'er unsheathed a sword,
And he in many a peril tried,
Alike resolved the brunt to bide,
And live or die by Bruce's side !

XX

O War ! thou hast thy fierce delight,
Thy gleams of joy, intensely bright ! 500
Such gleams as from thy polished shield
Fly dazzling o'er the battle-field !
Such transports wake, severe and high,
Amid the pealing conquest cry;
Scarce less, when after battle lost
Muster the remnants of a host,
And as each comrade's name they tell
Who in the well-fought conflict fell,
Knitting stern brow o'er flashing eye,
Vow to avenge them or to die ! — 510
Warriors ! — and where are warriors found,
If not on martial Britain's ground ?
And who, when waked with note of fire,
Love more than they the British lyre ?—
Know ye not, — hearts to honor dear !
That joy, deep-thrilling, stern, severe,
At which the heartstrings vibrate high,
And wake the fountains of the eye ?

And blame ye then the Bruce if trace
Of tear is on his manly face 520
When, scanty relics of the train
That hailed at Scone his early reign,
This patriot band around him hung,
And to his knees and bosom clung ? —
Blame ye the Bruce ? — His brother
    blamed,
But shared the weakness, while ashamed
With haughty laugh his head he turned,
And dashed away the tear he scorned.

XXI

'T is morning, and the convent bell
Long time had ceased its matin knell 530
    Within thy walls, Saint Bride !
An aged sister sought the cell
Assigned to Lady Isabel,
    And hurriedly she cried,
'Haste, gentle Lady, haste ! — there waits
A noble stranger at the gates;
Saint Bride's poor votaress ne'er has seen
A knight of such a princely mien;
His errand, as he bade me tell,
Is with the Lady Isabel.' 540
The princess rose, — for on her knee
Low bent she told her rosary, —
' Let him by thee his purpose teach;
I may not give a stranger speech.' —
' Saint Bride forefend, thou royal maid ! '
The portress crossed herself and said,
' Not to be Prioress might I
Debate his will, his suit deny.' —
' Has earthly show then, simple fool,
Power o'er a sister of thy rule ? 550
And art thou, like the worldly train,
Subdued by splendors light and vain ? '

XXII

' No, lady ! in old eyes like mine,
Gauds have no glitter, gems no shine;
Nor grace his rank attendants vain,
One youthful page is all his train.
It is the form, the eye, the word,
The bearing of that stranger lord;
His stature, manly, bold, and tall,
Built like a castle's battled wall, 560
Yet moulded in such just degrees,
His giant-strength seems lightsome ease.
Close as the tendrils of the vine
His locks upon his forehead twine,
Jet-black save where some touch of gray
Has ta'en the youthful hue away.
Weather and war their rougher trace
Have left on that majestic face; —

But 't is his dignity of eye !
There, if a suppliant, would I fly,   570
Secure, mid danger, wrongs, and grief,
Of sympathy, redress, relief —
That glance, if guilty, would I dread
More than the doom that spoke me dead !'
' Enough, enough,' the Princess cried,
' 'T is Scotland's hope, her joy, her pride !
To meaner front was ne'er assigned
Such mastery o'er the common mind —
Bestowed thy high designs to aid,
How long, O Heaven ! how long de-
    layed ! —   580
Haste, Mona, haste, to introduce
My darling brother, royal Bruce !'

XXIII

They met like friends who part in pain,
And meet in doubtful hope again.
But when subdued that fitful swell,
The Bruce surveyed the humble cell —
' And this is thine, poor Isabel ! —
That pallet-couch and naked wall,
For room of state and bed of pall;
For costly robes and jewels rare,   590
A string of beads and zone of hair;
And for the trumpet's sprightly call
To sport or banquet, grove or hall,
The bell's grim voice divides thy care,
'Twixt hours of penitence and prayer ! —
O ill for thee, my royal claim
From the First David's sainted name !
O woe for thee, that while he sought
His right, thy brother feebly fought !'

XXIV

' Now lay these vain regrets aside,   600
And be the unshaken Bruce !' she cried ;
' For more I glory to have shared
The woes thy venturous spirit dared,
When raising first thy valiant band
In rescue of thy native land,
Than had fair Fortune set me down
The partner of an empire's crown.
And grieve not that on pleasure's stream
No more I drive in giddy dream,
For Heaven the erring pilot knew,   610
And from the gulf the vessel drew,
Tried me with judgments stern and great,
My house's ruin, thy defeat,
Poor Nigel's death, till tamed I own
My hopes are fixed on Heaven alone;
Nor e'er shall earthly prospects win
My heart to this vain world of sin.'

XXV

' Nay, Isabel, for such stern choice
First wilt thou wait thy brother's voice;
Then ponder if in convent scene   620
No softer thoughts might intervene —
Say they were of that unknown knight,
Victor in Woodstock's tourney-fight —
Nay, if his name such blush you owe,
Victorious o'er a fairer foe !'
Truly his penetrating eye
Hath caught that blush's passing dye, —
Like the last beam of evening thrown
On a white cloud, — just seen and gone.
Soon with calm cheek and steady eye   630
The princess made composed reply:
' I guess my brother's meaning well;
For not so silent is the cell
But we have heard the islemen all
Arm in thy cause at Ronald's call,
And mine eye proves that knight unknown
And the brave Island Lord are one.
Had then his suit been earlier made,
In his own name with thee to aid —
But that his plighted faith forbade —   640
I know not — But thy page so near ? —
This is no tale for menial's ear.'

XXVI

Still stood that page, as far apart
  As the small cell would space afford;
With dizzy eye and bursting heart
  He leant his weight on Bruce's sword,
The monarch's mantle too he bore,
And drew the fold his visage o'er.
' Fear not for him — in murderous strife,'
Said Bruce, ' his warning saved my life;   650
Full seldom parts he from my side,
And in his silence I confide,
Since he can tell no tale again.
He is a boy of gentle strain,
And I have purposed he shall dwell
In Augustine the chaplain's cell
And wait on thee, my Isabel. —
Mind not his tears; I 've seen them flow,
As in the thaw dissolves the snow.
'T is a kind youth, but fanciful,   660
Unfit against the tide to pull,
And those that with the Bruce would
    sail
Must learn to strive with stream and
    gale.
But forward, gentle Isabel —
My answer for Lord Ronald tell.'

XXVII

'This answer be to Ronald given —
The heart he asks is fixed on heaven.
My love was like a summer flower
That withered in the wintry hour,
Born but of vanity and pride,   670
And with these sunny visions died.
If further press his suit — then say
He should his plighted troth obey,
Troth plighted both with ring and word,
And sworn on crucifix and sword. —
O, shame thee, Robert ! I have seen
Thou hast a woman's guardian been !
Even in extremity's dread hour,
When pressed on thee the Southern power,
And safety, to all human sight,   680
Was only found in rapid flight,
Thou heard'st a wretched female plain
In agony of travail-pain,
And thou didst bid thy little band
Upon the instant turn and stand,
And dare the worst the foe might do
Rather than, like a knight untrue,
Leave to pursuers merciless
A woman in her last distress.
And wilt thou now deny thine aid   690
To an oppressed and injured maid,
Even plead for Ronald's perfidy
And press his fickle faith on me ? —
So witness Heaven, as true I vow,
Had I those earthly feelings now
Which could my former bosom move
Ere taught to set its hopes above,
I 'd spurn each proffer he could bring
Till at my feet he laid the ring,
The ring and spousal contract both,   700
And fair acquittal of his oath,
By her who brooks his perjured scorn,
The ill-requited Maid of Lorn ! '

XXVIII

With sudden impulse forward sprung
The page and on her neck he hung;
Then, recollected instantly,
His head he stooped and bent his knee,
Kissed twice the hand of Isabel,
Arose, and sudden left the cell. —
The princess, loosened from his hold,   710
Blushed angry at his bearing bold;
  But good King Robert cried,
'Chafe not — by signs he speaks his mind,
He heard the plan my care designed,
  Nor could his transports hide. —
But, sister, now bethink thee well;
No easy choice the convent cell;

Trust, I shall play no tyrant part,
Either to force thy hand or heart,
Or suffer that Lord Ronald scorn   720
Or wrong for thee the Maid of Lorn.
But think, — not long the time has been,
That thou wert wont to sigh unseen,
And wouldst the ditties best approve
That told some lay of hapless love.
Now are thy wishes in thy power,
And thou art bent on cloister bower !
O, if our Edward knew the change,
How would his busy satire range,
With many a sarcasm varied still   730
On woman's wish and woman's will ! ' —

XXIX

'Brother, I well believe,' she said,
'Even so would Edward's part be played.
Kindly in heart, in word severe,
A foe to thought and grief and fear,
He holds his humor uncontrolled;
But thou art of another mould.
Say then to Ronald, as I say,
Unless before my feet he lay
The ring which bound the faith he
          swore,   740
By Edith freely yielded o'er,
He moves his suit to me no more.
Nor do I promise, even if now
He stood absolved of spousal vow,
That I would change my purpose made
To shelter me in holy shade. —
Brother, for little space, farewell !
To other duties warns the bell.'

XXX

'Lost to the world,' King Robert said,
When he had left the royal maid,   750
'Lost to the world by lot severe,
O, what a gem lies buried here,
Nipped by misfortune's cruel frost,
The buds of fair affection lost ! —
But what have I with love to do ?
Far sterner cares my lot pursue.
Pent in this isle we may not lie,
Nor would it long our wants supply.
Right opposite, the mainland towers   759
Of my own Turnberry court our powers —
Might not my father's beadsman hoar,
Cuthbert, who dwells upon the shore,
Kindle a signal-flame to show
The time propitious for the blow ?
It shall be so — some friend shall bear
Our mandate with despatch and care;

Edward shall find the messenger.
That fortress ours, the island fleet
May on the coast of Carrick meet. —
O Scotland ! shall it e'er be mine   770
To wreak thy wrongs in battle-line,
To raise my victor-head, and see
Thy hills, thy dales, thy people free, —
That glance of bliss is all I crave
Betwixt my labors and my grave ! '
Then down the hill he slowly went,
Oft pausing on the steep descent,
And reached the spot where his bold
        train
Held rustic camp upon the plain.

CANTO FIFTH

I

On fair Loch-Ranza streamed the early
        day,
Thin wreaths of cottage-smoke are up-
        ward curled
From the lone hamlet which her inland
        bay
And circling mountains sever from the
        world.
And there the fisherman his sail un-
        furled,
The goat-herd drove his kids to steep
        Ben-Ghoil,
Before the hut the dame her spindle
        twirled,
Courting the sunbeam as she plied her
        toil, —
For, wake where'er he may, man wakes to
        care and coil.

But other duties called each convent
        maid,   10
Roused by the summons of the moss-
        grown bell;
Sung were the matins and the mass was
        said,
And every sister sought her separate
        cell,
Such was the rule, her rosary to tell.
And Isabel has knelt in lonely prayer;
The sunbeam through the narrow lattice
        fell
Upon the snowy neck and long dark
        hair,
As stooped her gentle head in meek de-
        votion there.

II

She raised her eyes, that duty done,
When glanced upon the pavement-stone, 20
Gemmed and enchased, a golden ring,
Bound to a scroll with silken string,
With few brief words inscribed to tell,
' This for the Lady Isabel.'
Within the writing farther bore,
' 'T was with this ring his plight he swore,
With this his promise I restore;
To her who can the heart command
Well may I yield the plighted hand.
And O, for better fortune born,   30
Grudge not a passing sigh to mourn
Her who was Edith once of Lorn ! '
One single flash of glad surprise
Just glanced from Isabel's dark eyes,
But vanished in the blush of shame
That as its penance instant came.
' O thought unworthy of my race !
Selfish, ungenerous, mean, and base,
A moment's throb of joy to own
That rose upon her hopes o'erthrown ! — 40
Thou pledge of vows too well believed,
Of man ingrate and maid deceived,
Think not thy lustre here shall gain
Another heart to hope in vain !
For thou shalt rest, thou tempting gaud,
Where worldly thoughts are overawed,
And worldly splendors sink debased.'
Then by the cross the ring she placed.

III

Next rose the thought, — its owner far,
How came it here through bolt and
        bar ?   50
But the dim lattice is ajar.
She looks abroad, — the morning dew
A light short step had brushed anew,
    And there were footprints seen
On the carved buttress rising still,
Till on the mossy window-sill
    Their track effaced the green.
The ivy twigs were torn and frayed,
As if some climber's steps to aid. —
But who the hardy messenger   60
Whose venturous path these signs in-
        fer ? —
' Strange doubts are mine ! — Mona, draw
        nigh; —
Nought 'scapes old Mona's curious eye —
What strangers, gentle mother, say,
Have sought these holy walls to-day ?'
' None, lady, none of note or name;

Only your brother's foot-page came
At peep of dawn — I prayed him pass
To chapel where they said the mass;
But like an arrow he shot by,   70
And tears seemed bursting from his eye.'

IV

The truth at once on Isabel
As darted by a sunbeam fell:
'' T is Edith's self ! — her speechless woe,
Her form, her looks, the secret show ! —
Instant, good Mona, to the bay,
And to my royal brother say,
I do conjure him seek my cell
With that mute page he loves so well.'   79
' What ! know'st thou not his warlike host
At break of day has left our coast ?
My old eyes saw them from the tower.
At eve they couched in greenwood bower,
At dawn a bugle signal made
By their bold lord their ranks arrayed;
Up sprung the spears through bush and
          tree,
No time for benedicite !
Like deer that, rousing from their lair,
Just shake the dew-drops from their hair
And toss their armed crest aloft,   90
Such matins theirs !' — ' Good mother,
          soft —
Where does my brother bend his way ? ' —
' As I have heard, for Brodick Bay,
Across the isle — of barks a score
Lie there, 't is said, to waft them o'er,
On sudden news, to Carrick shore.' —
' If such their purpose, deep the need,'
Said anxious Isabel, ' of speed !
Call Father Augustine, good dame.' —
The nun obeyed, the father came.   100

' Kind father, hie without delay
Across the hills to Brodick Bay.
This message to the Bruce be given;
I pray him, by his hopes of Heaven,
That till he speak with me he stay !
Or, if his haste brook no delay,
That he deliver on my suit
Into thy charge that stripling mute.
Thus prays his sister Isabel
For causes more than she may tell —   110
Away, good father ! and take heed
That life and death are on thy speed.'
His cowl the good old priest did on,
Took his piked staff and sandalled shoon,
And, like a palmer bent by eld,
O'er moss and moor his journey held.

VI

Heavy and dull the foot of age,
And rugged was the pilgrimage;
But none were there beside whose care
Might such important message bear.   120
Through birchen copse he wandered slow,
Stunted and sapless, thin and low;
By many a mountain stream he passed,
From the tall cliffs in tumult cast,
Dashing to foam their waters dun
And sparkling in the summer sun.
Round his gray head the wild curlew
In many a fearless circle flew.
O'er chasms he passed where fractures
          wide
Craved wary eye and ample stride;   130
He crossed his brow beside the stone
Where Druids erst heard victims groan,
And at the cairns upon the wild
O'er many a heathen hero piled,
He breathed a timid prayer for those
Who died ere Shiloh's sun arose.
Beside Macfarlane's Cross he staid,
There told his hours within the shade
And at the stream his thirst allayed.
Thence onward journeying slowly still,   140
As evening closed he reached the hill
Where, rising through the woodland green,
Old Brodick's Gothic towers were seen.
From Hastings late, their English lord,
Douglas had won them by the sword.
The sun that sunk behind the isle
Now tinged them with a parting smile.

VII

But though the beams of light decay
'T was bustle all in Brodick Bay.
The Bruce's followers crowd the shore,   150
And boats and barges some unmoor,
Some raise the sail, some seize the oar;
Their eyes oft turned where glimmered
          far
What might have seemed an early star
On heaven's blue arch save that its light
Was all too flickering, fierce, and bright.
Far distant in the south the ray
Shone pale amid retiring day,
    But as, on Carrick shore,
Dim seen in outline faintly blue,   160
The shades of evening closer drew,
    It kindled more and more.
The monk's slow steps now press the sands,
And now amid a scene he stands
    Full strange to churchman's eye;
Warriors, who, arming for the fight,

Rivet and clasp their harness light,
And twinkling spears, and axes bright,
  And helmets flashing high.
Oft too with unaccustomed ears   170
A language much unmeet he hears,
  While, hastening all on board,
As stormy as the swelling surge
That mixed its roar, the leaders urge
Their followers to the ocean verge
  With many a haughty word.

VIII

Through that wild throng the father
    passed,
And reached the royal Bruce at last.
He leant against a stranded boat
That the approaching tide must float,   180
And counted every rippling wave
As higher yet her sides they lave,
And oft the distant fire he eyed,
And closer yet his hauberk tied,
And loosened in its sheath his brand.
Edward and Lennox were at hand,
Douglas and Ronald had the care
The soldiers to the barks to share. —
The monk approached and homage paid;
'And art thou come,' King Robert said,   190
'So far to bless us ere we part ? ' —
'My liege, and with a loyal heart ! —
But other charge I have to tell,' —
And spoke the hest of Isabel.
'Now by Saint Giles,' the monarch cried,
'This moves me much ! — this morning
    tide
I sent the stripling to Saint Bride
With my commandment there to bide.'
'Thither he came the portress showed,   199
But there, my liege, made brief abode.' —

IX

''T was I,' said Edward, 'found employ
Of nobler import for the boy.
Deep pondering in my anxious mind,
A fitting messenger to find
To bear thy written mandate o'er
To Cuthbert on the Carrick shore,
I chanced at early dawn to pass
The chapel gate to snatch a mass.
I found the stripling on a tomb
Low-seated, weeping for the doom   210
That gave his youth to convent gloom.
I told my purpose and his eyes
Flashed joyful at the glad surprise.
He bounded to the skiff, the sail
Was spread before a prosperous gale,

And well my charge he hath obeyed;
For see ! the ruddy signal made
That Clifford with his merry-men all
Guards carelessly our father's hall.'   219

X

'O wild of thought and hard of heart ! '
Answered the monarch, 'on a part
Of such deep danger to employ
A mute, an orphan, and a boy !
Unfit for flight, unfit for strife,
Without a tongue to plead for life !
Now, were my right restored by Heaven,
Edward, my crown I would have given
Ere, thrust on such adventure wild,
I perilled thus the helpless child.'
Offended half and half submiss, —   230
'Brother and liege, of blame like this,'
Edward replied, 'I little dreamed.
A stranger messenger, I deemed,
Might safest seek the beadsman's cell
Where all thy squires are known so well.
Noteless his presence, sharp his sense,
His imperfection his defence.
If seen, none can his errand guess;
If ta'en, his words no tale express —
Methinks, too, yonder beacon's shine   240
Might expiate greater fault than mine.'
'Rash,' said King Robert, ' was the deed —
But it is done. Embark with speed ! —
Good father, say to Isabel
How this unhappy chance befell;
If well we thrive on yonder shore,
Soon shall my care her page restore.
Our greeting to our sister bear,
And think of us in mass and prayer.'

XI

'Ay ! ' said the priest, 'while this poor
    hand   250
Can chalice raise or cross command,
While my old voice has accents' use,
Can Augustine forget the Bruce ! '
Then to his side Lord Ronald pressed,
And whispered, ' Bear thou this request,
That when by Bruce's side I fight
For Scotland's crown and freedom's right,
The princess grace her knight to bear
Some token of her favoring care;
It shall be shown where England's best   260
May shrink to see it on my crest.
And for the boy — since weightier care
For royal Bruce the times prepare,
The helpless youth is Ronald's charge,
His couch my plaid, his fence my targe.'

He ceased; for many an eager hand
Had urged the barges from the strand.
Their number was a score and ten,
They bore thrice threescore chosen men.
With such small force did Bruce at last 270
The die for death or empire cast!

XII

Now on the darkening main afloat,
Ready and manned rocks every boat;
Beneath their oars the ocean's might
Was dashed to sparks of glimmering light.
Faint and more faint, as off they bore,
Their armor glanced against the shore,
And, mingled with the dashing tide,
Their murmuring voices distant died. —
'God speed them!' said the priest, as dark
On distant billows glides each bark; 281
'O Heaven! when swords for freedom
shine
And monarch's right, the cause is thine!
Edge doubly every patriot blow!
Beat down the banners of the foe!
And be it to the nations known,
That victory is from God alone!'
As up the hill his path he drew,
He turned his blessings to renew,
Oft turned till on the darkened coast 290
All traces of their course were lost;
Then slowly bent to Brodick tower
To shelter for the evening hour.

XIII

In night the fairy prospects sink
Where Cumray's isles with verdant link
Close the fair entrance of the Clyde;
The woods of Bute, no more descried,
Are gone — and on the placid sea
The rowers ply their task with glee,
While hands that knightly lances bore 300
Impatient aid the laboring oar.
The half-faced moon shone dim and pale,
And glanced against the whitened sail;
But on that ruddy beacon-light
Each steersman kept the helm aright,
And oft, for such the king's command,
That all at once might reach the strand,
From boat to boat loud shout and hail
Warned them to crowd or slacken sail.
South and by west the armada bore, 310
And near at length the Carrick shore.
As less and less the distance grows,
High and more high the beacon rose;
The light that seemed a twinkling star
Now blazed portentous, fierce, and far.

Dark-red the heaven above it glowed,
Dark-red the sea beneath it flowed,
Red rose the rocks on ocean's brim,
In blood-red light her islets swim;
Wild scream the dazzled sea-fowl gave, 320
Dropped from their crags on plashing wave.
The deer to distant covert drew,
The black-cock deemed it day and crew.
Like some tall castle given to flame,
O'er half the land the lustre came.
'Now, good my liege and brother sage,
What think ye of mine elfin page?' —
'Row on!' the noble king replied,
'We 'll learn the truth whate'er betide;
Yet sure the beadsman and the child 330
Could ne'er have waked that beacon wild.'

XIV

With that the boats approached the land,
But Edward's grounded on the sand;
The eager knight leaped in the sea
Waist-deep and first on shore was he,
Though every barge's hardy band
Contended which should gain the land,
When that strange light, which seen afar
Seemed steady as the polar star,
Now, like a prophet's fiery chair, 340
Seemed travelling the realms of air.
Wide o'er the sky the splendor glows
As that portentous meteor rose;
Helm, axe, and falchion glittered bright,
And in the red and dusky light
His comrade's face each warrior saw,
Nor marvelled it was pale with awe.
Then high in air the beams were lost,
And darkness sunk upon the coast. —
Ronald to Heaven a prayer addressed, 350
And Douglas crossed his dauntless breast;
'Saint James protect us!' Lennox cried,
But reckless Edward spoke aside,
'Deem'st thou, Kirkpatrick, in that flame
Red Comyn's angry spirit came,
Or would thy dauntless heart endure
Once more to make assurance sure?'
'Hush!' said the Bruce; 'we soon shall
know
If this be sorcerer's empty show
Or stratagem of southern foe. 360
The moon shines out — upon the sand
Let every leader rank his band.'

XV

Faintly the moon's pale beams supply
That ruddy light's unnatural dye;
The dubious cold reflection lay

On the wet sands and quiet bay.
Beneath the rocks King Robert drew
His scattered files to order due,
Till shield compact and serried spear
In the cool light shone blue and clear. 370
Then down a path that sought the tide
That speechless page was seen to glide;
He knelt him lowly on the sand,
And gave a scroll to Robert's hand.
' A torch,' the monarch cried, ' What, ho !
Now shall we Cuthbert's tidings know.'
But evil news the letters bear,
The Clifford's force was strong and ware,
Augmented too, that very morn,
By mountaineers who came with Lorn. 380
Long harrowed by oppressor's hand,
Courage and faith had fled the land,
And over Carrick, dark and deep,
Had sunk dejection's iron sleep. —
Cuthbert had seen that beacon flame,
Unwitting from what source it came.
Doubtful of perilous event,
Edward's mute messenger he sent,
If Bruce deceived should venture o'er,
To warn him from the fatal shore. 390

XVI

As round the torch the leaders crowd,
Bruce read these chilling news aloud.
' What council, nobles, have we now ? —
To ambush us in greenwood bough,
And take the chance which fate may send
To bring our enterprise to end ?
Or shall we turn us to the main
As exiles, and embark again ? '
Answered fierce Edward, ' Hap what may,
In Carrick Carrick's lord must stay. 400
I would not minstrels told the tale
Wildfire or meteor made us quail.'
Answered the Douglas, ' If my liege
May win yon walls by storm or siege,
Then were each brave and patriot heart
Kindled of new for loyal part.'
Answered Lord Ronald, ' Not for shame
Would I that aged Torquil came
And found, for all our empty boast,
Without a blow we fled the coast. 410
I will not credit that this land,
So famed for warlike heart and hand,
The nurse of Wallace and of Bruce,
Will long with tyrants hold a truce.'
' Prove we our fate : the brunt we 'll bide !'
So Boyd and Haye and Lennox cried;
So said, so vowed the leaders all;
So Bruce resolved: ' And in my hall

Since the bold Southern make their home,
The hour of payment soon shall come, 420
When with a rough and rugged host
Clifford may reckon to his cost.
Meantime, through well-known bosk and
   dell
I 'll lead where we may shelter well.'

XVII

Now ask you whence that wondrous light,
Whose fairy glow beguiled their sight ? —
It ne'er was known — yet gray-haired eld
A superstitious credence held
That never did a mortal hand
Wake its broad glare on Carrick strand; 430
Nay, and that on the selfsame night
When Bruce crossed o'er still gleams the
   light.
Yearly it gleams o'er mount and moor
And glittering wave and crimsoned shore —
But whether beam celestial, lent
By Heaven to aid the king's descent,
Or fire hell-kindled from beneath
To lure him to defeat and death,
Or were it but some meteor strange
Of such as oft through midnight range, 440
Startling the traveller late and lone,
I know not — and it ne'er was known.

XVIII

Now up the rocky pass they drew,
And Ronald, to his promise true,
Still made his arm the stripling's stay,
To aid him on the rugged way.
' Now cheer thee, simple Amadine !
Why throbs that silly heart of thine ? '—
That name the pirates to their slave —
In Gaelic 't is the Changeling — gave — 450
' Dost thou not rest thee on my arm ?
Do not my plaid-folds hold thee warm ?
Hath not the wild bull's treble hide
This targe for thee and me supplied ?
Is not Clan-Colla's sword of steel ?
And, trembler, canst thou terror feel ?
Cheer thee, and still that throbbing heart;
From Ronald's guard thou shalt not
   part.' —
O ! many a shaft at random sent
Finds mark the archer little meant ! 460
And many a word at random spoken
May soothe or wound a heart that 's
   broken !
Half soothed, half grieved, half terrified,
Close drew the page to Ronald's side;
A wild delirious thrill of joy

Was in that hour of agony,
As up the steepy pass he strove,
Fear, toil, and sorrow, lost in love !

XIX

The barrier of that iron shore,
The rock's steep ledge, is now climbed
    o'er;   470
And from the castle's distant wall,
From tower to tower the warders call:
The sound swings over land and sea,
And marks a watchful enemy. —
They gained the Chase, a wide domain
Left for the castle's sylvan reign —
Seek not the scene; the axe, the plough,
The boor's dull fence, have marred it now,
But then soft swept in velvet green
The plain with many a glade between,   480
Whose tangled alleys far invade
The depth of the brown forest shade.
Here the tall fern obscured the lawn,
Fair shelter for the sportive fawn;
There, tufted close with copsewood green,
Was many a swelling hillock seen;
And all around was verdure meet
For pressure of the fairies' feet.
The glossy holly loved the park,
The yew-tree lent its shadow dark,   490
And many an old oak, worn and bare,
With all its shivered boughs was there.
Lovely between, the moonbeams fell
On lawn and hillock, glade and dell.
The gallant monarch sighed to see
These glades so loved in childhood free,
Bethinking that as outlaw now
He ranged beneath the forest bough.

XX

Fast o'er the moonlight Chase they sped.
Well knew the band that measured
    tread   500
When, in retreat or in advance,
The serried warriors move at once;
And evil were the luck if dawn
Descried them on the open lawn.
Copses they traverse, brooks they cross,
Strain up the bank and o'er the moss.
From the exhausted page's brow
Cold drops of toil are streaming now;
With effort faint and lengthened pause,
His weary step the stripling draws.   510
'Nay, droop not yet !' the warrior said;
'Come, let me give thee ease and aid !
Strong are mine arms, and little care
A weight so slight as thine to bear. —

What ! wilt thou not ? — capricious boy ! —
Then thine own limbs and strength employ.
Pass but this night and pass thy care,
I 'll place thee with a lady fair,
Where thou shalt tune thy lute to tell
How Ronald loves fair Isabel !'   520
Worn out, disheartened, and dismayed,
Here Amadine let go the plaid;
His trembling limbs their aid refuse,
He sunk among the midnight dews !

XXI

What may be done ? — the night is gone —
The Bruce's band moves swiftly on—
Eternal shame if at the brunt
Lord Ronald grace not battle's front ! —
' See yonder oak within whose trunk
Decay a darkened cell hath sunk;   530
Enter and rest thee there a space,
Wrap in my plaid thy limbs, thy face.
I will not be, believe me, far,
But must not quit the ranks of war.
Well will I mark the bosky bourne,
And soon, to guard thee hence, return. —
Nay, weep not so, thou simple boy !
But sleep in peace and wake in joy.'
In sylvan lodging close bestowed,
He placed the page and onward strode 540
With strength put forth o'er moss and
    brook,
And soon the marching band o'ertook.

XXII

Thus strangely left, long sobbed and wept
The page till wearied out he slept —
A rough voice waked his dream — ' Nay,
    here,
Here by this thicket passed the deer —
Beneath that oak old Ryno staid —
What have we here ? — A Scottish plaid
And in its folds a stripling laid ? —
Come forth ! thy name and business
    tell !   550
What, silent ? — then I guess thee well,
The spy that sought old Cuthbert's cell,
Wafted from Arran yester morn —
Come, comrades, we will straight return.
Our lord may choose the rack should teach
To this young lurcher use of speech.
Thy bow-string, till I bind him fast.' —
' Nay, but he weeps and stands aghast;
Unbound we 'll lead him, fear it not;
'T is a fair stripling, though a Scot.' 560
The hunters to the castle sped,
And there the hapless captive led.

XXIII

Stout Clifford in the castle-court
Prepared him for the morning sport;
And now with Lorn held deep discourse,
Now gave command for hound and horse.
War-steeds and palfreys pawed the ground,
And many a deer-dog howled around.
To Amadine Lorn's well-known word
Replying to that Southern lord,   570
Mixed with this clanging din, might seem
The phantasm of a fevered dream.
The tone upon his ringing ears
Came like the sounds which fancy hears
When in rude waves or roaring winds
Some words of woe the muser finds,
Until more loudly and more near
Their speech arrests the page's ear.

XXIV

'And was she thus,' said Clifford, 'lost ?
The priest should rue it to his cost !   580
What says the monk ?' — 'The holy sire
Owns that in masquer's quaint attire
She sought his skiff disguised, unknown
To all except to him alone.
But, says the priest, a bark from Lorn
Laid them aboard that very morn,
And pirates seized her for their prey.
He proffered ransom gold to pay
And they agreed — but ere told o'er,
The winds blow loud, the billows roar;   590
They severed and they met no more.
He deems — such tempests vexed the
    coast —
Ship, crew, and fugitive were lost.
So let it be, with the disgrace
And scandal of her lofty race !
Thrice better she had ne'er been born
Than brought her infamy on Lorn !'

XXV

Lord Clifford now the captive spied; —
'Whom, Herbert, hast thou there ?' he
    cried.
'A spy we seized within the Chase,   600
A hollow oak his lurking-place.' —
'What tidings can the youth afford ?' —
'He plays the mute.' — 'Then noose a
    cord —
Unless brave Lorn reverse the doom
For his plaid's sake.' — 'Clan - Colla's
    loom,'
Said Lorn, whose careless glances trace
Rather the vesture than the face,

'Clan-Colla's dames such tartans twine;
Wearer nor plaid claims care of mine.
Give him, if my advice you crave,   610
His own scathed oak; and let him wave
In air unless, by terror wrung,
A frank confession find his tongue. —
Nor shall he die without his rite;
Thou, Angus Roy, attend the sight,
And give Clan-Colla's dirge thy breath
As they convey him to his death.' —
'O brother ! cruel to the last !'
Through the poor captive's bosom passed
The thought, but, to his purpose true,   620
He said not, though he sighed, 'Adieu !'

XXVI

And will he keep his purpose still
In sight of that last closing ill,
When one poor breath, one single word,
May freedom, safety, life, afford ?
Can he resist the instinctive call
For life that bids us barter all ? —
Love, strong as death, his heart hath
    steeled,
His nerves hath strung — he will not
    yield !
Since that poor breath, that little word, 630
May yield Lord Ronald to the sword. —
Clan-Colla's dirge is pealing wide,
The griesly headsman's by his side;
Along the greenwood Chase they bend,
And now their march has ghastly end !
That old and shattered oak beneath,
They destine for the place of death.
What thoughts are his, while all in vain
His eye for aid explores the plain ?
What thoughts, while with a dizzy ear   640
He hears the death-prayer muttered near ?
And must he die such death accurst,
Or will that bosom-secret burst ?
Cold on his brow breaks terror's dew,
His trembling lips are livid blue;
The agony of parting life
Has nought to match that moment's strife !

XXVII

But other witnesses are nigh,
Who mock at fear, and death defy !
Soon as the dire lament was played   650
It waked the lurking ambuscade.
The Island Lord looked forth and spied
The cause, and loud in fury cried,
'By Heaven, they lead the page to die,
And mock me in his agony !
They shall aby it !' — On his arm

Bruce laid strong grasp, 'They shall not
    harm
A ringlet of the stripling's hair;
But till I give the word forbear. —
Douglas, lead fifty of our force   660
Up yonder hollow water-course,
And couch thee midway on the wold,
Between the flyers and their hold:
A spear above the copse displayed,
Be signal of the ambush made. —
Edward, with forty spearmen straight
Through yonder copse approach the gate,
And when thou hear'st the battle-din
Rush forward and the passage win,
Secure the drawbridge, storm the port, 670
And man and guard the castle-court. —
The rest move slowly forth with me,
In shelter of the forest-tree,
Till Douglas at his post I see.'

XXVIII

Like war-horse eager to rush on,
Compelled to wait the signal blown,
Hid, and scarce hid, by greenwood bough,
Trembling with rage stands Ronald now,
And in his grasp his sword gleams blue,
Soon to be dyed with deadlier hue. — 680
Meanwhile the Bruce with steady eye
Sees the dark death-train moving by,
And heedful measures oft the space
The Douglas and his band must trace,
Ere they can reach their destined ground.
Now sinks the dirge's wailing sound,
Now cluster round the direful tree
That slow and solemn company,
While hymn mistuned and muttered
    prayer
The victim for his fate prepare. — 690
What glances o'er the greenwood shade ?
The spear that marks the ambuscade ! —
'Now, noble chief ! I leave thee loose;
Upon them, Ronald !' said the Bruce.

XXIX

'The Bruce ! the Bruce !' to well-known
    cry
His native rocks and woods reply.
'The Bruce ! the Bruce !' in that dread
    word
The knell of hundred deaths was heard.
The astonished Southern gazed at first
Where the wild tempest was to burst 700
That waked in that presaging name.
Before, behind, around it came !
Half-armed, surprised, on every side

Hemmed in, hewed down, they bled and
    died.
Deep in the ring the Bruce engaged,
And fierce Clan-Colla's broadsword raged !
Full soon the few who fought were sped,
Nor better was their lot who fled
And met mid terror's wild career
The Douglas's redoubted spear ! 710
Two hundred yeomen on that morn
The castle left, and none return.

XXX

Not on their flight pressed Ronald's brand,
A gentler duty claimed his hand.
He raised the page where on the plain
His fear had sunk him with the slain:
And twice that morn surprise well near
Betrayed the secret kept by fear;
Once when with life returning came
To the boy's lip Lord Ronald's name, 720
And hardly recollection drowned
The accents in a murmuring sound;
And once when scarce he could resist
The chieftain's care to loose the vest
Drawn tightly o'er his laboring breast.
But then the Bruce's bugle blew,
For martial work was yet to do.

XXXI

A harder task fierce Edward waits.
Ere signal given the castle gates
    His fury had assailed; 730
Such was his wonted reckless mood,
Yet desperate valor oft made good,
Even by its daring, venture rude
    Where prudence might have failed.
Upon the bridge his strength he threw,
And struck the iron chain in two,
    By which its planks arose;
The warder next his axe's edge
Struck down upon the threshold ledge,
'Twixt door and post a ghastly wedge ! 740
    The gate they may not close.
Well fought the Southern in the fray,
Clifford and Lorn fought well that day,
But stubborn Edward forced his way
    Against a hundred foes.
Loud came the cry, 'The Bruce ! the
    Bruce !'
No hope or in defence or truce, —
    Fresh combatants pour in;
Mad with success and drunk with gore,
They drive the struggling foe before 750
    And ward on ward they win.
Unsparing was the vengeful sword,

And limbs were lopped and life - blood
    poured,
The cry of death and conflict roared,
    And fearful was the din !
The startling horses plunged and flung,
The clamored the dogs till turrets rung,
    Nor sunk the fearful cry
Till not a foeman was there found
Alive save those who on the ground   760
    Groaned in their agony !

XXXII

The valiant Clifford is no more;
On Ronald's broadsword streamed his gore.
But better hap had he of Lorn,
Who, by the foeman backward borne,
Yet gained with slender train the port
Where lay his bark beneath the fort,
    And cut the cable loose.
Short were his shrift in that debate,
That hour of fury and of fate,   770
    If Lorn encountered Bruce !
Then long and loud the victor shout
From turret and from tower rung out,
    The rugged vaults replied;
And from the donjon tower on high
The men of Carrick may descry
Saint Andrew's cross in blazonry
    Of silver waving wide !

XXXIII

The Bruce hath won his father's hall ! —
' Welcome, brave friends and comrades all,
    Welcome to mirth and joy !   781
The first, the last, is welcome here,
From lord and chieftain, prince and peer,
    To this poor speechless boy.
Great God ! once more my sire's abode
Is mine — behold the floor I trode
    In tottering infancy !
And there the vaulted arch whose sound
Echoed my joyous shout and bound
In boyhood, and that rung around   790
    To youth's unthinking glee !
O, first to thee, all-gracious Heaven,
Then to my friends, my thanks be
    given ! ' —
He paused a space, his brow he crossed —
Then on the board his sword he tossed,
Yet steaming hot; with Southern gore
From hilt to point 't was crimsoned o'er.

XXXIV

' Bring here,' he said, ' the mazers four
My noble fathers loved of yore.

Thrice let them circle round the board,   800
The pledge, fair Scotland's rights re-
    stored !
And he whose lip shall touch the wine
Without a vow as true as mine,
To hold both lands and life at nought
Until her freedom shall be bought, —
Be brand of a disloyal Scot
And lasting infamy his lot !
Sit, gentle friends ! our hour of glee
Is brief, we 'll spend it joyously !
Blithest of all the sun's bright beams,   810
When betwixt storm and storm he gleams.
Well is our country's work begun,
But more, far more, must yet be done.
Speed messengers the country through;
Arouse old friends and gather new;
Warn Lanark's knights to gird their mail,
Rouse the brave sons of Teviotdale,
Let Ettrick's archers sharp their darts,
The fairest forms, the truest hearts !
Call all, call all ! from Reedswair-Path   820
To the wild confines of Cape-Wrath;
Wide let the news through Scotland
    ring, —
The Northern Eagle claps his wing ! '

CANTO SIXTH

I

O who that shared them ever shall for-
    get
The emotions of the spirit-rousing time,
When breathless in the mart the couriers
    met
Early and late, at evening and at prime;
When the loud cannon and the merry
    chime
Hailed news on news, as field on field was
    won,
When Hope, long doubtful, soared at
    length sublime,
And our glad eyes, awake as day be-
    gun,
Watched Joy's broad banner rise to meet
    the rising sun !

O these were hours when thrilling joy
    repaid   10
A long, long course of darkness, doubts,
    and fears !
The heart-sick faintness of the hope de-
    layed,

The waste, the woe, the bloodshed, and
 the tears,
That tracked with terror twenty rolling
 years,
All was forgot in that blithe jubilee !
Her downcast eye even pale Affliction
 rears,
To sigh a thankful prayer amid the
 glee
That hailed the Despot's fall, and peace
 and liberty !

Such news o'er Scotland's hills trium-
 phant rode
When 'gainst the invaders turned the
 battle's scale,   20
When Bruce's banner had victorious
 flowed
O'er Loudoun's mountain and in Ury's
 vale;
When English blood oft deluged Doug-
 las-dale,
And fiery Edward routed stout Saint
 John,
When Randolph's war-cry swelled the
 southern gale,
And many a fortress, town, and tower
 was won,
And Fame still sounded forth fresh deeds
 of glory done.

II

Blithe tidings flew from baron's tower
To peasant's cot, to forest-bower,
And waked the solitary cell   30
Where lone Saint Bride's recluses dwell.
Princess no more, fair Isabel,
 A votaress of the order now,
Say, did the rule that bid thee wear
Dim veil and woollen scapulare,
And reft thy locks of dark-brown hair,
 That stern and rigid vow,
Did it condemn the transport high
Which glistened in thy watery eye
When minstrel or when palmer told 40
Each fresh exploit of Bruce the bold ? —
And whose the lovely form that shares
Thy anxious hopes, thy fears, thy prayers ?
No sister she of convent shade;
So say these locks in lengthened braid,
So say the blushes and the sighs,
The tremors that unbidden rise,
When, mingled with the Bruce's fame,
The brave Lord Ronald's praises came.

III

Believe, his father's castle won 50
And his bold enterprise begun,
That Bruce's earliest cares restore
The speechless page to Arran's shore:
Nor think that long the quaint disguise
Concealed her from a sister's eyes;
And sister-like in love they dwell
In that lone convent's silent cell.
There Bruce's slow assent allows
Fair Isabel the veil and vows;
And there, her sex's dress regained, 60
The lovely Maid of Lorn remained,
Unnamed, unknown, while Scotland far
Resounded with the din of war;
And many a month and many a day
In calm seclusion wore away.

IV

These days, these months, to years had
 worn
When tidings of high weight were borne
 To that lone island's shore;
Of all the Scottish conquests made
By the First Edward's ruthless blade 70
 His son retained no more,
Northward of Tweed, but Stirling's tow-
 ers,
Beleaguered by King Robert's powers;
 And they took term of truce,
If England's King should not relieve
The siege ere John the Baptist's eve,
 To yield them to the Bruce.
England was roused — on every side
Courier and post and herald hied
 To summon prince and peer, 80
At Berwick-bounds to meet their liege,
Prepared to raise fair Stirling's siege
 With buckler, brand, and spear.
The term was nigh — they mustered fast,
By beacon and by bugle-blast
 Forth marshalled for the field;
There rode each knight of noble name,
There England's hardy archers came,
The land they trode seemed all on flame
 With banner, blade, and shield ! 90
And not famed England's powers alone,
Renowned in arms, the summons own;
 For Neustria's knights obeyed,
Gascogne hath lent her horsemen good,
And Cambria, but of late subdued,
Sent forth her mountain-multitude,
And Connoght poured from waste and
 wood

Her hundred tribes, whose sceptre rude
Dark Eth O'Connor swayed.

V

Right to devoted Caledon   100
The storm of war rolls slowly on
  With menace deep and dread;
So the dark clouds with gathering power
Suspend awhile the threatened shower,
Till every peak and summit lower
  Round the pale pilgrim's head.
Not with such pilgrim's startled eye
King Robert marked the tempest nigh !
  Resolved the brunt to bide,
His royal summons warned the land   110
That all who owned their king's command
Should instant take the spear and brand
  To combat at his side.
O, who may tell the sons of fame
That at King Robert's bidding came
  To battle for the right !
From Cheviot to the shores of Ross,
From Solway-Sands to Marshal's-Moss,
  All bouned them for the fight.
Such news the royal courier tells   120
Who came to rouse dark Arran's dells;
But farther tidings must the ear
Of Isabel in secret hear.
These in her cloister walk next morn
Thus shared she with the Maid of Lorn: —

VI

' My Edith, can I tell how dear
Our intercourse of hearts sincere
  Hath been to Isabel ? —
Judge then the sorrow of my heart
When I must say the words, We part !   130
  The cheerless convent-cell
Was not, sweet maiden, made for thee;
Go thou where thy vocation free
  On happier fortunes fell.
Nor, Edith, judge thyself betrayed,
Though Robert knows that Lorn's high
      maid
And his poor silent page were one.
Versed in the fickle heart of man,
Earnest and anxious hath he looked   139
How Ronald's heart the message brooked
That gave him with her last farewell
The charge of Sister Isabel,
To think upon thy better right
And keep the faith his promise plight.
Forgive him for thy sister's sake
At first if vain repinings wake —
  Long since that mood is gone:

Now dwells he on thy juster claims,
And oft his breach of faith he blames —
  Forgive him for thine own ! ' —   150

VII

' No ! never to Lord Ronald's bower
Will I again as paramour ' —
' Nay, hush thee, too impatient maid,
Until my final tale be said ! —
The good King Robert would engage
Edith once more his elfin page,
By her own heart and her own eye
Her lover's penitence to try —
Safe in his royal charge and free,
Should such thy final purpose be,   160
Again unknown to seek the cell,
And live and die with Isabel.'
Thus spoke the maid — King Robert's eye
Might have some glance of policy;
Dunstaffnage had the monarch ta'en,
And Lorn had owned King Robert's reign;
Her brother had to England fled,
And there in banishment was dead;
Ample, through exile, death, and flight,
O'er tower and land was Edith's right;   170
This ample right o'er tower and land
Were safe in Ronald's faithful hand.

VIII

Embarrassed eye and blushing cheek
Pleasure and shame and fear bespeak !
Yet much the reasoning Edith made:
' Her sister's faith she must upbraid,
Who gave such secret, dark and dear,
In council to another's ear.
Why should she leave the peaceful cell ? —
How should she part with Isabel ? —   180
How wear that strange attire agen ? —
How risk herself midst martial men ? —
And how be guarded on the way ? —
At least she might entreat delay.'
Kind Isabel with secret smile
Saw and forgave the maiden's wile,
Reluctant to be thought to move
At the first call of truant love.

IX

O, blame her not ! — when zephyrs wake   189
The aspen's trembling leaves must shake;
When beams the sun through April's
      shower
It needs must bloom, the violet flower;
And Love, howe'er the maiden strive,
Must with reviving hope revive !
A thousand soft excuses came

To plead his cause 'gainst virgin shame.
Pledged by their sires in earliest youth,
He had her plighted faith and truth —
Then, 't was her liege's strict command,
And she beneath his royal hand   200
A ward in person and in land: —
And, last, she was resolved to stay
Only brief space — one little day —
Close hidden in her safe disguise
From all, but most from Ronald's eyes —
But once to see him more ! — nor blame
Her wish — to hear him name her name ! —
Then to bear back to solitude
The thought he had his falsehood rued !
But Isabel, who long had seen   210
Her pallid cheek and pensive mien,
And well herself the cause might know,
Though innocent, of Edith's woe,
Joyed, generous, that revolving time
Gave means to expiate the crime.
High glowed her bosom as she said,
' Well shall her sufferings be repaid ! '
Now came the parting hour — a band
From Arran's mountains left the land;
Their chief, Fitz-Louis, had the care   220
The speechless Amadine to bear
To Bruce with honor, as behoved
To page the monarch dearly loved.

X

The king had deemed the maiden bright
Should reach him long before the fight,
But storms and fate her course delay:
It was on eve of battle-day
When o'er the Gillie's-hill she rode.
The landscape like a furnace glowed,
And far as e'er the eye was borne   230
The lances waved like autumn-corn.
In battles four beneath their eye
The forces of King Robert lie.
And one below the hill was laid,
Reserved for rescue and for aid;
And three advanced formed vaward-line,
'Twixt Bannock's brook and Ninian's shrine.
Detached was each, yet each so nigh
As well might mutual aid supply.
Beyond, the Southern host appears,   240
A boundless wilderness of spears,
Whose verge or rear the anxious eye
Strove far, but strove in vain, to spy.
Thick flashing in the evening beam,
Glaives, lances, bills, and banners gleam;
And where the heaven joined with the hill,
Was distant armor flashing still,
So wide, so far, the boundless host
Seemed in the blue horizon lost.

XI

Down from the hill the maiden passed,   250
At the wild show of war aghast;
And traversed first the rearward host,
Reserved for aid where needed most.
The men of Carrick and of Ayr,
Lennox and Lanark too, were there,
    And all the western land;
With these the valiant of the Isles
Beneath their chieftains ranked their files
    In many a plaided band.
There in the centre proudly raised,   260
The Bruce's royal standard blazed,
And there Lord Ronald's banner bore
A galley driven by sail and oar.
A wild yet pleasing contrast made
Warriors in mail and plate arrayed
With the plumed bonnet and the plaid
    By these Hebrideans worn;
But O, unseen for three long years,
Dear was the garb of mountaineers
    To the fair Maid of Lorn !   270
For one she looked — but he was far
Busied amid the ranks of war —
Yet with affection's troubled eye
She marked his banner boldly fly,
Gave on the countless foe a glance,
And thought on battle's desperate chance.

XII

To centre of the vaward-line
Fitz-Louis guided Amadine.
Armed all on foot, that host appears
A serried mass of glimmering spears.   280
There stood the Marchers' warlike band,
The warriors there of Lodon's land;
Ettrick and Liddell bent the yew,
A band of archers fierce though few;
The men of Nith and Annan's vale,
And the bold Spears of Teviotdale; —
The dauntless Douglas these obey,
And the young Stuart's gentle sway.
Northeastward by Saint Ninian's shrine,
Beneath fierce Randolph's charge, com-   290
    bine
The warriors whom the hardy North
From Tay to Sutherland sent forth.
The rest of Scotland's war-array
With Edward Bruce to westward lay,
Where Bannock with his broken bank
And deep ravine protects their flank.
Behind them, screened by sheltering wood,
The gallant Keith, Lord Marshal, stood:
His men-at-arms bare mace and lance,
And plumes that wave and helms that
    glance.   300

Thus fair divided by the king,
Centre and right and leftward wing
Composed his front; nor distant far
Was strong reserve to aid the war.
And 't was to front of this array
Her guide and Edith made their way.

XIII

Here must they pause; for, in advance
As far as one might pitch a lance,
The monarch rode along the van,
The foe's approaching force to scan,   310
His line to marshal and to range,
And ranks to square, and fronts to change.
Alone he rode — from head to heel
Sheathed in his ready arms of steel;
Nor mounted yet on war-horse wight,
But, till more near the shock of fight,
Reining a palfrey low and light.
A diadem of gold was set
Above his bright steel basinet,
And clasped within its glittering twine   320
Was seen the glove of Argentine;
Truncheon or leading staff he lacks,
Bearing instead a battle-axe.
He ranged his soldiers for the fight
Accoutred thus, in open sight
Of either host. — Three bowshots far,
Paused the deep front of England's war,
And rested on their arms awhile,
To close and rank their warlike file,
And hold high council if that night   330
Should view the strife or dawning light.

XIV

O, gay yet fearful to behold,
Flashing with steel and rough with gold,
    And bristled o'er with bills and spears,
With plumes and pennons waving fair,
Was that bright battle-front ! for there
    Rode England's king and peers:
And who, that saw that monarch ride,
His kingdom battled by his side,
Could then his direful doom foretell ! —   340
Fair was his seat in knightly selle,
And in his sprightly eye was set
Some spark of the Plantagenet.
Though light and wandering was his
    glance,
It flashed at sight of shield and lance.
'Know'st thou,' he said, 'De Argentine,
Yon knight who marshals thus their
    line ? ' —
'The tokens on his helmet tell
The Bruce, my liege: I know him well.' —

'And shall the audacious traitor brave   350
The presence where our banners wave ? ' —
'So please my liege,' said Argentine,
'Were he but horsed on steed like mine,
To give him fair and knightly chance,
I would adventure forth my lance.' —
'In battle-day,' the king replied,
'Nice tourney rules are set aside. —
Still must the rebel dare our wrath ?
Set on him — Sweep him from our path ! '
And at King Edward's signal soon   360
Dashed from the ranks Sir Henry Boune.

XV

Of Hereford's high blood he came,
A race renowned for knightly fame.
He burned before his monarch's eye
To do some deed of chivalry.
He spurred his steed, he couched his lance,
And darted on the Bruce at once.
As motionless as rocks that bide
The wrath of the advancing tide,
The Bruce stood fast. — Each breast beat
    high   370
And dazzled was each gazing eye —
The heart had hardly time to think,
The eyelid scarce had time to wink,
While on the king, like flash of flame,
Spurred to full speed the war-horse came !
The partridge may the falcon mock,
If that slight palfrey stand the shock —
But, swerving from the knight's career,
Just as they met, Bruce shunned the spear.
Onward the baffled warrior bore   380
His course — but soon his course was
    o'er ! —
High in his stirrups stood the king,
And gave his battle-axe the swing.
Right on De Boune the whiles he passed
Fell that stern dint — the first — the
    last ! —
Such strength upon the blow was put
The helmet crashed like hazel-nut;
The axe-shaft with its brazen clasp
Was shivered to the gauntlet grasp.
Springs from the blow the startled
    horse,   390
Drops to the plain the lifeless corse;
First of that fatal field, how soon,
How sudden, fell the fierce De Boune !

XVI

One pitying glance the monarch sped
Where on the field his foe lay dead;
Then gently turned his palfrey's head,

And, pacing back his sober way,
Slowly he gained his own array.
There round their king the leaders crowd,
And blame his recklessness aloud   400
That risked 'gainst each adventurous
          spear
A life so valued and so dear.
His broken weapon's shaft surveyed
The king, and careless answer made,
' My loss may pay my folly's tax;
I 've broke my trusty battle-axe.'
'T was then Fitz-Louis bending low
Did Isabel's commission show;
Edith disguised at distance stands,
And hides her blushes with her hands.   410
The monarch's brow has changed its
          hue,
Away the gory axe he threw,
While to the seeming page he drew,
    Clearing war's terrors from his eye.
Her hand with gentle ease he took
With such a kind protecting look
    As to a weak and timid boy
Might speak that elder brother's care
And elder brother's love were there.

XVII

' Fear not,' he said, ' young Amadine !'   420
Then whispered, ' Still that name be thine.
Fate plays her wonted fantasy,
Kind Amadine, with thee and me,
And sends thee here in doubtful hour.
But soon we are beyond her power;
For on this chosen battle-plain,
Victor or vanquished, I remain.
Do thou to yonder hill repair;
The followers of our host are there,
And all who may not weapons bear. —   430
Fitz-Louis, have him in thy care. —
Joyful we meet, if all go well;
If not, in Arran's holy cell
Thou must take part with Isabel;
For brave Lord Ronald too hath sworn,
Not to regain the Maid of Lorn —
The bliss on earth he covets most —
Would he forsake his battle-post,
Or shun the fortune that may fall
To Bruce, to Scotland, and to all. —   440
But, hark ! some news these trumpets
          tell;
Forgive my haste — farewell ! — fare-
          well !'
And in a lower voice he said,
' Be of good cheer — farewell, sweet
          maid !'

XVIII

' What train of dust, with trumpet-sound
And glimmering spears, is wheeling round
Our leftward flank ? ' — the monarch cried
To Moray's Earl who rode beside.
' Lo ! round thy station pass the foes !
Randolph, thy wreath hath lost a rose.'   450
The Earl his visor closed, and said
' My wreath shall bloom, or life shall
          fade. —
Follow, my household !' and they go
Like lightning on the advancing foe.
' My liege,' said noble Douglas then,
' Earl Randolph has but one to ten:
Let me go forth his band to aid !' —
' Stir not. The error he hath made,
Let him amend it as he may;
I will not weaken mine array.'   460
Then loudly rose the conflict-cry,
And Douglas's brave heart swelled high, —
'My liege,' he said, ' with patient ear
I must not Moray's death-knell hear !' —
'Then go — but speed thee back again.'
Forth sprung the Douglas with his train:
But when they won a rising hill
He bade his followers hold them still. —
' See, see ! the routed Southern fly !
The Earl hath won the victory.   470
Lo ! where yon steeds run masterless,
His banner towers above the press.
Rein up; our presence would impair
The fame we come too late to share.'
Back to the host the Douglas rode,
And soon glad tidings are abroad
That, Dayncourt by stout Randolph slain,
His followers fled with loosened rein. —
That skirmish closed the busy day,
And couched in battle's prompt array,   480
Each army on their weapons lay.

XIX

It was a night of lovely June,
High rode in cloudless blue the moon,
    Demayet smiled beneath her ray;
Old Stirling's towers arose in light,
And, twined in links of silver bright,
    Her winding river lay.
Ah ! gentle planet ! other sight
Shall greet thee, next returning night,
Of broken arms and banners tore,   490
And marshes dark with human gore,
And piles of slaughtered men and horse,
And Forth that floats the frequent corse,
And many a wounded wretch to plain
Beneath thy silver light in vain !

But now from England's host the cry
Thou hear'st of wassail revelry,
While from the Scottish legions pass
The murmured prayer, the early mass ! —
Here, numbers had presumption given; 500
There, bands o'ermatched sought aid from
     Heaven.

XX

On Gillie's-hill, whose height commands
The battle-field, fair Edith stands
With serf and page unfit for war,
To eye the conflict from afar.
O, with what doubtful agony
She sees the dawning tint the sky ! —
Now on the Ochils gleams the sun,
And glistens now Demayet dun;
   Is it the lark that carols shrill,   510
      Is it the bittern's early hum ?
   No ! — distant but increasing still,
   The trumpet's sound swells up the
      hill,
      With the deep murmur of the drum.
Responsive from the Scottish host,
Pipe-clang and bugle-sound were tossed,
His breast and brow each soldier crossed
   And started from the ground;
Armed and arrayed for instant fight,   519
Rose archer, spearman, squire and knight,
And in the pomp of battle bright
   The dread battalia frowned.

XXI

Now onward and in open view
The countless ranks of England drew,
Dark rolling like the ocean-tide
When the rough west hath chafed his
   pride,
And his deep roar sends challenge wide
   To all that bars his way !
In front the gallant archers trode,
The men-at-arms behind them rode,   530
And midmost of the phalanx broad
   The monarch held his sway.
Beside him many a war-horse fumes,
Around him waves a sea of plumes,
Where many a knight in battle known,
And some who spurs had first braced on
And deemed that fight should see them
   won,
   King Edward's hests obey.
De Argentine attends his side,   539
With stout De Valence, Pembroke's pride,
Selected champions from the train
To wait upon his bridle-rein.

Upon the Scottish foe he gazed —
At once before his sight amazed
   Sunk banner, spear, and shield;
Each weapon-point is downward sent,
Each warrior to the ground is bent.
'The rebels, Argentine, repent !
   For pardon they have kneeled.' —
'Ay ! — but they bend to other powers,   550
And other pardon sue than ours !
See where yon barefoot abbot stands
And blesses them with lifted hands !
Upon the spot where they have kneeled
These men will die or win the field.' —
'Then prove we if they die or win !
Bid Gloster's Earl the fight begin.'

XXII

Earl Gilbert waved his truncheon high
   Just as the Northern ranks arose,
Signal for England's archery   560
   To halt and bend their bows.
Then stepped each yeoman forth a pace,
Glanced at the intervening space,
   And raised his left hand high;
To the right ear the cords they bring —
At once ten thousand bow-strings ring,
   Ten thousand arrows fly !
Nor paused on the devoted Scot
The ceaseless fury of their shot;
   As fiercely and as fast   570
Forth whistling came the gray-goose wing
As the wild hailstones pelt and ring
   Adown December's blast.
Nor mountain targe of tough bull-hide,
Nor lowland mail, that storm may bide;
Woe, woe to Scotland's bannered pride,
   If the fell shower may last !
Upon the right behind the wood,
Each by his steed dismounted stood
   The Scottish chivalry; —   580
With foot in stirrup, hand on mane,
Fierce Edward Bruce can scarce restrain
His own keen heart, his eager train,
Until the archers gained the plain;
   Then, ' Mount, ye gallants free ! '
He cried; and vaulting from the ground
His saddle every horseman found.
On high their glittering crests they toss,
As springs the wild-fire from the moss;
The shield hangs down on every breast,   590
   Each ready lance is in the rest,
      And loud shouts Edward Bruce,
' Forth, Marshal ! on the peasant foe !
We 'll tame the terrors of their bow,
      And cut the bow-string loose ! '

XXIII

Then spurs were dashed in chargers'
 flanks,
They rushed among the archer ranks,
No spears were there the shock to let,
No stakes to turn the charge were set,
And how shall yeoman's armor slight 600
Stand the long lance and mace of might?
Or what may their short swords avail
'Gainst barbed horse and shirt of mail?
Amid their ranks the chargers sprung,
High o'er their heads the weapons swung,
And shriek and groan and vengeful shout
Give note of triumph and of rout!
Awhile with stubborn hardihood
Their English hearts the strife made good.
Borne down at length on every side, 610
Compelled to flight they scatter wide. —
Let stags of Sherwood leap for glee,
And bound the deer of Dallom-Lee!
The broken vows of Bannock's shore
Shall in the greenwood ring no more!
Round Wakefield's merry May-pole now
The maids may twine the summer bough,
May northward look with longing glance
For those that wont to lead the dance,
For the blithe archers look in vain! 620
Broken, dispersed, in flight o'erta'en,
Pierced through, trode down, by thousands
 slain,
They cumber Bannock's bloody plain.

XXIV

The king with scorn beheld their flight.
'Are these,' he said, 'our yeomen wight?
Each braggart churl could boast before
Twelve Scottish lives his baldric bore!
Fitter to plunder chase or park
Than make a manly foe their mark. —
Forward, each gentleman and knight! 630
Let gentle blood show generous might
And chivalry redeem the fight!'
To rightward of the wild affray,
The field showed fair and level way;
 But in mid-space the Bruce's care
Had bored the ground with many a pit,
With turf and brushwood hidden yet,
 That formed a ghastly snare.
Rushing, ten thousand horsemen came,
With spears in rest and hearts on flame 640
 That panted for the shock!
With blazing crests and banners spread,
And trumpet-clang and clamor dread,
The wide plain thundered to their tread
 As far as Stirling rock.

Down! down! in headlong overthrow,
Horseman and horse, the foremost go,
 Wild floundering on the field!
The first are in destruction's gorge,
Their followers wildly o'er them
 urge; — 650
The knightly helm and shield,
The mail, the acton, and the spear,
Strong hand, high heart, are useless here!
Loud from the mass confused the cry
Of dying warriors swells on high,
And steeds that shriek in agony!
They came like mountain-torrent red
That thunders o'er its rocky bed;
They broke like that same torrent's wave
When swallowed by a darksome cave. 660
Billows on billows burst and boil,
Maintaining still the stern turmoil,
And to their wild and tortured groan
Each adds new terrors of his own!

XXV

Too strong in courage and in might
Was England yet to yield the fight.
 Her noblest all are here;
Names that to fear were never known,
Bold Norfolk's Earl De Brotherton,
 And Oxford's famed De Vere. 670
There Gloster plied the bloody sword,
And Berkley, Grey, and Hereford,
 Bottetourt and Sanzavere,
Ross, Montague, and Mauley came,
And Courtenay's pride, and Percy's fame —
Names known too well in Scotland's war
At Falkirk, Methven, and Dunbar,
Blazed broader yet in after years
At Cressy red and fell Poitiers.
Pembroke with these and Argentine 680
Brought up the rearward battle-line.
With caution o'er the ground they tread,
Slippery with blood and piled with dead,
Till hand to hand in battle set,
The bills with spears and axes met,
And, closing dark on every side,
Raged the full contest far and wide.
Then was the strength of Douglas tried,
Then proved was Randolph's generous
 pride,
And well did Stewart's actions grace 690
The sire of Scotland's royal race!
 Firmly they kept their ground;
As firmly England onward pressed,
And down went many a noble crest,
And rent was many a valiant breast,
 And Slaughter revelled round.

XXVI

Unflinching foot 'gainst foot was set,
Unceasing blow by blow was met;
　The groans of those who fell
Were drowned amid the shriller clang　700
That from the blades and harness rang,
　And in the battle-yell.
Yet fast they fell, unheard, forgot,
Both Southern fierce and hardy Scot;
And O, amid that waste of life
What various motives fired the strife !
The aspiring noble bled for fame,
The patriot for his country's claim;
This knight his youthful strength to prove,
And that to win his lady's love:　710
Some fought from ruffian thirst of blood,
From habit some or hardihood.
But ruffian stern and soldier good,
　The noble and the slave,
From various cause the same wild road,
On the same bloody morning, trode
　To that dark inn, the grave !

XXVII

The tug of strife to flag begins,
Though neither loses yet nor wins.
High rides the sun, thick rolls the dust,　720
And feebler speeds the blow and thrust.
Douglas leans on his war-sword now,
And Randolph wipes his bloody brow;
Nor less had toiled each Southern knight
From morn till mid-day in the fight.
Strong Egremont for air must gasp,
Beauchamp undoes his visor-clasp,
And Montague must quit his spear,
And sinks thy falchion, bold De Vere !
The blows of Berkley fall less fast,　730
And gallant Pembroke's bugle-blast
　Hath lost its lively tone;
Sinks, Argentine, thy battle-word,
And Percy's shout was fainter heard, —
　' My merry-men, fight on ! '

XXVIII

Bruce, with the pilot's wary eye,
The slackening of the storm could spy.
' One effort more and Scotland 's free !
Lord of the Isles, my trust in thee
　Is firm as Ailsa Rock;　740
Rush on with Highland sword and targe,
I with my Carrick spearmen charge;
　Now forward to the shock ! '
At once the spears were forward thrown,
Against the sun the broadswords shone;
The pibroch lent its maddening tone,

And loud King Robert's voice was
　known —
' Carrick, press on — they fail, they fail !
Press on, brave sons of Innisgail,
　The foe is fainting fast !　750
Each strike for parent, child, and wife,
For Scotland, liberty, and life, —
　The battle cannot last ! '

XXIX

The fresh and desperate onset bore
The foes three furlongs back and more,
Leaving their noblest in their gore.
Alone, De Argentine
Yet bears on high his red-cross shield,
Gathers the relics of the field,
Renews the ranks where they have
　reeled,　760
　And still makes good the line.
Brief strife but fierce his efforts raise,
A bright but momentary blaze.
Fair Edith heard the Southern shout,
Beheld them turning from the rout,
Heard the wild call their trumpets sent
In notes 'twixt triumph and lament.
That rallying force, combined anew,
Appeared in her distracted view
　To hem the Islesmen round;　770
' O God ! the combat they renew,
　And is no rescue found !
And ye that look thus tamely on,
And see your native land o'erthrown,
O, are your hearts of flesh or stone ? '

XXX

The multitude that watched afar,
Rejected from the ranks of war,
Had not unmoved beheld the fight
When strove the Bruce for Scotland's
　right;
Each heart had caught the patriot spark,　780
Old man and stripling, priest and clerk,
Bondsman and serf; even female hand
Stretched to the hatchet or the brand;
　But when mute Amadine they heard
　Give to their zeal his signal-word
　A frenzy fired the throng; —
' Portents and miracles impeach
Our sloth — the dumb our duties
　teach —
And he that gives the mute his speech
　Can bid the weak be strong.　790
To us as to our lords are given
A native earth, a promised heaven;
To us as to our lords belongs

The vengeance for our nation's wrongs;
The choice 'twixt death or freedom warms
Our breasts as theirs — To arms ! to
    arms !'
To arms they flew, — axe, club, or spear —
And mimic ensigns high they rear,
And, like a bannered host afar,
Bear down on England's wearied war.   800

XXXI

Already scattered o'er the plain,
Reproof, command, and counsel vain,
The rearward squadrons fled amain
Or made but doubtful stay; —
But when they marked the seeming show
Of fresh and fierce and marshalled foe,
    The boldest broke array.
O, give their hapless prince his due !
In vain the royal Edward threw
    His person mid the spears,   810
Cried, ' Fight !' to terror and despair,
Menaced and wept and tore his hair,
    And cursed their caitiff fears;
Till Pembroke turned his bridle rein
And forced him from the fatal plain.
With them rode Argentine until
They gained the summit of the hill,
    But quitted there the train: —
' In yonder field a gage I left,
I must not live of fame bereft;   820
    I needs must turn again.
Speed hence, my liege, for on your trace
The fiery Douglas takes the chase,
    I know his banner well.
God send my sovereign joy and bliss,
And many a happier field than this ! —
    Once more, my liege, farewell !'

XXXII

Again he faced the battle-field, —
Wildly they fly, are slain, or yield.
' Now then,' he said, and couched his
    spear,   830
' My course is run, the goal is near;
One effort more, one brave career,
    Must close this race of mine.'
Then in his stirrups rising high,
He shouted loud his battle-cry,
    ' Saint James for Argentine !'
And of the bold pursuers four
The gallant knight from saddle bore;
But not unharmed — a lance's point
Has found his breastplate's loosened
    joint,   840
    An axe has razed his crest;
Yet still on Colonsay's fierce lord,

Who pressed the chase with gory sword,
    He rode with spear in rest,
And through his bloody tartans bored
    And through his gallant breast.
Nailed to the earth, the mountaineer
Yet writhed him up against the spear,
    And swung his broadsword round !
Stirrup, steel-boot, and cuish gave way   850
Beneath that blow's tremendous sway,
    The blood gushed from the wound;
And the grim Lord of Colonsay
    Hath turned him on the ground,
And laughed in death-pang that his blade
The mortal thrust so well repaid.

XXXIII

Now toiled the Bruce, the battle done,
To use his conquest boldly won;
And gave command for horse and spear
To press the Southron's scattered rear,   860
Nor let his broken force combine,
When the war-cry of Argentine
    Fell faintly on his ear;
' Save, save his life,' he cried, ' O, save
The kind, the noble, and the brave !'
The squadrons round free passage gave,
    The wounded knight drew near;
He raised his red-cross shield no more,
Helm, cuish, and breastplate streamed with
    gore,
Yet, as he saw the king advance,   870
He strove even then to couch his lance —
    The effort was in vain!
The spur-stroke failed to rouse the horse;
Wounded and weary, in mid course
    He stumbled on the plain.
Then foremost was the generous Bruce
To raise his head, his helm to loose; —
    ' Lord Earl, the day is thine !
My sovereign's charge and adverse fate
Have made our meeting all too late;   880
    Yet this may Argentine
As boon from ancient comrade crave —
A Christian's mass, a soldier's grave.'

XXXIV

Bruce pressed his dying hand — its grasp
Kindly replied; but, in his clasp,
    It stiffened and grew cold —
' And, O farewell !' the victor cried,
' Of chivalry the flower and pride,
    The arm in battle bold,
The courteous mien, the noble race,   890
The stainless faith, the manly face ! —
Bid Ninian's convent light their shrine
For late-wake of De Argentine.

O'er better knight on death-bier laid
Torch never gleamed nor mass was said!'

XXXV

Nor for De Argentine alone
Through Ninian's church these torches
    shone
And rose the death-prayer's awful tone.
That yellow lustre glimmered pale
On broken plate and bloodied mail,   900
Rent crest and shattered coronet,
Of baron, earl, and banneret;
And the best names that England knew
Claimed in the death-prayer dismal due.
    Yet mourn not, Land of Fame!
Though ne'er the Leopards on thy shield
Retreated from so sad a field
    Since Norman William came.
Oft may thine annals justly boast
Of battles stern by Scotland lost;   910
    Grudge not her victory
When for her freeborn rights she strove;
Rights dear to all who freedom love,
    To none so dear as thee!

XXXVI

Turn we to Bruce whose curious ear
Must from Fitz-Louis tidings hear;
With him a hundred voices tell
Of prodigy and miracle,
  'For the mute page had spoke.'—
'Page!' said Fitz-Louis, 'rather say   920
An angel sent from realms of day
    To burst the English yoke.
I saw his plume and bonnet drop
When hurrying from the mountain top;
A lovely brow, dark locks that wave,
To his bright eyes new lustre gave,
A step as light upon the green,
As if his pinions waved unseen!'
'Spoke he with none?'—'With none—
    one word
Burst when he saw the Island Lord   930
Returning from the battle-field.'—
'What answer made the chief?'—'He
    kneeled,
Durst not look up, but muttered low
Some mingled sounds that none might
    know,
And greeted him 'twixt joy and fear
As being of superior sphere.'

XXVII

Even upon Bannock's bloody plain
Heaped then with thousands of the slain,

Mid victor monarch's musings high,
Mirth laughed in good King Robert's
    eye:—   940
'And bore he such angelic air,
Such noble front, such waving hair?
Hath Ronald kneeled to him?' he said;
'Then must we call the church to aid—
Our will be to the abbot known
Ere these strange news are wider blown,
To Cambuskenneth straight he pass
And deck the church for solemn mass,
To pay for high deliverance given
A nation's thanks to gracious Heaven.   950
Let him array besides such state,
As should on princes' nuptials wait.
Ourself the cause, through fortune's spite,
That once broke short that spousal rite,
Ourself will grace with early morn
The bridal of the Maid of Lorn.'

CONCLUSION

Go forth, my Song, upon thy venturous
    way;
Go boldly forth; nor yet thy master
    blame
Who chose no patron for his humble lay,
And graced thy numbers with no friendly
    name
Whose partial zeal might smooth thy path
    to fame.
There was—and O, how many sorrows
    crowd
Into these two brief words!—*there was*
    a claim
By generous friendship given—had fate
    allowed,
It well had bid thee rank the proudest of
    the proud!

All angel now—yet little less than all
While still a pilgrim in our world below!
What 'vails it us that patience to recall
Which hid its own to soothe all other
    woes;
What 'vails to tell how Virtue's purest
    glow
Shone yet more lovely in a form so fair:
And, least of all, what 'vails the world
    should know
That one poor garland, twined to deck
    thy hair,
Is hung upon thy hearse to droop and
    wither there!

THE FIELD OF WATERLOO

INTRODUCTORY NOTE

The brief Advertisement which was the sole preface Scott ever wrote to *The Field of Waterloo* intimates the circumstances under which it was written and the immediate purpose of its publication. 'It may be some apology for the imperfections of this poem, that it was composed hastily, and during a short tour upon the Continent, when the author's labors were liable to frequent interruption ; but its best apology is, that it was written for the purpose of assisting the Waterloo Subscription.'

The battle of Waterloo was fought in June, 1815, and Scott, fired by a spirited letter from one of the surgeons on the field to a brother in Edinburgh, suddenly resolved in the middle of July to go to Brussels and visit the battle-field. As an illustration of the slowness of travel at that time it may be noted that though he and his companions left Edinburgh 28 July, they did not reach Harwich till 4 August, when they hired a boat to take them to Helvoetsluys. The excursion was minutely chronicled in the prose *Paul's Letters to his Kinsfolk*, and gave rise to some animated personal letters printed by Lockhart. The poem also appears to have been begun and indeed practically completed *en route*.

Scott wrote to Mr. Morritt, under date of 2 October, 1815, the poem 'will be out this week, and you shall have a copy by the Carlisle coach, which pray judge favorably, and remember it is not always the grandest actions which are best adapted for the arts of poetry and painting. I believe I shall give offence to my old friends the Whigs, by not condoling with Buonaparte. Since his sentence of transportation, he has begun to look wonderfully comely in their eyes. I would they had hanged him, that he might have died a perfect Adonis.' Lockhart, at the close of chapter xxxv., gives a transcript of some notes written on the margin of the proof-sheets of the poem. John Ballantyne was at Abbotsford when the proof was ready, so his brother James sent the sheets to him with his own comments, and John entertained himself with recording below James's notes, the remarks which Scott made. Some of the more interesting of these points will be found in the *Notes* at the end of this volume.

The timeliness of the publication, and its manner, for it appeared in October, 1815, in a small volume, gave it immediate popularity. In writing to Lady Louisa Stuart, who had praised it enthusiastically, Scott was not disposed to be much elated by his success: 'I need hardly say,' he writes, 'that your applause is always gratifying to me, but more particularly so when it encourages me to hope I have got tolerably well out of a hazardous scrape. The Duke of Wellington himself told me there was nothing so dreadful as a battle *won* excepting only a battle *lost*. And lost or won, I can answer for it, they are almost as severe upon the bard who celebrates as the warrior who fights them. But I had committed myself in the present case, and like many a hot-headed man, had got into the midst of the fray without considering well how I was to clear myself out of it.' Scott went on in his letter to speak of the other tasks that had been employing him, concluding : ' If you ask me *why* I do these things, I would be much at a loss to give a good answer. I have been tempted to write for fame, and there have been periods when I have been compelled to write for money. Neither of these motives now exist — my fortune, though moderate, suffices my wishes, and I have heard so many blasts from the trumpet of Fame, both good and evil, that I am hardly tempted to solicit her notice anew. But the habit of throwing my ideas into rhyme is not easily conquered, and so, like Dogberry, I go on bestowing my tediousness upon the public.' The poem was issued in a cheap form and quickly surpassed in circulation both of the two long poems which were freshest in the memory of readers, *Rokeby* and *The Lord of the Isles.*

THE FIELD OF WATERLOO

Though Valois braved young Edward's gentle hand,
And Albert rushed on Henry's way-worn band,
With Europe's chosen sons, in arms renowned,
Yet not on Vere's bold archers long they looked,
Nor Audley's squires nor Mowbray's yeomen brooked, —
They saw their standard fall, and left their monarch bound.
AKENSIDE.

TO

HER GRACE

THE

DUCHESS OF WELLINGTON,

PRINCESS OF WATERLOO,

&c., &c., &c.,

THE FOLLOWING VERSES

ARE MOST RESPECTFULLY INSCRIBED BY

THE AUTHOR.

ADVERTISEMENT

It may be some apology for the imperfections of this poem, that it was composed hastily, and during a short tour upon the Continent, when the Author's labors were liable to frequent interruption; but its best apology is, that it was written for the purpose of assisting the Waterloo Subscription.
ABBOTSFORD, 1815.

I

FAIR Brussels, thou art far behind,
Though, lingering on the morning wind,
  We yet may hear the hour
Pealed over orchard and canal,
With voice prolonged and measured fall,
  From proud Saint Michael's tower;
Thy wood, dark Soignies, holds us now,
Where the tall beeches' glossy bough
  For many a league around,
With birch and darksome oak between,   10
Spreads deep and far a pathless screen
  Of tangled forest ground.
Stems planted close by stems defy
The adventurous foot — the curious eye
  For access seeks in vain;
And the brown tapestry of leaves,
Strewed on the blighted ground, receives
  Nor sun nor air nor rain.

No opening glade dawns on our way,
No streamlet glancing to the ray   20
  Our woodland path has crossed;
And the straight causeway which we tread
Prolongs a line of dull arcade,
Unvarying through the unvaried shade
  Until in distance lost.

II

A brighter, livelier scene succeeds;
In groups the scattering wood recedes,
Hedge-rows, and huts, and sunny meads,
  And corn-fields glance between;
The peasant at his labor blithe   30
Plies the hooked staff and shortened
  scythe: —
But when these ears were green,
Placed close within destruction's scope,
Full little was that rustic's hope

Their ripening to have seen!
And, lo! a hamlet and its fane: —
Let not the gazer with disdain
Their architecture view;
For yonder rude ungraceful shrine
And disproportioned spire are thine,   40
Immortal WATERLOO!

III

Fear not the heat, though full and high
The sun has scorched the autumn sky,
And scarce a forest straggler now
To shade us spreads a greenwood bough;
These fields have seen a hotter day
Than e'er was fired by sunny ray.
Yet one mile on — yon shattered hedge
Crests the soft hill whose long smooth
   ridge
  Looks on the field below,   50
And sinks so gently on the dale
That not the folds of Beauty's veil
  In easier curves can flow.
Brief space from thence the ground again
Ascending slowly from the plain
  Forms an opposing screen,
Which with its crest of upland ground
Shuts the horizon all around.
  The softened vale between
Slopes smooth and fair for courser's tread;
Not the most timid maid need dread   61
  To give her snow-white palfrey head
  On that wide stubble-ground;
Nor wood nor tree nor bush are there,
  Her course to intercept or scare,
  Nor fosse nor fence are found,
Save where from out her shattered bowers
Rise Hougomont's dismantled towers.

IV

Now, see'st thou aught in this lone scene
Can tell of that which late hath been? —   70
  A stranger might reply,
'The bare extent of stubble-plain
Seems lately lightened of its grain;
And yonder sable tracks remain
Marks of the peasant's ponderous wain
  When harvest-home was nigh.
On these broad spots of trampled ground
Perchance the rustics danced such round
  As Teniers loved to draw;
And where the earth seems scorched by
   flame,   80
To dress the homely feast they came,
And toiled the kerchiefed village dame
  Around her fire of straw.'

V

So deem'st thou — so each mortal deems
Of that which is from that which seems: —
  But other harvest here
Than that which peasant's scythe demands
Was gathered in by sterner hands,
  With bayonet, blade, and spear.
No vulgar crop was theirs to reap,   90
No stinted harvest thin and cheap!
Heroes before each fatal sweep
  Fell thick as ripened grain;
And ere the darkening of the day,
Piled high as autumn shocks there lay
The ghastly harvest of the fray,
  The corpses of the slain.

VI

Ay, look again — that line so black
And trampled marks the bivouac,   99
Yon deep-graved ruts the artillery's track,
  So often lost and won;
And close beside the hardened mud
Still shows where, fetlock-deep in blood,
The fierce dragoon through battle's flood
  Dashed the hot war-horse on.
These spots of excavation tell
The ravage of the bursting shell —
And feel'st thou not the tainted steam
That reeks against the sultry beam
  From yonder trenched mound?   110
The pestilential fumes declare
That Carnage has replenished there
  Her garner-house profound.

VII

Far other harvest-home and feast
Than claims the boor from scythe released
  On these scorched fields were known!
Death hovered o'er the maddening rout,
And in the thrilling battle-shout
Sent for the bloody banquet out
  A summons of his own.   120
Through rolling smoke the Demon's eye
Could well each destined guest espy.
Well could his ear in ecstasy
  Distinguish every tone
That filled the chorus of the fray —
From cannon-roar and trumpet-bray,
From charging squadrons' wild hurra,
From the wild clang that marked their
   way, —
  Down to the dying groan
And the last sob of life's decay   130
  When breath was all but flown.

VIII

Feast on, stern foe of mortal life,
Feast on ! — but think not that a strife
With such promiscuous carnage rife
  Protracted space may last;
The deadly tug of war at length
Must limits find in human strength,
  And cease when these are past.
Vain hope ! — that morn's o'erclouded sun
Heard the wild shout of fight begun   140
  Ere he attained his height,
And through the war-smoke volumed high
Still peals that unremitted cry,
  Though now he stoops to night.
For ten long hours of doubt and dread,
Fresh succors from the extended head
Of either hill the contest fed;
  Still down the slope they drew,
The charge of columns paused not,
Nor ceased the storm of shell and shot; 150
  For all that war could do
Of skill and force was proved that day,
And turned not yet the doubtful fray
  On bloody Waterloo.

IX

Pale Brussels ! then what thoughts were
    thine,
When ceaseless from the distant line
  Continued thunders came !
Each burgher held his breath to hear
These forerunners of havoc near,
  Of rapine and of flame.   160
What ghastly sights were thine to meet,
When, rolling through thy stately street,
The wounded showed their mangled plight
In token of the unfinished fight,
And from each anguish-laden wain
The blood-drops laid thy dust like rain !
How often in the distant drum
Heard'st thou the fell invader come,
While Ruin, shouting to his band,   169
Shook high her torch and gory brand ! —
Cheer thee, fair city ! From yon stand
Impatient still his outstretched hand
  Points to his prey in vain,
While maddening in his eager mood
And all unwont to be withstood,
  He fires the fight again.

X

' On ! On ! ' was still his stern exclaim;
' Confront the battery's jaws of flame !
  Rush on the levelled gun !

My steel-clad cuirassiers, advance !   180
Each Hulan forward with his lance,
My Guard — my chosen — charge for
    France,
  France and Napoleon ! '
Loud answered their acclaiming shout,
Greeting the mandate which sent out
Their bravest and their best to dare
The fate their leader shunned to share.
But HE, his country's sword and shield,
Still in the battle-front revealed
Where danger fiercest swept the field,   190
  Came like a beam of light,
In action prompt, in sentence brief —
' Soldiers, stand firm ! ' exclaimed the chief,
  ' England shall tell the fight ! '

XI

On came the whirlwind — like the last
But fiercest sweep of tempest-blast —
On came the whirlwind — steel - gleams
    broke
Like lightning through the rolling smoke;
  The war was waked anew,   199
Three hundred cannon-mouths roared loud,
And from their throats with flash and
    cloud
  Their showers of iron threw.
Beneath their fire in full career
Rushed on the ponderous cuirassier,
The lancer couched his ruthless spear,
And hurrying as to havoc near
  The cohorts' eagles flew.
In one dark torrent broad and strong
The advancing onset rolled along,
Forth harbingered by fierce acclaim,   210
That from the shroud of smoke and flame
Pealed wildly the imperial name.

XII

But on the British heart were lost
The terrors of the charging host;
For not an eye the storm that viewed
Changed its proud glance of fortitude,
Nor was one forward footstep staid,
As dropped the dying and the dead.
Fast as their ranks the thunders tear,   219
Fast they renewed each serried square;
And on the wounded and the slain
Closed their diminished files again,
Till from their lines scarce spears' lengths
    three
Emerging from the smoke they see
Helmet and plume and panoply —
  Then waked their fire at once !

Each musketeer's revolving knell,
As fast, as regularly fell,
As when they practise to display
Their discipline on festal day.   230
  Then down went helm and lance,
Down were the eagle banners sent,
Down reeling steeds and riders went,
Corselets were pierced and pennons rent;
  And to augment the fray,
Wheeled full against their staggering
    flanks,
The English horsemen's foaming ranks
  Forced their resistless way.
Then to the musket-knell succeeds
The clash of swords, the neigh of
    steeds,   240
As plies the smith his clanging trade,
Against the cuirass rang the blade;
And while amid their close array
The well-served cannon rent their way,
And while amid their scattered band
Raged the fierce rider's bloody brand,
Recoiled in common rout and fear
Lancer and guard and cuirassier,
Horsemen and foot, — a mingled host,
Their leaders fallen, their standards
    lost.   250

XIII

Then, WELLINGTON ! thy piercing eye
This crisis caught of destiny —
  The British host had stood
That morn 'gainst charge of sword and
    lance
As their own ocean-rocks hold stance,
But when thy voice had said, ' Advance ! '
  They were their ocean's flood. —
O thou whose inauspicious aim
Hath wrought thy host this hour of shame,
Think'st thou thy broken bands will
    bide   260
The terrors of yon rushing tide ?
Or will thy chosen brook to feel
The British shock of levelled steel ?
  Or dost thou turn thine eye
Where coming squadrons gleam afar,
And fresher thunders wake the war,
  And other standards fly ? —
Think not that in yon columns file
Thy conquering troops from distant
    Dyle —
  Is Blucher yet unknown ?   270
Or dwells not in thy memory still,
Heard frequent in thine hour of ill,
What notes of hate and vengeance thrill

  In Prussia's trumpet tone ? —
What yet remains ? — shall it be thine
To head the relics of thy line
  In one dread effort more ? —
The Roman lore thy leisure loved,
And thou canst tell what fortune proved
  That chieftain who of yore   280
Ambition's dizzy paths essayed,
And with the gladiators' aid
  For empire enterprised —
He stood the cast his rashness played,
Left not the victims he had made,
Dug his red grave with his own blade,
And on the field he lost was laid,
  Abhorred — but not despised.

XIV

But if revolves thy fainter thought
On safety — howsoever bought —   290
Then turn thy fearful rein and ride,
Though twice ten thousand men have died
  On this eventful day,
To gild the military fame
Which thou for life in traffic tame
  Wilt barter thus away.
Shall future ages tell this tale
Of inconsistence faint and frail ?
And art thou he of Lodi's bridge,
Marengo's field, and Wagram's ridge ! 300
  Or is thy soul like mountain-tide
That, swelled by winter storm and shower,
Rolls down in turbulence of power
  A torrent fierce and wide;
Reft of these aids, a rill obscure,
Shrinking unnoticed, mean and poor,
  Whose channel shows displayed
The wrecks of its impetuous course,
But not one symptom of the force
  By which these wrecks were made !   310

XV

Spur on thy way ! — since now thine ear
Has brooked thy veterans' wish to hear,
  Who as thy flight they eyed
Exclaimed — while tears of anguish came,
Wrung forth by pride and rage and
    shame —
  ' O, that he had but died ! '
But yet, to sum this hour of ill,
Look ere thou leavest the fatal hill
  Back on yon broken ranks —
Upon whose wild confusion gleams   320
The moon, as on the troubled streams
  When rivers break their banks,

And to the ruined peasant's eye
Objects half seen roll swiftly by,
　Down the dread current hurled —
So mingle banner, wain, and gun,
Where the tumultuous flight rolls on
Of warriors who when morn begun
　Defied a banded world.

XVI

List — frequent to the hurrying rout,　330
The stern pursuers' vengeful shout
Tells that upon their broken rear
Rages the Prussian's bloody spear.
　So fell a shriek was none
When Beresina's icy flood
Reddened and thawed with flame and
　blood
And, pressing on thy desperate way,
Raised oft and long their wild hurra
　The children of the Don.
Thine ear no yell of horror cleft　340
So ominous when, all bereft
Of aid, the valiant Polack left —
Ay, left by thee — found soldier's grave
In Leipsic's corpse-encumbered wave.
Fate, in these various perils past,
Reserved thee still some future cast;
On the dread die thou now hast thrown
Hangs not a single field alone,
Nor one campaign — thy martial fame,
Thy empire, dynasty, and name,　350
　Have felt the final stroke;
And now o'er thy devoted head
The last stern vial's wrath is shed,
　The last dread seal is broke.

XVII

Since live thou wilt — refuse not now
Before these demagogues to bow,
Late objects of thy scorn and hate,
Who shall thy once imperial fate
Make wordy theme of vain debate. —
Or shall we say thou stoop'st less low　360
In seeking refuge from the foe,
Against whose heart in prosperous life
Thine hand hath ever held the knife ?
　Such homage hath been paid
By Roman and by Grecian voice,
And there were honor in the choice,
　If it were freely made.
Then safely come — in one so low, —
So lost, — we cannot own a foe;
Though dear experience bid us end,　370
In thee we ne'er can hail a friend. —

Come, howsoe'er — but do not hide
Close in thy heart that germ of pride
Erewhile by gifted bard espied,
　That 'yet imperial hope;'
Think not that for a fresh rebound,
To raise ambition from the ground,
　We yield thee means or scope.
In safety come — but ne'er again
Hold type of independent reign;　380
　No islet calls thee lord,
We leave thee no confederate band,
No symbol of thy lost command,
To be a dagger in the hand
　From which we wrenched the sword.

XVIII

Yet, even in yon sequestered spot,
May worthier conquest be thy lot
　Than yet thy life has known;
Conquest unbought by blood or harm,
That needs nor foreign aid nor arm,　390
　A triumph all thine own.
Such waits thee when thou shalt control
Those passions wild, that stubborn soul,
　That marred thy prosperous scene: —
Hear this — from no unmoved heart,
Which sighs, comparing what THOU ART
　With what thou MIGHTST HAVE BEEN !

XIX

Thou too, whose deeds of fame renewed
Bankrupt a nation's gratitude,
To thine own noble heart must owe　400
More than the meed she can bestow.
For not a people's just acclaim,
Not the full hail of Europe's fame,
Thy prince's smiles, thy state's decree,
The ducal rank, the gartered knee,
Not these such pure delight afford
As that, when hanging up thy sword,'
Well mayst thou think, ' This honest steel
Was ever drawn for public weal;
And, such was rightful Heaven's de-
　cree,　410
Ne'er sheathed unless with victory ! '

XX

Look forth once more with softened heart
Ere from the field of fame we part;
Triumph and sorrow border near,
And joy oft melts into a tear.
Alas ! what links of love that morn
Has War's rude hand asunder torn !
For ne'er was field so sternly fought,
And ne'er was conquest dearer bought.

Here piled in common slaughter sleep   420
Those whom affection long shall weep:
Here rests the sire that ne'er shall strain
His orphans to his heart again;
The son whom on his native shore
The parent's voice shall bless no more;
The bridegroom who has hardly pressed
His blushing consort to his breast;
The husband whom through many a year
Long love and mutual faith endear.
Thou canst not name one tender tie   430
But here dissolved its relics lie !
O, when thou see'st some mourner's veil
Shroud her thin form and visage pale,
Or mark'st the matron's bursting tears
Stream when the stricken drum she hears,
Or see'st how manlier grief suppressed
Is laboring in a father's breast, —
With no inquiry vain pursue
The cause, but think on Waterloo !

XXI

Period of honor as of woes,   440
What bright careers 't was thine to
    close ! —
Marked on thy roll of blood what names
To Briton's memory and to Fame's
Laid there their last immortal claims !
Thou saw'st in seas of gore expire
Redoubted PICTON's soul of fire —
Saw'st in the mingled carnage lie
All that of PONSONBY could die —
DE LANCEY change Love's bridal-wreath
For laurels from the hand of Death —   450
Saw'st gallant MILLER's failing eye
Still bent where Albion's banners fly,
And CAMERON in the shock of steel
Die like the offspring of Lochiel;
And generous GORDON mid the strife
Fall while he watched his leader's life. —
Ah ! though her guardian angel's shield
Fenced Britain's hero through the field,
Fate not the less her power made known
Through his friends' hearts to pierce his
    own !   460

XXII

Forgive, brave dead, the imperfect lay !
Who may your names, your numbers,
    say ?
What high-strung harp, what lofty line,
To each the dear-earned praise assign,
From high-born chiefs of martial fame
To the poor soldier's lowlier name ?
Lightly ye rose that dawning day

From your cold couch of swamp and clay,
To fill before the sun was low
The bed that morning cannot know. —   470
Oft may the tear the green sod steep,
And sacred be the heroes' sleep
    Till time shall cease to run;
And ne'er beside their noble grave
May Briton pass and fail to crave
A blessing on the fallen brave
    Who fought with Wellington !

XXIII

Farewell, sad field ! whose blighted face
Wears desolation's withering trace;
Long shall my memory retain   480
Thy shattered huts and trampled grain,
With every mark of martial wrong
That scathe thy towers, fair Hougomont !
Yet though thy garden's green arcade
The marksman's fatal post was made,
Though on thy shattered beeches fell
The blended rage of shot and shell,
Though from thy blackened portals torn
Their fall thy blighted fruit-trees mourn,
Has not such havoc bought a name   490
Immortal in the rolls of fame ?
Yes — Agincourt may be forgot,
And Cressy be an unknown spot,
    And Blenheim's name be new;
But still in story and in song,
For many an age remembered long,
Shall live the towers of Hougomont
    And Field of Waterloo.

CONCLUSION

STERN tide of human time ! that know'st
    not rest,
But, sweeping from the cradle to the
    tomb,
Bear'st ever downward on thy dusky
    breast
Successive generations to their doom;
While thy capacious stream has equal
    room
For the gay bark where Pleasure's
    streamers sport
And for the prison-ship of guilt and
    gloom,
The fisher-skiff and barge that bears a
    court,
Still wafting onward all to one dark silent
    port; —

Stern tide of time ! through what mys-
  terious change
                                    10
Of hope and fear have our frail barks
  been driven !
For ne'er before vicissitude so strange
Was to one race of Adam's offspring given.
And sure such varied change of sea and
  heaven,
Such unexpected bursts of joy and woe,
Such fearful strife as that where we have
  striven,
Succeeding ages ne'er again shall know
Until the awful term when thou shalt cease
  to flow.

Well hast thou stood, my Country ! — the
  brave fight
Hast well maintained through good re-
  port and ill;
                                    20
In thy just cause and in thy native might,
And in Heaven's grace and justice con-
  stant still;
Whether the banded prowess, strength,
  and skill
Of half the world against thee stood
  arrayed,
Or when with better views and freer will
Beside thee Europe's noblest drew the
  blade,
Each emulous in arms the Ocean Queen to
  aid.

Well art thou now repaid — though
  slowly rose,
And struggled long with mists thy blaze
  of fame,
While like the dawn that in the orient
  glows
                                    30
On the broad wave its earlier lustre
  came;

Then eastern Egypt saw the growing
  flame,
And Maida's myrtles gleamed beneath
  its ray,
Where first the soldier, stung with generous shame,
Rivalled the heroes of the watery way,
And washed in foemen's gore unjust reproach away.

Now, Island Empress, wave thy crest on
  high,
And bid the banner of thy Patron flow,
Gallant Saint George, the flower of chiv-
  alry,
For thou hast faced like him a dragon
  foe,
                                    40
And rescued innocence from overthrow,
And trampled down like him tyrannic
  might,
And to the gazing world mayst proudly
  show
The chosen emblem of thy sainted knight,
Who quelled devouring pride and vindi-
  cated right.

Yet mid the confidence of just renown,
Renown dear-bought, but dearest thus
  acquired,
Write, Britain, write the moral lesson
  down:
'T is not alone the heart with valor fired,
The discipline so dreaded and admired,
In many a field of bloody conquest
  known ; —
                                    51
Such may by fame be lured, by gold be
  hired —
'T is constancy in the good cause alone
Best justifies the meed thy valiant sons
  have won.

HAROLD THE DAUNTLESS

INTRODUCTORY NOTE

In the Introduction to *The Lord of the Isles*,
which he prefixed to the 1830 edition of his
poems, Scott refers to the mystification which
he practised on the public by the anonymous
issue of *The Bridal of Triermain*, and the attempt to father it on Lord Kinedder. He
then says : 'Upon another occasion I sent up
another of these trifles, which, like schoolboys'
kites, served to show how the wind of popular
taste was setting. The manner was supposed
to be that of a rude minstrel or Scald, in opposition to *The Bridal of Triermain*, which was
designed to belong rather to the Italian school.
This new fugitive piece was called *Harold the
Dauntless ;* and I am still astonished at my
having committed the gross error of selecting
the very name which Lord Byron had made so
famous. It encountered rather an odd fate.
My ingenious friend, Mr. James Hogg, had
published, about the same time, a work called
The Poetic Mirror, containing imitations of the
principal living poets. There was in it a very

good imitation of my own style, which bore
such a resemblance to *Harold the Dauntless*
that there was no discovering the original from
the imitation; and I believe that many who
took the trouble of thinking upon the subject
were rather of opinion that my ingenious friend
was the true, and not the fictitious, Simon
Pure. Since this period, which was in the year
1817, the Author has not been an intruder on
the public by any poetical work of importance.'

Harold the Dauntless was indeed the last
poem of any length that Scott wrote. When it
appeared, in January, 1817, Scott was deep in
the multitudinous interests which swept him
away from poetry, — the enlargement of his domain, the writing of the Waverley Novels, contributions to the *Annual Register* and the various
literary enterprises into which he was drawn
by the Ballantynes. He kept *Harold* by him,
after finishing the *Bridal*, some two years,
making a plaything of it, something to take
up, as Lockhart says, 'whenever the coach
brought no proof-sheets to jog him as to serious
matters;' and poetry written under such conditions is hardly likely to repay the writer or
to treat him otherwise than as a jealous mistress
treats her lover.

It was published simply as by 'the author
of *The Bridal of Triermain*,' and no effort
seems to have been made to turn aside attention
to Erskine, Gillies, or any one else. Although
Scott professed in one or two instances an interest in his work, it is pretty evident that it
appealed but slightly to his mind, now so ab-
sorbed in larger ventures. 'I begin,' he wrote
to Morritt, 'to get too old and stupid, I think,
for poetry, and will certainly never again adventure on a grand scale;' and the next day he
wrote to Lady Louisa Stuart: 'I thought once
I should have made it something clever, but
it turned vapid upon my imagination; and I
finished it at last with hurry and impatience.
Nobody knows, that has not tried the feverish
trade of poetry, how much it depends upon
mood and whim; I don't wonder, that in dismissing all the other deities of Paganism, the
Muses should have been retained by common
consent; for, in sober reality, writing good
verses seems to depend upon something separate from the volition of the author.'

HAROLD THE DAUNTLESS

A POEM IN SIX CANTOS

INTRODUCTION

THERE is a mood of mind we all have known
On drowsy eve or dark and lowering day,
When the tired spirits lose their sprightly tone
And nought can chase the lingering hours away.
Dull on our soul falls Fancy's dazzling ray,
And Wisdom holds his steadier torch in vain,
Obscured the painting seems, mistuned the lay,
Nor dare we of our listless load complain,
For who for sympathy may seek that cannot tell of pain?

The jolly sportsman knows such drearihood   10
When bursts in deluge the autumnal rain,
Clouding that morn which threats the heath-cock's brood;
Of such in summer's drought the anglers plain,
Who hope the soft mild southern shower in vain;
But more than all the discontented fair,
Whom father stern and sterner aunt restrain
From county-ball or race occurring rare,
While all her friends around their vestments gay prepare.

Ennui! — or, as our mothers called thee, Spleen!   20
To thee we owe full many a rare device; —
Thine is the sheaf of painted cards, I ween,
The rolling billiard-ball, the rattling dice,
The turning lathe for framing gimcrack nice;

The amateur's blotched pallet thou mayst claim,
Retort, and air-pump, threatening frogs and mice —
Murders disguised by philosophic name —
And much of trifling grave and much of buxom game.

Then of the books to catch thy drowsy glance
Compiled, what bard the catalogue may quote !
Plays, poems, novels, never read but once ; —   30
But not of such the tale fair Edgeworth wrote,
That bears thy name and is thine antidote ;
And not of such the strain my Thomson sung,
Delicious dreams inspiring by his note,
What time to Indolence his harp he strung ; —
O, might my lay be ranked that happier list among !

Each hath his refuge whom thy cares assail.
For me, I love my study-fire to trim,
And con right vacantly some idle tale,
Displaying on the couch each listless limb,   40
Till on the drowsy page the lights grow dim
And doubtful slumber half supplies the theme ;
While antique shapes of knight and giant grim,
Damsel and dwarf, in long procession gleam,
And the romancer's tale becomes the reader's dream.

'T is thus my malady I well may bear,
Albeit outstretched, like Pope's own Paridel,
Upon the rack of a too-easy chair ;
And find to cheat the time a powerful spell
In old romaunts of errantry that tell,   50
Or later legends of the Fairy-folk,
Or Oriental tale of Afrite fell,
Of Genii, Talisman, and broad-winged Roc,
Though taste may blush and frown, and sober reason mock.

Oft at such season too will rhymes unsought
Arrange themselves in some romantic lay,
The which, as things unfitting graver thought,
Are burnt or blotted on some wiser day. —
These few survive — and, proudly let me say,
Court not the critic's smile nor dread his frown ;   60
They well may serve to while an hour away,
Nor does the volume ask for more renown
Than Ennui's yawning smile, what time she drops it down.

CANTO FIRST

I

LIST to the valorous deeds that were done
By Harold the Dauntless, Count Witikind's
    son !

Count Witikind came of a regal strain,
And roved with his Norsemen the land and
    the main.

Woe to the realms which he coasted ! for
    there
Was shedding of blood and rending of hair,
Rape of maiden and slaughter of priest,
Gathering of ravens and wolves to the feast :
When he hoisted his standard black,
Before him was battle, behind him wrack,   10
And he burned the churches, that heathen
    Dane,
To light his band to their barks again.

II

On Erin's shores was his outrage known,
The winds of France had his banners blown;
Little was there to plunder, yet still
His pirates had forayed on Scottish hill:
But upon merry England's coast
More frequent he sailed, for he won the
    most.
So wide and so far his ravage they knew,
If a sail but gleamed white 'gainst the
    welkin blue,   20
Trumpet and bugle to arms did call,
Burghers hastened to man the wall,
Peasants fled inland his fury to 'scape,
Beacons were lighted on headland and cape,
Bells were tolled out, and aye as they rung
Fearful and faintly the gray brothers sung,
'Bless us, Saint Mary, from flood and from
    fire,
From famine and pest, and Count Witi-
    kind's ire !'

III

He liked the wealth of fair England so well
That he sought in her bosom as native to
    dwell.   30
He entered the Humber in fearful hour
And disembarked with his Danish power.
Three earls came against him with all their
    train, —
Two hath he taken and one hath he slain.
Count Witikind left the Humber's rich
    strand,
And he wasted and warred in Northumber-
    land.
But the Saxon king was a sire in age,
Weak in battle, in council sage;
Peace of that heathen leader he sought,
Gifts he gave and quiet he bought;   40
And the count took upon him the peace-
    able style
Of a vassal and liegeman of Briton's broad
    isle.

IV

Time will rust the sharpest sword,
Time will consume the strongest cord;
That which moulders hemp and steel
Mortal arm and nerve must feel.
Of the Danish band whom Count Witikind
    led
Many waxed aged and many were dead:
Himself found his armor full weighty to
    bear,   49
Wrinkled his brows grew and hoary his hair;

He leaned on a staff when his step went
    abroad,
And patient his palfrey when steed he be-
    strode.
As he grew feebler, his wildness ceased,
He made himself peace with prelate and
    priest,
Made his peace, and stooping his head
Patiently listed the counsel they said:
Saint Cuthbert's Bishop was holy and
    grave,
Wise and good was the counsel he gave.

V

'Thou hast murdered, robbed, and spoiled,
Time it is thy poor soul were assoiled;   60
Priests didst thou slay and churches burn,
Time it is now to repentance to turn;
Fiends hast thou worshipped with fiendish
    rite,
Leave now the darkness and wend into light;
O, while life and space are given,
Turn thee yet, and think of Heaven !'
That stern old heathen his head he raised,
And on the good prelate he steadfastly
    gazed;
'Give me broad lands on the Wear and
    the Tyne,
My faith I will leave and I'll cleave unto
    thine.'   70

VI

Broad lands he gave him on Tyne and
    Wear,
To be held of the church by bridle and spear,
Part of Monkwearmouth, of Tynedale part,
To better his will and to soften his heart:
Count Witikind was a joyful man,
Less for the faith than the lands that he wan.
The high church of Durham is dressed for
    the day,
The clergy are ranked in their solemn array;
There came the count, in a bear-skin warm,
Leaning on Hilda his concubine's arm.   80
He kneeled before Saint Cuthbert's shrine
With patience unwonted at rites divine;
He abjured the gods of heathen race
And he bent his head at the font of grace.
But such was the grisly old proselyte's look,
That the priest who baptized him grew
    pale and shook;
And the old monks muttered beneath their
    hood,
'Of a stem so stubborn can never spring
    good !'

VII

Up then arose that grim convertite,   89
Homeward he hied him when ended the rite;
The prelate in honor will with him ride
And feast in his castle on Tyne's fair side.
Banners and banderols danced in the wind,
Monks rode before them and spearmen
    behind;
Onward they passed, till fairly did shine
Pennon and cross on the bosom of Tyne;
And full in front did that fortress lour
In darksome strength with its buttress and
    tower:
At the castle gate was young Harold
    there,
Count Witikind's only offspring and heir.

VIII

Young Harold was feared for his hardi-
    hood,   101
His strength of frame and his fury of mood.
Rude he was and wild to behold,
Wore neither collar nor bracelet of gold,
Cap of vair nor rich array,
Such as should grace that festal day:
His doublet of bull's hide was all un-
    braced,
Uncovered his head and his sandal un-
    laced:
His shaggy black locks on his brow hung
    low,
And his eyes glanced through them a
    swarthy glow;   110
A Danish club in his hand he bore,
The spikes were clotted with recent gore;
At his back a she-wolf and her wolf-cubs
    twain,
In the dangerous chase that morning slain.
Rude was the greeting his father he made,
None to the bishop, — while thus he
    said: —

IX

'What priest-led hypocrite art thou
With thy humbled look and thy monkish
    brow,
Like a shaveling who studies to cheat his
    vow ?
Canst thou be Witikind the Waster
    known,   120
Royal Eric's fearless son,
Haughty Gunhilda's haughtier lord,
Who won his bride by the axe and sword;
From the shrine of Saint Peter the chalice
    who tore,

And melted to bracelets for Freya and
    Thor;
With one blow of his gauntlet who burst
    the skull,
Before Odin's stone, of the Mountain
    Bull ?
Then ye worshipped with rites that to war-
    gods belong,
With the deed of the brave and the blow
    of the strong;
And now, in thine age to dotage sunk,   130
Wilt thou patter thy crimes to a shaven
    monk,
Lay down thy mail-shirt for clothing of
    hair, —
Fasting and scourge, like a slave, wilt thou
    bear ?
Or, at best, be admitted in slothful bower
To batten with priest and with paramour ?
O, out upon thine endless shame !
Each Scald's high harp shall blast thy
    fame,
And thy son will refuse thee a father's
    name !'

X

Ireful waxed old Witikind's look,
His faltering voice with fury shook: —   140
'Hear me, Harold of hardened heart !
Stubborn and wilful ever thou wert.
Thine outrage insane I command thee to
    cease,
Fear my wrath and remain at peace: —
Just is the debt of repentance I've paid,
Richly the church has a recompense made,
And the truth of her doctrines I prove
    with my blade,
But reckoning to none of my actions I owe,
And least to my son such accounting will
    show.
Why speak I to thee of repentance or
    truth,   150
Who ne'er from thy childhood knew rea-
    son or ruth ?
Hence ! to the wolf and the bear in her den;
These are thy mates, and not rational men.'

XI

Grimly smiled Harold and coldly replied,
'We must honor our sires, if we fear when
    they chide.
For me, I am yet what thy lessons have
    made,
I was rocked in a buckler and fed from a
    blade;

An infant, was taught to clasp hands and
  to shout
From the roofs of the tower when the flame
  had broke out;
In the blood of slain foemen my finger to
  dip,   160
And tinge with its purple my cheek and my
  lip. —
'T is thou know'st not truth, that hast bartered in eld
For a price the brave faith that thine ancestors held.
When this wolf ' — and the carcass he flung
  on the plain —
' Shall awake and give food to her nurslings
  again,
The face of his father will Harold review;
Till then, aged heathen, young Christian,
  adieu ! '

XII

Priest, monk, and prelate stood aghast,
As through the pageant the heathen passed.
A cross-bearer out of his saddle he flung,   170
Laid his hand on the pommel and into it
  sprung.
Loud was the shriek and deep the groan
When the holy sign on the earth was
  thrown !
The fierce old count unsheathed his brand,
But the calmer prelate stayed his hand.
' Let him pass free ! — Heaven knows its
  hour, —
But he must own repentance's power,
Pray and weep, and penance bear,
Ere he hold land by the Tyne and the
  Wear.'
Thus in scorn and in wrath from his father
  is gone   180
Young Harold the Dauntless, Count Witi-
  kind's son.

XIII

High was the feasting in Witikind's hall,
Revelled priests, soldiers, and pagans, and
  all;
And e'en the good bishop was fain to endure
The scandal which time and instruction
  might cure:
It were dangerous, he deemed, at the first
  to restrain
In his wine and his wassail a half-christened
  Dane.
The mead flowed around and the ale was
  drained dry,

Wild was the laughter, the song, and the
  cry;
With Kyrie Eleison came clamorously in 190
The war-songs of Danesmen, Norweyan,
  and Finn,
Till man after man the contention gave
  o'er,
Outstretched on the rushes that strewed
  the hall floor;
And the tempest within, having ceased its
  wild rout,
Gave place to the tempest that thundered
  without.

XIV

Apart from the wassail in turret alone
Lay flaxen-haired Gunnar, old Ermengarde's
  son;
In the train of Lord Harold that page was
  the first,
For Harold in childhood had Ermengarde
  nursed;
And grieved was young Gunnar his master
  should roam,   200
Unhoused and unfriended, an exile from
  home.
He heard the deep thunder, the plashing of
  rain,
He saw the red lightning through shot-hole
  and pane;
' And O ! ' said the page, ' on the shelterless
  wold
Lord Harold is wandering in darkness and
  cold !
What though he was stubborn and wayward
  and wild,
He endured me because I was Ermen-
  garde's child,
And often from dawn till the set of the sun
In the chase by his stirrup unbidden I run;
I would I were older, and knighthood could
  bear,   210
I would soon quit the banks of the Tyne
  and the Wear:
For my mother's command with her last
  parting breath
Bade me follow her nursling in life and to
  death.

XV

' It pours and it thunders, it lightens amain,
As if Lok the Destroyer had burst from
  his chain !
Accursed by the church and expelled by
  his sire,

Nor Christian nor Dane give him shelter
    or fire,
And this tempest what mortal may house-
    less endure ?
Unaided, unmantled, he dies on the moor !
Whate'er comes of Gunnar, he tarries not
    here.'   220
He leapt from his couch and he grasped to
    his spear,
Sought the hall of the feast.   Undisturbed
    by his tread,
The wassailers slept fast as the sleep of
    the dead:
'Ungrateful and bestial !' his anger broke
    forth,
'To forget mid your goblets the pride of
    the North !
And you, ye cowled priests who have plenty
    in store,
Must give Gunnar for ransom a palfrey and
    ore.'

XVI

Then, heeding full little of ban or of curse,
He has seized on the Prior of Jorvaux's
    purse:
Saint Meneholt's Abbot next morning has
    missed   230
His mantle, deep furred from the cape to
    the wrist:
The seneschal's keys from his belt he has
    ta'en —
Well drenched on that eve was old Hilde-
    brand's brain —
To the stable-yard he made his way
And mounted the bishop's palfrey gay,
Castle and hamlet behind him has cast
And right on his way to the moorland has
    passed.
Sore snorted the palfrey, unused to face
A weather so wild at so rash a pace;
So long he snorted, so long he neighed,   240
There answered a steed that was bound
    beside,
And the red flash of lightning showed there
    where lay
His master, Lord Harold, outstretched on
    the clay.

XVII

Up he started and thundered out, 'Stand !'
And raised the club in his deadly hand.
The flaxen-haired Gunnar his purpose told,
Showed the palfrey and proffered the gold.
'Back, back, and home, thou simple boy !

Thou canst not share my grief or joy:
Have I not marked thee wail and cry   250
When thou hast seen a sparrow die ?
And canst thou, as my follower should,
Wade ankle-deep through foeman's blood,
Dare mortal and immortal foe,
The gods above, the fiends below,
And man on earth, more hateful still,
The very fountain-head of ill ?
Desperate of life and careless of death,
Lover of bloodshed and slaughter and
    scathe,
Such must thou be with me to roam,   260
And such thou canst not be — back, and
    home !'

XVIII

Young Gunnar shook like an aspen bough,
As he heard the harsh voice and beheld
    the dark brow,
And half he repented his purpose and vow.
But now to draw back were bootless shame,
And he loved his master, so urged his
    claim:
'Alas ! if my arm and my courage be
    weak,
Bear with me awhile for old Ermengarde's
    sake;
Nor deem so lightly of Gunnar's faith
As to fear he would break it for peril of
    death.   270
Have I not risked it to fetch thee this
    gold,
This surcoat and mantle to fence thee from
    cold ?
And, did I bear a baser mind,
What lot remains if I stay behind ?
The priests' revenge, thy father's wrath,
A dungeon, and a shameful death.'

XIX

With gentler look Lord Harold eyed
The page, then turned his head aside;
And either a tear did his eyelash stain,
Or it caught a drop of the passing rain.   280
'Art thou an outcast, then ?' quoth he;
'The meeter page to follow me.'
'T were bootless to tell what climes they
    sought,
Ventures achieved, and battles fought;
How oft with few, how oft alone,
Fierce Harold's arm the field hath won.
Men swore his eye, that flashed so red
When each other glance was quenched with
    dread,

Bore oft a light of deadly flame
That ne'er from mortal courage came. 290
Those limbs so strong, that mood so stern,
That loved the couch of heath and fern,
Afar from hamlet, tower, and town,
More than to rest on driven down;
That stubborn frame, that sullen mood,
Men deemed must come of aught but good;
And they whispered the great Master Fiend
  was at one
With Harold the Dauntless, Count Witi-
  kind's son.

XX

Years after years had gone and fled,
The good old prelate lies lapped in lead; 300
In the chapel still is shown
His sculptured form on a marble stone,
With staff and ring and scapulaire,
And folded hands in the act of prayer.
Saint Cuthbert's mitre is resting now
On the haughty Saxon, bold Aldingar's
  brow;
The power of his crosier he loved to ex-
  tend
O'er whatever would break or whatever
  would bend;
And now hath he clothed him in cope and
  in pall,
And the Chapter of Durham has met at his
  call.   310
'And hear ye not, brethren,' the proud
  bishop said,
'That our vassal, the Danish Count Witi-
  kind's dead?
All his gold and his goods hath he given
To holy Church for the love of Heaven,
And hath founded a chantry with stipend
  and dole
That priests and that beadsmen may pray
  for his soul:
Harold his son is wandering abroad,
Dreaded by man and abhorred by God;
Meet it is not that such should heir
The lands of the Church on the Tyne and
  the Wear,   320
And at her pleasure her hallowed hands
May now resume these wealthy lands.'

XXI

Answered good Eustace, a canon old, —
'Harold is tameless and furious and bold;
Ever Renown blows a note of fame
And a note of fear when she sounds his
  name:

Much of bloodshed and much of scathe
Have been their lot who have waked his
  wrath.
Leave him these lands and lordships still,
Heaven in its hour may change his will; 330
But if reft of gold and of living bare,
An evil counsellor is despair.'
More had he said, but the prelate frowned,
And murmured his brethren who sate
  around,
And with one consent have they given their
  doom
That the Church should the lands of Saint
  Cuthbert resume.
So willed the prelate; and canon and dean
Gave to his judgment their loud amen.

CANTO SECOND

I

'TIS merry in greenwood — thus runs the
  old lay —
In the gladsome month of lively May,
When the wild birds' song on stem and
  spray
  Invites to forest bower;
Then rears the ash his airy crest,
Then shines the birch in silver vest,
And the beech in glistening leaves is drest,
And dark between shows the oak's proud
  breast
  Like a chieftain's frowning tower;
Though a thousand branches join their
  screen,   10
Yet the broken sunbeams glance between
And tip the leaves with lighter green,
  With brighter tints the flower:
Dull is the heart that loves not then
The deep recess of the wildwood glen,
Where roe and red-deer find sheltering den
  When the sun is in his power.

II

Less merry perchance is the fading leaf
That follows so soon on the gathered sheaf
  When the greenwood loses the name; 20
Silent is then the forest bound,
Save the redbreast's note and the rustling
  sound
Of frost-nipt leaves that are dropping
  round,
Or the deep-mouthed cry of the distant
  hound
  That opens on his game:

Yet then too I love the forest wide,
Whether the sun in splendor ride
And gild its many-colored side,
Or whether the soft and silvery haze   29
In vapory folds o'er the landscape strays,
And half involves the woodland maze,
  Like an early widow's veil,
Where wimpling tissue from the gaze
The form half hides and half betrays
  Of beauty wan and pale.

III

Fair Metelill was a woodland maid,
Her father a rover of greenwood shade,
By forest statutes undismayed,
  Who lived by bow and quiver;
Well known was Wulfstane's archery   40
By merry Tyne both on moor and lea,
Through wooded Weardale's glens so free,
Well beside Stanhope's wildwood tree,
  And well on Ganlesse river.
Yet free though he trespassed on wood-
      land game,
More known and more feared was the wiz-
      ard fame
Of Jutta of Rookhope, the Outlaw's dame;
Feared when she frowned was her eye of
      flame,
  More feared when in wrath she laughed;
For then, 't was said, more fatal true   50
To its dread aim her spell-glance flew
Than when from Wulfstane's bended yew
  Sprung forth the gray-goose shaft.

IV

Yet had this fierce and dreaded pair,
So Heaven decreed, a daughter fair;
  None brighter crowned the bed,
In Britain's bounds, of peer or prince,
Nor hath perchance a lovelier since
  In this fair isle been bred.
And nought of fraud or ire or ill   60
Was known to gentle Metelill, —
  A simple maiden she;
The spells in dimpled smile that lie,
And a downcast blush, and the darts that
      fly
With the sidelong glance of a hazel eye,
  Were her arms and witchery.
So young, so simple was she yet,
She scarce could childhood's joys forget,
And still she loved, in secret set
  Beneath the greenwood tree,   70
To plait the rushy coronet

And braid with flowers her locks of jet,
  As when in infancy; —
Yet could that heart so simple prove
The early dawn of stealing love:
  Ah! gentle maid, beware!
The power who, now so mild a guest,
Gives dangerous yet delicious zest
To the calm pleasures of thy breast,
Will soon, a tyrant o'er the rest,   80
  Let none his empire share.

V

One morn in kirtle green arrayed
Deep in the wood the maiden strayed,
  And where a fountain sprung
She sate her down unseen to thread
The scarlet berry's mimic braid,
  And while the beads she strung,
Like the blithe lark whose carol gay
Gives a good-morrow to the day,
  So lightsomely she sung.   90

VI

SONG

'Lord William was born in gilded bower,
The heir of Wilton's lofty tower;
Yet better loves Lord William now
To roam beneath wild Rookhope's brow;
And William has lived where ladies fair
With gawds and jewels deck their hair,
Yet better loves the dew-drops still
That pearl the locks of Metelill.

'The pious palmer loves, iwis,   99
Saint Cuthbert's hallowed beads to kiss;
But I, though simple girl I be,
Might have such homage paid to me;
For did Lord William see me suit
This necklace of the bramble's fruit,
He fain — but must not have his will —
Would kiss the beads of Metelill.

'My nurse has told me many a tale,
How vows of love are weak and frail;
My mother says that courtly youth
By rustic maid means seldom sooth.   110
What should they mean? it cannot be
That such a warning 's meant for me,
For nought — O, nought of fraud or ill
Can William mean to Metelill!'

VII

Sudden she stops — and starts to feel
A weighty hand, a glove of steel,

Upon her shrinking shoulders laid;
Fearful she turned, and saw dismayed
A knight in plate and mail arrayed,
His crest and bearing worn and frayed,   120
  His surcoat soiled and riven,
Formed like that giant race of yore
Whose long-continued crimes outwore
  The sufferance of Heaven.
Stern accents made his pleasure known,
Though then he used his gentlest tone:
' Maiden,' he said, ' sing forth thy glee.
Start not — sing on — it pleases me.'

VIII

Secured within his powerful hold,
To bend her knee, her hands to fold,   130
  Was all the maiden might;
And ' O, forgive,' she faintly said,
' The terrors of a simple maid,
  If thou art mortal wight !
But if — of such strange tales are told —
Unearthly warrior of the wold,
Thou comest to chide mine accents bold,
My mother, Jutta, knows the spell
At noon and midnight pleasing well
  The disembodied ear;   140
O, let her powerful charms atone
For aught my rashness may have done,
  And cease thy grasp of fear.'
Then laughed the knight — his laughter's
        sound
Half in the hollow helmet drowned;
His barred visor then he raised,
And steady on the maiden gazed.
He smoothed his brows, as best he might,
To the dread calm of autumn night,
  When sinks the tempest roar,   150
Yet still the cautious fishers eye
The clouds and fear the gloomy sky,
  And haul their barks on shore.

IX

' Damsel,' he said, ' be wise, and learn
Matters of weight and deep concern:
  From distant realms I come,
And wanderer long at length have planned
In this my native Northern land
  To seek myself a home.
Nor that alone — a mate I seek;   160
She must be gentle, soft, and meek, —
  No lordly dame for me;
Myself am something rough of mood
And feel the fire of royal blood,
And therefore do not hold it good

To match in my degree.
Then, since coy maidens say my face
Is harsh, my form devoid of grace,
  For a fair lineage to provide
'T is meet that my selected bride   170
  In lineaments be fair;
I love thine well — till now I ne'er
Looked patient on a face of fear,
But now that tremulous sob and tear
  Become thy beauty rare.
One kiss — nay, damsel, coy it not ! —
And now go seek thy parents' cot,
And say a bridegroom soon I come
To woo my love and bear her home.'

X

Home sprung the maid without a pause,   180
As leveret 'scaped from greyhound's jaws;
But still she locked, howe'er distressed,
The secret in her boding breast;
Dreading her sire, who oft forbade
Her steps should stray to distant glade.
Night came — to her accustomed nook
Her distaff aged Jutta took,
And by the lamp's imperfect glow
Rough Wulfstane trimmed his shafts and
        bow.
Sudden and clamorous from the ground   190
Upstarted slumbering brach and hound;
Loud knocking next the lodge alarms
And Wulfstane snatches at his arms,
When open flew the yielding door
And that grim warrior pressed the floor.

XI

' All peace be here — What ! none replies ?
Dismiss your fears and your surprise.
'T is I — that maid hath told my tale, —
Or, trembler, did thy courage fail ?
It recks not — it is I demand   200
Fair Metelill in marriage band;
Harold the Dauntless I, whose name
Is brave men's boast and caitiff's shame.'
The parents sought each other's eyes
With awe, resentment, and surprise:
Wulfstane, to quarrel prompt, began
The stranger's size and thews to scan;
But as he scanned his courage sunk,
And from unequal strife he shrunk,
Then forth to blight and blemish flies   210
The harmful curse from Jutta's eyes;
Yet, fatal howsoe'er, the spell
On Harold innocently fell !
And disappointment and amaze
Were in the witch's wildered gaze.

XII

But soon the wit of woman woke,
And to the warrior mild she spoke:
' Her child was all too young.' — ' A toy,
The refuge of a maiden coy.'
Again, ' A powerful baron's heir   220
Claims in her heart an interest fair.'
' A trifle — whisper in his ear
That Harold is a suitor here ! ' —
Baffled at length she sought delay:
' Would not the knight till morning stay ?
Late was the hour — he there might rest
Till morn, their lodge's honored guest.'
Such were her words — her craft might
          cast
Her honored guest should sleep his last:
' No, not to-night — but soon,' he swore,   230
' He would return, nor leave them more.'
The threshold then his huge stride crost,
And soon he was in darkness lost.

XIII

Appalled awhile the parents stood,
Then changed their fear to angry mood,
And foremost fell their words of ill
On unresisting Metelill:
Was she not cautioned and forbid,
Forewarned, implored, accused, and chid,
And must she still to greenwood roam   240
To marshal such misfortune home ?
' Hence, minion — to thy chamber hence —
There prudence learn and penitence.'
She went — her lonely couch to steep
In tears which absent lovers weep;
Or if she gained a troubled sleep,
Fierce Harold's suit was still the theme
And terror of her feverish dream.

XIV

Scarce was she gone, her dame and sire
Upon each other bent their ire;   250
' A woodsman thou and hast a spear,
And couldst thou such an insult bear ? '
Sullen he said, ' A man contends
With men, a witch with sprites and fiends;
Not to mere mortal wight belong
Yon gloomy brow and frame so strong.
But thou — is this thy promise fair,
That your Lord William, wealthy heir
To Ulrick, Baron of Witton-le-Wear,
Should Metelill to altar bear ?   260
Do all the spells thou boast'st as thine
Serve but to slay some peasant's kine,
His grain in autumn's storms to steep,
Or thorough fog and fen to sweep

And hag-ride some poor rustic's sleep ?
Is such mean mischief worth the fame
Of sorceress and witch's name ?
Fame, which with all men's wish conspires,
With thy deserts and my desires,
To damn thy corpse to penal fires ?   270
Out on thee, witch ! aroint ! aroint !
What now shall put thy schemes in joint ?
What save this trusty arrow's point,
From the dark dingle when it flies
And he who meets it gasps and dies ? '

XV

Stern she replied, ' I will not wage
War with thy folly or thy rage;
But ere the morrow's sun be low,
Wulfstane of Rookhope, thou shalt know
If I can venge me on a foe.   280
Believe the while that whatso'er
I spoke in ire of bow and spear,
It is not Harold's destiny
The death of pilfered deer to die.
But he, and thou, and yon pale moon —
That shall be yet more pallid soon,
Before she sink behind the dell —
Thou, she, and Harold too, shall tell
What Jutta knows of charm or spell.'
Thus muttering, to the door she bent   290
Her wayward steps and forth she went,
And left alone the moody sire
To cherish or to slake his ire.

XVI

Far faster than belonged to age
Has Jutta made her pilgrimage.
A priest has met her as she passed,
And crossed himself and stood aghast:
She traced a hamlet — not a cur
His throat would ope, his foot would stir;
By crouch, by trembling, and by groan,   300
They made her hated presence known !
But when she trode the sable fell,
Were wilder sounds her way to tell, —
For far was heard the fox's yell,
The black-cock waked and faintly crew,
Screamed o'er the moss the scared curlew;
Where o'er the cataract the oak
Lay slant, was heard the raven's croak;
The mountain-cat which sought his prey
Glared, screamed, and started from her
          way.   310
Such music cheered her journey lone
To the deep dell and rocking stone:
There with unhallowed hymn of praise
She called a god of heathen days.

XVII

INVOCATION

' From thy Pomeranian throne,
Hewn in rock of living stone,
Where, to thy godhead faithful yet,
Bend Esthonian, Finn, and Lett,
And their swords in vengeance whet,
That shall make thine altars wet,   320
Wet and red for ages more
With the Christian's hated gore, —
Hear me, Sovereign of the Rock !
Hear me, mighty Zernebock !

' Mightiest of the mighty known,
Here thy wonders have been shown;
Hundred tribes in various tongue
Oft have here thy praises sung;
Down that stone with Runic seamed
Hundred victims' blood hath streamed ! 330
Now one woman comes alone
And but wets it with her own,
The last, the feeblest of thy flock, —
Hear — and be present, Zernebock !

' Hark ! he comes ! the night-blast cold
Wilder sweeps along the wold;
The cloudless moon grows dark and dim,
And bristling hair and quaking limb
Proclaim the Master Demon nigh, —
Those who view his form shall die !   340
Lo ! I stoop and veil my head;
Thou who ridest the tempest dread,
Shaking hill and rending oak —
Spare me ! spare me, Zernebock !

' He comes not yet !   Shall cold delay
Thy votaress at her need repay ?
Thou — shall I call thee god or fiend ? —
Let others on thy mood attend
With prayer and ritual — Jutta's arms
Are necromantic words and charms;   350
Mine is the spell that uttered once
Shall wake thy Master from his trance,
Shake his red mansion-house of pain
And   burst   his   seven - times - twisted
         chain ! —
So ! com'st thou ere the spell is spoke ?
I own thy presence, Zernebock.' —

XVIII

' Daughter of   dust,' the   Deep   Voice
         said —
Shook while it spoke the vale for dread,
Rocked on the base that massive stone,

The Evil Deity to own, —   360
' Daughter of dust ! not mine the power
Thou seek'st on Harold's fatal hour.
'Twixt heaven and hell there is a strife
Waged for his soul and for his life,
And fain would we the combat win
And snatch him in his hour of sin.
There is a star now rising red
That threats him with an influence dread:
Woman, thine arts of malice whet,
To use the space before it set.   370
Involve him with the church in strife,
Push on adventurous chance his life;
Ourself will in the hour of need,
As best we may, thy counsels speed.'
So   ceased   the   Voice;   for seven leagues
         round
Each hamlet started at the sound,
But slept again as slowly died
Its thunders on the hill's brown side.

XIX

' And is this all,' said Jutta stern,
' That thou canst teach and I can learn ? 380
Hence ! to the land of fog and waste,
There fittest is thine influence placed,
Thou powerless, sluggish Deity !
But ne'er shall Briton bend the knee
Again before so poor a god.'
She struck the altar with her rod;
Slight was the touch as when at need
A damsel stirs her tardy steed;
But to the blow the stone gave place,
And, starting from its balanced base,   390
Rolled   thundering   down   the   moonlight
         dell, —
Re-echoed moorland, rock, and fell;
Into the moonlight tarn it dashed,
Their shores the sounding surges lashed,
      And there was ripple, rage, and foam;
But on that lake, so dark and lone,
Placid and pale the moonbeam shone
      As Jutta hied her home.

CANTO THIRD

I

GRAY towers of Durham ! there was
         once a time
I viewed your battlements with such
         vague hope
As brightens life in its first dawning
         prime;

Not that e'en then came within fancy's
   scope
A vision vain of mitre, throne, or cope;
Yet, gazing on the venerable hall,
Her flattering dreams would in perspec-
   tive ope
Some reverend room, some prebendary's
   stall, —
And thus Hope me deceived as she de-
   ceiveth all.

Well yet I love thy mixed and massive
   piles,   10
Half church of God, half castle 'gainst
   the Scot,
And long to roam these venerable aisles,
With records stored of deeds long since
   forgot;
There might I share my Surtees' happier
   lot,
Who leaves at will his patrimonial field
To ransack every crypt and hallowed
   spot,
And from oblivion rend the spoils they
   yield,
Restoring priestly chant and clang of
   knightly shield.

Vain is the wish — since other cares demand
Each vacant hour, and in another
   clime;   20
But still that northern harp invites my
   hand
Which tells the wonder of thine earlier
   time;
And fain its numbers would I now command
To paint the beauties of that dawning
   fair
When Harold, gazing from its lofty
   stand
Upon the western heights of Beaure-
   paire,
Saw Saxon Eadmer's towers begirt by
   winding Wear.

II

Fair on the half-seen streams the sunbeams danced,
Betraying it beneath the woodland bank,
And fair between the Gothic turrets
   glanced   30
Broad lights, and shadows fell on front
   and flank,

Where tower and buttress rose in martial rank,
And girdled in the massive donjon keep,
And from their circuit pealed o'er bush
   and bank
The matin bell with summons long and
   deep,
And echo answered still with long-resound-
   ing sweep.

III

The morning mists rose from the ground,
Each merry bird awakened round
   As if in revelry;
Afar the bugle's clanging sound   40
Called to the chase the lagging hound;
   The gale breathed soft and free,
And seemed to linger on its way
To catch fresh odors from the spray,
And waved it in its wanton play
   So light and gamesomely.
The scenes which morning beams reveal,
Its sounds to hear, its gales to feel
In all their fragrance round him steal,
It melted Harold's heart of steel,   50
And, hardly wotting why,
He doffed his helmet's gloomy pride
And hung it on a tree beside,
   Laid mace and falchion by,
And on the greensward sate him down
And from his dark habitual frown
   Relaxed his rugged brow —
Whoever hath the doubtful task
From that stern Dane a boon to ask
   Were wise to ask it now.   60

IV

His place beside young Gunnar took
And marked his master's softening look,
And in his eye's dark mirror spied
The gloom of stormy thoughts subside,
And cautious watched the fittest tide
   To speak a warning word.
So when the torrent's billows shrink,
The timid pilgrim on the brink
Waits long to see them wave and sink
   Ere he dare brave the ford,   70
And often after doubtful pause
His step advances or withdraws;
Fearful to move the slumbering ire
Of his stern lord, thus stood the squire
   Till Harold raised his eye,
That glanced as when athwart the shroud
Of the dispersing tempest-cloud
   The bursting sunbeams fly.

V

'Arouse thee, son of Ermengarde,
Offspring of prophetess and bard !   80
Take harp and greet this lovely prime
With some high strain of Runic rhyme,
Strong, deep, and powerful ! Peal it round
Like that loud bell's sonorous sound,
Yet wild by fits, as when the lay
Of bird and bugle hail the day.
Such was my grandsire Eric's sport
When dawn gleamed on his martial court.
Heymar the Scald with harp's high sound
Summoned the chiefs who slept around; 90
Couched on the spoils of wolf and bear,
They roused like lions from their lair,
Then rushed in emulation forth
To enhance the glories of the north. —
Proud Eric, mightiest of thy race,
Where is thy shadowy resting-place ?
In wild Valhalla hast thou quaffed
From foeman's skull metheglin draught,
Or wanderest where thy cairn was piled
To frown o'er oceans wide and wild ?   100
Or have the milder Christians given
Thy refuge in their peaceful heaven ?
Where'er thou art, to thee are known
Our toils endured, our trophies won,
Our wars, our wanderings, and our woes.'
He ceased, and Gunnar's song arose.

VI

SONG

'Hawk and osprey screamed for joy
O'er the beetling cliffs of Hoy,
Crimson foam the beach o'erspread,
The heath was dyed with darker red,   110
When o'er Eric, Inguar's son,
Dane and Northman piled the stone,
Singing wild the war-song stern,
" Rest thee, Dweller of the Cairn ! "

'Where eddying currents foam and boil
By Bersa's burgh and Græmsay's isle,
The seaman sees a martial form
Half-mingled with the mist and storm.
In anxious awe he bears away
To moor his bark in Stromna's bay,   120
And murmurs from the bounding stern,
" Rest thee, Dweller of the Cairn ! "

'What cares disturb the mighty dead ?
Each honored rite was duly paid;
No daring hand thy helm unlaced,

Thy sword, thy shield, were near thee
    placed;
Thy flinty couch no tear profaned:
Without, with hostile blood 't was stained;
Within, 't was lined with moss and fern, —
Then rest thee, Dweller of the Cairn !   130

'He may not rest: from realms afar
Comes voice of battle and of war,
Of conquest wrought with bloody hand
On Carmel's cliffs and Jordan's strand,
When Odin's warlike son could daunt
The turbaned race of Termagaunt.'

VII

'Peace,' said the knight, ' the noble Scald
Our warlike fathers' deeds recalled,
But never strove to soothe the son
With tales of what himself had done.   140
At Odin's board the bard sits high
Whose harp ne'er stooped to flattery,
But highest he whose daring lay
Hath dared unwelcome truths to say.'
With doubtful smile young Gunnar eyed
His master's looks and nought replied —
But well that smile his master led
To construe what he left unsaid.
'Is it to me, thou timid youth,   149
Thou fear'st to speak unwelcome truth !
My soul no more thy censure grieves
Than frosts rob laurels of their leaves.
Say on — and yet — beware the rude
And wild distemper of my blood;
Loath were I that mine ire should wrong
The youth that bore my shield so long,
And who, in service constant still,
Though weak in frame, art strong in
    will.' —
'O !' quoth the page, ' even there de-
    pends   159
My counsel — there my warning tends —
Oft seems as of my master's breast
Some demon were the sudden guest;
Then at the first misconstrued word
His hand is on the mace and sword,
From her firm seat his wisdom driven,
His life to countless dangers given.
O, would that Gunnar could suffice
To be the fiend's last sacrifice,
So that, when glutted with my gore,
He fled and tempted thee no more !'   170

VIII

Then waved his hand and shook his head
The impatient Dane while thus he said:

'Profane not, youth — it is not thine
To judge the spirit of our line —
The bold Berserkar's rage divine,
Through whose inspiring deeds are
        wrought
Past human strength and human thought.
When full upon his gloomy soul
The champion feels the influence roll,
He swims the lake, he leaps the wall — 180
Heeds not the depth, nor plumbs the
        fall —
Unshielded, mail-less, on he goes
Singly against a host of foes;
Their spears he holds like withered reeds,
Their mail like maiden's silken weeds;
One 'gainst a hundred will he strive,
Take countless wounds and yet survive.
Then rush the eagles to his cry
Of slaughter and of victory, —
And blood he quaffs like Odin's bowl, 190
Deep drinks his sword, — deep drinks his
        soul;
And all that meet him in his ire
He gives to ruin, rout, and fire;
Then, like gorged lion, seeks some den
And couches till he 's man agen. —
Thou know'st the signs of look and limb
When 'gins that rage to overbrim —
Thou know'st when I am moved and
        why;
And when thou see'st me roll mine eye,
Set my teeth thus, and stamp my foot, 200
Regard thy safety and be mute;
But else speak boldly out whate'er
Is fitting that a knight should hear.
I love thee, youth. Thy lay has power
Upon my dark and sullen hour; —
So Christian monks are wont to say
Demons of old were charmed away;
Then fear not I will rashly deem
Ill of thy speech, whate'er the theme.' 209

IX

As down some strait in doubt and dread
The watchful pilot drops the lead,
And, cautious in the midst to steer,
The shoaling channel sounds with fear;
So, lest on dangerous ground he swerved,
The page his master's brow observed,
Pausing at intervals to fling
His hand on the melodious string,
And to his moody breast apply
The soothing charm of harmony,
While hinted half, and half exprest, 220
This warning song conveyed the rest. —

SONG

'Ill fares the bark with tackle riven,
And ill when on the breakers driven, —
Ill when the storm-sprite shrieks in air,
And the scared mermaid tears her hair;
But worse when on her helm the hand
Of some false traitor holds command.

'Ill fares the fainting palmer, placed
Mid Hebron's rocks or Rana's waste, —
Ill when the scorching sun is high, 230
And the expected font is dry,
Worse when his guide o'er sand and heath,
The barbarous Copt, has planned his death.

'Ill fares the knight with buckler cleft,
And ill when of his helm bereft,
Ill when his steed to earth is flung,
Or from his grasp his falchion wrung;
But worse, of instant ruin token,
When he lists rede by woman spoken.' —

X

'How now, fond boy ? — Canst thou think
        ill,'
Said Harold, ' of fair Metelill ? ' 240

'She may be fair,' the page replied
        As through the strings he ranged, —
'She may be fair; but yet,' he cried,
        And then the strain he changed, —

SONG

'She may be fair,' he sang, ' but yet
        Far fairer have I seen
Than she, for all her locks of jet
        And eyes so dark and sheen.
Were I a Danish knight in arms, 250
        As one day I may be,
My heart should own no foreign charms —
        A Danish maid for me !

'I love my father's northern land,
        Where the dark pine-trees grow,
And the bold Baltic's echoing strand
        Looks o'er each grassy oe.
I love to mark the lingering sun,
        From Denmark loath to go,
And leaving on the billows bright, 260
To cheer the short-lived summer night,
        A path of ruddy glow.

'But most the northern maid I love,
        With breast like Denmark's snow

And form as fair as Denmark's pine,
Who loves with purple heath to twine
 Her locks of sunny glow;
And sweetly blend that shade of gold
 With the cheek's rosy hue,
And Faith might for her mirror hold   270
 That eye of matchless blue.

XI

' 'T is hers the manly sports to love
 That southern maidens fear,
To bend the bow by stream and grove,
 And lift the hunter's spear.
She can her chosen champion's flight
 With eye undazzled see,
Clasp him victorious from the strife,
Or on his corpse yield up her life, —
 A Danish maid for me !'   280

XI

Then smiled the Dane: ' Thou canst so well,
The virtues of our maidens tell,
Half could I wish my choice had been
Blue eyes, and hair of golden sheen,
And lofty soul; — yet what of ill
Hast thou to charge on Metelill ? '
' Nothing on her,' young Gunnar said,
' But her base sire's ignoble trade.
Her mother too — the general fame
Hath given to Jutta evil name,   290
And in her gray eye is a flame
Art cannot hide nor fear can tame. —
That sordid woodman's peasant cot
Twice have thine honored footsteps sought,
And twice returned with such ill rede
As sent thee on some desperate deed.'

XII

' Thou errest; Jutta wisely said,
He that comes suitor to a maid,
Ere linked in marriage, should provide
Lands and a dwelling for his bride —   300
My father's by the Tyne and Wear
I have reclaimed.' — ' O, all too dear
And all too dangerous the prize,
E'en were it won,' young Gunnar cries; —
' And then this Jutta's fresh device,
That thou shouldst seek, a heathen Dane,
From Durham's priests a boon to gain
When thou hast left their vassals slain
In their own halls !' — Flashed Harold's
 eye,
Thundered his voice — ' False page, you
 lie !'   310
The castle, hall and tower, is mine,
Built by old Witikind on Tyne.

The wild-cat will defend his den,
Fights for her nest the timid wren;
And think'st thou I 'll forego my right
For dread of monk or monkish knight ? —
Up and away, that deepening bell
Doth of the bishop's conclave tell.
Thither will I in manner due,
As Jutta bade, my claim to sue;   320
And if to right me they are loath,
Then woe to church and chapter both !'
Now shift the scene and let the curtain fall,
And our next entry be Saint Cuthbert's hall.

CANTO FOURTH

I

FULL many a bard hath sung the solemn
 gloom
Of the long Gothic aisle and stone-ribbed
 roof,
O'er-canopying shrine and gorgeous tomb,
Carved screen, and altar glimmering far
 aloof
And blending with the shade — a match-
 less proof
Of high devotion, which hath now waxed
 cold;
Yet legends say that Luxury's brute hoof
Intruded oft within such sacred fold,
Like step of Bel's false priest tracked in
 his fane of old.

Well pleased am I, howe'er, that when
 the rout   10
Of our rude neighbors whilome deigned
 to come,
Uncalled and eke unwelcome, to sweep out
And cleanse our chancel from the rags of
 Rome,
They spoke not on our ancient fane the
 doom
To which their bigot zeal gave o'er their
 own,
But spared the martyred saint and storied
 tomb,
Though papal miracles had graced the
 stone,
And though the aisles still loved the organ's
 swelling tone.

And deem not, though 't is now my part
 to paint
A prelate swayed by love of power and
 gold,   20

That all who wore the mitre of our Saint
Like to ambitious Aldingar I hold;
Since both in modern times and days of
old
It sate on those whose virtues might
atone
Their predecessors' frailties trebly told:
Matthew and Morton we as such may
own —
And such — if fame speak truth — the
honored Barrington.

II

But now to earlier and to ruder times,
As subject meet, I tune my rugged
rhymes, 29
Telling how fairly the chapter was met,
And rood and books in seemly order set;
Huge brass-clasped volumes which the
hand
Of studious priest but rarely scanned,
Now on fair carved desk displayed,
'T was theirs the solemn scene to aid.
O'erhead with many a scutcheon graced
And quaint devices interlaced,
A labyrinth of crossing rows,
The roof in lessening arches shows;
Beneath its shade placed proud and
high 40
With footstool and with canopy,
Sate Aldingar — and prelate ne'er
More haughty graced Saint Cuthbert's
chair;
Canons and deacons were placed below,
In due degree and lengthened row.
Unmoved and silent each sat there,
Like image in his oaken chair;
Nor head nor hand nor foot they stirred,
Nor lock of hair nor tress of beard;
And of their eyes severe alone 50
The twinkle showed they were not stone.

III

The prelate was to speech addressed,
Each head sunk reverent on each breast;
But ere his voice was heard — without
Arose a wild tumultuous shout,
Offspring of wonder mixed with fear,
Such as in crowded streets we hear
Hailing the flames that, bursting out,
Attract yet scare the rabble rout.
Ere it had ceased a giant hand 60
Shook oaken door and iron band
Till oak and iron both gave way,
Clashed the long bolts, the hinges bray,

And, ere upon angel or saint they can
call,
Stands Harold the Dauntless in midst of
the hall.

IV

'Now save ye, my masters, both rocket and
rood,
From bishop with mitre to deacon with
hood !
For here stands Count Harold, old Witi-
kind's son,
Come to sue for the lands which his ances-
tors won.'
The prelate looked round him with sore
troubled eye, 70
Unwilling to grant yet afraid to deny;
While each canon and deacon who heard
the Dane speak,
To be safely at home would have fasted a
week: —
Then Aldingar roused him and answered
again,
'Thou suest for a boon which thou canst
not obtain;
The Church hath no fiefs for an unchris-
tened Dane.
Thy father was wise, and his treasure hath
given
That the priests of a chantry might hymn
him to heaven;
And the fiefs which whilome he possessed
as his due
Have lapsed to the Church, and been
granted anew 80
To Anthony Conyers and Alberic Vere,
For the service Saint Cuthbert's blest ban-
ner to bear
When the bands of the North come to foray
the Wear;
Then disturb not our conclave with wran-
gling or blame,
But in peace and in patience pass hence as
ye came.'

V

Loud laughed the stern Pagan, 'They 're
free from the care
Of fief and of service, both Conyers and
Vere, —
Six feet of your chancel is all they will
need,
A buckler of stone and a corselet of lead. —
Ho, Gunnar ! — the tokens ! ' — and, sev-
ered anew,
90

A head and a hand on the altar he threw.
Then shuddered with terror both canon
and monk,
They knew the glazed eye and the counte-
nance shrunk,
And of Anthony Conyers the half-grizzled
hair,
And the scar on the hand of Sir Alberic
Vere.
There was not a churchman or priest that
was there
But grew pale at the sight and betook him
to prayer.

VI

Count Harold laughed at their looks of
fear:
'Was this the hand should your banner
bear ?   99
Was that the head should wear the casque
In battle at the Church's task ?
Was it to such you gave the place
Of Harold with the heavy mace ?
Find me between the Wear and Tyne
A knight will wield this club of mine, —
Give him my fiefs, and I will say
There's wit beneath the cowl of gray.'
He raised it, rough with many a stain
Caught from crushed skull and spouting
brain;
He wheeled it that it shrilly sung   110
And the aisles echoed as it swung,
Then dashed it down with sheer descent
And split King Osric's monument. —
'How like ye this music ? How trow ye
the hand
That can wield such a mace may be reft of
its land ?
No answer ? — I spare ye a space to agree,
And Saint Cuthbert inspire you, a saint if
he be.
Ten strides through your chancel, ten
strokes on your bell,
And again I am with you — grave fathers,
farewell.'

VII

He turned from their presence, he clashed
the oak door,   120
And the clang of his stride died away on
the floor;
And his head from his bosom the prelate
uprears
With a ghost-seer's look when the ghost
disappears:

'Ye Priests of Saint Cuthbert, now give
me your rede,
For never of counsel had bishop more
need !
Were the arch-fiend incarnate in flesh and
in bone,
The language, the look, and the laugh were
his own.
In the bounds of Saint Cuthbert there is
not a knight
Dare confront in our quarrel yon goblin in
fight;
Then rede me aright to his claim to
reply,   130
'T is unlawful to grant and 't is death to
deny.'

VIII

On venison and malmsie that morning had
fed
The Cellarer Vinsauf — 't was thus that he
said:
'Delay till to-morrow the Chapter's reply;
Let the feast be spread fair and the wine
be poured high:
If he's mortal he drinks, — if he drinks,
he is ours —
His bracelets of iron, — his bed in our
towers.'
This man had a laughing eye,
Trust not, friends, when such you spy;
A beaker's depth he well could drain,   140
Revel, sport, and jest amain —
The haunch of the deer and the grape's
bright dye
Never bard loved them better than I;
But sooner than Vinsauf filled me my
wine,
Passed me his jest, and laughed at mine,
Though the buck were of Bearpark, of
Bordeaux the vine,
With the dullest hermit I'd rather dine
On an oaken cake and a draught of the
Tyne.

IX

Walwayn the leech spoke next — he knew
Each plant that loves the sun and dew,   150
But special those whose juice can gain
Dominion o'er the blood and brain;
The peasant who saw him by pale moon-
beam
Gathering such herbs by bank and stream
Deemed his thin form and soundless tread
Were those of wanderer from the dead. —

'Vinsauf, thy wine,' he said, 'hath power,
Our gyves are heavy, strong our tower;
Yet three drops from this flask of mine,
More strong than dungeons, gyves, or
    wine,   160
Shall give him prison under ground
More dark, more narrow, more profound.
Short rede, good rede, let Harold have —
A dog's death and a heathen's grave.'
I have lain on a sick man's bed,
Watching for hours for the leech's tread,
As if I deemed that his presence alone
Were of power to bid my pain begone;
I have listed his words of comfort given,
As if to oracles from heaven;   170
I have counted his steps from my chamber
    door,
And blessed them when they were heard
    no more; —
But sooner than Walwayn my sick couch
    should nigh,
My choice were by leech-craft unaided to
    die.

X

'Such service done in fervent zeal
The Church may pardon and conceal,'
The doubtful prelate said, 'but ne'er
The counsel ere the act should hear. —
Anselm of Jarrow, advise us now,
The stamp of wisdom is on thy brow;   180
Thy days, thy nights, in cloister pent,
Are still to mystic learning lent; —
Anselm of Jarrow, in thee is my hope,
Thou well mayst give counsel to prelate or
    pope.'

XI

Answered the prior, — ''T is wisdom's use
Still to delay what we dare not refuse;
Ere granting the boon he comes hither to
    ask,
Shape for the giant gigantic task;
Let us see how a step so sounding can
    tread
In paths of darkness, danger, and dread; 190
He may not, he will not, impugn our decree
That calls but for proof of his chivalry;
And were Guy to return or Sir Bevis the
    Strong,
Our wilds have adventure might cumber
    them long —
The Castle of Seven Shields' — 'Kind
    Anselm, no more !
The step of the Pagan approaches the
    door.'

The churchmen were hushed. — In his
    mantle of skin
With his mace on his shoulder Count
    Harold strode in.
There was foam on his lips, there was fire
    in his eye,
For, chafed by attendance, his fury was
    nigh.   200
'Ho ! Bishop,' he said, 'dost thou grant
    me my claim ?
Or must I assert it by falchion and flame ? '

XII

'On thy suit, gallant Harold,' the bishop
    replied,
In accents which trembled, 'we may not
    decide
Until proof of your strength and your valor
    we saw —
'T is not that we doubt them, but such is
    the law.' —
'And would you, Sir Prelate, have Harold
    make sport
For the cowls and the shavelings that herd
    in thy court ?
Say what shall he do ? — From the shrine
    shall he tear
The lead bier of thy patron and heave it in
    air,   210
And through the long chancel make Cuth-
    bert take wing
With the speed of a bullet dismissed from
    the sling ? ' —
'Nay, spare such probation,' the cellarer
    said,
'From the mouth of our minstrels thy
    task shall be read.
While the wine sparkles high in the goblet
    of gold
And the revel is loudest, thy task shall be
    told;
And thyself, gallant Harold, shall, hearing
    it, tell
That the bishop, his cowls, and his shave-
    lings, meant well.'

XIII

Loud revelled the guests and the goblets
    loud rang,
But louder the minstrel, Hugh Meneville,
    sang;   220
And Harold, the hurry and pride of whose
    soul,
E'en when verging to fury, owned music's
    control,

Still bent on the harper his broad sable eye,
And often untasted the goblet passed by;
Than wine or than wassail to him was more
  dear
The minstrel's high tale of enchantment to
  hear;
And the bishop that day might of Vinsauf
  complain
That his art had but wasted his wine-casks
  in vain.

XIV

THE CASTLE OF THE SEVEN SHIELDS

A BALLAD

The Druid Urien had daughters seven,
Their skill could call the moon from hea-
  ven;   230
So fair their forms and so high their fame
That seven proud kings for their suitors
  came.

King Mador and Rhys came from Powis
  and Wales,
Unshorn was their hair and unpruned were
  their nails;
From Strath-Clyde was Ewain, and Ewain
  was lame,
And the red-bearded Donald from Galloway came.

Lot, King of Lodon, was hunchbacked from
  youth;
Dunmail of Cumbria had never a tooth;
But Adolf of Bambrough, Northumberland's heir,
Was gay and was gallant, was young and
  was fair.   240

There was strife 'mongst the sisters, for
  each one would have
For husband King Adolf, the gallant and
  brave;
And envy bred hate, and hate urged them
  to blows,
When the firm earth was cleft and the
  Arch-fiend arose !

He swore to the maidens their wish to fulfil —
They swore to the foe they would work by
  his will.
A spindle and distaff to each hath he given,
' Now hearken my spell,' said the Outcast
  of heaven.

' Ye shall ply these spindles at midnight
  hour,   249
And for every spindle shall rise a tower,
Where the right shall be feeble, the wrong
  shall have power,
And there shall ye dwell with your paramour.'

Beneath the pale moonlight they sate on
  the wold,
And the rhymes which they chanted must
  never be told;
And as the black wool from the distaff they
  sped,
With blood from their bosom they mois-
  tened the thread.

As light danced the spindles beneath the
  cold gleam,
The castle arose like the birth of a
  dream —
The seven towers ascended like mist from
  the ground,
Seven portals defend them, seven ditches
  surround.   260

Within that dread castle seven monarchs
  were wed,
But six of the seven ere the morning lay
  dead;
With their eyes all on fire and their daggers all red,
Seven damsels surround the Northumbrian's bed.

' Six kingly bridegrooms to death we have
  done,
Six gallant kingdoms King Adolf hath
  won,
Six lovely brides all his pleasure to do,
Or the bed of the seventh shall be husband-
  less too.'

Well chanced it that Adolf the night when
  he wed
Had confessed and had sained him e'er
  boune to his bed;   270
He sprung from the couch and his broadsword he drew,
And there the seven daughters of Urien he
  slew.

The gate of the castle he bolted and sealed,
And hung o'er each arch-stone a crown
  and a shield;

To the cells of Saint Dunstan then wended
  his way,
And died in his cloister an anchorite gray.

Seven monarchs' wealth in that castle lies
  stowed,
The foul fiends brood o'er them like raven
  and toad.
Whoever shall guesten these chambers
  within,
From curfew till matins, that treasure
  shall win.   280

But manhood grows faint as the world
  waxes old !
There lives not in Britain a champion so
  bold,
So dauntless of heart and so prudent of
  brain,
As to dare the adventure that treasure to
  gain.

The waste ridge of Cheviot shall wave
  with the rye,
Before the rude Scots shall Northumberland fly,
And the flint cliffs of Bambro' shall melt in
  the sun,
Before that adventure be perilled and won.

XV

'And is this my probation?' wild Harold
  he said,
'Within a lone castle to press a lone
  bed? —   290
Good even, my lord bishop, — Saint Cuth-
  bert to borrow,
The Castle of Seven Shields receives me
  to-morrow.'

CANTO FIFTH

I

DENMARK'S sage courtier to her princely
  youth,
Granting his cloud an ousel or a whale,
Spoke, though unwittingly, a partial
  truth;
For Fantasy embroiders Nature's veil.
The tints of ruddy eve or dawning pale,
Of the swart thunder-cloud or silver
  haze,
Are but the ground-work of the rich de-
  tail

Which Fantasy with pencil wild portrays,
Blending what seems and is in the wrapt
  muser's gaze.

Nor are the stubborn forms of earth and
  stone   10
Less to the Sorceress's empire given;
For not with unsubstantial hues alone,
Caught from the varying surge of vacant
  heaven,
From bursting sunbeam or from flashing
  levin,
She limns her pictures: on the earth, as
  air,
Arise her castles and her car is driven;
And never gazed the eye on scene so fair,
But of its boasted charms gave Fancy half
  the share.

II

Up a wild pass went Harold, bent to
  prove,
Hugh Meneville, the adventure of thy
  lay;   20
Gunnar pursued his steps in faith and
  love,
Ever companion of his master's way.
Midward their path, a rock of granite
  gray
From the adjoining cliff had made descent, —
A barren mass — yet with her drooping
  spray
Had a young birch-tree crowned its
  battlement,
Twisting her fibrous roots through cranny,
  flaw, and rent.

This rock and tree could Gunnar's
  thought engage
Till Fancy brought the tear-drop to his
  eye,
And at his master asked the timid
  page,   30
'What is the emblem that a bard should
  spy
In that rude rock and its green canopy?'
And Harold said, 'Like to the helmet
  brave
Of warrior slain in fight it seems to
  lie,
And these same drooping boughs do o'er
  it wave
Not all unlike the plume his lady's favor
  gave.'

'Ah, no!' replied the page; 'the ill-
starred love
Of some poor maid is in the emblem
shown,
Whose fates are with some hero's inter-
wove,
And rooted on a heart to love un-
known:　　　　　　　　　　40
And as the gentle dews of heaven alone
Nourish those drooping boughs, and as
the scathe
Of the red lightning rends both tree and
stone,
So fares it with her unrequited faith, —
Her sole relief is tears — her only refuge
death.'

III

'Thou art a fond fantastic boy,'
Harold replied, 'to females coy,
Yet prating still of love;
Even so amid the clash of war
I know thou lov'st to keep afar,　　　50
Though destined by thy evil star
With one like me to rove,
Whose business and whose joys are found
Upon the bloody battle-ground.
Yet, foolish trembler as thou art,
Thou hast a nook of my rude heart,
And thou and I will never part; —
Harold would wrap the world in flame
Ere injury on Gunnar came.'

IV

The grateful page made no reply,　　60
But turned to heaven his gentle eye,
And clasped his hands, as one who said,
'My toils — my wanderings are o'erpaid!'
Then in a gayer, lighter strain,
Compelled himself to speech again;
And, as they flowed along,
His words took cadence soft and slow,
And liquid, like dissolving snow,
They melted into song.

V

'What though through fields of carnage
wide　　　　　　　　　　70
I may not follow Harold's stride,
Yet who with faithful Gunnar's pride
Lord Harold's feats can see?
And dearer than the couch of pride
He loves the bed of gray wolf's hide,
When slumbering by Lord Harold's side
In forest, field, or lea.'

VI

'Break off!' said Harold, in a tone
Where hurry and surprise were shown,
With some slight touch of fear,　　80
'Break off, we are not here alone;
A palmer form comes slowly on!
By cowl and staff and mantle known,
My monitor is near.
Now mark him, Gunnar, heedfully;
He pauses by the blighted tree —
Dost see him, youth? — Thou couldst not see
When in the vale of Galilee
I first beheld his form,
Nor when we met that other while　　90
In Cephalonia's rocky isle
Before the fearful storm, —
Dost see him now?' — The page, dis-
traught
With terror, answered, 'I see nought,
And there is nought to see,
Save that the oak's scathed boughs fling
down
Upon the path a shadow brown
That, like a pilgrim's dusky gown,
Waves with the waving tree.'

VII

Count Harold gazed upon the oak　　100
As if his eyestrings would have broke,
And then resolvedly said,
'Be what it will yon phantom gray —
Nor heaven nor hell shall ever say
That for their shadows from his way
Count Harold turned dismayed:
I 'll speak him, though his accents fill
My heart with that unwonted thrill
Which vulgar minds call fear.
I will subdue it!' Forth he strode,　　110
Paused where the blighted oak-tree showed
Its sable shadow on the road,
And, folding on his bosom broad
His arms, said, 'Speak — I hear.'

VIII

The Deep Voice said, 'O wild of will,
Furious thy purpose to fulfil —
Heart-seared and unrepentant still,
How long, O Harold, shall thy tread
Disturb the slumbers of the dead?
Each step in thy wild way thou makest, 120
The ashes of the dead thou wakest;
And shout in triumph o'er thy path
The fiends of bloodshed and of wrath.
In this thine hour, yet turn and hear!
For life is brief and judgment near.'

IX

Then ceased the Voice. — The Dane re-
    plied
In tones where awe and inborn pride
For mastery strove, 'In vain ye chide
The wolf for ravaging the flock,
Or with its hardness taunt the rock, — 130
I am as they — my Danish strain
Sends streams of fire through every vein.
Amid thy realms of goule and ghost,
Say, is the fame of Eric lost,
Or Witikind's the Waster, known
Where fame or spoil was to be won;
Whose galleys ne'er bore off a shore
    They left not black with flame ? —
He was my sire, — and, sprung of him,
That rover merciless and grim, 140
    Can I be soft and tame?
Part hence and with my crimes no more
    upbraid me,
I am that Waster's son and am but what
    he made me.'

X

The Phantom groaned; — the mountain
    shook around,
The fawn and wild - doe started at the
    sound,
The gorse and fern did wildly round them
    wave,
As if some sudden storm the impulse gave.
'All thou hast said is truth — yet on the
    head
Of that bad sire let not the charge be laid
That he, like thee, with unrelenting pace 150
From grave to cradle ran the evil race: —
Relentless in his avarice and ire,
Churches and towns he gave to sword and
    fire;
Shed blood like water, wasted every land,
Like the destroying angel's burning brand;
Fulfilled whate'er of ill might be invented,
Yes, — all these things he did — he did,
    but he REPENTED !
Perchance it is part of his punishment still
That his offspring pursues his example of
    ill.
But thou, when thy tempest of wrath shall
    next shake thee, 160
Gird thy loins for resistance, my son, and
    awake thee;
If thou yield'st to thy fury, how tempted
    soever,
The gate of repentance shall ope for thee
    NEVER !'

XI

'He is gone,' said Lord Harold and gazed
    as he spoke;
'There is nought on the path but the shade
    of the oak.
He is gone whose strange presence my
    feeling oppressed,
Like the night-hag that sits on the slum-
    berer's breast.
My heart beats as thick as a fugitive's
    tread,
And cold dews drop from my brow and
    my head. —
Ho ! Gunnar, the flasket yon almoner
    gave; 170
He said that three drops would recall
    from the grave.
For the first time Count Harold owns
    leechcraft has power,
Or, his courage to aid, lacks the juice of a
    flower !'
The page gave the flasket, which Walwayn
    had filled
With the juice of wild roots that his heart
    had distilled —
So baneful their influence on all that had
    breath,
One drop had been frenzy and two had been
    death.
Harold took it, but drank not; for jubilee
    shrill
And music and clamor were heard on the
    hill,
And down the steep pathway o'er stock and
    o'er stone 180
The train of a bridal came blithesomely
    on ;
There was song, there was pipe, there was
    timbrel, and still
The burden was, 'Joy to the fair Metelill !'

XII

Harold might see from his high stance
Himself unseen, that train advance,
    With mirth and melody; —
On horse and foot a mingled throng,
Measuring their steps to bridal song
    And bridal minstrelsy;
And ever when the blithesome rout 190
Lent to the song their choral shout,
Redoubling echoes rolled about,
While echoing cave and cliff sent out
    The answering symphony
Of all those mimic notes which dwell
In hollow rock and sounding dell.

XIII

Joy shook his torch above the band,
By many a various passion fanned; —
As elemental sparks can feed
On essence pure and coarsest weed,   200
Gentle or stormy or refined,
Joy takes the colors of the mind.
Lightsome and pure but unrepressed,
He fired the bridegroom's gallant breast;
More feebly strove with maiden fear,
Yet still joy glimmered through the tear
On the bride's blushing cheek that shows
Like dew-drop on the budding rose;
While Wulfstane's gloomy smile declared
The glee that selfish avarice shared,   210
And pleased revenge and malice high
Joy's semblance took in Jutta's eye.
On dangerous adventure sped,
The witch deemed Harold with the dead,
For thus that morn her demon said: —
' If, ere the set of sun, be tied
The knot 'twixt bridegroom and his bride,
The Dane shall have no power of ill
O'er William and o'er Metelill.'
And the pleased witch made answer,
'Then   220
Must Harold have passed from the paths
of men !
Evil repose may his spirit have, —
May hemlock and mandrake find root in
his grave, —
May his death-sleep be dogged by dreams
of dismay,
And his waking be worse at the answer-
ing day !'

XIV

Such was their various mood of glee
Blent in one shout of ecstasy.
But still when Joy is brimming highest,
Of sorrow and misfortune nighest,
Of Terror with her ague cheek,   230
And lurking Danger, sages speak: —
These haunt each path, but chief they lay
Their snares beside the primrose way. —
Thus found that bridal band their path
Beset by Harold in his wrath.
Trembling beneath his maddening mood,
High on a rock the giant stood;
His shout was like the doom of death
Spoke o'er their heads that passed be-
neath.
His destined victims might not spy   240
The reddening terrors of his eye,
The frown of rage that writhed his face,

The lip that foamed like boar's in chase;
But all could see — and, seeing, all
Bore back to shun the threatened fall —
The fragment which their giant foe
Rent from the cliff and heaved to throw.

XV

Backward they bore — yet are there two
For battle who prepare: 249
No pause of dread Lord William knew
Ere his good blade was bare;
And Wulfstane bent his fatal yew,
But ere the silken cord he drew,
As hurled from Hecla's thunder flew
That ruin through the air !
Full on the outlaw's front it came,
And all that late had human name,
And human face, and human frame,
That lived and moved and had free will
To choose the path of good or ill,   260
Is to its reckoning gone;
And nought of Wulfstane rests behind
Save that beneath that stone,
Half-buried in the dinted clay,
A red and shapeless mass there lay
Of mingled flesh and bone !

XVI

As from the bosom of the sky
The eagle darts amain,
Three bounds from yonder summit high
Placed Harold on the plain.   270
As the scared wild-fowl scream and fly,
So fled the bridal train;
As 'gainst the eagle's peerless might
The noble falcon dares the fight,
But dares the fight in vain,
So fought the bridegroom; from his
hand
The Dane's rude mace has struck his
brand,
Its glittering fragments strew the sand,
Its lord lies on the plain.
Now, Heaven ! take noble William's
part,   280
And melt that yet unmelted heart,
Or, ere his bridal hour depart,
The hapless bridegroom 's slain !

XVII

Count Harold's frenzied rage is high,
There is a death-fire in his eye,
Deep furrows on his brow are trenched,
His teeth are set, his hand is clenched,
The foam upon his lip is white,

His deadly arm is up to smite !
But, as the mace aloft he swung,   290
To stop the blow young Gunnar sprung,
Around his master's knees he clung,
And cried, ' In mercy spare !
O, think upon the words of fear
Spoke by that visionary Seer,
The crisis he foretold is here, —
  Grant mercy, — or despair ! '
This word suspended Harold's mood,
Yet still with arm upraised he stood,
And visage like the headsman's rude   300
  That pauses for the sign.
' O mark thee with the blessed rood,'
The page implored : ' Speak word of
  good,
Resist the fiend or be subdued ! '
He signed the cross divine —
Instant his eye hath human light,
Less red, less keen, less fiercely bright;
His brow relaxed the obdurate frown,
The fatal mace sinks gently down,
  He turns and strides away;   310
Yet oft, like revellers who leave
Unfinished feast, looks back to grieve,
As if repenting the reprieve
  He granted to his prey.
Yet still of forbearance one sign hath he
  given,
And fierce Witikind's son made one step
  towards heaven.

XVIII

But though his dreaded footsteps part,
Death is behind and shakes his dart;
Lord William on the plain is lying,
Beside him Metelill seems dying ! — 320
Bring odors — essences in haste —
And lo ! a flasket richly chased, —
But Jutta the elixir proves
Ere pouring it for those she loves —
Then Walwayn's potion was not wasted,
For when three drops the hag had tasted
So dismal was her yell,
Each bird of evil omen woke,
The raven gave his fatal croak,
And shrieked the night-crow from the
  oak,   330
The screech-owl from the thicket broke,
  And fluttered down the dell !
So fearful was the sound and stern,
The slumbers of the full-gorged erne
Were startled, and from furze and fern
  Of forest and of fell
The fox and famished wolf replied —

For wolves then prowled the Cheviot
  side —
From mountain head to mountain head
The unhallowed sounds around were
  sped;   340
But when their latest echo fled
The sorceress on the ground lay dead.

XIX

Such was the scene of blood and woes
With which the bridal morn arose
  Of William and of Metelill;
But oft, when dawning 'gins to spread,
The summer morn peeps dim and red
  Above the eastern hill,
Ere, bright and fair, upon his road
The king of splendor walks abroad;   350
So, when this cloud had passed away,
Bright was the noontide of their day
And all serene its setting ray.

CANTO SIXTH

I

WELL do I hope that this my minstrel
  tale
Will tempt no traveller from southern
  fields,
Whether in tilbury, barouche, or mail,
To view the Castle of these Seven Proud
  Shields.
Small confirmation its condition yields
To Meneville's high lay, — no towers are
  seen
On the wild heath but those that Fancy
  builds,
And, save a fosse that tracks the moor
  with green,
Is nought remains to tell of what may there
  have been.

And yet grave authors, with the no small
  waste   10
Of their grave time, have dignified the spot
By theories, to prove the fortress placed
By Roman bands to curb the invading
  Scot.
Hutchinson, Horseley, Camden, I might
  quote,
But rather choose the theory less civil
Of boors, who, origin of things forgot,
Refer still to the origin of evil,
And for their master-mason choose that
  master-fiend the Devil.

II

Therefore, I say, it was on fiend-built
   towers
That stout Count Harold bent his wondering gaze   20
When evening dew was on the heather
   flowers,
And the last sunbeams made the mountain blaze
And tinged the battlements of other days
With the bright level light ere sinking
   down.
Illumined thus, the dauntless Dane surveys
The Seven Proud Shields that o'er the
   portal frown,
And on their blazons traced high marks of
   old renown.

A wolf North Wales had on his armor-
   coat,
And Rhys of Powis-land a couchant stag;
Strath-Clwyd's strange emblem was a
   stranded boat,   30
Donald of Galloway's a trotting nag;
A corn-sheaf gilt was fertile Lodon's
   brag;
A dudgeon - dagger was by Dunmail
   worn;
Northumbrian Adolf gave a sea-beat
   crag
Surmounted by a cross — such signs were
   borne
Upon these antique shields, all wasted now
   and worn.

III

These scanned, Count Harold sought the
   castle-door,
Whose ponderous bolts were rusted to
   decay;
Yet till that hour adventurous knight
   forbore
The unobstructed passage to essay.   40
More strong than armed warders in
   array,
And obstacle more sure than bolt or
   bar,
Sate in the portal Terror and Dismay,
While Superstition, who forbade to war
With foes of other mould than mortal
   clay,
Cast spells across the gate and barred the
   onward way.

Vain now those spells; for soon with
   heavy clank
The feebly-fastened gate was inward
   pushed,
And, as it oped, through that emblazoned
   rank
Of antique shields the wind of evening
   rushed   50
With sound most like a groan and then
   was hushed.
Is none who on such spot such sounds
   could hear
But to his heart the blood had faster
   rushed;
Yet to bold Harold's breast that throb
   was dear —
It spoke of danger nigh, but had no touch
   of fear.

IV

Yet Harold and his page no signs have
   traced
Within the castle that of danger showed;
For still the halls and courts were wild
   and waste,
As through their precincts the adventurers trode.
The seven huge towers rose stately, tall,
   and broad,   60
Each tower presenting to their scrutiny
A hall in which a king might make
   abode,
And fast beside, garnished both proud
   and high,
Was placed a bower for rest in which a
   king might lie.

As if a bridal there of late had been,
Decked stood the table in each gorgeous
   hall;
And yet it was two hundred years, I
   ween,
Since date of that unhallowed festival.
Flagons and ewers and standing cups
   were all
Of tarnished gold or silver nothing
   clear,   70
With throne begilt and canopy of pall,
And tapestry clothed the walls with
   fragments sear —
Frail as the spider's mesh did that rich
   woof appear.

V

In every bower, as round a hearse, was
  hung
A dusky crimson curtain o'er the bed,
And on each couch in ghastly wise were
  flung
The wasted relics of a monarch dead;
Barbaric ornaments around were spread,
Vests twined with gold and chains of
  precious stone,
And golden circlets, meet for monarch's
  head;   80
While grinned, as if in scorn amongst
  them thrown,
The wearer's fleshless skull, alike with dust
  bestrewn.

For these were they who, drunken with
  delight,
On pleasure's opiate pillow laid their
  head,
For whom the bride's shy footstep, slow
  and light,
Was changed ere morning to the murderer's tread.
For human bliss and woe in the frail
  thread
Of human life are all so closely twined
That till the shears of Fate the texture
  shred
The close succession cannot be dis-
  joined,   90
Nor dare we from one hour judge that
  which comes behind.

VI

But where the work of vengeance had
  been done,
In that seventh chamber, was a sterner
  sight;
There of the witch-brides lay each skeleton,
Still in the posture as to death when
  dight.
For this lay prone, by one blow slain
  outright;
And that, as one who struggled long in
  dying;
One bony hand held knife, as if to
  smite;
One bent on fleshless knees, as mercy
  crying;
One lay across the door, as killed in act of
  flying.   100

The stern Dane smiled this charnel-
  house to see, —
For his chafed thought returned to
  Metelill; —
And 'Well,' he said, 'hath woman's per-
  fidy,
Empty as air, as water volatile,
Been here avenged. — The origin of
  ill
Through woman rose, the Christian doc-
  trine saith;
Nor deem I, Gunnar, that thy minstrel
  skill
Can show example where a woman's
  breath
Hath made a true-love vow, and tempted
  kept her faith.'

VII

The minstrel-boy half smiled, half
  sighed,   110
And his half-filling eyes he dried,
And said, 'The theme I should but
  wrong,
Unless it were my dying song —
Our Scalds have said, in dying hour
The Northern harp has treble power —
Else could I tell of woman's faith,
Defying danger, scorn, and death.
Firm was that faith — as diamond stone
Pure and unflawed — her love unknown
And unrequited; — firm and pure,   120
Her stainless faith could all endure;
From clime to clime, from place to
  place,
Through want and danger and disgrace,
A wanderer's wayward steps could trace.
All this she did, and guerdon none
Required save that her burial-stone
Should make at length the secret known,
"Thus hath a faithful woman done." —
Not in each breast such truth is laid,
But Eivir was a Danish maid.'   130

VIII

'Thou art a wild enthusiast,' said
Count Harold, 'for thy Danish maid;
And yet, young Gunnar, I will own
Hers were a faith to rest upon.
But Eivir sleeps beneath her stone
And all resembling her are gone.
What maid e'er showed such constancy
In plighted faith, like thine to me?
But couch thee, boy; the darksome shade

Falls thickly round, nor be dismayed   140
  Because the dead are by.
They were as we; our little day
O'erspent, and we shall be as they.
Yet near me, Gunnar, be thou laid,
Thy couch upon my mantle made,
That thou mayst think, should fear in-
    vade,
  Thy master slumbers nigh.'
Thus couched they in that dread abode,
Until the beams of dawning glowed.

IX

An altered man Lord Harold rose,   150
When he beheld that dawn unclose —
  There 's trouble in his eyes,
And traces on his brow and cheek
Of mingled awe and wonder speak:
' My page,' he said, ' arise; —
Leave we this place, my page.' — No
    more
He uttered till the castle door
They crossed — but there he paused and
    said,
' My wildness hath awaked the dead —
  Disturbed the sacred tomb !   160
Methought this night I stood on high
Where Hecla roars in middle sky,
And in her caverned gulfs could spy
The central place of doom;
And there before my mortal eye
Souls of the dead came flitting by,
Whom fiends with many a fiendish cry
  Bore to that evil den !
My eyes grew dizzy and my brain
Was wildered, as the elvish train   170
With shriek and howl dragged on amain
Those who had late been men.

X

' With haggard eyes and streaming hair,
Jutta the Sorceress was there,
And there passed Wulfstane lately slain,
All crushed and foul with bloody stain. —
More had I seen, but that uprose
A whirlwind wild and swept the snows;
And with such sound as when at need
A champion spurs his horse to speed,   180
Three armed knights rush on who lead
Caparisoned a sable steed.
Sable their harness, and there came
Through their closed visors sparks of
    flame.
The first proclaimed, in sounds of fear,
" Harold the Dauntless, welcome here ! "

The next cried, " Jubilee ! we 've won
Count Witikind the Waster's son ! "
And the third rider sternly spoke,   189
" Mount, in the name of Zernebock ! —
From us, O Harold, were thy powers, —
Thy strength, thy dauntlessness, are
    ours;
Nor think, a vassal thou of hell,
With hell can strive." The fiend spoke
    true !
My inmost soul the summons knew,
  As captives know the knell
That says the headsman's sword is bare
And with an accent of despair
  Commands them quit their cell.
I felt resistance was in vain,   200
My foot had that fell stirrup ta'en,
My hand was on the fatal mane,
  When to my rescue sped
That palmer's visionary form,
And — like the passing of a storm —
  The demons yelled and fled !

XI

' His sable cowl flung back revealed
The features it before concealed;
  And, Gunnar, I could find
In him whose counsels strove to stay   210
So oft my course on wilful way
  My father Witikind !
Doomed for his sins and doomed for mine
  A wanderer upon earth to pine
Until his son shall turn to grace
And smooth for him a resting-place. —
Gunnar, he must not haunt in vain
This world of wretchedness and pain:
I 'll tame my wilful heart to live
In peace — to pity and forgive —   220
And thou, for so the Vision said,
Must in thy Lord's repentance aid.
Thy mother was a prophetess,
He said, who by her skill could guess
How close the fatal textures join
Which knit thy thread of life with mine;
Then dark he hinted of disguise
She framed to cheat too curious eyes
That not a moment might divide
Thy fated footsteps from my side.   230
Methought while thus my sire did teach
I caught the meaning of his speech,
Yet seems its purport doubtful now.'
His hand then sought his thoughtful
    brow —
Then first he marked, that in the tower
His glove was left at waking hour.

XII

Trembling at first and deadly pale,
Had Gunnar heard the visioned tale;
But when he learned the dubious close
He blushed like any opening rose,   240
And, glad to hide his tell-tale cheek,
Hied back that glove of mail to seek;
When soon a shriek of deadly dread
Summoned his master to his aid.

XIII

What sees Count Harold in that bower
So late his resting-place ? —
The semblance of the Evil Power,
Adored by all his race !
Odin in living form stood there,
His cloak the spoils of Polar bear;   250
For plumy crest a meteor shed
Its gloomy radiance o'er his head,
Yet veiled its haggard majesty
To the wild lightnings of his eye.
Such height was his as when in stone
O'er Upsal's giant altar shown:
So flowed his hoary beard;
Such was his lance of mountain-pine,
So did his sevenfold buckler shine;
But when his voice he reared,   260
Deep without harshness, slow and strong,
The powerful accents rolled along,
And while he spoke his hand was laid
On captive Gunnar's shrinking head.

XIV

' Harold,' he said, ' what rage is thine
To quit the worship of thy line,
To leave thy Warrior-God ? —
With me is glory or disgrace,
Mine is the onset and the chase,
Embattled hosts before my face   270
Are withered by a nod.
Wilt thou then forfeit that high seat
Deserved by many a dauntless feat
Among the heroes of thy line,
Eric and fiery Thorarine ? —
Thou wilt not.   Only I can give
The joys for which the valiant live,
Victory and vengeance — only I
Can give the joys for which they die,
The immortal tilt — the banquet full,   280
The brimming draught from foeman's
      skull.
Mine art thou, witness this thy glove,
The faithful pledge of vassal's love.'

XV

' Tempter,' said Harold, firm of heart,
' I charge thee, hence ! whate'er thou art,
I do defy thee — and resist
The kindling frenzy of my breast,
Waked by thy words; and of my mail
Nor glove nor buckler, splent nor nail,
Shall rest with thee — that youth release,
And, God or Demon, part in peace.'— 291
' Eivir,' the Shape replied, ' is mine,
Marked in the birth-hour with my sign.
Think'st thou that priest with drops of
      spray
Could wash that blood-red mark away ?
Or that a borrowed sex and name
Can abrogate a Godhead's claim ? '
Thrilled this strange speech through
      Harold's brain,
He clenched his teeth in high disdain,
For not his new-born faith subdued   300
Some tokens of his ancient mood. —
' Now, by the hope so lately given
Of better trust and purer heaven,
I will assail thee, fiend ! ' — Then rose
His mace, and with a storm of blows
The mortal and the demon close.

XVI

Smoke rolled above, fire flashed around,
Darkened the sky and shook the ground;
But not the artillery of hell,
The bickering lightning, nor the rock 310
Of turrets to the earthquake's shock,
Could Harold's courage quell.
Sternly the Dane his purpose kept,
And blows on blows resistless heaped,
Till quailed that demon form,
And — for his power to hurt or kill
Was bounded by a higher will —
Evanished in a storm.
Nor paused the Champion of the North,
But raised and bore his Eivir forth   320
From that wild scene of fiendish strife
To light, to liberty, and life !

XVII

He placed her on a bank of moss,
A silver runnel bubbled by,
And new-born thoughts his soul engross,
And tremors yet unknown across
His stubborn sinews fly,
The while with timid hand the dew
Upon her brow and neck he threw,
And marked how life with rosy hue   330

On her pale cheek revived anew
And glimmered in her eye.
Inly he said, ' That silken tress —
What blindness mine that could not
    guess !
Or how could page's rugged dress
That bosom's pride belie ?
O, dull of heart, through wild and wave
In search of blood and death to rave,
    With such a partner nigh ! '

XVIII

Then in the mirrored pool he peered, 340
Blamed his rough locks and shaggy beard,
The stains of recent conflict cleared, —
    And thus the Champion proved
That he fears now who never feared,
    And loves who never loved.
And Eivir — life is on her cheek
And yet she will not move or speak,
    Nor will her eyelid fully ope;
Perchance it loves, that half-shut eye,
Through its long fringe, reserved and
    shy,   350
Affection's opening dawn to spy;
And the deep blush, which bids its dye
O'er cheek and brow and bosom fly,
    Speaks shamefacedness and hope.

XIX

But vainly seems the Dane to seek
For terms his new-born love to speak, —
For words, save those of wrath and
    wrong,
Till now were strangers to his tongue;
So, when he raised the blushing maid,

In blunt and honest terms he said — 360
'T were well that maids, when lovers
    woo,
Heard none more soft, were all as true —
' Eivir ! since thou for many a day
Hast followed Harold's wayward way,
It is but meet that in the line
Of after-life I follow thine.
To-morrow is Saint Cuthbert's tide,
And we will grace his altar's side,
A Christian knight and Christian bride;
And of Witikind's son shall the marvel be
    said   370
That on the same morn he was christened
    and wed.'

CONCLUSION

AND now, Ennui, what ails thee, weary
    maid ?
And why these listless looks of yawning
    sorrow ?
No need to turn the page as if 't were
    lead,
Or fling aside the volume till to-mor-
    row. —
Be cheered — 't is ended — and I will
    not borrow,
To try thy patience more, one anecdote
From Bartholine or Perinskiold or
    Snorro.
Then pardon thou thy minstrel, who hath
    wrote
A tale six cantos long, yet scorned to add
    a note.   380

MISCELLANEOUS POEMS

From the time when Scott wrote the first of
his long poems, *The Lay of the Last Minstrel*,
till he deliberately abandoned the writing of
long poems in *Harold the Dauntless*, twelve
years later, he wrote about twoscore poems,
and in the twelve years which then followed
till he ceased writing altogether, only a dozen
more, and a large number of these were occasional. This does not take account, however,
of the bits of verse interspersed in the novels,
some of which were among his most characteristic pieces. In 1806, after publishing *The Lay*
of the Last Minstrel and before publishing
Marmion, Scott issued a collection of *Ballads
and Lyrical Pieces*, containing most of the
matter included in our division, *Early Ballads
and Lyrics ;* but not again was any collection
made till his distribution of all his writings toward the end of his life. It has seemed best,
in our arrangement, not to interrupt the series
of long poems by inserting these scattered
verses between them, but to group them all in
this general division, in as closely chronological order as seemed practicable.

THE DYING BARD

'The Welsh tradition,' says Scott, 'bears that a Bard, on his death-bed, demanded his harp, and played the air [Daffwdz Gangwen] to which these verses are adapted, requesting that it might be performed at his funeral.' Published in 1806.

DINAS EMLINN, lament; for the moment is
 nigh,
When mute in the woodlands thine echoes
 shall die:
No more by sweet Teivi Cadwallon shall
 rave,
And mix his wild notes with the wild dash-
 .ing wave.

In spring and in autumn thy glories of
 shade
Unhonored shall flourish, unhonored shall
 fade;
For soon shall be lifeless the eye and the
 tongue
That viewed them with rapture, with rapture that sung.

Thy sons, Dinas Emlinn, may march in
 their pride,
And chase the proud Saxon from Prestatyn's
 side;
But where is the harp shall give life to
 their name ?
And where is the bard shall give heroes
 their fame ?

And O, Dinas Emlinn ! thy daughters so
 fair,
Who heave the white bosom and wave the
 dark hair;
What tuneful enthusiast shall worship their
 eye,
When half of their charms with Cadwallon
 shall die ?

Then adieu, silver Teivi ! I quit thy loved
 scene
To join the dim choir of the bards who
 have been;
With Lewarch, and Meilor, and Merlin
 the Old,
And sage Taliessin, high harping to hold.

And adieu, Dinas Emlinn ! still green be
 thy shades,

Unconquered thy warriors and matchless
 thy maids !
And thou whose faint warblings my weakness can tell,
Farewell, my loved harp ! my last treasure, farewell !

THE NORMAN HORSE-SHOE

The Welsh, inhabiting a mountainous country, and possessing only an inferior breed of
horses, were usually unable to encounter the
shock of the Anglo-Norman cavalry. Occasionally, however, they were successful in re-
pelling the invaders ; and the following verses
are supposed to celebrate a defeat of Clare,
Earl of Striguil and Pembroke, and of Neville,
Baron of Chepstow, Lords-Marchers of Mon-
mouthshire. Published in 1806.

RED glows the forge in Striguil's bounds,
And hammers din, and anvil sounds,
And armorers with iron toil
Barb many a steed for battle's broil.
Foul fall the hand which bends the steel
Around the courser's thundering heel,
That e'er shall dint a sable wound
On fair Glamorgan's velvet ground !

From Chepstow's towers ere dawn of morn
Was heard afar the bugle-horn,
And forth in banded pomp and pride
Stout Clare and fiery Neville ride.
They swore their banners broad should
 gleam
In crimson light on Rymny's stream;
They vowed Caerphili's sod should feel
The Norman charger's spurning heel.

And sooth they swore — the sun arose,
And Rymny's wave with crimson glows;
For Clare's red banner, floating wide,
Rolled down the stream to Severn's tide !
And sooth they vowed — the trampled
 green
Showed where hot Neville's charge had
 been:
In every sable hoof-tramp stood
A Norman horseman's curdling blood !

Old Chepstow's brides may curse the toil
That armed stout Clare for Cambrian broil;
Their orphans long the art may rue,
For Neville's war-horse forged the shoe.

No more the stamp of armed steed
Shall dint Glamorgan's velvet mead;
Nor trace be there in early spring
Save of the Fairies' emerald ring:

THE MAID OF TORO

A later draft, 1806, of a song from 'The
House of Aspen.' See above, p. 10.

O, LOW shone the sun on the fair lake of
    Toro,
  And weak were the whispers that waved
    the dark wood,
All as a fair maiden, bewildered in sorrow,
  Sorely sighed to the breezes and wept to
    the flood.
' O saints, from the mansions of bliss lowly
    bending !
  Sweet Virgin, who hearest the suppliant's
    cry !
Now grant my petition in anguish ascending,
  My Henry restore or let Eleanor die !'

All distant and faint were the sounds of the
    battle,
  With the breezes they rise, with the
    breezes they fail,
Till the shout and the groan and the con-
    flict's dread rattle,
  And the chase's wild clamor, came load-
    ing the gale.
Breathless she gazed on the woodlands so
    dreary;
  Slowly approaching a warrior was seen;
Life's ebbing tide marked his footsteps so
    weary,
  Cleft was his helmet and woe was his
    mien.

' O, save thee, fair maid, for our armies are
    flying !
  O, save thee, fair maid, for thy guardian
    is low !
Deadly cold on yon heath thy brave Henry
    is lying,
  And fast through the woodland ap-
    proaches the foe.'
Scarce could he falter the tidings of sorrow,
  And scarce could she hear them, be-
    numbed with despair:
And when the sun sunk on the sweet lake
    of Toro,
  Forever he set to the Brave and the Fair.

THE PALMER

Published, 1806, in *Haydn's Collection of
Scottish Airs.*

' O OPEN the door, some pity to show,
  Keen blows the northern wind !
The glen is white with the drifted snow,
  And the path is hard to find.

' No outlaw seeks your castle gate,
  From chasing the king's deer,
Though even an outlaw's wretched state
  Might claim compassion here.

' A weary Palmer, worn and weak,
  I wander for my sin;
O, open, for Our Lady's sake !
  A pilgrim's blessing win !

' I 'll give you pardons from the Pope,
  And reliques from o'er the sea, —
Or if for these you will not ope,
  Yet open for charity.

' The hare is crouching in her form,
  The hart beside the hind;
An aged man amid the storm,
  No shelter can I find.

' You hear the Ettrick's sullen roar,
  Dark, deep, and strong is he,
And I must ford the Ettrick o'er,
  Unless you pity me.

' The iron gate is bolted hard,
  At which I knock in vain;
The owner's heart is closer barred,
  Who hears me thus complain.

' Farewell, farewell ! and Mary grant,
  When old and frail you be,
You never may the shelter want
  That 's now denied to me.'

The ranger on his couch lay warm,
  And heard him plead in vain;
But oft amid December's storm
  He 'll hear that voice again:

For lo ! when through the vapors dank
  Morn shone on Ettrick fair,
A corpse amid the alders rank,
  The Palmer weltered there.

THE MAID OF NEIDPATH

'There is a tradition in Tweeddale,' says Scott, 'that, when Neidpath Castle, near Peebles, was inhabited by the Earls of March, a mutual passion subsisted between a daughter of that noble family and a son of the Laird of Tushielaw, in Ettrick Forest. As the alliance was thought unsuitable by her parents, the young man went abroad. During his absence the lady fell into a consumption; and at length, as the only means of saving her life, her father consented that her lover should be recalled. On the day when he was expected to pass through Peebles, on the road to Tushielaw, the young lady, though much exhausted, caused herself to be carried to the balcony of a house in Peebles belonging to the family, that she might see him as he rode past. Her anxiety and eagerness gave such force to her organs, that she is said to have distinguished his horse's footsteps at an incredible distance. But Tushielaw, unprepared for the change in her appearance, and not expecting to see her in that place, rode on without recognizing her, or even slackening his pace. The lady was unable to support the shock; and, after a short struggle, died in the arms of her attendants.' Published, 1806, in *Haydn's Collection of Scottish Airs.*

O, LOVERS' eyes are sharp to see,
  And lovers' ears in hearing;
And love in life's extremity
  Can lend an hour of cheering.
Disease had been in Mary's bower,
  And slow decay from mourning,
Though now she sits on Neidpath's tower
  To watch her love's returning.

All sunk and dim her eyes so bright,
  Her form decayed by pining,
Till through her wasted hand at night
  You saw the taper shining;
By fits, a sultry hectic hue
  Across her cheek were flying;
By fits, so ashy pale she grew,
  Her maidens thought her dying.

Yet keenest powers to see and hear
  Seemed in her frame residing;
Before the watch-dog pricked his ear,
  She heard her lover's riding;
Ere scarce a distant form was kenned,
  She knew, and waved to greet him;
And o'er the battlement did bend,
  As on the wing to meet him.

He came — he passed — an heedless gaze,
  As o'er some stranger glancing;
Her welcome, spoke in faltering phrase,
  Lost in his courser's prancing —
The castle arch, whose hollow tone
  Returns each whisper spoken,
Could scarcely catch the feeble moan
  Which told her heart was broken.

WANDERING WILLIE

Published, 1806, in *Haydn's Collection of Scottish Airs.*

ALL joy was bereft me the day that you left
    me,
  And climbed the tall vessel to sail yon
    wide sea;
O weary betide it ! I wandered beside it,
  And banned it for parting my Willie and
    me.

Far o'er the wave hast thou followed thy
    fortune,
  Oft fought the squadrons of France and
    of Spain;
Ae kiss of welcome's worth twenty at
    parting,
  Now I hae gotten my Willie again.

When the sky it was mirk, and the winds
    they were wailing,
  I sat on the beach wi' the tear in my ee,
And thought o' the bark where my Willie
    was sailing,
  And wished that the tempest could a'
    blaw on me.

Now that thy gallant ship rides at her
    mooring,
  Now that my wanderer's in safety at
    hame,
Music to me were the wildest winds'
    roaring,
  That e'er o'er Inch-Keith drove the dark
    ocean faem.

When the lights they did blaze, and the
    guns they did rattle,
  And blithe was each heart for the great
    victory,
In secret I wept for the dangers of battle,
  And thy glory itself was scarce comfort
    to me.

But now shalt thou tell, while I eagerly
    listen,
  Of each bold adventure and every brave
    scar;
And trust me, I 'll smile, though my een
    they may glisten,
  For sweet after danger 's the tale of the
    war.

And O, how we doubt when there 's dis-
    tance 'tween lovers,
  When there 's naething to speak to the
    heart thro' the ee !
How often the kindest and warmest prove
    rovers,
  And the love of the faithfullest ebbs like
    the sea !

'Till, at times — could I help it ? — I pined
    and I pondered
  If love could change notes like the bird
    on the tree —
Now I 'll ne'er ask if thine eyes may hae
    wandered;
  Enough, thy leal heart has been constant
    to me.

Welcome, from sweeping o'er sea and
    through channel,
  Hardships and danger despising for
    fame,
Furnishing story for glory's bright an-
    nal,
  Welcome, my wanderer, to Jeanie and
    hame !

Enough now thy story in annals of glory
  Has humbled the pride of France, Hol-
    land, and Spain;
No more shalt thou grieve me, no more
    shalt thou leave me,
  I never will part with my Willie again.

HEALTH TO LORD MELVILLE

AIR — ' *Carrickfergus* '

' The impeachment of Lord Melville was
among the first measures of the new (Whig)
Government ; and personal affection and gratitude graced as well as heightened the zeal
with which Scott watched the issue of this, in
his eyes, vindictive proceeding ; but, though
the ex-minister's ultimate acquittal was, as to
all the charges involving his personal honor,
complete, it must now be allowed that the in-
vestigation brought out many circumstances
by no means creditable to his discretion ; and
the rejoicings of his friends ought not, therefore, to have been scornfully jubilant. Such
they were, however — at least in Edinburgh ;
and Scott took his share in them by inditing a
song, which was sung by James Ballantyne,
and received with clamorous applauses, at a
public dinner given in honor of the event, on
the 27th of June, 1806.' — Lockhart's *Life of
Scott*, Chapter xvi.

SINCE here we are set in array round the
    table,
  Five hundred good fellows well met in a
    hall,
Come listen, brave boys, and I 'll sing as
    I 'm able,
  How innocence triumphed and pride got
    a fall.
    But push round the claret —
    Come, stewards, don't spare it —
With rapture you 'll drink to the toast that
    I give;
      Here, boys,
      Off with it merrily —
Melville for ever, and long may he live !

What were the Whigs doing, when boldly
    pursuing,
  Pitt banished Rebellion, gave Treason a
    string;
Why, they swore on their honor, for
    Arthur O'Connor,
  And fought hard for Despard against
    country and king.
    Well, then, we knew, boys,
    Pitt and Melville were true boys,
And the tempest was raised by the friends
    of Reform.
      Ah ! woe !
      Weep to his memory;
Low lies the pilot that weathered the
    storm !

And pray, don't you mind when the Blues
    first were raising,
  And we scarcely could think the house
    safe o'er our heads ?
When villains and coxcombs, French poli-
    tics praising,
  Drove peace from our tables and sleep
    from our beds ?

Our hearts they grew bolder
When, musket on shoulder,
Stepped forth our old Statesmen example
to give.
　Come, boys, never fear,
　Drink the Blue grenadier —
Here 's to old Harry, and long may he
live !

They would turn us adrift, though rely,
sir, upon it,
Our own faithful chronicles warrant us
that
The free mountaineer and his bonny blue
bonnet
Have oft gone as far as the regular's
hat.
　We laugh at their taunting,
　For all we are wanting
Is license our life for our country to
give.
　Off with it merrily
　Horse, foot, and artillery,
Each loyal Volunteer, long may he live !

'T is not us alone, boys — the Army and
Navy
Have each got a slap 'mid their politic
pranks;
Cornwallis cashiered, that watched winters
to save ye,
And the Cape called a bauble unworthy
of thanks.
　But vain is their taunt,
　No soldier shall want
The thanks that his country to valor can
give:
　Come, boys,
　Drink it off merrily, —
Sir David and Popham, and long may they
live !

And then our revenue — Lord knows how
they viewed it,
While each petty statesman talked lofty
and big;
But the beer-tax was weak, as if Whit-
bread had brewed it,
And the pig-iron duty a shame to a
pig.
　In vain is their vaunting,
　Too surely there 's wanting
What judgment, experience, and steadiness
give:
　Come, boys,

　Drink about merrily, —
Health to sage Melville, and long may he
live !

Our King, too — our Princess — I dare not
say more, sir, —
May Providence watch them with mercy
and might !
While there 's one Scottish hand that can
wag a claymore, sir,
They shall ne'er want a friend to stand
up for their right.
　Be damned he that dare not, —
　For my part, I 'll spare not
To beauty afflicted a tribute to give.
　Fill it up steadily,
　Drink it off readily —
Here 's to the Princess, and long may she
live !

And since we must not set Auld Reekie in
glory,
And make her brown visage as light as
her heart;
Till each man illumine his own upper
story,
Nor law-book nor lawyer shall force us
to part.
　In Grenville and Spencer,
　And some few good men, sir,
High talents we honor, slight difference
forgive;
　But the Brewer we 'll hoax,
　Tallyho to the Fox,
And drink Melville for ever, as long as we
live !

HUNTING SONG

Published in *Edinburgh Annual Register*,
1808.

WAKEN, lords and ladies gay,
On the mountain dawns the day,
All the jolly chase is here,
With hawk and horse and hunting-spear !
Hounds are in their couples yelling,
Hawks are whistling, horns are knelling,
Merrily, merrily, mingle they,
' Waken, lords and ladies gay.'

Waken, lords and ladies gay,
The mist has left the mountain gray,
Springlets in the dawn are steaming,
Diamonds on the brake are gleaming:

And foresters have busy been
To track the buck in thicket green;
Now we come to chant our lay,
' Waken, lords and ladies gay.'

Waken, lords and ladies gay,
To the green-wood haste away;
We can show you where he lies,
Fleet of foot and tall of size;
We can show the marks he made,
When 'gainst the oak his antlers frayed;
You shall see him brought to bay,
' Waken, lords and ladies gay.'

Louder, louder chant the lay,
Waken, lords and ladies gay !
Tell them youth and mirth and glee
Run a course as well as we;
Time, stern huntsman, who can balk,
Stanch as hound and fleet as hawk ?
Think of this and rise with day,
Gentle lords and ladies gay.

SONG

1808

O, SAY not, my love, with that mortified air,
   That your spring-time of pleasure is
      flown,
Nor bid me to maids that are younger
      repair
   For those raptures that still are thine
      own.

Though April his temples may wreathe
      with the vine,
   Its tendrils in infancy curled,
'T is the ardor of August matures us the
      wine
   Whose life-blood enlivens the world.

Though thy form that was fashioned as
      light as a fay's
   Has assumed a proportion more round,
And thy glance that was bright as a fal-
      con's at gaze
   Looks soberly now on the ground, —

Enough, after absence to meet me again
   Thy steps still with ecstasy move;
Enough, that those dear sober glances
      retain
   For me the kind language of love.

THE RESOLVE

WRITTEN IN IMITATION OF AN OLD
ENGLISH POEM, 1809

Scott wrote of this to his brother Thomas,
who had guessed its authorship, when it was
published anonymously : ' It is mine : and it is
not — or, to be less enigmatical, it is an old
fragment, which I coopered up into its present
state with the purpose of quizzing certain
judges of poetry, who have been extremely delighted, and declare that no living poet could
write in the same exquisite taste.'

MY wayward fate I needs must plain,
   Though bootless be the theme;
I loved and was beloved again,
   Yet all was but a dream:
For, as her love was quickly got,
   So it was quickly gone;
No more I 'll bask in flame so hot,
   But coldly dwell alone.

Not maid more bright than maid was e'er
   My fancy shall beguile,
By flattering word or feigned tear,
   By gesture, look, or smile:
No more I 'll call the shaft fair shot,
   Till it has fairly flown,
Nor scorch me at a flame so hot —
   I 'll rather freeze alone.

Each ambushed Cupid I 'll defy
   In cheek or chin or brow,
And deem the glance of woman's eye
   As weak as woman's vow:
I 'll lightly hold the lady's heart,
   That is but lightly won;
I 'll steel my breast to beauty's art,
   And learn to live alone.

The flaunting torch soon blazes out,
   The diamond's ray abides;
The flame its glory hurls about,
   The gem its lustre hides;
Such gem I fondly deemed was mine,
   And glowed a diamond stone,
But, since each eye may see it shine,
   I 'll darkling dwell alone.

No waking dreams shall tinge my thought
   With dyes so bright and vain,
No silken net so slightly wrought
   Shall tangle me again:
No more I 'll pay so dear for wit,
   I 'll live upon mine own,

Nor shall wild passion trouble it, —
  I 'll rather dwell alone.

And thus I 'll hush my heart to rest, —
  ' Thy loving labor 's lost;
Thou shalt no more be wildly blest,
  To be so strangely crost:
The widowed turtles mateless die,
The phœnix is but one;
They seek no loves — no more will I —
  I 'll rather dwell alone.'

EPITAPH

DESIGNED FOR A MONUMENT IN LICH-
FIELD CATHEDRAL, AT THE BURIAL-
PLACE OF THE FAMILY OF MISS
SEWARD
1809

AMID these aisles where once his precepts
    showed
The heavenward pathway which in life he
    trode,
This simple tablet marks a Father's bier,
And those he loved in life in death are
    near;
For him, for them, a Daughter bade it rise,
Memorial of domestic charities.
Still wouldst thou know why o'er the mar-
    ble spread
In female grace the willow droops her
    head;
Why on her branches, silent and unstrung,
The minstrel harp is emblematic hung;
What poet's voice is smothered here in
    dust
Till waked to join the chorus of the just, —
Lo ! one brief line an answer sad supplies,
Honored, beloved, and mourned, here
    SEWARD lies !
Her worth, her warmth of heart, let
    friendship say, —
Go seek her genius in her living lay.

PROLOGUE

TO MISS BAILLIE'S PLAY OF 'THE
FAMILY LEGEND '

' The enclosed jangling verses,' Scott writes
to Lady Abercorn from Edinburgh January 21,
1810, ' are the only effort I have made in
rhyme since I came to Edinburgh for the winter. They were written within this hour and

are to be spoken to a beautiful tragedy of
Joanna Baillie, founded upon a Highland
story of the Old Time.'

'T IS sweet to hear expiring Summer's
    sigh,
Through forests tinged with russet, wail
    and die;
'T is sweet and sad the latest notes to hear
Of distant music, dying on the ear;
But far more sadly sweet on foreign strand
We list the legends of our native land,
Linked as they come with every tender tie,
Memorials dear of youth and infancy.

Chief thy wild tales, romantic Caledon,
Wake keen remembrance in each hardy
    son.
Whether on India's burning coasts he toil
Or till Acadia's winter-fettered soil,
He hears with throbbing heart and mois-
    tened eyes,
And, as he hears, what dear illusions rise !
It opens on his soul his native dell,
The woods wild waving and the water's
    swell;
Tradition's theme, the tower that threats
    the plain,
The mossy cairn that hides the hero slain;
The cot beneath whose simple porch were
    told
By gray-haired patriarch the tales of old,
The infant group that hushed their sports
    the while,
And the dear maid who listened with a
    smile.
The wanderer, while the vision warms his
    brain,
Is denizen of Scotland once again.

Are such keen feelings to the crowd
    confined,
And sleep they in the poet's gifted mind ?
O no ! For she, within whose mighty
    page
Each tyrant Passion shows his woe and
    rage,
Has felt the wizard influence they inspire,
And to your own traditions tuned her lyre.
Yourselves shall judge — whoe'er has
    raised the sail
By Mull's dark coast has heard this even-
    ing's tale.
The plaided boatman, resting on his oar,
Points to the fatal rock amid the roar

Of whitening waves, and tells whate'er to-
 night
Our humble stage shall offer to your sight;
Proudly preferred that first our efforts
 give
Scenes glowing from her pen to breathe
 and live;
More proudly yet, should Caledon approve
The filial token of a daughter's love.

THE POACHER

This imitation of Crabbe was published along
with *The Bridal of Triermain* and *Harold the
Dauntless* in the *Edinburgh Annual Register* for
1809. See *supra*, p. 283. Crabbe on seeing the
verses said : ' This man, whoever he is, can do
all that I can, and *something more.*'

WELCOME, grave stranger, to our green
 retreats
Where health with exercise and freedom
 meets !
Thrice welcome, sage, whose philosophic
 plan
By nature's limits metes the rights of
 man;
Generous as he who now for freedom
 bawls,
Now gives full value for true Indian
 shawls:
O'er court, o'er custom-house, his shoe
 who flings,
Now bilks excisemen and now bullies
 kings.
Like his, I ween, thy comprehensive mind
Holds laws as mouse-traps baited for man-
 kind: 10
Thine eye applausive each sly vermin sees,
That balks the snare yet battens on the
 cheese;
Thine ear has heard with scorn instead of
 awe
Our buckskinned justices expound the law,
Wire-draw the acts that fix for wires the
 pain,
And for the netted partridge noose the
 swain;
And thy vindictive arm would fain have
 broke
The last light fetter of the feudal yoke,
To give the denizens of wood and wild,
Nature's free race, to each her free-born
 child.   20

Hence hast thou marked with grief fair
 London's race,
Mocked with the boon of one poor Easter
 chase,
And longed to send them forth as free as
 when
Poured o'er Chantilly the Parisian train,
When musket, pistol, blunderbuss, com-
 bined,
And scarce the field-pieees were left be-
 hind !
A squadron's charge each leveret's heart
 dismayed,
On every covey fired a bold brigade;
La Douce Humanité approved the sport,
For great the alarm indeed, yet small the
 hurt;   30
Shouts patriotic solemnized the day,
And Seine re-echoed *Vive la Liberté!*
But mad *Citoyen*, meek *Monsieur* again,
With some few added links resumes his
 chain.
Then, since such scenes to France no more
 are known,
Come, view with me a hero of thine own,
One whose free actions vindicate the cause
Of sylvan liberty o'er feudal laws.

Seek we yon glades where the proud oak
 o'ertops   39
Wide-waving seas of birch and hazel copse,
Leaving between deserted isles of land
Where stunted heath is patched with ruddy
 sand,
And lonely on the waste the yew is seen,
Or straggling hollies spread a brighter
 green.
Here, little worn and winding dark and
 steep,
Our scarce marked path descends yon
 dingle deep:
Follow — but heedful, cautious of a trip —
In earthly mire philosophy may slip.
Step slow and wary o'er that swampy
 stream,
Till, guided by the charcoal's smothering
 steam,   50
We reach the frail yet barricaded door
Of hovel formed for poorest of the poor;
No hearth the fire, no vent the smoke re-
 ceives,
The walls are wattles and the covering
 leaves;
For, if such hut, our forest statutes say,
Rise in the progress of one night and day —

Though placed where still the Conqueror's
    hests o'erawe,
And his son's stirrup shines the badge of
    law —
The builder claims the unenviable boon,
To tenant dwelling, framed as slight and
    soon   60
As wigwam wild that shrouds the native
    frore
On the bleak coast of frost-barred Labrador.

Approach and through the unlatticed
    window peep —
Nay, shrink not back, the inmate is asleep;
Sunk mid yon sordid blankets till the sun
Stoop to the west, the plunderer's toils are
    done.
Loaded and primed and prompt for desper-
    ate hand,
Rifle and fowling-piece beside him stand;
While round the hut are in disorder laid
The tools and booty of his lawless trade; 70
For force or fraud, resistance or escape,
The crow, the saw, the bludgeon, and the
    crape.
His pilfered powder in yon nook he hoards,
And the filched lead the church's roof
    affords —
Hence shall the rector's congregation fret,
That while his sermon's dry his walls are
    wet.
The fish-spear barbed, the sweeping net are
    there,
Doe-hides, and pheasant plumes, and skins
    of hare,
Cordage for toils and wiring for the snare.
Bartered for game from chase or warren
    won,   80
Yon cask holds moonlight, run when moon
    was none;
And late-snatched spoils lie stowed in hutch
    apart
To wait the associate higgler's evening cart.

Look on his pallet foul and mark his rest:
What scenes perturbed are acting in his
    breast !
His sable brow is wet and wrung with pain,
And his dilated nostril toils in vain;
For short and scant the breath each effort
    draws,
And 'twixt each effort Nature claims a
    pause.
Beyond the loose and sable neckcloth
    stretched,   90

His sinewy throat seems by convulsion
    twitched,
While the tongue falters, as to utterance
    loath,
Sounds of dire import — watchword, threat,
    and oath.
Though, stupefied by toil and drugged with
    gin,
The body sleep, the restless guest within
Now plies on wood and wold his lawless
    trade,
Now in the fangs of justice wakes dis-
    mayed. —

'Was that wild start of terror and de-
    spair,
Those bursting eyeballs and that wildered
    air,   99
Signs of compunction for a murdered hare?
Do the locks bristle and the eyebrows
    arch
For grouse or partridge massacred in
    March ? '

No, scoffer, no ! Attend, and mark with
    awe,
There is no wicket in the gate of law !
He that would e'er so lightly set ajar
That awful portal must undo each bar:
Tempting occasion, habit, passion, pride,
Will join to storm the breach and force the
    barrier wide.

That ruffian, whom true men avoid and
    dread,
Whom bruisers, poachers, smugglers, call
    Black Ned,   110
Was Edward Mansell once; — the lightest
    heart
That ever played on holiday his part !
The leader he in every Christmas game,
The harvest-feast grew blither when he
    came,
And liveliest on the chords the bow did
    glance
When Edward named the tune and led the
    dance.
Kind was his heart, his passions quick and
    strong,
Hearty his laugh, and jovial was his song;
And if he loved a gun, his father swore,
' 'T was but a trick of youth would soon be
    o'er,   120
Himself had done the same some thirty
    years before.'

But he whose humors spurn law's awful
   yoke
Must herd with those by whom law's bonds
   are broke;
The common dread of justice soon allies
The clown who robs the warren or excise
With sterner felons trained to act more
   dread,
Even with the wretch by whom his fellow
   bled.
Then, as in plagues the foul contagions pass,
Leavening and festering the corrupted
   mass,
Guilt leagues with guilt while mutual mo-
   tives draw,   130
Their hope impunity, their fear the law;
Their foes, their friends, their rendezvous
   the same,
Till the revenue balked or pilfered game
Flesh the young culprit, and example leads
To darker villany and direr deeds.

Wild howled the wind the forest glades
   along,
And oft the owl renewed her dismal song;
Around the spot where erst he felt the
   wound,
Red William's spectre walked his midnight
   round.
When o'er the swamp he cast his blighting
   look,   140
From the green marshes of the stagnant
   brook
The bittern's sullen shout the sedges shook!
The waning moon with storm-presaging
   gleam
Now gave and now withheld her doubtful
   beam;
The old Oak stooped his arms, then flung
   them high,
Bellowing and groaning to the troubled sky,
'T was then that, couched amid the brush-
   wood sear,
In Malwood-walk young Mansell watched
   the deer:
The fattest buck received his deadly shot —
The watchful keeper heard and sought the
   spot.   150
Stout were their hearts, and stubborn was
   their strife;
O'erpowered at length the Outlaw drew
   his knife.
Next morn a corpse was found upon the
   fell —
The rest his waking agony may tell!

THE BOLD DRAGOON

OR, THE PLAIN OF BADAJOS

This song was written shortly after the battle of Badajos, April, 1812, for a Yeomanry
Cavalry dinner.

'T was a Maréchal of France, and he fain
   would honor gain,
And he longed to take a passing glance at
   Portugal from Spain;
   With his flying guns this gallant gay,
   And boasted corps d'armée —
O, he feared not our dragoons with their
   long swords boldly riding,
   Whack, fal de ral, etc.

To Campo Mayor come, he had quietly sat
   down,
Just a fricassee to pick while his soldiers
   sacked the town,
   When, 't was peste! morbleu! mon
   Général,
   Hear the English bugle-call!
And behold the light dragoons with their
   long swords boldly riding,
   Whack, fal de ral, etc.

Right about went horse and foot, artillery
   and all,
And, as the devil leaves a house, they tum-
   bled through the wall;
   They took no time to seek the door,
   But, best foot set before —
O, they ran from our dragoons with their
   long swords boldly riding,
   Whack, fal de ral, etc.

Those valiant men of France they had
   scarcely fled a mile,
When on their flank there soused at once
   the British rank and file;
   For Long, De Grey, and Otway then
   Ne'er minded one to ten,
But came on like light dragoons with their
   long swords boldly riding,
   Whack, fal de ral, etc.

Three hundred British lads they made
   three thousand reel,
Their hearts were made of English oak,
   their swords of Sheffield steel,
   Their horses were in Yorkshire bred,
   And Beresford them led;

So huzza for brave dragoons with their
  long swords boldly riding,
Whack, fal de ral, etc.

Then here's a health to Wellington, to
  Beresford, to Long,
And a single word of Bonaparte before I
  close my song:
The eagles that to fight he brings
Should serve his men with wings,
When they meet the bold dragoons with
  their long swords boldly riding,
  Whack, fal de ral, etc.

ON THE MASSACRE OF GLENCOE

1814

'O, TELL me, Harper, wherefore flow
Thy wayward notes of wail and woe
Far down the desert of Glencoe,
  Where none may list their melody?
Say, harp'st thou to the mists that fly,
Or to the dun-deer glancing by,
Or to the eagle that from high
  Screams chorus to thy minstrelsy?'

'No, not to these, for they have rest, —
The mist-wreath has the mountain-crest,
The stag his lair, the erne her nest,
  Abode of lone security.
But those for whom I pour the lay,
Not wild-wood deep nor mountain gray,
Not this deep dell that shrouds from
  day,
  Could screen from treacherous cruelty.

'Their flag was furled and mute their
  drum,
The very household dogs were dumb,
Unwont to bay at guests that come
  In guise of hospitality.
His blithest notes the piper plied,
Her gayest snood the maiden tied,
The dame her distaff flung aside
  To tend her kindly housewifery.

'The hand that mingled in the meal
At midnight drew the felon steel,
And gave the host's kind breast to feel
  Meed for his hospitality!
The friendly hearth which warmed that
  hand
At midnight armed it with the brand

That bade destruction's flames expand
  Their red and fearful blazonry.

'Then woman's shriek was heard in vain,
Nor infancy's unpitied plain,
More than the warrior's groan, could gain
  Respite from ruthless butchery!
The winter wind that whistled shrill,
The snows that night that cloked the hill,
Though wild and pitiless, had still
  Far more than Southern clemency.

'Long have my harp's best notes been gone,
Few are its strings and faint their tone,
They can but sound in desert lone
  Their gray-haired master's misery.
Were each gray hair a minstrel string,
Each chord should imprecations fling,
Till startled Scotland loud should ring,
  "Revenge for blood and treachery!"'

SONG

FOR THE ANNIVERSARY MEETING OF THE
PITT CLUB OF SCOTLAND

1814

O, DREAD was the time, and more dread-
  ful the omen,
  When the brave on Marengo lay slaugh-
    tered in vain,
And beholding broad Europe bowed down
  by her foemen,
  PITT closed in his anguish the map of
    her reign!
Not the fate of broad Europe could bend
  his brave spirit
  To take for his country the safety of
    shame;
O, then in her triumph remember his merit,
  And hallow the goblet that flows to his
    name.

Round the husbandman's head while he
  traces the furrow
  The mists of the winter may mingle with
    rain,
He may plough it with labor and sow it
  in sorrow,
  And sigh while he fears he has sowed it
    in vain;
He may die ere his children shall reap in
  their gladness,
  But the blithe harvest-home shall re-
    member his claim:

And their jubilee-shout shall be softened
    with sadness,
    While they hallow the goblet that flows
        to his name.

Though anxious and timeless his life was
        expended,
    In toils for our country preserved by his
        care,
Though he died ere one ray o'er the nations
        ascended,
    To light the long darkness of doubt and
        despair;
The storms he endured in our Britain's
        December,
    The perils his wisdom foresaw and o'er-
        came,
In her glory's rich harvest shall Britain
        remember,
    And hallow the goblet that flows to his
        name.

Nor forget His gray head who, all dark in
        affliction,
    Is deaf to the tale of our victories won,
And to sounds the most dear to paternal
        affection,
    The shout of his people applauding his
        Son;
By his firmness unmoved in success and
        disaster,
    By his long reign of virtue, remember
        his claim !
With our tribute to PITT join the praise of
        his Master,
    Though a tear stain the goblet that flows
        to his name.

Yet again fill the wine-cup and change the
        sad measure,
    The rites of our grief and our gratitude
        paid,
To our Prince, to our Heroes, devote the
        bright treasure,
    The wisdom that planned, and the zeal
        that obeyed !
Fill WELLINGTON'S cup till it beam like his
        glory,
    Forget not our own brave DALHOUSIE
        and GRÆME;
A thousand years hence hearts shall bound
        at their story,
    And hallow the goblet that flows to their
        fame.

LINES

ADDRESSED TO RANALD MACDONALD,
        ESQ., OF STAFFA

These lines were written in the album kept
at the Sound of Ulva Inn, in the month of August, 1814.

STAFFA, sprung from high Macdonald,
Worthy branch of old Clan-Ranald !
Staffa ! king of all kind fellows !
Well befall thy hills and valleys,
Lakes and inlets, deeps and shallows —
Cliffs of darkness, caves of wonder,
Echoing the Atlantic thunder;
Mountains which the gray mist covers,
Where the Chieftain spirit hovers,
Pausing while his pinions quiver,
Stretched to quit our land forever !
Each kind influence reign above thee !
Warmer heart 'twixt this and Staffa
Beats not than in heart of Staffa !

PHAROS LOQUITUR

Robert Stevenson, grandfather of Robert
Louis Stevenson, built, amongst others, the Bell
Rock Lighthouse. Scott visited the place with
Stevenson and the commissioners, July 30, 1814,
and wrote these lines in the album kept there.

FAR in the bosom of the deep,
O'er these wild shelves my watch I keep ;
A ruddy gem of changeful light,
Bound on the dusky brow of night,
The seaman bids my lustre hail,
And scorns to strike his timorous sail.

LETTER IN VERSE

ON THE VOYAGE WITH THE COMMISSION-
        ERS OF NORTHERN LIGHTS

'Of the letters which Scott wrote to his friends
during those happy six weeks, I have recovered only one, and it is, thanks to the leisure of
the yacht, in verse. The strong and easy hero-
ics of the first section prove, I think, that Mr.
Canning did not err when he told him that if
he chose he might emulate even Dryden's command of that noble measure ; and the dancing
anapæsts of the second show that he could
with equal facility have rivalled the gay graces

of Cotton, Anstey, or Moore.' — Lockhart, *Life*, Chapter xxxiii.

TO HIS GRACE THE DUKE OF BUCCLEUCH

LIGHTHOUSE YACHT IN THE SOUND OF LERWICK, ZETLAND, 8th August, 1814.

HEALTH to the chieftain from his clansman true !
From her true minstrel, health to fair Buccleuch !
Health from the isles where dewy Morning weaves
Her chaplet with the tints that Twilight leaves;
Where late the sun scarce vanished from the sight,
And his bright pathway graced the short-lived night,
Though darker now as autumn's shades extend
The north winds whistle and the mists ascend !
Health from the land where eddying whirl-winds toss
The storm-rocked cradle of the Cape of Noss;   10
On outstretched cords the giddy engine slides,
His own strong arm the bold adventurer guides,
And he that lists such desperate feat to try
May, like the sea-mew, skim 'twixt surf and sky,
And feel the mid-air gales around him blow,
And see the billows rage five hundred feet below.

Here, by each stormy peak and desert shore,
The hardy islesman tugs the daring oar,
Practised alike his venturous course to keep
Through the white breakers or the pathless deep,   20
By ceaseless peril and by toil to gain
A wretched pittance from the niggard main.
And when the worn-out drudge old ocean leaves,
What comfort greets him and what hut receives ?
Lady ! the worst your presence ere has cheered —

When want and sorrow fled as you appeared —
Were to a Zetlander as the high dome
Of proud Drumlanrig to my humble home.
Here rise no groves and here no gardens blow,
Here even the hardy heath scarce dares to grow;   30
But rocks on rocks, in mist and storm arrayed,
Stretch far to sea their giant colonnade,
With many a cavern seamed, the dreary haunt
Of the dun seal and swarthy cormorant.
Wild round their rifted brows, with frequent cry
As of lament, the gulls and gannets fly,
And from their sable base with sullen sound
In sheets of whitening foam the waves rebound.

Yet even these coasts a touch of envy gain
From those whose land has known oppression's chain;   40
For here the industrious Dutchman comes, once more
To moor his fishing craft by Bressay's shore,
Greets every former mate and brother tar,
Marvels how Lerwick 'scaped the rage of war,
Tells many a tale of Gallic outrage done,
And ends by blessing God and Wellington.
Here too the Greenland tar, a fiercer guest,
Claims a brief hour of riot, not of rest;
Proves each wild frolic that in wine has birth,
And wakes the land with brawls and boisterous mirth.   50
A sadder sight on yon poor vessel's prow
The captive Norseman sits in silent woe,
And eyes the flags of Britain as they flow.
Hard fate of war, which bade her terrors sway
His destined course and seize so mean a prey,
A bark with planks so warped and seams so riven
She scarce might face the gentlest airs of heaven:
Pensive he sits, and questions oft if none
Can list his speech and understand his moan;

In vain — no Islesman now can use the
    tongue   60
Of the bold Norse from whom their lineage
    sprung.
Not thus of old the Norsemen hither came,
Won by the love of danger or of fame;
On every storm-beat cape a shapeless
    tower
Tells of their wars, their conquests, and
    their power;
For ne'er for Grecia's vales nor Latian
    land
Was fiercer strife than for this barren
    strand;
A race severe, the isle and ocean lords
Loved for its own delight the strife of
    swords;
With scornful laugh the mortal pang de-
    fied,   70
And blest their gods that they in battle
    died.

    Such were the sires of Zetland's simple
    race,
And still the eye may faint resemblance
    trace
In the blue eye, tall form, proportion fair,
The limbs athletic, and the long light
    hair —
Such was the mien, as Scald and Minstrel
    sings,
Of fair-haired Harold, first of Norway's
    Kings; —
But their high deeds to scale these crags
    confined,
Their only welfare is with waves and wind.

    Why should I talk of Mousa's castle
    coast ?   80
Why of the horrors of the Sunburgh Rost ?
May not these bald disjointed lines suf-
    fice,
Penned while my comrades whirl the rat-
    tling dice —
While down the cabin skylight lessening
    shine
The rays, and eve is chased with mirth and
    wine ?
Imagined, while down Mousa's desert bay
Our well-trimmed vessel urged her nimble
    way,
While to the freshening breeze she leaned
    her side,
And bade her bowsprit kiss the foamy
    tide ?

Such are the lays that Zetland Isles
    supply;   90
Drenched with the drizzly spray and drop-
    ping sky,
Weary and wet, a sea-sick minstrel I.
           W. Scott.

POSTSCRIPTUM

KIRKWALL, ORKNEY, Aug. 13, 1814.

In respect that your Grace has com-
    missioned a Kraken,
You will please be informed that they sel-
    dom are taken;
It is January two years, the Zetland folks
    say,
Since they saw the last Kraken in Scallo-
    way bay;
He lay in the offing a fortnight or more,
But the devil a Zetlander put from the
    shore,
Though bold in the seas of the North to
    assail
The morse and the sea-horse, the grampus
    and whale.   100
If your Grace thinks I 'm writing the thing
    that is not,
You may ask at a namesake of ours, Mr.
    Scott —
He 's not from our clan, though his merits
    deserve it,
But springs, I 'm informed, from the Scotts
    of Scotstarvet; —
He questioned the folks who beheld it with
    eyes,
But they differed confoundedly as to its
    size.
For instance, the modest and diffident
    swore
That it seemed like the keel of a ship and
    no more —
Those of eyesight more clear or of fancy
    more high
Said it rose like an island 'twixt ocean and
    sky —   110
But all of the hulk had a steady opinion
That 't was sure a *live* subject of Neptune's
    dominion —
And I think, my Lord Duke, your Grace
    hardly would wish,
To cumber your house, such a kettle of fish,
Had your order related to night-caps or
    hose
Or mittens of worsted, there 's plenty of
    those.

Or would you be pleased but to fancy a
    whale ?
And direct me to send it — by sea or by
    mail ?
The season, I 'm told, is nigh over, but
    still
I could get you one fit for the lake at
    Bowhill.   120
Indeed, as to whales, there 's no need to
    be thrifty,
Since one day last fortnight two hundred
    and fifty,
Pursued by seven Orkneymen's boats and
    no more,
Betwixt Truffness and Luffness were
    drawn on the shore !
You 'll ask if I saw this same wonderful
    sight;
I own that I did not, but easily might —
For this mighty shoal of leviathans lay
On our lee-beam a mile, in the loop of the
    bay,
And the islesmen of Sanda were all at the
    spoil,
And *flinching* — so term it — the blubber
    to boil ; —   130
Ye spirits of lavender, drown the reflec-
    tion
That awakes at the thoughts of this odor-
    ous dissection. —
To see this huge marvel full fain would we
    go,
But Wilson, the wind, and the current
    said no.
We have now got to Kirkwall, and needs I
    must stare
When I think that in verse I have once
    called it *fair ;*
'T is a base little borough, both dirty and
    mean —
There is nothing to hear and there 's
    nought to be seen,
Save a church where of old times a prelate
    harangued,
And a palace that 's built by an earl that
    was hanged.   140
But farewell to Kirkwall — aboard we are
    going,
The anchor 's a-peak and the breezes are
    blowing ;
Our commodore calls all his band to their
    places,
And 't is time to release you — good-night
    to your Graces !

SONGS AND VERSES FROM WAVERLEY

So much of the preceding prose is given
with these separate pieces as will furnish the
needed setting.

I

'AND DID YE NOT HEAR OF A MIRTH BEFELL'

To the tune of ' I have been a Fiddler,' etc.

' The following song, which has been since
borrowed by the worshipful author of the famous " History of Fryar Bacon," has been with
difficulty deciphered. It seems to have been
sung on occasion of carrying home the bride. —
Appendix to General Preface.

AND did ye not hear of a mirth befell
    The morrow after a wedding day,
And carrying a bride at home to dwell ?
    And away to Tewin, away, away.

The quintain was set, and the garlands
    were made,
'T is pity old customs should ever decay ;
And woe be to him that was horsed on a
    jade,
    For he carried no credit away, away.

We met a concert of fiddle-de-dees ;
    We set them a-cockhorse, and made
    them play
The winning of Bullen, and Upsey-frees,
    And away to Tewin, away, away !

There was ne'er a lad in all the parish
    That would go to the plough that day ;
But on his fore-horse his wench he carries,
    And away to Tewin, away, away !

The butler was quick, and the ale he did
    tap,
    The maidens did make the chamber full
    gay ;
The servants did give me a fuddling cup,
    And I did carry 't away, away.

The smith of the town his liquor so took,
    That he was persuaded that the ground
    looked blue ;
And I dare boldly be sworn on a book,
    Such smiths as he there 's but a few.

A posset was made, and the women did sip,
　And simpering said, they could eat no
　　more;
Full many a maiden was laid on the lip, —
　I 'll say no more, but give o'er, give o'er.

II

'LATE, WHEN THE AUTUMN EVENING
FELL'

From Chapter v. 'His tutor, or, I should
say, Mr. Pembroke, for he scarce assumed the
name of tutor, picked up about Edward's
room some fragments of irregular verse, which
he appeared to have composed under the influence of the agitating feelings occasioned by
this sudden page being turned up to him in
the book of life, i. e., his being appointed captain in a regiment of dragoons.'

LATE, when the autumn evening fell
On Mirkwood-Mere's romantic dell,
The lake returned, in chastened gleam,
The purple cloud, the golden beam:
Reflected in the crystal pool,
Headland and bank lay fair and cool;
The weather-tinted rock and tower,
Each drooping tree, each fairy flower,
So true, so soft, the mirror gave,
As if there lay beneath the wave,
Secure from trouble, toil, and care,
A world than earthly world more fair.

But distant winds began to wake,
And roused the Genius of the Lake!
He heard the groaning of the oak,
And donned at once his sable cloak,
As warrior, at the battle cry,
Invests him with his panoply:
Then, as the whirlwind nearer pressed,
He 'gan to shake his foamy crest
O'er furrowed brow and blackened cheek,
And bade his surge in thunder speak.
In wild and broken eddies whirled,
Flitted that fond ideal world;
And, to the shore in tumult tost,
The realms of fairy bliss were lost.

Yet, with a stern delight and strange,
I saw the spirit-stirring change
As warred the wind with wave and wood.
Upon the ruined tower I stood,
And felt my heart more strongly bound,
Responsive to the lofty sound,
While, joying in the mighty roar,
I mourned that tranquil scene no more.

So, on the idle dreams of youth
Breaks the loud trumpet-call of truth,
Bids each fair vision pass away,
Like landscape on the lake that lay,
As fair, as flitting, and as frail,
As that which fled the autumn gale —
For ever dead to fancy's eye
Be each gay form that glided by,
While dreams of love and lady's charms
Give place to honor and to arms!

III

'THE KNIGHT'S TO THE MOUNTAIN'

From Chapter ix. '— The questioned party
replied, — and, like the witch of Thalaba,
"still his speech was song."'

THE knight 's to the mountain
　His bugle to wind;
The lady 's to greenwood
　Her garland to bind.
The bower of Burd Ellen
　Has moss on the floor,
That the step of Lord William
　Be silent and sure.

IV

'IT'S UP GLEMBARCHAN'S BRAES I GAED'

From Chapter xi. 'Balmwhapple could
hold no longer, but broke in what he called
a d—d good song, composed by Gibby Caeth-
rowit, the Piper of Cupar; and, without wasting
more time, struck up,' —

IT 's up Glembarchan's braes I gaed,
And o'er the bent of Killiebraid,
And mony a weary cast I made
　To cuittle the moor-fowl's tail.

If up a bonny black-cock should spring,
To whistle him down wi' a slug in his
　wing,
And strap him on to my lunzie string,
　Right seldom would I fail.

V

'HIE AWAY, HIE AWAY'

From Chapter xii. 'The stamping of horses
was now heard in the court, and Davie's voice
singing to the two large deer greyhounds,' —

HIE away, hie away,
Over bank and over brae,

Where the copsewood is the greenest,
Where the fountains glisten sheenest,
Where the lady-fern grows strongest,
Where the morning dew lies longest,
Where the black-cock sweetest sips it,
Where the fairy latest trips it:
   Hie to haunts right seldom seen,
   Lovely, lonesome, cool, and green,
   Over bank and over brae,
   Hie away, hie away.

VI

ST. SWITHIN'S CHAIR

From Chapter xiii. 'The view of the old tower, or fortalice, introduced some family anecdotes and tales of Scottish chivalry, which the Baron told with great enthusiasm. The projecting peak of an impending crag, which rose near it, had acquired the name of St. Swithin's Chair. It was the scene of a peculiar superstition, of which Mr. Rubrick mentioned some curious particulars, which reminded Waverley of a rhyme quoted by Edgar in King Lear; and Rose was called upon to sing a little legend in which they had been interwoven by some village poet, —

   " Who, nameless as the race from which he sprung,
     Saved other names, but left his own unsung."

'The sweetness of her voice, and the simple beauty of her music, gave all the advantage which the minstrel could have desired, and which his poetry so much wanted.'

On Hallow-Mass Eve, ere you boune ye to rest,
Ever beware that your couch be blessed;
Sign it with cross, and sain it with bead,
Sing the Ave and say the Creed.

For on Hallow-Mass Eve the Night-Hag will ride,
And all her nine-fold sweeping on by her side,
Whether the wind sing lowly or loud,
Sailing through moonshine or swathed in the cloud.

The Lady she sate in St. Swithin's Chair,
The dew of the night has damped her hair:
Her cheek was pale, but resolved and high
Was the word of her lip and the glance of her eye.

She muttered the spell of Swithin bold,
When his naked foot traced the midnight wold,
When he stopped the Hag as she rode the night,
And bade her descend and her promise plight.

He that dare sit on St. Swithin's Chair
When the Night-Hag wings the troubled air,
Questions three, when he speaks the spell,
He may ask, and she must tell.

The Baron has been with King Robert his liege,
These three long years in battle and siege;
News are there none of his weal or his woe,
And fain the Lady his fate would know.

She shudders and stops as the charm she speaks; —
Is it the moody owl that shrieks?
Or is that sound, betwixt laughter and scream,
The voice of the Demon who haunts the stream?

The moan of the wind sunk silent and low,
And the roaring torrent had ceased to flow;
The calm was more dreadful than raging storm,
When the cold gray mist brought the ghastly form!

.   .   .   .

VII

'YOUNG MEN WILL LOVE THEE MORE FAIR AND MORE FAST'

From Chapter xiv. 'The next day Edward arose betimes, and, in a morning walk around the house and its vicinity, came suddenly upon a small court in front of the dog-kennel, where his friend Davie was employed about his four-footed charge. One quick glance of his eye recognized Waverley, when, instantly turning his back, as if he had not observed him, he began to sing part of an old ballad.'

Young men will love thee more fair and more fast!
Heard ye so merry the little bird sing?

Old men's love the longest will last,
  *And the throstle-cock's head is under his
    wing.*

The young man's wrath is like light straw
    on fire;
  Heard ye so merry the little bird sing?
But like red-hot steel is the old man's ire,
  *And the throstle-cock's head is under his
    wing.*

The young man will brawl at the evening
    board;
  Heard ye so merry the little bird sing?
But the old man will draw at the dawning
    the sword,
  *And the throstle-cock's head is under his
    wing.*

VIII

FLORA MACIVOR'S SONG

From Chapter xxii.

THERE is mist on the mountain, and night
    on the vale,
But more dark is the sleep of the sons of
    the Gael.
A stranger commanded — it sunk on the
    land,
It has frozen each heart and benumbed
    every hand!

The dirk and the target lie sordid with
    dust,
The bloodless claymore is but reddened
    with rust;
On the hill or the glen if a gun should
    appear,
It is only to war with the heath-cock or
    deer.

The deeds of our sires if our bards should
    rehearse,
Let a blush or a blow be the meed of their
    verse!
Be mute every string and be hushed every
    tone
That shall bid us remember the fame that
    is flown!

But the dark hours of night and of slumber
    are past,
The morn on our mountains is dawning at
    last;

Glenaladale's peaks are illumed with the
    rays,
And the streams of Glenfinnan leap bright
    in the blaze.

O high-minded Moray! — the exiled — the
    dear! —
In the blush of the dawning the *Standard*
    uprear!
Wide, wide to the winds of the north let it
    fly,
Like the sun's latest flash when the tempest
    is nigh!

Ye sons of the strong, when that dawning
    shall break,
Need the harp of the aged remind you to
    wake?
That dawn never beamed on your fore-
    fathers' eye,
But it roused each high chieftain to van-
    quish or die.

O, sprung from the Kings who in Islay
    kept state,
Proud chiefs of Clan-Ranald, Glengary, and
    Sleat!
Combine like three streams from one
    mountain of snow,
And resistless in union rush down on the
    foe!

True son of Sir Evan, undaunted Lochiel,
Place thy targe on thy shoulder and burnish
    thy steel!
Rough Keppoch, give breath to thy bugle's
    bold swell,
Till far Coryarrick resound to the knell!

Stern son of Lord Kenneth, high chief of
    Kintail,
Let the stag in thy standard bound wild in
    the gale!
May the race of Clan-Gillian, the fearless
    and free,
Remember Glenlivet, Harlaw, and Dundee!

Let the clan of gray Fingon, whose offspring
    has given
Such heroes to earth and such martyrs to
    heaven,
Unite with the race of renowned Rorri
    More,
To launch the long galley and stretch to
    the oar!

How Mac-Shimei will joy when their chief
  shall display
The yew-crested bonnet o'er tresses of
  gray !
How the race of wronged Alpine and murdered Glencoe
Shall shout for revenge when they pour on
  the foe !

Ye sons of brown Dermid, who slew the
  wild boar,
Resume the pure faith of the great Callum-
  More !
Mac-Niel of the Islands, and Moy of the
  Lake,
For honor, for freedom, for vengeance
  awake !

Awake on your hills, on your islands awake,
Brave sons of the mountain, the frith, and
  the lake !
'T is the bugle — but not for the chase is
  the call;
'T is the pibroch's shrill summons — but not
  to the hall.

'T is the summons of heroes for conquest or
  death,
When the banners are blazing on mountain
  and heath;
They call to the dirk, the claymore, and the
  targe,
To the march and the muster, the line and
  the charge.

Be the brand of each chieftain like Fin's in
  his ire !
May the blood through his veins flow like
  currents of fire !
Burst the base foreign yoke as your sires
  did of yore !
Or die like your sires, and endure it no
  more !

IX

TO AN OAK TREE

IN THE CHURCHYARD OF ——, IN THE HIGH-
LANDS OF SCOTLAND, SAID TO MARK THE
GRAVE OF CAPTAIN WOGAN, KILLED IN 1649.

From Chapter xxix. ' The letter from the
Chief contained Flora's lines on the fate of
Captain Wogan, whose enterprising character
is so well drawn by Clarendon. He had originally engaged in the service of the Parliament,
but had abjured that party upon the execution
of Charles I. ; and upon hearing that the royal
standard was set up by the Earl of Glencairn
and General Middleton in the Highlands of
Scotland, took leave of Charles II., who was
then at Paris, passed into England, assembled
a body of cavaliers in the neighbourhood of
London, and traversed the kingdom, which had
been so long under domination of the usurper,
by marches conducted with such skill, dexterity, and spirit, that he safely united his
handful of horsemen with the body of Highlanders then in arms.   After several months of
desultory warfare, in which Wogan's skill and
courage gained him the highest reputation, he
had the misfortune to be wounded in a dangerous manner, and no surgical assistance being
within reach, he terminated his short but glorious career.'

EMBLEM of England's ancient faith,
  Full proudly may thy branches wave,
Where loyalty lies low in death,
  And valor fills a timeless grave.

And thou, brave tenant of the tomb !
  Repine not if our clime deny,
Above thine honored sod to bloom,
  The flowerets of a milder sky.

These owe their birth to genial May;
  Beneath a fiercer sun they pine,
Before the winter storm decay —
  And can their worth be type of thine ?

No ! for 'mid storms of Fate opposing,
  Still higher swelled thy dauntless heart,
And, while Despair the scene was clos-
  ing,
  Commenced thy brief but brilliant part.

'T was then thou sought'st on Albyn's hill,
  (When England's sons the strife re-
  signed,)
A rugged race resisting still,
  And unsubdued, though unrefined.

Thy death's hour heard no kindred wail,
  No holy knell thy requiem rung;
Thy mourners were the plaided Gael,
  Thy dirge the clamorous pibroch sung.

Yet who, in Fortune's summer-shine
  To waste life's longest term away,
Would change that glorious dawn of thine
  Though darkened ere its noontide day ?

Be thine the Tree whose dauntless boughs
  Brave summer's drought and winter's
    gloom !
Rome bound with oak her patriot's brows,
  As Albyn shadows Wogan's tomb.

X

'WE ARE BOUND TO DRIVE THE BUL-
LOCKS'

From Chapter xxxviii. 'The clan of Mac-
Farlane, occupying the fastnesses of the western side of Loch Lomond, were great depreda-
tors on the Low Country; and as their excursions
were made usually by night, the moon was
proverbially called their lantern. Their celebrated pibroch of *Hoggil nam Bo*, which is the
name of their gathering tune, intimates similar
practices, — the sense being ' —

WE are bound to drive the bullocks,
All by hollows, hirsts, and hillocks,
  Through the sleet and through the rain.
When the moon is beaming low
On frozen lake and hills of snow,
Bold and heartily we go,
  And all for little gain.

XI

'BUT FOLLOW, FOLLOW ME'

From Chapter lxiii.

BUT follow, follow me,
While glow-worms light the lea,
I'll show ye where the dead should be —
  Each in his shroud,
  While winds pipe loud,
And the red moon peeps dim through the
    cloud.

Follow, follow me:
Brave should he be
That treads by the night the dead man's
    lea.

FOR A' THAT AN' A' THAT

A NEW SONG TO AN OLD TUNE

Sung at the first meeting of the Pitt Club of
Scotland and published in the *Scots Magazine*
for July, 1814. Scott wrote two songs for the

anniversary of the death of Pitt, this and the
one on page 409. This one, though not printed
till July, 1814, was written for the celebration
in December, 1813.

THOUGH right be aft put down by
    strength,
  As mony a day we saw that,
The true and leilfu' cause at length
  Shall bear the grie for a' that !
For a' that an' a' that,
  Guns, guillotines, and a' that,
The Fleur-de-lis, that lost her right,
  Is queen again for a' that !

We 'll twine her in a friendly knot
  With England's Rose, and a' that;
The Shamrock shall not be forgot,
  For Wellington made bra' that.
The Thistle, though her leaf be rude,
  Yet faith we 'll no misca' that,
She sheltered in her solitude
  The Fleur-de-lis, for a' that.

The Austrian Vine, the Prussian Pine,
  (For Blucher's sake, hurra that,)
The Spanish Olive, too, shall join,
  And bloom in peace for a' that.
Stout Russia's Hemp, so surely twined
  Around our wreath we 'll draw that,
And he that would the cord unbind,
  Shall have it for his gra-vat !

Or, if to choke sae puir a sot,
  Your pity scorn to thraw that,
The Devil's elbo' be his lot,
  Where he may sit and claw that.
In spite of slight, in spite of might,
  In spite of brags and a' that,
The lads that battled for the right,
  Have won the day and a' that !

There 's ae bit spot I had forgot,
  America they ca' that !
A coward plot her rats had got
  Their father's flag to gnaw that:
Now see it fly top-gallant high,
  Atlantic winds shall blaw that,
And Yankee loon, beware your croun,
  There 's kames in hand to claw that !

For on the land, or on the sea,
  Where'er the breezes blaw that,
The British Flag shall bear the grie,
  And win the day for a' that !

FAREWELL TO MACKENZIE

HIGH CHIEF OF KINTAIL

FROM THE GAELIC

'The original verses,' says Scott, 'are arranged to a beautiful Gaelic air, of which the chorus is adapted to the double pull upon the oars of a galley, and which is therefore distinct from the ordinary jorums, or boat-songs. They were composed by the Family Bard upon the departure of the Earl of Sea-forth, who was obliged to take refuge in Spain, after an unsuccessful effort at insurrection in favor of the Stuart family, in the year 1718.' Written by Scott in 1815.

FAREWELL to Mackenneth, great Earl of the North,
The Lord of Lochcarron, Glenshiel, and Seaforth;
To the Chieftain this morning his course who began,
Launching forth on the billows his bark like a swan.
For a far foreign land he has hoisted his sail,
Farewell to Mackenzie, High Chief of Kintail!

O, swift be the galley and hardy her crew,
May her captain be skilful, her mariners true,
In danger undaunted, unwearied by toil,
Though the whirlwind should rise and the ocean should boil:
On the brave vessel's gunnel I drank his bonail,
And farewell to Mackenzie, High Chief of Kintail!

Awake in thy chamber, thou sweet south-land gale!
Like the sighs of his people, breathe soft on his sail;
Be prolonged as regret that his vassals must know,
Be fair as their faith and sincere as their woe:
Be so soft and so fair and so faithful, sweet gale,
Wafting onward Mackenzie, High Chief of Kintail!

Be his pilot experienced and trusty and wise,
To measure the seas and to study the skies:
May he hoist all his canvas from streamer to deck,
But O! crowd it higher when wafting him back —
Till the cliffs of Skooroora and Conan's glad vale
Shall welcome Mackenzie, High Chief of Kintail!

IMITATION

OF THE PRECEDING SONG

WRITTEN IN 1815

'These verses,' one of Scott's editors explains, 'were written shortly after the death of Lord Seaforth, the last male representative of his illustrious house. He was a nobleman of extraordinary talents, who must have made for himself a lasting reputation, had not his political exertions been checked by the painful natural infirmities alluded to in the fourth stanza.' The 'gentle dame' of the last stanza was Lady Hood, daughter of the last Lord Seaforth, widow of Admiral Sir Samuel Hood, and later Mrs. Stewart Mackenzie of Seaford and Glasserton.

So sung the old bard in the grief of his heart
When he saw his loved lord from his people depart.
Now mute on thy mountains, O Albyn, are heard
Nor the voice of the song nor the harp of the bard;
Or its strings are but waked by the stern winter gale,
As they mourn for Mackenzie, last Chief of Kintail.

From the far Southland Border a minstrel came forth,
And he waited the hour that some bard of the north
His hand on the harp of the ancient should cast,
And bid its wild numbers mix high with the blast;

But no bard was there left in the land of
    the Gael
To lament for Mackenzie, last Chief of
    Kintail.

' And shalt thou then sleep,' did the min-
    strel exclaim,
' Like the son of the lowly, unnoticed by
    fame ?
No, son of Fitzgerald ! in accents of
    woe
The song thou hast loved o'er thy coffin
    shall flow,
And teach thy wild mountains to join in
    the wail
That laments for Mackenzie, last Chief of
    Kintail.

' In vain, the bright course of thy talents
    to wrong,
Fate deadened thine ear and imprisoned
    thy tongue;
For brighter o'er all her obstructions arose
The glow of the genius they could not
    oppose;
And who in the land of the Saxon or
    Gael
Might match with Mackenzie, High Chief
    of Kintail ?

' Thy sons rose around thee in light and in
    love,
All a father could hope, all a friend could
    approve;
What 'vails it the tale of thy sorrows to
    tell, —
In the spring-time of youth and of promise
    they fell !
Of the line of Fitzgerald remains not a
    male
To bear the proud name of the Chief of
    Kintail.

' And thou, gentle dame, who must bear to
    thy grief
For thy clan and thy country the cares of
    a chief,
Whom brief rolling moons in six changes
    have left,
Of thy husband and father and brethren
    bereft,
To thine ear of affection how sad is the
    hail
That salutes thee the heir of the line of
    Kintail ! '

WAR–SONG OF LACHLAN

HIGH CHIEF OF MACLEAN

FROM THE GAELIC

Like the preceding this was translated in
1815 and prefaced thus by Scott: ' This song
appears to be imperfect, or, at least, like
many of the early Gaelic poems, makes a rapid
transition from one subject to another; from
the situation, namely, of one of the daughters
of the clan, who opens the song by lamenting
the absence of her lover, to an eulogium over
the military glories of the Chieftain. The
translator has endeavored to imitate the abrupt
style of the original.

A WEARY month has wandered o'er
Since last we parted on the shore;
Heaven ! that I saw thee, love, once more,
    Safe on that shore again ! —
'T was valiant Lachlan gave the word:
Lachlan, of many a galley lord:
He called his kindred bands on board,
    And launched them on the main.

Clan-Gillian is to ocean gone;
Clan-Gillian, fierce in foray known;
Rejoicing in the glory won
    In many a bloody broil:
For wide is heard the thundering fray,
The rout, the ruin, the dismay,
When from the twilight glens away
    Clan-Gillian drives the spoil.

Woe to the hills that shall rebound
Our bannered bag - pipes' maddening
    sound !
Clan-Gillian's onset echoing round,
    Shall shake their inmost cell.
Woe to the bark whose crew shall gaze
Where Lachlan's silken streamer plays !
The fools might face the lightning's blaze
    As wisely and as well !

SAINT CLOUD

This poem was written at Paris, 5th September. 1815, after an evening spent at St. Cloud,
with Lady Alvanley and her daughters, one of
whom was the songstress referred to in the last
stanza but one.

SOFT spread the southern summer night
    Her veil of darksome blue;
Ten thousand stars combined to light
    The terrace of Saint Cloud.

The evening breezes gently sighed,
  Like breath of lover true,
Bewailing the deserted pride
  And wreck of sweet Saint Cloud.

The drum's deep roll was heard afar,
  The bugle wildly blew
Good-night to Hulan and Hussar
  That garrison Saint Cloud.

The startled Naiads from the shade
  With broken urns withdrew,
And silenced was that proud cascade,
  The glory of Saint Cloud.

We sate upon its steps of stone,
  Nor could its silence rue,
When waked to music of our own
  The echoes of Saint Cloud.

Slow Seine might hear each lovely note
  Fall light as summer dew,
While through the moonless air they float,
  Prolonged from fair Saint Cloud.

And sure a melody more sweet
  His waters never knew,
Though music's self was wont to meet
  With princes at Saint Cloud.

Nor then with more delighted ear
  The circle round her drew.
Than ours, when gathered round to hear
  Our songstress at Saint Cloud.

Few happy hours poor mortals pass, —
  Then give those hours their due,
And rank among the foremost class
  Our evenings at Saint Cloud.

THE DANCE OF DEATH

In a letter to Morritt, October 2, 1815, Scott
writes, 'Out of my *Field of Waterloo* has
sprung an odd, wild sort of thing, which I intend to finish separately, and call it "The
Dance of Death."'

NIGHT and morning were at meeting
  Over Waterloo;
Cocks had sung their earliest greeting;
  Faint and low they crew,
For no paly beam yet shone
On the heights of Mount Saint John;

Tempest-clouds prolonged the sway
Of timeless darkness over day;
Whirlwind, thunder-clap, and shower
Marked it a predestined hour.   10
Broad and frequent through the night
Flashed the sheets of levin-light;
Muskets, glancing lightnings back,
Showed the dreary bivouac
  Where the soldier lay,
Chill and stiff and drenched with rain,
Wishing dawn of morn again,
  Though death should come with day.

'T is at such a tide and hour
Wizard, witch, and fiend have power,   20
And ghastly forms through mist and
    shower
  Gleam on the gifted ken;
And then the affrighted prophet's ear
Drinks whispers strange of fate and fear,
Presaging death and ruin near
  Among the sons of men; —
Apart from Albyn's war-array,
'T was then gray Allan sleepless lay;
Gray Allan, who for many a day
  Had followed stout and stern,   30
Where, through battle's rout and reel,
Storm of shot and edge of steel,
Led the grandson of Lochiel,
  Valiant Fassiefern.
Through steel and shot he leads no more,
Low laid mid friends' and foemen's gore —
But long his native lake's wild shore,
And Sunart rough, and high Ardgower,
  And Morven long shall tell,
And proud Bennevis hear with awe,   40
How upon bloody Quatre-Bras
Brave Cameron heard the wild hurra
  Of conquest as he fell.

Lone on the outskirts of the host,
The weary sentinel held post,
And heard through darkness far aloof
The frequent clang of courser's hoof,
Where held the cloaked patrol their course
And spurred 'gainst storm the swerving
    horse;
But there are sounds in Allan's ear   50
Patrol nor sentinel may hear,
And sights before his eye aghast
Invisible to them have passed,
  When down the destined plain,
'Twixt Britain and the bands of France,
Wild as marsh-borne meteor's glance,

Strange phantoms wheeled a revel dance
And doomed the future slain.
Such forms were seen, such sounds were
    heard,
When Scotland's James his march pre-
    pared   60
For Flodden's fatal plain;
Such, when he drew his ruthless sword,
As Choosers of the Slain, adored
The yet unchristened Dane.
An indistinct and phantom band,
They wheeled their ring-dance hand in
    hand
With gestures wild and dread:
The Seer, who watched them ride the
    storm,
Saw through their faint and shadowy form
The lightning's flash more red;   70
And still their ghastly roundelay
Was of the coming battle-fray
And of the destined dead.

SONG

Wheel the wild dance
While lightnings glance
    And thunders rattle loud,
And call the brave
To bloody grave,
    To sleep without a shroud.

Our airy feet,   80
So light and fleet,
    They do not bend the rye
That sinks its head when whirlwinds rave,
And swells again in eddying wave
    As each wild gust blows by;
But still the corn
At dawn of morn
    Our fatal steps that bore,
At eve lies waste,
A trampled paste   90
    Of blackening mud and gore.

Wheel the wild dance
While lightnings glance
    And thunders rattle loud,
And call the brave
To bloody grave,
    To sleep without a shroud.

Wheel the wild dance !
Brave sons of France,
    For you our ring makes room;   100

Make space full wide
For martial pride,
    For banner, spear, and plume.
Approach, draw near,
Proud cuirassier !
    Room for the men of steel !
Through crest and plate
The broadsword's weight
    Both head and heart shall feel.

Wheel the wild dance   110
While lightnings glance
    And thunders rattle loud,
And call the brave
To bloody grave,
    To sleep without a shroud.

Sons of the spear !
You feel us near
    In many a ghastly dream;
With fancy's eye
Our forms you spy,   120
    And hear our fatal scream.
With clearer sight
Ere falls the night,
    Just when to weal or woe
Your disembodied souls take flight
On trembling wing — each startled sprite
    Our choir of death shall know.

Wheel the wild dance
While lightnings glance
    And thunders rattle loud,   130
And call the brave
To bloody grave,
    To sleep without a shroud.

Burst ye clouds, in tempest showers,
Redder rain shall soon be ours —
    See the east grows wan —
Yield we place to sterner game,
Ere deadlier bolts and direr flame
Shall the welkin's thunders shame;
Elemental rage is tame   140
    To the wrath of man.

At morn, gray Allan's mates with awe
Heard of the visioned sights he saw,
    The legend heard him say;
But the Seer's gifted eye was dim,
Deafened his ear and stark his limb,
    Ere closed that bloody day —
He sleeps far from his Highland heath, —
But often of the Dance of Death
    His comrades tell the tale,   150

On picquet-post when ebbs the night,
And waning watch-fires glow less bright,
And dawn is glimmering pale.

ROMANCE OF DUNOIS

This and the two translations that follow were published by Scott in *Paul's Letters to his Kinsfolk*, in 1815, the book that grew out of his sudden visit to Waterloo. They were taken from a manuscript collection of French songs, probably compiled, says Scott, by some young officer, which was found stained with clay and blood on the field of Waterloo. The first is the well-known

'*Partant pour la Syrie*'

and both that and the second were written and set to music by Hortense Beauharnais, once queen of Holland.

IT was Dunois, the young and brave, was
    bound for Palestine,
But first he made his orisons before Saint
    Mary's shrine:
' And grant, immortal Queen of Heaven,'
    was still the soldier's prayer,
' That I may prove the bravest knight and
    love the fairest fair.'

His oath of honor on the shrine he graved
    it with his sword,
And followed to the Holy Land the banner
    of his Lord;
Where, faithful to his noble vow, his war-
    cry filled the air,
' Be honored aye the bravest knight, be-
    loved the fairest fair.'

They owed the conquest to his arm, and
    then his liege-lord said,
' The heart that has for honor beat by bliss
    must be repaid.
My daughter Isabel and thou shall be a
    wedded pair,
For thou art bravest of the brave, she fair-
    est of the fair.'

And then they bound the holy knot before
    Saint Mary's shrine
That makes a paradise on earth, if hearts
    and hands combine;
And every lord and lady bright that were
    in chapel there
Cried, 'Honored be the bravest knight, be-
    loved the fairest fair !'

THE TROUBADOUR

GLOWING with love, on fire for fame,
  A Troubadour that hated sorrow
Beneath his lady's window came,
  And thus he sung his last good-morrow:
' My arm it is my country's right,
  My heart is in my true love's bower;
Gayly for love and fame to fight
  Befits the gallant Troubadour.'

And while he marched with helm on head
  And harp in hand, the descant rung,
As, faithful to his favorite maid,
  The minstrel-burden still he sung:
' My arm it is my country's right,
  My heart is in my lady's bower;
Resolved for love and fame to fight,
  I come, a gallant Troubadour.'

Even when the battle-roar was deep,
  With dauntless heart he hewed his way,
Mid splintering lance and falchion-sweep,
  And still was heard his warrior-lay:
' My life it is my country's right,
  My heart is in my lady's bower;
For love to die, for fame to fight,
  Becomes the valiant Troubadour.'

Alas ! upon the bloody field
  He fell beneath the foeman's glaive,
But still reclining on his shield,
  Expiring sung the exulting stave:
' My life it is my country's right,
  My heart is in my lady's bower;
For love and fame to fall in fight,
  Becomes the valiant Troubadour.'

'IT CHANCED THAT CUPID ON A SEASON'

IT chanced that Cupid on a season,
  By Fancy urged, resolved to wed,
But could not settle whether Reason
  Or Folly should partake his bed.

What does he then ? — Upon my life,
  'T was bad example for a deity—
He takes me Reason for a wife,
  And Folly for his hours of gayety.

Though thus he dealt in petty treason,
  He loved them both in equal measure;
Fidelity was born of Reason,
  And Folly brought to bed of Pleasure.

SONG

ON THE LIFTING OF THE BANNER OF THE
HOUSE OF BUCCLEUCH, AT A GREAT
FOOT-BALL MATCH ON CARTERHAUGH

The foot-ball match took place December 5,
1815. The Ettrick Shepherd also celebrated it.

FROM the brown crest of Newark its sum-
    mons extending,
Our signal is waving in smoke and in
    flame;
And each forester blithe, from his moun-
    tain descending,
Bounds light o'er the heather to join in
    the game.
    Then up with the Banner, let forest winds
      fan her,
      She has blazed over Ettrick eight
      ages and more;
    In sport we'll attend her, in battle de-
      fend her,
      With heart and with hand, like our
      fathers before.

When the Southern invader spread waste
    and disorder,
At the glance of her crescents he paused
    and withdrew,
For around them were marshalled the
    pride of the Border,
The Flowers of the Forest, the Bands of
    BUCCLEUCH.

A stripling's weak hand to our revel has
    borne her,
No mail-glove has grasped her, no spear-
    men surround;
But ere a bold foeman should scathe or
    should scorn her
A thousand true hearts would be cold on
    the ground.

We forget each contention of civil dissen-
    sion,
And hail, like our brethren, HOME,
    DOUGLAS, and CAR:
And ELLIOT and PRINGLE in pastime shall
    mingle,
As welcome in peace as their fathers in
    war.

Then strip, lads, and to it, though sharp be
    the weather,
And if by mischance you should happen
    to fall,

There are worse things in life than a tum-
    ble on heather,
And life is itself but a game at foot-
    ball.

And when it is over we'll drink a blithe
    measure
To each laird and each lady that wit-
    nessed our fun,
And to every blithe heart that took part in
    our pleasure,
To the lads that have lost and the lads
    that have won.

May the Forest still flourish, both Borough
    and Landward,
From the hall of the peer to the herd's
    ingle-nook;
And huzza! my brave hearts, for BUC-
    CLEUCH and his standard,
For the King and the Country, the Clan
    and the Duke!
    Then up with the Banner, let forest winds
      fan her,
      She has blazed over Ettrick eight
      ages and more;
    In sport we'll attend her, in battle de-
      fend her,
      With heart and with hand, like our
      fathers before.

SONGS FROM GUY MANNERING

Published in 1815.

I

'CANNY MOMENT, LUCKY FIT'

From Chapter iii.

CANNY moment, lucky fit;
Is the lady lighter yet?
Be it lad, or be it lass,
Sign wi' cross, and sain wi' mass.

Trefoil, vervain, John's-wort, dill,
Hinders witches of their will;
Weel is them, that weel may
Fast upon St. Andrew's day.

Saint Bride and her brat,
Saint Colme and her cat,
Saint Michael and his spear,
Keep the house frae reif and wear.

II

'TWIST YE, TWINE YE! EVEN SO'

From Chapter iv.

TWIST ye, twine ye! even so,
Mingle shades of joy and woe,
Hope and fear and peace and strife,
In the thread of human life.

While the mystic twist is spinning,
And the infant's life beginning,
Dimly seen through twilight bending,
Lo, what varied shapes attending!

Passions wild and follies vain,
Pleasures soon exchanged for pain;
Doubt and jealousy and fear,
In the magic dance appear.

Now they wax and now they dwindle,
Whirling with the whirling spindle,
Twist ye, twine ye! even so,
Mingle human bliss and woe.

III

'WASTED, WEARY, WHEREFORE STAY'

From Chapter xxvii.

WASTED, weary, wherefore stay,
Wrestling thus with earth and clay?
From the body pass away; —
　　Hark! the mass is singing.

From thee doff thy mortal weed,
Mary Mother be thy speed,
Saints to help thee at thy need; —
　　Hark! the knell is ringing.

Fear not snow-drift driving fast,
Sleet or hail or levin blast;
Soon the shroud shall lap thee fast,
And the sleep be on thee cast
　　That shall ne'er know waking.

Haste thee, haste thee, to be gone,
Earth flits fast, and time draws on, —
Gasp thy gasp, and groan thy groan,
　　Day is near the breaking.

IV

'DARK SHALL BE LIGHT'

From Chapter xlix.

DARK shall be light,
　And wrong done to right,
When Bertram's right and Bertram's might
Shall meet on Ellangowan's height.

LULLABY OF AN INFANT CHIEF

AIR — '*Cadul gu lo*'

The words of the air signify 'Sleep on till day.' The lullaby was written for Mr. Terry's dramatization of *Guy Mannering*.

O, HUSH thee, my babie, thy sire was a knight,
Thy mother a lady both lovely and bright;
The woods and the glens, from the towers which we see,
They all are belonging, dear babie, to thee.
　　O ho ro, i ri ri, cadul gu lo,
　　O ho ro, i ri ri, etc.

O, fear not the bugle, though loudly it blows,
It calls but the warders that guard thy repose;
Their bows would be bended, their blades would be red,
Ere the step of a foeman draws near to thy bed.
　　O ho ro, i ri ri, etc.

O, hush thee, my babie, the time soon will come,
When thy sleep shall be broken by trumpet and drum;
Then hush thee, my darling, take rest while you may,
For strife comes with manhood and waking with day.
　　O ho ro, i ri ri, etc.

THE RETURN TO ULSTER

First published in Thomson's *Collection of Irish Airs*, 1816.

ONCE again, — but how changed since my wanderings began —
I have heard the deep voice of the Lagan and Bann,

And the pines of Clanbrassil resound to
    the roar
That wearies the echoes of fair Tullamore.
Alas ! my poor bosom, and why shouldst
    thou burn !
With the scenes of my youth can its rap-
    tures return ?
Can I live the dear life of delusion again,
That flowed when these echoes first mixed
    with my strain ?

It was then that around me, though poor
    and unknown,
High spells of mysterious enchantment
    were thrown;
The streams were of silver, of diamond the
    dew,
The land was an Eden, for fancy was new.
I had heard of our bards, and my soul was
    on fire
At the rush of their verse and the sweep
    of their lyre:
To me 't was not legend nor tale to the
    ear,
But a vision of noontide, distinguished and
    clear.

Ultonia's old heroes awoke at the call,
And renewed the wild pomp of the chase
    and the hall;
And the standard of Fion flashed fierce
    from on high,
Like a burst of the sun when the tempest
    is nigh.
It seemed that the harp of green Erin
    once more
Could renew all the glories she boasted of
    yore. —
Yet why at remembrance, fond heart,
    shouldst thou burn ?
They were days of delusion and cannot
    return.

But was she, too, a phantom, the maid
    who stood by,
And listed my lay while she turned from
    mine eye ?
Was she, too, a vision, just glancing to
    view,
Then dispersed in the sunbeam or melted
    to dew ?
O, would it had been so ! — O, would that
    her eye
Had been but a star - glance that shot
    through the sky,

And her voice that was moulded to
    melody's thrill,
Had been but a zephyr that sighed and
    was still !

O, would it had been so ! — not then this
    poor heart
Had learned the sad lesson, to love and to
    part;
To bear unassisted its burden of care,
While I toiled for the wealth I had no one
    to share.
Not then had I said, when life's summer
    was done
And the hours of her autumn were fast
    speeding on,
' Take the fame and the riches ye brought
    in your train,
And restore me the dream of my spring-
    tide again.'

JOCK OF HAZELDEAN

AIR — ' *A Border Melody* '

The first stanza is old. The others were
added to it for Campbell Albyn's *Anthology*,
1816.

' WHY weep ye by the tide, ladie ?
    Why weep ye by the tide ?
I 'll wed ye to my youngest son,
    And ye sall be his bride:
And ye sall be his bride, ladie,
    Sae comely to be seen ' —
But aye she loot the tears down fa'
    For Jock of Hazeldean.

' Now let this wilfu' grief be done,
    And dry that cheek so pale;
Young Frank is chief of Errington
    And lord of Langley-dale;
His step is first in peaceful ha',
    His sword in battle keen ' —
But aye she loot the tears down fa'
    For Jock of Hazeldean.

' A chain of gold ye sall not lack,
    Nor braid to bind your hair;
Nor mettled hound, nor managed hawk,
    Nor palfrey fresh and fair;
And you, the foremost o' them a',
    Shall ride our forest queen.' —
But aye she loot the tears down fa'
    For Jock of Hazeldean.

The kirk was decked at morning-tide,
  The tapers glimmered fair;
The priest and bridegroom wait the bride,
  And dame and knight are there.
They sought her baith by bower and ha';
  The ladie was not seen!
She's o'er the Border and awa'
  Wi' Jock of Hazeldean.

PIBROCH OF DONALD DHU

AIR — ' *Piobair of Donuil Dhuidh* '

This song was written for Albyn's *Anthology*, 1816, and contained the following preface by Scott : —
  'This is a very ancient pibroch belonging to Clan MacDonald, and supposed to refer to the expedition of Donald Balloch, who, in 1431, launched from the Isles with a considerable force, invaded Lochaber, and at Inverlochy defeated and put to flight the Earls of Mar and Caithness, though at the head of an army superior to his own. The words of the set, theme, or melody, to which the pipe variations are applied, run thus in Gaelic : —

" Piobaireachd Dhonuil Dhuidh, piobaireachd Dhonuil ;
Piobaireachd Dhonuil Dhuidh, piobaireachd Dhonuil ;
Piobaireachd Dhonuil Dhuidh, piobaireachd Dhonuil ;
Piob agus bratach air faiche Inverlochi."

" The pipe-summons of Donald the Black,
The pipe-summons of Donald the Black,
The war-pipe and the pennon are on the gathering-
    place at Inverlochy."

This readily suggests the gathering song in the third canto of *The Lady of the Lake*.

PIBROCH of Donuil Dhu,
  Pibroch of Donuil,
Wake thy wild voice anew,
  Summon Clan Conuil.
Come away, come away,
  Hark to the summons !
Come in your war array,
  Gentles and commons.

Come from deep glen and
  From mountain so rocky,
The war-pipe and pennon
  Are at Inverlochy.
Come every hill-plaid and
  True heart that wears one,
Come every steel blade and
  Strong hand that bears one.

Leave untended the herd,
  The flock without shelter;
Leave the corpse uninterred,
  The bride at the altar;
Leave the deer, leave the steer,
  Leave nets and barges:
Come with your fighting gear,
  Broadswords and targes.

Come as the winds come when
  Forests are rended;
Come as the waves come when
  Navies are stranded:
Faster come, faster come,
  Faster and faster,
Chief, vassal, page and groom,
  Tenant and master.

Fast they come, fast they come;
  See how they gather !
Wide waves the eagle plume,
  Blended with heather.
Cast your plaids, draw your blades,
  Forward each man set !
Pibroch of Donuil Dhu,
  Knell for the onset !

NORA'S VOW

AIR — ' *Cha teid mis a chaoidh* '

Written for Albyn's *Anthology*, 1816, with this note by Scott : —
  ' In the original Gaelic, the Lady makes protestations that she will not go with the Red Earl's son, until the swan should build in the cliff, and the eagle in the lake — until one mountain should change places with another, and so forth. It is but fair to add, that there is no authority for supposing that she altered her mind — except the vehemence of her protestation.'

HEAR what Highland Nora said,
' The Earlie's son I will not wed,
Should all the race of nature die
And none be left but he and I.
For all the gold, for all the gear,
And all the lands both far and near,
That ever valor lost or won,
I would not wed the Earlie's son.'

' A maiden's vows,' old Callum spoke,
' Are lightly made and lightly broke;
The heather on the mountain's height
Begins to bloom in purple light;
The frost-wind soon shall sweep away
That lustre deep from glen and brae;

Yet Nora ere its bloom be gone
May blithely wed the Earlie's son.'

'The swan,' she said, 'the lake's clear
　　breast
May barter for the eagle's nest;
The Awe's fierce stream may backward
　　turn,
Ben-Cruaichan fall and crush Kilchurn;
Our kilted clans when blood is high
Before their foes may turn and fly;
But I, were all these marvels done,
Would never wed the Earlie's son.'

Still in the water-lily's shade
Her wonted nest the wild-swan made;
Ben-Cruaichan stands as fast as ever,
Still downward foams the Awe's fierce
　　river;
To shun the clash of foeman's steel
No Highland brogue has turned the heel;
But Nora's heart is lost and won —
She 's wedded to the Earlie's son !

MACGREGOR'S GATHERING

Written for Albyn's *Anthology*, 1816.

AIR — '*Thain' a Grigalach*'

THE moon 's on the lake and the mist 's on
　　the brae,
And the Clan has a name that is nameless
　　by day;
　　Then gather, gather, gather, Grigalach!
　　Gather, gather, gather, etc.

Our signal for fight, that from monarchs
　　we drew,
Must be heard but by night in our vengeful
　　haloo !
　　Then haloo, Grigalach ! haloo, Griga-
　　lach !
　　Haloo, haloo, haloo, Grigalach, etc.

Glen Orchy's proud mountains, Coalchurn
　　and her towers,
Glenstrae and Glenlyon no longer are ours;
　　We 're landless, landless, landless,
　　Grigalach !
　　Landless, landless, landless, etc.

But doomed and devoted by vassal and lord,
MacGregor has still both his heart and his
　　sword !

Then courage, courage, courage, Grig-
　　alach !
Courage, courage, courage, etc.

If they rob us of name and pursue us with
　　beagles,
Give their roofs to the flame and their flesh
　　to the eagles !
　　Then vengeance, vengeance, vengeance,
　　Grigalach !
　　Vengeance, vengeance, vengeance, etc.

While there 's leaves in the forest and foam
　　on the river,
MacGregor, despite them, shall flourish
　　forever !
　　Come then, Grigalach, come then,
　　Grigalach !
　　Come then, come then, come then, etc.

Through the depths of Loch Katrine the
　　steed shall career,
O'er the peak of Ben-Lomond the galley
　　shall steer.
And the rocks of Craig-Royston like icicles
　　melt,
Ere our wrongs be forgot or our vengeance
　　unfelt.
　　Then gather, gather, gather, Griga-
　　lach !
　　Gather, gather, gather, etc.

VERSES

COMPOSED FOR THE OCCASION, ADAPTED
TO HAYDN'S AIR 'GOD SAVE THE EM-
PEROR FRANCIS,' AND SUNG BY A
SELECT BAND AFTER THE DINNER
GIVEN BY THE LORD PROVOST OF
EDINBURGH TO THE GRAND-DUKE
NICHOLAS OF RUSSIA, AND HIS SUITE,
19TH DECEMBER, 1816.

GOD protect brave ALEXANDER,
Heaven defend the noble Czar,
Mighty Russia's high Commander,
First in Europe's banded war;
For the realms he did deliver
From the tyrant overthrown,
Thou, of every good the Giver,
Grant him long to bless his own !
Bless him, mid his land's disaster
For her rights who battled brave;
Of the land of foemen master,
Bless him who their wrongs forgave.

O'er his just resentment victor,
Victor over Europe's foes,
Late and long supreme director,
Grant in peace his reign may close.
Hail ! then, hail ! illustrious stranger !
Welcome to our mountain strand;
Mutual interests, hopes, and danger,
Link us with thy native land.
Freemen's force or false beguiling
Shall that union ne'er divide,
Hand in hand while peace is smiling,
And in battle side by side.

VERSES FROM THE ANTIQUARY

Published in 1816.

I

'HE CAME, BUT VALOR HAD SO FIRED HIS EYE'

From Chapter vi.

He came — but valor had so fired his eye,
And such a falchion glittered on his thigh,
That, by the gods, with such a load of steel,
I thought he came to murder — not to
    heal.

II

'WHY SIT'ST THOU BY THAT RUINED HALL'

From Chapter x.

' Why sit'st thou by that ruined hall,
    Thou aged carle so stern and gray ?
Dost thou its former pride recall,
    Or ponder how it passed away ? '

' Know'st thou not me ? ' the Deep Voice
    cried:
' So long enjoyed, so oft misused —
Alternate, in thy fickle pride,
    Desired, neglected, and accused !

' Before my breath, like blazing flax,
    Man and his marvels pass away !
And changing empires wane and wax,
    Are founded, flourish, and decay.

' Redeem mine hours — the space is brief —
    While in my glass the sand - grains
    shiver,
And measureless thy joy or grief,
    When Time and thou shalt part forever!'

III

EPITAPH

From Chapter xi.

Heir lyeth John o' ye Girnell,
Erth has ye nit and heuen ye kirnell.
In hys tyme ilk wyfe's hennis clokit,
Ilka gud mannis herth wi' bairnis was
    stokit,
He deled a boll o' bear in firlottis fyve,
Four for ye halie kirke and ane for puir
    mennis wyvis.

IV

'THE HERRING LOVES THE MERRY MOON-LIGHT'

From Chapter xi. ' As the Antiquary lifted
the latch of the hut, he was surprised to hear
the shrill, tremulous voice of Elspeth chanting
forth an old ballad in a wild and doleful recita-
tive : ' —

The herring loves the merry moon-light,
    The mackerel loves the wind,
But the oyster loves the dredging sang,
    For they come of a gentle kind.

Now haud your tongue, baith wife and
    carle,
    And listen great and sma',
And I will sing of Glenallan's Earl
    That fought on the red Harlaw.

The cronach 's cried on Bennachie,
    And doun the Don and a',
And hieland and lawland may mournfu' be
    For the sair field of Harlaw. —

They saddled a hundred milk-white steeds,
    They hae bridled a hundred black,
With a chafron of steel on each horse's
    head,
    And a good knight upon his back.

They hadna ridden a mile, a mile,
    A mile but barely ten,
When Donald came branking down the
    brae
    Wi' twenty thousand men.

Their tartans they were waving wide,
    Their glaives were glancing clear,

The pibrochs rung frae side to side,
    Would deafen ye to hear.

The great Earl in his stirrups stood,
    That Highland host to see:
' Now here a knight that 's stout and good
    May prove a jeopardie:

' What would'st thou do, my squire so gay,
    That rides beside my reyne, —
Were ye Glenallan's Earl the day,
    And I were Roland Cheyne ?

' To turn the rein were sin and shame,
    To fight were wond'rous peril, —
What would ye do now, Roland Cheyne,
    Were ye Glenallan's Earl ? ' —

' Were I Glenallan's Earl this tide,
    And ye were Roland Cheyne,
The spur should be in my horse's side,
    And the bridle upon his mane.

' If they hae twenty thousand blades,
    And we twice ten times ten,
Yet they hae but their tartan plaids,
    And we are mail-clad men.

' My horse shall ride through ranks sae
        rude,
    As through the moorland fern, —
Then ne'er let the gentle Norman blude
    Grow cauld for Highland kerne.'

.   .   .   .

He turned him right and round again,
    Said, ' Scorn na at my mither;
Light loves I may get mony a ane,
    But minnie ne'er anither.'

VERSES FROM OLD MORTALITY

Published in 1816.

I

'AND WHAT THOUGH WINTER WILL
PINCH SEVERE '

From Chapter xix.

AND what though winter will pinch severe
    Through locks of gray and a cloak that 's
        old,
Yet keep up thy heart, bold cavalier,
    For a cup of sack shall fence the cold.

For time will rust the brightest blade,
    And years will break the strongest bow;
Was never wight so starkly made,
    But time and years would overthrow.

II

VERSES FOUND, WITH A LOCK OF HAIR, IN
BOTHWELL'S POCKET-BOOK

From Chapter xxiii.

THY hue, dear pledge, is pure and bright
As in that well-remembered night,
When first thy mystic braid was wove,
And first my Agnes whispered love.

Since then how often hast thou pressed
The torrid zone of this wild breast,
Whose wrath and hate have sworn to dwell
With the first sin that peopled hell;
A breast whose blood 's a troubled ocean,
Each throb the earthquake's wild commo-
        tion ! —
Oh, if such clime thou canst endure,
Yet keep thy hue unstained and pure,
What conquest o'er each erring thought
Of that fierce realm had Agnes wrought !
I had not wandered wild and wide,
With such an angel for my guide;
Nor heaven nor earth could then reprove
        me
If she had lived, and lived to love me.

Not then this world's wild joys had been
To me one savage hunting-scene,
My sole delight the headlong race,
And frantic hurry of the chase;
To start, pursue, and bring to bay,
Rush in, drag down and rend my prey,
Then — from the carcase turn away !
Mine ireful mood had sweetness tamed,
And soothed each wound which pride in-
        flamed !
Yes, God and man might now approve me,
If thou hadst lived, and lived to love me.

III

EPITAPH ON BALFOUR OF BURLEY

From Chapter xliv. ' Gentle reader, I did
request of mine honest friend Peter Proudfoot,
travelling merchant, known to many of this
land for his faithful and just dealings, as well
in muslins and cambrics as in small wares, to
procure me, on his next peregrinations to that

vicinage, a copy of the Epitaphion alluded to.
And, according to his report, which I see no
ground to discredit, it runneth thus : —

HERE lyes ane saint to prelates surly,
Being John Balfour, sometime of Burley,
Who, stirred up to vengeance take,
For solemn League and Cov'nant's sake,
Upon the Magus-Moor, in Fife,
Did tak' James Sharpe the apostate's life;
By Dutchman's hands was hacked and shot,
Then drowned in Clyde near this saam
    spot.

THE SEARCH AFTER HAPPINESS

OR, THE QUEST OF SULTAUN SOLIMAUN

The hint of this tale, which was published in
1817, was taken from a novel of Casti, *La
Camiscia Magica.*

O, FOR a glance of that gay Muse's eye
That lightened on Bandello's laughing
    tale,
And twinkled with a lustre shrewd and
    sly
When Giam Battista bade her vision
    hail ! —
Yet fear not, ladies, the *naïve* detail
Given by the natives of that land cano-
    rous;
Italian license loves to leap the pale,
We Britons have the fear of shame be-
    fore us,
And, if not wise in mirth, at least must be
    decorous.

In the far eastern clime, no great while
    since,   10
Lived Sultaun Solimaun, a mighty prince,
Whose eyes, as oft as they performed their
    round,
Beheld all others fixed upon the ground;
Whose ears received the same unvaried
    phrase,
' Sultaun ! thy vassal hears and he obeys ! '
All have their tastes — this may the fancy
    strike
Of such grave folks as pomp and grandeur
    like;
For me, I love the honest heart and warm
Of monarch who can amble round his farm,
Or, when the toil of state no more annoys, 20
In chimney corner seek domestic joys —

I love a prince will bid the bottle pass,
Exchanging with his subjects glance and
    glass;
In fitting time can, gayest of the gay,
Keep up the jest and mingle in the lay —
Such monarchs best our free-born humors
    suit,
But despots must be stately, stern, and
    mute.

This Solimaun Serendib had in sway —
And where 's Serendib ? may some critic
    say. —
Good lack, mine honest friend, consult the
    chart,   30
Scare not my Pegasus before I start !
If Rennell has it not, you 'll find mayhap
The isle laid down in Captain Sindbad's
    map —
Famed mariner, whose merciless narrations
Drove every friend and kinsman out of
    patience,
Till, fain to find a guest who thought them
    shorter,
He deigned to tell them over to a porter —
The last edition see, by Long, and Co.,
Rees, Hurst, and Orme, our fathers in the
    Row.

Serendib found, deem not my tale a fic-
    tion —   40
This Sultaun, whether lacking contradic-
    tion —
A sort of stimulant which hath its uses
To raise the spirits and reform the juices,
Sovereign specific for all sorts of cures
In my wife's practice and perhaps in
    yours —
The Sultaun lacking this same wholesome
    bitter,
Or cordial smooth for prince's palate fitter —
Or if some Mollah had hag-rid his dreams
With Degial, Ginnistan, and such wild
    themes
Belonging to the Mollah's subtle craft,   50
I wot not —but the Sultaun never laughed,
Scarce ate or drank, and took a melancholy
That scorned all remedy profane or holy;
In his long list of melancholies, mad
Or mazed or dumb, hath Burton none so bad.

Physicians soon arrived, sage, ware, and
    tried,
    As e'er scrawled jargon in a darkened
        room;

With heedful glance the Sultaun's tongue
     they eyed,
Peeped in his bath and God knows where
     beside,
   And then in solemn accent spoke their
      doom,   60
' His majesty is very far from well.'
Then each to work with his specific fell:
The Hakim Ibrahim *instanter* brought
His unguent Mahazzim al Zerdukkaut,
While Roompot, a practitioner more wily,
Relied on his Munaskif al fillfily.
More and yet more in deep array appear,
And some the front assail and some the
     rear;
Their remedies to reinforce and vary
Came surgeon eke, and eke apothecary; 70
Till the tired monarch, though of words
     grown chary,
Yet dropt, to recompense their fruitless
     labor,
Some hint about a bowstring or a sabre.
There lacked, I promise you, no longer
     speeches
To rid the palace of those learned leeches.

Then was the council called — by their
     advice —
They deemed the matter ticklish all and
     nice,
   And sought to shift it off from their
      own shoulders —
Tartars and couriers in all speed were
     sent,
To call a sort of Eastern Parliament   80
   Of feudatory chieftains and freehold-
      ers —
Such have the Persians at this very day,
My gallant Malcolm calls them *couroul-
     tai;* —
I 'm not prepared to show in this slight
     song
That to Serendib the same forms belong —
E'en let the learned go search, and tell me
     if I 'm wrong.

The Omrahs, each with hand on scimitar,
Gave, like Sempronius, still their voice for
     war —
' The sabre of the Sultaun in its sheath
Too long has slept nor owned the work of
     death;   90
Let the Tambourgi bid his signal rattle,
Bang the loud gong and raise the shout of
     battle !

This dreary cloud that dims our sovereign's
     day
Shall from his kindled bosom flit away,
When the bold Lootie wheels his courser
     round
And the armed elephant shall shake the
     ground.
Each noble pants to own the glorious sum-
     mons —
And for the charges — Lo ! your faithful
     Commons ! '   98
The Riots who attended in their places —
   Serendib language calls a farmer Riot —
Looked ruefully in one another's faces,
   From this oration auguring much dis-
     quiet,
Double assessment, forage, and free quar-
     ters;
And fearing these as Chinamen the Tartars,
Or as the whiskered vermin fear the
     mousers,
Each fumbled in the pocket of his trousers.

And next came forth the reverend Convo-
     cation,
   Bald heads, white beards, and many a
     turban green,   108
Imaum and Mollah there of every station,
   Santon, Fakir, and Calendar were seen.
Their votes were various — some advised
     a mosque
With fitting revenues should be erected,
With seemly gardens and with gay kiosque,
   To recreate a band of priests selected;
Others opined that through the realms a
     dole
   Be made to holy men, whose prayers
     might profit
The Sultaun's weal in body and in soul.
   But their long-headed chief, the Sheik
     Ul-Sofit,
More closely touched the point; — ' Thy
     studious mood,'
Quoth he, ' O Prince ! hath thickened
     all thy blood,   120
And dulled thy brain with labor beyond
     measure;
Wherefore relax a space and take thy
     pleasure,
And toy with beauty or tell o'er thy
     treasure;
From all the cares of state, my liege, en-
     large thee,
And leave the burden to thy faithful
     clergy.'

These counsels sage availed not a whit,
  And so the patient — as is not uncom-
    mon
Where grave physicians lose their time
    and wit —
  Resolved to take advice of an old
    woman;
His mother she, a dame who once was
    beauteous,   130
And still was called so by each subject
    duteous.
Now, whether Fatima was witch in earnest,
  Or only made believe, I cannot say —
But she professed to cure disease the stern-
    est,
  By dint of magic amulet or lay;
And, when all other skill in vain was shown,
She deemed it fitting time to use her own.

' *Sympathia magica* hath wonders done ' —
Thus did old Fatima bespeak her son —
' It works upon the fibres and the pores, 140
And thus insensibly our health restores,
And it must help us here. — Thou must
    endure
The ill, my son, or travel for the cure.
Search land and sea, and get where'er you
    can
The inmost vesture of a happy man,
I mean his SHIRT, my son; which, taken
    warm
And fresh from off his back, shall chase
    your harm,
Bid every current of your veins rejoice,
And your dull heart leap light as shepherd-
    boy's.
Such was the counsel from his mother
    came; —   150
I know not if she had some under-game,
As doctors have, who bid their patients
    roam
And live abroad when sure to die at home,
Or if she thought that, somehow or another,
Queen-Regent sounded better than Queen-
    Mother;
But, says the Chronicle — who will go look
    it —
That such was her advice — the Sultaun
    took it.

All are on board — the Sultaun and his
    train,
In gilded galley prompt to plough the main.
  The old Rais was the first who ques-
    tioned, ' Whither ? '   160

They paused — ' Arabia,' thought the pen-
    sive prince,
' Was called The Happy many ages since —
  For Mokha, Rais.' — And they came
    safely thither.
But not in Araby with all her balm,
Nor where Judea weeps beneath her palm,
Not in rich Egypt, not in Nubian waste,
Could there the step of happiness be traced.
One Copt alone professed to have seen her
    smile,
When Bruce his goblet filled at infant
    Nile:
She blessed the dauntless traveller as he
    quaffed,   170
But vanished from him with the ended
    draught.

' Enough of turbans,' said the weary King,
' These dolimans of ours are not the thing;
Try we the Giaours, these men of coat and
    cap, I
Incline to think some of them must be
    happy;
At least, they have as fair a cause as any
    can,
They drink good wine and keep no Rama-
    zan.
Then northward, ho ! ' — The vessel cuts
    the sea,
And fair Italia lies upon her lee. —
But fair Italia, she who once unfurled 180
Her eagle-banners o'er a conquered world,
Long from her throne of domination tum-
    bled;
Lay by her quondam vassals sorely hum-
    bled,
The Pope himself looked pensive, pale, and
    lean,
And was not half the man he once had
    been.
' While these the priest and those the noble
    fleeces,
Our poor old boot,' they said, ' is torn to
    pieces.
Its tops the vengeful claws of Austria feel,
And the Great Devil is rending toe and
    heel.
If happiness you seek, to tell you truly, 190
We think she dwells with one Giovanni
    Bulli;
A tramontane, a heretic — the buck,
Poffaredio ! still has all the luck;
By land or ocean never strikes his flag —
And then — a perfect walking money-bag.'

Off set our prince to seek John Bull's
    abode,
But first took France — it lay upon the
    road.

Monsieur Baboon after much late commo-
    tion
Was agitated like a settling ocean,
Quite out of sorts and could not tell what
    ailed him,   200
Only the glory of his house had failed him;
Besides, some tumors on his noddle biding
Gave indication of a recent hiding.
Our prince, though Sultauns of such things
    are heedless,
Thought it a thing indelicate and need-
    less
To ask if at that moment he was happy.
And Monsieur, seeing that he was *comme il
    faut,* a
Loud voice mustered up, for ' *Vive le Roi!* '
    Then whispered, ' Ave you any news of
       Nappy ? '
The Sultaun answered him with a cross
    question, —   210
    ' Pray, can you tell me aught of one John
       Bull,
That dwells somewhere beyond your
    herring-pool ? '
The query seemed of difficult digestion,
The party shrugged and grinned and took
    his snuff,
And found his whole good-breeding scarce
    enough.

Twitching his visage into as many puckers
As damsels wont to put into their tuckers
Ere liberal Fashion damned both lace and
    lawn,
And bade the veil of modesty be drawn —
Replied the Frenchman after a brief pause,
' Jean Bool ! — I vas not know him — Yes,
    I vas —   221
I vas remember dat, von year or two,
I saw him at von place called Vaterloo —
Ma foi ! il s'est très joliment battu,
Dat is for Englishman, — m'entendez-
    vous ?
But den he had wit him one damn son-gun,
Rogue I no like — dey call him Velling-
    ton.'
Monsieur's politeness could not hide his
    fret,
So Solimaun took leave and crossed the
    strait.

John Bull was in his very worst of
    moods,   230
Raving of sterile farms and unsold goods;
His sugar-loaves and bales about he threw,
And on his counter beat the devil's tattoo.
His wars were ended and the victory won,
But then 't was reckoning-day with honest
    John;
And authors vouch, 't was still this worthy's
    way,
' Never to grumble till he came to pay;
And then he always thinks, his temper's
    such,
The work too little and the pay too much.'
    Yet, grumbler as he is, so kind and
       hearty   240
That when his mortal foe was on the floor,
And past the power to harm his quiet
    more,
    Poor John had wellnigh wept for Bona-
       parte !
Such was the wight whom Solimaun sa-
    lamed, —
' And who are you,' John answered, ' and
    be d——d ? '

' A stranger, come to see the happiest
    man —
So, signior, all avouch — in Frangistan.'
' Happy ? my tenants breaking on my
    hand;
Unstocked my pastures and untilled my
    land;
Sugar and rum a drug, and mice and
    moths   250
The sole consumers of my good broad-
    cloths —
Happy ? — Why cursed war and racking
    tax
Have left us scarcely raiment to our backs.'
' In that case, signior, I may take my leave;
I came to ask a favor — but I grieve ' —
' Favor ? ' said John, and eyed the Sultaun
    hard,
' It 's my belief you came to break the
    yard ! —
But, stay, you look like some poor foreign
    sinner —
Take that to buy yourself a shirt and
    dinner.'
With that he chucked a guinea at his
    head;   260
But with due dignity the Sultaun said,
' Permit me, sir, your bounty to decline;
A *shirt* indeed I seek, but none of thine.

Signior, I kiss your hands, so fare you
well.'
'Kiss and be d——d,' quoth John, 'and go
to hell !'

Next door to John there dwelt his sister
Peg,
Once a wild lass as ever shook a leg
When the blithe bagpipe blew — but, so-
berer now,
She *doucely* span her flax and milked her
cow.
And whereas erst she was a needy slat-
tern,   270
Nor now of wealth or cleanliness a pat-
tern,
Yet once a month her house was partly
swept,
And once a week a plenteous board she
kept.
And whereas, eke, the vixen used her claws
And teeth of yore on slender provoca-
tion,
She now was grown amenable to laws,
A quiet soul as any in the nation;
The sole remembrance of her warlike joys
Was in old songs she sang to please her
boys.
John Bull, whom in their years of early
strife   280
She wont to lead a cat-and-doggish life,
Now found the woman, as he said, a
neighbor,
Who looked to the main chance, declined
no labor,
Loved a long grace and spoke a northern
jargon,
And was d——d close in making of a bar-
gain.

The Sultaun entered, and he made his
leg,
And with decorum curtsied sister Peg —
She loved a book, and knew a thing or
two,
And guessed at once with whom she had
to do.
She bade him ' Sit into the fire,' and
took   290
Her dram, her cake, her kebbuck from the
nook;
Asked him ' about the news from Eastern
parts;
And of her absent bairns, puir Highland
hearts !

If peace brought down the price of tea and
pepper,
And if the *nitmugs* were grown *ony*
cheaper; —
Were there nae *speerings* of our Mungo
Park —
Ye 'll be the gentleman that wants the
sark ?
If ye wad buy a web o' auld wife's spin-
ning,
I 'll warrant ye it 's a weel-wearing linen.'
Then up got Peg and round the house 'gan
scuttle   300
In search of goods her customer to nail,
Until the Sultaun strained his princely
throttle,
And holloed, ' Ma'am, that is not what
I ail.
Pray, are you happy, ma'am, in this snug
glen ?'
' Happy ?' said Peg; ' What for d' ye want
to ken ?
Besides, just think upon this by-gane year,
Grain wadna pay the yoking of the
pleugh.'
' What say you to the present ?' — ' Meal 's
sae dear,
To make their *brose* my bairns have
scarce aneugh.'
' The devil take the shirt,' said Soli-
maun,   310
' I think my quest will end as it began. —
Farewell, ma'am; nay, no ceremony, I
beg'—
' Ye 'll no be for the linen then ?' said
Peg.

Now, for the land of verdant Erin
The Sultaun's royal bark is steering,
The Emerald Isle where honest Paddy
dwells,
The cousin of John Bull, as story tells.
For a long space had John, with words of
thunder,
Hard looks, and harder knocks, kept Paddy
under,
Till the poor lad, like boy that 's flogged
unduly,   320
Had gotten somewhat restive and unruly.
Hard was his lot and lodging, you 'll allow,
A wigwam that would hardly serve a sow;
His landlord, and of middle - men two
brace,
Had screwed his rent up to the starving-
place;

His garment was a top-coat and an old
    one,
His meal was a potato and a cold one;
But still for fun or frolic and all that,
In the round world was not the match of
    Pat.

The Sultaun saw him on a holiday,   330
Which is with Paddy still a jolly day:
When mass is ended, and his load of sins
Confessed, and Mother Church hath from
    her binns
Dealt forth a bonus of imputed merit,
Then is Pat's time for fancy, whim, and
    spirit!
To jest, to sing, to caper fair and free,
And dance as light as leaf upon the tree.
'By Mahomet,' said Sultaun Solimaun,
'That ragged fellow is our very man!
Rush in and seize him — do not do him
    hurt,   340
But, will he nill he, let me have his *shirt*.'

Shilela their plan was wellnigh after balk-
    ing —
Much less provocation will set it a-walk-
    ing —
But the odds that foiled Hercules foiled
    Paddy Whack;
They seized, and they floored, and they
    stripped him — Alack!
Up-bubboo! Paddy had not — a shirt to his
    back!
And the king, disappointed, with sorrow
    and shame
Went back to Serendib as sad as he came.

LINES

WRITTEN FOR MISS SMITH

Miss Smith, afterward Mrs. Bartley, was an
actress who greatly pleased Scott, and he wrote
these lines for the night of her benefit at the
Edinburgh Theatre in 1817.

WHEN the lone pilgrim views afar
The shrine that is his guiding star,
With awe his footsteps print the road
Which the loved saint of yore has trod.
As near he draws and yet more near,
His dim eye sparkles with a tear;
The Gothic fane's unwonted show,
The choral hymn, the tapers' glow,

Oppress his soul; while they delight
And chasten rapture with affright.
No longer dare he think his toil
Can merit aught his patron's smile;
Too light appears the distant way,
The chilly eve, the sultry day —
All these endured no favor claim,
But murmuring forth the sainted name,
He lays his little offering down,
And only deprecates a frown.

We too who ply the Thespian art
Oft feel such bodings of the heart,
And when our utmost powers are strained
Dare hardly hope your favor gained.
She who from sister climes has sought
The ancient land where Wallace fought —
Land long renowned for arms and arts,
And conquering eyes and dauntless
    hearts —
She, as the flutterings *here* avow,
Feels all the pilgrim's terrors *now*;
Yet sure on Caledonian plain
The stranger never sued in vain.
'T is yours the hospitable task
To give the applause she dare not ask;
And they who bid the pilgrim speed,
The pilgrim's blessing be their meed.

MR. KEMBLE'S FAREWELL AD-
DRESS

ON TAKING LEAVE OF THE EDINBURGH
STAGE

Mr. Kemble recited these lines in the dress
of Macbeth, which he had just been acting,
March 29, 1817.

As the worn war-horse, at the trumpet's
    sound,
Erects his mane, and neighs, and paws the
    ground —
Disdains the ease his generous lord assigns,
And longs to rush on the embattled lines,
So I, your plaudits ringing on mine ear,
Can scarce sustain to think our parting near;
To think my scenic hour forever past,
And that those valued plaudits are my last.
Why should we part, while still some
    powers remain,
That in your service strive not yet in vain?
Cannot high zeal the strength of youth
    supply,
And sense of duty fire the fading eye;

And all the wrongs of age remain sub-
   dued
Beneath the burning glow of gratitude ?
Ah, no ! the taper, wearing to its close,
Oft for a space in fitful lustre glows;
But all too soon the transient gleam is
   past,
It cannot be renewed, and will not last;
Even duty, zeal, and gratitude can wage
But short-lived conflict with the frosts of
   age.
Yes ! It were poor, remembering what I
   was,
To live a pensioner on your applause,
To drain the dregs of your endurance dry,
And take, as alms, the praise I once could
   buy;
Till every sneering youth around enquires,
' Is this the man who once could please
   our sires ? '
And scorn assumes compassion's doubtful
   mien,
To warn me off from the encumbered
   scene.
This must not be; — and higher duties
   crave
Some space between the theatre and the
   grave,
That, like the Roman in the Capitol,
I may adjust my mantle ere I fall:
My life's brief act in public service flown,
The last, the closing scene, must be my
   own.

Here, then, adieu ! while yet some well-
   graced parts
May fix an ancient favorite in your hearts,
Not quite to be forgotten, even when
You look on better actors, younger men:
And if your bosoms own this kindly debt
Of old remembrance, how shall mine for-
   get —
O, how forget ! — how oft I hither came
In anxious hope, how oft returned with
   fame !
How oft around your circle this weak hand
Has waved immortal Shakespeare's magic
   wand,
Till the full burst of inspiration came,
And I have felt, and you have fanned the
   flame !
By mem'ry treasured, while her reign
   endures,
Those hours must live — and all their
   charms are yours.

O favored Land ! renowned for arts and
   arms,
For manly talent, and for female charms,
Could this full bosom prompt the sinking
   line,
What fervent benedictions now were thine !
But my last part is played, my knell is
   rung,
When e'en your praise falls faltering from
   my tongue;
And all that you can hear, or I can tell,
Is — Friends and Patrons, hail, and FARE
   YOU WELL.

THE SUN UPON THE WEIRDLAW
HILL

AIR — ' *Rimhin aluin 'stu mo run* '

' It was while struggling with such languor,
on one lovely evening of this autumn [1817],
that he composed the following beautiful
verses. They mark the very spot of their birth,
— namely, the then naked height overhanging
the northern side of the Cauldshields Loch,
from which Melrose Abbey to the eastward,
and the hills of Ettrick and Yarrow to the
west, are now visible over a wide range of rich
woodland, — all the work of the poet's hand.'
Lockhart's *Life*, Chapter xxxix.

THE sun upon the Weirdlaw Hill
   In Ettrick's vale is sinking sweet;
The westland wind is hush and still,
   The lake lies sleeping at my feet.
Yet not the landscape to mine eye
   Bears those bright hues that once it
     bore,
Though evening with her richest dye
   Flames o'er the hills of Ettrick's shore.

With listless look along the plain
   I see Tweed's silver current glide,
And coldly mark the holy fane
   Of Melrose rise in ruined pride.
The quiet lake, the balmy air,
   The hill, the stream, the tower, the
     tree —
Are they still such as once they were,
   Or is the dreary change in me ?

Alas ! the warped and broken board,
   How can it bear the painter's dye ?
The harp of strained and tuneless chord,
   How to the minstrel's skill reply ?

To aching eyes each landscape lowers,
  To feverish pulse each gale blows chill;
And Araby's or Eden's bowers
  Were barren as this moorland hill.

SONG FROM ROB ROY

Published in 1817.

TO THE MEMORY OF EDWARD THE BLACK PRINCE

O FOR the voice of that wild horn,
On Fontarabian echoes borne,
    The dying hero's call,
That told imperial Charlemagne,
How Paynim sons of swarthy Spain
    Had wrought his champion's fall.

Sad over earth and ocean sounding.
And England's distant cliffs astounding,
    Such are the notes should say
How Britain's hope, and France's fear,
Victor of Cressy and Poitier,
    In Bourdeaux dying lay.

' Raise my faint head, my squires,' he said,
' And let the casement be displayed,
    That I may see once more
The splendor of the setting sun
Gleam on thy mirror'd wave, Garonne,
    And Blaye's empurpled shore.'

' Like me, he sinks to Glory's sleep,
His fall the dews of evening steep,
    As if in sorrow shed.
So soft shall fall the trickling tear,
When England's maids and matrons hear
    Of their Black Edward dead.

' And though my sun of glory set,
Nor France nor England shall forget
    The terror of my name;
And oft shall Britain's heroes rise,
New planets in these southern skies,
    Through clouds of blood and flame.'

THE MONKS OF BANGOR'S MARCH

AIR — 'Ymdaith Mionge'

Written for Mr. George Thomson's Welsh
Melodies, in 1817, and provided by Scott with
this note, — ' Ethelfrid, or Olfrid, King of

Northumberland, having besieged Chester in
613, and Brockmael, a British Prince, advancing to relieve it, the religious of the neighboring Monastery of Bangor marched in procession,
to pray for the success of their countrymen.
But the British being totally defeated, the
heathen victor put the monks to the sword, and
destroyed their monastery. The tune to which
these verses are adapted is called the Monks'
March, and is supposed to have been played
at their ill-omened procession.'

WHEN the heathen trumpet's clang
Round beleaguered Chester rang,
Veiled nun and friar gray
Marched from Bangor's fair Abbaye;
High their holy anthem sounds,
Cestria's vale the hymn rebounds,
        Floating down the sylvan Dee,
            O miserere, Domine !

On the long procession goes,
Glory round their crosses glows,
And the Virgin-mother mild
In their peaceful banner smiled;
Who could think such saintly band
Doomed to feel unhallowed hand ?
        Such was the Divine decree,
            O miserere, Domine !

Bands that masses only sung,
Hands that censers only swung,
Met the northern bow and bill,
Heard the war-cry wild and shrill:
Woe to Brockmael's feeble hand,
Woe to Olfrid's bloody brand,
        Woe to Saxon cruelty,
            O miserere, Domine !

Weltering amid warriors slain,
Spurned by steeds with bloody mane,
Slaughtered down by heathen blade,
Bangor's peaceful monks are laid:
Word of parting rest unspoke,
Mass unsung and bread unbroke;
        For their souls for charity,
            Sing, O miserere, Domine !

Bangor ! o'er the murder wail !
Long thy ruins told the tale,
Shattered towers and broken arch
Long recalled the woful march:
On thy shrine no tapers burn,
Never shall thy priests return;
        The pilgrim sighs and sings for thee,
            O miserere, Domine !

EPILOGUE TO 'THE APPEAL'

The Appeal, a tragedy by John Galt, was played in Edinburgh and Mrs. Siddons spoke this epilogue February 16, 1818.

A CAT of yore — or else old Æsop lied —
Was changed into a fair and blooming
  bride,
But spied a mouse upon her marriage-day,
Forgot her spouse and seized upon her
  prey;
Even thus my bridegroom lawyer, as you
  saw,
Threw off poor me and pounced upon papa.
His neck from Hymen's mystic knot made
  loose,
He twisted round my sire's the literal
  noose.
Such are the fruits of our dramatic labor
Since the New Jail became our next-door
  neighbor.

Yes, times *are* changed; for in your
  father's age
The lawyers were the patrons of the stage;
However high advanced by future fate,
There stands the bench [*points to the Pit*]
  that first received their weight.
The future legal sage 't was ours to see
Doom though unwigged and plead without
  a fee.

But now, astounding each poor mimic
  elf,
Instead of lawyers comes the law herself;
Tremendous neighbor, on our right she
  dwells,
Builds high her towers and excavates her
  cells;
While on the left she agitates the town
With the tempestuous question, Up or
  down ?
'Twixt Scylla and Charybdis thus stand we,
Law's final end and law's uncertainty.
But, soft ! who lives at Rome the Pope
  must flatter,
And jails and lawsuits are no jesting matter.
Then — just farewell ! We wait with seri-
  ous awe
Till your applause or censure gives the
  law.
Trusting our humble efforts may assure ye,
We hold you Court and Counsel, Judge
  and Jury.

MACKRIMMON'S LAMENT

AIR — ' *Cha till mi tuille* '

This Lament was contributed by Scott to
Albyn's *Anthology* in 1818, with this preface:
' Mackrimmon, hereditary piper to the Laird of
Macleod, is said to have composed this Lament
when the Clan was about to depart upon a
distant and dangerous expedition. The Minstrel was impressed with a belief, which the
event verified, that he was to be slain in the
approaching feud ; and hence the Gaelic words,
" Cha till mi tuille ; ged thillis Macleod, cha
till Mackrimmon," " I shall never return ; although Macleod returns, yet Mackrimmon
shall never return ! " The piece is but too
well known, from its being the strain with
which the emigrants from the West Highlands
and Isles usually take leave of their native
shore.'

MACLEOD'S wizard flag from the gray
  castle sallies,
The rowers are seated, unmoored are the
  galleys;
Gleam war-axe and broadsword, clang target and quiver,
As Mackrimmon sings, ' Farewell to Dunvegan forever !
Farewell to each cliff on which breakers
  are foaming;
Farewell, each dark glen in which red-deer
  are roaming;
Farewell, lonely Skye, to lake, mountain,
  and river;
Macleod may return, but Mackrimmon
  shall never !

' Farewell the bright clouds that on Quil-
  lan are sleeping;
Farewell the bright eyes in the Dun that
  are weeping;
To each minstrel delusion, farewell ! — and
  forever —
Mackrimmon departs, to return to you
  never !
The *Banshee's* wild voice sings the death-
  dirge before me,
The pall of the dead for a mantle hangs
  o'er me;
But my heart shall not flag and my nerves
  shall not shiver,
Though devoted I go — to return again
  never !

'Too oft shall the notes of Mackrimmon's
   bewailing
Be heard when the Gael on their exile are
   sailing;
Dear land ! to the shores whence unwilling
   we sever
Return — return — return shall we never !
   Cha till, cha till, cha till sin tuille,
   Cha till, cha till, cha till sin tuille,
   Cha till, cha till, cha till sin tuille,
   Gea thillis Macleod, cha till Mackrimmon!'

DONALD CAIRD'S COME AGAIN

AIR— "*Malcolm Caird's come again.*"

This also was contributed to Albyn's *Anthology* in 1818.

CHORUS

Donald Caird's come again !
Donald Caird's come again !
Tell the news in brugh and glen,
Donald Caird's come again !

DONALD CAIRD can lilt and sing,
Blithely dance the Hieland fling.
Drink till the gudeman be blind,
Fleech till the gudewife be kind;
Hoop a leglin, clout a pan,
Or crack a pow wi' ony man;
Tell the news in brugh and glen,
Donald Caird's come again.
   Donald Caird's come again !
   Donald Caird's come again !
   Tell the news in brugh and glen,
   Donald Caird's come again.

Donald Caird can wire a maukin,
Kens the wiles o' dun-deer staukin',
Leisters kipper, makes a shift
To shoot a muir-fowl in the drift;
Water-bailiffs, rangers, keepers,
He can wauk when they are sleepers;
Not for bountith or reward
Dare ye mell wi' Donald Caird.
   Donald Caird's come again !
   Donald Caird's come again !
   Gar the bag-pipes hum amain,
   Donald Caird's come again.

Donald Caird can drink a gill
Fast as hostler-wife can fill;
Ilka ane that sells gude liquor
Kens how Donald bends a bicker;
When he's fou he's stout and saucy,

Keeps the cantle o' the cawsey;
Hieland chief and Lawland laird
Maun gie room to Donald Caird !
   Donald Caird's come again !
   Donald Caird's come again !
   Tell the news in brugh and glen,
   Donald Caird's come again.

Steek the amrie, lock the kist,
Else some gear may weel be mist;
Donald Caird finds orra things
Where Allan Gregor fand the tings;
Dunts of kebbuck, taits o' woo,
Whiles a hen and whiles a sow,
Webs or duds frae hedge or yard —
'Ware the wuddie, Donald Caird !
   Donald Caird's come again !
   Donald Caird's come again !
   Dinna let the Shirra ken
   Donald Caird's come again.

On Donald Caird the doom was stern,
Craig to tether, legs to airn;
But Donald Caird wi' mickle study
Caught the gift to cheat the wuddie;
Rings of airn, and bolts of steel,
Fell like ice frae hand and heel !
Watch the sheep in fauld and glen,
Donald Caird's come again !
   Donald Caird's come again !
   Donald Caird's come again !
   Dinna let the Justice ken
   Donald Caird's come again.

MADGE WILDFIRE'S SONGS

From *The Heart of Mid-Lothian*, published in 1818.

WHEN the gledd's in the blue cloud,
   The lavrock lies still;
When the hound's in the green-wood,
   The hind keeps the hill.

'O sleep ye sound, Sir James,' she said,
   'When ye suld rise and ride ?
There's twenty men, wi' bow and blade,
   Are seeking where ye hide.'

I glance like the wildfire thro' country and
   town;
I'm seen on the causeway — I'm seen on
   the down;

The lightning that flashes so bright and so
    free,
Is scarcely so blithe or so bonny as me.

What did ye wi' the bridal ring — bridal
    ring — bridal ring ?
What did ye wi' your wedding ring, ye
    little cutty quean, O ?
I gied it till a sodger, a sodger, a sodger,
I gied it till a sodger, an auld true love o'
    mine, O.

Good even, good fair moon, good even to
    thee;
I prithee, dear moon, now show to me
The form and the features, the speech and
    degree,
Of the man that true lover of mine shall
    be.

It is the bonny butcher lad,
    That wears the sleeves of blue;
He sells the flesh on Saturday,
    On Friday that he slew.

There's a bloodhound ranging Tinwald
    Wood,
    There's harness glancing sheen;
There's a maiden sits on Tinwald brae,
    And she sings loud between.

With my curtch on my foot, and my shoe
    on my hand,
I glance like the wildfire through brugh
    and through land.

In the bonnie cells of Bedlam,
    Ere I was ane and twenty,
I had hempen bracelets strong,
    And merry whips, ding-dong,
    And prayer and fasting plenty.

I'm Madge of the country, I'm Madge of
    the town,
And I'm Madge of the lad I am blithest
    to own, —

The Lady of Beever in diamonds may
    shine,
But has not a heart half so lightsome as
    mine.

I am Queen of the Wake, and I'm Lady
    of May,
And I lead the blithe ring round the May-
    pole to-day;
The wild-fire that flashes so fair and so
    free
Was never so bright, or so bonnie as me.

Our work is over — over now,
The goodman wipes his weary brow,
The last long wain wends slow away,
And we are free to sport and play.

The night comes on when sets the sun,
And labor ends when day is done.
When Autumn's gone, and Winter's come,
We hold our jovial harvest-home.

When the fight of grace is fought, —
When the marriage vest is wrought, —
When Faith has chased cold Doubt away —
And Hope but sickens at delay, —
When Charity, imprisoned here,
Longs for a more expanded sphere;
Doff thy robes of sin and clay;
Christian, rise, and come away.

Cauld is my bed, Lord Archibald,
    And sad my sleep of sorrow;
But thine sall be as sad and cauld,
    My fause true love ! to-morrow.

And weep ye not, my maidens free,
    Though death your mistress borrow;
For he for whom I die to-day,
    Shall die for me to-morrow.

Proud Maisie is in the wood,
    Walking so early;
Sweet Robin sits on the bush,
    Singing so rarely.

'Tell me, thou bonny bird,
    When shall I marry me ?' —

' When six braw gentlemen
    Kirkward shall carry ye.'

' Who makes the bridal bed,
    Birdie, say truly ? ' —
' The gray-headed sexton
    That delves the grave duly.

' The glow-worm o'er grave and stone
    Shall light thee steady.
The owl from the steeple sing,
    " Welcome, proud lady." '

THE BATTLE OF SEMPACH

These verses, which appeared in *Blackwood*
for February, 1818, are, says Scott, ' a literal
translation of an ancient Swiss ballad upon the
Battle of Sempach, fought 9th July, 1386, being
the victory by which the Swiss Cantons established their independence ; the author, Albert
Tchudi, denominated the Souter, from his profession of a shoemaker. He was a citizen of
Lucerne, esteemed highly among his countrymen, both for his powers as a *Meister-Singer*,
or minstrel, and his courage as a soldier ; so
that he might share the praise conferred by
Collins on Æschylus, that,—

" Not alone he nursed the poet's flame,
But reached from Virtue's hand the patriot steel." '

'T WAS when among our linden-trees
    The bees had housed in swarms —
And gray-haired peasants say that these
    Betoken foreign arms —

Then looked we down to Willisow,
    The land was all in flame;
We knew the Archduke Leopold
    With all his army came.

The Austrian nobles made their vow,
    So hot their heart and bold,   10
' On Switzer carles we 'll trample now,
    And slay both young and old.'

With clarion loud and banner proud,
    From Zurich on the lake,
In martial pomp and fair array
    Their onward march they make.

' Now list, ye lowland nobles all —
    Ye seek the mountain-strand,
Nor wot ye what shall be your lot
    In such a dangerous land.   20

' I rede ye, shrive ye of your sins
    Before ye farther go;
A skirmish in Helvetian hills
    May send your souls to woe.'

' But where now shall we find a priest
    Our shrift that he may hear ? ' —
' The Switzer priest has ta'en the field,
    He deals a penance drear.

' Right heavily upon your head
    He 'll lay his hand of steel,   30
And with his trusty partisan
    Your absolution deal.'

'T was on a Monday morning then,
    The corn was steeped in dew,
And merry maids had sickles ta'en,
    When the host to Sempach drew.

The stalwart men of fair Lucerne,
    Together have they joined;
The pith and core of manhood stern,
    Was none cast looks behind.   40

It was the Lord of Hare-castle,
    And to the Duke he said,
' Yon little band of brethren true
    Will meet us undismayed.' —

' O Hare-castle, thou heart of hare !'
    Fierce Oxenstern replied. —
' Shalt see then how the game will fare,'
    The taunted knight replied.

There was lacing then of helmets bright,
    And closing ranks amain;   50
The peaks they hewed from their boot-
        points
    Might well-nigh load a wain.

And thus they to each other said,
    ' Yon handful down to hew
Will be no boastful tale to tell,
    The peasants are so few.'

The gallant Swiss Confederates there,
    They prayed to God aloud,
And he displayed his rainbow fair
    Against a swarthy cloud.   60

Then heart and pulse throbbed more and more
    With courage firm and high,
And down the good Confederates bore
    On the Austrian chivalry.

The Austrian Lion 'gan to growl
  And toss his mane and tail,
And ball and shaft and crossbow bolt
  Went whistling forth like hail.

Lance, pike, and halbert mingled there,
  The game was nothing sweet;   70
The bows of many a stately tree
  Lay shivered at their feet.

The Austrian men-at-arms stood fast,
  So close their spears they laid;
It chafed the gallant Winkelreid,
  Who to his comrades said —

'I have a virtuous wife at home,
  A wife and infant son;
I leave them to my country's care, —
  This field shall soon be won.   80

'These nobles lay their spears right thick
  And keep full firm array,
Yet shall my charge their order break
  And make my brethren way.'

He rushed against the Austrian band,
  In desperate career,
And with his body, breast, and hand,
  Bore down each hostile spear.

Four lances splintered on his crest,
  Six shivered in his side;   90
Still on the serried files he pressed —
  He broke their ranks and died.

This patriot's self-devoted deed
  First tamed the Lion's mood,
And the four Forest Cantons freed
  From thraldom by his blood.

Right where his charge had made a lane
  His valiant comrades burst,
With sword and axe and partisan,
  And hack and stab and thrust.   100

The daunted Lion 'gan to whine
  And granted ground amain,
The Mountain Bull he bent his brows,
  And gored his sides again.

Then lost was banner, spear, and shield
  At Sempach in the flight,
The cloister vaults at Konig's-field
  Hold many an Austrian knight.

It was the Archduke Leopold,
  So lordly would he ride,   110
But he came against the Switzer churls,
  And they slew him in his pride.

The heifer said unto the bull,
  ' And shall I not complain ?
There came a foreign nobleman
  To milk me on the plain.

' One thrust of thine outrageous horn
  Has galled the knight so sore
That to the churchyard he is borne,
  To range our glens no more.'   120

An Austrian noble left the stour,
  And fast the flight 'gan take;
And he arrived in luckless hour
  At Sempach on the lake.

He and his squire a fisher called —
  His name was Hans von Rot —
' For love or meed or charity,
  Receive us in thy boat !'

Their anxious call the fisher heard,
  And, glad the meed to win,   130
His shallop to the shore he steered
  And took the flyers in.

And while against the tide and wind
  Hans stoutly rowed his way,
The noble to his follower signed
  He should the boatman slay.

The fisher's back was to them turned,
  The squire his dagger drew,
Hans saw his shadow in the lake,
  The boat he overthrew.   140

He whelmed the boat, and as they strove
  He stunned them with his oar,
' Now, drink ye deep, my gentle sirs,
  You 'll ne'er stab boatman more.

' Two gilded fishes in the lake
  This morning have I caught,
Their silver scales may much avail,
  Their carrion flesh is naught.'

It was a messenger of woe
  Has sought the Austrian land: 150
' Ah ! gracious lady, evil news !
  My lord lies on the strand.

'At Sempach, on the battle-field,
  His bloody corpse lies there.' —
'Ah, gracious God !' the lady cried,
  'What tidings of despair !'

Now would you know the minstrel wight
  Who sings of strife so stern,
Albert the Souter is he hight,
  A burgher of Lucerne.   160

A merry man was he, I wot,
  The night he made the lay,
Returning from the bloody spot
  Where God had judged the day.

THE NOBLE MORINGER

AN ANCIENT BALLAD

Lockhart, writing at the end of April, 1819, when Scott was recovering from an alarming illness, reports thus Scott's words to him : —
'"One day there was," he said, "when I certainly began to have great doubts whether the mischief was not getting at my mind — and I tell you how I tried to reassure myself on that score. I was quite unfit for anything like original composition ; but I thought if I could turn an old German ballad I had been reading into decent rhymes, I might dismiss my worst apprehensions — and you shall see what came of the experiment." He then desired his daughter Sophia to fetch the *MS.* of "The Noble Moringer," as it had been taken down from his dictation, partly by her, and partly by Mr. Laidlaw, during one long and painful day when he lay in bed.'

O, WILL you hear a knightly tale of old
  Bohemian day,
It was the noble Moringer in wedlock bed
  he lay;
He halsed and kissed his dearest dame
  that was as sweet as May,
And said, 'Now, lady of my heart, attend
  the words I say.

''T is I have vowed a pilgrimage unto a
  distant shrine,
And I must seek Saint Thomas-land and
  leave the land that 's mine;
Here shalt thou dwell the while in state,
  so thou wilt pledge thy fay
That thou for my return wilt wait seven
  twelvemonths and a day.'

Then out and spoke that lady bright, sore
  troubled in her cheer,
'Now tell me true, thou noble knight,
  what order takest thou here;   10
And who shall lead thy vassal band and
  hold thy lordly sway,
And be thy lady's guardian true when
  thou art far away ?'

Out spoke the noble Moringer, 'Of that
  have thou no care,
There 's many a valiant gentleman of me
  holds living fair;
The trustiest shall rule my land, my vassals, and my state,
And be a guardian tried and true to thee,
  my lovely mate.

'As Christian-man, I needs must keep the
  vow which I have plight,
When I am far in foreign land, remember
  thy true knight;
And cease, my dearest dame, to grieve, for
  vain were sorrow now,
But grant thy Moringer his leave, since
  God hath heard his vow.'   20

It was the noble Moringer from bed he
  made him boune,
And met him there his chamberlain with
  ewer and with gown:
He flung the mantle on his back, 't was
  furred with miniver,
He dipped his hand in water cold and
  bathed his forehead fair.

'Now hear,' he said, 'Sir Chamberlain,
  true vassal art thou mine,
And such the trust that I repose in that
  proved worth of thine,
For seven years shalt thou rule my towers
  and lead my vassal train,
And pledge thee for my lady's faith till I
  return again.'

The chamberlain was blunt and true, and
  sturdily said he,
'Abide, my lord, and rule your own, and
  take this rede from me;   30
That woman's faith 's a brittle trust —
  Seven twelvemonths didst thou
  say ?
I 'll pledge me for no lady's truth beyond
  the seventh fair day.'

The noble baron turned him round, his
heart was full of care,
His gallant esquire stood him nigh, he was
Marstetten's heir,
To whom he spoke right anxiously, ' Thou
trusty squire to me,
Wilt thou receive this weighty trust when
I am o'er the sea ?

' To watch and ward my castle strong, and
to protect my land,
And to the hunting or the host to lead my
vassal band;
And pledge thee for my lady's faith till
seven long years are gone,
And guard her as Our Lady dear was
guarded by Saint John.'   40

Marstetten's heir was kind and true, but
fiery, hot, and young,
And readily he answer made with too presumptuous tongue:
' My noble lord, cast care away and on
your journey wend,
And trust this charge to me until your pilgrimage have end.

' Rely upon my plighted faith, which shall
be truly tried,
To guard your lands, and ward your
towers, and with your vassals ride;
And for your lovely lady's faith, so virtuous and so dear,
I 'll gage my head it knows no change, be
absent thirty year.'

The noble Moringer took cheer when thus
he heard him speak,
And doubt forsook his troubled brow and
sorrow left his cheek;   50
A long adieu he bids to all — hoists top-
sails and away,
And wanders in Saint Thomas-land seven
twelvemonths and a day.

It was the noble Moringer within an
orchard slept,
When on the baron's slumbering sense a
boding vision crept;
And whispered in his ear a voice, ' 'T is
time, Sir Knight, to wake,
Thy lady and thy heritage another master
take.

' Thy tower another banner knows, thy
steeds another rein,
And stoop them to another's will thy gallant vassal train;
And she, the lady of thy love, so faithful
once and fair,
This night within thy fathers' hall she
weds Marstetten's heir.'   60

It is the noble Moringer starts up and
tears his beard,
' O, would that I had ne'er been born !
what tidings have I heard !
To lose my lordship and my lands the less
would be my care,
But, God ! that e'er a squire untrue should
wed my lady fair.

' O good Saint Thomas, hear,' he prayed,
' my patron saint art thou,
A traitor robs me of my land even while
I pay my vow !
My wife he brings to infamy that was so
pure of name,
And I am far in foreign land and must en-
dure the shame.'

It was the good Saint Thomas then who
heard his pilgrim's prayer,
And sent a sleep so deep and dead that it
o'erpowered his care;   70
He waked in fair Bohemian land outstretched beside a rill,
High on the right a castle stood, low on
the left a mill.

The Moringer he started up as one from
spell unbound,
And dizzy with surprise and joy gazed
wildly all around;
' I know my fathers' ancient towers, the
mill, the stream I know,
Now blessed be my patron saint who
cheered his pilgrim's woe !'

He leant upon his pilgrim staff and to the
mill he drew,
So altered was his goodly form that none
their master knew;
The baron to the miller said, ' Good friend,
for charity,
Tell a poor palmer in your land what tidings may there be ?'   80

The miller answered him again, ' He knew
of little news,
Save that the lady of the land did a new
bridegroom choose;
Her husband died in distant land, such is
the constant word,
His death sits heavy on our souls, he was
a worthy lord.

' Of him I held the little mill which wins
me living free,
God rest the baron in his grave, he still
was kind to me !
And when Saint Martin's tide comes round
and millers take their toll,
The priest that prays for Moringer shall
have both cope and stole.'

It was the noble Moringer to climb the hill
began,
And stood before the bolted gate a woe and
weary man;   90
' Now help me, every saint in heaven that
can compassion take,
To gain the entrance of my hall this woful
match to break.'

His very knock it sounded sad, his call was
sad and slow,
For heart and head, and voice and hand,
were heavy all with woe;
And to the warder thus he spoke: ' Friend,
to thy lady say,
A pilgrim from Saint Thomas-land craves
harbor for a day.

' I 've wandered many a weary step, my
strength is well-nigh done,
And if she turn me from her gate I 'll see
no morrow's sun;
I pray, for sweet Saint Thomas' sake, a
pilgrim's bed and dole,
And for the sake of Moringer's, her once-
loved husband's soul.'   100

It was the stalwart warder then he came
his dame before,
' A pilgrim, worn and travel-toiled, stands
at the castle-door;
And prays, for sweet Saint Thomas' sake,
for harbor and for dole,
And for the sake of Moringer, thy noble
husband's soul.'

The lady's gentle heart was moved: ' Do up
the gate,' she said,
' And bid the wanderer welcome be to banquet and to bed;
And since he names my husband's name,
so that he lists to stay,
These towers shall be his harborage a
twelvemonth and a day.'

It was the stalwart warder then undid the
portal broad,
It was the noble Moringer that o'er the
threshold strode;   110
' And have thou thanks, kind Heaven,' he
said, ' though from a man of sin,
That the true lord stands here once more
his castle-gate within.'

Then up the halls paced Moringer, his step
was sad and slow;
It sat full heavy on his heart none seemed
their lord to know;
He sat him on a lowly bench, oppressed
with woe and wrong,
Short space he sat, but ne'er to him seemed
little space so long.

Now spent was day and feasting o'er, and
come was evening hour,
The time was nigh when new-made brides
retire to nuptial bower;
' Our castle's wont,' a bridesman said, ' hath
been both firm and long
No guest to harbor in our halls till he shall
chant a song.'   120

Then spoke the youthful bridegroom there
as he sat by the bride,
' My merry minstrel folk,' quoth he, ' lay
shalm and harp aside;
Our pilgrim guest must sing a lay, the castle's rule to hold,
And well his guerdon will I pay with garment and with gold.'

' Chill flows the lay of frozen age,' 't was
thus the pilgrim sung,
' Nor golden meed nor garment gay unlocks
his heavy tongue;
Once did I sit, thou bridegroom gay, at
board as rich as thine,
And by my side as fair a bride with all her
charms was mine.

'But time traced furrows on my face and I
   grew silver-haired,
For locks of brown and cheeks of youth
   she left this brow and beard; 130
Once rich, but now a palmer poor, I tread
   life's latest stage,
And mingle with your bridal mirth the lay
   of frozen age.'

It was the noble lady there this woful lay
   that hears,
And for the aged pilgrim's grief her eye
   was dimmed with tears;
She bade her gallant cupbearer a golden
   beaker take,
And bear it to the palmer poor to quaff it
   for her sake.

It was the noble Moringer that dropped
   amid the wine
A bridal ring of burning gold so costly and
   so fine:
Now listen, gentles, to my song, it tells you
   but the sooth,
'T was with that very ring of gold he
   pledged his bridal truth. 140

Then to the cupbearer he said, 'Do me
   one kindly deed,
And should my better days return, full rich
   shall be thy meed;
Bear back the golden cup again to yonder
   bride so gay,
And crave her of her courtesy to pledge
   the palmer gray.'

The cupbearer was courtly bred nor was
   the boon denied,
The golden cup he took again and bore it
   to the bride;
'Lady,' he said, 'your reverend guest sends
   this, and bids me pray
That, in thy noble courtesy, thou pledge
   the palmer gray.'

The ring hath caught the lady's eye, she
   views it close and near,
Then might you hear her shriek aloud,
   'The Moringer is here!' 150
Then might you see her start from seat
   while tears in torrents fell,
But whether 't was for joy or woe the ladies
   best can tell.

But loud she uttered thanks to Heaven and
   every saintly power
That had returned the Moringer before the
   midnight hour;
And loud she uttered vow on vow that
   never was there bride
That had like her preserved her troth or
   been so sorely tried.

'Yes, here I claim the praise,' she said, 'to
   constant matrons due,
Who keep the troth that they have plight
   so steadfastly and true;
For count the term howe'er you will, so
   that you count aright,
Seven twelvemonths and a day are out
   when bells toll twelve to-night.' 160

It was Marstetten then rose up, his falchion
   there he drew,
He kneeled before the Moringer and down
   his weapon threw;
'My oath and knightly faith are broke,'
   these were the words he said,
'Then take, my liege, thy vassal's sword,
   and take thy vassal's head.'

The noble Moringer he smiled, and then
   aloud did say,
'He gathers wisdom that hath roamed
   seven twelvemonths and a day;
My daughter now hath fifteen years, fame
   speaks her sweet and fair,
I give her for the bride you lose and name
   her for my heir.

'The young bridegroom hath youthful
   bride, the old bridegroom the old,
Whose faith was kept till term and tide so
   punctually were told; 170
But blessings on the warder kind that oped
   my castle gate,
For had I come at morrow tide I came a
   day too late.'

EPITAPH ON MRS. ERSKINE

Mrs. Erskine was the wife of Scott's friend, William Erskine, afterward Lord Kinedder. She died in September, 1819, and the epitaph is on the stone over her grave at Saline, in the county of Fife.

PLAIN as her native dignity of mind,
Arise the tomb of her we have resigned;

Unflawed and stainless be the marble scroll,
Emblem of lovely form and candid soul. —
But, O, what symbol may avail to tell
The kindness, wit, and sense we loved so
    well !
What sculpture show the broken ties of life,
Here buried with the parent, friend, and
    wife !
Or on the tablet stamp each title dear
By which thine urn, EUPHEMIA, claims the
    tear !
Yet taught by thy meek sufferance to as-
    sume
Patience in anguish, hope beyond the tomb,
Resigned, though sad, this votive verse
    shall flow,
And brief, alas ! as thy brief span below.

SONGS FROM THE BRIDE OF LAMMERMOOR

I

'LOOK NOT THOU ON BEAUTY'S CHARM-ING'

From Chapter iii. 'The silver tones of Lucy
Ashton's voice mingled with the accompaniment in an ancient air, to which some one had
adapted the following words : '—

LOOK not thou on beauty's charming;
Sit thou still when kings are arming;
Taste not when the wine-cup glistens;
Speak not when the people listens;
Stop thine ear against the singer;
From the red gold keep thy finger;
Vacant heart and hand and eye,
Easy live and quiet die.

II

'THE MONK MUST ARISE WHEN THE MATINS RING'

From Chapter iii. 'And humming his rustic roundelay, the yeoman went on his road, the
sound of his rough voice gradually dying away
as the distance betwixt them increased.'

THE monk must arise when the matins ring,
The abbot may sleep to their chime;
But the yeoman must start when the bugles
    sing,
'T is time, my hearts, 't is time.

There 's bucks and raes on Billhope braes,
There 's a herd on Shortwood Shaw;
But a lily-white doe in the garden goes,
She 's fairly worth them a'.

III

'WHEN THE LAST LAIRD OF RAVENS-WOOD TO RAVENSWOOD SHALL RIDE'

From Chapter xviii. 'With a quivering voice,
and a cheek pale with apprehension, Caleb
faltered out the following lines : '—

WHEN the last Laird of Ravenswood to
    Ravenswood shall ride,
And woo a dead maiden to be his bride,
He shall stable his steed in the Kelpie's
    flow,
And his name shall be lost for evermoe !

SONGS FROM THE LEGEND OF MONTROSE

I

ANCIENT GAELIC MELODY

BIRDS of omen dark and foul,
Night-crow, raven, bat, and owl,
Leave the sick man to his dream —
All night long he heard you scream.
Haste to cave and ruined tower,
Ivy tod or dingled bower,
There to wink and mop, for, hark !
In the mid air sings the lark.

Hie to moorish gills and rocks,
Prowling wolf and wily fox, —
Hie ye fast, nor turn your view,
Though the lamb bleats to the ewe.
Couch your trains and speed your flight,
Safety parts with parting night;
And on distant echo borne,
Comes the hunter's early horn.

The moon's wan crescent scarcely gleams,
Ghost-like she fades in morning beams;
Hie hence, each peevish imp and fay
That scare the pilgrim on his way. —
Quench, kelpy ! quench, in bog and fen,
Thy torch that cheats benighted men;
Thy dance is o'er, thy reign is done,
For Benyieglo hath seen the sun.

Wild thoughts, that, sinful, dark, and
  deep,
O'erpower the passive mind in sleep,
Pass from the slumberer's soul away,
Like night-mists from the brow of day.
Foul hag, whose blasted visage grim
Smothers the pulse, unnerves the limb,
Spur thy dark palfrey and begone !
Thou darest not face the godlike sun.

II

THE ORPHAN MAID

NOVEMBER's hail-cloud drifts away,
  November's sun-beam wan
Looks coldly on the castle gray,
  When forth comes Lady Anne.

The orphan by the oak was set,
  Her arms, her feet, were bare;
The hail-drops had not melted yet
  Amid her raven hair.

'And, dame,' she said, 'by all the ties
  That child and mother know,
Aid one who never knew these joys, —
  Relieve an orphan's woe.'

The lady said, 'An orphan's state
  Is hard and sad to bear;
Yet worse the widowed mother's fate,
  Who mourns both lord and heir.

'Twelve times the rolling year has sped
  Since, while from vengeance wild
Of fierce Strathallan's chief I fled,
  Forth's eddies whelmed my child.'

'Twelve times the year its course has
  borne,'
  The wandering maid replied;
'Since fishers on Saint Bridget's morn
  Drew nets on Campsie side.

'Saint Bridget sent no scaly spoil;
  An infant, well-nigh dead,
They saved and reared in want and toil,
  To beg from you her bread.'

That orphan maid the lady kissed,
  'My husband's looks you bear;
Saint Bridget and her morn be blessed !
  You are his widow's heir.'

They 've robed that n⸻
  pale,
In silk and sandals r⸻
And pearls, for drops o⸻
Are glistening in her hair.

VERSES FROM IVANHOE

Published in 1819.

I

THE CRUSADER'S RETURN

From Chapter xvii.

HIGH deeds achieved of knightly fame,
From Palestine the champion came;
The cross upon his shoulders borne,
Battle and blast had dimmed and torn.
Each dint upon his battered shield
Was token of a foughten field;
And thus, beneath his lady's bower,
He sung, as fell the twilight hour:

'Joy to the fair ! — thy knight behold,
Returned from yonder land of gold;
No wealth he brings, nor wealth can
  need,
Save his good arms and battle-steed;
His spurs to dash against a foe,
His lance and sword to lay him low;
Such all the trophies of his toil
Such — and the hope of Tekla's smile !

'Joy to the fair ! whose constant knight
Her favor fired to feats of might !
Unnoted shall she not remain
Where meet the bright and noble train;
Minstrel shall sing, and herald tell —
" Mark yonder maid of beauty well,
'T is she for whose bright eyes was won
The listed field at Ascalon !

'" Note well her smile ! — it edged the
  blade
Which fifty wives to widows made,
When, vain his strength and Mahound's
  spell,
Iconium's turban'd Soldan fell.
See'st thou her locks, whose sunny glow
Half shows, half shades, her neck of snow ?
Twines not of them one golden thread,
But for its sake a Paynim bled."

y to the fair ! — my name unknown,
ach deed, and all its praise, thine own;
Then, oh ! unbar this churlish gate,
The night-dew falls, the hour is late.
Inured to Syria's glowing breath,
I feel the north breeze chill as death;
Let grateful love quell maiden shame,
And grant him bliss who brings thee fame.'

II

THE BAREFOOTED FRIAR

From Chapter xvii.

I 'LL give thee, good fellow, a twelvemonth
  or twain
To search Europe through from Byzantium
  to Spain;
But ne'er shall you find, should you search
  till you tire,
So happy a man as the Barefooted Friar.

Your knight for his lady pricks forth in
  career,
And is brought home at even-song pricked
  through with a spear;
I confess him in haste — for his lady de-
  sires
No comfort on earth save the Barefooted
  Friar's.

Your monarch ! — Pshaw ! many a prince
  has been known
To barter his robes for our cowl and our
  gown,
But which of us e'er felt the idle desire
To exchange for a crown the gray hood of
  a friar ?

The Friar has walked out, and where'er he
  has gone
The land and its fatness is marked for his
  own;
He can roam where he lists, he can stop
  where he tires,
For every man's house is the Barefooted
  Friar's.

He 's expected at noon, and no wight till
  he comes
May profane the great chair or the porridge
  of plums:

For the best of the cheer, and the seat by
  the fire,
Is the undenied right of the Barefooted
  Friar.

He 's expected at night, and the pasty's
  made hot,
They broach the brown ale and they fill the
  black pot;
And the good-wife would wish the good-
  man in the mire,
Ere he lacked a soft pillow, the Barefooted
  Friar.

Long flourish the sandal, the cord, and the
  cope,
The dread of the devil and trust of the
  Pope !
For to gather life's roses, unscathed by the
  briar,
Is granted alone to the Barefooted Friar.

III

' NORMAN SAW ON ENGLISH OAK '

From Chapter xxvii.

NORMAN saw on English oak,
On English neck a Norman yoke;
Norman spoon in English dish,
And England ruled as Normans wish;
Blithe world in England never will be more,
Till England 's rid of all the four.

IV

WAR-SONG

From Chapter xxxi. ' The fire was spreading
rapidly through all parts of the castle, when
Ulrica, who had first kindled it, appeared on a
turret, in the guise of one of the ancient furies,
yelling forth a war-song, such as was of yore
chanted on the field of battle by the scalds of
the yet heathen Saxons. Her long dishevelled
gray hair flew back from her uncovered head,
the inebriating delight of gratified vengeance
contended in her eyes with the fire of insanity,
and she brandished the distaff which she held
in her hand, as if she had been one of the Fatal
Sisters, who spin and abridge the thread of human life. Tradition has preserved some wild
strophes of the barbarous hymn which she

chanted wildly amid that scene of fire and slaughter.'

I

WHET the bright steel,
Sons of the White Dragon !
Kindle the torch,
Daughter of Hengist !
The steel glimmers not for the carving of the banquet,
It is hard, broad, and sharply pointed;
The torch goeth not to the bridal chamber,
It steams and glitters blue with sulphur.
Whet the steel, the raven croaks !
Light the torch, Zernebock is yelling !
Whet the steel, sons of the Dragon !
Kindle the torch, daughter of Hengist !

2

The black clouds are low over the thane's castle;
The eagle screams — he rides on their bosom.
Scream not, gray rider of the sable cloud,
Thy banquet is prepared !
The maidens of Valhalla look forth,
The race of Hengist will send them guests.
Shake your black tresses, maidens of Valhalla !
And strike your loud timbrels for joy !
Many a haughty step bends to your halls,
Many a helmed head.

3

Dark sits the evening upon the thane's castle,
The black clouds gather round;
Soon shall they be red as the blood of the valiant !
The destroyer of forests shall shake his red crest against them;
He, the bright consumer of palaces,
Broad waves he his blazing banner,
Red, white, and dusky,
Over the strife of the valiant;
His joy is in the clashing swords and broken bucklers;
He loves to lick the hissing blood as it bursts warm from the wound !

4

All must perish !
The sword cleaveth the helmet;
The strong armor is pierced by the lance:
Fire devoureth the dwelling of princes,
Engines break down the fences of the battle.
All must perish !
The race of Hengist is gone —
The name of Horsa is no more !
Shrink not then from your doom, sons of the sword !
Let your blades drink blood like wine;
Feast ye in the banquet of slaughter,
By the light of the blazing halls !
Strong be your swords while your blood is warm,
And spare neither for pity nor fear,
For vengeance hath but an hour;
Strong hate itself shall expire !
I also must perish.

V

REBECCA'S HYMN

From Chapter xxxix.

WHEN Israel of the Lord beloved
  Out from the land of bondage came,
Her fathers' God before her moved,
  An awful guide in smoke and flame.
By day, along the astonished lands
  The cloudy pillar glided slow;
By night, Arabia's crimsoned sands
  Returned the fiery column's glow.

There rose the choral hymn of praise,
  And trump and timbrel answered keen,
And Zion's daughters poured their lays,
  With priest's and warrior's voice between.
No portents now our foes amaze,
  Forsaken Israel wanders lone:
Our fathers would not know Thy ways,
  And Thou hast left them to their own.

But present still, though now unseen,
  When brightly shines the prosperous day,
Be thoughts of Thee a cloudy screen
  To temper the deceitful ray !
And O, when stoops on Judah's path
  In shade and storm the frequent night,
Be Thou, long-suffering, slow to wrath,
  A burning and a shining light !

Our harps we left by Babel's streams,
  The tyrant's jest, the Gentile's scorn;

No censer round our altar beams,
And mute are timbrel, harp, and horn.
But Thou hast said, The blood of goat,
The flesh of rams I will not prize;
A contrite heart, a humble thought,
Are mine accepted sacrifice.

VI

THE BLACK KNIGHT AND WAMBA

From Chapter xi. ' At the point of their journey at which we take them up, this joyous pair were engaged in singing a virelai, as it was called, in which the clown bore a mellow burthen to the better instructed Knight of the Fetterlock. And thus ran the ditty : ' —

ANNA-MARIE, love, up is the sun,
Anna-Marie, love, morn is begun,
Mists are dispersing, love, birds singing free,
Up in the morning, love, Anna-Marie.

Anna-Marie, love, up in the morn,
The hunter is winding blithe sounds on his horn,
The echo rings merry from rock and from tree,
'T is time to arouse thee, love, Anna-Marie.

WAMBA

O Tybalt, love, Tybalt, awake me not yet,
Around my soft pillow while softer dreams flit;
For what are the joys that in waking we prove,
Compared with these visions, O Tybalt, my love ?
Let the birds to the rise of the mist carol shrill,
Let the hunter blow out his loud horn on the hill,
Softer sounds, softer pleasures, in slumber I prove,
But think not I dreamed of thee, Tybalt, my love.

VII

ANOTHER CAROL BY THE SAME

' The Jester next struck into another carol, a sort of comic ditty, to which the Knight, catching up the tune, replied in the like manner.'

KNIGHT AND WAMBA

THERE came three merry men from south, west, and north,
Evermore sing the roundelay;
To win the Widow of Wycombe forth,
And where was the widow might say them nay ?

The first was a knight, and from Tynedale he came,
Evermore sing the roundelay;
And his fathers, God save us, were men of great fame,
And where was the widow might say him nay ?

Of his father the laird, of his uncle the squire,
He boasted in rhyme and in roundelay;
She bade him go bask by his sea-coal fire,
For she was the widow would say him nay.

WAMBA

The next that came forth, swore by blood and by nails,
Merrily sing the roundelay;
Hur 's a gentleman, God wot, and hur's lineage was of Wales,
And where was the widow might say him nay ?

Sir David ap Morgan ap Griffith ap Hugh
Ap Tudor Ap Rhice, quoth his roundelay;
She said that one widow for so many was too few,
And she bade the Welshman wend his way.

But then next came a yeoman, a yeoman of Kent,
Jollily singing his roundelay;
He spoke to the widow of living and rent,
And where was the widow could say him nay ?

BOTH

So the knight and the squire were both left in the mire,
There for to sing the roundelay;
For a yeoman of Kent, with his yearly rent,
There ne'er was a widow could say him nay.

VIII

FUNERAL HYMN

From Chapter xlii.

DUST unto dust,
To this all must;
    The tenant hath resigned
The faded form
To waste and worm —
    Corruption claims her kind.

Through paths unknown
Thy soul hath flown
    To seek the realms of woe,
Where fiery pain
Shall purge the stain
    Of actions done below.

In that sad place,
By Mary's grace,
    Brief may thy dwelling be !
Till prayers and alms,
And holy psalms,
    Shall set the captive free.

VERSES FROM THE MONASTERY

Published in 1820.

I

ANSWER TO INTRODUCTORY EPISTLE

TAKE thou no scorn,
Of fiction born,
    Fair fiction's muse to woo;
Old Homer's theme
Was but a dream,
    Himself a fiction too.

II

BORDER SONG

From Chapter xxv.

I

MARCH, march, Ettrick and Teviotdale,
    Why the deil dinna ye march forward in
        order ?
March, march, Eskdale and Liddesdale,

All the Blue Bonnets are bound for the
    Border.
        Many a banner spread,
        Flutters above your head,
Many a crest that is famous in story.
        Mount and make ready then,
        Sons of the mountain glen,
Fight for the Queen and our old Scottish
    glory.

2

Come from the hills where your hirsels are
    grazing,
    Come from the glen of the buck and the
        roe;
Come to the crag where the beacon is blaz-
    ing,
    Come with the buckler, the lance, and
        the bow.
        Trumpets are sounding,
        War-steeds are bounding,
Stand to your arms and march in good
    order;
        England shall many a day
        Tell of the bloody fray,
When the Blue Bonnets came over the
    Border.

III

SONGS OF THE WHITE LADY OF AVENEL

From Chapter v.

FORDING THE RIVER

I

MERRILY swim we, the moon shines
    bright,
Both current and ripple are dancing in
    light.
We have roused the night raven, I heard
    him croak,
As we plashed along beneath the oak
That flings its broad branches so far and so
    wide,
Their shadows are dancing in midst of the
    tide.
' Who wakens my nestlings ! ' the raven
    he said,
' My beak shall ere morn in his blood be
    red !

For a blue swollen corpse is a dainty meal,
And I 'll have my share with the pike and
the eel.'

2

Merrily swim we, the moon shines bright,
There 's a golden gleam on the distant height:
There 's a silver shower on the alders dank,
And the drooping willows that wave on the
bank.
I see the Abbey, both turret and tower,
It is all astir for the vesper hour;
The Monks for the chapel are leaving each
cell,
But where 's Father Philip should toll the
bell ?

3

Merrily swim we, the moon shines bright,
Downward we drift through shadow and
light.
Under yon rock the eddies sleep,
Calm and silent, dark and deep.
The Kelpy has risen from the fathomless
pool,
He has lighted his candle of death and of
dool:
Look, Father, look, and you 'll laugh to see
How he gapes and glares with his eyes on
thee !

4

Good luck to your fishing, whom watch ye
to-night ?
A man of mean or a man of might ?
Is it layman or priest that must float in
your cove,
Or lover who crosses to visit his love ?
Hark ! heard ye the Kelpy reply as we
passed,
' God's blessing on the warder, he locked
the bridge fast !
All that come to my cove are sunk,
Priest or layman, lover or monk.'

Landed — landed ! the black book hath
won,
Else had you seen Berwick with morning
sun !
Sain ye, and save ye, and blithe mot ye be,
For seldom they land that go swimming
with me.

IV

TO THE SUB-PRIOR

From Chapter ix.

GOOD evening, Sir Priest, and so late as
you ride,
With your mule so fair, and your mantle
so wide;
But ride you through valley, or ride you
o'er hill,
There is one that has warrant to wait on
you still.
Back, back,
The volume black !
I have a warrant to carry it back.

What, ho ! Sub-Prior, and came you but
here
To conjure a book from a dead woman's
bier ?
Sain you, and save you, be wary and
wise,
Ride back with the book, or you 'll pay for
your prize.
Back, back,
There 's death in the track !
In the name of my master, I bid thee bear
back.

' In the name of *my* Master,' said the astonished Monk, ' that name before which all things
created tremble, I conjure thee to say what
thou art that hauntest me thus ? '
The same voice replied, —

That which is neither ill nor well,
That which belongs not to heaven nor to
hell,
A wreath of the mist, a bubble of the
stream,
'Twixt a waking thought and a sleeping
dream;
A form that men spy
With the half-shut eye
In the beams of the setting sun, am I.

Vainly, Sir Prior, wouldst thou bar me my
right !
Like the star when it shoots, I can dart
through the night;
I can dance on the torrent, and ride on the
air,

And travel the world with the bonny night-
mare.
    Again, again,
    At the crook of the glen,
Where bickers the burnie, I 'll meet thee
again.

Men of good are bold as sackless,
Men of rude are wild and reckless.
    Lie thou still
    In the nook of the hill,
For those be before thee that wish thee ill.

V

HALBERT'S INCANTATION

From Chapter xi.

THRICE to the holly brake —
    Thrice to the well: —
I bid thee awake,
    White Maid of Avenel!

Noon gleams on the Lake —
    Noon glows on the Fell —
Wake thee, O wake,
    White Maid of Avenel.

VI

TO HALBERT

From Chapter xii.

THE WHITE MAID OF AVENEL

YOUTH of the dark eye, wherefore didst
    thou call me ?
Wherefore art thou here, if terrors can
    appall thee ?
He that seeks to deal with us must know
    nor fear, nor failing;
To coward and churl our speech is dark,
    our gifts are unavailing.
The breeze that brought me hither now
    must sweep Egyptian ground,
The fleecy cloud on which I ride for Araby
    is bound;
The fleecy cloud is drifting by, the breeze
    sighs for my stay,
For I must sail a thousand miles before
    the close of day.

What I am I must not show, —
What I am thou couldst not know —
Something betwixt heaven and hell —
Something that neither stood nor fell —
Something that through thy wit or will
May work thee good — may work thee
    ill.
Neither substance quite, nor shadow,
Haunting lonely moor and meadow,
Dancing by the haunted spring,
Riding on the whirlwind's wing;
Aping in fantastic fashion
Every change of human passion,
While o'er our frozen minds they pass,
Like shadows from the mirrored glass.
Wayward, fickle, is our mood,
Hovering betwixt bad and good,
Happier than brief-dated man,
Living twenty times his span;
Far less happy, for we have
Help nor hope beyond the grave !
Man awakes to joy or sorrow;
Ours the sleep that knows no morrow.
This is all that I can show —
This is all that thou may'st know.

Ay ! and I taught thee the word and the
    spell
To waken me here by the Fairies' Well.
But thou hast loved the heron and hawk,
More than to seek my haunted walk;
And thou hast loved the lance and the sword,
More than good text and holy word;
And thou hast loved the deer to track,
More than the lines and the letters black;
And thou art a ranger of moss and wood,
And scornest the nurture of gentle blood.

Thy craven fear my truth accused,
Thine idlehood my trust abused;
He that draws to harbor late,
Must sleep without, or burst the gate.
There is a star for thee which burned,
Its influence wanes, its course is turned;
Valor and constancy alone
Can bring thee back the chance that 's
    flown.

Within that awful volume lies
The mystery of mysteries !

Happiest they of human race,
To whom God has granted grace
To read, to fear, to hope, to pray,
To lift the latch, and force the way;
And better had they ne'er been born,
Who read to doubt, or read to scorn.

Many a fathom dark and deep
I have laid the book to sleep;
Ethereal fires around it glowing —
Ethereal music ever flowing —
The sacred pledge of Heaven
All things revere,
Each in his sphere,
      Save man for whom 't was given:
Lend thy hand, and thou shalt spy
Things ne'er seen by mortal eye.

Fearest thou to go with me?
Still it is free to thee
      A peasant to dwell;
Thou may'st drive the dull steer,
And chase the king's deer,
But never more come near
      This haunted well.

Here lies the volume thou hast boldly
      sought;
Touch it, and take it, 't will dearly be
      bought.

Rash thy deed,
Mortal weed
To immortal flames applying;
Rasher trust
Has thing of dust,
On his own weak worth relying:
Strip thee of such fences vain,
Strip, and prove thy luck again.

Mortal warp and mortal woof
Cannot brook this charmed roof;
All that mortal art hath wrought
In our cell returns to nought.
The molten gold returns to clay,
The polished diamond melts away;
All is altered, all is flown,
Nought stands fast but truth alone.

Not for that thy quest give o'er:
Courage! prove thy chance once more.

Alas! alas!
Not ours the grace
These holy characters to trace:
      Idle forms of painted air,
      Not to us is given to share
The boon bestowed on Adam's race.
      With patience bide,
      Heaven will provide
The fitting time, the fitting guide.

VII

TO THE SAME

From Chapter xvii. ' She spoke, and her
speech was still song, or rather measured
chant; but, as if now more familiar, it flowed
occasionally in modulated blank verse, and, at
other times, in the lyrical measure which she
had used at their former meeting.'

THIS is the day when the fairy kind
Sit weeping alone for their hopeless lot,
And the wood-maiden sighs to the sighing
      wind,
And the mermaiden weeps in her crystal
      grot;
For this is a day that the deed was
      wrought,
In which we have neither part nor share,
For the children of clay was salvation
      bought,
But not for the forms of sea or air!
And ever the mortal is most forlorn,
Who meeteth our race on the Friday morn.

Daring youth! for thee it is well,
Here calling me in haunted dell,
That thy heart has not quailed,
Nor thy courage failed,
And that thou couldst brook
The angry look
Of Her of Avenel.
Did one limb shiver,
Or an eyelid quiver,
Thou wert lost for ever.
Though I am formed from the ether
      blue,
And my blood is of the unfallen dew,

And thou art framed of mud and dust,
'T is thine to speak, reply I must.

A mightier wizard far than I
Wields o'er the universe his power;
Him owns the eagle in the sky,
The turtle in the bower.
Changeful in shape, yet mightiest still,
He wields the heart of man at will,
From ill to good, from good to ill,
In cot and castle-tower.

Ask thy heart, whose secret cell
Is filled with Mary Avenel !
Ask thy pride, why scornful look
In Mary's view it will not brook ?
Ask it, why thou seek'st to rise
Among the mighty and the wise, —
Why thou spurn'st thy lowly lot, —
Why thy pastimes are forgot, —
Why thou wouldst in bloody strife
Mend thy luck or lose thy life ?
Ask thy heart, and it shall tell,
Sighing from its secret cell,
'T is for Mary Avenel.
Do not ask me;
On doubts like these thou canst not task me.
We only see the passing show
Of human passions' ebb and flow;
And view the pageant's idle glance
As mortals eye the northern dance,
When thousand streamers, flashing bright,
Career it o'er the brow of night,
And gazers mark their changeful gleams,
But feel no influence from their beams.

By ties mysterious linked, our fated race
Holds strange connection with the sons of
men.
The star that rose upon the House of
Avenel,
When Norman Ulric first assumed the
name,
That star, when culminating in its orbit,
Shot from its spear a drop of diamond
dew,
And this bright font received it — and a
Spirit
Rose from the fountain, and her date of
life
Hath coexistence with the House of Ave-
nel,
And with the star that rules it.

Look on my girdle — on this thread of
gold —
'T is fine as web of lightest gossamer,
And, but there is a spell on 't, would not
bind,
Light as they are, the folds of my thin
robe.
But when 't was donned, it was a massive
chain,
Such as might bind the champion of the
Jews,
Even when his locks were longest — it
hath dwindled,
Hath 'minished in its substance and its
strength,
As sunk the greatness of the House of
Avenel.
When this frail thread gives way, I to the
elements
Resign the principles of life they lent
me.
Ask me no more of this ! — the stars for-
bid it.

Dim burns the once bright star of Ave-
nel,
Dim as the beacon when the morn is nigh,
And the o'er-wearied warder leaves the
lighthouse;
There is an influence sorrowful and fear-
ful,
That dogs its downward course. Disas-
trous passion,
Fierce hate and rivalry, are in the aspect
That lowers upon its fortunes.

Complain not on me, child of clay,
If to thy harm I yield the way.
We, who soar thy sphere above,
Know not aught of hate or love;
As will or wisdom rules thy mood,
My gifts to evil turn or good.
When Piercie Shafton boasteth high,

Let this token meet his eye.
The sun is westering from the dell,
Thy wish is granted — fare thee well !

VIII

TO THE SAME

From Chapter xx.

HE, whose heart for vengeance sued,
Must not shrink from shedding blood;
The knot that thou hast tied with word,
Thou must loose by edge of sword.

You have summoned me once, you have
    summoned me twice,
And without e'er a summons I come to you
    thrice;
Unasked for, unsued for, you came to my
    glen,
Unsued and unasked, I am with you again.

IX

TO MARY AVENEL

From Chapter xxx.

MAIDEN, whose sorrows wail the Living
    Dead,
    Whose eyes shall commune with the
    Dead Alive,
Maiden, attend ! Beneath my foot lies
    hid
    The Word, the Law, the Path which
    thou dost strive
To find, and canst not find.   Could Spirits
    shed
    Tears for their lot, it were my lot to
    weep,
Showing the road which I shall never
    tread,
    Though my foot points it.   Sleep, eter-
    nal sleep,
Dark, long, and cold forgetfulness my lot !
    But do not thou at human ills repine;
Secure there lies full guerdon in this spot
    For all the woes that wait frail Adam's
    line —
Stoop then and make it yours, — I may
    not make it mine !

X

TO EDWARD GLENDINNING

From Chapter xxxii.

THOU who seek'st my fountain lone,
With thoughts and hopes thou dar'st not
    own;
Whose heart within leaped wildly glad,
When most his brow seemed dark and sad;
Hie thee back, thou find'st not here
Corpse or coffin, grave or bier;
The Dead Alive is gone and fled:
Go thou and join the Living Dead !

The Living Dead, whose sober brow
Oft shrouds such thoughts as thou hast
    now,
Whose hearts within are seldom cured
Of passions by their vows abjured;
Where, under sad and solemn show,
Vain hopes are nursed, wild wishes glow.
Seek the convent's vaulted room,
Prayer and vigil be thy doom:
Doff the green, and don the grey,
To the cloister hence away !

XI

THE WHITE LADY'S FAREWELL

From Chapter xxxvii.

FARE thee well, thou Holly green !
Thou shalt seldom now be seen,
With all thy glittering garlands bending,
As to greet my slow descending,
Startling the bewildered hind,
Who sees thee wave without a wind.

Farewell, Fountain ! now not long
Shalt thou murmur to my song.
While thy crystal bubbles glancing,
Keep the time in mystic dancing,
Rise and swell, are burst and lost,
Like mortal schemes by fortune crossed.

The knot of fate at length is tied,
The Churl is Lord, the Maid is Bride !
Vainly did my magic sleight
Send the lover from her sight;
Wither bush, and perish well,
Fallen is lofty Avenel !

GOLDTHRED'S SONG

FROM KENILWORTH

Published in 1821.

From Chapter ii. 'After some brief interval, Master Goldthred, at the earnest instigation of mine host, and the joyous concurrence of his guests, indulged the company with the following morsel of melody :' —

OF all the birds on bush or tree,
  Commend me to the owl,
Since he may best ensample be
  To those the cup that trowl.
For when the sun hath left the west,
He chooses the tree that he loves the
  best,
And he whoops out his song, and he laughs
  at his jest;
Then though hours be late, and weather
  foul,
We'll drink to the health of the bonny,
  bonny owl.

The lark is but a bumpkin fowl,
  He sleeps in his nest till morn;
But my blessing upon the jolly owl,
  That all night blows his horn.
Then up with your cup till you stagger in
  speech,
And match me this catch though you swag-
  ger and screech,
And drink till you wink, my merry men
  each;
For though hours be late, and weather be
  foul,
We'll drink to the health of the bonny,
  bonny owl.

VERSES FROM THE PIRATE

Published in 1821.

I

THE SONG OF THE TEMPEST

From Chapter vi. 'A Norwegian invocation, still preserved in the island of Uist, under the name of the Song of the Reim-kennar, though some call it the Song of the Tempest. The following is a free translation, it being impossible to render literally many of the elliptical and metaphorical terms of expression peculiar to the ancient Northern poetry :' —

I

STERN eagle of the far northwest,
Thou that bearest in thy grasp the thunder-
  bolt,
Thou whose rushing pinions stir ocean to
  madness,
Thou the destroyer of herds, thou the scat-
  terer of navies,
Thou the breaker down of towers,
Amidst the scream of thy rage,
Amidst the rushing of thy onward wings,
Though thy scream be loud as the cry of
  a perishing nation,
Though the rushing of thy wings be like
  the roar of ten thousand waves,
Yet hear, in thine ire and thy haste,
Hear thou the voice of the Reim-kennar.

2

Thou hast met the pine-trees of Drontheim,
Their dark-green heads lie prostrate beside
  their uprooted stems;
Thou hast met the rider of the ocean,
The tall, the strong bark of the fearless
  rover,
And she has struck to thee the topsail
That she had not veiled to a royal ar-
  mada;
Thou hast met the tower that bears its crest
  among the clouds,
The battled massive tower of the Jarl of
  former days,
And the cope-stone of the turret
Is lying upon its hospitable hearth;
But thou too shalt stoop, proud compeller
  of clouds,
When thou hearest the voice of the Reim-
  kennar.

3

There are verses that can stop the stag in
  the forest,
Ay, and when the dark-colored dog is opening on his track;
There are verses can make the wild hawk
  pause on his wing,
Like the falcon that wears the hood and the
  jesses,
And who knows the shrill whistle of the
  fowler.
Thou who canst mock at the scream of the
  drowning mariner,

And the crash of the ravaged forest,
And the groan of the overwhelmed crowds,
When the church hath fallen in the mo-
    ment of prayer;
There are sounds which thou also must list,
When they are chanted by the voice of the
    Reim-kennar.

4

Enough of woe hast thou wrought on the
    ocean,
The widows wring their hands on the beach;
Enough of woe hast thou wrought on the
    land,
The husbandman folds his arms in despair;
Cease thou the waving of thy pinions,
Let the ocean repose in her dark strength;
Cease thou the flashing of thine eye,
Let the thunderbolt sleep in the armory of
    Odin;
Be thou still at my bidding, viewless racer
    of the northwestern heaven, —
Sleep thou at the voice of Norna the Reim-
    kennar.

5

Eagle of the far northwestern waters,
Thou hast heard the voice of the Reim-
    kennar,
Thou hast closed thy wide sails at her bid-
    ding,
And folded them in peace by thy side.
My blessing be on thy retiring path;
When thou stoopest from thy place on high,
Soft be thy slumbers in the caverns of the
    unknown ocean,
Rest till destiny shall again awaken thee;
Eagle of the northwest, thou hast heard
    the voice of the Reim-kennar.

II

HALCRO'S SONG

From Chapter xii.

FAREWELL to Northmaven,
    Grey Hillswicke, farewell !
To the calms of thy haven,
    The storms on thy fell —
To each breeze that can vary
    The mood of thy main,
And to thee, bonny Mary !
    We meet not again !

Farewell the wild ferry,
    Which Hacon could brave
When the peaks of the Skerry
    Were white in the wave.
There 's a maid may look over
    These wild waves in vain
For the skiff of her lover —
    He comes not again !

The vows thou hast broke,
    On the wild currents fling them;
On the quicksand and rock
    Let the mermaiden sing them:
New sweetness they 'll give her
    Bewildering strain;
But there 's one who will never
    Believe them again.

O, were there an island,
    Though ever so wild,
Where woman could smile, and
    No man be beguiled —
Too tempting a snare
    To poor mortals were given;
And the hope would fix there
    That should anchor on heaven.

III

SONG OF HAROLD HARFAGER

From Chapter xv.

THE sun is rising dimly red,
The wind is wailing low and dread;
From his cliff the eagle sallies,
Leaves the wolf his darksome valleys;
In the mist the ravens hover,
Peep the wild dogs from the cover,
Screaming, croaking, baying, yelling,
Each in his wild accents telling,
' Soon we feast on dead and dying,
Fair-haired Harold's flag is flying.'

Many a crest in air is streaming,
Many a helmet darkly gleaming,
Many an arm the axe uprears,
Doomed to hew the wood of spears.
All along the crowded ranks,
Horses neigh and armor clanks;
Chiefs are shouting, clarions ringing,
Louder still the bard is singing,
' Gather, footmen; gather, horsemen,
To the field, ye valiant Norsemen !

' Halt ye not for food or slumber,
View not vantage, count not number;
Jolly reapers, forward still,
Grow the crop on vale or hill,
Thick or scattered, stiff or lithe,
It shall down before the scythe.
Forward with your sickles bright,
Reap the harvest of the fight.
Onward footmen, onward horsemen,
To the charge, ye gallant Norsemen !

' Fatal Choosers of the Slaughter,
O'er you hovers Odin's daughter;
Hear the choice she spreads before ye —
Victory, and wealth, and glory;
Or old Valhalla's roaring hail,
Her ever-circling mead and ale,
Where for eternity unite
The joys of wassail and of fight.
Headlong forward, foot and horsemen,
Charge and fight, and die like Norsemen ! '

IV

SONG OF THE MERMAIDS AND MERMEN

From Chapter xvi.

MERMAID

FATHOMS deep beneath the wave,
    Stringing beads of glistering pearl,
Singing the achievements brave
    Of many an old Norwegian earl;
Dwelling where the tempest's raving
    Falls as light upon our ear,
As the sigh of lover, craving
    Pity from his lady dear,
Children of wild Thule, we,
From the deep caves of the sea,
As the lark springs from the lea,
Hither come, to share your glee.

MERMAN

From reining of the water-horse,
    That bounded till the waves were foaming,
Watching the infant tempest's course,
    Chasing the sea-snake in his roaming;
From winding charge-notes on the shell,
    When the huge whale and sword-fish
        duel,
Or tolling shroudless seamen's knell,
    When the winds and waves are cruel;
Children of wild Thule, we

Have ploughed such furrows on the sea,
As the steer draws on the lea,
And hither we come to share your glee.

MERMAIDS AND MERMEN

We heard you in our twilight caves,
    A hundred fathom deep below,
For notes of joy can pierce the waves,
    That drown each sound of war and woe.
Those who dwell beneath the sea
    Love the sons of Thule well;
Thus, to aid your mirth, bring we
    Dance and song and sounding shell.
Children of dark Thule, know,
Those who dwell by haaf and voe,
Where your daring shallops row,
Come to share the festal show.

V

NORNA'S VERSES

From Chapter xix.

FOR leagues along the watery way,
    Through gulf and stream my course has
        been;
The billows know my Runic lay,
    And smooth their crests to silent green.

The billows know my Runic lay,
    The gulf grows smooth, the stream is
        still;
But human hearts, more wild than they,
    Know but the rule of wayward will.

One hour is mine, in all the year,
    To tell my woes, and one alone;
When gleams this magic lamp, 't is here,
    When dies the mystic light, 't is gone.

Daughters of northern Magnus, hail !
    The lamp is lit, the flame is clear;
To you I come to tell my tale,
    Awake, arise, my tale to hear !

Dwellers of the mountain, rise,
Trolld the powerful, Haims the wise !
Ye who taught weak woman's tongue
Words that sway the wise and strong, —
Ye who taught weak woman's hand
How to wield the magic wand,
And wake the gales on Foulah's steep,

Or lull wild Sumburgh's waves to sleep !
Still are ye yet ?   Not yours the power
Ye knew in Odin's mightier hour.
What are ye now but empty names,
Powerful Trolld, sagacious Haims,
That, lightly spoken, and lightly heard,
Float on the air like thistle's beard ?

' When I awoke, I saw, through the dim
light which the upper aperture admitted, the
unshapely and indistinct form of Trolld the
dwarf. . . . He spoke, and his words were of
Norse, so old, that few, save my father or I
myself, could have comprehended their import.'

A thousand winters dark have flown,
Since o'er the threshold of my stone
A votaress passed, my power to own.
Visitor bold
Of the mansion of Trolld,
     Maiden haughty of heart.
Who hast hither presumed,
Ungifted, undoomed,
     Thou shalt not depart.
The power thou dost covet
     O'er tempest and wave,
Shall be thine, thou proud maiden,
     By beach and by cave. —
By stack, and by skerry, by noup, and by
     voe,
By air, and by wick, and by helyer and
     gio,
And by every wild shore which the northern
     winds know,
     And the northern tides lave.
But though this shall be given thee, thou
     desperately brave,
I doom thee that never the gift thou shalt
     have,
Till thou reave thy life's giver
Of the gift which he gave.

' I answered him in nearly the same strain.'

     Dark are thy words, and severe,
        Thou dweller in the stone;
     But trembling and fear
        To her are unknown,
     Who hath sought thee here,
        In thy dwelling lone.
     Come what comes soever,
        The worst I can endure;
     Life is but a short fever,
        And Death is the cure.

VI

HALCRO AND NORNA

From Chapter xxi.

CLAUD HALCRO

MOTHER darksome, Mother dread,
Dweller on the Fitful-head,
Thou canst see what deeds are done
Under the never-setting sun.
Look through sleet, and look through frost,
Look to Greenland's caves and coast, —
     By the iceberg is a sail
     Chasing of the swarthy whale;
     Mother doubtful, Mother dread,
     Tell us, has the good ship sped ?

NORNA

The thought of the aged is ever on gear,
On his fishing, his furrow, his flock, and
     his steer;
But thrive may his fishing, flock, furrow,
     and herd,
While the aged for anguish shall tear his
     gray beard.

The ship, well-laden as bark need be,
Lies deep in the furrow of the Iceland sea;
The breeze from Zetland blows fair and
     soft,
And gaily the garland is fluttering aloft:
Seven good fishes have spouted their last,
And their jaw-bones are hanging to yard
     and mast:
Two are for Lerwick, and two for Kirk-
     wall,
And three for Burgh-Westra, the choicest
     of all.

CLAUD HALCRO

Mother doubtful, Mother dread,
Dweller of the Fitful-head,
Thou hast conned full many a rhyme,
That lives upon the surge of time:
Tell me, shall my lays be sung,
Like Hacon's of the golden tongue,
Long after Halcro 's dead and gone ?
Or, shall Hialtland's minstrel own
One note to rival glorious John ?

NORNA

The infant loves the rattle's noise;
Age, double childhood, hath its toys;
But different far the descant rings,

As strikes a different hand the strings.
The eagle mounts the polar sky:
The Imber-goose, unskilled to fly,
Must be content to glide along,
Where seal and sea-dog list his song.

CLAUD HALCRO

Be mine the Imber-goose to play,
And haunt lone cave and silent bay;
The archer's aim so shall I shun;
So shall I 'scape the levelled gun;
Content my verses' tuneless jingle
With Thule's sounding tides to mingle,
While, to the ear of wondering wight,
Upon the distant headland's height,
Softened by murmur of the sea,
The rude sounds seem like harmony !

.   .   .   .

Mother doubtful, Mother dread,
Dweller of the Fitful-head,
A gallant bark from far abroad,
Saint Magnus hath her in his road,
With guns and firelocks not a few:
A silken and a scarlet crew,
Deep stored with precious merchandise
Of gold, and goods of rare device:
What interest hath our comrade bold
In bark and crew, in goods and gold ?

NORNA

Gold is ruddy, fair, and free,
Blood is crimson, and dark to see;
I looked out on Saint Magnus bay,
And I saw a falcon that struck her prey;
A gobbet of flesh in her beak she bore,
And talons and singles are dripping with
     gore;
Let him that asks after them look on his
     hand,
And if there is blood on 't, he 's one of
     their band.

CLAUD HALCRO

Mother doubtful, Mother dread,
Dweller of the Fitful-head,
Well thou know'st it is thy task
To tell what Beauty will not ask;
Then steep thy words in wine and milk,
And weave a doom of gold and silk;
For we would know, shall Brenda prove
In love, and happy in her love ?

NORNA

Untouched by love, the maiden's breast
Is like the snow on Rona's crest,

High seated in the middle sky,
In bright and barren purity;
But by the sunbeam gently kissed,
Scarce by the gazing eye 't is missed,
Ere, down the lonely valley stealing,
Fresh grass and growth its course reveal-
     ing,
It cheers the flock, revives the flower,
And decks some happy shepherd's bower.

MAGNUS TROIL

Mother, speak, and do not tarry,
Here 's a maiden fain would marry.
Shall she marry, ay or not ?
If she marry, what 's her lot ?

NORNA

Untouched by love, the maiden's breast
Is like the snow on Rona's crest;
So pure, so free from earthly dye,
It seems, whilst leaning on the sky,
Part of the heaven to which 't is nigh;
But passion, like the wild March rain,
May soil the wreath with many a stain.
We gaze — the lovely vision 's gone:
A torrent fills the bed of stone,
That, hurrying to destruction's shock,
Leaps headlong from the lofty rock.

VII

THE FISHERMEN'S SONG

From Chapter xxii. ' While they were yet
within hearing of the shore, they chanted an
ancient Norse ditty, appropriate to the occasion, of which Claud Halcro had executed the
following literal translation : ' —

FAREWELL, merry maidens, to song and to
     laugh,
For the brave lads of Westra are bound to
     the Haaf;
And we must have labor, and hunger, and
     pain,
Ere we dance with the maids of Dunross-
     ness again.

For now, in our trim boats of Noroway deal,
We must dance on the waves, with the
     porpoise and seal;
The breeze it shall pipe, so it pipe not too
     high,
And the gull be our songstress whene'er
     she flits by.

Sing on, my brave bird, while we follow,
  like thee,
By bank, shoal, and quicksand, the swarms
  of the sea;
And when twenty-score fishes are straining
  our line,
Sing louder, brave bird, for their spoils
  shall be thine.

We 'll sing while we bait, and we 'll sing
  when we haul,
For the deeps of the Haaf have enough
  for us all;
There is torsk for the gentle, and skate for
  the carle,
And there 's wealth for bold Magnus, the
  son of the earl.

Huzza ! my brave comrades, give way for
  the Haaf,
We shall sooner come back to the dance
  and the laugh;
For life without mirth is a lamp without oil;
Then, mirth and long life to the bold Magnus Troil !

VIII

CLEVELAND'S SONGS

LOVE wakes and weeps
  While Beauty sleeps:
O, for Music's softest numbers,
  To prompt a theme
  For Beauty's dream,
Soft as the pillow of her slumbers !

  Through groves of palm
  Sigh gales of balm,
Fire-flies on the air are wheeling;
  While through the gloom
  Comes soft perfume,
The distant beds of flowers revealing.

  O wake and live !
  No dream can give
A shadowed bliss, the real excelling;
  No longer sleep,
  From lattice peep,
And list the tale that Love is telling.

Farewell ! farewell ! the voice you hear
Has left its last soft tone with you, —

Its next must join the seaward cheer,
  And shout among the shouting crew.

The accents which I scarce could form
  Beneath your frown's controlling check
Must give the word, above the storm,
  To cut the mast and clear the wreck.

The timid eye I dared not raise, —
  The hand, that shook when pressed to
  thine,
Must point the guns upon the chase —
  Must bid the deadly cutlass shine.

To all I love, or hope, or fear, —
  Honor or own, a long adieu !
To all that life has soft and dear,
  Farewell ! save memory of you !

IX

HALCRO'S VERSES

From Chapter xxiii.

AND you shall deal the funeral dole;
  Ay, deal it, mother mine,
To weary body and to heavy soul,
  The white bread and the wine.

And you shall deal my horses of pride;
  Ay, deal them, mother mine;
And you shall deal my lands so wide,
  And deal my castles nine;

But deal not vengeance for the deed,
  And deal not for the crime;
The body to its place, and the soul to Hea-
  ven's grace,
  And the rest in God's own time.

Saint Magnus control thee, that martyr of
  treason;
Saint Ronan rebuke thee, with rhyme and
  with reason;
By the mass of Saint Martin, the might of
  Saint Mary,
Be thou gone, or thy weird shall be worse
  if thou tarry !
If of good, go hence and hallow thee;
If of ill, let the earth swallow thee;
If thou 'rt of air, let the gray mist fold thee;

If of earth, let the swart mine hold thee;
If a Pixie, seek thy ring;
If a Nixie, seek thy spring;
If on middle earth thou 'st been
Slave of sorrow, shame, and sin,
Hast ate the bread of toil and strife,
And dree'd the lot which men call life;
Begone to thy stone ! for thy coffin is scant
    of thee,
The worm, thy play-fellow, wails for the
    want of thee:
Hence, houseless ghost ! let the earth hide
    thee,
Till Michael shall blow the blast, see that
    there thou bide thee !
Phantom, fly hence ! take the Cross for a
    token,
Hence pass till Hallowmass ! — my spell is
    spoken.

Where corpse-light
Dances bright,
Be it by day or night,
Be it by light or dark,
There shall corpse lie stiff and stark.

Menseful maiden ne'er should rise,
Till the first beam tinge the skies;
Silk-fringed eyelids still should close,
Till the sun has kissed the rose;
Maiden's foot we should not view,
Marked with tiny print on dew,
Till the opening flowerets spread
Carpet meet for beauty's tread.

X

NORNA'S INCANTATIONS

From Chapter xxv.

CHAMPION, famed for warlike toil,
Art thou silent, Ribolt Troil ?
Sand, and dust, and pebbly stones,
Are leaving bare thy giant bones.
Who dared touch the wild bear's skin
Ye slumbered on, while life was in ?
A woman now, or babe, may come
And cast the covering from thy tomb.

Yet be not wrathful, Chief, nor blight
Mine eyes or ears with sound or sight !

I come not with unhallowed tread,
To wake the slumbers of the dead,
Or lay thy giant relics bare;
But what I seek thou well canst spare.
Be it to my hand allowed
To shear a merk's weight from thy shroud;
Yet leave thee sheeted lead enough
To shield thy bones from weather rough.

See, I draw my magic knife:
Never while thou wert in life
Laidst thou still for sloth or fear,
When point and edge were glittering near:
See, the cerements now I sever:
Waken now, or sleep for ever !
Thou wilt not wake: the deed is done !
The prize I sought is fairly won.

Thanks, Ribolt, thanks, — for this the
    sea
Shall smooth its ruffled crest for thee,
And while afar its billows foam,
Subside to peace near Ribolt's tomb.
Thanks, Ribolt, thanks — for this the might
Of wild winds raging at their height,
When to thy place of slumber nigh,
Shall soften to a lullaby.

She, the dame of doubt and dread,
Norna of the Fitful-head,
Mighty in her own despite,
Miserable in her might;
In despair and frenzy great,
In her greatness desolate;
Wisest, wickedest who lives,
Well can keep the word she gives.

XI

THE SAME, AT THE MEETING WITH MINNA

From Chapter xxviii.

THOU so needful, yet so dread,
With cloudy crest, and wing of red;
Thou, without whose genial breath
The North would sleep the sleep of death;
Who deign'st to warm the cottage hearth,
Yet hurls proud palaces to earth;
Brightest, keenest of the Powers,
Which form and rule this world of ours,
With my rhyme of Runic, I
Thank thee for thy agency.

Old Reimkennar, to thy art
Mother Hertha sends her part;
She, whose gracious bounty gives
Needful food for all that lives.
From the deep mine of the North,
Came the mystic metal forth,
Doomed amidst disjointed stones,
Long to cere a champion's bones,
Disinhumed my charms to aid:
Mother earth, my thanks are paid.

Girdle of our islands dear,
Element of Water, hear !
Thou whose power can overwhelm
Broken mounds and ruined realm
    On the lowly Belgian strand;
All thy fiercest rage can never
Of our soil a furlong sever
    From our rock-defended land;
Play then gently thou thy part,
To assist old Norna's art.

Elements, each other greeting,
Gifts and powers attend your meeting !

Thou, that over billows dark
Safely send'st the fisher's bark:
Giving him a path and motion
Through the wilderness of ocean;
Thou, that when the billows brave ye,
O'er the shelves canst drive the navy:
Didst thou chafe as one neglected,
While thy brethren were respected ?
To appease thee, see, I tear
This full grasp of grizzled hair;
Oft thy breath hath through it sung,
Softening to my magic tongue;
Now, 't is thine to bid it fly
Through the wide expanse of sky,
'Mid the countless swarms to sail
Of wild-fowl wheeling on thy gale;
Take thy portion and rejoice:
Spirit, thou hast heard my voice !

She who sits by haunted well,
Is subject to the Nixie's spell;
She who walks on lonely beach,
To the Mermaid's charmed speech;
She who walks round ring of green,
Offends the peevish Fairy Queen;
And she who takes rest in the Dwarfie's
    cave,
A weary weird of woe shall have.

By ring, by spring, by cave, by shore,
Minna Troil has braved all this and more;
And yet hath the root of her sorrow and
    ill
A source that 's more deep and more mys-
    tical still.
Thou art within a demon's hold,
More wise than Heims, more strong than
    Trolld;
No siren sings so sweet as he:
No fay springs lighter on the lea;
No elfin power hath half the art
To soothe, to move, to wring the heart:
Life-blood from the cheek to drain,
Drench the eye, and dry the vein.
Maiden, ere we farther go,
Dost thou note me, ay or no ?

MINNA

I mark thee, my mother, both word, look,
    and sign;
Speak on with thy riddle — to read it be
    mine.

NORNA

Mark me ! for the word I speak
Shall bring the color to thy cheek.
This leaden heart, so light of cost,
The symbol of a treasure lost,
Thou shalt wear in hope and in peace,
That the cause of your sickness and sorrow
    may cease,
When crimson foot meets crimson hand
In the Martyrs' Aisle, and in Orkney land.
Be patient, be patient, for Patience hath
    power
To ward us in danger, like mantle in
    shower;
A fairy gift you best may hold
In a chain of fairy gold;
The chain and the gift are each a true
    token,
That not without warrant old Norna hath
    spoken;
But thy nearest and dearest must never
    behold them,
Till time shall accomplish the truths I
    have told them.

XII

BRYCE SNAILSFOOT'S ADVERTISEMENT

From Chapter xxxii.

POOR sinners whom the snake deceives,
Are fain to cover them with leaves.
Zetland hath no leaves, 't is true,
Because that trees are none, or few;
But we have flax and taits of woo',
For linen cloth, and wadmaal blue;
And we have many of foreign knacks
Of finer waft than woo' or flax.
Ye gallanty Lambmas lads appear,
And bring your Lambmas sisters here,
Bryce Snailsfoot spares not cost or care,
To pleasure every gentle pair.

ON ETTRICK FOREST'S MOUNTAINS DUN

Written in 1822 after a week's shooting and fishing in which Scott had been engaged with some friends.

ON Ettrick Forest's mountains dun
'T is blithe to hear the sportsman's gun,
And seek the heath-frequenting brood
Far through the noonday solitude;
By many a cairn and trenched mound
Where chiefs of yore sleep lone and sound,
And springs where gray-haired shepherds tell
That still the fairies love to dwell.

Along the silver streams of Tweed
'T is blithe the mimic fly to lead,
When to the hook the salmon springs,
And the line whistles through the rings;
The boiling eddy see him try,
Then dashing from the current high,
Till watchful eye and cautious hand
Have led his wasted strength to land.

'T is blithe along the midnight tide
With stalwart arm the boat to guide;
On high the dazzling blaze to rear,
And heedful plunge the barbed spear;
Rock, wood, and scaur, emerging bright,
Fling on the stream their ruddy light,
And from the bank our band appears
Like Genii armed with fiery spears.

'T is blithe at eve to tell the tale
How we succeed and how we fail,
Whether at Alwyn's lordly meal,
Or lowlier board of Ashestiel;
While the gay tapers cheerly shine,
Bickers the fire and flows the wine —
Days free from thought and nights from care,
My blessing on the Forest fair.

THE MAID OF ISLA

AIR — ' *The Maid of Isla* '

Written for Mr. George Thomson's *Scottish Melodies*, and published in 1822.

O MAID of Isla, from the cliff
That looks on troubled wave and sky,
Dost thou not see yon little skiff
Contend with ocean gallantly ?
Now beating 'gainst the breeze and surge,
And steeped her leeward deck in foam,
Why does she war unequal urge ? —
O Isla's maid, she seeks her home.

O Isla's maid, yon sea-bird mark,
Her white wing gleams through mist and spray
Against the storm-cloud lowering dark,
As to the rock she wheels away; —
Where clouds are dark and billows rave,
Why to the shelter should she come
Of cliff, exposed to wind and wave ? —
O maid of Isla, 't is her home !

As breeze and tide to yonder skiff,
Thou 'rt adverse to the suit I bring,
And cold as is yon wintry cliff
Where seabirds close their wearied wing.
Yet cold as rock, unkind as wave,
Still, Isla's maid, to thee I come;
For in thy love or in his grave
Must Allan Vourich find his home.

FAREWELL TO THE MUSE

Also published in *Scottish Melodies* in 1822.

ENCHANTRESS, farewell, who so oft has decoyed me
At the close of the evening through woodlands to roam,

Where the forester lated with wonder es-
    pied me
Explore the wild scenes he was quitting
    for home.
Farewell, and take with thee thy num-
    bers wild speaking
The language alternate of rapture and
    woe:
O ! none but some lover whose heart-strings
    are breaking
The pang that I feel at our parting can
    know !

Each joy thou couldst double, and when
    there came sorrow
Or pale disappointment to darken my
    way,
What voice was like thine, that could sing
    of to-morrow
Till forgot in the strain was the grief of
    to-day !
But when friends drop around us in life's
    weary waning,
The grief, Queen of Numbers, thou canst
    not assuage;
Nor the gradual estrangement of those yet
    remaining,
The languor of pain and the chillness of
    age.

'T was thou that once taught me in accents
    bewailing
To sing how a warrior lay stretched on
    the plain,
And a maiden hung o'er him with aid un-
    availing,
And held to his lips the cold goblet in vain;
As vain thy enchantments, O Queen of
    wild Numbers,
To a bard when the reign of his fancy is
    o'er,
And the quick pulse of feeling in apathy
    slumbers —
Farewell, then, Enchantress; — I meet
    thee no more.

NIGEL'S INITIATION AT WHITE-FRIARS

From Chapter xvii. of *The Fortunes of Nigel*,
published in 1822.

Your suppliant, by name
Nigel Grahame,

In fear of mishap
From a shoulder-tap;
And dreading a claw
From the talons of law,
    That are sharper than briars;
His freedom to sue
And rescue by you:
Through weapon and wit,
From warrant and writ,
From bailiff's hand,
From tipstaff's wand,
    Is come hither to Whitefriars.

By spigot and barrel,
    By bilboe and buff;
Thou art sworn to the quarrel
    Of the blades of the Huff.
For Whitefriars and its claims
    To be champion or martyr,
And to fight for its dames
    Like a Knight of the Garter.

From the touch of the tip,
    From the blight of the warrant,
From the watchmen who skip
    On the Harman Beck's errand,
From the bailiff's cramp speech,
    That makes man a thrall,
I charm thee from each,
    And I charm thee from all.
Thy freedom 's complete
    As a blade of the Huff,
To be cheated and cheat,
    To be cuffed and to cuff;
To stride, swear, and swagger,
    To drink till you stagger,
    To stare and to stab,
And to brandish your dagger
    In the cause of your drab;
To walk wool-ward in winter,
    Drink brandy, and smoke,
And go *fresco* in summer
    For want of a cloak;
To eke out your living
    By the wag of your elbow,
By fulham and gourd,
    And by baring of bilboe;
To live by your shifts,
    And to swear by your honor
Are the freedom and gifts
    Of which I am the donor.

CARLE, NOW THE KING'S COME

BEING NEW WORDS TO AN AULD SPRING

This imitation of an old Jacobite ditty was written on the appearance, in the Frith of Forth, of the fleet which conveyed his Majesty King George the Fourth to Scotland, in August, 1822, and was published as a broadside. The reader will recall the enthusiasm of Scott over this royal visit as set forth graphically by Lockhart in Chapter lvi. of the *Life*.

PART FIRST

THE news has flown frae mouth to mouth,
The North for ance has banged the South;
The deil a Scotsman 's die o' drouth,
    Carle, now the King 's come !

CHORUS

    Carle, now the King 's come !
    Carle, now the King 's come !
    Thou shalt dance, and I will sing,
    Carle, now the King 's come !

Auld England held him lang and fast;
And Ireland had a joyfu' cast;
But Scotland's turn is come at last:
    Carle, now the King 's come :

Auld Reekie, in her rokelay gray,
Thought never to have seen the day;
He 's been a weary time away —
    But, Carle, now the King 's come !

She 's skirling frae the Castle-hill;
The Carline's voice is grown sae shrill,
Ye 'll hear her at the Canon-mill:
    Carle, now the King's come !

' Up, bairns !' she cries, 'baith grit and sma',
And busk ye for the weapon-shaw !
Stand by me, and we 'll bang them a' —
    Carle, now the King 's come !

' Come from Newbattle's ancient spires,
Bauld Lothian, with your knights and squires,
And match the mettle of your sires:
    Carle, now the King 's come !

' You 're welcome hame, my Montagu !
Bring in your hand the young Buccleuch;

I 'm missing some that I may rue:
    Carle, now the King 's come;

' Come, Haddington, the kind and gay,
You 've graced my causeway mony a day;
I 'll weep the cause if you should stay:
    Carle, now the King 's come !

' Come, premier Duke, and carry doun
Frae yonder craig his ancient croun;
It 's had a lang sleep and a soun':
    But, Carle, now the King 's come!

' Come, Athole, from the hill and wood,
Bring down your clansmen like a cloud;
Come, Morton, show the Douglas' blood:
    Carle, now the King 's come !

' Come, Tweeddale, true as sword to sheath;
Come, Hopetoun, feared on fields of death;
Come, Clerk, and give your bugle breath;
    Carle, now the King's come !

' Come, Wemyss, who modest merit aids;
Come, Rosebery, from Dalmeny shades;
Breadalbane, bring your belted plaids;
    Carle, now the King 's come !

' Come, stately Niddrie, auld and true,
Girt with the sword that Minden knew;
We have o'er few such lairds as you:
    Carle, now the King 's come !

' King Arthur 's grown a common crier,
He 's heard in Fife and far Cantire:
" Fie, lads, behold my crest of fire ! "
    Carle, now the King 's come !'

' Saint Abb roars out, " I see him pass,
Between Tantallon and the Bass ! "
Calton, get out your keeking-glass,
    Carle, now the King 's come !'

The Carline stopped; and, sure I am,
For very glee had ta'en a dwam,
But Oman helped her to a dram.
    Cogie, now the King 's come !

CHORUS

    Cogie, now the King 's come !
    Cogie, now the King 's come !
    I 'se be fou', and ye 's be toom,
    Cogie, now the King 's come !

PART SECOND

A Hawick gill of mountain dew
Heised up Auld Reekie's heart, I trow,
It minded her of Waterloo:
　　Carle, now the King's come!

Again I heard her summons swell,
For, sic a dirdum and a yell,
It drowned Saint Giles's jowing bell:
　　Carle, now the King's come!

'My trusty Provost, tried and tight,
Stand forward for the Good Town's right,
There's waur than you been made a knight:
　　Carle, now the King's come!

'My reverend Clergy, look ye say
The best of thanksgivings ye ha'e,
And warstle for a sunny day —
　　Carle, now the King's come!

'My Doctors, look that you agree,
Cure a' the town without a fee;
My Lawyers, dinna pike a plea:
　　Carle, now the King's come!

'Come forth each sturdy Burgher's bairn,
That dints on wood or clanks on airn,
That fires the o'en, or winds the pirn —
　　Carle, now the King's come!

'Come forward with the Blanket Blue,
Your sires were loyal men and true,
As Scotland's foemen oft might rue:
　　Carle, now the King's come!

'Scots downa loup, and rin and rave,
We're steady folks and something grave,
We'll keep the causeway firm and brave:
　　Carle, now the King's come!

'Sir Thomas, thunder from your rock,
Till Pentland dinnles wi' the shock,
And lace wi' fire my snood o' smoke:
　　Carle, now the King's come!

'Melville, bring out your bands of blue,
A' Louden lads, baith stout and true,
With Elcho, Hope, and Cockburn, too:
　　Carle, now the King's come!

'And you, who on yon bluidy braes
Compelled the vanquished Despot's praise,
Rank out, rank out, my gallant Greys:
　　Carle, now the King's come!

'Cock of the North, my Huntly bra',
Where are you with the Forty-twa?
Ah! waes my heart that ye're awa':
　　Carle, now the King's come!

'But yonder come my canty Celts,
With durk and pistols at their belts,
Thank God, we've still some plaids and
　　　kilts:
　　Carle, now the King's come!

'Lord, how the pibrochs groan and yell!
Macdonell's ta'en the field himsell,
Macleod comes branking o'er the fell:
　　Carle, now the King's come!

'Bend up your bow each Archer spark,
For you're to guard him light and dark;
Faith, lads, for ance ye've hit the mark:
　　Carle, now the King's come!

'Young Errol, take the sword of state,
The Sceptre, Pane-Morarchate;
Knight Mareschal, see ye clear the gate:
　　Carle, now the King's come!

'Kind cummer, Leith, ye've been mis-
　　　set,
But dinna be upon the fret:
Ye 'se hae the handsel of him yet,
　　Carle, now the King's come!

'My daughters, come with een sae blue,
Your garlands weave, your blossoms strew;
He ne'er saw fairer flowers than you:
　　Carle, now the King's come!

'What shall we do for the propine:
We used to offer something fine,
But ne'er a groat's in pouch of mine:
　　Carle, now the King's come!

'Deil care — for that I'se never start,
We'll welcome him with Highland heart;
Whate'er we have he's get a part:
　　Carle, now the King's come!

'I'll show him mason-work this day:
Nane of your bricks of Babel clay,
But towers shall stand till Time's away:
　　Carle, now the King's come!

'I'll show him wit, I'll show him lair,
And gallant lads and lasses fair,
And what wad kind heart wish for mair?
　　Carle, now the King's come!

'Step out, Sir John, of projects rife,
Come win the thanks of an auld wife,
And bring him health and length of life:
    Carle, now the King's come!'

THE BANNATYNE CLUB

This club of bibliophiles was founded by Sir Walter, who was its first president and wrote these verses for the first anniversary dinner, March, 1823.

ASSIST me, ye friends of Old Books and
    Old Wine,
To sing in the praises of sage Banna-
    tyne,
Who left such a treasure of old Scottish
    lore
As enables each age to print one volume
    more.
    One volume more, my friends, one
      volume more,
    We'll ransack old Banny for one vol-
      ume more.

And first, Allan Ramsay, was eager to
    glean
From Bannatyne's *Hortus* his bright Ever-
    green;
Two light little volumes — intended for
    four —
Still leave us the task to print one volume
    more.
    One volume more, etc.

His ways were not ours, for he cared not
    a pin
How much he left out or how much he put
    in;
The truth of the reading he thought was a
    bore,
So this accurate age calls for one volume
    more.
    One volume more, etc.

Correct and sagacious, then came my Lord
    Hailes,
And weighed every letter in critical scales,
But left out some brief words which the
    prudish abhor,
And castrated Banny in one volume more.
    One volume more, my friends, one
      volume more;
    We'll restore Banny's manhood in one
      volume more.

John Pinkerton next, and I'm truly con-
    cerned
I can't call that worthy so candid as
    learned;
He railed at the plaid and blasphemed the
    claymore,
And set Scots by the ears in his one volume
    more.
    One volume more, my friends, one
      volume more,
    Celt and Goth shall be pleased with
      one volume more.

As bitter as gall and as sharp as a razor,
And feeding on herbs as a Nebuchadnezzar;
His diet too acid, his temper too sour,
Little Ritson came out with his two volumes
    more.
    But one volume, my friends, one vol-
      ume more,
    We'll dine on roast-beef and print one
      volume more.

The stout Gothic yeditur, next on the roll,
With his beard like a brush and as black
    as a coal;
And honest Greysteel that was true to the
    core,
Lent their hearts and their hands each to
    one volume more.
    One volume more, etc.

Since by these single champions what won-
    ders were done,
What may not be achieved by our Thirty
    and One?
Law, Gospel, and Commerce, we count in
    our corps,
And the Trade and the Press join for one
    volume more.
    One volume more, etc.

Ancient libels and contraband books, I
    assure ye,
We'll print as secure from Exchequer or
    Jury;
Then hear your Committee and let them
    count o'er
The Chiels they intend in their three vol-
    umes more.
    Three volumes more, etc.

They'll produce you King Jamie, the sa-
    pient and Sext,
And the Rob of Dumblane and her Bishops
    come next;

One tome miscellaneous they 'll add to
    your store,
Resolving next year to print four volumes
    more.
Four volumes more, my friends, four
    volumes more;
Pay down your subscriptions for four
    volumes more.

COUNTY GUY

From Chapter iv. of *Quentin Durward*, published in 1823.

AH ! County Guy, the hour is nigh,
    The sun has left the lea,
The orange flower perfumes the bower,
    The breeze is on the sea.
The lark his lay who thrilled all day
    Sits hushed his partner nigh;
Breeze, bird, and flower confess the hour,
    But where is County Guy ?

The village maid steals through the shade,
    Her shepherd's suit to hear;
To beauty shy by lattice high,
    Sings high-born Cavalier.
The star of Love, all stars above,
    Now reigns o'er earth and sky;
And high and low the influence know —
    But where is County Guy ?

EPILOGUE

TO THE DRAMA FOUNDED ON SAINT RONAN'S WELL

This drama appeared in 1824, promptly after
the publication of the novel. Lockhart remarks of the epilogue, ' though it caused great
merriment at the time in Edinburgh, the allusions are so exclusively local and temporary,
that I fear no commentary could ever make it
intelligible elsewhere.'

[*Enter* MEG DODDS, *encircled by a crowd of unruly boys, whom a town's-officer is driving off.*]

THAT 's right, friend — drive the gaitlings
    back,
And lend yon muckle ane a whack;
Your Embro' bairns are grown a pack,
    Sae proud and saucy,
They scarce will let an auld wife walk
    Upon your causey.

I 've seen the day they would been scaured
Wi' the Tolbooth or wi' the Guard,
Or maybe wud hae some regard
    For Jamie Laing —
The Water-hole was right weel wared
    On sic a gang.

But whar 's the gude Tolbooth gane now ?
Whar 's the auld Claught, wi' red and
    blue ?
Whar 's Jamie Laing ? and whar 's John
    Doo ?
    And whar 's the Weigh-house ?
Deil hae't I see but what is new,
    Except the Playhouse !

Yoursells are changed frae head to heel,
There 's some that gar the causeway
    reel
With clashing hufe and rattling wheel,
    And horses canterin',
Wha's fathers' daundered hame as weel
    Wi' lass and lantern.

Mysell being in the public line,
I look for howfs I kenned lang syne,
Whar gentles used to drink gude wine
    And eat cheap dinners;
But deil a soul gangs there to dine
    Of saints or sinners !

Fortune's and Hunter's gane, alas !
And Bayle's is lost in empty space;
And now if folk would splice a brace
    Or crack a bottle,
They gang to a new-fangled place
    They ca' a Hottle.

The deevil hottle them for Meg !
They are sae greedy and sae gleg,
That if ye 're served but wi' an egg —
    And that 's puir picking —
In comes a chiel and makes a leg,
    And charges chicken !

' And wha may ye be,' gin ye speer,
' That brings your auld - warld clavers
    here ? '
Troth, if there 's onybody near
    That kens the roads,
I 'll haud ye Burgundy to beer
    He kens Meg Dodds.

I came a piece frae west o' Currie;
And, since I see you 're in a hurry,

Your patience I 'll nae langer worry,
But be sae crouse
As speak a word for ane Will Murray
That keeps this house.

Plays are auld-fashioned things in truth,
And ye 've seen wonders mair uncouth;
Yet actors shouldna suffer drouth
Or want of dramock,
Although they speak but wi' their mouth,
Not with their stamock.

But ye take care of a' folk's pantry;
And surely to hae stooden sentry
Ower this big house — that 's far frae rent-
free —
For a lone sister,
Is claims as gude 's to be a ventri—
How'st ca'd —loquister.

Weel, sirs, gude'en, and have a care
The bairns mak fun o' Meg nae mair;
For gin they do, she tells you fair
And without failzie,
As sure as ever ye sit there,
She 'll tell the Bailie.

EPILOGUE

When Scott was collecting his stray poems
for a definitive edition, he wrote thus to Constable, October 22, 1824: 'I recovered the
above with some difficulty. I believe it was
never spoken, but written for some play, afterwards withdrawn, in which Mrs. H. Siddons
was to have spoken it in the character of Queen
May:' —

THE sages — for authority, pray, look
Seneca's morals or the copy-book —
The sages to disparage woman's power,
Say beauty is a fair but fading flower; —
I cannot tell — I 've small philosophy —
Yet if it fades it does not surely die,
But, like the violet, when decayed in
bloom,
Survives through many a year in rich per-
fume.
Witness our theme to-night; two ages gone,
A third wanes fast, since Mary filled the
throne.
Brief was her bloom with scarce one sunny
day
'Twixt Pinkie's field and fatal Fotherin-
gay:

But when, while Scottish hearts and blood
you boast,
Shall sympathy with Mary's woes be
lost ?
O'er Mary's memory the learned quarrel,
By Mary's grave the poet plants his laurel,
Time's echo, old tradition, makes her
name
The constant burden of his faltering
theme;
In each old hall his gray-haired heralds
tell
Of Mary's picture and of Mary's cell,
And show — my fingers tingle at the
thought —
The loads of tapestry which that poor
queen wrought.
In vain did fate bestow a double dower
Of every ill that waits on rank and power,
Of every ill on beauty that attends —
False ministers, false lovers, and false
friends.
Spite of three wedlocks so completely
curst,
They rose in ill from bad to worse and
worst,
In spite of errors — I dare not say more,
For Duncan Targe lays hand on his clay-
more.
In spite of all, however humors vary,
There is a talisman in that word Mary,
That unto Scottish bosoms all and some
Is found the genuine *open sesamum!*
In history, ballad, poetry, or novel,
It charms alike the castle and the hovel,
Even you — forgive me — who, demure and
shy,
Gorge not each bait nor stir at every fly,
Must rise to this, else in her ancient reign
The Rose of Scotland has survived in vain.

VERSES FROM REDGAUNTLET

Published in 1824.

I

A CATCH OF COWLEY'S ALTERED

From Letter x.

FOR all our men were very very merry,
And all our men were drinking:
There were two men of mine,
Three men of thine,

And three that belonged to old Sir Thom
o' Lyne.
As they went to the ferry, they were very
very merry,
And all our men were drinking.

Jack looked at the sun, and cried, Fire,
fire, fire!
Tom stabled his keffel in Birkendale mire;
Jem started a calf, and hallooed for a stag;
Will mounted a gate-post instead of his
nag:
For all our men were very very merry,
And all our men were drinking;
There were two men of mine,
Three of thine,
And three that belonged to old Sir Thom
o' Lyne.
As they went to the ferry, they were very
very merry,
For all our men were drinking.

II

'AS LORDS THEIR LABORERS' HIRE DE-
LAY'

From Chapter ix.

As lords their laborers' hire delay,
Fate quits our toil with hopes to come,
Which, if far short of present pay,
Still owns a debt and names a sum.

Quit not the pledge, frail sufferer, then,
Although a distant date be given;
Despair is treason towards man,
And blasphemy to Heaven.

LINES

ADDRESSED TO MONSIEUR ALEXANDRE,
THE CELEBRATED VENTRILOQUIST

This M. Alexandre is better known now as
M. Alexandre Vattemaire, who initiated a system of international literary exchanges.
'When Monsieur Alexandre, the celebrated
ventriloquist, was in Scotland, in 1824, he
paid a visit to Abbotsford, where he entertained his distinguished host, and the other
visitors, with his unrivalled imitations. Next
morning, when he was about to depart, Sir
Walter felt a good deal embarrassed, as to the

sort of acknowledgment he should offer; but
at length, resolving that it would probably be
most agreeable to the young foreigner to be
paid in professional coin, if in any, he stepped
aside for a few minutes, and, on returning,
presented him with this epigram. The reader
need hardly be reminded, that Sir Walter
Scott held the office of Sheriff of the county
of Selkirk.' — Scotch Newspaper, 1830.

Of yore, in old England, it was not
thought good
To carry two visages under one hood;
What should folk say to *you?* who have
faces such plenty,
That from under one hood, you last night
showed us twenty!
Stand forth, arch-deceiver, and tell us in
truth,
Are you handsome or ugly, in age or in
youth?
Man, woman, or child — a dog or a
mouse?
Or are you, at once, each live thing in the
house?
Each live thing, did I ask? each dead im-
plement, too,
A work-shop in your person, — saw, chisel,
and screw!
Above all, are you one individual? I know
You must be at least Alexandre and Co.
But I think you 're a troop, an assemblage,
a mob,
And that I, as the Sheriff, should take up
the job;
And instead of rehearsing your wonders in
verse,
Must read you the Riot-Act, and bid you
disperse.

TO J. G. LOCKHART, ESQ.

ON THE COMPOSITION OF MAIDA'S EPI-
TAPH

In October, 1824, died Maida, the most celebrated of all Sir Walter's faithful dogs and
companions, and his master had inscribed upon
his monument the following epitaph: —

'Maidæ marmoreâ dormis sub imagine Maida
Ad januam domini; sit tibi terra levis.'

'Thus Englished,' says Sir Walter in a letter
to his son Charles, 'by an eminent hand: ' —

'Beneath the sculptured form which late you wore,
Sleep soundly, Maida, at your master's door.'

'The monument here mentioned,' says Lockhart, was a *leaping-on-stone* to which the skill of Scott's master-mason had given the shape of Maida recumbent. It had stood by the gate of Abbotsford a year or more before the dog died.' The Latin was Lockhart's, the English, Sir Walter's, but James Ballantyne, who was an over zealous admirer of his great author, saw the inscription, and when he went back to Edinburgh printed it in a newspaper with pride, the Latin verses as Sir Walter's. It happened that Lockhart's inscription had a false quantity *januam*, but Ballantyne not only did not discover this; his memory played him false, and in repeating the inscription he put *jaces* for *dormis*. At once the newspaper paragraphist raised a laugh over 'Sir Walter's false quantities.' Scott, in his generous nature, refused to shield himself behind Lockhart, and much pother was made over the matter. The verses which follow savor, as Lockhart says, of Scott's 'recent overhauling of Swift and Sheridan's doggrel epistles.'

DEAR JOHN, — I some time ago wrote to inform his
Fat worship of *jaces*, misprinted for *dormis ;*
But that several Southrons assured me the *januam*
Was a twitch to both ears of Ass Priscian's cranium.
You perhaps may observe that one Lionel Berguer,
In defence of our blunder appears a stout arguer.
But at length I have settled, I hope, all these clatters,
By a *rowt* in the papers, fine place for such matters.
I have therefore to make it for once my command, sir,
That my gudeson shall leave the whole thing in my hand, sir,
And by no means accomplish what James says you threaten, —
Some banter in Blackwood to claim your dog-Latin.
I have various reasons of weight, on my word, sir,
For pronouncing a step of this sort were absurd, sir.
Firstly, erudite sir, 't was against your advising
I adopted the lines this monstrosity lies in;
For you modestly hinted my English translation

Would become better far such a dignified station.
Second, how, in God's name, would my bacon be saved
By not having writ what I clearly engraved ?
On the contrary, I, on the whole, think it better
To be whipped as the thief, than his lousy resetter.
Thirdly, don't you perceive that I don't care a boddle
Although fifty false metres were flung at my noddle,
For my back is as broad and as hard as Benlomon's,
And I treat as I please both the Greeks and the Romans;
Whereas the said heathens might rather look serious
At a kick on their drum from the scribe of Valerius.
And, fourthly and lastly, it is my good pleasure
To remain the sole source of that murderous measure.
So, *stet pro ratione voluntas*, — be tractile,
Invade not, I say, my own dear little dactyl;
If you do, you 'll occasion a breach in our intercourse.
To-morrow will see me in town for the winter-course,
But not at your door, at the usual hour, sir,
My own pye-house daughter's good prog to devour, sir.
Ergo, peace ! — on your duty your squeamishness throttle,
And we 'll soothe Priscian's spleen with a canny third bottle.
A fig for all dactyls, a fig for all spondees,
A fig for all dunces and Dominie Grundys;
A fig for dry thrapples, south, north, east, and west, sir,
Speats and raxes ere five for a famishing guest, sir;
And as Fatsman and I have some topics for haver, he 'll
Be invited, I hope, to meet me and Dame Peveril,
Upon whom, to say nothing of Oury and Anne, you a
Dog shall be deemed if you fasten your *Janua.*

SONGS FROM THE BETROTHED

Published in 1825.

I

'SOLDIER, WAKE!'

From Chapter xix.

SOLDIER, wake! the day is peeping,
Honor ne'er was won in sleeping;
Never when the sunbeams still
Lay unreflected on the hill:
'T is when they are glinted back
From axe and armor, spear and jack,
That they promise future story
Many a page of deathless glory.
Shields that are the foeman's terror,
Ever are the morning's mirror.

Arm and up! the morning beam
Hath called the rustic to his team,
Hath called the falc'ner to the lake,
Hath called the huntsman to the brake;
The early student ponders o'er
His dusty tomes of ancient lore.
Soldier, wake! thy harvest, fame;
Thy study, conquest; war, thy game.
Shield, that would be foeman's terror,
Still should gleam the morning's mirror.

Poor hire repays the rustic's pain;
More paltry still the sportsman's gain:
Vainest of all, the student's theme
Ends in some metaphysic dream:
Yet each is up, and each has toiled,
Since first the peep of dawn has smiled:
And each is eagerer in his aim
Than he who barters life for fame.
Up, up, and arm thee, son of terror!
Be thy bright shield the morning's mirror.

II

WOMAN'S FAITH

From Chapter xx.

WOMAN's faith, and woman's trust:
Write the characters in dust,
Stamp them on the running stream,
Print them on the moon's pale beam,
And each evanescent letter
Shall be clearer, firmer, better,

And more permanent, I ween,
Than the things those letters mean.

I have strained the spider's thread
'Gainst the promise of a maid;
I have weighed a grain of sand
'Gainst her plight of heart and hand;
I told my true love of the token,
How her faith proved light, and her word
    was broken:
Again her word and truth she plight,
And I believed them again ere night.

III

'I ASKED OF MY HARP'

From Chapter xxxi. 'A lay, of which we
can offer only a few fragments, literally translated from the ancient language in which they
were chanted, premising that they are in that
excursive symbolical style of poetry, which
Taliessin, Llewarch Hen, and other bards, had
derived perhaps from the time of the Druids.'

I ASKED of my harp, 'Who hath injured
    thy chords?'
And she replied, 'The crooked finger, which
    I mocked in my tune.'
A blade of silver may be bended — a blade
    of steel abideth:
Kindness fadeth away, but vengeance en-
    dureth.

The sweet taste of mead passeth from the
    lips,
But they are long corroded by the juice of
    wormwood;
The lamb is brought to the shambles, but
    the wolf rangeth the mountain;
Kindness fadeth away, but vengeance en-
    dureth.

I asked the red-hot iron, when it glim-
    mered on the anvil,
'Wherefore glowest thou longer than the
    fire-brand?'
'I was born in the dark mine, and the
    brand in the pleasant greenwood.'
Kindness fadeth away, but vengeance en-
    dureth.

I asked the green oak of the assembly,
    wherefore its boughs were dry and
    seared like the horns of the stag?

And it showed me that a small worm had
gnawed its roots.
The boy who remembered the scourge, undid the wicket of the castle at midnight.
Kindness fadeth away, but vengeance en-
dureth.

Lightning destroyeth temples, though their
spires pierce the clouds;
Storms destroy armadas, though their sails
intercept the gale.
He that is in his glory falleth, and that by
a contemptible enemy.
Kindness fadeth away, but vengeance en-
dureth.

IV

'WIDOWED WIFE AND WEDDED MAID'

From the last Chapter.

WIDOWED wife and wedded maid,
Betrothed, betrayer, and betrayed,
All is done that has been said;
Vanda's wrong hath been y-wroken:
Take her pardon by this token.

VERSES FROM THE TALISMAN

Published in 1825.

I

'DARK AHRIMAN, WHOM IRAK STILL'

From Chapter iii.

DARK Ahriman, whom Irak still
Holds origin of woe and ill!
When, bending at thy shrine,
We view the world with troubled eye,
Where see we, 'neath the extended sky,
An empire matching thine!

If the Benigner Power can yield
A fountain in the desert field,
Where weary pilgrims drink;
Thine are the waves that lash the rock,
Thine the tornado's deadly shock,
Where countless navies sink!

Or if He bid the soil dispense
Balsams to cheer the sinking sense,
How few can they deliver

From lingering pains, or pang intense,
Red Fever, spotted Pestilence,
The arrows of thy quiver!

Chief in Man's bosom sits thy sway,
And frequent, while in words we pray
Before another throne,
Whate'er of specious form be there,
The secret meaning of the prayer
Is, Ahriman, thine own.

Say, hast thou feeling, sense, and form,
Thunder thy voice, thy garments storm,
As Eastern Magi say;
With sentient soul of hate and wrath,
And wings to sweep thy deadly path,
And fangs to tear thy prey?

Or art thou mixed in Nature's source,
An ever-operating force,
Converting good to ill;
An evil principle innate,
Contending with our better fate,
And oh! victorious still?

Howe'er it be, dispute is vain.
On all without thou hold'st thy reign,
Nor less on all within;
Each mortal passion's fierce career,
Love, hate, ambition, joy, and fear,
Thou goadest into sin.

Whene'er a sunny gleam appears,
To brighten up our vale of tears,
Thou art not distant far;
Mid such brief solace of our lives,
Thou whett'st our very banquet-knives
To tools of death and war.

Thus, from the moment of our birth,
Long as we linger on the earth,
Thou rul'st the fate of men;
Thine are the pangs of life's last hour,
And — who dare answer? — is thy power,
Dark Spirit! ended THEN?

II

'WHAT BRAVE CHIEF SHALL HEAD THE
FORCES'

From Chapter xi. 'A hearing was at length
procured the poet preferred, who sung, in
high German, stanzas which may be thus translated:' —

WHAT brave chief shall head the forces,
  Where the red-cross legions gather ?
Best of horsemen, best of horses,
  Highest head and fairest feather.

Ask not Austria why, 'midst princes,
  Still her banner rises highest;
Ask as well the strong-wing'd eagle
  Why to heaven he soars the nighest.

III

THE BLOODY VEST

From Chapter xxvi. ' The song of Blondel
was, of course, in the Norman language ; but
the verses which follow express its meaning
and its manner.'

'T WAS near the fair city of Benevent,
When the sun was setting on bough and
    bent,
And knights were preparing in bower and
    tent,
On the eve of the Baptist's tournament;
When in Lincoln green a stripling gent,
Well seeming a page by a princess sent,
Wandered the camp, and, still as he went,
Inquired for the Englishman, Thomas à
    Kent.

Far hath he fared, and farther must fare,
Till he finds his pavilion nor stately nor
    rare, —
Little save iron and steel was there:
And, as lacking the coin to pay armorer's
    care,
With his sinewy arms to the shoulders
    bare,
The good knight with hammer and file did
    repair
The mail that to-morrow must see him
    wear,
For the honor of Saint John and his lady
    fair.

' Thus speaks my lady,' the page said
    he,
And the knight bent lowly both head and
    knee:
' She is Benevent's Princess so high in
    degree,
And thou art as lowly as knight may well
    be —
He that would climb so lofty a tree,

Or spring such a gulf as divides her from
    thee,
Must dare some high deed, by which all
    men may see
His ambition is backed by his hie chivalrie.

' Therefore thus speaks my lady,' the fair
    page he said,
And the knight lowly louted with hand and
    with head:
' Fling aside the good armor in which thou
    art clad,
And don thou this weed of her night-gear
    instead,
For a hauberk of steel, a kirtle of thread:
And charge thus attired, in the tournament
    dread,
And fight, as thy wont is, where most blood
    is shed,
And bring honor away, or remain with the
    dead.'

Untroubled in his look, and untroubled in
    his breast,
The knight the weed hath taken, and re-
    verently hath kissed:
' Now blessed be the moment, the messenger
    be blest !
Much honored do I hold me in my lady's
    high behest;
And say unto my lady, in this dear night-
    weed dressed,
To the best armed champion I will not veil
    my crest;
But if I live and bear me well, 't is her turn
    to take the test.'
Here, gentles, ends the foremost fytte of
    the Lay of the Bloody Vest.

FYTTE SECOND

The Baptist's fair morrow beheld gallant
    feats:
There was winning of honor, and losing of
    seats:
There was hewing with falchions, and
    splintering of staves,
The victors won glory, the vanquished won
    graves.
Oh, many a knight there fought bravely
    and well,
Yet one was accounted his peers to excel,
And 't was he whose sole armor on body and
    breast
Seemed the weed of a damsel when bound
    for her rest.

There were some dealt him wounds, that
were bloody and sore,
But others respected his plight, and fore-
bore.
'It is some oath of honor,' they said, 'and
I trow,
'T were unknightly to slay him achieving
his vow.'
Then the Prince, for his sake, bade the
tournament cease,
He flung down his warder, the trumpets
sung peace;
And the judges declare, and competitors
yield,
That the Knight of the Night-gear was first
in the field.

The feast it was nigh, and the mass it was
nigher,
When before the fair Princess low louted a
squire,
And delivered a garment unseemly to view,
With sword-cut and spear-thrust, all hacked
and pierced through;
All rent and all tattered, all clotted with
blood,
With foam of the horses, with dust, and
with mud;
Not the point of that lady's small finger, I
ween,
Could have rested on spot was unsullied
and clean.

'This token my master, Sir Thomas à
Kent,
Restores to the Princess of fair Benevent:
He that climbs the tall tree has won right
to the fruit,
He that leaps the wide gulf should prevail
in his suit;
Through life's utmost peril the prize I have
won,
And now must the faith of my mistress be
shown;
For she who prompts knights on such dan-
ger to run,
Must avouch his true service in front of the
sun.

'I restore,' says my master, 'the garment
I 've worn,
And I claim of the Princess to don it in
turn,
For its stains and its rents she should prize
it the more,

Since by shame 't is unsullied, though crimsoned with gore.'
Then deep blushed the Princess, yet kissed
she and pressed
The blood-spotted robes to her lips and her
breast.
'Go tell my true knight, church and chamber shall show
If I value the blood on this garment or no.'

And when it was time for the nobles to
pass,
In solemn procession to minster and
mass,
The first walked the Princess in purple and
pall,
But the blood-besmeared night-robe she
wore over all;
And eke, in the hall, where they all sat at
dine,
When she knelt to her father and proffered
the wine,
Over all her rich robes and state jewels she
wore
That wimple unseemly bedabbled with gore.

Then lords whispered ladies, as well you
may think,
And ladies replied, with nod, titter, and
wink:
And the Prince, who in anger and shame had
looked down,
Turned at length to his daughter, and
spoke with a frown:
'Now since thou hast published thy folly
and guilt,
E'en atone with thy hand for the blood
thou hast spilt;
Yet sore for your boldness you both will
repent,
When you wander as exiles from fair Benevent.'

Then out spoke stout Thomas, in hall
where he stood,
Exhausted and feeble, but dauntless of
mood;
'The blood that I lost for this daughter of
thine,
I poured forth as freely as flask gives its
wine:
And if for my sake she brooks penance and
blame,
Do not doubt I will save her from suffering
and shame;

And light will she reck of thy princedom
    and rent,
When I hail her, in England, the Countess
    of Kent.'

VERSES FROM WOODSTOCK

Published in 1826.

I

'BY PATHLESS MARCH, BY GREENWOOD
TREE'

From Chapter xiv.

By pathless march, by greenwood tree,
It is thy weird to follow me:
To follow me through the ghastly moon-
    light,
To follow me through the shadows of night,
To follow me, comrade, still art thou bound:
I conjure thee by the unstanched wound,
I conjure thee by the last words I spoke,
When the body slept and the spirit awoke,
In the very last pangs of the deadly stroke !

II

GLEE FOR KING CHARLES

From Chapter xx.

Bring the bowl which you boast,
    Fill it up to the brim;
'T is to him we love most,
    And to all who love him.
Brave gallants, stand up,
    And avaunt ye, base carles !
Were there death in the cup,
Here's a health to King Charles !

Though he wanders through dangers,
    Unaided, unknown,
Dependent on strangers,
    Estranged from his own;
Though 't is under our breath
    Amidst forfeits and perils,
Here's to honor and faith,
    And a health to King Charles !

Let such honors abound
    As the time can afford,
The knee on the ground,
    And the hand on the sword;

But the time shall come round
    When, 'mid Lords, Dukes, and Earls,
The loud trumpet shall sound,
    Here's a health to King Charles !

III

'AN HOUR WITH THEE'

From Chapter xxvi.

An hour with thee ! When earliest day
Dapples with gold the eastern gray,
Oh, what can frame my mind to bear
The toil and turmoil, cark and care,
New griefs, which coming hours unfold,
And sad remembrance of the old ?
            One hour with thee

One hour with thee ! When burning June
Waves his red flag at pitch of noon;
What shall repay the faithful swain
His labor on the sultry plain;
And more than cave or sheltering bough,
Cool feverish blood, and throbbing brow ?
            One hour with thee !

One hour with thee ! When sun is set,
Oh ! what can teach me to forget
The thankless labors of the day;
The hopes, the wishes, flung away;
The increasing wants and lessening gains,
The master's pride who scorns my pains ? —
            One hour with thee !

IV

'SON OF A WITCH'

From Chapter xxx.

Son of a witch,
    Mayst thou die in a ditch,
With the butchers who back thy quarrels;
    And rot above ground,
    While the world shall resound
A welcome to Royal King Charles.

LINES TO SIR CUTHBERT SHARP

Lockhart, in Chapter lxxv. of the *Life*,
writes : 'Sir Cuthbert Sharp, who had been
particularly kind and attentive to Scott when
at Sunderland, happened, in writing to him on

some matter of business, to say he hoped he had not forgotten his friends in that quarter. Sir Walter's answer to Sir Cuthbert [October, 1827] (who had been introduced to him by his old and dear friend, Mr. Surtees of Mainsforth) begins thus: ' —

FORGET thee! No! my worthy fere!
Forget blithe mirth and gallant cheer!
Death sooner stretch me on my bier!
          Forget thee? No.

Forget the universal shout
When ' canny Sunderland' spoke out:
A truth which knaves affect to doubt:
          Forget thee? No.

Forget you? No: though nowaday
I've heard your knowing people say,
' Disown the debt you cannot pay,
You'll find it far the thriftiest way ' —
          But I? — O no.

Forget your kindness found for all room,
In what, though large, seemed still a small room,
Forget my *Surtees* in a ball-room:
          Forget you? No.

Forget your sprightly dumpty-diddles,
And beauty tripping to the fiddles,
Forget my lovely friends the *Liddells:*
          Forget you? No.

VERSES FROM CHRONICLES OF THE CANONGATE

Published in 1827.

I

OLD SONG

From *The Highland Widow*, Chapter ii.

OH, I'm come to the Low Country,
    Och, och, ohonochie,
Without a penny in my pouch
    To buy a meal for me.
I was the proudest of my clan,
    Long, long may I repine;
And Donald was the bravest man,
    And Donald he was mine.

II

THE LAY OF POOR LOUISE

From Chapter x. of *The Fair Maid of Perth.*

AH, poor Louise! the livelong day
She roams from cot to castle gay;
And still her voice and viol say,
Ah, maids, beware the woodland way,
          Think on Louise.

Ah, poor Louise! The sun was high,
It smirched her cheek, it dimmed her eye,
The woodland walk was cool and nigh,
Where birds with chiming streamlets vie
          To cheer Louise.

Ah, poor Louise! The savage bear
Made ne'er that lovely grove his lair;
The wolves molest not paths so fair —
But better far had such been there
          For poor Louise.

Ah, poor Louise! In woody wold
She met a huntsman fair and bold;
His baldrick was of silk and gold,
And many a witching tale he told
          To poor Louise.

Ah, poor Louise! Small cause to pine
Hadst thou for treasures of the mine;
For peace of mind, that gift divine,
And spotless innocence were thine,
          Ah, poor Louise!

Ah, poor Louise! Thy treasure's reft!
I know not if by force or theft,
Or part by violence, part by gift;
But misery is all that's left
          To poor Louise.

Let poor Louise some succor have!
She will not long your bounty crave,
Or tire the gay with warning stave —
For Heaven has grace, and earth a grave,
          For poor Louise.

III

DEATH CHANT

From Chapter xxii. ' Ere he guessed where he was going, the leech was hurried into the house of the late Oliver Proudtute, from which he heard the chant of the women, as they swathed and dressed the corpse of the umquhile Bonnet-maker, for the ceremony of next morning, of which chant, the following verses may be received as a modern imitation : —

VIEWLESS Essence, thin and bare,
Well-nigh melted into air;
Still with fondness hovering near
The earthly form thou once didst wear;

Pause upon thy pinion's flight,
Be thy course to left or right;
Be thou doomed to soar or sink,
Pause upon the awful brink.

To avenge the deed expelling
Thee untimely from thy dwelling,
Mystic force thou shalt retain
O'er the blood and o'er the brain.

When the form thou shalt espy
That darkened on thy closing eye;
When the footstep thou shalt hear
That thrilled upon thy dying ear;

Then strange sympathies shall wake,
The flesh shall thrill, the nerves shall quake;
The wounds renew their clottered flood,
And every drop cry blood for blood.

IV

SONG OF THE GLEE-MAIDEN

From Chapter xxx. ' The maiden sung a melancholy dirge in Norman French; the words, of which the following is an imitation, were united to a tune as doleful as they are themselves : ' —

YES, thou mayst sigh,
And look once more at all around,
At stream and bank, and sky and ground ;
Thy life its final course has found,
And thou must die.

Yes, lay thee down,
And while thy struggling pulses flutter,
Bid the grey monk his soul-mass mutter
And the deep bell its death-tone utter:
Thy life is gone.

Be not afraid,
'T is but a pang, and then a thrill,

A fever fit, and then a chill;
And then an end of human ill:
For thou art dead.

THE DEATH OF KEELDAR

These verses, written in 1828, were published in *The Gem*, an annual edited by Hood. They accompanied an engraving from a painting by Cooper, suggested by the incident.

UP rose the sun o'er moor and mead;
Up with the sun rose Percy Rede;
Brave Keeldar, from his couples freed,
 Careered along the lea;
The Palfrey sprung with sprightly bound,
As if to match the gamesome hound;
His horn the gallant huntsman wound:
 They were a jovial three !

Man, hound, or horse, of higher fame,
To wake the wild deer never came
Since Alnwick's Earl pursued the game
 On Cheviot's rueful day:
Keeldar was matchless in his speed,
Than Tarras ne'er was stancher steed,
A peerless archer, Percy Rede;
 And right dear friends were they.

The chase engrossed their joys and woes.
Together at the dawn they rose,
Together shared the noon's repose
 By fountain or by stream;
And oft when evening skies were red
The heather was their common bed,
Where each, as wildering fancy led,
 Still hunted in his dream.

Now is the thrilling moment near
Of sylvan hope and sylvan fear;
Yon thicket holds the harbored deer,
 The signs the hunters know:
With eyes of flame and quivering ears
The brake sagacious Keeldar nears;
The restless palfrey paws and rears;
 The archer strings his bow.

The game 's afoot ! — Halloo ! Halloo !
Hunter and horse and hound pursue; —
But woe the shaft that erring flew —
 That e'er it left the string !
And ill betide the faithless yew !
The stag bounds scathless o'er the dew,
And gallant Keeldar's life-blood true
 Has drenched the gray-goose wing.

The noble hound — he dies, he dies;
Death, death has glazed his fixed eyes;
Stiff on the bloody heath he lies
　Without a groan or quiver.
Now day may break and bugle sound,
And whoop and hollow ring around,
And o'er his couch the stag may bound,
　But Keeldar sleeps forever.

Dilated nostrils, staring eyes,
Mark the poor palfrey's mute surprise;
He knows not that his comrade dies,
　Nor what is death — but still
His aspect hath expression drear
Of grief and wonder mixed with fear,
Like startled children when they hear
　Some mystic tale of ill.

But he that bent the fatal bow
Can well the sum of evil know,
And o'er his favorite bending low
　In speechless grief recline;
Can think he hears the senseless clay
In unreproachful accents say,
' The hand that took my life away,
　Dear master, was it thine ?

' And if it be, the shaft be blessed
Which sure some erring aim addressed,
Since in your service prized, caressed,
　I in your service die;
And you may have a fleeter hound
To match the dun-deer's merry bound,
But by your couch will ne'er be found
　So true a guard as I.'

And to his last stout Percy rued
The fatal chance, for when he stood
'Gainst fearful odds in deadly feud
　And fell amid the fray,
E'en with his dying voice he cried,
' Had Keeldar but been at my side,
Your treacherous ambush had been spied —
　I had not died to-day ! '

Remembrance of the erring bow
Long since had joined the tides which
　flow,
Conveying human bliss and woe
　Down dark oblivion's river;
But Art can Time's stern doom arrest
And snatch his spoil from Lethe's breast,
And, in her Cooper's colors drest,
　The scene shall live forever.

THE SECRET TRIBUNAL

From *Anne of Geierstein*, published in 1829.

From Chapter xx. ' Philipson could perceive
that the lights proceeded from many torches,
borne by men muffled in black cloaks, like
mourners at a funeral, or the Black Friars of
Saint Francis's Order, wearing their cowls
drawn over their heads, so as to conceal their
features. They appeared anxiously engaged
in measuring off a portion of the apartment ;
and, while occupied in that employment, they
sung, in the ancient German language, rhymes
more rude than Philipson could well understand, but which may be imitated thus : ' —

MEASURERS of good and evil,
Bring the square, the line, the level, —
Rear the altar, dig the trench,
Blood both stone and ditch shall drench.
Cubits six, from end to end,
Must the fatal bench extend;
Cubits six, from side to side,
Judge and culprit must divide.
On the east the Court assembles,
On the west the Accused trembles:
Answer, brethren, all and one,
Is the ritual rightly done ?

On life and soul, on blood and bone,
One for all, and all for one,
We warrant this is rightly done.

How wears the night ? Doth morning
　shine
In early radiance on the Rhine ?
What music floats upon his tide ?
Do birds the tardy morning chide ?
Brethren, look out from hill and height,
And answer true, how wears the night ?

The night is old; on Rhine's broad breast
Glance drowsy stars which long to rest.
　No beams are twinkling in the east.
There is a voice upon the flood,
The stern still call of blood for blood;
　'T is time we listen the behest.

Up, then, up ! When day 's at rest,
'T is time that such as we are watchers;

Rise to judgment, brethren, rise !
Vengeance knows not sleepy eyes,
He and night are matchers.

THE FORAY

Printed in Thomson's *Scottish Collection*,
1830, and set to music by John Whitefield,
Mus. Doc. Cam.

THE last of our steers on the board has
been spread,
And the last flask of wine in our goblet is
red;
Up ! up, my brave kinsmen ! belt swords
and begone,
There are dangers to dare and there's spoil
to be won.

The eyes that so lately mixed glances with
ours
For a space must be dim, as they gaze
from the towers,
And strive to distinguish through tempest
and gloom
The prance of the steed and the toss of the
plume.

The rain is descending; the wind rises
loud;
And the moon her red beacon has veiled
with a cloud;
'T is the better, my mates ! for the warder's dull eye
Shall in confidence slumber nor dream we
are nigh.

Our steeds are impatient ! I hear my
blithe Gray !
There is life in his hoof-clang and hope in
his neigh;
Like the flash of a meteor, the glance of
his mane
Shall marshal your march through the
darkness and rain.

The drawbridge has dropped, the bugle
has blown;
One pledge is to quaff yet — then mount
and begone ! —
To their honor and peace that shall rest
with the slain;
To their health and their glee that see
Teviot again!

INSCRIPTION

FOR THE MONUMENT OF THE REV. GEORGE SCOTT

George Scott was the son of Hugh Scott of
Harden. He died at Kentisbeare, in Devon-
shire, where he was rector of the church, in
1830. The verses are on his tomb.

To youth, to age, alike, this tablet pale
Tells the brief moral of its tragic tale.
Art thou a parent ? Reverence this bier,
The parents' fondest hopes lie buried here.
Art thou a youth, prepared on life to start,
With opening talents and a generous heart;
Fair hopes and flattering prospects all thine
own ?
Lo ! here their end — a monumental stone.
But let submission tame each sorrowing
thought,
Heaven crowned its champion ere the fight
was fought.

SONGS FROM THE DOOM OF DEVORGOIL

Scott's play, *The Doom of Devorgoil*, though
not published till 1830, was sketched, and apparently written as early as 1817, and the song of
Bonny Dundee was written, Scott notes in his
diary, in December, 1825. He notes also that
the first song was abridged into *County Guy*.

I

' THE SUN UPON THE LAKE '

THE sun upon the lake is low,
The wild birds hush their song,
The hills have evening's deepest glow,
Yet Leonard tarries long.
Now all whom varied toil and care
From home and love divide,
In the calm sunset may repair
Each to the loved one's side.

The noble dame, on turret high
Who waits her gallant knight,
Looks to the western beam to spy
The flash of armor bright.
The village maid, with hand on brow
The level ray to shade,
Upon the footpath watches now
For Colin's darkening plaid.

Now to their mates the wild swans row,
By day they swam apart;

And to the thicket wanders slow
The hind beside the hart.
The woodlark at his partner's side
Twitters his closing song —
All meet whom day and care divide,
But Leonard tarries long.

II

' WE LOVE THE SHRILL TRUMPET '

WE love the shrill trumpet, we love the
drum's rattle,
They call us to sport, and they call us to
battle;
And old Scotland shall laugh at the threats
of a stranger,
While our comrades in pastime are comrades in danger.

If there's mirth in our house, 't is our
neighbor that shares it —
If peril approach, 't is our neighbor that
dares it;
And when we lead off to the pipe and the
tabor,
The fair hand we press is the hand of a
neighbor.

Then close your ranks, comrades, the bands
that combine them,
Faith, friendship, and brotherhood, joined
to entwine them;
And we'll laugh at the threats of each insolent stranger,
While our comrades in sport are our comrades in danger.

III

'ADMIRE NOT THAT I GAINED THE PRIZE'

ADMIRE not that I gained the prize
From all the village crew;
How could I fail with hand or eyes
When heart and faith were true ?

And when in floods of rosy wine
My comrades drowned their cares,
I thought but that thy heart was mine,
My own leapt light as theirs.

My brief delay then do not blame,
Nor deem your swain untrue;

My form but lingered at the game,
My soul was still with you.

IV

' WHEN THE TEMPEST '

WHEN the tempest 's at the loudest
On its gale the eagle rides;
When the ocean rolls the proudest
Through the foam the sea-bird glides —
All the rage of wind and sea
Is subdued by constancy.

Gnawing want and sickness pining,
All the ills that men endure,
Each their various pangs combining,
Constancy can find a cure —
Pain and Fear and Poverty
Are subdued by constancy.

Bar me from each wonted pleasure,
Make me abject, mean, and poor,
Heap on insults without measure,
Chain me to a dungeon floor —
I 'll be happy, rich, and free,
If endowed with constancy.

V

BONNY DUNDEE

AIR — ' *The Bonnets of Bonny Dundee* '

To the Lords of Convention 't was Clav-
er'se who spoke,
' Ere the King's crown shall fall there are
crowns to be broke;
So let each Cavalier who loves honor and
me,
Come follow the bonnet of Bonny Dundee.
Come fill up my cup, come fill up my
can,
Come saddle your horses and call up
your men;
Come open the West Port and let me
gang free,
And it 's room for the bonnets of Bonny
Dundee ! '

Dundee he is mounted, he rides up the
street,
The bells are rung backward, the drums
they are beat;

But the Provost, douce man, said, 'Just
    e'en let him be,
The Gude Town is weel quit of that Deil
    of Dundee.'
Come fill up my cup, etc.

As he rode down the sanctified bends of
    the Bow,
Ilk carline was flyting and shaking her
    pow;
But the young plants of grace they looked
    couthie and slee,
Thinking, luck to thy bonnet, thou Bonny
    Dundee!
Come fill up my cup, etc.

With sour-featured Whigs the Grassmar-
    ket was crammed
As if half the West had set tryst to be
    hanged;
There was spite in each look, there was
    fear in each e'e,
As they watched for the bonnets of Bonny
    Dundee.
Come fill up my cup, etc.

These cowls of Kilmarnock had spits and
    had spears,
And lang-hafted gullies to kill Cava-
    liers;
But they shrunk to close-heads and the
    causeway was free,
At the toss of the bonnet of Bonny Dundee.
Come fill up my cup, etc.

He spurred to the foot of the proud Castle
    rock,
And with the gay Gordon he gallantly
    spoke;
'Let Mons Meg and her marrows speak
    twa words or three,
For the love of the bonnet of Bonny Dun-
    dee.'
Come fill up my cup, etc.

The Gordon demands of him which way he
    goes —
'Where'er shall direct me the shade of
    Montrose!
Your Grace in short space shall hear tidings
    of me,
Or that low lies the bonnet of Bonny Dun-
    dee.
Come fill up my cup, etc.

'There are hills beyond Pentland and lands
    beyond Forth,
If there 's lords in the Lowlands, there 's
    chiefs in the North;
There are wild Duniewassals three thou-
    sand times three,
Will cry hoigh! for the bonnet of Bonny
    Dundee.
Come fill up my cup, etc.

'There 's brass on the target of barkened
    bull-hide;
There 's steel in the scabbard that dangles
    beside;
The brass shall be burnished, the steel
    shall flash free,
At a toss of the bonnet of Bonny Dundee.
Come fill up my cup, etc.

'Away to the hills, to the caves, to the
    rocks —
Ere I own an usurper, I 'll couch with the
    fox;
And tremble, false Whigs, in the midst of
    your glee,
You have not seen the last of my bonnet
    and me!'
Come fill up my cup, etc.

He waved his proud hand and the trumpets
    were blown,
The kettle-drums clashed, and the horse-
    men rode on,
Till on Ravelston's cliffs and on Clermis-
    ton's lee
Died away the wild war-notes of Bonny
    Dundee.
Come fill up my cup, come fill up my
    can,
Come saddle the horses and call up
    the men;
Come open your gates and let me gae
    free,
For it 's up with the bonnets of Bonny
    Dundee!

VI

'WHEN FRIENDS ARE MET'

WHEN friends are met o'er merry cheer,
And lovely eyes are laughing near,
And in the goblet's bosom clear
    The cares of day are drowned;

When puns are made and bumpers quaffed,
And wild Wit shoots his roving shaft,
And Mirth his jovial laugh has laughed,
  Then is our banquet crowned,
    Ah ! gay,
  Then is our banquet crowned.

When glees are sung and catches trolled,
And bashfulness grows bright and bold,
And beauty is no longer cold,
  And age no longer dull;
When chimes are brief and cocks do crow
To tell us it is time to go,
Yet how to part we do not know,
  Then is our feast at full,
    Ah ! gay,
  Then is our feast at full.

'HITHER WE COME'

A song from the drama of *Auchindrane;* or
The Ayrshire Tragedy, published in 1830.

HITHER we come,
Once slaves to the drum,
But no longer we list to its rattle;
  Adieu to the wars,
  With their slashes and scars,
The march, and the storm, and the battle.

There are some of us maimed,
And some that are lamed,
And some of old aches are complaining;
  But we 'll take up the tools
  Which we flung by like fools,
'Gainst Don Spaniard to go a-campaigning.

Dick Hathorn doth vow
To return to the plough,
Jack Steele to his anvil and hammer;
  The weaver shall find room
  At the wight-wapping loom,
And your clerk shall teach writing and
    grammar.

THE DEATH OF DON PEDRO

Lockhart included this ballad in his *Ancient
Spanish Ballads*, published in 1823, and credits
the translation to Sir Walter. He reminds the
reader that it was quoted more than once by
Cervantes in his *Don Quixote*.

HENRY and King Pedro clasping,
  Hold in straining arms each other;
Tugging hard and closely grasping,
  Brother proves his strength with
    brother.

Harmless pastime, sport fraternal,
  Blends not thus their limbs in strife;
Either aims, with rage infernal,
  Naked dagger, sharpened knife.

Close Don Henry grapples Pedro,
  Pedro holds Don Henry strait;
Breathing, this, triumphant fury,
  That, despair and mortal hate.

Sole spectator of the struggle,
  Stands Don Henry's page afar,
In the chase, who bore his bugle,
  And who bore his sword in war.

Down they go in deadly wrestle,
  Down upon the earth they go,
Fierce King Pedro has the vantage,
  Stout Don Henry falls below.

Marking then the fatal crisis,
  Up the page of Henry ran,
By the waist he caught Don Pedro,
  Aiding thus the fallen man.

'King to place, or to depose him,
  Dwelleth not in my desire,
But the duty which he owes him,
  To his master pays the squire.'

Now Don Henry has the upmost,
  Now King Pedro lies beneath,
In his heart his brother's poniard,
  Instant finds its bloody sheath.

Thus with mortal gasp and quiver,
  While the blood in bubbles welled,
Fled the fiercest soul that ever
  In a Christian bosom dwelled.

LINES ON FORTUNE

'Another object of this journey was to consult, on the advice of Dr. Ebenezer Clarkson,
a skilful mechanist, by name *Fortune*, about a
contrivance for the support of the lame limb,
which had of late given him much pain, as
well as inconvenience. Mr. Fortune produced

a clever piece of handiwork, and Sir Walter felt at first great relief from the use of it : inasmuch that his spirits rose to quite the old pitch, and his letter to me upon the occasion overflows with merry applications of sundry maxims and verses about *Fortune.* "*Fortes Fortuna adjuvat*" — he says — "never more sing I!"' Lockhart, Chapter lxxix. The first stanza is an old Elizabethan song. The second, Scott's palinode, appears to be his last effort in verse. The incident was in February, 1831.

FORTUNE, my Foe, why dost thou frown
    on me ?
And will my Fortune never better be ?

Wilt thou, I say, forever breed my
    pain ?
And wilt thou ne'er return my joys
    again ?

No — let my ditty be henceforth —

Fortune, my friend, how well thou favor-
    est me !
A kinder Fortune man did never see !
Thou propp'st my thigh, thou ridd'st my
    knee of pain,
I 'll walk, I 'll mount — I 'll be a man
    again. —

APPENDIX

APPENDIX

I. JUVENILE LINES

A TRANSLATION FROM VIRGIL

' The autobiography tells us that his translations in verse from Horace and Virgil were
often approved by Dr. Adam. One of these
little pieces, written in a weak boyish scrawl,
within pencilled marks still visible, had been
carefully preserved by his mother ; it was
found folded up in a cover, inscribed by the
old lady — " *My Walter's first lines*, 1782." ' —
Lockhart, *Life of Scott*, Chapter iii.

In awful ruins Ætna thunders nigh,
And sends in pitchy whirlwinds to the sky
Black clouds of smoke, which still as they as-
    pire,
From their dark sides there bursts the glowing
    fire ;
At other times huge balls of fire are tossed,
That lick the stars, and in the smoke are lost ;
Sometimes the mount, with vast convulsions
    torn,
Emits huge rocks, which instantly are borne
With loud explosions to the starry skies,
The stones made liquid as the huge mass flies,
Then back again with greater weight recoils,
While Ætna thundering from the bottom boils.

ON A THUNDER-STORM

' In Scott's Introduction to the Lay, he
alludes to an original effusion of these " school-
boy days," prompted by a thunder-storm, which
he says " was much approved of, until a malevolent critic sprung up in the shape of an apothecary's blue-buskined wife ; she affirmed that
my most sweet poetry was copied from an old
magazine." ' — Lockhart, Chapter iii. The
lines were written in 1783.

Loud o'er my head though awful thunders roll,
And vivid lightnings flash from pole to pole,
Yet 't is thy voice, my God, that bids them
    fly,
Thy arm directs those lightnings through the
    sky.
Then let the good thy mighty name revere,
And hardened sinners thy just vengeance fear.

ON THE SETTING SUN

' These lines, as well as the foregoing, were
found wrapped in a paper with the inscription,
by Dr. Adam, — " Walter Scott, July, 1783." '
— Lockhart, Chapter iii.

Those evening clouds, that setting ray,
And beauteous tints, serve to display
    Their great Creator's praise ;
Then let the short-lived thing called man,
Whose life 's comprised within a span,
    To Him his homage raise.

We often praise the evening clouds,
    And tints so gay and bold,
But seldom think upon our God,
    Who tinged these clouds with gold.

II. MOTTOES FROM THE NOVELS

' The scraps of poetry, which have been in
most cases tacked to the beginning of chapters in these novels, are sometimes quoted
either from reading or from memory, but, in
the general case, are pure invention. I found
it too troublesome to turn to the collection of
the British Poets to discover apposite mottoes,
and in the situation of the theatrical machinist,
who, when the white paper which represented
his shower of snow was exhausted, continued
the shower by snowing brown, I drew on my
memory as long as I could, and when that
failed, eked it out with invention. I believe
that in some cases, where actual names are affixed to the supposed quotations, it would be
to little purpose to seek them in the works of
the authors referred to. In some cases I have
been entertained when Dr. Watts and other
graver authors have been ransacked in vain for
stanzas for which the novelist alone was responsible.' — *Introduction to Chronicles of the
Canongate.*
' It may be worth noting that it was in correcting the proof-sheets of *The Antiquary* that
Scott first took to equipping his characters
with mottoes of his own fabrication. On one
occasion he happened to ask John Ballantyne,
who was sitting by him, to hunt for a particu-

lar passage in Beaumont and Fletcher. John
did as he was bid, but did not succeed in discovering the lines. " Hang it, Johnnie ! " cried
Scott, "I believe I can make a motto sooner
than you will find one." He did so accordingly; and from that hour, whenever memory
failed to suggest an appropriate epigraph, he
had recourse to the inexhaustible mines of " *old
play* " or " *old ballad*," to which we owe some
of the most exquisite verse that ever flowed
from his pen.' — Lockhart's *Life of Scott*, Chapter xxvii.

From The Antiquary

I KNEW Anselmo. He was shrewd and pru-
        dent,
Wisdom and cunning had their shares of him ;
But he was shrewish as a wayward child,
And pleased again by toys which childhood
        please ;
As book of fables graced with print of wood,
Or else the jingling of a rusty medal,
Or the rare melody of some old ditty
That first was sung to please King Pepin's
        cradle.

' BE brave,' she cried, ' you yet may be our
        guest.
Our haunted room was ever held the best :
If then your valor can the fight sustain
Of rustling curtains and the clinking chain,
If your courageous tongue have powers to talk
When round your bed the horrid ghost shall
        walk,
If you dare ask it why it leaves its tomb,
I 'll see your sheets well aired and show the
        room.'
                                True Story.

SOMETIMES he thinks that Heaven this vision
        sent,
And ordered all the pageants as they went ;
Sometimes that only 't was wild Fancy's play,
The loose and scattered relics of the day.

BEGGAR ! — the only freemen of your Common-
        wealth,
Free above Scot-free, that observe no laws,
Obey no governor, use no religion
But what they draw from their own ancient
        customs
Or constitute themselves, yet they are no rebels.
                                Brome.

HERE has been such a stormy encounter
Betwixt my cousin Captain and this soldier,
About I know not what ! — nothing, indeed ;
Competitions, degrees, and comparatives
Of soldiership ! —
                        A Faire Quarrel.

IF you fail honor here,
Never presume to serve her any more ;
Bid farewell to the integrity of arms,
And the honorable name of soldier

Fall from you, like a shivered wreath of laurel
By thunder struck from a desertlesse forehead.
                        A Faire Quarrel.

THE Lord Abbot had a soul
Subtile and quick, and searching as the fire :
By magic stairs he went as deep as hell,
And if in devils' possession gold be kept,
He brought some sure from thence — 't is hid in
        caves,
Known, save to me, to none —
                The Wonder of a Kingdome.

MANY great ones
Would part with half their states, to have the
        plan
And credit to beg in the first style. —
                        Beggar's Bush.

WHO is he ? — One that for the lack of land
Shall fight upon the water — he hath challenged
Formerly the grand whale ; and by his titles
Of Leviathan, Behemoth, and so forth.
He tilted with a sword-fish — Marry, sir,
Th' aquatic had the best — the argument
Still galls our champion's breech.
                                Old Play.

TELL me not of it, friend — when the young
        weep,
Their tears are lukewarm brine ; — from our
        old eyes
Sorrow falls down like hail-drops of the North,
Chilling the furrows of our withered cheeks,
Cold as our hopes and hardened as our feeling —
Theirs, as they fall, sink sightless — ours recoil,
Heap the fair plain and bleaken all before us.
                                Old Play.

REMORSE — she ne'er forsakes us ! —
A bloodhound stanch — she tracks our rapid
        step
Through the wild labyrinth of youthful frenzy,
Unheard, perchance, until old age hath tamed
        us ;
Then in our lair, when Time hath chilled our
        joints
And maimed our hope of combat or of flight,
We hear her deep-mouthed bay, announcing all
Of wrath and woe and punishment that bides
        us.
                                Old Play.

STILL in his dead hand clenched remain the
        strings
That thrill his father's heart — e'en as the limb,
Lopped off and laid in grave, retains, they tell
        us,
Strange commerce with the mutilated stump,
Whose nerves are twinging still in maimed ex-
        istence.
                                Old Play.

LIFE, with you,
Glows in the brain and dances in the arteries ;
'T is like the wine some joyous guest hath
        quaffed,

That glads the heart and elevates the fancy: —
Mine is the poor residuum of the cup,
Vapid and dull and tasteless, only soiling
With its base dregs the vessel that contains it.
Old Play.

YES! I love Justice well — as well as you do —
But, since the good dame's blind, she shall ex-
    cuse me,
If, time and reason fitting, I prove dumb ; —
The breath I utter now shall be no means
To take away from me my breath in future.
Old Play.

WELL, well, at worst, 't is neither theft nor
    coinage,
Granting I knew all that you charge me with.
What tho' the tomb hath borne a second birth
And given the wealth to one that knew not on 't,
Yet fair exchange was never robbery,
Far less pure bounty —
Old Play.

LIFE ebbs from such old age, unmarked and
    silent,
As the slow neap-tide leaves yon stranded galley.
Late she rocked merrily at the least impulse
That wind or wave could give ; but now her
    keel
Is settling on the sand, her mast has ta'en
An angle with the sky from which it shifts not.
Each wave receding shakes her less and less,
Till, bedded on the strand, she shall remain
Useless as motionless.
Old Play.

So, while the Goose, of whom the fable told,
Incumbent brooded o'er her eggs of gold,
With hand outstretched impatient to destroy,
Stole on her secret nest the cruel Boy,
Whose gripe rapacious changed her splendid
    dream
For wings vain fluttering and for dying scream.
The Loves of the Sea-Weeds.

LET those go see who will — I like it not —
For, say he was a slave to rank and pomp,
And all the nothings he is now divorced from
By the hard doom of stern necessity ;
Yet is it sad to mark his altered brow,
Where Vanity adjusts her flimsy veil
O'er the deep wrinkles of repentant Anguish.
Old Play.

FORTUNE, you say, flies from us — She but
    circles,
Like the fleet sea-bird round the fowler's skiff,
Lost in the mist one moment, and the next
Brushing the white sail with her whiter wing,
As if to court the aim. — Experience watches,
And has her on the wheel. —
Old Play.

From The Black Dwarf

THE bleakest rock upon the loneliest heath
Feels in its barrenness some touch of spring ;

And, in the April dew or beam of May,
Its moss and lichen freshen and revive ;
And thus the heart, most seared to human
    pleasure,
Melts at the tear, joys in the smile of woman.
Beaumont.

'T WAS time and griefs
That framed him thus : Time, with his fairer
    hand,
Offering the fortunes of his former days,
The former man may make him — Bring us to
    him,
And chance it as it may.
Old Play.

From Old Mortality

AROUSE thee, youth ! — it is no common call, —
God's Church is leaguered — haste to man the
    wall;
Haste where the Red-cross banners wave on
    high
Signals of honored death or victory.
James Duff.

MY hounds may a' rin masterless,
    My hawks may fly frae tree to tree,
My lord may grip my vassal lands,
    For there again maun I never be !
Old Ballad.

SOUND, sound the clarion, fill the fife !
    To all the sensual world proclaim,
One crowded hour of glorious life
    Is worth an age without a name.
Anonymous.

From Rob Roy

IN the wide pile, by others heeded not,
Hers was one sacred solitary spot,
Whose gloomy aisles and bending shelves con-
    tain
For moral hunger food, and cures for moral
    pain.
Anonymous.

DIRE was his thought who first in poison steeped
The weapon formed for slaughter — direr his,
And worthier of damnation, who instilled
The mortal venom in the social cup,
To fill the veins with death instead of life.
Anonymous.

LOOK round thee, young Astolpho : Here 's the
    place
Which men — for being poor — are sent to
    starve in —
Rude remedy, I trow, for sore disease.
Within these walls, stifled by damp and stench,
Doth Hope's fair torch expire; and at the snuff,
Ere yet 't is quite extinct, rude, wild, and way-
    ward,

The desperate revelries of wild despair,
Kindling their hell-born cressets, light to deeds
That the poor captives would have died ere
  practised,
Till bondage sunk his soul to his condition.
                    The Prison, Act I. Scene 3.

FAR as the eye could reach no tree was seen,
Earth, clad in russet, scorned the lively green;
No birds, except as birds of passage, flew;
No bee was heard to hum, no dove to coo;
No streams, as amber smooth, as amber clear,
Were seen to glide, or heard to warble here.
                    Prophecy of Famine.

'WOE to the vanquished!' was stern Brenno's
  word,
When sunk proud Rome beneath the Gallic
  sword—
'Woe to the vanquished!' when his massive
  blade
Bore down the scale against her ransom
  weighed,
And on the field of foughten battle still,
Who knows no limit save the victor's will.
                    The Gaulliad.

AND be he safe restored ere evening set,
Or, if there 's vengeance in an injured heart
And power to wreak it in an armed hand,
Your land shall ache for 't.
                    Old Play.

FAREWELL to the land where the clouds love to
  rest,
Like the shroud of the dead, on the mountain's
  cold breast:
To the cataract's roar where the eagles reply,
And the lake her lone bosom expands to the
  sky.

From The Heart of Midlothian

To man, in this his trial state,
  The privilege is given,
When lost by tides of human fate,
  To anchor fast in Heaven.
                    Watts' Hymns.

LAW, take thy victim!—May she find the mercy
In yon mild heaven which this hard world denies her!

AND Need and Misery, Vice and Danger, bind
In sad alliance each degraded mind.

                    I BESEECH you—
These tears beseech you, and these chaste
  hands woo you,
That never yet were heaved but to things holy—
Things like yourself—You are a God above
  us;
Be as a God then, full of saving mercy!
                    The Bloody Brother.

HAPPY thou art! then happy be,
  Nor envy me my lot:
Thy happy state I envy thee,
  And peaceful cot.
                    Lady C—— C——l.

From The Bride of Lammermoor

THE hearth in hall was black and dead,
  No board was dight in bower within,
Nor merry bowl nor welcome bed;
  'Here 's sorry cheer,' quoth the Heir of
    Linne.
                    Old Ballad
          (Altered from 'The Heir of Linne').

As, to the Autumn breeze's bugle-sound,
Various and vague the dry leaves dance their
  round;
Or from the garner-door, on æther borne,
The chaff flies devious from the winnowed
  corn;
So vague, so devious, at the breath of heaven,
From their fixed aim are mortal councils driven.
                    Anonymous.

          HERE is a father now,
Will truck his daughter for a foreign venture,
Make her the stop-gap to some cankered feud,
Or fling her o'er, like Jonah, to the fishes,
To appease the sea at highest.
                    Anonymous.

SIR, stay at home and take an old man's counsel:
Seek not to bask you by a stranger's hearth;
Our own blue smoke is warmer than their fire.
Domestic food is wholesome, though 't is
  homely,
And foreign dainties poisonous, though tasteful.
                    The French Courtezan.

TRUE-LOVE, an thou be true,
  Thou hast ane kittle part to play,
For fortune, fashion, fancy, and thou
  Maun strive for many a day.

I 've kend by mony a friend's tale,
  Far better by this heart of mine,
What time and change of fancy avail,
  A true love-knot to untwine.
                    Hendersoun.

WHY, now I have Dame Fortune by the fore-
  lock,
And if she 'scapes my grasp the fault is mine;
He that hath buffeted with stern adversity,
Best knows to shape his course to favoring
  breezes.
                    Old Play.

From The Legend of Montrose

DARK on their journey loured the gloomy day,
Wild were the hills and doubtful grew the way;

More dark, more gloomy, and more doubtful
    showed
The mansion which received them from the
    road.
           The Travellers, a Romance.

Is this thy castle, Baldwin ? Melancholy
Displays her sable banner from the donjon,
Darkening the foam of the whole surge beneath.
Were I a habitant, to see this gloom
Pollute the face of nature, and to hear
The ceaseless sound of wave and sea-bird's
    scream,
I 'd wish me in the hut that poorest peasant
Ere framed to give him temporary shelter.
                  Browne.

THIS was the entry, then, these stairs — but
    whither after ?
Yet he that 's sure to perish on the land
May quit the nicety of card and compass,
And trust the open sea without a pilot.
          Tragedy of Brennovalt.

From Ivanhoe

AWAY ! our journey lies through dell and
    dingle,
Where the blithe fawn trips by its timid mother,
Where the broad oak with intercepting boughs
Chequers the sun-beam in the greensward
    alley —
Up and away ! for lovely paths are these
To tread, when the glad sun is on his throne ;
Less pleasant and less safe when Cynthia's
    lamp
With doubtful glimmer lights the dreary forest.
             Ettrick Forest.

WHEN autumn nights were long and drear,
    And forest walks were dark and dim,
How sweetly on the pilgrim's ear
    Was wont to steal the hermit's hymn !

Devotion borrows Music's tone,
    And Music took Devotion's wing,
And, like the bird that hails the sun,
    They soar to heaven, and soaring sing.
      The Hermit of Saint Clement's Well.

THE hottest horse will oft be cool,
    The dullest will show fire ;
The friar will often play the fool,
    The fool will play the friar.
               Old Song.

THIS wandering race, severed from other men,
Boast yet their intercourse with human arts;
The seas, the woods, the deserts, which they
    haunt,
Find them acquainted with their secret trea-
    sures;
And unregarded herbs and flowers and blossoms
Display undreamed-of powers when gathered
    by them.
                The Jew.

APPROACH the chamber, look upon his bed.
His is the passing of no peaceful ghost,
Which, as the lark arises to the sky,
Mid morning's sweetest breeze and softest dew,
Is winged to heaven by good men's sighs and
    tears !
Anselm parts otherwise.
                Old Play.

TRUST me, each state must have its policies:
Kingdoms have edicts, cities have their charters;
Even the wild outlaw in his forest-walk
Keeps yet some touch of civil discipline.
For not since Adam wore his verdant apron
Hath man with man in social union dwelt,
But laws were made to draw that union closer.
                Old Play.

AROUSE the tiger of Hyrcanian deserts,
Strive with the half-starved lion for his prey;
Lesser the risk than rouse the slumbering fire
Of wild Fanaticism.
              Anonymous.

SAY not my art is fraud — all live by seeming.
The beggar begs with it, and the gay courtier
Gains land and title, rank and rule, by seeming:
The clergy scorn it not, and the bold soldier
Will eke with it his service. — All admit it,
All practise it ; and he who is content
With showing what he is shall have small
    credit
In church or camp or state. — So wags the world.
                Old Play.

STERN was the law which bade its votaries leave
At human woes with human hearts to grieve ;
Stern was the law which at the winning wile
Of frank and harmless mirth forbade to smile;
But sterner still when high the iron-rod
Of tyrant power she shook, and called that
    power of God.
            The Middle Ages.

From The Monastery

O AY ! the Monks, the Monks, they did the mis-
    chief !
Theirs all the grossness, all the superstition
Of a most gross and superstitious age. —
May HE be praised that sent the healthful
    tempest,
And scattered all these pestilential vapors;
But that we owed them *all* to yonder Harlot
Throned on the seven hills with her cup of gold,
I will as soon believe, with kind Sir Roger,
That old Moll White took wing with cat and
    broomstick,
And raised the last night's thunder.
                Old Play.

IN yon lone vale his early youth was bred.
Not solitary then — the bugle-horn
Of fell Alecto often waked its windings,
From where the brook joins the majestic river

To the wild northern bog, the curlieu's haunt,
Where oozes forth its first and feeble streamlet.
Old Play.

A PRIEST, ye cry, a priest ! — lame shepherds
    they,
How shall they gather in the straggling flock ?
Dumb dogs which bark not — how shall they
    compel
The loitering vagrants to the Master's fold ?
Fitter to bask before the blazing fire,
And snuff the mess neat-handed Phillis dresses,
Than on the snow-wreath battle with the wolf.
The Reformation.

Now let us sit in conclave. That these weeds
Be rooted from the vineyard of the Church,
That these foul tares be severed from the wheat,
We are, I trust, agreed. Yet how to do this,
Nor hurt the wholesome crop and tender vine-
    plants,
Craves good advisement.
The Reformation.

NAY, dally not with time, the wise man's trea-
    sure,
Though fools are lavish on 't — the fatal Fisher
Hooks souls while we waste moments.
Old Play.

You call this education, do you not ?
Why, 't is the forced march of a herd of bullocks
Before a shouting drover. The glad van
Move on at ease, and pause awhile to snatch
A passing morsel from the dewy greensward,
While all the blows, the oaths, the indignation,
Fall on the croupe of the ill-fated laggard
That cripples in the rear.
Old Play.

THERE 's something in that ancient superstition,
Which, erring as it is, our fancy loves.
The spring that, with its thousand crystal bub-
    bles,
Bursts from the bosom of some desert rock
In secret solitude, may well be deemed
The haunt of something purer, more refined,
And mightier than ourselves.
Old Play.

NAY, let me have the friends who eat my
    victuals
As various as my dishes. The feast 's naught,
Where one huge plate predominates. — John
    Plaintext,
He shall be mighty beef, our English staple;
The worthy Alderman, a buttered dumpling;
Yon pair of whiskered Cornets, ruffs and rees,
Their friend the Dandy, a green goose in sippets.
And so the board is spread at once and filled
On the same principle — Variety.
New Play.

HE strikes no coin, 't is true, but coins new
    phrases,
And vends them forth as knaves vend gilded
    counters,

Which wise men scorn and fools accept in pay-
    ment.
Old Play.

A COURTIER extraordinary, who by diet
Of meats and drinks, his temperate exercise,
Choice music, frequent bath, his horary shifts
Of shirts and waistcoats, means to immortalize
Mortality itself, and makes the essence
Of his whole happiness the trim of court.
Magnetic Lady.

Now choose thee, gallant, betwixt wealth and
    honor ;
There lies the pelf, in sum to bear thee through
The dance of youth and the turmoil of manhood,
Yet leave enough for age's chimney-corner ;
But an thou grasp to it, farewell Ambition !
Farewell each hope of bettering thy condition,
And raising thy low rank above the churls
That till the earth for bread !
Old Play.

INDIFFERENT, but indifferent — pshaw ! he
    doth it not
Like one who is his craft's master — ne'ertheless
I have seen a clown confer a bloody coxcomb
On one who was a master of defence.
Old Play.

YES, life hath left him — every busy thought,
Each fiery passion, every strong affection,
The sense of outward ill and inward sorrow,
Are fled at once from the pale trunk before
    me ;
And I have given that which spoke and moved,
Thought, acted, suffered, as a living man,
To be a ghastly form of bloody clay,
Soon the foul food for reptiles.
Old Play.

'T IS when the wound is stiffening with the cold,
The warrior first feels pain — 't is when the heat
And fiery fever of his soul is past,
The sinner feels remorse.
Old Play.

I 'LL walk on tiptoe ; arm my eye with caution,
My heart with courage, and my hand with
    weapon,
Like him who ventures on a lion's den.
Old Play.

Now, by Our Lady, Sheriff, 't is hard reckoning
That I, with every odds of birth and barony,
Should be detained here for the casual death
Of a wild forester, whose utmost having
Is but the brazen buckle of the belt
In which he sticks his hedge-knife.
Old Play.

You call it an ill angel — it may be so ;
But sure I am, among the ranks which fell,
'T is the first fiend e'er counselled man to rise,
And win the bliss the sprite himself had for-
    feited.
Old Play.

AT school I knew him — a sharp-witted youth,
Grave, thoughtful, and reserved amongst his
  mates,
Turning the hours of sport and food to labor,
Starving his body to inform his mind.
Old Play.

Now on my faith this gear is all entangled,
Like to the yarn-clew of the drowsy knitter,
Dragged by the frolic kitten through the cabin
While the good dame sits nodding o'er the fire —
Masters, attend; 't will crave some skill to
  clear it.
Old Play.

IT is not texts will do it — Church artillery
Are silenced soon by real ordnance,
And canons are but vain opposed to cannon.
Go, coin your crosier, melt your church plate
  down,
Bid the starved soldier banquet in your halls,
And quaff your long-saved hogsheads. — Turn
  them out
Thus primed with your good cheer, to guard
  your wall,
And they will venture for 't.
Old Play.

From The Abbot

IN the wild storm
The seaman hews his mast down, and the mer-
  chant
Heaves to the billows wares he once deemed
  precious:
So prince and peer, mid popular contentions,
Cast off their favorites.
Old Play.

THOU hast each secret of the household, Francis.
I dare be sworn thou hast been in the but-
  tery,
Steeping thy curious humor in fat ale,
And in the butler's tattle — ay, or chatting
With the glib waiting-woman o'er her comfits —
These bear the key to each domestic mystery.
Old Play.

THE sacred tapers' lights are gone,
Gray moss has clad the altar stone,
The holy image is o'erthrown,
  The bell has ceased to toll.
The long ribbed aisles are burst and shrunk,
The holy shrines to ruin sunk,
Departed is the pious monk,
  God's blessing on his soul !
Rediviva.

LIFE hath its May, and all is mirthful then:
The woods are vocal and the flowers all odor;
Its very blast has mirth in 't, and the maidens,
The while they don their cloaks to skreen their
  kirtles,
Laugh at the rain that wets them.
Old Play.

NAY, hear me, brother — I am elder, wiser,
And holier than thou; and age and wisdom
And holiness have peremptory claims,
And will be listened to.
Old Play.

NOT the wild billow, when it breaks its bar-
  rier —
Not the wild wind, escaping from its cavern —
Not the wild fiend, that mingles both together
And pours their rage upon the ripening harvest,
Can match the wild freaks of this mirthful
  meeting —
Comic, yet fearful — droll, and yet destructive.
The Conspiracy.

YOUTH ! thou wear'st to manhood now;
Darker lip and darker brow,
Statelier step, more pensive mien,
In thy face and gait are seen:
Thou must now brook midnight watches,
Take thy food and sport by snatches !
For the gambol and the jest
Thou wert wont to love the best,
Graver follies must thou follow,
But as senseless, false, and hollow.
Life, a Poem.

IT is and is not — 't is the thing I sought for,
Have kneeled for, prayed for, risked my fame
  and life for,
And yet it is not — no more than the shadow
Upon the hard, cold, flat, and polished mirror,
Is the warm, graceful, rounded, living substance
Which it presents in form and lineament.
Old Play.

GIVE me a morsel on the greensward rather,
Coarse as you will the cooking — let the fresh
  spring
Bubble beside my napkin — and the free birds,
Twittering and chirping, hop from bough to
  bough,
To claim the crumbs I leave for perquisites —
Your prison-feasts I like not.
The Woodman, a Drama.

'T IS a weary life this —
Vaults overhead, and grates and bars around
  me,
And my sad hours spent with as sad compan-
  ions,
Whose thoughts are brooding o'er their own
  mischances,
Far, far too deeply to take part in mine.
The Woodman.

AND when Love's torch hath set the heart in
  flame,
Comes Seignior Reason, with his saws and cau-
  tions,
Giving such aid as the old gray-beard Sexton,
Who from the church-vault drags his crazy
  engine,
To ply its dribbling ineffectual streamlet
Against a conflagration.
Old Play.

YES, it is she whose eyes looked on thy child-
hood,
And watched with trembling hope thy dawn of
youth,
That now, with these same eyeballs, dimmed
with age,
And dimmer yet with tears, sees thy dishonor.
Old Play.

IN some breasts passion lies concealed and silent,
Like war's swart powder in a castle vault,
Until occasion, like the linstock, lights it;
Then come at once the lightning and the thun-
der,
And distant echoes tell that all is rent asunder.
Old Play.

DEATH distant? — No, alas! he's ever with us,
And shakes the dart at us in all our actings:
He lurks within our cup while we're in health:
Sits by our sick-bed, mocks our medicines;
We cannot walk, or sit, or ride, or travel,
But Death is by to seize us when he lists.
The Spanish Father.

AY, Pedro, — come you here with mask and
lantern,
Ladder of ropes, and other moonshine tools —
Why, youngster, thou mayst cheat the old
Duenna,
Flatter the waiting-woman, bribe the valet;
But know, that I her father play the Gryphon,
Tameless and sleepless, proof to fraud or bribe,
And guard the hidden treasure of her beauty.
The Spanish Father.

IT is a time of danger, not of revel,
When churchmen turn to masquers.
The Spanish Father.

AY, sir — our ancient crown, in these wild times,
Oft stood upon a cast — the gamester's ducat,
So often staked and lost and then regained,
Scarce knew so many hazards.
The Spanish Father.

From Kenilworth

NOT serve two masters? — Here's a youth will
try it —
Would fain serve God, yet give the devil his due;
Says grace before he doth a deed of villany,
And returns his thanks devoutly when 't is
acted.
Old Play.

HE was a man
Versed in the world as pilot in his compass.
The needle pointed ever to that interest
Which was his loadstar, and he spread his sails
With vantage to the gale of others' passion.
The Deceiver, a Tragedy.

THIS is he
Who rides on the court-gale; controls its tides;

Knows all their secret shoals and fatal eddies;
Whose frown abases and whose smile exalts.
He shines like any rainbow — and, perchance,
His colors are as transient.
Old Play.

THIS is rare news thou tell'st me, my good fel-
low;
There are two bulls fierce battling on the green
For one fair heifer — if the one goes down,
The dale will be more peaceful, and the herd,
Which have small interest in their brulziement,
May pasture there in peace.
Old Play.

WELL, then, our course is chosen; spread the
sail, —
Heave oft the lead and mark the soundings well;
Look to the helm, good master; many a shoal
Marks this stern coast, and rocks where sits the
siren
Who, like ambition, lures men to their ruin.
The Shipwreck.

Now God be good to me in this wild pilgrimage!
All hope in human aid I cast behind me.
O, who would be a woman? who that fool,
A weeping, pining, faithful, loving woman?
She hath hard measure still where she hopes
kindest,
And all her bounties only make ingrates.
Love's Pilgrimage.

HARK! the bells summon and the bugle calls,
But she the fairest answers not; the tide
Of nobles and of ladies throngs the halls,
But she the loveliest must in secret hide.
What eyes were thine, proud prince, which in
the gleam
Of yon gay meteors lost that better sense
That o'er the glow-worm doth the star esteem,
And merit's modest blush o'er courtly inso-
lence?
The Glass Slipper.

WHAT, man, ne'er lack a draught when the full
can
Stands at thine elbow and craves emptying! —
Nay, fear not me, for I have no delight
To watch men's vices, since I have myself
Of virtue naught to boast of, — I'm a striker,
Would have the world strike with me, pellmell,
all.
Pandæmonium.

Now fare thee well, my master! if true service
Be guerdoned with hard looks, e'en cut the
tow-line,
And let our barks across the pathless flood
Hold different courses.
Shipwreck.

Now bid the steeple rock — she comes, she
comes!
Speak for us, bells! speak for us, shrill-tongued
tuckets!

Stand to the linstock, gunner; let thy cannon
Play such a peal as if a Paynim foe
Came stretched in turbaned ranks to storm the
    ramparts.
We will have pageants too; but that craves wit,
And I 'm a rough-hewn soldier.
The Virgin-Queen, a Tragi-Comedy.

THE wisest sovereigns err like private men,
And royal hand has sometimes laid the sword
Of chivalry upon a worthless shoulder,
Which better had been branded by the hang-
    man.
What then? Kings do their best, — and they
    and we
Must answer for the intent, and not the event.
Old Play.

HERE stands the victim — there the proud be-
    trayer,
E'en as the hind pulled down by strangling dogs
Lies at the hunter's feet, who courteous proffers
To some high dame, the Dian of the chase,
To whom he looks for guerdon, his sharp blade
To gash the sobbing throat.
The Woodman.

HIGH o'er the eastern steep the sun is beaming,
And darkness flies with her deceitful shadows;
So truth prevails o'er falsehood.
Old Play.

From The Pirate

'T IS not alone the scene — the man, Anselmo.
The man finds sympathies in these wild wastes
And roughly tumbling seas, which fairer views
And smoother waves deny him.
Ancient Drama.

SHE does no work by halves, yon raving ocean;
Engulfing those she strangles, her wild womb
Affords the mariners whom she hath dealt on
Their death at once and sepulchre.
Old Play.

THIS is a gentle trader and a prudent —
He 's no Autolycus, to blear your eye
With quips of worldly gauds and gamesome-
    ness,
But seasons all his glittering merchandise
With wholesome doctrine suited to the use,
As men sauce goose with sage and rosemary.
Old Play.

ALL your ancient customs
And long-descended usages I 'll change.
Ye shall not eat, nor drink, nor speak, nor move,
Think, look, or walk, as ye were wont to do;
Even your marriage-beds shall know mutation;
The bride shall have the stock, the groom the
    wall;
For all old practice will I turn and change,
And call it reformation — marry, will I!
'T is Even that we 're at Odds.

WE 'LL keep our customs — what is law it-
    self
But old established custom? What religion —
I mean, with one half of the men that use it —
Save the good use and wont that carries them
To worship how and where their fathers wor-
    shipped?
All things resolve in custom — we 'll keep ours.
Old Play.

I DO love these ancient ruins!
We never tread upon them but we set
Our foot upon some reverend history,
And questionless, here in this open court —
Which now lies naked to the injuries
Of stormy weather — some men lie interred,
Loved the Church so well and gave so largely
    to it,
They thought it should have canopied their
    bones
Till doomsday; — but all things have their
    end —
Churches and cities, which have diseases like
    to men,
Must have like death which we have.
Duchess of Malfy.

SEE yonder woman, whom our swains revere
And dread in secret, while they take her coun-
    sel
When sweetheart shall be kind, or when cross
    dame shall die;
Where lurks the thief who stole the silver
    tankard,
And how the pestilent murrain may be cured; —
This sage adviser 's mad, stark mad, my friend;
Yet in her madness hath the art and cunning
To wring fools' secrets from their inmost
    bosoms,
And pay inquirers with the coin they gave her.
Old Play.

WHAT ho, my jovial mates! come on! we 'll
    frolic it
Like fairies frisking in the merry moonshine,
Seen by the curtal friar, who, from some chris-
    tening
Or some blithe bridal, hies belated cell-ward —
He starts, and changes his bold bottle swagger
To churchman's pace professional, — and, ran-
    sacking
His treacherous memory for some holy hymn,
Finds but the roundel of the midnight catch.
Old Play.

I STRIVE like to the vessel in the tide-way,
Which, lacking favoring breeze, hath not the
    power
To stem the powerful current. — Even so,
Resolving daily to forsake my vices,
Habit, strong circumstance, renewed tempta-
    tion,
Sweep me to sea again. — O heavenly breath,
Fill thou my sails, and aid the feeble vessel,
Which ne'er can reach the blessed port without
    thee!
'T is Odds when Evens meet.

PARENTAL love, my friend, has power o'er
    wisdom,
And is the charm, which like the falconer's
    lure,
Can bring from heaven the highest soaring
    spirits. —
So, when famed Prosper doffed his magic
    robe
It was Miranda plucked it from his shoul-
    ders.
                    Old Play.

HARK to the insult loud, the bitter sneer,
The fierce threat answering to the brutal jeer;
Oaths fly like pistol-shots, and vengeful words
Clash with each other like conflicting swords. —
The robber's quarrel by such sounds is shown,
And true men have some chance to gain their
    own.
                  Captivity, a Poem.

OVER the mountains and under the waves,
Over the fountains and under the graves,
    Over floods that are deepest,
      Which Neptune obey,
    Over rocks that are steepest,
    Love will find out the way.
                  Old Song.

From The Fortunes of Nigel

Now Scot and English are agreed,
And Saunders hastes to cross the Tweed,
Where, such the splendors that attend him,
His very mother scarce had kenned him.
His metamorphosis behold
From Glasgow frieze to cloth of gold;
His back-sword with the iron-hilt,
To rapier fairly hatched and gilt;
Was ever seen a gallant braver!
His very bonnet's grown a beaver.
                The Reformation.

THIS, sir, is one among the Seigniory,
Has wealth at will, and will to use his wealth,
And wit to increase it. Marry, his worst folly
Lies in a thriftless sort of charity,
That goes a-gadding sometimes after objects
Which wise men will not see when thrust upon
    them.
                The Old Couple.

AY, sir, the clouted shoe hath ofttimes craft
    in 't,
As says the rustic proverb; and your citizen,
In 's grogram suit, gold chain, and well-blacked
    shoes,
Bears under his flat cap ofttimes a brain
Wiser than burns beneath the cap and feather,
Or seethes within the statesman's velvet night-
    cap.
              Read me my Riddle.

WHEREFORE come ye not to court?
Certain 't is the rarest sport;
There are silks and jewels glistening,

Prattling fools and wise men listening,
Bullies among brave men justling,
Beggars amongst nobles bustling;
Low-breathed talkers, minion lispers,
Cutting honest throats by whispers;
Wherefore come ye not to court?
Skelton swears 't is glorious sport.
          Skelton Skeltonizeth.

O, I DO know him — 't is the mouldy lemon
Which our court wits will wet their lips withal,
When they would sauce their honied conversa-
    tion
With somewhat sharper flavor. — Marry, sir,
That virtue 's wellnigh left him — all the juice
That was so sharp and poignant is squeezed
    out;
While the poor rind, although as sour as ever,
Must season soon the draff we give our grunters,
For two-legged things are weary on 't.
        The Chamberlain, a Comedy.

THINGS needful we have thought on; but the
    thing
Of all most needful — that which Scripture
    terms,
As if alone it merited regard,
The ONE thing needful — that 's yet unconsid-
    ered.
              The Chamberlain.

AH! mark the matron well — and laugh not,
    Harry,
At her old steeple-hat and velvet guard —
I 've called her like the ear of Dionysius;
I mean that ear-formed vault, built o'er the
    dungeon
To catch the groans and discontented murmurs
Of his poor bondsmen. — Even so doth Martha
Drink up for her own purpose all that passes,
Or is supposed to pass, in this wide city —
She can retail it too, if that her profit
Shall call on her to do so; and retail it
For your advantage, so that you can make
Your profit jump with hers.
              The Conspiracy.

BID not thy fortune troll upon the wheels
Of yonder dancing cups of mottled bone;
And drown it not, like Egypt's royal harlot,
Dissolving her rich pearl in the brimmed wine-
    cup.
These are the arts, Lothario, which shrink acres
Into brief yards — bring sterling pounds to
    farthings,
Credit to infamy: and the poor gull,
Who might have lived an honored, easy life,
To ruin and an unregarded grave.
              The Changes.

          THIS is the very barn-yard
Where muster daily the prime cocks o' the
    game,
Ruffle their pinions, crow till they are hoarse,
And spar about a barleycorn. Here, too,
    chickens,
The callow unfledged brood of forward folly,

Learn first to rear the crest, and aim the spur,
And tune their note like full-plumed Chanti-
    cleer.
The Bear Garden.

LET the proud salmon gorge the feathered hook,
Then strike, and then you have him. — He will
    wince ;
Spin out your line that it shall whistle from you
Some twenty yards or so, yet you shall have
    him —
Marry ! you must have patience — the stout rock
Which is his trust hath edges something sharp ;
And the deep pool hath ooze and sludge enough
To mar your fishing — 'less you are more care-
    ful.
Albion, or the Double Kings.

GIVE way — give way — I must and will have
    justice,
And tell me not of privilege and place ;
Where I am injured, there I 'll sue redress.
Look to it, every one who bars my access ;
I have a heart to feel the injury,
A hand to right myself, and, by my honor,
That hand shall grasp what gray-beard Law
    denies me.
The Chamberlain.

COME hither, young one — Mark me ! Thou art
    now
'Mongst men o' the sword, that live by reputa-
    tion
More than by constant income — Single-suited
They are, I grant you ; yet each single suit
Maintains, on the rough guess, a thousand fol-
    lowers —
And they be men who, hazarding their all,
Needful apparel, necessary income,
And human body, and immortal soul,
Do in the very deed but hazard nothing —
So strictly is that ALL bound in reversion ;
Clothes to the broker, income to the usurer, —
And body to disease, and soul to the foul fiend ;
Who laughs to see Soldadoes and fooladoes
Play better than himself his game on earth.
The Mohocks.

Mother. What ! dazzled by a flash of Cupid's
    mirror,
With which the boy, as mortal urchins wont,
Flings back the sunbeam in the eye of passen-
    gers —
Then laughs to see them stumble !
Daughter.   Mother ! no —
It was a lightning-flash which dazzled me,
And never shall these eyes see true again.
Beef and Pudding, an Old English Comedy.

BY this good light, a wench of matchless mettle !
This were a leaguer-lass to love a soldier,
To bind his wounds, and kiss his bloody brow,
And sing a roundel as she helped to arm him,
Though the rough foeman's drums were beat
    so nigh
They seemed to bear the burden.
Old Play.

CREDIT me, friend, it hath been ever thus
Since the ark rested on Mount Ararat.
False man hath sworn, and woman hath be-
    lieved —
Repented and reproached, and then believed
    once more.
The New World.

ROVE not from pole to pole — the man lives
    here
Whose razor 's only equalled by his beer ;
And where, in either sense, the cockney-put
May if he pleases, get confounded *cut*.
On the Sign of an Alehouse kept by a Barber.

CHANCE will not do the work — Chance sends
    the breeze ;
But if the pilot slumber at the helm,
The very wind that wafts us towards the port
May dash us on the shelves. — The steersman's
    part is vigilance,
Blow it or rough or smooth.
Old Play.

THIS is the time — Heaven's maiden-sentinel
Hath quitted her high watch — the lesser
    spangles
Are paling one by one ; give me the ladder
And the short lever — bid Anthony
Keep with his carabine the wicket-gate ;
And do thou bare thy knife and follow me,
For we will in and do it — darkness like this
Is dawning of our fortunes.
Old Play.

DEATH finds us mid our playthings — snatches
    us,
As a cross nurse might do a wayward child,
From all our toys and baubles. His rough call
Unlooses all our favorite ties on earth ;
And well if they are such as may be answered
In yonder world, where all is judged of truly.
Old Play.

GIVE us good voyage, gentle stream — we stun
    not
Thy sober ear with sounds of revelry,
Wake not the slumbering echoes of thy banks
With voice of flute and horn — we do but seek
On the broad pathway of thy swelling bosom
To glide in silent safety.
The Double Bridal.

THIS way lie safety and a sure retreat ;
Yonder lie danger, shame, and punishment.
Most welcome danger then — nay, let me say,
Though spoke with swelling heart — welcome
    e'en shame ;
And welcome punishment — for, call me guilty,
I do but pay the tax that's due to justice ;
And call me guiltless, then that punishment
Is shame to those alone who do inflict it.
The Tribunal.

How fares the man on whom good men would
    look
With eyes where scorn and censure combated,

But that kind Christian love hath taught the
   lesson —
That they who merit most contempt and hate
Do most deserve our pity —
                     Old Play.

MARRY, come up, sir, with your gentle blood !
Here 's a red stream beneath this coarse blue
   doublet
That warms the heart as kindly as if drawn
From the far source of old Assyrian kings,
Who first made mankind subject to their sway.
                     Old Play.

WE are not worse at once — the course of evil
Begins so slowly and from such slight source,
An infant's hand might stem its breach with
   clay ;
But let the stream get deeper, and philosophy —
Ay, and religion too — shall strive in vain
To turn the headlong torrent.
                     Old Play.

From *Peveril of the Peak*

WHY then, we will have bellowing of beeves,
Broaching of barrels, brandishing of spigots ;
Blood shall flow freely, but it shall be gore
Of herds and flocks and venison and poultry,
Joined to the brave heart's-blood of John-a-
   Barleycorn !
                     Old Play.

No, sir, I will not pledge — I'm one of those
Who think good wine needs neither bush nor
   preface
To make it welcome. If you doubt my word,
Fill the quart-cup, and see if I will choke on 't.
                     Old Play.

YOU shall have no worse prison than my chamber,
Nor jailer than myself.
                 The Captain.

Ascasto.   Can she not speak ?
Oswald. If speech be only in accented sounds,
Framed by the tongue and lips, the maiden 's
   dumb ;
But if by quick and apprehensive look,
By motion, sign, and glance, to give each mean-
   ing,
Express as clothed in language, be termed
   speech,
She hath that wondrous faculty ; for her eyes,
Like the bright stars of heaven, can hold dis-
   course,
Though it be mute and soundless.
                     Old Play.

THIS is a love meeting ? See the maiden mourns,
And the sad suitor bends his looks on earth.
There 's more hath passed between them than
   belongs
To Love's sweet sorrows.
                     Old Play.

Now, hoist the anchor, mates — and let the
   sails
Give their broad bosom to the buxom wind,
Like lass that woos a lover.
                     Anonymous.

HE was a fellow in a peasant's garb ;
Yet one could censure you a woodcock's carv-
   ing,
Like any courtier at the ordinary.
                The Ordinary.

WE meet, as men see phantoms in a dream,
Which glide and sigh and sign and move their
   lips,
But make no sound ; or, if they utter voice,
'T is but a low and undistinguished moaning,
Which has nor word nor sense of uttered sound.
                The Chieftain.

THE course of human life is changeful still
As is the fickle wind and wandering rill ;
Or, like the light dance which the wild-breeze
   weaves
Amidst the faded race of fallen leaves ;
Which now its breath bears down, now tosses
   high,
Beats to the earth, or wafts to middle sky.
Such, and so varied, the precarious play
Of fate with man, frail tenant of a day !
                 Anonymous.

NECESSITY — thou best of peacemakers,
As well as surest prompter of invention —
Help us to composition !
                     Anonymous.

THIS is some creature of the elements
Most like your sea-gull. He can wheel and
   whistle
His screaming song, e'en when the storm is
   loudest —
Take for his sheeted couch the restless foam
Of the wild wave-crest — slumber in the calm,
And dally with the storm. Yet 't is a gull,
An arrant gull, with all this.
                The Chieftain.

I FEAR the devil worst when gown and cas-
   sock,
Or in the lack of them, old Calvin's cloak,
Conceals his cloven hoof.
                     Anonymous.

'T IS the black ban-dog of our jail — pray look
   on him,
But at a wary distance — rouse him not —
He bays not till he worries.
          The Black Dog of Newgate.

'SPEAK not of niceness, when there 's chance of
   wreck,'
The captain said, as ladies writhed their
   neck
To see the dying dolphin flap the deck :
'If we go down, on us these gentry sup ;
We dine upon them, if we haul them up.

Wise men applaud us when we eat the eaters,
As the devil laughs when keen folks cheat the
   cheaters.'
The Sea Voyage.

CONTENTIONS fierce,
Ardent, and dire, spring from no petty cause.
Albion.

HE came amongst them like a new-raised spirit,
To speak of dreadful judgments that impend,
And of the wrath to come.
The Reformer.

AND some for safety took the dreadful leap ;
Some for the voice of Heaven seemed calling on
   them ;
Some for advancement, or for lucre's sake —
I leaped in frolic.
The Dream.

HIGH feasting was there there — the gilded
   roofs
Rung to the wassail-health — the dancer's step
Sprung to the chord responsive — the gay game-
   ster
To fate's disposal flung his heap of gold,
And laughed alike when it increased or les-
   sened :
Such virtue hath court-air to teach us patience
Which schoolmen preach in vain.
Why come ye not to Court ?

HERE stand I tight and trim,
Quick of eye, though little of limb ;
He who denieth the word I have spoken,
Betwixt him and me shall lances be broken.
Lay of the Little John de Saintré.

From Quentin Durward

PAINTERS show Cupid blind — hath Hymen
   eyes ?
Or is his sight warped by those spectacles
Which parents, guardians, and advisers lend
   him
That he may look through them on lands and
   mansions,
On jewels, gold, and all such rich donations,
And see their value ten times magnified ? —
Methinks 't will brook a question.
The Miseries of Enforced Marriage.

THIS is a lecturer so skilled in policy
That — no disparagement to Satan's cunning —
He well might read a lesson to the devil,
And teach the old seducer new temptations.
Old Play.

I SEE thee yet, fair France — thou favored
   land
Of art and nature — thou art still before me ;
Thy sons, to whom their labor is a sport,
So well thy grateful soil returns its tribute ;
Thy sun-burnt daughters, with their laughing
   eyes

And glossy raven-locks. But, favored France,
Thou hast had many a tale of woe to tell,
In ancient times as now.
Anonymous.

HE was a son of Egypt, as he told me,
And one descended from those dread magicians
Who waged rash war, when Israel dwelt in
   Goshen,
With Israel and her Prophet — matching rod
With his the son of Levi's — and encounter-
   ing
Jehovah's miracles with incantations,
Till upon Egypt came the Avenging Angel,
And those proud sages wept for their first-
   born,
As wept the unlettered peasant.
Anonymous.

RESCUE or none, Sir Knight, I am your captive ;
Deal with me what your nobleness suggests —
Thinking the chance of war may one day place
   you
Where I must now be reckoned — i' the roll
Of melancholy prisoners.
Anonymous.

No human quality is so well wove
In warp and woof but there 's some flaw in it ;
I 've known a brave man fly a shepherd's cur,
A wise man so demean him drivelling idiocy
Had wellnigh been ashamed on 't. For your
   crafty,
Your worldly-wise man, he, above the rest,
Weaves his own snares so fine he 's often caught
   in them.
Old Play.

WHEN Princes meet, astrologers may mark it
An ominous conjunction, full of boding,
Like that of Mars with Saturn.
Old Play.

THY time is not yet out — the devil thou servest
Has not as yet deserted thee. He aids
The friends who drudge for him, as the blind
   man
Was aided by the guide, who lent his shoulder
O'er rough and smooth, until he reached the
   brink
Of the fell precipice — then hurled him down-
   ward.
Old Play.

OUR counsels waver like the unsteady bark,
That reels amid the strife of meeting cur-
   rents.
Old Play.

HOLD fast thy truth, young soldier. — Gentle
   maiden,
Keep you your promise plight — leave age its
   subtleties,
And gray-haired policy its maze of falsehood ;
But be you candid as the morning sky,
Ere the high sun sucks vapors up to stain it.
The Trial.

From Saint Ronan's Well

QUIS novus hic hospes ?
    Dido apud Virgilium.

CH'M-MAID ! — The Gen'man in the front parlor !
    Boots's free Translation of the Æneid.

THERE must be government in all society —
Bees have their Queen, and stag herds have
    their leader ;
Rome had her Consuls, Athens had her Archons,
And we, sir, have our Managing Committee.
    The Album of Saint Ronan's.

COME, let me have thy counsel, for I need it ;
Thou art of those, who better help their friends
With sage advice, than usurers with gold,
Or brawlers with their swords — I 'll trust to
    thee,
For I ask only from thee words, not deeds.
    The Devil hath met his Match.

NEAREST of blood should still be next in love ;
And when I see these happy children playing,
While William gathers flowers for Ellen's ring-
    lets
And Ellen dresses flies for William's angle,
I scarce can think that in advancing life
Coldness, unkindness, interest, or suspicion
Will e'er divide that unity so sacred,
Which Nature bound at birth.
    Anonymous.

OH ! you would be a vestal maid, I warrant,
The bride of Heaven — Come — we may shake
    your purpose :
For here I bring in hand a jolly suitor
Hath ta'en degrees in the seven sciences
That ladies love best — He is young and noble,
Handsome and valiant, gay and rich, and
    liberal.
    The Nun.

IT comes — it wrings me in my parting hour,
The long-hid crime — the well-disguised guilt.
Bring me some holy priest to lay the spectre !
    Old Play.

Sedet post equitem atra cura —

STILL though the headlong cavalier,
O'er rough and smooth, in wild career,
    Seems racing with the wind ;
His sad companion — ghastly pale,
And darksome as a widow's veil,
    CARE — keeps her seat behind.
    Horace.

WHAT sheeted ghost is wandering through the
    storm ?
For never did a maid of middle earth
Choose such a time or spot to vent her sorrows.
    Old Play.

HERE come we to our close — for that which
    follows
Is but the tale of dull, unvaried misery.

Steep crags and headlong lins may court the
    pencil
Like sudden haps, dark plots, and strange ad-
    ventures ;
But who would paint the dull and fog-wrapt
    moor
In its long tract of sterile desolation ?
    Old Play.

From The Betrothed

IN Madoc's tent the clarion sounds,
    With rapid clangor hurried far ;
Each hill and dale the note rebounds,
    But when return the sons of war ?
Thou, born of stern Necessity,
Dull Peace ! the valley yields to thee,
And owns thy melancholy sway.
    Welsh Poem.

O, SADLY shines the morning sun
    On leaguered castle wall,
When bastion, tower, and battlement
    Seem nodding to their fall.
    Old Ballad.

Now, all ye ladies of fair Scotland,
    And ladies of England that happy would
    prove,
Marry never for houses, nor marry for land,
    Nor marry for nothing but only love.
    Family Quarrels.

Too much rest is rust,
    There 's ever cheer in changing ;
We tyne by too much trust,
    So we 'll be up and ranging.
    Old Song.

RING out the merry bells, the bride approaches.
The blush upon her cheek has shamed the
    morning,
For that is dawning palely. Grant, good saints,
These clouds betoken naught of evil omen !
    Old Play.

Julia.   Gentle sir,
You are our captive — but we 'll use you so,
That you shall think your prison joys may
    match
Whate'er your liberty hath known of plea-
    sure.
    Roderick. No, fairest, we have trifled here
    too long :
And, lingering to see your roses blossom,
I 've let my laurels wither.
    Old Play.

From The Talisman

THIS is the Prince of Leeches ; fever, plague,
Cold rheum, and hot podagra, do but look on
    him,
And quit their grasp upon the tortured sinews.
    Anonymous.

ONE thing is certain in our Northern land,
Allow that birth or valor, wealth or wit,
Give each precedence to their possessor,
Envy, that follows on such eminence
As comes the lyme-hound on the roebuck's
    trace,
Shall pull them down each one.
Sir David Lindsay.

YOU talk of Gayety and Innocence !
The moment when the fatal fruit was eaten,
They parted ne'er to meet again ; and Malice
Has ever since been playmate to light Gayety
From the first moment when the smiling in-
    fant
Destroys the flower or butterfly he toys with,
To the last chuckle of the dying miser,
Who on his death-bed laughs his last to hear
His wealthy neighbor has become a bankrupt.
Old Play.

'T IS not her sense — for sure, in that
    There 's nothing more than common ;
And all her wit is only chat,
    Like any other woman.
Song.

WERE every hair upon his head a life,
And every life were to be supplicated
By numbers equal to those hairs quadrupled,
Life after life should out like waning stars
Before the daybreak — or as festive lamps,
Which have lent lustre to the midnight revel,
Each after each are quenched when guests
    depart. *Old Play.*

MUST we then sheath our still victorious sword ;
Turn back our forward step, which ever trode
O'er foemen's necks the onward path of glory ;
Unclasp the mail, which with a solemn vow
In God's own house we hung upon our shoul-
    ders ;
That vow, as unaccomplished as the promise
Which village nurses make to still their chil-
    dren,
And after think no more of ?
The Crusade, a Tragedy.

WHEN beauty leads the lion in her toils,
Such are her charms he dare not raise his mane,
Far less expand the terror of his fangs ;
So great Alcides made his club a distaff,
And spun to please fair Omphale.
Anonymous.

MID these wild scenes Enchantment waves her
    hand,
To change the face of the mysterious land ;
Till the bewildering scenes around us seem
The vain productions of a feverish dream.
Astolpho, a Romance.

A GRAIN of dust
Soiling our cup, will make our sense reject
Fastidiously the draught which we did thirst
    for ;
A rusted nail, placed near the faithful compass,

Will sway it from the truth and wreck the
    argosy.
Even this small cause of anger and disgust
Will break the bonds of amity 'mongst princes
And wreck their noblest purposes.
The Crusade.

THE tears I shed must ever fall !
    I weep not for an absent swain,
For time may happier hours recall,
    And parted lovers meet again.

I weep not for the silent dead,
    Their pains are past, their sorrows o'er,
And those that loved their steps must tread,
    When death shall join to part no more.

But worse than absence, worse than death,
    She wept her lover's sullied fame,
And, fired with all the pride of birth,
    She wept a soldier's injured name.
Ballad.

From Woodstock

COME forth, old man — thy daughter's side
    Is now the fitting place for thee :
When Time hath quelled the oak's bold pride,
    The youthful tendril yet may hide
    The ruins of the parent tree.

Now, ye wild blades, that make loose inns your
    stage,
To vapor forth the acts of this sad age,
Stout Edgehill fight, the Newberries and the
    West,
And northern clashes, where you still fought
    best ;
Your strange escapes, your dangers void of
    fear,
When bullets flew between the head and ear,
Whether you fought by Damme or the Spirit,
    Of you I speak.
Legend of Captain Jones.

YON path of greensward
Winds round by sparry grot and gay pavilion ;
There is no flint to gall thy tender foot,
There 's ready shelter from each breeze or
    shower. —
But Duty guides not that way — see her stand,
With wand entwined with amaranth, near yon
    cliffs.
Oft where she leads thy blood must mark thy
    footsteps,
Oft where she leads thy head must bear the
    storm,
And thy shrunk form endure heat, cold, and
    hunger ;
But she will guide thee up to noble heights,
Which he who gains seems native of the sky,
While earthly things lie stretched beneath his
    feet,
Diminished, shrunk, and valueless —
Anonymous.

My tongue pads slowly under this new language,
And starts and stumbles at these uncouth
    phrases.
They may be great in worth and weight, but
    hang
Upon the native glibness of my language
Like Saul's plate-armor on the shepherd boy,
Encumbering and not arming him.
                                    J. B.

Here we have one head
Upon two bodies — your two-headed bullock
Is but an ass to such a prodigy.
These two have but one meaning, thought, and
    counsel ;
And when the single noddle has spoke out,
The four legs scrape assent to it.
                                Old Play.

Deeds are done on earth
Which have their punishment ere the earth
    closes
Upon the perpetrators.   Be it the working
Of the remorse-stirred fancy, or the vision,
Distinct and real, of unearthly being,
All ages witness that beside the couch
Of the fell homicide oft stalks the ghost
Of him he slew, and shows the shadowy wound.
                                Old Play.

We do that in our zeal
Our calmer moments are afraid to answer.
                                Anonymous.

The deadliest snakes are those which, twined
    'mongst flowers,
Blend their bright coloring with the varied
    blossoms,
Their fierce eyes glittering like the spangled
    dew-drop ;
In all so like what nature has most harmless,
That sportive innocence, which dreads no dan-
    ger,
Is poisoned unawares.
                                Old Play.

From Chronicles of the Canongate

Were ever such two loving friends ! —
How could they disagree ?

O, thus it was: he loved him dear,
    And thought but to requite him ;
And, having no friend left but he,
    He did resolve to fight him.
                                Duke upon Duke.

There are times
When Fancy plays her gambols, in despite
Even of our watchful senses, when in sooth
Substance seems shadow, shadow substance
    seems,
When the broad, palpable, and marked parti-
    tion
'T wixt that which is and is not, seems dissolved,
As if the mental eye gained power to gaze

Beyond the limits of the existing world.
Such hours of shadowy dreams I better love
Than all the gross realities of life.
                                Anonymous.

From The Fair Maid of Perth

The ashes here of murdered kings
    Beneath my footsteps sleep ;
And yonder lies the scene of death
    Where Mary learned to weep.
                        Captain Marjoribanks.

' Behold the Tiber ! ' the vain Roman cried,
Viewing the ample Tay from Baiglie's side ;
But where 's the Scot that would the vaunt re-
    pay,
And hail the puny Tiber for the Tay.
                                Anonymous.

Fair is the damsel, passing fair —
    Sunny at distance gleams her smile !
Approach — the cloud of woful care
    Hangs trembling in her eye the while.
                            Lucinda, a Ballad.

O for a draught of power to steep
The soul of agony in sleep !
                                Bertha.

Lo ! where he lies embalmed in gore,
    His wound to Heaven cries ;
The floodgates of his blood implore
    For vengeance from the skies.
                            Uranus and Psyche.

From Anne of Geierstein

Cursed be the gold and silver which persuade
Weak man to follow far fatiguing trade.
The lily, peace, outshines the silver store,
And life is dearer than the golden ore.
Yet money tempts us o'er the desert brown
To every distant mart and wealthy town.
                        Hassan, or the Camel-Driver.

I was one
Who loved the greenwood bank and lowing
    herd,
The russet prize, the lowly peasant's life,
Seasoned with sweet content, more than the
    halls
Where revellers feast to fever-height.   Believe
    me,
There ne'er was poison mixed in maple bowl.
                                Anonymous.

When we two meet, we meet like rushing tor-
    rents ;
Like warring winds, like flames from various
    points,
That mate each other's fury — there is naught
Of elemental strife, were fiends to guide it,
Can match the wrath of man.
                                Frenaud.

WE know not when we sleep nor when we wake.
Visions distinct and perfect cross our eye,
Which to the slumberer seem realities;
And while they waked, some men have seen
such sights
As set at naught the evidence of sense,
And left them well persuaded they were dream-
ing.
Anonymous.

THESE be the adept's doctrines — every ele-
ment
Is peopled with its separate race of spirits.
The airy Sylphs on the blue ether float;
Deep in the earthy cavern skulks the Gnome;
The sea-green Naiad skims the ocean-billow,
And the fierce fire is yet a friendly home
To its peculiar sprite — the Salamander.
Anonymous.

UPON the Rhine, upon the Rhine they cluster,
The grapes of juice divine,
Which make the soldier's jovial courage mus-
ter;
'O, blessed be the Rhine!
Drinking Song.

TELL me not of it — I could ne'er abide
The mummery of all that forced civility.
'Pray, seat yourself, my lord.' With cringing
hams
The speech is spoken, and with bended knee
Heard by the smiling courtier. — 'Before you,
sir?
It must be on the earth, then.' Hang it all!
The pride which cloaks itself in such poor fashion
Is scarcely fit to swell a beggar's bosom.
Old Play.

A MIRTHFUL man he was — the snows of age
Fell, but they did not chill him. Gayety,
Even in life's closing, touched his teeming brain
With such wild visions as the setting sun
Raises in front of some hoar glacier,
Painting the bleak ice with a thousand hues.
Old Play.

AY, this is he who wears the wreath of bays
Wove by Apollo and the Sisters Nine,
Which Jove's dread lightning scathes not. He
hath doft
The cumbrous helm of steel, and flung aside
The yet more galling diadem of gold;
While, with a leafy circlet round his brows,
He reigns the King of Lovers and of Poets.

WANT you a man
Experienced in the world and its affairs?
Here he is for your purpose. — He's a monk.
He hath forsworn the world and all its work —
The rather that he knows it passing well,
'Special the worst of it, for he's a monk.
Old Play.

TOLL, toll the bell!
Greatness is o'er,
The heart has broke,

To ache no more;
An unsubstantial pageant all —
Drop o'er the scene the funeral pall.
Old Poem.

HERE's a weapon now
Shall shake a conquering general in his tent,
A monarch on his throne, or reach a prelate,
However holy be his offices,
E'en while he serves the altar.
Old Play.

From Count Robert of Paris

Othus. This superb successor
Of the earth's mistress, as thou vainly speakest,
Stands midst these ages as, on the wide ocean,
The last spared fragment of a spacious land,
That in some grand and awful ministration
Of mighty nature has engulfed been,
Doth lift aloft its dark and rocky cliffs
O'er the wild waste around, and sadly frowns
In lonely majesty.
Constantine Paleologus, Scene 1.

HERE, youth, thy foot unbrace,
Here, youth, thy brow unbraid,
Each tribute that may grace
The threshold here be paid.
Walk with the stealthy pace
Which Nature teaches deer,
When, echoing in the chase,
The hunter's horn they hear.
The Court.

THE storm increases — 'tis no sunny shower,
Fostered in the moist breast of March or April,
Or such as parched Summer cools his lip with;
Heaven's windows are flung wide; the inmost
deeps
Call in hoarse greeting one upon another;
On comes the flood in all its foaming horrors,
And where's the dike shall stop it!
The Deluge, a Poem.

VAIN man! thou mayst esteem thy love as fair
As fond hyperboles suffice to raise.
She may be all that's matchless in her person,
And all-divine in soul to match her body;
But take this from me — thou shalt never call
her
Superior to her sex while *one* survives
And I am her true votary.
Old Play.

THROUGH the vain webs which puzzle sophists'
skill,
Plain sense and honest meaning work their
way;
So sink the varying clouds upon the hill
When the clear dawning brightens into day.
Dr. Watts.

BETWEEN the foaming jaws of the white torrent
The skilful artist draws a sudden mound;

By level long he subdivides their strength,
Stealing the waters from their rocky bed,
First to diminish what he means to conquer ;
Then, for the residue he forms a road,
Easy to keep, and painful to desert,
And guiding to the end the planner aimed at.
The Engineer.

THESE were wild times — the antipodes of ours :
Ladies were there who oftener saw themselves
In the broad lustre of a foeman's shield
Than in a mirror, and who rather sought
To match themselves in battle than in dalliance
To meet a lover's onset. — But though Nature
Was outraged thus, she was not overcome.
Feudal Times.

WITHOUT a ruin, broken, tangled, cumbrous,
Within it was a little paradise,
Where Taste had made her dwelling. Statuary.
First-born of human art, moulded her images
And bade men mark and worship.
Anonymous.

THE parties met. The wily, wordy Greek,
Weighing each word, and canvassing each syl-
lable,
Evading, arguing, equivocating.
And the stern Frank came with his two-hand
sword,
Watching to see which way the balance sways,
That he may throw it in and turn the scales.
Palestine.

STRANGE ape of man ! who loathes thee while
he scorns thee ;
Half a reproach to us and half a jest.
What fancies can be ours ere we have pleasure
In viewing our own form, our pride and passions,
Reflected in a shape grotesque as thine !
Anonymous.

'T IS strange that in the dark sulphureous mine
Where wild ambition piles its ripening stores
Of slumbering thunder, Love will interpose
His tiny torch, and cause the stern explosion
To burst when the deviser 's least aware.
Anonymous.

ALL is prepared — the chambers of the mine
Are crammed with the combustible, which,
harmless
While yet unkindled as the sable sand,
Needs but a spark to change its nature so
That he who wakes it from its slumbrous mood
Dreads scarce the explosion less than he who
knows
That 't is his towers which meet its fury.
Anonymous.

HEAVEN knows its time ; the bullet has its
billet,
Arrow and javelin each its destined purpose ;
The fated beasts of Nature's lower strain
Have each their separate task.
Old Play.

From Castle Dangerous

A TALE of sorrow, for your eyes may weep ;
A tale of horror, for your flesh may tingle ;
A tale of wonder, for the eyebrows arch,
And the flesh curdles if you read it rightly.
Old Play.

WHERE is he ? Has the deep earth swallowed
him ?
Or hath he melted like some airy phantom
That shuns the approach of morn and the young
sun ?
Or hath he wrapt him in Cimmerian darkness,
And passed beyond the circuit of the sight
With things of the night's shadows ?
Anonymous.

THE way is long, my children, long and rough —
The moors are dreary and the woods are dark ;
But he that creeps from cradle on to grave,
Unskilled save in the velvet course of fortune,
Hath missed the discipline of noble hearts.
Old Play.

HIS talk was of another world — his bodements
Strange, doubtful, and mysterious ; those who
heard him
Listened as to a man in feverish dreams,
Who speaks of other objects than the present,
And mutters like to him who sees a vision.
Old Play.

CRY the wild war-note, let the champions pass,
Do bravely each, and God defend the right ;
Upon Saint Andrew thrice can they thus cry,
And thrice they shout on height,
And then marked them on the Englishmen,
As I have told you right.
Saint George the bright, our ladies' knight,
To name they were full fain ;
Our Englishmen they cried on height,
And thrice they shout again.
Old Ballad.

III. NOTES AND ILLUSTRATIONS

[These notes, except when enclosed in brack-
ets, are from editions prepared or supervised by
Scott.]

Page 5. THE WILD HUNTSMAN.
The tradition upon which it is founded bears,
that formerly a Wildgrave, or keeper of a royal
forest, named Faulkenburg, was so much addicted to the pleasures of the chase, and otherwise so extremely profligate and cruel, that he
not only followed this unhallowed amusement
on the Sabbath, and other days consecrated to
religious duty, but accompanied it with the
most unheard-of oppression upon the poor peasants, who were under his vassalage. When
this second Nimrod died, the people adopted a
superstition, founded probably on the many va-

rious uncouth sounds heard in the depth of a German forest, during the silence of the night. They conceived they still heard the cry of the Wildgrave's hounds; and the well-known cheer of the deceased hunter, the sounds of his horses' feet, and the rustling of the branches before the game, the pack, and the sportsmen, are also distinctly discriminated; but the phantoms are rarely, if ever, visible. Once, as a benighted *Chasseur* heard this infernal chase pass by him, at the sound of the halloo, with which the Spectre Huntsman cheered his hounds, he could not refrain from crying, ' *Gluck zu Falkenburgh!* ' (Good sport to ye, Falkenburgh!) 'Dost thou wish me good sport?' answered a hoarse voice; ' thou shalt share the game;' and there was thrown at him what seemed to be a huge piece of foul carrion. The daring *Chasseur* lost two of his best horses soon after, and never perfectly recovered the personal effects of this ghostly greeting. This tale, though told with some variations, is universally believed all over Germany.

The French had a similar tradition concerning an aërial hunter who infested the forest of Fontainebleau. He was sometimes visible; when he appeared as a huntsman, surrounded with dogs, a tall grisly figure. Some account of him may be found in Sully's *Memoirs*, who says he was called *Le Grand Veneur*. At one time he chose to hunt so near the palace, that the attendants, and, if I mistake not, Sully himself, came out into the court, supposing it was the sound of the king returning from the chase. This phantom is elsewhere called St. Hubert.

The superstition seems to have been very general, as appears from the following fine poetical description of this phantom chase, as it was heard in the wilds of Ross-shire: —

' Ere since of old, the haughty thanes of Ross —
So to the simple swain tradition tells —
Were wont with clans, and ready vassals thronged,
To wake the bounding stag, or guilty wolf,
There oft is heard, at midnight, or at noon,
Beginning faint, but rising still more loud,
And nearer, voice of hunters, and of hounds,
And horns, hoarse winded, blowing far and keen : —
Forthwith the hubbub multiplies; the gale
Labors with wilder shrieks, and rifer din
Of hot pursuit; the broken cry of deer
Mangled by throttling dogs; the shouts of men,
And hoofs, thick beating on the hollow hill.
Sudden the grazing heifer in the vale
Starts at the noise, and both the herdsman's ears
Tingle with inward dread. Aghast, he eyes
The mountain's height, and all the ridges round,
Yet not one trace of living wight discerns,
Nor knows, o'erawed, and trembling as he stands,
To what, or whom, he owes his idle fear,
To ghost, to witch, to fairy, or to fiend ;
But wonders, and no end of wondering finds.'
Albania — reprinted in *Scottish Descriptive Poems*,
     pp. 167, 168.

A posthumous miracle of Father Lesley, a Scottish capuchin, related to his being buried on a hill haunted by these unearthly cries of hounds and huntsmen. After his sainted relics had been deposited there, the noise was never

heard more. The reader will find this, and other miracles, recorded in the life of Father Bonaventura, which is written in the choicest Italian.

WAR-SONG.
Page 9, line 16. *Oh! had they marked the avenging call.*
The allusion is to the massacre of the Swiss Guards on the fatal 10th August, 1792. It is painful, but not useless, to remark, that the passive temper with which the Swiss regarded the death of their bravest countrymen, mercilessly slaughtered in discharge of their duty, encouraged and authorized the progressive injustice, by which the Alps, once the seat of the most virtuous and free people upon the continent, have, at length, been converted into the citadel of a foreign and military despot. A state degraded is half enslaved. [Written in 1812.]

GLENFINLAS.
Page 11, line 13. *How blazed Lord Ronald's beltane-tree.*
The fires lighted by the Highlanders, on the first of May, in compliance with a custom derived from the Pagan times, are termed *The Beltane-tree.* It is a festival celebrated with various superstitious rites, both in the north of Scotland and in Wales.
Page 12, line 26. *The seer's prophetic spirit found.*
I can only describe the second sight, by adopting Dr. Johnson's definition, who calls it ' an impression, either by the mind upon the eye, or by the eye upon the mind, by which things distant and future are perceived and seen as if they were present.' To which I would only add, that the spectral appearances, thus presented, usually presage misfortune; that the faculty is painful to those who suppose they possess it; and that they usually acquire it while themselves under the pressure of melancholy.
Line 87. *Will good Saint Oran's rule prevail?*
St. Oran was a friend and follower of St. Columba, and was buried at Icolmkill. His pretensions to be a saint were rather dubious. According to the legend, he consented to be buried alive, in order to propitiate certain demons of the soil, who obstructed the attempts of Columba to build a chapel. Columba caused the body of his friend to be dug up, after three days had elapsed; when Oran, to the horror and scandal of the assistants, declared that there was neither a God, a judgment, nor a future state! He had no time to make further discoveries, for Columba caused the earth once more to be shovelled over him with the utmost despatch. The chapel, however, and the cemetery, was called *Relig Ouran;* and, in memory of his rigid celibacy, no female was permitted to pay her devotions or be buried in that place. This is the rule alluded to in the poem.
Page 14, line 218. *And thrice Saint Fillan's powerful prayer.*
St. Fillan has given his name to many chap-

els, holy fountains, etc., in Scotland. He was, according to Camerarius, an Abbot of Pitten-weem, in Fife ; from which situation he retired, and died a hermit in the wilds of Glenurchy, A. D. 649. While engaged in transcribing the Scriptures, his left hand was observed to send forth such a splendor as to afford light to that with which he wrote, — a miracle which saved many candles to the convent, as St. Fillan used to spend whole nights in that exercise. The 9th of January was dedicated to this saint, who gave his name to Kilfillan, in Renfrew, and St. Phillans, or Forgend, in Fife.

THE EVE OF ST. JOHN.
Page 14, line 1. *The Baron of Smaylho'me rose with day.*
Smaylholme or Smallholm Tower, the scene of the ballad, is situated on the northern bound-ary of Roxburghshire, among a cluster of wild rocks, called Sandiknow-Crags, the property of Hugh Scott, Esq., of Harden. [It was at the farmhouse of Sandy-Knowe, one is glad to re-member, that Scott spent his earliest boyhood, with his paternal grandfather, as recorded by him in his autobiographic sketch.] The tower is a high square building, surrounded by an outer wall, now ruinous. The circuit of the outer court, being defended on three sides by a precipice and morass, is accessible only from the west, by a steep and rocky path. The apartments, as is usual in a Border keep, or fortress, are placed one above another, and communicate by a narrow stair ; on the roof are two bartizans, or platforms, for defence or plea-sure. The inner door of the tower is wood, the outer an iron gate ; the distance between them being nine feet, the thickness, namely, of the wall. From the elevated situation of Smayl-holme Tower, it is seen many miles in every direction. Among the crags by which it is sur-rounded, one, more eminent, is called the *Watchfold*, and is said to have been the station of a beacon, in the times of war with England. Without the tower-court is a ruined chapel. Brotherstone is a heath, in the neighborhood of Smaylholme Tower.
Page 15, lines 17, 18.
He came not from where Ancram Moor
Ran red with English blood.
[Sir Ralph Evers and Sir Brian Laboun, during the year 1544, committed heavy ravages upon the Scottish border. For this Sir Ralph was made a Lord of Parliament and the next year the two reëntered Scotland with a larger army and repeated their bloody work. As they re-turned toward Jedburgh they were followed by the Earl of Angus at the head of a thousand horse, who was shortly after joined by the fa-mous Norman Lesley, with a body of Fife-men. A fierce battle ensued on Ancram Moor, in which Lord Evers and his son Sir Brian and 800 Englishmen were slain, and a thousand pris-oners were taken.]
Page 16, line 79. *So, by the black rood-stone and by holy Saint John.*

The black rood of Melrose was a crucifix of black marble, and of superior sanctity.
Line 108. *All under the Eildon-tree.*
Eildon is a high hill, terminating in three conical summits, immediately above the town of Melrose, where are the admired ruins of a magnificent monastery. Eildon-tree is said to be the spot where Thomas the Rhymer uttered his prophecies. See also note, p. 513.
Page 17, line 193. *That nun who ne'er beholds the day.*
The circumstance of the nun ' who never saw the day,' is not entirely imaginary. About fifty years ago, an unfortunate female wan-derer took up her residence in a dark vault, among the ruins of Dryburgh Abbey, which, during the day, she never quitted. When night fell, she issued from this miserable habita-tion, and went to the house of Mr. Haliburton of Newmains, the Editor's great-grandfather, or to that of Mr. Erskine of Sheilfield, two gentlemen of the neighborhood. From their charity she obtained such necessaries as she could be prevailed upon to accept. At twelve, each night, she lighted her candle, and returned to her vault, assuring her friendly neighbors that during her absence her habitation was arranged by a spirit, to whom she gave the uncouth name of *Fatlips*; describing him as a little man, wearing heavy iron shoes, with which he trampled the clay floor of the vault, to dispel the damps. This circumstance caused her to be regarded, by the well-informed, with compassion, as deranged in her understanding ; and by the vulgar, with some degree of terror. The cause of her adopting this extraordinary mode of life she would never explain. It was, however, believed to have been occasioned by a vow that during the absence of a man to whom she was attached, she would never look upon the sun. Her lover never returned. He fell during the civil war of 1745–46, and she never-more would behold the light of day.
The vault, or rather dungeon, in which this unfortunate woman lived and died, passes still by the name of the supernatural being with which its gloom was tenanted by her disturbed imagination, and few of the neighboring peas-ants dare enter it by night.

THE GRAY BROTHER.
Page 18, lines 17, 18.
The breath of one of evil deed
Pollutes our sacred day.
The scene with which the ballad opens, was suggested by the following curious passage, ex-tracted from the *Life of Alexander Peden*, one of the wandering and persecuted teachers of the sect of Cameronians, during the reign of Charles II. and his successor, James. This person was supposed by his followers, and, perhaps, really believed himself, to be possessed of supernatural gifts ; for the wild scenes which they frequented, and the constant dangers which were incurred through their proscription, deep-ened upon their minds the gloom of superstition, so general in that age.

' About the same time he [Peden] came to Andrew Normand's house, in the parish of Alloway, in the shire of Ayr, being to preach at night in his barn. After he came in, he halted a little, leaning upon a chair-back, with his face covered ; when he lifted up his head he said, " They are in this house that I have not one word of salvation unto ; " he halted a little again, saying, " This is strange, that the devil will not go out, that we may begin our work ! " Then there was a woman went out, ill-looked upon almost all her life, and to her dying hour, for a witch, with many presumptions of the same. It escaped me, in the former passages, what John Muirhead (whom I have often mentioned) told me, that when he came from Ireland to Galloway, he was at family-worship, and giving some notes upon the Scripture read, when a very ill-looking man came, and sat down within the door, at the back of the *hallan* [partition of the cottage]: immediately he halted and said, " There is some unhappy body just now come into this house. I charge him to go out, and not stop my mouth ! " This person went out, and he *insisted* [went on], yet he saw him neither come in nor go out.'

Page 18, line 66.   *By blast of bugle free.*

The barony of Pennycuick, the property of Sir George Clerk, Bart., is held by a singular tenure ; the proprietor being bound to sit upon a large rocky fragment, called the Buckstane, and wind three blasts of a horn, when the king shall come to hunt on the Borough Muir, near Edinburgh. Hence, the family have adopted, as their crest, a demi-forester proper, winding a horn, with the motto, *Free for a Blast.*

Line 67.   *To Auchendinny's hazel glade.*

[Auchendinny, situated upon the Eske, below Pennycuick, when Scott wrote, was the residence of H. Mackenzie, author of the *Man of Feeling, &c.*]

Line 70.   *And Roslin's rocky glen.*

[The rocky glen is less an object of interest than the marvellous chapel with an elaborateness of sculptured story which to the modern tourist seems singularly unidiomatic in Scotland.]

Line 71.   *Dalkeith, which all the virtues love.*

[In Scott's time the place once belonging to the Earl of Morton, was endeared to him by being the residence of the family of Buccleuch.]

Line 72.   *And classic Hawthornden.*

Hawthornden, the residence of the poet Drummond. A house, of more modern date, is enclosed, as it were, by the ruins of the ancient castle, and overhangs a tremendous precipice, upon the banks of the Eske, perforated by winding caves, which, in former times, were a refuge to the oppressed patriots of Scotland. Here Drummond received Ben Jonson, who journeyed from London, on foot, in order to visit him.

Upon the whole, tracing the Eske from its source, till it joins the sea at Musselburgh, no stream in Scotland can boast such a varied succession of the most interesting objects, as well as of the most romantic and beautiful scenery.

Page 26.   CADYOW CASTLE.

The ruins of Cadyow, or Cadzow Castle, the ancient baronial residence of the family of Hamilton, are situated upon the precipitous banks of the river Evan, about two miles above its junction with the Clyde. It was dismantled, in the conclusion of the Civil Wars, during the reign of the unfortunate Mary, to whose cause the house of Hamilton devoted themselves with a generous zeal, which occasioned their temporary obscurity, and, very nearly, their total ruin. The situation of the ruins, embosomed in wood, darkened by ivy and creeping shrubs, and overhanging the brawling torrent, is romantic in the highest degree. In the immediate vicinity of Cadyow is a grove of immense oaks, the remains of the Caledonian Forest, which anciently extended through the south of Scotland, from the eastern to the Atlantic Ocean. Some of these trees measure twenty-five feet, and upwards, in circumference ; and the state of decay in which they now appear shows that they have witnessed the rites of the Druids. The whole scenery is included in the magnificent and extensive park of the Duke of Hamilton. There was long preserved in this forest the breed of the Scottish wild cattle, until their ferocity occasioned their being extirpated, about forty years ago. Their appearance was beautiful, being milk-white, with black muzzles, horns, and hoofs. The bulls are described by ancient authors as having white manes ; but those of latter days had lost their peculiarity, perhaps by intermixture with the tame breed.

In detailing the death of the Regent Murray, which is made the subject of the ballad, it would be injustice to my reader to use other words than those of Dr. Robertson, whose account of that memorable event forms a beautiful piece of historical painting.

' Hamilton of Bothwellhaugh was the person who committed this barbarous action. He had been condemned to death soon after the battle of Langside, as we have already related, and owed his life to the Regent's clemency. But part of his estate had been bestowed upon one of the Regent's favorites [Sir James Bellenden, Lord Justice-Clerk], who seized his house and turned out his wife, naked, in a cold night, into the open fields, where, before next morning, she became furiously mad. This injury made a deeper impression on him than the benefit he had received, and from that moment he vowed to be revenged of the Regent. Party rage strengthened and inflamed his private resentment. His kinsmen, the Hamiltons, applauded the enterprise. The maxims of that age justified the most desperate course he could take to obtain vengeance. He followed the Regent for some time, and watched for an opportunity to strike the blow. He resolved at last to wait till his enemy should arrive at Linlithgow, through which he was to pass in his way from Stirling to Edinburgh. He took his stand in a wooden gallery, which had a window towards the street ; spread a feather-bed on the floor to hinder the noise of his feet from being heard ; hung up a black cloth behind him, that his shadow might not be observed from without ; and, after all this preparation, calmly expected the Regent's approach, who had lodged, during the night, in a house not far distant. Some indistinct information of the danger which threatened him had been conveyed to the Regent, and he paid so much regard to it that he resolved to return by the same gate through which he had entered, and to fetch a compass round the town. But as the crowd about the gate was great, and he himself unacquainted with fear, he proceeded directly along the street ; and the throng of people obliging him to move very slowly, gave the assassin time to take so true an aim, that he shot him, with a single bullet, through the lower part of his belly, and killed the horse of a gentleman who rode on his other side. His followers instantly endeavored to break into the house whence the blow had come ; but they found the door strongly barricadoed, and, before it could be forced open, Hamilton had mounted a fleet horse which stood ready for him at a back passage, and was got far beyond their reach. The Regent died the same night [January 23, 1569] of his wound ' (*History of Scotland*, book v.).

' Bothwellhaugh rode straight to Hamilton, where he was received in triumph ; for the ashes of the houses in Clydesdale, which had been burned by Murray's army, were yet smoking ; and party prejudice, the habits of the age, and the enormity of the provocation, seemed to his kinsmen to justify the deed. After a short abode at Hamilton, this fierce and determined man left Scotland, and served in France, under the patronage of the family of Guise, to whom he was doubtless recommended by having avenged the cause of their niece, Queen Mary, upon her ungrateful brother. De Thou has recorded that an attempt was made to engage him to assassinate Gaspar de Coligni, the famous Admiral of France, and the buckler of the Huguenot cause. But the character of Bothwellhaugh was mistaken. He was no mercenary trader in blood, and rejected the offer with contempt and indignation. He had no authority, he said, from Scotland to commit murders in France, he had avenged his own just quarrel, but he would neither, for price nor prayer, avenge that of another man ' (*Thuanus*, cap. 46).

Page 27, line 45. *First of his troop, the chief rode on.*
The head of the family of Hamilton at this period, was James, Earl of Arran, Duke of Chatelherault, in France, and first peer of the Scottish realm. In 1569, he was appointed by Queen Mary her lieutenant-general in Scotland, under the singular title of her adopted father.

Line 81. *Stern Claud replied with darkening face.*
Lord Claud Hamilton, second son of the Duke of Chatelherault, and commendator of the Ab-

bey of Paisley, acted a distinguished part during the troubles of Queen Mary's reign, and remained unalterably attached to the cause of that unfortunate princess. He led the van of her army at the fatal battle of Langside, and was one of the commanders at the Raid of Stirling, which had so nearly given complete success to the queen's faction.

Line 85. *Few suns have set since Woodhouselee.*
This barony, stretching along the banks of the Esk, near Auchendinny, belonged to Bothwellhaugh, in right of his wife. The ruins of the mansion, from whence she was expelled in the brutal manner which occasioned her death, are still to be seen in a hollow glen beside the river. Popular report tenants them with the restless ghost of the Lady Bothwellhaugh ; whom, however, it confounds with Lady Anne Bothwell, whose *Lament* is so popular. This spectre is so tenacious of her rights, that, a part of the stones of the ancient edifice having been employed in building or repairing the present Woodhouselee, she has deemed it a part of her privilege to haunt that house also ; and, even of very late years, has excited considerable disturbance and terror among the domestics. This is a more remarkable vindication of the *rights of ghosts*, as the present Woodhouselee is situated on the slope of the Pentland hills, distant at least four miles from her proper abode. She always appears in white, and with her child in her arms.

Page 28, line 112. *Drives to the leap his jaded steed.*
Birrel informs us, that Bothwellhaugh, being closely pursued, ' after that spur and wand had failed him, he drew forth his dagger, and strocke his horse behind, whilk caused the horse to leap a very brode stanke [*i. e.* ditch], by whilk means he escapit, and gat away from all the rest of the horses ' (*Diary*, p. 18).

Line 129. *From the wild Border's humbled side.*
Murray's death took place shortly after an expedition to the Borders.

Line 137. *With hackbut bent, my secret stand.*
With gun cocked. The carbine with which the Regent was shot is preserved at Hamilton Palace. It is a brass piece, of a middling length, very small in the bore, and, what is rather extraordinary, appears to have been rifled or indented in the barrel. It had a matchlock, for which a modern firelock has been injudiciously substituted.

Line 141. *Dark Morton, girt with many a spear.*
He was concerned in the murder of David Rizzio, and at least privy to that of Darnley.

Line 144. *The wild Macfarlanes' plaided clan.*
This clan of Lennox Highlanders were attached to the Regent Murray.

Line 145. *Glencairn and stout Parkhead were nigh.*
The Earl of Glencairn was a steady adherent of the Regent. George Douglas of Parkhead was a natural brother of the Earl of Morton, whose horse was killed by the same ball by which Murray fell.

Line 147. *And haggard Lindesay's iron eye.*
Lord Lindsay, of the Byres, was the most ferocious and brutal of the Regent's faction, and, as such, was employed to extort Mary's signature to the deed of resignation presented to her in Lochleven Castle. He discharged his commission with the most savage rigor; and it is even said that when the weeping captive, in the act of signing, averted her eyes from the fatal deed, he pinched her arm with the grasp of his iron glove.

Line 152. *So close the minions crowded nigh.*
Not only had the Regent notice of the intended attempt upon his life, but even of the very house from which it was threatened. With that infatuation at which men wonder, after such events have happened, he deemed it would be a sufficient precaution to ride briskly past the dangerous spot. But even this was prevented by the crowd; so that Bothwellhaugh had time to take a deliberate aim. *Spottiswoode*, p. 233.

Page 29, line 178. *Spread to the wind thy bannered tree.*
An oak, half-sawn, with the motto *through*, is an ancient cognizance of the family of Hamilton.

THE REIVER'S WEDDING.
Page 29, line 50. *Beneath the trysting tree.*
At Linton, in Roxburghshire, there is a circle of stones surrounding a smooth plot of turf, called the *tryst*, or place of appointment, which tradition avers to have been the rendezvous of the neighboring warriors. The name of the leader was cut in the turf, and the arrangement of the letters announced to his followers the course which he had taken.

CHRISTIE'S WILL.
Page 31, line 2. *And sae has he down by the Grey Mare's Tail.*
A cataract above Moffat.

Line 13. *Bethink how he sware, by the salt and the bread.*
'He took bread and salt, by this light, that he would never open his lips.' — *The Honest Whore*, Act v. scene ii.

Page 32, line 67. *And, hunting over Middleton Moor.*
Middleton Moor is about fifteen miles from Edinburgh on the way to the Border.

Line 87. *Or that the gipsies glamoured gang.*
Besides the prophetic powers ascribed to the gipsies in most European countries, the Scottish peasants believe them possessed of the power of throwing upon bystanders a spell, to fascinate their eyes, and cause them to see the thing that is not. Thus in the old ballad of Johnie Faa, the elopement of the Countess of Cassillis, with a gipsy leader, is imputed to fascination: —

' As sune as they saw her weel-far'd face,
They cast the *glamour* ower her.'

Line 95. *I have tar-barrelled mony a witch.*
Human nature shrinks from the brutal scenes produced by the belief in witchcraft. Under the idea that the devil imprinted upon the body of his miserable vassals a mark, which was insensible to pain, persons were employed to run needles into the bodies of the old women who were suspected of witchcraft.

THOMAS THE RHYMER.
Page 33, line 24. *All underneath the Eildon Tree.*
The Eildon Tree, from beneath the shade of which Thomas the Rhymer delivered his prophecies, now no longer exists; but the spot is marked by a large stone, called Eildon Tree Stone. A neighboring rivulet takes the name of the Bogle Burn (Goblin Brook) from the Rhymer's supernatural visitants.

Line 66. *And she pu'd an apple frae a tree.*
The traditional commentary upon this ballad informs us, that the apple was the produce of the fatal tree of knowledge, and that the garden was the terrestrial paradise. The repugnance of Thomas to be debarred the use of falsehood, when he might find it convenient, has a comic effect.

Page 34, line 27. *Where a king lay stiff beneath his steed.*
King Alexander, killed by a fall from his horse, near Kinghorn.

Line 42. *My doom is not to die this day.*
The uncertainty which long prevailed in Scotland concerning the fate of James IV. is well known.

Line 56. *Is by a burn, that 's called of bread.*
One of Thomas's rhymes, preserved by tradition, runs thus: —

' The burn of breid
Shall run fou reid.'

Bannock-burn is the brook here meant. The Scots give the name of *bannock* to a thick round cake of unleavened bread.

Page 35, line 3. *And Ruberslaw showed high Dunyon.*
Ruberslaw and Dunyon are two hills near Jedburgh.

Line 5. *Then all by bonny Coldingknow.*
An ancient tower near Ercildoune, belonging to a family of the name of Home. One of Thomas's prophecies is said to have run thus: —

' Vengeance! Vengeance! when and where?
On the house of Coldingknow, now and evermair!'

The spot is rendered classical by its having given name to the beautiful melody called the 'Broom o' the Cowdenknows.'

Page 36, line 112. *As white as snow on Fairnalie.*
An ancient seat upon the Tweed, in Selkirkshire. In a popular edition of the first part of 'Thomas the Rhymer,' the Fairy Queen thus addresses him: —

' Gin ye wad meet wi' me again,
Gang to the bonny banks of Fairnalie.'

THE BARD'S INCANTATION.
Page 37, line 21. *The Spectre with his Bloody Hand.*
The forest of Glenmore is haunted by a spirit called Lhamdearg, or Red-hand.
Line 32. *On Bloody Largs and Loncarty.*
Where the Norwegian invader of Scotland received two bloody defeats.

THE LAY OF THE LAST MINSTREL.
Page 46, line 27. *He passed where Newark's stately tower.*
'A massive square tower, now unroofed and ruinous, surrounded by an outward wall, defended by round flanking turrets. It is most beautifully situated, about three miles from Selkirk, upon the banks of the Yarrow, a fierce and precipitous stream, which unites with the Ettrick about a mile beneath the castle. . . . The castle continued to be an occasional seat of the Buccleuch family for more than a century; and here, it is said, the Duchess of Monmouth and Buccleuch was brought up.' Schetky's *Illustrations of the Lay of the Last Minstrel.*
Line 37. *The Duchess marked his weary pace.*
Anne, Duchess of Buccleuch and Monmouth, representative of the ancient Lords of Buccleuch, and widow of the unfortunate James, Duke of Monmouth, who was beheaded in 1685.
Page 47, line 49. *Of good Earl Francis, dead and gone.*
Francis Scott, Earl of Buccleuch, father of the Duchess.
Line 50. *And of Earl Walter, rest him, God!*
Walter, Earl of Buccleuch, grandfather of the Duchess, and a celebrated warrior.
Line 1. *The feast was over in Branksome tower.*
In the reign of James I., Sir William Scott of Buccleuch, chief of the clan bearing that name, exchanged, with Sir Thomas Inglis of Manor, the estate of Murdiestone, in Lanarkshire, for one-half of the barony of Branksome, or Brankholm, lying upon the Teviot, about three miles above Hawick. He was probably induced to this transaction from the vicinity of Branksome to the extensive domain which he possessed in Ettrick Forest and in Teviotdale. In the former district he held by occupancy the estate of Buccleuch, and much of the forest land on the river Ettrick. In Teviotdale, he enjoyed the barony of Eckford, by a grant from Robert II. to his ancestor, Walter Scott of Kirkurd, for the apprehending of Gilbert Ridderford, confirmed by Robert III., 3d May, 1424. Tradition imputes the exchange betwixt Scott and Inglis to a conversation, in which the latter, a man, it would appear, of a mild and forbearing nature, complained much of the injuries which he was exposed to from the English Borderers, who frequently plundered his lands of Branksome. Sir William Scott instantly offered him the estate of Murdiestone, in exchange for that which was subject to such egregious inconvenience. When the bargain was completed, he dryly remarked that the

cattle in Cumberland were as good as those of Teviotdale; and proceeded to commence a system of reprisals upon the English, which was regularly pursued by his successors. In the next reign, James II. granted to Sir Walter Scott of Branksome, and to Sir David, his son, the remaining half of the barony of Branksome, to be held in blanche for the payment of a red rose. The cause assigned for the grant is, their brave and faithful exertions in favor of the King against the house of Douglas, with whom James had been recently tugging for the throne of Scotland.
Branksome Castle continued to be the principal seat of the Buccleuch family, while security was any object in their choice of a mansion. It has since been the residence of the Commissioners, or Chamberlains of the family. From the various alterations which the building has undergone, it is not only greatly restricted in its dimensions, but retains little of the castellated form, if we except one square tower of massy thickness, the only part of the original building which now remains.
Lines 16, 17.
   Nine-and-twenty knights of fame
   Hung their shields in Branksome Hall.
The ancient Barons of Buccleuch, both from feudal splendor and from their frontier situation, retained in their household, at Branksome, a number of gentlemen of their own name, who held lands from their chief, for the military service of watching and warding his castle.
Line 39. *And with Jedwood-axe at saddlebow.*
'Of a truth,' says Froissart, 'the Scottish cannot boast great skill with the bow, but rather bear axes, with which, in time of need, they give heavy strokes.' The Jedwood-axe was a sort of partisan, used by horsemen, as appears from the arms of Jedburgh, which bear a cavalier mounted, and armed with this weapon. It is also called a Jedwood or Jeddart staff.
Page 48, line 50. *Threaten Branksome's lordly towers.*
Branksome Castle was continually exposed to the attacks of the English, both from its situation and the restless military disposition of its inhabitants, who were seldom on good terms with their neighbors.
Lines 57, 58.
   Bards long shall tell
   How Lord Walter fell!
Sir Walter Scott of Buccleuch succeeded to his grandfather, Sir David, in 1492. He was a brave and powerful baron, and Warden of the West Marches of Scotland. His death was the consequence of a feud betwixt the Scotts and Kerrs, which, in spite of all means used to bring about an agreement, raged for many years upon the Borders.
Line 69. *No! vainly to each holy shrine.*
Among other expedients resorted to for stanching the feud betwixt the Scotts and the Kerrs, there was a bond executed in 1529, between the heads of each clan, binding them-

selves to perform reciprocally the four principal pilgrimages of Scotland for the benefit of the souls of those of the opposite name who had fallen in the quarrel. But either it never took effect, or else the feud was renewed shortly afterwards.

Line 105. *With Carr in arms had stood.*

The family of Ker, Kerr, or Carr, was very powerful on the Border. Cessford Castle, the ancient baronial residence of the family, is situated near the village of More-battle, within two or three miles of the Cheviot Hills. It has been a place of great strength and consequence, but is now ruinous.

Line 109. *Before Lord Cranstoun she should wed.*

The Cranstouns, Lord Cranstoun, are an ancient Border family, whose chief seat was at Crailing, in Teviotdale. They were at this time at feud with the clan of Scott; for it appears that the Lady of Buccleuch, in 1557, beset the Laird of Cranstoun, seeking his life. Nevertheless, the same Cranstoun, or perhaps his son, was married to a daughter of the same lady.

Line 113. *Of Bethune's line of Picardie.*

The Bethunes were of French origin, and derived their name from a small town in Artois. There were several distinguished families of the Bethunes in the neighboring province of Picardy; they numbered among their descendants the celebrated Duc de Sully; and the name was accounted among the most noble in France. The family of Bethune, or Beaton, in Fife, produced three learned and dignified prelates; namely, Cardinal Beaton, and two successive Archbishops of Glasgow, all of whom flourished about the date of the romance. Of this family was descended Dame Janet Beaton, Lady Buccleuch, widow of Sir Walter Scott, of Branksome. She was a woman of masculine spirit, as appeared from her riding at the head of her son's clan after her husband's murder. She also possessed the hereditary abilities of her family in such a degree, that the superstition of the vulgar imputed them to supernatural knowledge. With this was mingled, by faction, the foul accusation of her having influenced Queen Mary to the murder of her husband.

Line 115. *In Padua, far beyond the sea.*

Padua was long supposed, by the Scottish peasants, to be the principal school of necromancy.

Line 120. *His form no darkening shadow traced.*

The shadow of a necromancer is independent of the sun. Glycas informs us, that Simon Magus caused his shadow to go before him, making people believe it was an attendant spirit (Heywood's *Hierarchie*, p. 475.) The vulgar conceive, that when a class of students have made a certain progress in their mystic studies, they are obliged to run through a subterraneous hall where the devil literally catches the hindmost in the race, unless he crosses the hall so speedily, that the arch-enemy

can only apprehend his shadow. In the latter case, the person of the sage never after throws any shade; and those who have thus *lost their shadow* always prove the best magicians. [In Chamisso's story of *Peter Schlemihl*, which appeared not long after the *Lay*, the shadow is parted with by a sale to the Devil.]

Line 125. *The viewless forms of air.*

The Scottish vulgar, without having any very defined notion of their attributes, believe in the existence of an intermediate class of spirits, residing in the air or in the waters; to whose agency they ascribe floods, storms, and all such phenomena as their own philosophy cannot readily explain. They are supposed to interfere in the affairs of mortals, sometimes with a malevolent purpose, and sometimes with milder views.

Page 49, line 197. *A fancied moss-trooper.*

This was the usual appellation of the marauders upon the Border; a profession diligently pursued by the inhabitants on both sides, and by none more actively and successfully than by Buccleuch's clan. Long after the union of the crowns, the moss-troopers, although sunk in reputation, and no longer enjoying the pretext of national hostility, continued to pursue their calling. [Fuller in his *Worthies* derives the name from their 'dwelling in the mosses and riding in troops together.']

Line 208. *Exalt the Crescents and the Star.*

The arms of the Kerrs of Cessford were *Vert* on a chevron, betwixt three unicorns' heads erased *argent*, three mullets *sable*; crest, a unicorn's head erased *proper.* The Scotts of Buccleuch bore, *Or*, on a bend azure; a star of six points betwixt two crescents of the first.

Page 50, line 214. *She called to her William of Deloraine.*

The lands of Deloraine are joined to those of Buccleuch in Ettrick Forest. They were immemorially possessed by the Buccleuch family, under the strong title of occupancy, although no charter was obtained from the crown until 1545.

Line 219. *By wily turns, by desperate bounds.*

The kings and heroes of Scotland, as well as the Border-riders, were sometimes obliged to study how to evade the pursuit of bloodhounds. Barbour informs us that Robert Bruce was repeatedly tracked by sleuth-dogs. On one occasion he escaped by wading a bow-shot down a brook, and ascending into a tree by a branch which overhung the water; thus, leaving no trace on land of his footsteps, he baffled the scent.

Line 258. *Were 't my neck-verse at Hairibee.*

Hairibee was the place of executing the Border marauders at Carlisle. The *neck-verse* is the beginning of the 51st Psalm, *Miserere mei*, etc., anciently read by criminals claiming the benefit of clergy.

Line 267. *Dimly he viewed the Moat-hill's mound.*

This is a round artificial mount near Hawick, which, from its name (*Mot*, A. S. *Concilium, Conventus*), was probably anciently used as a place for assembling a national council of the adjacent tribes. There are many such mounds in Scotland, and they are sometimes, but rarely, of a square form.

Line 287. *On Minto-crags the moonbeams glint.*
A romantic assemblage of cliffs, which rise suddenly above the vale of Teviot, in the immediate vicinity of the family-seat from which Lord Minto takes his title. A small platform, on a projecting crag, commanding a most beautiful prospect, is termed ' Barnhills' Bed.' This Barnhills is said to have been a robber, or outlaw. There are remains of a strong tower beneath the rocks, where he is supposed to have dwelt, and from which he derived his name.

Line 300. *To ancient Riddell's fair domain.*
The family of Riddell have been very long in possession of the barony called Riddell, or Ryedale, part of which still bears the latter name. [At a later date, the family of Riddell parted with all their Scottish estates.]

Page 51, line 321. *As glanced his eye o'er Halidon.*
An ancient seat of the Kerrs of Cessford, now demolished. About a quarter of a mile to the northward lay the field of battle betwixt Buccleuch and Angus, which is called to this day the Skirmish Field.

Line 334. *Old Melros' rose and fair Tweed ran.*
Melrose Abbey. The ancient and beautiful monastery of Melrose was founded by King David I. Its ruins afford the finest specimen of Gothic architecture and Gothic sculpture which Scotland can boast. The stone of which it is built, though it has resisted the weather for so many ages, retains perfect sharpness, so that even the most minute ornaments seem as entire as when newly wrought. In some of the cloisters there are representations of flowers, vegetables, etc., carved in stone, with accuracy and precision so delicate, that we almost distrust our senses, when we consider the difficulty of subjecting so hard a substance to such intricate and exquisite modulation. This superb convent was dedicated to St. Mary, and the monks were of the Cistercian order. At the time of the Reformation, they shared in the general reproach of sensuality and irregularity, thrown upon the Roman churchmen.

Line 2. *Go visit it by the pale moonlight.*
[In a letter to Joanna Baillie, Nov. 27, 1816, Scott, possibly in allusion to this oft-quoted injunction, speaks jestingly of ' recommending to others to catch cold by visiting old abbeys by moonlight, which he never happened to see under the chaste moonbeam himself.']

Line 16. *Then view Saint David's ruined pile.*
David I. of Scotland purchased the reputation of sanctity by founding, and liberally endowing, not only the monastery of Melrose, but those of Kelso, Jedburgh, and many others ; which led to the well-known observation of his successor, that he was *a sore saint for the crown.*

Page 52, line 30. *Had gifted the shrine for their souls' repose.*

The Buccleuch family were great benefactors to the Abbey of Melrose. As early as the reign of Robert II., Robert Scott, Baron of Murdieston and Rankleburn (now Buccleuch), gave to the monks the lands of Hinkery, in Ettrick Forest, *pro salute animæ suæ.*

Line 66. *Save to patter an Ave Mary.*
The Borderers were, as may be supposed, very ignorant about religious matters. But we learn from Lesley that, however deficient in real religion, they regularly told their beads, and never with more zeal than when going on a plundering expedition.

Line 79. *And beneath their feet were the bones of the dead.*
The cloisters were frequently used as places of sepulture. An instance occurs in Dryburgh Abbey where the cloister has an inscription bearing, *Hic jacet frater Archibaldus.*

Line 88. *So had he seen, in fair Castile.*
' " By my faith " sayd the Duke of Lancaster (to a Portuguese squire) " of all the feates of armes that the Castellyans, and they of your countrey doth use, the castynge of their derkes best pleaseth me, and gladly I wold se it: for, as I hear say, if they strike one aryghte, without he be well armed, the dart will pierce him thrughe." — " By my fayth, sir," sayd the squyer, " ye say troth ; for I have seen many a grete stroke given with them, which at one time cost us deerly ; for, at the said skyrmishe, Sir John Laurence of Coygne was stricken with a dart in such wise, that the head perced all the plates of his cote of mayle, and a sacke stoffed with sylke, and passed thrughe his body, so that he fell down dead." ' Froissart, chap. 44. This mode of fighting with darts was imitated in the military game called *Jengo de las canas,* which the Spaniards borrowed from their Moorish invaders.

Page 53, line 109. *O gallant Chief of Otterburne!*
The famous and desperate battle of Otterburne was fought 15th August, 1388, betwixt Henry Percy, called Hotspur, and James, Earl of Douglas. Both these renowned champions were at the head of a chosen body of troops, and they were rivals in military fame. The issue of the conflict is well known: Percy was made prisoner, and the Scots won the day, dearly purchased by the death of their gallant general, the Earl of Douglas, who was slain in the action. He was buried at Melrose beneath the high altar.

Line 110. *And thine, dark knight of Liddesdale!*
William Douglas, called the Knight of Liddesdale, flourished during the reign of David II., and was so distinguished by his valor that he was called the Flower of Chivalry. Nevertheless, he tarnished his renown by the cruel murder of Sir Alexander Ramsay of Dalhousie, originally his friend and brother in arms. The King had conferred upon Ramsay the sheriffdom of Teviotdale, to which Douglas pretended some claim. In revenge of this preference, the

Knight of Liddesdale came down upon Ramsay, while he was administering justice at Hawick, seized and carried him off to his remote and inaccessible castle of Hermitage, where he threw his unfortunate prisoner, horse and man, into a dungeon, and left him to perish of hunger. It is said the miserable captive prolonged his existence for several days by the corn which fell from a granary above the vault in which he was confined. So weak was the royal authority, that David, although highly incensed at this atrocious murder, found himself obliged to appoint the Knight of Liddesdale successor to his victim, as Sheriff of Teviotdale. But he was soon after slain, while hunting in Ettrick Forest, by his own godson and chieftain, William, Earl of Douglas, in revenge, according to some authors, of Ramsay's murder; although a popular tradition, preserved in a ballad quoted by Godscroft, and some parts of which are still preserved, ascribes the resentment of the Earl to jealousy. The place where the Knight of Liddesdale was killed is called, from his name, William-Cross, upon the ridge of a hill called William-Hope, betwixt Tweed and Yarrow. His body, according to Godscroft, was carried to Lindean church the first night after his death, and thence to Melrose, where he was interred with great pomp, and where his tomb is still shown.

Line 138. *To meet the wondrous Michael Scott.*

Sir Michael Scott of Balwearie flourished during the thirteenth century, and was one of the ambassadors sent to bring the Maid of Norway to Scotland upon the death of Alexander III. By a poetical anachronism, he is here placed in a later era. He was a man of much learning, chiefly acquired in foreign countries. He wrote a commentary upon Aristotle, printed at Venice in 1496: and several treatises upon natural philosophy, from which he appears to have been addicted to the abstruse studies of judicial astrology, alchemy, physiognomy, and chiromancy. Hence he passed among his contemporaries for a skilful magician. Dempster informs us, that he remembers to have heard in his youth that the magic books of Michael Scott were still in existence, but could not be opened without danger, on account of the malignant fiends who were thereby invoked. Tradition varies concerning the place of his burial; some contend for Holme Coltrame, in Cumberland, others for Melrose Abbey. But all agree that his books of magic were interred in his grave, or preserved in the convent where he died.

Line 140. *That when, in Salamanca's cave.*

Spain, from the relics, doubtless, of Arabian learning and superstition, was accounted a favorite residence of magicians. Pope Sylvester, who actually imported from Spain the use of the Arabian numerals, was supposed to have learned there the magic for which he was stigmatized by the ignorance of his age. There were public schools where magic, or rather the sciences supposed to involve its mysteries, were

regularly taught, at Toledo, Seville, and Salamanca. In the latter city, they were held in a deep cavern; the mouth of which was walled up by Queen Isabella, wife of King Ferdinand.

Line 142. *The bells would ring in Notre Dame.*

Michael Scott was chosen, it is said, to go upon an embassy, to obtain from the King of France satisfaction for certain piracies committed by his subjects upon those of Scotland. Instead of preparing a new equipage and splendid retinue, the ambassador retreated to his study, opened his book and evoked a fiend in the shape of a huge black horse, mounted upon his back, and forced him to fly through the air towards France. As they crossed the sea, the devil insidiously asked his rider what it was that the old women of Scotland muttered at bed-time. A less experienced wizard might have answered that it was the Pater Noster, which would have licensed the devil to precipitate him from his back. But Michael sternly replied, ' What is that to thee? Mount, Diabolus, and fly! ' When he arrived at Paris, he tied his horse to the gate of the palace, entered, and boldly delivered his message. An ambassador, with so little of the pomp and circumstance of diplomacy, was not received with much respect, and the king was about to return a contemptuous refusal to his demand, when Michael besought him to suspend his resolution till he had seen his horse stamp three times. The first stamp shook every steeple in Paris, and caused all the bells to ring; the second threw down three of the towers of the palace; and the infernal steed had lifted his hoof to give the third stamp, when the king rather chose to dismiss Michael, with the most ample concessions, than to stand to the probable consequences.

Line 145. *The words that cleft Eildon Hills in three.*

Michael Scott was, once upon a time, much embarrassed by a spirit, for whom he was under the necessity of finding constant employment. He commanded him to build a *cauld*, or damhead, across the Tweed at Kelso; it was accomplished in one night, and still does honor to the infernal architect. Michael next ordered that Eildon Hill, which was then a uniform cone, should be divided into three. Another night was sufficient to part its summit into the three picturesque peaks which it now bears. At length the enchanter conquered this indefatigable demon, by employing him in the hopeless and endless task of making ropes out of sea-sand.

Line 186. *That lamp shall burn unquenchably.*

Baptista Porta, and other authors who treat of natural magic, talk much of eternal lamps, pretended to have been found burning in ancient sepulchres. One of these perpetual lamps is said to have been discovered in the tomb of Tulliola, the daughter of Cicero. The wick was supposed to be composed of asbestos. Kircher enumerates three different recipes for constructing such lamps, and wisely concludes that the thing is nevertheless impossible.

Page 54, line 245. *He thought, as he took it, the dead man frowned.*

William of Deloraine might be strengthened in this belief by the well-known story of the Cid Ruy Diaz. When the body of that famous Christian champion was sitting in state by the high altar of the cathedral church of Toledo, where it remained for ten years, a certain malicious Jew attempted to pull him by the beard ; but he had no sooner touched the formidable whiskers, than the corpse started up, and half unsheathed his sword. The Israelite fled ; and so permanent was the effect of his terror, that he became Christian. Heywood's *Hierarchie*, p. 480, quoted from Sebastian Cobarruvia's *Crozee*.

Page 56, line 353. *The Baron's dwarf his courser held.*

The idea of Lord Cranstoun's Goblin Page is taken from a being called Gilpin Horner, who appeared, and made some stay, at a farmhouse among the Border-mountains. An old man, of the name of Anderson, who was born, and lived all his life, at Todshaw-hill in Eskedale-muir, said that two men, late in the evening, when it was growing dark, heard a voice, at some distance, crying, ' *Tint! tint! tint!* ' One of the men, named Moffat, called out, ' What deil has tint you ? Come here.' Immediately a creature, of something like a human form, appeared. It was surprisingly little, distorted in features, and misshapen in limbs. As soon as the two men could see it plainly, they ran home in a great fright, imagining they had met with some goblin. By the way Moffat fell, and it ran over him, and was home at the house as soon as either of them, and staid there a long time ; but it is not stated how long. It was real flesh and blood, and ate and drank, was fond of cream, and, when it could get at it, would destroy a great deal. It seemed a mischievous creature ; and any of the children whom it could master, it would beat and scratch without mercy. It was once abusing a child belonging to the same Moffat, who had been so frightened by its first appearance ; and he, in a passion, struck it so violent a blow upon the side of the head, that it tumbled upon the ground ; but it was not stunned ; for it set up its head directly, and exclaimed, ' Ah hah, Will o' Moffat, you strike sair ! ' (i. e., *sore*.) After it had staid there long, one evening, when the women were milking the cows in the loan, it was playing among the children near by them, when suddenly they heard a loud shrill voice cry, three times, ' *Gilpin Horner !* ' It started, and said, ' *That is me, I must away,*' and instantly disappeared, and was never heard of more. Besides constantly repeating the word *tint! tint!* Gilpin Horner was often heard to call upon Peter Bertram, or Bete-ram, as he pronounced the word ; and when the shrill voice called Gilpin Horner, he immediately acknowledged it was the summons of the said Peter Bertram, who seems therefore to have been the devil who had *tint*, or lost, the little imp. As much as has been objected to

Gilpin Horner on account of his being supposed rather a device of the author than a popular superstition, I can only say, that no legend which I ever heard seemed to be more universally credited, and that many persons of very good rank and considerable information are well known to repose absolute faith in the tradition.

Line 390. *But the Ladye of Branksome gathered a band.*

' Upon 25th June, 1557, Dame Janet Beatoune, Lady Buccleuch, and a great number of the name of Scott, delaitit (accused) for coming to the kirk of St. Mary of the Lowes, to the number of two hundred persons bodin in feire of weire (arrayed in armor) and breaking open the door of the said kirk, in order to apprehend the Laird of Cranstoune for his destruction.' On the 20th July, a warrant from the Queen is presented, discharging the justice to proceed against the Lady Buccleuch while new calling. — *Abridgment of Books of Adjournal*, in Advocates Library. No farther procedure seems to have taken place. It is said, that upon this rising, the kirk of St. Mary was burnt by the Scotts.

Page 57, line 33. *He marked the crane on the Baron's crest.*

The crest of the Cranstouns, in allusion to their name, is a crane dormant, holding a stone in his foot, with an emphatic Border motto, *Thou shalt want ere I want.*

Page 58, line 90. *Like a book-bosomed priest should ride.*

At Unthank, two miles N. E. from the church of Ewes, there are the ruins of a chapel for divine service, in time of Popery. There is a tradition, that friars were wont to come from Melrose, or Jedburgh, to baptize and marry in this parish ; and from being in use to carry the mass-book in their bosoms, they were called, by the inhabitants, *Book-a-bosomes.*

Page 58, line 110. *All was delusion, nought was truth.*

Glamour, in the legends of Scottish superstition, means the magic power of imposing on the eyesight of the spectators, so that the appearance of an object shall be totally different from the reality. The transformation of Michael Scott by the witch of Falsehope, already mentioned, was a genuine operation of glamour. To a similar charm the ballad of *Johnny Fa'* imputes the fascination of the lovely Countess, who eloped with that gypsy leader : —

' Sae soon as they saw her weel-far'd face,
    They cast the *glamour* o'er her.'

Line 155. *The running stream dissolved the spell.*

It is a firm article of popular faith, that no enchantment can subsist in a living stream. Nay, if you can interpose a brook betwixt you and witches, spectres, or even fiends, you are in perfect safety. Burns's inimitable *Tam o' Shanter* turns entirely upon such a circumstance. The belief seems to be of antiquity. Brompton informs us that certain Irish wizards could, by spells, convert earthen clods or stones into fat pigs, which they sold in the market, but which always reassumed their proper form when driven by the deceived purchaser across a running stream.

Page 59, line 227. *He never counted him a man.*

Imitated from Drayton's account of Robin Hood and his followers (*Polyolbion*, Song 26): —

' A hundred valiant men had this brave Robin Hood,
Still ready at his call, that bowmen were right good :
All clad in Lincoln green, with caps of red and blue,
His fellow's winded horn not one of them but knew.
When setting to their lips their bugles shrill,
The warbling echoes waked from every dale and hill;
Their bauldrics set with studs athwart their shoulders cast,
To which under their arms their sheafs were buckled fast,
A short sword at their belt, a buckler scarce a span,
Who struck below the knee not counted then a man.
All made of Spanish yew, their bows were wondrous strong,
They not an arrow drew but was a clothyard long.
Of archery they had the very perfect craft,
With broad arrow, or but, or prick, or roving shaft.'

To wound an antagonist in the thigh, or leg, was reckoned contrary to the law of arms.

Page 60, line 291. *And with a charm she stanched the blood.*

See several charms for this purpose in Reginald Scott's *Discovery of Witchcraft*, p. 273.

' Tom Potts was but a serving man,
But yet he was a doctor good ;
He bound his handkerchief on the wound,
And with some kinds of words he stanched the blood.'
Pieces of Ancient Popular Poetry, London, 1791, p. 131.

Line 326. *O, 't is the beacon-blaze of war.*

The Border beacons, from their number and position, formed a sort of telegraphic communication with Edinburgh. The Act of Parliament, 1455, c. 48, directs that one bale or fagot shall be warning of the approach of the English in any manner ; two bales, that they are coming indeed ; four bales blazing beside each other, that the enemy are in great force.

Page 61, line 387. *On many a cairn's gray pyramid.*

The cairns, or piles of loose stones, which crown the summit of most of our Scottish hills, and are found in other remarkable situations, seem usually, though not universally, to have been sepulchral monuments. Six flat stones are commonly found in the centre, forming a cavity of greater or smaller dimensions, in which an urn is often placed. The author is possessed of one, discovered beneath an immense cairn at Roughlee, in Liddesdale. It is of the most barbarous construction; the middle of the substance alone having been subjected to the fire, over which, when hardened, the artist had laid an inner and outer coat of unbaked clay, etched with some very rude ornaments ; his skill apparently being inadequate to baking the vase, when completely finished. The contents were bones and ashes, and a quantity of beads made of coal. This seems to

have been a barbarous imitation of the Roman fashion of Sepulture.

Page 62, line 20. *Fell by the side of great Dundee.*

The Viscount of Dundee, slain in the battle of Killiecrankie.

Line 28. *For pathless marsh and mountain cell.*

The morasses were the usual refuge of the Border herdsmen, on the approach of an English army. Caves, hewed in the most dangerous and inaccessible places, also afforded an occasional retreat. Such caverns may be seen in the precipitous banks of the Teviot at Sunlaws, upon the Ale at Ancram, upon the Jed at Hundalee, and in many other places upon the Border. The banks of the Esk at Gorton and Hawthornden are hollowed into similar recesses. But even these dreary dens were not always secure places of concealment.

Line 40. *Watt Tinlinn, from the Liddel-side.*

This person was, in my younger days, the theme of many a fireside tale. He was a retainer of the Buccleuch family, and held for his Border service a small tower on the frontiers of Liddesdale. Watt was, by profession, a *sutor*, but, by inclination and practice, an archer and warrior. Upon one occasion, the Captain of Bewcastle, military governor of that wild district of Cumberland, is said to have made an incursion into Scotland, in which he was defeated and forced to fly. Watt Tinlinn pursued him closely through a dangerous morass ; the captain, however, gained the firm ground ; and seeing Tinlinn dismounted, and floundering in the bog, used these words of insult : ' Sutor Watt, ye cannot sew your boots ; the heels *risp* [creak], and the seams *rive*.' ' If I cannot sew,' retorted Tinlinn, discharging a shaft, which nailed the captain's thigh to his saddle, ' if I cannot sew, I can *yerk*,' i. e. twitch, as shoemakers do in securing the stitches of their work.

Line 51. *I think 't will prove a Warden-raid.*

An inroad commanded by the warden in person.

Line 60. *Of silver brooch and bracelet proud.*

As the Borderers were indifferent about the furniture of their habitations, so much exposed to be burned and plundered, they were proportionally anxious to display splendor in decorating and ornamenting their females.

Line 74. *Belted Will Howard is marching here.*

Lord William Howard, third son of Thomas, Duke of Norfolk, succeeded to Naworth Castle, and a large domain annexed to it, in right of his wife Elizabeth, sister of George Lord Dacre, who died without heirs-male, in the 11th of Queen Elizabeth. By a poetical anachronism, he is introduced into the romance a few years earlier than he actually flourished. He was warden of the Western Marches; and, from the rigor with which he repressed the Border excesses, the name of Belted Will Howard is still famous in our traditions. In the castle of Naworth, his apartments, containing a bedroom, oratory, and library, are still shown. They impress us with an unpleasing idea of the life of a lord warden of the Marches. Three or four strong doors, separating these rooms from the rest of the castle, indicate the apprehensions of treachery from his garrison; and the secret winding passages, through which he could privately descend into the guard-room, or even into the dungeons, imply the necessity of no small degree of secret superintendence on the part of the governor. As the ancient books and furniture have remained undisturbed, the venerable appearance of these apartments, and the armor scattered around the chamber, almost lead us to expect the arrival of the warden in person. Naworth Castle is situated near Brampton, in Cumberland. Lord William Howard is ancestor of the Earls of Carlisle.

Line 75. *And hot Lord Dacre, with many a spear.*

The well-known name of Dacre is derived from the exploits of one of their ancestors at the siege of Acre, or Ptolemais, under Richard Cœur-de-Lion.

Line 76. *And all the German hackbut-men.*

In the wars with Scotland, Henry VIII. and his successors employed numerous bands of mercenary troops. At the battle of Pinky, there were in the English army six hundred hackbutters on foot, and two hundred on horseback, composed chiefly of foreigners. From the battle-pieces of the ancient Flemish painters, we learn that the Low Country and German soldiers marched to an assault with their right knees bared. And we may also observe, in such pictures, the extravagance to which they carried the fashion of ornamenting their dress with knots of ribbon.

Page 63, line 119. *'Ready, aye ready,' for the field.*

Sir John Scott of Thirlestane flourished in the reign of James V., and possessed the estates of Thirlestane, Gamescleuch, etc., lying upon the river of Ettrick, and extending to St. Mary's Loch, at the head of Yarrow. It appears that when James had assembled his nobility, and their feudal followers, at Fala, with the purpose of invading England, and was, as is well known, disappointed by the obstinate refusal of his peers, this baron alone declared himself ready to follow the King wherever he should lead. In memory of his fidelity, James granted to his family a charter of arms, entitling them to bear a border of fleurs-de-luce similar to the tressure in the royal arms, with a bundle of spears for the crest; motto, *Ready, aye ready.*

Line 120. *An aged knight, to danger steeled.*

The family of Harden are descended from a younger son of the Laird of Buccleuch, who flourished before the estate of Murdieston was acquired by the marriage of one of those chieftains with the heiress, in 1296. Walter Scott of Harden, who flourished during the reign of Queen Mary, was a renowned Border freebooter. His castle was situated upon the very brink of a dark and precipitous dell, through which a scanty rivulet steals to meet the Borthwick. In

the recess of this glen he is said to have kept his spoil, which served for the daily maintenance of his retainers, until the production of a pair of clean spurs, in a covered dish, announced to the hungry band that they must ride for a supply of provisions. He was married to Mary Scott, daughter of Philip Scott of Dryhope, and called in song the Flower of Yarrow. He possessed a very extensive estate, which was divided among his five sons.

Line 145. *Scotts of Eskdale, a stalwart band.*

In this and the following stanzas, some account is given of the mode in which the property in the valley of Esk was transferred from the Beattisons, its ancient possessors, to the name of Scott. It is needless to repeat the circumstances, which are given in the poem literally as they have been preserved by tradition. Lord Maxwell, in the latter part of the sixteenth century, took upon himself the title of Earl of Morton. The descendants of Beattison of Woodkerrick, who aided the earl to escape from his disobedient vassals, continued to hold these lands within the memory of man, and were the only Beattisons who had property in the dale. The old people give locality to the story by showing the Galliard's Haugh, the place where Buccleuch's men were concealed, etc.

Page 64, line 229. *Their gathering word was Bellenden.*

Bellenden is situated near the head of Borthwick Water, and being in the centre of the possessions of the Scotts, was frequently used as their place of rendezvous and gathering word.

Page 65, line 365. *Bore high a gauntlet on his spear.*

A glove upon a lance was the emblem of faith among the ancient Borderers, who were wont, when any one broke his word, to expose this emblem, and proclaim him a faithless villain at the first Border meeting. This ceremony was much dreaded.

Page 66, line 409. *That he may suffer march-treason pain.*

Several species of offences, peculiar to the Border, constituted what was called march-treason. Among others, was the crime of riding, or causing to ride, against the opposite country during the time of truce.

Line 437. *Will cleanse him by oath of march-treason stain.*

In dubious cases, the innocence of Border criminals was occasionally referred to their own oath. The form of excusing bills, or indictments, by Border-oath, ran thus : ' You shall swear by heaven above you, hell beneath you, by your part of Paradise, by all that God made in six days and seven nights, and by God himself, you are whart out sackless of art, part, way, witting, ridd, kenning, having, or recetting of any of the goods and cattels named in this bill. So help you God.'

Line 442. *Knighthood he took of Douglas' sword.*

The dignity of knighthood, according to the original institution, had this peculiarity, that it did not flow from the monarch, but could be conferred by one who himself possessed it, upon any squire who, after due probation, was found to merit the honor of chivalry. Latterly, this power was confined to generals, who were wont to create knights bannerets after or before an engagement. Even so late as the reign of Queen Elizabeth, Essex highly offended his jealous sovereign by the indiscriminate exertion of this privilege.

Line 443. *When English blood swelled Ancram ford.*

The battle of Ancram Moor, or Penielheuch, was fought A. D. 1545. The English, commanded by Sir Ralph Evers, and Sir Brian Latoun, were totally routed, and both their leaders slain in the action. The Scottish army was commanded by Archibald Douglas, Earl of Angus, assisted by the Laird of Buccleuch, and Norman Lesley.

Page 67, line 505. *Said the Blanche Lion e'er fall back.*

This was the cognizance of the noble house of Howard in all its branches. The crest, or bearing, of a warrior was often used as a *nom de guerre.* Thus Richard III. acquired his well-known epithet, *The Boar of York.* In the violent satire on Cardinal Wolsey, written by Roy, the Duke of Buckingham is called the *Beautiful Swan,* and the Duke of Norfolk, or Earl of Surrey, the *White Lion.*

Page 68, line 570. *But he, the jovial harper, taught.*

The person here alluded to, is one of our ancient Border minstrels, called Rattling Roaring Willie. This *sobriquet* was probably derived from his bullying disposition ; being, it would seem, such a roaring boy as is frequently mentioned in old plays. While drinking at Newmill, upon Teviot, about five miles above Hawick, Willie chanced to quarrel with one of his own profession, who was usually distinguished by the odd name of Sweet Milk, from a place on Rule Water so called. They retired to a meadow on the opposite side of the Teviot, to decide the contest with their swords, and Sweet Milk was killed on the spot. A thorn-tree marks the scene of the murder, which is still called Sweet Milk Thorn. Willie was taken and executed at Jedburgh, bequeathing his name to the beautiful Scotch air, called 'Rattling Roaring Willie.'

Line 574. *Of Black Lord Archibald's battle-laws.*

The most ancient collection of Border regulations.

Page 69, line 51. *The Bloody Heart blazed in the van.*

The chief of this potent race of heroes, about the date of the poem, was Archibald Douglas, seventh Earl of Angus, a man of great courage and activity. The Bloody Heart was the well-known cognizance of the House of Douglas, assumed from the time of good Lord James, to whose care Robert Bruce committed his heart, to be carried to the Holy Land.

Line 54. *Where the Seven Spears of Wedderburne.*

Sir David Home, of Wedderburn, who was slain in the fatal battle of Flodden, left seven sons by his wife Isabel. They were called the Seven Spears of Wedderburn.

Line 58. *Of Clarence's Plantagenet.*

At the battle of Beauge, in France, Thomas, Duke of Clarence, brother to Henry V., was unhorsed by Sir John Swinton of Swinton, who distinguished him by a coronet set with precious stones, which he wore around his helmet. The family of Swinton is one of the most ancient in Scotland, and produced many celebrated warriors.

Line 65. *And shouting still, ' A Home ! a Home.'*

The Earls of Home, as descendants of the Dunbars, ancient Earls of March, carried a lion rampant, argent ; but, as a difference, changed the color of the shield from gules to vert, in allusion to Greenlaw, their ancient possession. The slogan, or war-cry, of this powerful family, was, 'A Home ! a Home !' It was anciently placed in an escrol above the crest. The helmet is armed with a lion's head erased gules, with a cap of state gules, turned up ermine. The *Hepburns,* a powerful family in East Lothian, were usually in close alliance with the Homes. The chief of this clan was Hepburn, Lord of Hailes, a family which terminated in the too famous Earl of Bothwell.

Line 110. *Pursued the football play.*

The football was anciently a very favorite sport all through Scotland, but especially upon the Borders. Sir John Carmichael of Carmichael, Warden of the Middle Marches, was killed in 1600 by a band of the Armstrongs, returning from a football match. Sir Robert Carey, in his Memoirs, mentions a great meeting, appointed by the Scotch riders to be held at Kelso for the purpose of playing at football, but which terminated in an incursion upon England.

Page 70, line 122. *Twixt truce and war, such sudden change.*

Notwithstanding the constant wars upon the Borders, and the occasional cruelties which marked the mutual inroads, the inhabitants on either side do not appear to have regarded each other with that violent and personal animosity, which might have been expected. On the contrary, like the outposts of hostile armies, they often carried on something resembling friendly intercourse, even in the middle of hostilities ; and it is evident, from various ordinances against trade and intermarriages, between English and Scottish Borderers, that the governments of both countries were jealous of their cherishing too intimate a connection.

The Border meetings of truce which, although places of merchandise and merriment, often witnessed the most bloody scenes, may serve to illustrate the description in the text. They are vividly portrayed in the old ballad of the Reidsquair. Both parties came armed to a meeting of the wardens, yet they intermixed fearlessly and peaceably with each other in mutual sports and familiar intercourse, until a casual fray arose : —

'Then was there nought but bow and spear
And every man pulled out a brand.'

In the 29th stanza of this canto, there is an
attempt to express some of the mixed feelings
with which the Borderers on each side were led
to regard their neighbors.

Page 74, line 494. *Cheer the dark bloodhound
on his way.*

The pursuit of Border maurauders was followed by the injured party and his friends with
bloodhounds and bugle-horn, and was called the
hot-trod. He was entitled, if his dog could trace
the scent, to follow the invaders into the opposite kingdom ; a privilege which often occasioned bloodshed. The breed was kept up by
the Buccleuch family on their Border estates
till within the eighteenth century.

Page 75, line 68. *She wrought not by forbidden
spell.*

Popular belief, though contrary to the doctrines of the Church, made a favorable distinction betwixt magicians and necromancers, or
wizards ; the former were supposed to command
the evil spirits, and the latter to serve, or at
least to be in league and compact with, those
enemies of mankind. The arts of subjecting
the demons were manifold ; sometimes the
fiends were actually swindled by the magicians.

Line 79. *A merlin sat upon her wrist.*

A merlin, or sparrow-hawk, was actually carried by ladies of rank, as a falcon was, in time
of peace, the constant attendant of a knight or
baron. Godscroft relates, that when Mary of
Lorraine was regent, she pressed the Earl of
Angus to admit a royal garrison into his Castle
of Tantallon. To this he returned no direct
answer ; but, as if apostrophizing a goshawk,
which sat on his wrist, and which he was feeding during the Queen's speech, he exclaimed,
' The devil 's in this greedy glede, she will never
be full.' Barclay complains of the common and
indecent practice of bringing hawks and hounds
into churches.

Lines 90, 91.

*And princely peacock's gilded train,
And o'er the boar-head garnished brave.*

The peacock, it is well known, was considered,
during the times of chivalry, not merely as an
exquisite delicacy, but as a dish of peculiar
solemnity. After being roasted, it was again
decorated with its plumage, and a sponge,
dipped in lighted spirits of wine, was placed
in its bill. When it was introduced on days
of grand festival, it was the signal for the adventurous knights to take upon them vows to
do some deed of chivalry, ' before the peacock
and the ladies.'

The boar's head was also a usual dish of
feudal splendor. In Scotland it was sometimes
surrounded with little banners, displaying the
colors and achievements of the baron at whose
board it was served.

Line 92. *And cygnet from Saint Mary's wave.*

There are often flights of swans upon St.
Mary's Lake, at the head of the river Yarrow.

[Wordsworth's ' Yarrow Visited ' will be re-
called : —
' The swan on still Saint Mary's Lake
Floats double, swan and shadow.']

Line 120. *Smote with his gauntlet stout Hunthill.*

The Rutherfords of Hunthill were an ancient
race of Border Lairds, whose names occur in
history, sometimes as defending the frontier
against the English, sometimes as disturbing the
peace of their own country. Dickon Draw-the-
sword was son to the ancient warrior, called in
tradition the Cock of Hunthill, remarkable for
leading into battle nine sons, gallant warriors,
all sons of the aged champion.

Line 128. *But bit his glove and shook his head.*

To bite the thumb, or the glove, seems not to
have been considered, upon the Border, as a
gesture of contempt, though so used by Shakespeare, but as a pledge of mortal revenge. It
is yet remembered that a young gentleman of
Teviotdale, on the morning after a hard drinking-bout, observed that he had bitten his glove.
He instantly demanded of his companion, with
whom he had quarrelled ? And, learning that
he had had words with one of the party, insisted
on instant satisfaction, asserting that though he
remembered nothing of the dispute, yet he was
sure he never would have bit his glove unless he
had received some unpardonable insult. He
fell in the duel, which was fought near Selkirk,
in 1721.

Page 76, line 144. *The pledge to Arthur Fire-
the-Braes.*

The person bearing this redoubtable *nom de
guerre* was an Elliot, and resided at Thorles-
hope, in Liddesdale. He occurs in the list of
Border riders, in 1597.

Line 154. *Since old Buccleuch the name did
gain.*

A tradition preserved by Scott of Satchells
gives the following romantic origin of that name.
Two brethren, natives of Galloway, having been
banished from that country for a riot, or insurrection, came to Rankleburn, in Ettrick Forest,
where the keeper, whose name was Brydone,
received them joyfully, on account of their skill
in winding the horn, and in the other mysteries
of the chase. Kenneth MacAlpin, then King of
Scotland, came soon after to hunt in the royal
forest, and pursued a buck from Ettrickheuch
to the glen now called Buckcleuch, about two
miles above the junction of Rankleburn with
the river Ettrick. Here the stag stood at bay ;
and the king and his attendants, who followed
on horseback, were thrown out by the steep-
ness of the hill and the morass. John, one of
the brethren from Galloway, had followed the
chase on foot ; and now coming in, seized the
buck by the horns, and, being a man of great
strength and activity, threw him on his back,
and ran with his burden about a mile up the
steep hill, to a place called Cracra-Cross, where
Kenneth had halted, and laid the buck at the
sovereign's feet.

Line 181. *And first stepped forth old Albert
Græme.*

John Grahame, second son of *Malice*, Earl of *Monteith*, commonly surnamed *John with the Bright Sword*, upon some displeasure risen against him at court, retired with many of his clan and kindred into the English Borders, in the reign of King Henry the Fourth, where they seated themselves; and many of their posterity have continued there ever since. Mr. Sandford, speaking of them, says (which indeed was applicable to most of the Borderers on both sides): 'They were all stark moss-troopers, and arrant thieves: Both to England and Scotland outlawed: yet sometimes connived at, because they gave intelligence forth of Scotland, and would raise 400 horse at any time upon a raid of the English into Scotland. A saying is recorded of a mother to her son (which is now become proverbial), *Ride, Rowley, hough's i' the pot*: that is, the last piece of beef was in the pot, and therefore it was high time for him to go and fetch more.' *History of Cumberland*, introd.

The residence of the Græmes being chiefly in the Debatable Land, so called because it was claimed by both kingdoms, their depredations extended both to England and Scotland with impunity; for as both wardens accounted them the proper subjects of their own prince, neither inclined to demand reparation for their excesses from the opposite officers, which would have been an acknowledgment of his jurisdiction over them.

Page 77, line 229. *The gentle Surrey loved his lyre.*

The gallant and unfortunate Henry Howard, Earl of Surrey, was unquestionably the most accomplished cavalier of his time; and his sonnets display beauties which would do honor to a more polished age. He was beheaded on Tower-hill in 1546; a victim to the mean jealousy of Henry VIII., who could not bear so brilliant a character near his throne.

The song of the supposed bard is founded on an incident said to have happened to the Earl in his travels. Cornelius Agrippa, the celebrated alchemist, showed him, in a looking-glass, the lovely Geraldine, to whose service he had devoted his pen and his sword. The vision represented her as indisposed, and reclining upon a couch, reading her lover's verses by the light of a waxen taper.

Page 78, line 312. *Where erst Saint Clairs held princely sway.*

The St. Clairs are of Norman extraction, being descended from William de St. Clair, second son of Walderne Compte de St. Clair, and Margaret, daughter to Richard, Duke of Normandy. He was called, for his fair deportment, the Seemly St. Clair; and, settling in Scotland during the reign of Malcolm Calnmore, obtained large grants of land in Mid-Lothian.

Line 314. *Still nods their palace to its fall.*

The Castle of Kirkwall was built by the St. Clairs while Earls of Orkney. It was dismantled by the Earl of Caithness about 1615, having been garrisoned against the government by Robert Stewart, natural son to the Earl of Orkney.

Line 329. *Their barks the dragons of the wave.*

The chief of the *Vakingr* or Scandinavian pirates assumed the title of Sækonungs, or Sea-kings. Ships, in the inflated language of the Skalds, are often termed the serpents of the ocean.

Line 336. *Of that Sea-snake, tremendous curled.*

The *jormungandr*, or Snake of the Ocean, whose folds surround the earth, is one of the wildest fictions of the Edda. It was very nearly caught by the god Thor, who went to fish for it with a hook baited with a bull's head. In the battle betwixt the evil demons and the divinities of Odin, which is to precede the *Ragnarockr*, or Twilight of the Gods, this Snake is to act a conspicuous part.

Line 338. *Of those dread Maids whose hideous yell.*

These were the *Valkyrier*, or Selectors of the Slain, despatched by Odin from Valhalla, to choose those who were to die, and to distribute the contest. They are well known to the English reader as Gray's Fatal Sisters.

Line 340. *Of chiefs who, guided through the gloom.*

The Northern warriors were usually entombed with their arms and their other treasures. Thus Angantyr, before commencing the duel in which he was slain, stipulated that if he fell, his sword Tyrfing should be buried with him. His daughter, Hervor, afterwards took it from his tomb. The dialogue which passed betwixt her and Angantyr's spirit on this occasion has been often translated. The whole history may be found in the Hervarar-Saga. Indeed, the ghosts of the Northern warriors were not wont tamely to suffer their tombs to be plundered; and hence the mortal heroes had an additional temptation to attempt such adventures; for they held nothing more worthy of their valor than to encounter supernatural beings.

Line 355. *That mourns the lovely Rosabelle.*

This was a family name in the house of St. Clair. Henry St. Clair, the second of the line, married Rosabelle, fourth daughter of the Earl of Stratherne.

Line 358. *Rest thee in Castle Ravensheuch.*

A large and strong castle, situated betwixt Kirkaldy and Dysart, on a steep crag, washed by the Frith of Forth. It was conferred on Sir William St. Clair, as a slight compensation for the earldom of Orkney, by a charter of King James III., dated in 1471.

Page 79, line 455. *Who spoke the spectre-hound in Man.*

The ancient castle of Peel-town in the Isle of Man is surrounded by four churches, now ruinous. They say that an apparition, called, in the Mankish language, the *Mauthe Doog*, in the shape of a large black spaniel, with curled shaggy hair, was used to haunt Peel-castle; and has been frequently seen in every room, but particularly in the guard-chamber, where, as soon as candles were lighted, it came and lay down before the fire, in presence of all the soldiers, who, at length, by being so much accustomed to the sight of it, lost great part of the terror they were seized with at its first appearance. But though they endured the shock of such a guest when all together in a body, none cared to be left alone with it. It being the custom, therefore, for one of the soldiers to lock the gates of the castle at a certain hour, and carry the keys to the captain, to whose apartment . . . the way led through the church, they agreed among themselves, that whoever was to succeed the ensuing night his fellow in this errand, should accompany him that went first, and by this means no man would be exposed singly to the danger. One night a fellow, being drunk, laughed at the simplicity of his companions ; and though it was not his turn to go with the keys, would needs take that office upon him, to testify his courage. All the soldiers endeavored to dissuade him ; but the more they said, the more resolute he seemed, and swore that he desired nothing more than that the *Mauthe Doog* would follow him as it had done the others ; for he would try if it were dog or devil. After having talked in a very reprobate manner for some time, he snatched up the keys, and went out of the guard-room. In some time after his departure, a great noise was heard, but nobody had the boldness to see what occasioned it, till, the adventurer returning, they demanded the knowledge of him ; but as loud and noisy as he had been at leaving them, he was now become sober and silent enough ; for he was never heard to speak more ; and though all the time he lived, which was three days, he was entreated by all who came near him, either to speak, or, if he could not do that, to make some signs, by which they might understand what had happened to him, yet nothing intelligible could be got from him, only that, by the distortion of his limbs and features, it might be guessed that he died in agonies more than is common in a natural death.

Page 80, line 469. *Did to Saint Bride of Douglas make.*

This was a favorite saint of the house of Douglas, and of the Earl of Angus in particular, as we learn from Godscroft, who says: 'The Queen-Regent had proposed to raise a rival noble to the ducal dignity ; and discoursing of her purpose with Angus, he answered, "Why not, madam ? we are happy that have such a princess, that can know and will acknowledge men's services, and is willing to recompense it ; but, by the might of God" (this was his oath when he was serious and in anger ; at other times, it was by St. Bryde of Douglas), "if he be a Duke, I will be a Drake !" So she desisted from prosecuting of that purpose.'

MARMION: A TALE OF FLODDEN FIELD.
Page 89, line 72. *Who victor died on Gadite wave.*
Nelson.
Line 130. *For talents mourn, untimely lost.*
[The Introductory Note has a reference to the first form which the twelve lines beginning

thus, took. The lines as originally written by Scott before revision at the suggestion of Lord Abercorn were as follows : —

'If genius high, and judgment sound,
  And wit that loved to play, not wound,
And all the reasoning powers divine,
To penetrate, resolve, combine,
Could save one mortal of the herd
From error — Fox had never erred.']

Page 91, line 258. *As when the champion of the lake.*

[Launcelot du Lac. When Scott wrote, the romances of King Arthur were not so familiar to readers as they have since become, both through the frequent issues of Sir Thomas Malory's *Morte d'Arthur*, and through the popularization effected by Tennyson. He illustrated this and other passages in the Introduction to Canto First, by copious extracts from Malory.]

Line 275. *And Dryden in immortal strain.*

Dryden's melancholy account of his projected Epic Poem, blasted by the selfish and sordid parsimony of his patrons, is contained in an *Essay on Satire*, addressed to the Earl of Dorset, and prefaced to the *Translation of Juvenal*. After mentioning a plan of supplying machinery from the guardian angels of kingdoms, mentioned in the Book of Daniel, he adds: 'Thus, my Lord, I have, as briefly as I could, given your lordship, and by you the world, a rude draft of what I have been long laboring in my imagination, and what I had intended to have put in practice (though far unable for the attempt of such a poem); and to have left the stage, to which my genius never much inclined me, for a work which would have taken up my life in the performance of it. This, too, I had intended chiefly for the honor of my native country, to which a poet is particularly obliged. Of two subjects, both relating to it, I was doubtful whether I should choose that of King Arthur conquering the Saxons, which, being further distant in time, gives the greater scope to my invention ; or that of Edward the Black Prince, in subduing Spain, and restoring it to the lawful prince, though a great tyrant, Don Pedro the Cruel ; which, for the compass of time, including only the expedition of one year, for the greatness of the action, and its answerable event, for the magnanimity of the English hero, opposed to the ingratitude of the person whom he restored, and for the many beautiful episodes which I had interwoven with the principal design, together with the characters of the chiefest English persons (wherein, after Virgil and Spenser, I would have taken occasion to represent my living friends and patrons of the noblest families, and also shadowed the events of future ages in the succession of our imperial line), — with these helps, and those of the machines which I have mentioned, I might perhaps have done as well as some of my predecessors, or at least chalked out a way for others to amend my errors in a like design ; but being encouraged only with fair words by King Charles II., my little salary ill paid, and no prospect of a future subsistence, I was then discouraged in the beginning of my attempt ; and now age has overtaken me ; and want, a more insufferable evil, through the change of the times, has wholly disabled me.'

Line 312. *Ytene's oaks — beneath whose shade.*
The New Forest in Hampshire, anciently so called.

Line 314. *Of Ascapart, and Bevis bold.*
[Ascapart, or Ascabart, was a giant who figures in the *History of Bevis of Hampton*, by whom he was conquered. The images of the two are still to be seen on either side of an old gate at Southampton.]

Line 325. *Partenopex's mystic love.*
[Mr. Rose published in 1808 a poem entitled *Partenopex de Blois.*]

Line 1. *Day set on Norham's castled steep.*
The ruinous castle of Norham (anciently called Ubbanford) is situated on the southern bank of the Tweed, about six miles above Berwick, and where that river is still the boundary between England and Scotland. The extent of its ruins, as well as its historical importance, show it to have been a place of magnificence, as well as strength. Edward I. resided there when he was created umpire of the dispute concerning the Scottish succession. It was repeatedly taken and retaken during the wars between England and Scotland ; and, indeed, scarce any happened in which it had not a principal share. Norham Castle is situated on a steep bank which overhangs the river. The repeated sieges which the castle had sustained rendered frequent repairs necessary. In 1164 it was almost rebuilt by Hugh Pudsey, Bishop of Durham, who added a huge keep or donjon ; notwithstanding which, King Henry II., in 1174, took the castle from the bishop, and committed the keeping of it to William de Neville. After this period it seems to have been chiefly garrisoned by the king, and considered as a royal fortress. The Greys of Chillinghame Castle were frequently the castellans or captains of the garrison. Yet, as the castle was situated in the patrimony of Saint Cuthbert, the property was in the see of Durham till the Reformation.
The ruins of the castle consist of a large shattered tower, with many vaults, and fragments of other edifices, enclosed within an outward wall of great circuit.

Line 4. *The battled towers, the donjon keep.*
It is perhaps unnecessary to remind my readers that *donjon*, in its proper signification, means the strongest part of a feudal castle ; a high square tower, with walls of tremendous thickness, situated in the centre of the other buildings, from which, however, it was usually detached. Here, in case of the outward defences being gained, the garrison retreated to make their last stand. The donjon contained the great hall, and principal rooms of state for solemn occasions, and also the prison of the fortress ; from which last circumstance we derive the modern and restricted use of the word *dungeon*.

Page 92, line 29. *O'er Horncliff-hill, a plump of spears.*
This word properly applies to a flight of water-fowl ; but is applied, by analogy, to a body of horse.

'There is a knight of the North Country
Which leads a lusty *plump* of spears.'
Flodden Field.

Line 79. *In mail and plate of Milan steel.*
The artists of Milan were famous in the middle ages for their skill in armory, as appears from the following passage, in which Froissart gives an account of the preparations made by Henry, Earl of Hereford, afterwards Henry IV., and Thomas, Duke of Norfolk, Earl Marischal, for their proposed combat in the lists at Coventry : 'These two lords made ample provision of all things necessary for the combat ; and the Earl of Derby sent off messengers to Lombardy, to have armor from Sir Galeas, Duke of Milan. The duke complied with joy, and gave the knight, called Sir Francis, who had brought the message, the choice of all his armor for the Earl of Derby. When he had selected what he wished for in plated and mail armor, the Lord of Milan, out of his abundant love for the earl, ordered four of the best armorers in Milan to accompany the knight to England, that the Earl of Derby might be more completely armed.'

Line 88. *Who checks at me, to death is dight.*
The crest and motto of Marmion are borrowed from the following story : Sir David de Lindesay, first Earl of Cranford, was, among other gentlemen of quality, attended, during a visit to London, in 1390, by Sir William Dalzell, who was, according to my authority, Bower, not only excelling in wisdom, but also of a lively wit. Chancing to be at the court, he there saw Sir Piers Courtenay, an English knight, famous for skill in tilting, and for the beauty of his person, parading the palace, arrayed in a new mantle, bearing for device an embroidered falcon, with this rhyme, —

'I bear a falcon, fairest of flight,
Whoso pinches at her, his death is dight,
In graith.'

The Scottish knight, being a wag, appeared next day in a dress exactly similar to that of Courtenay, but bearing a magpie instead of a falcon, with a motto ingeniously contrived to rhyme to the vaunting inscription of Sir Piers : —

'I bear a pie picking at a peice,
Whoso picks at her, I shall pick at his nese,
In faith.'

This affront could only be expiated by a joust with sharp lances. In the course, Dalzell left his helmet unlaced, so that it gave way at the touch of his antagonist's lance, and he thus avoided the shock of the encounter. This happened twice : in the third encounter, the handsome Courtenay lost two of his front teeth. As the Englishman complained bitterly of Dalzell's fraud in not fastening his helmet, the Scottish-man agreed to run six courses more, each champion staking in the hand of the king two hundred pounds, to be forfeited if, on entering the lists, any unequal advantage should be detected. This being agreed to, the wily Scot demanded that Sir Piers, in addition to the loss of his teeth, should consent to the extinction of one of his eyes, he himself having lost an eye in the fight of Otterburn. As Courtenay demurred to this equalization of optical powers, Dalzell demanded the forfeit, which, after much altercation, the king appointed to be paid to him, saying he surpassed the English both in wit and valor.

Page 93, line 156. *They hailed Lord Marmion.*

Lord Marmion, the principal character of the present romance, is entirely a fictitious personage. In earlier times, indeed, the family of Marmion, Lords of Fontenay, in Normandy, was highly distinguished. Robert de Marmion, Lord of Fontenay, a distinguished follower of the Conqueror, obtained a grant of the castle and town of Tamworth, and also of the manor of Scrivelby, in Lincolnshire. One or both of these noble possessions was held by the honorable service of being the royal champion, as the ancestors of Marmion had formerly been to the Dukes of Normandy. But after the castle and demesne of Tamworth had passed through four successive barons from Robert, the family became extinct in the person of Philip de Marmion, who died in 20th Edward I. without issue male. He was succeeded in his castle of Tamworth by Alexander de Freville, who married Mazera, his granddaughter. Baldwin de Freville, Alexander's descendant, in the reign of Richard I., by the supposed tenure of his castle of Tamworth, claimed the office of royal champion, and to do the service appertaining; namely, on the day of coronation to ride, completely armed, upon a barbed horse, into Westminster Hall, and there to challenge the combat against any who would gainsay the king's title. But this office was adjudged to Sir John Dymoke, to whom the manor of Scrivelby had descended by another of the coheiresses of Robert de Marmion; and it remains in that family, whose representative is Hereditary Champion of England at the present day. The family and possessions of Freville have merged in the Earls of Ferrars. I have not, therefore, created a new family, but only revived the titles of an old one in an imaginary personage.

Line 163. *Now, largesse, largesse, Lord Marmion.*

This was the cry with which heralds and pursuivants were wont to acknowledge the bounty received from the knights. The heralds, like the minstrels, were a race allowed to have great claims upon the liberality of the knights, of whose feats they kept a record, and proclaimed them aloud, as in the text, upon suitable occasions. At Berwick, Norham, and other Border fortresses of importance, pursuivants usually resided, whose inviolable character rendered them the only persons that could, with perfect assurance of safety, be sent on necessary embassies into Scotland. This is alluded to in stanza xxi. below.

Line 194. *And Captain of the Hold.*

Were accuracy of any consequence in a fictitious narrative, this castellan's name ought to have been William; for William Heron of Ford was husband to the famous Lady Ford, whose siren charms are said to have cost our James IV. so dear. Moreover, the said William Heron was, at the time supposed, a prisoner in Scotland, being surrendered by Henry VIII., on account of his share in the slaughter of Sir Robert Kerr of Cessford. His wife, represented in the text as residing at the Court of Scotland, was, in fact, living in her own castle at Ford.

Page 94, line 264. *I left him sick in Lindisfarne.*

Lindisfarne, an isle on the coast of Northumberland, was called *Holy Island*, from the sanctity of its ancient monastery, and from its having been the Episcopal seat of the see of Durham during the early ages of British Christianity. A succession of holy men held that office; but their merits were swallowed up in the superior fame of Saint Cuthbert, who was sixth bishop of Durham, and who bestowed the name of his 'patrimony' upon the extensive property of the see. The ruins of the monastery upon Holy Island betoken great antiquity. The arches are, in general, strictly Saxon; and the pillars which support them, short, strong, and massy. In some places, however, there are pointed windows, which indicate that the building has been repaired at a period long subsequent to the original foundation. The exterior ornaments of the building, being of a light sandy stone, have been wasted, as described in the text. Lindisfarne is not properly an island, but rather, as the Venerable Bede has termed it, a semi-isle; for, although surrounded by the sea at full tide, the ebb leaves the sands dry between it and the opposite coast of Northumberland, from which it is about three miles distant.

Line 298. *Warbeck, that Flemish counterfeit.*

The story of Perkin Warbeck, or Richard, Duke of York, is well known. In 1496 he was received honorably in Scotland; and James IV., after conferring upon him in marriage his own relation, the Lady Catherine Gordon, made war on England in behalf of his pretensions. To retaliate an invasion of England, Surrey advanced into Berwickshire at the head of considerable forces, but retreated after taking the inconsiderable fortress of Ayton.

Line 304. *For here be some have pricked as far.*

The garrisons of the English castles of Wark, Norham, and Berwick were, as may be easily supposed, very troublesome neighbors to Scotland. Sir Richard Maitland of Ledington wrote a poem, called 'The Blind Baron's Comfort,' when his barony of Blythe, in Lauderdale, was *harried* by Rowland Foster, the English captain of Wark, with his company, to the number of 300 men. They spoiled the poetical knight of 5,000 sheep, 200 nolt, 30 horses and mares ; the whole furniture of his house of Blythe, worth 100 pounds Scots, and everything else that was portable. ' This spoil was committed the 16th day of May, 1570 (and the said Sir Richard was threescore and fourteen years of age, and grown blind), in time of peace ; when nane of that country *lippened* [expected] such a thing.'

Page 95, line 309. *And given them light to set their hoods.*

The line contains a phrase by which the Borderers jocularly intimated the burning of a house. When the Maxwells, in 1685, burned the castle of Lockwood, they said they did so to give the Lady Johnstone ' light to set her hood.' Nor was the phrase inapplicable ; for, in a letter to which I have mislaid the reference, the Earl of Northumberland writes to the king and council, that he dressed himself, at midnight, at Warwick, by the blaze of the neighboring villages burned by the Scottish marauders.

Line 342. *The priest of Shoreswood — he could rein.*

This churchman seems to have been akin to Welsh, the vicar of St. Thomas of Exeter, a leader among the Cornish insurgents in 1549. ' This man,' says Holinshed, ' had many good things in him. He was of no great stature, but well set, and mightilie compact : he was a very good wrestler ; shot well, both in the long-bow, and also in the cross-bow ; he handled his hand-gun and peece very well ; he was a very good woodman, and a hardie, and such a one as would not give his head for the poling, or his beard for the washing. He was a companion in any exercise of activitie, and of a courteous and gentle behaviour. He descended of a good, honest parentage, being borne at Peneverin in Cornwall ; and yet, in this rebellion, an arch-captain, and a principal doer.' This model of clerical talents had the misfortune to be hanged upon the steeple of his own church.

Page 96, line 407. *Saint Rosalie retired to God.*

' Saint Rosalie was of Palermo, and born of a very noble family, and, when very young, abhorred so much the vanities of this world, and avoided the converse of mankind, resolving to dedicate herself wholly to God Almighty, that she, by divine inspiration, forsook her father's house, and never was more heard of, till her body was found in that cleft of a rock, on that almost inaccessible mountain, where now the chapel is built ; and they affirm she was carried up there by the hands of angels ; for that place was not formerly so accessible (as now it is) in the days of the Saint ; and even now it is a very bad, and steepy, and breakneck way. In this frightful place, this holy woman lived a great many years feeding only on what she found growing on that barren mountain, and creeping into a narrow and dreadful cleft in a

rock, which was always dropping wet, and was her place of retirement, as well as prayer ; having worn out even the rock with her knees, in a certain place, which is now opened on purpose to show it to those who come here.' — *Voyage to Sicily and Malba*, by Mr. John Dryden (son to the poet).

Line 459. *This Palmer to the castle-hall.*

A *Palmer*, opposed to a *Pilgrim*, was one who made it his sole business to visit different holy shrines, travelling incessantly, and subsisting by charity ; whereas the Pilgrim retired to his usual home and occupations, when he had paid his devotions at the particular spot which was the object of his pilgrimage.

Page 97, line 506. *Where good Saint Rule his holy lay.*

St. Regulus (*Scottice*, St. Rule) ; a monk of Patrae, in Achaia, warned by a vision, is said, A. D. 370, to have sailed westward, until he landed at St. Andrew's, in Scotland, where he founded a chapel and tower. The latter is still standing ; and, though we may doubt the precise date of its foundation, is certainly one of the most ancient edifices in Scotland. A cave, nearly fronting the ruinous castle of the Archbishops of St. Andrew's, bears the name of this religious person. It is difficult of access, and the rock in which it is hewed is washed by the German ocean. It is nearly round, about ten feet in diameter, and the same in height. On one side is a sort of stone altar ; on the other an aperture into an inner den, where the miserable ascetic, who inhabited this dwelling, probably slept. At full tide, egress and regress is hardly practicable.

Line 509. *Thence to Saint Fillan's blessed well.*

St. Fillan was a Scottish saint of some reputation. . . . There are in Perthshire several wells and springs dedicated to St. Fillan, which are still places of pilgrimage and offerings, even among the Protestants. They are held powerful in cases of madness ; and, in some of very late occurrence, lunatics have been left all night bound to the holy stone, in confidence that the saint would cure and unloose them before morning. [See also note to page 14, line 218].

Line 1. *The scenes are desert now and bare.*

Ettrick Forest, now a range of mountainous sheep-walks, was anciently reserved for the pleasure of the royal chase. Since it was disparked, the wood has been, by degrees, almost totally destroyed, although, wherever protected from the sheep, copses soon arise without any planting. When the king hunted there, he often summoned the array of the country to meet and assist his sport. Thus, in 1528, James V. ' made proclamation to all lords, barons, gentlemen, landwardmen, and freeholders, that they should compear at Edinburgh, with a month's victuals, to pass with the king where he pleased, to danton the thieves of Tiviotdale, Annandale, Liddisdale, and other parts of that country ; and also warned all gentlemen that had good dogs, to bring them, that he might hunt in the said country as he pleased : The whilk the Earl of Argyle, the Earl of Huntley, the Earl of Athole, and so all the rest of the gentlemen of the Highland, did, and brought their hounds with them in like manner, to hunt with the king, as he pleased.

' The second day of June the king passed out of Edinburgh to the hunting, with many of the nobles and gentlemen of Scotland with him, to the number of twelve thousand men ; and then past to Meggitland, and hounded and hawked all the country and bounds ; that is to say, Crammat, Pappert-law, St. Mary-laws, Carlavirick, Chapel, Ewindoores, and Longhope. I heard say, he slew, in these bounds, eighteen score of harts ' (Pitscottie's *History of Scotland*, folio ed. p. 143).

These huntings had, of course, a military character, and attendance upon them was a part of the duty of a vassal. The act for abolishing ward or military tenures in Scotland enumerates the services of hunting, hosting, watching, and warding, as those which were in future to be illegal.

Line 32. *Then oft from Newark's riven tower.*
The tale of the Outlaw Murray, who held out Newark Castle and Ettrick Forest against the king, may be found in the *Border Minstrelsy*, vol. i. In the Macfarlane MS., among other causes of James the Fifth's charter to the burgh, is mentioned that the citizens assisted him to suppress this dangerous outlaw. [See also note to page 46, line 27.]

Page 98, line 73. *Thy bowers, untenanted Bowhill !*
A seat of the Duke of Buccleuch on the Yarrow, in Ettrick Forest.

Line 115. *I called his ramparts holy ground.*
There is, on a high mountainous ridge above the farm of Ashestiel, a fosse called Wallace's Trench.

Page 99, line 147. *By lone Saint Mary's silent lake.*
This beautiful sheet of water forms the reservoir from which the Yarrow takes its source. It is connected with a smaller lake, called the Loch of the Lowes, and surrounded by mountains. In the winter it is still frequented by flights of wild swans ; hence my friend Mr. Wordsworth's lines : —

' The swans on sweet Saint Mary's lake
Float double, swan and shadow.'

Near the lower extremity of the lake are the ruins of Dryhope Tower, the birthplace of Mary Scott, daughter of Philip Scott of Dryhope, and famous by the traditional name of the Flower of Yarrow. She was married to Walter Scott of Harden, no less renowned for his depredations than his bride for her beauty. Her romantic appellation was, in latter days, with equal justice, conferred on Miss Mary Lilias Scott, the last of the elder branch of the Harden family.

Line 177. *Hath laid Our Lady's chapel low.*
The Chapel of Saint Mary of the Lowes (*de lacubus*) was situated on the eastern side of the

lake, to which it gives name. It was injured by the clan of Scott, in a feud with the Cranstouns, but continued to be a place of worship during the seventeenth century. The vestiges of the building can now scarcely be traced ; but the burial-ground is still used as a cemetery. A funeral, in a spot so very retired, has an uncommonly striking effect. The vestiges of the chaplain's house are yet visible. Being in a high situation, it commanded a full view of the lake, with the opposite mountain of Bourhope, belonging, with the lake itself, to Lord Napier. On the left hand is the tower of Dryhope, mentioned in the preceding note.

Line 202. *To sit upon the Wizard's grave.*
At one corner of the burial-ground of the demolished chapel, but without its precincts, is a small mound, called *Binram's corse*, where tradition deposits the remains of a necromantic priest, the former tenant of the chaplainry.

Line 239. *Like that which frowns round dark Loch-skene.*
A mountain lake of considerable size, at the head of the Moffat-water. The character of the scenery is uncommonly savage, and the earn, or Scottish eagle, has for many ages built its nest yearly upon an islet in the lake. Lochskene discharges itself into a brook, which, after a short and precipitate course, falls from a cataract of immense height and gloomy grandeur, called, from its appearance, the ' Gray Mare's Tail.' The ' Giant's Grave,' afterwards mentioned, is a sort of trench which bears that name, a little way from the foot of the cataract. It has the appearance of a battery, designed to command the pass.

Page 100, line 264. *Marriott, thy harp, on Isis strung.*
[Mr. Marriott himself was the author of several ballads which may be found in Scott's collection, *The Border Minstrelsy*.]

Line 9. *Where, from high Whitby's cloistered pile.*
The Abbey of Whitby, on the coast of Yorkshire, was founded A. D. 657, in consequence of a vow of Oswy, King of Northumberland. It contained both monks and nuns of the Benedictine order ; but, contrary to what was usual in such establishments, the abbess was superior to the abbot. The monastery was afterwards ruined by the Danes, and rebuilded by William Percy, in the reign of the Conqueror.

Line 10. *Bound to Saint Cuthbert's Holy Isle.*
[See note to page 94, line 264.]

Page 102, lines 233, 234.
How to their house three barons bold
Must menial service do.
The popular account of this curious service, which was probably considerably exaggerated, is thus given in *A True Account*, printed and circulated at Whitby : ' In the fifth year of the reign of Henry II., after the conquest of England by William, Duke of Normandy, the Lord of Uglebarnby, then called William de Bruce, the Lord of Smeaton, called Ralph de Percy, with a gentleman and freeholder called Allatson, did, on the 16th of October, 1159, appoint to

meet and hunt the wild boar, in a certain wood, or desert place, belonging to the Abbot of Whitby: the place's name was Eskdale-side; and the abbot's name was Sedman. Then, these young gentlemen being met, with their hounds and boar-staves, in the place before mentioned, and there having found a great wild boar, the hounds ran him well near about the chapel and hermitage of Eskdale-side, where was a monk of Whitby, who was an hermit. The boar, being very sorely pursued, and dead-run, took in at the chapel door, there laid him down, and presently died. The hermit shut the hounds out of the chapel, and kept himself within at his meditations and prayers, the hounds standing at bay without. The gentlemen, in the thick of the wood, being put behind their game, followed the cry of their hounds, and so came to the hermitage, calling on the hermit, who opened the door, and came forth; and within they found the boar lying dead: for which the gentlemen, in a very great fury, because the hounds were put from their game, did most violently and cruelly run at the hermit with their boar-staves, whereby he soon after died. Thereupon the gentlemen perceiving and knowing that they were in peril of death, took sanctuary at Scarborough; but at that time the abbot being in very great favor with the king, removed them out of the sanctuary; whereby they came in danger of the law, and not to be privileged, but likely to have the severity of the law, which was death for death. But the hermit being a holy and devout man, and at the point of death, sent for the abbot, and desired him to send for the gentlemen who had wounded him. The abbot so doing, the gentlemen came; and the hermit being very sick and weak, said unto them, "I am sure to die of those wounds you have given me." The abbot answered, "They shall as surely die for the same." But the hermit answered, "Not so, for I will freely forgive them my death, if they will be content to be enjoined the penance I shall lay on them for the safeguard of their souls." The gentlemen being present, bade him save their lives. Then said the hermit: "You and yours shall hold your lands of the Abbot of Whitby, and his successors, in this manner: That, upon Ascension-day, you, or some of you, shall come to the wood of the Strayheads, which is in Eskdale-side, the same day at sun-rising, and there shall the abbot's officer blow his horn, to the intent that you may know where to find him; and he shall deliver unto you, William de Bruce, ten stakes, eleven strout stowers, and eleven yethers, to be cut by you, or some for you, with a knife of one penny price; and you, Ralph de Percy, shall take twenty-one of each sort, to be cut in the same manner; and you, Allatson, shall take nine of each sort, to be cut as aforesaid; and to be taken on your backs, and carried to the town of Whitby, and to be there before nine of the clock the same day before mentioned. At the same hour of nine of the clock, if it be full sea, your labor and service shall cease; and, if low water, each of you shall set your stakes to the

brim, each stake one yard from the other, and so yether them on each side with your yethers; and so stake on each side with your strout stowers, that they may stand three tides, without removing by the force thereof. Each of you shall do, make, and execute the said service, at that very hour, every year, except it be full sea at that hour; but when it shall so fall out, this service shall cease. You shall faithfully do this, in remembrance that you did most cruelly slay me; and that you may have better call to God for mercy, repent unfeignedly of your sins, and do good works. The officer of Eskdale-side shall blow *Out on you! Out on you! Out on you!* for this heinous crime. If you or your successors shall refuse this service, so long as it shall not be full sea at the aforesaid hour, you or yours shall forfeit your lands to the Abbot of Whitby, or his successors. This I intreat, and earnestly beg, that you may have lives and goods preserved for this service; and I request of you to promise, by your parts in Heaven, that it shall be done by you and your successors, as is aforesaid requested; and I will confirm it by the faith of an honest man."

Then the hermit said: "My soul longeth for the Lord; and I do as freely forgive these men my death, as Christ forgave the thieves on the cross." And, in the presence of the abbot and the rest, he said moreover these words: "In manus tuos, Domine, commendo spiritum meum, a vinculis enim mortis redemisti me, Domine veritatis. Amen." So he yielded up the ghost the eighth day of December, anno Domini 1159, whose soul God have mercy upon. Amen.'

Line 244. *The lovely Edelfled.*

She was the daughter of King Oswy, who, in gratitude to Heaven for the great victory which he won in 655, against Penda, the pagan King of Mercia, dedicated Edelfleda, then but a year old, to the service of God, in the monastery of Whitby, of which Saint Hilda was then abbess. She afterwards adorned the place of her education with great magnificence.

Line 245. *And how, of thousand snakes, each one.*

These two miracles are much insisted upon by all ancient writers, who have occasion to mention either Whitby or St. Hilda. The reliques of the snakes which infested the precincts of the convent, and were, at the abbess's prayer, not only beheaded, but petrified, are still found about the rocks, and are termed by Protestant fossilists *Ammonitæ*.

The other miracle is thus mentioned by Camden: 'It is also ascribed to the power of her sanctity, that these wild geese, which, in the winter, fly in great flocks to the lakes and rivers unfrozen in the southern parts, to the great amazement of every one, fall down suddenly upon the ground, when they are in their flight over certain neighboring fields hereabouts: a relation I should not have made, if I had not received it from several credible men. But those who are less inclined to heed superstition, attribute it to some occult quality in the ground, and to somewhat of antipathy between it and the geese, such as they say is between wolves and scylla-roots. For that such hidden tendencies and aversions, as we call sympathies and antipathies, are implanted in many things by provident nature for the preservation of them, is a thing so evident that everybody grants it.'

Line 256. *His body's resting-place, of old.*

St. Cuthbert was, in the choice of his sepulchre, one of the most mutable and unreasonable saints in the Calendar. He died A. D. 688, in a hermitage upon the Farne Islands, having resigned the bishopric of Lindisfarne, or Holy Island, about two years before. His body was brought to Lindisfarne, where it remained until a descent of the Danes, about 793, when the monastery was nearly destroyed. The monks fled to Scotland, with what they deemed their chief treasure, the relics of St. Cuthbert. The saint was, however, a most capricious fellow-traveller; which was the more intolerable, as, like Sinbad's Old Man of the Sea, he journeyed upon the shoulders of his companions. They paraded him through Scotland for several years, and came as far west as Whithern, in Galloway, whence they attempted to sail for Ireland, but were driven back by tempests. the at length made a halt at Norham; from Hence he went to Melrose, where he remained stationary for a short time, and then caused himself to be launched upon the Tweed in a stone coffin, which landed him at Tilmouth, in Northumberland. This boat is finely shaped, ten feet long, three feet and a half in diameter, and only four inches thick; so that, with very little assistance, it might certainly have swam. It still lies, or at least did so a few years ago, in two pieces, beside the ruined chapel of Tilmouth. From Tilmouth, Cuthbert wandered into Yorkshire; and at length made a long stay at Chester-le-Street, to which the bishop's see was transferred. At length, the Danes continuing to infest the country, the monks removed to Ripon for a season; and it was in returning from thence to Chester-le-Street, that, passing through a forest called Dunholme, the saint and his carriage became immovable at a place named Wardlaw, or Wardilaw. Here the saint chose his place of residence; and all who have seen Durham must admit that, if difficult in his choice, he evinced taste in at length fixing it. [The editor of a later edition notes that in 1827 the discovery of the remains was made under a blue stone in the middle of the shrine of St. Cuthbert at the eastern extremity of the choir of Durham Cathedral. The bones were restored to the grave in a new coffin, and the various insignia of gold and silver were deposited in the library of the Dean and chapter.]

Page 103, line 287. *Even Scotland's dauntless king and heir.*

Every one has heard that when David I., with his son Henry, invaded Northumberland in 1136, the English host marched against them under the holy banner of St. Cuthbert; to the efficacy of which was imputed the great victory which they obtained in the bloody battle of Northallerton, or Cuton-moor.

Line 293. *'T was he, to vindicate his reign.*

Cuthbert, we have seen, had no great reason to spare the Danes, when opportunity offered. Accordingly, I find in Simeon of Durham, that the saint appeared in a vision to Alfred, when lurking in the marshes of Glastonbury, and promised him assistance and victory over his heathen enemies: a consolation which, as was reasonable, Alfred, after the victory of Ashendown, rewarded by a royal offering at the shrine of the saint. As to William the Conqueror, the terror spread before his army, when he marched to punish the revolt of the Northumbrians, in 1096, had forced the monks to fly once more to Holy Island with the body of the saint. It was, however, replaced before William left the North; and, to balance accounts, the Conqueror having intimated an indiscreet curiosity to view the saint's body, he was, while in the act of commanding the shrine to be opened, seized with heat and sickness, accompanied with such a panic terror that, notwithstanding there was a sumptuous dinner prepared for him, he fled without eating a morsel (which the monkish historian seems to have thought no small part both of the miracle and the penance), and never drew his bridle till he got to the river Tees.

Line 300. *Saint Cuthbert sits, and toils to frame.*

Although we do not learn that Cuthbert was, during his life, such an artificer as Dunstan, his brother in sanctity, yet since his death he has acquired the reputation of forging those *Entrochi* which are found among the rocks of Holy Island, and pass there by the name of St. Cuthbert's Beads. While at this task, he is supposed to sit during the night upon a certain rock, and use another as his anvil.

Line 316. *Old Colwulf built it, for his fault.*

Ceolwulf, or Colwulf, King of Northumberland, flourished in the eighth century. He was a man of some learning; for the Venerable Bede dedicates to him his *Ecclesiastical History*. He abdicated the throne about 738, and retired to Holy Island, where he died in the odor of sanctity. Saint as Colwulf was, however, I fear the foundation of the penance-vault does not correspond with his character; for it is recorded among his *memorabilia*, that, finding the air of the island raw and cold, he indulged the monks, whose rule had hitherto confined them to milk or water, with the comfortable privilege of using wine or ale. If any rigid antiquary insists on this objection, he is welcome to suppose the penance-vault was intended, by the founder, for the more genial purposes of a cellar. These penitential vaults were the *Geissel-gewölbe* of German convents. In the earlier and more rigid times of monastic discipline, they were sometimes used as a cemetery for the lay benefactors of the convent whose unsanctified corpses were then seldom permitted to pollute the choir. They also served as places of meeting for the chapter, when measures of uncommon severity were to be adopted. But their most frequent use, as implied by the name, was as places for performing penances, or undergoing punishment.

Page 104, line 371. *Is Tynemouth's haughty Prioress.*

That there was an ancient priory at Tynemouth is certain. Its ruins are situated on a high rocky point ; and, doubtless, many a vow was made at the shrine by the distressed mariners, who drove towards the iron-bound coast of Northumberland in stormy weather. It was anciently a nunnery ; for Virca, Abbess of Tynemouth, presented St. Cuthbert (yet alive) with a rare winding-sheet, in emulation of a holy lady called Tuda, who had sent him a coffin. But, as in the case of Whitby, and of Holy Island, the introduction of nuns at Tynemouth, in the reign of Henry VIII., is an anachronism. The nunnery at Holy Island is altogether fictitious. Indeed, St. Cuthbert was unlikely to permit such an establishment ; for, notwithstanding his accepting the mortuary gifts above mentioned, and his carrying on a visiting acquaintance with the Abbess of Coldingham, he certainly hated the whole female sex ; and, in revenge of a slippery trick played to him by an Irish princess, he, after death, inflicted severe penances on such as presumed to approach within a certain distance of his shrine.

Page 105, line 468. *Alive within the tomb.*

It is well known that the religious who broke their vows of chastity were subjected to the same penalty as the Roman vestals in a similar case. A small niche, sufficient to enclose their bodies, was made in the massive wall of the convent ; a slender pittance of food and water was deposited in it, and the awful words, *Vade in pacem*, were the signal for immuring the criminal. It is not likely that, in latter times, this punishment was often resorted to ; but, among the ruins of the abbey of Coldingham, were some years ago discovered the remains of a female skeleton, which, from the shape of the niche and position of the figure, seemed to be that of an immured nun.

Page 107, line 81. *Or of the Red-Cross hero teach.*

[Sir Sidney Smith].
Line 95. *Who snatched on Alexandria's sand.*

[Sir Ralph Abercromby].
Line 103. *When she, the bold Enchantress, came.*

[Joanna Baillie.]
Page 108, line 178. *And still I thought that shattered tower.*

[See note to page 14, line 1. These lines in the Introduction to Canto Third connect the author's thought with his ballad ' The Eve of St. Johns.']

Page 109, lines 216, 217.
Whose doom discording neighbors sought Content with equity unbought.

Upon revising the poem, it seems proper to mention that these lines have been uncon-

sciously borrowed from a passage in Dryden's beautiful epistle to John Driden of Chesterton.
Line 218. *To him the venerable priest.*

[Mr. John Martin, minister of Mertoun, the parish containing Smailholm Tower.]
Line 33. *The village inn seemed large, though rude.*

The accommodations of a Scottish hostelrie, or inn, in the sixteenth century, may be collected from Dunbar's admirable tale of *The Friars of Berwick*. Simon Lawder, ' the gay ostler,' seems to have lived very comfortably ; and his wife decorated her person with a scarlet kirtle, and a belt of silk and silver, and rings upon her fingers ; and feasted her paramour with rabbits, capons, partridges, and Bourdeaux wine. At least, if the Scottish inns were not good, it was not for want of encouragement from the Legislature ; who, so early as the reign of James I., not only enacted that in all boroughs and fairs there be hostellaries, having stables and chambers, and provision for man and horse, but by another statute, ordained that no man, travelling on horse or foot, should presume to lodge anywhere except in these hostellaries; and that no person, save innkeepers, should receive such travellers, under the penalty of forty shillings, for exercising such hospitality.

Page 111, line 211. *Seemed in mine ear a death peal rung.*

Among other omens to which faithful credit is given among the Scottish peasantry, is what is called the ' dead-bell,' explained by my friend James Hogg to be that tinkling in the ear which the country people regard as the secret intelligence of some friend's decease.

Page 112, line 333. *The founder of the Goblin-Hall.*

A vaulted hall under the ancient castle of Gifford, or Yester (for it bears either name indifferently), the construction of which has, from a very remote period, been ascribed to magic.

Page 113, line 354. *There floated Haco's banner trim.*

In 1263, Haco, King of Norway, came into the Firth of Clyde with a powerful armament, and made a descent at Largs, in Ayrshire. Here he was encountered and defeated, on the 2d October, by Alexander III. He retreated to Orkney, where he died soon after this disgrace to his arms. There are still existing, near the place of battle, many barrows, some of which, having been opened, were found, as usual, to contain bones and urns.

Line 362. *But, in his wizard habit strange.*

' Magicians, as is well known, were very curious in the choice and form of their vestments. Their caps are oval, or like pyramids, with lappets on each side, and fur within. Their gowns are long, and furred with fox-skins, under which they have a linen garment reaching to the knee. Their girdles are three inches broad, and have many cabalistical names, with crosses, trines, and circles inscribed on them. Their shoes should be of new russet leather, with a cross cut upon them. Their knives are dagger-fashion ; and their swords have neither guard nor scabbard.' — Reginald Scot's *Discovery of Witchcraft*.

Line 369. *Upon his breast a pentacle.*

Scott again cites Reginald Scot : ' A pentacle is a piece of fine linen, folded with five corners, according to the five senses, and suitably inscribed with characters. This the magician extends towards the spirits which he invokes, when they are stubborn and rebellious, and refuse to be conformable unto the ceremonies and rites of magic.'

Line 407. *As born upon that blessed night.*

It is a popular article of faith, that those who are born on Christmas or Good-Friday have the power of seeing spirits, and even of commanding them. The Spaniards imputed the haggard and downcast looks of their Philip II. to the disagreeable visions to which this privilege subjected him.

Page 114, line 484. *A royal city, tower and spire.*

[The reference is to the expedition to Copenhagen in 1801.]

Line 502. *The Elfin Warrior doth wield.*

Gervase of Tilbury relates the following popular story concerning a fairy knight : ' Osbert, a bold and powerful baron, visited a noble family in the vicinity of Wandlebury, in the bishopric of Ely. Among other stories related in the social circle of his friends, who, according to custom, amused each other by repeating ancient tales and traditions, he was informed that if any knight, unattended, entered an adjacent plain by moonlight, and challenged an adversary to appear, he would be immediately encountered by a spirit in the form of a knight. Osbert resolved to make the experiment, and set out, attended by a single squire, whom he ordered to remain without the limits of the plain, which was surrounded by an ancient entrenchment. On repeating the challenge he was instantly assailed by an adversary, whom he quickly unhorsed, and seized the reins of his steed. During this operation his ghostly opponent sprung up, and, darting his spear, like a javelin, at Osbert, wounded him in the thigh. Osbert returned in triumph with the horse, which he committed to the care of his servants. The horse was of a sable color, as well as his whole accoutrements, and apparently of great beauty and vigor. He remained with his keeper till cockcrowing, when, with eyes flashing fire, he reared, spurned the ground, and vanished. On disarming himself, Osbert perceived that he was wounded, and that one of his top-boots was full of blood.' Gervase adds that, as long as he lived, the scar of his wound opened afresh on the anniversary of the eve on which he encountered the spirit.

Page 116, line 91. *The morn may find the stiffened swain.*

I cannot help here mentioning, that, on the night in which these lines were written, suggested, as they were, by a sudden fall of snow, beginning after sunset, an unfortunate man perished exactly in the manner here described,

and his body was next morning found close to his own house. The accident happened within five miles of the farm of Ashestiel.

Line 132. *Scarce had lamented Forbes paid.*

Sir William Forbes of Pitsligo, Baronet ; unequalled, perhaps, in the degree of individual affection entertained for him by his friends, as well as in the general respect and esteem of Scotland at large. His *Life of Beattie*, whom he befriended and patronized in life, as well as celebrated after his decease, was not long published, before the benevolent and affectionate biographer was called to follow the subject of his narrative. This melancholy event very shortly succeeded the marriage of the friend to whom this introduction is addressed, with one of Sir William's daughters.

Page 117, line 174. *Pandour and Camp, with eyes of fire.*

[Raeburn introduced Scott's bull - terrier, Camp, into his portrait of the poet.]

Line 191. *Then he, whose absence we deplore.*

[Colin Mackenzie, of Portmore.]

Line 195. *And one whose name I may not say.*

[The son of Sir William Forbes, mentioned above. He also was a member of the volunteer corps and club which included Scott, Sir William Rae of St. Catharine's, Mr. Skene and Mr. Mackenzie with others.]

Page 118, line 31. *Been lantern-led by Friar Rush.*

Alias, ' Will o' the wisp.' This personage is a strolling demon, or *esprit follet*, who, once upon a time, got admittance into a monastery as a scullion, and played the monks many pranks. He was a sort of Robin Goodfellow, and Jack o'Lantern.

Page 119, line 153. *Sir David Lindesay of the Mount.*

I am uncertain if I abuse poetical license by introducing Sir David Lindesay in the character of Lion-Herald sixteen years before he obtained that office. At any rate, I am not the first who has been guilty of the anachronism ; for the author of *Flodden Field* despatches *Dallamount*, which can mean nobody but Sir David de Ia Mont, to France, on the message of defiance from James IV. to Henry VIII. It was often an office imposed on the Lion King-at-arms, to receive foreign embassadors ; and Lindesay himself did this honor to Sir Ralph Sadler in 1539–40. Indeed, the oath of the Lion, in its first article, bears reference to his frequent employment upon royal messages and embassies.

Line 194. *Where Crichtoun Castle crowns the bank.*

A large ruinous castle on the banks of the Tyne, about seven miles from Edinburgh. As indicated in the text, it was built at different times and with a very differing regard to splendor and accommodation. The oldest part of the building is a narrow keep, or tower, such as formed the mansion of a lesser Scottish baron ; but so many additions have been made to it that there is now a large court-yard, surrounded by buildings of different ages. The eastern front of the court is raised above a portico, and decorated with entablatures bearing anchors. All the stones of this front are cut into diamond facets, the angular projections of which have an uncommonly rich appearance. The inside of this part of the building appears to have contained a gallery of great length, and uncommon elegance. Access was given to it by a magnificent staircase, now quite destroyed.

Page 120, line 232. *The darkness of thy Massy More.*
The Castle of Crichtoun has a dungeon vault, called the Massy More. The epithet, which is not uncommonly applied to the prisons of other old castles in Scotland, is of Saracenic origin. It occurs twice in the *Epistolæ Itinerariæ* of Tollius, ' *carcer subterraneus, sive, ut Mauri appellant, Mazmorra.*' The same word applies to the dungeons of the ancient Moorish castles in Spain, and serves to show from what nation the Gothic style of castle-building was originally derived.

Line 248. *Earl Adam Hepburn,— he who died.*
He was the second Earl of Bothwell and fell in the field of Flodden, where, according to an ancient English poet, he distinguished himself by a furious attempt to retrieve the day.

Lines 254, 255.
> *Before the name*
> *Of hated Bothwell stained their fame.*

Adam was grandfather to James, Earl of Bothwell, too well known in the history of Queen Mary.

Line 278. *For that a messenger from heaven.*
This story is told by Pitscottie with characteristic simplicity: ' The king, seeing that France could get no support of him for that time, made a proclamation, full hastily, through all the realm of Scotland, both east and west, south and north, as well in the Isles as in the firm land, to all manner of man betwixt sixty and sixteen years, that they should be ready, within twenty days, to pass with him, with forty days victual, and to meet at the Burrow-muir of Edinburgh, and there to pass forward where he pleased. His proclamations were hastily obeyed, contrary the Council of Scotland's will; but every man loved his prince so well, that they would on no ways disobey him; but every man caused make his proclamation so hastily, conform to the charge of the king's proclamation.

' The king came to Lithgow, where he happened to be for the time at the council, very sad and dolorous, making his devotion to God, to send him good chance and fortune in his voyage. In this mean time, there came a man clad in a blue gown in at the kirk-door, and belted about him in a roll of linen cloth ; a pair of brotikings on his feet, to the great of his legs ; with all other hose and clothes conform thereto: but he had nothing on his head, but syde red yellow hair behind, and on his haffets, which wan down to his shoulders ; but his forehead was bald and bare. He seemed to be a man of two-and-fifty years, with a great pike-staff in his hand, and came first forward among the lords, crying and speiring for the king, saying, he desired to speak with him. While, at the last, he came where the king was sitting in the desk at his prayers ; but when he saw the king, he made him little reverence or salutation, but leaned down grofling on the desk before him, and said to him in this manner, as after follows: "Sir king, my mother hath sent me to you, desiring you not to pass, at this time, where thou art purposed ; for if thou does, thou wilt not fare well in thy journey, nor none that passeth with thee. Further, she bade thee mell with no woman, nor use their counsel, nor let them touch thy body, nor thou theirs ; for, if thou do it, thou wilt be confounded and brought to shame."

' By this man had spoken thir words unto the king's grace, the evening song was near done, and the king paused on thir words, studying to give him an answer ; but, in the mean time, before the king's eyes, and in the presence of all the lords that were about him for the time, this man vanished away, and could no ways be seen nor comprehended, but vanished away as he had been a blink of the sun, or a whip of the whirlwind, and could no more be seen. I heard say, Sir David Lindesay, lyonherauld, and John Inglis the marshal, who were, at that time, young men, and special servants to the king's grace, were standing presently beside the king, who thought to have laid hands on this man, that they might have speired further tidings at him. But all for nought ; they could not touch him ; for he vanished away betwixt them, and was no more seen.'

Line 287. *Linlithgow is excelling.*
The situation of Linlithgow Palace is eminently beautiful. It stands on a promontory of some elevation, which advances almost into the midst of the lake. The form is that of a square court, composed of buildings of four stories high, with towers at the angles. The fronts within the square, and the windows, are highly ornamented, and the size of the rooms, as well as the width and character of the staircases, are upon a magnificent scale. One banquet-room is ninety-four feet long, thirty feet wide, and thirty-three feet high, with a gallery for music. The king's wardrobe, or dressing-room, looking to the west, projects over the walls, so as to have a delicious prospect on three sides, and is one of the most enviable boudoirs we have ever seen.

Line 291. *The wild buck bells from ferny brake.*
I am glad of an opportunity to describe the cry of the deer by another word than *braying*, although the latter has been sanctified by the use of the Scottish metrical translation of the Psalms. *Bell* seems to be an abbreviation of *bellow*. This sylvan sound conveyed great delight to our ancestors, chiefly, I suppose, from association. A gentle knight in the reign of Henry VIII., Sir Thomas Wortley, built Wantley Lodge, in Wancliffe Forest, for the pleasure (as an ancient inscription testifies) of ' listening to the hart's *bell*.'

Line 298. *June saw his father's overthrow.*
The rebellion against James III. was signalized by the cruel circumstance of his son's pre-

sence in the hostile army. When the king saw his own banner displayed against him, and his son in the faction of his enemies, he lost the little courage he ever possessed, fled out of the field, fell from his horse, as it started at a woman and water-pitcher, and was slain, it is not well understood by whom. James IV., after the battle, passed to Stirling, and hearing the monks of the chapel royal deploring the death of his father, their founder, he was seized with deep remorse, which manifested itself in severe penances. The battle of Sauchie-burn, in which James III. fell, was fought 18th June, 1488.

Page 123, line 521. *Spread all the Borough-moor below.*

The Borough, or common Moor of Edinburgh, was of very great extent, reaching from the southern walls of the city to the bottom of Braid Hills. It was anciently a forest ; and, in that state, was so great a nuisance, that the inhabitants of Edinburgh had permission granted to them of building wooden galleries, projecting over the street, in order to encourage them to consume the timber ; which they seem to have done very effectually. When James IV. mustered the array of the kingdom there, in 1513, the Borough-moor was, according to Hawthornden, 'a field spacious, and delightful by the shade of many stately and aged oaks.' Upon that, and similar occasions, the royal standard is traditionally said to have been displayed from the Hare Stone, a high stone, now built into the wall, on the left hand of the highway leading towards Braid, not far from the head of Bruntsfield-links. The Hare Stone probably derives its name from the British word *Har*, signifying an army.

Line 557. *And there were Borthwick's Sisters Seven.*

Seven culverins, so called, cast by one Borthwick.

Line 566. *Scroll, pennon, pencil, bandrol, there.*

Each of these feudal ensigns intimated the different rank of those entitled to display them.

Line 578. *The ruddy lion ramped in gold.*

The well-known arms of Scotland. If you will believe Boethius and Buchanan, the double tressure round the shield was first assumed by Achaius, King of Scotland, contemporary of Charlemagne, and founder of the celebrated League with France ; but later antiquaries make poor Eochy, or Achy, little better than a sort of King of Brentford, whom old Grig (who also has swelled into Gregorius Magnus) associated with himself in the important duty of governing some part of the northeastern coast of Scotland.

Page 125, line 37. *True, Caledonia's Queen is changed.*

The Old Town of Edinburgh was secured on the north side by a lake, now drained, and on the south by a wall, which there was some attempt to make defensible even so late as 1745. The gates, and the greater part of the wall, have been pulled down, in the course of the late extensive and beautiful enlargement of the city.

Page 126, line 118. *To Henry meek she gave repose.*

Henry VI., with his queen, his heir, and the chiefs of his family, fled to Scotland after the fatal battle of Towton.

Line 120. *Great Bourbon's relics sad she saw.*

[In January, 1796, the exiled Count d'Artois, afterwards Charles X. of France, took up his residence in Holyrood, where he remained until August, 1799. When again driven from his country by the Revolution of July, 1830, the same unfortunate prince, with all the immediate members of his family, sought refuge once more in the ancient palace of the Stuarts, and remained there until 18th September, 1832.]

Line 180. *Till Windsor's oaks and Ascot plain.*

[Scott wrote part of the first two cantos of this poem at Ellis's seat, Sunning-hill, near Windsor.]

Page 127, line 18. *The cloth-yard arrows flew like hail.*

This is no poetical exaggeration. In some of the counties of England, distinguished for archery, shafts of this extraordinary length were actually used. Thus, at the battle of Blackheath, between the troops of Henry VII. and the Cornish insurgents, in 1496, the bridge of Dartford was defended by a picked band of archers from the rebel army, 'whose arrows,' says Holinshed, 'were in length a full cloth yard.' The Scottish, according to Ascham, had a proverb, that every English archer carried under his belt twenty-four Scots, in allusion to his bundle of unerring shafts.

Line 36. *He saw the hardy burghers there.*

The Scottish burgesses were, like yeomen, appointed to be armed with bows and sheaves, sword, buckler, knife, spear, or a good axe instead of a bow, if worth £100 ; their armor to be of white or bright harness. They wore *white hats;* that is, bright steel caps, without crest or visor. By an act of James IV., their *weapon-schawings* are appointed to be held four times a year, under the aldermen or bailiffs.

Line 53. *His arms were halbert, axe, or spear.*

Bows and quivers were in vain recommended to the peasantry of Scotland, by repeated statutes ; spears and axes seem universally to have been used instead of them. Their defensive armor was the plate-jack, hauberk, or brigantine ; and their missile weapons cross-bows and culverins. All wore swords of excellent temper, according to Patten ; and a voluminous handkerchief round their neck, 'not for cold, but for cutting.' The mace also was much used in the Scottish army. When the feudal array of the kingdom was called forth, each man was obliged to appear with forty days' provision. When this was expended, which took place before the battle of Flodden, the army melted away of course. Almost all the Scottish forces, except a few knights, men-at-arms, and the Border-prickers, who formed excellent light cavalry, acted upon foot.

Page 128, line 165. *A banquet rich and costly wines.*

In all transactions of great or petty importance, and among whomsoever taking place, it would seem that a present of wine was a uniform and indispensable preliminary. It was not to Sir John Falstaff alone that such an introductory preface was necessary, however well judged and acceptable on the part of Mr. Brook ; for Sir Ralph Sadler, while on an embassy to Scotland in 1539-40, mentions, with complacency, 'the same night came Rothesay (the herald so called) to me again, and brought me wine from the King, both white and red.'

Page 129, line 247. *The pressure of his iron belt.*

Few readers need to be reminded of this belt, to the weight of which James added certain ounces every year that he lived. Pitscottie founds his belief that James was not slain in the battle of Flodden, because the English never had this token of the iron belt to show to any Scottishman. The person and character of James are delineated according to our best historians. His romantic disposition, which led him highly to relish gayety approaching to license, was, at the same time, tinged with enthusiastic devotion. The propensities sometimes formed a strange contrast. He was wont, during his fits of devotion, to assume the dress, and conform to the rules, of the order of Franciscans ; and when he had thus done penance for some time in Stirling, to plunge again into the tide of pleasure. Probably, too, with no unusual inconsistency, he sometimes laughed at the superstitious observances to which he at other times subjected himself.

Line 260. *O'er James's heart the courtiers say.*

It has been already noticed that King James's acquaintance with Lady Heron of Ford did not commence until he marched into England. Our historians impute to the king's infatuated passion the delays which led to the fatal defeat of Flodden. The author of *The Genealogy of the Heron Family* endeavors, with laudable anxiety, to clear the Lady Ford from this scandal : that she came and went, however, between the armies of James and Surrey, is certain. Heron of Ford had been, in 1511, in some sort accessory to the slaughter of Sir Robert Kerr of Cessford, Warden of the Middle Marches. It was committed by his brother the bastard, Lilburn and Starked, three Borderers. Lilburn and Heron of Ford were delivered up by Henry to James, and were imprisoned in the fortress of Fastcastle, where the former died. Part of the pretence of Lady Ford's negotiations with James was the liberty of her husband.

Line 269. *For the fair Queen of France.*

' Also the Queen of France wrote a love-letter to the King of Scotland, calling him her love, showing him that she had suffered much rebuke in France for the defending of his honor. She believed surely that he would recompense her again with some of his kingly support in her necessity ; that is to say, that he would raise her an army, and come three foot of ground on English ground, for her sake. To that effect she sent him a ring off her finger, with fourteen thousand French crowns to pay his expenses.' — Pitscottie, p. 110.

Page 130. LOCHINVAR.

This ballad is in a very slight degree founded on a ballad called ' Katharine Ianfarie.'

Line 332. *Love swells like the Solway, but ebbs like its tide.*

[An editor of Scott reminds the reader of the detailed picture of some of the extraordinary phenomena of the spring-tides in the Solway Firth which Scott drew in *Redgauntlet*.]

Page 131, line 398. *Of Archibald Bell-the-Cat.*

Archibald Douglas, Earl of Angus, a man remarkable for strength of body and mind, acquired the popular name of *Bell-the-Cat* upon the following remarkable occasion : James the Third, of whom Pitscottie complains that he delighted more in music and ' policies of building,' than in hunting, hawking, and other noble exercises, was so ill advised as to make favorites of his architects and musicians, whom the same historian irreverently terms masons and fiddlers. His nobility, who did not sympathize in the king's respect for the fine arts, were extremely incensed at the honors conferred on those persons, particularly on Cochran, a mason, who had been created Earl of Mar ; and seizing the opportunity, when, in 1482, the king had convoked the whole array of the country to march against the English, they held a midnight council in the church of Lauder, for the purpose of forcibly removing these minions from the king's person. When all had agreed on the propriety of this measure, Lord Gray told the assembly the apologue of the Mice, who had formed a resolution that it would be highly advantageous to their community to tie a bell round the cat's neck, that they might hear her approach at a distance ; but which public measure unfortunately miscarried, from no mouse being willing to undertake the task of fastening the bell. ' I understand the moral,' said Angus, ' and, that what we propose may not lack execution, I will *bell the cat.*'

Line 414. *And chafed his royal lord.*

Angus was an old man when the war against England was resolved upon. He earnestly spoke against that measure from its commencement, and, on the eve of the battle of Flodden, remonstrated so freely upon the impolicy of fighting, that the king said to him, with scorn and indignation, ' if he was afraid, he might go home.' The earl burst into tears at this insupportable insult, and retired accordingly, leaving his sons, George, Master of Angus, and Sir William of Glenbervie, to command his followers. They were both slain in the battle, with two hundred gentlemen of the name of Douglas. The aged earl, broken-hearted at the calamities of his house and his country, retired into a religious house, where he died about a year after the field of Flodden.

Line 429. *Then rest you in Tantallon hold.*

The ruins of Tantallon Castle occupy a high

rock projecting into the German Ocean, about two miles east of North Berwick. The building is not seen till a close approach, as there is rising ground betwixt it and the land. The circuit is of large extent, fenced upon three sides by the precipice which overhangs the sea, and on the fourth by a double ditch and very strong outworks. Tantallon was a principal castle of the Douglas family, and when the Earl of Angus was banished, in 1527, it continued to hold out against James V. The king was forced to raise the siege, and only afterwards obtained possession of Tantallon by treaty with the governor, Simeon Panango. When the Earl of Angus returned from banishment, upon the death of James, he again obtained possession of Tantallon, and it actually afforded refuge to an English ambassador, under circumstances similar to those described in the text. This was no other than the celebrated Sir Ralph Sadler, who resided there for some time under Angus's protection, after the failure of his negotiation for matching the infant Mary with Edward VI.

Line 432. *He wears their motto on his blade.*

A very ancient sword, in possession of Lord Douglas, bears, among a great deal of flourishing, two hands pointing to a heart, which is placed betwixt them, and the date 1329, being the year in which Bruce charged the Good Lord Douglas to carry his heart to the Holy Land. This curious and valuable relic was lost during the Civil War of 1745–46, being carried away from Douglas Castle by some of those in arms for Prince Charles. But great interest having been made by the Duke of Douglas among the chief partisans of the Stuart, it was at length restored. It resembles a Highland claymore, of the usual size, is of an excellent temper, and admirably poised.

Page 132, line 501. *Lords, to the dance,— a hall! a hall!*

The ancient cry to make room for a dance, or pageant.

Page 133, line 587. *And had made league with Martin Swart.*

A German general who commanded the auxiliaries sent by the Duchess of Burgundy under Lambert Simnel. He was defeated and killed at Stokefield. His name is preserved by that of the field of battle, which is called, after him, Swart-moor.

Page 134, line 709. *Dun-Edin's Cross, a pillared stone.*

The Cross of Edinburgh was an ancient and curious structure. The lower part was an octagonal tower, sixteen feet in diameter, and about fifteen feet high. At each angle there was a pillar, and between them an arch, of the Grecian shape. Above these was a projecting battlement, with a turret at each corner, and medallions, of rude but curious workmanship, between them. Above this rose the proper Cross, a column of one stone, upwards of twenty feet high, surmounted with an unicorn. This pillar is preserved at the House of Drum, near Edinburgh. The Magistrates of Edin-

burgh, in 1756, with consent of the Lords of Session (*proh pudor!*), destroyed this curious monument, under a wanton pretext that it encumbered the street. [Since the above was written the shaft of the old Cross has been set up within the railings of St. Giles's Church, very near its original site. — W. J. R.] From the tower of the Cross, so long as it remained, the heralds published the acts of Parliament; and its site, marked by radii, diverging from a stone centre, in the High Street, is still the place where proclamations are made.

Line 735. *This awful summons came.*

This supernatural citation is mentioned by all our Scottish historians. It was, probably, like the apparition at Linlithgow, an attempt, by those averse to the war, to impose upon the superstitious temper of James IV.

Page 135, line 838. *Before a venerable pile.*

The convent alluded to is a foundation of Cistercian nuns near North Berwick, of which there are still some remains. It was founded by Duncan, Earl of Fife, in 1216.

Page 136, line 914. *Drove the monks forth of Coventry.*

This relates to the catastrophe of a real Robert de Marmion, in the reign of King Stephen, whom William of Newbury describes with some attributes of my fictitious hero. '*Homo bellicosus, ferocia et astucia fere nullo suo tempore impar.*' This baron, having expelled the monks from the church of Coventry, was not long of experiencing the divine judgment, as the same monks, no doubt, termed his disaster. Having waged a feudal war with the Earl of Chester, Marmion's horse fell, as he charged in the van of his troop, against a body of the earl's followers: the rider's thigh being broken by the fall, his head was cut off by a common foot-soldier, ere he could receive any succor.

Page 137, line 6. *Even, heathen yet, the savage Dane.*

The Iol of the heathen Danes (a word still applied to Christmas in Scotland) was solemnized with great festivity. The humor of the Danes at table displayed itself in pelting each other with bones; and Torfæus tells a long and curious story, in the history of Hrolfe Kraka, of one Hottus, an inmate of the Court of Denmark, who was so generally assailed with these missiles that he constructed, out of the bones with which he was overwhelmed, a very respectable entrenchment against those who continued the raillery. The dances of the Northern warriors round the great fires of pine-trees are commemorated by Olaus Magnus, who says they danced with such fury, holding each other by the hands, that if the grasp of any failed, he was pitched into the fire with the velocity of a sling. The sufferer on such occasions was instantly plucked out, and obliged to quaff off a certain measure of ale, as a penalty for 'spoiling the king's fire.'

Page 138, line 74. *Who lists may in their mumming see.*

It seems certain that the Mummers of England who (in Northumberland at least) used to go about in disguise to the neighboring houses, bearing the then useless ploughshare ; and the *Guisards* of Scotland, not yet in total disuse, present, in some indistinct degree, a shadow of the old mysteries, which were the origin of the English drama. In Scotland (*me ipso teste*), we were wont, during my boyhood, to take the characters of the apostles, at least of Peter, Paul, and Judas Iscariot, which last carried the bag, in which the dole of our neighbor's plum-cake was deposited. One played a Champion, and recited some traditional rhymes ; another was

> ' Alexander, king of Macedon,
> Who conquered all the world but Scotland alone;
> When he came to Scotland his courage grew cold,
> To see a little nation courageous and bold. '

These, and many such verses, were repeated, but by rote, and unconnectedly. There was also occasionally, I believe, a Saint George. In all there was a confused resemblance of the ancient mysteries, in which the characters of Scripture, the Nine Worthies, and other popular personages were usually exhibited.

Line 95, 96.
Where my great-grandsire came of old
With amber beard and flaxen hair.
Mr. Scott of Harden, my kind and affectionate friend, and distant relation, has the original of a poetical invitation, addressed from his grandfather to my relative, from which a few lines in the text are imitated. They are dated, as the epistle in the text, from Mertoun-house, the seat of the Harden family.

> ' With amber beard, and flaxen hair,
> And reverend apostolic air,
> Free of anxiety and care,
> Come hither, Christmas-day, and dine;
> We 'll mix sobriety with wine,
> And easy mirth with thoughts divine.
> We Christians think it holiday.
> On it no sin to feast or play ;
> Others, in spite, may fast and pray.
> No superstition in the use
> Our ancestors made of a goose ;
> Why may not we, as well as they,
> Be innocently blithe that day,
> On goose or pie, on wine or ale,
> And scorn enthusiastic zeal ?
> Pray come, and welcome, or plague rott
> Your friend and landlord, Walter Scott.'

Page 139, line 160. *The Highlander, whose red claymore.*
The *Daoine shi'*, or *Men of Peace*, of the Scottish Highlanders, rather resemble the Scandinavian *Duergar* than the English Fairies. Notwithstanding their name, they are, if not absolutely malevolent, at least peevish, discontented, and apt to do mischief on slight provocation. The belief of their existence is deeply impressed on the Highlanders, who think they are particularly offended with mortals who talk of them, who wear their favorite color green, or in any respect interfere with their affairs. This is particularly to be avoided on Friday, when, whether as dedicated to Venus, with

whom, in Germany, this subterraneous people are held nearly connected, or for a more solemn reason, they are more active, and possessed of greater power.
Line 169. *Beneath the towers of Franchémont.*
The journal of the friend to whom the Fourth Canto of the Poem is inscribed, furnished me with the following account of a striking superstition : —
' Passed the pretty little village of Franchémont (near Spaw), with the romantic ruins of the old castle of that name. The road leads through many delightful vales, on a rising ground ; at the extremity of one of them stands the ancient castle, now the subject of many superstitious legends. It is firmly believed by the neighboring peasantry, that the last Baron of Franchémont deposited, in one of the vaults of the castle, a ponderous chest, containing an immense treasure in gold and silver, which, by some magic spell, was intrusted to the care of the Devil, who is constantly found sitting on the chest in the shape of a huntsman. Any one adventurous enough to touch the chest is instantly seized with the palsy. Upon one occasion a priest of noted piety was brought to the vault : he used all the arts of exorcism to persuade his infernal majesty to vacate his seat, but in vain ; the huntsman remained immovable. At last, moved by the earnestness of the priest, he told him that he would agree to resign the chest if the exorcisor would sign his name with blood. But the priest understood his meaning and refused, as by that act he would have delivered over his soul to the Devil. Yet if anybody can discover the mystic words used by the person who deposited the treasure, and pronounce them, the fiend must instantly decamp. I had many stories of a similar nature from a peasant, who had himself seen the Devil, in the shape of a great cat.'
Line 207. *My song the messenger from heaven.*
[See page 120, line 278, note thereto.]
Page 142, line 280. *The rest were all in Twisel glen.*
Where James encamped before taking post on Flodden.
Page 143, line 327. *A bishop by the altar stood.*
The well-known Gawain Douglas, Bishop of Dunkeld, son of Archibald Bell-the-cat, Earl of Angus. He was author of a Scottish metrical version of the Æneid, and of many other poetical pieces of great merit. He had not at this period attained the mitre.
Line 341. *Upon the huge and sweeping brand.*
Angus had strength and personal activity corresponding to his courage. Spens of Kilspindie, a favorite of James IV., having spoken of him lightly, the earl met him while hawking, and compelling him to single combat, at one blow cut asunder his thigh-bone and killed him on the spot. But ere he could obtain James's pardon for this slaughter, Angus was obliged to yield his castle of Hermitage, in exchange for that of Bothwell, which was some diminution to the family greatness. The sword with which he struck so remarkable a blow was presented

by his descendant, James, Earl of Morton, afterwards Regent of Scotland, to Lord Lindesay of the Byres, when he defied Bothwell to single combat on Carberry-hill.

Page 144, line 431. *Fierce he broke forth, — 'And darest thou then?'*

This ebullition of violence in the potent Earl of Angus is not without its examples in the real history of the house of Douglas, whose chieftains possessed the ferocity with the heroic virtues of a savage state. The most curious instance occurred in the case of Maclellan, tutor of Bomby, who, having refused to acknowledge the preëminence claimed by Douglas over the gentlemen and Barons of Galloway, was seized and imprisoned by the earl, in his castle of the Thrieve, on the borders of Kirkcudbright-shire. Sir Patrick Gray, commander of King James the Second's guard, was uncle to the tutor of Bomby, and obtained from the king 'a sweet letter of supplication,' praying the earl to deliver his prisoner into Gray's hand. When Sir Patrick arrived at the castle, he was received with all the honor due to a favorite servant of the king's household ; but while he was at dinner, the earl, who suspected his errand, caused his prisoner to be led forth and beheaded. After dinner, Sir Patrick presented the king's letter to the earl, who received it with great affectation of reverence ; 'and took him by the hand, and led him forth to the green, where the gentleman was lying dead, and showed him the manner, and said, "Sir Patrick, you are come a little too late ; yonder is your sister's son lying, but he wants the head : take his body, and do with it what you will." Sir Patrick answered again with a sore heart, and said, "My lord, if ye have taken from him his head, dispone upon the body as ye please : " and with that called for his horse, and leaped thereon ; and when he was on horseback, he said to the earl on this manner: "My lord, if I live, you shall be rewarded for your labors, that you have used at this time, according to your demerits." At this saying the earl was highly offended, and cried for horse. Sir Patrick, seeing the earl's fury, spurred his horse, but he was chased near Edinburgh ere they left him: and had it not been his lead horse was so tried and good, he had been taken.' — Pitscottie's *History.*

Line 457. *Did ever knight so foul a deed ?*

Lest the reader should partake of the Earl's astonishment, and consider the crime as inconsistent with the manners of the period, I have to remind him of the numerous forgeries (partly executed by a female assistant) devised by Robert of Artois, to forward his suit against the Countess Matilda ; which, being detected, occasioned his flight into England, and proved the remote cause of Edward the Third's memorable wars in France. John Harding, also, was expressly hired by Edward IV. to forge such documents as might appear to establish the claim of fealty asserted over Scotland by the English monarchs.

Page 145, line 500. *The earl did much the Master pray.*

His eldest son, the Master of Angus.

Line 540. *Where Lennel's convent closed their march.*

This was a Cistercian house of religion, now almost entirely demolished. It is situated near Coldstream, almost opposite to Cornhill, and consequently very near to Flodden Field.

Line 573. *The Till by Twisel Bridge.*

On the evening previous to the memorable battle of Flodden, Surrey's head-quarters were at Barmore-wood, and King James held an inaccessible position on the ridge of Flodden-hill, one of the last and lowest eminences detached from the ridge of Cheviot. The Till, a deep and slow river, winded between the armies. On the morning of the 9th September, 1513, Surrey marched in a northwesterly direction, and crossed the Till, with his van and artillery, at Twisel-bridge, nigh where that river joins the Tweed, his rear-guard column passing about a mile higher, by a ford. This movement had the double effect of placing his army between King James and his supplies from Scotland, and of striking the Scottish monarch with surprise, as he seems to have relied on the depth of the river in his front. But as the passage, both over the bridge and through the ford, was difficult and slow, it seems possible that the English might have been attacked to great advantage, while struggling with these natural obstacles.

Page 146, line 681. *Hence might they see the full array.*

The reader cannot here expect a full account of the Battle of Flodden ; but, so far as is necessary to understand the romance, I beg to remind him, that, when the English army, by their skilful countermarch, were fairly placed between King James and his own country, the Scottish monarch resolved to fight ; and, setting fire to his tents, descended from the ridge of Flodden to secure the neighboring eminence of Brankstone, on which that village is built. Thus the two armies met, almost without seeing each other, when, according to the old poem of 'Flodden Field' —

> 'The English line stretched east and west,
> And southward were their faces set;
> The Scottish northward proudly prest,
> And manfully their foes they met.'

The English army advanced in four divisions. On the right, when first engaged, were the sons of Earl Surrey, namely, Thomas Howard, the Admiral of England, and Sir Edmund, the Knight Marshal of the army. Their divisions were separated from each other ; but, at the request of Sir Edmund, his brother's battalion was drawn very near to his own. The centre was commanded by Surrey in person ; the left wing by Sir Edward Stanley, with the men of Lancashire, and of the palatinate of Chester. Lord Dacres, with a large body of horse, formed a reserve. When the smoke, which the wind had driven between the armies, was somewhat dispersed, they perceived the Scots, who had moved down the hill in a similar order of battle, and in deep silence. The Earls of Huntly and of Home commanded their left wing, and charged Sir Edmund Howard with such success, as entirely to defeat his part of the English right wing. Sir Edmund's banner was beaten down, and he himself escaped with difficulty to his brother's division. The Admiral, however, stood firm; and Dacre advancing to his support with the reserve of cavalry, probably between the interval of the divisions commanded by the brothers Howard, appears to have kept the victors in effectual check. Home's men, chiefly Borderers, began to pillage the baggage of both armies; and their leader is branded, by the Scottish historians, with negligence or treachery. On the other hand, Huntly, on whom they bestow many encomiums, is said, by the English historians, to have left the field after the first charge. Meanwhile the Admiral, whose flank these chiefs ought to have attacked, availed himself of their inactivity, and pushed forward against another large division of the Scottish army in his front, headed by the Earls of Crawford and Montrose, both of whom were slain, and their forces routed. On the left, the success of the English was yet more decisive; for the Scottish right wing, consisting of undisciplined Highlanders, commanded by Lennox and Argyle, was unable to sustain the charge of Sir Edward Stanley, and especially the severe execution of the Lancashire archers. The king and Surrey, who commanded the respective centres of their armies, were meanwhile engaged in close and dubious conflict. James, surrounded by the flower of his kingdom, and impatient of the galling discharge of arrows, supported also by his reserve under Bothwell, charged with such fury, that the standard of Surrey was in danger. At that critical moment, Stanley, who had routed the left wing of the Scottish, pursued his career of victory, and arrived on the right flank, and in the rear of James's division, which, throwing itself into a circle, disputed the battle till night came on. Surrey then drew back his forces; for the Scottish centre not having been broken, and their left wing being victorious, he yet doubted the event of the field. The Scottish army, however, felt their loss, and abandoned the field of battle in disorder, before dawn. They lost, perhaps, from eight to ten thousand men; but that included the very prime of their nobility, gentry, and even clergy. Scarce a family of eminence but has an ancestor killed at Flodden; and there is no province in Scotland, even at this day, where the battle is mentioned without a sensation of terror and sorrow. The English lost also a great number of men, perhaps within one third of the vanquished, but they were of inferior note. — See the only distinct detail of the field of Flodden in Pinkerton's *History,* Book xi., all former accounts being full of blunders and inconsistency.

The spot from which Clara views the battle must be supposed to have been on a hillock commanding the rear of the English right wing,

which was defeated, and in which conflict Marmion is supposed to have fallen.

Page 147, line 717. *With Brian Tunstall, stainless knight.*

Sir Brian Tunstall, called, in the romantic language of the time, Tunstall the Undefiled, was one of the few Englishmen of rank slain at Flodden. He figures in the ancient English poem, to which I may safely refer my reader; as an edition, with full explanatory notes, has been published by my friend Mr. Henry Weber. Tunstall perhaps derived his epithet of *undefiled* from his white armor and banner, the latter bearing a white cock about to crow, as well as from his unstained loyalty and knightly faith.

Page 150, line 1081. *And fell on Flodden plain.*

There can be no doubt that King James fell in the battle of Flodden. He was killed, says the curious French *Gazette,* within a lance's length of the Earl of Surrey; and the same account adds, that none of his division were made prisoners, though many were killed, — a circumstance that testifies the desperation of their resistance. The Scottish historians record many of the idle reports which passed among the vulgar of their day. Home was accused, by the popular voice, not only of failing to support the king but even of having carried him out of the field, and murdered him. Other reports gave a still more romantic turn to the king's fate, and averred that James, weary of greatness after the carnage among his nobles, had gone on a pilgrimage, to merit absolution for the death of his father and the breach of his oath of amity to Henry. Stowe has recorded a degrading story of the disgrace with which the remains of the unfortunate monarch were treated in his time. An unhewn column marks the spot where James fell, still called the King's Stone.

Line 1095. *'T was levelled when fanatic Brook.* This storm of Lichfield Cathedral, which had been garrisoned on the part of the king, took place in the great civil war. Lord Brook, who, with Sir John Gill, commanded the assailants, was shot with a musket-ball through the visor of his helmet. The royalists remarked that he was killed by a shot fired from Saint Chad's Cathedral, and upon Saint Chad's Day, and received his death-wound in the very eye with which he had said he hoped to see the ruin of all the cathedrals in England. The magnificent church in question suffered cruelly upon this and other occasions; the principal spire being ruined by the fire of the besiegers.

THE LADY OF THE LAKE.

Page 157, line 53. *Sought the wild heaths of Uam-Var.*

Ua-Var, as the name is pronounced, or more properly *Uaigh-mor,* is a mountain to the northeast of the village of Callander, in Menteith, deriving its name, which signifies the great den, or cavern, from a sort of retreat among the rocks on the south side, said, by tradition,

to have been the abode of a giant. In latter
times it was the refuge of robbers and banditti,
who have been only extirpated within these
forty or fifty years. Strictly speaking, this
stronghold is not a cave, as the name would
imply, but a sort of small enclosure, or recess,
surrounded with large rocks and open above
head.

Line 120. *Two dogs of black Saint Hubert's breed.*

Scott quotes Tubervile here: 'The hounds
which we call St. Hubert's hounds are commonly all blacke, yet neuerthelesse, the race is
so mingled at these days, that we find them
of all colours. These are the hounds which
the abbots of St. Hubert haue always kept
some of their race or kind, in honour or remembrance of the saint, which was a hunter
with St. Eustace. Whereupon we may conceiue
that (by the grace of God) all good huntsmen
shall follow them into paradise.'

Line 137. *For the death-wound, and death-halloo.*

When the stag turned to bay, the ancient
hunter had the perilous task of going in upon,
and killing, or disabling, the desperate animal.
At certain times of the year this was held particularly dangerous, a wound received from a
stag's horn being then deemed poisonous, and
more dangerous than one from the tusks of a
boar, as the old rhyme testifies: —

' If thou be hurt with hart, it brings thee to thy bier,
But barber's hand will boar's hurt heal, therefore thou
need'st not fear.'

At all times, however, the task was dangerous,
and to be adventured upon wisely and warily,
either by getting behind the stag while he was
gazing on the hounds, or by watching an opportunity to gallop roundly in upon him and kill
him with the sword.

Page 159, line 254. *And now, to issue from the
glen.*

Until the present road was made through the
romantic pass which I have presumptuously attempted to describe in the preceding stanzas,
there was no mode of issuing out of the defile
called the Trosachs, excepting by a sort of ladder, composed of the branches and roots of
trees.

Line 313. *To meet with Highland plunderers
here.*

The clans who inhabited the romantic regions
in the neighborhood of Loch Katrine were, even
until a late period, much addicted to predatory
excursions upon their Lowland neighbors.

Page 161, line 459. *A gray-haired sire, whose
eye intent.*

If force of evidence could authorize us to believe facts inconsistent with the general laws of
nature, enough might be produced in favor of
the existence of the second-sight. It is called
in Gaelic *Taishitaraugh*, from *Taish*, an unreal
or shadowy appearance ; and those possessed of
the faculty are called *Taishatrin*, which may be
aptly translated visionaries. Martin, a steady

believer in the second-sight, gives the following
account of it : —

' The second-sight is a singular faculty of seeing an otherwise invisible object without any
previous means used by the person that uses it
for that end : the vision makes such a lively
impression upon the seers, that they neither see
nor think of anything else, except the vision, as
long as it continues ; and then they appear pensive or jovial, according to the object that was
represented to them.

' At the sight of a vision, the eyelids of the
person are erected, and the eyes continue staring until the object vanish. This is obvious to
others who are by when the persons happen to
see a vision, and occurred more than once to my
own observation, and to others that were with
me. . . .

' If a woman is seen standing at a man's left
hand, it is a presage that she will be his wife,
whether they be married to others, or unmar-
ried at the time of the apparition.

' To see a spark of fire fall upon one's arm or
breast is a forerunner of a dead child to be seen
in the arms of those persons ; of which there
are several fresh instances. . . .

' To see a seat empty at the time of one's sitting in it is a presage of that person's death
soon after.' — Martin's *Description of the Western Islands*, 1716, 8vo, p. 300 *et seq.*

To these particulars innumerable examples
might be added, all attested by grave and credible authors. But, in despite of evidence which
neither Bacon, Boyle, nor Johnson was able to
resist, the *Taish*, with all its visionary properties, seems to be now universally abandoned to
the use of poetry. The exquisitely beautiful
poem of *Lochiel* will at once occur to the recollection of every reader.

Line 504. *Here for retreat in dangerous hour.*

The Celtic chieftains, whose lives were continually exposed to peril, had usually, in the
most retired spot of their domains, some place
of retreat for the hour of necessity, which, as
circumstances would admit, was a tower, a cavern, or a rustic hut, in a strong and secluded
situation. One of these last gave refuge to the
unfortunate Charles Edward, in his perilous
wanderings after the battle of Culloden.

Page 162, line 573. *Of Ferragus or Ascabart.*

These two sons of Anak flourished in romantic fable. The first is well known to the ad-
mirers of Ariosto by the name of Ferrau. He
was an antagonist of Orlando, and was at length
slain by him in single combat. . . . Ascapart,
or Ascabart, makes a very material figure in
the *History of Bevis of Hampton*, by whom he
was conquered. His effigies may be seen guarding one side of the gate at Southampton, while
the other is occupied by Bevis himself.

Line 585. *Though all unasked his birth and
name.*

The Highlanders, who carried hospitality to
a punctilious excess, are said to have considered
it as churlish to ask a stranger his name or lineage before he had taken refreshment. Feuds
were so frequent among them, that a contrary

rule would in many cases have produced the discovery of some circumstance which might have excluded the guest from the benefit of the assistance he stood in need of.

Page 164, line 7. *Morn's genial influence roused a minstrel gray.*

Highland chieftains, to a late period, retained in their service the bard, as a family officer.

Page 165, line 109. *Pour forth the glory of the Græme.*

The ancient and powerful family of Graham (which, for metrical reasons, is here spelled after the Scottish pronunciation) held extensive possessions in the counties of Dumbarton and Stirling. Few families can boast of more historical renown, having claim to three of the most remarkable characters in the Scottish annals. Sir John the Græme, the faithful and undaunted partaker of the labors and patriotic warfare of Wallace, fell in the unfortunate field of Falkirk, in 1298. The celebrated Marquis of Montrose, in whom De Retz saw realized his abstract idea of the heroes of antiquity, was the second of these worthies. And, notwithstanding the severity of his temper, and the rigor with which he executed the oppressive mandates of the princes whom he served, I do not hesitate to name as the third, John Græme, of Claverhouse, Viscount of Dundee, whose heroic death, in the arms of victory, may be allowed to cancel the memory of his cruelty to the nonconformists, during the reigns of Charles II. and James II.

Line 131. *This harp, which erst Saint Modan swayed.*

I am not prepared to show that St. Modan was a performer on the harp. It was, however, no unsaintly accomplishment ; for St. Dunstan certainly did play upon that instrument, which retaining, as was natural, a portion of the sanctity attached to its master's character, announced future events by its spontaneous sound.

Line 142. *Ere Douglases, to ruin driven.*

The downfall of the Douglases of the house of Angus, during the reign of James V., is the event alluded to in the text. The Earl of Angus, it will be remembered, had married the queen-dowager, and availed himself of the right which he thus acquired, as well as of his extensive power, to retain the king in a sort of tutelage, which approached very near to captivity. Several open attempts were made to rescue James from this thraldom, with which he was well known to be deeply disgusted ; but the valor of the Douglases, and their allies, gave them the victory in every conflict. At length, the king, while residing at Falkland, contrived to escape by night out of his own court and palace, and rode full speed to Stirling Castle, where the governor, who was of the opposite faction, joyfully received him.

Page 166, line 221. *In Holy-Rood a knight he slew.*

This was by no means an uncommon occurrence in the Court of Scotland ; nay, the presence of the sovereign himself scarcely restrained the ferocious and inveterate feuds which were the perpetual source of bloodshed among the Scottish nobility.

Line 229. *The Douglas, like a stricken deer.*

The exiled state of this powerful race is not exaggerated in this and subsequent passages. The hatred of James against the race of Douglas was so inveterate, that numerous as their allies were, and disregarded as the regal authority had usually been in similar cases, their nearest friends, even in the most remote part of Scotland, durst not entertain them, unless under the strictest and closest disguise.

Page 167, line 260. *A votaress in Maronnan's cell.*

The parish of *Kilmaronock*, at the eastern extremity of Loch Lomond, derives its name from a *cell*, or chapel, dedicated to Saint Maronock, or Marnock, or Maronnan, about whose sanctity very little is now remembered.

Line 270. *But wild as Bracklinn's thundering wave.*

This beautiful cascade is on the Keltie, a mile from Callander. The height of the fall is about fifty feet.

Line 306. *For Tine-man forged by fairy-lore.*

Archibald, the third Earl of Douglas, was so unfortunate in all his enterprises, that he acquired the epithet of ' tine-man,' because he tined, or lost, his followers in every battle which he fought. He was vanquished, as every reader must remember, in the bloody battle of Homildon-hill, near Wooler, where he himself lost an eye, and was made prisoner by Hotspur. He was no less unfortunate when allied with Percy, being wounded and taken at the battle of Shrewsbury. He was so unsuccessful in an attempt to besiege Roxburgh Castle, that it was called the 'Foul Raid,' or disgraceful expedition. His ill fortune left him indeed at the battle of Beaugé, in France ; but it was only to return with double emphasis at the subsequent action of Vernoil, the last and most unlucky of his encounters, in which he fell, with the flower of the Scottish chivalry, then serving as auxiliaries in France, and about two thousand common soldiers, A. D. 1424.

Line 309. *Did, self-unscabbarded, foreshow.*

The ancient warriors, whose hope and confidence rested chiefly in their blades, were accustomed to deduce omens from them, especially from such as were supposed to have been fabricated by enchanted skill, of which we have various instances in the romances and legends of the time.

Lord Lovat is said, by the author of the *Letters from Scotland*, to have affirmed that a number of swords that hung in the hall of the mansion-house, leaped of themselves out of the scabbard at the instant he was born.

Page 168, line 363. *Those thrilling sounds, that call the might.*

The connoisseurs in pipe-music affect to discover in a well-composed pibroch the imitative sounds of march, conflict, flight, pursuit, and all the ' current of a heady fight.'

Line 408. *Roderigh Vich Alpine dhu, ho!
ieroe!*

Besides his ordinary name and surname, which were chiefly used in the intercourse with the Lowlands, every Highland chief had an epithet expressive of his patriarchal dignity as head of the clan, and which was common to all his predecessors and successors, as Pharaoh to the kings of Egypt, or Arsaces to those of Parthia. This name was usually a patronymic, expressive of his descent from the founder of the family. Thus the Duke of Argyll is called MacCallum More, or the *son of Colin the Great.* Sometimes, however, it is derived from armorial distinctions, or the memory of some great feat; thus Lord Seaforth, as chief of the Mackenzies, or Clan-Kennet, bears the epithet of Caber-fae, or *Buck's Head,* as representative of Colin Fitzgerald, founder of the family, who saved the Scottish king when endangered by a stag. But besides this title, which belonged to his office and dignity, the chieftain had usually another peculiar to himself, which distinguished him from the chieftains of the same race. This was sometimes derived from complexion, as *dhu* or *roy;* sometimes from size, as *beg* or *more;* at other times, from some peculiar exploit, or from some peculiarity of habit or appearance. The line of the text therefore signifies, —

Black Roderick, the descendant of Alpine.

The song itself is intended as an imitation of the *jorrams,* or boat songs of the Highlanders, which were usually composed in honor of a favorite chief. They are so adapted as to keep time with the sweep of the oars, and it is easy to distinguish between those intended to be sung to the oars of a galley, where the stroke is lengthened and doubled, as it were, and those which were timed to the rowers of an ordinary boat.

Line 422. *And the best of Loch Lomond lie dead on her side.*

The Lennox, as the district is called which encircles the lower extremity of Loch Lomond, was peculiarly exposed to the incursions of the mountaineers, who inhabited the inaccessible fastnesses at the upper end of the lake, and the neighboring district of Loch Katrine. These were often marked by circumstances of great ferocity.

Page 170, line 616. *Boasts to have tamed the Border-side.*

In 1529, James V. made a convention at Edinburgh for the purpose of considering the best mode of quelling the Border robbers, who, during the license of his minority, and the troubles which followed, had committed many exorbitances. Accordingly, he assembled a flying army of ten thousand men, consisting of his principal nobility and their followers, who were directed to bring their hawks and dogs with them, that the monarch might refresh himself with sport during the intervals of military execution. With this array he swept through Ettrick Forest, where he hanged over the gate of

his own castle Piers Cockburn of Henderland, who had prepared, according to tradition, a feast for his reception. He caused Adam Scott of Tushielaw also to be executed, who was distinguished by the title of King of the Border. But the most noted victim of justice, during that expedition, was John Armstrong of Gilnockie, famous in Scottish song, who, confiding in his own supposed innocence, met the king with a retinue of thirty-six persons, all of whom were hanged at Carlenrig, near the source of the Teviot.

Page 172, lines 801, 802.

> *Pity 't were
> Such cheek should feel the midnight air.*

Hardihood was in every respect so essential to the character of a Highlander, that the reproach of effeminacy was the most bitter which could be thrown upon him. Yet it was sometimes hazarded on what we might presume to think slight grounds. It is reported of old Sir Ewen Cameron, of Lochiel, when upwards of seventy, that he was surprised by night on a hunting or military expedition. He wrapped him in his plaid, and lay contentedly down upon the snow, with which the ground happened to be covered. Among his attendants, who were preparing to take their rest in the same manner, he observed that one of his grandsons, for his better accommodation, had rolled a large snow-ball, and placed it below his head. The wrath of the ancient chief was awakened by a symptom of what he conceived to be degenerate luxury. 'Out upon thee,' said he. kicking the frozen bolster from the head which it supported; 'art thou so effeminate as to need a pillow?'

Page 173, line 18. *And while the Fiery Cross glanced, like a meteor, round.*

When a chieftain designed to summon his clan upon any sudden or important emergency, he slew a goat, and making a cross of any light wood, seared its extremities in the fire, and extinguished them in the blood of the animal. This was called the *Fiery Cross,* also *Crean Tarigh,* or the *Cross of Shame,* because disobedience to what the symbol implied, inferred infamy. It was delivered to a swift and trusty messenger, who ran full speed with it to the next hamlet, where he presented it to the principal person, with a single word, implying the place of rendezvous. He who received the symbol was bound to send it forward, with equal despatch, to the next village; and thus it passed with incredible celerity through all the district which owed allegiance to the chief, and also among his allies and neighbors, if the danger was common to them. At sight of the Fiery Cross, every man, from sixteen years old to sixty, capable of bearing arms, was obliged instantly to repair, in his best arms and accoutrements, to the place of rendezvous. He who failed to appear suffered the extremities of fire and sword, which were emblematically denounced to the disobedient by the bloody and burnt marks upon this warlike signal. During the civil war of 1745–46, the Fiery Cross often made its circuit ; and upon one occasion it passed through the whole district of Breadalbane, a tract of thirty-two miles, in three hours. The late Alexander Stewart, Esq., of Invernahyle, described to me his having sent round the Fiery Cross through the district of Appine, during the same commotion. The coast was threatened by a descent from two English frigates, and the flower of the young men were with the army of Prince Charles Edward, then in England; yet the summons was so effectual that even old age and childhood obeyed it ; and a force was collected in a few hours so numerous and so enthusiastic that all attempt at the intended diversion upon the country of the absent warriors was in prudence abandoned as desperate.

Page 174, line 71.   *That monk, of savage form and face.*

The state of religion in the middle ages afforded considerable facilities for those whose mode of life excluded them from regular worship, to secure, nevertheless, the ghostly assistance of confessors, perfectly willing to adapt the nature of their doctrine to the necessities and peculiar circumstances of their flock. Robin Hood, it is well known, had his celebrated domestic chaplain Friar Tuck.

Line 91.   *Of Brian's birth strange tales were told.*

[Scott says that the legend which follows is not of his invention, and goes on to show that it is taken with slight variation from ' the geographical collections made by the Laird of Macfarlane.']

Line 114.   *No hunter's hand her snood untied.*

The *snood*, or riband, with which a Scottish lass braided her hair, had an emblematical signification, and applied to her maiden character. It was exchanged for the *curch, toy,* or coif, when she passed, by marriage, into the matron state. But if the damsel was so unfortunate as to lose pretensions to the name of maiden without gaining a right to that of matron, she was neither permitted to use the snood, nor advanced to the graver dignity of the curch.

Line 149.   *The desert gave him visions wild.*

In adopting the legend concerning the birth of the Founder of the Church of Kilmallie, the author has endeavored to trace the effects which such a belief was likely to produce in a barbarous age on the person to whom it related. It seems likely that he must have become a fanatic or an impostor, or that mixture of both which forms a more frequent character than either of them, as existing separately. It was a natural attribute of such a character as the supposed hermit, that he should credit the numerous superstitions with which the minds of ordinary Highlanders are always imbued. A few of these are slightly alluded to in this stanza. The River Demon, or Riverhorse, for it is that form which he commonly assumes, is the Kelpy of the Lowlands, an evil and malicious spirit, delighting to forebode and to witness calamity. He frequents most Highland lakes and rivers ; and one of his most

memorable exploits was performed upon the banks of Loch Vennachar, in the very district which forms the scene of our action ; it consisted in the destruction of a funeral procession with all its attendants. The ' noontide hag,' called in Gaelic *Glas-lich,* a tall, emaciated, gigantic female figure, is supposed in particular to haunt the district of Knoidart. A goblin dressed in antique armor, and having one hand covered with blood, called from that circumstance *Lhamdeerg,* or Red-hand, is a tenant of the forests of Glenmore and Rothiemurcus.

Page 175, line 168.   *The fatal Ben-Shie's boding scream.*

Most great families in the Highlands were supposed to have a tutelar, or rather a domestic, spirit, attached to them, who took an interest in their prosperity, and intimated, by its wailings, any approaching disaster. That of Grant of Grant was called *May Moullach,* and appeared in the form of a girl, who had her arm covered with hair. Grant of Rothiemurcus had an attendant called *Bodach-an-dun,* or the Ghost of the Hill ; and many other examples might be mentioned. The Ben-Shie implies the female fairy whose lamentations were often supposed to precede the death of a chieftain of particular families. When she is visible, it is in the form of an old woman, with a blue mantle and streaming hair. A superstition of the same kind is, I believe, universally received by the inferior ranks of the native Irish.

Line 169.   *Sounds, too, had come in midnight blast.*

A presage of the kind alluded to in the text is still believed to announce death to the ancient Highland family of M'Lean of Lochbuy. The spirit of an ancestor slain in battle is heard to gallop along a stony bank, and then to ride thrice around the family residence, ringing his fairy bridle, and thus intimating the approaching calamity.

Line 191.   *Whose parents in Inch-Cailliach wave.*

The Isle of Nuns, or of Old Women, is a most beautiful island at the lower extremity of Loch Lomond. The church belonging to the former nunnery was long used as the place of worship for the parish of Buchanan, but scarce any vestiges of it now remain. The burial-ground continues to be used, and contains the family places of sepulture of several neighboring clans.

Page 176, line 300.   *Speed, Malise, speed ! the dun deer's hide.*

The present *brogue* of the Highlanders is made of half-dried leather, with holes to admit and let out the water ; for walking the moors dry-shod is a matter altogether out of question. The ancient buskin was still ruder, being made of undressed deer's hide, with the hair outwards, — a circumstance which procured the Highlanders the well-known epithet of *Redshanks.*

Page 177, line 369.   *The dismal coronach resound.*

The *Coronach* of the Highlanders, like the *Ululatus* of the Romans, and the *Ululoo* of the Irish, was a wild expression of lamentation, poured forth by the mourners over the body of a departed friend. When the words of it were articulate, they expressed the praises of the deceased, and the loss the clan would sustain by his death.

Page 178, line 452. *Benledi saw the cross of fire.*

The first stage of the Fiery Cross is to Duncraggan, a place near the Brigg of Turk, where a short stream divides Loch Achray from Loch Vennachar. From thence it passes towards Callander, and then, turning to the left up the pass of Leny, is consigned to Norman at the Chapel of Saint Bride, which stood on a small and romantic knoll in the middle of the valley, called Strath-Ire. Tombea and Arnandave, or Ardmandave, are names of places in the vicinity. The alarm is then supposed to pass along the Lake of Lubnaig, and through the various glens in the district of Balquidder, including the neighboring tracts of Glenfinlas and Strath-Gartney.

Page 179, line 570. *Balquidder, speeds the midnight blaze.*

It may be necessary to inform the Southern reader that the heath on the Scottish moorlands is often set fire to, that the sheep may have the advantage of the young herbage produced, in room of the tough old heather plants. This custom (execrated by sportsmen) produces occasionally the most beautiful nocturnal appearances, similar almost to the discharge of a volcano. This simile is not new to poetry. The charge of a warrior, in the fine ballad of *Hardyknute*, is said to be ' like fire to heather set.'

Line 622. *Has Coir-nan-Uriskin been sung.*

This is a very steep and most romantic hollow in the mountain of Benvenue, overhanging the southeastern extremity of Loch Katrine. It is surrounded with stupendous rocks, and overshadowed with birch-trees, mingled with oaks, the spontaneous production of the mountain, even where its cliffs appear denuded of soil. A dale in so wild a situation, and amid a people whose genius bordered on the romantic, did not remain without appropriate deities. The name literally implies the Corri, or Den, of the Wild or Shaggy Men. Tradition has ascribed to the *Urisk*, who gives name to the cavern, a figure between a goat and a man ; in short, however much the classical reader may be startled, precisely that of the Grecian Satyr. The *Urisk* seems not to have inherited, with the form, the petulance of the sylvan deity of the classics ; his occupation, on the contrary, resembled those of Milton's Lubbar Fiend, or of the Scottish Brownie, though he differed from both in name and appearance.

Page 180, line 673. *Alone attended on his lord.*

A Highland chief, being as absolute in his patriarchal authority as any prince, had a corresponding number of officers attached to his person. 1. The Henchman. 2. The Bard. 3.

Bladier, or spokesman. 4. Gillie - more, or sword - bearer. 5. Gillie-casflue, who carried the chief, if on foot, over the fords. 6. Gilliecomstraine, who leads the chief's horse. 7. Gillie-Trushanarinsh, the baggageman. 8. The piper. 9. The piper's gillie, or attendant who carries the bagpipe.

Page 182, line 63. *The Taghairm called ; by which, afar.*

The Highlanders, like all rude people, had various superstitious modes of inquiring into futurity. One of the most noted was the *Taghairm*, mentioned in the text. A person was wrapped up in the skin of a newly slain bullock, and deposited beside a waterfall, or at the bottom of a precipice, or in some other strange, wild, and unusual situation, where the scenery around him suggested nothing but objects of horror. In this situation he revolved in his mind the question proposed; and whatever was impressed upon him by his exalted imagination, passed for the inspiration of the disembodied spirits who haunt these desolate recesses.

Line 84. *Tradition calls the Hero's Targe.*

There is a rock so named in the Forest of Glenfinlas, by which a tumultuary cataract takes its course. This wild place is said in former times to have afforded refuge to an outlaw, who was supplied with provisions by a woman, who lowered them down from the brink of the precipice above. His water he procured for himself, by letting down a flagon tied to a string into the black pool beneath the fall.

Line 98. *That, watching while the deer is broke.*

Everything belonging to the chase was matter of solemnity among our ancestors ; but nothing was more so than the mode of cutting up, or, as it was technically called, *breaking*, the slaughtered stag. The forester had his allotted portion ; the hounds had a certain allowance ; and, to make the division as general as possible, the very birds had their share also.

Line 132. *Which spills the foremost foeman's life.*

Though this be in the text described as a response of the Taghairm, or Oracle of the Hide, it was of itself an augury frequently attended to. The fate of the battle was often anticipated, in the imagination of the combatants, by observing which party first shed blood. It is said that the Highlanders under Montrose were so deeply imbued with this notion, that on the morning of the battle of Tippermoor they murdered a defenceless herdsman, whom they found in the fields, merely to secure an advantage of so much consequence to their party.

Page 184, line 306. *The fairies' fatal green.*

As the *Daoine Shi'*, or Men of Peace, wore green habits, they were supposed to take offence when any mortals ventured to assume their favorite color. Indeed, from some reason, which has been perhaps originally a general superstition, *green* is held in Scotland to be unlucky to particular tribes and counties. The Caithness men, who hold this belief, allege as a reason that their bands wore that color when they were cut off at the battle of Flodden; and for the same reason they avoid crossing the Ord on a Monday, being the day of the week on which their ill-omened array set forth. Green is also disliked by those of the name of Ogilvy; but more especially it is held fatal to the whole clan of Grahame. It is remembered of an aged gentleman of that name that when his horse fell in a fox-chase, he accounted for it at once by observing that the whipcord attached to his lash was of this unlucky color.

Line 308. *For thou wert christened man.*

The Elves were supposed greatly to envy the privileges acquired by Christian initiation, and they gave to those mortals who had fallen into their power a certain precedence, founded upon this advantageous distinction.

Page 185, line 356. *To the joyless Elfin bower.*

The subjects of Fairy-land were recruited from the regions of humanity by a sort of *crimping* system, which extended to adults as well as to infants.

Page 188, line 594. *It was a stag, a stag of ten.*

Having ten branches on his antlers.

Page 189, line 747. *Who ever recked, where, how, or when.*

St. John actually used this illustration when engaged in confuting the plea of law proposed for the unfortunate Earl of Strafford: 'It was true, we gave laws to hares and deer, because they are beasts of chase; but it was never accounted either cruelty or foul play to knock foxes or wolves on the head as they can be found, because they are beasts of prey. In a word, the law and humanity were alike: the one being more fallacious, and the other more barbarous, than in any age had been vented in such an authority.' — Clarendon's *History of the Rebellion.*

Line 762. *The hardened flesh of mountain deer.*

The Scottish Highlanders, in former times, had a concise mode of cooking their venison, or rather of dispensing with cooking it, which appears greatly to have surprised the French whom chance made acquainted with it. The Vidame of Chartres, when a hostage in England, during the reign of Edward VI., was permitted to travel into Scotland, and penetrated as far as the remote Highlands. After a great hunting party, at which a most wonderful quantity of game was destroyed, he saw these *Scottish savages* devour a part of their venison raw, without any further preparation than compressing it between two batons of wood, so as to force out the blood, and render it extremely hard. This they reckoned a great delicacy; and when the Vidame partook of it, his compliance with their taste rendered him extremely popular.

Page 191, line 124. *While Albany with feeble hand.*

There is scarcely a more disorderly period of

Scottish history than that which succeeded the battle of Flodden, and occupied the minority of James V. Feuds of ancient standing broke out like old wounds, and every quarrel among the independent nobility, which occurred daily, and almost hourly, gave rise to fresh bloodshed.

Line 164. *The Gael, of plain and river heir.*

So far indeed was a *Creagh*, or foray, from being held disgraceful, that a young chief was always expected to show his talents for command so soon as he assumed it, by leading his clan on a successful enterprise of this nature, either against a neighboring sept, for which constant feuds usually furnished an apology, or against the *Sassenach*, Saxons, or Lowlanders, for which no apology was necessary. The Gael, great traditional historians, never forgot that the Lowlands had, at some remote period, been the property of their Celtic forefathers, which furnished an ample vindication of all the ravages that they could make on the unfortunate districts which lay within their reach.

Page 192, lines 270, 271.

> *I only meant*
> *To show the reed on which you leant.*

This incident, like some other passages in the poem, illustrative of the character of the ancient Gael, is not imaginary, but borrowed from fact. The Highlanders, with the inconsistency of most nations in the same state, were alternately capable of great exertions of generosity and of cruel revenge and perfidy. Early in the last century, John Gunn, a noted Highland robber, infested Inverness-shire, and levied *black-mail* up to the walls of the provincial capital. A garrison was then maintained in the castle of that town, and their pay (country banks being unknown) was usually transmitted in specie under the guard of a small escort. It chanced that the officer who commanded this little party was unexpectedly obliged to halt, about thirty miles from Inverness, at a miserable inn. About nightfall, a stranger in the Highland dress, and of very prepossessing appearance, entered the same house. Separate accommodation being impossible, the Englishman offered the newly arrived guest a part of his supper, which was accepted with reluctance. By the conversation he found his new acquaintance knew well all the passes of the country, which induced him eagerly to request his company on the ensuing morning. He neither disguised his business and charge, nor his apprehensions of that celebrated freebooter, John Gunn. The Highlander hesitated a moment, and then frankly consented to be his guide. Forth they set in the morning; and in travelling through a solitary and dreary glen, the discourse again turned on John Gunn. 'Would you like to see him?' said the guide; and without waiting an answer to this alarming question he whistled, and the English officer, with his small party, were surrounded by a body of Highlanders, whose numbers put resistance out of question, and who were all well armed. 'Stranger,' resumed the guide, 'I am that very John Gunn by whom you feared to be intercepted, and not without cause; for I came to the inn last night with the express purpose of learning your route, that I and my followers might ease you of your charge by the road. But I am incapable of betraying the trust you reposed in me, and having convinced you that you were in my power, I can only dismiss you unplundered and uninjured.' He then gave the officer directions for his journey, and disappeared with his party as suddenly as they had presented themselves.

Page 193, line 298. *Which, daughter of three mighty lakes.*

The torrent which discharges itself from Loch Vennachar, the lowest and eastmost of the three lakes which form the scenery adjoining to the Trosachs, sweeps through a flat and extensive moor, called Bochastle. Upon a small eminence called the *Dun* of Bochastle, and indeed on the plain itself, are some intrenchments which have been thought Roman.

Line 315. *See, here all vantageless I stand.*

The duellists of former times did not always stand upon those punctilios respecting equality of arms, which are now judged essential to fair combat. It is true, that in formal combats in the lists, the parties were, by the judges of the field, put as nearly as possible in the same circumstances. But in private duel it was often otherwise. In that desperate combat which was fought between Luelus, a minion of Henry III. of France, and Antraguet, with two seconds on each side, from which only two persons escaped alive, Luelus complained that his antagonist had over him the advantage of a poinard, which he used in parrying, while his left hand, which he was forced to employ for the same purpose, was cruelly mangled. When he charged Antraguet with this odds, 'Thou hast done wrong,' answered he, 'to forget thy dagger at home. We are here to fight, and not to settle punctilios of arms.' In a similar duel, however, a younger brother of the house of Aubanye, in Angoulesme, behaved more generously on the like occasion, and at once threw away his dagger when his enemy challenged it as an undue advantage. But at this time hardly anything can be conceived more horridly brutal and savage than the mode in which private quarrels were conducted in France. Those who were most jealous of the point of honor, and acquired the title of *Ruffinés*, did not scruple to take every advantage of strength, numbers, surprise, and arms, to accomplish their revenge.

Page 194, line 380. *That on the field his targe he threw.*

A round target of light-wood, covered with strong leather and studded with brass or iron, was a necessary part of a Highlander's equipment. In charging regular troops they received the thrust of the bayonet in this buckler, twisted it aside, and used the broadsword against the encumbered soldier. In the civil war of 1745 most of the front rank of the clans were thus armed; and Captain Grose (*Military Antiquities*, vol. i. p. 164) informs us that in 1747 the privates of the 42d regiment, then in Flanders, were for the most part permitted to carry

targets. A person thus armed had a considerable advantage in private fray.

Line 384. *Fitz-James's blade was sword and shield.*

The use of defensive armor, and particularly of the buckler or target, was general in Queen Elizabeth's time, although that of the single rapier seems to have been occasionally practised much earlier. Rowland Yorke, however, who betrayed the fort of Zutphen to the Spaniards, for which good service he was afterward poisoned by them, is said to have been the first who brought the rapier-fight into general use.

Page 195, line 551. *And thou, O sad and fatal mound !*

An eminence on the northeast of the Castle, where state criminals were executed. Stirling was often polluted with noble blood. This 'heading-hill,' as it was sometimes termed, bears commonly the less terrible name of Hurly-hacket, from its having been the scene of a courtly amusement alluded to by Sir David Lindesay, who says of the pastimes in which the young king was engaged

    ' Some harled him to the Hurly-hacket ; '

which consisted in sliding, in some sort of chair, it may be supposed, from top to bottom of a smooth bank.

Page 195, line 564. *The burghers hold their sports to-day.*

Every burgh of Scotland of the least note, but more especially the considerable towns, had their solemn *play*, or festival, when feats of archery were exhibited, and prizes distributed to those who excelled in wrestling, hurling the bar, and the other gymnastic exercises of the period. Stirling, a usual place of royal residence, was not likely to be deficient in pomp upon such occasions, especially since James V. was very partial to them. His ready participation in these popular amusements was one cause of his acquiring the title of the King of the Commons, or *Rex Plebeiorum*, as Lesley has latinized it. The usual prize to the best shooter was a silver arrow.

Page 196, line 614. *Bold Robin Hood and all his band.*

The exhibition of this renowned outlaw and his band was a favorite frolic at such festivals as we are describing. This sporting, in which kings did not disdain to be actors, was prohibited in Scotland upon the Reformation, by a statute of the 6th parliament of Queen Mary, c. 61, A. D. 1555, which ordered, under heavy penalties, that 'na manner of person be chosen Robert Hude, nor Little John, Abbot of Unreason, Queen of May, nor otherwise.' But in 1561 the 'rascal multitude,' says John Knox, 'were stirred up to make a Robin Hude, whilk enormity was of mony years left and damned by statute and act of Parliament; yet would they not be forbidden.' Accordingly they raised a very serious tumult, and at length made prisoners the magistrates who endeavored to suppress it, and would not release them till they extorted a formal promise that no one should be punished for his share of the disturbance. It would seem, from the complaints of the General Assembly of the Kirk, that these profane festivities were continued down to 1592 (*Book of the Universal Kirk*, p. 414).

Line 631. *The monarch gave the arrow bright.*

The Douglas of the poem is an imaginary person, a supposed uncle of the Earl of Angus. But the king's behavior during an unexpected interview with the Laird of Kilspindie, one of the banished Douglasses, under circumstances similar to those in the text, is imitated from a real story told by Home of Godscroft.

Line 641. *To Douglas gave a golden ring.*

The usual prize of a wrestling was a ram and a ring, but the animal would have embarrassed my story.

Page 199, line 887. *Where stout Earl William was of old.*

Stabbed by James II. in Stirling Castle.

Line 47. *Adventurers they, from far who roved.*

The Scottish armies consisted chiefly of the nobility and barons, with their vassals, who held lands under them for military service by themselves and their tenants. The patriarchal influence exercised by the heads of clans in the Highlands and Borders was of a different nature, and sometimes at variance with feudal principles. It flowed from the *Patria Potestas*, exercised by the chieftain as representing the original father of the whole name, and was often obeyed in contradiction to the feudal superior. James V. seems first to have introduced, in addition to the militia furnished from these sources, the service of a small number of mercenaries, who formed a body-guard, called the Foot-Band.

Page 200, line 131. *The leader of a juggler band.*

The *jongleurs*, or jugglers, as we learn from the elaborate work of the late Mr. Strutt, on the sports and pastimes of the people of England, used to call in the aid of various assistants, to render these performances as captivating as possible. The glee-maiden was a necessary attendant. Her duty was tumbling and dancing; and therefore the Anglo-Saxon version of St. Mark's Gospel states Herodias to have vaulted or tumbled before King Herod. In Scotland, these poor creatures seem, even at a late period, to have been bondswomen to their masters.

Page 203, line 348. *Strike it! — and then, — for well thou canst.*

There are several instances, at least in tradition, of persons so much attached to particular tunes as to require to hear them on their death-bed. Such an anecdote is mentioned by the late Mr. Riddel of Glenriddel, in his collection of Border tunes, respecting an air called the *Dandling of the Bairns*, for which a certain Gallovidian laird is said to have evinced this strong mark of partiality. It is popularly told of a famous freebooter, that he composed the tune known by the name of *Macpherson's Rant* while under sentence of death, and played it at the gallows-tree. Some spirited words have been adapted to it by Burns. A similar story is recounted of a Welsh bard, who composed and played on his death-bed the air called *Dafyddy Garregg Wen.*

Canto xv. *Battle of Bea'l an Duine.*

A skirmish actually took place at a pass thus called in the Trosachs, and closed with the remarkable incident mentioned in the text. It was greatly posterior in date to the reign of James V.

Page 204, line 452. *As their Tinchel cows the game.*

A circle of sportsmen, who, by surrounding a great space, and gradually narrowing, brought immense quantities of deer together, which usually made desperate efforts to break through the *Tinchel.*

Page 207, line 740. *And Snowdoun's Knight is Scotland's King.*

This discovery will probably remind the reader of the beautiful Arabian tale of *Il Bondocani.* Yet the incident is not borrowed from that elegant story, but from Scottish tradition. James V., of whom we are treating, was a monarch whose good and benevolent intentions often rendered his romantic freaks venial, if not respectable, since, from his anxious attention to the interests of the lower and most oppressed class of his subjects, he was, as we have seen, popularly termed the *King of the Commons.* For the purpose of seeing that justice was regularly administered, and frequently from the less justifiable motive of gallantry, he used to traverse the vicinage of his several palaces in various disguises. The two excellent comic songs entitled *The Gaberlunzie Man* and *We'll gae nae mair a roving* are said to have been founded upon the success of his amorous adventures when travelling in the disguise of a beggar. The latter is perhaps the best comic ballad in any language.

Line 789. *Of yore the name of Snowdoun claims.*

William of Worcester, who wrote about the middle of the fifteenth century, calls Stirling Castle Snowdoun. Sir David Lindesay bestows the same epithet upon it in his *Complaint of the Papingo:* —

'Adieu, fair Snawdoun, with thy towers high,
　Thy chaple-royal, park, and table round;
　May, June, and July, would I dwell in thee,
　Were I a man, to hear the birdis sound,
　Whilk doth agane thy royal rock rebound.'

Mr. Chalmers, in his late excellent edition of Sir David Lindesay's works, has refuted the chimerical derivation of Snawdoun from *snedding*, or cutting. It was probably derived from the romantic legend which connected Stirling with King Arthur, to which the mention of the Round Table gives countenance. The ring within which jousts were formerly practised, in the castle park, is still called the Round Table. Snawdoun is the official title of one of the Scottish heralds, whose epithets seem in all countries to have been fantastically adopted from ancient history or romance. It appears that the real name by which James was actually distinguished in his private excursions was the *Good-*

man of Ballenquick, derived from a steep pass leading up to the Castle of Stirling, so called.

THE VISION OF DON RODERICK.
Page 211, line 35. *And Cattreath's glens with voice of triumph rung.*

This locality may startle those readers who do not recollect that much of the ancient poetry preserved in Wales refers less to the history of the Principality to which that name is now limited, than to events which happened in the northwest of England, and southwest of Scotland, where the Britons for a long time made a stand against the Saxons. The battle of Cattreath, lamented by the celebrated Aneurin, is supposed, by the learned Dr. Leyden, to have been fought on the skirts of Ettrick Forest. It is known to the English reader by the paraphrase of Gray, beginning, —

'Had I but the torrent's might,
With headlong rage and wild affright,' etc.

But it is not so generally known that the champions, mourned in this beautiful dirge, were the British inhabitants of Edinburgh, who were cut off by the Saxons of Deiria, or Northumberland, about the latter part of the sixth century.

Line 67. *Or round the marge of Minchmore's haunted spring.*

A belief in the existence and nocturnal revels of the fairies still lingers among the vulgar in Selkirkshire. A copious fountain upon the ridge of Minchmore, called the Cheesewell, is supposed to be sacred to these fanciful spirits, and it was customary to propitiate them by throwing in something upon passing it. A pin was the usual oblation; and the ceremony is still sometimes practised, though rather in jest than earnest.

Page 212, line 76. *In verse spontaneous chants some favored name.*

The flexibility of the Italian and Spanish languages, and perhaps the liveliness of their genius, renders these countries distinguished for the talent of improvisations, which is found even among the lowest of the people. It is mentioned by Baretti and other travellers.

Line 79. *Or whether, kindling at the deeds of Græme.*

Over a name sacred for ages to heroic verse, a poet may be allowed to exercise some power. I have used the freedom, here and elsewhere, to alter the orthography of the name of my gallant countryman, in order to apprise the Southern reader of its legitimate sound ; — Grahame being, on the other side of the Tweed, usually pronounced as a dissyllable.

Page 213, line 31. *What ! will Don Roderick here till morning stay.*

Almost all the Spanish historians, as well as the voice of tradition, ascribe the invasion of the Moors to the forcible violation committed by Roderick upon Florinda, called by the Moors, Caba or Cava. She was the daughter of Count Julian, one of the Gothic monarch's principal lieutenants, who, when the crime was perpetrated, was engaged in the defence of Ceuta against the Moors. In his indignation at the ingratitude of his sovereign, and the dishonor of his daughter, Count Julian forgot the duties of a Christian and a patriot, and, forming an alliance with Musa, then the Caliph's lieutenant in Africa, he countenanced the invasion of Spain by a body of Saracens and Africans, commanded by the celebrated Tarik ; the issue of which was the defeat and death of Roderick, and the occupation of almost the whole peninsula by the Moors.

Line 59. '*Thus royal Witiza was slain,*' he said.

The predecessor of Roderick upon the Spanish throne, and slain by his connivance, as is affirmed by Rodriguez of Toledo, the father of Spanish history.

Page 215, line 168. *The Tecbir war-cry and the Lelie's yell.*

The Tecbir (derived from the words *Alla acbar*, God is most mighty) was the original warcry of the Saracens. It is celebrated by Hughes in the Siege of Damascus : —

'We heard the Tecbir ; so these Arabs call
Their shout of onset, when, with loud appeal,
They challenge Heaven, as if demanding conquest.'

The *Lelie*, well known to the Christians during the crusades, is the shout of *Alla illa Alla*, the Mahometan confession of faith. It is twice used in poetry by my friend Mr. W. Stewart Rose, in the romance of *Partenopex*, and in the *Crusade of Saint Lewis.*

Line 181. *By Heaven, the Moors prevail ! the Christians yield !*

Count Julian, the father of the injured Florinda, with the connivance and assistance of Oppas, Archbishop of Toledo, invited, in 713, the Saracens into Spain. A considerable army arrived under the command of Tarik, or Tarif, who bequeathed the well-known name of Gibraltar (*Gibel al Tarik*, or the mountain of Tarik) to the place of his landing. He was joined by Count Julian, ravaged Andalusia, and took Seville. In 714, they returned with a still greater force, and Roderick marched into Andalusia at the head of a great army, to give them battle.

Orelia, the courser of Don Roderick, was celebrated for her speed and form. She is mentioned repeatedly in Spanish romance, and also by Cervantes.

Page 218, line 293. *When for the light bolero ready stand.*

The *bolero* is a very light and active dance, much practised by the Spaniards, in which castanets are always used. *Mozo and muchacha* is equivalent to our phrase of *lad and lass.*

Page 219, line 382. *While trumpets rang, and heralds cried ' Castile ! '*

The heralds, at the coronation of a Spanish monarch, proclaim his name three times, and repeat three times the word *Castilla, Castilla, Castilla ;* which, with all other ceremonies, was carefully copied in the mock inauguration of Joseph Bonaparte.

Page 223, line 563. *Then, though the Vault of Destiny be gone.*

Before finally dismissing the enchanted cavern of Don Roderick, it may be noticed that the legend occurs in one of Calderon's plays, entitled *La Virgin del Sagrario.*

Line 15. *While downward on the land his legions press.*

I have ventured to apply to the movements of the French army that sublime passage in the prophecies of Joel (ii. 2–10) which seems applicable to them in more respects than that I have adopted in the text. One would think their ravages, their military appointments, the terror which they spread among invaded nations, their military discipline, their arts of political intrigue and deceit, were distinctly pointed out.

Page 224, line 68. *Vainglorious fugitive, yet turn again!*

The French conducted this memorable retreat with much of the *fanfarronade* proper to their country, by which they attempt to impose upon others, and perhaps on themselves, a belief that they are triumphing in the very moment of their discomfiture. On the 30th March, 1811, their rear-guard was overtaken near Pega by the British cavalry. Being well posted, and conceiving themselves safe from infantry (who were indeed many miles in the rear) and from artillery, they indulged themselves in parading their bands of music, and actually performed 'God save the King.' Their minstrelsy was, however, deranged by the undesired accompaniment of the British horse-artillery, on whose part in the concert they had not calculated. The surprise was sudden, and the rout complete ; for the artillery and cavalry did execution upon them for about four miles, pursuing at the gallop as often as they got beyond the range of the guns.

Line 83. *Vainly thy squadrons hide Assuava's plain.*

In the severe action of Fuentes d'Honoro ['Honor's Fountain,' l. 70] upon 5th May, 1811, the grand mass of the French cavalry attacked the right of the British position, covered by two guns of the horse-artillery, and two squadrons of cavalry. After suffering considerably from the fire of the guns, which annoyed them in every attempt at formation, the enemy turned their wrath entirely towards them, distributed brandy among their troopers, and advanced to carry the fieldpieces with the desperation of drunken fury. They were in no wise checked by the heavy loss which they sustained in this daring attempt, but closed, and fairly mingled with the British cavalry, to whom they bore the proportion of ten to one. Captain Ramsay, who commanded the two guns, dismissed them at the gallop, and, putting himself at the head of the mounted artillerymen, ordered them to fall upon the French, sabre-in-hand. This very unexpected conversion of artillerymen into dragoons contributed greatly to the defeat of the enemy already disconcerted by the reception they had met from the two British squadrons ; and the appearance of some small reinforcements, notwithstanding the immense disproportion of force, put them to absolute rout.

Line 86. *And what avails thee that, for Cameron slain.*

The gallant Colonel Cameron was wounded mortally during the desperate contest in the streets of the village called Fuentes d'Honoro. He fell at the head of his native Highlanders, the 71st and 79th, who raised a dreadful shriek of grief and rage. They charged, with irresistible fury, the finest body of French grenadiers ever seen, being a part of Bonaparte's selected guard. The officer who led the French, a man remarkable for stature and symmetry, was killed on the spot. The Frenchman who stepped out of his rank to take aim at Colonel Cameron was also bayoneted, pierced with a thousand wounds, and almost torn to pieces by the furious Highlanders, who, under the command of Colonel Cadogan, bore the enemy out of the contested ground at the point of the bayonet.

Page 225, line 118. *O who shall grudge him Albuera's bays.*

Nothing during the war of Portugal seems, to a distinct observer, more deserving of praise, than the self-devotion of Field-Marshal Beresford, who was contented to undertake all the hazard of obloquy which might have been founded upon any miscarriage in the highly important experiment of training the Portuguese troops to an improved state of discipline.

Page 226, line 153. *Than when wild Ronda learned the conquering shout of Græme!*

This stanza alludes to the various achievements of the warlike family of Græme, or Grahame. They are said, by tradition, to have descended from the Scottish chief under whose command his countrymen stormed the wall built by the Emperor Severus between the Friths of Forth and Clyde, the fragments of which are still popularly called Græme's Dyke. Sir John the Græme, 'the hardy, wight, and wise,' is well known as the friend of Sir William Wallace. Alderne, Kilsythe, and Tibbermuir were scenes of the victories of the heroic Marquis of Montrose. The pass of Killycrankie is famous for the action between King William's forces and the Highlanders in 1689.

'Where glad Dundee in faint huzzas expired.'

It is seldom that one line can number so many heroes, and yet more rare when it can appeal to the glory of a living descendant in support of its ancient renown.

ROKEBY.

Page 231, line 5. *On Barnard's towers, and Tees's stream.*

'Barnard Castle,' saith old Leland, 'standeth stately upon Tees.' It is founded upon a very high bank, and its ruins impend over the river, including within the area a circuit of six acres and upwards. This once magnificent fortress derives its name from its founder.

Barnard Baliol, the ancestor of the short and unfortunate dynasty of that name, which succeeded to the Scottish throne under the patronage of Edward I. and Edward III. Baliol's Tower, afterwards mentioned in the poem, is a round tower of great size, situated at the western extremity of the building. It bears marks of great antiquity, and was remarkable for the curious construction of its vaulted roof, which has been lately greatly injured by the operations of some persons, to whom the tower has been leased for the purpose of making patent shot! The prospect from the top of Baliol's Tower commands a rich and magnificent view of the wooded valley of the Tees.

Page 232, line 96. *The morion's plumes his visage hide.*

The use of complete suits of armor was fallen into disuse during the Civil War, though they were still worn by leaders of rank and importance. 'In the reign of King James I.,' says our military antiquary, 'no great alterations were made in the article of defensive armor, except that the buff-coat, or jerkin, which was originally worn under the cuirass, now became frequently a substitute for it, it having been found that a good buff leather would of itself resist the stroke of a sword; this, however, only occasionally took place among the light-armed cavalry and infantry, complete suits of armor being still used among the heavy horse. Buff-coats continued to be worn by the city trained-bands till within the memory of persons now living, so that defensive armor may, in some measure, be said to have terminated in the same materials with which it began, that is, the skins of animals, or leather.' — Grose's *Military Antiquities*, Lond. 1801, 4to, vol. ii. p. 323.

Line 141. *On his dark face a scorching clime.*

In this character I have attempted to sketch one of those West Indian adventurers, who, during the course of the seventeenth century, were popularly known by the name of Buccaneers. The successes of the English in the predatory incursions upon Spanish America during the reign of Elizabeth had never been forgotten; and, from that period downward, the exploits of Drake and Raleigh were imitated, upon a smaller scale indeed, but with equally desperate valor, by small bands of pirates, gathered from all nations, but chiefly French and English. The engrossing policy of the Spaniards tended greatly to increase the number of these free-booters, from whom their commerce and colonies suffered, in the issue, dreadful calamity.

Page 233, line 223. *Would'st hear the tale? — On Marston heath.*

The well-known and desperate battle of Long-Marston Moor, which terminated so unfortunately for the cause of Charles, commenced under very different auspices. Prince Rupert had marched with an army of twenty thousand men for the relief of York, then besieged by Sir Thomas Fairfax, at the head of the Parliamentary army, and the Earl of

Leven, with the Scottish auxiliary forces. In this he so completely succeeded, that he compelled the besiegers to retreat to Marston Moor, a large open plain, about eight miles distant from the city. Thither they were followed by the Prince, who had now united to his army the garrison of York, probably not less than ten thousand men strong, under the gallant Marquis (then Earl) of Newcastle.

Lord Clarendon informs us that the King, previous to receiving the true account of the battle, had been informed, by an express from Oxford, ' that Prince Rupert had not only relieved York, but totally defeated the Scots, with many particulars to confirm it, all which was so much believed there, that they had made public fires of joy for the victory.'

Page 236, line 436. *Monckton and Mitton told the news.*

Monckton and Mitton are villages near the river Ouse, and not very distant from the field of battle. The particulars of the action were violently disputed at the time.

Line 445. *Stout Cromwell has redeemed the day.*

Cromwell, with his regiment of cuirassiers, had a principal share in turning the fate of the day at Marston Moor; which was equally matter of triumph to the Independents, and of grief and heart-burning to the Presbyterians and to the Scottish.

Line 461. *Of Percy Rede the tragic song.*

In a poem, entitled *The Lay of the Reedwater Minstrel*, Newcastle, 1809, this tale, with many others peculiar to the valley of the Reed, is commemorated : ' The particulars of the traditional story of Parcy Reed of Troughend, and the Halls of Girsonfield, the author had from a descendant of the family of Reed. From his account, it appears that Percival Reed, Esquire, a keeper of Reedsdale, was betrayed by the Halls (hence denominated the false-hearted Ha's) to a band of moss-troopers of the name of Crosier, who slew him at Batinghope, near the source of the Reed.

' The Halls were, after the murder of Parcy Reed, held in such universal abhorrence and contempt by the inhabitants of Reedsdale, for their cowardly and treacherous behavior, that they were obliged to leave the country.' In another passage we are informed that the ghost of the injured Borderer is supposed to haunt the banks of a brook called the Pringle. These Redes of Troughend were a very ancient family, as may be conjectured from their deriving their surname from the river on which they had their mansion. An epitaph on one of their tombs affirms that the family held their lands of Troughend, which are situated on the Reed, nearly opposite to Otterburn, for the incredible space of nine hundred years.

Line 466. *And near the spot that gave me name.*

Risingham, upon the river Reed, near the beautiful hamlet of Woodburn, is an ancient Roman station, formerly called Habitancum. Camden says, that in his time the popular account bore that it had been the abode of a deity, or giant, called Magon; and appeals, in support of this tradition, as well as to the etymology of Risingham, or Reisenham, which signifies, in German, the habitation of the giants, to two Roman altars taken out of the river, inscribed DEO MOGONTI CADENORUM. About half a mile distant from Risingham, upon an eminence covered with scattered birch-trees and fragments of rock, there is cut upon a large rock, in *alto relievo*, a remarkable figure, called Robin of Risingham, or Robin of Redesdale. It presents a hunter, with his bow raised in one hand, and in the other what seems to be a hare. There is a quiver at the back of the figure, and he is dressed in a long coat or kirtle, coming down to the knees, and meeting close, with a girdle bound round him. Dr. Horseley, who saw all monuments of antiquity with Roman eyes, inclines to think this figure a Roman archer; and certainly the bow is rather of the ancient size than of that which was so formidable in the hand of the English archers of the middle ages. But the rudeness of the whole figure prevents our founding strongly upon mere inaccuracy of proportion. The popular tradition is, that it represents a giant, whose brother resided at Woodburn, and he himself at Risingham. It adds, that they subsisted by hunting, and that one of them, finding the game become too scarce to support them, poisoned his companion, in whose memory the monument was engraved.

Line 491. *The statutes of the buccaneer.*

The 'statutes of the Buccaneers' were, in reality, more equitable than could have been expected from the state of society under which they had been formed. They chiefly related, as may readily be conjectured, to the distribution and the inheritance of their plunder. When the expedition was completed, the fund of prize-money acquired was thrown together, each party taking his oath that he had retained or concealed no part of the common stock. If any one transgressed in this important particular, the punishment was, his being set ashore on some desert key or island, to shift for himself as he could. The owners of the vessel had then their share assigned for the expenses of the outfit. These were generally old pirates, settled at Tobago, Jamaica, St. Domingo, or some other French or English settlement. The surgeon's and carpenter's salaries, with the price of provisions and ammunition, were also defrayed. Then followed the compensation due to the maimed and wounded, rated according to the damage they had sustained; as six hundred pieces of eight, or six slaves, for the loss of an arm or leg, and so in proportion. The remainder of the booty was divided into as many shares as there were Buccaneers. The commander could only lay claim to a single share, as the rest; but they complimented him with two or three, in proportion as he had acquitted himself to their satisfaction.

Page 239, line 22. *Down his deep woods the course of Tees.*

The view from Barnard Castle commands the rich and magnificent valley of Tees. Immediately adjacent to the river, the banks are very thickly wooded; at a little distance they are more open and cultivated; but, being interspersed with hedgerows, and with isolated trees of great size and age, they still retain the richness of woodland scenery. The river itself flows in a deep trench of solid rock, chiefly limestone and marble.

Page 240, line 80. *And Egliston's gray ruins passed.*

The ruins of this abbey, or priory, are beautifully situated upon the angle formed by a little dell called Thorsgill at its junction with the Tees. Egliston was dedicated to St. Mary and St. John the Baptist, and is supposed to have been founded by Ralph de Multon about the end of Henry the Second's reign.

Line 98. *Raised by that Legion long renowned.*

Close behind the George Inn at Greta Bridge, there is a well-preserved Roman encampment, surrounded with a triple ditch, lying between the river Greta and a brook called the Tutta. The four entrances are easily to be discerned. Very many Roman altars and monuments have been found in the vicinity.

Line 108. *Awoke when Rokeby's turrets high.*

This ancient manor long gave name to a family by whom it is said to have been possessed from the Conquest downward, and who are at different times distinguished in history. It was the Baron of Rokeby who finally defeated the insurrection of the Earl of Northumberland, *tempore* Hen. IV. The Rokeby, or Rokesby family, continued to be distinguished until the great Civil War, when, having embraced the cause of Charles I., they suffered severely by fines and confiscations.

Page 241, line 135. *A stern and lone yet lovely road.*

What follows is an attempt to describe the romantic glen, or rather ravine, through which the Greta finds a passage between Rokeby and Mortham; the former situated upon the left bank of Greta, the latter on the right bank, about half a mile nearer to its junction with the Tees. The river runs with very great rapidity over a bed of solid rock, broken by many shelving descents, down which the stream dashes with great noise and impetuosity.

Page 242, line 251. *How whistle rash bids tempests roar.*

That this is a general superstition, is well known to all who have been on shipboard, or who have conversed with seamen.

Line 253. *Of Erick's cap and Elmo's light.*

'This Ericus, King of Sweden, in his time was held second to none in the magical art; and he was so familiar with the evil spirits, which he exceedingly adored, that which way soever he turned his cap, the wind would presently blow that way. From this occasion he was called Windy Cap; and many men believed that Regnerus, King of Denmark, by the conduct of this Ericus, who was his nephew, did happily extend his piracy into the most remote parts of the earth, and conquered many countries and fenced cities by his cunning, and at last was his coadjutor; that by the consent of the nobles, he should be chosen King of Sweden, which continued a long time with him very happily, until he died of old age.' — *Olaus Magnus*, p. 45.

Line 263. *The Demon Frigate braves the gale.*
This is an allusion to a well-known nautical superstition concerning a fantastic vessel, called by sailors the 'Flying Dutchman,' and supposed to be seen about the latitude of the Cape of Good Hope. She is distinguished from earthly vessels by bearing a press of sail when all others are unable, from stress of weather, to show an inch of canvas. The cause of her wandering is not altogether certain; but the general account is, that she was originally a vessel loaded with great wealth, on board of which some horrid act of murder and piracy had been committed; that the plague broke out among the wicked crew who had perpetrated the crime, and that they sailed in vain from port to port, offering, as the price of shelter, the whole of their ill-gotten wealth; that they were excluded from every harbor, for fear of the contagion which was devouring them; and that, as a punishment of their crimes, the apparition of the ship still continues to haunt those seas in which the catastrophe took place, and is considered by the mariners as the worst of all possible omens.

Line 268. *How, by some desert isle or key.*
What contributed much to the security of the Buccaneers about the Windward Islands was the great number of little islets, called in that country *keys*. These are small sandy patches, appearing just above the surface of the ocean, covered only with a few bushes and weeds, but sometimes affording springs of water, and, in general, much frequented by turtle. Such little uninhabited spots afforded the pirates good harbors, either for refitting or for the purpose of ambush; they were occasionally the hiding-place of their treasure, and often afforded a shelter to themselves.

Page 243, line 363. *Before the gate of Mortham stood.*
The castle of Mortham, which Leland terms 'Mr. Rokesby's Place, in *ripa citer*, scant a quarter of a mile from Greta Bridge, and not a quarter of a mile beneath into Tees,' is a picturesque tower, surrounded by buildings of different ages, now converted into a farmhouse and offices. The situation of Mortham is eminently beautiful, occupying a high bank, at the bottom of which the Greta winds out of the dark, narrow, and romantic dell, which the text has attempted to describe, and flows onward through a more open valley to meet the Tees about a quarter of a mile from the castle.

Line 424. *There dig and tomb your precious heap.*
If time did not permit the Buccaneers to lavish away their plunder in their usual debaucheries, they were wont to hide it, with many superstitious solemnities, in the desert

islands and keys which they frequented, and where much treasure, whose lawless owners perished without reclaiming it, is still supposed to be concealed. They killed a Negro or Spaniard, and buried him with the treasure, believing that his spirit would haunt the spot, and terrify away all intruders. I cannot produce any other authority on which this custom is ascribed to them than that of maritime tradition, which is, however, amply sufficient for the purposes of poetry.

Page 244, line 444. *And force him as by magic spell.*
All who are conversant with the administration of criminal justice must remember many occasions in which malefactors appear to have conducted themselves with a species of infatuation, either by making unnecessary confidences respecting their guilt, or by sudden and involuntary allusions to circumstances by which it could not fail to be exposed. A remarkable instance occurred in the celebrated case of Eugene Aram. It happened to the author himself, while conversing with a person accused of an atrocious crime, for the purpose of rendering him professional assistance upon his trial, to hear the prisoner, after the most solemn and reiterated protestations that he was guiltless, suddenly, and, as it were, involuntarily, in the course of his communications, make such an admission as was altogether incompatible with innocence.

Page 246, line 632. *Of Brackenbury's dismal tower.*
This tower is situated near the northeastern extremity of the wall which encloses Barnard Castle, and is traditionally said to have been the prison.

Line 693. *Right heavy shall his ransom be.*
After the battle of Marston Moor, the Earl of Newcastle retired beyond sea in disgust, and many of his followers laid down their arms and made the best composition they could with the Committees of Parliament. Fines were imposed upon them in proportion to their estates and degrees of delinquency, and these fines were often bestowed upon such persons as had deserved well of the Commons. In some circumstances it happened that the oppressed cavaliers were fain to form family alliances with some powerful person among the triumphant party.

Page 247, line 27. *Now covering with the withered leaves.*
The patience, abstinence, and ingenuity exerted by the North American Indians, when in pursuit of plunder or vengeance, is the most distinguished feature in their character; and the activity and address which they display in their retreat is equally surprising.

Line 33. *In Redesdale his youth had heard.*
The inhabitants of the valleys of Tyne and Reed were, in ancient times, so inordinately addicted to these depredations, that in 1564 the Incorporated Merchant-adventurers of Newcastle made a law that none born in these districts should be admitted apprentice. The inhabitants are stated to be so generally addicted

to rapine that no faith should be reposed in those proceeding from 'such lewde and wicked progenitors.' This regulation continued to stand unrepealed until 1771. A beggar, in an old play, describes himself as 'born in Redesdale, in Northumberland, and come of a wight-riding surname called the Robsons, good honest men and true, *saving a little shifting for their living, God help them!*' — a description which would have applied to most Borderers on both sides.

Line 35. *When Rooken-edge and Redswair high.*

Reidswair, famed for a skirmish to which it gives name, is on the very edge of the Carter-fell, which divides England from Scotland. The *Rooken* is a place upon Reedwater.

Line 90. *Hiding his face, lest foemen spy.*

After one of the recent battles, in which the Irish rebels were defeated, one of their most active leaders was found in a bog, in which he was immersed up to the shoulders, while his head was concealed by an impending ledge of turf. Being detected and seized, notwithstanding his precaution, he became solicitous to know how his retreat had been discovered. ' I caught,' said the Sutherland Highlander by whom he was taken, 'the sparkle of your eye.'

Page 248, line 184. *And throatwort with its azure bell.*

The *Campanula Latifolia*, grand throatwort, or Canterbury bells, grows in profusion upon the beautiful banks of the River Greta, where it divides the manors of Brignall and Scargill, about three miles above Greta Bridge. [The reader instinctively recalls Mr. Morritt's account of Scott's notebook with memoranda jotted down for the local color of this poem.]

Page 249, line 274. *Of my marauding on the clowns.*

The troops of the king, when they first took the field, were as well disciplined as could be expected from circumstances. But as the circumstances of Charles became less favorable, and his funds for regularly paying his forces decreased, habits of military license prevailed among them in greater excess. Lacy the player, who served his master during the Civil War, brought out after the Restoration a piece called *The Old Troop*, in which he seems to have commemorated some real incidents which occurred in his military career. The names of the officers of the Troop sufficiently express their habits. We have Flea-flint Plunder-Master - General, Captain Ferret - farm, and Quarter-Master Burndrop. The officers of the Troop are in league with these worthies, and connive at their plundering the country for a suitable share in the booty. All this was undoubtedly drawn from the life, which Lacy had an opportunity to study.

Page 250, line 339. *And Brignall's woods and Scargill's wave.*

The banks of the Greta, below Rutherford Bridge, abound in seams of grayish slate, which are wrought in some places to a very great depth under ground, thus forming artificial caverns, which, when the seam has been ex-

hausted, are gradually hidden by the underwood which grows in profusion upon the romantic banks of the river. In times of public confusion, they might be well adapted to the purposes of banditti.

Page 252, line 504. *When Spain waged warfare with our land.*

There was a short war with Spain in 1625-26, which will be found to agree pretty well with the chronology of the poem. But probably Bertram held an opinion very common among the maritime heroes of the age, that ' there was no peace beyond the Line.' The Spanish *guarda-costas* were constantly employed in aggressions upon the trade and settlements of the English and French ; and, by their own severities, gave room for the system of buccaneering, at first adopted in self-defence and retaliation, and afterwards persevered in from habit and thirst of plunder.

Line 571. *And once amid our comrade's strife.*

The laws of the Buccaneers, and their successors the Pirates, however severe and equitable, were, like other laws, often set aside by the stronger party. Their quarrels about the division of the spoil fill their history, and they as frequently arose out of mere frolic, or the tyrannical humor of their chiefs.

Page 254, line 697. *And adieu for evermore.*

The last verse of this song is taken from the fragment of an old Scottish ballad which seems to express the fortunes of some follower of the Stuart family.

Line 735. *Who at Rere-cross on Stanmore meets Allen-a-Dale!*

This is a fragment of an old cross, with its pediment, surrounded by an intrenchment, upon the very summit of the waste ridge of Stanmore, near a small house of entertainment called the *Spittal*. The situation of the cross, and the pains taken to defend it, seem to indicate that it was intended for a landmark of importance.

Line 756. *Speak, Hamlin! hast thou lodged our deer ?*

The duty of the ranger, or pricker, was first to lodge, or harbor the deer ; i. e., to discover his retreat, and then to make his report to his prince, or master.

Page 255, line 1. *When Denmark's raven soared on high.*

About the year of God 866 the Danes, under their celebrated leaders Inguar (more properly Agnar) and Hubba, — sons, it is said, of the still more celebrated Regnar Lodbrog, — invaded Northumberland, bringing with them the magical standard, so often mentioned in poetry, called *Reafen*, or *Rumfan*, from its bearing the figure of a raven. The Danes renewed and extended their incursions, and began to colonize, establishing a kind of capital at York, from which they spread their conquests and incursions in every direction. Stanmore, which divides the mountains of Westmoreland and Cumberland, was probably the boundary of the Danish kingdom in that direction. The district to the west, known in ancient British history by the name of Reged, had never been conquered by the Saxons, and continued to maintain a precarious independence until it was ceded to Malcolm, King of Scots, by William the Conqueror.

Line 9. *Beneath the shade the Northmen came.*

The heathen Danes have left several traces of their religion in the upper part of Teesdale. Balder-garth, which derives its name from the unfortunate son of Odin, is a tract of waste land on the very ridge of Stanmore ; and a brook, which falls into the Tees near Barnard Castle, is named after the same deity. A field upon the banks of the Tees is also termed Woden-Croft, from the supreme deity of the Edda. Thorsgill, of which a description is attempted in stanza 2, is a beautiful little brook and dell, running up behind the ruins of Egliston Abbey.

Page 256, line 131. *Who has not heard how brave O'Neale.*

The O'Neale here meant, for more than one succeeded to the chieftainship during the reign of Elizabeth, was Hugh, the grandson of Con O'Neale, called Con Bacco, or the Lame. His father, Matthew O'Kelly, was illegitimate, and, being the son of a blacksmith's wife, was usually called Matthew the Blacksmith. His father, nevertheless, destined his succession to him ; and he was created, by Elizabeth, Baron of Dungannon. Upon the death of Con Bacco, this Matthew was slain by his brother. Hugh narrowly escaped the same fate, and was protected by the English. Shane O'Neale, his uncle, called Shane-Dymas, was succeeded by Turlough Lynogh O'Neale ; after whose death Hugh, having assumed the chieftainship, became nearly as formidable to the English as any by whom it had been possessed. Lord Mountjoy succeeded in finally subjugating O'Neale ; but it was not till the succession of James, to whom he made personal submission, and was received with civility at court.

Line 145. *The Tanist he to great O'Neale.*

'It is a custom amongst all the Irish, that presently after the death of one of their chiefe lords or captaines, they doe presently assemble themselves to a place generally appointed and knowne unto them, to choose another in his stead, where they do nominate and elect, for the most part not the eldest sonne, nor any of the children of the lord deceased, but the next to him in blood, that is, the eldest and worthiest, as commonly the next brother unto him, if he have any, or the next cousin, or so forth, as any is elder in that kindred or sept ; and then next to them doe they choose the next of the blood to be Tanist, who shall next succeed him in the said captainry, if he live thereunto ' (Spenser's *Ireland*). The Tanist, therefore, of O'Neale, was the heir-apparent of his power. This kind of succession appears also to have regulated, in very remote times, the succession to the crown of Scotland. It would have been imprudent, if not impossible, to have asserted a minor's right of succession in those stormy days.

Line 177. *His plaited hair in elf-locks spread.*

There is here an attempt to describe the ancient Irish dress, which was (the bonnet excepted)

very similar to that of the Scottish Highlanders. The want of a covering on the head was supplied by the mode of plaiting and arranging the hair, which was called the *glibbe*.

Page 257, line 244. *His foster father was his guide.*

There was no tie more sacred among the Irish than that which connected the foster-father, as well as the nurse herself, with the child they brought up.

Page 258, line 344. *Great Nial of the Pledges Nine.*

Neal Naighvallach, or Of the Nine Hostages, is said to have been monarch of all Ireland during the end of the fourth or beginning of the fifth century. He exercised a predatory warfare on the coast of England and of Bretagne, or Armorica ; and from the latter country brought off the celebrated Saint Patrick, a youth of sixteen, among other captives, whom he transported to Ireland. Neal derived his epithet from nine nations, or tribes, whom he held under his subjection, and from whom he took hostages.

Line 345. *Shane-Dymas wild, and Geraldine.*

This Shane-Dymas, or John the Wanton, held the title and power of O'Neale in the earlier part of Elizabeth's reign, against whom he rebelled repeatedly. When reduced to extremity by the English, and forsaken by his allies, this Shane-Dymas fled to Clandeboy, then occupied by a colony of Scottish Highlanders of the family of MacDonell. He was at first courteously received ; but by degrees they began to quarrel about the slaughter of some of their friends whom Shane-Dymas had put to death, and advancing from words to deeds, fell upon him with their broadswords, and cut him to pieces. After his death a law was made that none should presume to take the name and title of O'Neale. The O'Neales were closely allied with the powerful and warlike family of Geraldine ; for Henry Owen O'Neale married the daughter of Thomas, Earl of Kildare, and their son Con More married his cousin-german, a daughter of Gerald, Earl of Kildare. This Con More cursed any of his posterity who should learn the English language, sow corn, or build houses, so as to invite the English to settle in their country. Others ascribe this anathema to his son Con Bacco.

Line 379. *And named his page, the next degree.*

Originally, the order of chivalry embraced three ranks: 1. The Page ; 2. The Squire ; 3. The Knight, — a gradation which seems to have been imitated in the mystery of freemasonry. But, before the reign of Charles I., the custom of serving as a squire had fallen into disuse, though the order of the page was still, to a certain degree, in observance. This state of servitude was so far from inferring anything degrading, that it was considered as the regular school for acquiring every quality necessary for future distinction.

Page 263, line 52. *Seemed half-abandoned to decay.*

The ancient castle of Rokeby stood exactly

upon the site of the present mansion, by which a part of its walls is enclosed. It is surrounded by a profusion of fine wood, and the park in which it stands is adorned by the junction of the Greta and of the Tees.

Page 265, line 225. *Naught knowest thou of the Felon Sow.*

The ancient minstrels had a comic as well as a serious strain of romance. The comic romance was a sort of parody upon the usual subjects of minstrel poetry. One of the very best of these mock romances, and which has no small portion of comic humor, is the Hunting of the Felon Sow of Rokeby by the Friars of Richmond.

Line 247. *The Filea of O'Neale was he.*

The Filea, or Ollamh Re Dan, was the proper bard, or, as the name literally implies, poet. Each chieftain of distinction had one or more in his service, whose office was usually hereditary.

Line 258. *Ah, Clandeboy! thy friendly floor.*

Clandeboy is a district of Ulster, formerly possessed by the sept of the O'Neales, and Slieve-Donard a romantic mountain in the same province. The clan was ruined after Tyrone's great rebellion, and their places of abode laid desolate. The ancient Irish, wild and uncultivated in other respects, did not yield even to their descendants in practising the most free and extended hospitality.

Page 266, line 326. *On Marwood-chase and Toller Hill.*

Marwood-chase is the old park extending along the Durham side of the Tees, attached to Barnard Castle. Toller Hill is an eminence on the Yorkshire side of the river, commanding a superb view of the ruins.

Page 267, line 414. *The ancient English minstrel's dress.*

Among the entertainments presented to Elizabeth at Kenilworth Castle was the introduction of a person designed to represent a travelling minstrel, who entertained her with a solemn story out of the Acts of King Arthur.

Page 282, line 884. *A horseman armed at headlong speed,* etc.

This, and what follows, is taken from a real achievement of Major Robert Philipson, called from his desperate and adventurous courage, Robin the Devil.

THE BRIDAL OF TRIERMAIN.

Page 288, line 2. *That may match with the Baron of Triermain?*

Triermain was a fief of the Barony of Gilsland, in Cumberland ; it was possessed by a Saxon family at the time of the Conquest, but, ' after the death of Gilmore, Lord of Tryermaine and Torcrossock, Hubert Vaux gave Tryermaine and Torcrossock to his second son, Ranulph Vaux ; which Ranulph afterwards became heir to his elder brother Robert, the founder of Lanercost, who died without issue. Ranulph, being Lord of all Gilsland, gave Gilmore's lands to his younger son, named Roland, and let the Barony descend to his eldest son Robert, son of Ranulph. Roland had issue

Alexander, and he, Randolph, after whom succeeded Robert, and they were named Rolands successively, that were lords thereof, until the reign of Edward the Fourth.' Burn's *Antiquities of Westmoreland and Cumberland,* vol. ii. p. 482.

Page 289, line 91. *And his who sleeps at Dunmailraise.*

This is one of the grand passes from Cumberland into Westmoreland. It takes its name from a cairn, or pile of stones, erected, it is said, to the memory of Dunmail, the last King of Cumberland.

Page 290, line 114. *He passed Red Penrich's Table Round.*

A circular intrenchment, about half a mile from Penrith, is thus popularly termed. The circle within the ditch is about one hundred and sixty paces in circumference, with openings, or approaches, directly opposite to each other. As the ditch is on the inner side, it could not be intended for the purpose of defence, and it has reasonably been conjectured, that the enclosure was designed for the solemn exercise of feats of chivalry, and the embankment around for the convenience of the spectators.

Line 116. *Left Mayburgh's mound and stones of power.*

Higher up the river Eamont than Arthur's Round Table, is a prodigious enclosure of great antiquity, formed by a collection of stones upon the top of a gently sloping hill, called Mayburgh. In the plain which it encloses there stands erect an unhewn stone of twelve feet in height. Two similar masses are said to have been destroyed during the memory of man. The whole appears to be a monument of Druidical times.

Line 162. *The surface of that sable tarn.*

The small lake called Scales-tarn lies so deeply embosomed in the recesses of the huge mountain called Saddleback, more poetically Glaramara, is of such great depth, and so completely hidden from the sun, that it is said its beams never reach it, and that the reflection of the stars may be seen at mid-day.

Page 291, line 282. *On Caliburn's resistless brand.*

This was the name of King Arthur's well-known sword, sometimes also called Excalibur.

Page 292, line 321. *The terrors of Tintagel's spear.*

Tintagel Castle, in Cornwall, is reported to have been the birthplace of King Arthur.

Page 295, line 175. *Scattering a shower of fiery dew.*

The author has an indistinct recollection of an adventure, somewhat similar to that which is here ascribed to King Arthur, having befallen one of the ancient Kings of Denmark. The horn in which the burning liquor was presented to that monarch is said still to be preserved in the Royal Museum at Copenhagen.

Line 184. *The monarch, breathless and amazed,* etc.

' We now gained a view of the Vale of St. John's, a very narrow dell, hemmed in by mountains, through which a small brook makes many meanderings, washing little enclosures of grass-ground, which stretch up the rising of the hills. In the widest part of the dale you are struck with the appearance of an ancient ruined castle, which seems to stand upon the summit of a little mount, the mountains around forming an amphitheatre. This massive bulwark shows a front of various towers, and makes an awful, rude, and Gothic appearance, with its lofty turrets and ragged battlements; we traced the galleries, the bending arches, the buttresses. The greatest antiquity stands characterized in its architecture; the inhabitants near it assert it is an antediluvian structure.

'The traveller's curiosity is roused, and he prepares to make a nearer approach, when that curiosity is put upon the rack by his being assured that if he advances, certain genii who govern the place, by virtue of their supernatural art and necromancy, will strip it of all its beauties, and by enchantment transform the magic walls. The vale seems adapted for the habitation of such beings; its gloomy recesses and retirements look like haunts of evil spirits. There was no delusion in the report; we were soon convinced of its truth; for this piece of antiquity, so venerable and noble in its aspect, as we drew near, changed its figure, and proved no other than a shaken massive pile of rocks, which stand in the midst of this little vale, disunited from the adjoining mountains, and have so much the real form and resemblance of a castle, that they bear the name of the Castle Rocks of St. John.' — Hutchinson's *Excursion to the Lakes*, p. 121.

Line 198. *Twelve bloody fields with glory fought.*

Arthur is said to have defeated the Saxons in twelve pitched battles, and to have achieved the other feats alluded to in the text.

Page 296, line 359. *Sir Carodac to fight that prize.*

See the comic tale of *The Boy and the Mantle*, in the third volume of Percy's *Reliques of Ancient Poetry*, from the Breton or Norman original of which Ariosto is supposed to have taken his *Tale of the Enchanted Cup.*

Page 300, line 690. *Whose logic is from ' Single-Speech.'*

See *Parliamentary Logic*, etc., by the Right Honorable William Gerard Hamilton (1808), commonly called 'Single-Speech Hamilton.'

THE LORD OF THE ISLES.

Page 314, line 47. *Thy rugged halls, Artornish, rung.*

The ruins of the castle of Artornish are situated upon a promontory on the Morven, or mainland side of the Sound of Mull, a name given to the deep arm of the sea which divides that island from the continent. The situation is wild and romantic in the highest degree, having on the one hand a high and precipitous chain of rocks overhanging the sea, and on the other the narrow entrance to the beautiful salt-water lake, called Loch Alline, which is in many places

finely fringed with copsewood. The ruins of Artornish are not now very considerable, and consist chiefly of the remains of an old keep, or tower, with fragments of outward defences. But in former days it was a place of great consequence, being one of the principal strongholds which the Lords of the Isles, during the period of their stormy independence, possessed upon the mainland of Argyleshire.

Line 76. *Rude Heiskar's seal through surges dark.*

The seal displays a taste for music, which could scarcely be expected from his habits and local predilections. They will long follow a boat in which any musical instrument is played, and even a tune simply whistled has attractions for them. The Dean of the Isles says of Heiskar, a small uninhabited rock, about twelve (Scottish) miles from the isle of Uist, that an infinite slaughter of seals takes place there.

Page 315, line 177. *O'erlooked, dark Mull, thy mighty Sound.*

The Sound of Mull, which divides that island from the continent of Scotland, is one of the most striking scenes which the Hebrides afford to the traveller. Sailing from Oban to Aros, or Tobermory, through a narrow channel, yet deep enough to bear vessels of the largest burden, he has on his left the bold and mountainous shores of Mull; on the right those of that district of Argyleshire called Morven or Morvern, successively indented by deep salt-water lochs, running up many miles inland. To the southeastward arise a prodigious range of mountains, among which Cruachan-Ben is preëminent. And to the northeast is the no less huge and picturesque range of the Ardnamurchan hills. Many ruinous castles, situated generally upon cliffs overhanging the ocean, add interest to the scene. Still passing on to the northward, Artornish and Aros become visible upon the opposite shores; and, lastly, Mingarry, and other ruins of less distinguished note. In fine weather, a grander and more impressive scene, both from its natural beauties and associations with ancient history and tradition, can hardly be imagined. When the weather is rough, the passage is both difficult and dangerous, from the narrowness of the channel, and in part from the number of inland lakes, out of which sally forth a number of conflicting and thwarting tides, making the navigation perilous to open boats. The sudden flaws and gusts of wind which issue without a moment's warning from the mountain glens, are equally formidable. So that in unsettled weather, a stranger, if not much accustomed to the sea, may sometimes add to the other sublime sensations excited by the scene, that feeling of dignity which arises from a sense of danger.

Line 181. *Round twice a hundred islands rolled.*

The number of the western isles of Scotland exceeds two hundred, of which St. Kilda is the most northerly, anciently called Hirth, or Hirt, probably from ' earth,' being in fact the whole globe to its inhabitants. Ilay, which now belongs almost entirely to Walter Campbell, Esq., of Shawfield, is by far the most fertile of the Hebrides, and has been greatly improved under the spirited and sagacious management of the present proprietor. This was in ancient times the principal abode of the Lords of the Isles, being, if not the largest, the most important island of their archipelago.

Line 188. *From where Mingarry sternly placed.*

The castle of Mingarry is situated on the sea-coast of the district of Ardnamurchan. The ruins, which are tolerably entire, are surrounded by a very high wall, forming a kind of polygon, for the purpose of adapting itself to the projecting angles of a precipice overhanging the sea, on which the castle stands. It was anciently the residence of the MacIans, a clan of MacDonalds, descended from Ian, or John, a grandson of Angus Og, Lord of the Isles.

Page 316, line 197. *The heir of mighty Somerled?*

Somerled was thane of Argyle and Lord of the Isles, about the middle of the twelfth century. He seems to have exercised his authority in both capacities, independent of the crown of Scotland, against which he often stood in hostility. He made various incursions upon the western lowlands during the reign of Malcolm IV., and seems to have made peace with him upon the terms of an independent prince, about the year 1157. In 1164 he resumed the war against Malcolm, and invaded Scotland with a large but probably a tumultuary army, collected in the isles, in the mainland of Argyleshire, and in the neighboring provinces of Ireland. He was defeated and slain in an engagement with a very inferior force, near Renfrew.

Line 200. *Lord of the Isles, whose lofty name.*

The representative of this independent principality — for such it seems to have been, though acknowledging occasionally the preëminence of the Scottish crown — was, at the period of the poem, Angus, called Angus Og; but the name has been, *euphoniæ gratia*, exchanged for that of Ronald, which frequently occurs in the genealogy. Angus was a protector of Robert Bruce, whom he received in his castle of Dunnaverty, during the time of his greatest distress.

Line 267. *A daughter of the House of Lorn.*

The House of Lorn was, like the Lord of the Isles, descended from a son of Somerled, slain at Renfrew, in 1164. This son obtained the succession of his mainland territories, comprehending the greater part of the three districts of Lorn, in Argyleshire, and of course might rather be considered as petty princes than feudal barons. They assumed the patronymic appellation of MacDougal, by which they are distinguished in the history of the middle ages. The Lord of Lorn, who flourished during the wars of Bruce, was Allaster (or Alexander) MacDougal called Allaster of Argyle. He had married the third daughter of John, called the Red Comyn, who was slain by Bruce in the Dominican church at Dumfries, and hence he

was a mortal enemy of that prince, and more than once reduced him to great straits during the early and distressed period of his reign, as we shall have repeated occasion to notice. Bruce, when he began to obtain an ascendency in Scotland, took the first opportunity in his power to requite these injuries. He marched into Argyleshire to lay waste the country. John of Lorn, son of the chieftain, was posted with his followers in the formidable pass between Dalmally and Bunawe. It is a narrow path along the verge of the huge and precipitous mountain, called Cruachan-Ben, and guarded on the other side by a precipice overhanging Loch Awe. The pass seems to the eye of a soldier as strong, as it is wild and romantic to that of an ordinary traveller. But the skill of Bruce had anticipated this difficulty. While his main body, engaged in a skirmish with the men of Lorn, detained their attention to the front of their position, James of Douglas, with Sir Alexander Fraser, Sir William Wiseman, and Sir Andrew Grey, ascended the mountain with a select body of archery, and obtained possession of the heights which commanded the pass. A volley of arrows descending upon them directly warned the Argyleshire men of their perilous situation, and their resistance, which had hitherto been bold and manly, was changed into a precipitate flight. The deep and rapid river of Awe was then (we learn the fact from Barbour with some surprise) crossed by a bridge. This bridge the mountaineers attempted to demolish, but Bruce's followers were too close upon their rear; they were, therefore, without refuge and defence, and were dispersed with great slaughter. John of Lorn, suspicious of the event, had early betaken himself to the galleys which he had upon the lake; but the feelings which Barbour assigns to him, while witnessing the rout and slaughter of his followers, exculpate him from the charge of cowardice.

Page 318, line 451. *The mimic fires of ocean glow.*

The phenomenon called by sailors Sea-fire is one of the most beautiful and interesting which is witnessed in the Hebrides. At times the ocean appears entirely illuminated around the vessel, and a long train of lambent coruscations are perpetually bursting upon the sides of the vessel, or pursuing her wake through the darkness.

Page 319, line 499. *Sought the dark fortress by a stair.*

The fortress of a Hebridean chief was almost always on the sea-shore, for the facility of communication which the ocean afforded. Nothing can be more wild than the situations which they chose, and the devices by which the architects endeavored to defend them. Narrow stairs and arched vaults were the usual mode of access; and the drawbridge appears at Dunstaffnage, and elsewhere, to have fallen from the gate of the building to the top of such a staircase; so that any one advancing with hostile purpose, found himself in a state of exposed and precarious elevation, with a gulf between him and the object of his attack.

Page 321, line 37. *And that keen knight, De Argentine.*

Sir Egidius, or Giles de Argentine, was one of the most accomplished knights of the period. He had served in the wars of Henry of Luxemburg with such high reputation that he was, in popular estimation, the third worthy of the age. Those to whom fame assigned precedence over him were, Henry of Luxemburg himself, and Robert Bruce. Argentine had warred in Palestine, encountered thrice with the Saracens, and had slain two antagonists in each engagement: an easy matter, he said, for one Christian knight to slay two Pagan dogs. His death corresponded with his high character. With Aymer de Valence, Earl of Pembroke, he was appointed to attend immediately upon the person of Edward II. at Bannockburn. When the day was utterly lost they forced the king from the field. De Argentine saw the king safe from immediate danger, and then took his leave of him ; ' God be with you, sir,' he said, ' it is not my wont to fly.' So saying, he turned his horse, cried his war-cry, plunged into the midst of the combatants, and was slain.

Line 54. *' Fill me the mighty cup,' he said.*

A Hebridean drinking-cup, of the most ancient and curious workmanship, has been long preserved in the castle of Dunvegan, in Skye, the romantic seat of MacLeod of MacLeod, the chief of that ancient and powerful clan. This very curious piece of antiquity is nine inches and three quarters in inside depth, and ten and a half in height on the outside, the extreme measure over the lips being four inches and a half. The cup is divided into two parts by a wrought ledge, beautifully ornamented, about three fourths of an inch in breadth. Beneath this ledge the shape of the cup is rounded off, and terminates in a flat circle, like that of a teacup ; four short feet support the whole. Above the projecting ledge the shape of the cup is nearly square, projecting outward at the brim. The cup is made of wood, (oak to all appearance,) but most curiously wrought and embossed with silver work, which projects from the vessel. There are a number of regular projecting sockets, which appear to have been set with stones ; two or three of them still hold pieces of coral, the rest are empty. At the four corners of the projecting ledge, or cornice, are four sockets, much larger, probably for pebbles or precious stones. The workmanship of the silver is extremely elegant, and appears to have been highly gilded. The ledge brim and legs of the cup are of silver.

Page 322, line 150. *With Carrick's outlawed Chief.*

It must be remembered by all who have read Scottish history, that after he had slain Comyn at Dumfries, and asserted his right to the Scottish crown, Robert Bruce was reduced to the greatest extremity by the English and their adherents. He was crowned at Scone by the general consent of the Scottish barons, but

his authority endured but a short time. According to the phrase said to have been used by his wife, he was for that year ' a summer king, but not a winter one.'

Line 180. *Whence the brooch of burning gold.*

Robert Bruce, after his defeat at Methven, being hard pressed by the English, endeavored, with the dispirited remnant of his followers, to escape from Breadalbane and the mountains of Perthshire into the Argyleshire Highlands. But he was encountered and repulsed, after a very severe engagement, by the Lord of Lorn. Bruce's personal strength and courage were never displayed to greater advantage than in this conflict. There is a tradition in the family of the MacDougals of Lorn, that their chieftain engaged in personal battle with Bruce himself, while the latter was employed in protecting the retreat of his men ; that MacDougal was struck down by the king, whose strength of body was equal to his vigor of mind, and would have been slain on the spot, had not two of Lorn's vassals, a father and son, whom tradition terms MacKeoch, rescued him, by seizing the mantle of the monarch, and dragging him from above his adversary. Bruce rid himself of these foes by two blows of his redoubted battle-axe, but was so closely pressed by the other followers of Lorn, that he was forced to abandon the mantle, and brooch which fastened it, clasped in the dying grasp of the MacKeochs. A studded brooch, said to have been that which King Robert lost upon this occasion, was long preserved in the family of MacDougal, and was lost in a fire which consumed their temporary residence.

Page 323, line 212. *Vain was then the Douglas brand.*

The gallant Sir James, called the Good Lord Douglas, the most faithful and valiant of Bruce's adherents, was wounded at the battle of Dalry. Sir Nigel, or Neil Campbell, was also in that unfortunate skirmish. He married Marjorie, sister to Robert Bruce, and was among his most faithful followers.

Line 214. *Vain Kirkpatrick's bloody dirk.*

The proximate cause of Bruce's asserting his right to the crown of Scotland was the death of John, called the Red Comyn. (See canto i. st. 27.) The causes of this act of violence, equally extraordinary from the high rank both of the perpetrator and sufferer, and from the place where the slaughter was committed, are variously related by the Scottish and English historians, and cannot now be ascertained. The fact that they met at the high altar of the Minorites, or Greyfriars Church in Dumfries, that their difference broke out into high and insulting language, and that Bruce drew his dagger and stabbed Comyn, is certain. Rushing to the door of the church, Bruce met two powerful barons, Kirkpatrick of Closeburn, and James de Lindsay, who eagerly asked him what tidings ? ' Bad tidings,' answered Bruce ; ' I doubt I have slain Comyn.' — ' Doubtest thou ? ' said Kirkpatrick ; ' I make sicker ' (*i. e.* sure). With these words, he and Lindsay rushed into the church, and despatched the wounded Comyn. The Kirkpatricks of Closeburn assumed, in memory of this deed, a hand holding a dagger, with the memorable words, ' I make sicker ' (i. e. ' secure ').

Line 216. *Barendown fled fast away.*

These knights are enumerated by Barbour among the small number of Bruce's adherents, who remained in arms with him after the battle of Methven.

Line 239. *To praise the hand that pays thy pains!*

The character of the Highland bards, however high in an earlier period of society, seems soon to have degenerated. The Irish affirm that in their kindred tribes severe laws became necessary to restrain their avarice. In the Highlands they seem gradually to have sunk into contempt, as well as the orators, or men of speech, with whose office that of family poet was often united. — ' The orators, in their language called Isdane, were in high esteem both in these islands and the continent ; until within these forty years, they sat always among the nobles and chiefs of families in the streah, or circle. Their houses and little villages were sanctuaries, as well as churches, and they took place before doctors of physick. The orators, after the Druids were extinct, were brought in to preserve the genealogy of families, and to repeat the same at every succession of chiefs ; and upon the occasion of marriages and births, they made epithalamiums and panegyricks, which the poet or bard pronounced. The orators, by the force of their eloquence, had a powerful ascendant over the greatest men in their time ; for if any orator did but ask the habit, arms, horse, or any other thing belonging to the greatest man in these islands, it was readily granted them, sometimes out of respect, and sometimes for fear of being exclaimed against by a satyre, which, in those days, was reckoned a great dishonor. But these gentlemen becoming insolent, lost ever since both the profit and esteem which was formerly due to their character ; for neither their panegyricks nor satyres are regarded to what they have been, and they are now allowed but a small salary. I must not omit to relate their way of study, which is very singular : They shut their doors and windows for a day's time, and lie on their backs, with a stone upon their belly, and plads about their heads, and their eyes being covered, they pump their brains for rhetorical encomium or panegyrick ; and indeed they furnish such a style from this dark cell as is understood by very few ; and if they purchase a couple of horses as the reward of their meditation, they think they have done a great matter. The poet, or bard, had a title to the bridegroom's upper garb, that is, the plad and bonnet ; but now he is satisfyed with what the bridegroom pleases to give him on such occasions.' — Martin's *Western Isles.*

Page 325, line 459. *Was 't not enough to Ronald's bower.*

It was anciently customary in the Highlands to bring the bride to the house of the husband. Nay, in some cases the complaisance was stretched so far that she remained there upon trial for a twelvemonth ; and the bridegroom, even after this period, retained an option of refusing to fulfil his engagement.

Line 477. *Since matchless Wallace first had been.*

There is something singularly doubtful about the mode in which Wallace was taken. That he was betrayed to the English is indubitable ; and popular fame charges Sir John Menteith with the indelible infamy. ' Accursed,' says Arnold Blair, ' be the day of nativity of John de Menteith, and may his name be struck out of the book of life.' But John de Menteith was all along a zealous favorer of the English interest, and was governor of Dumbarton Castle by commission from Edward the First ; and therefore, as the accurate Lord Hailes has observed, could not be the friend and confidant of Wallace, as tradition states him to be. The truth seems to be that Menteith, thoroughly engaged in the English interest, pursued Wallace closely, and made him prisoner through the treachery of an attendant, whom Peter Langtoft calls Jack Short.

Line 481. *Where 's Nigel Bruce ? and De la Haye ?*

When these lines were written, the author was remote from the means of correcting his indistinct recollection concerning the individual fate of Bruce's followers, after the battle of Methven. Hugh de la Haye, and Thomas Somerville of Lintoun and Cowdally, ancestor of Lord Somerville, were both made prisoners at that defeat, but neither was executed.

Sir Nigel Bruce was the younger brother of Robert, to whom he committed the charge of his wife and daughter, Marjorie, and the defence of his strong castle of Kildrummie, near the head of the Don, in Aberdeenshire. Kildrummie long resisted the arms of the Earls of Lancaster and Hereford, until the magazine was treacherously burnt. The garrison was then compelled to surrender at discretion, and Nigel Bruce, a youth remarkable for personal beauty, as well as for gallantry, fell into the hands of the unrelenting Edward. He was tried by a special commission at Berwick, was condemned, and executed.

Christopher Seatoun shared the same unfortunate fate. He also was distinguished by personal valor, and signalized himself in the fatal battle of Methven. Robert Bruce adventured his person in that battle like a knight of romance. He dismounted Aymer de Valence, Earl of Pembroke, but was in his turn dismounted by Sir Philip Mowbray. In this emergence Seatoun came to his aid, and remounted him. Langtoft mentions, that in this battle the Scottish wore white surplices, or shirts, over their armor, that those of rank might not be known. In this manner both Bruce and Seatoun escaped. But the latter was afterwards betrayed to the English, through means, according to Barbour, of one MacNabi

' a disciple of Judas,' in whom the unfortunate knight reposed entire confidence. There was some peculiarity respecting his punishment; because, according to Matthew of Westminster, he was considered not as a Scottish subject, but an Englishman. He was therefore taken to Dumfries, where he was tried, condemned, and executed, for the murder of a soldier slain by him. His brother, John de Seton, had the same fate at Newcastle; both were considered as accomplices in the slaughter of Comyn; but in what manner they were particularly accessary to that deed does not appear.

The fate of Sir Simon Fraser, or Frizel, ancestor of the family of Lovat, is dwelt upon at great length, and with savage exultation, by the English historians. This knight, who was renowned for personal gallantry, and high deeds of chivalry, was also made prisoner, after a gallant defence, in the battle of Methven.

Line 491. *Was not the life of Athole shed.*

John de Strathbogie, Earl of Athole, had attempted to escape out of the kingdom, but a storm cast him upon the coast, when he was taken, sent to London, and executed, with circumstances of great barbarity, being first half strangled, then let down from the gallows while yet alive, barbarously dismembered, and his body burnt. It may surprise the reader to learn that this was a *mitigated* punishment; for in respect that his mother was a granddaughter of King John, by his natural son Richard, he was not drawn on a sledge to execution, ' that point was forgiven,' and he made the passage on horseback. Matthew of Westminster tells us that King Edward, then extremely ill, received great ease from the news that his relative was apprehended. ' *Quo audito, Rex Angliæ, etsi gravissimo morbo tunc langueret, levius tamen tulit dolorem.*' To this singular expression the text alludes.

Line 494. *Be nought but quarter, hang, and slay!*

This alludes to a passage in Barbour, singularly expressive of the vindictive spirit of Edward I. The prisoners taken at the castle of Kildrummie had surrendered upon condition that they should be at King Edward's disposal. ' But his will,' says Barbour, ' was always evil toward Scottishmen.' The news of the surrender of Kildrummie arrived when he was in his mortal sickness at Burgh-upon-Sands.

Page 326, line 500. *By Woden wild — my grandsire's oath.*

The MacLeods, and most other distinguished Hebridean families, were of Scandinavian extraction, and some were late or imperfect converts to Christianity. The family names of Torquil, Thormod, etc. are all Norwegian.

Line 566. *While I the blessed cross advance.*

Bruce uniformly professed, and probably felt, compunction for having violated the sanctuary of the church by the slaughter of Comyn; and finally, in his last hours, in testimony of his faith, penitence, and zeal, he requested James Lord Douglas to carry his heart to Jerusalem, to be there deposited in the Holy Sepulchre.

Line 589. *De Bruce! I rose with purpose dread.*

So soon as the notice of Comyn's slaughter reached Rome, Bruce and his adherents were excommunicated. It was published first by the Archbishop of York, and renewed at different times, particularly by Lambyrton, Bishop of St. Andrews, in 1308; but it does not appear to have answered the purpose which the English monarch expected. Indeed, for reasons which it may be difficult to trace, the thunders of Rome descended upon the Scottish mountains with less effect than in more fertile countries. Many of the Scottish prelates, Lambyrton the primate particularly, declared for Bruce, while he was yet under the ban of the church, although he afterwards again changed sides.

Line 596. *A power that will not be repressed.*

Bruce, like other heroes, observed omens, and one is recorded by tradition. After he had retreated to one of the miserable places of shelter, in which he could venture to take some repose after his disasters, he lay stretched upon a handful of straw, and abandoned himself to his melancholy meditations. He had now been defeated four times, and was upon the point of resolving to abandon all hopes of further opposition to his fate, and to go to the Holy Land. It chanced his eye, while he was thus pondering, was attracted by the exertions of a spider, who, in order to fix his web, endeavored to swing himself from one beam to another above his head. Involuntarily he became interested in the pertinacity with which the insect renewed his exertions, after failing six times; and it occurred to him that he would decide his own course according to the success or failure of the spider. At the seventh effort the insect gained his object; and Bruce, in like manner, persevered and carried his own. Hence it has been held unlucky or ungrateful, or both, in one of the name of Bruce to kill a spider.

Page 329, line 160. ' *Alas! dear youth, the unhappy time.*'

I have followed the vulgar and inaccurate tradition, that Bruce fought against Wallace and the array of Scotland, at the fatal battle of Falkirk. The story, which seems to have no better authority than that of Blind Harry, bears, that having made much slaughter during the engagement, he sat down to dine with the conquerors without washing the filthy witness from his hands.

Page 330, line 245. *These are the savage wilds that lie.*

The extraordinary piece of scenery which I have here attempted to describe is, I think, unparalleled in any part of Scotland, at least in any which I have happened to visit. It lies just upon the frontier of the Laird of MacLeod's country, which is thereabouts divided from the estate of Mr. Maccalister of Strath-Aird, called Strathnardill by the Dean of the Isles. [Scott gives a full account of his visit in his Journal under date of 25 August, 1814. See Lockhart, chap. xxxi.]

Page 331, line 400. *Men were they all of evil mien.*

The story of Bruce's meeting the banditti is copied, with such alterations as the fictitious narrative rendered necessary, from a striking incident in the monarch's history, told by Barbour.

Page 333, line 628. *And mermaid's alabaster grot.*

Imagination can hardly conceive anything more beautiful than the extraordinary grotto discovered not many years since upon the estate of Alexander MacAllister, Esq., of Strathaird. It has since been much and deservedly celebrated, and a full account of its beauties has been published by Dr. MacLeay of Oban. [Scott, again, in the same passage of his Journal just referred to, gives a description of this cave.]

Page 335, line 62. *Yet to no sense of selfish wrongs.*

The generosity which does justice to the character of an enemy often marks Bruce's sentiments, as recorded by the faithful Barbour. He seldom mentions a fallen enemy without praising such good qualities as he might possess.

Page 336, line 78. *Such hate was his on Solway's strand.*

To establish his dominion in Scotland had been a favorite object of Edward's ambition, and nothing could exceed the pertinacity with which he pursued it, unless his inveterate resentment against the insurgents, who so frequently broke the English yoke when he deemed it most firmly riveted. After the battles of Falkirk and Methven, and the dreadful examples which he had made of Wallace and other champions of national independence, he probably concluded every chance of insurrection was completely annihilated. This was in 1306, when Bruce, as we have seen, was utterly expelled from Scotland: yet, in the conclusion of the same year, Bruce was again in arms and formidable; and in 1307, Edward, though exhausted by a long and wasting malady, put himself at the head of the army destined to destroy him utterly. But even his spirit of vengeance was unable to restore his exhausted strength. He reached Burgh-upon-Sands, a petty village of Cumberland, on the shores of the Solway Firth, and there, 6th July, 1307, expired in sight of the detested and devoted country of Scotland. His dying injunctions to his son required him to continue the Scottish war, and never to recall Gaveston.

Page 337, line 175. *From Canna's tower, that, steep and gray.*

The little island of Canna, or Cannay, adjoins to those of Rum and Muick, with which it forms one parish. In a pretty bay opening towards the east, there is a lofty and slender rock detached from the shore. Upon the summit are the ruins of a very small tower, scarcely accessible by a steep and precipitous path. Here, it is said, one of the kings, or Lords of the Isles, confined a beautiful lady, of whom he was jealous. The ruins are of course haunted by her restless spirit, and many romantic stories are told by the aged people of the island concerning her fate in life, and her appearances after death.

Line 219. *And Ronin's mountains dark have sent.*

Ronin (popularly called Rum) is a very rough and mountainous island, adjacent to those of Eigg and Cannay. There is almost no arable ground upon it.

Line 225. *On Scooreigg next a warning light.*

These, and the following lines of the stanza, refer to a dreadful tale of feudal vengeance. Scoor-Eigg is a high peak in the centre of the small Isle of Eigg, or Egg. The MacDonalds of the Isle of Egg, a people dependent on Clan Ranald, had done some injury to the Laird of MacLeod. The tradition of the isle says that it was by a personal attack on the chieftain, in which his back was broken. But that of the other isles bears, more probably, that the injury was offered to two or three of the MacLeods, who, landing upon Eigg, and using some freedom with the young women, were seized by the islanders, bound hand and foot, and turned adrift in a boat, which the winds and waves safely conducted to Skye. To avenge the offence given, MacLeod sailed with such a body of men as rendered resistance hopeless. The natives, fearing his vengeance, concealed themselves in this cavern, and, after a strict search, the MacLeods went on board their galleys, after doing what mischief they could, concluding the inhabitants had left the isle, and betaken themselves to the Long Island, or some of Clan Ranald's other possessions. But next morning they espied from the vessels a man upon the island, and immediately landing again, they traced his retreat by the marks of his footsteps, a light snow being unhappily on the ground. MacLeod then surrounded the cavern, summoned the subterranean garrison, and demanded that the individuals who had offended him should be delivered up to him. This was peremptorily refused. The chieftain then caused his people to divert the course of a rill of water, which, falling over the entrance of the cave, would have prevented his purposed vengeance. He then kindled, at the entrance of the cavern, a huge fire, composed of turf and fern, and maintained it with unrelenting assiduity, until all within were destroyed by suffocation.

Page 338, line 293. *Scenes sung by him who sings no more.*

The ballad, entitled *Macphail of Colonsay, and the Mermaid of Corrievrekin,* was composed by John Leyden, from a tradition which he found while making a tour through the Hebrides about 1801, soon before his fatal departure for India, where he died a martyr to his zeal for knowledge, in the island of Java, immediately after the landing of our forces near Batavia, in August, 1811.

Line 305. *Up Tarbat's western lake they bore.*

The peninsula of Cantire is joined to South Knapdale by a very narrow isthmus, formed by the western and eastern Loch of Tarbat. These two salt-water lakes, or bays, encroach so far upon the land, and the extremities come so near to each other, that there is not above a mile of land to divide them.

Line 326. *Ben-Ghoil*, ' *the Mountain of the Wind*.'

Loch Ranza is a beautiful bay, on the northern extremity of Arran, opening towards East, Tarbat Loch. Ben-Ghaoil, ' the mountain of the winds, is generally known by its English, and less poetical, name of Goatfield.

Page 339, line 469. *That blast was winded by the king!*

The passage in Barbour describing the landing of Bruce, and his being recognized by Douglas and those of his followers who had preceded him, by the sound of his horn, is in the original singularly simple and affecting. — The king arrived in Arran with thirty-three small row-boats. He interrogated a female if there had arrived any warlike men of late in that country. ' Surely, sir,' she replied, ' I can tell you of many who lately came hither, discomfited the English governor, and blockaded his castle of Brodick. They maintain themselves in a wood at no great distance.' The king, truly conceiving that this must be Douglas and his followers, who had lately set forth to try their fortune in Arran, desired the woman to conduct him to the wood. She obeyed.

> ' The king then blew his horn on high ;
> And gert his men that were him by,
> Hold them still, and all privy ;
> And syne again his horne blew he.
> James of Dowglas heard him blow,
> And at the last alone gan know,
> And said, " Soothly yon is the king ;
> I know long while since his blowing."
> The third time therewithall he blew,
> And then Sir Robert Boid it knew ;
> And said, " Yon is the king, but dread,
> Go we forth till him, better speed."
> Then went they till the king in hye,
> And him inclined courteously.
> And blithly welcomed them the king,
> And was joyful of their meeting,
> And kissed them ; and speared syne
> How they had fared in hunting ?
> And they him told all, but lesing ;
> Syne laud they God of their meeting.
> Syne with the king till his harbourye
> Went both joyfu' and jolly.'
>
> BARBOUR'S *Bruce*, Book v. pp. 115, 116.

Page 340, line 525. *Blame ye the Bruce ? His brother blamed.*

The kind and yet fiery character of Edward Bruce is well painted by Barbour, in the account of his behavior after the battle of Bannockburn. Sir Walter Ross, one of the very few Scottish nobles who fell in that battle, was so dearly beloved by Edward, that he wished the victory had been lost, so Ross had lived.

Page 342, line 682. *Thou heard'st a wretched female plain.*

This incident, which illustrates so happily the chivalrous generosity of Bruce's character,

is one of the many simple and natural traits recorded by Barbour. It occurred during the expedition which Bruce made to Ireland, to support the pretensions of his brother Edward to the throne of that kingdom. Bruce was about to retreat, and his host was arrayed for moving.

Page 344, line 129. *O'er chasms he passed where fractures wide.*

The interior of the Island of Arran abounds with beautiful Highland scenery. The hills, being very rocky and precipitous, afford some cataracts of great height, though of inconsiderable breadth. There is one pass over the river Machrai, renowned for the dilemma of a poor woman, who, being tempted by the narrowness of the ravine to step across, succeeded in making the first movement, but took fright when it became necessary to move the other foot, and remained in a posture equally ludicrous and dangerous, until some chance passenger assisted her to extricate herself. It is said she remained there some hours.

Line 132. *Where Druids erst heard victims groan.*

The Isle of Arran, like those of Man and Anglesea, abounds with many relics of heathen, and probably Druidical, superstition. There are high erect columns of unhewn stone, circles of rude stones, and cairns, or sepulchral piles, within which are usually found urns enclosing ashes.

Line 143. *Old Brodick's Gothic towers were seen.*

Brodick or Brathwick Castle, in the Isle of Arran, is an ancient fortress, near an open roadstead called Brodick-Bay, and not far distant from a tolerable harbor, closed in by the Island of Lamlash. This important place had been assailed a short time before Bruce's arrival in the island. James Lord Douglas, who accompanied Bruce to his retreat in Rachrine, seems, in the spring of 1306, to have tired of his abode there, and set out accordingly, in the phrase of the times, to see what adventure God would send him. Sir Robert Boyd accompanied him ; and his knowledge of the localities of Arran appears to have directed his course thither. They landed in the island privately, and appear to have laid an ambush for Sir John Hastings, the English governor of Brodwick, and surprised a considerable supply of arms and provisions, and nearly took the castle itself. Indeed, that they actually did so, has been generally averred by historians, although it does not appear from the narrative of Barbour. On the contrary, it would seem that they took shelter within a fortification of the ancient inhabitants, a rampart called *Tor an Schian*. When they were joined by Bruce, it seems probable that they had gained Brodick Castle. At least tradition says, that from the battlements of the tower he saw the supposed signal-fire on Turnberry-nook.

Page 345, line 171. *A language much unmeet he hears.*

Barbour, with great simplicity, gives an anecdote, from which it would seem that the vice of profane swearing, afterwards too general among the Scottish nation, was, at this time, confined to military men. As Douglas, after Bruce's return to Scotland, was roving about the mountainous country of Tweeddale, near the water of Line, he chanced to hear some persons in a farm-house say 'the devil.' Concluding, from this hardy expression, that the house contained war-like guests, he immediately assailed it, and had the good fortune to make prisoners Thomas Randolph, afterwards the famous Earl of Murray, and Alexander Stuart, Lord Bonkle. Both were then in the English interest, and had come into that country with the purpose of driving out Douglas. They afterwards ranked among Bruce's most zealous adherents.

Page 347, line 425. *Now ask you whence that wondrous light.*

'The only tradition now remembered of the landing of Robert the Bruce in Carrick, relates to the fire seen by him from the Isle of Arran. It is still generally reported, and religiously believed by many, that this fire was really the work of supernatural power, unassisted by the hand of any mortal being ; and it is said that for several centuries the flame rose yearly on the same hour of the same night of the year on which the king first saw it from the turrets of Brodick Castle ; and some go so far as to say that if the exact time were known, it would be still seen. That this superstitious notion is very ancient, is evident from the place where the fire is said to have appeared, being called the Bogles' Brae, beyond the remembrance of man. In support of this curious belief, it is said that the practice of burning heath for the improvement of land was then unknown ; that a spunkie [Jack o'lanthorn] could not have been seen across the breadth of the Forth of Clyde, be-tween Ayrshire and Arran ; and that the courier of Bruce was his kinsman, and never suspected of treachery.' — Letter from Mr. Joseph Train of Newton Stuart.

Page 348, line 471. *And from the castle's dis-tant wall.*

The castle of Turnberry, on the coast of Ayrshire, was the property of Robert Bruce, in right of his mother. Lord Hailes mentions the following remarkable circumstance concerning the mode in which he became proprietor of it: 'Martha, Countess of Carrick in her own right, the wife of Robert Bruce, Lord of Annandale, bare him a son, afterwards Robert I. (11 July, 1274). The circumstances of her marriage were singular: happening to meet Robert Bruce in her domains, she became enamored of him, and with some violence led him to her castle of Turnberry. A few days after she married him, without the knowledge of the relations of either party, and without the requisite consent of the king. The king instantly seized her castle and whole estates. She afterwards atoned by a fine for her feudal delinquency. Little did Alexan-der foresee that, from this union, the restorer of the Scottish monarchy was to arise.' — *Annals of Scotland*, ii. 180.

Page 351, line 779. *The Bruce hath won his father's hall!*

I have followed the flattering and pleasing tradition, that the Bruce, after his descent upon the coast of Ayrshire, actually gained posses-sion of his maternal castle. But the tradition is not accurate. The fact is, that he was only strong enough to alarm and drive in the out-posts of the English garrison, then commanded, not by Clifford, as assumed in the text, but by Percy. Neither was Clifford slain upon this occasion, though he had several skirmishes with Bruce. He fell afterwards in the battle of Bannockburn. Bruce, after alarming the castle of Turnberry, and surprising some part of the garrison, who were quartered without the walls of the fortress, retreated into the mountainous part of Carrick, and there made himself so strong that the English were obliged to evacuate Turnberry, and at length the castle of Ayr.

Line 798. *'Bring here,' he said, 'the mazers four.'*

These mazers were large drinking-cups, or goblets.

Line 815. *Arouse old friends and gather new.*

As soon as it was known in Kyle, says ancient tradition, that Robert Bruce had landed in Carrick, with the intention of recovering the crown of Scotland, the Laird of Craigie, and forty-eight men in his immediate neighborhood, declared in favor of their legitimate prince.

Line 818. *Let Ettrick's archers sharp their darts.*

The forest of Selkirk, or Ettrick, at this period, occupied all the district which retains that denomination, and embraced the neighbor-ing dales of Tweeddale, and at least the upper ward of Clydesdale.

Page 352, line 21. *When Bruce's banner had victorious flowed.*

The first important advantage gained by Bruce, after landing at Turnberry, was over Aymer de Valence, Earl of Pembroke, the same by whom he had been defeated near Methven. They met, as has been said, by ap-pointment, at Loudonhill, in the west of Scot-land. Pembroke sustained a defeat; and from that time Bruce was at the head of a consider-able flying army. Yet he was subsequently obliged to retreat into Aberdeenshire, and was there assailed by Comyn, Earl of Buchan, de-sirous to avenge the death of his relative, the Red Comyn, and supported by a body of Eng-lish troops under Philip de Moubray. Bruce was ill at the time of a scrofulous disorder, but took horse to meet his enemies, although obliged to be supported on either side. He was victori-ous, and it is said that the agitation of his spirits restored his health.

Line 23. *When English blood oft deluged Doug-las-dale.*

The 'good Lord James of Douglas,' during these commotions, often took from the English his own castle of Douglas ; but being unable to garrison it, contented himself with destroying the fortifications and retiring into the moun-tains. As a reward to his patriotism, it is said to have been prophesied that how often soever Douglas Castle should be destroyed, it should always again arise more magnificent from its ruins. Upon one of these occasions he used fearful cruelty, causing all the store of provisions, which the English had laid up in his castle, to be heaped together, bursting the wine and beer casks among the wheat and flour, slaughtering the cattle upon the same spot, and upon the top of the whole cutting the throats of the English prisoners. This pleasantry of the 'good Lord James' is commemorated under the name of the *Douglas's Larder.*

Line 24. *And fiery Edward routed stout Saint John.*

'John de Saint John, with 15,000 horsemen, had advanced to oppose the inroad of the Scots. By a forced march he endeavored to surprise them ; but intelligence of his motions was timeously received. The courage of Edward Bruce, approaching to temerity, frequently enabled him to achieve what men of more judicious valor would never have attempted. He ordered the infantry, and the meaner sort of his army, to entrench themselves in strong narrow ground. He himself, with fifty horsemen well harnessed, issued forth under cover of a thick mist, surprised the English on their march, attacked and dispersed them.' — Dalrymple's *Annals of Scotland.*

Line 25. *When Randolph's war-cry swelled the southern gale.*

Thomas Randolph, Bruce's sister's son, a renowned Scottish chief, was in the early part of his life not more remarkable for consistency than Bruce himself. He espoused his uncle's party when Bruce first assumed the crown, and was made prisoner at the fatal battle of Methven, in which his relative's hopes appeared to be ruined. Randolph accordingly not only submitted to the English, but took an active part against Bruce ; appeared in arms against him ; and in the skirmish where he was so closely pursued by the bloodhound it is said his nephew took his standard with his own hand. But Randolph was afterwards made prisoner by Douglas in Tweeddale, and brought before King Robert. Some harsh language was exchanged between the uncle and nephew, and the latter was committed for a time to close custody. Afterwards, however, they were reconciled, and Randolph was created Earl of Moray about 1312. After this period he eminently distinguished himself, first by the surprise of Edinburgh Castle, and afterwards by many similar enterprises, conducted with equal courage and ability.

Line 72. *Northward of Tweed, but Stirling's towers.*

When a long train of success, actively improved by Robert Bruce, had made him master of almost all Scotland, Stirling Castle continued to hold out. The care of the blockade was committed by the king to his brother Edward, who concluded a treaty with Sir Philip Mowbray, the governor, that he should surrender the fortress, if it were not succored by the King of Eng-

land before St. John the Baptist's day. The consequence was, of course, that each kingdom mustered its strength for the expected battle ; and as the space agreed upon reached from Lent to Midsummer, full time was allowed for that purpose.

Line 95. *And Cambria, but of late subdued.*

Edward the First, with the usual policy of a conqueror, employed the Welsh, whom he had subdued, to assist him in his Scottish wars, for which their habits, as mountaineers, particularly fitted them. But this policy was not without its risks. Previous to the battle of Falkirk, the Welsh quarrelled with the English men-at-arms, and after bloodshed on both parts, separated themselves from his army, and the feud between them, at so dangerous and critical a juncture, was reconciled with difficulty. Edward II. followed his father's example in this particular, and with no better success. They could not be brought to exert themselves in the cause of their conquerors. But they had an indifferent reward for their forbearance. Without arms, and clad only in scanty dresses of linen cloth, they appeared naked in the eyes even of the Scottish peasantry ; and after the rout of Bannockburn were massacred by them in great numbers, as they retired in confusion towards their own country.

Line 97. *And Connoght poured from waste and wood.*

There is in the *Fœdera* an invitation to Eth O'Connor, chief of the Irish of Connaught, setting forth that the king was about to move against his Scottish rebels, and therefore requesting the attendance of all the force he could muster, either commanded by himself in person, or by some nobleman of his race. These auxiliaries were to be commanded by Richard de Burgh, Earl of Ulster.

Page 354, line 220. *Their chief, Fitz-Louis, had the care.*

Fitz-Louis, or MacLouis, otherwise called Fullarton, is a family of ancient descent in the Isle of Arran. They are said to be of French origin, as the name intimates. They attached themselves to Bruce upon his first landing ; and Fergus MacLouis, or Fullarton, received from the grateful monarch a charter, dated 26th November, in the second year of his reign, 1307, for the lands of Kilmichel, and others.

Line 258. *Beneath their chieftains ranked their files.*

The men of Argyle, the islanders, and the Highlanders in general, were ranked in the rear. They must have been numerous, for Bruce had reconciled himself with almost all their chieftains, excepting the obnoxious MacDougals of Lorn.

Page 355, line 309. *The monarch rode along the van.*

The English vanguard, commanded by the Earls of Gloucester and Hereford, came in sight of the Scottish army upon the evening of the 23d of June. Bruce was then riding upon a little palfrey, in front of his foremost line, putting his host in order. It was then that the personal encounter took place betwixt him and Sir Henry de Bohun, a gallant English knight, the issue of which had a great effect upon the spirits of both armies. The Scottish leaders remonstrated with the king upon his temerity. He only answered, ' I have broken my good battle-axe.' The English vanguard retreated after witnessing this single combat. Probably their generals did not think it advisable to hazard an attack while its unfavorable issue remained upon their minds.

Page 357, line 516. *Pipe-clang and bugle-sound were tossed.*

There is an old tradition, that the well-known Scottish tune of ' Hey, tutti taitti,' was Bruce's march at the battle of Bannockburn. The late Mr. Ritson, no granter of propositions, doubts whether the Scots had any martial music, quotes Froissart's account of each soldier in the host bearing a little horn, on which, at the onset, they would make such a horrible noise, as if all the devils of hell had been among them. He observes that these horns are the only music mentioned by Barbour, and concludes that it must remain a moot point whether Bruce's army were cheered by the sound even of a solitary bagpipe.

Line 552. *See where yon barefoot abbot stands.*

' Maurice, Abbot of Inchaffray, placing himself on an eminence, celebrated mass in sight of the Scottish army. He then passed along the front barefooted, and bearing a crucifix in his hands, and exhorting the Scots, in few and forcible words, to combat for their rights and their liberty. The Scots kneeled down. " They yield," cried Edward ; " see, they implore mercy." — " They do," answered Ingelram de Umfraville, " but not ours. On that field they will be victorious, or die." ' — *Annals of Scotland*, vol. ii. p. 47.

Line 593. *Forth, Marshal, on the peasant foe !*

The English archers commenced the attack with their usual bravery and dexterity. But against a force, whose importance he had learned by fatal experience, Bruce was provided. A small but select body of cavalry were detached from the right, under command of Sir Robert Keith. They rounded, as I conceive, the marsh called Milntown bog, and, keeping the firm ground, charged the left flank and rear of the English archers. As the bowmen had no spears nor long weapons fit to defend themselves against horse, they were instantly thrown into disorder, and spread through the whole English army a confusion from which they never fairly recovered.

Page 358, line 627. *Twelve Scottish lives his baldric bore !*

Roger Ascham quotes a similar Scottish proverb, ' whereby they give the whole praise of shooting honestly to Englishmen, saying thus, " that every English archer beareth under his girdle twenty-four Scottes." Indeed, Toxophilus says before, and truly of the Scottish nation, " The Scottes surely be good men of warre in theyre owne feates as can be ; but as for shoot-

inge, they can neither use it to any profite, nor yet challenge it for any praise." '

Line 646. *Down ! down ! in headlong overthrow.*

It is generally alleged by historians, that the English men-at-arms fell into the hidden snare which Bruce had prepared for them. Barbour does not mention the circumstance. According to his account, Randolph, seeing the slaughter made by the cavalry on the right wing among the archers, advanced courageously against the main body of the English, and entered into close combat with them. Douglas and Stuart, who commanded the Scottish centre, led their division also to the charge, and the battle becoming general along the whole line, was obstinately maintained on both sides for a long space of time ; the Scottish archers doing great execution among the English men-at-arms, after the bowmen of England were dispersed.

Line 656. *And steeds that shriek in agony !*

I have been told that this line requires an explanatory note ; and, indeed, those who witness the silent patience with which horses submit to the most cruel usage, may be permitted to doubt that in moments of sudden and intolerable anguish, they utter a most melancholy cry. Lord Erskine, in a speech made in the House of Lords, upon a bill for enforcing humanity towards animals, noticed this remarkable fact, in language which I will not mutilate by attempting to repeat it. It was my fortune, upon one occasion, to hear a horse, in a moment of agony, utter a thrilling scream, which I still consider the most melancholy sound I ever heard.

Page 359, line 739. *Lord of the Isles, my trust in thee.*

When the engagement between the main bodies had lasted some time, Bruce made a decisive movement by bringing up the Scottish reserve. It is traditionally said that at this crisis he addressed the Lord of the Isles in a phrase used as a motto by some of his descendants, ' My trust is constant in thee.'

Page 360, line 797. *To arms they flew, — axe, club, or spear.*

The followers of the Scottish camp observed, from the Gillies' Hill in the rear, the impression produced upon the English army by the bringing up of the Scottish reserve, and, prompted by the enthusiasm of the moment, or the desire of plunder, assumed, in a tumultuary manner, such arms as they found nearest, fastened sheets to tent-poles and lances, and showed themselves like a new army advancing to battle. The unexpected apparition of what seemed a new army completed the confusion which already prevailed among the English, who fled in every direction, and were pursued with immense slaughter. The brook of Bannock, according to Barbour, was so choked with the bodies of men and horses that it might have been passed dry-shod.

Line 808. *O, give their hapless prince his due !*

Edward II., according to the best authorities, showed, in the fatal field of Bannockburn, personal gallantry not unworthy of his great sire and greater son. He remained on the field till forced away by the Earl of Pembroke, when all was lost. He then rode to the Castle of Stirling, and demanded admittance; but the governor, remonstrating upon the imprudence of shutting himself up in that fortress, which must so soon surrender, he assembled around his person five hundred men-at-arms, and, avoiding the field of battle and the victorious army, fled towards Linlithgow, pursued by Douglas with about sixty horse. They were augmented by Sir Lawrence Abernethy with twenty more, whom Douglas met in the Torwood upon their way to join the English army, and whom he easily persuaded to desert the defeated monarch, and to assist in the pursuit. They hung upon Edward's flight as far as Dunbar, too few in number to assail him with effect, but enough to harass his retreat so constantly, that whoever fell an instant behind, was instantly slain, or made prisoner. Edward's ignominious flight terminated at Dunbar, where the Earl of March, who still professed allegiance to him, 'received him full gently.' From thence, the monarch of so great an empire, and the late commander of so gallant and numerous an army, escaped to Bamborough in a fishing vessel.

THE FIELD OF WATERLOO.
Page 363, line 31. *Plies the hooked staff and shortened scythe.*
The reaper in Flanders carries in his left hand a stick with an iron hook, with which he collects as much grain as he can cut at one sweep with a short scythe, which he holds in his right hand. They carry on this double process with great spirit and dexterity.
Page 364, line 71. *A stranger might reply.*
[On the margin of the proof sheets submitted by Ballantyne and preserved by him appeared the following: —
'*James.* — My objection to this is probably fantastical, and I state it only because, from the first moment to the last, it has always made me boggle. I don't like a *stranger* — Query, " the questioned," — " the spectator " — " gazer," etc.
'*Scott.* — *Stranger* is appropriate — it means stranger to the circumstances.'
Line 113. *Her garner-house profound.*
'*James.* — You had changed " garner-house profound," which I think quite admirable, to " garner under ground " which I think quite otherwise. I have presumed not to make the change — must I?
'*Scott.* — I acquiesce, but with doubts: *profound* sounds affected.']
Page 365, line 155. *Pale Brussels! then what thoughts were thine.*
It was affirmed by the prisoners of war that Bonaparte had promised his army, in case of victory, twenty-four hours' plunder of the city of Brussels.
Line 177. ' *On! On!* ' *was still his stern exclaim.*
The characteristic obstinacy of Napoleon was

never more fully displayed than in what we may be permitted to hope will prove the last of his fields. He would listen to no advice and allow of no obstacles. An eyewitness has given the following account of his demeanor towards the end of the action: —
' It was near seven o'clock; Bonaparte, who till then had remained upon the ridge of the hill whence he could best behold what passed, contemplated with a stern countenance the scene of this horrible slaughter. The more that obstacles seemed to multiply, the more his obstinacy seemed to increase. He became indignant at these unforeseen difficulties; and, far from fearing to push to extremities an army whose confidence in him was boundless, he ceased not to pour down fresh troops, and to give orders to march forward — to charge with the bayonet — to carry by storm. He was repeatedly informed, from different points, that the day went against him, and that the troops seemed to be disordered; to which he only replied, " *En-avant! En-avant!* " '
Line 187. *The fate their leader shunned to share.*
It has been reported that Bonaparte charged at the head of his guards, at the last period of this dreadful conflict. This, however, is not accurate. He came down, indeed, to a hollow part of the high-road leading to Charleroi, within less than a quarter of a mile of the farm of La Haye Sainte, one of the points most fiercely disputed. Here he harangued the guards, and informed them that his preceding operations had destroyed the British infantry and cavalry, and that they had only to support the fire of the artillery, which they were to attack with the bayonet. This exhortation was received with shouts of *Vive l'Empereur*, which were heard over all our line, and led to an idea that Napoleon was charging in person. But the guards were led on by Ney; nor did Bonaparte approach nearer the scene of action than the spot already mentioned, which the rising banks on each side rendered secure from all such balls as did not come in a straight line.
Line 194. *England shall tell the fight!*
In riding up to a regiment which was hard pressed, the duke called to the men, 'Soldiers, we must never be beat, — what will they say in England?' It is needless to say how this appeal was answered.
Page 366, line 241. *As plies the smith his clanging trade.*
A private soldier of the 95th regiment compared the sound which took place immediately upon the British cavalry mingling with those of the enemy, to ' a thousand tinkers at work mending pots and kettles.'
Line 255. *As their own ocean-rocks hold stance.*
[In the marginal notes, John Ballantyne writes: ' I do not know such an English word as *stance*,' and Scott rejoins, ' Then we 'll make it one for the *nance*.']
Page 368, line 440. *Period of honor as of woes.*
[Sir Thomas Picton, Sir William Ponsonby,

and Sir William de Lancey were among the lost. The last-named was married in the preceding April. Colonel Miller, when mortally wounded, desired to see the colors of the regiment once more ere he died. They were waved over his head, and the expiring officer declared himself satisfied. Colonel Cameron, of Fassiefern, so often distinguished in Lord Wellington's despatches from Spain, fell in the action at Quatre Bras (16th June, 1815), while leading the 92d or Gordon Highlanders, to charge a body of cavalry supported by infantry. Colonel Alexander Gordon fell by the side of his chief.]

Line 446. *Redoubled Picton's soul of fire.*
['*James.* — From long association, this epithet strikes me as conveying a semi-ludicrous idea. '*Scott.* — It is here appropriate, and your objection seems merely personal to your own association.']

HAROLD THE DAUNTLESS.

Page 381, line 8. *Some reverend room, some prebendary's stall.*
[It is possible that in these introductory lines, Scott did have a half sly purpose of throwing readers off the scent as to the authorship of the poem. Nobody would suspect Scott of such dreams, though the sentiment might easily have been attached to Erskine, a son of an Episcopal clergyman, and by his temper and predilections, quite likely to entertain such hopes.]

Line 14. *There might I share my Surtees' happier lot.*
[Robert Surtees of Mainsforth. A Fellow of the Society of Antiquaries, and author of *The History and Antiquities of the County Palatine of Durham.* He was an early and dear friend of Scott's. A club for the publication of documents connected with the history of the English border was formed, named *The Surtees Club.*]

Page 385, line 27. *And such — if fame speak truth — the honored Barrington.*
[Shute Barrington, Bishop of Durham, was a friend of Scott's. The lives of Bishops Matthew and Morton are recorded by Surtees in his *History of the Bishopric of Durham.*]

Page 398, line 380. *A tale six cantos long, yet scorned to add a note.*
[Scott here gives a sly dig at the Scott, whose name was not attached to *Harold the Dauntless,* and whose predilection for notes was well known.]

THE NORMAN HORSE-SHOE.

Page 399, line 14. *In crimson light on Rymny's stream.*
Rymny is a stream which divides the counties of Monmouth and Glamorgan. Caerphili, the scene of the supposed battle, is a vale upon its banks, dignified by the ruins of a very ancient castle.

THE POACHER.

Page 407, line 62. *On the bleak coast of frost-barred Labrador.*
Such is the law in the New Forest, Hamp-

shire, tending greatly to increase the various settlements of thieves, smugglers, and deerstealers, who infest it. In the forest courts the presiding judge wears as a badge of office an antique stirrup, said to have been that of William Rufus. See Mr. William Rose's spirited poem, entitled 'The Red King.'

Line 81. *Yon cask holds moonlight, run when moon was none.*
A cant term for smuggled spirits.

THE BOLD DRAGOON.

Page 408, line 14. *And, as the devil leaves a house, they tumbled through the wall.*
In their hasty evacuation of Campo Mayor, the French pulled down a part of the rampart, and marched out over the glacis.

LETTER IN VERSE.

Page 412, line 104. *But spring, I 'm informed, from the Scotts of Scotstarvet.*
The Scotts of Scotstarvet, and other families of the name in Fife and elsewhere, claim no kindred with the great clan of the Border, and their armorial bearings are different.

SONG ON THE LIFTING OF THE BANNER OF THE HOUSE OF BUCCLEUCH.

Page 424, line 13. *A stripling's weak hand to our revel has borne her.*
[This was Scott's eldest son, Walter.]

THE RETURN TO ULSTER.

Page 426, line 20. *Like a burst of the sun when the tempest is nigh.*
In ancient Irish poetry, the standard of Fion, or Fingal, is called the *Sun-burst,* an epithet feebly rendered by the *Sun-beam* of Macpherson.

THE SEARCH AFTER HAPPINESS.

Page 434, line 239. *The work too little and the pay too much.*
See the *True-Born Englishman,* by Daniel Defoe.

EPILOGUE TO 'THE APPEAL.'

Page 439, line 10. *Since the New Jail became our next-door neighbor.*
It is necessary to mention, that the allusions in this piece are all local, and addressed only to the Edinburgh audience. The new prisons of the city, on the Calton Hill, are not far from the theatre.

Line 22. *With the tempestuous question, Up or down?*
At this time, the public of Edinburgh was much agitated by a lawsuit betwixt the magistrates and many of the inhabitants of the city, concerning a range of new buildings on the western side of the North Bridge, which the latter insisted should be removed as a deformity.

THE BATTLE OF SEMPACH.

Page 442, line 27. *The Switzer priest has ta'en the field.*

All the Swiss clergy who were able to bear arms fought in this patriotic war.

Line 52. *Might well-nigh load a wain.*

This seems to allude to the preposterous fashion, during the middle ages, of wearing boots with the points or peaks turned upwards, and so long, that in some cases they were fastened to the knees of the wearer with small chains. When they alighted to fight upon foot, it would seem that the Austrian gentlemen found it necessary to cut off these peaks that they might move with the necessary activity.

THE NOBLE MORINGER.

Page 444. The original of these verses occurs in a collection of German popular songs, entitled *Sammlung Deustcher Volkslieder*, Berlin, 1807, published by Messrs. Busching and Von der Hagen, both, and more especially the last, distinguished for their acquaintance with the ancient popular poetry and legendary history of Germany.

In the German editor's notice of the ballad, it is stated to have been extracted from a manuscript Chronicle of Nicolaus Thomann, chaplain to Saint Leonard in Weisenhorn, which bears the date 1533; and the song is stated by the author to have been generally sung in the neighborhood at that early period. Thomann, as quoted by the German editor, seems faithfully to have believed the event he narrates. He quotes tombstones and obituaries to prove the existence of the personages of the ballad, and discovers that there actually died, on the 11th May, 1349, a Lady Von Neuffen, Countess of Marstetten, who was, by birth, of the house of Moringer. This lady he supposes to have been Moringer's daughter, mentioned in the ballad. He quotes the same authority for the death of Berckhold Von Neuffen, in the same year. The editors, on the whole, seem to embrace the opinion of Professor Smith, of Ulm, who, from the language of the ballad, ascribes its date to the 15th century.

CARLE, NOW THE KING'S COME.

Page 469, line 47. *Come, Clerk, and give your bugle breath.*

Sir George Clerk, of Pennycuik, Bart. The Baron of Pennycuik is bound by his tenure, whenever the king comes to Edinburgh, to receive him at the Harestone (in which the standard of James IV. was erected when his army encamped on the Boroughmuir, before his fatal expedition to England), now built into the park-wall at the end of Tipperlin Lone, near the Boroughmuirhead ; and, standing thereon, to give three blasts on a horn.

Page 470, line 25. *Come forward with the Blanket Blue.*

[' The Blue Blanket is the standard of the incorporated trades of Edinburgh, and is kept by their convener, "at whose appearance therewith," observes Maitland, "'t is said, that not only the artificers of Edinburgh are obliged to repair to it, but all the artificers or craftsmen within Scotland are bound to follow it, and fight under the convener of Edinburgh, as aforesaid." ']

THE BANNATYNE CLUB.

Page 471. [' This club was instituted in 1822 for the publication of rare and curious works connected with the history and antiquities of Scotland. It consisted, at first, of a very few members, — gradually extended to one hundred. They assume the name from George Bannatyne, of whom little is known beyond that prodigious effort which produced his present honors, and is, perhaps, one of the most singular instances of its kind which the literature of any country exhibits. His labors as an amanuensis were undertaken during the time of pestilence, in 1568. The dread of infection had induced him to retire into solitude, and under such circumstances he had the energy to form and execute the plan of saving the literature of the whole nation ; and, undisturbed by the general mourning for the dead, and general fears of the living, to devote himself to the task of collecting and recording the triumphs of human genius in the poetry of his age and country ; — thus, amid the wreck of all that was mortal, employing himself in preserving the lays by which immortality is at once given to others, and obtained for the writer himself. He informs us of some of the numerous difficulties he had to contend with in this self-imposed task. The volume containing his labors, deposited in the Library of the Faculty of Advocates at Edinburgh, is no less than eight hundred pages in length, and very neatly and closely written, containing nearly all the ancient poetry of Scotland now known to exist.']

To J. G. LOCKHART, Esq.

Page 475, line 2. *Fat worship.*

[So also at foot of the page ; *Fatsman*, one of the many *aliases* of Mr. James Ballantyne. *Speats and raxes* are ' spits and ranges.']

IV. GLOSSARY

abbaye, abbey.
acton, buckram vest worn under armor.
air, sand-bank.
almagest, astronomical or astrological treatise.
Almayn, German.
amice, ecclesiastical vestment.
angel, a gold coin.
arquebus, hagbut, or heavy musket.
aventayle, movable front of helmet.

baldric, belt.
bale, beacon-fire.
ballium, fortified court.
bandelier, belt for carrying ammunition.
ban-dog, watch-dog.
bandrol, a kind of banner or ensign.
barbican, fortification at castle-gate.
barded, armored (of horses).
barding, horse-armor.
barret-cap, cloth cap.
bartizan, small overhanging turret.
basnet, light helmet.
bassened, having a white stripe down the face.
battalia, battalion, army (*not* a plural).
battle, army.
beadsman, one hired to offer prayers for another.
beaver, movable front of helmet.
Beltane, the first of May (a Celtic festival).
bend, bind.
bend (noun), heraldic term.
bent, slope.
beshrew, may evil befall ; confound.
bill, a kind of battle-axe or halberd.
billmen, troops armed with the bill.
black-jack, leather jug or pitcher.
blaze, blazon, proclaim.
bonail, i. e. *bonallez*, a god-speed, parting with a friend.
bonnet-pieces, gold coins with the king's cap (bonnet) on them.
boune, *bowne*, prepare, make ready.
boune, ready, prepared.
bourd, jest.
bower, chamber, lodging-place ; lady's apartments.
brae, hillside.
braid, broad.
bratchet, slowhound.
brigantine, a kind of body armor.
brigg, bridge.
brock, badger.
broke, quartered (the cutting up of a deer).
brotikins, buskins.
buff, a thick cloth.
buxom, lively.
by times, betimes, early.

caird, tinker.
cairn, heap of stones.
canna, cotton-grass.
cap of maintenance, cap worn by the king-at-arms or chief herald.
carp, talk.

cast, pair (of hawks).
chanters, the *pipes* of the bagpipe.
check at, meditate attack (in falconry).
cheer, face, countenance.
claymore, a large sword.
clerk, scholar.
clip, clasp, embrace.
combust, astrological term.
corbel, bracket.
coronach, dirge.
correi, hollow in hillside, resort of game.
crabs, crab-apples.
crenell, aperture for shooting arrows through.
cresset, hanging lamp or chandelier.
culver, small cannon.
cumber, trouble.
curch, matron's coif, or head-dress.
cushat-dove, wood-pigeon.

darkling, in the dark.
deas, dais, platform.
deft, skilful.
demi-volt, movement in horsemanship.
dern, hid.
dight, decked, dressed.
donjon, main tower or *keep* of a castle.
doom, judgment, arbitration.
double tressure, a kind of border in heraldry.
dought, could.
down, hill.
drie, suffer, endure.

earn (see *erne*).
eburnine, made of ivory.
embossed, foaming at the mouth (hunter's term).
emprise, enterprise.
ensenzie, ensign, war-cry.
erne, eagle.
even, spotless.

falcon, a kind of small cannon.
fang, to catch.
far yaud, the signal made by a shepherd to his dog, when he is to drive away some sheep at a distance.
fauld, sheep-fold.
fay, faith.
ferlie, marvel.
flemens-firth, asylum for outlaws.
force, waterfall.
fosse, ditch, moat.
fretted, adorned with raised work.
fro, from.
frounced, flounced, plaited.

galliard, a lively dance.
gallowglasses, heavy-armed soldiers (Celtic).
gar, to make.
gazehound, a hound that pursues by sight rather than scent.
ghast, ghastly.
gipon, doublet or jacket worn under armor.
glaive, broadsword.
glamour, magical illusion.

glee-maiden, dancing-girl.
glidders, slippery stones.
glozing, flattering.
gorged, having the throat cut.
gorget, armor for the throat.
graith, armor.
gramarye, magic.
gramercy, great thanks (French, *grand merci*).
gree, prize.
gripple, grasping, miserly.
grisly, horrible, grim.
guarded, edged, trimmed.
gules, red (heraldic).

hackbuteer, soldier armed with hackbut or hagbut.
haffets, cheeks.
hag, broken ground in a bog.
hagbut (*hackbut, haquebut, arquebus, harquebuss,* etc.), a heavy musket.
halberd (*halbert*), combined spear and battle-axe.
hale, haul, drag.
hanger, short broadsword.
harried, plundered, sacked.
hearse, canopy over tomb, or the tomb itself.
heeze, hoist.
hent, seize.
heriot, tribute due to a lord from a vassal.
heron-shew, young heron.
hight, called, named.
holt, wood, woodland.
hosen, hose (old plural).

idlesse, idleness.
imp, child.
inch, island.

jack, leather jacket, a kind of armor for the body.
jennet, a small Spanish horse.
jerkin, a kind of short coat.

kale, broth.
keek, peep.
kern, light-armed soldier (Celtic).
kill, cell.
kirn, Scottish harvest-home.
kirtle, skirt, gown.
knosp, knob (architectural).

lair, to stick in the mud.
largesse, largess, liberality, gift.
lauds, midnight service of the Catholic Church.
launcegay, a kind of spear.
laverock, lark.
leaguer, camp.
leash, thong for leading greyhound ; also the hounds so led.
leven, lawn, an open space between or among woods.
levin, lightning, thunderbolt.
Lincoln green, a cloth worn by huntsmen.
linn, waterfall ; pool below fall ; precipice.
linstock (*lintstock*), handle for *lint*, or match used in firing cannon.
lists, enclosure for tournament.
litherlie, mischievous, vicious.

lorn, lost.
lourd, rather.
lout, bend, stoop.
lurch, rob.
lurcher, a dog that *lurches* (lurks), or lies in wait for game.
lurdane, blockhead.
lyke-wake, watching of corpse before burial.

make, do.
malison, malediction, curse.
Malvoisie, Malmsey wine.
march, border, frontier.
march-treason, offences committed on the Border.
massy, massive.
mavis, thrush.
melle, mell, meddle.
merle, blackbird.
mewed, shut up, confined.
mickle, much, great.
minion, favorite.
miniver, a kind of fur.
mirk, dark.
morion, steel cap, helmet.
morrice-pike, long heavy spear.
morris, a kind of dance.
morsing-horns, powder-flasks.
mot (*mote*), must, might.
muir, moor, heath.

need-fire, beacon-fire.
nese, nose.

oe, island.
O hone, alas !
Omrahs, nobles (Turkish).
or, gold (heraldic).
owches, jewels.

pallioun, pavilion.
palmer, pilgrim to Holy Land.
pardoner, seller of priestly indulgences.
partisan, halberd.
peel, Border tower.
pensils, small pennons or streamers.
pentacle, magic diagram.
pibroch, Highland air on bagpipe.
pied, variegated.
pinnet, pinnacle.
placket, stomacher, petticoat, slit in petticoat, etc.
plate-jack, coat-armor.
plump, body of cavalry ; group, company.
poke, sack, pocket.
port, martial bagpipe music.
post and pair, an old game at cards.
presence, royal presence-chamber.
pricked, spurred.
pryse, the note blown at the death of the game.
pursuivant, attendant on herald.

quaigh, wooden cup, composed of staves hooped together.
quarry, game (hunter's term).
quatre-feuille, quatrefoil (Gothic ornament).
quit, requite.

rack, floating cloud.
racking, flying, like breaking cloud.
rade, rode (old form).
rais, master of a vessel.
reads, counsels.
reave, tear away.
rede, story ; counsel, advice.
retrograde, astrological term.
rie, prince or chief, *O hone a rie*, alas for the chief !
risp, creak.
rochet, bishop's short surplice.
rood, cross (as in *Holy-Rood*).
room, piece of land.
rowan, mountain-ash.
ruth, pity, compassion.

sack, Sherry or Canary wine.
sackless, innocent.
saga, Scandinavian epic.
saltier, stirrup.
salvo-shot, salute of artillery.
saye, say, assertion.
scalds, Scandinavian minstrels.
scapular, ecclesiastical scarf.
scathe, harm, injury.
scaur, cliff, precipice.
scrae, bank of loose stones.
scrogg, shady wood.
sea-dog, seal.
selcouth, strange, uncouth.
selle, saddle.
seneschal, steward of castle.
sewer, officer who serves up a feast.
shalm, shawm, musical instrument.
sheeling, shepherd's hut.
sheen, bright, shining.
shent, shamed.
shrieve, shrive, absolve.
shroud, garment, plaid.
sleights, tricks, stratagems.
slogan, Highland battle-cry.
snood, maiden's hair-band or fillet.
soland, solan-goose, gannet.
sooth, true, truth.
sped, despatched, ' done for.'
speer, speir, ask.
spell, make out, study out.
sperthe, a battle-axe.
springlet, small spring.
spule, shoulder.
spurn, kick.
stag of ten, one having ten branches on his antlers.
stance, station.
sterte, started.
stirrup-cup, parting cup.
stole, ecclesiastical scarf (sometimes robe).
stoled, wearing the *stole*.
store (adjective), stored up.
stowre, battle, tumult.
strain, stock, race.
strath, broad river-valley.
strathspey, a Highland dance.
streight, strait.
strook, struck, stricken.
stumah, faithful.

swith, haste.
syde, long.
syne, since.

tabard, herald's coat.
tarn, mountain lake.
tartan, the full Highland dress, made of the checquered stuff so termed.
telt, a plait or plaited knot.
throstle, thrush.
tide, time.
tint, lost.
tire, head-dress.
tottered, tattered, ragged.
train, allure, entice.
tressure, border (heraldic).
trews, Highland trousers.
trine, astrological term.
trow, believe, trust.
tyke, dog.
tyne, to lose.

uneath, not easily, with difficulty.
unsparred, unbarred.
upsees, Bacchanalian cry or interjection, borrowed from the Dutch.
urchin, elf.

vail, avail.
vail, lower, let fall.
vair, fur of squirrel.
vantage-coign, advantageous corner.
vaunt-brace, or *warn-brace*, armor for the body.
vaward, van, front.
vilde, vile.

wan, won (old form).
Warden-raid, a raid commanded by a Border Warden in person.
warlock, a wizard.
warped, frozen.
warrison, ' note of assault ' (Scott).
wassail, spiced ale ; drinking-bout.
weapon-schaw, military array of a county ; muster.
weed, garment.
weird, fate, doom.
whenas, when.
whilere (*while-ere*), erewhile, a while ago.
whilom (*whilome*), formerly.
whin, gorse, furze.
whingers, knives, poniards.
whinyard, hunter's knife.
wight, active, gallant, war-like.
wildering, bewildering.
wimple, veil.
woe-worth, woe be to.
woned, dwelt.
wraith, apparition, spectre.
wreak, avenge.

yare, ready.
yate, gate.
yaud, see *far yaud*.
yerk, jerk.
yode, went (archaic).

INDEX OF FIRST LINES

[Including the first Lines of Songs contained in the longer Poems]

INDEX OF TITLES

[The Titles of Major Works and General Divisions are set in SMALL CAPITALS]